A complete checklist of the
Birds of the World

Richard Howard
Alick Moore

A complete checklist of the
Birds of the World

With a Foreword by
Leslie Brown

Oxford New York Toronto Melbourne

OXFORD UNIVERSITY PRESS

1980

Oxford University Press, Walton Street, Oxford OX2 6DP

Oxford London Glasgow
New York Toronto Melbourne Wellington
Kuala Lumpur Singapore Hong Kong Tokyo
Delhi Bombay Calcutta Madras Karachi
Nairobi Dar Es Salaam Cape Town

© Richard Howard and Alick Moore 1980

British Library Cataloguing in Publication Data

Howard, Richard
A complete checklist of the birds of the world.
1. Birds
I Title   II Moore, Alick
598.2'021'6   QL673   79–41431
ISBN 0-19-217681-1

Printed in Great Britain by
Richard Clay (The Chaucer Press) Ltd.
Bungay, Suffolk

Contents

Foreword by Leslie Brown   vii

Introduction   1

Acknowledgements   3

Arrangement of orders and families   4

References   8

CHECKLIST   49

Index   643

Foreword

A great many people enjoy making lists of birds they have seen, very often once only, on some distant journey, with very little likelihood of being able to see and watch the same bird again. Certainly, knowing what a bird is and where it occurs is the first step towards the wider interest that may stem from merely ticking a bird off on a list — twitching, as the vulgar parlance has it. If a bird does not occur where it ought to then one may question why, and that leads to further thoughts of the why and wherefore.

Most available lists cover a district, a country, a region or a continent, perhaps an ocean. Here is one that covers the whole world, down to subspecies level. As the authors remark, the need for an authoritative world list has been in the minds of professional ornithologists and amateurs for many years, and this need has never yet been adequately satisfied for amateurs. There is, and long has been, an official world list for the professionals, the Peters' list, compiled long ago and revised since by many different authorities. It is, however, a multi-volume work, not all of it up to date, and it is not the sort of thing that a traveller can carry around in his or her luggage. Wisely, the authors of the present list have based theirs largely on the Peters' list, incorporating various new ideas, and thereby avoid making confusion worse confounded by riding their own hobby-horse. There have been several other world lists prepared in recent times but at least one of these departs radically from any generally accepted systematic order and they all pursue a somewhat differing approach which may appeal to the author but not always to others.

The authors have made a great effort to supply what is wanted in this present list. Having helped to prepare a checklist myself I know only too well how difficult it is, and how much unexpected work arises from trying to reconcile differing approaches and conflicting ideas resulting in varying treatment of families, genera, species, and subspecies. The present list is based on the sequence of families proposed by Ernst Mayr, often called the father of modern systematics, and it builds on the Peters' list. It should meet with the general approval of many taxonomists and professional ornithologists while its contents are not too difficult or academic for an ordinary birdwatcher to understand. Thorough cross-referencing to other authorities will enable anyone interested to dig deeper among other sources of information.

The fact that there is as yet no absolute agreement on the order in which species, genera, even families should be placed is really a reflection of the fact that we are dealing with some 8500 species of highly mobile living beings, themselves still in the process of evolution. Many, too, are still very little-known and a few new species are discovered almost every year — there have been three in Ethiopia alone in the last two decades. Research in museums and in the field is constantly throwing up new ideas and facts that may suggest different or fresh relationships. Thus it is really asking too much, at our present state of knowledge, to say that the last 'i' has been dotted and the last 't' crossed, and that such a bird is without doubt thus and thus now and forever more. One has only to think of the common and widespread Little Grebe which is given a different generic name in three standard reference books that I own. The authors of this list have done their best to crystallize what is known now of species and their relationships with one another and within families; and they have adopted a geographical approach to subspecies more useful for the ordinary ornithologist than argument about whether such a sub-species is or is not valid, or even should be considered a good species (some probably should). They have consulted widely with experts all over the world, or on particular groups and they have, above all, wisely eschewed that counsel of despair, listing in alphabetical order – quite seriously advocated by some eminent authorities only about a decade ago – which absolutely obscures the relationships of one species to another.

I have never myself been much of a lister. I have on the whole concentrated on deeper study of a few families or species which have taken my fancy. However, I know that most birdwatchers are interested in seeing and identifying as many birds as they can, and association with some such people has often shown me how ignorant I am. I have very little sympathy with those who tick a bird off on a list and thereafter forget it. They've seen it, it's number so and so, and that's that. Every bird seen and clearly identified should be unforgettable and one should record where and when one saw it. If one has never seen it, and recorded the fact, one can have no idea about its habits except at second hand. Possession of a handy, compact list will help those going to a new area to be aware of what they might see, or have heard of. For those interested in particular families or groups it pinpoints objects and areas of study, and can save much valuable hard won time and money.

I will certainly look forward to using this list as it is meant to be used, as a handy reference tool for recording species seen, and where and when. It will be scribbled over, as it should be, and I shall undoubtedly use it to draw up that long-deferred life list of my own – simply because I have never previously had all the species available in one volume. It will be interesting to see if I am even approximately right about my own guess of the number of species I think I have seen, and probably humbling too. Many of us think we know more about birds than we do and the hard fact on the printed page can bring us up short with a jerk. Have I or have I not *seen* a Prothonotary Warbler? Yes, I have, and I can tell you where, too, but I wouldn't be certain that I could infallibly recognize it again!

Leslie Brown
Karen, Kenya 1980

Introduction

The late Professor David Lack once presented a proposal for an 'official' authoritative list of the orders, families, subfamilies, genera, and species of the birds of the world and, of course, in an agreed order. This was an idea likely to be accepted much more readily by amateur ornithologists than by professional taxonomists and thus it did not ever get a start. During the past four years, however, no fewer than five checklists of the world's birds have been published, four in the United States and one in Britain. A comparison of these lists reveals some of the difficulties, disagreements, and varying opinions and points of view that arise in compiling such a list. It also reveals the need for a more accurate and authoritative world list for the use of both amateur and professional ornithologists.

This list was started in 1972 and very quickly we perceived the need to go to subspecific level to do justice to the correct status of a species, and to cover adequately the geographical distribution. How often in lists of European birds do we see both *Corvus corone* and *Corvus cornix* included, not because the author really believes they are separate species, but to be able to document a large black and grey bird which would otherwise be described and pictured as all black? Therefore, we attempt now to list all the birds of the world, including their generally recognized subspecies, that are definitely not extinct, in the best accepted order, and following those whom we believe to be the best available authorities.

Order of families

At once we run into a major dispute involving the most eminent ornithologists. We have opted for the order described by Ernst Mayr, partly because we believe this to be the easiest to comprehend and partly owing to the fact that the authority to which we refer most, the JL Peters' *Checklist of the Birds of the World,* also follows Mayr in what has become known as the Basel sequence.

Order of genera and species

These again generally bear most reference to Peters' *Checklists,* but where that list has been updated and revised, then the more recent version has been used.

Subspecies

These are listed in common geographical order which is to say generally from north-west to south-east, though there are naturally many places where the order of subspecies is arguable and doubtless readily acceptable if changed.

Inevitably the question now arises of what is a valid or recognised subspecies, and we then become involved in another area of contention, but we have tried to select the most generally accepted subspecies and certainly have attempted to include those erected during most recent years. Of course, it is recognized that clinal variations of size or plumage colour make the arbitrary selection of subspecies very difficult, but once again we have tried to follow authorities in these matters.

Other taxonomic divisions have, as far as possible, and for the sake of simplicity, been avoided. The suborder is only used where the relevant authority followed deems it necessary, and subfamilies are adhered to according to the Basel sequence. Many authors subscribe to tribes, and though in compiling this list we have disagreed with this taxonomic refinement, we have found it necessary on a few occasions. Much work has been done on the existence of subgenera and super-species, groups of species sufficiently similar to be grouped together away from near-relatives, yet not sufficiently dissimilar from those near-relatives to be placed within another genus. Additionally, there are subspecies closer to one another in groups to be classed separately from other subspecies within the same species. There is without question validity for recognizing these subdivisions, but their use does very much complicate a simple and clear list.

References

For each family or large subfamily we have given a list of the references used in the compilation of that family. At the head of each list of references is the name of the book or journal publication used as the principal authority and after this follow the books and articles used to update and refine the family.

Geographical distribution

The names of countries are as up to date as we can make them; many have changed since we started the list and no doubt many more will change within a short time of publication. In the interests of clarity and general knowledge we have deliberately disregarded some more recent changes. We refer, for instance, to New Guinea rather than differentiating between Papua New Guinea and West Irian. We still refer to Celebes instead of Sulawesi, and Borneo is still the whole island, but Malaya we call Malaysia without the distinction of being Malaysia West.

Where the migration of a bird takes it well outside its breeding area, the migration area is indicated by »

North, south, east, and west etc. are abbreviated to N, S, E, and W throughout and central becomes C so that south-central would be SC. Island(s) is abbreviated to I(s). a ? indicates that a bird's distribution is uncertain.

English names

We have given every species an English name, but this is a hazardous task and wide open to argument. There is no doubt that many English names could and should be improved, and in particular shortened and clarified. Generally, when a bird becomes well known its English name becomes more reasonable. There must be some better English name for *Hemispingus superciliaris* than Superciliaried Hemispingus, and the translation of guttulatus as 'guttulated' is not helpful.

Extinct birds

Where a bird is known to be extinct it is omitted from the list. Where some doubt still exists, and the bird is possibly or even probably extinct, it is included and marked by **e?**

General references

Several reference books of a general nature have been used throughout the compilation of the list, and in writing this introduction.

J.L. Peters & successors 1931–72 *Checklist of the Birds of the World* vols. I–VII, IX, X, XII–XV. (Harvard University Press & Mus. Comp. Zool., Cambridge. Mass.)

Mayr & Zimmer 1943 'Species described 1938–41' *Auk* 60

Mayr & Amadon 1951 *'Classification of Recent Birds' Amer. Mus. Novit.* 1964

Verhuyen 1951 'New Classification of Non-passerine Birds' *Bull. instr. r. Sci. Bolg.* 37

Mayr & Greenway 1956 *Breviora Mus. Comp. Zool.* 58

Mayr 1957 'Species described 1941–55' *Journ. f. Orn.* 98

Stresemann 1959 'Status of Avian Systematics' *Auk* 76

Greenway 1967 *Extinct and Vanishing Birds of the World* (Dover, New York)

Austin 1967 *Auk* 84

Mayr 1969 *Principles of Systematic Zoology* (Amer. Mus. Nat. Hist., New York)

Mayr & Short 1970 'Species Taxa of North American Birds' *Publ. Nuttall Orn. Cl.* 9

Mayr 1971 'Species described 1956–65' *Journ. f. Om.* 112

Voous 1973 'List of Recent Holarctic Bird Species, Non-passerines' *Ibis* 115

Lack 1975 *Evolution illustrated by Waterfowl* (Blackwell, Oxford)

Moroney, Bock & Farrand 1975 *Reference List of the Birds of the World* (Amer. Mus. Nat. Hist., New York)

Gruson 1975 *Checklist of the Birds of the World* (Collins, London) *Zoological Record* (London)

Acknowledgements

The authors would like to express their appreciation of the help given by Dr. Amadon, Michael Everett, and Dr. D. W. Snow and would also like to thank Howard Brokaw, Trevor Gunton, and Dr. C. M. Perrins for their comments and encouragement.

Arrangement of orders and families

Class **AVES**

Order **Struthioniformes**

1 STRUTHIONIDAE	OSTRICHES

Order **Rheiiformes**

2 RHEIDAE	RHEAS

Order **Casuariiformes**

3 CASUARIIDAE	CASSOWARIES
4 DROMAIIDAE	EMUS

Order **Apterygiformes**

5 APTERYGIDAE	KIWIS

Order **Tinamiformes**

6 TINAMIDAE	TINAMOUS

Order **Sphenisciformes**

7 SPHENISCIDAE	PENGUINS

Order **Gaviiformes**

8 GAVIIDAE	DIVERS

Order **Podicipediformes**

9 PODICIPEDIDAE	GREBES

Order **Procellariiformes**

10 DIOMEDEIDAE	ALBATROSSES
11 PROCELLARIIDAE	PETRELS, SHEARWATERS
12 HYDROBATIDAE	STORM PETRELS
13 PELECANOIDIDAE	DIVING PETRELS

Order **Pelecaniformes**

14 PHAETHONTIDAE	TROPIC BIRDS
15 PELECANIDAE	PELICANS
16 SULIDAE	GANNETS, BOOBIES
17 PHALACROCORACIDAE	CORMORANTS
18 ANHINGIDAE	ANHINGAS
19 FREGATIDAE	FRIGATE BIRDS

Order **Ciconiiformes**

20 ARDEIDAE	HERONS, BITTERNS
21 BALAENICIPITIDAE	WHALE HEADED STORK
22 SCOPIDAE	HAMMERKOP
23 CICONIIDAE	STORKS
24 THRESKIORNITHIDAE	IBISES, SPOONBILLS
25 PHAENICOPTERIDAE	FLAMINGOS

Order **Anseriformes**

26 ANHIMIDAE	SCREAMERS
27 ANATIDAE	DUCKS, GEESE, SWANS

Order **Falconiformes**

28 CATHARTIDAE	NEW WORLD VULTURES
29 PANDIONIDAE	OSPREYS
30 ACCIPITRIDAE	HAWKS, EAGLES
31 SAGITTARIIDAE	SECRETARY BIRD
32 FALCONIDAE	FALCONS, CARACARAS

Order **Galliformes**

33 MEGAPODIIDAE	MEGAPODES
34 CRACIDAE	CURASSOWS, GUANS
35 PHASIANIDAE	PHEASANTS, GROUSE
36 OPISTHOCOMIDAE	HOATZIN

Order **Gruiformes**

37 MESITORNITHIDAE	MESITES
38 TURNICIDAE	BUTTON QUAILS
39 PEDIONOMIDAE	PLAINS WANDERER
40 GRUIDAE	CRANES
41 ARAMIDAE	LIMPKIN
42 PSOPHIIDAE	TRUMPETERS
43 RALLIDAE	RAILS, COOTS
44 HELIORNITHIDAE	SUNGREBES
45 RHYNOCHETIDAE	KAGU
46 EURYPYGIDAE	SUNBITTERNS
47 CARIAMIDAE	SERIEMAS
48 OTIDIDAE	BUSTARDS

Order **Charadriiformes**

49 JACANIDAE	JACANAS
50 ROSTRATULIDAE	PAINTED SNIPE
51 DROMADIDAE	CRAB-PLOVER
52 HAEMATOPODIDAE	OYSTER-CATCHERS
53 IBIDORHYNCHIDAE	IBIS-BILL
54 RECURVIROSTRIDAE	AVOCETS, STILTS
55 BURHINIDAE	STONE CURLEWS
56 GLAREOLIDAE	COURSERS, PRATINCOLES
57 CHARADRIIDAE	PLOVERS
58 SCOLOPACIDAE	SANDPIPERS, SNIPE
59 THINOCORIDAE	SEED SNIPE
60 CHIONIDIDAE	SHEATHBILLS
61 STERCORARIIDAE	SKUAS
62 LARIDAE	GULLS, TERNS
63 RYNCHOPIDAE	SKIMMERS
64 ALCIDAE	AUKS

Order **Columbiformes**

65 PTEROCLIDIDAE	SANDGROUSE
66 COLUMBIDAE	DOVES, PIGEONS

Order **Psittaciformes**

67 LORIIDAE	LORIES
68 CACATUIDAE	COCKATOOS
69 PSITTACIDAE	PARROTS

Order **Cuculiformes**

| 70 | MUSOPHAGIDAE | TURACOS |
| 71 | CUCULIDAE | CUCKOOS |

Order **Strigiformes**

| 72 | TYTONIDAE | BARN OWLS |
| 73 | STRIGIDAE | OWLS |

Order **Caprimulgiformes**

74	STEATORNITHIDAE	OILBIRD
75	PODARGIDAE	FROGMOUTHS
76	NYCTIBIIDAE	POTOOS
77	AEGOTHELIDAE	OWLET-NIGHTJARS
78	CAPRIMULGIDAE	NIGHTJARS

Order **Apodiformes**

79	APODIDAE	SWIFTS
80	HEMIPROCNIDAE	TREE SWIFTS
81	TROCHILIDAE	HUMMING BIRDS

Order **Coliiformes**

| 82 | COLIIDAE | MOUSEBIRDS |

Order **Trogoniformes**

| 83 | TROGONIDAE | TROGONS |

Order **Coraciiformes**

84	ALCEDINIDAE	KINGFISHERS
85	TODIDAE	TODIES
86	MOMOTIDAE	MOTMOTS
87	MEROPIDAE	BEE EATERS
88	CORACIIDAE	ROLLERS
89	BRACHYPTERACIIDAE	GROUND ROLLERS
90	LEPTOSOMATIDAE	COUROLS
91	UPUPIDAE	HOOPOES
92	PHOENICULIDAE	WOOD HOOPOES
93	BUCEROTIDAE	HORNBILLS

Order **Piciformes**

94	GALBULIDAE	JACAMARS
95	BUCCONIDAE	PUFFBIRDS
96	CAPITONIDAE	BARBETS
97	INDICATORIDAE	HONEYGUIDES
98	RAMPHASTIDAE	TOUCANS
99	PICIDAE	WOODPECKERS

Order **Passeriformes**

100	EURYLAIMIDAE	BROADBILLS
101	DENDROCOLAPTIDAE	WOODCREEPERS
102	FURNARIIDAE	OVENBIRDS
103	FORMICARIIDAE	ANTBIRDS
104	CONOPOPHAGIDAE	GNATEATERS
105	RHINOCRYPTIDAE	TAPACULOS
106	COTINGIDAE	COTINGAS
107	PIPRIDAE	MANAKINS

108	TYRANNIDAE	TYRANT FLYCATCHERS
109	OXYRUNCIDAE	SHARPBILL
110	PHYTOTOMIDAE	PLANTCUTTERS
111	PITTIDAE	PITTAS
112	XENICIDAE	NEW ZEALAND WRENS
113	PHiLEPITTIDAE	ASITIES
114	MENURIDAE	LYREBIRDS
115	ATRICHORNITHIDAE	SCRUB BIRDS
116	ALAUDIDAE	LARKS
117	HIRUNDINIDAE	SWALLOWS, MARTINS
118	MOTACILLIDAE	WAGTAILS, PIPITS
119	CAMPEPHAGIDAE	CUCKOO SHRIKES
120	PYCNONOTIDAE	BULBULS
121	IRENIDAE	LEAFBIRDS, IORAS
122	LANIIDAE	SHRIKES
123	VANGIDAE	VANGA SHRIKES
124	BOMBYCILLIDAE	WAXWINGS
125	DULIDAE	PALM CHAT
126	CINCLIDAE	DIPPERS
127	TROGLODYTIDAE	WRENS
128	MIMIDAE	MOCKING BIRDS, THRASHERS
129	PRUNELLIDAE	ACCENTORS
130–142	MUSCICAPIDAE	THRUSHES, WARBLERS ETC.
143	AEGITHALIDAE	LONGTAILED TITS
144	REMIZIDAE	PENDULINE TITS
145	PARIDAE	TITS, CHICKADEES
146	SITTIDAE	NUTHATCHES
147	CERTHIIDAE	TREE CREEPERS
148	RHABDORNITHIDAE	PHILIPPINE CREEPERS
149	CLIMACTERIDAE	AUSTRALIAN CREEPERS
150	DICAEIDAE	FLOWERPECKERS
151	NECTARINIIDAE	SUNBIRDS
152	ZOSTEROPIDAE	WHITE EYES
153	MELIPHAGIDAE	HONEYEATERS
154–158	EMBERIZIDAE	BUNTINGS, TANAGERS
159	PARULIDAE	NEW WORLD WARBLERS
160	DREPANIDIDAE	HAWAIIAN HONEYCREEPERS
161	VIREONIDAE	VIREOS
162	ICTERIDAE	NEW WORLD BLACKBIRDS
163	FRINGILLIDAE	FINCHES
164	ESTRILDIDAE	WAXBILLS
165	PLOCEIDAE	WEAVERS, SPARROWS
166	STURNIDAE	STARLINGS
167	ORIOLIDAE	ORIOLES
168	DICRURIDAE	DRONGOS
169	CALLAEIDAE	WATTLEBIRDS
170	GRALLINIDAE	MAGPIE LARKS
171	ARTAMIDAE	WOOD SWALLOWS
172	CRACTICIDAE	BUTCHER BIRDS
173	PTILONORHYNCHIDAE	BOWER BIRDS
174	PARADISAEIDAE	BIRDS OF PARADISE
175	CORVIDAE	CROWS, JAYS

References

Family STRUTHIONIDAE

J.L. Peters, 1931, *Checklist of the Birds of the World* I (Harvard University Press, Cambridge, Mass.)

C. Vaurie, 1965, *Birds of the Palaearctic Fauna* II (Witherby, London)
C.M.N. White, 1965, *Revised Checklist of African Non-passerine Birds* (Govt. Printer, Lusaka)

Family RHEIDAE

J.L. Peters, 1931, *Checklist of the Birds of the World* I

R. Meyer de Schauensee, 1966, *The Species of Birds of South America* (Acad. Nat. Sci., Philadelphia)
E.R. Blake, 1977, *Manual of Neotropical Birds* I (Chicago University Press, Chicago)

Family CASUARIIDAE

J.L. Peters, 1931, *Checklist of the Birds of the World* I

E. Mayr, 1940, *Amer. Mus. Novit.* 1056
A.L. Rand & E.T. Gilliard, 1967, *Handbook of New Guinea Birds* (Weidenfeld & Nicholson, London)

Family DROMAIIDAE

J.L. Peters, 1931, *Checklist of the Birds of the World* I

1965, *Bull. Zool. Nomencl.* 22
H.T. Condon, 1975, *Checklist of the Birds of Australia* Pt. I (R.A.O.U., Melbourne)

Family APTERYGIDAE

J.L. Peters, 1931, *Checklist of the Birds of the World* I

O.S.N.Z. 1970, *Annotated Checklist of the Birds of New Zealand* (Reed, Wellington)

Family TINAMIDAE

J.L. Peters, 1931, *Checklist of the Birds of the World* I

E.R. Blake, 1977, *Manual of Neotropical Birds* I (Chicago University Press, Chicago)
C.E. Hellmayr & Conover, 1942, *Field Mus. Nat. Hist. Zool.* Ser. 13.1
A. Wetmore, 1951, *Proc. Biol. Soc. Wash.* 68
E. Eisenmann, 1955, 'The Species of Middle American Birds', *Trans. Lin. Soc. N.Y.* 7
C.C. Olrog, 1959, *Neotropica* 5
M. Koepcke, 1962, *Journ. f. Orn.* 103
W.H. Phelps and Phelps, 1963, *Boll. Soc. Venez. Cienc. Nat.* 12.19.24
R. Meyer de Schauensee, 1964, *Birds of Colombia* (Livingston, Narberth, Pennsylvania)
R. Meyer de Schauensee, 1966, *The Species of Birds of South America* (Acad. Nat. Sci., Philadelphia)
J.R. Jehl, 1971, *Trans. San Diego Soc. Nat. Hist.* 16

Family SPHENISCIDAE

J.L. Peters, 1931, *Checklist of the Birds of the World* I

G.M. Mathews & T. Iredale, 1921, *Austr. Av. Rec.* 4
N.W. Cayley, 1925, *Emu* 25
R.C. Murphy, 1947, *Auk* 64

V. Serventy & Whittell, 1952, *Emu* 52
W.R.B. Oliver, 1953, *Emu* 53
W.B. Alexander, 1963, *Birds of the Ocean* 2nd edn. (Putnam, New York)
R.A. Falla *et al*, 1966, *Field Guide to the Birds of New Zealand* (Collins, London)
R.A. Falla *et al*, 1970, *Notornis* 17
O.S.N.Z., 1970, *Annotated Checklist of the Birds of New Zealand* (Reed, Wellington)
B. Stonehouse, 1970, *Ibis* 112
B. Stonehouse, 1971, *Ibis* 113
H.T. Condon, 1975, *Checklist of the Birds of Australia* Pt. I (R.A.O.U., Melbourne)

Family **GAVIIDAE**

J.L. Peters, 1931, *Checklist of the Birds of the World* I

1956, *ICZN; Opinion* 401
C. Vaurie, 1965, *Birds of the Palaearctic Fauna* II (Witherby, London)

Family **PODICIPEDIDAE**

J.L. Peters, 1931, *Checklist of the Birds of the World* I

J. Delacour, 1932, *Ois. Rev. Fr. Orn.* 2.6
E. Mayr, 1943, *Emu* 43
E. Mayr, 1945, *Emu* 44
1956, *ICZN; Opinion* 401
K.E.L. Simmons, 1962, *Bull. B.O.C.* 82
R.W. Storer, 1963, *Proc. 13th Int. Orn. Cong.* 126
C. Vaurie, 1965, *Birds of the Palaearctic Fauna* II (Witherby, London)
K.H. Voous & Payne, 1965, *Ardea* 53
R. Meyer de Schauensee, 1966, *The Species of Birds of South America* (Acad. Nat. Sci., Philadelphia)
K.E.L. Simmons, 1968, *British Birds* 61
1972, *Bull. Zool. Nomencl.* 29
L. Rumboll, 1974, *Comm. Mus. Arg. Cienc. Nat. Bernardino Rivadavia* 4 (5) 33
H.T. Condon, 1975, *Checklist of the Birds of Australia* Pt. I (R.A.O.U., Melbourne)
D.R. Wells & Lord Medway, 1976, *Bull. B.O.C.* 96

Family **DIOMEDEIDAE**

J.L. Peters, 1931, *Checklist of the Birds of the World* I
W.B. Alexander, 1963, *Birds of the Ocean* 2nd edn. (Putnam, New York)

R.C. Murphy, 1930, *Amer. Mus. Novit.* 419
W.H. Bierman & K.H. Voous, 1950, *Ardea* 37
A.M. Bailey & J.H. Sorensen, 1962, *Proc. Denver Mus. Nat. Hist.* 10
W.B. Alexander *et al*, 1965, *Ibis* 107
P.A. Clancey, 1965, *Ostrich* 36
O.S.N.Z., 1970, *Annotated Checklist of the Birds of New Zealand* (Reed, Wellington)
V. Serventy *et al*, 1971, *Handbook of Australian Seabirds* (Sydney)
G.E. Watson *et al*, 1971, *Birds of the Antarctic and Subantarctic* (Amer. Geog. Soc., New York)
H.T. Condon, 1975, *Checklist of the Birds of Australia* Pt. I (R.A.O.U., Melbourne)
S. Cramp, *et al*, 1977, *Handbook of the Birds of Europe, the Middle East, and North Africa* I (Oxford University Press, Oxford)

Family **PROCELLARIIDAE**

J.L. Peters, 1931, *Checklist of the Birds of the World* I
W.B. Alexander, 1963, *Birds of the Ocean* 2nd edn. (Putnam, New York)
H.T. Condon, 1975, *Checklist of the Birds of Australia* Pt. I (R.A.O.U., Melbourne)

R.A. Falla, 1942, *Emu* 42
K.H. Voous, 1949, *Ardea* 37

R.C. Murphy, 1951, *Amer. Mus. Novit.* 1512
R.C. Murphy & Pennoyer, 1952, *Amer. Mus. Novit.* 1580
H.T. Condon, 1955, *Emu* 55
C. Jouanin, 1955, *L'Oiseau* 25
W.W.A. Phillips & Sims, 1958, *Journ. Bombay Nat. Hist. Soc.* 55
J. Warham, 1962, *Auk* 79
Bartle, 1963, *Notornis,* 15
C. Jouanin, 1963, *Bull. Mus. Nat. Hist. Paris* 35(2)
W.R.P. Bourne, 1964, *Notornis* 11
W.B. Alexander, *et al,* 1965, *Ibis* 107
R.C. Murphy, 1965, *Amer. Mus. Novit.* 1586
W.R.P. Bourne & J. Warham, 1966, *Ardea* 54
C. Jouanin & Gill, 1967, *L'Oiseau* 37
I.A. Strange, 1968, *Ibis* 110
M.J. Imber & Crockett, 1970, *Notornis* 17
O.S.N.Z., 1970, *Annotated Checklist of the Birds of New Zealand* (Reed, Wellington)
W.R.P. Bourne, 1971, *Sea Swallow* 21
G.E. Watson, *et al,* 1971, *Birds of the Antarctic and Subantarctic* (Amer. Geog. Soc., New York)
S. Cramp, *et al,* 1977, *Handbook of the Birds of Europe, the Middle East, and North Africa* I
  (Oxford University Press, Oxford)

Family **HYDROBATIDAE**

J.L. Peters, 1931, *Checklist of the Birds of the World* I
W.B. Alexander, 1963, *Birds of the Ocean* 2nd edn. (Putnam, New York)

G.M. Mathews, 1933, *Novit Zool.* 39
R.C. Murphy & S. Irving, 1951, *Amer. Mus. Novit.* 1506
O.L. Austin, 1952, *Bull. Mus. Comp. Zool.* 107
R.C. Murphy & J.P. Snyder, 1952, *Amer. Mus. Novit.* 1596
W.B. Alexander, *et al,* 1965, *Ibis* 107
C. Vaurie, 1965, *Birds of the Palaearctic Fauna* II (Witherby, London)
G.E. Watson, *et al,* 1971, *Birds of the Antarctic and Subantarctic (Amer. Geog. Soc., New York)*
H.T. Condon, 1975, *Checklist of the Birds of Australia* Pt. 1 (R.A.O.U., Melbourne)

Family **PELECANOIDIDAE**

J.L. Peters, 1931, *Checklist of the Birds of the World* I

W.B. Alexander, 1963, *Birds of the Ocean* 2nd edn. (Putnam, New York)
W.R.P. Bourne, 1968, *Bull. B.O.C.* 88

Family **PHAETHONTIDAE**

J.L. Peters, 1931, *Checklist of the Birds of the World* I

W.B. Alexander, 1963, *Birds of the Ocean* 2nd edn. (Putnam, New York)

Family **PELECANIDAE**

J.L. Peters, 1931, *Checklist of the Birds of the World* I

W.B. Alexander, 1963, *Birds of the Ocean* 2nd edn. (Putnam, New York)

Family **SULIDAE**

J.L. Peters, 1931, *Checklist of the Birds of the World* I

W.B. Alexander, 1963, *Birds of the Ocean* 2nd edn. (Putnam, New York)

Family **PHALACROCORACIDAE**

J.L. Peters, 1931, *Checklist of the Birds of the World* I

W.B. Alexander, 1963, *Birds of the Ocean* 2nd edn. (Putnam, New York)
P.A. Clancey, 1965–6, *Durban Mus. Novit.* 7
G.F. van Tets, 1965, *Orn. Monogr.* 2
J.G. Williams, 1966, *Bull. B.O.C. 86*
J-F, Voisin, 1973, *Notomis* 20(3)
H.T. Condon, 1975, *Checklist of the Birds of Australia* Pt. I (R.A.O.U., Melbourne)

Family **ANHINGIDAE**

J.L. Peters, 1931, *Checklist of the Birds of the World* I

E. Mayr & Short, 1970, *Publ. Nuttall Orn. Cl.* 9

Family **FREGATIDAE**

J.L. Peters, 1931, *Checklist of the Birds of the World* I

W.B. Alexander, 1963, *Birds of the Ocean* 2nd edn. (Putnam, New York)

Family **ARDEIDAE**

J. Hancock & H. Elliott, 1978, *Herons of the World* (London Editions)
W.J. Bock, 1956, *Amer. Mus. Novit.* 1779
J.L. Peters, 1931, *Checklist of the Birds of the World* I

K.C. Parkes, 1955, *Ann. Carnegie Mus.* 33
C.W. Mackworth Praed & C.H.B. Grant, 1962, *African Handbook of Birds* Ser. 1—3 (Longmans, London)
R.A. Falla, 1963, *Notornis* 10
P.S. Humphrey & K.C. Parkes, 1963, *Proc. 13th Inst. Orn. Cong.* 84
E. Eisenmann, 1965, *Hornero* 10
R. Meyer de Schauensee, 1966, *The Species of Birds of South America* (Acad. Nat. Sci., Philadelphia)
O.S.N.Z., 1970, *Annotated Checklist of Birds of New Zealand* (Reed, Wellington)
C.W. Benson, R.K. Brooke, & M.P.S. Irwin, 1971, *Bull. B.O.C.* 91
K. Curry-Lindahl, 1971, *Ostrich* Suppl. 9
R.K. Murton, 1972, *Biol. Conserv.* 4(2)
R.W. Dickerman, 1973, *Bull. B.O.C.* 93
R.B. Payne, 1974, *Bull. B.O.C.* 94
H.T. Condon, 1975, *Checklist of the Birds of Australia* Pt. I (R.A.O.U., Melbourne)
M.P.S. Irwin, 1975, *Bonn. Zool. Beitr.* 26
R.B. Payne & C.J. Risley, 1976, *Univ. Mich. Mus. Zool. Misc. Publ.* 150
D.R. Wells & Lord Medway, 1976, *Bull. B.O.C.* 96
S. Cramp, *et al*, 1977, *Handbook of the Birds of Europe, The Middle East, and North Africa* 1 (Oxford University Press, Oxford)

Family **BALAENICIPITIDAE**

J.L. Peters, 1931, *Checklist of the Birds of the World* I

C.M.N. White, 1965, *Revised Checklist of African Non-passerine Birds* (Govt. Printer, Lusaka)

Family **SCOPIDAE**

J.L. Peters, 1931, *Checklist of the Birds of the World* I

A.L. Rand, 1936, *Bull. Amer. Mus. Nat. Hist.* 72
C.M.N. White, 1965, *Revised Checklist of African Non-passerine Birds* (Govt. Printer, Lusaka)

Family **CICONIIDAE**

M.P. Kahl, 1972, *Journ. Zool.* 167

J.L. Peters, 1931, *Checklist of the Birds of the World* I
M.P. Kahl, 1971, *Living Birds* 10
M.P. Kahl & Schüz, 1972, *Vogelwarte* 26

Family **THRESKIORNITHIDAE**

J.L. Peters, 1931, *Checklist of the Birds of the World* I

D. Amadon & Woolfenden, 1953, *Amer. Mus. Novit.* 1564
D. Holyoak, 1970, *Bull. B.O.C.* 90

Family **PHOENICOPTERIDAE**

J.L. Peters, 1931, *Checklist of the Birds of the World* I

R. Meyer de Schauensee, 1966, *The Species of Birds of South America* (Acad. Nat. Sci., Philadelphia)
C.G. Sibley, *et al*, 1969, *Condor* 71
C.G. Sibley & J.E. Ahlqvist, 1972, *Bull. Peabody Mus. Nat. Hist.* 39
J. Kear & N. Duplaix-Hall, 1975, *Flamingoes* (Berkhampstead)

Family **ANHIMIDAE**

J.L. Peters, 1931, *Checklist of the Birds of the World* I

R. Meyer de Schauensee, 1966, *The Species of Birds of South America* (Acad. Nat. Sci., Philadelphia)

Family **ANATIDAE**

P.A. Johnsgard, 1965, *Handbook of Waterfowl Behaviour,* (Cornell, New York)
J. Delacour, 1954, *Waterfowl of the World* 1–4 (Country Life, London)

J.L. Peters, 1931, *Checklist of the Birds of the World* I
E. Mayr, 1940, *Amer. Mus. Novit.* 1056
J. Delacour & Mayr, 1945, *Wilson Bull.* 57
H. Friedmann, 1947, *Condor,* 49
R.E. Stewart & J.W. Aldrich, 1956, *Proc. Biol. Soc. Wash.* 69
P. Scott, 1957, *Coloured Key to the Wildfowl of the World,* (Wildfowl Trust, Slimbridge)
S.D. Ripley, 1964, *Bull. Peabody Mus. Nat. Hist.* 19
H.J. Frith, 1967, *Waterfowl of Australia* (A.H. & A.W. Reed, Sydney)
H.T. Condon, 1975, *Checklist of the Birds of Australia* Pt. I (R.A.O.U., Melbourne)
S. Cramp, *et al.* 1977, *Handbook of the Birds of Europe, the Middle east, and North Africa* 1 (Oxford University Press, Oxford)

Family **CATHARTIDAE**

L. Brown & D. Amadon, 1968, *Eagles, Hawks and Falcons of the World* (Country Life, London)

Family **PANDIONIDAE**

L. Brown & D. Amadon, 1968, *Eagles, Hawks and Falcons of the World* (Country Life, London)

Family **ACCIPITRIDAE**

L. Brown & D. Amadon, 1968, *Eagles, Hawks and Falcons of the World* (Country Life, London)

J.L. Peters, 1931, *Checklist of the Birds of the World* I

A.C.V. van Bemmell, 1948, *Treubia* 19
C.E. Hellmayr, 1949, *Catalogue of Birds of the Americas* 1.4
D. Amadon, 1953, *Ibis* 492
C. Vaurie, 1965, *Birds of the Palaearctic Fauna* II (Witherby, London)
C.M.N. White, 1965, *Revised Checklist of African Non-passerine Birds* (Govt. Printer, Lusaka)
A.L. Rand & E.T. Gilliard, 1967, *Handbook of New Guinea Birds* (Weidenfeld & Nicholson, London)
M. Desfayes, 1973, *Bull. B.O.C.* 94
K.C. Parkes, 1973, *Nemouria* 11
H.T. Condon, 1975, *Checklist of the Birds of Australia* Pt. I (R.A.O.U., Melbourne)

Family **SAGITTARIIDAE**

L. Brown & D. Amadon, 1968, *Eagles, Hawks and Falcons of the World* (Country Life, London)

Family **FALCONIDAE**

L. Brown & D. Amadon, 1968, *Eagles, Hawks and Falcons of the World* (Country Life, London)

J.L. Peters, 1931, *Checklist of the Birds of the World* I
C.W. Mackworth-Praed & C.H.B. Grant, 1933, *Bull. B.O.C.* 54
H.T. Condon, 1950, *Emu* 50
D. Amadon, 1964, *Amer. Mus. Novit.* 2166
C. Vaurie, 1965, *Birds of the Palaearctic Fauna* II (Witherby, London)
C.M.N. White, 1965, *Revised Checklist of African Non-passerine Birds* (Govt. Printer, Lusaka)
A.L. Rand & E.T. Gilliard, 1967, *Handbook of New Guinea Birds* (Weidenfeld & Nicholson, London)
P. Schwartz, 1972, *Condor* 74

Family **MEGAPODIIDAE**

J.L. Peters, 1934, *Checklist of the Birds of the World* II (Harvard University Press, Cambridge, Mass.)

E. Mayr, 1938, *Amer. Mus. Novit.* 1006
D. Amadon, 1942, *Amer. Mus. Novit.* 1175
H.J. Frith, 1956, *Ibis* 98
A.L. Rand & E.T. Gilliard, 1967, *Handbook of New Guinea Birds* (Weidenfeld & Nicholson, London)

Family **CRACIDAE**

J. Delacour & D. Amadon, 1973, *Curassows and Related Birds* (Amer. Mus. Nat. Hist., New York)

J.L. Peters, 1934, *Checklist of the Birds of the World* II
C. Vaurie, 1964–5, *Amer. Mus. Novit.* 2197, 2222, 2232, 2237
Vuilleumier, 1965, *Bull. Mus. Comp Zool.* 134
C. Vaurie, 1966, *Amer. Mus. Novit.* 2251
C. Vaurie, 1967, *Amer. Mus. Novit.* 2296, 2299, 2305, 2307
C. Vaurie, 1968, *Bull. Amer. Mus. Nat. Hist.* 138
E.R. Blake, 1977, *Manual of Neotropical Birds* I (Chicago University Press, Chicago)

Family **PHASIANIDAE**

P.A. Johnsgard, 1973, *Grouse and Quails of North America* (Nebraska University Press, Lincoln)
J. Delacour, 1977, *Pheasants of the World* 2nd edn. (Spur, Hindhead)

J.L. Peters, 1934, *Checklist of the Birds of the World* II
M. Hachisuka, 1941, *Zoologica* 26
A. Dugand, 1943, *Caldasia* 2
F. Ludlow, 1944, *Ibis* 86
R. Meyer de Schauensee, 1946, *Proc. Acad. Nat. Sci. Phil.* 91
C.W. Mackworth-Praed & C.H.B. Grant, 1951, *Ibis* 92
C.M.N. White, 1952, *Ibis* 94
C.M.N. White, 1958, *Bull. B.O.C.* 78
S.D. Ripley, 1961, *Synopsis of the Birds of India and Pakistan* (Nat. Hist. Soc, Bombay)
G.E. Watson, 1962, *Ibis* 104
B.P. Hall, 1963, *Bull. Brit. Mus. Nat. Hist.* 10(2)
A. Wetmore, 1963, *Smiths. Misc. Coll.* 145(6)
C. Vaurie, 1965, *Birds of the Palaearctic Fauna* II (Witherby, London)
C.M.N. White, 1965, *Revised Checklist of African Non-passerine Birds* (Govt. Printer, Lusaka)
R. Meyer de Schauensee, 1966, *The Species of Birds of South America* (Acad. Nat. Sci., Philadelphia)
Short, 1967, *Amer. Mus. Novit.* 2289
J. Farrand Jr. & S.L. Olsen, 1973, *Bull. B.O.C.* 93(2)
A.M. Rea, 1973, *Condor* 75(3)
G.W.H. Davison, 1974, *Bull. B.O.C.* 94(4)
D.G. Roles, 1976, *Rare Pheasants of the World* (Spur Publications, Liss, Hampshire)

Family **OPISTHOCOMIDAE**

J.L. Peters, 1934, *Checklist of the Birds of the World* II

C.G. Sibley & J.E. Ahlqvist, 1973, *Auk 90*

Family **MESITORNITHIDAE**

J.L. Peters, 1934, *Checklist of the Birds of the World* II

A.L. Rand, 1936, *Bull. Amer. Mus. Nat. Hist.* 72

Family **TURNICIDAE**

J.L. Peters, 1934, *Checklist of the Birds of the World* II

E. Hartert, 1928, *Novit. Zool.* 34
E. Mayr, 1938, *Amer. Mus. Novit.* 1007
E. Mayr, 1944, *Bull. Amer. Mus. Nat. Hist.* 83
J.D. Macdonald, 1971, *Sunbird* 2
H.T. Condon, 1975, *Checklist of the Birds of Australia* Pt. I (R.A.O.U., Melbourne)

Family **PEDIONOMIDAE**

J.L. Peters, 1934, *Checklist of the Birds of the World* II

W.J. Bock & McEvey, 1969, *Proc. R. Soc. Victoria* 82(2)

Family **GRUIDAE**

J.L. Peters, 1934, *Checklist of the Birds of the World* II

T.H. Cheng, 1955, *Distributional List of Chinese Birds* Pt. I (Acad. Sin., Peking)
C. Vaurie, 1965, *Birds of the Palaearctic Fauna* II (Witherby, London)
J.W. Aldrich, 1972, *Proc. Biol. Soc. Wash.* 85
L. Walkinshaw, 1973, *Cranes of the World* (Winchester, New York)

Family **ARAMIDAE**

A.O.U., 1957, *Checklist of North American Birds* (A.O.U., Baltimore)

J.L. Peters, 1934, *Checklist of the Birds of the World* II

J. Bond, 1971, *Birds of the West Indies* (Collins, London)

Family **PSOPHIIDAE**

J.L. Peters, 1934, *Checklist of the Birds of the World* II

R. Meyer de Schauensee, 1966, *The Species of Birds of South America* (Acad. Nat. Sci., Philadelphia)

Family **RALLIDAE**

S.D. Ripley, 1977, *Rails of the World* (Feheley, Toronto)

E. Mayr, 1933, *Amer. Mus. Novit.* 590
H.B. Conover, 1934, *Auk* 51(3)
J.L. Peters, 1934, *Checklist of the Birds of the World* II
C.E. Hellmayr & Conover, 1942, *Field Mus. Nat. Hist.* 12–13
J.T. Zimmer & W.H. Phelps, 1944, *Amer. Mus. Novit.* 1270
E. Mayr, 1950, *Amer. Mus. Novit.* 1417(3)
A.M. Lysaght, 1953, *Bull. B.O.C.* 73
W.W.A. Phillips & R.W. Sims, 1958, *Bull. B.O.C.* 78
K.C. Parkes & D. Amadon, 1959, *Wilson Bull.* 71(4)
F.B. Gill, 1964, *Condor* 66
R. Meyer de Schauensee, 1966, *The Species of Birds of South America* (Acad. Nat. Sci., Philadelphia)
A.L. Rand & E.T. Gilliard, 1967, *Handbook of New Guinea Birds* (Weidenfeld & Nicholson, London)
H.T. Hendrickson, 1969, *Ibis* 111
L.B. Keith, C.W. Benson, & M.P.S. Irwin, 1970, *Bull. Amer. Mus. Nat. Hist.* 143
O.S.N.Z., 1970, *Annotated Checklist of Birds of New Zealand* (Reed, Wellington)
S.L. Olsen, 1973, *Wilson Bull.* 85
G.M. Storr, 1973, 'List of Queensland Birds' *Spec. Publs. W. Aust. Mus.* 5
H.T. Condon, 1975, *Checklist of the Birds of Australia* Pt. I (R.A.O.U., Melbourne)
S.L. Olson, 1975, *Emu* 75

Family **HELIORNITHIDAE**

J.L. Peters, 1934, *Checklist of the Birds of the World* II

C.M.N. White, 1965, *Revised Checklist of African Non-passerine Birds* (Govt. Printer, Lusaka)
R. Meyer de Schauensee, 1966, *The Species of Birds of South America* (Acad. Nat. Sci., Philadelphia)

Family **RHYNOCHETIDAE**

J.L. Peters, 1934, *Checklist of the Birds of the World* II

E. Mayr, 1945, *Birds of the Southwest Pacific* (Macmillan, New York)

Family **EURYPYGIDAE**

J.L. Peters, 1934, *Checklist of the Birds of the World* II

R. Meyer de Schauensee, 1966, *The Species of Birds of South America* (Acad. Nat. Sci., Philadelphia)

Family **CARIAMIDAE**

J.L. Peters, 1934, *Checklist of the Birds of the World* II

R. Meyer de Schauensee, 1966, *The Species of Birds of South America* (Acad. Nat. Sci., Philadelphia)

Family **OTIDAE**

J.L. Peters, 1934, *Checklist of the Birds of the World* II

A. Roberts, 1937, *Ostrich* 8
J. Vincent, 1949, *Ostrich* 20
S.D. Ripley, 1961, *Synopsis of the Birds of India and Pakistan* (Nat. Hist. Soc., Bombay)
C.M. N. White, 1965, *Revised Checklist of African Non-passerine Birds* (Govt. Printer, Lusaka)

Family **JACANIDAE**

J.L. Peters, 1934, *Checklist of the Birds of the World* II

A. Wetmore, 1965, *Smiths. Misc. Coll.* 150(1)
J.R. Jehl, 1968, *Mem. San Diego Soc. Nat. Hist.* 3

Family **ROSTRATULIDAE**

J.L. Peters, 1934, *Checklist of the Birds of the World* II

C. Vaurie, 1965, *Birds of the Palaearctic Fauna* II (Witherby, London)
R. Meyer de Schauensee, 1966, *The Species of Birds of South America* (Acad. Nat. Sci., Philadelphia)

Family **DROMADIDAE**

J.L. Peters, 1934, *Checklist of the Birds of the World* II

C.M.N. White, 1965, *Revised Checklist of African Non-passerine Birds* (Govt. Printer, Lusaka)

Family **HAEMATOPODIDAE**

J.L. Peters, 1934, *Checklist of the Birds of the World* II

J.R. Jehl, 1968, *Mem. San Diego Soc. Nat. Hist.* 3
E. Mayr & Short, 1970, *Publ. Nuttall Orn. Cl.* 9
O.S.N.Z., 1970, *Annotated Checklist of the Birds of New Zealand* (Reed, Wellington)
H.T. Condon, 1975, *Checklist of the Birds of Australia* Pt. I (R.A.O.U., Melbourne)

Family **IBIDORHYNCHIDAE**

J.L. Peters, 1934, *Checklist of the Birds of the World* II

S.D. Ripley, 1961, *Synopsis of the Birds of India and Pakistan* (Nat. Hist. Soc., Bombay)

Family **RECURVIROSTRIDAE**

J.L. Peters, 1934, *Checklist of the Birds of the World* II

S.D. Ripley, 1961, *Synopsis of the Birds of India and Pakistan* (Nat. Hist. Soc., Bombay)
R. Meyer de Schauensee, 1966, *The Species of Birds of South America* (Acad. Nat. Sci., Philadelphia)
E. Mayr & Short, 1970, *Publ. Nuttall Orn. Cl.* 9
H.T. Condon, 1975, *Checklist of the Birds of Australia* Pt. 2 (R.A.O.U., Melbourne)

Family **BURHINIDAE**

J.L. Peters, 1934, *Checklist of the Birds of the World* II

C. Vaurie, 1965, *Birds of the Palaearctic Fauna* II (Witherby, London)
C.M.N. White, 1965, *Revised Checklist of African Non-passerine Birds* (Govt. Printer, Lusaka)
R. Meyer de Schauensee, 1966, *The Species of Birds of South America* (Acad. Nat. Sci., Philadelphia)

Family **GLAREOLIDAE**

J.L. Peters, 1934, *Checklist of the Birds of the World* II

W.J. Bock, 1959, *Bull. Mus. Comp. Zool.* 118(2)
C.M.N. White, 1965, *Revised Checklist of African Non-passerine Birds* (Govt. Printer, Lusaka)
J.R. Jehl, 1968, *Mem. San Diego Soc. Nat. Hist.* 3

Family **CHARADRIIDAE**

W.J. Bock, 1958, *Bull. Mus. Comp. Zool. Harvard* 118(2)
J.L. Peters, 1934, *Checklist of the Birds of the World* II

W. Serle, 1956, *Bull. B.O.C.* 76
A.O.U., 1957, *Checklist of North American Birds* (A.O.U., Baltimore)
J. Warham, 1960, *Emu* 60
C. Vaurie, 1964, *Amer. Mus. Novit.* 2177
C. Vaurie, 1964, *Bull. Amer. Mus. Nat. Hist.* 127
C. Vaurie, 1965, *Birds of the Palaearctic Fauna* II (Witherby, London)
C.M.N. White, 1965, *Revised Checklist of African Non-passerine Birds* (Govt. Printer, Lusaka)
G.F. van Tets *et al,* 1967, *Emu* 67
J.R. Jehl, 1968, *Mem. San Diego Soc. Nat..Hist.* 3
E. Mayr & Short, 1970, *Publ. Nuttall Orn. Cl.* 9
R.L. Zusi & J.R. Jehl, 1970, *Auk* 87
H.E. Walters, 1974, *Bonn. Zool. Beitr.* 25(4)
H.T. Condon, 1975, *Checklist of the Birds of Australia* Pt. I (R.A.O.U., Melbourne)

Family **SCOLOPACIDAE**

J.R. Jehl, 1968, *Mem. San Diego Soc. Nat. Hist.* 3
J.L. Peters, 1934, *Checklist of the Birds of the World* II

1956, *Bull. Zool. Nomencl. Dir.* 39
A.O.U., 1957, *Checklist of North American Birds* (A.O.U., Baltimore)
C. Vaurie, 1965, *Birds of the Palaearctic Fauna* II (Witherby, London)
R.L. Zusi & J.R. Jehl, 1970, *Auk* 87
H.T. Condon, 1975, *Checklist of the Birds of Australia* Pt. I (R.A.O.U., Melbourne)

Family **THINOCORIDAE**

J.L. Peters, 1934, *Checklist of the Birds of the World* II

R. Meyer de Schauensee, 1966, *The Species of Birds of South America* (Acad. Nat. Sci.,
  Philadelphia)

Family **CHIONIDIDAE**

J.L. Peters, 1934, *Checklist of the Birds of the World* II

Family **STERCORARIIDAE**

W.B. Alexander, 1963, *Birds of the Ocean* 2nd edn. (Putnam, New York)
J.L. Peters, 1937, *Checklist of the Birds of the World*

Family **LARIDAE**

W.B. Alexander, 1963, *Birds of the Ocean* 2nd edn. (Putnam, New York)
J.L. Peters, 1934, *Checklist of the Birds of the World* II

M. Moynihan, 1959, *Amer. Mus. Novit.* 1928
C. Vaurie, 1965, *Birds of the Palaearctic Fauna* II (Witherby, London)
E. Mayr & Short, 1970, *Publ. Nuttall Orn. Cl.* 9

F. Goethe, 1973, *Stuttgarter Beitr. Naturk.* 261
Schnell, 1970, *Syst. Zool.* 19
D.R. Wells & Lord Medway, 1976, **Bull. B.O.C.** 96

Family **RYNCHOPIDAE**

W.B. Alexander, 1963, *Birds of the Ocean* 2nd edn. (Putnam, New York)
J.L. Peters, 1934, *Checklist of the Birds of the World* II

A.O.U., 1957, *Checklist of North American Birds* (A.O.U., Baltimore)
S.D. Ripley, 1961, *Synopsis of the Birds of India and Pakistan* (Nat. Hist. Soc., Bombay)
C. Vaurie, 1965, *Birds of the Palaearctic Fauna* II (Witherby, London)

Family **ALCIDAE**

W.B. Alexander, 1963, *Birds of the Ocean* 2nd edn. (Putnam, New York)
J.L. Peters, 1934, *Checklist of the Birds of the World* II

A.O.U., 1957, *Checklist of North American Birds* (A.O.U., Baltimore)
C. Vaurie, 1965, *Birds of the Palaearctic Fauna* II (Witherby, London)

Family **PTEROCLIDIDAE**

J.L. Peters, 1937, *Checklist of the Birds of the World* III (Harvard University Press, Cambridge, Mass.)

C.W. Benson, 1947, *Bull. B.O.C.* 67
C.M.N. White, 1965, *Revised Checklist of African Non-passerine Birds* (Govt. Printer, Lusaka)
M. Maclean, 1967, *Journ. f. Orn.* 108

Family **COLUMBIDAE**

D. Goodwin, 1970, *Pigeons and Doves of the World* (Brit. Mus. Nat. Hist., London)
J.L. Peters, 1937, *Checklist of the Birds of the World* III

C.W. Benson, 1943, *Bull. B.O.C.* 63
E. Mayr, 1945, *Birds of the Southwest Pacific* (Macmillan, New York)
W.E.C. Todd, 1947, *Proc. Biol. Soc. Wash.* 60
A.J. van Rossem, 1947, *Proc. Biol. Soc. Wash.* 60
E. Mayr, 1951, *Emu* 51
D. Amadon, 1953, *Bull. Amer. Mus. Nat. Hist.* 100
A.J. Cain, 1954, *Bull. Brit. Mus. Nat. Hist. Zool.* 2
S.D. Ripley, 1961, *Synopsis of the Birds of India and Pakistan* (Nat. Hist. Soc., Bombay)
C. Vaurie, 1965, *Birds of the Palaearctic Fauna* II (Witherby, London)
C.M.N. White, 1965, *Revised Checklist of African Non-passerine Birds* (Govt. Printer, Lusaka)
A.L. Rand & E.T. Gilliard, 1967, *Handbook of New Guinea Birds* (Weidenfeld & Nicholson, London)
D. Goodwin, 1969, *Bull. B.O.C.* 89
T.H. Cheng, *et al*, 1973, *Acta. Zool. Sin.* 19(8)
D. Holyoak, 1974, *Bull. B.O.C.* 94
H.T. Condon, 1975, *Checklist of the Birds of Australia* Pt. I (R.A.O.U., Melbourne)
P.A. Clancey, 1976, *Bull. B.O.C.* 96
M.D. Bruce, 1976, *Bull. B.O.C.* 96

Family **LORIIDAE**

J.M. Forshaw, 1973, *Parrots of the World* (Lansdowne, Melbourne)

J.L. Peters, 1937, *Checklist of the Birds of the World* III
E. Mayr & Condon, 1968, *Bull. Zool. Nom.* 25
A.W. Diamond, 1972, *Publ. Nuttall Orn. Cl.* 12
H.T. Condon, 1975, *Checklist of the Birds of Australia* Pt. I (R.A.O.U., Melbourne)

Family **CACATUIDAE**

J.M. Forshaw, 1973, *Parrots of the World* (Lansdowne, Melbourne)

J.L. Peters, 1937, *Checklist of the Birds of the World* III
H.M. Whittell, 1950, *West Aust. Nat.* 2
E. Mayr, Keast, & Serventy, 1964, *Bull. Zool. Nom.* 21(5)
J.M. Forshaw, 1968, *Emu* 67
H.T. Condon, 1975, *Checklist of the Birds of Australia* Pt. I (R.A.O.U., Melbourne)

Family **PSITTACIDAE**

J.M. Forshaw, 1973, *Parrots of the World* (Lansdowne, Melbourne)

J.L. Peters, 1937, *Checklist of the Birds of the World* III
H.T. Condon, 1941, *Rec. S. Aust. Mus.* 7
A.J. Cain, 1955, *Ibis* 97
C.M.N. White, 1965, *Revised Checklist of African Non-passerine Birds* (Govt. Printer, Lusaka)
R. Meyer de Schauensee, 1966, *The Species of Birds of South America* (Acad. Nat. Sci., Philadelphia)
J.M. Forshaw, 1966, *Mem. Qd. Mus.* 14
J.M. Forshaw, 1967, *Mem. Qd. Mus.* 15
A.L. Rand & E.T. Gilliard, 1967, *Handbook of New Guinea Birds* (Weidenfeld & Nicholson, London)
E. Mayr & Condon, 1968, *Bull. Zool. Nom.* 25
D. Holyoak, 1970, *Emu* 70
A.W. Diamond, 1972, *Publ. Nuttall Orn. Cl.* 12
D. Holyoak, 1973, *Emu* 73
G.M. Storr, 1973, *Spec. Publs. W.Aust. Mus.* 5
H.T. Condon, 1975, *Checklist of the Birds of Australia* Pt. I (R.A.O.U., Melbourne)
K.C. Parkes, 1976, *Bull. B.O.C.* 96

Family **MUSOPHAGINAE**

R.E. Moreau, 1958, *Ibis* 100(1 and 2)

C.M.N. White, 1965, *Revised Checklist of African Non-passerine Birds* (Govt. Printer, Lusaka)
C.W. Benson, *et al,* 1971, *Birds of Zambia* (Collins, London)

Family **CUCULIDAE**

J.L. Peters, 1940, *Checklist of the Birds of the World* IV (Harvard University Press, Cambridge, Mass.)

A.L. Rand, 1936, *Bull. Amer. Mus. Nat. Hist.* 72
W.W.A. Phillips, 1949, *Bull. B.O.C.* 69
A.J. Berger, 1955, *U.S. Nat. Mus. Bull.* 103
E. Stresemann, 1961, *Journ. f. Orn.* 102
C. Vaurie, 1965, *Birds of the Palaearctic Fauna* II (Witherby, London)
C.M.N. White, 1965, *Revised Checklist of African Non-passerine Birds* (Govt. Printer, Lusaka)
R. Meyer de Schauensee, 1966, *The Species of Birds of South America* (Acad. Nat. Sci., Philadelphia)
A.L. Rand & E.T. Gilliard, 1967, *Handbook of New Guinea Birds* (Weidenfeld & Nicholson, London)
C.W. Mackworth-Praed & C.H.B. Grant, 1970, *African Handbook of Birds* III (Longmans, London)
J.E. DuPont, 1971, *Philippine Birds* (Mus. Nat. Hist., Greenville, Del.)
H.T. Condon, 1975, *Checklist of the Birds of Australia* Pt. 1 (R.A.O.U., Melbourne)
Becking, 1975, *Ibis* 117
R. Woodell, 1976, *Bull. B.O.C.* 96

Family **TYTONIDAE**

J.L. Peters, 1940, *Checklist of the Birds of the World* IV

H. Schouteden, 1952, *Rev. Zool. Bot. Afr.* 46
W.H. Marshall, 1966, *Nat. Hist. Bull. Siam Soc.* 21
Sparks & Soper, 1970, *Owls* (David & Charles, Newton Abbott)
A.W. Diamond, 1972, *Publ. Nuttall Orn. Cl.* 12

Family **STRIGIDAE**

J.L. Peters, 1940, *Checklist of the Birds of the World* IV

R.T. Moore, 1947, *Proc. Biol. Soc. Wash.* 60
W.E.C. Todd, 1947, *Proc. Biol. Soc. Wash.* 60
W.N. Koelz, 1950, *Amer. Mus. Novit.* 1452
C. Vaurie, 1960–3, *Amer. Mus. Novit.* 2000, 2015, 2021, 2132
Marshall, 1966, *Nat. Hist. Bull, Siam Soc.* 21
S.D. Ripley, 1966, *Ibis* 108(1)
J. Sparks & T. Soper, 1970, *Owls* (David & Charles, Newton Abbott)
A.A. Soares, 1973, *Archives Mus. Bocage* 2 Ser. 3(2, 5)
J.P. O'Neill & G.R. Graves, 1977, *Auk* 94

Family **STEATORNITHIDAE**

J.L. Peters, 1940, *Checklist of the Birds of the World* IV

R. Meyer de Schauensee, 1966, *The Species of Birds of South America* (Acad. Nat. Sci., Philadelphia)
R. ffrench, 1973, *Guide to the Birds of Trinidad and Tobago* (Livingston, Wynnewood)

Family **PODARGIDAE**

J.L. Peters, 1940, *Checklist of the Birds of the World* IV

H.T. Condon, 1975, *Checklist of the Birds of Australia* Pt. I (R.A.O.U., Melbourne)

Family **NYCTIBIIDAE**

J.L. Peters, 1940, *Checklist of the Birds of the World* IV

R. Meyer de Schauensee, 1966, *The Species of Birds of South America* (Acad. Nat. Sci., Philadelphia)

Family **AEGOTHELIDAE**

J.L. Peters, 1940, *Checklist of the Birds of the World* IV

G.C.A. Junge, 1953, *Zool. Verh.* 20
A.L. Rand & E.T. Gilliard, 1967, *Handbook of New Guinea Birds* (Weidenfeld & Nicholson, London)
A.W. Diamond, 1972, *Publ. Nuttall Orn. Cl.* 12
H.T. Condon, 1975, *Checklist of the Birds of Australia* Pt. I (R.A.O.U., Melbourne)

Family **CAPRIMULGIDAE**

J.L. Peters, 1940, *Checklist of the Birds of the World* IV

E. Mayr, 1941, 'List of New Guinea Birds', *Amer. Mus. Nat. Hist.* 82
C. Vaurie, 1960, *Amer. Mus. Novit.* 1985
A.H. Davis, 1962, *Tex. Journ. Sci.* 14(1)
C.M.N. White, 1965, *Revised Checklist of African Non-passerine Birds* (Govt. Printer, Lusaka)
R. Meyer de Schauensee, 1966, *The Species of Birds of South America* (Acad. Nat. Sci., Philadelphia)
J. Bond, 1971, *Birds of the West Indies* (Collins, London)

Family **APODIDAE**

R.K. Brooke, 1970, *Durban Mus. Novit.* 8

C.M.N. White, *1965, Revised Checklist of African Non-passerine Birds* (Govt. Printer, Lusaka)

R. Meyer de Schauensee, 1966, *The Species of Birds of South America* (Acad. Nat. Sci., Philadelphia)

H.G. Deignan, 1955, *Bull. B.O.C.* 75
D. Lack, 1955, *Ibis* 98
D. Lack, 1956, *Auk* 73
D. Lack, 1956, *Bull. B.O.C.* 76
D. Lack, 1957, *Auk* 74
R.W. Sims, 1961, *Ibis* 103
H.G. Deignan, 1962, *Bull. B.O.C.* 82
E. Eisenmann & Lehmann, 1962, *Amer. Mus. Novit.* 2117
B.P. Hall & R.E. Moreau, 1962, *Bull. Brit. Mus. Nat. Hist. Zool.* 8
Orr, 1963, *Proc. 13th Int. Orn. Cong.* 126
Lord Medway, 1966, *Proc. Linn. Soc. London* 177(2)
C.W. Benson, 1967, *Bull. B.O.C.* 87
P. Somadikarta, 1967, *Proc. U.S. Nat. Mus.* 124
de Roo, 1968, *Rev. Zool. Bot. Afr.* 77
R.K. Brooke, 1971, *Ostrich Suppl.* 8
C.T. Collins, 1972, *Contr. Sci. L.A. County Mus.* 229(4)
A.W. Diamond, 1972, *Publ. Nuttall Orn. Cl.* 12
Behle, 1973, *Auk* 90
W.H. Phelps. 1973, *Bol. Soc. Venez. Cienc. Nat.* 30.124
D. Holyoak, 1974, *Bull. B.O.C.* 94(4) 146
D. Holyoak & Thibault, 1978, *Bull. B.O.C.* 98

Family **HEMIPROCNIDAE**

J.L. Peters, 1940, *Checklist of the Birds of the World* IV

R.K. Brooke, 1969, *Bull. B.O.C.* 89(6)

Family **TROCHILIDAE**

J.L. Peters, 1945, *Checklist of the Birds of the World* V (Harvard University Press, Cambridge, Mass.)

A. Wetmore, 1947, *Smiths. Misc. Coll.* 106
H. Friedman, Griscom, & Moore, 1950, *Pacific Coast Avifauna* 29(1)
E. Eisenmann, 1955, 'The Species of Middle American Birds', *Trans. Lin. Soc. N.Y.* 7
W.H. Phelps, 1956, *Proc. Biol. Soc. Wash.* 69
W.H. Phelps & Phelps, 1963, *Bol. Soc. Venez. Cienc. Nat.* 24
A. Wetmore, 1963, *Smiths. Misc. Coll.* 145
R. Meyer de Schauensee, 1964, *Birds of Colombia* (Livingston, Narbeth, Penn.)
Rowley & Orr, 1964, *Condor* 66(2)
J. Berlioz, 1965, *L'Oiseau* 35(1)
R. Meyer de Schauensee, 1966, *The Species of Birds of South America* (Acad. Nat. Sci., Philadelphia)
R. Meyer de Schauensee, 1967, *Not. Nat.* 402
Grantsau, 1968, *Pap. Avuls Zool.* 22(7)
Grantsau, 1969, *Pap. Avuls Zool.* 22(23)
J. Bond, 1971, *Birds of the West Indies* (Collins, London)
Ruschi, 1972, *Bol. Mus. Biol. Mello Leitao* 35
R. ffrench, 1973, *Guide to the Birds of Trinidad and Tobago* (Livingston, Wynnewood)
Ruschi, 1973, *Bol. Mus. Biol. Mello Leitao* 36
J. Berlioz, 1974, *L'Oiseau* 44(4)
J.S. Weske & J.W. Terborgh, 1977, *Condor* 79

R. Meyer de Schauensee & W.H. Phelps, 1978, *Birds of Venezuela* (Princeton University Press, Princeton)

Family **COLIIDAE**

J.L. Peters, 1945, *Checklist of the Birds of the World* V (Harvard University Press, Cambridge, Mass.)

C.M.N. White, 1965, *Revised Checklist of African Non-passerine Birds* (Govt. Printer, Lusaka)

Family **TROGONIDAE**

J.L. Peters, 1945, *Checklist of the Birds of the World* V

C.M.N. White, 1965, *Revised Checklist of African Non-passerine Birds* (Govt. Printer, Lusaka)
R. Meyer de Schauensee, 1966, *The Species of Birds of South America* (Acad. Nat. Sci., Philadelphia)

Family **ALCEDINIDAE**

J.L. Peters, 1945, *Checklist of the Birds of the World* V

C.M.N. White, 1965, *Revised Checklist of African Non-passerine Birds* (Govt. Printer, Lusaka)
A.L. Rand & E.T. Gilliard, 1967, *Handbook of New Guinea Birds* (Weidenfeld & Nicholson, London)
C.W. Benson, 1974, *L'Oiseau* 44(2)
D. Holyoak, 1974, *Bull. B.O.C.* 94(4) 147
H.T. Condon, 1975, *Checklist of the Birds of Australia* Pt. I (R.A.O.U., Melbourne)

Family **TODIDAE**

J.L. Peters, 1945, *Checklist of the Birds of the World* V

J. Bond, 1971, *Birds of the West Indies* (Collins, London)

Family **MOMOTIDAE**

J.L. Peters, 1945, *Checklist of the Birds of the World* V

A. Wetmore, 1947, *Smiths. Misc. Coll.* 106.16
A. Wetmore, 1968, *Smiths. Misc. Coll.* 150. 2

Family **MEROPIDAE**

C. Fry, 1969, *Ibis* 111
J.L. Peters, 1945, *Checklist of the Birds of the World* V

C.H.B. Grant & C.W. Mackworth-Praed, 1937, *Bull. B.O.C.* 57
H.G. Deignan, 1955, *Bull. B.O.C.* 75
C.M.N. White, 1965, *Revised Checklist of African Non-passerine Birds* (Govt. Printer, Lusaka)

Family **CORACIIDAE**

J.L. Peters, 1945, *Checklist of the Birds of the World* V

A.L. Rand, 1936, *Bull. Amer. Mus. Nat. Hist.* 72
C.M.N. White, 1965, *Revised Checklist of African Non-passerine Birds* (Govt. Printer, Lusaka)
J. Cracraft, 1971, *Auk* 88

Family **BRACHYPTERACIIDAE**

J.L. Peters, 1945, *Checklist of the Birds of the World* V

A.L. Rand, 1936, *Bull. Amer. Mus. Nat. Hist.* 72
J. Cracraft, 1971, *Auk* 88

Family **LEPTOSOMATIDAE**

J.L. Peters, 1945, *Checklist of the Birds of the World* V

A.L. Rand, 1936, *Bull. Amer. Mus. Nat. Hist.* 72

Family **UPUPIDAE**

J.L. Peters, 1945, *Checklist of the Birds of the World* V

C.M.N. White, 1965, *Revised Checklist of African Non-passerine Birds* (Govt. Printer, Lusaka)

Family **PHOENICULIDAE**

J.L. Peters, 1945, *Checklist of the Birds of the World* V

J.D. Macdonald, 1947, *Bull. B.O.C.* 67
W. Serle, 1949, *Bull. B.O.C.* 69
C.M.N. White, 1965, *Revised Checklist of African Non-passerine Birds* (Govt. Printer, Lusaka)

Family **BUCEROTIDAE**

J.L. Peters, 1945, *Checklist of the Birds of the World* V

C.H.B. Grant, 1957, *Bull. B.O.C.* 67
K. Sanft, 1960, *Das Tierreich* 76.1
S.D. Ripley, 1961, *Synopsis of the Birds of India and Pakistan* (Nat. Hist. Soc., Bombay)
C.M.N. White, 1965, *Revised Checklist of African Non-passerine Birds* (Govt. Printer, Lusaka)
J.E. DuPont, 1971, Philippine Birds (Mus. Nat. Hist., Greenville, Del.)

Family **GALBULIDAE**

J.L. Peters, 1948, *Checklist of the Birds of the World* VI (Harvard University Press, Cambridge, Mass.)

W.E.C. Todd, 1943, *Ann. Carnegie Mus.* 30
R. Meyer de Schauensee, 1966, *The Species of Birds of South America* (Acad. Nat. Sci., Philadelphia)
J. Haffer, 1974, *Publ. Nuttall Orn. Cl.* 14

Family **BUCCONIDAE**

J.L. Peters, 1948, *Checklist of the Birds of the World* VI

W.H. Phelps, 1955, *Proc. Biol. Soc. Wash.* 60
R. Meyer de Schauensee, 1966, *The Species of Birds of South America* (Acad. Nat. Sci., Philadelphia)

Family **CAPITONIDAE**

J.L. Peters, 1948, *Checklist of the Birds of the World* VI

W. Serle, 1949, *Bull. B.O.C.* 69
M.A. Traylor, 1951, *Auk* 68
Mukheriee, 1952, *Bull. B.O.C.* 72
S.D. Ripley, 1953, *Ibis* 95
C.W. Benson, 1956, *Bull. B.O.C.* 76
P.A. Clancey, 1956, *Durban Mus. Novit.* 4. 15
H.G. Deignan, 1956, *Proc. Biol. Soc. Wash.* 59
S.D. Ripley, 1961, *Synopsis of the Birds of India and Pakistan* (Nat. Hist. Soc., Bombay)
C.W. Benson & M.P.S. Irwin, 1965, *Bull. B.O.C.* 85(1)
C.M.N. White, 1965, *Revised Checklist of African Non-passerine Birds* (Govt. Printer, Lusaka)

R. Meyer de Schauensee, 1966, *The Species of Birds of South America* (Acad. Nat. Sci., Philadelphia)
Wickler, 1973, *Journ. f. Orn.* 114. 123
C. Erard, 1976, *Bull. B.O.C.* 96

Family **INDICATORIDAE**

J.L. Peters, 1948, *Checklist of the Birds of the World* VI

J.P. Chapin, 1958, *Bull. B.O.C.* 78
B.P. Hall, 1958, *Bull. B.O.C.* 78
J.P. Chapin, 1962, *Ibis* 104
C.M.N. White, 1965, *Revised Checklist of African Non-passerine Birds* (Govt. Printer, Lusaka)

Family **RAMPHASTIDAE**

J. Haffer, 1974, *Publ. Nuttall Orn. Cl.* 14

R. Meyer de Schauensee, 1945, *Proc. Acad. Nat. Sci. Phil.* 97
J.L. Peters, 1948, *Checklist of the Birds of the World* VI
R. Meyer de Schauensee, 1966, *The Species of Birds of South America* (Acad. Nat. Sci., Philadelphia)
R. Meyer de Schauensee & Phelps, 1978, *Birds of Venezuela* (Princeton University Press, Princeton)

Family **PICIDAE**

J.J. Moroney Jr., W.J. Bock, & J. Farrand Jr., 1975, *Reference List of the Birds of the World* (Amer. Mus. Nat. Hist., New York)

J.L. Peters, 1948, *Checklist of the Birds of the World* VI
R. Meinertzhagen, 1949, *Bull. B.O.C.* 69
T.H. Cheng, 1955, *Distributional List of Chinese Birds* Pt. I (Acad. Sin., Peking)
T.H. Cheng, 1956, *Act. Sinica* 8.2
K.C. Parkes, 1960, *Bull. B.O.C.* 80
B.E. Smythies, 1960, *Birds of Borneo* (Oliver & Boyd, Edinburgh)
S.D. Ripley, 1961, *Synopsis of the Birds of India and Pakistan* (Nat. Hist. Soc., Bombay)
C. Vaurie, 1965, *Birds of the Palaearctic Fauna* II (Witherby, London)
C.M.N. White, 1965, *Revised Checklist of African Non-passerine Birds* (Govt. Printer, Lusaka)
R. Meyer de Schauensee, 1966, *The Species of Birds of South America* (Acad. Nat. Sci., Philadelphia)
K.E. Stager, 1968, *Contr. Sci. L.A. County Mus.* 153.1
J.E. DuPont, 1971, *Philippine Birds* (Mus. Nat. Hist., Greenville, Del.)
L.L. Short, 1971, *Bull. Amer. Mus. Nat. Hist.* 145
W.R. Goodge, 1972, *Auk* 89
L.L. Short, 1972, *Amer. Mus. Novit.* 2487
L.L. Short, 1972, *Bull. Amer. Mus. Nat. Hist.* 149
L.L. Short, 1973, *Wilson Bull.* 85(4)
O.H. Garrido, 1973, *Poeyana* 119
W.H. Phelps, 1973, *Bol. Soc. Venez. Cienc. Nat.* 30.124
G.F. Mees, 1974, *Zool. Meded. Leiden* 48(7)
R. Meyer de Schauensee & W.H. Phelps, 1978, *Birds of Venezuela* (Princeton University Press, Princeton)

Family **EURYLAIMIDAE**

J.L. Peters, 1951, Checklist of the Birds of the World VII (Harvard University Press, Cambridge, Mass.)

T.H. Cheng, 1958, *Distributional List of Chinese Birds* II (Acad. Sin., Peking)

B.E. Smythies, 1960, *Birds of Borneo (Oliver & Boyd, Edinburgh)*
S.D. Ripley, 1961, *A Synopsis of the Birds of India and Pakistan* (Nat. Hist. Soc., Bombay)
C.M.N. White, 1961, *Revised Checklist of African Broadbills etc.*(Govt. Printer, Lusaka)
P.A. Clancey, 1970, *Bull. B.O.C.* 90
B.P. Hall & R.E. Moreau, 1970, *An Atlas of Speciation in African Passerine Birds* (Brit. Mus. Nat. Hist., London)
S.L. Olsen, 1971, *Ibis* 113

Family **DENDROCOLAPTIDAE**

J.L. Peters, 1951, *Checklist of the Birds of the World* VII

E. Eisenmann, 1955, *Trans. Lin. Soc. N.Y.* 7
J.T. Zimmer & W.H. Phelps, 1955, *Amer. Mus. Novit.* 1709
W.H. Phelps & W.H. Phelps, 1963, *Bol. Soc. Venez. Cienc. Nat.* 24
R. Meyer de Schauensee, 1964, *Birds of Colombia* (Livingston, Narberth, Pennsylvania)
L.C. Binford, 1965, *Occ. Pap. Mus. Zool. La. St. Univ.* 30
R. Meyer de Schauensee, 1966, *The Species of Birds of South America* (Acad. Nat. Sci., Philadelphia)
A. Wetmore, 1970, *Proc. Biol. Soc. Wash.* 82
E.R. Blake, 1972, *Birds of Mexico* (Chicago University Press, Chicago)
A. Feduccia, 1973, *Orn. Monog.* 13
G.F. Mees, 1974, *Zool. Meded. Leiden* 48(7)
O. Pinto, 1974, *Pap. Avuls. S. Paulo* 27(14)
R. Meyer de Schauensee & W.H. Phelps, 1978, *Birds of Venezuela* (Princeton University Press, Princeton)

Family **FURNARIIDAE**

C. Vaurie, 1971, *Classification of the Ovenbirds* (Witherby, London)

J.L. Peters, 1951, *Checklist of the Birds of the World* VII
M. Koepcke, 1953, *Beitr. Neotrop. Fauna* 1
E. Eisenmann, 1955, *Trans. Lin. Soc. N.Y.* 7
W.H. Phelps & Phelps, 1963, *Bol. Soc. Venez. Cienc. Nat.* 24
R. Meyer de Schauensee, 1964, *Birds of Colombia* (Livingston, Narberth, Penn.)
M. Koepcke, 1965, *Beitr. Neotrop. Fauna* 4
R. Meyer de Schauensee, 1966, *The Species of Birds of South America* (Acad. Nat. Sci., Philadelphia)
H. Sick, 1969, *Beitr. Neotrop. Fauna* 4
E.R. Blake, 1971, *Auk* 88
E. Mayr, 1971, *Journ. f. Orn.* 112
C. Vaurie, 1971, *Ibis* 113
C.C. Olrog, 1972, *Neotropica* 18
C. Vaurie, Weske, & Terborgh, 1972, *Bull. B.O.C.* 92
A. Feduccia, 1973, *Orn. Monog.* 13
W.H. Phelps, 1973, *Bol. Soc. Venez. Cienc. Nat.* 30.124
J.P. O'Neill & T.A. Parker III, 1976, *Bull. B.O.C.* 96
R. Meyer de Schauensee & W.H. Phelps, 1978, *Birds of Venezuela* (Princeton University Press, Princeton)

Family **FORMICARIIDAE**

J.L. Peters, 1951, *Checklist of the Birds of the World* VII

E. Eisenmann, 1955, *Trans. Lin. Soc. N.Y.* 7.128
W.H. Phelps & Phelps, 1963, *Bol. Soc. Venez. Cienc. Nat.* 24
R. Meyer de Schauensee, 1964, *Birds of Colombia* (Livingston, Narbeth, Penn.)
R. Meyer de Schauensee, 1966, *The Species of Birds of South America* (Acad. Nat. Sci., Philadelphia)
G.H. Lowery & O'Neill, 1969, *Auk* 86

E.R. Blake, 1972, *Birds of Mexico* (Chicago University Press, Chicago)
R. ffrench, 1973, *Guide to the Birds of Trinidad and Tobago* (Livingston, Wynnewood)
G.F. Mees, 1974, *Bull. B.O.C.* 59
R. Meyer de Schauensee & W.H. Phelps, 1978, *Birds of Venezuela* (Princeton University Press, Princeton)

Family **CONOPOPHAGIDAE**

J.L. Peters, 1951, *Checklist of the Birds of the World* VII

W.H. Phelps & Phelps, 1963, *Bol. Soc. Venez. Cienc. Nat.* 24
R. Meyer de Schauensee, 1964, *Birds of Colombia* (Livingston, Narberth, Penn.)
R. Meyer de Schauensee, 1966, *The Species of Birds of South America* (Acad. Nat. Sci., Philadelphia)
M.A. Heimerdinger & P.L. Ames, 1967, *Postilla* 105
P.L. Ames, *et al*, 1968, *Postilla* 114

Family **RHINOCRYPTIDAE**

J.L. Peters, 1951, *Checklist of the Birds of the World* VII

W.H. Phelps & Phelps, 1963, *Bol. Soc. Venez. Cienc. Nat.* 24
R. Meyer de Schauensee, 1964, *Birds of Colombia* (Livingston, Narberth, Penn.)
R. Meyer de Schauensee, 1966, *The Species of Birds of South America* (Acad. Nat. Sci., Philadelphia)
A. Wetmore, 1972, *Smiths. Misc. Coll.* 150
A. Wetmore, 1972, *Birds of Panama* III (Smiths. Inst., Washington)

Family **COTINGIDAE**

D.W. Snow, 1973, *Breviora* 409

J.T. Zimmer, 1936, *Amer. Mus. Novit.* 893/4
W.H. Phelps & E.T. Gilliard, 1941, *Amer. Mus. Novit.* 1153
C.E. Hellmayr & Conover, 1942, *Catalogue of Birds of the Americas* (Chicago University Press, Chicago)
W.H. Phelps & Phelps, 1949, *Proc. Biol. Soc. Wash.* 62
R. Meyer de Schauensee, 1950, *Not. Nat.* 221
N. Gyldenstolpe, 1951, *Ark. Zool.* (2)2
R. Meyer de Schauensee, 1953, *Proc. Acad. Nat. Sci. Phil.* 105
W.H. Phelps & Phelps, 1953, *Proc. Biol. Soc. Wash.* 66
E. Eisenmann, 1955, *Trans. Lin. Soc. N.Y.* 7
W.H. Phelps & Phelps, 1955, *Proc. Biol. Soc. Wash.* 68
W.H. Phelps & Phelps, 1963, *Bol. Soc. Venez. Cienc. Nat.* 24
R. Meyer de Schauensee, 1964, *Birds of Colombia* (Livingston, Narberth, Penn.)
R. Meyer de Schauensee, 1966, *The Species of Birds of South America (Acad. Nat. Sci., Philadelphia)*
A.R. Phillips, 1966, *Bull. B.O.C.* 86
E.R. Blake, 1972, *Birds of Mexico* (Chicago University Press, Chicago)
R. ffrench, 1973, *Guide to the Birds of Trinidad and Tobago* (Livingston, Wynnewood)
A. Wetmore, 1973, *Birds of Panama* III (Smiths. Inst., Washington)
J.J. Moroney Jr., W.J. Bock, & J. Farrand Jr., 1975, *Reference Book of Birds of the World* (Amer. Mus. Nat. Hist., New York)
R. Meyer de Schauensee & Phelps, 1978, *Birds of Venezuela* (Princeton University Press, Princeton)

Family **PIPRIDAE**

D.W. Snow, 1975, *Bull. B.O.C.* 95

C.B. Cory, C.E. Hellmayr, *et al*, 1927, *Catalogue of Birds of the Americas* (Chicago University Press, Chicago)

E. Eisenmann, 1955, *Trans. Lin. Soc. N.Y.* 7
W.H. Phelps & Phelps, 1963, *Bol. Soc. Venez. Cienc. Nat.* 24
R. Meyer de Schauensee, 1964, *Birds of Colombia* (Livingston, Narberth, Penn.)
Novaes, 1964, *Bol. Mus. Paraense Emilio Goeldi (Zool.)* 47
R. Meyer de Schauensee, 1966, *The Species of Birds of South America* (Acad. Nat. Sci., Philadelphia)
R. ffrench, 1973, *Guide to the Birds of Trinidad and Tobago* (Livingston, Wynnewood)
R. Meyer de Schauensee & W.H. Phelps, 1978, *Birds of Venezuela* (Princeton University Press, Princeton)

Family **TYRANNIDAE/OXYRUNCIDAE**

C.B. Cory, C.E. Hellmayr, *et al,* 1927, *Catalogue of Birds of the Americas* (Chicago University Press, Chicago)

R. Meyer de Schauensee, 1966, *Species of Birds of South America* (Acad. Nat. Sci., Philadelphia)

W.P. Brodkorb, 1943, *Occ. Pap. Mus. Zool. Mich.* 478
W.P. Brodkorb, 1950, *Auk* 67
W.E.C. Todd, 1952, *Ann. Carnegie Mus.* 32
J.T. Zimmer, 1953, *Amer. Mus. Novit.* 1605
W. Meise, 1954, *Auk* 71
E. Eisenmann, 1955, *Trans. Lin. Soc. N.Y.* 7:128
J.T. Zimmer, 1955, *Amer. Mus. Novit.* 1749
J.T. Zimmer & W.H. Phelps, 1955, *Amer. Mus. Novit.* 1709
A.O.U., 1957, *Checklist of the Birds of North America* (A.O.U., Baltimore)
W.E. Lanyon, 1963, *Amer. Mus. Novit.* 2129
W.H. Phelps & Phelps, 1963, *Bol. Soc. Venez. Cienc. Nat.* 24
R. Meyer de Schauensee, 1964, *Birds of Colombia* (Livingston, Narberth, Penn.)
L.C. Binford, 1965, *Occ. Pap. Mus. Zool. La. St. Univ.* 30
A.H. Howell, 1965, *Auk* 82
Olivares, 1965, *Caldasia* 9
C.C. Olrog & Contino, 1966, *Neotropica* 12
A.R. Phillips, 1966, *Bull. B.O.C.* 86
W.E. Lanyon, 1967, *Bull. Amer. Mus. Nat. Hist.* 136
L.L. Short, 1969, *Auk* 86
E. Mayr & Short, 1970, 'Species Taxa of N. American Birds', *Publ. Nuttall Orn. Cl.* 9
J. Bond, 1971, *Birds of the West Indies* (Collins, London)
E. Eisenmann & W.H. Phelps, 1971, *Ornitologia* XXIX
E. Eisenmann & W.H. Phelps, 1971, *Bol. Soc. Venez. Cienc. Nat.* 29
Palerm, 1971, *Bol. Soc. Zool. Uruguay* 1
F. Vuilleumier, 1971, *Bull. Mus. Comp. Zool. Harv.* 141
E.R. Blake, 1972, *Birds of Mexico* (Chicago University Press, Chicago)
A. Wetmore, 1972, *Birds of Panama* III (Smiths. Inst., Washington)
E. Eisenmann & W.H. Phelps, 1973, *Bol. Soc. Venez. Cienc. Nat.* 29.119
E. Eisenmann, 1973, *Auk* 90
O.H. Garrido, 1973, *Poeyana* 119
R. ffrench, 1973, *Guide to the Birds of Trinidad and Tobago* (Livingston, Wynnewood)
D.W. Snow, 1973, *Breviora* 409
J.P. O'Neill & T.A. Parker III, 1976, *Bull. B.O.C.* 96
R. Meyer de Schauensee & W.H. Phelps, 1978, *Birds of Venezuela* (Princeton University Press, Princeton)
G.F. Mees, 1974, *Zool. Meded. Leiden* 48(7)

Family **PHYTOTOMIDAE**

C.B. Cory, C.E. Hellmayr, *et al,* 1927, *Catalogue of Birds of the Americas* (Chicago University Press, Chicago)

28

R. Meyer de Schauensee, 1966, *The Species of Birds of South America* (Acad. Nat. Sci., Philadelphia)

Family **PITTIDAE**

J.J. Moroney Jr., W.J. Bock, & J. Farrand Jr., 1975, *Reference List of the Birds of the World* (Amer. Mus. Nat. Hist., New York)

B.B. Rensch, 1929, *Journ. f. Orn.* Erg. III
B.B. Rensch, 1931, *Mitt. Zool. Mus. Berl.* 17
E. Stresemann, 1939–41, 'Die Vögel von Celebes', *J. f. Orn.* 87. 88. 89
S.D. Ripley, 1941, *Occ. Pap. N.H.S. Boston* 8
H.M. Whittell, 1943, *Emu* 43
H.G. Deignan, 1945, *Smiths. Inst. Bull.* 186
E. Mayr, 1945, *Birds of the Southwest Pacific* (Macmillan, New York)
J. Delacour, 1947, *Birds of Malaysia* (Hamilton, New York)
A.C.V. van Bemmell, 1948, *Treubia* 19
B.E. Smythies, 1953, *Birds of Burma* (Oliver & Boyd, Edinburgh)
E. Mayr, 1955, *Amer. Mus. Novit.* 1707
T.H. Cheng, 1958, *Distributional List of Chinese Birds* Pt. II (Acad. Sin., Peking)
J. Delacour & Jabouille, 1960, *L'Oiseau* 10
B.E. Smythies, 1960, *Birds of Borneo* (Oliver & Boyd, Edinburgh)
S.D. Ripley, 1961, *Synopsis of the Birds of India and Pakistan* (Nat. Hist. Soc., Bombay)
C.M.N. White, 1961, *Revised Checklist of African Broadbills etc.* (Govt. Printer, Lusaka)
S.D. Ripley & Rabor, 1962, 'New Birds from Culion Is. and Palawan', *Postilla* 73
A.L. Rand & E.T. Gilliard, 1967, *Handbook of New Guinea Birds* (Weidenfeld & Nicholson, London)
V. Serventy, 1968, *Bull. B.O.C.* 88
B.P. Hall & R.E. Moreau, 1970, *Atlas of Speciation in African Passerine Birds* (Brit. Mus. Nat. Hist., London)
J.E. DuPont, 1971, *Philippine Birds* (Mus. Nat. Hist., Greenville, Del.)
K.C. Parkes, 1971, *Bull. B.O.C.* 91
R. Schodde, 1975, *Interim List of Australian Songbirds, Passerines* (R.A.O.U., Melbourne)
B. King, 1978, *Bull. B.O.C.* 98

Family **XENICIDAE**

O.S.N.Z., 1970, *Annotated Checklist of the Birds of New Zealand* (Reed, Wellington)

R.A. Falla, Sibson, & Turbot, 1966, *Field Guide to the Birds of New Zealand* (Collins, London)

Family **PHILEPITTIDAE**

A.L. Rand, 1936, *Bull. Amer. Mus. Nat. Hist.* 72

D. Amadon, 1951, *L'Oiseau* 21
A.L. Thomson, 1964, *New Dictionary of Birds* (McGraw-Hill, New York)

Family **MENURIDAE**

R. Schodde, 1975, *Interim List of Australian Songbirds, Passerines* (R.A.O.U., Melbourne)

J.D. Macdonald, 1973, *Birds of Australia* (Witherby, London)
P. Slater, 1975, *Field Guide to Australian Birds, Passerines* (S.A.P., Edinburgh)

Family **ATRICHORNITHIDAE**

R. Schodde, 1975, *Interim List of Australian Songbirds, Passerines* (R.A.O.U., Melbourne)

J.D. Macdonald, 1973, *Birds of Australia* (Witherby, London)
P. Slater, 1975, *Field Guide to Australian Birds, Passerines* (S.A.P., Edinburgh)

Family **ALAUDIDAE**

J.L. Peters, 1960, *Checklist of the Birds of the World* IX (Harvard University Press, Cambridge, Mass.)

C.W. Mackworth-Praed & C.H.B. Grant, 1933–70, *African Handbook of Birds* Ser. 1–3 (Longmans, London)
C.W. Mackworth-Praed & C.H.B. Grant, 1939, *Bull. B.O.C.* 59
A.O.U., 1957, *Checklist of North American Birds* (A.O.U., Baltimore)
T.H. Cheng, 1958, *Distributional List of Chinese Birds* Pr. II (Acad. Sin., Peking)
C. Vaurie, 1959, *Birds of the Palaearctic Fauna* I (Witherby, London)
C.M.N. White, 1960, *Bull. B.O.C.* 80
S.D. Ripley, 1961, *Synopsis of the Birds of India and Pakistan* (Nat. Hist. Soc., Bombay)
C.M.N. White, 1961, *Revised Checklist of African Broadbills etc.* (Govt. Printer, Lusaka)
C.W. Benson & M.P.S. Irwin, 1965, *Arnoldia* 37
A.A. Da Rosa Pinto, 1965, *Mem. Inst. Invest. Cient. Mozambique* 5
Winterbottom 1965 *L'Oiseau* 35
C. W. Benson 1966 *Bull. B.O.C.* 86
P. A. Clancey 1966 *Durban Mus. Novit.* 7
R. Meyer De Schauensee 1966 *The Species of Birds of South America* (Acad. Nat. Sci., Philadelphia)
R. D. Etchecopar & Hüe 1964 *Les Oiseaux du Nord de l'Afrique* (Boubée, Paris)
L. S. Stepanyan 1967 *Acta. Orn.* 10(4)
H. Kumerloeve 1969 *Journ. Orn. Leipzig* 110
B. P. Hall & R. E. Moreau 1970 *Atlas of Speciation in African Passerine Birds* (Brit. Mus. Nat. Hist., London)
H. Kumerloeve 1970 *Beitr. Vogelk.* 16
G. Rudebeck 1970 *Ornis. Scand.* 1
E. R. Blake 1972 *Birds of Mexico* (Chicago University Press, Chicago)
P. A. Clancey 1972 *Durban Mus. Novit.* 9
A. R. Phillips 1972 *Bull. B.O.C.* 90
J. M. Winterbottom 1972 *Ostrich* 43
C. Erard & G. Jarry 1973 *Bull. B.O.C.* 93
C. Erard & R. De Naurois 1973 *Bull. B.O.C.* 93

Family **HIRUNDINIDAE**

J. L. Peters 1960 *Checklist of the Birds of the World* IX

C.W. Mackworth-Praed & C.H.B. Grant 1933–70 *African Handbook of Birds* Ser. 1–3 (Longmans, London)
C. M. N. White 1937 *Bull. B.O.C.* 57
E. Mayr & Bond 1943 *Ibis* 85
E. Eisenmann 1955 *Trans. Lin. Soc.* N.Y. 7.
A.O.U. 1957 *Checklist of North American Birds* (A.O.U., Baltimore)
C. Vaurie, 1959, *Birds of the Palaearctic Fauna* I (Witherby, London)
S.D. Ripley, 1960, *Postilla* 43
S.D. Ripley, 1961, *Synopsis of the Birds of India and Pakistan* (Nat. Hist. Soc., Bombay)
C.M.N. White, 1961, *Revised Checklist of African Broadbills etc.* (Govt. Printer, Lusaka)
P.A. Clancey & Irwin, 1966, *Durban Mus. Novit.* 8
R. Meyer de Schauensee, 1966, *The Species of Birds of South America* (Acad. Nat. Sci., Philadelphia)
E.T. Gilliard & Lecroy, 1967, *Bull. Amer. Mus. Nat. Hist.* 135
K. Thonglongya, 1968, *Thai. Mus. Sci. Pap. Fauna* 1
P.A. Clancey, 1969, *Durban Mus. Novit.* 8
J. Bond, 1971, *Birds of the West Indies* (Collins, London)
K.C. Parkes, 1971, *Nemouria* 4
H.E. Wolters, 1971, *Bonn. Zool. Beitr.* 22
R.K. Brooke, 1972, *Bull. B.O.C.* 92
R.K. Brooke, 1974, *Durban Mus. Novitates* 10(a)
L.S. Stepanyan, 1974, *Zool. Zh.* 53.8
R. Schodde, 1975, *Interim List of Australian Songbirds, Passerines* (R.A.O.U., Melbourne)

Family **MOTACILLIDAE**

J.L. Peters, 1960, *Checklist of the Birds of the World* IX

B.E. Smythies, 1953, *Birds of Burma* (Oliver & Boyd, Edinburgh)
T.H. Cheng, 1958, *Distributional List of Chinese Birds* II (Acad. Sin., Peking)
C. Vaurie, 1959, *Birds of the Palaearctic Fauna* I (Witherby, London)
B.P. Hall, 1961, *Bull. Amer. Mus. Nat. Hist.* 7(5)
C.M.N. White, 1961, *Revised Checklist of African Broadbills etc.* (Govt. Printer, Lusaka)
R. Meyer de Schauensee, 1966, *The Species of Birds of South America* (Acad. Nat. Sci., Philadelphia)
B.P. Hall & R.E. Moreau, 1970, *Atlas of Speciation in African Passerine Birds* (Brit. Mus. Nat. Hist., London)
O.S.N.Z., 1970, *Annotated Checklist of the Birds of New Zealand* (Reed, Wellington)

Family **CAMPEPHAGIDAE**

J.L. Peters, Mayr, & Deignan, 1960, in J.L. Peters *Checklist of the Birds of the World* IX

B. Rensch, 1929, *Journ. f. Orn.* Erg. III
E. Mayr, 1940, *Emu* 40
S.D. Ripley, 1941, *Auk* 58
E. Mayr, 1945, *Birds of the Southwest Pacific* (Macmillan, New York)
A.C.V. van Bemmell, 1948, *Treubia* 19
K.H. Voous & van Marle, 1949, *Bijdr. Dierk* 28
E. Mayr, 1955, *Amer. Mus. Novit.* 1707
A.J. Keast, 1958, *Aust. Journ. Zool.* 6
S.D. Ripley, 1961, *Synopsis of the Birds of India and Pakistan* (Nat. Hist. Soc., Bombay)
I.C.J. Galbraith & E.H. Galbraith, 1962, *Bull. Brit. Mus. Nat. Hist.* 9
C.M.N. White, 1962, *Revised Checklist of African Shrikes etc.* (Govt. Printer, Lusaka)
F. Salamonsen, 1964, *Noona Dan Pap.* 9
E.T. Gilliard & Lecroy, 1967, *Bull. Amer. Mus. Nat. Hist.* 135(4)
A.L. Rand & E.T. Gilliard, 1967, *Handbook of New Guinea Birds* (Weidenfeld & Nicholson, London)
A.W. Diamond, 1969, *Amer. Mus. Novit.* 2362
I.C.J. Galbraith, 1969, *Emu* 69
K.C. Parkes, 1971, *Nemouria* 4
J.E. DuPont, 1972, *Nemouria* 7
K.C. Parkes, 1974, *Annals Carn. Mus.* 45.3
R. Schodde, 1975, *Interim Checklist of Australian Songbirds, Passerines* (R.A.O.U., Melbourne)

Family **PYCNONOTIDAE**

A.L. Rand & Deignan, 1960, in J.L. Peters *Checklist of the Birds of the World* IX

C.W. Mackworth-Praed & C.H.B. Grant, 1933–70, *African Handbook of Birds*, Ser. 1–3 (Longmans, London)
A.L. Rand, 1958, *Fieldiana* 35
C.M.N. White, 1962, *Revised Checklist of African Shrikes etc.* (Govt. Printer, Lusaka)
H.G. Deignan, 1963, *Checklist of the Birds of Thailand* (Smiths. Inst., Washington)
A. Hoogerwerf, 1965, *Bull. B.O.C.* 85
De Roo, 1967, *Rev. Zool. Bot. Afr.* 75
P.A. Clancey, 1969, *Durban Mus. Novit.* 8
A. Prigogine, 1969, *Rev. Zool. Bot. Afr.* 79
A.L. Rand & Rabor, 1969, *Fieldiana, Zool.* 51
B.P. Hall & R.E. Moreau, 1970, *Atlas of Speciation in African Passerine Birds* (Brit. Mus. Nat. Hist., London)
P.R. Colston, 1972, *Ibis* 114(1)
A. Prigogine, 1972, *Bull. B.O.C.* 92(5)

Family **IRENIDAE**

J. Delacour, 1960, in J.L. Peters *Checklist of the Birds of the World* IX

Marien, 1952, *Amer. Mus. Novit.* 1589
B.P. Hall, 1957, *Ibis* 74
S.D. Ripley, 1961, *Synopsis of the Birds of India and Pakistan* (Nat. Hist. Soc., Bombay)
Prescott, 1970, *Bull. B.O.C.* 90
J.E. Dupont, 1972, *Philippine Birds* (Mus. Nat. Hist., Greenville, Del.)

Family **LANIIDAE**

A.L. Rand, 1960, in J.L. Peters *Checklist of the Birds of the World* IX

E. Mayr, 1943, *Ibis* 57
C. Vaurie, 1959, *Birds of the Palaearctic Fauna* I (Witherby, London)
S.D. Ripley, 1961, *Synopsis of the Birds of India and Pakistan* (Nat. Hist. Soc., Bombay)
C.M.N. White, 1962, *Revised Checklist of African Shrikes etc.* (Govt. Printer, Lusaka)
P.A. Clancey, 1965, *Arnoldia* 23
A.A. Da Rosa Pinto, 1965, *Mem. Inst. Invest. Cient. Mozambique* 5
P.A. Clancey, 1969, *Durban Mus. Novit.* 8
P.A. Clancey, 1970, *Durban Mus. Novit.* 9
B.P. Hall & R.E. Moreau, 1970, *Atlas of Speciation in African Passerine Birds* (Brit. Mus. Nat. Hist., London)
C.W. Benson, *et al,* 1971, *Birds of Zambia* (Collins, London)
G.D. Field, 1979, *Bull. B.O.C.* 99.2

Family **VANGIDAE**

A.L. Rand, 1960, in J.L. Peters *Checklist of the Birds of the World* IX

A.L. Rand, 1936, *Bull. Amer. Mus. Nat. Hist.* 72

Family **BOMBYCILLIDAE**

J.C. Greenway, 1960, in J.L. Peters *Checklist of the Birds of the World* IX

O.L. Austin & N. Kuroda, 1953, *Bull. Mus. Comp. Zool.* 109(4)
R. Meinertzhagen, 1954, *Birds of Arabia* (Oliver & Boyd, Edinburgh)
A.O.U., 1957, *Checklist of the Birds of North America* (A.O.U., Baltimore)
C. Vaurie, 1959, *Birds of the Palaearctic Fauna* I (Witherby, London)
E.R. Blake, 1972, *Birds of Mexico* (Chicago University Press, Chicago)
A.R. Phillips, 1966, *Bull. B.O.C.* 86

Family **DULIDAE**

J.C. Greenway, 1960, in J.L. Peters *Checklist of the Birds of the World* IX

J. Bond, 1971, *Birds of the West Indies* (Collins, London)

Family **CINCLIDAE**

J.C. Greenway, 1960, in J.L. Peters *Checklist of the Birds of the World* IX

C. Vaurie, 1955, *Amer. Mus. Novit.* 1751
J.C. Greenway & C. Vaurie, 1958, *Mus. Comp. Zool.* 89
C. Vaurie, 1959, *Birds of the Palaearctic Fauna* I (Witherby, London)
R. Meyer de Schauensee, 1966, *The Species of Birds of South America* (Acad. Nat. Sci., Philadelphia)
A.R. Phillips, 1966, *Bull. B.O.C.* 86

Family **TROGLODYTIDAE**

R.A. Paynter & C. Vaurie, 1960, in J.L. Peters *Checklist of the Birds of the World* IX

W.H. Phelps & Phelps, 1963, *Bol. Soc. Venez. Cienc. Nat.* 24
R. Meyer de Schauensee, 1964, *Birds of Columbia* (Livingstone, Narberth, Penn.)
P. Slud, 1964, *Bull. Amer. Mus. Nat. Hist.* 128
R. Meyer de Schauensee, 1966, *The Species of Birds of South America* (Acad. Nat. Sci., Philadelphia)
A.R. Phillips, 1966, *Bull. B.O.C.* 86
E.R. Blake, 1972, *Birds of Mexico* (Chicago University Press, Chicago)
L. Irby Davies, 1972, *Field Guide to the Birds of Mexico and Central America* (Texas University, Austin)
R.S. Crossin & C.A. Ely, 1973, *Condor* 75(2)
R.W. Dickermann, 1973, *Condor* 75(3)
H.M. Stevenson, 1973, *Auk* 90
A. Wetmore, 1973, *Birds of Panama* III (Smiths. Inst., Washington)
R.W. Dickermann, 1975, *Amer. Mus. Novit.* 2569
R. Meyer de Schauensee & W.H. Phelps, 1978, *Birds of Venezuela* (Princeton University Press, Princeton)

Family **MIMIDAE**

J. Davis & A.H. Miller, 1960, in J.L. Peters *Checklist of the Birds of the World* IX

A.R. Phillips, 1964, *Revta. Soc. Mex. Hist. Nat.* 25
R. Meyer de Schauensee, 1966, *The Species of Birds of South America* (Acad. Nat. Sci., Philadelphia)
J. Bond, 1971, *Birds of the West Indies* (Collins, London)
E.R. Blake, 1972, *Birds of Mexico* (Chicago University Press, Chicago)
L. Irby Davis, 1972, *Field Guide to the Birds of Mexico and Central America* (Texas University, Austin)

Family **PRUNELLIDAE**

S.D. Ripley, 1964, in J.L. Peters *Checklist of the Birds of the World* X (Harvard, University Press, Cambridge, Mass.)

C. Vaurie, 1959, *Birds of the Palaearctic Fauna* I (Witherby, London)
H.G. Deignan, 1964, *Bull. B.O.C.* 84
Mauersberger, 1971, *Journ. f. Orn.* 112

Subfamily TURDINAE

S.D. Ripley, 1964, in J.L. Peters *Checklist of the Birds of the World* X (Mus. Comp. Zool., Cambridge, Mass.)

E. Stresemann, 1940, *Journ. f. Orn.* 88
J. Dorst, 1950, *Ois. Rev. Fr. Orn.* 20
J.P. Chapin, 1953, *Bull. Amer. Mus. Nat. Hist.* 75A
G.P. Dementiev & Gladkov (eds.), 1954, *Birds of the Soviet Union* (Moscow)
R. Meinertzhagen, 1954, *Birds of Arabia* (Oliver & Boyd, Edinburgh)
C. Vaurie, 1955, *Amer. Mus. Novit.* 1731
J.T. Zimmer & W.H. Phelps, 1955, *Amer. Mus. Novit.* 1709
S.D. Ripley, 1958, *Postilla* 37
C. Vaurie, 1959, *Birds of the Palaearctic Fauna* I (Witherby, London)
B.P. Hall, 1961, *Bull. B.O.C.* 81
C.M.N. White, 1961, *Bull. B.O.C.* 81
I.C.J. Galbraith & E.H. Galbraith, 1962, *Bull. Brit. Mus. Nat. Hist.* 9
S.D. Ripley, 1962, *Postilla* 63

C.M.N. White, 1962, *Revised Checklist of African Shrikes etc.* (Govt. Printer, Lusaka)
A.H. Howell, 1965, *Auk* 82
N. Kuroda, 1965, *Misc. Rep. Yamashina Inst. Orn. Zool.* 4
Phillips & Rook, 1965, *Condor* 67
L.S. Stepanyan, 1965, *Trudy Zool. Mus. Moscow* 9
P.A. Clancey, 1966, *Durban Mus. Novit.* 7
R. Meyer de Schauensee, 1966, *The Species of Birds of South America* (Acad. Nat. Sci., Philadelphia)
A.R. Phillips, 1966, *Bull. B.O.C.* 86
S.D. Ripley & Heinrich, 1966, *Postilla* 95
E.T. Gilliard & Lecroy, 1967, *Bull. Amer. Mus. Nat. Hist.* 135(4)
C.G. Sibley, 1968, *Postilla* 125
P.A. Clancey, 1969, *Durban Mus. Novit.* 8
P.A. Clancey & Lawson, 1969, *Bull. B.O.C.* 89
A.R. Phillips, 1969, *Auk* 86
A. Prigogine, 1969, *Rev. Zool. Bot. Afr.* 79
A. Berlioz & W. Roche, 1970, *Monitore Zool. Ital.* Suppl. 3.12
B.R. Hall & R.E. Moreau, 1970, *Atlas of Speciation in African Passerine Birds* (Brit. Mus. Nat. Hist., London)
T. Farkas, 1971, *Ostrich* 42(9)
H.E. Wolters, 1971, *Bonn. Zoo. Beitr.* 22
P.A. Clancey, 1972, *Durban Mus. Novit.* 9
T. Farkas, 1972, *Ostrich* 43
T. Farkas, 1973, *Bull. B.O.C.* 93
Olrog, 1973, *Acta. Zool. Lilloana* 30
J.D. Webster, 1973, *Auk* 90
P.A. Clancey, 1974, *Durban Mus. Novit.* 10
P.A. Clancey, 1974, *Arnoldia* 6(28)
M.P.S. Irwin & P.A. Clancey, 1974, *Arnoldia* 6(34)
Harrison, 1977, *Bull. B.O.C.* 97
A. Prigogine, 1977, *Bull. B.O.C.* 97
Orenstein, 1979, *Ibis,* 121

Subfamily ORTHONYCHINAE

H.G. Deignan, 1964, in J.L. Peters *Checklist of the Birds of the World* X

H.T. Condon, 1962, *Rec. South Austr. Mus.* 14
A.L. Rand & E.T. Gilliard, 1967, *Handbook of New Guinea Birds* (Weidenfeld & Nicholson, London)
J.D. Macdonald, 1968, *Emu* 68
A.W. Diamond, 1969, *Amer. Mus. Novit.* 2362
J. Ford, 1971, *Emu* 71
J. Ford & Parker, 1973, *Emu* 73
J. Ford, 1974, *Emu* 74
R. Schodde, 1975, *Interim List of Australian Songbirds, Passerines* (R.A.O.U., Melbourne)
J. Ford, 1977, *Proc. 16th Int. Orn Cong.*

Subfamily TIMALIINAE

H.G. Deignan, 1964, in J.L. Peters *Checklist of the Birds of the World* X

J.P. Chapin, 1953, *Bull. Amer. Mus. Nat. Hist.* 75A
B.E. Smythies, 1953, *The Birds of Burma* (Oliver & Boyd, Edinburgh)
T.H. Cheng, 1958, *Distributional List of Chinese Birds* Pt. II (Acad. Sin., Peking)
C. Vaurie, 1959, *Birds of the Palaearctic Fauna* I (Witherby, London)
H.G. Deignan, 1960, *Emu* 60
B.E. Smythies, 1960, *The Birds of Borneo* (Oliver & Boyd, Edinburgh)
S.D. Ripley, 1961, *Synopsis of the Birds of India and Pakistan* (Nat. Hist. Soc., Bombay)
C.M.N. White, 1962, *Revised Checklist of African Shrikes etc.* (Govt. Printer, Lusaka)
R.B. Cowles, 1964, *Emu* 64

A. Prigogine, 1964, *Rev. Zool. Bot. Afr.* 70
C. Vaurie, 1965, *L'Oiseau* 34
A. Hoogerwerf, 1966, *Misc. Rep. Yamashina Inst. Orn.* 4
S.D. Ripley & Heinrich 1966, *Postilla* 95
S. Ali & S.D. Ripley, 1971, *Birds of India and Pakistan* VI (Oxford University Press, Oxford)
J.E. DuPont, 1971, *Philippine Birds* (Mus. Nat. Hist., Greenville, Del.)
J.E. DuPont, 1971, *Nemouria* 3
J. Ford, 1971, *Emu* 71
J.E. Dupont & Rabor, 1973, *Nemouria* 9
P.A. Clancey, 1974, *Durban Mus. Novit.* X.2
T.H. Cheng, 1974, *Acta. Zool. Sin.* 20(1)
D.R. Wells & Lord Medway, 1976, *Bull. B.O.C.* 96
C.F. Mann, *et al*, 1978, *Bull. B.O.C.* 98

Subfamily PANURINAE

H.G. Deignan, 1964, in J.L. Peters *Checklist of the Birds of the World* X

C. Vaurie, 1954, *Amer. Mus. Novit.* 1669
T.H. Cheng, 1958, *Distributional List of Chinese Birds* Pt. II (Acad. Sin., Peking)
C. Vaurie, 1959, *Birds of the Palaearctic Fauna* I (Witherby, London)
T.H. Cheng, 1973, *Acta. Zool. Sin.* 19(1)

Subfamily PICATHARTINAE

H.G. Deignan, 1964, in J.L. Peters *Checklist of the Birds of the World* X

C.M.N. White, 1960, *Revised Checklist of African Muscicapidae etc.* (Govt. Printer, Lusaka)

Subfamily POLIOPTILINAE

R.A. Paynter, 1964, in J.L. Peters *Checklist of the Birds of the World* X

W.H. Phelps & Phelps, 1950, *Bol. Soc. Venez. Cienc. Nat.* 12
R. Meyer de Schauensee, 1951, *Caldasia* 5
E.R. Blake, 1953, *Birds of Mexico* (Chicago University Press, Chicago)
A.L. Rand & Traylor, 1953, *Auk* 70
E. Eisenmann, 1955, 'The Species of Middle American Birds', *Trans. Lin. Soc. N.Y.* 7
A.H. Miller, *et al*, 1957, 'Pacific Coast Avifauna', *Cooper Orn. Soc.* 33
R. Meyer de Schauensee, 1966, *A Guide to the Birds of South America* (Livingston, Wynnewood, Pennsylvania)
K.C. Parkes, 1979, *Bull. B.O.C.* 99(2)

Subfamily SYLVIINAE

J.J. Moroney Jr., W.J. Bock, & J. Farrand Jr., 1975, *Reference List of the Birds of the World* (Amer. Mus. Nat. Hist., New York)
C. Vaurie, 1959, *Birds of the Palaearctic Fauna* Pt. I (Witherby, London)

B. Rensch, 1929, *Journ. f. Orn. Erg.* III
H. Lynes, 1930, *Ibis* 12(6)
G.M. Mathews, 1930, *Syst. Avium Austr.* Pt. II (B.O.U., London)
A.L. Rand, 1936, *Bull. Amer. Mus. Nat. Hist.* 72
C.B. Ticehurst, 1938, *The Genus Phylloscopus* (Brit. Mus. Nat. Hist., London)
H.F. Witherby, *et al*, 1938, *Handbook of British Birds* II
E. Stresemann, 1939–41, *Journ. f. Orn.* 87(3). 88(1). 88(3). 89(1)
S.D. Ripley, 1941, *Occ. Pap. N.H.S. Boston* 8
E. Mayr, 1944, *Bull. Amer. Mus. Nat. Hist.* 83(2)
E. Mayr, 1945, *Birds of the Southwest Pacific* (Macmillan, New York)
J. Delacour, 1947, *Birds of Malaysia* (Macmillan, New York)

E. Mayr, 1948, *Emu* 47
A.C.V. van Bemmell, 1948, *Treubia* 19(2)
E. Stresemann & J. Arnold, 1949, *Journ. Bombay Nat. Hist. Soc.* 48
J. Baker, 1951, *Univ. Kan. Pub. Mus. Nat. Hist.* 3(1)
J. Delacour, 1952, *Ibis* 94
H. Schouteden, 1952, *Rev. Zool. Bot. Afr.* XLVI
B.E. Smythies, 1953, *Birds of Burma* (Oliver & Boyd, Edinburgh)
G.P. Dementiev & Gladkov (eds.), 1954, *Birds of the Soviet Union* (Moscow)
C.W. Mackworth-Praed & C.H.B. Grant, 1955–73, *African Handbook of Birds* Ser. 1–3 (Longmans, London)
E. Mayr, 1955, *Amer. Mus. Novit.* 1707
C. Vaurie, 1956, *Ibis* 99
T.H. Cheng, 1958, *Distributional List of Chinese Birds* Pt. II (Acad. Sin., Peking)
C.W. Benson, 1960, *Ibis* 103 b
E.T. Gilliard, 1960, *Amer. Mus. Novit.* 2008
G.C. Munro, 1960, *Birds of Hawaii* (Bridgeway Press, Rutland, Vermont)
B.E. Smythies, 1960, *Birds of Borneo* (Oliver & Boyd, Edinburgh)
C.M.N. White, 1960, 'Checklist of Ethiopian Musc. (Sylv.) 1 + 2', *Occ. Pap. Nat. Mus. Sci. Rhodesia*
A.J. Keast, 1961, *Bull. Amer. Mus. Nat. Hist.* 123(8)
S.D. Ripley, 1961, *Synopsis of the Birds of India and Pakistan* (Nat. Hist. Soc., Bombay)
I.C.J. Galbraith & E.H. Galbraith, 1962, *Bull. Brit. Mus. Nat. Hist.* 9
H.G. Deignan, 1963, *Bull. U.S. Nat. Mus.* 226
E. Mayr, 1963, *Emu* 63
A.R. Phillips, 1964, *Revta. Soc. Mex. Hist. Nat.* 25
P.A. Clancey, 1965, *Durban Mus. Novit.* VII
F. Salomonsen, 1965, *Vidensk. Meddr. dansk naturh Foren* 128
C.W. Benson & M.P.S. Irwin, 1966, *Arnoldia* (2)27
M.P.S. Irwin, 1966, *Bull. Brit. Orn. Cl.* 86
M.P.S. Irwin, 1966, *Durban Mus. Novit.* VIII
S.D. Ripley & Heinrich, 1966, *Postilla* 95/96
E.T. Gilliard & Lecroy, 1967, *Bull. Amer. Mus. Nat. Hist.* 135(4)
A.L. Rand & E.T. Gilliard, 1967, *Handbook of New Guinea Birds* (Weidenfeld & Nicholson, London)
G.M. Storr, 1967, *Spec. Publs. West Aust. Mus.* 4
C.W. Benson & Penny, 1968, *Bull. B.O.C.* 88
Phillips, 1968, *Journ. Bombay Nat. Hist. Soc.* 65
P.A. Clancey, 1969, *Bull. B.O.C.* 89
P.A. Clancey, 1970, *Durban Mus. Novit.* VIII
de Roo, 1970, *Rev. Zool. Bot. Afr.* 82
B.P. Hall & R.E. Moreau, 1970, *Atlas of Speciation in African Passerine Birds* (Brit. Mus. Nat. Hist., London)
O.S.N.Z., 1970, *Annotated Checklist of the Birds of New Zealand* (Reed, Wellington)
K.C. Parkes, 1970, *Bull. B.O.C.* 90
L.S. Stepanyan, 1970, *Biol. Nauki* 1970 (11)
P.A. Clancey, 1971, *Durban Mus. Novit.* IX
J.E. DuPont, 1971, *Philippine Birds* (Mus. Nat. Hist., Greenville, Del.)
K.C. Parkes, 1971, *Nemouria* 4
A.W. Diamond, 1972, *Publ. Nuttall Orn. Cl.* 12
L.S. Stepanyan, 1972, *Zool. Zhurn.* 51(12)
C. Chappuis & C. Erard, 1973, *Bull. B.O.C.* 93
P.A. Clancey, 1973, *Durban Mus. Novit.* X(i)
B.A. Kazakov, 1973, *Zoologicheskij Zh.* 52(4)
P.A. Clancey, 1973, *Arnoldia* 6
A. Prigogine, 1973, *Rev. Zool. Bot. Afr.* 87(3)
P.A. Clancey, 1974, *Durban Mus. Novit.* IX(ii)
P.A. Clancey, 1974, *Durban Mus. Novit.* X(VII)
C. Erard, 1974, *Bull. B.O.C.* 94(1)
C. Erard, 1974, *Bonn Zool. Beitr.* 25(1–3)
Ford & Parker, 1974, *Emu* 74
C.H. Fry, K, Williamson & I.J. Ferguson Lees, 1974, *Ibis* 116(3)
L.G. Grimes, 1974, *Bull. B.O.C.* 94(3)

B.A. Kazokov, 1974, *Vestriik Zool.* 1974(2)
Kinsky, 1975, *Bull. B.O.C.* 95
C. Erard, 1978, *Bull. B.O.C. 98*
D.T. Holyoak & J-C Thibault, 1978, *Bull. B.O.C.* 98
D.B. Hanmer, 1979, *Bull. B.O.C.* 99

Subfamily MALURINAE

J.J. Moroney Jr., W.J. Bock, & J. Farrand Jr., 1975, *Reference List of the Birds of the World* (Amer. Mus. Nat. Hist., New York)

R. Schodde, 1975, *Interim List of Australian Songbirds, Passerines* (R.A.O.U., Melbourne)

G.M. Mathews, 1930, *Syst. Avium Aust.* Pt. II (B.O.U., London)
W. Meise, 1931, *Novit. Zool.* 36
G. Mack, 1934, *Mem. Natn. Mus. Vict.* 8
G. Mack, 1936, *Mem. Natn. Mus. Vict.* 10
E. Mayr, 1937, *Amer. Mus. Novit.* 904
E. Mayr & Serventy, 1938, *Emu* 38
H.T. Condon, 1951, *S. Aust. Orn.* 20
A.J. Keast, 1957, *Proc. R. Zool. Soc. N.S.W.* 1955–6
A.J. Keast, 1957, *Aust. Journ. Zool.* 6
A.J. Keast, 1961, *Bull. Mus. Comp. Zool.* 123(8)
G.F. Mees, 1961, *Journ. Proc. R. Soc. West Aust.* 44
A.H. Miller, 1964, *Auk* 81(2)
J. Ford, 1966, *Emu* 66
J.C. Greenway, 1966, *Amer. Mus. Novit.* 2258
A.L. Rand & E.T. Gilliard, 1967, *Handbook of New Guinea Birds* (Weidenfeld & Nicholson, London)
N.J. Favaloro & McEvey, 1968, *Mem. Natn. Mus. Vict.* 28
H.T. Condon, 1969, *Mem. Qd. Mus.* 15
A.W. Diamond, 1969, *Amer. Mus. Novit.* 2362
J. Ford, 1969, *Emu* 68
J. Ford, 1970, *Emu* 70
E.T. Gilliard & Lecroy, 1970, *Amer. Mus. Novit.* 2420
A.R. McGill, 1970, *Australian Warblers* (B.O.C., Melbourne)
O.S.N.Z. 1970, *Annotated Checklist of the Birds of New Zealand* (Reed, Wellington)
A.W. Diamond, 1972, *Publ. Nuttall Orn. Cl.* 12
C.J.O. Harrison, 1972, *Bull. Brit. Mus. Nat. Hist. (Zool.)* 21
S. Parker, 1972, *Emu* 72
J. Ford & Parker, 1974, *Emu* 74

Subfamily MUSCICAPINAE/PLATYSTEIRINAE

C. Vaurie, 1953, *Bull. Amer. Mus. Nat. Hist.* 100(4)

J.J. Moroney Jr., W.J. Bock, & J. Farrand Jr., 1975, *Reference List of the Birds of the World* (Amer. Mus. Nat. Hist., New York)

B. Rensch, 1929, *Journ. f. Orn.* Erg. II
A.L. Rand, 1936, *Bull. Amer. Mus. Nat. Hist.* 72
E. Stresemann, 1939–41, *Journ. f. Orn.* 87. 88. 89
J. Delacour & Jabouille, 1941, *L'Oiseau* 11
E. Mayr, 1941, *Amer. Mus. Novit.* 1133
E. Mayr, 1944, *Bull. Amer. Mus. Nat. Hist.* 83(2)
E. Mayr, 1945, *Birds of the Southwest Pacific* (Macmillan, New York)
H.G. Deignan, 1947, *Auk* 64
J. Delacour, 1947, *Birds of Malaya* (Macmillan, New York)
A.C.V. van Bemmell, 1948, *Treubia* 19
C.A. Fleming, 1950, *R.S.N.Z.* 78

J. Baker, 1951, *Univ. Kan. Pub. Mus. Nat. Hist.* 3
C. Vaurie, 1952, *Amer. Mus. Novit.* 1570
B.E. Smythies, 1953, *Birds of Burma* (Oliver & Boyd, Edinburgh)
G.P. Dementiev & Gladkov, 1954, *Birds of the Soviet Union* (Moscow)
C.W. Mackworth-Praed & C.H.B. Grant, 1955–70, *African Handbook of Birds* Ser. 1–3 (Longmans, London)
P.A. Clancey, 1957, *Ibis* 99
H.G. Deignan, 1957, *Ibis* 99
C. Vaurie, 1957, *Ibis* 99
A.J. Keast, 1958, *Rec. Aust. Mus.* XXIV/8
G.M. Storr, 1958, *Emu* 58
C. Vaurie, 1959, *Birds of the Palaearctic Fauna* I (Witherby, London)
B.E. Smythies, 1960, *Birds of Borneo* (Oliver & Boyd, Edinburgh)
S.D. Ripley, 1961, *Synopsis of the Birds of India and Pakistan* (Nat. Hist. Soc., Bombay)
I.C.J. Galbraith & E.H. Galbraith, 1962, *Bull. Brit. Mus. Nat. Hist.* 9
S.D. Ripley & Rabor, 1962, *Postilla* 1973
H.G. Deignan, 1963, *Bull. U.S. Nat. Mus.* 226
P.A. Clancey, 1966, *Ostrich* 37
W.J. Lawson, 1966, *Bull. B.O.C.* 86
E.T. Gilliard & Lecroy, 1967, *Bull. Amer. Mus. Nat. Hist.* 135(4)
A.L. Rand & E.T. Gilliard, 1967, *Handbook of New Guinea Birds* (Weidenfeld & Nicholson, London)
S.D. Ripley & Marshall, 1967, *Proc. Biol. Soc. Wash.* 80
H.R. Officer, 1969, *Australian Flycatchers* (B.O.C., Melbourne)
D. Amadon & J.E. Dupont, 1970, *Occ. Pap. Delaware Mus. N.H.* 1
A.D. Forbes-Watson, 1970, *Bull. B.O.C.* 90
B.P. Hall & R.E. Moreau, 1970, *Atlas of Speciation in African Passerine Birds* (Brit. Mus. Nat. Hist., London)
M.A. Traylor, 1970, *Bull. B.O.C.* 90
M.A. Traylor, 1970, *Ibis* 112
J.E. DuPont, 1971, *Nemouria* 3
J.E. DuPont, 1971, *Philippine Birds* (Mus. Nat. Hist., Greenville, Del.)
J. Ford, 1971, *Emu* 71
K.C. Parkes, 1971, *Nemouria* 4
P. Bruner, 1972, *Birds of French Polynesia* (Pac. Sci. Inf. Ctr., B.P. Bishop Mus., Hawaii)
A.W. Diamond, 1972, *Publ. Nuttall Orn. Cl.* 12
K.C. Parkes, 1973, *Emu* 73
R. Schodde, 1975, *Interim List of Australian Songbirds, Passerines* (R.A.O.U., Melbourne)
P.A. Clancey, 1976, *Bull. B.O.C.* 96

Subfamily MONARCHINAE/RHIPIDURINAE

J.J. Moroney Jr., W.J. Bock, & J. Farrand Jr., 1975, *Reference List of the Birds of the World* (Amer. Mus. Nat. Hist., New York)

G.M. Mathews, 1930, *Syst. Avium Aust.* Pt. II (B.O.U., London)
J. Delacour & Jabouille, 1941, *L'Oiseau* 11
E. Mayr & Moynihan, 1946, *Amer. Mus. Novit. 1321*
C.G. Sibley, 1946, *Condor* 46
A.C.V. van Bemmell, 1948, *Treubia* 19
C. Vaurie, 1951, *Bull. B.O.C.* 71
E. Mayr, 1955, *Amer. Mus. Novit.* 1707
A.J. Cain & I.C.J. Galbraith, 1956, *Ibis* 98
A.J. Keast, 1958, *Rec. Aust. Mus.* XXIV/8
K.C. Parkes, 1958, *Amer. Mus. Novit.* 1891
F. Salomonsen, 1964, *Noona Dan Papers* 9
G.F. Mees, 1965, *Zool.* 31
A.W. Diamond, 1967, *Amer. Mus. Novit.* 2284
A.L. Rand & E.T. Gilliard, 1967, *Handbook of New Guinea Birds* (Weidenfeld & Nicholson, London)

R. Schodde & Hitchcock, 1968, *Div. Wildlife Res. Tech. Pap.* 13
A.L. Rand & Rabor, 1969, *Fieldiana Zool.* 51
A.L. Rand, 1970, *Nat. Hist. Bull. Siam Soc.* 23
J.R. Ford, 1971, *Emu* 71
A.W. Diamond, 1972, *Publ. Nuttall Orn. Cl.* 12
G.F. Mees, 1973, *Zool. Meded* 46 (12)
R. Schodde, 1975, *Interim List of Australian Songbirds, Passerines* (R.A.O.U., Melbourne)

Subfamily PACHYCEPHALINAE

E, Mayr, 1967, J.L. Peters *Checklist of the Birds of the World* XII (Mus. Comp. Zool., Cambridge, Mass.)

B. Rensch, 1929, *Journ. f. Orn. Erg.* II
E. Mayr, 1941, 'List of New Guinea Birds', *Amer. Mus. Nat. Hist.* 82
A.L. Rand, 1941, *Amer. Mus. Novit.* 1102
P.J. Oliver, 1945, *Emu* 45
E. Mayr, 1953, *Emu* 53
E. Mayr, 1954, *Amer. Mus. Novit.* 1653
E. Mayr & E.T. Gilliard, 1954, *Bull. Amer. Mus. Nat. Hist.* 103
E. Mayr, 1955, *Amer. Mus. Novit.* 1707
I.C.J. Galbraith, 1956, *Bull. Brit. Mus. Nat. Hist.* 4/4
J.C. Greenway, 1966, *Amer. Mus. Novit.* 2258
K.C. Parkes, 1966, *Bull. B.O.C.* 86
Galbraith, 1967, *Emu* 66
A.L. Rand & E.T. Gilliard, 1967, *Handbook of New Guinea Birds* (Weidenfeld & Nicholson, London)
J. Ford, 1971, *Emu* 71
A.W. Diamond, 1972, *Publ. Nuttall Orn. Cl.* 12
R. Schodde, 1975, *Interim List of Australian Songbirds, Passerines* (R.A.O.U., Melbourne)

Family **CERTHIIDAE**

J.C. Greenway, 1967, in J.L. Peters *Checklist of the Birds of the World* XII

C. Vaurie, 1950, *Amer. Mus. Novit.*, 1472
C. Vaurie, 1959, *Birds of the Palaearctic Fauna* I (Witherby, London)
S.D. Ripley, 1961, *Synopsis of the Birds of India and Pakistan* (Nat. Hist. Soc., Bombay)
C.M.N. White, 1963, *Revised Checklist of African Flycatchers etc.* (Govt. Printer, Lusaka)
A.R. Phillips, 1966, *Bull. B.O.C.* 86
E.R. Blake, 1972, *Birds of Mexico* (Chicago University Press, Chicago)
P.A. Clancey, 1975, *Durban Mus. Novit.* X

Family **RHABDORNITHIDAE**

J.C. Greenway, 1967, in J.L. Peters *Checklist of the Birds of the World* XII

J. Delacour & Mayr, 1946, *Birds of the Philippines* (Macmillan, New York)
J.E. DuPont, 1971, *Philippine Birds* (Mus. Nat. Hist., Greenville, Del.)
K.C. Parkes, 1973, *Nemouria* 11

Family **CLIMACTERIDAE**

J.C. Greenway, 1967, in J.L. Peters *Checklist of the Birds of the World* XII

A.J. Keast, 1957, *Aust. Journ. Zool.* 5
A.J. Keast, 1961, *Bull. Mus. Comp. Zool Harvard* 123
J.D. Macdonald, 1966, *Emu* 66
Harrison, 1970, *Emu,* 70
J. Ford, 1971, *Emu* 71
R. Schodde, 1975, *Interim List of Australian Songbirds, Passerines* (R.A.O.U., Melbourne)

Family **SITTIDAE**

J.C. Greenway, 1967, in J.L. Peters *Checklist of the Birds of the World* XII

E. Mayr, 1950, *Emu* 49
C. Vaurie, 1957, *Amer. Mus. Novit.* 1854
S.D. Ripley, 1959, *Postilla* 42
Löhrl, 1960, *Journ. f. Orn.* 101
A.L. Rand, 1960, *Fieldiana Zool.* 35
J.D. Macdonald, 1969, *Emu* 69
J. Ford & Parker, 1974, *Emu* 74
R. Schodde, 1975, *Interim List of Australian Songbirds, Passerines* (R.A.O.U., Melbourne)
Vieilliard, 1976, *Alauda* 44

Family **AEGITHALIDAE**

D.W. Snow, 1967, in J.L. Peters *Checklist of the Birds of the World* XII

C. Vaurie, 1957, *Amer. Mus. Novit.* 1853
C. Vaurie, 1959, *Birds of the Palaearctic Fauna* I (Witherby, London)
E.R. Blake, 1972, *Birds of Mexico* (Chicago University Press, Chicago)
E. Eisenmann, *et al,* 1973, *Auk* 90

Family **REMIZIDAE**

D.W. Snow, 1967, in J.L. Peters *Checklist of the Birds of the World* XII

C. Vaurie, 1957, *Amer. Mus. Novit.* 1853
C. Vaurie, 1959, *Birds of the Palaearctic Fauna* I (Witherby, London)
C.M.N. White, 1963, *Revised Checklist of African Flycatchers etc.* (Govt. Printer, Lusaka)

Family **PARIDAE**

D.W. Snow, 1967 in J.L. Peters *Checklist of the Birds of the World* XII

C. Vaurie, 1956, *Amer. Mus. Novit.* 1833
C. Vaurie & Snow, 1957, *Amer. Mus. Novit.* 1852
K.C. Parkes, 1958, *Proc. Biol. Soc. Wash.* 71
C. Vaurie, 1959, *Birds of the Palaearctic Fauna* I (Witherby, London)
C.M.N. White, 1963, *Revised Checklist of African Flycatchers etc.* (Govt. Printer, Lusaka)
P.A. Clancey, 1964, *Durban Mus. Novit.* 7
Kniprath, 1967, *Journ. f. Orn.* 108
B.P. Hall & R.E. Moreau, 1970, *Atlas of Speciation in African Passerine Birds* (Brit. Mus. Nat. Hist., London)
Martens, 1971, *Journ. f. Orn.* 112
K.C. Parkes, 1971, *Nemouria* 4
E.R. Blake, 1972, *Birds of Mexico* (Chicago University Press, Chicago)
P.A. Clancey, 1972, *Durban Mus. Novit.* 9
L.S. Stepanyan, 1974, *By. Mosk. Ob. Isp. Priv.* 99(6)

Family **DICAEIDAE**

F. Salomonsen, 1967, in J.L. Peters *Checklist of the Birds of the World* XII

B. Rensch, 1931, *Mitt. Zool. Mus. Berlin* 17
K.A. Hindwood & Mayr, 1946, *Emu* 46
E. Mayr & Amadon, 1947, *Amer. Mus. Novit.* 1360
F. Salomonsen, 1960, *Amer. Mus. Novit.* 1960, 1990/1, 2016
F. Salomonsen, 1961, *Amer. Mus. Novit.* 2057, 2067, 2068
G.F. Mees, 1965, *Emu* 65
C.J.O. Harrison & S.A. Parker, 1966, *Bull. B.O.C.* 86
S.D. Ripley & Rabor, 1966, *Proc. Biol. Soc. Wash.* 79

E.T. Gilliard & Lecroy, 1967, *Bull. Amer. Mus. Nat. Hist.* 135(4)
A.L. Rand & E.T. Gilliard, 1967, *Handbook of New Guinea Birds* (Weidenfeld & Nicholson, London)
J.D. Macdonald, 1969, *Emu* 69
A.L. Rand & Rabor, 1969, *Fieldiana Zool.* 51
J.E. DuPont, 1971, *Philippine Birds* (Mus. Nat. Hist., Greenville, Del.)
K.C. Parkes, 1971, *Nemouria* 4
R. Schodde, 1975, *Interim List of Australian Songbirds, Passerines* (R.A.O.U., Melbourne)

Family **NECTARINIIDAE**

A. L. Rand, 1967, in J.L. Peters *Checklist of the Birds of the World* XII

J. Delacour, 1944, *Zoologica (N.Y.)* 39
C.W. Mackworth-Praed & C.H.B. Grant, 1955–70, *African Handbook of Birds* Ser. 1–3 (Longmans, London)
H.G. Deignan, 1961, *Bull. U.S. Nat. Mus.* 221
S.D. Ripley, 1961, *Synopsis of the Birds of India and Pakistan* (Nat. Hist. Soc., Bombay)
C.M.N. White, 1963, *Revised Checklist of African Flycatchers etc.* (Govt. Printer, Lusaka)
G.F. Mees, 1966, *Zool. Meded* 41
E.T. Gilliard & Lecroy, 1967, *Bull. Amer. Mus. Nat. Hist.* 135(4)
A.L. Rand & E.T. Gilliard, 1967, *A Handbook of New Guinea Birds* (Weidenfeld & Nicholson, London)
P.A. Clancey, 1970, *Durban Mus. Novit.* VIII, IX
B.P. Hall & R.E. Moreau, 1970, *Atlas of Speciation in African Passerine Birds* (Brit. Mus. Nat. Hist., London)
J.E. DuPont, 1971, *Nemouria* 3
K.C. Parkes, 1971, *Nemouria* 4
P.A. Clancey, 1973, *Durban Mus. Novit.* X
P.A. Clancey, 1975, *Durban Mus. Novit.* XI

Family **ZOSTEROPIDAE**

E. Mayr & R.E. Moreau, 1967, in J.L. Peters *Checklist of the Birds of the World* XII

E. Mayr, 1945, *Birds of the Southwest Pacific* (Macmillan, New York)
J. Delacour & Mayr, 1946, *Birds of the Philippines* (Macmillan, New York)
R.E. Moreau, 1953, *Bull. B.O.C.* 73
G.F. Mees, 1957, *Zool. Verh. Rijksmus. Nat. Hist. Leiden* 35
R.E. Moreau, 1957, *Bull. Brit. Mus. Nat. Hist. (Zool.)* 4
T.H. Cheng, 1958, *Distributional List of Chinese Birds* Pt. II (Acad. Sin., Peking)
T. Mishima, 1959, *Tori* 15
G.F. Mees, 1961, *Zool. Verh. Rijksmus. Nat. Hist. Leiden* 50
S.D. Ripley, 1961, *Synopsis of the Birds of India and Pakistan* (Nat. Hist. Soc., Bombay)
C.M.N. White, 1963, *Revised Checklist of African Flycatchers etc.* (Govt. Printer, Lusaka)
E. Mayr, 1965, *Breviora Mus. Comp. Zool. Harvard* 228
P.A. Clancey, 1966, *Durban Mus. Novit.* VII
R.W. Storer & Gill, 1966, *Occ. Pap. Mus. Zool. Univ. Michigan* 648
A.L. Rand & E.T. Gilliard, 1967, *Handbook of New Guinea Birds* (Weidenfeld & Nicholson, London)
G.F. Mees, 1969, *Zool. Verh. Rijksmus. Nat. Hist. Leiden* 102
J.E. DuPont, 1971, *Nemouria* 3
K.C. Parkes, 1971, *Nemouria* 4
G.M. Storr, 1973, *List of Queensland Birds* (Spec. Publs. W. Aust. Mus.)

Family **MELIPHAGIDAE**

F. Salomonsen, 1967, in J.L. Peters *Checklist of the Birds of the World* XII

E. Mayr, 1944, *Bull. Amer. Mus. Nat. Hist.* 83
E. Mayr & E.T. Gilliard, 1954, *Bull. Amer. Mus. Nat. Hist.* 103

E. Mayr, 1955, *Amer. Mus. Novit.* 1707
E.T. Gilliard, 1959, *Amer. Mus. Novit.* 1959
D.L. Serventy & H.M. Whittell, 1962, *Birds of Western Australia* 3rd edn. (Lamb Publs., Perth)
H.R. Officer, 1964, *Australian Honeyeaters* (R.A.O.U., Melbourne)
D.M. Skead, 1964, *Ostrich* 35
F. Salomonsen, 1966, *Breviora Mus. Comp. Zool. Harvard* 254
A.W. Diamond, 1967, *Amer. Mus. Novit.* 2284
A.L. Rand & E.T. Gilliard, 1967, *Handbook of New Guinea Birds* (Weidenfeld & Nicholson, London)
A.W. Diamond, 1969, *Amer. Mus. Novit.* 2362
A.L. Rand & Rabor, 1969, *Fieldiana Zool.* 51
A.W. Diamond, 1971, *Condor* 73
J. Ford, 1971, *Emu* 71
S. Parker, 1971, *Emu* 71
S. Parker, 1971, *Sunbird* 2
A.W. Diamond, 1972, *Publ. Nuttall Orn. Cl.* 12
F.H.J. Crome, 1973, *Emu* 73
R. Schodde, 1975, *Interim List of Australian Songbirds, Passerines* (R.A.O.U., Melbourne)

Subfamily EMBERIZINAE/CARDINALINAE

R.A. Paynter, 1970, in J.L. Peters *Checklist of the Birds of the World* XIII (Mus. Comp. Zool., Cambridge, Mass.)

D. Lack, 1947, *Darwin's Finches* (Cambridge University Press)
R. Meyer de Schauensee, 1952, *Proc. Acad. Nat. Sci., Phil.* 104
K.C. Parkes, 1954, *Condor* 56
A.L. Rand, 1955, *Fieldiana Zool. (Chicago)* 37
R.W. Storer, 1955, *Condor* 57
C. Vaurie, 1956, *Amer. Mus. Novit.* 1795
M. Koepcke, 1957, *Scientia* 4
T.H. Cheng, 1958, *Distributional List of Chinese Birds* Pt. II (Acad. Sin., Peking)
C. Vaurie, 1959, *Birds of the Palaearctic Fauna* I (Witherby, London)
J.D. Webster, 1959, *Condor* 61
D.M. Skead, *et al*, 1960, *Canaries, Seedeaters and Buntings of South Africa* (S.A. Bird Book Fund, Johannesburg)
K.H. Voous, 1960, *Atlas of European Birds* (Nelson, London)
S.D. Ripley, 1961, *Synopsis of the Birds of India and Pakistan* (Nat. Hist. Soc., Bombay)
W.H. Phelps & Phelps, 1963, *Bol. Soc. Venez. Cienc. Nat.* 24
C.M.N. White, 1963, *Revised Checklist of African Flycatchers etc.* (Govt. Printer, Lusaka)
P.A. Clancey, 1964, *Bull. B.O.C.* 84
R. Meyer de Schauensee, 1964, *Birds of Colombia* (Livingston, Narberth, Penn.)
R.A. Paynter, 1964, *Condor* 66
A.R. Phillips, J. Marshall, & G. Monson, 1964, *Birds of Arizona* (University of Arizona, Tucson)
P.A. Clancey, 1965, *Ostrich* 36
W.E. Godfrey, 1965, *Auk* 82
P.A. Clancey, 1966, *Durban Mus. Novit.* VII
R. Meyer de Schauensee, 1966, *The Species of Birds of South America* (Acad. Nat. Sci., Philadelphia)
R.W. Dickerman & Phillips, 1967, *Condor* 69
R.A. Paynter, 1967, *Breviora Mus. Comp. Zool. Harvard* 278
J.C. Bent, *et al*, 1968, *Bull. Amer. Mus. Nat. Hist.* 237
L.L. Short, 1969, *Wilson Bull.* 81
R. Meyer de Schauensee, 1970, *Notulae Naturae* 428
E.R. Blake, 1972, *Birds of Mexico* (Chicago University Press, Chicago)
Johnson & Brush, 1972, *Syst. Zool.* 21
Martins, 1972, *Bonn. Zool. Beitr.* 23
B. Matousek, 1972, *Annotationes Zool. bot. Bratislava* 82
B. Matousek, 1973, *Zbornik slov. narod. Mus.* 17(1)
K.C. Parkes, 1974, *Wilson Bull.* 86(3)

L.L. Short, 1974, *Bull. Amer. Mus. Nat. Hist.* 154
P.R. Colston, 1978, *Bull. B.O.C.* 98

Subfamily THRAUPINAE/CATAMBLYRHNCHINAE/TERSINAE

R.W. Storer, 1970, in J.L. Peters *Checklist of the Birds of the World* XIII

J.T. Zimmer, 1942, *Amer. Mus. Novit.* 1193
J.T. Zimmer, 1943, *Amer. Mus. Novit.* 1225
J.T. Zimmer, 1944, *Amer. Mus. Novit.* 1262
J. Bond, 1947, *Auk* 64
J.T. Zimmer, 1947, *Amer. Mus. Novit.* 1367
E. Eisenmann, 1955, *Trans. Lin. Soc. N.Y.* 7
J. Bond, 1956, *Checklist of Birds of the West Indies* 4th edn. (Acad. Nat. Sci., Philadelphia)
E. Eisenmann, 1957, *Condor* 59
Novaes, 1959, *Bol. Mus. Goeldi* 22
W.H. Phelps & Phelps, 1964, *Bol. Soc. Venez. Cienc. Nat.* 24
R. Meyer de Schauensee, 1964, *Birds of Colombia* (Livingston, Narberth, Penn.)
R. Meyer de Schauensee, 1966, *The Species of Birds of South America* (Acad. Nat. Sci., Philadelphia)
A.R. Phillips, 1966, *Bull. B.O.C.* 86
A.W. Johnson, 1967, *Birds of Chile* 2
E. Mayr & Phelps, 1967, *Bull. Amer. Mus. Nat. Hist.* 136
F. Haverschmidt, 1968, *List of the Birds of Surinam* (Oliver & Boyd, Edinburgh)
K.C. Parkes, 1969, *Bull. B.O.C.* 89
K.C. Parkes, 1969, *Auk* 86
R.W. Storer, 1969, *Living Bird* 8
E.R. Blake & Hocking, 1974, *Wilson Bull.* 86(4)
J.S. Weske, 1974, *Wilson Bull.* 86(2)
J.S. Weske & J.W. Terborgh, 1974, *Wilson Bull.* 86(2)
K.C. Parkes, 1977, *Bull. B.O.C.* 97
R. Meyer de Schauensee & W.H. Phelps, 1978, *Birds of Venezuela* (Princeton University Press, Princeton)

Family **PARULIDAE**

G.H. Lowery & B.L. Monroe, 1968, in J.L. Peters *Checklist of the Birds of the World* XIV (Mus. Comp. Zool., Cambridge, Mass.)

R. Meyer de Schauensee, 1946, *Notulae Naturae* 167
J.T. Zimmer, 1949, *Amer. Mus. Novit.* 1428
J.C. Bent, 1953, *Bull. U.S. Nat. Mus.* 203
A.O.U., 1957, *Checklist of North American Birds* (A.O.U., Baltimore)
L. Griscom & A. Sprunt Jr. (eds.), 1957, *Warblers of North America* (Devin-Adair, New York)
J. Bond, 1961, *Birds of the West Indies* (Collins, London)
K.C. Parkes, 1961, *Wilson Bull.* 73
J.D. Webster, 1961, *Auk* 78
E. Eisenmann, 1962, *Auk* 79
George, 1962, *Amer. Mus. Novit.* 2103
A.F. Skutch, 1962, *Condor* 64
J.D. Webster, 1962, *Wilson Bull.* 74
W.H. Phelps & Phelps, 1963, *Bol. Soc. Venez. Cienc. Nat.* 24
R. Meyer de Schauensee, 1964, *Birds of Colombia* (Livingston, Narberth, Penn.)
R. Meyer de Schauensee, 1966, *The Species of Birds of South America* (Acad. Nat. Sci., Philadelphia)
J. Bond, 1967, *Checklist of Birds of the West Indies* Suppl. 12 (Acad. Nat. Sci., Philadelphia)
R.W. Storer, 1967, in J.L. Peters *Checklist of the Birds of the World* XIII
Orr & J.D. Webster, 1968, *Proc. Biol. Soc. Wash.* 81
C.G. Sibley, 1968, *Postilla* 125
R.W. Dickerman, 1970, *Condor* 72

E.R. Blake, 1972, *Birds of Mexico* (Chicago University Press, Chicago)
A.W. Johnson & W.R. Millie, 1972, *Supplement to The Birds of Chile* p. 6. Platt Est. Graf., Buenos Aires
C.B. Kepler & K.C. Parkes, 1972, *Auk* 89
S.L. Olsen, 1975, *Bull. B.O.C.* 95
R. Meyer de Schauensee & W.H. Phelps, 1978, *Birds of Venezuela* (Princeton University Press, Princeton)

Family **DREPANIDIDAE**

G.C. Munro, 1944, *Birds of Hawaii*

G.C. Munro, 1945, *Elepaio (Journ. Honolulu Audubon Soc.)* 5
D. Amadon, 1950, *Bull. Amer. Mus. Nat. Hist.* 95
J.C. Greenway, 1968, in J.L. Peters *Checklist of the Birds of the World* XIV
T.L.C. Casey & J.D. Jacobi, 1974, *Occ. Pap. Bernice P. Bishop Mus.* 24
W.J. Bock, 1977, *Ibis* 120

Family **VIREONIDAE**

E.R. Blake, 1968, in J.L. Peters *Checklist of the Birds of the World* XIV

J. Bond, 1953, *Notulae Naturae* 255
A.F. Skutch, 1960, *Pacific Coast Avifauna* 34
J. Bond, 1961, *Caribbean Journ. Sci.* 1
T.H. Hamilton, 1962, *Wilson Bull.* 70
W.H. Phelps & Phelps, 1963, *Bol. Soc. Venez. Cienc. Nat.* 24
R. Meyer de Schauensee, 1964, *Birds of Colombia* (Livingston, Narberth, Penn.)
R. Meyer de Schauensee, 1966, *The Species of Birds of South America* (Acad. Nat. Sci., Philadelphia)
O.H. Garrido, 1971, *Poeyana* 81
E.R. Blake, 1972, *Birds of Mexico* (Chicago University Press, Chicago)
O.H. Garrido, 1973, *Poeyana* 119
G.F. Mees, 1974, *Zool. Meded. Leiden* 48(7)

Family **ICTERIDAE**

E.R. Blake, 1968, in J.L. Peters *Checklist of he Birds of the World* XIV

E. Eisenmann, 1955, 'The Species of Middle American Birds , *Trans. Lin. Soc., N.Y.* 7
J.C. Bent, 1958, *Bull. U.S. Nat. Mus.* 211
W.H. Phelps & Phelps, 1963, *Bol. Soc. Venez. Cienc. Nat.* 24
R. Meyer de Schauensee, 1964, *Birds of Colombia* (Livingston, Narberth, Penn.)
K.C. Parkes & Blake, 1965, *Fieldiana Zool. (Chicago)* 44
R. Meyer de Schauensee, 1966, *The Species of Birds of South America* (Acad. Nat. Sci., Philadelphia)
L.L. Short, 1968, Amer. Mus. Novit. 2349
L.L. Short, 1969, *Occ. Pap. Mus. Zool. La. State Univ.* 36
R.W. Dickerman & Phillips, 1970, *Condor* 72
O.H. Garrido, 1970, *Poeyana* 68
Markham, 1971, *Ann. Inst. Patagonia* 2
R.W. Dickerman, 1974, *Amer. Mus. Novit.* 2538

Family **FRINGILLIDAE**

E. Mayr, 1968, in J.L. Peters *Checklist of the Birds of the World* XIV

K.H. Voous, 1949, *Condor* 51
C. Vaurie, 1956, *Amer. Mus. Novit.* 1775, 1786, 1788
T.H. Cheng, 1958, *Distributional List of Chinese Birds* Pt. II Passeriformes (Acad. Sin., Peking)
J. Nicolai, 1959, *Zool. Jahrb. Abt. Syst.* 87
C. Vaurie, 1959, *Birds of the Palaearctic Fauna* I Passeriformes (Witherby, London)

D.M. Skead, et al, 1960, *Canaries, Seedeaters & Buntings of South Africa* (S.A. Bird Book Fund, Johannesburg)

S.D. Ripley & Rabor, 1961, *Postilla* 50

S.D. Ripley, 1961, *Synopsis of the Birds of India and Pakistan* (Nat. Hist. Soc., Bombay)

B.P. Hall & R.E. Moreau, 1962, *Bull. Brit. Mus. Nat. Hist. Zool.* 8

D. Amadon, 1965, *Ibis* 107

P.A. Clancey, 1966, *Durban Mus. Novit.* VII

R. Meyer de Schauensee, 1966, *The Species of Birds of South America* (Acad. Nat. Sci., Philadelphia)

Ackermann, 1967, *Journ. f. Orn.* 108

H.E. Wolters, 1967, *Bonn. Zool. Beitr.* 18

T.R. Howell, R.A. Paynter, & A.L. Rand, 1968, in J.L. Peters *Checklist of the Birds of the World* XII

A.L. Rand, 1968, *Fieldiana Zool. (Chicago)* 50

B.P. Hall & R.E. Moreau, 1970, *Atlas of Speciation in African Passerine Birds* (Brit. Mus. Nat. Hist., London)

E.R. Blake, 1972, *Birds of Mexico* (Chicago University Press, Chicago)

M.A. Traylor, 1972, *Bull. B.O.C.* 90

A.G. Knox, 1976, *Bull. B.O.C.* 96

K.H. Voous, 1977, *Ibis* 119

J.S. Ash, 1979, *Ibis* 121

Family **ESTRILDIDAE**

E. Mayr, R.A. Paynter, & M.A. Traylor, 1968, in J.L. Peters *Checklist of the Birds of the World* XIV

S.D. Ripley, 1961, *Synopsis of the Birds of India and Pakistan* (Nat. Hist. Soc., Bombay)

C.M.N. White, 1963, Revised Checklist of African Flycatchers etc. (Govt. Printer, Lusaka)

K. Immelman, 1965, *Australian Finches* (Angus & Robertson, Sydney)

H.E. Wolters, 1966, *Ostrich* Suppl. 6

A.L. Rand & E.T. Gilliard, 1967, *Handbook of New Guinea Birds* (Weidenfeld & Nicholson, London)

Zisweiler, 1967, *Zool. Jahrb. Abt. Syst.* 94

E. Mayr, 1968, *Breviora Mus. Comp. Zool. Harvard* 287

P.A. Clancey, 1969, *Durban Mus. Novit.* VIII

Hald Mortensen, 1970, *Dansk Orn. Foren. Tids. skr.* 64

B.P. Hall & R.E. Moreau, 1970, *Atlas of Speciation in African Passerine Birds* (Brit. Mus. Nat. Hist., London)

P.A. Clancey, 1971, *Durban Mus. Novit.* IX

J.E. DuPont, 1972, *Wilson Bull.* 84

H.E. Wolters, 1972, *Bonn. Zool. Beitr.* 23

Zisweiler, Guttinger, & Bregulla, 1972, *Bonn. Zool. Monogr.* 12

P.A. Clancey, 1974, *Arnoldia* 6(28)

Family **PLOCEIDAE**

M.A. Traylor, J.C. Greenway, & R.E. Moreau, 1962/8, in J.L. Peters *Checklist of the Birds of the World* XIV, XV

A.L. Rand, 1936, *Bull. Amer. Mus. Nat. Hist.* 72

T.H. Cheng, 1958, *Distributional List of Chinese Birds* Pt. II (Acad. Sin., Peking)

C. Vaurie, 1959, *Birds of the Palaearctic Fauna* I. Passeriformes (Witherby, London)

R.E. Moreau, 1960, *Ibis* 102

S.D. Ripley, 1961, *Synopsis of the Birds of India and Pakistan* (Nat. Hist. Soc., Bombay)

C.M.N. White, 1963, *Revised Checklist of African Flycatchers etc.* (Govt. Printer, Lusaka)

J. Nicolai, 1967, *Journ. f. Orn.* 108

R.B. Payne, 1968, *Bull. B.O.C.* 88

P.A. Clancey, 1970, *Durban Mus. Novit.* VIII

B.P. Hall & R.E. Moreau, 1970, *Atlas of Speciation in African Passerine Birds* (Brit. Mus. Nat. Hist., London)

P.A. Clancey, 1972, *Durban Mus. Novit.* IX
J. Nicolai, 1972, *Journ. f. Orn.* 113
J.C. Benson, *et al.* 1973, *Birds of Zambia* (Collins, London)
R.B. Payne, 1973, *Ornithological Monograms* 11 (A.O.U.)
P.A. Clancey, 1974, *Durban Mus. Novit.* X
H.E. Wolters, 1974, *Bonn. Zool. Beitr.* 25(4)

Family **STURNIDAE**

D. Amadon, 1962, in J.L. Peters *Checklist of the Birds of the World* XV (Mus. Comp. Zool. Cambridge, Mass.)

S.B. Wilson, 1907, *Ibis* 3
E. Mayr, 1945, *Birds of the Southwest Pacific* (Macmillan, New York)
J. Delacour, 1974, *Birds of Malaysia* (Hamilton, New York)
B.E. Smythies, 1953, *Birds of Burma* (Oliver & Boyd, Edinburgh)
D. Amadon, 1956, *Amer. Mus. Novit.* 1803
T.H. Cheng, 1958, *Distributional List of Chinese Birds* Pt. II (Acad. Sin., Peking)
C. Vaurie, 1959, *Birds of the Palaearctic Fauna* I. Passerines (Witherby, London)
S.D. Ripley, 1961, *Synopsis of the Birds of India and Pakistan* (Nat. Hist. Soc., Bombay)
C.M.N. White, 1962, *Revised Checklist of African Shrikes etc.* (Govt. Printer, Lusaka)
A.L. Rand & E.T. Gilliard, 1967, *Handbook of New Guinea Birds* (Weidenfeld & Nicholson, London)
J.E. DuPont, 1971, *Philippine Birds* (Mus. Nat. Hist., Greenville, Del.)
P.A. Clancey, 1973, *Durban Mus. Novit.* IX
Brooke, 1976, *Bull. B.O.C.* 96
P.A. Clancey, 1976, *Bull. B.O.C.* 96

Family **ORIOLIDAE**

J.C. Greenway, 1962, in J.L. Peters *Checklist of the Birds of the World* XV

A.J. Keast, 1956, *Proc. R. Soc. N.S.W.* 1954/5
T.H. Cheng, 1958, *Distributional List of Chinese Birds* Pt. II (Acad. Sin., Peking)
S.D. Ripley, 1961, *Synopsis of the Birds of India and Pakistan* (Nat. Hist. Soc., Bombay)
H.G. Deignan, 1963, *Checklist of the Birds of Thailand* (Smiths. Inst., Washington)
A.L. Rand & E.T. Gilliard, 1967, *Handbook of New Guinea Birds* (Weidenfeld & Nicholson, London)
W.J. Lawson, 1969, *Bull. B.O.C.* 89
Wolters & Clancey, 1969, *Bull. B.O.C.* 89
B.P. Hall & R.E. Moreau, 1970, *Atlas of Speciation in African Passerine Birds* (Brit. Mus. Nat. Hist., London)
K.C. Parkes, 1971, *Nemouria* 4
J. Ford, 1975, *Emu* 75

Family **DICRURIDAE**

C. Vaurie, 1962, in J.L. Peters *Checklist of the Birds of the World* XV

C. Vaurie, 1958, *Amer. Mus. Novit.* 1869

Family **CALLAEIDAE**

D. Amadon, 1962, in J.L. Peters *Checklist of the Birds of the World* XV

O.S.N.Z., 1970, *Annotated Checklist of the Birds of New Zealand* (Reed, Wellington)

Family **GRALLINIDAE**

E. Mayr, 1962, in J.L. Peters *Checklist of the Birds of the World* XV

D. Amadon, 1950, *Emu* 50

A.L. Rand & E.T. Gilliard, 1967, *Handbook of New Guinea Birds* (Weidenfeld & Nicholson, London)
R. Schodde, 1975, *Interim List of Australian Songbirds, Passerines* (R.A.O.U., Melbourne)

Family **ARTAMIDAE**

E. Mayr, 1962, in J.L. Peters *Checklist of the Birds of the World* XV

T.H. Cheng, 1958, *Distributional List of Chinese Birds* Pt. II (Acad. Sin., Peking)
A.J. Keast, 1958, *Emu* 58
A.L. Rand & E.T. Gilliard, 1967, *Handbook of New Guinea Birds* (Weidenfeld & Nicholson, London)
R. Schodde, 1975, *Interim List of Australian Songbirds, Passerines* (R.A.O.U., Melbourne)

Family **CRACTICIDAE**

D. Amadon, 1962, in J.L. Peters *Checklist of the Birds of the World* XV

D. Amadon, 1951, *Amer. Mus. Novit.* 1504
A.L. Rand & E.T. Gilliard, 1967, *Handbook of New Guinea Birds* (Weidenfeld & Nicholson, London)
O.S.N.Z., 1970, *Annotated Checklist of the Birds of New Zealand* (Reed, Wellington)
G.M. Storr, 1973, *Spec. Publs. West. Aust. Mus.* 5
R. Schodde, 1975, *Interim List of Australian Songbirds, Passerines* (R.A.O.U., Melbourne)

Family **PTILINORHYNCHIDAE**

W.J. Cooper & J.M. Forshaw, 1977, *Birds of Paradise and Bowerbirds* (Collins, London)

E. Mayr & Jennings, 1952, *Amer. Mus. Novit.* 1602
A.J. Marshall, 1954, *Bowerbirds: their Displays and Breeding Cycles* (Oxford University Press)
E. Mayr, 1962, in J.L. Peters *Checklist of the Birds of the World* XV
W.J. Bock, 1963, *Condor* 65
A.L. Rand & E.T. Gilliard, 1967, *Handbook of New Guinea Birds* (Weidenfeld & Nicholson, London)
E.T. Gilliard, 1969, *Birds of Paradise and Bowerbirds* (Weidenfeld & Nicholson, London)
R. Schodde & McKean, 1973, *Emu* 73

Family **PARADISAEIDAE**

W.J. Cooper & J.M. Forshaw, 1977, *Birds of Paradise and Bowerbirds* (Collins, London)

E. Mayr, 1962, in J.L. Peters *Checklist of the Birds of the World* XV
W.J. Bock, 1963, *Condor* 65
A.L. Rand & E.T. Gilliard, 1967, *Handbook of New Guinea Birds* (Weidenfeld & Nicholson, London)
A.W. Diamond, 1969, *Amer. Mus. Novit.* 2362
E.T. Gilliard, 1969, *Birds of Paradise and Bowerbirds* (Weidenfeld & Nicholson, London)
A.W. Diamond, 1972, *Publ. Nuttall Orn. Cl.* 12
R. Schodde & McKean, 1972, *Emu* 72
R. Schodde & McKean, 1973, *Emu* 73

Family **CORVIDAE**

C. Vaurie & Blake, 1962, in J.L. Peters *Checklist of the Birds of the World* XV
D. Goodwin, 1976, *Crows of the World* (Brit. Mus. Nat. Hist., London)

E. Mayr, 1944, *Bull. Amer. Mus. Nat. Hist.* 83

E. Mayr, 1945, *Birds of the Southwest Pacific* (Macmillan, New York)

J. Dorst, 1947, *Ois. Rev. Fr. Orn.* 17

G.P. Dementiev & Gladkov, 1954, *Birds of the Soviet Union* (Moscow)

C. Vaurie, 1954, *Amer. Mus. Novit.* 1668

L.I. Davis, 1958, *Wilson Bull.* 70

R.K. Selander & D.R. Giller, 1959, *Condor* 61

C. Vaurie, 1959, *Birds of the Palaearctic Fauna* I. Passerines (Witherby, London)

S.D. Ripley, 1961, *Synopsis of the Birds of India and Pakistan* (Nat. Hist. Soc., Bombay)

C.M.N. White, 1963, *Revised Checklist of African Shrikes etc.* (Govt. Printer, Lusaka)

R. Meyer de Schauensee, 1966, *The Species of Birds of South America* (Acad. Nat. Sci., Philadelphia)

E.T. Gilliard & Lecroy, 1967, *Bull. Amer. Mus. Nat. Hist.* 135

I. Rowley, 1967, *Emu* 67

J.W. Hardy, 1969, *Condor* 71

I. Rowley, 1970, *CSIRO Wildlife Res.* 15

J. Bond, 1971, *Birds of the West Indies* (Collins, London)

E.R. Blake, 1972, *Birds of Mexico* (Chicago University Press, Chicago)

A. Keve, 1973, *Zool. Abh. St. Mus. Tierk. Dresden* 32(12)

R. Schodde, 1975, *Interim List of Australian Songbirds, Passerines* (R.A.O.U., Melbourne)

CHECKLIST

Struthioniformes

1 STRUTHIONIDAE (OSTRICHES)

STRUTHIO
Struthio camelus (Ostrich)
S. c. camelus
   N Africa, Sudan
S. c. spatzi
   Rio de Oro
S. c. syriacus
   Syrian & Arabian deserts
S. c. molybdophanes
   Somalia, NE Kenya
S. c. massaicus
   E Kenya, E Tanzania
S. c. australis
   Southern Africa

Rheiformes

2 RHEIDAE (RHEAS)

RHEA
Rhea americana (Greater Rhea)
R. a. americana
   N & E Brazil
R. a. intermedia
   S Brazil, Uruguay
R. a. albescens
   N Argentina

PTEROCNEMIA
Pterocnemia pennata (Lesser Rhea)
P. p. garleppi
   SE Peru, Bolivia, NW Argentina
P. p. tarapacensis
   N Chile
P. p. pennata
   S Argentina

Casuariiformes

3 CASUARIIDAE (CASSOWARIES)

CASUARIUS
Casuarius casuarius (Double-wattled Cassowary)
C. c. casuarius
   Ceram I

C. c. bicarunculatus
   Aru Is, NW New Guinea
C. c. tricarunculatus
   Geelvink Bay, New Guinea
C. c. lateralis
   N New Guinea
C. c. sclaterii
   S New Guinea
C. c. aruensis
   Wokan I
C. c. violicollis
   Trangan I
C. c. johnsonii
   N Queensland
Casuarius bennetti (Dwarf Cassowary)
C. b. papuanus
   NW New Guinea
C. b. goodfellowi
   Japen I
C. b. claudii
   NC New Guinea
C. b. hecki
   NE New Guinea
C. b. picticollis
   SE New Guinea
C. b. bennetti
   New Britain
C. b. shawmayeri
   Krätke Mts (New Britain)
Casuarius unappendiculatus (One-wattled Cassowary)
C. u. rothschildi
   W New Guinea
C. u. philipi
   Sepik river, New Guinea
C. u. unappendiculatus
   Salawati I, Misol I
C. u. occipitalis
   Japen I
C. u. rufotinctus
   N New Guinea
C. u. aurantiacus
   NE New Guinea

4 DROMAIIDAE (EMUS)

DROMAIUS
Dromaius novaehollandiae (Emu)
D. n. woodwardi
   NW & Western Australia, Northern Territory
D. n. rothschildi
   SW Australia

D. n. novaehollandiae
   C & S Queensland to Victoria, S Australia

Apterygiformes

5 APTERYGIDAE (KIWIS)

APTERYX
Apteryx australis (Brown Kiwi)
   A. a. mantelli
      S North I (New Zealand)
   A. a. novaezelandiae
      N North I (New Zealand)
   A. a. australis
      South I (New Zealand)
   A. a. lawryi
      Stewart I
Apteryx owenii (Little Spotted Kiwi)
   A. o. iredalei
      North I (New Zealand)
   A. o. owenii
      South I (New Zealand)
Apteryx haastii (Great Spotted Kiwi)
   W South I (New Zealand)

Tinamiformes

6 TINAMIDAE (TINAMOUS)

TINAMUS
Tinamus tao (Grey Tinamou)
   T. t. septentrionalis
      Colombia, Venezuela, Guyana
   T. t. larensis
      C Colombia, Venezuela
   T. t. tao
      N & C Brazil
   T. t. kleei
      N Bolivia, E Peru
Tinamus solitarius (Solitary Tinamou)
   T. s. pernambucensis
      E Brazil
   T. s. solitarius
      C Brazil, Paraguay
Tinamus osgoodi (Black Tinamou)
   T. o. herschkovitzi
      S Columbia
   T. o. osgoodi
      Peru
Tinamus major (Great Tinamou)
   T. m. robustus
      EC Guatemala to N Nicaragua
   T. m. percautus
      S Mexico, Guatemala
   T. m. fuscipennis
      E Nicaragua to Panama

T. m. brunneiventris
   C Panama
T. m. castaneiceps
   SW Costa Rica, W Panama
T. m. saturatus
   E Panama, N Colombia
T. m. latifrons
   W Colombia, W Ecuador
T. m. zuliensis
   E Colombia, W Venezuela
T. m. major
   the Guianas, N Brazil
T. m. olivascens
   E Brazil
T. m. peruvianus
   E Colombia, E Ecuador, E Peru
T. m. serratus
   S Venezuela, W Brazil
Tinamus guttatus (White-throated Tinamou)
   E Ecuador & N Bolivia to E Brazil

NOTHOCERCUS
Nothocercus bonapartei (Highland Tinamou)
   N. b. frantzii
      Costa Rica, W Panama
   N. b. intercedens
      W Colombia
   N. b. discrepans
      Colombia
   N. b. bonapartei
      E Colombia, W Venezuela
   N. b. plumbeiceps
      E Ecuador
Nothocercus julius (Tawny-breasted Tinamou)
   W Venezuela & Colombia to S Peru
Nothocercus nigrocapillus (Hooded Tinamou)
   N. n. cadwaladeri
      N Peru
   N. n. nigrocapillus
      C Bolivia

CRYPTURELLUS
Crypturellus cinereus (Cinereous Tinamou)
   C. c. berlepschi
      NW Colombia, N Ecuador
   C. c. cinereus
      the Guianas to E Peru
Crypturellus soui (Little Tinamou)
   C. s. meserythrus
      S Mexico to Honduras
   C. s. modestus
      Nicaragua to W Panama
   C. s. capnodes
      NW Panama

C. s. panamensis
Pearl Is (Panama)
C. s. caucae
W Colombia
C. s. harterti
NW Colombia, W Ecuador
C. s. mustelinus
NE Colombia
C. s. caquetae
SE Colombia
C. s. nigriceps
E Ecuador
C. s. soui
E Colombia, Venezuela, the Guianas,
N Brazil
C. s. andrei
Trinidad
C. s. albigularis
E Brazil
C. s. inconspicuus
C Bolivia
Crypturellus ptaritepui (Tepui Tinamou)
SE Venezuela
Crypturellus obsoletus (Brown Tinamou)
C. o. cerviniventris
Venezuela
C. o. castaneus
E Colombia, E Ecuador, N Peru
C. o. ochraceiventris
C Peru
C. o. punensis
S Peru, W Bolivia
C. o. griseiventris
Santarem, Brazil
C. o. obsoletus
S Brazil, Paraguay, NE Argentina
C. o. traylori
E Peru
C. o. hypochracea
SW Brazil
**Crypturellus undulatus (Undulated
Tinamou)**
C. u. manapiare
S Venezuela
C. u. simplex
S Guyana
C. u. adspersus
N Brazil
C. u. yapura
E Ecuador, E Peru, W Brazil
C. u. vermiculatus
E Brazil
C. u. undulatus
E Bolivia, SW Brazil, Paraguay
**Crypturellus transfasciatus (Pale-browed
Tinamou)**
W Ecuador, W Peru

**Crypturellus strigulosus (Brazilian
Tinamou)**
Brazil
**Crypturellus duidae (Grey-legged
Tinamou)**
SE Venezuela
**Crypturellus erythropus (Red-footed
Tinamou)**
C. e. colombianus
NC Colombia
C.e. saltuarius
NC Colombia
C. e. idoneus
NE Colombia, W Venezuela
C. e. cursitans
N Colombia, NW Venezuela
C. e. spencei
N Venezuela
C. e. margaritae
Margarita I
C. e. erythrops
E Venezuela, Guyana, Surinam, N Brazil
**Crypturellus noctivagus (Yellow-legged
Tinamou)**
C. n. zabele
NE Brazil
C. n. noctivagus
SE Brazil
**Crypturellus atrocapillus (Black-capped
Tinamou)**
C. a. atrocapillus
SE Peru
C. a. garleppi
N Bolivia
**Crypturellus cinnamomeus (Thicket
Tinamou)**
C. c. occidentalis
W coast of Mexico
C. c. mexicanus
NE Mexico
C. c. sallaei
S Mexico
C. c. goldmani
SE Mexico, N Belize
C. c. soconuscensis
C Chiapas
C. c. cinnamomeus
El Salvador to Nicaragua
C. c. vicinior
Chiapas to C Honduras
C. c. delattrei
Nicaragua
C. c. praepes
NW Costa Rica
**Crypturellus boucardi (Slaty-breasted
Tinamou)**
C. b. boucardi
S Mexico to N Nicaragua

C. b. costaricensis
E Honduras to Costa Rica
Crypturellus kerriae (Choco Tinamou)
Colombia
Crypturellus variegatus (Variegated Tinamou)
Amazonia, E Brazil
Crypturellus brevirostris (Rusty Tinamou)
E Peru, W Brazil, French Guiana
Crypturellus bartletti (Bartlett's Tinamou)
E Peru
Crypturellus parvirostris (Small-billed Tinamou)
SE Peru to S Brazil & NE Argentina
Crypturellus casiquiare (Barred Tinamou)
E Colombia, S Venezuela
Crypturellus tataupa (Tataupa Tinamou)
C. t. inops
NW Peru
C. t. peruviana
WC Peru
C. t. lepidotus
NE Brazil
C. t. tataupa
S Brazil, E Bolivia, Paraguay

RHYNCHOTUS
Rhynchotus rufescens (Red-winged Tinamou)
R. r. catingae
C Brazil
R. r. rufescens
E Bolivia to NE Brazil and Uruguay
R. r. pallescens
N Argentina
R. r. maculicollis
W & S Bolivia to W Argentina

NOTHOPROCTA
Nothoprocta taczanowskii (Taczanowski's Tinamou)
C & S Peru
Nothoprocta kalinowskii (Kalinowski's Tinamou)
C Peru
Nothoprocta ornata (Ornate Tinamou)
N. o. branickii
C Peru
N. o. ornata
SE Peru, Bolivia
N. o. rostrata
W Argentina
Nothoprocta perdicaria (Chilian Tinamou)
N. p. perdicaria
N & C Chile
N. p. sanborni
W Argentina, S Chile

Nothoprocta cinerascens (Brushland Tinamou)
N. c. cinerascens
W Argentina
N. c. parvimaculata
La Rioja (Argentina)
Nothoprocta pentlandii (Andean Tinamou)
N. p. ambigua
S Ecuador
N. p. oustaleti
S Ecuador, NW Peru
N. p. niethammeri
central coast of Peru
N. p. fulvescens
SE Peru
N. p. pentlandii
Bolivia to NW Argentina
N. p. doeringi
C Argentina
N. p. mendozae
WC Argentina
Nothoprocta curvirostris (Curve-billed Tinamou)
N. c. curvirostris
C Ecuador
N. c. peruviana
C Peru

NOTHURA
Nothura boraquira (White-bellied Nothura)
NE Brazil, E Bolivia, Paraguay
Nothura minor (Lesser Nothura)
S Brazil
Nothura darwinii (Darwin's Nothura)
N. d. peruviana
S Peru
N. d. agassizii
SE Peru, W Bolivia
N. d. boliviana
W Bolivia
N. d. salvadorii
W Argentina
N. d. darwinii
SC Argentina
Nothura maculosa (Spotted Nothura)
N. m. cearensis
S Ceara, Brazil
N. m. major
E Brazil
N. m. paludivaga
C Paraguay, NC Argentina
N. m. maculosa
SE Brazil, E Paraguay, Uruguay
NE Argentina
N. m. pallida
NW Argentina
N. m. annectens
E Argentina

N. m. submontana
  SW Argentina
N. m. nigroguttata
  S Argentina
Nothura chacoensis (Chaco Nothura)
  Paraguay, N Argentina

TAONISCUS
Taoniscus nanus (Dwarf Tinamou)
  Paraguay, SW Brazil

EUDROMIA
Eudromia elegans (Elegant Crested-Tinamou)
  E. e. intermedia
    NW Argentina
  E. e. magnistriata
    NW Argentina
  E. e. riojana
    NW Argentina
  E. e. albida
    W Argentina
  E. e. elegans
    C Argentina
  E. e. multiguttata
    EC Argentina
  E. e. devia
    SW Argentina
  E. e. patagonica
    S Chile, S Argentina

Eudromia formosa (Quebracho Crested-Tinamou)
  N Argentina

TINAMOTIS
Tinamotis pentlandii (Puna Tinamou)
  C Peru, W Argentina, N Chile
Tinamotis ingoufi (Patagonian Tinamou)
  S Chile, S Argentina

Sphenisciformes

7 SPHENISCIDAE (PENGUINS)

APTENODYTES
Aptenodytes patagonica (King Penguin)
  A. p. patagonica
    Staten I, S Georgia I, Falkland Is
  A. p. halli
    Macquarie I, Kerguelen I, Crozet Is, Marion I
Aptenodytes forsteri (Emperor Penguin)
  Antarctica

PYGOSCELIS
Pygoscelis papua (Gentoo Penguin)
  P. p. papua
    Falkland Is, S Georgia I
  P. p. taeniata
    Macquarie I, Heard I, Kerguelen I, Marion I

P. p. ellsworthi
  S Orkney Is, Deception I, S Shetlands Is
Pygoscelis adeliae (Adelie Penguin)
  Antarctica, S Orkney Is, S Shetland Is
Pygoscelis antarctica (Bearded Penguin)
  Antarctic Ocean, S Atlantic

EUDYPTES
Eudyptes pachyrhynchus (Victoria Penguin)
  E. p. pachyrhynchus
    New Zealand, Stewart I
  E. p. atratus
    Snares I
Eudyptes robustus (Snares I. Penguin)
  Snares I
Eudyptes sclateri (Big-crested Penguin)
  Auckland Is, Antipodes Is
Eudyptes crestatus (Rockhopper Penguin)
  E. c. crestatus
    Tierra del Fuego, Falkland Is
  E. c. filholi
    Kerguelen I & islands S of New Zealand
  E. c. moseleyi
    Tristan da Cunha I, St Paul I, Amsterdam I,
Eudyptes schlegeli (Royal Penguin)
  Macquarie I.
Eudyptes chrysolophus (Macaroni Penguin)
  S Georgia I, Kerguelen I, Falkland Is
  S Orkney Is, S Shetland Is

MEGADYPTES
Megadyptes antipodes (Yellow-eyed Penguin)
  South I, New Zealand & southern islands

EUDYPTULA
Eudyptula minor (Little Penguin)
  E. m. novaehollandiae
    Tasmania, S Australian islands
  E. m. minor
    New Zealand, Stewart I, Chatham I.
Eudyptula albosignata (White-flippered Penguin)
  E South I, New Zealand

SPHENISCUS
Spheniscus demersus (Jackass Penguin)
  coast of S Africa and islands
Spheniscus humboldti (Humboldt Penguin)
  W coast of S America & islands
Spheniscus magellanicus (Magellanic Penguin)
  S South America & islands
Spheniscus mendiculus (Galapagos Penguin)
  Galapagos Is

Gaviiformes

8 GAVIIDAE (DIVERS)

GAVIA
Gavia stellata (Red-throated Diver)
Holarctic, Circumpolar » S Europe
S China, Florida
Gavia arctica (Black-throated Diver)
G. a. arctica
N Europe, N Russia
G. a. suschkini
W Siberia to EC Asia
G. a. viridigularis
NE Siberia to W Alaska
Gavia pacifica (Pacific Diver)
Arctic of N America, Alaska » W North
America
Gavia immer (Great Northern Diver)
G. i. immer
N North America, N Europe » N Mexico
Florida, North Sea
G. i. elasson
W Canada, N Dakota
Gavia adamsii (White-billed Diver)
Arctic, E Siberia, N North America
» Norway, S Alaska

Podicipediformes

9 PODICIPEDIDAE (GREBES)

TACHYBAPTUS
Tachybaptus ruficollis (Little Grebe)
T. r. ruficollis
Europe to Urals, NW Africa
T. r. iraquensis
Iraq, SW Iran
T. r. capensis
Caucasus to Burma, Ghana to Ethiopia
& Cape Province
T. r. poggei
E China, Hainan I, Malaysia
T. r. kunikyonis
C Riukiu Is
T. r. philippensis
Taiwan, Borneo, Philippine Is
T. r. cotabato
Mindanao I
T. r. javanicus
Java
T. r. vulcanorum
Bali I to Timor I
T. r. tricolor
Celebes to Solomon Is.

Tachybaptus novaehollandiae (Australian Dabchick)
New Guinea, Australia, New Caledonia
Tachybaptus pelzelni (Madagascar Little Grebe)
Madagascar
Tachybaptus rufolarvatus (Delacour's Little Grebe)
Madagascar

PODILYMBUS
Podilymbus podiceps (Pied-billed Grebe)
P. p. podiceps
Canada & USA » Panama & Cuba
P. p. antillarum
Gtr & Lssr Antilles
P. p. antarcticus
Colombia & Venezuela to S Argentina
Podilymbus gigas (Atitlan Grebe)
Lake Atitlan, Guatemala

ROLLANDIA
Rollandia rolland (White-tufted Grebe)
R. r. morrisoni
C Peru
R. r. chilensis
S Brazil & S Peru to Tierra del Fuego
R. r. rolland
Falkland Is
Rollandia micropterum (Short-winged Grebe)
Lake Titicaca, Bolivia

PODICEPS
Podiceps major (Great Grebe)
Amazonia to S Chile
Podiceps poliocephalus (Hoary-headed Grebe)
Australia, Tasmania
Podiceps rufopectus (New Zealand Dabchick)
New Zealand
Podiceps dominicus (Least Grebe)
P. d. brachypterus
S Texas to Panama
P. d. bangsi
S Baja California
P. d. dominicus
Gtr Antilles, S. Mexico to Argentina
P. d. speciosus
Columbia
Podiceps grisegena (Red-necked Grebe)
P. g. grisegena
Holarctic, Scandinavia to Siberia» N. Africa and Iran
P. g. holbollii
N America, NE Asia » China, Japan, S USA

Podiceps cristatus (Great Crested Grebe)
　　P. c. cristatus
　　　Europe to China, India, N Africa
　　P. c. infuscatus
　　　Senegal to Ethiopia & Cape Province
　　P. c. australis
　　　S Australia, Tasmania, South I, New
　　　Zealand
Podiceps auritus (Slavonian Grebe)
　　N America, N Europe, N Asia
　　　» Mediterranean, E China, S USA
Podiceps nigricollis (Black-necked Grebe)
　　P. n. nigricollis
　　　Europe, Russia
　　P. n. gurneyi
　　　S Angola to Ethiopia & Cape Province
　　P. n. californicus
　　　W Canada, W USA » Guatemala
　　P. n. andinus
　　　C Colombia
Podiceps occipitalis (Silvery Grebe)
　　P. o. juninensis
　　　Peru, Bolivia
　　P. o. occipitalis
　　　NW Argentina to Tierra del Fuego
Podiceps taczanowskii (Puna Grebe)
　　Lake Junin, Peru
Podiceps gallardoi (Hooded Grebe)
　　NW Argentina

AECHMOPHORUS
Aechmophorus occidentalis (Western
Grebe)
　　W Canada, NW USA » SW USA
　　& C Mexico

Procellariiformes

10 DIOMEDEIDAE (ALBATROSSES)

DIOMEDEA
Diomedea exulans (Wandering Albatross)
　　D. e. exulans
　　　Southern Ocean, South Georgia I
　　D. e. dabbenena
　　　Tristan da Cunha, Gough I
　　D. e. chionoptera
　　　S Indian Ocean, Macquarie I
Diomedea epomophora (Royal Albatross)
　　D. e. sanfordi
　　　South I, New Zealand, Chatham I
　　D. e. epomophora
　　　Auckland I to S Australia, S South America
Diomedea irrorata (Waved Albatross)
　　Peru, Galapagos Is
Diomedea albatrus (Short-tailed Albatross)
　　N Pacific, Riukiu Is, Bonin Is

Diomedea nigripes (Black-footed
Albatross)
　　N Pacific, Hawaii Is, Marshall Is
Diomedea immutabilis (Laysan Albatross)
　　NW Hawaii Is
Diomedea melanophrys (Black-browed
Albatross)
　　D. m. impavida
　　　islands S of New Zealand
　　D. m. melanophrys
　　　S South America
Diomedea bulleri (Buller's Albatross)
　　South Pacific, Snares I
Diomedea cauta (Shy Albatross)
　　D. c. cauta
　　　Bass Strait, Albatross I
　　D. c. eremita
　　　Chatham I
　　D. c. salvini
　　　S South America, Snares I, Bounty I
Diomedea chlororhynchos (Yellow-nosed
Albatross)
　　Tristan da Cunha, Gough I
Diomedea chrysostoma (Grey-headed
Albatross)
　　S Georgia, Marion I, Crozet Is, Kerguelen I

PHOEBETRIA
Phoebetria fusca (Sooty Albatross)
　　Tristan da Cunha, Gough I, St Paul I
Phoebetria palpebrata (Light-mantled
Sooty Albatross)
　　P. p. palpebrata
　　　South Georgia I
　　P. p. huttoni
　　　Kerguelen I, Crozet Is, Heard I, Antipodes
　　　Is, Macquarie I

11 PROCELLARIIDAE (PETRELS,
SHEARWATERS)

MACRONECTES
Macronectes giganteus (Giant Petrel)
　　Southern Ocean
Macronectes halli (Hall's Giant Petrel)
　　Southern Ocean (N of *M. giganteus*)?

FULMARUS
Fulmarus glacialis (Fulmar)
　　F. g. glacialis
　　　Greenland, Br Isles, Iceland, Norway
　　F. g. rodgersii
　　　NE Asian Is, Bering Sea
　　F. g. minor
　　　N Greenland
Fulmarus glacialoides (Silver-Grey Petrel)
　　Antarctic, New Zealand

THALASSOICA
Thalassoica antarctica (Antarctic Petrel)
Antarctic

DAPTION
Daption capense (Pintado Petrel)
D. c. capense
Antarctica, S Georgia I
D. c. australe
Snares I, Antipodes Is, Bounty I

PAGODROMA
Pagodroma nivea (Snow Petrel)
Antarctica, S Georgia I, S Orkney Is

PTERODROMA
Pterodroma macroptera (Great-winged Petrel)
P. m. macroptera
Tristan da Cunha, Crozet Is, Marion I,
Kerguelen I
P. m. gouldi
SW Australia, North I, New Zealand
Pterodroma aterrima (Mascarene Black Petrel)
Reunion I
Pterodroma lessoni (White-headed Petrel)
Auckland I, Kerguelen I, Antipodes Is,
Macquarie I,
Pterodroma hasitata (Black-capped Petrel)
Dominica, Caribbean Sea
Pterodroma cahow (Cahow)
Bermuda I
Pterodroma incerta (Schlegel's Petrel)
Tristan da Cunha, S Atlantic
Pterodroma rostrata (Tahiti Petrel)
P. r. rostrata
Marquesas Is, Society Is
P. r. trouessarti
New Caledonia
P. r. becki
Solomon Is
Pterodroma alba (Phoenix Petrel)
Christmas I, Phoenix I, Tonga I,
Marquesas Is
Pterodroma inexpectata (Peale's Petrel)
New Zealand, Chatham I
Pterodroma solandri (Solander's Petrel)
Lord Howe I, Austral I
Pterodroma brevirostris (Kerguelen Petrel
Gough I, Kerguelen I, Marion I
Pterodroma ultima (Murphy's Petrel)
S Pacific, Tuamotu I, Austral I
Pterodroma neglecta (Kermadec Petrel)
P. n. neglecta
Lord Howe I, Kermadec I, Tuamotu I,
Austral I
P. n. juana
Juan Fernandez Is

Pterodroma magentae (Chatham Island Taiko)
Chatham I
Pterodroma arminjoniana (Trinidade Petrel)
P. a. arminjoniana
Mauritius I, S Trinidad I (Brazil)
P. a. heraldica
Tonga I, Marquesas Is, Tuamotu I
P. a. paschae
Easter I
Pterodroma mollis (Soft-plumaged Petrel)
P. m. mollis
Tristan da Cunha, Gough I, St Paul I,
Kerguelen I
P. m. feae
Cape Verde Is
P. m. deserta
Deserta I
P. m. madeira
Madeira I
Pterodroma baraui (Barau's Petrel)
Reunion I
Pterodroma phaeopygia (Hawaiian Petrel)
P. p. phaeopygia
Galapagos Is
P. p. sandwichensis
Hawaiian Is
Pterodroma externa (White-necked Petrel)
P. e. cervicalis
Kermadec Is
P. e. externa
Masafuera I, Juan Fernandez Is
P. e. tristani
Tristan da Cunha
Pterodroma cookii (Cook's Petrel)
P. c. cookii
Little Barrier I, New Zealand
P. c. orientalis
W South America
P. c. defilippiana
Juan Fernandez Is
Pterodroma leucoptera (White-winged Petrel)
P. l. leucoptera
Pt Stephens (NS Wales)
P. l. masafuerae
Masafuera I
Pterodroma brevipes (Collared Petrel)
New Caledonia, New Hebrides, Fiji Is
Pterodroma hypoleuca (Bonin Petrel)
Bonin Is, W Hawaiian Is
Pterodroma nigripennis (Black-winged Petrel)
Lord Howe I, Kermadec Is
Pterodroma axillaris (Chatham Island Petrel)
Chatham I

Pterodroma longirostris (Stejneger's Petrel)
Masafuera I
Pterodroma pycrofti (Pycroft's Petrel)
New Zealand
Pterodroma macgillivrayi (Macgillivray's Petrel)
Fiji Is.

HALOBAENA
Halobaena caerulea (Blue Petrel)
Kerguelen I, Crozet Is, Falkland Is

PACHYPTILA
Pachyptila vittata (Broad-billed Prion)
P. v. vittata
Tristan da Cunha, S Georgia I, Chatham I, SW New Zealand
P. v. macgillivrayi
Amsterdam I, St Pauls I
Pachyptila salvini (Salvin's Prion)
P. s. salvini
Marion I
P. s. crozeti
Crozet Is
Pachyptila desolata (Dove Prion)
P. d. desolata
Kerguelen I
P. d. peringueyi
S Africa
P. d. alexanderi
SW Australia
P. d. macquariensis
Macquarie I
P. d. alter
Auckland I, Heard I
P. d. banksi
S Georgia I, S Orkney Is
Pachyptila belcheri (Slender-billed Prion)
Kerguelen I, Falkland Is
Pachyptila turtur (Fairy Prion)
SE Australia, New Zealand, Falkland Is
Pachyptila crassirostris (Thick-billed Prion)
P. c. eatoni
Kerguelen I, Heard I, Antipodes Is
P. c. crassirostris
Bounty I
P. c. pyramidalis
Chatham I

BULWERIA
Bulweria bulwerii (Bulwer's Petrel)
Pacific & Atlantic Oceans
Bulweria fallax (Jouanin's Petrel)
Indian Ocean

PROCELLARIA
Procellaria cinerea (Brown Petrel)
Tristan de Cunha, Gough I, Kerguelen I, Macquarie I

Procellaria aequinoctialis (White-chinned Petrel)
P. a. aequinoctialis
S Georgia I, Falkland Is, Crozet Is, Kerguelen I
P. a. conspicillata
Inaccessible I, Tristan da Cunha
P. a. steadi
Auckland I, Antipodes Is, Campbell I, Macquarie I
Procellaria parkinsoni (Black Petrel)
New Zealand
Procellaria westlandica (Westland Petrel)
South I, New Zealand

CALONECTRIS
Calonectris leucomelas (White-faced Shearwater)
NW Pacific Ocean
Calonectris diomedea (Cory's Shearwater)
C. d. diomedea
Mediterranean Islands
C. d. borealis
Portugal, Canary Is, Madeira I, Azores Is
C. d. edwardsi
Cape Verde Is
C. d. flavirostris
W Indian Ocean, Kerguelen I

PUFFINUS
Puffinus creatopus (Pink-footed Shearwater)
E Pacific, Juan Fernandez Is
Puffinus carneipes (Pale-footed Shearwater)
P. c. carneipes
SW Australia
P. c. hullianus
Lord Howe I, New Zealand
Puffinus gravis (Greater Shearwater)
Tristan da Cunha, Gough I, Falkland Is
Puffinus pacificus (Wedge-tailed Shearwater)
P. p. chlororhynchus
W Australian islands
P. p. pacificus
Kermadec I
P. p. cuneatus
Bonin Is, Hawaiian Is
P. p. royanus
E Australian islands
Puffinus bulleri (Grey-backed Shearwater)
islands off New Zealand
Puffinus griseus (Sooty Shearwater)
South I, New Zealand to Chile, Falkland Is
Puffinus tenuirostris (Short-tailed Shearwater
SE Australia, Tasmania

Puffinus heinrothi (Heinroth's Shearwater)
New Britain
Puffinus nativitatis (Christmas Island Shearwater)
Hawaii Is, Christmas I, Tuamotu I
Puffinus puffinus (Manx Shearwater)
P. p. puffinus
E North Atlantic
P. p. yelkouan
E Mediterranean
P. p. mauretanicus
W Mediterranean
Puffinus gavia (Fluttering Shearwater)
islands off New Zealand
Puffinus huttoni (Hutton's Shearwater)
South I, New Zealand
Puffinus opisthomelas (Black-vented Shearwater)
W North America
Puffinus auricularis (Townsend's Shearwater)
W Mexico
Puffinus assimilis (Dusky Shearwater)
P. a. baroli
Azores Is, Madeira I, Canary Is
P. a. boydi
Cape Verde Is
P. a. elegans
Tristan da Cunha, Gough I
P. a. tunneyi
islands off SW Australia
P. a. assimilis
Lord Howe I, Norfolk I
P. a. haurakiensis
New Zealand
P. a. munda
Chatham I
P. a. kermadecensis
Kermadec Is
Puffinus lherminieri (Audubon's Shearwater)
P. l. bailloni
Mauritius I, Reunion I, Seychelles
P. l. bannermani
Bonin Is
P. l. nugax
New Hebrides
P. l. dichrous
Palau Is, Phoenix I, Christmas Is
P. l. polynesiae
Samoa Is, Society Is, Marquesas Is, Tuamotu I
P. l. subalaris
Galapagos Is
P. l. lherminieri
West Indies, Bahama Is, Bermuda I
P. l. persicus
NW India, Iran

P. l. loyemilleri
Costa Rica to Guyana

12 HYDROBATIDAE (STORM-PETRELS)

OCEANITES
Oceanites oceanicus (Wilson's Petrel)
Sub-antarctic Islands
Oceanites gracilis (Elliot's Storm Petrel)
O. g. gracilis
W South America
O. g. galapagoensis
Galapagos Is

GARRODIA
Garrodia nereis (Grey-backed Storm Petrel)
S Georgia I, Falkland Is, Kerguelen I, Chatham I

PELAGODROMA
Pelagodroma marina (White-faced Storm Petrel)
P. m. hypoleuca
Madeira I, Canary Is, Cape Verde Is
P. m. marina
Tristan da Cunha
P. m. dulciae
W & S Australia
P. m. maoriana
New Zealand, Auckland I, Chatham I
P. m. albiclunis
Kermadec Is

FREGETTA
Fregetta grallaria (White-bellied Storm Petrel)
F. g. royana
Lord Howe I
F. g. titan
Austral I
F. g. grallaria
Juan Fernandez Is
Fregetta tropica (Black-bellied Storm Petrel)
F. t. tropica
Tristan da Cunha
F. t. melanogaster
Kerguelen I, Crozet Is
F. t. lineata
Samoa Is

NESOFREGETTA
Nesofregetta fuliginosa (White-throated Storm Petrel)
N. f. fuliginosa
Christmas I, Marquesas Is, Fiji Is, New Hebrides
N. f. moestissima
Samoa Is

HYDROBATES
Hydrobates pelagicus (British Storm Petrel)
E North Atlantic, Mediterranean

HALOCYPTENA
Halocyptena microsoma (Least Storm Petrel)
W Mexico to Ecuador

OCEANODROMA
Oceanodroma tethys (Galapagos Storm Petrel)
O. t. tethys
Galapagos Is
O. t. kelsalli
coast of Peru
Oceanodroma castro (Madeiran Storm Petrel)
O. c. cryptoleucura
North Pacific, Hawaiian Is
O. c. bangsi
South Pacific, Cocos Is, Galapagos Is
O. c. castro
E Atlantic islands, St Helena I
Oceanodroma leucorhoa (Leach's Storm Petrel)
O. l. leucorhoa
N Pacific & N Atlantic coasts
O. l. beali
SE Alaska to California
O. l. kaedingi
Guadelupe I (Baja California)
Oceanodroma markhami (Sooty Storm Petrel)
O. m. markhami
W South America
O. m. owstoni
Hawaiian Is
Oceanodroma matsudairae (Matsudaira's Storm Petrel)
Volcano I
Oceanodroma tristrami (Stejneger's Storm Petrel)
Japan, Laysan I, Midway I
Oceanodroma monorhis (Swinhoe's Storm Petrel)
O. m. monorhis
E North Pacific, Taiwan, Japan
O. m. socorroensis
W North Pacific, Baja California
Oceanodroma homochroa (Ashy Storm Petrel)
California, Santa Barbara I
Oceanodroma hornbyi (Ringed Storm Petrel)
W South America
Oceanodroma furcata (Fork-tailed Storm Petrel)
N Pacific Ocean

Oceanodroma melania (Black Storm Petrel)
E Pacific, Baja California

13 PELECANOIDIDAE (DIVING PETRELS)

PELECANOIDES
Pelecanoides garnoti (Peruvian Diving Petrel)
coasts of Peru & Chile
Pelecanoides magellani (Magellan Diving Petrel)
S Chile, Cape Horn
Pelecanoides georgicus (Georgian Diving Petrel)
P. g. georgicus
South Georgia I
P. g. novus
Macquarie I
Pelecanoides urinatrix (Common Diving Petrel)
P. u. berard
Falkland Is
P. u. coppingeri
S Chile
P. u. dacunhae
Tristan da Cunha
P. u. elizabethae
Gough I
P. u. urinatrix
SE Australia, Tasmania, New Zealand
P. u. chathamensis
Chatham I, Antipodes Is, Snares I
P. u. exsul
Crozet Is, Marion I, Heard I,
Kerguelen I, Auckland I

Pelecaniformes

14 PHAETHONTIDAE (TROPIC BIRDS)

PHAETHON
Phaethon aethereus (Red-billed Tropic Bird)
P. a. limatus
Tower I, Galapagos Is
P. a. mesonauta
Daphne I, Lesser Antilles to Cape Verde Is
P. a. aethereus
Fernando Noronha I, St Helena I, Ascension I
P. a. indicus
Persian Gulf, Gulf of Aden
Phaethon rubricauda (Red-tailed Tropic Bird)
P. r. rubricauda
Mauritius I, Aldabra I

P. r. westralis
Christmas I, Cocos Keeling Is,
NW Australia
P. r. roseotincta
Lord Howe I, Norfolk I, Kermadec Is
P. r. melanorhynchus
Society Is, Palmerston I
P. r. rothschildi
Bonin Is, Hawaiian Is
Phaethon lepturus (White-tailed Tropic Bird)
P. l. catesbyi
West Indies, Bahama Is, Bermuda I
P. l. ascensionis
Fernando Noronha I, Ascension I,
Gulf of Guinea
P. l. lepturus
Mascarene Is, Seychelles, Andaman Is
P. l. fulvus
Christmas I (Java)
P. l. dorotheae
SW Pacific islands

15 PELECANIDAE (PELICANS)

PELECANUS
Pelecanus onocrotalus (Eastern White Pelican)
S Europe, Africa, C Asia
Pelecanus roseus (White Pelican)
China, Persian Gulf
Pelecanus rufescens (Pink-backed Pelican)
C & S Africa
Pelecanus philippensis (Grey Pelican)
S Asia, Iran to Philippine Is
Pelecanus crispus (Dalmatian Pelican)
SE Europe to China
Pelecanus conspicillatus (Australian Pelican)
Australia, Tenimber Is, New Guinea
Pelecanus erythrorhynchos (American White Pelican)
North & C America, W Indies
Pelecanus occidentalis (Brown Pelican)
P. o. occidentalis
West Indies
P. o. carolinensis
coasts of S Carolina to Venezuela
P.o. californicus
coast of California, W Mexico
P. o. murpheyi
coasts of W Columbia & Ecuador
P. o. urinator
Galapagos Is
P. o. thagus
coasts of Peru & Chile

16 SULIDAE (GANNETS, BOOBIES)

MORUS
Morus bassanus (Northern Gannet)
E Canada, Iceland, Br Isles
Morus capensis (Cape Gannet)
Southern Africa
Morus serrator (Australian Gannet)
M. s. serrator
S Australian coast, Tasmania, Bass Str
M. s. rex
North I, New Zealand

SULA
Sula nebouxii (Blue-footed Booby)
S. n. nebouxii
California to Peru
S. n. excisa
Galapagos Is
Sula variegata (Peruvian Booby)
coasts of Peru & Chile
Sula abbotti (Abbott's Booby)
Tropical Indian Ocean
Sula dactylatra (Blue-faced Booby)
S. d. dactylatra
Caribbean, Bahama Is, Acension I
S. d. melanops
W Indian Ocean, Seychelles Is
S. d. californica
W Mexico Islands
S. d. granti
Galapagos Is
S. d. bedouti
Christmas I (Java), Lesser Sunda Is
S. d. personata
N Australian & Pacific Is
Sula sula (Red-footed Booby)
S. s. sula
Caribbean Is & South Trinidad I,
(Brazil)
S. s. rubripes
Indian Ocean & Pacific islands
S. s. websteri
Galapagos Is
Sula leucogaster (Brown Booby)
S. l. leucogaster
Caribbean & Atlantic Is
S. l. brewsteri
coast of California & W Mexico
S. l. etesiaca
C American & Colombian islands
S. l. plotus
Indian & W Pacific Ocean Islands & Java
to N Australia
S. l. nesiotes
Clipperton I

17 PHALACROCORACIDAE (CORMORANTS)

PHALACROCORAX

Phalacrocorax auritus (Double-crested Cormorant)
P. a. cincinatus
Alaska to Oregon
P. a. albociliatus
California to W Mexico
P. a. auritus
C & E Canada, E USA
P. a. floridanus
S USA to Bahama Is & Honduras

Phalacrocorax olivaceus (Olivaceous Cormorant)
P. o. mexicanus
S USA to Nicaragua & Cuba
P. o. olivaceus
Panama to Patagonia
P. o. choncho
Sonora (NW Mexico)
P. o. hornensis
Tierra del Fuego

Phalacrocorax sulcirostris (Little Black Cormorant)
P. s. territori
Malaysia to New Guinea & N Australia
P. s. sulcirostris
E & S Australia, Tasmania
P. s. purpuragula
New Zealand

Phalacrocorax carbo (Common Cormorant)
P. c. carbo
E Canada to Br Isles
P. c. maroccanus
N Africa
P. c. lugubris
NE Africa
P. c. sinensis
C Europe to India & China
P. c. hanedae
Japan
P. c. novaehollandiae
Australia & Tasmania
P. c. steadi
New Zealand, Chatham I

Phalacrocorax lucidus (White-breasted Cormorant)
Cape Verde Is, Senegal to E & S Africa

Phalacrocorax fuscicollis (Indian Cormorant)
India, Sri Lanka, Burma

Phalacrocorax capensis (Cape Cormorant)
coasts of South Africa

Phalacrocorax nigrogularis (Socotra Cormorant)
S Red Sea, Persian Gulf

Phalacrocorax neglectus (Bank Cormorant)
coasts of South Africa

Phalacrocorax capillatus (Japanese Cormorant)
NE Asia to China, Japan

Phalacrocorax penicillatus (Brandt's Cormorant)
S Alaska to NW Mexico

Phalacrocorax aristotelis (Shag)
P. a. aristotelis
Iceland & Lapland to Portugal
P. a. desmaresti
C Mediterranean
P. a. riggenbachi
coast of Morocco

Phalacrocorax pelagicus (Pelagic Cormorant)
P. p. pelagicus
N Pacific islands
P. p. resplendens
British Columbia to Mexico

Phalacrocorax urile (Red-faced Cormorant)
Bering Sea to Taiwan

Phalacrocorax magellanicus (Magellan Cormorant)
Tierra del Fuego, Falkland Is

Phalacrocorax bougainvillei (Guanay Cormorant)
coasts of Peru & Chile

Phalacrocorax featherstoni (Chatham Cormorant)
Chatham I

Phalacrocorax varius (Pied Cormorant)
Australia, Tasmania, New Zealand

Phalacrocorax fuscescens (Black-faced Cormorant)
S Australia, Tasmania

Phalacrocorax carunculatus (Rough-faced Cormorant)
P. c. carunculatus
South I, New Zealand
P. c. chalconotus
Stewart I
P. c. onslowi
Chatham I

Phalacrocorax campbelli (Campbell Is Cormorant)
P. c. campbelli
Campbell I
P. c. colensoi
Auckland I
P. c. ranfurlyi
Bounty I

Phalacrocorax verrucosus (Kerguelen Cormorant)
Kerguelen I, Marion I

Phalacrocorax gaimardi (Red-legged Cormorant)
coasts of S South America

Phalacrocorax punctatus (Spotted Cormorant)
P. p. punctatus
New Zealand
P. p. oliveri
Stewart I

Phalacrocorax atriceps (Blue-eyed Cormorant)
P. a. atriceps
S South America
P. a. nivalis
Heard I

Phalacrocorax georgianus (South Georgia Cormorant)
South Georgia I

Phalacrocorax albiventer (King Cormorant)
P. a. albiventer
Patagonia, Falkland Is
P. a. melanogenis
Crozet Is
P. a. purpurascens
Macquarie I

HALIETOR

Haliëtor melanoleucos (Little Pied Cormorant)
H. m. melvillensis
Malaysia to N Australia
H. m. melanoleucos
S Australia, Tasmania
H. m. brevirostris
New Zealand
H. m. brevicauda
Rennell I

Haliëtor africanus (Reed Cormorant)
H. a. africanus
Senegal to Egypt & Cape Province
H. a. pictilis
Madagascar
H. a. coronatus
Namibia

Haliëtor niger (Javanese Cormorant)
India to Java and Borneo

Haliëtor pygmeus (Pigmy Cormorant)
C Europe, N Africa to C Asia

NANNOPTERUM

Nannopterum harrisi (Flightless Cormorant)
Galapagos Is

18 ANHINGIDAE (ANHINGAS)

ANHINGA

Anhinga rufa (African Darter)

A. r. rufa
Senegal to Cape Province
A. r. vulsini
Madagascar
A. r. chantrei
Tigris & Euphrates rivers
A. r. papua
New Guinea

Anhinga melanogaster (Indian Darter)
India to Philippine Is & Celebes

Anhinga novaehollandiae (Australian Darter)
New Guinea, Australia

Anhinga anhinga (American Darter)
A. a. anhinga
Brazil, Argentina
A. e. leucogaster
SE USA to Colombia

19 FREGATIDAE (FRIGATE BIRDS)

FREGATA

Fregata aquila (Ascension Frigate Bird)
Ascension I

Fregata andrewsi (Christmas I Frigate Bird)
E Indian Ocean, Christmas I

Fregata magnificens (Magnificent Frigate Bird)
F. m. magnificens
Galapagos Is
F. m. rothschildi
SE USA, C America, W Indies
F. m. lowei
Cape Verde Is

Fregata minor (Great Frigate Bird)
F. m. aldabrensis
Seychelles, Aldabra I
F. m. minor
Christmas I, Cocos Keeling Is
F. m. peninsulae
Raine I (Queensland)
F. m. palmerstoni
C & S Pacific
F. m. strumosa
Hawaiian Is
F. m. ridgwayi
Galapagos Is
F. m. nicolli
S Trinidad I (Brazil)

Fregata ariel (Lesser Frigate Bird)
F. a. iredalei
W Indian Ocean, Aldebra I
F. a. ariel
Philippine Is to N Australia, S Pacific
F. a. trinitatis
S Trinidad I (Brazil)

Ciconiiformes

20 ARDEIDAE (HERONS, BITTERNS)

BOTAURINAE

BOTAURUS
Botaurus stellaris (Eurasian Bittern)
  B. s. stellaris
   Europe to E Asia » N & C Africa
  B. s. capensis
   C Botswana to Natal & Cape Province
Botaurus poiciloptilus (Australian Bittern)
   Australia, Tasmania, New Zealand
Botaurus lentiginosus (American Bittern)
   Canada to SW & NE USA » C America
Botaurus pinnatus (Pinnated Bittern)
  B. p. pinnatus
   Colombia to SE Brazil
  B.p. caribaeus
   SE Mexico, Belize

IXOBRYCHUS
Ixobrychus exilis (Least Bittern)
  I. e. exilis
   North America to W Indies » Brazil
  I. e. pullus
   S Sonora
  I. e. bogotensis
   C Colombia
  I. e. erythromelas
   Trinidad, the Guianas to Paraguay
  I. e. limoncochae
   E Ecuador
  I. e. peruvianus
   coast of Peru
Ixobrychus minutus (Little Bittern)
  I. m. minutus
   C & S Europe to C Asia and NW India
    » Africa
  I. m. payesii
   Senegal to Aden » Cape Province
  I. m. podiceps
   Madagascar
  I. m. dubius
   E & SW Australia
  I. m. novaezelandiae
   New Zealand
Ixobrychus sinensis (Chinese Little Bittern)
   Manchuria, Japan » India, Sunda Is,
   Philippine Is
Ixobrychus involucris (Stripe-backed Bittern)
   S. Brazil to Patagonia
Ixobrychus eurhythmus (Schrenk's Little Bittern)
   E Asia » Malaysia, Sunda Is, Philippine Is

Ixobrychus cinnamomeus (Cinnamon Bittern)
   India to China, Phil Is & Celebes
Ixobrychus sturmii (Dwarf Bittern)
   Senegal to Sudan & Cape Province
Ixobrychus flavicollis (Black Bittern)
  I. f. flavicollis
   C China to India, Malaysia, Celebes
  I. f. australis
   Timor I
  I. f. nesophilus
   New Britain, New Ireland
  I. f. woodfordi
   Solomon Is
  I. f. gouldi
   Moluccas, New Guinea, Australia
  I. f. pallidior
   Rennell I

ARDEINAE

TIGRIORNITHINI

ZONERODIUS
Zonerodius heliosylus (Forest Bittern)
   New Guinea, Aru Is

TIGRIORNIS
Tigriornis leucolophus (African Tiger Bittern)
   Sierra Leone to SW & NE Zaire

TIGRISOMA
Tigrisoma lineatum (Rufescent Tiger Heron)
  T. l. lineatum
   Honduras to NW South America
  T. l. marmoratum
   Brazil, Paraguay, N. Argentina
Tigrisoma fasciatum (Fasciated Tiger Heron)
  T. f. fasciatum
   SE Brazil
  T. f. salmoni
   Colombia, Ecuador
  T. f. bolivianum
   Bolivia, N Argentina
  T. f. pallescens
   NW Argentina
Tigrisoma mexicanum (Bare-throated Tiger Heron)
  T. m. fremitus
   S Sonora
  T. m. mexicanum
   W Mexico to E Panama, NW Colombia

ZEBRILUS
Zebrilus undulatus (Zigzag Heron)
   the Guianas to C Brazil

GORSACHIUS
Gorsachius goisagi (Japanese Night Heron)
E China, Japan, Philippine Is
Gorsachius melanolophus (Tiger Bittern)
G. m. melanolophus
S India, S China to Sumatra, Java
G. m. minor
Nicobar Is
G. m. kutteri
Philippine Is
G. m. rufolineatus
Palawan I
Gorsachius magnificus (Magnificent Night Heron)
SE China, Hainan I
Gorsachius leuconotus (White-backed Night Heron)
Senegal to Sudan & Natal

NYCTICORAX
Nycticorax nycticorax (Black-crowned Night Heron)
N. n. nycticorax
Holland to Japan, Sudan Is, Africa
N. n. hoactli
SE Canada to Argentina, Hawaii Is
N. n. obscurus
S Peru to Tierra del Fuego
N. n. falklandicus
Falkland Is
Nycticorax caledonicus (Rufous Night Heron)
N. c. manillensis
Philippine Is, N Borneo
N. c. minahassae
Celebes
N. c. pelewensis
Palau Is
N. c. mandibularis
Solomon Is
N. c. caledonicus
New Caledonia
H. c. hilli
Moluccas, New Guinea, Australia
N. c. cancrivorus
Bismarck Archipelago
Nycticorax violaceus (Yellow-crowned Night Heron)
N. v. violaceus
EC USA, ECentral America, W Indies
N. v. bancrofti
W Baja California
N. v. gravirostris
Socorro I.

N. v. caliginis
Colombia
N. v. cayennensis
S Colombia to Peru & S Brazil
N. v. pauper
Galapagos Is

COCHLEARIINI

COCHLEARIUS
Cochlearius cochlearius (Boat-billed Heron)
C. c. zeledoni
W Mexico
C. c. phillipsi
S Mexico, Belize
C. c. ridgwayi
Guatemala, Honduras
C. c. panamensis
S Costa Rica, Panama
C. c. cochlearius
Trinidad, N & C South America

PILHERODIUS
Pilherodius pileatus (Capped Heron)
E Panama to E Peru & S Brazil

ARDEINI

ARDEOLA
Ardeola ralloides (Squacco Heron)
S Europe to Iran & Africa
Ardeola idae (Madagascar Squacco Heron)
E Africa, Madagascar
Ardeola grayii (Indian Pond Heron)
A. g. grayii
Iran to India, Burma, Sri Lanka
A. g. phillipsi
S Maldive Is
Ardeola bacchus (Chinese Pond Heron)
China to Malaysia & Borneo
Ardeola speciosa (Javanese Pond Heron)
Borneo Celebes, Sumatra, Java
Ardeola rufiventis (Rufous-bellied Heron)
S Angola to Tanzania & Cape Province

BUBULCUS
Bubulcus ibis (Cattle Egret)
B. i. ibis
Spain to Iran, N & C Africa, E North America, C & N South America
B. i. coromandus
India to S Japan, Philippine Is, Moluccas
B. i. seychellarum
Seychelle

SYRIGMA
Syrigma sibilator (Whistling Heron)
S. s. fostersmithi
NW Venezuela, NE Colombia
S. s. sibilator
S Brazil, Paraguay, Uruguay

BUTORIDES
Butorides striatus (Striated (Green) Heron)
B. s. anthonyi
  SW USA, W Mexico
B. s. frazari
  S Baja California
B. s. virescens
  E North America » Panama
B. s. bahamensis
  Bahama Is
B. s. maculatus
  W Indies, EC America
B. s. margaritophilus
  Pearl Is (Panama)
B. s. curacensis
  Curaçao I
B. s. patens
  C Panama
B. s. striatus
  E Panama to S Brazil
B. s. robinsoni
  Margarita I
B. s. sundevalli
  Galapagos Is
B. s. cyanurus
  Paraguay, Uruguay, N Argentina
B. s. fuscicollis
  Bolivia
B. s. brevipes
  Somalia, Red Sea Coast
B. s. atricapillus
  Senegal to Sudan & Cape Province
B. s. rutenbergi
  Madagascar, Réunion I
B. s. rhizophorae
  Comoro Is
B. s. degens
  Seychelle
B. s. crawfordi
  Assumption I, Aldabra I
B. s. albolimbatus
  Diego Garcia I
B. s. didii
  C & N Maldive Is
B. s. albidulus
  S Maldive Is
B. s. chloriceps
  India, Sri Lanka
B. s. spodiogaster
  Andaman Is, Nicobar Is, W Sumatran
  islands
B. s. amurensis
  NE Asia » Philippine Is, Sunda Is
B. s. abbotti
  Malaysia
B. s. connectens
  China

B. s. actophilus
  S China, N Indochina » Indonesia
B. s. javanicus
  E India to Philippine Is & Sunda Is
B. s. moluccarum
  S Moluccas
B. s. solomonensis
  Solomon Is
B. s. papuensis
  NW New Guinea
B. s. macrorhynchus
  S New Guinea E Australia
B. s. stagnatilis
  N & NW Australia
B. s. patruelis
  Tahiti I
B. s. rogersi
  WC Australia

EGRETTA
Egretta picata (Pied Heron)
  Celebes to New Guinea, N Australia
Egretta ardesiaca (Black Heron)
  Senegal to Sudan & Natal
Egretta vinaceigula (Red-throated Heron)
  Transvaal
Egretta caerulea (Little Blue Heron)
  S USA to C South America
Egrette tricolor (Louisiana Heron)
E. t. ruficollis
  SE USA to NW South America
E. t. tricolor
  French Guiana, Surinam, NE Brazil
E. t. rufimentum
  Trinidad.
Egretta rufescens (Reddish Egret)
E. r. rufescens
  S USA, Mexico, Cuba, Jamaica,
  Hispaniola
E. r. colorata
  Yucatan peninsula
E. r. dickeyi
  San Luis I
Egretta sacra (Eastern Reef Heron)
E. s. sacra
  SE Asia to Australia, New Zealand
E. s. albolineata
  New Caledonia
Egretta eulophotes (Swinhoe's Egret)
  S & C China, Taiwan, Celebes
Egretta thula (Snowy Egret)
E. t. brewsteri
  W USA
E. t. thula
  SE USA to N Chile, N Argentina
Egretta gularis (Western Reef Heron)
E. g. gularis
  Senegal to Gabon

E. g. asha
Red Sea to W Indian coast
E. g. dimorpha
Madagascar, Aldabra I
Egretta garzetta (Little Egret)
E. g. garzetta
S Europe to Japan & Africa
E. g. nigripes
Sunda Is, Philippine Is to New Guinea,
Australia
Egretta intermedia (Intermediate Egret)
E. i. brachyrhyncha
Sudan to Cape Province
E. i. intermedia
S India to Japan & Gtr Sunda Is
E. i. plumifera
S Moluccas, New Guinea, Australia
Egretta alba (Great Egret)
E. a. alba
SE Europe, N Asia » N Africa, India
S China
E. a. modestus
India to Japan & Australia
E. a. maorianus
South I, New Zealand
E. a. melanorhynchos
Senegal to Sudan & Cape Province
E. a. egretta
S USA to Patagonia

ARDEA
Ardea purpurea (Purple Heron)
A. p. purpurea
S Europe to Iran, Africa
A. p. bournei
Cape Verde Is
A. p. madagascariensis
Madagascar
A. p. manilensis
India, China, Gtr Sunda Is
Ardea novaehollandiae (White-faced Heron)
A. n. novaehollandiae
Lombok I to Timor I, Australia, New
Zealand
A. n. parryi
NW Australia
Ardea pacifica (White-necked Heron)
Australia, Tasmania
Ardea cinerea (Grey Heron)
A. c. cinerea
Europe to W China, Africa
A. c. monicae
Banc d'Arguin Is, Mauretania
A. c. rectirostris
E Siberia, Japan, Taiwan, E China
A. c. firasa
Madagascar, Aldebra I, Comoro Is

A. c. altirostris
Java, Sumatra
Ardea herodias (Great Blue Heron)
A. h. fannini
W Canada
A. h. hyperonca
W USA
A. h. treganzai
WC USA, NW Mexico
A. h. herodias
NE North America » C America
A. h. wardi
SE USA
A. h. sanctilucae
Baja California
A. h. cognata
Galapagos Is
A. h. occidentalis
SE USA, Cuba, Jamaica
Ardea cocoi (Cocoi Heron)
South America
Ardea melanocephala (Black-headed Heron)
Gambia to Sudan & Cape Province
Ardea humbloti (Madagascar Heron)
E Madagascar, Aldabra I
Ardea goliath (Goliath Heron)
Senegal to Sudan & Cape Province
Ardea imperialis (Great White-bellied Heron)
Sikkim to C Burma
Ardea sumatrana (Dusky-grey Heron)
Burma, Malaysia to Philippine Is, New
Guinea, N Australia

AGAMIA
Agamia agami (Chestnut-bellied Heron)
E Mexico to Peru & Brazil

21 BALAENICIPITIDAE (WHALE-HEADED STORK)

BALAENICEPS
Balaeniceps rex (Whale-headed Stork)
Sudan to Zambia

22 SCOPIDAE (HAMMERKOP)

SCOPUS
Scopus umbretta (Hammerkop)
S. u. umbretta
Senegal to Nigeria
S. u. minor
coast from Sierra Leone to Nigeria
S. u. bannermanni
Cameroun to Aden & Cape Province

23 CICONIIDAE (STORKS)

MYCTERIINI

MYCTERIA
Mycteria americana (American Wood Ibis)
    SE USA to C South America
Mycteria cinerea (Milky Stork)
    Malaysia, Sumatra, Java
Mycteria ibis (Yellow-billed Stork)
    Senegal to Sudan & Cape Province
Mycteria leucocephala (Painted Stork)
    India to SW China, Indochina

ANASTOMUS
Anastomus oscitans (Asian Open-bill Stork)
    India to Indochina
Anastomus lamelligerus (African Open-bill Stork)
    A. l. lamelligerus
        Senegal to Sudan & Rhodesia
    A. l. madagascariensis
        Madagascar

CICONIINI

CICONIA
Ciconia nigra (Black Stork)
    Europe to N China » Africa, India
Ciconia abdimii (Abdim's Stork)
    Ethiopia to Angola & Transvaal
Ciconia episcopus (Woolly-necked Stork)
    C. e. microscelis
        Senegal to Sudan & Cape Province
    C. e. episcopus
        India, Sri Lanka, Burma
    C. e. neglecta
        Malaysia to Philippine Is, Sunda Is
    C. e. stormi
        Borneo
Ciconia maguari (Maguari Stork)
    the Guianas to Chile & S Argentina
Ciconia ciconia (White Stork)
    C. c. ciconia
        Europe, N Africa » S Africa
    C. c. asiatica
        C Asia » India
    C. c. boyciana
        NE Asia, Japan

LEPTOPTILINI

EPHIPPIORHYNCHUS
Ephippiorhynchus asiaticus (Black-necked Stork)
    E. a. asiaticus
        India to Malaysia & Indochina
    E. a. australis
        New Guinea, N & E Australia

Ephippiorhynchus senegalensis (Saddle-bill Stork)
    Senegal to Sudan & Transvaal

JABIRU
Jabiru mycteria (Jabiru)
    S Mexico to C Argentina

LEPTOPTILOS
Leptoptilos javanicus (Lesser Adjutant Stork)
    C India to S China, Gtr Sunda Is
Leptoptilos dubius (Greater Adjutant Stork)
    India to Indochina, Gtr Sunda Is
Leptoptilos crumeniferus (Marabou Stork)
    Senegal to Sudan & Transvaal

24 THRESKIORNITHIDAE (IBISES, SPOONBILLS)

THRESKIORNITHINAE

THRESKIORNIS
Threskiornis aethiopicus (Sacred Ibis)
    T. a. aethiopicus
        Africa, Saudi Arabia
    T. a. abbotti
        Aldabra I
    T. a. bernieri
        Madagascar
Threskiornis melanocephalus (Oriental Ibis)
    India to China, Japan
Threskiornis molucca (Australian White Ibis)
    T. m. molucca
        W Papuan Is, Kei Is, New Guinea
    T. m. strictipennis
        Australia

CARPHIBIS
Carphibis spinicollis (Straw-necked Ibis)
    Australia, Tasmania

PSEUDIBIS
Pseudibis papillosa (Black Ibis)
    N India
Pseudibis davisoni (Davison's Ibis)
    E Burma to S Indochina

THAUMATIBIS
Thaumatibis gigantea (Giant Ibis)
    S Thailand, S Indochina

GERONTICUS
Geronticus eremita (Hermit Ibis) (Waldrapp)
    N Africa, Ethiopia
Geronticus calvus (Bald Ibis)
    S Africa

NIPPONIA
Nipponia nippon (Japanese Crested Ibis)
NE Asia, Japan

LAMPRIBIS
Lampribis olivacea (Olive Ibis)
L. o. olivacea
Sierra Leone, Liberia
L. o. cupreipennis
S Cameroun to W Zaire
L. o. rothschildi
Principé I **e?**
L. o. bocagei
Sao Thomé I
L. o. akleyorum
Kenya
Lampribis rara (Spot-breasted Ibis)
Liberia to E Zaire & Angola

HAGEDASHIA
Hagedashia hagedash (Hadada Ibis)
H. h. brevirostris
Gambia to Zaire
H. h. nilotica
Ethiopia to Uganda
H. h. erlangeri
Somalia to Malawi
H. h. hagedash
Southern Africa

BOSTRYCHIA
Bostrychia carunculata (Wattled Ibis)
Ethiopia

HARPIPRION
Harpiprion caerulescens (Plumbeous Ibis)
C Brazil to N Argentina

THERISTICUS
Theristicus caudatus (Buff-necked Ibis)
T. c. caudatus
E Panama to French Guiana
T. c. hyperorious
C South America
Theristicus branickii (Branicki's Ibis)
Ecuador, Peru, N Bolivia
Theristicus melanopis (Black-faced Ibis)
S Chile, S Argentina

CERCIBIS
Cercibis oxycerca (Sharp-tailed Ibis)
SE Colombia to Surinam, N Brazil

MESEMBRINIBIS
Mesembrinibis cayennensis (Green Ibis)
Panama to NE Argentina

PHIMOSUS
Phimosus infuscatus (Bare-faced Ibis)
P. i. berlepschi
N South America
P. i. nudifrons
C & S Brazil

P. i. infuscatus
Paraguay, Uruguay, NE Argentina

EUDOCIMUS
Eudocimus albus (White Ibis)
S USA to N South America
Eudocimus ruber (Scarlet Ibis)
N South America, Trinidad

PLEGADIS
Plegadis falcinellus (Glossy Ibis)
P. f. falcinellus
S Europe, Asia, Africa, Central America
P. f. peregrinus
Philippine Is, Celebes, Java to Australia
Plegadis chihi (White-faced Ibis)
NW USA to SC South America
Plegadis ridgwayi (Puna Ibis)
Peru, Bolivia

LOPHOTIBIS
Lophotibis cristata (Crested Wood Ibis)
L. c. cristata
E Madagascar
L. c. urschi
W Madagascar

PLATALEINAE

PLATALEA
Platalea leucorodia (White Spoonbill)
P. l. leucorodia
Holland, S Europe to Asia Minor » Africa
P. l. major
C Asia to Japan, Egypt, India, Taiwan
P. l. balsaci
Mauretania
P. l. archeri
Red Sea coasts, Somalia
Platalea minor (Black-faced Spoonbill)
S Japan to S China, Taiwan
Platalea alba (African Spoonbill)
Gambia to Sudan, Cape Province
Platalea regia (Royal Spoonbill)
Australia to New Guinea, Celebes, New Zealand

PLATIBIS
Platibis flavipes (Yellow-billed Spoonbill)
Australia

AJAIA
Ajaia ajaja (Roseate Spoonbill)
S USA to C Argentina & C Chile

25 PHOENICOPTERIDAE (FLAMINGOS)

PHOENICOPTERUS
Phoenicopterus ruber (Greater Flamingo)
P. r. ruber
Atlantic, Central & South America, W Indies

P. r. roseus
    S Europe, C Asia, NW India, S Africa
Phoenicopterus chilensis (Chilian Flamingo)
    Peru, Uruguay to Tierra del Fuego

PHOENICONAIAS
Phoeniconaias minor (Lesser Flamingo)
    S & E Africa, NW India, Madagascar

PHOENICOPARRUS
Phoenicoparrus andinus (Andean Flamingo)
    Chile & NW Argentina
Phoenicoparrus jamesi (James' Flamingo)
    S Peru, N Chile, NW Argentina

Anseriformes

26 ANHIMIDAE (SCREAMERS)

ANHIMA
Anhima cornuta (Horned Screamer)
    N South America

CHAUNA
Chauna torquata (Crested Screamer)
    Paraguay, S Brazil, N & E Argentina
Chauna chavaria (Northern Screamer)
    N Colombia, N Venezuela

27 ANATIDAE (DUCKS, GEESE, SWANS)

ANSERANATINAE

ANSERANAS
Anseranas semipalmata (Magpie Goose)
    S New Guinea, N Australia

ANSERINAE

DENDROCYGNINI

DENDROCYGNA
Dendrocygna guttata (Spotted Whistling Duck)
    Mindanao I to Celebes & New Guinea
Dendrocygna eytoni (Plumed Whistling Duck)
    Australia, Tasmania
Dendrocygna bicolor (Fulvous Whistling Duck)
    D. b. helva
        S USA, N Mexico
    D. b. bicolor
        N South America, E Africa, India
Dendrocygna arcuata (Wandering Whistling Duck)
    D. a. arcuata
        Sumatra to Philippine Is, Timor I, Moluccas
    D. a. australis
        Australia, New Guinea

D. a. pygmaea
    New Britain, Fiji Is
Dendrocygna javanica (Indian Whistling Duck)
    India to Java & Indochina
Dendrocygna viduata (White-faced Whistling Duck)
    S America, C Africa
Dendrocygna arborea (Black-billed Whistling Duck)
    West Indies
Dendrocygna autumnalis (Red-billed Whistling Duck)
    D. a. autumnalis
        SE Texas to Panama
    D. a. discolor
        E Panama to Ecuador & N Argentina

ANSERINI

CYGNUS
Cygnus olor (Mute Swan)
    Europe to C Asia » N Africa, India
Cygnus atratus (Black Swan)
    Australia, Tasmania
Cygnus melanocoryphus (Black-necked Swan)
    S South America, Falkland Is
Cygnus cygnus (Whooper Swan)
    C. c. cygnus
        N Europe, N Asia » C Europe, C Asia, China
    C. c. islandicus
        S Greenland, Iceland
    C. c. buccinator
        N Canada, N USA » USA
Cygnus columbianus (Whistling Swan)
    C. c. columbianus
        N Canada » coasts of USA
    C. c. bewickii
        N Russia, N Siberia » N Europe, C Asia
    C. c. jankowskii
        NE Asia » China, Japan

COSCOROBA
Coscoroba coscoroba (Coscoroba Swan)
    S South America

ANSER
Anser cygnoides (Swan Goose)
    NC Asia & Siberia » China
Anser fabalis (Bean Goose)
    A. f. fabalis
        Lapland to Ural Mts » W & E Europe
    A. f. johanseni
        W Siberia
    A. f. middendorffi
        E Siberia » E China & Japan
    A. f. rossicus
        N Russia, NW Siberia » WC Europe, C Asia

A. f. serrirostris
N Siberia » China, Japan

A. f. brachyrhynchus
Greenland, Iceland, Spitzbergen »
W Europe

Anser albifrons (White-fronted Goose)

A. a. albifrons
N Europe, N Asia » W Europe, S Russia,
India, China

A. a. frontalis
E Siberia, N Canada » W USA, China,
Japan

A. a. flavirostris
NW Greenland » British Isles

A. a. gambelli
NW Canada » C California

A. a. elgasi
Alaska

Anser erythropus (Lesser White-fronted Goose)
N Russia, N Asia » SE Europe & China

Anser anser (Greylag Goose)

A. a. anser
N Europe, N Asia » NW Africa

A. a. rubrirostris
C & E Asia » NW India, China

Anser indicus (Bar-headed Goose)
C Asia » N India, N Burma

Anser caerulescens (Snow Goose)

A. c. caerulescens
N Canada » S USA

A. c. atlanticus
N Greenland » NE USA

Anser rossi (Ross's Goose)
N Canada » N California

Anser canagicus (Emperor Goose)
NE Siberia, NW Alaska » Aleutian Is

BRANTA

Branta sandvicensis (Hawaiian Goose)
Hawaii

Branta canadensis (Canada Goose)

B. c. leucopareia
Aleutian Is » Japan & W USA

B. c. minima
W Alaska » W USA

B. c. occidentalis
Gulf of Alaska

B. c. fulva
S Alaska, W British Colombia

B. c. taverneri
N Canada » SW USA, Mexico

B. c. parvipes
Interior Canada » SC USA

B. c. moffitti
SW Canada » NW USA

B. c. hutchinsii
NC Canada » Texas, Mexico

B. c. interior
C & E Canada » E USA

B. c. canadensis
(Introduced Europe, New Zealand,
E Canada » E USA

Branta leucopsis (Barnacle Goose)
NE Greenland, Spitzbergen to W Europe

Branta bernicla (Brent Goose)

B. b. bernicla
N Europe, NW Asia » W Europe

B. b. hrota
E Canada, Greenland » NE USA,
NW Europe

B. b. nigricans
NE Canada » New Jersey

B. b. orientalis
E Siberia, W Canada » E Asia, W USA

Branta ruficollis (Red-breasted Goose)
N Siberia » S Russia

CEREOPSIS

Cereopsis novaehollandiae (Cereopsis Goose)
Islands off S Australia

STICTONETTINI

STICTONETTA

Stictonetta naevosa (Freckled Duck)
Southern Australia, Tasmania

ANATINAE

TADORNINI

CYANOCHEN

Cyanochen cyanopterus (Blue-winged Goose)
Ethiopia

CHLOEPHAGA

Chloephaga melanoptera (Andean Goose)
Peru to Tierra del Fuego

Chloephaga picta (Magellan Goose)

C. p. picta
S Chile, S Argentina

C. p. leucoptera
Falkland Is

Chloephaga hybrida (Kelp Goose)

C. h. hybrida
S Chile

C. h. malvinarum
Falkland Is

Chloephaga poliocephala (Ashy-headed Goose)
S Chile, Argentina

Chloephaga rubidiceps (Ruddy-headed Goose)
Tierra del Fuego, Falkland Is

NEOCHEN

Neochen jubatus (Orinoco Goose)
Orinoco & Amazon basins

ALOPOCHEN
Alopochen aegyptiacus (Eygptian Goose)
Africa (Introduced UK)

TADORNA
Tadorna ferruginea (Ruddy Shelduck)
SE Europe & C Asia » India & S China
Tadorna cana (South African Shelduck)
Transvaal, Cape Province
Tadorna variegata (Paradise Shelduck)
New Zealand
Tadorna tadornoides (Australian Shelduck)
Southern Australia, Tasmania
Tadorna tadorna (Common Shelduck)
W Europe to E Asia » N Africa, India,
S China
Tadorna radjah (Radjah Shelduck)
T. r. radjah
S Moluccas, Aru Is, New Guinea
T. r. rufitergum
N & E Australia

TACHYERINI

TACHYERES
Tachyeres patachonicus (Flying Steamer Duck)
S South America
Tachyeres pteneres (Flightless Steamer Duck)
S South America
Tachyeres brachypterus (Falkland Is Flightless Steamer Duck)
Falkland Is

CAIRININI

PLECTROPTERUS
Plectropterus gambensis (Spur-winged Goose)
P. g. gambensis
Gambia to Sudan & Rhodesia
P. g. niger
Southern Africa

CAIRINA
Cairina moschata (Muscovy Duck)
Mexico to Peru & Uruguay
Cairina scutulata (White-winged Wood Duck)
Assam & Thailand to Sumatra & Java

SARKIDIORNIS
Sarkidiornis melanotos (Comb Duck)
S. m. melanotos
Africa, India, SE China
S. m. sylvatica
Colombia
S. m. carunculatus
Venezuela to N Argentina

PTERONETTA
Pteronetta hartlaubii (Hartlaub's Duck)

P. h. hartlaubii
Liberia to E Zaire
P. h. albifrons
EC Africa

NETTAPUS
Nettapus pulchellus (Green Pygmy Goose)
S Moluccas, S New Guinea, N Australia
Nettapus coromandelianus (Cotton Pygmy Goose)
N. c. coromandelianus
India to S China & NW Indonesia
N. c. albipennis
NE Australia
Nettapus auritus (African Pygmy Goose)
Gambia to Kenya & Cape Province

CALLONETTA
Callonetta leucophrys (Ringed Teal)
C South America

AIX
Aix sponsa (Wood Duck)
S Canada, USA, Cuba
Aix galericulata (Mandarin)
NE Asia, E China, Japan

CHENONETTA
Chenonetta jubata (Maned Goose)
Australia, Tasmania

AMAZONETTA
Amazonetta brasiliensis (Brazilian Teal)
A. b. brasiliensis
Venezuela to N Argentina
A. b. ipecutiri
C & S Argentina

ANATINI

HYMENOLAIMUS
Hymenolaimus malacorhynchus (Mountain Duck)
New Zealand

MERGANETTA
Merganetta armata (Torrent Duck)
M. a. colombiana
W Venezuela, Colombia, Ecuador
M. a. leucogenis
C & S Ecuador, Peru
M. a. turneri
S Peru
M. a. garleppi
Bolivia
M. a. berlepschi
NW Argentina
M. a. armata
C Chile, W Argentina
M. a. fraenata
SC Chile

ANAS
Anas waigiuensis (Salvadori's Duck)
New Guinea, Waigeu I

Anas sparsa (African Black Duck)
  A. s. maclatchyi
    Cameroun, Gabon
  A. s. leucostigma
    Sudan & Ethiopia to Tanzania
  A. s. sparsa
    Angola, Malawi to Cape Province
Anas penelope (European Wigeon)
  N Europe, N Asia » N Africa, India, Japan
Anas americana (American Wigeon)
  W Canada, USA » Costa Rica, W Indies
Anas sibilatrix (Chiloe Wigeon)
  S South America
Anas falcata (Falcated Teal)
  NE Asia » E & S China
Anas strepera (Gadwall)
  Europe, Asia, W North America » N Africa,
    India, China, Mexico
Anas formosa (Baikal Teal)
  NE Asia » China, Japan
Anas crecca (Green-winged Teal)
  A. c. crecca
    Europe, Asia » N Africa, India, China
  A. c. nimia
    Aleutian Is
  A. c. carolinensis
    N Canada » S USA, Central America,
    W Indies
Anas flavirostris (Chilean Teal)
  A. f. flavirostris
    C Chile, NW Argentina to Tierra del Fuego
  A. f. andium
    C & S Colombia, Ecuador
  A. f. altipetens
    W Venezuela, E Colombia
  A. f. oxyptera
    N Peru to N Chile, Argentina
Anas capensis (Cape Teal)
  S Ethiopia to Botswana, Cape Province
Anas gibberifrons (Grey Teal)
  A. g. gibberifrons
    Java to Celebes, Timor I, Wetar I
  A. g. remissa
    Rennell I
  A. g. gracilis
    New Guinea, Australia, New Zealand
  A. g. albogularis
    Andaman Is, Cocos Is
Anas bernieri (Madagascar Teal)
  W Madagascar
Anas castanea (Chestnut-breasted Teal)
  Southern Australia, Tasmania
Anas aucklandica (New Zealand Teal)
  A. a. aucklandica
    Auckland I
  A. a. nesiotis
    Campbell I
  A. a. chlorotis
    New Zealand

Anas platyrhynchos (Mallard)
  A. p. platyrhynchos
    Europe, Asia, N America » N Africa, India,
    Mexico
  A. p. conboschas
    Greenland
  A. p. wyvilliana
    Hawaiian Is
  A. p. laysanensis
    Laysan I
  A. p. fulvigula
    SE USA
  A. p. diazi
    N & C Mexico
  A. p. maculosa
    Mexico
Anas rubripes (North American Black Duck)
  NE North America to SE USA
Anas melleri (Meller's Duck)
  E Madagascar
Anas undulata (African Yellow-bill)
  A. u. ruppelli
    Ethiopia, Sudan
  A. u. undulata
    Angola to Uganda, Cape Province
Anas poecilorhyncha (Spotbill Duck)
  A. p. poecilorhyncha
    India, Sri Lanka
  A. p. haringtoni
    Burma, SW China
  A. p. zonorhyncha
    NE Asia, China
  A. p. pelewensis
    Palau Is, Solomon Is, Fiji Is, N New Guinea
  A. p. percna
    Sunda Is, Celebes
  A. p. superciliosa
    S New Guinea, Australia, Tasmania, New
    Zealand
Anas luzonica (Philippine Duck)
  Philippine Is
Anas specularis (Bronze-winged Duck)
  S Chile, S Argentina
Anas specularioides (Crested Duck)
  A. s. alticola
    C Peru, Bolivia, N Chile
  A. s. specularioides
    C & S Chile, WC Argentina
Anas acuta (Pintail)
  A. a. acuta
    N Europe, Asia, N America » Africa, China,
    Central America
  A. a. eatoni
    Kerguelen I
  A. a. drygalskii
    Crozet Is
Anas georgica (Georgian Teal)
  A. g. niceforoi
    EC Colombia

A. g. spinicauda
S Colombia to Tierra del Fuego
A. g. georgica
South Georgia I
Anas bahamensis (Bahama Pintail)
A. b. bahamensis
Bahama Is, Gtr Antilles, N South
America
A. b. rubrirostris
S Brazil to C Peru
A. b. galapagensis
Galapagos Is
Anas erythrorhyncha (Red-billed Pintail)
S & E Africa
Anas versicolor (Versicolor Teal)
A. v. versicolor
Bolivia to C Chile, C Argentina
A. v. fretensis
S Chile, S Argentina
A. v. puna
Highlands of C Peru to N Chile
Anas punctata (Hottentot Teal)
Uganda to Cape Province, Madagascar
Anas querquedula (Garganey)
W Europe to Japan » Africa, India,
Indonesia
Anas discors (Blue-winged Teal)
A. d. discors
S Canada, C USA » Central America &
N South America
A. d. orphna
SE Canada, E USA » W Indies, South
America
Anas cyanoptera (Cinnamon Teal)
A. c. septentrionalium
W North America to N South America
A. c. tropica
Lowlands of Colombia
A. c. borreroi
Highlands of Colombia
A. c. orinomus
Peru, Bolivia, N Chile
A. c. cyanoptera
S Brazil to Tierra del Fuego
Anas platalea (Argentine Shoveller)
Peru, S Brazil to Tierra del Fuego
Anas smithi (Cape Shoveller)
Angola, Transvaal to Cape Province
Anas rhynchotis (Australian Shoveller)
A. r. rhynchotis
Australia, Tasmania
A. r. variegata
New Zealand
Anas clypeata (Common Shoveller)
Europe, Asia, N America » E Africa, India,
China, Mexico

MALACORHYNCHUS
**Malacorhynchus membranaceus
(Pink-eared Duck)**
Australia, Tasmania **e?**

MARMARONETTA
**Marmaronetta angustirostris (Marbled
Teal)**
S Spain to NW India

AYTHYINI

RHODONESSA
**Rhodonessa caryophyllacea (Pink-headed
Duck)**
NE & E India **e?**

NETTA
Netta rufina (Red-crested Pochard)
E Europe, C Asia » N Africa, India
Netta erythrophthalma (Southern Pochard)
N. e. brunnea
Angola to Ethiopia & Cape Province
N. e. erythrophthalma
W South America
Netta peposaca (Rosybill)
C Chile, N & C Argentina, Paraguay

AYTHYA
Aythya valisineria (Canvasback)
WC Canada, WC USA » S USA, Mexico
Aythya ferina (European Pochard)
W Europe to C Asia » N Africa, India,
S China
Aythya americana (Redhead)
W Canada, W USA » NW Mexico
Aythya collaris (Ring-necked Duck)
W Canada, NW USA » S USA,
Central America, W Indies
**Aythya australis (Australian White-eyed
Duck)**
A. a. australis
Australia, Tasmania, New Zealand
A. a. extima
New Hebrides
A. a. papuana
W New Guinea
Aythya baeri (Baer's Pochard)
NE Asia » China, Burma, Japan
Aythya nyroca (Ferruginous Duck)
S & E Europe to C Asia » NE Africa, Iran,
Burma
Aythya innotata (Madagascar Pochard)
N & E Madagascar
**Aythya novaeseelandiae (New Zealand
Scaup)**
New Zealand, Auckland I
Aythya fuligula (Tufted Duck)
Europe, Asia » India, S China, Philippine Is
Aythya marila (Greater Scaup)

A. m. marila
 N Europe, Asia » W & S Europe,
 NW India
A. m. marilioides
 Bering Is » China, Korea, Japan
A. m. nearctica
 N & W Canada » W & E USA, W Indies
Aythya affinis (Lesser Scaup)
 W & C Canada, W USA » S USA, Panama,
 W Indies

MERGINI

SOMATERIA
Somateria mollissima (Eider)
 S. m. v-nigra
 Alaska, NE Asia » Aleutian Is
 S. m. borealis
 N Canada, W Greenland » Maine
 S. m. dresseri
 NE Canada » Newfoundland
 S. m. mollissima
 Iceland to Novaya Zemlya » NW Europe
 S. m. sedentaria
 Hudson Bay
 S. m. faroeensis
 Faroe Is
Somateria spectabilis (King Eider)
 N Europe, N Asia, N Canada
Somateria fischeri (Spectacled Eider)
 NE Siberia, Alaska » Aleutian Is

POLYSTICTA
Polysticta stelleri (Steller's Eider)
 NE Siberia, Alaska » Aleutian Is

HISTRIONICUS
Histrionicus histrionicus (Harlequin Duck)
 H. h. histrionicus
 Iceland, Greenland, N Labrador
 H. h. pacificus
 E Siberia, Alaska, W USA to Japan,
 California

CLANGULA
Clangula hyemalis (Long-tailed Duck)
 N Europe, Asia, N America » W Europe,
 Japan, S USA

MELANITTA
Melanitta nigra (Common Scoter)
 M. n. nigra
 N Europe, N Asia, » W Europe to Black Sea
 M. n. americana
 NE Asia, W Alaska » China, Gt Lakes,
 California
Melanitta perspicillata (Surf Scoter)
 N Canada, NE Siberia to coasts of USA
Melanitta fusca (Velvet Scoter)
 M. f. fusca
 N Europe, NW Asia to W Europe, SW Asia
 M. f. stejnegeri
 C & E Asia » China & Japan

M. f. dixoni
 W Alaska » W USA
M. f. deglandi
 NW Canada, NW USA to Gt Lakes, E USA

BUCEPHALA
Bucephala albeola (Bufflehead)
 N & W Canada » USA
Bucephala islandica (Barrow's Goldeneye)
 SC Alaska to Iceland » coasts of USA
Bucephala clangula (Goldeneye)
 B. c. clangula
 N Europe, N Asia » S Europe, India, Japan
 B. c. americana
 Canada » California, S Carolina

MERGUS
Mergus cucullatus (Hooded Merganser)
 SC Canada to SE USA » S USA
Mergus albellus (Smew)
 N Europe, N Asia » N India, China, Japan
**Mergus octosetaceus (Brazilian
Merganser)**
 S Brazil, E Paraguay, NE Argentina
Mergus serrator (Red-breasted Merganser)
 M. s. serrator
 N Europe, Asia, N America » China,
 Mexico
 M. s. schioleri
 Greenland
Mergus squamatus (Chinese Merganser)
 NE Asia » China
Mergus merganser (Goosander)
 M. m. merganser
 Iceland to NE Asia » Mediterranean &
 China
 M. m. orientalis
 C Asia to Himalayas » Assam & Japan
 M. m. americanus
 Canada, W USA » E & S USA

OXYURINI

HETERONETTA
**Heteronetta atricapilla (Black-headed
Duck)**
 C Chile, Paraguay, N & C Argentina

OXYURA
Oxyura dominica (Masked Duck)
 Gtr Antilles, N & C South America
Oxyura jamaicensis (Ruddy Duck)
 O. j. rubida
 W Canada, W USA » Mexico, E & S USA
 O. j. jamaicensis
 W Indies
 O. j. andina
 Colombia
 O. j. ferruginea
 Peru, Bolivia
Oxyura leucocephala (White-headed Duck)
 Mediterranean to C Asia to Egypt, N India

Oxyura maccoa (Maccoa Duck)
S Ethiopia to Cape Province
Oxyura vittata (Argentine Lake Duck)
N Chile, S Brazil to Tierra del Fuego
Oxyura australis (Australian Blue-billed Duck)
S Australia, Tasmania

BIZIURA
Biziura lobata (Musk Duck)
S Australia, Tasmania

THALASSORNIS
Thalassornis leuconotos (White-backed Duck)
T. l. leuconotos
E Cameroun, to S Ethiopia & Cape Province
T. l. insularis
Madagascar

Falconiformes
Cathartae

28 CATHARTIDAE (NEW WORLD VULTURES)

CATHARTES
Cathartes aura (Turkey Vulture)
C. a. aura
S Canada to Costa Rica & Cuba
C. a. septentrionalis
E North America
C. a. ruficollis
Panama to N Argentina, Trinidad
C. a. jota
Colombia to Patagonia, Falkland Is
Cathartes burrovianus (Lesser Yellow-headed Vulture)
E Mexico to N Argentina
Cathartes melambrotus (Greater Yellow-headed Vulture)
C South America

CORAGYPS
Coragyps atratus (American Black Vulture)
C. a. atratus
W & S USA, N Mexico
C. a. brasiliensis
C Mexico to Peru & Brazil
C. a. foetens
Ecuador to C Chile & Patagonia

SARCORHAMPHUS
Sarcorhamphus papa (King Vulture)
C Mexico to N Argentina, Trinidad

GYMNOGYPS
Gymnogyps californianus (Californian Condor)
S California

Vultur gryphus (Andean Condor)
Andes from W Venezuela to Tierra del Fuego

Accipitres

29 PANDIONIDAE (OSPREY)
PANDION

Pandion haliaetus (Osprey)
P. h. haliaetus
Europe, Asia » S Africa, India, Sunda Is
P. h. carolinensis
N America » C South America
P. h. ridgwayi
Bahama Is, E Belize
P. h. melvillensis
Philippine Is to Sumatra & C Australia
P. h. microhaliaetus
New Caledonia, N Australia
P. h. cristatus
S Australia, Tasmania

30 ACCIPITRIDAE (HAWKS, EAGLES)

AVICEDA
Aviceda cuculoides (African Cuckoo Falcon)
A. c. cuculoides
Gambia to N Zaire
A. c. verreauxi
Angola to Uganda & Cape Province
A. c. batesi
Guinea to Cameroun
A. c. emini
NE Zaire
Aviceda madagascariensis (Madagascar Cuckoo Falcon)
Madagascar
Aviceda jerdoni (Jerdon's Baza)
A. j. jerdoni
E Himalayas, N India
A. j. ceylonensis
S India, Sri Lanka
A. j. borneensis
Borneo
A. j. magnirostris
Philippine Is
A. j. celebensis
Celebes, Banggai I, Sula Is
Aviceda subcristata (Crested Baza)
A. s. timorlaonsis
Lombok I to Timor I & Babar I
A. s. rufa
Obi Is, N Moluccas
A. s. stresemanni
Buru I
A. s. reinwardtii
Ceram I, Ambon I

A. s. pallida
Kei Is
A. s. obscura
Biak I
A. s. waigeuensis
Waigeu I
A. s. stenozona
W New Guinea, Aru Is, Misol I
A. s. megala
E New Guinea, Fergusson I, Goodenough I
A. s. bismarckii
New Britain, New Ireland, New Hanover
A. s. coultasi
Admiralty Is, Manus I
A. s. gurneyi
San Cristobal I, Ugi I, Santa Anna I,
Malaita I, Guadaicanal I
A. s. robusta
Choiseul I, Ysabel I
A. s. proxima
Bougainville I, Shortland I
A.s. njikena
NW Australia
A. s. subcristata
NE & E Australia
Aviceda leuphotes (Black Baza)
A. l. leuphotes
Himalayas to SW India
A. l. burmana
Burma, Malaysia & Indochina
A. l. sayama
Nepal, S China » Indo China
A. l. wolfi
Szechwan
A. l. andamanica
Andaman Is

LEPTODON
Leptodon cayanensis (Grey-headed Kite)
EC Mexico to N Argentina, Trinidad

CHONDROHIERAX
Chondrohierax uncinatus (Hook-billed Kite)
C. u. uncinatus
S Mexico to N Argentina, Trinidad
C. u. aquilonis
Mexico
C. u. mirus
Grenada
C. u. wilsonii
E Cuba

HENICOPERNIS
Henicopernis longicauda (Long-tailed Honey Buzzard)
H. l. longicauda
New Guinea
H. l. minimus
islands off W New Guinea

H. l. fraterculus
Japen I
Henicopernis infuscata (Black Honey Buzzard)
New Britain

PERNIS
Pernis apivorus (Honey Buzzard)
Europe, N Asia » Africa
Pernis ptilorhynchus (Oriental Honey Buzzard)
P. p. orientalis
E Siberia » Burma, China
P. p. ruficollis
India, Burma, SW China
P. p. torquatus
Malaysia, Thailand, Sumatra, Borneo
P. p. ptilorynchus
Java
P. p. palawanensis
Palawan I
P. p. philippensis
Philippine Is
Pernis celebensis (Barred Honey Buzzard)
P. c. celebensis
Celebes
P. c. steerei
Philippine Is

ELANOIDES
Elanoides forficatus (Swallow-tailed Kite)
E. f. forficatus
S USA, N Mexico
E. f. yetapa
S Mexico to N Argentina

MACHAERHAMPHUS
Machaerhamphus alcinus (Bat Hawk)
M. a. alcinus
Malaysia, Sumatra, Borneo
M. a. papuanus
SE New Guinea
M. a. anderssoni
Gambia to Somalia & Natal

GAMPSONYX
Gampsonyx swainsonii (Pearl Kite)
G. s. leonae
W Nicaragua, N South America
G. s. swainsonii
C Brazil to N Argentina
G. s. magnus
S Ecuador, N Peru

ELANUS
Elanus leucurus (White-tailed Kite)
E. l. majusculus
S USA & E Mexico
E. l. leucurus
N South America to C Chile
Elanus caeruleus (Black-shouldered Kite)

E. c. caeruleus
Africa, S Asia
E. c. sumatranus
Sumatra
E. c. hypoleucus
Java to Philippine Is & Celebes
E. c. wahgiensis
E & C New Guinea
***Elanus notatus* (Australian Black-shouldered Kite)**
Australia
***Elanus scriptus* (Letter-winged Kite)**
C Australia

CHELICTINIA
***Chelictinia riocourii* (African Swallow-tailed Kite)**
Senegal to Somalia & N Kenya

ROSTRHAMUS
***Rostrhamus sociabilis* (Everglade Kite)**
R. s. plumbeus
Florida
R. s. levis
Cuba, Isle of Pines
R. s. major
E Mexico, Guatemala
R. s. sociabilis
Nicaragua to Argentina
***Rostrhamus hamatus* (Slender-billed Kite)**
E Panama to Peru & E Brazil

HARPAGUS
***Harpagus bidentatus* (Double-toothed Kite)**
H. b. fasciatus
S Mexico to W Colombia & Ecuador
H. b. bidentatus
E Bolivia to E Colombia & E Brazil
***Harpagus diodon* (Rufous-thighed Kite)**
the Guianas to Paraguay & N Argentina

ICTINIA
***Ictinia plumbea* (Plumbeous Kite)**
EC Mexico to Paraguay & N Argentina
***Ictinia misisippiensis* (Mississippi Kite)**
S USA to C South America

LOPHOICTINIA
***Lophoictinia isura* (Square-tailed Kite)**
Australia

HAMIROSTRA
***Hamirostra melanosternon* (Black-breasted Buzzard Kite)**
N & C Australia

MILVUS
***Milvus migrans* (Black Kite)**
M. m. migrans
Europe, Middle East, W Asia
M. m. tenebrosus
Cape Verde Is, Madeira

M. m. arabicus
Egypt
M. m. aegyptius
N Africa, Somalia, S Yemen
M. m. parasitus
Senegal to Sudan & Cape Province
M. m. lineatus
C & E Asia, Japan to Himalayas
M. m. govinda
India to Indochina & Malaysia
M. m. formosanus
Hainan I, Taiwan
M. m. affinis
Lombok I to Timor I, Celebes, New Guinea, Australia
***Milvus milvus* (Red Kite)**
M. m. milvus
Europe, Asia Minor, NW Africa, Canary Is
M. m. fasciicauda
Cape Verde Is

HALIASTUR
***Haliastur sphenurus* (Whistling Hawk)**
E New Guinea, New Caledonia, Australia
***Haliastur indus* (Brahminy Kite)**
H. i. indus
India, Sri Lanka to S China, Indochina
H. i. intermedius
Malaysia, Philippine Is, Borneo, Indonesia
H. i. girrenera
Australia, New Guinea, Bismarck Archipelago
H. i. flavirostris
Solomon Is

HALIAEETUS
***Haliaeetus leucogaster* (White-bellied Sea Eagle)**
India to China & Australia
***Haliaeetus sanfordi* (Sanford's Sea Eagle)**
Solomon Is
***Haliaeetus vocifer* (African Fish Eagle)**
Senegal to Ethiopia & Cape Province
***Haliaeetus vociferoides* (Madagascar Fish Eagle)**
Madagascar
***Haliaeetus leucoryphus* (Pallas' Sea Eagle)**
C Asia to Iraq, N India & Burma
***Haliaeetus leucocephalus* (American Bald Eagle)**
H. l. alascensis
Alaska, W Canada
H. i. leucocephalus
C & S USA
***Haliaeetus albicilla* (White-tailed Sea Eagle)**
H. a. albicilla
Europe, N Asia, Japan to India, China
H. a. groenlandicus
Greenland

Haliaeetus pelagicus (Steller's Sea Eagle)
  H. p. pelagicus
    NE Asia, N China, Japan
  H. p. niger
    Korea

ICHTHYOPHAGA
Ichthyophaga nana (Lesser Fishing Eagle)
  I. n. plumbea
    Himalayas to N Vietnam, Hainan I
  I. n. nana
    Thailand to Malaysia, Sumatra to Celebes
Ichthyophaga ichthyaetus (Grey-headed Fishing Eagle)
    India to Borneo & Philippine Is

GYPOHIERAX
Gypohierax angolensis (Palm-nut Vulture)
    Senegal to Kenya & Cape Province

NEOPHRON
Neophron percnopterus (Egyptian Vulture)
  N. p. percnopterus
    S Europe, Middle East, Africa
  N. p. ginginianus
    Himalayas to S India

GYPAETUS
Gypaetus barbatus (Lammergeier)
  G. b. aureus
    S Europe, Middle East, C Asia
  G. b. haemachalanus
    E Asia
  G. b. barbatus
    NW Africa to Egypt
  G. b. meridionalis
    Yemen, Ethiopia to S Africa

NECROSYRTES
Necrosyrtes monachus (Hooded Vulture)
  N. m. monachus
    Senegal to Sudan
  N. m. pileatus
    E Sudan & Angola to CapeProvince

GYPS
Gyps bengalensis (Indian White-backed Vulture)
    India to Indochina
Gyps africanus (African White-backed Vulture)
    Senegal to Sudan & Transvaal
Gyps indicus (Indian Griffon)
  G. i. indicus
    N & S India to Indochina
  G. i. nudiceps
    NE India
Gyps rüeppellii (Rüppell's Griffon)
  G. r. rüepellii
    Egypt, Senegal to Uganda, Tanzania
  G. r. erlangeri
    Ethiopia, Somalia

Gyps himalayensis (Himalayan Griffon)
    C Asia to N India
Gyps fulvus (Griffon Vulture)
  G. f. fulvus
    S Europe, N Africa to C. Asia
  G. f. fulvescens
    Afghanistan, NW India
Gyps coprotheres (Cape Vulture)
    SW Rhodesia, South Africa

TORGOS
Torgos tracheliotus (Lappet-faced Vulture)
    NW Sahara to Ethiopia & Cape Province

AEGYPIUS
Aegypius monachus (European Black Vulture)
    Spain to C Asia » N Africa, India & China
Aegypius occipitalis (White-headed Vulture)
    Senegal to Sudan & Cape Province

SARCOGYPS
Sarcogyps calvus (Asiatic King Vulture)
    India to Laos & SW China

CIRCAETUS
Circaetus gallicus (Short-toed Eagle)
  C. g. gallicus
    S Europe, N Africa to India & China
  C. g. heptneri
    E Asia
  C. g. beaudouini
    Senegal to Sudan & W Kenya
  C. g. pectoralis
    E & S Africa
Circaetus cinereus (Brown Harrier Eagle)
    Senegal to Ethiopia & Cape Province
Circaetus fasciolatus (Southern Banded Snake Eagle)
    E Kenya to Natal
Circaetus cinerascens (Smaller Banded Snake Eagle)
    Guinea to Ethiopia & Tanzania

TERATHOPIUS
Terathopius ecaudatus (Bateleur)
    Senegal to Iraq & Cape Province

SPILORNIS
Spilornis holospilus (Philippine Serpent Eagle)
    Philippine Is
Spilornis rufipectus (Celebes Serpent Eagle)
  S. r. rufipectus
    Celebes
  S. r. sulaensis
    Sula Is
Spilornis cheela (Crested Serpent Eagle)
  S. c. cheela
    N India

S. c. melanotis
  S India
S. c. spilogaster
  Sri Lanka
S. c. burmanicus
  Burma to C & S Indochina
S. c. ricketti
  SE China, N Indochina
S. c. malayensis
  S Burma, Malaysia, N Sumatra
S. c. davisoni
  Andaman Is
S. c. rutherfordi
  Hainan I
S. c. hoya
  Taiwan
S. c. perplexus
  S Riukiu Is
S. c. pallidus
  Borneo
S. c. kinabaluensis
  Borneo
S. c. natunensis
  Bunguran I, Billiton I
S. c. sipora
  Mentawei Is, Sipora I
S. c. batu
  Batu I, S Sumatra
S. c. asturinus
  Nias I
S. c. abbottii
  Simalur I
S. c. bido
  Java, Bali I
S. c. baweanus
  Bawean I
S. c. palawanensis
  Palawan I, Balabac I, Calamian I
S. c. minimus
  C Nicobar Is
Spilornis klossi (Nicobar Serpent Eagle)
  Gt Nicobar I
Spilornis elgini (Andaman Serpent Eagle)
  Andaman Is

DRYOTRIORCHIS
Dryotriorchis spectabilis (Congo Serpent Eagle)
D. s. spectabilis
  Liberia to N Cameroun
D. s. batesi
  S Cameroun & Gabon to C Zaire

EUTRIORCHIS
Eutriorchis astur (Madagascar Serpent Eagle)
  Madagascar

POLYBOROIDES
Polyboroides typus (African Harrier Hawk)

P. t. typus
  Sudan to Angola & Cape Province
P. t. pectoralis
  Gambia to Gabon & W Zaire
Polyboroides radiatus (Madagascar Harrier Hawk)
  Madagascar

GERANOSPIZA
Geranospiza caerulescens (Crane Hawk)
G. c. livens
  NW Mexico
G. c. nigra
  Mexico to C Panama
G. c. balzarensis
  E Panama to NW Peru
G. c. caerulescens
  E Ecuador & Colombia to the Guianas, N Brazil
G. c. gracilis
  NE Brazil
G. c. flexipes
  S Brazil & Bolivia to N Argentina

CIRCUS
Circus assimilis (Spotted Harrier)
  Celebes, Timor I & W N & E Australia
Circus aeruginosus (Marsh Harrier)
C. a. aeruginosus
  Europe, Israel, C Asia
C. a. harterti
  Morocco & Algeria
C. a. spilonotus
  E Asia to Japan, Philippine Is & Borneo
C. a. macrosceles
  Madagascar, Comoro Is
C. a. maillardi
  Reunion I
C. a. spilothorax
  W New Guinea
C. a. approximans
  New Caledonia, Fiji Is, Tonga, New Hebrides
C. a. gouldi
  SE New Guinea, E & S Australia, New Zealand
Circus ranivorus (African Marsh Harrier)
  Angola & Kenya to Cape Province
Circus maurus (Black Harrier)
  Natal & Cape Province
Circus cyaneus (Hen Harrier)
C. c. cyaneus
  Europe, Asia, N Africa
C. c. hudsonius
  North & Central America
Circus cinereus (Cinereous Harrier)
  W & S South America, Falkland Is
Circus macrourus (Pallid Harrier)
  E Europe & C Asia to Africa & India

Circus pygargus **(Montagu's Harrier)**
W Europe & EC Asia to Africa, China
Circus melanoleucus **(Pied Harrier)**
E Siberia to India & Indochina
Circus buffoni **(Long-winged Harrier)**
Colombia, Trinidad, the Guianas to
C Argentina

MELIERAX
Melierax metabates (Dark Chanting Goshawk)
M. m. metabates
Senegal to Ethiopia
M. m. theresae
SW Morocco
M. m. neumanni
Mali to N Sudan
M. m. ignoscens
Yemen
M. m. mechowi
Angola & N Namibia to Kenya & Rhodesia
Melierax canorus (Pale Chanting Goshawk)
M. c. poliopterus
Somalia to Tanzania
M. c. canorus
South Africa
Melierax gabar (Gabar Goshawk)
Senegal to Yemen & Cape Province

MEGATRIORCHIS
Megatriorchis doriae (Doria's Goshawk)
New Guinea
ERYTHROTRIORCHIS
Erythrotriorchis radiatus (Red Goshawk)
NC Australia

ACCIPITER
Accipiter gentilis (Northern Goshawk)
A. g. gentilis
Europe, SW Asia, Morocco
A. g. buteoides
N Scandinavia, N Russia
A. g. albidus
NE Siberia
A. g. arrigonii
Corsica, Sardinia
A. g. schvedowi
SE Russia to W China
A. g. fujiyamae
Japan
A. g. atricapillus
North America
A. g. laingi
British Columbian islands
A. g. apache
SW USA, NW Mexico
Accipiter henstii (Henst's Goshawk)
Madagascar
Accipiter melanoleucus (Great Sparrow Hawk)

A. m. melanoleucus
Central African Republic & Ethiopia to
Cape Province
A. m. temminckii
Ghana to Gabon, Cape Verde Is
Accipiter meyerianus (Meyer's Goshawk)
Moluccas, New Britain, Solomon Is
Accipiter buergersi (Bürger's Sparrow Hawk)
E New Guinea
Accipiter ovampensis (Ovampo Sparrow Hawk)
Ghana & Ethiopia to E Transvaal
Accipiter madagascariensis (Madagascar Sparrow Hawk)
Madagascar
Accipiter gularis (Japanese Lesser Sparrow Hawk)
NE Asia, Japan to S China & Philippine Is
Accipiter virgatus (Besra Sparrow Hawk)
A. v. affinis
W Himalayas to W & S China, Indochina
A. v. besra
S India, Sri Lanka, Andaman Is
A. v. confusus
Philippine Is
A. v. quegga
Leyte I
A. v. rufotibialis
N Borneo
A. v. vanbemmeli
Sumatra
A. v. virgatus
Java
Accipiter nanus (Celebes Little Sparrow Hawk)
Celebes
Accipiter rhodogaster (Vinous-breasted Sparrow Hawk)
A. r. rhodogaster
Celebes
A. r. butonensis
Muna I, Buton I
A. r. sulaensis
Peling I, Sula Is
Accipiter erythrauchen (Moluccan Sparrow Hawk)
A. e. erythrauchen
Batjan I, Halmahera I, Morotai I, Obi Is
A. e. ceramensis
Ceram I, Buru I
Accipiter cirrhocephalus (Collared Sparrow Hawk)
A. c. papuanus
New Guinea, Aru Is, Waigeu I, Japen I
A. c. rosselianus
Louisiades Archipelago, Rossel I

A. c. quaesitandus
  Cape York Peninsular, & N Australia
A. c. cirrhocephalus
  S Australia, Tasmania
Accipiter brachyurus (New Britain Sparrow Hawk)
  New Britain
Accipiter nisus (European Sparrow Hawk)
A. n. nisus
  Europe to C Russia & Iran
A. n. punicus
  Morocco, Algeria, Tunisia
A. n. granti
  Madeira, Canary Is
A. n. wolterstorffi
  Corsica, Sardinia
A. n. nisosimilis
  N Iran to Manchuria & Japan
A. n. melaschistos
  Himalayas to W China
Accipiter rufiventris (Rufous-breasted Sparrow Hawk)
A. r. rufiventris
  C Zaire to Kenya & Cape Province
A. r. perspicillaris
  Ethiopia
Accipiter striatus (Sharp-shinned Hawk)
A. s. perobscurus
  Queen Charlotte Is (British Columbia)
A. s. velox
  Canada, USA
A. s. suttoni
  N Mexico
A. s. madrensis
  SW Mexico
A. s. chionogaster
  S Mexico, Guatemala to Nicaragua
A. s. fringilloides
  Cuba
A. s. striatus
  Hispaniola
A. s. venator
  Puerto Rico
A. s. ventralis
  W Venezuela & Colombia to W Bolivia
A. s. erythronemius
  E Bolivia & S Brazil to Uruguay, N Argentina
Accipiter erythropus (Red-thighed Sparrow Hawk)
A. e. erythropus
  Gambia to Togo
A. e. zenkeri
  Cameroun to S Angola & Uganda
Accipiter minullus (African Little Sparrow Hawk)
  Ethiopia to Angola & Cape Province

Accipiter castanilus (Chestnut-bellied Sparrow Hawk)
A. c. castanilus
  Nigeria to W Zaire
A. c. beniensis
  E Zaire
Accipiter tachiro (African Goshawk)
A. t. macroscelides
  Sierra Leone to W Cameroun
A. t. lopezi
  Fernando Po I
A. t. toussenelii
  Cameroun, Gabon, N & W Zaire
A. t. canescens
  E Zaire
A. t. unduliventer
  E & S Ethiopia
A. t. croizati
  SW Ethiopia
A. t. sparsimfasciatus
  Uganda & S Zaire to Somalia & Tanzania
A. t. tachiro
  S Angola & Mozambique to Cape Province
Accipiter trivirgatus (Crested Goshawk)
A. t. peninsulae
  SW India
A. t. layardi
  Sri Lanka
A. t. indicus
  NE India to S China, Malaysia
A. t. trivirgatus
  Sumatra
A. t. niasensis
  Nias I
A. t. javanicus
  Java
A. t. microstictus
  Borneo
A. t. palawanus
  Palawan I, Calamian Is
A. t. castroi
  Polillo Is
A. t. extimus
  Negros I, Samar I, Leyte I, Mindanao I
Accipiter griseiceps (Celebes Crested Goshawk)
  Celebes, Muna I, Buton I
Accipiter trinotatus (Spot-tailed Accipiter)
  Celebes, Muna I, Buton I
Accipiter luteoschistaceus (Blue and Grey Sparrow Hawk)
  New Britain
Accipiter fasciatus (Australian Goshawk)
A. f. natalis
  Christmas I
A. f. wallacei
  Lombok I to Wetar I, Damar I, Moa I

A. f. tjendanae
Sumba I

A. f. stresemanni
Djampea I, Tukangbesi Is

A. f. savu
Savu I

A. f. hellmayri
Alor I, Samao I, Timor I

A. f. buruensis
Buru I

A. f. dogwa
S New Guinea

A. f. polycryptus
E New Guinea

A. f. vigilax
New Caledonia, New Hebrides

A. f. didimus
N coast of Australia

A. f. fasciatus
Rennell I, Australia, Tasmania

Accipiter henicogrammus (Gray's Goshawk)
Batjan I, Halmahera I, Morotai I

Accipiter novaehollandiae (White Goshawk)

A. n. misoriensis
Biak I

A. n. hiogaster
Ceram I, Ambon I

A. n. albiventris
Kei Is

A. n. pallidiceps
Buru I

A. n. matthiae
South Matthias Is

A. n. manusi
Admiralty Is

A. n. lavongai
New Hanover

A. n. rubianae
New Georgia, Rendova I, Vellalavella I

A. n. rufoschistaceus
Ysabel I, Choiseul I

A. n. bougainvillei
Faure I, Bougainville I

A. n. malaitae
Malaita I

A. n. pulchellus
Guadalcanal I

A. n. sylvestris
Sumbawa I, Flores I, Pantar I, Alor I

A. n. dampieri
Rook I

A. n. lihirensis
Lihir Is, Tanga I

A. n. misulae
Louisiade Archipelago

A. n. leucosomus
New Guinea & islands

A. n. polionotus
Babar I, Damar I, Timorlaut I, Banda Is

A. n. pallidimas
D'Entrecasteaux Archipelago

A. n. novaehollandiae
N & E Australia, Tasmania

Accipiter griseogularis (Grey-throated Goshawk)

A. g. mortyi
Morotai I

A. g. griseogularis
C Moluccas

A. g. obiensis
Obi Is

Accipiter melanochlamys (Black-mantled Accipiter)
New Guinea

Accipiter imitator (Imitator Sparrow Hawk
Choiseul I, Ysabel I

Accipiter albogularis (Pied Goshawk)

A. a. woodfordi
Bougainville I, Guadalcanal I, Malaita I, Choiseul I

A. a. gilvus
New Georgia I, Rendova I, Vellalavella I

A. a. albogularis
San Cristobal I, Ugi I, Santa Anna I

A. a. eichorni
Feni I

A. a. sharpei
Vanikoro I, Utupua I

Accipiter haplochrous (New Caledonia Sparrow Hawk)
New Caledonia

Accipiter rufitorques (Fiji Goshawk)
Fiji Is

Accipiter poliocephalus (New Guinea Grey headed Goshawk)
New Guinea & islands

Accipiter princeps (New Britain Grey-headed Goshawk)
New Britain

Accipiter soloensis (Grey Frog Hawk)
S & NE China to Indonesia

Accipiter brevipes (Levant Sparrow Hawk)
Balkans to S Russia & Egypt

Accipiter badius (Shikra)

A. b. sphenurus
Gambia to Ethiopia & Tanzania

A. b. polyzonoides
S Tanzania & S Zaire to Cape Province

A. b. cenchroides
Transcaucasia, N Iran to Tien Shan

A. b. dussumieri
Himalayas, N India

A. b. badius
S India, Sri Lanka

A. b. polyopsis
Assam to Taiwan & Indochina
Accipiter butleri (Nicobar Shikra)
A. b. butleri
Car Nicobar Is
A. b. obsoletus
S Nicobar Is
Accipiter francesii (France's Sparrow Hawk)
A. f. francesii
Madagascar
A. f. griveaudi
Gd Comoro I
A. f. pusillus
Anjouan I
A. f. brutus
Mayotte I
Accipiter collaris (American Collared Sparrow Hawk)
W Venezuela, E & S Colombia, Ecuador
Accipiter superciliosus (Tiny Sparrow Hawk)
A. s. fontanieri
SE Nicaragua to W Colombia, Ecuador
A. s. superciliosus
E Peru to Venezuela, the Guianas & N Argentina
Accipiter gundlachii (Gundlach's Hawk)
Cuba **e?**
Accipiter cooperii (Cooper's Hawk)
S Canada to N Central America
Accipiter bicolor (Bicoloured Sparrow Hawk)
A. b. bicolor
S Mexico to E Bolivia
A. b. fidens
SW Mexico
A. b. pileatus
S Brazil
A. b. guttifer
S Bolivia, Paraguay, N Argentina
A. b. chilensis
Andes of Chile, Argentina to Tierra del Fuego
Accipiter poliogaster (Grey-bellied Goshawk)
N & C South America

UROTRIORCHIS
Urotriorchis macrourus (African Long-tailed Hawk)
Ghana to C Zaire

BUTASTUR
Butastur rufipennis (Grasshopper Buzzard-Eagle)
Senegal to Ethiopia & Tanzania
Butastur liventer (Rufous-winged Buzzard-Eagle)
S Burma to Java & Sula I

Butastur teesa (White-eyed Buzzard) 83
India, Burma
Butastur indicus (Grey-faced Buzzard-Eagle)
NE Asia, Japan, Philippine Is

KAUPIFALCO
Kaupifalco monogrammicus (Lizard Buzzard)
K. m. monogrammicus
Senegal to Ethiopia & Kenya
K. m. meridionalis
Angola to Tanzania & Natal

LEUCOPTERNIS
Leucopternis schistacea (Slate-coloured Hawk)
Amazonia
Leucopternis plumbea (Plumbeous Hawk)
E Panama to NW Peru
Leucopternis princeps (Prince's Hawk)
Costa Rica to N Ecuador
Leucopternis melanops (Black-faced Hawk)
N Amazonia
Leucopternis kuhli (White-browed Hawk)
S Amazonia
Leucopternis lacernulata (White-necked Hawk)
E & S Brazil
Leucopternis semiplumbea (Semi-plumbeous Hawk)
Honduras to NW Ecuador
Leucopternis albicollis (White Hawk)
L. a. ghiesbreghti
S Mexico to Nicaragua
L. a. costaricensis
Honduras to NW Colombia
L. a. williaminae
NW Colombia to W Venezuela
L. a. albicollis
Trinidad, C Venezuela & the Guianas to S Brazil
Leucopternis occidentalis (Grey-backed Hawk)
W Ecuador
Leucopternis polionota (Mantled Hawk)
E & S Brazil to N Argentina

BUTEOGALLUS
Buteogallus anthracinus (Common Black Hawk)
B. a. anthracinus
SW USA to NW Guyana, St Vincent I
B. a. subtilis
coast from S Mexico to NW Peru
B. a. utilensis
Bay I, Honduras
B. a. gundlachii
Cuba, Isle of Pines

Buteogallus aequinoctialis (Rufous Crab Hawk)
Venezuela to SE Brazil

Buteogallus urubitinga (Great Black Hawk)
B. u. ridgwayi
N Mexico to Panama
B. u. urubitinga
N & C South America, Trinidad

Buteogallus meridionalis (Savannah Hawk)
E Panama to C Argentina

HARPYHALIAETUS

Harpyhaliaetus solitarius (Black Solitary Eagle)
NW Mexico to Venezuela & Peru

Harpyhaliaetus coronatus (Crowned Solitary Eagle)
S Brazil to E Bolivia & C Argentina

BUSARELLUS

Busarellus nigricollis (Fishing Buzzard)
B. n. nigricollis
Mexico to N Argentina
B. n. leucocephalus
Paraguay, NC Argentina

GERANOAETUS

Geranoaetus melanoleucus (Grey Eagle-Buzzard)
G. m. australis
Venezuela, W South America, Tierra del Fuego
G. m. melanoleucus
S Brazil, Uruguay, Paraguay, N Argentina

PARABUTEO

Parabuteo unicinctus (Harris's Hawk)
P. u. harrisi
S Texas to N Peru
P. u. superior
SE California, W Mexico
P. u. unicinctus
South America

ASTURINA

Asturina nitida (Grey Hawk)
A. n. plagiata
S USA to NW Costa Rica
A. n. costaricensis
SW Costa Rica to W Ecuador
A. n. nitida
Trinidad, N Amazonia
A. n. pallida
S Brazil, E Bolivia to NC Argentina

BUTEO

Buteo magnirostris (Large-billed Hawk)
B. m. griseocauda
Mexico to W Panama
B. m. conspectus
SE Mexico, N Belize

B. m. gracilis
Cozumel I, Holbox I
B. m. sinushonduri
Bonacca I, Ruatan I, (Honduras)
B. m. petulans
SW Costa Rica, SW Panama
B. m. alius
Pearl Is (Panama)
B. m. magnirostris
South America (N of R Amazon)
B. m. occiduus
E Peru, W Brazil
B. m. saturatus
Bolivia to W Argentina
B. m. nattereri
NE Brazil
B. m. magniplumis
S Brazil, NW Argentina
B. m. pucherani
E Argentina, Paraguay

Buteo leucorrhous (Rufous-thighed Hawk)
Venezuela to Bolivia & NE Argentina

Buteo ridgwayi (Ridgway's Hawk)
Hispaniola

Buteo lineatus (Red-shouldered Hawk)
B. l. lineatus
E North America
B. l. alleni
Florida to E Texas
B. l. extimus
S Florida & Keys
B. l. texanus
SC Texas to C Mexico
B. l. elegans
S Oregon to Baja California

Buteo platypterus (Broad-winged Hawk)
B. p. platypterus
SE Canada, E USA to Peru & Brazil
B. p. cubanensis
Cuba
B. p. brunnescens
Puerto Rico
B. p. insulicola
Antigua I
B. p. rivierei
Dominica I, Martinique I, St Lucia I
B. p. antillarum
Barbados I, St Vincent I, Grenada I, Tobago I

Buteo brachyurus (Short-tailed Hawk)
B. b., fuliginosus
S Florida to Panama
B. b. brachyurus
South America (below 7000ft)
B. b. albigula
Andes from Colombia to C Chile

Buteo swainsonii (Swainson's Hawk)
W Canada & W USA & C Argentina

Buteo galapagoensis (Galapagos Hawk)
   Galapagos Is
Buteo albicaudatus (White-tailed Hawk)
   B. a. hypospodius
      Texas to N Colombia, W Venezuela
   B. a. colonus
      E Colombia to Surinam
   B. a. albicaudatus
      S Brazil to C Argentina
Buteo polyosoma (Red-backed Buzzard)
   B. p. polyosoma
      NW Colombia to Tierra del Fuego,
      Falkland Is
   B. p. exsul
      Masafuera I
Buteo poecilochrous (Gurney's Buzzard)
   SW Colombia to N Chile
Buteo albonotatus (Zone-tailed Hawk)
   SW USA to N South America
Buteo solitarius (Hawaiian Hawk)
   Hawaii Is
Buteo ventralis (Red-tailed Buzzard)
   S Chile, S Argentina
Buteo jamaicensis (Red-tailed Hawk)
   B. j. borealis
      E North America to N Mexico
   B. j. calurus
      W North America » Central America
   B. j. harlani
      N British Columbia, N Alberta » S USA
   B. j. alascensis
      SE Alaska
   B. j. kriderii
      SC Canada, NC USA » S USA
   B. j. fuertesi
      SW USA, NW Mexico
   B. j. umbrinus
      S Florida, Bahama Is
   B. j. hadropus
      N to SC Mexico
   B. j. socorroensis
      Socorro I
   B. j. fumosus
      Tres Marias Is
   B. j. solitudinis
      Cuba, Isle of Pines
   B. j. jamaicensis
      Jamaica, Hispaniola, Puerto Rico
   B. j. kiemsiesi
      S Mexico to Nicaragua
   B. J. costaricensis
      Costa Rica, W Panama
Buteo buteo (Common Buzzard)
   B. b. buteo
      W & S Europe, Atlantic islands
   B. b. vulpinus
      N & E Europe, C Asia, E & S Africa

B. b. menetriesi
   Caucasus & Elburz Mts
B. b. japonicus
   Transbaikalia & Tibet to Japan, Indochina
B. b. toyoshimae
   Bonin Is, Izu Is
Buteo oreophilus (African Mountain Buzzard)
   B. o. oreophilus
      S Ethiopia to C Tanzania
   B. o. trizonatus
      S Natal, E Cape Province
Buteo brachypterus (Madagascar Buzzard)
   Madagascar
Buteo lagopus (Rough-legged Buzzard)
   B. l. lagopus
      Europe, C Asia
   B. l. menzbieri
      NE Asia
   B. l. kamchatkensis
      Kamchatka, N Kurile Is
   B. l. sanctijohannis
      Canada, N USA
Buteo rufinus (Long-legged Buzzard)
   B. r. rufinus
      C Europe to C Asia
   B. r. cirtensis
      Morocco to Egypt
Buteo hemilasius (Upland Buzzard)
   C & E Asia
Buteo regalis (Ferruginous Hawk)
   SW Canada, WC USA
Buteo auguralis (African Red-tailed Buzzard)
   Sierra Leone to Ethiopia & Angola
Buteo rufofuscus (Augur Buzzard)
   B. r. archeri
      Somalia
   B. r. augur
      S Ethiopia to Angola & Mozambique
   B. r. rufofuscus
      Namibia, South Africa

MORPHNUS
Morphnus guianensis (Guiana Crested Eagle)
   Honduras to N Paraguay & Argentina

HARPIA
Harpia harpyja (Harpy Eagle)
   S Mexico to E Bolivia & N Argentina

HARPYOPSIS
Harpyopsis novaeguineae (New Guinea Harpy Eagle)
   New Guinea

PITHECOPHAGA
Pithecophaga jefferyi (Monkey-eating Eagle)
   Luzon I, Mindanao I

ICTINAETUS
Ictinaetus malayensis (Indian Black Eagle)
  I. m. perniger
    India, Sri Lanka
  I. m. malayensis
    Burma to S China & Moluccas

AQUILA
Aquila pomarina (Lesser Spotted Eagle)
  A. p. pomarina
    C & E Europe, Caucasus, Transcaucasia
  A. p. hastata
    India, N Burma
Aquila clanga (Greater Spotted Eagle)
  E Europe to E Asia, & NE Africa to S China
Aquila rapax (Tawny Eagle)
  A. r. orientalis
    E Europe, C Asia to C Africa
  A. r. nipalensis
    EC Asia & India
  A. r. vindhiana
    Baluchistan, India, N Burma
  A. r. belisarius
    Morocco to Nigeria & Ethiopia
  A. r. rapax
    SC & South Africa
Aquila heliaca (Imperial Eagle)
  A. h. adalberti
    Spain
  A. h. heliaca
    Greece to C Siberia » NE Africa, India
Aquila wahlbergi (Wahlberg's Eagle)
  Gambia to Ethiopia to N Cape Province
Aquila gurneyi (Gurney's Eagle)
  N Moluccas, New Guinea
Aquila chrysaetos (Golden Eagle)
  A. c. chrysaetos
    Scotland, Alps, N Europe, W Asia
  A. c. daphanea
    Russian Turkestan to SW China
  A. c. japonica
    Korea, C Japan
  A. c. canadensis
    NE Siberia, N Mongolia, Canada, W USA
  A. c. homeyeri
    Spain, N Africa
Aquila audax (Wedge-tailed Eagle)
  A. a. audax
    S New Guinea, Australia
  A. a. fleayi
    Tasmania
Aquila verreauxii (Verreaux's Eagle)
  Ethiopia, Sudan to Cape Province

HIERAAETUS
Hieraaetus fasciatus (Bonelli's Eagle)
  H. f. fasciatus
    S Europe, N Africa to India & China

  H. f. spilogaster
    Gambia to Ethiopia & Cape Province
  H. f. renschii
    Lesser Sunda Is
Hieraaetus pennatus (Booted Eagle)
  H. p. pennatus
    S Europe to N Africa & Caucasus
  H. p. harterti
    SW & C Asia
Hieraaetus morphnoides (Little Eagle)
  H. m. morphnoides
    Australia
  H. m. weiskei
    New Guinea
Hieraaetus dubius (Ayres' Hawk Eagle)
  Nigeria to Ethiopia & Cape Province
Hieraaetus kienerii (Chestnut-bellied Hawk Eagle)
  H. k. kienerii
    S Himalayas, W India, Sri Lanka
  H. k. formosus
    Burma to Philippine Is, Celebes & Java

SPIZASTUR
Spizastur melanoleucus (Black & White Hawk Eagle)
  E & S Mexico to Paraguay & NE Argentina

LOPHAETUS
Lophaetus occipitalis (Long-crested Eagle)
  Senegal to Ethiopia & Cape Province

SPIZAETUS
Spizaetus africanus (Cassin's Hawk Eagle)
  Togo to C Zaire & Uganda
Spizaetus cirrhatus (Crested Hawk Eagle)
  S. c. cirrhatus
    India
  S. c. ceylanensis
    Sri Lanka
  S. c. limnaetus
    NE India to Mindanao, Borneo & Java
  S. c. andamanensis
    Andaman Is
  S. c. vanheurni
    Simalur I
  S. c. floris
    Sumbawa I, Flores I
Spizaetus nipalensis (Mountain Hawk Eagle)
  S. n. nipalensis
    W India, Himalayas to SE China
  S. n. kelaarti
    Sri Lanka
  S. n. orientalis
    Japan
Spizaetus bartelsi (Java Hawk Eagle)
  W Java

Spizaetus lanceolatus (Celebes Hawk Eagle)
  Sula I & Celebes
Spizaetus philippensis (Philippine Hawk Eagle)
  Philippine Is, Palawan
Spizaetus alboniger (Blyth's Hawk Eagle)
  S Burma to Sumatra & Borneo
Spizaetus nanus (Wallace's Hawk Eagle)
  S. n. nanus
    Malaysia, Borneo, Sumatra
  S. n. stresemanni
    Nias I
Spizaetus tyrannus (Black Hawk Eagle)
  S. t. serus
    C Mexico to E Peru
  S. t. tyrannus
    E & S Brazil
Spizaetus ornatus (Ornate Hawk Eagle)
  S. o. vicarius
    Mexico to Colombia, W Ecuador
  S. o. ornatus
    C Colombia to Guianas & N Argentina

STEPHANOAETUS
Stephanoaetus coronatus (Crowned Eagle)
  Guinea to Ethiopia and Cape Province

OROAETUS
Oroaetus isidori (Isidor's Eagle)
  W Venezuela to Bolivia & NW Argentina

POLEMAETUS
Polemaetus bellicosus (Martial Eagle)
  Senegal to Somalia & Cape Province

31 SAGITTARIIDAE (SECRETARY BIRD)

SAGITTARIUS
Sagittarius serpentarius (Secretary Bird)
  Senegal to Somalia & Cape Province

32 FALCONIDAE (FALCONS, CARACARAS)

DAPTRIUS
Daptrius ater (Yellow-throated Caracara)
  Amazonia
Daptrius americanus (Red-throated Caracara)
  S Mexico to C Peru & S Brazil

PHALCOBOENUS
Phalcoboenus carunculatus (Carunculated Caracara)
  Andes of Ecuador & SW Colombia
Phalcoboenus megalopterus (Mountain Caracara)
  Andes of Peru to N Chile

Phalcoboenus albogularis (White-throated Caracara)
  S Chile, S Argentina
Phalcoboenus australis (Forster's Caracara)
  Falkland Is, Cape Horn islands

POLYBORUS
Polyborus plancus (Common Caracara)
  P. p. auduboni
    S USA to W Panama, Cuba
  P. p. pallidus
    Tres Marias Is
  P. p. cheriway
    E Panama & South America
    (N of R Amazon)
  P. p. plancus
    S South America, Falkland Is

MILVAGO
Milvago chimango (Chimango)
  M. c. chimango
    Paraguay & Uruguay to S Argentina
  M. c. temucoensis
    S Chile, Tierra del Fuego
Milvago chimachima (Yellow-headed Caracara)
  Panama to E Bolivia & N Argentina

HERPETOTHERES
Herpetotheres cachinnans (Laughing Falcon)
  H. c. cachinnans
    NW Mexico to N Argentina
  H. c. fulvescens
    W Panama to N Peru

MICRASTUR
Micrastur ruficollis (Barred Forest Falcon)
  M. r. guerilla
    Mexico to Nicaragua
  M. r. interstes
    Costa Rica to W Colombia & Ecuador
  M. r. zonothorax
    N Venezuela, E Colombia
  M. r. gilvicollis
    S Venezuela, the Guianas, Amazonia
  M. r. pelzelni
    W Brazil, E Peru
  M. r. ruficollis
    E Brazil, Paraguay, N Argentina
  M. r. olrogi
    NW Argentina
Micrastur plumbeus (Sclater's Forest Falcon)
  W Colombia, NW Ecuador
Micrastur mirandollei (Slaty-backed Forest Falcon)
  E Costa Rica to E Peru & SE Brazil

Micrastur semitorquatus (Collared Forest Falcon)
> *M. s. naso*
> > Mexico to NW Peru
> *M. s. semitorquatus*
> > E Colombia & N Peru to Brazil &
> > N Argentina

Micrastur buckleyi (Traylor's Forest Falcon)
> E Ecuador, NE Peru

SPIZIAPTERYX
Spiziapteryx circumcinctus (Spot-winged Falconet)
> N & W Argentina

POLIHIERAX
Polihierax semitorquatus (African Pigmy Falcon)
> *P. s. castanotus*
> > E Zaire & Ethiopia to C Tanzania
> *P. s. semitorquatus*
> > S Angola, Namibia, Botswana, W South
> > Africa

Polihierax insignis (Fieldens Falconet)
> *P. i. insignis*
> > N Burma
> *P. i. cinereiceps*
> > S Burma, Thailand, N Indochina
> *P. i. harmandi*
> > S Laos, S Vietnam

MICROHIERAX
Microhierax caerulescens (Red-legged Falconet)
> *M. c. caerulescens*
> > Himalayas, N India
> *M. c. burmanicus*
> > Burma to Indochina

Microhierax fringillarius (Black-legged Falconet)
> S Burma to Bali I & Sumatra

Microhierax latifrons (Bornean Falconet)
> NW Borneo

Microhierax erythrogonys (Philippine Falconet)
> Philippine Is

Microhierax melanoleucus (Pied Falconet)
> Assam, SE China, N Indochina

FALCO
Falco naumanni (Lesser Kestrel)
> S Europe to China » S Africa

Falco rupicoloides (Greater Kestrel)
> *F. r. fieldi*
> > Somalia, N Kenya
> *F. r. arthuri*
> > C & S Kenya, N Tanzania
> *F. r. rupicoloides*
> > S Tanzania & Angola to S Transvaal

Falco alopex (Fox Kestrel)
> Ghana to Sudan & W Kenya

Falco sparverius (American Kestrel)
> *F. s. sparverius*
> > Alaska & Canada to S Mexico
> *F. s. paulus*
> > SE USA
> *F. s. peninsularis*
> > Baja California, NW Mexico
> *F. s. tropicalis*
> > S Mexico, Guatemala, N Honduras
> *F. s. nicaraguensis*
> > NW Honduras, Nicaragua
> *F. s. sparveroides*
> > S Bahama Is, Cuba
> *F. s. dominicensis*
> > Hispaniola
> *F. s. caribearum*
> > Puerto Rico, Virgin Is, Lesser Antilles
> *F. s. brevipennis*
> > Netherlands West Indies
> *F. s. isabellinus*
> > the Guianas, E Venezuela, N Brazil
> *F. s. ochraceus*
> > E Colombia, NW Venezuela
> *F. s. aequatorialis*
> > NW Colombia, N Ecuador
> *F. s. peruvianus*
> > SW Ecuador, Peru, N Chile
> *F. s. cinnamominus*
> > SE Peru to Paraguay & Tierra del Fuego
> *F. s. fernandensis*
> > Mastierra I, Juan Fernandez Is
> *F. s. cearae*
> > S Brazil

Falco tinnunculus (Common Kestrel)
> *F. t. tinnunculus*
> > Europe to NE Asia, » C Africa & India
> *F. t. canariensis*
> > Madeira, W Canary Is
> *F. t. dacotiae*
> > Lanzarote, E Canary Is
> *F. t. neglectus*
> > N Cape Verde Is
> *F. t. alexanderi*
> > S Cape Verde Is
> *F. t. rupicolaeformis*
> > Egypt, S Yemen
> *F. t. archeri*
> > Socotra I, Somalia, NE Kenya
> *F. t. rufescens*
> > Guinea & N Angola to Ethiopia & Tanzania
> *F. t. rupicolus*
> > C Angola & S Tanzania to Cape Province
> *F. t. interstinctus*
> > Himalayas to Japan & Philippine Is
> *F. t. objurgatus*
> > S India

Falco newtoni (Madagascar Kestrel)
   F. n. newtoni
      Madagascar
   F. n. aldabranus
      Aldabra I, Anjouan I
Falco punctatus (Mauritius Kestrel)
   Mauritius
Falco araea (Seychelles Kestrel)
   Seychelles
Falco moluccensis (Moluccan Kestrel)
   F. m. moluccensis
      Ambon I, Ceram I, Buru I
   F. m. bernsteini
      N Moluccas
   F. m. timorensis
      Timor I, Tenimber Is
   F. m. microbalia
      Lombok I to Alor I, Celebes, Solombo
      Besar I
   F. m. renschii
      Sumba I
   F. m. javensis
      Java, Bali I, Kangean I
Falco cenchroides (Australian Kestrel)
   F. c. baru
      C New Guinea
   F. c. cenchroides
      Australia, Tasmania
Falco ardosiaceus (Grey Kestrel)
   Senegal to Ethiopia & S Tanzania
Falco dickinsoni (Dickinson's Kestrel)
   Angola to Tanzania & Natal
Falco zoniventris (Madagascar Banded Kestrel)
   Madagascar
Falco vespertinus (Red-footed Falcon)
   F. v. vespertinus
      C Europe to C Asia » W & SW Africa
   F. v. amurensis
      E Siberia, N China » E & S Asia
Falco chicquera (Red-headed Falcon)
   F. c. chicquera
      Pakistan, India
   F. c. ruficollis
      Gambia to Ethiopia » Zambia
   F. c. horsbrughi
      Rhodesia, South Africa
Falco columbarius (Merlin)
   F. c. subaesalon
      Iceland to Britain & Belgium
   F. c. aesalon
      Europe to N Russia & W Siberia
   F. c. insignis
      E Siberia to Japan, Indochina, India
   F. c. pallidus
      Transcaucasia to SC Asia
   F. c. lymani
      E Altai, Tien Shan to W China

   F. c. columbarius
      Alaska to Newfoundland & N South
      America
   F. c. suckleyi
      W British Columbia to N California
   F. c. richardsoni
      SW C Canada to WC USA
Falco berigora (Brown Hawk)
   F. b. novaeguineae
      New Guinea, Dampier I
   F. b. berigora
      humid parts of Australia
   F. b. centralis
      dry interior of Australia
   F. b. tasmanica
      Tasmania
Falco novaezeelandiae (New Zealand Falcon)
   New Zealand
Falco subbuteo (European Hobby)
   F. s. subbuteo
      Europe to Japan » Africa & India
   F. s. streichi
      C & S China, Laos
Falco cuvierii (African Hobby)
   Ghana to Ethiopia & Cape Province
Falco severus (Oriental Hobby)
   F. s. severus
      E Himalayas to Philippine Is & N Borneo
   F. s. papuanus
      Celebes to New Guinea & Solomon Is
Falco longipennis (Australian Hobby)
   F. l. murchisonianus
      dry Northern Australia
   F. l. longipennis
      SE & SW Australia, Tasmania
Falco eleonorae (Eleonora's Falcon)
   Canary Is, Mediterranean Is »
      Madagascar
Falco concolor (Sooty Falcon)
   NE Africa » Madagascar
Falco rufigularis (Bat Falcon)
   F. r. petrophilus
      W Mexico
   F. r. rufigularis
      C Mexico, all E South America to
      N Argentina
Falco femoralis (Aplomado Falcon)
   F. f. septentrionalis
      SW USA & Mexico
   F. f. pichinchae
      Andes from Colombia to Chile
   F. f. femoralis
      Central & South America
Falco hypoleucos (Grey Falcon)
   C N & Western Australia
Falco subniger (Black Falcon)
   Australia

***Falco biarmicus* (Lanner Falcon)**
F. b. feldeggi
SE Europe, Asia minor
F. b. erlangeri
NW Africa
F. b. tanypterus
NE Africa, Arabia, Iraq
F. b. abyssinicus
Ghana to N Zaire, Uganda, Ethiopia
F. b. biarmicus
E Zaire & Kenya to Angola & Cape
Province
***Falco mexicanus* (Prairie Falcon)**
SW Canada, W USA, NW Mexico
***Falco jugger* (Laggar Falcon)**
Baluchistan, Himalayas, N & C India
***Falco cherrug* (Saker Falcon)**
F. c. cyanopus
C Europe, W Russia
F. c. cherrug
C Asia, NW Mongolia to N Africa, N India
F. c. milvipes
SC Asia
F. c. altaicus
mountains of C Asia
***Falco rusticolus* (Gyrfalcon)**
Arctic Europe, Asia, N America
***Falco deiroleucus* (Orange-breasted Falcon)**
Central America to N Argentina
***Falco fasciinucha* (Taita Falcon)**
S Ethiopia to Zambia & Malawi
***Falco kreyenborgi* (Kleinschmidt's Falcon)**
S Chile, Tierra del Fuego
***Falco peregrinus* (Peregrine Falcon)**
F. p. pealei
coast of W Canada, W USA
F. p. anatum
N Central & South America
F. p. cassini
S Chile, Tierra del Fuego, Falkland Is
F. p. peregrinus
Europe to N Russia & Caucasus
F. p. calidus
N Russia, N Siberia to Southern Africa
& New Guinea
F. p. japonensis
E Siberia, Japan, Taiwan
F. p. brookei
Mediterranean, Asia Minor
F. p. pelegrinoides
North Africa, N Sudan
F. p. babylonicus
Iraq to Mongolia, N India
F. p. peregrinator
India, Sri Lanka to S China
F. p. minor
Ghana to Ethiopia » Cape Province

F. p. submelanogenys
SW Australia
F. p. macropus
Australia (except SW)
F. p. madens
Cape Verde Is
F. p. radama
Madagascar, Comoro Is
F. p. furuitii
Volcano I
F. p. ernesti
Indonesia, Philippine Is, New Guinea
F. p. nesiotes
New Hebrides, Loyalty Is, New Caledonia

Galliformes

33 MEGAPODIIDAE (MEGAPODES)

MEGAPODIUS
***Megapodius freycinet* (Common Scrub Hen)**
M. f. nicobariensis
N Nicobar Is
M. f. abbotti
Gt & Little Nicobar Is
M. f. pusillus
Philippine Is
M. f. tabon
Mindanao I
M. f. cumingii
Palawan I, Balabac I
M. f. sanghirensis
Sanghir Is, Talaut Is
M. f. gilbertii
Celebes
M. f. bernsteinii
Sula Is
M. f. perrufus
Peling I
M. f. tenimberensis
Tenimber Is
M. f. aruensis
Aru Is
M. f. affinis
N New Guinea
M. f. duperryii
W & S New Guinea
M. f. reinwardt
Lesser Sunda Is
M. f. buruensis
Buru I
M. f. forstenii
S Moluccas
M. f. macgillivrayi
Louisiade & D'Entrecasteaux Archipelago
M. f. tumulus
Melville I, Northern Territory

M. f. yorki
  N Queensland
M. f. eremita
  Admiralty Is, Bismarck Archipelago
M. f. brenchleyi
  Solomon Is
M. f. freycinet
  N Moluccas, W Papuan Is
M. f. geelvinkianus
  Biak I, Numfor I, Meosnum I, Japen I
M. f. castanonotus
  N & C Queensland
M. f. layardi
  Banks I, N New Hebrides
Megapodius laperouse (Marianas Scrub Hen)
M. l. senex
  Palau Is
M. l. laperouse
  Mariana Is
Megapodius pritchardii (Polynesian Scrub Hen)
  Friendly Is

Eulipoa wallacei (Moluccas Scrub Hen)
  Moluccas, Misol I

LEIPOA
Leipoa ocellata (Mallee Fowl)
  Southern Australia

ALECTURA
Alectura lathami (Brush Turkey)
A. l. purpureicollis
  N Queensland
A. l. lathami
  C & S Queensland, N South Wales

TALEGALLA
Talegalla cuvieri (Red-billed Brush Turkey)
  NW New Guinea, Salawati I, Misol I
Talegalla fuscirostris (Black-billed Brush Turkey)
T. f. fuscirostris
  S & E New Guinea
T. f. occidentis
  Aru Is, SW New Guinea
Talegalla jobiensis (Brown-collared Brush Turkey)
T. j. jobiensis
  Japen I, N New Guinea
T. j. longicaudus
  SE New Guinea

AEPYPODIUS
Aepypodius arfakianus (Wattled Brush Turkey)
A. a. arfakianus
  NW New Guinea

A. a. misoliensis
  Misol I
Aepypodius bruijnii (Bruijn's Brush Turkey)
  Waigeu I

MACROCEPHALON
Macrocephalon maleo (Maleo Fowl)
  Celebes

34 CRACIDAE (CURASSOWS, GUANS)

ORTALIS
Ortalis vetula (Plain Chachalaca)
O. v. mccallii
  S Texas, SE Mexico
O. v. vetula
  E Mexico to C Nicaragua
O. v. pallidiventris
  N Yucatan
O. v. deschauenseei
  Utila I (Honduras)
Ortalis cinereiceps (Grey-headed Chachalaca)
  SE Honduras to NW Colombia
Ortalis garrula (Chestnut-winged Chachalaca)
O. g. mira
  Panama
O. g. chocoensis
  NW Colombia
O. g. garrula
  N Colombia
Ortalis ruficauda (Rufous-vented Chachalaca)
O. r. ruficrissa
  N Colombia, NW Venezuela
O. r. lamprophonia
  Guajira peninsula
O. r. baliolus
  Lake Maracaibo
O. r. ruficauda
  Venezuela, Tobago I, Lesser Antilles Is
Ortalis erythroptera (Rufous-headed Chachalaca)
  W Ecuador, NW Peru
Ortalis poliocephala (West Mexican Chachalaca)
O. p. wagleri
  NW Mexico
O. p. lajuelae
  C Mexico
O. p. poliocephala
  W Mexico
Ortalis canicollis (Chaco Chachalaca)
O. c. canicollis
  E Bolivia, W Paraguay, N Argentina
O. c. pantanalensis
  SW Brazil

Ortalis leucogastra (White-bellied Chachalaca)
SE Mexico to NW Nicaragua
Ortalis motmot (Variable Chachalaca)
O. m. motmot
S Venezuela, the Guianas, N Brazil
O. m. ruficeps
NC Brazil
O. m. superciliaris
NE Brazil
O. m. araucuan
E Brazil
O. m. squamata
SE Brazil
O. m. caucae
N Colombia
O. m. colombiana
SC Colombia, NW Upper Amazonia
O. m. guttata
W Upper Amazonia
O. m. subaffinis
NE & E Bolivia, W Brazil

PENELOPE
Penelope argyrotis (Band-tailed Guan)
P. a. mesaeus
W Venezuela, N Colombia
P. a. albicauda
W Venezuela, NE Colombia
P. a. colombiana
Santa Marta Mts
P. a. argyrotis
NW Colombia, N Venezuela
P. a. olivaceiceps
N Venezuela
Penelope barbata (Bearded Guan)
S Ecuador, NW Peru
Penelope montagnii (Andean Guan)
P. m. montagnii
N & C Colombia
P. m. atrogularis
S Colombia, WC Ecuador
P. m. brookei
S Colombia, EC Ecuador
P. m. plumosa
C Peru
P. m. sclateri
C Bolivia, NW Argentina
Penelope ortoni (Orton's Guan)
W Colombia, W Ecuador
Penelope marail (Marail Guan)
P. m. jacupeba
SE Venezuela, N Brazil
P. m. marail
E Venezuela, the Guianas
Penelope superciliaris (Rusty-margined Guan)
P. s. superciliaris
NC & E Brazil

P. s. jacupemba
C & S Brazil
P. s. major
S Brazil, E Paraguay, NE Argentina
Penelope dabbenei (Red-faced Guan)
S Bolivia, NW Argentina
Penelope obscura (Dusky-legged Guan)
P. o. bronzina
E Brazil
P. o. obscura
S Brazil, E Paraguay, Uruguay, NE Argentina
P. o. bridgesi
C Bolivia, NW Argentina
Penelope jacquaçu (Spix's Guan)
P. j. granti
E Venezuela, Guyana
P. j. orienticola
NW Brazil, SE Venezuela
P. j. jacquaçu
Upper Amazonia
P. j. speciosa
C & E Bolivia
Penelope perspicax (Cauca Guan)
W & C Colombia
Penelope purpurascens (Crested Guan)
P. p. purpurascens
NE & NW Mexico to Honduras, Nicaragua
P. p. aequatorialis
S Honduras to NW Colombia
P. p. brunnescens
N Colombia, E Venezuela
Penelope jacucaca (White-browed Guan)
NE Brazil
Penelope ochrogaster (Chestnut-bellied Guan)
SC Brazil
Penelope pileata (White-crested Guan)
NC Brazil

ABURRIA
Aburria pipile (Common Piping Guan)
A. p. pipile
Trinidad
A. p. cumanensis
the Guianas to C Colombia & NW Peru, W Brazil
A. p. grayi
E Bolivia, NE Paraguay, SW Brazil
A. p. nattereri
S & W Amazonia
A. p. cujubi
NC Brazil
Aburria jacutinga (Black-fronted Piping Guan)
SE Brazil, SE Paraguay
Aburria aburri (Wattled Guan)
N Colombia, E Venezuela to SC Peru

CHAMAEPETES
Chamaepetes unicolor (Black Guan)
  Costa Rica, Panama
Chamaepetes goudotii (Sickle-winged Guan)
  C. g. goudotii
    C & W Colombia
  C. g. sanctaemarthae
    Santa Marta Mts
  C. g. fagani
    SW Colombia, W Ecuador
  C. g. tschudii
    EC Ecuador, N Peru
  C. g. rufiventris
    EC Peru

PENELOPINA
Penelopina nigra (Highland Guan)
  S Mexico to N Nicaragua

OREOPHASIS
Oreophasis derbianus (Horned Guan)
  SE Mexico, SW Guatemala

NOTHOCRAX
Nothocrax urumutum (Nocturnal Curassow)
  Upper Amazonia

CRAX
Crax tomentosa (Crestless Curassow)
  SE Colombia to Guyana, NW Brazil
Crax salvini (Salvin's Curassow)
  SW Colombia, E Ecuador, NE Peru
Crax mitu (Razor-billed Curassow)
  C. m. tuberosa
    S Amazonia
  C. m. mitu
    E Brazil **e?**
Crax pauxi (Northern Helmeted Curassow)
  C. p. pauxi
    NC to W Venezuela
  C. p. gilliardi
    Venezuela-Colombia border
Crax unicornis (Southern Helmeted Curassow)
  C. u. unicornis
    NE Bolivia
  C. u. koepckeae
    E Peru
Crax rubra (Great Curassow)
  C. r. rubra
    E Mexico to W Colombia & W Ecuador
  C. r. griscomi
    Cozumel I
Crax alberti (Blue-bellied Curassow)
  N Colombia
Crax daubentoni (Yellow-knobbed Curassow)
  N Venezuela

Crax alector (Black Curassow)
  E Colombia to the Guianas, N Brazil
Crax globulosa (Wattled Curassow)
  W Upper Amazonia
Crax fasciolata (Bare-faced Curassow)
  C. f. fasciolata
    C & SW Brazil, Paraguay
  C. f. pinima
    NE Brazil
  C. f. grayi
    E Bolivia
Crax blumenbachii (Red-billed Curassow)
  SE Brazil

35 PHASIANIDAE (PHEASANTS, GROUSE)

MELEAGRIDINAE

MELEAGRIS
Meleagris gallopavo (Common Turkey)
  M. g. silvestris
    SE USA
  M. g. osceola
    S Florida
  M. g. intermedia
    N Texas to NE Mexico
  M. g. onusta
    NW Mexico
  M. g. mexicana
    NC Mexico
  M. g. merriami
    SW USA, NW Mexico
  M. g. gallopavo
    WC Mexico

AGRIOCHARIS
Agriocharis ocellata (Ocellated Turkey)
  SE Mexico, Belize, Guatemala

TETRAONINAE

DENDRAGAPUS
Dendragapus falcipennis (Siberian Spruce Grouse)
  NE Asia, Sakhalin
Dendragapus canadensis (Spruce Grouse)
  D. c. osgoodi
    Alaska
  D. c. atratus
    S Alaska
  D. c. canadensis
    C Alberta to Labrador
  D. c. torridus
    Nova Scotia
  D. c. canace
    SE Canada, N & NE USA
Dendragapus obscurus (Dusky Grouse)
  D. o. sitkensis
    SE Alaska

D. o. fuliginosus
S Yukon to NW California
D. o. sierrae
Oregon to NC California
D. o. howardi
C California
D. o. richardsonii
N British Columbia to SE Idaho
D. o. pallidus
SE British Columbia to NE Oregon
D. o. obscurus
Utah to New Mexico

LAGOPUS
Lagopus lagopus (Willow/Red Grouse)
L. l. scoticus
Scotland, Wales, N England
L. l. hibernicus
Outer Hebrides, Ireland
L. l. lagopus
Circumpolar, N Europe, N Asia, N Canada
L. l. birulai
N Siberian islands
L. l. leucopterus
islands N of N America
L. l. rossicus
European Russia
L. l. maior
SE Russia
L. l. brevirostris
S Siberia
L. l. kozlowae
C Asia, N Mongolia
L. l. alexandrae
S & SE Alaska islands, NW British
Columbia
L. l. alleni
Newfoundland
Lagopus mutus (Rock Ptarmigan)
L. m. hyperboreus
Spitzbergen, Franz Josef Land
L. m. mutus
N Scandinavia, N Russia
L. m. millaisi
Scotland
L. m. helveticus
Alps
L. m. pyrenaicus
Pyrenees
L. m. komensis
N Ural Mts
L. m. pleskei
N Siberia
L. m. macrorhynchus
Tarbagatai
L. m. nadezdae
Altai, C Asia
L. m. transbaicalicus
SE Siberia

L. m. ridgwayi
Commander Is
L. m. kurilensis
N & C Kurile Is
L. m. japonicus
Honshu I, Japan
L. m. evermanni
Attu I (Aleutian Is)
L. m. townsendi
Kiska I (Aleutian Is)
L. m. sanfordi
Tanaga I (Aleutian Is)
L. m. chamberlaini
Adak I (Aleutian Is)
L. m. atkhensis
Atka I (Aleutian Is)
L. m. nelsoni
Unimak I, Unalaska I, to S Alaska
L. m. gabrielsoni
C Alaska
L. m. dixoni
Glacier Bay islands
L. m. rupestris
N North America
L. m. saturatus
W Greenland
L. m. welchi
Newfoundland
L. m. reinhardi
SW Greenland
L. m. captus
E Greenland
L. m. islandorum
Iceland
**Lagopus leucurus (White-tailed
Ptarmigan)**
L. l. peninsularis
C Alaska, Yukon
L. l. leucurus
N British Columbia to Vancouver I
L. l. rainierensis
Mt Rainier, C & S Washington
L. l. saxatilis
Vancouver I
L. l. altipetens
Rocky Mts from Montana to New Mexico

TETRAO
**Tetrao mlokosiewiczi (Georgian Black
Grouse)**
Caucasus
Tetrao tetrix (Black Grouse)
T. t. britannicus
Scotland, N England
T. t. tetrix
Scandinavia & France to N Siberia
T. t. viridanus
SE Russia, SW Siberia

T. t. tschusii
S Siberia
T. t. baikalensis
N Mongolia, W Manchuria
T. t. mongolicus
C Tien Shan, W Altai
T. t. ussuriensis
N Manchuria, NE Korea
***Tetrao parvirostris* (Siberian Capercaillie)**
T. p. turensis
NC Siberia
T. p. janensis
NE Siberia
T. p. parvirostris
E Siberia, Sakhalin
T. p. macrurus
C Asia, N Mongolia
T. p. kamschaticus
Kamchatka
***Tetrao urogallus* (Capercaillie)**
T. u. aquitanicus
Pyrenees & N Spain
T. u. urogallus
Scandinavia, Scotland
T. u. major
C Europe, W Russia
T. u. lugens
Finland, NW Russia
T. u. pleskei
N Russia
T. u. volgensis
C Russia
T. u. uralensis
C Ural Mts
T. u. grisescens
S Ural Mts
T. u. kureikensis
Lower Yenisei valley
T. u. taczanowskii
C Siberia, NW Mongolia

BONASA
***Bonasa sewerzowi* (Severtzov's Hazel Grouse)**
B. s. sewerzowi
Kansu
B. s. secunda
W Szechwan
***Bonasa bonasia* (Hazel Grouse)**
B. b. bonasia
Scandinavia to Ural Mts
B. b. griseonota
N Sweden
B. b. rupestris
C Germany to Alps & Bulgaria
B. p. horicei
E Carpathians
B. b. volgensis
C Poland to C Russia

B. b. sibiricus
C Siberia, N Mongolia
B. b. kolymensis
E Siberia
B. b. amurensis
Korea, S Amur, N Manchuria
B. b. vicinitas
Sakhalin, Hokkaido
***Bonasa umbellus* (Ruffed Grouse)**
B. u. yukonensis
Alaska, NW Canada
B. u. umbelloides
S British Columbia to Manitoba
& N Colorado
B. u. castaneus
Olympic Mt, Washington
B. u. affinis
British Columbia, Oregon
B. u. obscura
N Ontario
B. u. sabini
coast of British Columbia to California
B. u. brunnescens
Vancouver I
B. u. togata
NC & NE USA
B. u. medianus
Minnesota
B. u. phaios
Idaho
B. u. incanus
Utah
B. u. monticola
W Virginia
B. u. umbellus
EC USA
B. u. thayeri
Nova Scotia

CENTROCERCUS
***Centrocercus urophasianus* (Sage Hen)**
S British Columbia to E California
& Nebraska

TYMPANUCHUS
***Tympanuchus phasianellus* (Sharp-tailed Grouse)**
T. p. kennicottii
NW Canada
T. p. phasianellus
EC Canada
T. p. columbianus
British Columbia to N California & Utah
T. p. jamesi
EC Colorado
T. p. campestris
C Canada to Wisconsin
***Tympanuchus cupido* (Prairie Chicken)**
T. c. pinnatus
SC Canada to NE Texas

T. c. attwateri
coast of Texas & SW Louisiana
T. c. pallidicinctus
Kansas to New Mexico
(*T.c. cupido* — extinct)

ODONTOPHORINAE

DENDRORTYX
Dendrortyx barbatus (Bearded Wood Partridge)
Vera Cruz (Mexico)
Dendrortyx macroura (Long-tailed Wood Partridge)
D. m. macroura
Vera Cruz (Mexico)
D. m. griseipectus
Morales (Mexico)
D. m. diversus
NW Jalisco
D. m. striatus
Michoacan & Colima (Mexico),
Guerrero (Mexico)
D. m. oaxacae
E Oaxaca (Mexico)
Dendrortyx leucophrys (Buffy-crowned Wood Partridge)
D. l. leucophrys
SE Mexico, Guatemala
D. l. nicaraguae
Honduras, Nicaragua
D. l. hypospodius
Costa Rica

OREORTYX
Oreortyx picta (Mountain Quail)
O. p. palmeri
coast from SW Washington to California
O. p. picta
Columbia river to California
O. p. russelli
California
O. p. confinis
Baja California

CALLIPEPLA
Callipepla squamata (Scaled Quail)
C. s. pallida
SW USA, NW Mexico
C. s. squamata
NC & C Mexico
C. s. castanogastris
S Texas, NE Mexico
C. s. hargravei
New Mexico

LOPHORTYX
Lophortyx californica (California Quail)
L. c. brunnescens
coast from SW Oregon to C California

L. c. canfieldae
EC California
L. c. decolorata
Baja California
L. c. californica
E Oregon to Baja California
L. c. catalinensis
Santa Catalina I (Los Coronados Is)
L. c. achrustera
S Baja California
Lophortyx gambelii (Gambel's Quail)
L. g. gambelii
SW USA, NW Mexico
L. g. sana
W Colorado
L. g. friedmann
coast of NW Mexico
L. g. fulvipectus
SW Sonora
L. g. pembertoni
Tiburon I
Lophortyx douglasii (Elegant Quail)
L. d. bensoni
Sonora
L. d. douglasii
Sinaloa, Jalisco
L. d. languens
C Chihuahua
L. d. impedita
Nayarit
L. d. teres
NW Jalisco

PHILORTYX
Philortyx fasciatus (Banded Quail)
Colima, Guerrero, Puebla (SW Mexico)

COLINUS
Colinus virginianus (Bobwhite)
C. v. virginianus
C & E USA
C. v. floridanus
Florida, Bahama Is
C. v. cubanensis
Cuba
C. v. ridgwayi
N & SC Sonora
C. v. texanus
NE Mexico
C. v. maculatus
C Mexico
C. v. aridus
NC Mexico
C. v. graysoni
WC Mexico
C. v. nigripectus
SC Mexico
C. v. pectoralis
C Vera Cruz

C. v. godmani
E Vera Cruz

C. v. minor
NE Chiapas

C. v. insignis
NW Guatemala, W Chiapas

C. v. salvini
S Chiapas

C. v. coyolcos
S Mexico

C. v. thayeri
NE Oaxaca

C. v. atriceps
W Oaxaca

C. v. nelsoni
C Chiapas

Colinus nigrogularis (Black-throated Bobwhite)

C. n. caboti
Campeche (Mexico)

C. n. persiccus
N Yucatan

C. n. nigrogularis
Yucatan

C. n. segoviensis
Guatemala, Honduras

Colinus leucopogon (White-faced Bobwhite)

C. l. incanus
Guatemala

C. l. hypoleucus
W Guatemala, W El Salvador

C. l. leucopogon
El Salvador

C. l. sclateri
W Honduras, W Nicaragua

C. l. dickeyi
SW Nicaragua, W Costa Rica

Colinus cristatus (Crested Bobwhite) ι

C. c. panamensis
W Panama

C. c. decoratus
N Colombia

C. c. bogotensis
C Colombia

C. c. badius
C Colombia

C. c. leucotis
S Colombia

C. c. parvicristatus
EC Colombia

C. c. littoralis
NE Colombia

C. c. cristatus
E Colombia, W Venezuela, Aruba I, Curaçao

C. c. horvathi
Venezuela

C. c. sonnini
E Venezuela, the Guianas, N Brazil

C. c. mocquerysi
NE Venezuela, Margarita I

C. c. mariae
W Panama

C. c. continentis
NW Venezuela

C. c. barnesi
NC Venezuela

ODONTOPHORUS

Odontophorus gujanensis (Marbled Wood Quail)

O. g. castigatus
SW Costa Rica, NW Panama

O. g. marmoratus
N Colombia, E Panama

O. g. polionotus
NW Venezuela

O. g. gujanensis
E Venezuela, the Guianas

O. g. medius
Mt Duida (S Venezuela)

O. g. buckleyi
SE Colombia, E Ecuador, W Brazil

O. g. rufogularis
NE Peru

O. g. pachyrhynchus
E Peru

O. g. simonsi
NW Bolivia

Odontophorus capueira (Spot-winged Wood Quail)
E Brazil, Paraguay

Odontophorus erythrops (Rufous-fronted Wood Quail)

O. e. verecundus
Honduras

O. e. melanotis
Nicaragua, N & E Costa Rica

O. e. coloratus
W Panama

O. e. erythrops
W Ecuador

O. e. parambae
W Colombia, NW Ecuador

Odontophorus atrifrons (Black-fronted Wood Quail)

O. a. atrifrons
Santa Marta Mts (Colombia)

O. a. variegatus
E Colombia

O. a. navai
W Venezuela

Odontophorus melanonotus (Black-backed Wood Quail)
W Ecuador

98

Odontophorus hyperythrus (Chestnut Wood Quail)
Andes of Colombia
Odontophorus speciosus (Rufous-breasted Wood Quail)
O. s. söderströrnii
C Ecuador
O. s. speciosus
E Ecuador, E Peru
O. s. loricatus
C Bolivia
Odontophorus strophium (Gorgeted Wood Quail)
C Colombia
Odontophorus dialeucos (Black-crowned Wood Quail)
Panama
Odontophorus colombianus (Venezuela Wood Quail)
N Venezuela
Odontophorus leucolaemus (White-throated Wood Quail)
N Costa Rica, W Panama
Odontophorus balliviani (Stripe-faced Wood Quail)
Peru, Bolivia
Odontophorus stellatus (Starred Wood Quail)
E Ecuador, E Peru
Odontophorus guttatus (Spotted Wood Quail)
S Mexico to W Panama

DACTYLORTYX
Dactylortyx thoracicus (Singing Quail)
D. t. thoracicus
E coast of Mexico
D. t. sharpei
Yucatan peninsula
D. t. devius
W Mexico
D. t. lineolatus
S Mexico
D. t. chiapensis
W Guatemala, C Chiapas
D. t. fuscus
E Chiapas to S Honduras
D. t. salvadoranus
C El Salvador
D. t. taylori
N El Salvador, S Honduras
D. t. colophonus
W Guatamela
D. t. rufescens
Honduras
D. t. conoveri
EC Honduras

CYRTONYX
Cyrtonyx montezumae (Montezuma's Quail)
C. m. mearnsi
S USA, NW Mexico
C. m. montezumae
N & C Mexico
C. m. merriami
Mt Orizaba (Vera Cruz, Mexico)
Cyrtonyx sallei (Salle's Quail)
SW Mexico
Cyrtonyx ocellatus (Ocellated Quail)
C. o. ocellatus
SW Mexico, W Guatemala
C. o. differens
W Honduras, N Nicaragua

RHYNCHORTYX
Rhynchortyx cinctus (Tawny-faced Quail)
R. c. pudibundus
N Honduras
R. c. cinctus
Nicaragua to SE Panama
R. c. hypopius
NE Panama
R. c. australis
W Colombia, NW Ecuador

PHASIANINAE

LERWA
Lerwa lerwa (Snow Partridge)
Afghanistan, Himalayas, W China

AMMOPERDIX
Ammoperdix griseogularis (See See Partridge)
A.g. peraticus
W Afghanistan
A. g. griseogularis
S Russia, Iran to NW India
Ammoperdix heyi (Sand Partridge)
A. h. heyi
River Jordan to Sinai
A. h. nicolli
N Egypt
A. h. cholmleyi
River Nile to Red Sea
A. h. intermedia
S Arabia

TETRAOGALLUS
Tetraogallus caucasicus (Caucasian Snowcock)
Caucasus
Tetraogallus caspius (Caspian Snowcock)
T. c. caspius
Taurus Mts to N Iran
T. c. semenowtianschanskii
Zagros Mts (Iran)
Tetraogallus tibetanus (Tibetan Snowcock)
T. t. tibetanus
Pamir Mts (W Tibet)

T. t. tschimenensis
N Tibet
T. t. centralis
NE & C Tibet
T. t. przewalskii
E Tibet, W Kansu
T. t. henrici
W China
T. t. aquilonifer
S Tibet, Sikkim
Tetraogallus altaicus (Altai Snowcock)
T. a. altaicus
Altai Mts, Sajan Mts
T. a. orientalis
NW Mongolia
Tetraogallus himalayensis (Himalayan Snowcock)
T. h. sewerzowi
SE Turkestan
T. h. himalayensis
W Himalayas, E Afghanistan
T. h. bendi
NW Afghanistan
T. h. grombczewskii
W Kwenlun Mts
T. h. koslowi
Humboldt & S Kokonor Mts

TETRAOPHASIS
Tetraophasis obscurus (Verreaux's Monal Partridge)
NE Tibet, W China
Tetraophasis szechenyii (Szechenyi's Monal Partridge)
E Tibet, SW China

ALECTORIS
Alectoris graeca (Rock Partridge)
A. g. saxatilis
Alps
A. g. graeca
SE Europe
A. g. scotti
Crete
A. g. sinaica
Syria to Sinai
A. g. daghestanica
N Caucasus
A. g. caucasica
S Caucasus
A. g. werae
SW Iran
A. g. koroviakovi
E & S Iran
A. g. shestoperovi
S Transcaspia
A. g. subpallida
Kyzylkum Mts

A. g. falki
W & C Tien Shan Mts
A. g. dzungarica
Tarbagatai Mts
A. g. fallax
E Tien Shan Mts
A. g. pallida
S Chinese Turkestan
A. g. pallescens
N India
A. g. obscurata
W Tannu Ola Mts
Alectoris chukar (Chukar Partridge)
A. c. kleini
E Greece
A. c. cypriotes
Cyclades, Asia Minor
A. c. kurdestanica
S Kurdistan
A. c. chukar
Himalayas
A. c. potanini
W Mongolia
A. c. pubescens
S Manchuria, N China
Alectoris magna (Przewalski's Rock Partridge)
E Tibet, W Kansu
Alectoris philbyi (Philby's Rock Partridge)
SW Arabia
Alectoris barbara (Barbary Partridge)
A. b. barbara
N Morocco, N Algeria, N Tunisia
A. b. theresae
S Morocco
A. b. koenigi
Canary Is
A. b. spatzi
S Algeria, S Tunisia
A. b. barbata
Libya
Alectoris rufa (Red-legged Partridge)
A. r. rufa
SC Europe
A. r. hispanica
NW Spain & N Portugal
A. r. intercedens
S Spain
A. r. corsa
Corsica
A. r. australis
Gran Canaria I
Alectoris melanocephala (Arabian Chukar)
A. m. melanocephala
SW Arabia

A. m. guichardi
  E Hadhramaut

ANUROPHASIS
Anurophasis monorthonyx (Snow Mountain Quail)
  Oranje Mts (New Guinea)

FRANCOLINUS
Francolinus francolinus (Black Partridge)
F. f. francolinus
  Cyprus to Caucasia & N Iran
F. f. billypaynei
  Syria
F. f. arabistanicus
  S Iraq, W Iran
F. f. bogdanovi
  S Iran
F. f. henrici
  Pakistan
F. f. asiae
  N India
F. f. melanonotus
  E Himalayas, Assam
Francolinus pictus (Painted Partridge)
F. p. pallidus
  NC India
F. p. pictus
  S India
F. p. watsoni
  Sri Lanka
Francolinus pintadeanus (Chinese Francolin)
F. p. phayrei
  NE India to S China, Indochina
F. p. pintadeanus
  SE China
Francolinus afer (Bare-throated Francolin)
F. a. nyanzae
  Uganda, W Kenya, W Tanzania
F. a. harterti
  Rwanda, Burundi
F. a. cranchii
  N Angola, N Zambia, W Tanzania
F. a. leucoparaeus
  E Kenya, N Tanzania
F. a. böhmi
  W Tanzania
F. a. itigi
  C Tanzania
F. a. intercedens
  SE Zaire, S Tanzania, N Zambia
F. a. castaneiventer
  E Cape Province
F. a. loangwae
  NE Zambia
F. a. benguellensis
  W Angola

F. a. punctulatus
  C Angola
F. a. afer
  S Angola
F. a. cunenensis
  S Angola, N Namibia
F. a. humboldtii
  S Malawi, W Mozambique
F. a. swynnertoni
  Rhodesia, S Mozambique
F. a. lehmanni
  E Transvaal
F. a. krebsi
  SE Cape Province, S Natal
F. a. notatus
  S Cape Province
Francolinus swainsonii (Swainson's Francolin)
F. s. gilli
  N Namibia, N Botswana, W Zambia
F. s. damarensis
  Waterburg, Namibia
F. s. chobiensis
  NE Botswana, Rhodesia, W Mozambique
F. s. swainsonii
  S Botswana, Transvaal, S Mozambique
Francolinus rufopictus (Painted Francolin)
  SE Lake Victoria
Francolinus leucoscepus (Yellow-necked Francolin)
F. l. leucoscepus
  E Ethiopia, N Somalia
F. l. muhamedbenabdullah
  S Somalia, N Kenya
F. l. infuscatus
  NE Uganda, S Ethiopia to N Tanzania
Francolinus erckelii (Erckel's Francolin)
F. e. erckelii
  Ethiopia
F. e. pentoni
  NE Sudan
Francolinus ochropectus (Pale-bellied Francolin)
  Somalia
Francolinus castaneicollis (Chestnut-naped Francolin)
F. c. ogoensis
  Somalia
F. c. castaneicollis
  E Ethiopia
F. c. bottegi
  S Ethiopia
F. c. kaffanus
  W Ethiopia
F. c. gofanus
  SW Ethiopia
F. c. atrifrons
  S Ethiopia

Francolinus jacksoni **(Jackson's Francolin)**
F. j. jacksoni
　Higher Aberdare Mts
F. j. pollenorum
　Mt Kenya
F. j. gurae
　Lower Aberdare Mts
Francolinus nobilis **(Handsome Francolin)**
F. n. nobilis
　E Zaire, SW Uganda
F. n. chapini
　Ruwenzori Mts (E Zaire)
Francolinus camerunensis **(Cameroun Mountain Francolin)**
　Cameroun Mts
Francolinus swierstrai **(Swierstra's Francolin)**
　S Angola
Francolinus ahantensis **(Ahanta Francolin)**
F. a. hopkinsoni
　Gambia, Guinea
F. a. ahantensis
　Guinea to Nigeria
Francolinus squamatus **(Scaly Francolin)**
F. s. squamatus
　S Nigeria to N Zaire
F. s. schuetti
　Angola to Ethiopia, W Kenya
F. s. zappeyi
　Uganda, W Kenya
F. s. tetraoninus
　W Ethiopia
F. s. maranensis
　S Kenya
F. s. usambarae
　Usambara Mts (Tanzania)
F. s. uzungwensis
　Uzungwe Mts (Tanzania)
F. s. doni
　Vipya plateau (W Malawi)
Francolinus griseostriatus **(Grey-striped Francolin)**
　N Angola
Francolinus bicalcaratus **(Double-spurred Francolin)**
F. b. ayesha
　W Morocco
F. b. bicalcaratus
　Senegal to Niger & N Nigeria
F. b. thornei
　Sierra Leone to Benin
F. b. adamauae
　N Nigeria, Cameroun
F. b. ogilvie-granti
　Cameroun

Francolinus icterorhynchus **(Yellow-billed Francolin)**
F. i. icterorhynchus
　Central African Republic to SW Sudan
F. i. dybowskii
　NE Zaire, W Uganda
F. i. ugandensis
　C Uganda
Francolinus clappertoni **(Clapperton's Francolin)**
F. c. clappertoni
　Mali to W Sudan
F. c. heuglini
　SW Sudan
F. c. cavei
　SE Sudan
F. c. gedgii
　Mt Elgon
F. c. sharpii
　E Ethiopia
F. c. testis
　Ethiopia
F. c. nigrosquamatus
　Ethiopia
Francolinus hildebrandti **(Hildebrandt's Francolin)**
F. h. helleri
　N Kenya
F. h. altumi
　W Kenya
F. h. hildebrandti
　E Kenya to NE Zambia & W Malawi
F. h. fischeri
　C Tanzania
F. h. grotei
　SE Tanzania
F. h. johnstoni
　S Tanzania, E Zambia, S Malawi, Mozambique
Francolinus natalensis **(Natal Francolin)**
F. n. neavei
　NE Zambia, W Mozambique
F. n. natalensis
　S Zambia to Natal
Francolinus hartlaubi **(Hartlaub's Francolin)**
F. h. hartlaubi
　Angola
F. h. bradfieldi
　N Namibia
F. h. crypticus
　Onguato area, C Namibia
Francolinus harwoodi **(Harwood's Francolin)**
　S Ethiopia
Francolinus adspersus **(Red-billed Francolin)**
　S Angola, Namibia, Botswana
Francolinus capensis **(Cape Francolin)**
　Cape Province

Francolinus sephaena (Crested Francolin)
F. s. somaliensis
Somalia
F. s. grantii
Ethiopia to C Tanzania
F. s. rovuma
E Tanzania & E Mozambique
F. s. sephaena
E Rhodesia to Mozambique & N Natal
F. s. zambesiae
Namibia to S Malawi

Francolinus streptophorus (Ring-necked Francolin)
Cameroun, W Kenya, NW Tanzania

Francolinus psilolaemus (Montane Francolin)
C Ethiopia

Francolinus shelleyi (Shelley's Francolin)
F. s. elgonensis
Kenya
F. s. theresae
Mt Kenya
F. s. shelleyi
Uganda to Natal
F. s. trothae
W Tanzania
F. s. whytei
SE Zaire, Zambia, N Malawi

Francolinus africanus (Greywing Francolin)
F. a. gutteralis
N Ethiopia
F. a. eritreae
NE Ethiopia
F. a. lorti
Somalia
F. a. ellenbecki
C Ethiopia
F. a. archeri
SC Ethiopia
F. a. triedmanni
S Ethiopia
F. a. uluensis
C Kenya
F. a. macarthuri
SE Kenya
F. a. africanus
South Africa

Francolinus levalliantoides (Archer's Greywing Francolin)
F. l. jugularis
S Angola
F. l. cunenensis
S Angola, N Namibia
F. l. pallidior
Etosha Pan, N Namibia
F. l. wattii
C Namibia
F. l. kalaharica
C Botswana
F. l. langi
NE Botswana
F. l. levalliantoides
E Botswana, Orange Free State
F. l. ludwigi
SW Transvaal
F. l. gariepensis
S Transvaal, N Orange Free State

Francolinus levaillantii (Red-winged Francolin)
F. l. kikuyuensis
Uganda, Kenya
F. l. crawshayi
N Malawi
F. l. benguellensis
S Angola
F. l. clayi
W Zambia
F. l. levaillantii
Transvaal, Natal, NE Cape Province

Francolinus finschi (Finsch's Francolin)
SW Zaire, Angola

Francolinus coqui (Coqui Francolin)
F. c. buckleyi
Ghana to S Nigeria
F. c. spinetorum
Mali to Nigeria
F. c. maharao
S Ethiopia
F. c. angolensis
Gabon to Angola & Zambia
F. c. ruahdae
S Uganda
F. c. hubbardi
W Kenya
F. c. thikae
C Kenya
F. c. coqui
Kenya to Botswana & Natal
F. c. kasaicus
C Zaire
F. c. vernayi
Botswana
F. c. hoeschianus
N Namibia

Francolinus albogularis (White-throated Francolin)
F. a. albogularis
Senegal, Gambia
F. a. buckleyi
Ghana to Cameroun
F. a. dewittei
SE Zaire
F. a. meinertzhageni
E Angola, NW Zambia

***Francolinus schlegelii* (Schlegel's Francolin)**
S Central African Republic to SW Sudan
***Francolinus lathami* (Latham's Francolin)**
F. l. lathami
Sierra Leone to Gabon & NW Zaire
F. l. schubotzi
NE Zaire to SW Sudan & Uganda
***Francolinus nahani* (Nahan's Forest Francolin)**
NE Zaire, Uganda
***Francolinus pondicerianus* (Indian Grey Francolin)**
F. p. mecranensis
S Iran to Pakistan
F. p. interpositus
N India
F. p. pondicerianus
S India
F. p. ceylonensis
Sri Lanka
***Francolinus gularis* (Swamp Partridge)**
NE India, Assam

PERDIX
***Perdix perdix* (Grey Partridge)**
P. p. perdix
British Isles, W & C Europe
P. p. armoricana
NW France
P. p. sphagnetorum
NE Holland, NW Germany
P. p. hispaniensis
Pyrenees, N Spain
P. p. italica
Italy
P. p. lucida
NE Europe
P. p. robusta
NW Russia
P. p. arenicola
WC Russia
P. p. furvescens
SW Russia, N Iran
P. p. canescens
Transcaucasia to NW Iran
***Perdix dauuricae* (Daurian Partridge)**
P. d. dauuricae
EC Asia, Mongolia, N China
P. d. castaneothorax
S Manchuria
P. d. turcomana
E Turkestan, E Tien Shan
P. d. przewalskii
E Nanshans, NW China
P. d. suschkini
C Amur, Ussuriland
***Perdix hodgsoniae* (Tibetan Partridge)**

P. h. koslowi
W Nanshans, S Kokonor Mts
P. h. sifanica
E Nanshans, SE Tibet, W China
P. h. caraganae
E Ladak, W Himalayas
P. h. hodgsoniae
Tibet, E Himalayas, Assam

RHIZOTHERA
***Rhizothera longirostris* (Long-billed Wood Partridge)**
R. l. longirostris
Malaysia, Sumatra, W Borneo
R. l. dulitensis
N Borneo

MARGAROPERDIX
***Margaroperdix madagarensis* (Madagascar Partridge)**
Madagascar

MELANOPERDIX
***Melanoperdix nigra* (Black Wood Partridge)**
M. n. nigra
Malaysia, Sumatra
M. n. borneensis
Borneo

COTURNIX
***Coturnix coturnix* (Common Quail)**
C. c. coturnix
Europe, W Asia to C Africa & India
C. c. ussuriensis
NE Asia, Mongolia
C. c. conturbans
Azores
C. c. confisa
Madeira, Canary Is
C. c. inopinata
Cape Verde Is
C. c. africana
Southern Africa, Madagascar
***Coturnix japonica* (Japanese Quail)**
Sakhalin, Japan to Indochina
***Coturnix coromandelica* (Black-breasted Quail)**
India, Sri Lanka, Burma
***Coturnix delegorguei* (Harlequin Quail)**
C. d. delegorguei
Senegal to Ethiopia & S Africa
C. d. histrionica
Sao Thomé I
C. d. arabica
S Arabia
***Coturnix pectoralis* (Pectoral Quail)**
Australia, Tasmania

SYNOICUS
***Synoicus ypsilophorus* (Brown Quail)**

S. y. raaltenii
Flores I, Timor I
S. y. pallidior
Sumba I, Savu I
S. y. saturatior
N New Guinea
S. y. lamonti
C New Guinea
S. y. dogwa
S New Guinea
S. y. mafulu
SE New Guinea
S. y. castaneus
Lesser Sunda Is
S. y. plumbeus
SE New Guinea
S. y. cervinus
NW Australia
S. y. queenslandicus
N Queensland
S. y. australis
SW Australia & S Queensland to Victoria
S. y. ypsilophorus
SE Australia, Tasmania

EXCALFACTORIA
Excalfactoria adansonii (Blue Quail)
Ethiopia to Sierra Leone & E Cape Province
Excalfactoria chinensis (Indian Blue Quail)
E. c. chinensis
India to Malaysia, S China & Indochina
E. c. trinkutensis
Nicobar Is
E. c. palmeri
Sumatra, Java
E. c. lineata
Philippine Is, Borneo, Celebes
E. c. lineatula
Lombok I, Sumba I, Flores I, Timor I
E. c. lepida
Bismarck Archipelago
E. c. papuensis
SE New Guinea
E. c. australis
Queensland to Victoria
E. c. colletti
Northern Territory

PERDICULA
Perdicula asiatica (Jungle Bush Quail)
Himalayas, N & C India
Perdicula argoondah (Rock Bush Quail)
SE India
Perdicula erythrorhyncha (Painted Bush Quail)
P. e. erythrorhyncha
SW India
P. e. blewitti
C India

Perdicula manipurensis (Manipur Bush Quail)
P. m. inglisi
N Assam
P. m. manipurensis
S Assam

ARBOROPHILA
Arborophila torqueola (Common Hill Partridge)
A. t. millardi
NW India
A. t. torqueola
N & E India, S Tibet
A. t. batemani
N Burma
A. t. griseata
W N Vietnam
Arborophila rufogularis (Rufous-throated Hill Partridge)
A. r. rufogularis
N India
A. r. intermedia
Assam to NW Burma
A. r. tickelli
S Burma to SW Laos
A. r. euroa
S China, N Laos
A. r. guttata
C Vietnam
A. r. annamensis
S Vietnam
Arborophila atrogularis (White-cheeked Hill Partridge)
Assam, N Burma
Arborophila crudigularis (White-throated Hill Partridge)
Taiwan
Arborophila mandellii (Red-breasted Hill Partridge)
Sikkim to E Assam
Arborophila brunneopectus (Brown-breasted Hill Partridge)
A. b. brunneopectus
E Assam & S Yunnan to S Thailand
A. b. henrici
N & C Vietnam
A. b. albigula
S Vietnam
Arborophila rufipectus (Boulton's Hill Partridge)
W Szechwan
Arborophila gingica (Rickett's Hill Partridge)
SE China
Arborophila davidi (David's Tree Partridge)
S Vietnam

Arborophila cambodiana (Chestnut-headed Tree Partridge)
  A. c. cambodiana
    Cambodia
  A. c. diversa
    SE Thailand
Arborophila orientalis (Sumatran Hill Partridge)
  A. o. campbelli
    Malaysia
  A. c. rolli
    NW Sumatra
  A. o. sumatrana
    C Sumatra
  A. o. orientalis
    E Java
Arborophila javanica (Chestnut-bellied Tree Partridge)
  A. j. javanica
    W Java
  A. j. bartelsi
    C Java
  A. j. lawuana
    C Java
Arborophila rubrirostris (Red-billed Tree Partridge)
    Sumatra
Arborophila hyperythra (Red-breasted Tree Partridge)
    NW Borneo
Arborophila ardens (Hainan Hill Partridge)
    Hainan I

TROPICOPERDIX
Tropicoperdix charltonii (Chestnut-breasted Tree Partridge)
  T. c. charltonii
    S Thailand, Malaysia
  T. c. atjehensis
    N Sumatra
  T. c. tonkinensis
    N Vietnam
  T. c. graydoni
    Borneo
Tropicoperdix chloropus (Green-legged Hill Partridge)
  T. c. chloropus
    N Burma to W & S Thailand
  T. c. olivacea
    Laos, Cambodia
  T. c. cognacqi
    S Vietnam
Tropicoperdix merlini (Annamese Hill Partridge)
  T. m. merlini
    C Vietnam
  T. m. vivida
    EC Vietnam

CALOPERDIX
Caloperdix oculea (Ferruginous Wood Partridge)
  C. o. oculea
    S Thailand, Malaysia
  C. o. sumatrana
    Sumatra
  C. o. borneensis
    Borneo

HAEMATORTYX
Haematortyx sanguiniceps (Crimson-headed Wood Partridge)
    N Borneo

ROLLULUS
Rollulus roulroul (Crested Wood Partridge)
    S Thailand, Malaysia, Sumatra, Borneo

PTILOPACHUS
Ptilopachus petrosus (Stone Partridge)
  P. p. petrosus
    Gambia to Cameroun
  P. p. saturatior
    NC Cameroun
  P. p. brehmi
    Lake Chad to Sudan
  P. p. major
    N Ethiopia
  P. p. florentiae
    S Sudan to NE Zaire, Uganda & Kenya

BAMBUSICOLA
Bambusicola fytchii (Bamboo Partridge)
  B. f. fytchii
    W China, Burma, N Vietnam
  B. f. hopkinsoni
    Assam, S Burma
Bambusicola thoracica (Chinese Bamboo Partridge)
  B. t. thoracica
    China
  B. t. sonorivox
    Taiwan

GALLOPERDIX
Galloperdix spadicea (Red Spurfowl)
  G. s. spadicea
    W Nepal to SE India
  G. s. caurina
    Rajputana
  G. s. stewarti
    C & S Travancore
Galloperdix lunulata (Painted Spurfowl)
    India
Galloperdix bicalcarata (Ceylon Spurfowl)
    Sri Lanka

Ophrysia superciliosa (Himalayan Mountain Quail)
　NW Himalayas

ITHAGINIS
Ithaginis cruentus (Blood Pheasant)
　I. c. cruentus
　　Nepal, Sikkim, W Bhutan
　I. c. affinis
　　Sikkim
　I. c. tibetanus
　　E Bhutan, SE Tibet
　I. c. kuseri
　　E Assam to Yunnan
　I. c. holoptilus
　　Yunnan
　I. c. rocki
　　W Yunnan
　I. c. clarkei
　　W Yunnan
　I. c. annae
　　NW Szechwan
　I. c. beicki
　　N Kansu
　I. c. marionae
　　NE Burma
　I. c. geoffroyi
　　SE Tibet to W Szechwan
　I. c. berezowskii
　　S Kansu, N Szechwan
　I. c. sinensis
　　Shensi
　I. c. michaëlis
　　W Kansu

TRAGOPAN
Tragopan melanocephalus (Western Tragopan)
　NW Himalayas
Tragopan satyra (Satyr Tragopan)
　C & E Himalayas
Tragopan blythii (Blyth's Tragopan)
　T. b. molesworthi
　　SE Tibet
　T. b. blythii
　　Assam, NW Burma
Tragopan temminckii (Temminck's Tragopan)
　SE Tibet, W China, N Vietnam
Tragopan caboti (Cabot's Tragopan)
　SE China

PUCRASIA
Pucrasia macrolopha (Koklass Pheasant)
　P. m. castanea
　　Afghanistan, N Pakistan
　P. m. biddulphi
　　N Kashmir, Ladakh

P. m. macrolopha
　W Himalayas
P. m. bethelae
　Punjab
P. m. nipalensis
　W Nepal
P. m. meyeri
　SE Tibet, W Yunnan
P. m. ruficollis
　Kansu, W Shansi
P. m. xanthospila
　SE Mongolia
P. m. joretiana
　W Anhwei
P. m. darwini
　Hupeh & E China

LOPHOPHORUS
Lophophorus impeyanus (Himalayan Monal Pheasant)
　Himalayas
Lophophorus sclateri (Sclater's Monal Pheasant)
　L. s. sclateri
　　E Assam, N Burma, W Yunnan
　L. s. orientalis
　　Myitkyina, Burma
Lophophorus lhuysii (Chinese Monal Pheasant)
　W & NW Szechwan

GALLUS
Gallus gallus (Red Junglefowl)
　G. g. murghi
　　Kashmir to Assam & C India
　G. g. gallus
　　S Indochina, Thailand, Sumatra
　G. g. spadiceus
　　SW Yunnan, N Indochina, Burma, Malaysia
　G. g. jabouillei
　　N Vietnam
　G. g. bankiva
　　Java
Gallus lafayettei (Ceylon Jungle-fowl)
　Sri Lanka
Gallus sonneratii (Grey Jungle-fowl)
　W & S India
Gallus varius (Green Junglefowl)
　Java to Sumba & Flores

LOPHURA
Lophura leucomelana (Kalij Pheasant)
　L. l. hamiltonii
　　W Himalayas
　L. l. moffitti
　　C Bhutan
　L. l. leucomelana
　　Nepal

L. l. melanotus
E Nepal
L. l. lathami
E Bhutan, Assam, W Burma
L. l. williamsi
N Burma
L. l. oatesi
S Burma
L. l. lineatus
E Burma, Thailand
L. l. crawfurdi
S & W Thailand
ophura nycthemera (Silver Pheasant)
L. n. occidentalis
NW Yunnan, NE Burma
L. n. rufipes
SW Yunnan, N Burma
L. n. jonesi
SW Yunnan, C Thailand, C Burma
L n. ripponi
S Burma
L. n. beaulieui
SE Yunnan, N Indochina
L. n. omeiensis
Szechwan
L. n. fokiensis
NW Fokien
L. n. nycthemera
S China, NE Vietnam
L. n. berliozi
WC Indochina
L. n. beli
C Vietnam
L. n. annamensis
S Vietnam
L. n. lewisi
Cambodia
L. n. engelbachi
S Laos
L. n. whiteheadi
Hainan I
ophura imperialis (Imperial Pheasant)
NC Indochina
ophura edwardsi (Edwards' Pheasant)
C Vietnam
ophura swinhoii (Swinhoe's Pheasant)
Taiwan
ophura inornata (Salvadori's Pheasant)
L. i. hoogewerfi
N Sumatra
L. i. inornata
W Sumatra
ophura erythrophthalma (Crestless Fireback Pheasant)
L. e. erythrophthalma
S Malaysia, NE Sumatra
L. e. pyronota
N Borneo

Lophura ignita (Crested Fireback Pheasant) 107
L. i. rufa
S Thailand, Malaysia, N & C Sumatra
L. i. macartneyi
SE Sumatra
L. i. nobilis
N Borneo
L. i. ignita
S Borneo
Lophura diardi (Siamese Fireback Pheasant)
Burma, Thailand, C & S Indochina
Lophura bulweri (Bulwer's Pheasant)
Borneo

CROSSOPTILON
Crossoptilon crossoptilon (White Eared-Pheasant)
C. c. dolani
S Kokonor
C. c. crossoptilon
C Szechwan, NW Yunnan
C. c. lichiangense
NW Yunnan
C. c. drouynii
SE Tibet
C. c. harmani
SE Tibet
Crossoptilon mantchuricum (Brown Eared-Pheasant)
NE China
Crossoptilon auritum (Blue Eared-Pheasant)
W China

CATREUS
Catreus wallichii (Cheer Pheasant)
Himalayas

SYRMATICUS
Syrmaticus ellioti (Elliot's Pheasant)
SE China
Syrmaticus humiae (Mrs Hume's Pheasant)
S. h. humiae
N Burma
S. h. burmanicus
SW Yunnan, NE Burma
Syrmaticus mikado (Mikado Pheasant)
Taiwan
Syrmaticus soemmerringi (Copper Pheasant)
S. s. scintillans
Honshu I
S. s. subrufus
W Honshu I
S. s. intermedius
SW Honshu I, Shikoku I
S. s. soemmerringi
N & C Kyushu I

S. s. ijimae
SE Kyushu I
Syrmaticus reevesii (Reeves' Pheasant)
N & C China

PHASIANUS
Phasianus colchicus (Ring-necked Pheasant)
P. c. septentrionalis
N Caucasus, W Caspian Sea
P. c. colchicus
Transcaucasia, E & SE Black Sea
P. c. talischensis
SW & S Caspian Sea
P. c. persicus
SW Transcaspia
P. c. principalis
S Turkestan, N Afghanistan
P. c. chrysomelas
Russian Turkestan
P. c. zarudnyi
Russian Turkestan
P. c. bianchii
Pamir, Hindukush Mts
P. c. zerafschanicus
Samarkand
P. c. bergii
Aral Sea
P. c. turcestanicus
Russian Turkestan
P. c. mongolicus
NE Russian Turkestan,S Dzungaria
P. c. shawii
Chinese Turkestan
P. c. tarimensis
E Chinese Turkestan
P. c. vlangalii
E Zaidam
P. c. satscheuensis
W Kansu
P. c. edzinensis
C Gobi
P. c. sohokotensis
Soho-khoto Oasis
P. c. alaschanicus
C Alaschan Mts
P. c. hagenbecki
W Mongolia
P. c. pallasi
SE Siberia, C Manchuria
P. c. karpowi
S Manchuria, Korea
P. c. kiangsuensis
SE Mongolia, N Shansi, N Shensi
P. c. strauchi
Kansu, C & S Shensi, NE Szechwan
P. c. süehschanensis
NW Szechwan

P. c. elegans
SW Szechwan to N Burma
P. c. rothschildi
SE Yunnan, N Vietnam
P. c. decollatus
WC China
P. c. torquatus
E China
P. c. takatsukasae
NE Vietnam
P. c. formosanus
Taiwan
Phasianus versicolor (Japanese Pheasant)
P. v. robustipes
Sado I, NW Honshu
P. v. versicolor
Kyushu, E & S Honshu, Shikoku
P. v. tanensis
S peninsulas & islands off Honshu

CHRYSOLOPHUS
Chrysolophus pictus (Golden Pheasant)
C China
Chrysolophus amherstiae (Lady Amherst's Pheasant)
SE Tibet, SW China, N Burma

POLYPLECTRON
Polyplectron chalcurum (Sumatran Peacock-Pheasant)
P. c. scutulatum
N Sumatra
P. c. chalcurum
S Sumatra
Polyplectron inopinatum (Rothschild's Peacock-Pheasant)
C Malaysia
Polyplectron germaini (Germain's Peacock-Pheasant)
S Vietnam
Polyplectron bicalcaratum (Burmese Peacock-Pheasant)
P. b. bakeri
Sikkim to E Assam
P. b. bicalcaratum
C & S Burma to Laos
P. b. bailyi
N Thailand
P. b. ghigii
N Vietnam
P. b. katsumatae
Hainan I
Polyplectron malacense (Malay Peacock-Pheasant)
P. m. malacense
SW Thailand, Malaysia, Sumatra
P. m. schleiermacheri
Borneo

Polyplectron emphanum (Palawan Peacock-Pheasant)
    Palawan I

RHEINARTIA
Rheinartia ocellata (Rheinard's Pheasant)
    C Vietnam
Rheinartia nigrescens (Malay Ocellated Pheasant)
    C Malaysia

ARGUSIANUS
Argusianus argus (Great Argus Pheasant)
    A. a. grayi
      C Borneo
    A. a. argus
      SW Thailand, Malaysia, Sumatra

PAVO
Pavo cristatus (Common Peafowl)
    India, Sri Lanka
Pavo muticus (Green Peafowl)
    P. m. spicifer
      SE Assam, W Burma
    P. m. imperator
      E Burma, Thailand, Indochina
    P. m. muticus
      Java, Malaysia

AFROPAVO
Afropavo congensis (Congo Peafowl)
    Ituri Forest, EC Zaire

NUMIDINAE
PHASIDUS
Phasidus niger (Black Guineafowl)
    S Cameroun to C Zaire

AGELASTES
Agelastes meleagrides (White-breasted Guineafowl)
    Liberia, Ghana

NUMIDA
Numida meleagris (Helmet Guineafowl)
    N. m. sabyi
      W Morocco
    N. m. galeata
      Cape Verde Is, Senegal to Air & Cameroun
    N. m. marchei
      Gabon, Central African Republic
    N. m. strasseni
      E Cameroun, N Central African Republic
    N. m. meleagris
      Chad, Sudan, N Ethiopia, SW Arabia
    N. m. somaliensis
      SE Ethiopia, Somalia, N Kenya
    N. m. major
      NE Zaire, S Ethiopia, NW Kenya, N Uganda

N. m. toruensis
    E Zaire, W Uganda
N. m. intermedia
    SW Uganda
N. m. mitrata
    S Kenya to Rhodesia, Madagascar
N. m. macroceras
    W Kenya
N. m. reichenowi
    SW Kenya, NW Tanzania
N. m. uhehensis
    SC Tanzania
N. m. callewaerte
    N Angola to SC Zaire
N. m. marungensis
    S Zaire, Zambia
N. m. maxima
    S Angola
N. m. rikwae
    SW Tanzania
N. m. papillosa
    S Angola
N. m. damarensis
    N Namibia
N. m. transvaalensis
    W Transvaal
N. m. coronata
    E Transvaal, Natal, E Cape Province

GUTTERA
Guttera plumifera (Plumed Guineafowl)
    G. p. plumifera
      Cameroun, Gabon, N Angola
    G. p. schubotzi
      N Zaire
Guttera edouardi (Crested Guineafowl)
    G. e. verreauxi
      Guinea to Togo
    G. e. sclateri
      W Cameroun
    G. e. schoutedeni
      S Zaire
    G. e. chapini
      S Angola
    G. e. sethsmithi
      E Zaire, NW Tanzania
    G. e. suahelica
      C Tanzania
    G. e. barbata
      SW Tanzania, W Mozambique
    G. e. kathleenae
      W Zambia
    G. e. edouardi
      S Malawi, E Transvaal, Natal
Guttera pucherani (Kenya Crested Guineafowl)
    SE Somalia, E Kenya, NE Tanzania, Zanzibar

ACRYLLIUM

Acryllium vulturinum (Vulturine Guineafowl)
E Uganda, S Somalia, E Kenya, NE Tanzania

36 OPISTHOCOMIDAE (HOATZIN)

OPISTHOCOMUS
Opisthocomus hoatzin (Hoatzin)
Northern Amazonian forest

Gruiformes

37 MESITORNITHIDAE (MESITES)

MESITORNIS
Mesitornis variegata (White-breasted Mesite)
E Madagascar
Mesitornis unicolor (Brown Mesite)
E Madagascar

MONIAS
Monias benschi (Bensch's Monia)
SW Madagascar

38 TURNICIDAE (BUTTON QUAILS)

TURNIX
Turnix sylvatica (Little Button Quail)
T. s. sylvatica
S Iberia, NW Africa
T. s. lepurana
Senegal to Sudan & Cape Province
T. s. dussumier
India, Burma
T. s. mikado
Thailand, S China, N Indochina, Taiwan
T. s. davidi
S Indochina
T. s. bartelsorum
Java
T. s. whiteheadi
Luzon I
T. s. celestinoi
Bohol I
T. s. masaaki
Mindanao I
T. s. suluensis
Sulu Is
T. s. kinneari
Peling I
T. s. beccarii
Celebes, Tukang Besi Is
T. s. maculosa
Lesser Sunda Is, Kei Is
T. s. everetti

Sumba I.
T. s. saturata
New Britain, Duke of York I
T. s. furva
New Guinea
T. s. giluwensis
C New Guinea
T. s. savuensis
Savu Is
T. s. sumbana
Sumba I
T. s. floresiana
Flores I
T. s. horsbrughi
S New Guinea, Sudest I
T. s. salamonis
Guadalcanal I, Bismarck Archipelago
T. s. pseutes
NW Australia
Turnix worcesteri (Worcester's Button Quail)
Luzon I
Turnix nana (Natal Button Quail)
T. n. nana
Ghana to Uganda & SE Cape Province
T. n. luciana
C Kenya
Turnix hottentotta (Hottentot Button Quail)
SW Cape Province
Turnix tanki (Yellow-legged Button Quail)
T. t. tanki
India, Nicobar & Andaman Is
T. t. blanfordii
Manchuria to Burma, S China, Indochina
Turnix suscitator (Bustard Quail)
T. s. plumbipes
Nepal to N Burma
T. s. bengalensis
NE India
T. s. taigoor
India
T. s. leggei
Sri Lanka
T. s. blakistoni
S China, N Indochina
T. s. rostrata
Taiwan
T. s. pallescens
SC Burma
T. s. thai
C Thailand
T. s. interrumpens
S Burma, S Thailand
T. s. atrogularis
Malaysia, N Sumatra

T. s. machetes
C Sumatra

T. s. suscitator
SE Sumatra, Java, Bali I

T. s. kuiperi
Billiton I

T. s. okinavensis
Okinawa I

T. s. fasciata
Palawan I, N & W Philippine Is

T. s. nigrescens
Negros I, Cebu I

T. s. rufilata
Celebes

T. s. powelli
Lesser Sunda islands

Turnix nigricollis (Madagascar Button Quail)
Madagascar

Turnix ocellata (Spotted Button Quail)
Luzon I

Turnix melanogaster (Black-breasted Button Quail)
Queensland, New South Wales

Turnix varia (Painted Button Quail)

T. v. scintillans
Houtman (Abrolhos) Is

T. v. varia
Australia

T. v. novaecaledoniae
New Caledonia

Turnix castanota (Chestnut-backed Button Quail)

T. c. castanota
NW Australia, Northern Territory, Melville I

T. c. olivii
N Queensland

Turnix pyrrhothorax (Red-chested Button Quail)
N, E & SE Australia

Turnix velox (Little Quail)
Australia

ORTYXELOS

Ortyxelos meiffrenii (Quail Plover)
Senegal to C Sudan, N Kenya

39 PEDIONOMIDAE (PLAINS WANDERER)

PEDIONOMUS

Pedionomus torquatus (Plains Wanderer)
New South Wales, Victoria, South Australia

40 GRUIDAE (CRANES)

GRUINAE

GRUS

Grus grus (Common Crane)

G. g. grus
N & E Europe, W Russia » NE Africa

G. g. lilfordi
C & E Asia, China, N India

Grus nigricollis (Black-necked Crane)
C Asia to Assam, S China

Grus monacha (Hooded Crane)
SE Siberia, N China, Japan

Grus canadensis (Sandhill Crane)

G. c. canadensis
E Siberia, NW Canada to NW USA

G. c. tabida
SW Canada, W USA, N Mexico

G. c. pratensis
SE USA

G. c. nesiotes
Isle of Pines, W Cuba

Grus japonensis (Manchurian Crane)
Manchuria » E China

Grus americana (Whooping Crane)
N Sasketchewan » SE Texas

Grus vipio (Japanese White-necked Crane)
NW Mongolia » E China

Grus antigone (Sarus Crane)

G. a. antigone
N India

G. a. sharpii
E Assam, Burma to S Indochina

Grus rubicunda (Brolga)
S New Guinea, N, E & S Australia

Grus leucogeranus (Great White Crane)
SE Russia, Siberia » NW India & China

BUGERANUS

Bugeranus carunculatus (Wattled Crane)
Somalia to Angola & South Africa

ANTHROPOIDES

Anthropoides virgo (Demoiselle Crane)
SE Europe, NE Africa to C Asia & China

Anthropoides paradisea (Stanley Crane)
Southern Africa

BALEARICINAE

BALEARICA

Balearica pavonina (Crowned Crane)

B. p. pavonina
Senegal to Chad & N Zaire

B. p. ceciliae
Sudan, Ethiopia

B. p. gibbericeps
E Zaire, Uganda, Kenya, N Tanzania

Balearica regulorum (South African Crowned Crane)
Southern Africa

41 ARAMIDAE (LIMPKIN)

ARAMUS
Aramus guarauna (Limpkin)
  A. g. pictus
    SE USA, Cuba, Jamaica
  A. g. elucus
    Hispaniola, Puerto Rico
  A. g. dolosus
    S Mexico to Panama
  A. g. guarauna
    N South America to Paraguay &
    Argentina

42 PSOPHIIDAE (TRUMPETERS)

PSOPHIA
Psophia crepitans (Common Trumpeter)
  P. c. crepitans
    S Venezuela, the Guianas, NE Brazil
  P. c. napensis
    N Upper Amazonia
Psophia leucoptera (White-winged Trumpeter)
  P. l. leucoptera
    E Peru, N Bolivia, W Brazil
  P. l. ochroptera
    NW Brazil
Psophia viridis (Green-winged Trumpeter)
  P. v. viridis
    N Brazil
  P. v. dextralis
    NC Brazil
  P. v. interjecta
    C Brazil
  P. v. obscura
    NE Brazil

43 RALLIDAE (RAILS, COOTS)

HIMANTORNIS
Himantornis haematopus (Nkulengu Rail)
  H. h. haematopus
    Liberia to S Cameroun
  H. h. petiti
    Gabon to N Angola
  H. h. whitesidei
    C Zaire

CANIRALLUS
Canirallus oculeus (Grey-throated Rail)
  C. o. oculeus
    Liberia to Nigeria
  C. o. batesi
    S Cameroun to C Zaire
Canirallus kioloides (Madagascar Grey-throated Rail)
  C. k. berliozi
    NW Madagascar

  C. k. kioloides
    E Madagascar
Canirallus cuvieri (White-throated Rail)
  C. c. cuvieri
    Madagascar, Mauritius I
  C. c. aldabranus
    Aldabra I

EULABEORNIS
Eulabeornis castaneoventris (Chestnut-bellied Rail)
  E. c. sharpei
    Aru Is
  E. c. castaneoventris
    coast of N & NE Australia
Eulabeornis plumbeiventris (Bare-eyed Rail)
  E. p. plumbeiventris
    N Moluccas, New Ireland, N New Guinea
  E. p. hoeveni
    S New Guinea, Aru Is
Eulabeornis rosenbergii (Bald-faced Rail)
    N & C Celebes
Eulabeornis calopterus (Red-winged Wood Rail)
    E Ecuador, E Peru
Eulabeornis saracura (Slaty-breasted Wood Rail)
    SE Brazil, Paraguay
Eulabeornis ypecaha (Giant Wood Rail)
    E Brazil to C Argentina
Eulabeornis wolfi (Brown Wood Rail)
    Colombia to SW Ecuador
Eulabeornis mangle (Little Wood Rail)
    E Brazil
Eulabeornis cajaneus (Grey-necked Wood Rail)
  E. c. mexicanus
    S Mexico
  E. c. vanrossemi
    Guatemala, El Salvador
  E. c. albiventris
    Yucatan to Belize
  E. c. pacificus
    Honduras, Nicaragua
  E. c. plumbeicollis
    NE Costa Rica
  E. c. cajaneus
    Costa Rica to Paraguay & N Argentina
  E. c. latens
    San Miguel I, Pearl Is (Panama)
  E. c. morrisoni
    Pearl Is (Panama)
Eulabeornis axillaris (Rufous-necked Wood Rail)
    S Mexico to Guyana & Ecuador
Eulabeornis concolor (Uniform Crake)
  E. c. guatemalensis
    S Mexico to Ecuador

E. c. castaneus
    NE South America
    (*E. c. concolor — extinct*)

RALLUS
Rallus plateni (Platen's Celebes Rail)
    Celebes
Rallus wallacii (Wallace's Rail)
    Halmahera I
Rallus insignis (New Britain Rail)
    New Britain
Rallus lafresnayanus (New Caledonian Wood Rail)
    New Caledonia **e?**
Rallus sylvestris (Lord Howe Wood Rail)
    Lord Howe I
Rallus poecilopterus (Barred Wing Rail)
    R. p. poecilopterus
        Taveuni I, Viti Levu I **e?**
    R. p. woodfordi
        Guadalcanal I
    R. p. immaculatus
        Ysabel I
    R. p. tertius
        Bougainville I
Rallus sanguinolentus (Plumbeous Rail)
    R. s. simonsi
        NW Peru, N Chile
    R. s. tschudii
        C Peru
    R. s. zelebori
        Rio de Janeiro, Brazil
    R. s. sanguinolentus
        S Brazil, W Argentina
    R. s. landbecki
        C Chile
    R. s. luridus
        Tierra del Fuego
Rallus nigricans (Blackish Rail)
    R. n. nigricans
        E Ecuador to E Brazil and E Argentina
    R. n. caucae
        Cauca valley, Colombia
Rallus maculatus (Spotted Rail)
    R. m. insolitus
        S Mexico to Costa Rica
    R. m. maculatus
        Venezuela to C Argentina, Trinidad, Cuba
Rallus philippensis (Banded Rail)
    R. p. philippensis
        Celebes, Mindoro I, Luzon I, Batan I
    R. p. xerophilus
        Banda Sea islands
    R. p. wilkinsoni
        S Flores I
    R. p. andrewsi
        Cocos Keeling Is

    R. p. admiralitatis
        Admiralty Is
    R. p. praedo
        Skoki I
    R. p. lesouefi
        New Hanover
    R. p. meyeri
        Witu I, New Britain
    R. p. anchoretae
        Anchorite I
    R. p. pelewensis
        Palau Is
    R. p. christophori
        E Solomon Is
    R. p. randi
        Mt Wilhelmina (New Guinea)
    R. p. lacustris
        Sentani Lake (W New Guinea)
    R. p. reductus
        NE New Guinea
    R. p. wahgiensis
        SE New Guinea
    R. p. yorki
        W & S New Guinea, N Queensland
    R. p. australis
        E & S Australia, Tasmania
    R. p. mellori
        Sandy Hooks I, SW Australia
    R. p. assimilis
        New Zealand
    R. p. norfolkensis
        Norfolk I
    R. p. swindellsi
        New Caledonia
    R. p. sethsmithi
        New Hebrides, Fiji Is
    R. p. goodsoni
        Samoa Is
    R. p. ecaudatus
        Tonga
Rallus striatus (Blue-breasted Banded Rail)
    R. s. gularis
        Java
    R. s. albiventer
        India, Burma, N Malaysia
    R. s. obscurior
        Andman Is, Nicobar Is
    R. s. jouyi
        SE China
    R. s. taiwanus
        Taiwan
    R. s. striatus
        Borneo, Celebes, Philippine Is
    R. s. paratermus
        Samar I

Rallus torquatus (Barred Rail)
  R. t. torquatus
    Philippine Is
  R. t. celebensis
    Celebes
  R. t. sulcirostris
    Peling I, Sula Is
  R. t. kuehni
    Tukang Besi Is
  R. t. limarius
    Salawati I, NW New Guinea
Rallus owstoni (Guam Rail)
    Guam I
Rallus pectoralis (Slate-breasted Rail)
  R. p. exsul
    Flores I
  R. p. mayri
    NW New Guinea
  R. p. insulsus
    Hertzog Mts (New Guinea)
  R. p. captus
    Mt Hagen (New Guinea)
  R. p. alberti
    S C New Guinea
  R. p. pectoralis
    SW, S & E Australia
  R. p. brachipus
    Tasmania
  R. p. muelleri
    Adams I, S New Zealand
  R. p. mirificus
    Luzon I
Rallus caerulescens (Kaffir Rail)
    N Angola to Ethiopia & Cape Province
Rallus madagascariensis (Madagascar Rail)
    E Madagascar
Rallus aquaticus (Water Rail)
  R. a. aquaticus
    W Europe to W Siberia, NW Africa
  R. a. hibernans
    Iceland
  R. a. korejewi
    Turkey to NW India
  R. a. indicus
    Siberia to Japan, N India & China
Rallus semiplumbeous (Bogota Rail)
    Colombia, Ecuador, Peru
Rallus longirostris (Clapper Rail)
  R. l. obsoletus
    N California
  R. l. levipes
    S California
  R. l. yumanensis
    SW USA, N Mexico
  R. l. beldingi
    S Mexico to N Colombia

R. l. tenuirostris
    SC Mexico
R. l. pallidus
    Yucatan
R. l. grossi
    Quintana Roo
R. l. belizensis
    Belize
R. l. elegans
    C & E USA
R. l. crepitans
    E Coast USA, Connecticut to N Carolina
R. l. waynei
    S Carolina to Florida
R. l. saturatus
    coast of Texas, Alabama
R. l. scotti
    W Florida
R. l. insularum
    Florida Keys
R. l. coryi
    Bahama Is
R. l. ramsdeni
    Cuba
R. l. leucophaeus
    Isle of Pines
R. l. caribaeus
    Cuba, Jamaica, Hispaniola, Puerto Rico, Antigua I
R. l. margaritae
    N Venezuela
R. l. phelpsi
    Colombia, Venezuela
R. l. pelodramus
    Trinidad
R. l. longirostris
    Coast of the Guianas
R. l. crassirostris
    Coast of Brazil
R. l. cypereti
    W Ecuador, N Peru
Rallus wetmorei (Plain-flanked Rail)
    N Venezuela
Rallus limicola (Virginia Rail)
  R. l. limicola
    USA, N Mexico
  R. l. friedmanni
    C Mexico
  R. l. aequatorialis
    Colombia, Ecuador, Peru
  R. l. antarcticus
    C & S Chile, S Argentina

ATLANTISIA
Atlantisia rogersi (Inaccessible Island Rail)
    Inaccessible I

GALLIRALLUS
Gallirallus australis (Weka Rail)
  G. a. greyi
    North I, New Zealand
  G. a. australis
    N & W South I, New Zealand
  G. a. hectori
    E South I, New Zealand
  G. a. scotti
    Stewart I

ROUGETIUS
Rougetius rougetii (Rouget's Rail)
  N Ethiopia

CYANOLIMNAS
Cyanolimnas cerverai (Zapata Rail)
  S Cuba

RALLINA
Rallina rubra (New Guinea Chestnut Rail)
  R. r. rubra
    NW New Guinea
  R. r. telefolminensis
    WC New Guinea
  R. r. klossi
    C & SW New Guinea
Rallina leucospila (White-striped Chestnut Rail)
  NW & W New Guinea
Rallina forbesi (Forbes' Chestnut Rail)
  R. f. forbesi
    SE New Guinea
  R. f. dryas
    Huon peninsula, New Guinea
  R. f. steini
    C New Guinea
Rallina mayri (Mayr's Chestnut Rail)
  R. m. mayri
    Cyclops Mts (New Guinea)
  R. m. carmichaeli
    NE New Guinea
Rallina castaneiceps (Chestnut-headed Crake)
  R. c. coccineipes
    SW Colombia, NE Ecuador
  R. c. castaneiceps
    E Ecuador, N Peru
Rallina tricolor (Red-necked Crake)
  R. t. tricolor
    N Queensland, New Guinea & islands
  R. t. victor
    Damar I, Tenimber Is, St Matthias I
  R. t. convicta
    New Hanover, New Ireland
Rallina canningi (Andaman Banded Crake)
  Andaman Is
Rallina fasciata (Red-legged Crake)
  S Burma to Philippine Is, Moluccas, Java
Rallina eurizonoides (Banded Crake)

  R. e. amauroptera
    India » Sri Lanka
  R. e. telmatophila
    Burma to Indochina & Java
  R. e. sepiaria
    Riukiu Is
  R. e. formosana
    Taiwan
  R. e. eurizonoides
    Philippine Is
  R. e. minahasa
    Celebes, Sula Is
Rallina paykullii (Band-bellied Crake)
  NE Asia, China » Borneo, Java

COTURNICOPS
Coturnicops rufa (Red-chested Crake)
  C. r. bonapartii
    Sierra Leone to Gabon
  C. r. elizabethae
    NE Zaire, Uganda, N Kenya
  C. r. rufa
    Angola, South Africa
Coturnicops pulchra (White-spotted Crake)
  C. p. pulchra
    Sierra Leone to NW Cameroun
  C. p. zenkeri
    S Cameroun
  C. p. batesi
    S Cameroun
  C. p. centralis
    SE Cameroun to N Kenya, N Angola
Coturnicops lugens (Chestnut-headed Crake)
  C. l. lugens
    Angola to NE Zaire, Tanzania
  C. l. lynesi
    NE Zambia
Coturnicops boehmi (Streaky-breasted Crake)
  Guinea to N Kenya & Malawi
Coturnicops elegans (Buff-spotted Crake)
  C. e. reichenovi
    Liberia to Angola & Uganda
  C. e. elegans
    Somalia to E Cape Province
Coturnicops affinis (Chestnut-tailed Crake)
  C. a. antonii
    Sudan to Zambia & Malawi
  C. a. affinis
    Rhodesia to Natal, E Cape Province
Coturnicops insularis (Madagascar Crake)
  Madagascar
Coturnicops watersi (Waters' Crake)
  Madagascar
Coturnicops ayresi (White-winged Crake)
  Ethiopia & E South Africa
Coturnicops schomburgkii (Ocellated Crake)

116

C. s. schomburgkii
Venezuela, Guyana, French Guiana
C. s. chapmani
S Brazil
Coturnicops notata (Darwins Rail)
Guyana, Uruguay to S Argentina
Coturnicops noveboracensis (Yellow Rail)
C. n. noveboracensis
E Canada to SW USA
C. n. goldmani
Lerma, Mexico
C. n. exquisitus
Siberia to Japan, China

LATERALLUS
Laterallus fasciatus (Black-banded Crake)
SE Colombia, NE Peru, NW Brazil
Laterallus levraudi (Rusty-flanked Crake)
N Venezuela
Laterallus ruber (Ruddy Crake)
C Mexico to N Nicaragua
Laterallus viridis (Russet-crowned Crake)
L. v. brunnescens
C Colombia
L. v. viridis
E Peru, the Guianas, Brazil
Laterallus exilis (Grey-breasted Crake)
Peru to the Guianas, Trinidad
Laterallus spilonotus (Galapagos Rail)
Galapagos Is
Laterallus melanophaius (Rufous-sided Crake)
L. m. oenops
E Colombia, E Ecuador
L. m. melanophaius
Guyana to C Argentina
Laterallus albigularis (White-throated Crake)
L. a. cinereiceps
Nicaragua to W Panama
L. a. albigularis
SW Costa Rica to W Ecuador
L. a. cerdaleus
E Colombia
Laterallus leucopyrrhus (Red & White Crake)
S Brazil, Paraguay, Uruguay
Laterallus jamaicensis (Black Rail)
L. j. jamaicensis
C & E USA, Jamaica, Cuba
L. j. coturniculus
S California
L. j. murivagans
W Peru
L. j. salinasi
C Chile
Laterallus xenopterus (Rufous-faced Crake)
Paraguay

CREX
Crex crex (Corncrake)
Europe, N Africa to C Asia
PORZANA
Porzana egregia (African Crake)
Gambia to E Ethiopia & Natal
Porzana flavirostra (Black Crake)
Senegal to Sucan & Cape Province
Porzana olivieri (Olivier's Rail)
W Madagascar
Porzana flaviventer (Yellow-breasted Crake)
P. f. gossii
Cuba, Jamaica
P.f. hendersoni
Hispaniola, Puerto Rico
P. f. woodi
El Salvador
P. f. bangsi
NC Colombia
P. f. flaviventer
SW Colombia to French Guiana
Porzana cinerea (White-browed Rail)
P. c. cinerea
Malaysia, Sumatra to Sumbawa I,
Moluccas
P. c. ocularis
Philippine Is, Celebes
P. c. micronesiae
Guam I, Yap I, Truk I
P. c. leucophrys
Bismarck Archipelago, New Guinea,
N Australia
P. c. meeki
St Matthias I
P. c. tannensis
New Caledonia, New Hebrides, Fiji Is,
Samoa Is
Porzana spiloptera (Dot-winged Crake)
Uruguay, NE Argentina
Porzana albicollis (White-throated Crake)
P. a. olivacea
N Colombia, the Guianas, Venezuela
P. a. albicollis
E Brazil, E Bolivia, Paraguay,
NW Argentina
Porzana marginalis (Striped Crake)
Irregular distribution throughout Africa
Porzana erythrops (Paint-billed Crake)
P. e. olivascens
Venezuela, the Guianas to NW Argentin
P. e. erythrops
Peru, Brazil, N Argentina
Porzana columbiana (Colombian Crake)
P. c. ripleyi
S Panama, NW Colombia
P. c. columbiana
N Colombia, NW Ecuador

Porzana tabuensis (Sooty Crake)
  P. t. tabuensis
    Fiji Is, New Caledonia, Samoa Is, Tonga,
    Marquesas Is
  P. t. edwardi
    EC New Guinea
  P. t. richardsoni
    C New Guinea
  P. t. plumbea
    Chatham I, S Australia, Tasmania
Porzana atra (Henderson Island Crake)
  Henderson I
Porzana parva (Little Crake)
  E & S Europe to W India
Porzana pusilla (Baillon's Crake)
  P. p. intermedia
    W Europe to Iran & N Africa
  P. p. pusilla
    C Asia to India & China
  P. p. obscura
    Uganda to Angola & Cape Province,
    Madagascar
  P. p. mira
    Borneo, Malaysia, Sumatra
  P. p. mayri
    New Guinea
  P. p. palustris
    Australia, Tasmania
  P. p. affinis
    New Zealand
Porzana fluminea (Australian Spotted Crake)
  SW to E Australia, Tasmania
Porzana porzana (Spotted Crake)
  W Europe, N Africa to C Asia, India
Porzana carolina (Sora Rail)
  Canada to Venezuela, Peru, W Indies
Porzana fusca (Ruddy-breasted Crake)
  P. f. fusca
    N India to Philippine Is, Celebes, Flores I
  P. f. erythrothorax
    Japan, China
  P. f. phaeopyga
    Riukiu Is
  P. f. zeylonica
    SW India, Sri Lanka
AMAURORNIS
Amaurornis olivaceus (Rufous-tailed Moorhen)
  A. o. moluccanus
    N & E New Guinea, Moluccas
  A. o. olivaceus
    Philippine Is
  A. o. nigrifrons
    Bismarck Archipelago, Solomon Is
  A. o. ultimus
    Gower I

  A. o. ruficrissus
    SE New Guinea, Northern Territory,
    N Queensland
Amaurornis isabellinus (Celebes Water Hen)
  N & SE Celebes
Amaurornis ineptus (New Guinea Flightless Rail)
  A. e. ineptus
    N Coast & SW Coast, New Guinea
  A. e. pallidus
    S New Guinea
Amaurornis akool (Brown Crake)
  A. a. akool
    N India
  A. a. coccineipes
    SE China, NE Indochina
Amaurornis bicolor (Elwes' Crake)
  Nepal to W China, N Indochina
Amaurornis phoenicurus (White-breasted Water Hen)
  A. p. phoenicurus
    Philippine Is, Indochina to S India, Sri
    Lanka
  A. p. insularis
    Andaman Is, Nicobar Is
  A. p. leucomelanus
    Celebes, Lesser Sunda Is
GALLICREX
Gallicrex cinerea (Water Cock)
  India to Japan, Philippine Is, Celebes
GALLINULA
Gallinula ventralis (Black-tailed Native Hen)
  Australia
Gallinula m. mortierii (Tasmanian Native Hen)
  Tasmania (other sub spp extinct)
Gallinula silvestris (San Cristobal Mountain Rail)
  San Cristobal I
Gallinula pacifica (Samoan Wood Rail)
  Samoa e?
Gallinula nesiotis comeri (Gough Is Coot)
  Gough Is
  (G. n. Nesiotis — extinct)
Gallinula tenebrosa (Dusky Moorhen)
  G. t. frontata
    SE Borneo, Celebes, S Moluccas, S New
    Guinea
  G. t. neumanni
    N New Guinea
  G. t. tenebrosa
    Australia
Gallinula chloropus (Moorhen)
  G. c. correiana
    Azores Is
  G. c. chloropus
    Europe, N Africa, Mid East, Russia

G. c. indica
India to Japan, Taiwan, Malaysia
G. c. pyrrhorhoa
Madagascar, Reunion I, Mauritius I
G. c. orientalis
Africa (S of Sahara) & S Malaysia to
Philippine Is
G. c. guami
Mariana Is
G. c. sandvicensis
Hawaii Is
G. c. cachinnans
USA, Bermuda I, Galapagos Is
G. c. cerceris
Gtr & Lesser Antilles
G. c. pauxilla
N & W Colombia, W Ecuador, NW Peru
G. c. garmani
Peru, Bolivia, N Chile, NW Argentina
G. c. galeata
the Guianas, Uruguay, N Argentina,
Trinidad
Gallinula angulata (Lesser Moorhen)
Senegal to Sudan, Cape Province
**Gallinula melanops (Spot-flanked
Gallinule)**
G. m. bogotensis
C Colombia
G. m. melanops
E Brazil to Paraguay, N Argentina
G. m. crassirostris
C Chile
Gallinula flavirostris (Azure Gallinule)
the Guianas, N & C Brazil, Paraguay
Gallinula alleni (Allen's Gallinule)
Senegal to Sudan, Cape Province
Gallinula martinica (Purple Gallinule)
SE USA to Argentina, W Indies

PORPHYRIO
Porphyrio porphyrio (Purple Swamphen)
P. p. porphyrio
SW Europe, NW Africa
P. p. madagascariensis
E & S Africa, Madagascar
P. p. seistanicus
E Turkey, E Iran
P. p. poliocephalus
Iraq to Thailand, Andaman Is, Nicobar Is
P. p. viridis
Burma, Malaysia, S China, Indochina
P. p. indicus
Sumatra to Bali I, Borneo, Celebes
P. p. melanopterus
Timor I, Moluccas, New Guinea
P. p. bellus
SW Australia
P. p. chathamensis
Chatham I

P. p. melanotus
S New Guinea, E Australia
P. p. pulverulentus
Philippine Is
P. p. pelewensis
Palau Is
P. p. samoensis
Western Pacific Islands
Porphyrio mantelli (Takahe)
P. m. mantelli
North Island, New Zealand
P. m. hochstetteri
SE South Island, New Zealand

FULICA
Fulica armillata (Red-gartered Coot)
Paraguay & S Brazil to Cape Horn
Fulica leucoptera (White-winged Coot)
Bolivia & S Brazil to Cape Horn
Fulica rufifrons (Red-fronted Coot)
N Chile & Uruguay to S Argentina
Fulica gigantea (Giant Coot)
Peru, Bolivia, N Chile
Fulica cornuta (Horned Coot)
Bolivia, N Chile, NW Argentina
Fulica caribaea (Caribbean Coot)
W Indies, Trinidad, NE Venezuela
Fulica americana (American Coot)
F. a. alai
Hawaii Is
F. a. americana
Canada to Nicaragua, West Indies
F. a. colombiana
C Colombia to N Ecuador
F. a. ardesiaca
Ecuador to N Chile
Fulica atra (Common Coot)
F. a. atra
Europe to SE Asia, N Africa
F. a. lugubris
Java
F. a. novaeguineae
NW & C New Guinea
F. a. australis
Buru I, Australia, Tasmania
Fulica cristata (Red-knobbed Coot)
S Spain, Ethiopia to Cape Province
Madagascar

44 HELIORNITHIDAE (SUNGREBES)

PODICA
Podica senegalensis (Peters' Finfoot)
P. s. senegalensis
Senegal to N Zaire
P. s. camerunensis
Cameroun, Gabon to C Zaire
P. s. albipectus
W Angola

P. s. petersii
    N Kenya to Cape Province

HELIOPAIS
***Heliopais personata* (Masked Finfoot)**
    NE India to Malaysia, Sumatra

HELIORNIS
***Heliornis fulica* (American Finfoot)**
    S Mexico to Paraguay & NE Argentina

45 RHYNOCHETIDAE (KAGU)

RHYNOCHETOS
***Rhynochetos jubatus* (Kagu)**
    New Caledonia

46 EURYPYGIDAE (SUN BITTERNS)

EURYPYGA
***Eurypyga helias* (Sun-Bittern)**
    E. h. major
        Guatemala to Colombia, E Ecuador
    E. h. meridionalis
        SC Peru
    E. h. helias
        Upper Amazonia, the Guianas, N Brazil

47 CARIAMIDAE (SERIEMAS)

CARIAMA
***Cariama cristata* (Red-legged Seriema)**
    C Brazil to NW Argentina & Paraguay

CHUNGA
***Chunga burmeisteri* (Black-legged Seriema)**
    NW Argentina

48 OTIDAE (BUSTARDS)

TETRAX
***Tetrax tetrax* (Little Bustard)**
    T. t. tetrax
        NW France to NW Africa
    T. t. orientalis
        E Europe to C Asia

OTIS
***Otis tarda* (Great Bustard)**
    O. t. tarda
        C & S Europe, W Asia
    O. t. korejewi
        Turkestan, C Tien Shan
    O. t. dybowskii
        Altai & Amur to China

NEOTIS
***Neotis cafra* (Barrow's Bustard)**
    N. c. denhami
        Guinea & Mauretania to Ethiopia
    N. c. jacksoni
        Angola, S Zaire to Kenya & Malawi

N. c. cafra
    Botswana, E South Africa
N. c. mackenziei
    SW Zaire, Zambia
***Neotis ludwigii* (Ludgwig's Bustard)**
    Namibia, W South Africa
***Neotis burchellii* (Burchell's Bustard)**
    E Sudan
***Neotis nuba* (Nubian Bustard)**
    Niger to N Sudan
***Neotis heuglinii* (Heuglin's Bustard)**
    Somalia

CHORIOTIS
***Choriotis arabs* (Arabian Bustard)**
    C. a. lynesi
        NW Morocco
    C. a. stieberi
        E Gambia, Ivory Coast to Sudan
    C. a. butleri
        S Sudan
    C. a. arabs
        S Arabia, E Sudan, Somalia
***Choriotis kori* (Kori Bustard)**
    C. k. struthiunculus
        Ethiopia to Uganda & C Tanzania
    C. k. kori
        Rhodesia, Transvaal
***Choriotis nigriceps* (Great Indian Bustard)**
    C India
***Choriotis australis* (Australian Bustard)**
    S New Guinea, Australia

CHLAMYDOTIS
***Chlamydotis undulata* (Houbara Bustard)**
    C. u. fuertaventurae
        Canary Is
    C. u. undulata
        N Sahara to Nile valley
    C. u. macqueenii
        Syria to C Asia, N India

LOPHOTIS
***Lophotis savilei* (Lynes' Bustard)**
    Senegal to S Sudan
***Lophotis ruficrista* (Crested Bustard)**
    L. r. hilgerti
        N & C Somalia
    L. r. gindiana
        S Somalia, NE Kenya
    L. r. ruficrista
        Southern Africa

AFROTIS
***Afrotis atra* (Little Black Bustard)**
    A. a. etoschae
        NW Namibia
    A. a. mababiensis
        Lake Ngami area
    A. a. afraoides
        Transvaal to N Cape Province

A. a. atra
S Cape Province
A. a. kalaharica
Kalahari Desert
A. a. damarensis
N & C Namibia, Botswana

EUPODOTIS
Eupodotis vigorsii (Black-throated Bustard)
E. v. scolopacea
S Botswana, W Cape Province
E. v. vigorsii
Transvaal, C Cape Province
E. v. orangensis
W Cape Province
E. v. harei
E Namibia
E. v. barlowi
C Namibia
E. v. karrooensis
W Cape Province
Eupodotis rueppellii (Rüppell's Bustard)
E. r. picturata
NW Namibia
E. r. rueppellii
NE Namibia
E. r. fitzsimmonsi
S Namibia
Eupodotis humilis (Little Brown Bustard)
N Somalia
Eupodotis senegalensis (White-bellied Bustard)
E. s. senegalensis
Senegal to Nile valley
E. s. barrowii
Botswana, Transvaal, Cape Province
E. s. somaliensis
Ethiopia to W Kenya
E. s. canicollis
E Kenya, E Tanzania
Eupodotis caerulescens (Blue Bustard)
S Africa

LISSOTIS
Lissotis melanogaster (Black-bellied Bustard)
L. m. melanogaster
Senegal to Ethiopia, Angola, Zambia
L. m. notophila
SE Africa
Lissotis hartlaubii (Hartlaub's Bustard)
E Sudan to Uganda & C Tanzania

HOUBAROPSIS
Houbaropsis bengalensis (Bengal Florican)
H. b. bengalensis
Himalayas, N India
H. b. blandini
Cambodia

SYPHEOTIDES
Sypheotides indica (Lesser Florican)
India

Charadriiformes

49 JACANIDAE (JACANAS)

MICROPARRA
Microparra capensis (Smaller Jacana)
Sudan to Natal & Cape Province

ACTOPHILORNIS
Actophilornis africana (African Jacana)
Senegal to Sudan & Cape Province
Actophilornis albinucha (Madagascar Jacana)
Madagascar

IREDIPARRA
Irediparra gallinacea (Comb-crested Jacana)
I. g. gallinacea
S Borneo, Mindanao I to Moluccas & Timor
I. g. novaeguinae
Misol I, Aru Is, N & C New Guinea
I. g. novaehollandiae
S New Guinea, N & E Australia

HYDROPHASIANUS
Hydrophasianus chirurgus (Pheasant-tailed Jacana)
India to Philippine Is, Taiwan & Java

METOPIDIUS
Metopidius indicus (Bronze-winged Jacana)
India to Cambodia, Java, Sumatra

JACANA
Jacana spinosa (Northern Jacana)
J. s. gymnostoma
S Mexico
J. s. violacea
Cuba, Jamaica, Hispaniola
J. s. spinosa
Guatemala to W Panama
Jacana jacana (Wattled Jacana)
J. j. hypomelaena
E Panama, N Colombia
J. j. melanopygia
W Colombia, W Venezuela
J. j. intermedia
N Venezuela
J. j. jacana
Trinidad, the Guianas to E Bolivia & N Argentina
J. j. scapularis
W Ecuador
J. j. peruviana
E Peru

50 ROSTRATULIDAE (PAINTED SNIPES)

ROSTRATULA
Rostratula benghalensis (Painted Snipe)
    R. b. benghalensis
        Africa, S Asia to Java & Philippine Is
    R. b. australis
        Australia & Tasmania

NYCTICRYPHES
Nycticryphes semicollaris (South American Painted Snipe)
    C Chile to N Argentina & Uruguay

51 DROMADIDAE (CRAB PLOVER)

DROMAS
Dromas ardeola (Crab Plover)
    E Africa, Indian Ocean, Andaman Is

52 HAEMATOPODIDAE (OYSTER-CATCHERS)

HAEMATOPUS
Haematopus ostralegus (Oystercatcher)
    H. o. palliatus
        E Coast N & Central America, West Indies
    H. o. pratti
        Bahama Is
    H. o. galapagensis
        Galapagos Is
    H. o. pitanay
        W coast of South America
    H. o. durnfordi
        E coast of South America
    H. o. malacophaga
        Iceland, Faroe Is
    H. o. occidentalis
        British Isles
    H. o. ostralegus
        Europe, Asia Minor, N Africa
    H. o. longipes
        Russia, Siberia
    H. o. osculans
        NE Asia, China, Japan
    H. o. meade-waldoi
        E Canary Is
    H. o. longirostris
        Aru Is, S New Guinea, Australia
    H. o. finschi
        South I, New Zealand
Haematopus bachmani (American Black Oystercatcher)
    H. b. bachmani
        Aleutian Is to N Baja California
    H. b. frazeri
        S Baja California, W Mexico

Haematopus moquini (African Black Oystercatcher)
    Gabon to Natal
Haematopus unicolor (New Zealand Sooty Oystercatcher)
    H. u. unicolor
        New Zealand
    H. u. chathamensis
        Chatham I
Haematopus leucopodus (Magellanic Oystercatcher)
    South America, Falkland Is
Haematopus ater (Blackish Oystercatcher)
    South America, Falkland Is
Haematopus fuliginosus (Sooty Oyster-catcher)
    H. f. fuliginosus
        coast of Australia
    H. f. ophthalmicus
        coast of N Australia

53 IBIDORHYNCHIDAE (IBIS BILL)

IBIDORHYNCHA
Ibidorhyncha struthersii (Ibis Bill)
    C Asia, Himalayas, N India

54 RECURVIROSTRIDAE (AVOCETS, STILTS)

HIMANTOPUS
Himantopus himantopus (Black-winged Stilt)
    S Europe to China, India, C Africa
Himantopus leucocephalus (Australian Stilt)
    Philippine Is to Java & Australia
Himantopus melanurus (Black-tailed Stilt)
    Peru to C Argentina, C Chile
Himantopus mexicanus (Black-necked Stilt)
    USA to N South America, West Indies
Himantopus ceylonensis (Sri Lanka Stilt)
    Sri Lanka
Himantopus knudseni (Hawaiian Stilt)
    Hawaii
Himantopus novaezelandiae (New Zealand Stilt)
    New Zealand
Himantopus meridionalis (South African Stilt)
    South Africa

CLADORHYNCHUS
Cladorhynchus leucocephalus (Banded Stilt)
    Australia

Recurvirostra avosetta (Avocet)
Europe to China, India, S Africa
Recurvirostra americana (American Avocet)
W USA to Guatemala
Recurvirostra novaehollandiae (Red-necked Avocet)
Australia, Tasmania
Recurvirostra andina (Andean Avocet)
S Peru to N Chile, NW Argentina '

55 BURHINIDAE (STONE-CURLEWS)

BURHINUS
Burhinus oedicnemus (Stone-Curlew)
B. o. distinctus
W Canary Is
B. o. insularum
E Canary Is
B. o. jordansi
Balearic Is
B. o. oedicnemus
Europe, SW Asia to N & E Africa
B. o. theresae
W Morocco
B. o. saharae
N Africa to Israel
B. o. astutus
Afghanistan, Pakistan
B. o. indicus
India, Sri Lanka to S Indochina
Burhinus senegalensis (Senegal Stone-Curlew)
B. s. senegalensis
Senegal to Central African Republic & Angola
B. s. inornatus
Egypt to N Uganda, Ethiopia
Burhinus vermiculatus (Water Dikkop)
B. v. buttikoferi
Liberia to N Zaire
B. v. vermiculatus
Kenya to Cape Province
Burhinus capensis (Cape Dikkop)
B. c. maculosus
Senegal to Niger, N Nigeria
B. c. affinis
Sudan, Ethiopia, Uganda, Somalia
B. c. ehrenbergi
Dahlak Is
B. c. dodsoni
S Arabia, N Somalia
B. c. capensis
Angola to Kenya & Cape Province
B. c. damarensis
Namibia
Burhinus bistriatus (Double-striped Stone-Curlew)

B. b. bistriatus
S Mexico to W Costa Rica
B. b. vocifer
N Colombia to Guyana & N Brazil
B. b. pediacus
N Colombia
B. b. dominicensis
Hispaniola
Burhinus superciliaris (Peruvian Stone-Curlew)
Ecuador to S Peru
Burhinus magnirostris (Australian Stone-Curlew)
B. m. rufescens
NW Australia, Northern Territory
B. m. ramsayi
N Queensland
B. m. magnirostris
S Queensland to SW Australia, Tasmania

ESACUS
Esacus recurvirostris (Great Stone Plover)
India, Burma, Sri Lanka
Esacus magnirostris (Great Australian Stone Plover)
Malaysia to New Guinea & Australia

56 GLAREOLIDAE (COURSERS, PRATINCOLES)

CURSORIINAE

PLUVIANUS
Pluvianus aegyptius (Egyptian Plover)
P. a. aegyptius
Senegal to N Zaire & Egypt
P. a. angolae
N Angola, W Zaire

CURSORIUS
Cursorius cursor (Cream-coloured Courser)
C. c. bogolubovi
N & E Iran
C. c. cursor
N Africa to NW India
C. c. bannermani
Canary Is, W Morocco
C. c. exsul
Cape Verde Is
C. c. dahlakensis
Dahlak Is
C. c. somalensis
N Somalia
C. c. littoralis
S Somalia, Kenya
C. c. meruensis
C Kenya
C. c. theresae
NW Cape Province

C. c. rufus
  Botswana, Transvaal, Cape Province
Cursorius coromandelicus (Indian Courser)
  India, N Sri Lanka
Cursorius temminckii (Temminck's Courser)
  C. t. temminckii
    Senegal to Ethiopia & Cape Province
  C. t. damarensis
    Namibia

RHINOPTILUS
Rhinoptilus africanus (Two-banded Courser)
  R. a. raffertyi
    C Ethiopia
  R. a. hartingi
    Somalia
  R. a. gracilis
    C Kenya, N Tanzania
  R. a. illustris
    C Tanzania
  R. a. bisignatus
    Angola
  R. a. sharpei
    Namibia
  R. a. africanus
    S Namibia, W Cape Province
  R. a. granti
    Transvaal, C Cape Province
Rhinoptilus cinctus (Heuglin's Courser)
  R. c. cinctus
    Sudan, Somalia to N Tanzania
  R. c. emini
    islands in Lake Victoria
  R. c. seebohmi
    S Angola, Namibia to Rhodesia
Rhinoptilus chalcopterus (Bronze-winged Courser)
  R. c. chalcopterus
    Senegal to Sudan & Kenya
  R. c. albofasciatus
    Angola & Tanzania to Cape Province
Rhinoptilus bitorquatus (Jerdon's Courser)
  C India **e?**

GLAREOLINAE

STILTIA
Stiltia isabella (Australian Pratincole)
  Australia to Borneo, Java, New Guinea

GLAREOLA
Glareola pratincola (Pratincole)
  G. p. pratincola
    Mediterranean to NW India & N Africa
  G. p. boweni
    Senegal to Chad & Gabon
  G. p. limbata
    Sudan, Ethiopia, Somalia, S Arabia

  G. p. erlangeri
    S Somalia, N Kenya
  G. p. fulleborni
    E Zaire, C Kenya to Cape Province
Glareola maldivarus (Large Indian Pratincole)
  C & E Asia to Indochina, Malaysia
Glareola nordmanni (Black-winged Pratincole)
  SE Europe, C Asia, Africa
Glareola ocularis (Madagascar Pratincole)
  E Africa, Madagascar
Glareola nuchalis (White-collared Pratincole)
  G. n. liberiae
    Sierra Leone to W Cameroun
  G. n. nuchalis
    Chad to Ethiopia & Mozambique
Glareola cinerea (Cream-coloured Pratincole)
  G. c. cinerea
    Ghana to C Zaire
  G. c. colorata
    Upper Niger river
Glareola lactea (Small Indian Pratincole)
  India, Sri Lanka to S Indochina

57 CHARADRIIDAE (PLOVERS)

VANELLUS
Vanellus vanellus (Lapwing)
  W Europe to China & Japan
Vanellus crassirostris (Long-toed Lapwing)
  V. c. crassirostris
    Sudan, Uganda
  V. c. hybrida
    Kenya to Malawi
  V. c. leucoptera
    Mozambique, N Natal
Vanellus spinosus (Spur-winged Plover)
  Middle East, C & E Africa
Vanellus duvaucelii (River Lapwing)
  N India to Indochina
Vanellus tectus (Blackhead Plover)
  V. t. tectus
    Senegal to Ethiopia
  V. t. latifrons
    S Somalia to E Kenya
Vanellus malabaricus (Yellow-wattled Lapwing)
  India, Sri Lanka
Vanellus albiceps (White-crowned Wattled Plover)
  Liberia to Sudan & Rhodesia
Vanellus lugubris (Senegal Plover)
  Sierra Leone to Uganda & Natal
Vanellus melanopterus (Black-winged Plover)
  V. m. minor
    Kenya to Cape Province

V. m. melanopterus
S Arabia, Ethiopia
Vanellus coronatus (Crowned Plover)
V. c. demissus
Somalia
V. c. coronatus
Ethiopia to Angola & Cape Province
Vanellus senegallus (Senegal Wattled Plover)
V. s. senegallus
Senegal to Sudan & Uganda
V. s. major
W Ethiopia
V. s. lateralis
E Zaire, Uganda to Angola & Natal
Vanellus melanocephalus (Spot-breasted Plover)
N Ethiopia
Vanellus superciliosus (Brown-chested Wattled Plover)
Benin to Uganda & Kenya
Vanellus gregarius (Sociable Plover)
C Asia to NE Africa, N India
Vanellus leucurus (White-tailed Plover)
W & C Asia, NE Africa, NW India
Vanellus cayanus (Cayenne Plover)
S Venezuela, the Guianas, Upper Amazonia
Vanellus chilensis (Chilian Lapwing)
V. c. cayennensis
Colombia, Venezuela, the Guianas, N Brazil
V. c. lampronotus
S Brazil to C Argentina, Uruguay
V. c. chilensis
C Chile, SW Argentina
V. c. fretensis
S Chile, S Argentina
Vanellus resplendens (Andean Lapwing)
Ecuador to N Chile, NW Argentina
Vanellus cinereus (Grey-headed Lapwing)
China, Japan, Indochina
Vanellus indicus (Red-wattled Lapwing)
V. i. aigneri
Middle East to Pakistan
V. i. indicus
India, Sri Lanka
V. i. atronuchalis
Burma, Malaysia, Indochina
Vanellus macropterus (Javanese Wattled Lapwing)
Java
Vanellus tricolor (Banded Plover)
S Australia, Tasmania
Vanellus miles (Masked Plover)
V. m. miles
S Moluccas, Kei Is, S New Guinea, N Australia
V. m. novaehollandiae
E Australia

ANITIBYX
Anitibyx armatus (Blacksmith Plover)
S Angola to Kenya & Natal

PLUVIALIS
Pluvialis apricaria (Golden Plover)
P. a. apricaria
N Europe & N Asia » Mediterranean, N India
P. a. oreophilos
N & W British Isles, Denmark, Germany
Pluvialis dominica (American Golden Plover)
P. d. fulva
N Siberia, NE Asia, Alaska, » SE Asia & Australia
P. d. dominica
N Canada » C South America
Pluvialis squatarola (Grey Plover)
Circumpolar » Africa, Australia & South America
Pluvialis obscura (New Zealand Dotterel)
New Zealand

CHARADRIUS
Charadrius hiaticula (Ringed Plover)
C. h. psammodroma
NE Canada, Greenland, Iceland
C. h. hiaticula
British Isles, Sweden to Mediterranean
C. h. tundrae
N Europe, N Asia » Iran, E Africa
Charadrius semipalmatus (Semi-palmated Plover)
N Canada » C & South America
Charadrius placidus (Long-billed Ring Plover)
NE Asia » China, Burma, Indochina
Charadrius dubius (Little Ringed Plover)
C. d. curonicus
Europe, N Asia » S Africa, India, China
C. d. jerdoni
India » Indochina & Lssr Sunda Is
C. d. papuanus
New Ireland, New Guinea
C. d. dubius
S Japan, S China, Philippine Is
Charadrius wilsonia (Wilson's Plover)
C. w. wilsonia
S & SE USA, E Central America
C. w. rufinucha
Bahama Is, Gtr Antilles, N Lesser Antilles
C. w. beldingi
Baja California to Peru
C. w. cinnamominus
Colombia to French Guiana, Arubu I, Trinidad

***Charadrius vociferus* (Killdeer Plover)**
  C. v. vociferus
    W Canada, USA » West Indies, N South
    America
  C. v. ternominatus
    Gtr Antilles
  C. v. peruvianus
    W Peru
***Charadrius melodus* (Piping Plover)**
  S Canada, E USA, N Mexico
***Charadrius thoracicus* (Black-banded Sand Plover)**
  Madagascar
***Charadrius pecuarius* (Kittlitz's Sand Plover)**
  C. p. allenbyi
    Nile valley
  C. p. pecuarius
    Senegal to Sudan & Cape Province,
    Madagascar
***Charadrius sanctaehelenae* (St Helena Sand Plover)**
  St Helena I
***Charadrius tricollaris* (Three-banded Plover)**
  C. t. forbesi
    Guinea to S Zaire
  C. t. tricollaris
    Sudan to Angola & Cape Province
  C. t. bifrontatus
    Madagascar
***Charadrius alexandrinus* (Kentish Plover)**
  C. a. alexandrinus
    W Europe to C Asia » Africa, China
  C. a. spatzi
    W African coast
  C. a. dealbatus
    S Japan » Indochina & S Thailand
  C. a. seebohmi
    Sri Lanka
  C. a. javanicus
    Java
  C. a. hesperius
    Liberia to Central African Republic
***Charadrius marginatus* (White-fronted Sand Plover)**
  C. m. pons
    S Somalia
  C. m. tenellus
    E Africa to Natal, Madagascar
  C. m. marginatus
    Angola to Cape Province
***Charadrius occidentalis* (Snowy Plover)**
  C. c. nivosus
    W USA, W Mexico
  C. c. tenuirostris
    C & SE USA, Cuba, Hispaniola, Puerto
    Rico

  C. c. occidentalis
    Peru to Chile
***Charadrius ruficapillus* (Red-capped Dotterel)**
  S New Guinea, Australia, Tasmania
***Charadrius peronii* (Malaysian Sand Plover)**
  Philippine Is, Celebes, Java, Borneo
***Charadrius venustus* (Chestnut-banded Sand Plover)**
  C. v. pallidus
    Angola to S Cape Province
  C. v. venustus
    S Kenya, Tanzania
***Charadrius collaris* (Collared Plover)**
  S Mexico to N Argentina, Trinidad
***Charadrius bicinctus* (Double-banded Plover)**
  Australia, Tasmania, New Zealand
***Charadrius falklandicus* (Two-banded Plover)**
  S South America, Falkland Is
***Charadrius mongolus* (Mongolian Plover)**
  C. m. atrifrons
    C Asia » India, Malaysia, E Africa
  C. m. mongolus
    E Siberia, Japan » Australia
  C. m. stegmani
    Bering Is
***Charadrius leschenaultii* (Great Sand Plover)**
  E Asia & Red Sea » S Africa, Australia
***Charadrius asiaticus* (Caspian Plover)**
  SE Russia & Iran » India, E & S Africa
***Charadrius veredus* (Eastern Sand Plover)**
  N China » Celebes & Australia
***Charadrius modestus* (Rufous-chested Dotterel)**
  S Chile, Argentina, Falkland Is
***Charadrius montanus* (Mountain Plover)**
  W USA to C Mexico
***Charadrius melanops* (Black-fronted Plover)**
  Australia, Tasmania
***Charadrius cinctus* (Red-kneed Dotterel)**
  Australia
***Charadrius rubricollis* (Hooded Plover)**
  S Australia, Tasmania
***Charadrius novaeseelandiae* (Long-billed Plover)**
  Chatham I

ANARHYNCHUS
***Anarhynchus frontalis* (Wry-bill)**
  New Zealand

PHEGORNIS
***Phegornis mitchellii* (Mitchell's Plover)**
  Peru to N Chile, W Argentina

PELTOHYAS
Peltohyas australis (Australian Courser)
 SW Australia to Victoria & New South
 Wales

EUDROMIAS
Eudromias morinellus (Dotterel)
 N Europe & N Asia » Med & Iran
**Eudromias ruficollis (Tawny-throated
 Dotterel)**
 E. r. pallidus
 N Peru
 E. r. ruficollis
 Peru & E Argentina to Tierra del Fuego

PLUVIANELLUS
Pluvianellus socialis (Magellanic Plover)
 Straits of Magellan

58 SCOLOPACIDAE (SANDPIPERS, SNIPE)

TRINGINAE

LIMOSA
Limosa limosa (Black-tailed Godwit)
 L. l. limosa
 Europe, W Asia » N Africa & India
 L. l. melanuroides
 NE Asia » China, N Australia
Limosa haemastica (Hudsonian Godwit)
 NW Canada » S South America
Limosa lapponica (Bar-tailed Godwit)
 L. l. lapponica
 N Europe, N Asia » tropical Africa, N India
 L. l. baueri
 NE Asia, NW Canada » Australia, Pacific
 islands
Limosa fedoa (Marbled Godwit)
 WC Canada » S USA & Peru

NUMENIUS
Numenius minutus (Little Curlew)
 C & E Siberia » Moluccas, Australia
Numenius borealis (Eskimo Curlew)
 N Canada » S South America **e?**
Numenius phaeopus (Whimbrel)
 N. p. phaeopus
 N Europe, N Asia» Africa, NW India
 N. p. variegatus
 E Siberia » Australia, Pacific Is
 N. p. hudsonicus
 N Canada » N South America
**Numenius tahitiensis (Bristle-thighed
 Curlew)**
 W Alaska » Hawaii, Society Is
**Numenius tenuirostris (Slender-billed
 Curlew)**
 SW Siberia to E Europe » Iran
Numenius arquata (Curlew)
 N. a. arquata
 N Europe & Russia » Africa & NW India

 N. a. orientalis
 C Asia » E Africa, India, Indochina
**Numenius madagascariensis (Far Eastern
 Curlew)**
 E Siberia » China & Australia
**Numenius americanus (Long-billed
 Curlew)**
 N. a. occidentalis
 WC Canada to N Mexico
 N. a. americanus
 WC USA to Guatemala

BARTRAMIA
Bartramia longicauda (Upland Sandpiper)
 W & S Canada, NC USA » C South
 America

TRINGA
Tringa erythropus (Spotted Red-shank)
 N Europe, N Russia » Africa & China
Tringa totanus (Redshank)
 T. t. robusta
 Iceland to W Europe, » W Africa
 T. t. britannica
 British Isles to W Europe
 T. t. totanus
 N Europe & W Siberia » Africa & W Asia
 T. t. eurhinus
 C & E Asia » India, China, Celebes
Tringa stagnatilis (Marsh Sandpiper)
 SE Europe to Mongolia » Africa, Australia
Tringa nebularia (Greenshank)
 N Palaearctic » Africa, India to
 New Zealand
Tringa guttifer (Spotted Greenshank)
 E Siberia » India, Malaysia
Tringa melanoleuca (Greater Yellowlegs)
 N Canada » C & South America
Tringa flavipes (Lesser Yellowlegs)
 N Canada » South America
Tringa ochropus (Green Sandpiper)
 N Palaearctic » C Africa to Philippine Is
Tringa solitaria (Solitary Sandpiper)
 T. s. cinnamonea
 NW Canada » C South America
 T. s. solitaria
 C Canada » West Indies & N South
 America
Tringa glareola (Wood Sandpiper)
 N Palaearctic » Africa, SE Asia, Australia

CATOPTROPHORUS
Catoptrophorus semipalmatus (Willet)
 C. s. inornatus
 S Canada, W USA » Peru
 C. s. semipalmatus
 E Canada, E USA, Cuba, Puerto Rico

XENUS
Xenus cinereus (Terek Sandpiper)
 NE Europe, W Siberia » E Africa, India
 to Australia

ACTITIS
Actitis hypoleucos (Common Sandpiper)
Palaearctic » Africa, NE Asia to Australia
Actitis macularia (Spotted Sandpiper)
North America » West Indies, C South
America

HETEROSCELUS
Heteroscelus brevipes (Grey-rumped Sandpiper)
E Siberia » China, Australia
Heteroscelus incanus (Wandering Tattler)
NW Canada » W USA, Pacific islands

PROSOBONIA
Prosobonia cancellata (Tuamotu Sandpiper)
Tuamotu Is

ARENARIINAE

ARENARIA
Arenaria interpres (Turnstone)
A. i. interpres
N Palaearctic » Africa, SE Asia, Australia,
South America
A. i. morinella
N Canada » SE USA, West Indies,
E South America
Arenaria melanocephala (Black Turnstone)
Alaska to W USA

PHALAROPODINAE

PHALAROPUS
Phalaropus tricolor (Wilson's Phalarope)
SW Canada, W USA » S South America
Phalaropus lobatus (Red-necked Phalarope)
N America, N Palaearctic » Southern coasts
Phalaropus fulicarius (Grey Phalarope)
N Holarctic » coasts of Africa & Chile

SCOLOPACINAE

SCOLOPAX
Scolopax rusticola (Woodcock)
Palaearctic » India, S China
Scolopax mira (Amami Woodcock)
Amami-Oshima (Riukiu Is)
Scolopax saturata (East Indian Woodcock)
S. s. saturata
Sumatra, Java
S. s. rosenbergii
New Guinea
Scolopax celebensis (Celebes Woodcock)
S. c. heinrichi
N Celebes
S. c. celebensis
C Celebes
Scolopax rochussenii (Obi Woodcock)
Obi I

Scolopax minor (American Woodcock) 127
S Canada, SE USA, Gulf coast

GALLINAGONINAE

COENOCORYPHA
Coenocorypha aucklandica (Sub-Antarctic Snipe)
C. a. pusilla
Mangare I
C. a. iredalei
Jack Lees I
C. a. huegeli
Snares I
C. a. meinertzhagenae
Antipodes Is
C. a. aucklandica
Auckland Is

GALLINAGO
Gallinago solitaria (Solitary Snipe)
G. s. solitaria
C Asia, Himalayas, N Burma
G. s. japonica
E Asia, Japan, E China
Gallinago hardwickii (Japanese Snipe)
Kurile Is, Japan, Australia
Gallinago nemoricola (Wood Snipe)
Himalayas, Burma, S India
Gallinago stenura (Pintail Snipe)
NE Asia » India, S China & Timor I
Gallinago megala (Swinhoe's Snipe)
EC Asia » Burma, Borneo, Australia
Gallinago nigripennis (African Snipe)
G. n. nigripennis
Ethiopia to Namibia & Cape Province
G. n. angolensis
Angola, Zambia, Botswana
Gallinago macrodactyla (Madagascar Snipe)
Madagascar, Mauritius
Gallinago media (Great Snipe)
N Europe, W Asia » E Africa
Gallinago gallinago (Common Snipe)
G. g. faroeensis
Iceland, Faroe Is
G. g. gallinago
N Palaearctic » E Africa, India, China
G. g. delicato
N Canada » SW USA, Central America
West Indies
Gallinago paraguaiae (Paraguayan Snipe)
G. p. paraguaiae
Colombia to Uruguay
G. p. magellanica
S South America, Tierra del Fuego
G. p. andina
Peru, N Chile
G. p. innotata
N Chile

Gallinago nobilis (Noble Snipe)
C & E Colombia, N Ecuador
Gallinago undulata (Giant Snipe)
G. u. undulata
Guyana, French Guiana, Surinam
G. u. gigantea
Brazil, Paraguay, N & E Argentina
Gallinago stricklandii (Strickland's Snipe)
S Chile, Falkland Is
Gallinago jamesoni (Jameson's Snipe)
N Colombia to Bolivia
Gallinago imperialis (Banded Snipe)
C Colombia

LYMNOCRYPTES
Lymnocryptes minima (Jack Snipe)
N Europe, W Asia » N Africa, Iran, India

LIMNODROMUS
Limnodromus griseus (Short-billed Dowitcher)
L. g. caurinus
Alaska, W USA » Peru
L. g. griseus
NE Canada » E Caribbean
Limnodromus scolopaceus (Long-billed Dowitcher)
NW Canada, » S USA to Ecuador, Cuba, Jamaica
Limnodromus semipalmatus (Semi-palmated Snipe)
W Siberia, Mongolia » China, Japan, Indochina

CALIDRIDINAE

APHRIZA
Aphriza virgata (Surf-bird)
SC Alaska, W coast to S Chile

CALIDRIS
Calidris canutus (Knot)
C. c. canutus
Spitzbergen, Taimyr Peninsula » Africa
C. c. rogersi
Siberian islands, E Asia» Australia
C. c. rufus
Greenland, N Canada » S South America
Calidris tenuirostris (Great Knot)
NE Siberia » China, India & Australia
Calidris alba (Sanderling)
N Holarctic » South America, India & Australia
Calidris pusilla (Semipalmated Sandpiper)
N Canada » South America, West Indies
Calidris mauri (Western Sandpiper)
NW Canada » W South America, Trinidad
Calidris ruficollis (Rufous-necked Sandpiper)
NE Siberia, Alaska » China, Australia

Calidris minuta (Little Stint)
N Europe » S Africa, W India
Calidris temminckii (Temminck's Stint)
N Europe, N Asia » NE Africa to China
Calidris subminuta (Long-toed Stint)
E Siberia » India, China, Philippine Is
Calidris minutilla (Least Sandpiper)
N North America » S USA & N South America
Calidris fuscicollis (White-rumped Sandpiper)
N Canada » S South America
Calidris bairdii (Baird's Sandpiper)
E Siberia & N Canada » S South America
Calidris melanotos (Pectoral Sandpiper)
E Siberia & N Canada » SC South America
Calidris acuminata (Sharp-tailed Sandpiper)
NE Asia » Australia, Pacific Is
Calidris maritima (Purple Sandpiper)
Arctic America & Europe » NE USA, W Europe
Calidris ptilocnemis (Rock Sandpiper)
C. p. couesi
NE Siberia, Alaska, W Canada
C. p. ptilocnemis
Bering Sea, SE Alaska
C. p. quarta
Commander Is
C. p. kurilensis
Kurile Is
Calidris alpina (Dunlin)
C. a. arctica
E Greenland
C. a. alpina
N Europe, NW Asia » NE Africa, SW Asia
C. a. schinzii
British Isles, Holland
C. a. centralis
N Siberia, Mongolia » India
C. a. pacifica
NE Asia, NW Canada » E China, W USA & SE USA
Calidris ferruginea (Curlew Sandpiper)
N Asia to Europe, » Africa, India & Australia

EURYNORHYNCHUS
Eurynorhynchus pygmeus (Spoon-billed Sandpiper)
NE Asia » S China

LIMICOLA
Limicola falcinellus (Broad-billed Sandpiper)
L. f. falcinellus
N Europe, N Russia » Middle East, W India

L. f. sibirica
  NE Siberia » E India & Australia

MICROPALAMA
Micropalama himantopus (Stilt Sandpiper)
  N Canada » C South America & West Indies

TRYNGITES
Tryngites subruficollis (Buff-breasted Sandpiper)
  N Canada » SC South America

PHILOMACHUS
Philomachus pugnax (Ruff)
  N Europe & Asia » Africa, India, Burma

59 THINOCORIDAE (SEED SNIPE)

ATTAGIS
Attagis gayi (Rufous-bellied Seedsnipe)
  A. g. latreillii
    Ecuador
  A. g. simonsi
    Peru, N Bolivia
  A. g. gayi
    Chile, Argentina
Attagis malouinus (White-bellied Seedsnipe)
  A. m. cheeputi
    C Argentina
  A. m. malouinus
    Tierra del Fuego

THINOCORUS
Thinocorus orbignyianus (Grey-breasted Seedsnipe)
  T. o. ingae
    S Peru, W Bolivia
  T. o. orbignyianus
    C & S Chile, S Argentina
Thinocorus rumicivorus (Least Seedsnipe)
  T. r. pallidus
    SW Ecuador
  T. r. cuneicauda
    W Peru, N Chile
  T. r. bolivianus
    SW Bolivia
  T. r. rumicivorus
    C Chile, C Argentina, Uruguay
  T. r. patagonicus
    S Argentina

60 CHIONIDIDAE (SHEATHBILLS)

CHIONIS
Chionis alba (Snowy Sheathbill)
  S Georgia, S Orkneys, Falkland Is
Chionis minor (Black-faced Sheathbill)
  C. m. marionensis
    Prince Edward I, Marion I

C. m. crozettensis
  Crozet I, Possession I
C. m. minor
  Kerguelen I
C. m. nasicornis
  Heard I

61 STERCORARIIDAE (SKUAS)

CATHARACTA
Catharacta skua (Great Skua)
  C. s. skua
    NW Europe to E Canada & SW Europe
  C. s. chilensis
    S Chile to W USA & E Argentina
  C. s. antarctica
    Falkland Is, Tristan da Cunha
  C. s. clarkei
    S Georgia, S Orkney Is, S Shetland Is
  C. s. lonnbergi
    South I New Zealand to S Australia
  C. s. intercedens
    Kerguelen I to S Africa
Catharacta maccormicki (McCormick's Skua)
    Ross Sea, Weddell Sea, S Shetland Is to New Zealand

STERCORARIUS
Stercorarius pomarinus (Pomarine Skua)
  N Holarctic » Peru, S Africa, India, N Australia
Stercorarius parasiticus (Arctic Skua)
  N Holarctic » S South America, S Africa, India, Australia
Stercorarius longicaudus (Long-tailed Skua)
  N Holarctic » W Africa, S South America, Mediterranean & Japan

62 LARIDAE (GULLS, TERNS)

LARINAE

GABIANUS
Gabianus pacificus (Pacific Gull)
  S coast Australia, Tasmania
Gabianus scoresbii (Magellan Gull)
  S coast America, Falkland Is

PAGOPHILA
Pagophila alba (Ivory Gull)
  Circumpolar to N Europe, N Asia, N America
LARUS
Larus fuliginosus (Dusky Gull)
  Galapagos Is
Larus modestus (Grey Gull)
  coast of Peru & Chile
Larus heermanni (Heermann's Gull)
  W USA, W Mexico

Larus leucophthalmus (White-eyed Gull)
S Red Sea, Somali coast

Larus hemprichii (Sooty Gull)
S Red Sea, Iran & E Africa coast

Larus belcheri (Band-tailed Gull)
L. b. belcheri
coast of Peru
L. b. atlanticus
coast of Argentina

Larus crassirostris (Japanese Gull)
coasts of Japan Sea, China Sea

Larus audouinii (Audouin's Gull)
Mediterranean Is

Larus delawarensis (Ring-billed Gull)
Canada & USA coasts to S Mexico, Cuba

Larus canus (Common Gull)
L. c. canus
NW Europe to Mediterranean
L. c. brachyrhynchus
Alaska, W Canada, W USA

Larus kamtschatschensis (Eastern Common Gull)
E Siberia to China, Japan

Larus argentatus (Herring-Gull)
L. a. smithsonianus
Canada to W Mexico
L. a. argentatus
NW Europe, Mediterranean
L. a. omissus
White Sea islands
L. a. birulae
Arctic Ocean islands
L. a. heuglini
N Siberia to Persian Gulf
L. a. vegae
NE Siberia to China, Japan
L. a. atlantis
Azores, Madeira, Canary Is
L. a. michahelles
W & C Mediterranean
L. a. cachinnans
S Russia, SC Asia, N Red Sea

Larus thayeri (Thayer's Gull)
Arctic Canada, W USA

Larus fuscus (Lesser Black-backed Gull)
L. f. fuscus
Scandinavia to W & E Africa
L. f. graellsii
British Isles to W Mediterranean & W Africa

Larus californicus (California Gull)
W USA, W Mexico

Larus occidentalis (Western Gull)
L. o. occidentalis
W USA
L. o. wymani
S California, Baja California

L. o. livens
Gulf of California islands

Larus dominicanus (Southern Black-backed Gull)
S South America, S Africa, New Zealand

Larus schistisagus (Slaty-backed Gull)
NE Asia to Alaska & Japan

Larus marinus (Great Black-backed Gull)
N Atlantic to Cuba, Azores, Mediterranean

Larus glaucescens (Glaucous-winged Gull)
NE Asia & Alaska to W USA & China

Larus hyperboreus (Glaucous Gull)
Circumpolar to W Europe, China, USA

Larus glaucoides (Iceland Gull)
NE Canada, Greenland, N Siberia, Baltic

Larus ichthyaetus (Great Black-headed Gull)
S Russia, Mongolia to Red Sea, India

Larus atricilla (Laughing Gull)
Maine to Brazil & W Central America

Larus brunnicephalus (Indian Black-headed Gull)
C & S Asia

Larus cirrocephalus (Grey-headed Gull)
L. c. cirrocephalus
EC South America
L. c. poiocephalus
Ethiopia to Malawi, S Madagascar

Larus serranus (Andean Gull)
coast of Peru & Andean Lakes

Larus pipixcan (Franklin's Gull)
S Canada, NC USA to W South America

Larus novaehollandiae (Silver Gull)
L. n. forsteri
New Caledonia, N Australia
L. n. novaehollandiae
S Australia, Tasmania
L. n. scopulinus
New Zealand, Chatham I
L. n. hartlaubii
W Cape Province

Larus melanocephalus (Mediterranean Gull)
SE Europe, C & W Asia

Larus relictus (Relict Gull)
C Asia

Larus bulleri (Buller's Gull)
New Zealand

Larus maculipennis (Brown-hooded Gull)
S South America, Falkland Is

Larus ridibundus (Black-headed Gull)
Europe, Asia to N Africa, India, Phillipine I

Larus genei (Slender-billed Gull)
Mediterranean, Black Sea, Asia Minor

Larus philadelphia (Bonaparte's Gull)
W Canada, W & E USA

***Larus minutus* (Little Gull)**
    N Europe, Siberia to Mediterranean, Black
    Sea
***Larus saundersi* (Saunders' Gull)**
    Mongolia, N China, Japan

RHODOSTETHIA
***Rhodostethia rosea* (Ross's Gull)**
    N Siberia, Alaska, Greenland

RISSA
***Rissa tridactyla* (Kittiwake)**
    R. t. tridactyla
        NE Canada, NW Europe to Azores, USA,
        W Africa
    R. t. pollicaris
        Bering Sea & islands, Japan, W USA
***Rissa brevirostris* (Red-legged Kittiwake)**
    Pribilov Is, Commander Is

CREAGRUS
***Creagrus furcatus* (Swallow-tailed Gull)**
    Galapagos Is

XEMA
***Xema sabini* (Sabine's Gull)**
    Arctic Regions » W Africa and W Americas

STERNINAE

CHLIDONIAS
***Chlidonias hybrida* (Whiskered Tern)**
    C. h. hybrida
        S Europe, SW Asia » E & W Africa
    C. h. swinhoei
        S China, Taiwan, Indochina
    C. h. indica
        Iran to India
    C. h. sclateri
        Kenya to Cape Province, Madagascar
    C. h. javanica
        Sri Lanka, Malaysia, Java, Celebes
    C. h. fluviatilis
        Moluccas, New Guinea, Australia
***Chlidonias leucoptera* (White-winged Black Tern)**
    S E Europe, C Asia » S Africa, India, China,
    Australia
***Chlidonias nigra* (Black Tern)**
    C. n. nigra
        Europe, W Asia » SC Africa
    C. n. surinamensis
        Canada, N USA » South America

PHAETUSA
***Phaetusa simplex* (Large-billed Tern)**
    P. s. simplex
        N & E South America
    P. s. chloropoda
        SC & S South America

GELOCHELIDON
***Gelochelidon nilotica* (Gull-billed Tern)**
    G. n. nilotica
        Europe, C Asia » N & E Africa & India

G. n. addenda
    S China
G. n. macrotarsa
    Australia
G. n. aranea
    E USA, Cuba, Gulf Coast
G. n. vanrossemi
    S California, W Mexico to Ecuador
G. n. grönvoldi
    Mexiana I, SE Brazil

HYDROPROGNE
***Hydroprogne caspia* (Caspian Tern)**
    H. c. caspia
        N America, Europe, Africa, C & S Asia
    H. c. strenua
        W & S Australia, New Zealand

STERNA
***Sterna aurantia* (Indian River Tern)**
    Iran, India, Malaysia
***Sterna hirundinacea* (South American Tern)**
    Peru, N Brazil to Tierra del Fuego
***Sterna hirundo* (Common Tern)**
    S. h. hirundo
        N America, Europe, W Asia, » South America,
        W Africa
    S. h. tibetana
        Turkestan, Tibet » India & Malaysia
    S. h. minussensis
        C Asia, N Mongolia
    S. h. longipennis
        NE Asia » Japan, China, New Guinea
***Sterna paradisaea* (Arctic Tern)**
    Arctic regions » Chile, S Africa &
    Antarctica
***Sterna vittata* (Swallow-tailed Tern)**
    S. v. vittata
        Ascension I, St Helena I, Gough I,
        Kerguelen I
    S. v. tristanensis
        Tristan da Cunha
    S. v. georgiae
        S Georgia, S Orkneys
    S. v. gaini
        S Shetlands
    S. v. bethunei
        Sub-Antarctic islands of New Zealand
***Sterna virgata* (Kerguelen Tern)**
    S Indian Ocean islands
***Sterna forsteri* (Forster's Tern)**
    W Canada, USA, N Central America
***Sterna trudeaui* (Trudeau's Tern)**
    S South America
***Sterna dougallii* (Roseate Tern)**
    S. d. dougallii
        E & W North Atlantic coasts » Brazil,
        Azores, S Africa
    S. d. korustes
        Sri Lanka, Andaman Is

S. d. arideensis
Seychelles, Mascarane Is
S. d. bangsi
Riukiu Is, Philippine Is, Kei Is,
Solomon Is
S. d. gracilis
Moluccas, N & W coasts of Australia
Sterna striata (White-fronted Tern)
S. s. striata
New Zealand
S. s. incerta
Tasmania to SE Australia
S. s. aucklandorna
Auckland Is, Chatham I, Snares I
Sterna repressa (White-cheeked Tern)
S Red Sea to Kenya & Persian Gulf
Sterna sumatrana (Black-naped Tern)
S. s. sumatrana
E Indian & Pacific Ocean islands,
N Australia
S. s. mathewsi
W Indian Ocean islands
Sterna melanogaster (Black-bellied Tern)
India, Burma, S Indochina
Sterna aleutica (Aleutian Tern)
Bering Sea to Japan
Sterna lunata (Spectacled Tern)
Moluccas & Fiji to Hawaiian Is
Sterna anaethetus (Bridled Tern)
S. a. anaethetus
Taiwan to Japan and Australia
S. a. fuligula
S Red Sea to E Africa & W India
S. a. antarctica
Seychelles, Mauritius, Maldive Is
S. a. rogersi
N Western Australia
S. a. novaehollandiae
Queensland
S. a. nelsoni
W coast of Mexico & Central America
S. a. melanoptera
West Indies
Sterna fuscata (Sooty Tern)
S. f. fuscata
West Indies, W African islands
S. f. crissalis
W Mexican islands, Galapagos Is
S. f. oahuensis
Hawaii, Bonin Is
S. f. kermadeci
Kermadec Is
S. f. serrata
Australia, New Guinea, N Caledonia
S. f. somaliensis
Mait I, Gulf of Aden
S. f. nubilosa
Indian Ocean & China Sea islands,
Riukiu Is

Sterna nereis (Fairy Tern)
S. n. horni
Western Australia
S. n. nereis
S Australia, Victoria, Tasmania
S. n. davisae
New Zealand
S. n. exsul
New Caledonia
Sterna albistriata (Black-fronted Tern)
New Zealand
Sterna superciliaris (Amazon Tern)
E South America
Sterna balaenarum (Damara Tern)
SW Africa
Sterna lorata (Chilean Tern)
W South America
Sterna albifrons (Little Tern)
S. a. albifrons
Europe, W Asia » N Africa, NW India
S. a. guineae
Ghana to Gabon
S. a. innominata
Persian Gulf islands
S. a. pusilla
N India, Burma, Java, Sumatra
S. a. sinensis
Japan & Indochina » Philippine Is & New
Guinea
S. a. placens
Australia
S. a. antillarum
E USA » West Indies & NE Brazil
S. a. mexicana
Sonora, Sinaloa
S. a. browni
W American coast from California to Peru
Sterna saundersii (Black-shafted Tern)
S Red Sea, Somalia to NW India

THALASSEUS
Thalasseus bergii (Crested Tern)
T. b. bergii
Southern Africa coast, Madagascar
T. b. thalassinus
Seychelles, Aldabra I, Rodriguez I
T. b. velox
NE Africa to Sri Lanka, Red Sea
T. b. cristatus
Malaysia to Riukiu Is & E Australia
T. b. gwendolenae
W & NW Australia
Thalasseus maximus (Royal Tern)
T. m. maximus
California to Peru, Florida to Argentina,
West Indies
T. m. albidorsalis
coast of W Africa

***Thalasseus bengalensis* (Lesser Crested Tern)**
T. b. par
  N & E Africa, Madagascar
T. b. bengalensis
  Persian Gulf to Singapore » Celebes
T. b. torresii
  Aru Is, N Australia
***Thalasseus bernsteini* (Chinese Crested Tern)**
  E China, Philippine Is
***Thalasseus eurygnatha* (Cayenne Tern)**
  E South America, Trinidad
***Thalasseus elegans* (Elegant Tern)**
  California to Chile
***Thalasseus sandvicensis* (Sandwich Tern)**
T. s. sandvicensis
  W & S Europe » Africa, NW India
T. s. acuflavidus
  Florida, Gulf Coast » Brazil, West Indies

LAROSTERNA
***Larosterna inca* (Inca Tern)**
  coast of Peru & Chile

PROCELSTERNA
***Procelsterna cerulea* (Blue-grey Noddy)**
P. c. saxatilis
  W Hawaiian Is, Marcus I
P. c. cerulea
  Christmas I, Marquesas Is
P. c. nebouxi
  Phoenix I, Ellis Is, Samoa Is
P. c. teretirostris
  Tuamotu I, Society Is
P. c. albivitta
  Kermadec Is, Friendly Is, Norfolk I
P. c. skottsbergii
  Easter I
P. c. imitatrix
  St Ambrose I (Chile)

ANOÜS
***Anoüs stolidus* (Common Noddy)**
A. s. stolidus
  Caribbean & Tropical Atlantic islands
A. s. plumbeigularis
  S Red Sea
A. s. pileatus
  Seychelles to Hawaian Is & N Australia
A. s. ridgwayi
  islands of W Mexico & W Central America
A. s. galapagensis
  Galapagos Is
***Anoüs tenuirostris* (Lesser Noddy)**
A. t. tenuirostris
  Seychelles, Madagascar, Mascarene Is
A. t. melanops
  Houtman Abrolhos Is (W Australia)

***Anoüs minutus* (White-capped Noddy)** 133
A. m. minutus
  islands from Tuamotu to New Guinea
A. m. worcesteri
  Cavilli I (Sulu Sea)
A. m. marcusi
  Marcus I & Wake I to Caroline Is
A. m. melanogenys
  Hawaiian Is
A. m. diamesus
  Clipperton I, Cocos I
A. m. americanus
  islands off Belize, Central America
A. m. atlanticus
  Tropical South Atlantic islands

GYGIS
***Gygis alba* (White Tern)**
G. a. alba
  South Atlantic Ocean islands
G. a. monte
  Seychelles, Madagascar, Mascarene Is
G. a. royana
  Norfolk I, Kermadec Is
G. a. candida
  S W Pacific Ocean islands
G. a. rothschildi
  Laysan I
G. a. microrhyncha
  Marquesas Is
G. a. pacifica
  S Pacific Ocean islands

63 RYNCHOPIDAE (SKIMMERS)

RYNCHOPS
***Rynchops niger* (Black Skimmer)**
R. n. niger
  New Jersey to Gulf Coast & N Brazil
R. n. cinerascens
  N & E South America
R. n. intercedens
  E & S South America
***Rynchops flavirostris* (African Skimmer)**
  Senegal to Sudan & Transvaal
***Rynchops albicollis* (Indian Skimmer)**
  India, Burma, Indochina

64 ALCIDAE (AUKS)

ALLE
***Alle alle* (Little Auk)**
A. a. alle
  N Atlantic Ocean » New Jersey &
    W Europe
A. a. polaris
  Franz Josef Land, Barents Sea

ALCA
Alca torda (Razorbill)
  A. t. pica
    NE Canada, NE USA
  A. t. islandica
    Iceland, Faroe Is, British Isles
  A. t. torda
    Baltic Sea islands

URIA
Urialomvia (Brunnich's Guillemot)
  U. l. lomvia
    Arctic Sea & N Atlantic Ocean
  U. l. arra
    Bering Sea, N Pacific ocean
Uria aalge (Common Guillemot)
  U. a. aalge
    Labrador to Orkneys & Norway
  U. a. hyperborea
    Bear I
  U. a. spiloptera
    Faroe Is
  U. a. albionis
    British Isles to Portugal
  U. a. intermedia
    Islands in Baltic Sea
  U. a. inornata
    Bering Sea, N Pacific ocean
  U. a. californica
    California

CEPPHUS
Cepphus grylle (Black Guillemot)
  C. g. mandtii
    Arctic Sea, Spitzbergen to N Greenland
  C. g. arcticus
    N Labrador, S Greenland
  C. g. grylle
    North Atlantic, Baltic & White Sea
Cepphus columba (Pigeon Guillemot)
  C. c. columba
    Bering Sea, N Pacific Ocean
  C. c. snowi
    Kurile Is, N Hokkaido I
Cepphus carbo (Spectacled Guillemot)
  Kurile Is, Okhotsk Sea to N Japan

BRACHYRAMPHUS
Brachyramphus marmoratus (Marbled Murrelet)
  B. m. perdix
    Kamchatka to Kurile Is, Hokkaido I
  B. m. marmoratus
    Alaska to California
Brachyramphus brevirostris (Kittlitz's Murrelet)
  Bering Sea, N Pacific ocean
Brachyramphus hypoleucus (Xantus' Murrelet)
  California & islands

Brachyramphus craveri (Craveri's Murrelet)
  Gulf of California, Raza I

SYNTHLIBORAMPHUS
Synthliboramphus antiquus (Ancient Murrelet)
  Bering Sea, N Pacific ocean
Synthliboramphus wumizusume (Crested Murrelet)
  coast of Japan

PTYCHORAMPHUS
Ptychoramphus aleuticus (Cassin's Auklet)
  Aleutian Is to S California

CYCLORRHYNCHUS
Cyclorrhynchus psittacula (Paroquet Auklet)
  Bering Sea, N Pacific ocean

AETHIA
Aethia cristatella (Crested Auklet)
  Bering Sea, N Pacific ocean
Aethia pusilla (Least Auklet)
  Bering Sea, N Pacific ocean
Aethia pygmaea (Whiskered Auklet)
  Kurile Is, Aleutian Is to N Japan

CERORHINCA
Cerorhinca monocerata (Rhinoceros Auklet)
  Aleutian Is, & N Pacific coasts

FRATERCULA
Fratercula arctica (Atlantic Puffin)
  F. a. naumanni
    Greenland to Novaya Zemlya
  F. a. arctica
    NE Canada to N Norway
  F. a. grabae
    Faroe Is, British Isles, S Norway
Fratercula corniculata (Horned Puffin)
  Bering Sea, N Pacific ocean

LUNDA
Lunda cirrhata (Tufted Puffin)
  Bering Sea, N Pacific Ocean & coasts

Columbiformes

65 PTEROCLIDIDAE (SANDGROUSE)

SYRRHAPTES
Syrrhaptes tibetanus (Tibetan Sandgrouse)
  C Asia, India
Syrrhaptes paradoxus (Pallas' Sandgrouse)
  C Asia, N China » NE China

PTEROCLES
Pterocles alchata (Pintailed Sandgrouse)
  P. a. alchata
    S Spain, S France

P. a. caudacutus
  N Africa, Israel to C Asia & India
**Pterocles namaqua (Namaqua
Sandgrouse)**
  Namibia to Transvaal & W Cape Province
**Pterocles exustus (Chestnut-bellied
Sandgrouse)**
  P. e. exustus
    Senegal to Ethiopia
  P. e. floweri
    Egypt
  P. e. ellioti
    NE Africa to Kenya
  P. e. olivascens
    Kenya
  P. e. erlangeri
    SW Saudi Arabia
  P. e. hindustan
    Iraq, India
Pterocles senegallus (Spotted Sandgrouse)
  NE Africa, Middle East, India
**Pterocles orientalis (Black-bellied
Sandgrouse)**
  P. o. aragonica
    Spain, Canary Is, Morocco
  P. o. orientalis
    N Africa, Middle East, India
  P. o. arenarius
    S Russia, N Afghanistan
**Pterocles coronatus (Crowned
Sandgrouse)**
  P. c. coronatus
    Algeria & Niger to Egypt
  P. c. vastitas
    Sinai
  P. c. saturatus
    E Saudi Arabia
  P. c. atratus
    Iraq to India
  P. c. ladas
    Sind
**Pterocles gutturalis (Yellow-throated
Sandgrouse)**
  P. g. saturatior
    N Ethiopia to N Tanzania
  P. g. tanganjicae
    Tanzania
  P. g. gutturalis
    Zambia to Mozambique & Transvaal
**Pterocles burchelli (Variegated
Sandgrouse)**
  P. b. makarikari
    Namibia, N Botswana
  P. b. burchelli
    E Botswana, W Transvaal
**Pterocles personatus (Madagascar
Sandgrouse)**
  W Madagascar

**Pterocles decoratus (Black-faced
Sandgrouse)**
  P. d. ellenbecki
    S Somalia, N Kenya
  P. d. decoratus
    S Kenya
  P. d. katharinae
    N Tanzania
  P. d. loveridgei
    C Tanzania
**Pterocles lichtensteinii (Lichtenstein's
Sandgrouse)**
  P. l. targius
    S Algeria, Niger
  P. l. lichtensteinii
    Ethiopia, N Sudan, Egypt
  P. l. ingramsi
    S Saudi Arabia
  P. l. sukensis
    Kenya
  P. l. arabicus
    E Saudi Arabia to Afghanistan &
    Pakistan
**Pterocles bicinctus (Double-banded
Sandgrouse)**
  P. b. ansorgei
    S Angola
  P. b. elizabethae
    W Namibia
  P. b. bicinctus
    C & E Namibia to SW Zambia
  P. b. usheri
    E Zambia, S Malawi
  P. b. multicolor
    S Zambia, Rhodesia, Mozambique,
    Transvaal
Pterocles indicus (Painted Sandgrouse)
  India
**Pterocles quadricinctus (Four-banded
Sandgrouse)**
  P. q. quadricinctus
    Senegal & Gambia to N Nigeria
  P. q. lowei
    Chad to Sudan, Uganda, NW Kenya

66 COLUMBIDAE (DOVES, PIGEONS)

COLUMBA
Columba livia (Feral Rock Dove)
  C. l. livia
    W Europe, NW Africa
  C. l. atlantis
    Cape Verde Is, Madeira, Azores
  C. l. canariensis
    Canary Is
  C. l. gymnocyclus
    Senegal, Ghana

C. l. targia
Air to Darfur
C. l. lividior
Mali
C. l. butleri
NE Sudan
C. l. daklae
Dakla & Kharga Oases, Libya
C. l. schimperi
Nile valley
C. l. palestinae
Israel, Sinai, W Arabia
C. l. gaddi
Asia Minor, Iraq
C. l. neglecta
Turkestan, Pakistan
C. l. intermedia
S India, Sri Lanka
C. l. nigricans
Mongolia, N China
Columba rupestris (Eastern Rock Pigeon)
C. r. turkestanica
C Asia, Himalayas
C. r. rupestris
N China, Manchuria
Columba leuconota (Snow Pigeon)
C. l. leuconota
Himalayas, W China
C. l. gradaria
C China
Columba guinea (Speckled Pigeon)
C. g. guinea
Senegal to Ethiopia, Tanzania
C. g. phaeonota
S Africa
C. g. bradfieldi
C Namibia
Columba albitorques (White-collared Pigeon)
C & E Ethiopia
Columba oenas (Stock Dove)
C. o. oenas
Europe, N Africa, Asia Minor
C. o. hyrcana
N Iran
C. o. yarkandensis
E Turkestan, Tien Shan
Columba eversmanni (Yellow-eyed Stock Dove)
Turkestan to NW India
Columba oliviae (Somali Stock Dove)
Somalia
Columba palumbus (Wood Pigeon)
C. p. palumbus
Europe, W Russia
C. p. madarensis
Madeira

C. p. azorica
Azores
C. p. excelsa
N Africa
C. p. iranica
Iran
C. p. casiotis
N India
Columba trocaz (Trocaz Pigeon)
Madeira
Columba bollii (Boll's Pigeon)
Canary Is
Columba unicincta (African Wood Pigeon)
Liberia to Zaire, Uganda
Columba junoniae (Laurel Pigeon)
Palma, Gonera (Canary Is)
Columba arquatrix (Olive Pigeon)
Ethiopia & Angola to E South Africa
Columba sjöstedi (Cameroun Olive Pigeon)
SE Nigeria, Cameroun
Columba thomensis (Sao Thomé Olive Pigeon)
Sao Thomé I
Columba pollenii (Comoro Olive Pigeon)
Comoro Is
Columba hodgsonii (Speckled Wood Pigeon)
Himalayas, Burma, W China
Columba albinucha (White-naped Pigeon)
E Zaire, W Uganda
Columba pulchricollis (Ashy Wood Pigeon)
Tibet, N Burma, N Thailand
Columba elphinstonii (Nilgiri Wood Pigeon)
SW India
Columba torringtoni (Sri Lanka Wood Pigeon)
Sri Lanka
Columba punicea (Purple Wood Pigeon)
NE India to N Malaysia, Vietnam
Columba argentina (Silver Pigeon)
islands W of Sumatra & N of Borneo
Columba palumboides (Andaman Wood Pigeon)
Andaman Is, Nicobar Is
Columba janthina (Black Wood Pigeon)
C. j. janthina
S Japanese Is, N Riukiu Is
C. j. stejnegeri
S Riukiu Is
C. j. nitens
Bonin Is, Volcano I
Columba vitiensis (White-throated Pigeon)
C. v. halmaheira
Moluccas, New Guinea, Solomon Is
C. v. leopoldi
New Hebrides

C. v. hypoenochroa
New Caledonia
C. v. griseogularis
Philippine Is, N Bornean Is
C. v. anthracinus
Palawan
C. v. mendeni
Sula Is
C. v. metallica
Lesser Sunda Is
C. v. vitiensis
Fiji Is
C. v. castaneiceps
Samoa
Columba leucomela (White-headed Pigeon)
E Australia
Columba jouyi (Silver-banded Black Pigeon)
Okinawa I **e?**
Columba pallidiceps (Yellow-legged Pigeon)
Solomon Is, Bismarck Arch
Columba leucocephala (White-crowned Pigeon)
West Indies, S Florida
Columba squamosa (Red-necked Pigeon)
Gtr, Lesser & Dutch Antilles
Columba speciosa (Scaled Pigeon)
S Mexico to Brazil & Paraguay
Columba picazuro (Picazuro Pigeon)
C. p. marginalis
NE Brazil
C. p. picazuro
E Brazil to NE Argentina
Columba corensis (Bare-eyed Pigeon)
N Colombia, N Venezuela, Dutch Antilles
Columba maculosa (Spotted Pigeon)
C. m. albipennis
S Peru, W Bolivia
C. m. maculosa
N Argentina, Uruguay, Paraguay
Columba fasciata (Band tailed pigeon)
C. f. fasciata
W North America
C. f. monilis
N Baja California
C. f. vioscae
S Baja California
C. f. letonai
Honduras, El Salvador
C. f. parva
N Nicaragua
C. f. crissalis
Costa Rica, W Panama
C. f. albilinea
N & W Colombia to E Bolivia

C. f. roraimae
Mt Duida, Mt Roraima (Venezuela)
Columba araucana (Chilean Pigeon)
C & S Chile
Columba caribaea (Jamaican Band-tailed Pigeon)
Jamaica
Columba cayennensis (Rufous Pigeon)
C. c. pallidicrissa
S Mexico to Colombia
C. c. cayennensis
Venezuela, the Guianas, N Brazil
C. c. sylvestris
E Peru to N Argentina
C. c. occidentalis
W Colombia
C. c. tamboensis
SW Colombia
Columba flavirostris (Red-billed Pigeon)
C. f. flavirostris
Texas, E & S Mexico to El Salvador
C. f. madrensis
Tres Marias Is
C. f. restricta
W Mexico
C. f. minima
W Costa Rica
Columba oenops (Salvin's Pigeon)
N Peru
Columba inornata (Plain Pigeon)
C. i. inornata
Cuba, Hispaniola, Isle of Pines
C. i. exigua
Jamaica
C. i. wetmorei
Puerto Rico
Columba plumbea (Plumbeous Pigeon)
C. p. bogotensis
Colombia to N Peru
C. p. chapmani
W Ecuador
C. p. pallescens
SE Ecuador to E Brazil
C. p. baeri
C Brazil
C. p. wallacei
Lower Amazon, the Guianas
C. p. plumbea
SE Brazil, Paraguay
Columba subvinacea (Ruddy Pigeon)
C. s. subvinacea
Costa Rica, W Panama
C. s. berlepschi
E Panama to S Ecuador
C. s. ruberrima
NW Colombia
C. s. peninsularis
N Venezuela

C. s. zuliae
W Venezuela
C. s. purpureotincta
E Colombia, E Venezuela, the Guianas
C. s. anolaimae
SC Colombia
C. s. ogilvie-granti
SE Colombia
Columba nigrirostris (Short-billed Pigeon)
SE Mexico to E Panama
Columba goodsoni (Goodson's Pigeon)
W Colombia, W Ecuador
Columba delegorguei (Delegorgue's Pigeon)
C. d. sharpei
S Sudan, Kenya, Tanzania
C. d. delegorguei
Natal
Columba iriditorques (Bronze-naped Pigeon)
Sierra Leone to Angola, E Zaire
Columba malherbii (Sao Thomé Bronze-naped Pigeon)
Sao Thomé I, Principé I, Annobon I
Columba mayeri (Pink Pigeon)
Mauritius I

STREPTOPELIA
Streptopelia turtur (Turtle Dove)
S. t. turtur
Europe, Asia Minor, Azores Is
S. t. arenicola
N Africa, SW Asia
S. t. hoggara
S Sahara
S. t. isabellina
E Libya, N Egypt
Streptopelia lugens (Dusky Turtle Dove)
S. l. bishaensis
SW Arabia
S. l. lugens
Ethiopia, Somalia
S. l. funebrea
Uganda to Tanzania, Malawi
Streptopelia hypopyrrha (Pink-bellied Turtle Dove)
E Nigeria, Cameroun
Streptopelia orientalis (Eastern Turtle Dove)
S. o. meena
W Himalayas
S. o. erythrocephala
S India
S. o. agricola
Burma, NE India
S. o. orientalis
Siberia, China, Japan
S. o. stimpsoni
Riukiu Is

S. o. orii
Taiwan
Streptopelia bitorquata (Javanese Collared Dove)
S. b. dusumieri
Philippine Is, N Borneo
S. b. bitorquata
Java to Timor I
Streptopelia decaocto (Collared Dove)
S. d. decaocto
Europe to W China
S. d. stoliczkae
Chinese Turkestan
S. d. xanthocyclus
Burma to E China
Streptopelia roseogrisea(African Collared Dove)
S. r. bornuensis
Mali, N Nigeria, Chad
S. r. roseogrisea
Sudan, W Ethiopia
S. r. arabica
E Ethiopia, Somalia, Arabia
Streptopelia reichenowi (White-winged Collared Dove)
S Somalia, NE Kenya
Streptopelia decipiens (Mourning Collared Dove)
S. d. decipiens
E Chad, Sudan, Ethiopia
S. d. shelleyi
Senegal to N Nigeria
S. d. logonensis
E Cameroun, N Zaire
S. d. ambigua
Angola, S Zaire, W Zambia
S. d. perspicillata
Somalia to Malawi, Mozambique
Streptopelia semitorquata (Red-eyed Dove)
S. s. semitorquata
Angola to Ethiopia & N Mozambique
S. s. minor
S Somalia, E Kenya, NE Tanzania
S. s. australis
S Mozambique, Rhodesia, South Africa
Streptopelia capicola (Ring-necked Dove)
S. c. hilgerti
N Somalia
S. c. electa
S Ethiopia
S. c. somalica
S Ethiopia, S Somalia, E Kenya
S. c. anceps
S Kenya, C Tanzania
S. c. tropica
Uganda, W Tanzania to Mozambique

S. c. dryas
  E Zaire
S. c. bailunduensis
  Angola
S. c. ongouati
  Namibia
S. c. damarensis
  C & W South Africa
S. c. capicola
  Transvaal, Natal, Cape Province
Streptopelia vinacea (Vinaceous Dove)
S. v. vinacea
  Senegal to Sudan
S. v. grotei
  Chad, N Cameroun
S. v. savannae
  Sierra Leone to N Zaire
Streptopelia tranquebarica (Red-collared Dove)
S. t. humilis
  N Tibet to Indochina & N Philippine Is
S. t. murmensis
  E Nepal, Sikkim, NE India
S. t. tranquebarica
  India
Streptopelia picturata (Madagascar Turtle Dove)
S. p. picturata
  Madagascar
S. p. coppingeri
  Glorioso Is
S. p. comorensis
  Anjouan I (Comoro)
S. p. aldabrana
  Aldabra I
S. p. assumptionis
  Assumption I
S. p. saturata
  Amirante I
S. p. rostrata
  Seychelles
S. p. chuni
  Diego Garcia I
Streptopelia chinensis (Spotted Dove)
S. c. ceylonensis
  Sri Lanka
S. c. suratensis
  India
S. c. forresti
  NE Burma, NW Yunnan
S. c. chinensis
  E China
S. c. formosa
  Taiwan
S. c. hainana
  Hainan I
S. c. vacillans
  SE Yunnan

S. c. tigrina   139
  Burma to Palawan, Borneo & Sumatra
Streptopelia senegalensis (Laughing Dove)
S. s. phoenicophila
  Morocco, Algeria, Tunisia
S. s. daklae
  Dakhla Oasis, Libya
S. s. aegyptiaca
  Nile valley, Egypt
S. s. senegalensis
  Senegal to Ethiopia & Cape Province
S. s. thomé
  Sao Thomé I
S. s. sokotrae
  Socotra I
S. s. cambayensis
  Iran, India
S. s. ermanni
  Afghanistan, Turkestan

APLOPELIA
Aplopelia larvata (Lemon Dove)
A. l. bronzina
  Ethiopia
A. l. larvata
  SE Sudan to Cape Province
A. l. jacksoni
  E Zaire, Uganda, W Tanzania
A. l. plumbescens
  S Cameroun
A. l. samaliyae
  Angola, NW Zambia
A. l. inornata
  Cameroun Mt, E Nigeria
A. l. poensis
  Fernando Po
A. l. principalis
  Principé I
A. l. simplex
  Sao Thomé I
A. l. hypoleuca
  Annobon I

MACROPYGIA
Macropygia unchall (Bar tailed Cuckoo Dove)
M. u. tusalia
  Himalayas, W China, N Burma
M. u. minor
  SE China, N Indochina, Hainan I
M. u. unchall
  Malaysia, Sumatra, Java, Lombok I
Macropygia amboinensis (Pink-breasted Cuckoo Dove)
M. a. sanghirensis
  Sanghir Is, Talaut Is
M. a. albicapilla
  Celebes
M. a. sedecima
  Sula Is

M. a. batchianensis
N Moluccas
M. a. amboinensis
S Moluccas
M. a. keyensis
Kei Is
M. a. doreya
NW New Guinea, W Papuan Is
M. a. maforensis
Numfor I
M. a. griseinucha
Meos Num I
M. a. kerstingi
N New Guinea, Japen I
M. a. meeki
Vulcan I
M. a. cinereiceps
D'Entrecasteaux Arch
M. a. cunctata
Louisiade Archipelago
M. a. carteretia
Bismarck Archipelago
M. a. hüskeri
New Hanover
Macropygia phasianella (Large Brown Cuckoo Dove)
M. p. septentrionalis
Botel Tobago I, Batan I
M. p. phaea
Calayan I
M. p. tenuirostris
Philippine Is, Palawan, Sulu Arch
M. p. borneensis
N Borneo
M. p. hypopercna
Simalur I
M. p. modiglianii
Nias I
M. p. elassa
Mentawi I
M. p. cinnamomea
Enggano I
M. p. emiliana
Sumatra to Flores I
M. p. megala
Kangean I
M. p. robinsoni
N Australia
M. p. phasianella
S Queensland, New South Wales
Macropygia magna (Large Cuckoo Dove)
M. m. macassariensis
S Celebes, Saleyer I
M. m. longa
Djampea I
M. m. magna
Timor I, Alor I, Wetar I

M. m. timorlaoënsis
Tenimber Is
Macropygia rufipennis (Andaman's Cuckc Dove)
Andaman Is, Nicobar Is
Macropygia nigrirostris (Lesser Bar-tailed Cuckoo Dove)
New Guinea & NE Islands
Macropygia mackinlayi (Mackinlay's Cuckoo Dove)
M. m. mackinlayi
Santa Cruz, Banks I, N Hebrides
M. m. arossi
Solomon Is
M. m. krakari
Karkar I
M. m. goodsoni
St Matthias Is, NE New Guinea
Macropygia ruficeps (Little Cuckoo Dove)
M. r. assimilis
S Burma, NW Thailand
M. r. malayana
Malaysia
M. r. engelbachi
N Indochina
M. r. nana
Borneo
M. r. sumatrana
Sumatra
M. r. simalurensis
Simalur I
M. r. ruficeps
Java, Bali I
M. r. orientalis
Sumbawa I, Flores I, Timor I

REINWARDTOENA
Reinwardtoena reinwardtsi (Reinwardt's Long-tailed Pigeon)
R. r. reinwardtsi
Moluccas
R. r. griseotincta
New Guinea, W New Guinea Is
R. r. brevis
Biak I
Reinwardtoena browni (Brown's Long-tailed Pigeon)
New Britain, Duke of York I
Reinwardtoena crassirostris (Crested Long-tailed Pigeon)
Solomon Is

TURACOENA
Turacoena manadensis (White-faced Pigeon)
T. m. manadensis
Celebes

T. m. sulaënsis
    Peling I, Sula Is
Turacoena modesta (Timor Black Pigeon)
    Timor I, Wetar I

Turtur chalcospilos (Emerald-spotted Wood Dove)
T. c. chalcospilos
    Somalia to Angola & Cape Province
T. c. volkmanni
    Namibia
Turtur abyssinicus (Black-billed Wood Dove)
    Senegal to N Ethiopia
Turtur afer (Blue-spotted Wood Dove)
    Senegal to Ethiopia & Transvaal
Turtur tympanistria (Tambourine Dove)
T. t. fraseri
    Sierra Leone to Ethiopia & Tanzania
T. t. tympanistria
    E Rhodesia, Natal, E Cape Province
Turtur brehmeri (Blue-headed Wood Dove
T. b. infelix
    Sierra Leone to Cameroun Mt
T. b. brehmeri
    S Cameroun, Gabon, Zaire

Oena capensis (Namaqua Dove)
O. c. capensis
    Senegal to Arabia & Cape Province
O. c. aliena
    Madagascar

Chalcophaps indica (Emerald Dove)
C. i. indica
    India to the Philippine Is, Moluccas, Gtr
    Sunda Is
C. i. robinsoni
    Sri Lanka
C. i. maxima
    Andaman Is
C. i. natalis
    Christmas I
C. i. formosanus
    Taiwan
C. i. yamashinae
    Riukiu Is
C. i salimali
    Kerala (S India)
C. i. minima
    Numfor I, Biak I, Meos Num I
C. i. timorensis
    Lesser Sunda Is
C. i. chrysochlora
    New Guinea & islands, E Australia

C. i. sandwichensis
    Santa Cruz Is, New Hebrides, New
    Caledonia
C. i. longirostris
    Northern Territory, (Australia)
C. i. melvillensis
    Melville I
Chalcophaps stephani (Brown-backed Emerald Dove)
C. s. wallacei
    Celebes
C. s. stephani
    New Guinea & surrounding islands
C. s. mortoni
    Solomon Is

Henicophaps albifrons (Black Bronzewing)
H. a. albifrons
    New Guinea, Waigeu I, Misol I, Japen I
H. a. schlegeli
    Aru Is
Henicophaps foersteri (New Britain Bronzewing)
    New Britain

Phaps chalcoptera (Common Bronzewing)
P. c. murchisoni
    mid Western & SW Australia
P. c. consobrina
    N Australia
P. c. chalcoptera
    S Queensland to Tasmania, S Australia
Phaps elegans (Brush Bronzewing)
P. e. neglecta
    Southern Australia
P. e. elegans
    Tasmania
Phaps histrionica (Flock Pigeon)
P. h. alisteri
    NW Australia
P. h. histrionica
    W Queensland, W New South Wales

Ocyphaps lophotes (Crested Pigeon)
O. l. whitlocki
    WC Australia
O. l. lophotes
    C & EC Australia

Petrophassa plumifera (White-bellied Plumed Pigeon)
P. p. plumifera
    N Western Australia to NW Queensland
P. p. mungi
    Derby District N Western Australia

P. p. proxima
Upper Fitzroy river, N Western Australia
P. p. leucogaster
N South Australia, S Northern Territory
Petrophassa ferruginea (Red-Plumed Pigeon)
NW Australia
Petrophassa scripta (Partridge Bronzewing)
P. s. peninsulae
N Queensland
P. s. scripta
C Queensland, C New South Wales
Petrophassa smithii (Bare-eyed Partridge Bronzewing)
N & NW Australia
Petrophassa rufipennis (Chestnut-quilled Rock Pigeon)
N Territory (Australia)
Petrophassa albipennis (White-quilled Rock Pigeon)
P. a. albipennis
N Western Australia
P. a. boothi
N Northern Territory

GEOPELIA
Geopelia cuneata (Diamond Dove)
N & C Australia
Geopelia striata (Zebra Dove)
G. s. striata
S Burma to Philippine Is, Borneo, Lombok I
G. s. papua
S New Guinea
G. s. maugeus
Sumbawa I to Timor I
G. s. audacis
Tenimber Is, Kei Is
G. s. placida
N Australia
G. s. tranquilla
C Australia
G. s. clelandi
mid Western Australia
Geopelia humeralis (Bar-shouldered Dove)
G. h. gregalis
S New Guinea
G. h. humeralis
N & NE Australia

LEUCOSARCIA
Leucosarcia melanoleuca (Wonga Pigeon)
Queensland to Victoria

ZENAIDA
Zenaida macroura (Mourning Dove)
Z. m. marginella
W North America & Central America

Z. m. carolinensis
E North America, Bahama Is
Z. m. macroura
Cuba, Isle of Pines, Hispaniola
Z. m. tresmariae
Tres Marias Is
Z. m. clarionensis
Clarion I
Z. m. graysoni
Socorro I (Revillagigedo Is)
Zenaida auriculata (Eared Dove)
Z. a. caucae
W Colombia
Z. a. vulcania
C Colombia
Z. a. hypoleuca
W Ecuador, W Peru
Z. a. auriculata
Chile, W Argentina
Z. a. chrysauchenia
Bolivia to Uruguay & S Argentina
Z. a. noronha
NE Brazil
Z. a. marajoensis
River Amazon Estuary
Z. a. stenura
Grenada I, Trinidad, NE South America
Z. a. penthera
E Colombia, NW Venezuela
Z. a. antioquiae
NC Colombia
Z. a. vinaceorufa
Curaçao I, Aruba I, Bonaire I
Zenaida aurita (Zenaida Dove)
Z. a. salvadorii
Yucatan coast & islands
Z. a. zenaida
Bahama Is, Gtr Antilles, Virgin Is
Z. a. aurita
Lesser Antilles
Zenaida galapagoensis(Galapagos Dove)
Z. g. galapagoensis
Galapagos Is
Z. g. exsul
Culpepper I, Wenman I
Zenaida asiatica (White-winged Dove)
Z. a. mearnsi
SW USA, W Mexico, Tres Marias Is
Z. a. asiatica
S USA, E Mexico, Gtr Antilles Is
Z. a. australis
W Costa Rica
Z. a. meloda
SW Ecuador to N Chile

COLUMBINA
Columbina passerina (Scaly-breasted Ground Dove)

C. p. passerina
SE Coast of USA
C. p. bahamensis
Bahama Is, Bermuda I
C. p. insularis
Gtr Antilles, Cayman Is
C. p. jamaicensis
Jamaica
C. p. navassae
Navassa I
C. p. exigua
Gt Inagua I, Mona I
C. p. portoricensis
Puerto Rico, Virgin Is
C. p. nigrirostris
St Croix I, N Lesser Antilles
C. p. trochila
Martinique I
C. p. antillarum
S Lesser Antilles
C. p. pallescens
S USA to Guatemala & Belize
C. p. socorroensis
Socorro I
C. p. neglecta
Honduras to Costa Rica
C. p. albivitta
N Colombia, N Venezuela, Dutch
Antilles
C. p. parvula
NC Colombia
C. p. nana
W Colombia
C. p. quitensis
C Ecuador
C. p. griseola
S Venezuela, the Guianas, N Brazil
C. p. tortugensis
Los Hermanos I, La Tortuga I
**Columbina minuta (Plain-breasted
Ground Dove)**
C. m. interrupta
SE Mexico, Guatemala, Belize
C. m. elaeodes
SW Costa Rica, WC Columbia
C. m. minuta
Venezuela, the Guianas, Peru, Brazil,
Paraguay
**Columbina buckleyi (Buckley's Ground
Dove)**
NW Ecuador, NW Peru
Columbina talpacoti (Ruddy Ground Dove)
C. t. eluta
W Mexico
C. t. rufipennis
SE Mexico to N Colombia, N Venezuela,
Trinidad

C. t. caucae
Cauca valley, Colombia
C. t. talpacoti
C & E South America from the Guianas to
C Argentina
Columbina picui (Picui Dove)
C. p. strepitans
NE Brazil
C. p. picui
Bolivia & S Brazil to C Chile & Argentina
**Columbina cruziana (Gold-billed Ground
Dove)**
N Ecuador to NW Chile
**Columbina cyanopis (Blue-eyed Ground
Dove)**
C Brazil

CLARAVIS
Claravis pretiosa (Blue Ground Dove)
SE Mexico to Paraguay & N Argentina
**Claravis godefrida (Purple-barred Ground
Dove)**
SE Brazil, E Paraguay
**Claravis mondetoura (Purple-breasted
Ground Dove)**
SE Mexico to Venezuela & E Peru

METRIOPELIA
**Metriopelia ceciliae (Barefaced Ground
Dove)**
M. c. ceciliae
W Peru
M. c. obsoleta
E Peru
M. c. gymnops
S Peru, Bolivia, N Chile
**Metriopelia morenoi (Moreno's Barefaced
Ground Dove)**
NW Argentina
**Metriopelia melanoptera (Black-winged
Ground Dove)**
M. m. saturatior
S Colombia, Ecuador
M. m. melanoptera
Peru to Chile or W Argentina
**Metriopelia aymara (Bronze-winged
Ground Dove)**
S Peru to Chile, W Argentina

SCARDAFELLA
Scardafella inca (Inca Dove)
Arizona to N Costa Rica
Scardafella squammata (Scaly Dove)
S. s. ridgwayi
coast of Colombia & Venezuela, Trinidad
S. s. squammata
E & S Brazil

Uropelia campestris (Mauve-spotted Ground Dove)
  E Bolivia, C Brazil

LEPTOTILA
Leptotila verreauxi (White-fronted Dove)
  L. v. capitalis
    Tres Marias Is
  L. v. angelica
    N & C Mexico
  L. v. fulviventris
    S Mexico, E Guatemala, Belize
  L. v. bangsi
    W Guatemala to W Nicaragua
  L. v. nuttingi
    Ometepe I (Lake Nicaragua)
  L. v. verreauxi
    SW Nicaragua to N Venezuela,
      Dutch Antilles
  L. v. insularis
    Trinidad
  L. v. tobagensis
    Tobago I
  L. v. decolor
    W Colombia, W Ecuador, N Peru
  L. v. brasiliensis
    the Guianas, N Brazil
  L. v. approximans
    E Brazil
  L. v. decipiens
    E Peru, E Bolivia, W Brazil
  L. v. chalcauchenia
    S Bolivia, Uruguay, N Argentina
Leptotila megalura (White-faced Dove)
  L. m. megalura
    N & C Bolivia
  L. m. saturata
    S Bolivia, NW Argentina
Leptotila rufaxilla (Grey-fronted Dove)
  L. r. pallida
    W Colombia, SW Ecuador
  L. r. pallidipectus
    E Colombia
  L. r. dubusi
    E Ecuador to E Venezuela
  L. r. rufaxilla
    E Venezuela, French Guiana
  L. r. hellmayri
    N Venezuela, Trinidad
  L. r. bahiae
    E Brazil
  L. r. reichenbachii
    C Brazil to Paraguay & Uruguay
Leptotila plumbeiceps (Grey-headed Dove)
  L. p. plumbeiceps
    SE Mexico to W Costa Rica
  L. p. notius
    W Panama

  L. p. malae
    Mala peninsula, W Panama
  L. p. battyi
    Coiba I
Leptotila pallida (Pallid Dove)
  W Colombia, SW Ecuador
Leptotila wellsi (Grenada Dove)
  Grenada I
Leptotila jamaicensis (White-bellied Dove)
  L. j. gaumeri
    N Yucatan peninsula & islands
  L. j. collaris
    Gd Cayman I
  L. j. jamaicensis
    Jamaica
  L. j. neoxena
    St Andrews I
Leptotila cassini (Cassin's Dove)
  L. c. cerviniventris
    E Guatemala to Panama
  L. c. rufinucha
    SW Costa Rica, W Panama
  L. c. cassini
    E Panama, N Colombia
Leptotila ochraceiventris (Buff-bellied Dove)
  SW Ecuador
Leptotila conoveri (Conover's Dove)
  C Colombia

GEOTRYGON
Geotrygon lawrencii (Lawrence's Quail Dove)
  G. l. carrikeri
    Vera Cruz, Mexico
  G. l. lentipes
    NW Costa Rica
  G. l. lawrencii
    E Costa Rica, W Panama
Geotrygon costaricensis (Costa Rican Quail Dove)
  Costa Rica, W Panama
Geotrygon goldmani (Goldman's Quail Dove)
  G. g. goldmani
    E Darien (E Panama)
  G. g. oreas
    Quebrada (E Panama)
Geotrygon saphirina (Purple Quail Dove)
  G. s. purpurata
    W Colombia, W Ecuador
  G. s. saphirina
    E Ecuador
  G. s. rothschildi
    Marcapata valley, Peru
Geotrygon caniceps (Grey-faced Quail Dove)

G. c. caniceps
  Cuba
G. c. leucometopius
  Hispaniola
Geotrygon versicolor (Crested Quail Dove)
  Jamaica
Geotrygon veraguensis (Veragua Quail Dove)
  E Costa Rica to NW Ecuador
Geotrygon linearis (White-faced Quail Dove)
  G. l. albifacies
    SE Mexico, NE Guatemala
  G. l. rubida
    Guerrero, Mexico
  G. l. anthonyi
    S Mexico, W Guatemala
  G. l. silvestris
    El Salvador, Honduras, N Nicaragua
  G. l. chiriquensis
    Costa Rica, W Panama
  G. l. infusca
    Santa Marta, Colombia
  G. l. linearis
    E Colombia, W Venezuela
  G. l. trinitatis
    NE Venezuela, Trinidad
Geotrygon frenata (Pink-faced Quail Dove)
  G. f. bourcieri
    Colombia, Ecuador
  G. f. subgrisea
    SW Ecuador
  G. f. frenata
    Peru, Bolivia
Geotrygon chrysia (Key West Quail Dove)
  Bahama Is, Cuba, Hispaniola
Geotrygon mystacea (Bridled Quail Dove)
  Virgin Is, Lesser Antilles
Geotrygon violacea (Violaceous Quail Dove)
  G. v. albiventer
    Nicaragua to N Colombia
  G. v. violacea
    Surinam to Paraguay
Geotrygon montana (Ruddy Quail Dove)
  G. m. martinica
    Lesser Antilles Is
  G. m. montana
    Mexico to N Argentina, Gtr Antilles, Trinidad

STARNOENAS
Starnoenas cyanocephala (Blue-headed Quail Dove)
  Cuba, Isle of Pines

CALOENAS
Caloenas nicobarica (Nicobar Pigeon)

C. n. nicobarica
  Nicobar Is to Luzon I, New Guinea, Solomon Is
C. n. pelewensis
  Palau Is

GALLICOLUMBA
Gallicolumba luzonica (Luzon Bleeding Heart)
  Luzon I, Polillo Is
Gallicolumba criniger (Bartlett's Bleeding Heart)
  Mindanao, Leyte I, Samar I, Basilan I
Gallicolumba platenae (Mindoro Bleeding Heart)
  Mindoro I
Gallicolumba keayi (Negros Bleeding Heart)
  Negros I
Gallicolumba menagei (Tawitawi Bleeding Heart)
  Tawitawi Is
Gallicolumba rufigula (Golden Heart)
  G. r. helviventris
    Aru Is
  G. r. rufigula
    W New Guinea
  G. r. septentrionalis
    N New Guinea
  G. r. alaris
    S New Guinea
  G. r. orientalis
    SE New Guinea
Gallicolumba tristigmata (Celebes Quail Dove)
  G. t. tristigmata
    N Celebes
  G. t. auripectus
    C & SE Celebes
  G. t. bimaculata
    S Celebes
Gallicolumba jobiensis (White-breasted Ground Pigeon)
  G. j. jobiensis
    New Guinea, Bismarck Archipelago
  G. j. chalconota
    Vella Lavella I, Guadalcanal (Solomon Is)
Gallicolumba kubaryi (Truk Is Ground Dove)
  E Caroline Is
Gallicolumba erythroptera (Society Is Ground Dove)
  Society Is, Tuamotu Is
Gallicolumba xanthonura (White-throated Dove)
  Mariana Is, Yap I
Gallicolumba stairi (Friendly Quail Dove)
  Fiji, Tonga, Samoan Is

Gallicolumba sanctaecrucis (Santa Cruz Ground Dove)
Santa Cruz Is

Gallicolumba salamonis (Thick-billied Ground Dove)
San Cristobal I, Ramos I

Gallicolumba rubescens (Marquesas Ground Dove)
Marquesas Is

Gallicolumba beccarii (Grey-breasted Quail Dove)
G. b. eichhorni
St Matthias Is
G. b. admiralitatis
Admiralty Is
G. b. johannae
Bismarck Archipelago, Dampier I
G. b. beccarii
New Guinea
G. b. intermedia
W Solomon Is
G. b. solomonensis
Rennell I, E Solomon Is

Gallicolumba canifrons (Palau Ground Dove)
Palau Is

Gallicolumba hoedtii (Wetar Is Ground Dove)
Wetar I

TRUGON

Trugon terrestris (Thick-billed Ground Pigeon)
T. t. terrestris
NW New Guinea, Salawati I
T. t. mayri
N New Guinea
T. t. leucopareia
S New Guinea

MICROGOURA

Microgoura meeki (Solomon Is Ground Pigeon)
Choiseul I **e?**

OTIDIPHAPS

Otidiphaps nobilis (Pheasant Pigeon)
O. n. nobilis
W New Guinea
O. n. cervicalis
E & SE New Guinea
O. n. insularis
Fergusson I
O. n. aruensis
Aru Is

GOURA

Goura cristata (Blue Crowned Pigeon)
G. c. cristata
NW New Guinea
G. c. minor
W Papuan islands

Goura scheepmakeri (Maroon-breasted Crowned Pigeon)
G. s. sclaterii
S New Guinea
G. s. wadai
S New Guinea
G. s. scheepmakeri
SE New Guinea

Goura victoria (Victoria Crowned Pigeon)
G. v. victoria
Japen I, Biak I
G. v. beccarii
N New Guinea

DIDUNCULUS

Didunculus strigirostris (Tooth-billed Pigeon)
Upolu I, Savaii (Samoa)

PHAPITRERON

Phapitreron leucotis (Lesser Brown Fruit Dove)
P. l. leucotis
Catanduanes I, Luzon I, Mindoro I
P. l. nigrorum
Tablas I, Masbate I, Panay I, Negros I, Cebu I
P. l. albifrons
Bohol I, Samar I, Siquijor I
P. l. brevirostris
Leyte I, Mindanao I
P. l. occipitalis
Basilan I, Sulu Is

Phapitreron amethystina (Greater Brown Fruit Dove)
P. a. amethystina
Luzon I, Samar I, Leyte I, Bohol I, Mindanao I
P. a. maculipectus
Negros I
P. a. frontalis
Cebu I
P. a. brunneiceps
Basilan I
P. a. cinereiceps
Tawitawi Is

TRERON

Treron fulvicollis (Cinnamon-headed Green Pigeon)
T. f. fulvicollis
Malaysia, Sumatra, S Borneo
T. f. oberholseri
Natuna Is
T. f. melopogenys
Nias I
T. f. baramensis
N Borneo & islands

Treron olax (Little Green Pigeon)
Malaysia, Sumatra, Borneo, Java

Treron vernans (Pink-necked Green Pigeon)
  T. v. griseicapilla
    Malaysia, S Indochina, W Java, N Borneo
  T. v. parva
    NE Sumatra
  T. v. miza
    Simalur I
  T. v. mesochloa
    Nias I, Siberut I, Enggano I, Pagi I
  T. v. adina
    Natuna Is, Anamba Is
  T. v. purpurea
    S Borneo, Java to Sumbawa I
  T. v. vernans
    Philippine Is, Palawan I
  T. v. zalepta
    Celebes

Treron bicincta (Orange-breasted Green Pigeon)
  T. b. bicincta
    India to Indochina & Malaysia
  T. b. leggei
    Sri Lanka
  T. b. domvilii
    Hainan I
  T. b. javana
    Java

Treron pompadora (Pompadour Green Pigeon)
  T. p. pompadora
    Sri Lanka
  T. p. affinis
    W India
  T. p. phayrei
    E India to Thailand & S Indochina
  T. p. chloroptera
    Andaman Is, Nicobar Is
  T. p. axillaris
    Philippine Is
  T. p. everetti
    Sulu Archipelago
  T. p. pallidior
    Djampea I, Kalao I
  T. p. ada
    Madu I, Kalao Tua I
  T. p. aromatica
    Buru I

Treron curvirostra (Thick-billed Green Pigeon)
  T. c. nipalensis
    W Nepal to Thailand & Indochina
  T. c. curvirostris
    Malaysia, Sumatra
  T. c. harterti
    NE Sumatra
  T. c. hainana
    Hainan I
  T. c. erimacra
    Philippine Is

  T. c. nasica
    Borneo
  T. c. haliploa
    Simalur I
  T. c. pega
    Nias I
  T. c. smicra
    Sipora I, Siberut I, Batu I
  T. c. hypothapsina
    Enggano I

Treron griseicauda (Grey-faced Thick-billed Green Pigeon)
  T. g. sanghirensis
    Sanghir Is
  T. g. griseicauda
    Celebes
  T. g. goodsoni
    Tukang Besi Is
  T. g. pulverulenta
    S Sumatra, Java, Bali
  T. g. vordermani
    Kangean I

Treron teysmanni (Sumba Is Green Pigeon)
  Sumba I·

Treron floris (Flores Green Pigeon)
  Lesser Sunda Is from Lombok I to Alor I

Treron psittacea (Timor Green Pigeon)
  Timor I, Samau I

Treron capellei (Large Green Pigeon)
  T. c. magnirostris
    Malaysia, N Sumatra, Borneo
  T. c. capellei
    S Sumatra, Java

Treron phoenicoptera (Yellow-legged Green Pigeon)
  T. p. phoenicoptera
    N India
  T. p. chlorigaster
    S India
  T. p. phillipsi
    Sri Lanka
  T. p. viridifrons
    Burma, W Thailand
  T. p. annamensis
    E Thailand, Indochina

Treron waalia (Yellow-bellied Green Pigeon)
  Senegal to S Arabia

Treron australis (Madagascar Green Pigeon)
  T. a. australis
    E Madagascar
  T. a. xenia
    W Madagascar
  T. a. griveaudi
    Moheli I (Comoro Is)

Treron calva (African Green Pigeon)
  T. c. nudirostris
    Senegal to Guinea
  T. c. sharpei
    Sierra Leone to N Cameroun

T. c. calva
Gabon, N Angola, W Zaire
T. c. poensis
Fernando Po
T. c. virescens
Principé I
T. c. uellensis
N Zaire, Uganda
T. c. brevicera
SW Ethiopia, E Kenya
T. c. salvadorii
Lake Kivu area, NE Zaire
T. c. gibberifrons
S Zaire, W Kenya
T. c. wakefieldii
E Kenya, NE Tanzania
T. c. orientalis
S Tanzania, Mozambique
T. c. schalowi
Zambia, S Zaire
T. c. chobiensis
NW Zambia
T. c. ansorgei
S Angola
T. c. damarensis
N Namibia
T. c. vylderi
NE Namibia
T. c. granti
E Kenya to N Malawi
T. c. delalandii
Mozambique to Natal
Treron pembaensis (Pemba I Green Pigeon)
Pemba I
Treron sanctithomae (Sao Thomé Green Pigeon)
Sao Thomé I
Treron apicauda (Pin-tailed Green Pigeon)
T. a. apicauda
Himalayas, W Burma
T. a. laotinus
N Indochina
T.a.lowei
S Vietnam
Treron oxyura (Yellow-bellied Pin-tailed Green Pigeon)
Sumatra, W Java
Treron seimundi (White-bellied Pin-tailed Green Pigeon)
T. s. seimundi
S Thailand, Malaysia
T. s. modestus
C Vietnam
Treron sphenura (Wedge-tailed Green Pigeon)
T. s. sphenura
Kashmir to Burma

T. s. yunnanensis
SW China, N Vietnam
T. s. annamensis
C Vietnam
T. s. oblitus
Hainan I
T. s. robinsoni
Malaysia
T. s. korthalsi
Sumatra, Java, Lombok I
Treron sieboldii (White-bellied Wedge-tailed Green Pigeon)
T. s. fopingenis
Shensi
T. s. sieboldii
Japan
T. s. sororius
Taiwan
T. s. murielae
N & C Vietnam
Treron formosae (Formosan Green Pigeon)
T. f. permagna
N Riukiu Is
T. f. medioximus
S Riukiu Is
T. f. formosae
Taiwan, Botel Tobago I
T. f. australis
Batan I, Calayan I, Camiguin I (Phil Is)

PTILINOPUS
Ptilinopus cincta (Black-backed Fruit Dove)
P. c. albocincta
Bali I to Flores I
P. c. everetti
Pantar I, Alor I
P. c. cincta
Timor I, Wetar I, Roma I
P. c. lettiensis
Letti I, Moa I, Luang I, Sermatta I
P. c. ottonis
Damar I, Babar I
Ptilinopus alligator (Black-banded Pigeon)
N Territory (Australia)
Ptilinopus dohertyi (Red-naped Fruit Dove)
Sumba I
Ptilinopus porphyrea (Pink-necked Fruit Dove)
Sumatra, Java, Bali
Ptilinopus marchei (Marche's Fruit Dove)
Luzon I, Polillo Is
Ptilinopus merrilli (Merrill's Fruit Dove)
P. m. faustinoi
Mt Tabuan (N Luzon I)
P. m. merrilli
E & S Luzon I, Polillo Is

Ptilinopus occipitalis (Yellow-breasted
Fruit Dove)
  Philippine Is
Ptilinopus fischeri (Fischer's Fruit Dove)
  P. f. fischeri
    N Celebes
  P. f. centralis
    C & SE Celebes
  P. f. meridionalis
    S Celebes
Ptilinopus jambu (Jambu Fruit Dove)
  Malaysia, Sumatra, Borneo
Ptilinopus subgularis (Dark-chinned Fruit
Dove)
  P. s. epia
    Celebes
  P. s. subgularis
    Peling I, Banggai I
  P. s. mangoliensis
    Sula Mangoli I
Ptilinopus leclancheri (Black-chinned
Fruit Dove)
  P. l. leclancheri
    Philippine Is
  P. l. gironieri
    Palawan I
Ptilinopus formosus (Scarlet-breasted
Fruit Dove)
  N Moluccas
Ptilinopus magnificus (Magnificent Fruit
Dove)
  P. m. puella
    NW New Guinea & islands
  P. m. interposita
    WC & SW New Guinea
  P. m. septentrionalis
    N & NE New Guinea, Japen I, Dampier I
  P. m. poliura
    SE New Guinea
  P. m. assimilis
    N Queensland
  P. m. keri
    Bellenden Ker, Queensland
  P. m. magnificus
    S Queensland to Victoria
Ptilinopus perlatus (Pink-spotted Fruit
Dove)
  P. p. perlatus
    NW New Guinea & islands
  P. p. plumbeicollis
    NE New Guinea
  P. p. zonurus
    SE New Guinea, Aru Is, Fergusson I
Ptilinopus ornatus (Ornate Fruit Dove)
  P. o. ornatus
    NW New Guinea
  P. o. gestroi
    C & E New Guinea

  P. o. kaporensis
    SW New Guinea
Ptilinopus tannensis (Silver-shouldered
Fruit Dove)
  New Hebrides, Banks Is
Ptilinopus aurantiifrons (Orange-fronted
Fruit Dove)
  New Guinea & NW islands
Ptilinopus wallacii (Wallace's Fruit Dove)
  Babar I, Kei I, Aru Is, SW New Guinea
Ptilinopus superbus (Superb Fruit Dove)
  P. s. temminckii
    Celebes, Sulu Arch
  P. s. superbus
    Moluccas to Solomon Is, NE Australia
Ptilinopus perousii (Many-coloured Fruit
Dove)
  P. p. perousii
    Samoan Is
  P. p. mariae
    Tonga, Fiji Is
Ptilinopus porphyraceus (Purple-capped
Fruit Dove)
  P. p. fasciatus
    Samoan Is
  P. p. graeffei
    Uvea I
  P. p. ponapensis
    Caroline Is
  P. p. porphyraceus
    Tonga, Fiji Is
Ptilinopus pelewensis (Palau Fruit Dove)
  Palau Is
Ptilinopus rarotongensis (Rarotongan
Fruit Dove)
  P. r. rarotongensis
    Rarotonga I
  P. r. goodwini
    Cook Is
Ptilinopus roseicapilla (Marianas Fruit
Dove)
  Mariana Is
Ptilinopus regina (Pink-capped Fruit Dove)
  P. r. roseipileum
    Wetar I, Roma I, Kissar I, Moa I
  P. r. xanthogaster
    Banda Is, Kei Is, Damar I, Babar I
  P. r. flavicollis
    Flores I, Samoa Is, Timor I
  P. r. ewingii
    Northern Territory, Melville I
  P. r. regina
    Cape York to New South Wales
Ptilinopus richardsii (Silver-capped Fruit
Dove)
  P. r. richardsii
    E Solomon Is

P. r. cyanopterus
Rennell I

Ptilinopus purpuratus (Grey-green Fruit Dove)
 P. p. chrysogaster
 W Society Is
 P. p. frater
 Moorea I
 P. p. purpuratus
 Tahiti
 P. p. chalcurus
 Mahatea I
 P. p. coralensis
 Tuamotu Is

Ptilinopus greyii (Grey's Fruit Dove)
 Santa Cruz Is, New Hebrides, New
 Caledonia

Ptilinopus huttoni (Rapa I Fruit Dove)
 Rapa I

Ptilinopus dupetithouarsii (White-capped Fruit Dove)
 P. d. viridior
 N Marquesas Is
 P. d. dupetithouarsii
 S Marquesas Is

Ptilinopus mercierii (Red-moustached Fruit Dove)
 P. m. mercierii
 Nukuhiva I
 P. m. tristrami
 Hivaoa I

Ptilinopus insularis (Henderson I Fruit Dove)
 Henderson I (Pitcairn Is)

Ptilinopus coronulatus (Lilac-capped Fruit Dove)
 P. c. trigeminus
 NW New Guinea, Salawati I
 P. c. geminus
 N New Guinea, Japen I
 P. c. quadrigeminus
 N New Guinea, Vulcan I
 P. c. huonensis
 SE New Guinea
 P. c. coronulatus
 S New Guinea, Aru Is

Ptilinopus pulchellus (Crimson-capped Fruit Dove)
 P. p. pulchellus
 New Guinea & western Islands
 P. p. decorus
 N New Guinea

Ptilinopus monacha (Blue-capped Fruit Dove)
 N Moluccas

Ptilinopus rivoli (White-bibbed Fruit Dove)
 P. r. buruanus
 Buru I

P. r. prasinorrhous
Moluccas, Kei Is, W Papuan Is
P. r. rivoli
Bismarck Archipelago
P. r. strophium
Louisiade Archipelago, Egum Atoll
P. r. miquelii
Japen I, Meos Num I
P. r. bellus
New Guinea, Admiralty Is

Ptilinopus solomonensis (Yellow-bibbed Fruit Dove)
 P. s. johannis
 St Matthias Is, New Hanover
 P. s. meyeri
 New Britain, Rook I
 P. s. neumanni
 Nissan I
 P. s. bistictus
 Bougainville I
 P. s. vulcanorum
 C Solomon Is
 P. s. ocularis
 Guadalcanal I
 P. s. ambiguus
 Malaita I
 P. s. solomonensis
 San Cristobal I, Ugi I
 P. s. speciosus
 Numfor I, Biak I

Ptilinopus viridis (Red-bibbed Fruit Dove)
 P. v. viridis
 S Moluccas
 P.v. vicinus
 Trobriand Is, D'Entrecasteaux Archipelago
 P. v. lewisii
 W Solomon Is
 P. v. geelvinkiana
 islands of Geelvink Bay
 P. v. pseudogeelvinkiana
 Meos Num I
 P. v. pectoralis
 W Papuan Is, NW New Guinea
 P. v. salvadorii
 N New Guinea

Ptilinopus eugeniae (White-headed Fruit Dove)
 San Cristobal I, Ugi I

Ptilinopus iozonus (Orange-bellied Fruit Dove)
 P. i. humeralis
 W Papuan Is, NW New Guinea
 P. i. jobiensis
 Japen I, Vulcan I, N New Guinea
 P. i. pseudohumeralis
 C New Guinea
 P. i. finschii
 SE New Guinea

P. i. iozonus
Aru Is
Ptilinopus insolitus (Knob-billed Fruit Dove)
P. i. insolitus
New Ireland, New Britain, Lihir Is
P. i. inferior
St Matthias Is
Ptilinopus hyogastra (Grey-headed Fruit Dove)
Halmahera I, Batjan I
Ptilinopus granulifrons (Carunculated Fruit Dove)
Obi Major I
Ptilinopus melanospila (Black-naped Fruit Dove)
P. m. bangueyensis
Philippine Is, N Bornean Is
P. m. talautensis
Talaut Is
P. m. xanthorrhoa
Sangir Is
P. m. melanospila
Celebes, Togian I
P. m. aurescentior
Tukang Besi Is
P. m. pelingensis
Peling I, Banggai I
P. m. chrysorrhoa
Sula Is, Ceram I
P. m. margaretha
Kalaotoa I, Madu I
P. m. massoptera
Pulo Mata Siri I
P. m. melanauchen
Java, Bali to Alor I, Kangean I
Ptilinopus naina (Dwarf Fruit Dove)
P. n. minimus
W Papuan Is
P. n. naina
S New Guinea
Ptilinopus arcanus (Ripley's Fruit Dove)
NC Negros I
Ptilinopus victor (Orange Dove)
Fiji Is
Ptilinopus luteovirens (Golden Dove)
Fiji Is
Ptilinopus layardi (Yellow-headed Dove)
Kandavu I (Fiji Is)

DREPANOPTILA
Drepanoptila holosericea (Cloven-feathered Dove)
New Caledonia I

ALECTROENAS
Alectroenas madagascariensis (Madagascar Blue Pigeon)
Madagascar

Alectroenas sganzini (Comoro Blue Pigeon)
A. s. minor
Aldabra I
A. s. sganzini
Comoro Is
Alectroenas pulcherrima (Seychelles Blue Pigeon)
Seychelles

DUCULA
Ducula poliocephala (Philippine Zone-tailed Pigeon)
Philippine Is
Ducula forsteni (Green & White Zone-tailed Pigeon)
Celebes
Ducula mindorensis (Mindoro Zone-tailed Pigeon)
Mindoro I
Ducula radiata (Grey-headed Zone-tailed Pigeon)
Celebes
Ducula carola (Grey-necked Fruit Pigeon)
D. c. carola
Luzon I, Mindoro I
D. c. nigrorum
Negros I
D. c. mindanensis
Mindanao I
Ducula aenea (Green Imperial Pigeon)
D. a. pusilla
S India, Sri Lanka
D. a. sylvatica
N India, Thailand, Indochina
D. a. nicobarica
Nicobar Is
D. a. aenea
Malaysia, Borneo, Sumatra to Alor I
D. a. mista
Simalur I
D. a. babiensis
Pulo Babi I
D. a. consobrina
Nias I
D. a. vicina
Mentawi Is
D. a. palawanensis
S Philippine Is
D. a. chalybura
N Philippine Is
D. a. paulina
Celebes, Talaut Is
D. a. sulana
Sula Is
D. a. aneothorax
Engano I

Ducula perspicillata (White-eyed Imperial Pigeon)
  D. p. perspicillata
    N Moluccas
  D. p. neglecta
    S Moluccas
Ducula concinna (Blue-tailed Imperial Pigeon)
  D. c. intermedia
    Talaut Is
  D. c. concinna
    Islands E of Celebes
  D. c. aru
    Aru Is
  D. c. separata
    Tenimber Is, Kei Is
Ducula pacifica (Pacific Pigeon)
  D. p. tarrali
    N New Guinea Is, New Hebrides
  D. p. pacifica
    Ellis Is, Tonga I
  D. p. intensitincta
    Fiji Is
  D. p. microcera
    Samoa Is
  D. p. sejuncta
    Bismarck Archipelago
Ducula oceanica (Micronesian Pigeon)
  D. o. monacha
    Yap I, Palau Is
  D. o. tereokai
    Truk I
  D. o. townsendi
    Ponapé I
  D. o. oceanica
    Kusaie I, Marshall Is
  D. o. ratakensis
    Arno I, Wotje I (Marshall Is)
Ducula aurorae (Society Is Pigeon)
  Society Is
Ducula galeata (Marquesas Pigeon)
  Nukuhiva I
Ducula rubricera (Red-knobbed Pigeon)
  D. r. rubricera
    Bismarck Archipelago, Lihir Is
  D. r. rufigula
    Solomon Is
Ducula myristicivora (Black-knobbed Pigeon)
  D. m. myristicivora
    W Papuan Is
  D. m. geelvinkiana
    Meos Num I, Numfor I, Biak I
Ducula rufigaster (Rufous-bellied Fruit Pigeon)
  D. r. rufigaster
    W Papuan Is, W New Guinea
  D. r. pallida
    S New Guinea

  D. r. uropygialis
    N New Guinea
Ducula basilica (Moluccan Rufous-bellied Fruit Pigeon)
  D. b. basilica
    N Moluccas
  D. b. obiensis
    Obi I
Ducula finschii (Finsch's Rufous-bellied Fruit Pigeon)
  Bismarck Archipelago
Ducula chalconota (Mountain Rufous-bellied Fruit Pigeon)
  D. c. chalconota
    NW New Guinea
  D. c. smaragdina
    New Guinea
Ducula pistrinaria (Island Imperial Pigeon)
  D. p. rhodinolaema
    Admiralty Is, New Hanover
  D. p. vanwyckii
    Bismarck Archipelago
  D. p. postrema
    Islands off SE New Guinea
  D. p. pistrinaria
    Solomon Is, Lihir Is
Ducula rosacea (Pink-headed Imperial Pigeon)
  D. r. rosacea
    Lesser Sunda Is from Duizend I to Sudest
  D. r. zamydra
    Arends I, Colombo Besar I (Java Sea)
Ducula whartoni (Christmas I Imperial Pigeon)
  Christmas I
Ducula pickeringii (Grey Imperial Pigeon)
  D. p. pickeringii
    N Bornean Is, Sulu Archipelago, Talaut Is
  D. p. langhornei
    Bolod I, Loran I
  D. p. palmasensis
    Palmas I
Ducula latrans (Peale's Pigeon)
  Fiji Is
Ducula brenchleyi (Chestnut-bellied Pigeon)
  Solomon Is
Ducula bakeri (Baker's Pigeon)
  New Hebrides
Ducula goliath (New Caledonian Pigeon)
  New Caledonia
Ducula pinon (Pinon Imperial Pigeon)
  D. p. pinon
    W Papuan Is, SW New Guinea
  D. p. rubiensis
    C & S New Guinea
  D. p. jobiensis
    N New Guinea, Japen I, Dampier I

D. p. salvadorii
D'Entrecasteaux & Louisiade Archi-
pelago
**Ducula melanochroa (Black Imperial
Pigeon)**
Bismarck Archipelago
**Ducula mullerii (Black-collared Fruit
Pigeon)**
D. m. aurantia
N New Guinea
D. m. mullerii
S New Guinea, Aru Is
Ducula zoeae (Banded Imperial Pigeon)
New Guinea & SW & SE islands
Ducula badia (Mountain Imperial Pigeon)
D. b. insignis
Himalayas
D. b. cuprea
SW India
D. b. griseicapilla
Burma, Thailand, Indochina
D. b. obscurata
SE Thailand
D. b. badia
Malaysia, Sumatra, Borneo
D. b. capistrata
W Java
**Ducula lacernulata (Dark-backed Imperial
Pigeon)**
D. l. lacernulata
W & C Java
D. l. williami
E Java, Bali I
D. l. sasakensis
Lombok I, Flores I
Ducula cineracea (Timor Imperial Pigeon)
D. c. cineracea
Timor I
D. c. schistacea
Wetar I
Ducula bicolor (Pied Imperial Pigeon)
D. b. bicolor
Andaman Is to Philippine Is & Lesser
Sunda Is
D. b. melanura
Moluccas
**Ducula luctuosa (Celebes Pied Imperial
Pigeon)**
Celebes, Sula Is
**Ducula spilorrhoa (Australian Pied Imperial
Pigeon)**
D. s. subflavescens
Bismarck Archipelago, Admiralty Is
D. s. spilorrhoa
Aru Is, W New Guinea & islands
D. s. tarara
S New Guinea

D. s. melvillensis
SE New Guinea, N & NE Australia, Lord
Howe I
LOPHOLAIMUS
**Lopholaimus antarcticus (Top-knot
Pigeon)**
N Queensland to Victoria

HEMIPHAGA
**Hemiphaga novaeseelandiae (New Zealand
Pigeon)**
H. n. novaeseelandiae
New Zealand
H. n. chathamensis
Chatham I

CRYPTOPHAPS
**Cryptophaps poecilorrhoa (Celebes Dusky
Pigeon)**
N & SE Celebes

GYMNOPHAPS
**Gymnophaps albertisii (Bare-eyed
Mountain Pigeon)**
G. a. exsul
Batjan I (Moluccas)
G. a. albertisii
New Guinea, Bismarck Archipelago
**Gymnophaps mada (Long-tailed Mountain
Pigeon)**
G. m. mada
Buru I
G. m. stalkeri
Ceram I
**Gymnophaps solomonensis (Pale
Mountain Pigeon)**
Solomon Is

Psittaciformes

67 LORIIDAE (LORIES)

CHALCOPSITTA
Chalcopsitta atra (Black Lory)
C. a. bernsteini
Misol I
C. a. atra
Batanta I, Salawati I, NW New Guinea
C. a. insignis
Amberpon, NW New Guinea
C. a. spectabilis
NW New Guinea
**Chalcopsitta duivenbodei (Duyvenbode's
Lory)**
C. d. duivenbodei
coast of NW New Guinea
C. d. syringanuchalis
coast of NE New Guinea

Chalcopsitta sintillata (Yellow-streaked Lory)
  C. s. rubrifrons
    Aru Is
  C. s. sintillata
    S New Guinea
  C. s. chloroptera
    SE New Guinea
Chalcopsitta cardinalis (Cardinal Lory)
  Islands NW of New Ireland, Solomon Is

EOS
Eos cyanogenia (Black-winged Lory)
  Islands in Geelvink Bay
Eos squamata (Violet-necked Lory)
  E. s. obiensis
    Obi I
  E. s. atrocaerulea
    Maju I
  E. s. riciniata
    N Moluccas
  E. s. squamata
    W Papuan islands
Eos reticulata (Blue-streaked Lory)
  Tenimber Is, Kei Is, Damar I
Eos histrio (Red and Blue Lory)
  E. h. histrio
    Gt Sangi I, Siao I
  E. h. talautensis
    Talaut Is
  E.h. challengeri
    Nenusa I
Eos bornea (Red Lory)
  E. b. bornea
    Ambon I, Saparua I
  E.b. cyanonothus
    Buru I
  E.b. rothschildi
    Ceram I
  E. b. bernsteini
    Kei Is
Eos semilarvata (Blue-eared Lory)
  C̄ Ceram I

PSEUDEOS
Pseudeos fuscata (Dusky Lory)
  Salawati I, Japen I, New Guinea

TRICHOGLOSSUS
Trichoglossus ornatus (Ornate Lory)
  Celebes
Trichoglossus haematodus (Rainbow Lory)
  T. h. mitchellii
    Bali I, Lombok I
  T. h. forsteni
    Sumbawa I
  T. h. djampeanus
    Djampea I
  T. h. stresemanni
    Kalaotua I

T. h. fortis
  Sumba I
T. h. weberi
  Flores I
T. h. capistratus
  Timor I
T. h. flavotectus
  Wetar I, Roma I
T. h. haematodus
  S Moluccas, W New Guinea
T. h. rosenbergii
  Biak I
T. h. intermedius
  N New Guinea
T. h. micropteryx
  E New Guinea
T. h. caeruleiceps
  S New Guinea
T. h. nigrogularis
  E Kei Is, Aru Is
T. h. brooki
  Trangan I (Aru Is)
T. h. massena
  New Hebrides, Bismarck Archipelago,
  Solomon Is
T. h. flavicans
  New Hanover, Admiralty Is
T. h. nesophilus
  Ninigo I
T. h. deplanchii
  New Caledonia, Loyalty Is
T. h. moluccanus
  E Australia, Tasmania
T. h. rubritorquis
  N Australia
Trichoglossus rubiginosus (Ponapé Lory)
  Ponapé I
Trichoglossus johnstoniae (Johnstone's Lorikeet)
  T. j. johnstoniae
    C & SE Mindanao
  T. j. pistra
    W Mindanao
Trichoglossus flavoviridis (Yellow and Green Lorikeet)
  T. f. meyeri
    Celebes
  T. f. flavoviridis
    Sula Is
Trichoglossus chlorolepidotus (Scaly-breasted Lorikeet)
  NE Australia
Trichoglossus euteles (Perfect Lorikeet)
  Timor I, Lomblen I to Babar I
Trichoglossus versicolor (Varied Lorikeet)
  N Australia
Trichoglossus iris (Iris Lorikeet)
  T. i. iris
    W Timor I

T. i. rubripileum
E Timor I
T. i. wetterensis
Wetar I
Trichoglossus goldiei (Goldie's Lorikeet)
C New Guinea

LORIUS
Lorius hypoinochrous (Purple-bellied Lory)
L. h. devittatus
Bismark Archipelago, SE New Guinea & islands
L. h. hypoinochrous
Misima I, Tagula I
L. h. rosselianus
Rossel I
Lorius lory (Black-capped Lory)
L. l. lory
NW New Guinea & islands
L. l. erythrothorax
C New Guinea
L. l. somu
S New Guinea
L. l. salvadorii
NE New Guinea
L. l. viridicrissalis
N New Guinea
L. l. jobiensis
Japen I, Meos Num I
L. l. cyanuchen
Biak I
Lorius albidinuchus (White-naped Lory)
New Ireland
Lorius amabilis (Stresemann's Lory)
New Britain
Lorius chlorocercus (Yellow-bibbed Lory)
E Solomon islands
Lorius domicellus (Purple-naped Lory)
Ceram I, Ambon I
Lorius tibialis (Blue-thighed Lory)
unknown
Lorius garrulus (Chattering Lory)
L. g. garrulus
Halmahera I, Weda I
L. g. flavopalliatus
Batjan I, Obi I
L. g. morotaianus
Morotai I

PHIGYS
Phigys solitarius (Collared Lory)
Fiji Is

VINI
Vini australis (Blue-crowned Lory)
Samoa Is, Tonga I, Lau Archipelago
Vini kuhlii (Kuhl's Lory)
Rimıtara I, Tubuai I
Vini stepheni (Stephen's Lory)
Henderson I

Vini peruviana (Tahitian Lory)
Cook Is, Society Is
Vini ultramarina (Ultramarine Lory)
Marquesas Is

GLOSSOPSITTA
Glossopsitta concinna (Musk Lorikeet)
E & SE Australia, Tasmania
Glossopsitta pusilla (Little Lorikeet)
E & SE Australia, Tasmania
Glossopsitta porphyrocephala (Purple-crowned Lorikeet)
SW & SE Australia

CHARMOSYNA
Charmosyna palmarum (Palm Lorikeet)
New Hebrides, Banks Is
Charmosyna rubrigularis (Red-chinned Lorikeet)
C. r. rubrigularis
New Britain, New Ireland
C. r. krakari
Karkar I
Charmosyna meeki (Meek's Lorikeet)
Solomon Is
Charmosyna toxopei (Blue-fronted Lorikeet)
Buru I
Charmosyna multistriata (Striated Lorikeet)
WC New Guinea
Charmosyna wilhelminae (Wilhelmina's Lorikeet)
C New Guinea
Charmosyna rubronotata (Red-spotted Lorikeet)
C. r. rubronotata
Salawati I, NW New Guinea
C. r. kordoana
Biak I
Charmosyna placentis (Red-flanked Lorikeet)
C. p. intensior
N Moluccas
C. p. placentis
S Moluccas, Kei Is, Aru Is, S New Guinea
C. p. ornata
NW New Guinea & islands
C. p. subplacens
E New Guinea
C. p. pallidior
Bismarck Archipelago, W Solomon Is
Charmosyna diadema (New Caledonian Lorikeet)
New Caledonia **e?**
Charmosyna amabilis (Red-throated Lorikeet)
Viti Levu I, Ovalau I, Taviuni I

***Charmosyna margarethae* (Duchess Lorikeet)**
Solomon Is

***Charmosyna pulchella* (Fairy Lorikeet)**
C. p. pulchella
NW, C & SE New Guinea
C. p. rothschildi
NC New Guinea
C. p. bella
SE New Guinea

***Charmosyna josefinae* (Josephine's Lory)**
C. j. josefinae
NW New Guinea
C. j. sepikiana
Sepik Mtn area, New Guinea
C. j. cyclopum
Cyclops Mtns, New Guinea

***Charmosyna papou* (Papuan Lory)**
C. p. papou
NW New Guinea
C. p. stellae
SE New Guinea
C. p. goliathina
C New Guinea
C. p. wahnesi
Huon peninsula, New Guinea

OREOPSITTACUS
***Oreopsittacus arfaki* (Whiskered Lorikeet)**
O. a. arfaki
NW New Guinea
O. a. major
C New Guinea
O. a. grandis
SE New Guinea

NEOPSITTACUS
***Neopsittacus musschenbroekii* (Musschenbroek's Lorikeet)**
N. m. musschenbroekii
NW New Guinea
N. m. medius
W New Guinea
N. m. major
SE New Guinea

***Neopsittacus pullicauda* (Emerald Lorikeet)**
N. p. alpinus
W New Guinea
N. p. socialis
EC New Guinea
N. p. pullicauda
SE New Guinea

68 CACATUIDAE (COCKATOOS)

CACATUINAE

PROBOSCIGER
***Prosciger aterrimus* (Palm Cockatoo)**
P. a. goliath
W Papuan Is, NW to SE New Guinea

P. a. stenolophus
Japen I, N New Guinea
P. a. aterrimus
Aru Is, Misol I, S New Guinea, Cape York, Queensland

CALYPTORHYNCHUS
***Calyptorhynchus funereus* (Black Cockatoo)**
C. f. baudinii
SW Australia
C. f. tenuirostris
SW Australia
C. f. funereus
E Australia
C. f. xanthonotus
SE Australia, Tasmania

***Calyptorhynchus magnificus* (Red-tailed Cockatoo)**
C. m. naso
SW Australia
C. m. samueli
SW Queensland, W New South Wales
C. m. macrorhynchus
N Australia
C. m. magnificus
Queensland to S New South Wales, W Victoria

***Calyptorhynchus lathami* (Glossy Cockatoo)**
C Queensland to E Victoria, Kangaroo I

CALLOCEPHALON
***Callocephalon fimbriatum* (Gang-gang Cockatoo)**
SE Australia, N Tasmania

EOLOPHUS
***Eolophus roseicapillus* (Galah)**
E. r. kuhli
NW Australia
E. r. assimilis
Western Australia
E. r. roseicapillus
NC & E Australia

CACATUA
***Cacatua leadbeateri* (Major Mitchell's Cockatoo)**
C. l. mollis
mid-Western Australia
C. l. leadbeateri
interior of Australia

***Cacatua sulphurea* (Lesser Sulphur-crested Cockatoo)**
C. s. sulphurea
Celebes, Buton I
C. s. djampeana
Alor I to Madu I, Tukangbesi Is
C. s. abbotti
Solombo Besar I

C. s. occidentalis
  Lombok I, Sumbawa I, Flores I
C. s. parvula
  Timor I, Samao I
C. s. citrinocristata
  Sumba I
Cacatua galerita (Sulphur-crested Cockatoo)
C. g. eleonora
  Aru Is
C. g. triton
  New Guinea & N & E islands
C. g. fitzroyi
  N Australia to W Queensland
C. g. galerita
  E & SE Australia
Cacatua ophthalmica (Blue-eyed Cockatoo)
  New Britain, New Ireland
Cacatua moluccensis (Salmon-crested Cockatoo)
  S Moluccas
Cacatua alba (White Cockatoo)
  N & C Moluccas
Cacatua haematuropygia (Red-vented Cockatoo)
  Philippine Is, Palawan I
Cacatua goffini (Goffin's Cockatoo)
  Tenimber Is
Cacatua sanguinea (Little Corella)
C. s. normantoni
  S. New Guinea, NW Queensland
C. s. sanguinea
  W, NW & EC Australia
Cacatua tenuirostris (Long-billed Corella)
C. t. pastinator
  SW Australia
C. t. tenuirostris
  SE Australia
Cacatua ducorps (Ducorp's Cockatoo)
  E Solomon Is

NYMPHICINAE

NYMPHICUS
Nymphicus hollandicus (Cockatiel)
  Australia (mainly interior)

69 PSITTACIDAE (PARROTS)

NESTORINAE

NESTOR
Nestor notabilis (Kea)
  C South I, New Zealand
Nestor meridionalis (Kaka)
  New Zealand

MICROPSITTA
Micropsitta pusio (Buff-faced Pygmy Parrot)
M. p. beccarii
  N New Guinea
M. p. pusio
  SE New Guinea, Bismarck Archipelago
M. p. harterti
  Fergusson I
M. p. stresemanni
  Misima I, Tagula I
Micropsitta keiensis (Yellow-capped Pygmy Parrot)
M. k. keiensis
  Kei Is, Aru Is
M. k. chloroxantha
  W Papuan islands, NW New Guinea
M. k. viridipectus
  S New Guinea
Micropsitta geelvinkiana (Geelvink Pygmy Parrot)
M. g. geelvinkiana
  Numfor I
M. g. misoriensis
  Biak I
Micropsitta meeki (Meek's Pygmy Parrot)
M. m. meeki
  Admiralty Is
M. m. proxima
  St Matthias Is, Squally I
Micropsitta finschii (Finsch's Pygmy Parrot)
M. f. viridifrons
  New Hanover, New Ireland, Lihir Is
M. f. finschii
  Ugi I, San Cristobal I, Rennell I
M. f. aolae
  Guadalcanal I, Malaita I, Russell I
M. f. tristami
  Vella Lavella I, Kulambangra I, Rendova I
M. f. nanina
  Bougainville I, Choiseul I, Ysabel I
Micropsitta bruijnii (Red-breasted Pygmy Parrot)
M. b. pileata
  Buru I, Ceram I
M. b. bruijnii
  New Guinea
M. b. necopinata
  New Britain, New Ireland
M. b. rosea
  Bougainville I, Guadalcanal I, Kulambangra I

OPOPSITTA

Opopsitta gulielmitertii (Orange-breasted Fig Parrot)

O. g. gulielmitertii
Salawati I, NW New Guinea

O. g. nigrifrons
N New Guinea

O. g. ramuensis
Ramu R, N New Guinea

O. g. amabilis
NE New Guinea

O. g. suavissima
SE New Guinea

O. g. fuscifrons
S New Guinea

O. g. melanogenia
Aru Is

Opopsitta diophthalma (Double-eyed Fig Parrot)

O. d. diophthalma
W New Guinea & islands

O. d. festetichi
E & NE New Guinea

O. d. aruensis
Aru Is, S New Guinea

O. d. virago
Goodenough I, Fergusson I

O. d. inseparabilis
Tagula I

O. d. marshalli
Cape York Peninsula

O. d. macleayana
coast of N Queensland

O. d. coxeni
coast of N New South Wales

PSITTACULIROSTRIS

Psittaculirostris desmarestii (Desmarest's Fig Parrot)

P. d. blythii
Misol I

P. d. occidentalis
Salawati I, Batanta I, NW New Guinea

P. d. desmarestii
NW New Guinea

P. d. intermedia
Onin peninsula, NW New Guinea

P. d. godmani
S New Guinea

P. d. cervicalis
SE New Guinea

Psittaculirostris edwardsii (Edwards' Fig Parrot)
NE New Guinea

Psittaculirostris salvadorii (Salvadori's Fig Parrot)
NW New Guinea

BOLBOPSITTACUS

Bolbopsittacus lunulatus (Guaiabero)

B. l. lunulatus
Luzon I

B. l. intermedius
Leyte I

B. l. callainipictus
Samar I

B. l. mindanensis
Mindanao I, Panaon I

PSITTINUS

Psittinus cyanurus (Blue-rumped Parrot)

P. c. cyanurus
SW Thailand, Malaysia, Sumatra, Borneo

P. c. pontius
Siberut I, Sipora I, Mentawei Is

P. c. abbotti
Simalur I, Siumat I

PSITTACELLA

Psittacella brehmii (Brehm's Parrot)

P. b. brehmii
NW New Guinea

P. b. intermixta
WC New Guinea

P. b. harterti
E New Guinea

P. b. pallida
S & SE New Guinea

Psittacella picta (Painted Parrot)

P. p. picta
SE New Guinea

P. p. excelsa
C New Guinea

P. p. lorentzi
WC New Guinea

Psittacella modesta (Modest Parrot)

P. m. modesta
NW New Guinea

P. m. collaris
WC New Guinea

P. m. subcollaris
C New Guinea

Psittacella madaraszi (Maderasz's Parrot)

P. m. major
WC New Guinea

P. m. hallstromi
C New Guinea

P. m. huonensis
E New Guinea

P. m. maderaszi
SE New Guinea

GEOFFROYUS

Geoffroyus geoffroyi (Red-cheeked Parrot)

G. g. floresianus
Lombok I, Sumbawa I, Flores I, Sumba I

G. g. geoffroyi
Timor I, Wetar I

G. g. cyanicollis
  N Moluccas
G. g. obiensis
  C Moluccas
G.g. rhodops
  S Moluccas
G. g. explorator
  Goram I
G. g. keyensis
  Kei Is
G. g. timorlaoensis
  Tenimber Is
G. g. aruensis
  Aru Is, S New Guinea, NE Queensland
G. g. orientalis
  NE New Guinea
G. g. sudestiensis
  Misima I, Tagula I
G. g. cyanicarpus
  Rossel I
G. g. minor
  N New Guinea
G. g. jobiensis
  Japen I, Meos Num I
G. g. mysoriensis
  Biak I, Numfor I
G. g. pucherani
  W Papuan islands, NW New Guinea
***Geoffroyus simplex* (Blue-collared Parrot)**
G. s. simplex
  NW New Guinea
G. s. buergersi
  C & SE New Guinea
***Geoffroyus heteroclitus* (Singing Parrot)**
G. h. heteroclitus
  Lihir Is, New Ireland, New Britain, Solomon Is
G. h. hyacinthus
  Rennell I

***Prioniturus luconensis* (Green Racket-tailed Parrot)**
  Luzon I, Marinduque I
***Prioniturus discurus* (Blue-crowned Racket-tailed Parrot)**
P. d. discurus
  Mindanao I, Basilan I, Luzon I
P. d. whiteheadi
  Negros I, Bohol I, Samar I, Leyte I, Masbate I, Cebu I
P. d. nesophilus
  Catanduanes I, Sibuyan I, Tablas I
P. d. mindorensis
  Mindoro I
P. d. platenae
  Palawan I, Balabac I
***Prioniturus montanus* (Mountain Racket-tailed Parrot)**

P. m. montanus
  Luzon I
P. m. verticalis
  Sulu Archipelago
P. m. waterstradti
  Mindanao I
P. m. malindangensis
  Mt Malindang, Mindanao I
***Prioniturus flavicans* (Red-spotted Racket-tailed Parrot)**
  N Celebes
***Prioniturus platurus* (Golden-mantled Racket-tailed Parrot)**
P. p. platurus
  Celebes, Togian I, Peleng I, Banggai I
P. p. talautensis
  Talaut Is
P. p. sinerubris
  Taliabu I
***Prioniturus mada* (Buru Racket-tailed Parrot)**
  Buru I

***Tanygnathus megalorhynchos* (Great-billed Parrot)**
T. m. megalorhynchos
  Talaut Is, Sanghir Is, N & C Moluccas
T. m. affinis
  S Moluccas
T. m. subaffinis
  Tenimber Is
T. m. hellmayri
  W Timor I, Semao I
T. m. viridipennis
  Kalaotua I, Madu I
T. m. djampeae
  Djampea I, Kalao I
T. m. floris
  Flores I
T. m. sumbensis
  Sumba I
***Tanygnathus lucionensis* (Blue-naped Parrot)**
T. l. lucionensis
  Luzon I, Mindoro I
T. l. hybridus
  Polillo Is
T. l. talautensis
  C & S Philippine Is, Palawan I, Sulu Archipelago
***Tanygnathus sumatranus* (Müller's Parrot)**
T. s. duponti
  Luzon I
T. s. freeri
  Polillo Is
T. s. everetti
  Panay I, Samar I, Leyte I, Negros I, Mindanao I

T. s. burbidgii
Sulu Archipelago

T. s. sangirensis
Sanghir Is, Talaut Is

T. s. sumatranus
Celebes, Banggai I, Muna I, Buton I

Tanygnathus heterurus (Rufous-tailed Parrot)
Celebes?

Tanygnathus gramineus (Blacklored Parrot)
Buru I

ECLECTUS

Eclectus roratus (Eclectus Parrot)

E. r. vosmaeri
N & C Moluccas

E. r. roratus
S Moluccas

E. r. westermani
not known

E. r. cornelia
Sumba I

E. r. riedeli
Tenimber Is

E. r. polychloros
Kei Is, New Guinea & islands

E. r. biaki
Biak I

E. r. aruensis
Aru Is

E. r. macgillivrayi
NE Queensland

E. r. solomonensis
Admiralty Is, Bismarck Archipelago, Solomon Is

PSITTRICHAS

Psittrichas fulgidus (Pesquet's Parrot)
Mts of New Guinea

PROSOPEIA

Prosopeia tabuensis (Red Shining Parrot)

P. t. atrogularis
Vanua Levu I, Kio I

P. t. koroensis
Koro I

P. t. taviunensis
Taviuni I, Ngamea I

P. t. tabuensis
Ngau I, Eua I

P. t. splendens
Kandavu I

Prosopeia personata (Masked Shining Parrot)
Viti Levu I

ALISTERUS

Alisterus scapularis (Australian King Parrot)

A. s. minor
NE Queensland

A. s. scapularis
Eastern Australia

Alisterus chloropterus (Green-winged King Parrot)

A. c. moszkowskii
N New Guinea

A. c. callopterus
C New Guinea

A. c. chloropterus
E New Guinea

Alisterus amboinensis (Amboina King Parrot)

A. a. amboinensis
Ambon I, Ceram I

A. a. sulaensis
Sula Is

A. a. versicolor
Peleng I

A. a. buruensis
Buru I

A. a. hypophonius
Halmahera I

A. a. dorsalis
NW New Guinea & islands

APROSMICTUS

Aprosmictus erythropterus (Red-winged Parrot)

A. e. papua
S New Guinea

A. e. coccineopterus
N Australia

A. e. erythropterus
interior Eastern Australia

Aprosmictus jonquillaceus (Timor Red-winged Parrot)

A. j. jonquillaceus
Timor I

A. j. wetterensis
Wetar I

POLYTELIS

Polytelis swainsonii (Superb Parrot)
interior New South Wales, N Victoria

Polytelis anthopeplus (Regent Parrot)

P. a. anthopeplus
NW Victoria

P. a. westralis
SW Australia

Polytelis alexandrae (Princess Parrot)
interior C & Western Australia

PURPUREICEPHALUS

Purpureicephalus spurius (Red-capped Parrot)
SW Australia

BARNARDIUS

Barnardius barnardi (Mallee Ringneck Parrot)
  B. b. macgillivrayi
    NW Queensland, E Northern Territory
  B. b. whitei
    Flinders Range, South Australia
  B. b. barnardi
    interior of SE Australia
Barnardius zonarius (Port Lincoln Parrot)
  B. z. occidentalis
    NW Western Australia
  B. z. semitorquatus
    SW Western Australia
  B.z. dundasi
    SW Australia
  B. z. myrtae
    C Australia
  B. z. zonarius
    S Australia

PLATYCERCUS

Platycercus caledonicus (Green Rosella)
    Tasmania, Bass Strait
Platycercus elegans (Crimson Rosella)
  P. e. nigrescens
    NE Queensland
  P. e. elegans
    SE Queensland to SE South Australia
  P. e. melanoptera
    Kangaroo I
  P. e. fleurieuensis
    Fleurieu Peninsula, S Australia
Platycercus flaveolus (Yellow Rosella)
    interior of SE Australia
Platycercus adelaidae (Adelaide Rosella)
    S South Australia
Platycercus eximius (Eastern Rosella)
  P. e. ceciliae
    SE Queensland, NE New South Wales
  P. e. eximius
    SE Australia
  P. e. diemenensis
    Tasmania
Platycercus adscitus (Pale-headed Rosella)
  P. a. adscitus
    N Queensland
  P. a. mackaiensis
    NE Queensland
  P. a. amathusiae
    NE Queensland
  P. a. palliceps
    C Queensland to N New South Wales
Platycercus venustus (Northern Rosella)
    NW & N Australia
Platycercus icterotis (Western Rosella)
  P. i. icterotis
    coast of SW Australia

  P. i. xanthogenys
    interior of SW Australia

PSEPHOTUS

Psephotus haematonotus (Red-rumped Parrot)
  P. h. caeruleus
    Innamincka, South Australia
  P. h. haematonotus
    interior of SE Australia
Psephotus varius (Mulga Parrot)
  P. v. varius
    interior of S Australia
  P. v. orientalis
    SW New South Wales, W Victoria
Psephotus haematogaster (Blue Bonnet)
  P. h. narethae
    SE Western Australia
  P. h. pallescens
    Lake Eyre Basin
  P. h. haematorrhous
    S Queensland, N New South Wales
  P. h. haematogaster
    W & S New South Wales, NW Victoria, SE South Australia
Psephotus chrysopterygius (Golden-shouldered Parrot)
  P. c. chrysopterygius
    S Cape York Peninsula
  P. c. dissimilis
    NE Northern Territory
Psephotus pulcherrimus (Paradise Parrot)
    C & S Queensland, N New South Wales

CYANORAMPHUS

Cyanoramphus unicolor (Antipodes Green Parakeet)
    Antipodes Is
Cyanoramphus novaezelandiae (Red-fronted Parakeet)
  C. n. novaezelandiae
    New Zealand, Auckland I
  C. n. cyanurus
    Kermadec Is
  C. n. chathamensis
    Chatham I
  C. n. hochstetteri
    Antipodes Is
  C. n. cookii
    Norfolk I
  C. n. saissetti
    New Caledonia
Cyanoramphus auriceps (Yellow-fronted Parakeet)
  C. a. auriceps
    New Zealand, Stewart I, Auckland I
  C. a. forbesi
    Chatham I

Cyanoramphus malherbi (Orange-fronted Parakeet)
South I, New Zealand

Cyanoramphus cornutus (Horned Parakeet)
C. c. cornutus
New Caledonia
C. c. uvaeensis
Ouvea I

NEOPHEMA
Neophema bourkii (Bourke's Parrot)
interior of C & S Australia

Neophema chrysostoma (Blue-winged Parrot)
SE Australia, Tasmania

Neophema elegans (Elegant Parrot)
SW & SE Australia

Neophema petrophila (Rock Parrot)
N. p. petrophila
coast of W Australia
N. p. zietzi
coast of S Australia

Neophema chrysogaster (Orange-bellied Parrot)
Tasmania, coast of W Victoria

Neophema pulchella (Turquoise Parrot)
SE Queensland to N Victoria

Neophema splendida (Scarlet-chested Parrot)
interior of S Australia

LATHAMUS
Lathamus discolor (Swift Parrot)
SE Australia, Tasmania

MELOPSITTACUS
Melopsittacus undulatus (Budgerigar)
Australia

PEZOPORUS
Pezoporus wallicus (Ground Parrot)
P. w. flaviventris
coast of SW Australia
P. w. wallicus
SE Australia, W Tasmania

GEOPSITTACUS
Geopsittacus occidentalis (Night Parrot)
interior of Australia

CORACOPSIS
Coracopsis vasa (Vasa Parrot)
C. v. drouhardi
W Madagascar
C. v. vasa
E Madagascar
C. v. comorensis
Great Comoro I, Moheli I, Anjouan I

Coracopsis nigra (Black Parrot)
C. n. libs
W Madagascar

C. n. nigra
E Madagascar
C. n. sibilans
Great Comoro I, Anjouan I
C. n. barklyi
Praslin I

PSITTACUS
Psittacus erithacus (Grey Parrot)
P. e. timneh
S Guinea to Ivory Coast
P. e. erithacus
SE Ivory Coast to W Kenya & N Angola
P. e. princeps
Principé I, Fernando Po I

POICEPHALUS
Poicephalus robustus (Cape Parrot)
P. r. fuscicollis
Gambia to N Ghana & Togo
P. r. suahelicus
Angola to S Zaire, Tanzania & Mozambique
P. r. robustus
E Cape Province to N Natal

Poicephalus gulielmi (Jardine's Parrot)
P. g. fantiensis
Liberia to Cameroun
P. g. gulielmi
S Cameroun to N Angola
P. g. permistus
C Kenya
P. g. massaicus
S Kenya, N Tanzania

Poicephalus cryptoxanthus (Brown-headed Parrot)
P. c. tanganyikae
C. Tanzania
P. c. zanzibaricus
Zanzibar I, Pemba I
P. c. cryptoxanthus
Natal to SE Kenya

Poicephalus crassus (Niam-Niam Parrot)
E Cameroun to SW Sudan

Poicephalus senegalus (Senegal Parrot)
P. s. senegalus
Senegal to Guinea, S Mali
P. s. versteri
Ivory Coast, Ghana to Nigeria
P. s. mesotypus
E & NE Nigeria, SW Chad, N Cameroun

Poicephalus rufiventris (Red-bellied Parrot)
P. r. rufiventris
C Ethiopia to NE Tanzania
P. r. pallidus
Somalia, E Ethiopia

Poicephalus meyeri (Meyer's Parrot)
P. m. meyeri
S Chad, NE Cameroun to W Ethiopia

P. m. saturatus
  Uganda, Kenya, W Tanzania
P. m. matschiei
  SE Kenya to Zambia, Malawi
P. m. transvaalensis
  N Mozambique, Transvaal
P. m. reichenowi
  N & C Angola, SW Zaire
P. m. damarensis
  S Angola, SW Africa
Poicephalus rueppellii (Rüppell's Parrot)
  S Angola, N Namibia
Poicephalus flavifrons (Yellow-faced Parrot)
P. f. flavifrons
  N & C Ethiopia
P. f. aurantiiceps
  SW Ethiopia

AGAPORNIS
Agapornis cana (Grey-headed Lovebird)
A. c. cana
  coast of Madagascar
A. c. ablectanea
  SW Madagascar
Agapornis pullaria (Red-faced Lovebird)
A. p. guineensis
  Guinea to N Zaire
A. p. pullaria
  S Ethiopia & S Sudan to NW Tanzania
A. p. ugandae
  SW Ethiopia to NW Tanzania
Agapornis taranta (Black-winged Lovebird)
  Ethiopia
Agapornis swinderniana (Black-collared Lovebird)
A. s. swinderniana
  Liberia
A. s. zenkeri
  Cameroun, Gabon to C Zaire
A. s. emini
  E Zaire, W Uganda
Agapornis roseicollis (Peach-faced Lovebird)
A. r. roseicollis
  Namibia, NW Cape Province
A. r. catumbella
  S Angola
Agapornis fischeri (Fischer's Lovebird)
  S Kenya, N Tanzania
Agapornis personata (Masked Lovebird)
  NE Tanzania
Agapornis lilianae (Nyasa Lovebird)
  NW Mozambique to E Zambia
Agapornis nigrigenis (Black-cheeked Lovebird)
  SW Zambia

Loriculus vernalis (Vernal Hanging Parrot)
  SW India to S Vietnam
Loriculus beryllinus (Ceylon Hanging Parrot)
  Sri Lanka
Loriculus philippensis (Philippine Hanging Parrot)
L. p. philippensis
  Luzon I, Marinduque I
L. p. mindorensis
  Mindoro I
L. p. bournsi
  Tablas I, Romblon I, Sibuyan I
L. p. panayensis
  Ticao I, Masbate I, Panay I
L. p. regulus
  Guimaras I, Negros I
L. p. chrysonotus
  Cebu I
L. p. worcesteri
  Samar I, Leyte I, Bohol I
L. p. siquijorensis
  Siquijor I
L. p. apicalis
  Mindanao I
L. p. dohertyi
  Basilan I
L. p. bonapartei
  Jolo I, Bongas I, Tawitawi Is
Loriculus galgulus (Blue-crowned Hanging Parrot)
  Malaysia, Borneo, Sumatra
Loriculus stigmatus (Celebes Hanging Parrot)
L. s. stigmatus
  Celebes
L. s. quadricolor
  Togian I
L. s. croconotus
  Butung I, Muna I
Loriculus amabilis (Moluccan Hanging Parrot)
L. a. amabilis
  Halmahera I, Batjan I
L. a. catamene
  Gt Sangi I
L. a. sclateri
  Sula Is
L. a. ruber
  Peling I, Banggai I
Loriculus exilis (Green Hanging Parrot)
  N & SE Celebes
Loriculus flosculus (Wallace's Hanging Parrot)
  Flores I

Loriculus pusillus (Yellow-throated Hanging Parrot)
Java, Bali I
Loriculus aurantiifrons (Orange-fronted Hanging Parrot)
L. a. aurantiifrons
Misol I
L. a. batavorum
Waigeu I, W Papuan Is, NW New Guinea
L. a. meeki
New Guinea, Fergusson I, Goodenough I
L. a. tener
Bismarck Archipelago

PSITTACULA
Psittacula eupatria (Alexandrine Parakeet)
P. e. eupatria
Sri Lanka, S India
P. e. nipalensis
E Afghanistan to Assam
P. e. magnirostris
Andaman Is
P. e. avensis
E Assam, Burma
P. e. siamensis
N & W Thailand, Indochina
Psittacula krameri (Rose-ringed Parakeet)
P. k. krameri
Senegal to S Sudan
P. k. parvirostris
Sudan to NW Somalia
P. k. borealis
W Pakistan, N India to C Burma
P. k. manillensis
S India, Sri Lanka
Psittacula echo (Mauritius Parakeet)
Mauritius
Psittacula himalayana (Slatyheaded Parakeet)
P. h. himalayana
E Afghanistan to N Assam
P. h. finschii
S Assam to SW China, N Indochina
Psittacula cyanocephala (Plum-headed Parakeet)
India, Sri Lanka
Psittacula roseata (Blossom-headed Parakeet)
P. r. roseata
N Assam, N Burma
P. r. juneae
S Assam, S Burma to Indochina
Psittacula intermedia (Intermediate Parrot)
N India
Psittacula columboides (Malabar Parakeet)
SW India

Psittacula calthorpae (Emerald-collared Parakeet)
Sri Lanka
Psittacula derbiana (Derbyan Parakeet)
NE Assam, SE Tibet
Psittacula alexandri (Moustached Parakeet)
P. a. alexandri
Java, Bali I
P. a. fasciata
N India to S China, Indochina
P. a. abbotti
Andaman Is
P. a. cala
Simalur I
P. a. major
Lasia I, Babi I
P. a. perionca
Nias I
P. a. dammermani
Karimon Java I
P. a. kangeanensis
Kangean I
Psittacula caniceps (Blyth's Parakeet)
Nicobar Is
Psittacula longicauda (Long-tailed Parakeet)
P. l. tytleri
Andaman Is
P. l. nicobarica
Nicobar Is
P. l. longicauda
Malaysia, Borneo, Sumatra
P. l. defontainei
Natuna Is, Riau Archipelago
P. l. modesta
Enggano I

ANODORHYNCHUS
Anodorhynchus hyacinthinus (Hyacinth Macaw)
SC Brazil
Anodorhynchus glaucus (Glaucous Macaw)
Paraguay, NE Argentina
Anodorhynchus leari (Lear's Macaw)
NE Brazil

CYANOPSITTA
Cyanopsitta spixii (Spix's Macaw)
EC Brazil

ARA
Ara ararauna (Blue and Yellow Macaw)
E Panama to Paraguay & S Brazil
Ara caninde (Caninde Macaw)
Bolivia, Paraguay, N Argentina
Ara militaris (Military Macaw)

A. m. mexicana
  N & C Mexico
A. m. militaris
  W Colombia, NE Ecuador, N Peru
A. m. boliviana
  Bolivia, NW Argentina
Ara ambigua (Buffon's Macaw)
  A. a. ambigua
    Nicaragua to W Colombia
  A. a, guayaquilensis
    W Ecuador
Ara macao (Scarlet Macaw)
  SC Mexico to Bolivia & C Brazil
Ara chloroptera (Green-winged Macaw)
  E Panama & N Argentina
Ara rubrogenys (Red-fronted Macaw)
  Bolivia
Ara auricollis (Yellow-collared Macaw)
  S Brazil, NW Argentina
Ara severa (Chestnut-fronted Macaw)
  A. s. castaneifrons
    E Panama to N Bolivia, C Brazil
  A. s. severa
    E Venezuela, the Guianas, NW Brazil
Ara manilata (Red-bellied Macaw)
  S Colombia to N & C Brazil
Ara maracana (Illiger's Macaw)
  E Brazil, NE Argentina
Ara couloni (Blue-headed Macaw)
  E Peru
Ara nobilis (Red-shouldered Macaw)
  A. n. nobilis
    the Guianas, E Venezuela, NE Brazil
  A. n. cumanensis
    C Brazil
  A. n. longipennis
    S Brazil

ARATINGA
Aratinga acuticaudata (Blue-crowned Conure)
  A. a. haemorrhous
    E Colombia, N Venezuela to C & SW Brazil
  A. a. neoxena
    Margarita I
  A. a. acuticaudata
    E Bolivia to N Argentina & Uruguay
  A. a. neumanni
    C Bolivia
Aratinga guarouba (Golden Conure)
  NE Brazil
Aratinga holochlora (Green Conure)
  A. h. brewsteri
    NW Mexico
  A. h. strenua
    W Mexico to NW Nicaragua
  A. h. holochlora
    E & S Mexico

A. h. rubritorquis
  E Guatemala, N Nicaragua
A. h. brevipes
  Socorro I
Aratinga finschi (Finsch's Conure)
  S Nicaragua to W Panama
Aratinga wagleri (Red-fronted Conure)
  A. w. wagleri
    NW Venezuela, Colombia
  A. w. transilis
    N Venezuela, E Colombia
  A. w. frontata
    W Ecuador, W Peru
  A. w. minor
    C & S Peru
Aratinga mitrata (Mitred Conure)
  A. m. mitrata
    C Peru to NW Argentina
  A. m. alticola
    C Peru
Aratinga erythrogenys (Red-masked Conure)
  W Ecuador, NW Peru
Aratinga leucophthalmus (White-eyed Conure)
  A. l. leucophthalmus
    the Guianas to Paraguay, Uruguay
  A. l. callogenys
    E Ecuador, NE Peru, NW Brazil
  A. l. propinquus
    SE Brazil, NE Argentina
  A. l. nicefori
    S Colombia
Aratinga chloroptera (Hispaniolan Conure)
  Hispaniola
Aratinga euops (Cuban Conure)
  Cuba
Aratinga auricapilla (Golden-capped Conure)
  A. a. auricapilla
    NE Brazil
  A. a. aurifrons
    SE Brazil
Aratinga jandaya (Jandaya Conure)
  NE Brazil
Aratinga solstitialis (Sun Conure)
  the Guianas, NE Brazil
Aratinga weddellii (Dusky-headed Conure)
  W Amazonia
Aratinga nana (Olive-throated Conure)
  A. n. nana
    Jamaica
  A. n. astec
    E Mexico to SE Costa Rica
  A. n. vicinalis
    NE Mexico
Aratinga canicularis (Orange-fronted Conure)

A. c. eburnirostrum
SW Mexico

A. c. clarae
WC & SW Mexico

A. c. canicularis
SW Mexico to W Costa Rica

Aratinga pertinax (Brown-throated Conure)

A. p. ocularis
W Panama

A. p. pertinax
Curaçao I

A. p. xanthogenia
Bonaire I

A. p. arubensis
Aruba I

A. p. aeruginosa
N Colombia, NW Venezuela

A. p. griseipecta
NE Colombia

A. p. lehmanni
E Colombia

A. p. tortugensis
Tortuga I

A. p. margaritensis
Margarita I, Los Frailes I

A. p. venezuelae
Venezuela

A. p. chrysophrys
SE Venezuela, S Guyana, NE Brazil

A. p. surinama
NE Venezuela, French Guiana, Surinam

A. p. chrysogenys
NW Brazil

A. p. paraensis
NC Brazil

Aratinga cactorum (Cactus Conure)

A. c. caixana
NE Brazil

A. c. cactorum
NE Brazil (South of *A. c. caixana*)

Aratinga aurea (Peach-fronted Conure)

A. a. aurea
C & S Brazil, E Bolivia

A. a. major
S Bolivia, NW Argentina

NANDAYUS
Nandayus nenday (Nanday Conure)
SE Bolivia, Paraguay, N Argentina

LEPTOSITTACA
Leptosittaca branickii (Golden-plumed Conure)
Colombia, Ecuador, Peru

OGNORHYNCHUS
Ognorhynchus icterotis (Yellow-eared Conure)
S Colombia, N Ecuador

RHYNCHOPSITTA
Rhynchopsitta pachyrhyncha (Thick-billed Panot)

R. p. pachyrhyncha
NW & C Mexico

R. p. terrisi
Nuevo Leon, Mexico

CYANOLISEUS
Cyanoliseus patagonus (Patagonian Conure)

C. p. byroni
C Chile

C. p. andinus
NW Argentina

C. p. patagonus
C & S Argentina

PYRRHURA
Pyrrhura cruentata (Blue-throated Conure)
E Brazil

Pyrrhura devillei (Blaze-winged Conure)
E Bolivia, SW Brazil

Pyrrhura frontalis (Maroon-bellied Conure)

P. f. frontalis
SE Brazil

P. f. kriegi
S & SE Brazil

P. f. chiripepe
Paraguay, Uruguay, N Argentina

Pyrrhura perlata (Pearly Conure)

P. p. lepida
NE Brazil

P. p. coerulescens
NE Brazil

P. p. anerythra
C Brazil

P. p. perlata
unknown

Pyrrhura rhodogaster (Crimson-bellied Conure)
C Brazil

Pyrrhura molinae (Green-cheeked Conure)

P. m. molinae
E Bolivia

P. m. phoenicura
NE Bolivia, SW Brazil

P. m. sordida
S Brazil

P. m. restricta
Chiquitos, Bolivia

P. m. australis
S Bolivia, NW Argentina

Pyrrhura hypoxantha (Yellow-sided Conure)
SW Brazil

Pyrrhura leucotis (White-eared Conure)

P. l. emma
N Venezuela

P. l. auricularis
NE Venezuela
P.l. pfrimeri
NE Brazil
P. l. griseipectus
NE Brazil
P. l. leucotis
E & SE Brazil
Pyrrhura picta (Painted Conure)
P. p. subandina
NW Colombia
P. p. caeruliceps
N Colombia
P. p. roseifrons
NW Brazil
P. p. picta
E Venezuela, the Guianas, N Brazil
P. p. amazonum
N Brazil
P. p. pantchenkoi
NW Venezuela
P. p. microtera
NC Brazil
P. p. lucianii
E Peru, Bolivia, W Brazil
Pyrrhura viridicata (Santa Marta Conure)
N Colombia
Pyrrhura egregia (Fiery-shouldered Conure)
P. e. egregia
W Guyana, SE Venezuela
P. e. obscura
Roraima, N Brazil
Pyrrhura melanura (Maroon-tailed Conure)
P. m. pacifica
SW Colombia
P.m. melanura
NE Peru, NW Brazil, S Venezuela
P. m. souancei
S Colombia, E Ecuador, N Peru
P. m. berlepschi
E Peru
P. m. chapmani
S Colombia
Pyrrhura rupicola (Black-capped Conure)
P. r. rupicola
C Peru
P. r. sandiae
SE Peru, W Brazil, N Bolivia
Pyrrhura albipectus (White-necked Conure)
SE Ecuador
Pyrrhura calliptera (Brown-breasted Conure)
C Colombia
Pyrrhura hoematotis (Red-eared Conure)
P. h. immarginata
N Venezuela

P. h. hoematotis
NC Venezuela
Pyrrhura rhodocephala (Rose-crowned Conure)
W Venezuela
Pyrrhura hoffmanni (Hoffman's Conure)
P. h. hoffmanni
S Costa Rica
P. h. gaudens
W Panama

ENICOGNATHUS
Enicognathus ferrugineus (Austral Conure)
E. f. minor
S Chile, SW Argentina
E. f. ferrugineus
S Chile, S Argentina, Tierra del Fuego
Enicognathus leptorhynchus (Slender-billed Conure)
C Chile

MYIOPSITTA
Myiopsitta monachus (Monk Parakeet)
M. m. luchsi
C Bolivia
M. m. cotorra
SE Bolivia, S Brazil, N Argentina
M. m. calita
W Argentina
M. m. monachus
SE Brazil, Uruguay, NE Argentina

BOLBORHYNCHUS
Bolborhynchus aymara (Sierra Parakeet)
E Andes from C Bolivia to NW Argentina
Bolborhynchus aurifrons (Mountain Parakeet)
B. a. robertsi
NW Peru
B. a. aurifrons
coast of W Andes of C Peru
B. a. margaritae
S Peru to N Chile & NW Argentina
B. a. rubrirostris
WC Argentina, C Chile
Bolborhynchus lineola (Barred Parakeet)
B. l. lineola
S Mexico to W Panama
B. l. tigrinus
NW Venezuela to SW Colombia, C Peru
Bolborhynchus orbygnesius (Andean Parakeet)
Peru & N Bolivia
Bolborhynchus ferrugineifrons (Rufous-fronted Parakeet)
WC Colombia

Forpus cyanopygius (Mexican Parrotlet)
   F. c. insularis
     Tres Marias Is
   F. c. pallidus
     SE Sonora, NW Mexico
   F. c. cyanopygius
     NW Mexico
Forpus passerinus (Green-rumped Parrotlet)
   F. p. cyanophanes
     N Colombia
   F. p. viridissimus
     Trinidad, N Venezuela
   F. p. passerinus
     the Guianas
   F. p. cyanochlorus
     N Brazil
   F. p. deliciosus
     NC & E Brazil
Forpus xanthopterygius (Blue-winged Parrotlet)
   F. x. spengeli
     NW Colombia
   F. x. crassirostris
     SE Colombia, NE Peru, NW Brazil
   F. x. olallae
     NW Brazil
   F. x. flavissimus
     NE Brazil
   F. x. flavescens
     SE & E Peru, E Bolivia
   F. x. xanthopterygius
     C & EC Brazil to Paraguay & NE Argentina
Forpus conspicillatus (Spectacled Parrotlet)
   F. c. conspicillatus
     E Panama, N & C Colombia
   F. c. metae
     C Colombia to W Venezuela
   F. c. caucae
     SW Colombia
Forpus sclateri (Sclater's Parrotlet)
   F. s. eidos
     S Venezuela & the Guianas, N Brazil,
      E Colombia
   F. s. sclateri
     N & W Brazil to S Colombia, E Peru &
      N Bolivia
Forpus coelestis (Pacific Parrotlet)
   W Ecuador, NW Peru
Forpus xanthops (Yellow-faced Parrotlet)
   NE Peru

BROTOGERIS
Brotogeris tirica (Plain Parakeet)
   E & SE Brazil
Brotogeris versicolurus (Canary-winged Parakeet)

   B. v. versicolurus
     E Ecuador to S French Guiana & N Brazil
   B. v. chiriri
     N Bolivia, N Argentina to E & S Brazil
   B. v. behni
     C & S Bolivia, NW Argentina
Brotogeris pyrrhopterus (Grey-cheeked Parakeet)
   W Ecuador, NW Peru
Brotogeris jugularis (Orange-chinned Parakeet)
   B. j. jugularis
     SW Mexico to N Colombia &
      NW Venezuela
   B. j. exsul
     SE Colombia, W Venezuela
Brotogeris cyanoptera (Cobalt-winged Parakeet)
   B. c. cyanoptera
     W Upper Amazonia
   B. c. gustavi
     N Peru
   B. c. beniensis
     N Bolivia
Brotogeris chrysopterus (Golden-winged Parakeet)
   B. c. chrysopterus
     E Venezuela, N Brazil, the Guianas
   B. c. tuipara
     N & NE Brazil
   B. c. chrysosema
     Madeira River, N Brazil
   B. c. solimoensis
     Upper Amazon River, N Brazil
   B. c. tenuifrons
     NW Brazil
Brotogeris sanctithomae (Tui Parakeet)
   B. s. sanctithomae
     C & W Brazil, SE Colombia, NE Peru
   B. s. takatsukasae
     NE Brazil

NANNOPSITTACA
Nannopsittaca panychlora (Tepui Parrotlet)
   E Venezuela, W Guyana

TOUIT
Touit batavica (Seven-coloured Parrotlet)
   N Venezuela, the Guianas, Trinidad
Touit huetii (Scarlet-shouldered Parrotlet)
   C Colombia, N Venezuela, NE Brazil,
     E Ecuador
Touit dilectissima (Red-winged Parrotlet)
   T. d. costaricensis
     SE Costa Rica, W Panama
   T. d. dilectissima
     E Panama, N & W Colombia, NW Ecuador
Touit purpurata (Sapphire-rumped Parrotlet)

T. p. purpurata
  S Venezuela, the Guianas, NE Brazil
T. p. viridiceps
  SE Colombia, NW & NC Brazil
Touit melanonota (Brown-backed Parrrotlet)
  SE Brazil
Touit surda (Golden-tailed Parrotlet)
T. s. ruficauda
  Recife, E Brazil
T. s. surda
  SE Brazil
Touit stictoptera (Spot-winged Parrotlet)
  SW Colombia, W Ecuador

PIONITES
Pionites melanocephala (Black-headed Caique)
P. m. pallida
  S Colombia to NE Peru
P. m. melanocephala
  E & S Venezuela, the Guianas, N Brazil
Pionites leucogaster (White-bellied Caique)
P. l. leucogaster
  N Brazil
P. l. xanthurus
  NW Brazil
P. l. xanthomeria
  W Brazil, E Ecuador

PIONOPSITTA
Pionopsitta pileata (Pileated Parrot)
  SE Brazil, E Paraguay, NE Argentina
Pionopsitta haematotis (Brown-hooded Parrot)
P. h. haematotis
  S Mexico to W Panama
P. h. coccinicollaris
  E Panama, NW Colombia
Pionopsitta pulchra (Rose-faced Parrot)
  W Colombia, W Ecuador
Pionopsitta barrabandi (Barraband's Parrot)
P. b. barrabandi
  N Upper Amazonia
P. b. aurantiigena
  W Upper Amazonia
Pionopsitta pyrilia (Saffron-headed Parrot)
  E Panama, N Colombia
Pionopsitta caica (Caica Parrot)
  E Venezuela, the Guianas, NE Brazil

GYPOPSITTA
Gypopsitta vulturina (Vulturine Parrot)
  Guyana, NE Brazil

HAPALOPSITTACA
Hapalopsittaca melanotis (Black-winged Parrot)

H. m. peruviana
  C Peru
H. m. melanotis
  WC Bolivia
Hapalopsittaca amazonina (Rusty-faced Parrot)
H. a. amazonina
  C Colombia to NW Venezuela
H. a. theresae
  NW Venezuela
H. a. fuertesi
  C Colombia
H. a. pyrrhops
  W Ecuador

GRAYDIDASCALUS
Graydidascalus brachyurus (Short-tailed Parrot)
  E Ecuador to NE Brazil

PIONUS
Pionus menstruus (Blue-headed Parrot)
P. m. rubrigularis
  S Costa Rica to W Ecuador
P. m. menstruus
  the Guianas, Upper Amazonia, E Peru
P. m. reichenowi
  NE Brazil
Pionus sordidus (Red-billed Parrot)
P. s. ponsi
  N Colombia, NW Venezuela
P. s. sordidus
  NW Venezuela
P. s. saturatus
  N Colombia
P. s. antelius
  NE Venezuela
P. s. corallinus
  C Colombia to N Bolivia
P. s. mindoensis
  W Ecuador
Pionus maximiliani (Scaly-headed Parrot)
P. m. maximiliani
  NE Brazil
P. m. melanoblepharus
  C Brazil, E Paraguay, NE Argentina
P. m. siy
  S Brazil, E Bolivia, Paraguay
P. m. lacerus
  NW Argentina
Pionus tumultuosus (Plum-crowned Parrot)
  Andes of E Peru & Bolivia
Pionus seniloides (White-headed Parrot)
  NW Venezuela to SW Ecuador
Pionus senilis (White-capped Parrot)
  E Mexico to W Panama
Pionus chalcopterus (Bronze-winged Parrot)
P. c. chalcopterus
  NW Venezuela, NE & C Colombia

P. c. cyanescens
SW Colombia, W Ecuador, NW Peru
Pionus fuscus (Dusky Parrot)
NE Colombia, S Venezuela, the Guianas,
NE Brazil

AMAZONA
Amazona collaria (Yellow-billed Amazon)
Jamaica
Amazona leucocephala (Cuban Amazon)
A. l. palmarum
W Cuba, Isle of Pines
A. l. leucocephala
C & E Cuba
A. l. bahamensis
Bahama Is
A. l. caymanensis
Gd Cayman I
A. l. hesterna
Little Cayman I, Cayman Brac I
Amazona ventralis (Hispaniolan Amazon)
Hispaniola
**Amazona albifrons (White-fronted
Amazon)**
A. a. saltuensis
NW Mexico
A. a. albifrons
WC Mexico to SW Guatemala
A. a. nana
SE Mexico to NW Costa Rica
**Amazona xantholora (Yellow-lored
Amazon)**
Yucatan, SE Mexico & Belize
Amazona agilis (Black-billed Amazon)
Jamaica
Amazona vittata (Puerto Rican Amazon)
Puerto Rico
Amazona tucumana (Tucuman Amazon)
SE Bolivia, N Argentina
Amazona pretrei (Red-spectacled Amazon)
SE Brazil, N Uruguay, NE Argentina
**Amazona viridigenalis (Green-cheeked
Amazon)**
NE Mexico
Amazona finschi (Lilac-crowned Amazon)
A. f. woodi
NW Mexico
A. f. finschi
WC & SW Mexico
Amazona autumnalis (Red-lored Amazon)
A. a. autumnalis
E Mexico to N Nicaragua
A. a. salvini
SE Nicaragua to W Colombia
A. a. lilacina
W Ecuador
A. a. diadema
NW Brazil
Amazona brasiliensis (Red-tailed Amazon)
SE Brazil
**Amazona dufresniana (Blue-cheeked
Amazon)**

A. d. dufresniana
SE Venezuela, the Guianas
A. d. rhodocorytha
E Brazil
Amazona festiva (Festive Amazon)
A. f. bodini
C Venezuela, NW Guyana
A. f. festiva
E Ecuador, NE Peru to C Brazil
Amazona xanthops (Yellow-faced Amazon)
E & C Brazil
**Amazona barbadensis (Yellow-shouldered
Amazon)**
A. b. barbadensis
coast of Venezuela, Aruba I
A. b. rothschildi
Bonaire I, Margarita I
Amazona aestiva (Blue-fronted Amazon)
A. a. aestiva
E Brazil
A. a. xanthopteryx
N & E Bolivia, Paraguay, N Argentina
**Amazona ochrocephala (Yellow-crowned
Amazon)**
A. o. oratrix
SW & S Mexico
A. o. tresmariae
Tres Marias Is
A. o. auropalliata
S Mexico to NW Costa Rica
A. o. parvipes
E Honduras, NE Nicaragua
A. o. belizensis
Belize
A. o. panamensis
W Panama, N Colombia, Pearl Is
A. o. nattereri
S Colombia to E Peru, W Brazil
A. o. xantholaema
Marajo I (N Brazil)
A. o. ochrocephala
W Colombia to Surinam, N Brazil,
Trinidad
**Amazona amazonica (Orange-winged
Amazon)**
A. a. amazonica
Colombia to N Bolivia & C & E Brazil
A. a. tobagensis
Trinidad, Tobago I
**Amazona mercenaria (Scaly-naped
Amazon)**
A. m. canipalliata
NW Venezuela, Colombia, C Ecuador
A. m. mercenaria
N Peru to N Bolivia
Amazona farinosa (Mealy Amazon)
A. f. guatemalae
S Mexico to Honduras

A. f. virenticeps
  Nicaragua to W Panama
A. f. inornata
  E Panama to NW Ecuador & W Venezuela
A. f. chapmani
  SE Colombia to NE Bolivia
A. f. farinosa
  S Venezuela, the Guianas, C & E Brazil,
  N Bolivia
Amazona vinacea (Vinaceous Amazon)
  SE Brazil, NE Argentina
Amazona versicolor (St Lucia Amazon)
  St Lucia I
Amazona arausica (Red-necked Amazon)
  Dominica I
Amazona guildingii (St Vincent Amazon)
  St Vincent I
Amazona imperialis (Imperial Amazon)
  Dominica I

DEROPTYUS
**Deroptyus accipitrinus (Hawk-headed
Parrot)**
  D. a. accipitrinus
    the Guianas, S Venezuela, N Brazil,
    NE Peru
  D. a. fuscifrons
    C & NE Brazil

TRICLARIA
**Triclaria malachitacea (Purple-bellied
Parrot)**
  SE Brazil

STRIGOPINAE

STRIGOPS
Strigops habroptilus (Kakapo)
  S South I, New Zealand

Cuculiformes

70 MUSOPHAGIDAE (TURACOS)

CORYTHAEOLA
Corythaeola cristata (Great Blue Turaco)
  Portuguese Guinea to N Angola &
  W Kenya

CRINIFER
Crinifer piscator (Grey Plantain-eater)
  Senegal to N Zaire
**Crinifer zonurus (Eastern Grey Plantain-
eater)**
  N Zaire, Ethiopia, NW Tanzania

CORYTHAIXOIDES
Corythaixoides concolor (Go-away Bird)
  C. c. pallidiceps
    Cabinda to C Namibia

C. c. concolor
  S Zaire & Tanzania to S Africa
**Corythaixoides personata (Bare-faced
Go-away Bird)**
  C. p. personata
    Ethiopia
  C. p. leopoldi
    E Zaire, Kenya to Zambia, Malawi
**Corythaixoides leucogaster (White-bellied
Go-away Bird)**
  Ethiopia to E Tanzania

MUSOPHAGA
Musophaga violacea (Violet Turaco)
  Gambia to Nigeria
Musophaga rossae (Lady Ross's Turaco)
  N Cameroun to Sudan, N Angola, Zambia

TAURACO
Tauraco corythaix (Knysna Turaco)
  T. c. buffoni
    Gambia to Sierra Leone
  T. c. persa ·
    Ivory Coast to N Angola
  T. c. zenkeri
    S Cameroun, N Gabon
  T. c. schuetii
    N Zaire
  T. c. emini
    NE Zaire, Uganda, SW Sudan
  T. c. fischeri
    Juba River & SE Kenya
  T. c. schalowi
    SW Kenya (isolate), C Angola, S Zaire
    to Malawi
  T. c. chalcolophus
    NC Tanzania
  T. c. zanzibaricus
    Zanzibar I
  T. c. livingstonii
    E Tanzania to N Natal & SE Zaire (isolate)
  T. c. phoebus
    E Transvaal
  T. c. corythaix
    Natal, SE Cape Province
**Tauraco erythrolophus (Red-crested
Turaco)**
  SW Zaire, Angola
**Tauraco bannermani (Bannerman's
Turaco)**
  N Cameroun
Tauraco macrorhynchus (Crested Turaco)
  T. m. macrorhynchus
    Sierra Leone to Ivory Coast
  T. m. verreauxi
    S Nigeria to W Zaire
Tauraco hartlaubi (Hartlaub's Turaco)
  Kenya, N Tanzania
Tauraco leucotis (White-cheeked Turaco)

T. l. leucotis
Ethiopia
T. l. donaldsoni
E Ethiopia, W Somalia
Tauraco ruspolii (Prince Ruspoli's Turaco)
S Ethiopia
Tauraco leucolophus (White-crested Turaco)
Central African Republic to S Sudan
Tauraco porphyreolophus (Violet-crested Turaco)
T. p. chlorochlamys
S Kenya to Mozambique
T. p. porphyreolophus
Rhodesia, E Transvaal, Natal
Tauraco johnstoni (Ruwenzori Turaco)
T. j. johnstoni
Ruwenzori Mtns
T. j. kivuensis
Kivu area, E Zaire
T. j. bredoi
Mt Kabobo

71 CUCULIDAE (CUCKOOS)

CUCULINAE

CLAMATOR
Clamator glandarius (Great Spotted Cuckoo)
Spain to Iran, NE & S Africa
Clamator coromandus (Red-winged Crested Cuckoo)
Himalayas to S China, Java, Borneo
Clamator jacobinus (Black & White Cuckoo)
C. j. serratus
Sengal to S Africa, N India, Burma
C. j. jacobinus
S India, Sri Lanka
Clamator levaillanti (Levaillant's Cuckoo)
Senegal to Somalia & S Africa

PACHYCOCCYX
Pachycoccyx audeberti (Thick-billed Cuckoo)
P. a. validus
Guinea to S Sudan, S Zaire, NE Tanzania
P. a. canescens
Angola to Malawi & N Cape Province
P. a. audeberti
Madagascar

CUCULUS
Cuculus crassirostris (Celebes Hawk Cuckoo)
N & C Celebes
Cuculus sparverioides (Large Hawk Cuckoo)
C. s. sparverioides
Himalayas, SE Asia, to Philippine Is & Celebes

C. s. bocki
Malaysia, Sumatra, Borneo
Cuculus varius (Common Hawk Cuckoo)
C. v. varius
India (except NW)
C. v. ciceliae
Sri Lanka
Cuculus vagans (Small Hawk Cuckoo)
Malaysia, Thailand, Java, Borneo
Cuculus fugax (Fugitive Hawk Cuckoo)
C. f. hyperythrus
NE Asia, China, Indochina
C. f. nisicolor
E Himalayas to Malaysia, Sumatra
C. f. pectoralis
Luzon I, Cebu I, Mindoro I
C. f. fugax
Malaysia, Sumatra, Java, Borneo
Cuculus solitarius (Red-chested Cuckoo)
Guinea to Ethiopia & Cape Province
Cuculus cafer (Black Cuckoo)
C. c. cafer
Gambia to Ethiopia & South Africa
C. c. gabonensis
Nigeria to N Zaire, Uganda
Cuculus micropterus (Short-winged Cuckoo)
C. m. micropterus
India to E Asia & E Asian islands
C. m. ognevi
NE Asia
C. m. concretus
Sumatra, Java, Borneo
Cuculus canorus (European Cuckoo)
C. c. canorus
Europe & W Siberia » E & S Africa
C. c. bangsi
Iberia, N Africa
C. c. kleinschmidti
Corsica, Sardinia
C. c. johanseni
C Asia
C. c. telephonus
NE Asia & Japan » India & New Guinea
C. c. fallax
C & S China
C. c. bakeri
NW China, Burma, Indochina
C. c. subtelephonus
Transcaspia to W Chinese Turkestan
C. c. gularis
Gambia to Sudan & N South Africa
Cuculus saturatus (Oriental Cuckoo)
C. s. horsfieldi
C & E Asia » SE Asia
C. s. lepidus
Malaysia & Sumatra to Timor I

C. s. saturatus
 S Himalayas to S China
Cuculus poliocephalus (Little Cuckoo)
 C. p. rochii
  Madagascar
 C. p. poliocephalus
  Himalayas to India, C China, Japan
 C. p. insulindae
  Borneo
Cuculus pallidus (Pallid Cuckoo)
 C. p. occidentalis
  W Australia, Northern Territory
 C. p. pallidus
  E & S Australia, Tasmania

CERCOCOCCYX
Cercococcyx mechowi (Dusky Long-tailed Cuckoo)
 Sierra Leone to N Uganda & N Angola
Cercococcyx olivinus (Olive Long-tailed Cuckoo)
 Ghana, Cameroun to N Angola
Cercococcyx montanus (Mountain Long-tailed Cuckoo)
 C. m. montanus
  Ruwenzori Mtns
 C. m. patulus
  N Tanzania

PENTHOCERYX
Penthoceryx sonneratii (Banded Bay Cuckoo)
 P. s. sonneratii
  India, Burma, Thailand, S Indochina
 P. s. waiti
  Sri Lanka
 P. s. malayanus
  N & C Malaysia
 P. s. fasciolatus
  S Malaysia, Sumatra, Borneo, Philippine Is
 P. s. musicus
  Java

CACOMANTIS
Cacomantis merulinus (Plaintive Cuckoo)
 C. m. passerinus
  W Himalayas, India, Sri Lanka
 C. m. querulus
  E Himalayas to S China, Indochina
 C. m. threnodes
  Malaysia, Sumatra, Borneo
 C. m. subpallidus
  Nias I
 C. m. lanceolatus
  Java
 C. m. merulinus
  Philippine Is
 C. m. celebensis
  Celebes

Cacomantis variolosus (Brush Cuckoo)
 C. v. sepulcralis
  Malaysia, Borneo, Sumatra to Flores I, Philippine Is
 C. v. everetti
  Basilan I, Sulu Archipelago
 C. v. virescens
  Celebes, Tukangbesi Is
 C. v. oblitus
  N Moluccas
 C. v. aeruginosus
  Buru I
 C. v. stresemanni
  Ceram I, Ambon I
 C. v. infaustus
  W Papuan Is, N & C New Guinea
 C. v. chivae
  Biak I
 C. v. obscuratus
  Numfor I
 C. v. fortior
  Goodenough I, Fergusson I
 C. v. oreophilus
  S New Guinea
 C. v. blandus
  Admiralty Is
 C. v. websteri
  New Hanover
 C. v. macrocercus
  New Britain, New Ireland
 C. v. addendus
  Kulambangra I, Malaita I, Rubiana I
 C. v. variolosus
  N & E Australia » Moluccas, New Guinea
Cacomantis castaneiventris (Chestnut-breasted Cuckoo)
 C. c. arfakianus
  W Papuan Is, NW New Guinea
 C. c. weiskei
  C & E New Guinea
 C. c. castaneiventris
  Cape York Peninsula
Cacomantis heinrichi (Heinrich's Brush Cuckoo)
 Halmahera I, Batjan I
Cacomantis pyrrhophanus (Fan-tailed Cuckoo)
 C. p. prionurus
  E & S Australia, Tasmania
 C. p. excitus
  New Guinea
 C. p. meeki
  Solomon Is
 C. p. schistaceigularis
  New Hebrides
 C. p. pyrrhophanus
  New Caledonia, Loyalty Is
 C. p. simus
  Fiji Is

Rhamphomantis megarhynchus (Little Long-billed Cuckoo)
R. m. sanfordi
Waigeu I
R. m. megarhynchus
NW & N New Guinea, Aru Is

MISOCALIUS
Misocalius osculans (Black-eared Cuckoo)
Interior of Australia

CHRYSOCOCCYX
Chrysococcyx cupreus (African Emerald Cuckoo)
C. c. cupreus
Gambia to S Ethiopia
C. c. intermedius
Cameroun to S Zaire, N Kenya
C. c. sharpei
S Angola to Zambia & Cape Province
Chrysococcyx flavigularis (Yellow-throated Green Cuckoo)
Sierra Leone to N & C Zaire
Chrysococcyx klaas (Klaas' Cuckoo)
C. k. klaas
Senegal to Ethiopia & Cape Province
C. k. arabicus
S Arabia
Chrysococcyx caprius (Didric Cuckoo)
Senegal to Ethiopia & Cape Province

CHALCITES
Chalcites maculatus (Emerald Cuckoo)
Himalayas to China, SE Asia
Chalcites xanthorhynchus (Violet Cuckoo)
C. x. xanthorhynchus
NE India to SE Asia, Borneo & Java
C. x. limborgi
S Burma
C. x. bangueyensis
Banguey I
C. x. amethystinus
Philippine Is
Chalcites basalis (Horsfield's Bronze Cuckoo)
S Australia » Gtr Sunda Is
Chalcites lucidus (Golden-Bronze Cuckoo)
C. l. plagosus
S Australia to Lesser Sunda Is & New Guinea
C. l. lucidus
New Zealand to Solomon Is
C. l. layardi
New Caledonia, Loyalty Is
C. l. aeneus
New Hebrides, Banks Is
C. l. harterti
Rennell I, Bellona I

Chalcites malayanus (Malay Emerald Cuckoo)
C. m. malayanus
Malaysia, Sumatra, Philippine Is
C. m. albifrons
Java
C. m. aheneus
Borneo
C. m. jungei
C & S Celebes
C. m. rufomerus
Lesser Sunda Is
C. m. salvadorii
Babar I
C. m. misoriensis
Biak I
C. m. poecilurus
W Papuan Is, New Guinea
C. m. russatus
Cape York Peninsula
C. m. minutillus
Melville I, N Australia
Chalcites crassirostris (Moluccan Bronze Cuckoo)
Moluccas, Kei Is, New Guinea
Chalcites ruficollis (Reddish-throated Bronze Cuckoo)
NW New Guinea
Chalcites meyeri (Meyer's Bronze Cuckoo)
NW New Guinea

CALIECHTHRUS
Caliechthrus leucolophus (White-crowned Koel)
Salawati I, New Guinea

SURNICULUS
Surniculus lugubris (Drongo-Cuckoo)
S. l. dicruroïdes
N & C India to S China, Indochina
S. l. stewarti
SW India, Sri Lanka
S. l. barussarum
Malaysia, Sumatra, Borneo
S. l. minimus
Palawan I, Balabac I
S. l. lugubris
Java, Bali I
S. l. velutinus
Philippine Is
S. l. musschenbroeki
Celebes

MICRODYNAMIS
Microdynamis parva (Black-capped Cuckoo)
M. p. parva
SW & E New Guinea
M. p. grisescens
N New Guinea

EUDYNAMYS
Eudynamys scolopacea (Koel)
  E. s. scolopacea
    India, Sri Lanka, Nicobar Is
  E. s. chinensis
    W & S China, Indochina
  E. s. harterti
    Hainan I
  E. s. simalurensis
    Simalur I, Babi I
  E. s. malayana
    Assam to Thailand, Malaysia, Sumatra to
    Flores I
  E. s. paraguena
    Palawan I, Busuanga I
  E. s. dolosa
    Andaman Is
  E. s. mindanensis
    Philippine Is, Sangir Is, Talaut Is
  E. s. frater
    Calayan I, Fuga I
  E. s. melanorhyncha
    Celebes, Togian I, Peling I
  E. s. facialis
    Sula Is
  E. s. everetti
    Sumba I to Timor I & Roma I, Kei Is
  E. s. corvina
    N Moluccas
  E. s. orientalis
    S Moluccas
  E. s. salvadorii
    Bismarck Archipelago
  E. s. alberti
    Solomon Is
  E. s. rufiventer
    W Papuan Is, & N & C New Guinea
  E. s. minima
    S New Guinea
Eudynamys cyanocephala (Australian Koel)
  E. s. subcyanocephala
    NW Australia, W Queensland
  E. s. cyanocephala
    N Queensland, N New South Wales

URODYNAMIS
Urodynamis taitensis (Long-tailed Koel)
  New Zealand & SW Pacific Is

SCYTHROPS
Scythrops novaehollandiae (Channel-billed Cuckoo)
  Flores I to E Australia

PHAENICOPHAEINAE

COCCYZUS
Coccyzus pumilus (Dwarf Cuckoo)
  W Venezuela, E Colombia

Coccyzus cinereus (Ash-coloured Cuckoo)
  Paraguay, S Brazil to C Argentina
Coccyzus erythrophthalmus (Black-billed Cuckoo)
  S Canada » NW South America
Coccyzus americanus (Yellow-billed Cuckoo)
  C. a. americanus
    C & E USA » N South America
  C. a. occidentalis
    SW Canada » W Mexico
Coccyzus euleri (Pearly-breasted Cuckoo)
  NE South America
Coccyzus minor (Mangrove Cuckoo)
  C. m. palloris
    coast of W Mexico to E Panama, Tres
    Marias Is
  C. m. continentalis
    coast of E Mexico to Panama
  C. m. cozumelae
    Cozumel I
  C. m. maynardi
    S Florida, Bahama Is
  C. m. caymanensis
    Cayman Is
  C. m. nesiotes
    Jamaica
  C. m. teres
    Greater Antilles
  C. m. rileyi
    Barbuda I, Antigua I
  C. m. dominicae
    Montserrat I, Guadeloupe I, Dominica I
  C. m. vincentis
    Martinique I, St Lucia I, St Vincent I
  C. m. grenadensis
    Grenada I, Bequia I
  C. m. abbotti
    Old Providence I, St Andrews I
  C. m. minor
    N South America
  C. m. ferrugineus
    Cocos I (E Pacific)
Coccyzus melacoryphus (Dark-billed Cuckoo)
  South America, Galapagos Is
Coccyzus lansbergi (Grey-capped Cuckoo)
  Colombia, Venezuela, W Ecuador

PIAYA
Piaya rufigularis (Rufous-breasted Cuckoo)
  Hispaniola
Piaya pluvialis (Chestnut-bellied Cuckoo)
  Jamaica
Piaya cayana (Squirrel Cuckoo)
  P. c. extima
    NW Mexico

P. c. mexicana
W Mexico
P. c. stirtoni
W coast of Guatemala to NW Costa Rica
P. c. thermophila
E Mexico to Panama
P. c. mesura
E Colombia, E Ecuador
P. c. nigricrissa
W Colombia, W Ecuador, NW & EC Peru
P. c. mehleri
NE Colombia, N Venezuela
P. c. circe
W Venezuela
P. c. insulana
Trinidad
P. c. cayana
E & S Venezuela, the Guianas, N Brazil
P. c. boliviana
EC Peru to N Bolivia
P. c. obscura
C Brazil
P. c. hellmayri
C & E Brazil
P. c. pallescens
E Brazil
P. c. cearae
Ceara, Brazil
P. c. cabanisi
SC Brazil
P. c. macroura
SE Brazil, NE Argentina, Paraguay,
Uruguay
P. c. mogenseni
S Bolivia, NW Argentina
Piaya melanogaster (Black-bellied Cuckoo)
P. m. melanogaster
N & C Amazonia
P. m. ochracea
SE Colombia, S Peru
Piaya minuta (Little Cuckoo)
P. m. panamensis
E Panama
P. m. gracilis
W Colombia, W Ecuador
P. m. minuta
N & W Amazonia
P. m. chaparensis
N Bolivia

SAUROTHERA
Saurothera merlini (Great Lizard Cuckoo)
S. m. bahamensis
New Providence I, Eleuthera I
S. m. andria
Andros I
S. m. merlini
Cuba

S. m. decolor
Isle of Pines
Saurothera vetula (Jamaican Lizard Cuckoo)
S. v. vetula
Jamaica
S. v. petersi
Gonave I
S. v. longirostris
Hispaniola, Tortuga I
S. v. saonae
Saona I
S. v. vieilloti
Puerto Rico

CEUTHMOCHARES
Ceuthmochares aereus (Yellow-bill)
C. a. flavirostris
Senegal to W Nigeria
C. a. aereus
Nigeria to N Angola
C. a. intermedius
N Zaire & Uganda to W Tanzania
C. a. australis
Kenya to Malawi & Natal

RHOPODYTES
Rhopodytes diardi (Lesser Green-billed Malcoha)
R. d. diardi
S Malaysia, Sumatra
R. d. borneensis
Borneo
Rhopodytes sumatranus (Rufous-bellied Malcoha)
R. s. sumatranus
S Burma, Malaysia, Sumatra
R. s. minor
Borneo
Rhopodytes tristis (Greater Green-billed Malcoha)
R. t. tristis
W Himalayas to N Burma
R. t. saliens
Burma, N Indochina, S China
R. t. longicaudatus
S Burma, Malaysia, S Indochina
R. t. hainanus
Hainan I
R. t. elongatus
Sumatra
R. t. kangeangensis
Kangean I
Rhopodytes viridirostris (Small Green-billed Malcoha)
S India, Sri Lanka

TACCOCUA
Taccocua leschenaultii (Sirkeer Cuckoo)

T. l. sirkee
  NW India
T. l. infuscata
  W Himalayas
T. l. affinis
  NE India
T. l. leschenaultii
  S India

RHINORTHA
Rhinortha chlorophaea (Raffles' Malcoha)
  R. c. chlorophaea
    S Burma, Malaysia, Sumatra
  R. c. fuscigularis
    N Borneo & islands
  R. c. mayri
    S Borneo

ZANCLOSTOMUS
Zanclostomus javanicus (Red-billed Malcoha)
  Z. j. pallidus
    S Burma, Malaysia, Sumatra, Borneo
  Z. j. factus
    Tanahmasa I
  Z. j. javanicus
    Java
  Z. j. natunensis
    Natuna Is

RHAMPHOCOCCYX
Rhampococcyx calyorhynchus (Celebes Malcoha)
  R. c. calyorhynchus
    N Celebes, Togian I
  R. c. centralis
    C Celebes
  R. c. meridionalis
    S Celebes
  R. c. rufiloris
    Buton I
Rhamphococcyx curvirostris (Chestnut-breasted Malcoha)
  R. c. erythrognathus
    S Burma, Malaysia, Sumatra
  R. c. oeneicaudus
    Islands off SW Sumatra
  R. c. curvirostris
    W & C Java
  R. c. deningeri
    E Java, Bali I
  R. c. borneensis
    Borneo, Natuna Is
  R. c. harringtoni
    Palawan I, Balabac I

PHAENICOPHAEUS
Phaenicophaeus pyrrhocephalus (Red-faced Malcoha)
  S India, Sri Lanka

DASYLOPHUS
Dasylophus superciliosus (Rough-crested Cuckoo)
  N Philippine Is

LEPIDOGRAMMUS
Lepidogrammus cumingi (Scale-feathered Cuckoo)
  Luzon I, Marinduque I

CROTOPHAGINAE

CROTOPHAGA
Crotophaga major (Greater Ani)
  E Panama to N Argentina, Trinidad
Crotophaga ani (Smooth-billed Ani)
  Bahama Is, Antilles, N South America
Crotophaga sulcirostris (Groove-billed Ani)
  C. s. pallidula
    S Baja California
  C. s. sulcirostris
    Mexico to C South America, Curaçao I, Trinidad

GUIRA
Guira guira (Guira Cuckoo)
  S & E Brazil, N Argentina, Uruguay

NEOMORPHINAE

TAPERA
Tapera naevia (Striped Cuckoo)
  T. n. excellens
    SE Mexico to Panama
  T. n. naevia
    N South America, Trinidad
  T. n. chochi
    S Brazil, N Argentina

MOROCOCCYX
Morococcyx erythropygus (Lesser Ground Cuckoo)
  M. e. dilutus
    W Mexico
  M. e. simulans
    Guerrero, Mexico
  M. e. mexicanus
    SW & S Mexico
  M. e. erythropygus
    S Mexico to N Costa Rica
  M. e. macrourus
    Guatemala

DROMOCOCCYX
Dromococcyx phasianellus (Pheasant Cuckoo)
  D. p. rufigularis
    SE Mexico to Colombia
  D. p. phasianellus
    C & S Brazil, Paraguay, Bolivia

Dromococcyx pavoninus (Pavonine Cuckoo)
  D. p. perijanus
    NW Venezuela
  D. p. pavoninus
    N South America, intermittently

GEOCOCCYX
Geococcyx california (Road-runner)
  S USA to CS Mexico
Geococcyx velox (Lesser Road-runner)
  G. v. melanchima
    W Mexico
  G. v. velox
    EC Mexico
  G. v. affinis
    El Salvador, W Guatemala
  G. v. pallidus
    Yucatan, E Guatemala
  G. v. longisignum
    Honduras, N Nicaragua

NEOMORPHUS
Neomorphus geoffroyi (Rufous-vented Ground Cuckoo)
  N. g. salvini
    Nicaragua to W Colombia
  N. g. aequatorialis
    E Ecuador
  N. g. australis
    S Peru, NW Bolivia
  N. g. geoffroyi
    C & S Brazil
  N. g. dulcis
    E Brazil
Neomorphus squamiger (Scaled Ground Cuckoo)
  N. s. squamiger
    EC Brazil
  N. s. iungens
    C Brazil
Neomorphus radiolosus (Banded Ground Cuckoo)
  NW Ecuador
Neomorphus rufipennis (Rufous-winged Ground Cuckoo)
  N. r. rufipennis
    NE Venezuela
  N. r. nigrogularis
    S Venezuela, Guyana, N Brazil
Neomorphus pucheranii (Red-billed Ground Cuckoo)
  N. p. pucheranii
    W Brazil, E Ecuador, NE Peru
  N. p. lepidophanes
    E Peru, SW Brazil

CARPOCOCCYX
Carpococcyx radiceus (Ground Cuckoo)
  C. r. radiceus
    Borneo

  C. r. viridis
    Sumatra
Carpococcyx renauldi (Coral-billed Ground Cuckoo)
  SE Thailand, Indochina

COUINAE

COUA
Coua gigas (Giant Madagascar Coucal)
  W & S Madagascar
Coua coquereli (Coquerel's Madagascar Coucal)
  W Madagascar
Coua serriana (Rufous-breasted Madagascar Coucal)
  NE Madagascar
Coua reynaudii (Red-footed Madagascar Coucal)
  NW & E Madagascar
Coua cursor (Running Coucal)
  SW Madagascar
Coua ruficeps (Red-capped Madagascar Coucal)
  C. r. ruficeps
    NW Madagascar
  C. r. olivaceiceps
    SW Madagascar
Coua cristata (Crested Madagascar Coucal)
  C. c. dumonti
    W Madagascar
  C. c. cristata
    N & E Madagascar
  C. c. pyropyga
    SW Madagascar
  C. c. maxima
    SE Madagascar
Coua verreauxi (Southern Crested Madagascar Coucal)
  SW Madagascar
Coua caerulea (Blue Madagascar Coucal)
  NW & E Madagascar

CENTROPODINAE

CENTROPUS
Centropus milo (Buff-headed Coucal)
  C. m. albidiventris
    Vella Lavella I, Kulambangra I, Gizo I, Rendova I
  C. m. milo
    Florida I, Guadalcanal I
Centropus goliath (Large Coucal)
  N Moluccas
Centropus violaceus (Violet Coucal)
  New Ireland, New Britain
Centropus menbecki (Greater Coucal)
  C. m. menbecki
    W Papuan islands, New Guinea
  C. m. jobiensis
    Japen I

C. m. aruensis
Aru Is
Centropus ateralbus (New Britain Coucal)
New Britain, New Ireland
Centropus chalybeus (Biak Island Coucal)
Biak I, Numfor I
Centropus phasianius (Pheasant Coucal)
C. p. propinquus
N New Guinea
C. p. nigricans
SE New Guinea
C. p. obscuratus
Goodenough I, Fergusson I, E New Guinea
C. p. thierfelderi
S New Guinea
C. p. phasianius
NE Australia
C. p. macrourus
N & mid Western Australia
Centropus spilopterus (Moluccan Coucal)
Kei Is
Centropus bernsteini (Bernstein's Coucal)
C. b. manam
Vulcan I
C. b. bernsteini
W New Guinea
Centropus chlororhynchus (Ceylon Coucal)
SW Sri Lanka
Centropus rectunguis (Short-toed Coucal)
Malaysia, Sumatra, Borneo
Centropus steerii (Steere's Coucal)
Mindoro I
Centropus sinensis (Common Crow-Pheasant)
C. s. parroti
C & S India, Sri Lanka
C. s. sinensis
N India to S China
C. s. intermedius
Burma, S Thailand, Indochina, Hainan I
C. s. eurycercus
Malaysia, Sumatra, Borneo, Palawan I
C. s. bubutus
Java, Bali I
C. s. anonymous
C Philippine Is
C. s. kangeanensis
Kangean I
C. s. andamanensis
Cocos I, Andaman Is
Centropus nigrorufus (Sunda Coucal)
Sumatra, Java
Centropus viridis (Philippine Coucal)
C. v. viridis
Philippine Is
C. v. carpenteri
Batan I

C. v. mindorensis
Mindoro I, Semirara I
Centropus toulou (Black Coucal)
C. t. toulou
Madagascar
C. t. insularis
Aldabra I
C. t. assumptionis
Assumption I **e?**
Centropus bengalensis (Lesser Coucal)
C. b. bengalensis
India, Burma to Indochina
C. b. lignator
SE China, Taiwan
C. b. javanensis
Malaysia, Sumatra, Java, Borneo, Philippine Is
C. b. sarasinorum
Celebes, Lesser Sunda Is
C. b. medius
Moluccas
Centropus grillii (Black-chested Coucal
C. g. grillii
Guinea to Kenya & Malawi
C. g. caeruleiceps
S Ethiopia
C. g. wahlbergi
Natal
Centropus epomidis (Rufous-bellied Coucal)
Ghana, S Nigeria
Centropus leucogaster (Black-throated Coucal)
C. l. leucogaster
Sierra Leone to Nigeria
C. l. efulenensis
W Cameroun, Gabon
C. l. neumanni
N Zaire
Centropus anselli (Gabon Coucal)
S Cameroun to Angola, S Zaire
Centropus monachus (Blue-headed Coucal)
C. m. occidentalis
Ghana to NE Zaire
C. m. angolensis
N Angola
C. m. fischeri
Sudan, Uganda, N Kenya
C. m. monachus
Ethiopia, Kenya
C. m. songweensis
S Tanzania, N Malawi
C. m. cupreicaudus
S Angola to S Tanzania, Namibia
Centropus senegalensis (Senegal Coucal)
C. s. aegyptius
Egypt

C. s. senegalensis
Senegal to Sudan, Angola, Tanzania
C. s. incertus
NW Kenya
C. s. flecki
Botswana, Rhodesia, Transvaal
Centropus superciliosus (White-browed Coucal)
C. s. loandae
Angola to Uganda & Malawi
C. s. superciliosus
Sudan to Somalia & Tanzania
C. s. sokotrae
Socotra I
C. s. burchellii
S Tanzania to Cape Province
Centropus melanops (Black-faced Coucal)
C. m. melanops
Leyte I, Bohol I, Mindanao I, Basilan I
C. m. banken
Samar I
Centropus celebensis (Celebes Coucal)
C. c. celebensis
N Celebes
C. c. rufescens
C & S Celebes
Centropus unirufus (Rufous Coucal)
C. u. unirufus
Luzon I
C. u. polillensis
Polillo Is

Strigiformes

72 TYTONIDAE (BARN OWLS)

TYTONINAE

TYTO
Tyto soumagnei (Madagascar Grass Owl)
Madagascar
Tyto alba (Barn Owl)
T. a. schmitzi
Madeira
T. a. gracilirostris
E Canary Is
T. a. alba
W Europe
T. a. ernesti
Corsica, Sardinia
· T. a. guttata
C Europe
T. a. detorta
Cape Verde Is
T. a. affinis
Gambia to Sudan & Cape Province
T. a. poensis
Fernando Po I

T. a. thomensis
Sao Thomé I
T. a. erlangeri
Arabia to Syria & Iraq
T. a. hypermetra
Comoro Is, Madagascar
T. a. stertens
India, N Burma, Sri Lanka
T. a. javanica
Burma to Indochina, Java to Timor I
T. a. deroepstorffi
S Andaman Is
T. a. sumbaensis
Sumba I
T. a. everetti
Savu Is
T. a. kuehni
Kisar I
T. a. bellonae
Bellona I
T. a. meeki
SE New Guinea, Vulcan I, Dampier I
T. a. delicatula
Australia, Solomon Is
T. a. crassirostris
Boang I
T. a. interposita
Santa Cruz I, Banks Is, New Hebrides
T. a. lulu
New Caledonia, Fiji Is, Tonga I, Samoa Is
T. a. pratincola
C & NE USA to E Nicaragua
T. a. guatemalae
W Guatemala to Panama
T. a. lucayana
Bahama Is
T. a. furcata
Cuba, Cayman Is, Jamaica
T. a. bargei
Curaçao I
T. a. subandeana
Colombia, Ecuador
T. a. contempta
W Colombia to Venezuela & Peru
T. a. hellmayri
the Guianas, N Brazil
T. a. tuidara
C Brazil to Chile, Argentina
T. a. glaucops
Tortuga I, Hispaniola
T. a. nigrescens
Dominica I
T. a. insularis
S Lesser Antilles
T. a. punctatissima
Galapagos Is

Tyto *rosenbergii* (Celebes Barn Owl)
  Celebes
Tyto *nigrobrunnea* (Sula Is Barn Owl)
  Sula Is
Tyto *inexspectata* (Minahassa Barn Owl)
  N Celebes
Tyto *novaehollandiae* (Masked Owl)
  T. n. sorocula
    Tenimber Is
  T. n. cayelii
    Buru I
  T. n. manusi
    Manus I
  T. n. kimberli
    S New Guinea, N Australia
  T. n. novaehollandiae
    SE Australia
  T. n. perplexa
    SW Australia
  T. n. castanops
    Tasmania
Tyto *aurantia* (New Britain Barn Owl)
  New Britain
Tyto *tenebricosa* (Sooty Owl)
  T. t. arfaki
    New Guinea, Japen I
  T. t. tenebricosa
    E & S Australia
Tyto *capensis* (Grass Owl)
  T. c. cameroonensis
    Cameroun
  T. c. liberatus
    Kenya
  T. c. damarensis
    S Angola, N Namibia
  T. c. capensis
    SE Zaire to Cape Province
Tyto *longimembris* (Eastern Grass Owl)
  T. l. longimembris
    India, possibly to Indochina
  T. l. melli
    Kwangsi, Kwangtung
  T. l. chinensis
    Fukien
  T. l. amauronota
    Philippine Is
  T. l. walleri
    N & E Australia, Celebes? Fiji?
  T. l. papuensis
    SE New Guinea

PHODILINAE

PHODILUS
Phodilus *badius* (Bay Owl)
  P. b. saturatus
    Nepal to Indochina
  P. b. parvus
    Billiton I

  P. b. badius
    C Burma to Malaysia, Sumatra, Java,
    Borneo
  P. b. assimilis
    Sri Lanka
  P. b. arixuthus
    Bunguran I
Phodilus *prigoginei* (Tanzanian Bay Owl)
  E Zaire, NW Tanzania

73 STRIGIDAE (OWLS)

BUBONINAE

OTUS
Otus *sagittatus* (White-fronted Scops Owl)
  S Burma, Thailand, Malaysia
Otus *rufescens* (Rufous Scops Owl)
  O. r. malayensis
    Malaysia
  O. r. rufescens
    Sumatra, Java, Borneo
  O. r. burbidgei
    Jolo I
Otus *icterorhynchus* (Sandy Scops Owl)
  O. i. icterorhynchus
    Ghana
  O. i. holerythrus
    S Cameroun to N Zaire
Otus *ireneae* (Sokoke Scops Owl)
  SE Kenya
Otus *spilocephalus* (Spotted Scops Owl)
  O. s. huttoni
    W Himalayas
  O. s. spilocephalus
    E Himalayas to Burma
  O. s. latouchei
    SE China, N Indochina
  O. s. hambroecki
    Taiwan
  O. s. siamensis
    Thailand, S Indochina
  O. s. vulpes
    Malaysia
  O. s. stresemanni
    Sumatra
  O. s. angelinae
    Java
  O. s. luciae
    Borneo
Otus *balli* (Andaman Scops Owl)
  Andaman Is
Otus *alfredi* (Flores Scops Owl)
  Flores I
Otus *brucei* (Striated Scops Owl)
  Middle East to Pakistan
Otus *scops* (Scops Owl)
  O. s. scops
    W Europe to Russia & C Africa

O. s. cycladum
Cyclades Is, Crete
O. s. cyprius
Cyprus
O. s. turanicus
Transcaspia, N Iran
O. s. pulchellus
Caucasus, Russia to C Asia & NW India
O. s. stictonotus
Manchuria to China, Taiwan
O. s. japonicus
N Japan
O. s. modestus
Assam to S China, Indochina
O. s. malayanus
Malaysia
O. s. sunia
Himalayas, N India
O. s. rufipennis
C & S India
O. s. leggei
Sri Lanka
O. s. interpositus
Borodino Is
O. s. elegans
Riukiu Is (?)
O. s. botelensis
Botel Tobago I
O. s. calayensis
Calayan I
O. s. longicornis
Luzon I
O. s. mindorensis
Mindoro I
O. s. romblonis
Banton I, Romblon I
O. s. cuyensis
Cuyo I
O. s. mantananensis
Mantanani I
Otus umbra (Mentaur Scops Owl)
O. u. umbra
Simalur I
O. u. enganensis
Enggano I
Otus senegalensis (African Scops Owl)
O. s. senegalensis
Senegal to Sudan
O. s. pygmea
S Sudan, NW Ethiopia
O. s. caecus
C & S Ethiopia, Somalia, N Kenya
O. s. socotranus
Socotra I
O. s. pamelae
Saudi Arabia
O. s. ugandae
W Uganda, N & NE Zaire

O. s. feae
Annobon I
O. s. graueri
E Kenya, Tanzania
O. s. hendersonii
Angola, SW Zaire
O. s. pusillus
Mozambique, E Malawi, E Rhodesia
O. s. intermedius
Namibia to S Mozambique & N Natal
O. s. latipennis
Cape Province
Otus flammeolus (Flammulated Owl)
O. f. flammeolus
SW Canada to W Mexico
O. f. rarus
Guatemala
Otus brookii (Rajah's Scops Owl)
O. b. brookii
Java, Borneo
O. b. solokensis
Sumatra
Otus rutilus (Madagascar Scops Owl)
O. r. pembaensis
Pemba I
O. r. capnodes
Anjouan I **e?**
O. r. rutilus
Madagascar
Otus manadensis (Celebes Scops Owl)
O. m. sibutuensis
Sibutu I
O. m. steerei
Tumindao I
O. m. manadensis
Celebes
O. m. mendeni
Peling I
O. m. siaoensis
Siao I
O. m. sulaensis
Sula Mangoli I
O. m. kalidupae
Kalidupa I
O. m. morotensis
Morotai I, Ternate I
O. m. leucospilus
Halmahera I, Batjan I
O. m. bouruensis
Buru I
O. m. magicus
Ceram I, Ambon I
O. m. albiventris
Lombok I, Sumbawa I, Flores I, Lomblen I
O. m. tempestatis
Wetar I
Otus beccarii (Biak I Scops Owl)
Biak I

Otus silvicola (Lesser Sunda Scops Owl)
Flores I, Sumbawa I
Otus whiteheadi (Whitehead's Scops Owl)
Luzon I
Otus insularis (Bare-legged Scops Owl)
Mahé I **e?**
Otus bakkamoena (Collared Scops Owl)
O. b. ussuriensis
S Manchuria to Korea, Sakhalin I
O. b. semitorques
Kurile Is, Japan, Quelpart I
O. b. pryeri
Hachijo I, Okinawa I
O. b. aurorae
N China
O. b. erythrocampe
S China, N Vietnam
O. b. glabripes
Taiwan
O. b. umbratilis
Hainan I
O. b. lettia
E Himalayas to Burma, N Thailand
O. b. manipurensis
Manipur, Assam
O. b. plumipes
NW Himalayas
O. b. deserticolor
SE Saudi Arabia, S Iran, Pakistan
O. b. gangeticus
NW & NC India
O. b. marathae
C India
O. b. bakkamoena
S India, Sri Lanka
O. b. condorensis
Pulo Condor I
O. b. kangeana
Kangean I
O. b. cnephaeus
Malaysia
O. b. hypnodes
Singapore, Sumatra
O. b. lempiji
Java, Bali, Borneo
O. b. mentawi
Siberut I, Sipora I, Pagi Is
O. b. fuliginosus
Palawan I
O. b. boholensis
Bohol I
O. b. everetti
Samar I, Mindanao I, Basilan I
Otus asio (Screech Owl)
O. a. kennicotti
SE Alaska to W Washington
O. a. brewsteri
S Washington to NW California

183

O. a. bendirei
W California
O. a. macfarlanei
S British Columbia to Idaho
O. a. inyoensis
E California to N Utah
O. a. maxwelliae
E Montana to C Colorado
O. a. aikeni
C Colorado to N Mexico
O. a. swenki
SC Canada to Oklahoma
O. a. naevius
EC Canada to Georgia
O. a. asio
E Virginia to Kansas
O. a. floridanus
Florida & Gulf Coast
O. a. hasbroucki
C Oklahoma to N Texas
O. a. mychophilus
NC Utah, N Arizona
O. a. mccallii
S Texas, NE Mexico
O. a. cineraceus
C Arizona to NW Texas
O. a. cardonensis
W Baja California
O. a. yumanensis
SW Arizona
O. a. clazus
S California
O. a. quercinus
SW California
O. a. xantusi
S Baja California
O. a. vinaceus
NE Sinaloa
O. a. sinaloensis
SE Sonora, NW Sinaloa
Otus trichopsis (Whiskered Owl)
O. t. aspersus
SE Arizona, NW Mexico
O. t. pinosus
E Mexico
O. t. trichopsis
W & S Mexico
O. t. guerrerensis
S W Mexico
O. t. mesamericanus
Guatemala, El Salvador
O. t. pumilus
Honduras
Otus barbarus (Bearded Screech Owl)
N Guatemala
Otus guatemalae (Vermiculated Screech Owl)

O. g. tomlini
NW Mexico
O. g. hastatus
W Mexico
O. g. cassini
N Vera Cruz
O. g. fuscus
C Vera Cruz
O. g. thompsoni
Yucatan, Campeche
O. g. guatemalae
SE Vera Cruz, Guatemala, Honduras
U. g. dacrysistactus
N Nicaragua
O. g. vermiculatus
Costa Rica, Panama
O. g. napensis
E Ecuador
O. g. roraimae
SE Venezuela, S Guyana
Otus roboratus (West Peruvian Screech Owl)
NW Peru
Otus cooperi (Pacific Screech Owl)
O. c. chiapensis
S Mexico
O. c. cooperi
El Salvador, NW Costa Rica
Otus choliba (Tropical Screech Owl)
O. c. luctisonus
Costa Rica to NW Colombia
O. c. margaritae
N Colombia, N Venezuela, Margarita I
O. c. crucigerus
Upper Amazonia, C Brazil
O. c. alticola
C Colombia
O. c. duidae
SE Venezuela
O. c. decussatus
SC & E Brazil
O. c. choliba
S Brazil, Paraguay, N Argentina, Uruguay
O. c. wetmorei
SE Bolivia, W Paraguay, NW Argentina
Otus atricapillus (Long-tufted Screech Owl)
C & SE Brazil
Otus ingens (Rufescent Screech Owl)
O. i. colombianus
C Colombia
O. i. ingens
Ecuador
O. i. venezuelanus
W Venezuela
Otus watsonii (Tawny-bellied Screech Owl)
O. w. watsonii
Northern & Upper Amazonia

O. w. usta
C Brazil to N Argentina
Otus nudipes (Puerto Rico Screech Owl)
O. n. nudipes
Puerto Rico
O. n. newtoni
St Thomas I, St John I, St Croix I
Otus clarkii (Bare-legged Screech Owl)
Costa Rica, Panama
Otus albogularis (White-throated Screech Owl)
O. a. albogularis
Colombia, N Ecuador
O. a. obscurus
NW Venezuela
O. a. meridensis
W Venezuela
O. a. aequatorialis
E Ecuador
Otus minimus (Least Screech Owl)
W Bolivia
Otus leucotis (White-faced Scops Owl)
O. l. leucotis
Senegal to Ethiopia & Kenya
O. l. margarethae
Sudan
O. l. granti
S Zaire & Tanzania to Cape Province
Otus hartlaubi (Sao Thomé Scops Owl)
Sao Thomé I

PYRROGLAUX
Pyrroglaux podargina (Palau Scops Owl)
Palau Is
MIMIZUKU
Mimizuku gurneyi (Giant Scops Owl)
Marinduque I, Mindanao I
JUBULA
Jubula lettii (Akun Scops Owl)
Liberia to N Zaire
LOPHOSTRIX
Lophostrix cristata (Crested Owl)
L. c. stricklandi
S Mexico to W Colombia
L. c. wedeli
E Panama
L. c. cristata
the Guianas, N & W Brazil
BUBO
Bubo virginianus (Great Horned Owl)
B. v. algistus
W Alaska
B. v. lagophonus
C Alaska to NE Oregon & Idaho
B. v. saturatus
SW Alaska to California
B. v. pacificus
S Oregon, California

B. v. wapacuthu
  W & C Canada
B. v. occidentalis
  WC Canada to WC USA
B. v. pallescens
  SW USA to NC Mexico
B. v. heterocnemis
  E Canada
B. v. virginianus
  SE Canada, EC USA
B. v. elachistus
  S Baja California
B. v. mayensis
  C Mexico to W Panama
B. v. elutus
  E Colombia
B. v. colombianus
  C Colombia
B. v. nigrescens
  W Ecuador
B. v. scotinus
  E Venezuela
B. v. deserti
  E Brazil
B. v. nacurutu
  Peru & NW Brazil to Tierra del Fuego

Bubo bubo (Eagle Owl)
B. b. bubo
  Scandinavia, W Europe to W Russia
B. b. hispanus
  Iberian peninsula
B. b. interpositus
  SW Russia to Syria
B. b. ruthenus
  SE Russia
B. b. sibiricus
  WC & C Asia
B. b. yenisseensis
  C & EC Siberia
B. b. dauricus
  N Mongolia
B. b. jakutensis
  NE Siberia
B. b. ussuriensis
  Lower Amur, Ussuriland
B. b. inexpectatus
  Manchuria, N China
B. b. tenuipes
  Korea, S Kurile Is, Hokkaido I
B. b. borissowi
  Sakhalin I
B. b. turcomanus
  Turkestan
B. b. zaissanensis
  SC Asia
B. b. nikolskii
  Iran, Iraq

B. b. tibetanus
  C Tibet to NW China
B. b. kiautschensis
  C & E China
B. b. jarlandi
  SE Yunnan
B. b. swinhoei
  SE China
B. b. hemachalana
  W Tien Shan, W Himalayas
B. b. bengalensis
  N & C India
B. b. ascalaphus
  semi desert of N Africa
B. b. desertorum
  desert of N Africa
Bubo capensis (Cape Eagle Owl)
B. c. dillonii
  Ethiopia
B. c. mackinderi
  Kenya, Tanzania
B. c. capensis
  Natal, Cape Province
Bubo africanus (Spotted Eagle Owl)
B. a. cinerascens
  French Guinea to Somalia
B. a. africanus
  Uganda & Kenya to Angola
B. a. milesi
  S Saudi Arabia
Bubo poensis (Nduk Eagle Owl)
B. p. poensis
  Ghana to N Zaire
B. p. vosseleri
  N Tanzania
Bubo nipalensis (Forest Eagle Owl)
B. n. nipalensis
  Himalayas to C Burma, India
B. n. blighi
  Sri Lanka
Bubo sumatrana (Malay Eagle Owl)
B. s. sumatrana
  S Burma, Malaysia, Sumatra
B. s. strepitans
  Java, Bali, Borneo
Bubo shelleyi (Banded Eagle Owl)
  Liberia to S Cameroun
Bubo lacteus (Verreaux's Eagle Owl)
  Senegal to Ethiopia to Cape Province
Bubo coromandus (Dusky Eagle Owl)
B. c. coromandus
  N & C India
B. c. klossii
  S Burma, Malaysia
Bubo leucostictus (Akun Eagle Owl)
  Sierra Leone to Zaire

Pseudoptynx philippensis (Philippine Horned Owl)
P. p. philippensis
Luzon I, Cebu I
P. p. mindanensis
Mindanao I

KETUPA
Ketupa blakistoni (Blakiston's Fish Owl)
K. b. piscivorus
W Manchuria
K. b. doerriesi
NE Asia
K. b. karafutonis
Sakhalin I
K. b. blakistoni
Hokkaido I
Ketupa zeylonensis (Brown Fish Owl)
K. z. semenowi
Israel to NW India
K. z. leschenault
India, Burma, Thailand
K. z. zeylonensis
Sri Lanka
K. z. orientalis
NE Burma to SE China, Indochina
Ketupa flavipes (Tawny Fish Owl)
Himalayas to W China, Indochina
Ketupa ketupu (Malay Fish Owl)
K. k. ketupu
Malaysia, Sumatra, Java, Borneo
K. k. aagaardi
S Assam to S Thailand & Vietnam
K. k. pageli
NE Borneo
K. k. minor
Nias I

SCOTOPELIA
Scotopelia peli (Pel's Fishing Owl)
Senegal to Ethiopia & Cape Province
Scotopelia ussheri (Rufous Fishing Owl)
Sierra Leone to Ghana
Scotopelia bouvieri (Vermiculated Fishing Owl)
S Cameroun, Congo, N Angola

PULSATRIX
Pulsatrix perspicillata (Spectacled Owl)
P. p. saturata
S Mexico to W Panama
P. p. chapmani
E Costa Rica to W Ecuador
P. p. perspicillata
N South America
P. p. trinitatis
Trinidad
P. p. pulsatrix
E Brazil, Paraguay
P. p. boliviana
S Bolivia, N Argentina
Pulsatrix koeniswaldiana (Tawny-browed Owl)
S Brazil, NE Argentina
Pulsatrix melanota (Band-bellied Owl)
P. m. melanota
E Ecuador, E Peru
P. m. philoscia
Bolivia

NYCTEA
Nyctea scandiaca (Snowy Owl)
N Asia, N Canada, Holarctic Region

SURNIA
Surnia ulula (Hawk Owl)
S. u. ulula
N Europe, N Asia
S. u. tianschanica
Tien Shan
S. u. caparoch
W & C Canada, N USA

GLAUCIDIUM
Glaucidium passerinum (Eurasian Pygmy Owl)
G. p. passerinum
N Europe, W Asia
G. p. orientale
E Siberia, Manchuria
Glaucidium gnoma (Northern Pygmy Owl)
G. g. grinnelli
SE Alaska to N California
G. g. swarthi
Vancouver I
G. g. californicum
C British Columbia to S California
G. g. pinicola
WC USA
G. g. hoskinsii
Baja California
G. g. gnoma
N & C Mexico
G. g. cobanense
Guatemala
Glaucidium siju (Cuban Pygmy Owl)
G. s. siju
Cuba
G. s. vittatum
Isle of Pines
Glaucidium minutissimum (Least Pygmy Owl)
G. m. oberholseri
C & S Sinaloa
G. m. palmarum
W Mexico
G. m. griseiceps
E Guatemala, Belize, E Honduras

G. m. rarum
  Costa Rica, Panama
G. m. minutissimum
  Guyana, Surinam, Brazil
G. m. griscomi
  SW Morelos, NE Guerrero
G. m. occultum
  E Oaxaca, Chiapas
G. m. sanchezi
  S San Luis Potosi
Glaucidium jardinii (Jardine's Pygmy Owl)
G. j. jardinii
  Colombia, Ecuador, Peru, Venezuela
G. j. costaricanum
  Costa Rica, Panama
Glaucidium brasilianum (Ferruginous Pygmy Owl)
G. b. cactorum
  S Arizona, W Mexico
G. b. ridgwayi
  S Texas to C Panama
G. b. medianum
  N Colombia
G. b. phaloenoides
  N Venezuela, Trinidad
G. b. olivaceum
  Mt Augun-tepui (Venezuela)
G. b. margaritae
  Margarita I
G. b. duidae
  Mt Duida (Venezuela)
G. b. ucayalae
  SE Colombia to Peru
G. b. brasilianum
  W & S Amazonia, NE Argentina
G. b. pallens
  E Bolivia, W Paraguay, NW Argentina
G. b. tucumanum
  W Argentina
G. b. nanum
  S Chile, S Argentina
Glaucidium perlatum (Pearl-spotted Owlet)
G. p. perlatum
  Senegal to Cameroun
G. p. kilimense
  E & NE Africa
G. p. licua
  Southern Africa
Glaucidium tephronotum (Red-chested Owlet)
G. t. tephronotum
  Ghana
G. t. pycrafti
  S Cameroun
G. t. medje
  N Zaire

G. t. lukolelae
  C Zaire
G. t. kivuense
  E Zaire
G. t. elgonense
  Mt Elgon (Kenya)
Glaucidium capense (Barred Owlet)
G. c. castaneum
  E Zaire
G. c. scheffleri
  SE Kenya, NE Tanzania
G. c. ngamiense
  S Zaire, NE Angola
G. c. robertsi
  W Tanzania, W Mozambique
G. c. capense
  Angola, Southern Africa
Glaucidium brodiei (Collared Pygmy Owl)
G. b. brodiei
  Himalayas to N Indochina & Malaysia
G. b. pardalotum
  Taiwan
G. b. peritum
  Sumatra
G. b. borneense
  Borneo
Glaucidium radiatum (Jungle Owlet)
G. r. radiatum
  India, Sri Lanka
G. r. malabaricum
  SW India
Glaucidium cuculoides (Cuckoo Owl)
G. c. castanonotum
  Sri Lanka
G. c. cuculoides
  W Himalayas
G. c. rufescens
  NE India, N Burma
G. c. brügeli
  S Burma, S Thailand
G. c. austerum
  NE Assam
G. c. delacouri
  N Indochina
G. c. deignani
  SE Thailand, S Indochina
G. c. whitelyi
  W, C & SE China, NE Vietnam
G. c. persimile
  Hainan I
G. c. castanopterum
  Java, Bali
Glaucidium sjostedti (Sjostedt's Barred Owlet)
  Cameroun to C Zaire

XENOGLAUX
Xenoglaux loweryi (Long-whiskered Owlet)
N Peru

MICRATHENE
Micrathene whitneyi (Elf Owl)
M. w. whitneyi
  SW USA, NW Mexico
M. w. idonea
  Texas, C Mexico
M. w. sanfordi
  Baja California
M. w. graysoni
  Socorro I

UROGLAUX
Uroglaux dimorpha (Papuan Hawk Owl)
New Guinea, Japen I

NINOX
Ninox rufa (Rufous Owl)
N. r. humeralis
  New Guinea, Waigeu I
N. r. aruensis
  Aru Is
N. r. rufa
  N Australia
N. r. queenslandica
  E Queensland
Ninox strenua (Powerful Owl)
New South Wales, Victoria
Ninox connivens (Barking Owl)
N. c. rufostrigata
  N Moluccas
N. c. assimilis
  E New Guinea, Vulcan I, Dampier I
N. c. occidentalis
  NW Australia, N Territory
N. c. peninsularis
  Cape York Peninsula
N. c. enigma
  C North Queensland
N. c. addenda
  SW Australia
N. c. connivens
  S & E Australia
Ninox novaeseelandiae (Boobook Owl)
N. n. rudolfi
  Sumba I
N. n. plesseni
  Alor I
N. n. fusca
  Timor I
N. n. cinnamomina
  Babar I
N. n. remigialis
  Kei Is
N. n. pusilla
  S New Guinea

N. n. ocellata
  N Australia, Melville I
N. n. marmorata
  S & SW Australia
N. n. lurida
  NE Queensland
N. n. boobook
  E Australia
N. n. leucopsis
  Tasmania
N. n. albaria
  Lord Howe I
N. n. undulata
  Norfolk I
N. n. venatica
  North I, New Zealand
N. n. novaeseelandiae
  South I, New Zealand
Ninox scutulata (Brown Hawk Owl)
N. s. ussuriensis
  NE Asia
N. s. scutulata
  Japan, E China to Lesser Sunda Is
N. s. burmanica
  S Assam to Malaysia & Indochina
N. s. lugubris
  N & C India
N. s. hirsuta
  S India, Sri Lanka
N. s. obscura
  Andaman Is, Nicobar Is
N. s. malaccensis
  S Malaysia, Sumatra, Bangka I
N. s. javanensis
  W Java
N. s. borneensis
  Borneo, N Natuna Is
N. s. randi
  Philippine Is
Ninox affinis (Andaman Brown Hawk Owl)
N. a. affinis
  Andaman Is
N. a. isolata
  Nicobar Is
Ninox superciliaris (White-browed Owl)
W Madagascar
Ninox philippensis (Philippine Hawk Owl)
N. p. philippensis
  Luzon I, Marinduque I, Leyte I
N. p. proxima
  Ticao I, Masbate I
N. p. centralis
  Panay I, Guimaras I, Negros I, Siquijor I
Ninox spilonota (Spotted Hawk Owl)
Mindoro I, Tablas I, Sibuyan I
Ninox spilocephala (Tweeddale's Hawk Owl)

N. s. mindorensis
  Mindoro I
N. s. spilocephala
  Mindanao I, Basilan I
N. s. reyi
  Jolo I, Bongao I
N. s. everetti
  Siasi I

Ninox perversa (Ochre-bellied Hawk Owl)
  Celebes

Ninox squamipila (Indonesian Hawk Owl)
N. s. hypogramma
  N Moluccas
N. s. hantu
  Buru I
N. s. squamipila
  Ceram I
N. s. forbesi
  Tenimber Is
N. s. natalis
  Christmas I

Ninox theomacha (Brown Owl)
N. t. hoedtii
  Waigeu I, Misol I
N. t. goldii
  D'Entrecasteaux Archipelago
N. t. theomacha
  New Guinea
N. t. rosseliana
  Louisiade Archipelago

Ninox punctulata (Speckled Hawk Owl)
  Celebes

Ninox meeki (Admiralty Is Hawk Owl)
  Admiralty Is

Ninox solomonis (New Ireland Hawk Owl)
N. s. superior
  New Hanover
N. s. solomonis
  New Britain, New Ireland

Ninox odiosa (New Britain Hawk Owl)
  New Britain

Ninox jacquinoti (Solomon Is Hawk Owl)
N. j. eichhorni
  Bougainville I, Choiseul I
N. j. mono
  Mono I
N. j. jacquinoti
  Ysabel I, St George I
N. j. floridae
  Florida I
N. j. granti
  Guadalcanal I
N. j. malaitae
  Malaita I
N. j. roseoaxillaris
  San Cristobal I

GYMNOGLAUX
Gymnoglaux lawrencii (Bare-legged Owl)
G. l. exsul
  W Cuba, Isle of Pines
G. l. lawrencii
  C & E Cuba

SCELOGLAUX
Sceloglaux albifacies (White-faced Owl)
  South I, New Zealand

ATHENE
Athene noctua (Little Owl)
A. n. vidalii
  W Europe
A. n. noctua
  C Europe
A. n. sarda
  Sardinia
A. n. indigena
  N Iran, Greece, S Russia
A. n. glaux
  N Africa
A. n. saharae
  S Morocco to N Saudi Arabia
A. n. solitudinis
  C Sahara
A. n. lilith
  Syria, Israel
A. n. bactriana
  Transcaspia to Pakistan
A. n. orientalis
  NE Russian & Chinese Turkestan
A. n. ludlowi
  Tibet
A. n. impasta
  Kokonor, W Kansu
A. n. plumipes
  EC Asia
A. n. spilogastra
  E Sudan, NE Ethiopia
A. n. somaliensis
  E Ethiopia, Somalia

Athene brama (Spotted Little Owl)
A. b. albida
  Iran
A. b. indica
  N & C India
A. b. brama
  S India
A. b. pulchra
  Burma to SW Indochina

Athene blewitti (Forest Spotted Owlet)
  C India

SPEOTYTO
Speotyto cunicularia (Burrowing Owl)
S. c. hypugaea
  SW Canada to W Mexico

S. c. rostrata
Clarion I
S. c. floridana
C & S Florida, Bahama Is
S. c. troglodytes
Hispaniola, Gonave I
S. c. arubensis
Aruba I
S. c. brachyptera
Margarita I, N Venezuela
S. c. minor
S Guyana, S Surinam, NE Brazil
S. c. carrikeri
E Colombia
S. c. tolimae
W Colombia
S. c. pichinchae
W Ecuador
S. c. punensis
SW Ecuador, NW Peru
S. c. intermedia
W Peru
S. c. apurensis
NC Venezuela
S. c. juninensis
C Peru, W Bolivia
S. c. boliviana
Bolivia
S. c. nanodes
SW Peru
S. c. grallaria
E & S Brazil
S. c. cunicularia
S Bolivia & S Brazil to Tierra del Fuego

CICCABA
Ciccaba virgata (Mottled Owl)
C. v. tamaulipensis
S Tamaulipas
C. v. squamulata
W Mexico
C. v. centralis
S Mexico to W Panama
C. v. virgata
E Panama to Venezuela & Ecuador,
Trinidad
C. v. macconnelli
the Guianas
C. v. superciliaris
NC & NE Brazil
C. v. minuscula
W Colombia
C. v. borelliana
S Brazil, Paraguay, NE Argentina
Ciccaba nigrolineata (Black & White Owl)
S Mexico to W Ecuador
Ciccaba huhula (Black-banded Owl)
the Guianas to C & S Brazil
Ciccaba albitarsus (Rufous-banded Owl)

C. a. albitarsus
Colombia, Ecuador, Venezuela
C. a. tertia
Bolivia
Ciccaba woodfordii (African Wood Owl)
C. w. umbrina
Ethiopia
C. w. nigricantior
Kenya, Tanzania
C. w. nuchalis
Sierra Leone to N Angola
C. w. bohndorffi
Central African Republic to Sudan
& S Zaire
C. w. woodfordii
Zambia & Malawi to Cape Province

STRIGINAE

STRIX
Strix butleri (Hume's Tawny Owl)
SW Asia
Strix seloputo (Spotted Wood Owl)
S. s. seloputo
S Burma to S Indochina, Malaysia, Java
S. s. baweana
Bawean I
S. s. wiepkeni
Palawan I
Strix ocellata (Mottled Wood Owl)
S. o. ocellata
Himalayas, N India
S. o. grandis
W India
S. o. grisescens
NC India
Strix leptogrammica (Brown Wood Owl)
S. l. newarensis
Himalayas, N Burma, N Thailand
S. l. indranee
S India
S. l. connectens
C India
S. l. ochrogenys
Sri Lanka
S. l. maingayi
S Burma, S Thailand, Malaysia
S. l. ticehursti
SE China, N Indochina
S. l. laotiana
S Indochina
S. l. caligata
Taiwan, Hainan I
S. l. myrtha
Sumatra
S. l. nyctiphasma
Banjak I
S. l. niasensis
Nias I

S. l. chaseni
  Billiton I
S. l. bartelsi
  W & C Java
S. l. vaga
  N Borneo
S. l. leptogrammica
  S & C Borneo
Strix aluco (Tawny Owl)
S. a. sylvatica
  Britain, W Europe
S. a. mauritanica
  N Africa, Syria, Israel
S. a. aluco
  Scandinavia, C & E Europe
S. a. volhyniae
  SW Russia
S. a. siberiae
  E Russia, W Siberia
S. a. willkonskii
  Caucasus
S. a. obscurata
  S Russia, N Iran
S. a. sanctinicolae
  Iraq, W & SW Iran
S. a. härmsi
  Russian Turkestan
S. a. biddulphi
  Pakistan, NW India
S. a. nivicola
  Himalayas, S & W China
S. a. yamadae
  S Taiwan
S. a. ma
  NE China, Korea
Strix occidentalis (Spotted Owl)
S. o. caurina
  S British Colombia to N California
S. o. occidentalis
  S California
S. o. lucida
  SW USA to C Mexico
Strix varia (Barred Owl)
S. v. varia
  S Canada, EC USA
S. v. georgica
  S & SE USA
S. v. helveola
  SC Texas
S. v. sartorii
  N & C Mexico
S. v. fulvescens
  S Mexico, W Guatemala, Honduras
Strix hylophila (Rusty Barred Owl)
  Brazil, Paraguay, N Argentina
Strix rufipes (Rufous-legged Owl)
S. r. chacoensis
  Paraguay, N Argentina

S. r. sanborn
  Chiloe I
S. r. rufipes
  S Chile, S Argentina
Strix uralensis (Ural Owl)
S. u. liturata
  N Scandinavia to C Russia
S. u. uralensis
  E Russia to W Siberia
S. u. yenisseensis
  C Siberia
S. u. daurica
  Lake Baikal to W Amurland
S. u. nikolskii
  Sea of Okhotsk to E Amurland
S. u. tatibanai
  Sakhalin I
S. u. coreensis
  SE Manchuria, Korea, Hokkaido I
S. u. hondoensis
  N Honshu I
S. u. momiyamae
  C. Honshu I
S. u. fuscescens
  S Honshu I, Kyushu I
Strix davidi (David's Wood Owl)
  W Szechwan
Strix nebulosa (Great Grey Owl)
S. n. nebulosa
  N North America
S. n. lapponica
  N Europe, N Asia, Sakhalin I
S. n. elisabethae
  N Mongolia

RHINOPTYNX
Rhinoptynx clamator (Striped Owl)
R. c. clamator
  SE Mexico to C South America
R. c. oberi
  Tobago I
R. c. midas
  S Brazil, Paraguay, Uruguay, N Argentina

ASIO
Asio otus (Long-eared Owl)
A. o. otus
  Europe, Asia, NW Africa
A. o. canariensis
  Canary Is
A. o. tuftsi
  Canada
A. o. wilsonianus
  S Canada, W & C USA
Asio stygius (Stygian Owl)
A. s. lambi
  NW Mexico
A. s. robustus
  E Mexico, Guatemala, Nicaragua

A. s. siguapa
Cuba, Isle of Pines
A. s. noctipetens
Hispaniola, Gonave I
A. s. stygius
C & S Brazil
A. s. barberoi
Paraguay, N Argentina
Asio abyssinicus (Abyssinian Long-eared Owl)
A. a. abyssinicus
Ethiopia
A. a. graueri
E Zaire, Mt Kenya
Asio madagascariensis (Madagascar Long-eared Owl)
Madagascar
Asio flammeus (Short-eared Owl)
A. f. flammeus
Europe, N Asia, N Africa, North America
A. f. bogotensis
Colombia, Ecuador
A. f. pallidicaudus
Venezuela
A. f. suinda
S Peru, S Brazil to Tierra del Fuego
A. f. sanfordi
Falkland Is
A. f. sandwichensis
Hawaiian Is
A. f. ponapensis
Ponapé I
A. f. domingensis
Hispaniola
A. f. portoricensis
Puerto Rico
A. f. galapagoensis
Galapagos Is
Asio capensis (African Marsh Owl)
A. c. tingitanus
NW Africa, Senegal to Cameroun
A. c. capensis
Ethiopia to Angola & Cape Province
A. c. hova
Madagascar

PSEUDOSCOPS
Pseudoscops grammicus (Jamaican Owl)
Jamaica

NESASIO
Nesasio solomonensis (Fearful Owl)
Bougainville I, Choiseul I, Ysabel I

AEGOLIUS
Aegolius funereus (Tengmalm's Owl)
A. f. funereus
N & C Europe, W Siberia
A. f. caucasicus
N Caucasus

A. f. sibiricus
NC & NE Asia
A. f. pallens
Tien Shan, Tarbagatai
A. f. jakutorum
C Siberia
A. f. beickianus
N Kansu
A. f. magnus
NE Siberia
A. f. richardsoni
N Canada to N USA
Aegolius acadicus (Saw-whet Owl)
A. a. acadicus
Canada, W USA, N Mexico
A. a. brooksi
Queen Charlotte Is
Aegolius ridgwayi (Unspotted Saw-whet Owl)
A. r. tacanensis
S Mexico
A. r. rostratus
Guatemala
A. r. ridgwayi
Costa Rica
Aegolius harrisii (Buff-fronted Owl)
A. h. harrisii
Colombia, Ecuador, Venezuela
A. h. iheringi
SE Brazil, Paraguay, N Argentina

Caprimulgiformes

74 STEATORNITHDAE (OILBIRD)

STEATORNIS
Steatornis caripensis (Oilbird)
Peru, Ecuador to the Guianas, Trinidad

75 PODARGIDAE (FROGMOUTHS)

PODARGUS
Podargus strigoides (Tawny Frogmouth)
P. s. phalaenoides
NW Australia, Northern Territory, Melville I
P. s. lilae
Groote Eylandt I
P. s. gouldi
W Cape York Peninsula
P. s. cornwalli
E Queensland
P. s. brachypterus
NW Victoria, C Australia
P. s. strigoides
SE Queensland, New South Wales
P. s. victoriae
S New South Wales, E South Australia
P. s. cuvieri
Tasmania

Podargus papuensis (Papuan Frogmouth)
New Guinea & Is, Cape York Peninsula
Podargus ocellatus (Marbled Frogmouth)
P. o. ocellatus
New Guinea & islands
P. o. marmoratus
Cape York Peninsula
P. o. intermedius
Triobriand Is, Fergusson I, Goodenough I
P. o. meeki
Tagula I
P. o. inexpectatus
Solomon Is

BATRACHOSTOMUS
Batrachostomus auritus (Large Frogmouth)
Malaysia, Sumatra, Borneo
Batrachostomus harterti (Dulit Frogmouth)
C Borneo
Batrachostomus septimus (Philippine Frogmouth)
B. s. microrhynchus
N Luzon I
B. s. menagei
Panay I, Negros I
B. s. septimus
Mindanao I, Basilan I
Batrachostomus stellatus (Gould's Frogmouth)
Malaysia, Sumatra, Borneo
Batrachostomus moniliger (Ceylon Frogmouth)
SW India, Sri Lanka
Batrachostomus hodgsoni (Hodgson's Frogmouth)
B. h. hodgsoni
Sikkim to Assam & N Burma
B. h. indochinae
C Burma to Indochina
Batrachostomus poliolophus (Pale-headed Frogmouth)
Sumatra
Batrachostomus mixtus (Sharpe's Frogmouth)
Borneo
Batrachostomus javensis (Javan Frogmouth)
B. j. continentalis
S Burma, SE Thailand
B. j. javensis
W & C Java
B. j. cornutus
Sumatra, Bangka I, Billiton I, Borneo
B. j. chaseni
Palawan I, Banguey I
Batrachostomus affinis (Blyth's Frogmouth)
Malaysia, Sumatra, Borneo

NYCTIBIUS
Nyctibius grandis (Grand Potoo)
Panama to Peru & S Brazil
Nyctibius aethereus (Long-tailed Potoo)
N. a. chocoensis
W Colombia
N. a. longicaudatus
E Ecuador, E Peru to Guyana
N. a. aethereus
SE Brazil, Paraguay
Nyctibius griseus (Common Potoo)
N. g. mexicanus
S Mexico to Honduras
N. g. costaricensis
Nicaragua to W Panama
N. g. panamensis
C Panama to Peru
N. g. cornutus
C & S Brazil, Paraguay, N Argentina
N. g. griseus
N Brazil, the Guianas, Trinidad
N. g. jamaicensis
Jamaica
N. g. abbotti
Hispaniola, Gonave I
Nyctibius leucopterus (White-winged Potoo)
N. l. maculosus
E Colombia, E Ecuador
N. l. leucopterus
E Brazil
Nyctibius bracteatus (Rufous Potoo)
Guyana, S Colombia, E Ecuador, E Peru

77 AEGOTHELIDAE (OWLET-NIGHTJARS)

AEGOTHELES
Aegotheles crinifrons (Halmahera Owlet-Nightjar)
Halmahera I, Batjan I
Aegotheles insignis (Large Owlet-Nightjar)
A. i. insignis
NW & N New Guinea
A. i. tatei
S New Guinea
A. i. pulcher
SE New Guinea
Aegotheles cristatus (Owlet-Nightjar)
A. c. major
S New Guinea
A. c. leucogaster
N Australia
A. c. cristatus
C & S Australia
A. c. tasmanicus
Tasmania

Aegotheles savesi (New Caledonian Owlet-Nightjar)
New Caledonia
Aegotheles bennettii (Barred Owlet-Nightjar)
A. b. affinis
NW New Guinea
A. b. wiedenfeldi
N New Guinea
A. b. terborghi
EC New Guinea
A. b. bennettii
SE New Guinea
A. b. plumiferus
Fergusson I, Goodenough I
Aegotheles wallacii (Wallace's Owlet-Nightjar)
A. w. wallacii
W New Guinea, Aru Is
A. w. gigas
WC New Guinea
A. w. manni
SW New Guinea
Aegotheles albertisi (Mountain Owlet-Nightjar)
A. a. albertisi
NW New Guinea
A. a. wondiwoi
C New Guinea
A. a. salvadorii
C & S New Guinea
Aegotheles archboldi (Eastern Mountain Owlet-Nightjar)
EC New Guinea

78 CAPRIMULGIDAE (NIGHTJARS)

CHORDEILINAE

LUROCALIS
Lurocalis semitorquatus (Semi-collared Nighthawk)
L. s. stonei
Nicaragua
L. s. noctivagus
Panama
L. s. semitorquatus
N Colombia to the Guianas, N Brazil
L. s. schaeferi
NC Venezuela
L. s. nattereri
C & S Brazil
L. s. rufiventris
W Venezuela, E Colombia to Peru

CHORDEILES
Chordeiles pusillus (Least Nighthawk)
C. p. septentrionalis
NW Brazil, E Venezuela, Guyana
C. p. pusillus
CE & S Brazil

C. p. esmeraldae
Venezuela
Chordeiles rupestris (Sand-coloured Nighthawk)
C. r. xyostictus
C Colombia
C. r. rupestris
Upper Amazonia
Chordeiles acutipennis (Lesser Nighthawk)
C. a. texensis
SW USA » C America
C. a. inferior
Baja California
C. a. micromeris
S Mexico, Guatemala
C. a. acutipennis
N South America
C. a. aequatorialis
W Ecuador
C. a. exilis
W Peru
C. a. crissalis
C Colombia
Chordeiles minor (Common Nighthawk)
C. m. minor
Canada, C & E USA » C South America
C. m. hesperis
SW Canada, W USA » C South America
C. m. sennetti
NW USA » C South America
C. m. howelli
WC USA » C South America
C. m. henryi
SW USA » C South America
C. m. aserriensis
SE Texas » C South America
C. m. chapmani
SE USA » C South America
C. m. panamensis
Panama
C. m. vicinus
Bahama Is
C. m. gundlachii
Cuba, Jamaica, Puerto Rico

NYCTIPROGNE
Nyctiprogne leucopyga (Band-tailed Nighthawk)
N. l. exigua
E Colombia, Venezuela
N. l. pallida
WC Venezuela
N. l. majuscula
C Brazil
N. l. leucopyga
E Venezuela, the Guianas, E & S Brazil
N. l. latifascia
C Venezuela

PODAGER
Podager nacunda (Nacunda Nighthawk)
P. n. minor
N & NE South America
P. n. nacunda
E Peru & C Brazil to Patagonia

CAPRIMULGINAE

EUROSTOPODUS
Eurostopodus guttatus (Spotted Night-jar)
E. g. insulanus
Babar I
E. g. harterti
NW Australia
E. g. gilberti
Groote Eylandt I
E. g. guttatus
E Australia, Aru Is
Eurostopodus mystacalis (White-throated Nightjar)
E. m. mystacalis
E Australia, New Guinea
E. m. nigripennis
Solomon Is
E. m. exul
New Caledonia
Eurostopodus diabolicus (Devilish Nightjar)
N Celebes
Eurostopodus papuensis (Papuan Nightjar)
E. p. papuensis
Salawati I, W New Guinea
E. p. astrolabae
E New Guinea
Eurostopodus archboldi (Archbold's Nightjar)
New Guinea
Eurostopodus temminckii (Malaysian Eared Nightjar)
Malaysia, Sumatra, Borneo
Eurostopodus macrotis (Great Eared Nightjar)
E. m. cerviniceps
Assam to N Malaysia, W China, Indochina
E. m. bourdilloni
S India
E. m. macrotis
Luzon I, Mindoro I, Mindanao I
E. m. jacobsoni
Simalur I
E. m. macropterus
Celebes

VELES
Veles binotatus (Brown Nightjar)
Ghana to E Cameroun

NYCTIDROMUS
Nyctidromus albicollis (Pauraque)
N. a. insularis
Tres Marias Is
N. a. merrilli
S Texas, E Mexico
N. a. yucatanensis
NW Mexico to Guatemala
N. a. albicollis
W Guatemala to Peru & E Brazil
N. a. gilvus
N Colombia
N. a. derbyanus
C & S Brazil, Paraguay

PHALAENOPTILUS
Phalaenoptilus nuttallii (Poorwill)
P. n. nuttallii
W & WC USA » C Mexico
P. n. californicus
W California
P. n. hueyi
SE California, SW Arizona
P. n. dickeyi
S Baja California
P. n. centralis
C Mexico

SIPHONORHIS

Siphonorhis brewsteri (Least Pauraque)
Hispaniola, Gonave I

OTOPHANES
Otophanes mcleodii (Eared Poorwill)
O. m. mcleodii
Chihuahua, Jalisco
O. m. rayi
Guerrero
Otophanes yucatanicus (Yucatan Poorwill)
SE Mexico, N Guatemala

NYCTIPHRYNUS
Nyctiphrynus ocellatus (Ocellated Poorwill)
N. o. lautus
NE Nicaragua
N. o. rosenbergi
W Colombia, NW Ecuador
N. o. ocellatus
E Ecuador, C Brazil to NE Argentina

CAPRIMULGUS
Caprimulgus carolinensis (Chuck Will's Widow)
EC & S USA » Central America
Caprimulgus rufus (Rufous Nightjar)
C. r. minimus
Panama to Venezuela
C. r. otiosus
St Lucia I
C. r. rufus
the Guianas, NE Brazil

C. r. noctivigulus
C Colombia
C. r. rutilus
S Brazil, Paraguay
Caprimulgus cubanensis (Greater Antillean Nightjar)
C. c. cubanensis
Cuba, Isle of Pines
C. c. ekmani
Hispaniola
Caprimulgus sericocaudatus (Silky-tailed Nightjar)
C. s. sericocaudatus
Peru
C. s. mengeli
Upper Amazonia
Caprimulgus salvini (Tawny-collared Nightjar)
E Mexico
Caprimulgus badius (Yucatan Tawny-collared Nightjar)
Yucatan, Belize
Caprimulgus ridgwayi (Ridgway's Whippoorwill)
C. r. ridgwayi
W Mexico
C. r. troglodytes
Guatemala, Honduras
Caprimulgus vociferus (Whippoorwill)
C. v. vociferus
S Canada, E USA » Honduras
C. v. arizonae
SW USA, N Mexico
C. v. setosus
E Mexico
C. v. oaxacae
SC Mexico
C. v. chiapensis
S Mexico, Guatemala
C. v. vermiculatus
Honduras, El Salvador
C. v. noctitherus
Puerto Rico **e?**
Caprimulgus saturatus (Dusky Nightjar)
Costa Rica, W Panama
Caprimulgus longirostris (Band-winged Nightjar)
C. l. ruficervix
Colombia, Venezuela, Ecuador
C. l. roraimae
Mt Duida, Mt Roraima (Venezuela)
C. l. decussatus
W Peru
C. l. atripunctatus
Peru, Bolivia, N Chile
C. l. bifasciatus
C Chile
C. l. longirostris
Argentina

Caprimulgus cayennensis (White-tailed Nightjar)
C. c. albicauda
Costa Rica to N Colombia
C. c. apertus
W Colombia
C. c. insularis
Curaçao I, Bonaire I, Margarita I, N Venezuela
C. c. leopetes
Trinidad, Tobago I
C. c. cayennensis
E Colombia, S Venezuela, The Guianas, N Brazil
Caprimulgus candicans (White-winged Nightjar)
C Brazil, Paraguay
Caprimulgus maculicaudus (Spot-tailed Nightjar)
N & W Amazonia
Caprimulgus parvulus (Little Nightjar)
C. p. anthonyi
W Ecuador
C. p. heterurus
N Colombia
C. p. parvulus
E Peru to E Brazil & C Argentina
Caprimulgus maculosus (Cayenne Nightjar)
French Guiana
Caprimulgus nigrescens (Blackish Nightjar)
W & N Amazonia
Caprimulgus whitelyi (Roraiman Nightjar)
Mt Roraima (Venezuela)
Caprimulgus hirundinaceus (Pygmy Nightjar)
C. h. cearae
E Brazil
C. h. hirundinaceus
E Brazil
Caprimulgus ruficollis (Red-necked Nightjar)
C. r. ruficollis
Portugal, S Spain, Morocco
C. r. desertorum
Algeria, Tunisia » S Sahara
Caprimulgus indicus (Jungle Nightjar)
C. i. hazarae
Himalayas, Burma, Malaysia
C. i. indicus
India
C. i. kelaarti
Sri Lanka
C. i. jotaka
NE Asia, N China, Japan » Java, Borneo
C. i. phalaena
Palau Is
Caprimulgus europaeus (European Nightjar)

C. e. europaeus
  N Europe, Russia, » C & S Africa
C. e. meridionalis
  S Europe, N Africa, Caucasus » W Africa
C. e. sarudnyi
  W Siberia, C Asia
C. e. unwini
  SW Asia, Iran, Afghan » E Africa, NW India
C. e. plumipes
  E Turkestan » SW Africa
Caprimulgus mahrattensis (Sykes'
Nightjar)
  Afghanistan to NW India
Caprimulgus centralasicus (Vaurie's
Nightjar)
  W China
Caprimulgus nubicus (Nubian Nightjar)
  C. n. tamaricis
    Dead Sea to Aden
  C. n. nubicus
    N Sudan
  C. n. torridus
    Somalia to N Tanzania
  C. n. jonesi
    Socotra I
Caprimulgus aegyptius (Egyptian Nightjar)
  C. a. aegyptius
    S Russia, Iran » Egypt & Sudan
  C. a. saharae
    N Sahara
Caprimulgus eximius (Golden Nightjar)
  C. e. simplicior
    N Niger, N Chad
  C. e. eximius
    W & N Sudan
Caprimulgus madagascariensis
(Madagascar Nightjar)
  C. m. aldabrensis
    Aldabra I
  C. m. madagascariensis
    Madagascar
Caprimulgus macrurus (Long-tailed
Nightjar)
  C. m. albonotatus
    N & NE India
  C. m. atripennis
    S India
  C. m. aequabilis
    Sri Lanka
  C. m. ambiguus
    Burma, Thailand, S Indochina
  C. m. bimaculatus
    Malaysia, Sumatra
  C. m. andamanicus
    Andaman Is
  C. m. macrurus
    Java, Borneo, Palawan I
  C. m. hainanus
    Hainan I

C. m. manillensis
  Philippine Is
C. m. delacouri
  Mindanao I
C. m. jungei
  Sula Is
C. m. celebensis
  Celebes, Wetar I
C. m. oberholseri
  Lombok I, Sumbawa I, Djampea I,
    Saleyer I
C. m. mesophanis
  S Moluccas
C. m. kuehni
  Babar I, Tenimber Is, Kei Is
C. m. schillmölleri
  Halmahera I, W Papuan Is
C. m. yorki
  New Britain, Aru Is, New Guinea,
    N Australia
C. m. meeki
  Tagula I
Caprimulgus pectoralis (Dusky Nightjar)
  C. p. nigriscapularis
    Guinea to E Zaire, Uganda
  C. p. fervidus
    Angola to Tanzania & Natal
  C. p. pectoralis
    Namibia, S Natal, Cape Province
Caprimulgus rufigena (Rufous-cheeked
Nightjar)
  C. r. fraenatus
    Ethiopia to S Kenya
  C. r. quanzae
    Angola
  C. r. rufigena
    Southern Africa » W Africa
Caprimulgus donaldsoni (Donaldson
Smith's Nightjar)
  W Somalia & Kenya
Caprimulgus poliocephalus (Abyssinian
Nightjar)
  C. p. poliocephalus
    Ethiopia to N Tanzania
  C. p. ruwenzorii
    E Zaire, Rwanda
  C. p. guttifer
    C Tanzania
  C. p. koesteri
    W Angola
Caprimulgus asiaticus (Indian Nightjar)
  C.a. asiaticus
    India to S Indochina
  C. a. eidos
    Sri Lanka
  C. a. siamensis
    N Thailand
Caprimulgus natalensis (African White-
tailed Nightjar)

198

C. n. accrae
Liberia to W Cameroun
C. n. chadensis
Chad to Sudan, N Zaire
C. n. gabonensis
Gabon to C Zaire
C. n. carpi
Caprivi Strip, Namibia
C. n. fulviventris
Angola
C. n. mpusa
Zambia
C. n. natalensis
Natal
Caprimulgus inornatus (Plain Nightjar)
C. i. vinaceabrunneus
S Niger, N Nigeria
C. i. inornatus
Niger & Nigeria to Tanzania & Yemen
C. i. malbranti
Ennedi Mts
Caprimulgus stellatus (Star-spotted Nightjar)
C. s. stellatus
W Ethiopia, Somalia & Kenya
C. s. simplex
S Ethiopia
Caprimulgus ludovicianus (Ludovic's Nightjar)
SW Ethiopia
Caprimulgus monticolus (Franklin's Nightjar)
C. m. monticolus
India
C. m. burmanicus
E Himalayas to Thailand
C. m. amoyensis
SE China
C. m. stictomus
Indochina, Taiwan
Caprimulgus affinis (Allied Nightjar)
C. a. affinis
Sumatra, Borneo, Java
C. a. kasuidori
Savu I, Sumba I
C. a. griseatus
Luzon I, Mindoro I, Negros I, Cebu I
C. a. mindanensis
Mindanao I
C. a. propinquus
C & S Celebes
C. a. undulatus
Lesser Sunda Is
C. a. timorensis
Timor I
Caprimulgus tristigma (Freckled Nightjar)
C. t. sharpei
Senegal to S Sudan

C. t. tristigma
E Sudan & Ethiopia to S Kenya
C. t. lentiginosus
Angola to Tanzania & Transvaal
Caprimulgus concretus (Bonaparte's Nightjar)
Sumatra, Borneo, Billiton I
Caprimulgus pulchellus (Salvadori's Nightjar)
C. p. pulchellus
Sumatra
C. p. bartelsi
Java
Caprimulgus enarratus (Collared Nightjar)
NW & E Madagascar
Caprimulgus batesi (Bates' Nightjar)
S Cameroun to C Zaire
SCOTORNIS
Scotornis fossii (Gabon Nightjar)
Cameroun to Zaire & Mozambique
Scotornis climacurus (Long-tailed Nightjar)
S. c. clarus
Ethiopia to C Tanzania
S. c. climacurus
Senegal to Sudan
S. c. nigricans
W Sudan
S. c. leoninus
Sierra Leone
S. c. sclateri
Nigeria to C Zaire
MACRODIPTERYX
Macrodipteryx longipennis (Standard-winged Nightjar)
Senegal to Ethiopia
SEMEIOPHORUS
Semeiophorus vexillarius (Pennant-winged Nightjar)
Angola to Transvaal » Nigeria & Uganda
HYDROPSALIS
Hydropsalis climacocerca (Ladder-tailed Nightjar)
H. c. schomburgki
E Venezuela, Guyana, Surinam
H. c. climacocerca
Upper Amazonia
H. c. pallidior
C Brazil
H. c. intercedens
C Brazil
H. c. canescens
C Brazil
Hydropsalis brasiliana (Scissor-tailed Nightjar)
H. b. brasiliana
C & E Brazil

H. b. furcifera
  E Bolivia, S Brazil, Uruguay

N. n. niger
  West Indies, Trinidad

UROPSALIS
Uropsalis segmentata (Swallow-tailed Nightjar)
  U. s. segmentata
    Colombia, Ecuador, Peru, Bolivia
  U. s. kalinowskii
    C Peru
Uropsalis lyra (Lyre-tailed Nightjar)
  U. l. lyra
    Colombia, Ecuador, Venezuela
  U. l. peruana
    Peru

MACROPSALIS
Macropsalis creagra (Long-trained Nightjar)
  SE Brazil

ELEOTHREPTUS
Eleothreptus anomalus (Sickle-winged Nightjar)
  Paraguay, N Argentina, SE Brazil

Apodiformes

79 APODIDAE (SWIFTS)

CYPSELOIDINAE

CYPSELOIDES
Cypseloides fumigatus (Sooty Swift)
  E Panama to S Brazil
Cypseloides cherriei (Spot-fronted Swift)
  Costa Rica
Cypseloides cryptus (White-chinned Swift)
  Costa Rica, Guyana, Peru
Cypseloides lemosi (White-chested Swift)
  Cauca (Colombia)
Cypseloides major (Great Swift)
  S Bolivia, NW Argentina
Cypseloides phelpsi (Tepui Swift)
  S Venezuela
Cypseloides rutilus (Chestnut-collared Swift)
  C. r. griseifrons
    W Mexico
  C. r. brunnitorques
    SE Mexico to Peru
  C. r. rutilus
    the Guianas, Trinidad

NEPHOECETES
Nephoecetes niger (Black Swift)
  N. n. borealis
    SE Alaska to SW USA » Mexico
  N. n. costaricensis
    Honduras to Costa Rica

AERORNIS
Aerornis senex (Great Dusky Swift)
  S Brazil, Paraguay, NE Argentina

STREPTOPROCNE
Streptoprocne zonaris (White-collared Swift)
  S. z. mexicana
    S Mexico, Belize to El Salvador
  S. z. pallidifrons
    Greater Antilles
  S. z. albicincta
    Honduras to NW & C South America
  S. z. altissima
    Colombia, Ecuador
  S. z. zonaris
    S Brazil, Bolivia, W Argentina
Streptoprocne biscutatus (Biscutate Swift)
  E Brazil
Streptoprocne semicollaris (White-naped Swift)
  C Mexico

APODINAE

COLLOCALIINI

COLLOCALIA
Collocalia gigas (Giant Swiftlet)
  Malaysia, Sumatra, Java
Collocalia spodiopygia (White-rumped Swiftlet)
  C. s. sororum
    C S & SE Celebes
  C. s. infuscata
    N Moluccas
  C. s. ceramensis
    S Moluccas
  C. s. eichhorni
    Bismarck Archipelago
  C. s. reichenowi
    Guadalcanal I
  C. s. terraereginae
    N Queensland
  C. s. leucopygia
    Loyalty Is, New Hebrides, New Caledonia
  C. s. assimilis
    Fiji Is
  C. s. townsendi
    Tonga I
  C. s. spodiopygia
    Samoa Is
Collocalia francica (Grey-rumped Swiftlet)
  C. f. francica
    Mauritius, Réunion I
  C. f. inexpectata
    Andaman Is, Nicobar Is

C. f. germani
Malaysia, Indochina, N Borneo
C. f. amechana
Anamba Is
C. f. amelis
Luzon I, Cebu I, Mindanao I
C. f. perplexa
E Bornean islands
C. f. bartelsi
Java, Kangean I
C. f. dammermanni
Lesser Sunda Is, Bali I to Flores I
C. f. micans
Sumba I, Savu I, Timor I
C. f. pelewensis
Palau Is
C. f. bartschi
Guam I
Collocalia elaphra (Seychelles Cave Swiftlet)
Seychelles
Collocalia unicolor (Indian Edible-nest Swiftlet)
SW India, Sri Lanka
Collocalia vanikorensis (Uniform Swiftlet)
C. v. aenigma
C & SE Celebes
C. v. heinrichi
S Celebes
C. v. moluccarum
Moluccas, Kei Is
C. v. coultasi
Admiralty Is
C. v. lihirensis
St Matthias Is, Lihir Is
C. v. waigeuensis
Waigeo I
C. v. steini
Numfor I
C. v. granti
S & E New Guinea, Fergusson I
C. v. tagulae
Louisiade Archipelago, Tagula I, Misima I
C. v. yorki
Cape York Peninsula
C. v. vanikorensis
Solomon Is, Santa Cruz I, New Hebrides, New Caledonia
Collocalia inquieta (Carolines Swiftlet)
C. i. rukensis
Caroline Is, Truk I, Yap I
C. i. ponapensis
Ponapé I
C. i. inquieta
Kusaie I
Collocalia salangana (Mossy Swiftlet)
C. s. salangana
India, China, Indochina

C. s. natunae
N Borneo, Natuna Is
Collocalia hirundinacea (Mountain Swiftlet)
C. h. baru
Japen I
C. h. hirundinacea
New Guinea, Dampier I, Goodenough I
C. h. excelsa
Snowy Mts, New Guinea
Collocalia leucophaea(Tahitian Swiftlet)
Society Is
Collocalia ocista (Marquesan Swiftlet)
Marquesas Is
Collocalia sawtelli (Cook Is Swiftlet)
Cook Is
Collocalia brevirostris (Himalayan Swiftlet)
C. b. innominata
C & W China to Malaysia, N Vietnam
C. b. rogersi
NW Thailand, N Laos
C. b. brevirostris
Himalayas, N Burma, SE Tibet
Collocalia whiteheadi (Whitehead's Swiftlet)
C. w. tsubame
Palawan I
C. w. whiteheadi
Philippine Is, New Guinea
C. w. origenis
Mindanao I
C. w. apoensis
Mt Apo (Mindanao I)
Collocalia nuditarsus (Schrader Mountain Swiftlet)
NC New Guinea
Collocalia papuensis (Idenburg River Swiftlet)
New Guinea
Collocalia orientalis (Guadalcanal Swiftlet)
Guadalcanal I
Collocalia fuciphaga (Thunberg's Swiftlet)
Java
Collocalia maxima (Lowe's Swiftlet)
C. m. maxima
Malaysia, Anamba Is
C. m. lowi
Sumatra, Nias I, Labuan I, N & W Borneo
C. m. tichelmani
SE Borneo
C. m. palawanensis
Palawan I
C. m. vulcanorum
Java
Collocalia esculenta (White-bellied Swiftlet)

C. e. affinis
  Andaman Is, Nicobar Is
C. e. elachyptera
  S Thailand, Mergui Archipelago
C. e. cyanoptila
  Malaysia, E Sumatra, Billiton I, Borneo
C. e. oberholseri
  W Sumatra, Nias I, Mentawi Is
C. e. linchi
  SE Sumatra, Java to Lombok I, Kangean I
C. e. natalis
  Christmas I
C. e. dodgei
  N Borneo
C. e. isonota
  Luzon I, Mindoro I, Mindanao I
C. e. bagobo
  Mt Apo (Mindanao I)
C. e. sumbawae
  Sumbawa I, Flores I, Sumba I
C. e. minuta
  Tanahdjampea I, Kalao I
C. e. neglecta
  Alor I to Damar I, Timor I
C. e. esculenta
  Celebes, Moluccas, New Guinea
C. e. erwini
  S New Guinea
C. e. stresemanni
  Admiralty Is, Bismarck Archipelago
C. e. becki
  N & C Solomon Is
C. e. makirensis
  San Cristobal I
C. e. desiderata
  Rennell I
C. e. uropygialis
  New Caledonia, New Hebrides
Collocalia marginata (Philippine Swiftlet)
C. m. marginata
  Luzon I, Mindoro I, Masbate I, Cebu I,
  Bohol I, Palawan I
C. m. septentrionalis
  Babuyan I, Calayan I, Camiguin I (North)
Collocalia troglodytes (Pygmy Swiftlet)
  Philippine Is, Palawan I

SCHOUTEDENAPUS
Schoutedenapus myioptilus (Scarce Swift)
S. m. poensis
  Fernando Po I
S. m. myioptilus
  Kenya to Malawi
S. m. chapini
  E Zaire
**Schoutedenapus schoutedeni
(Schouteden's Swift)**
  E Zaire

MEARNSIA
**Mearnsia picina (Philippine Spinetailed
  Swift)**
  Leyte I, Cebu I, Mindanao I
**Mearnsia novaeguineae (New Guinea
  Spinetailed Swift)**
M. n. bürgersi
  New Guinea
M. n. novaeguineae
  S New Guinea

ZOONAVENA
**Zoonavena grandidieri (Madagascar
  Spinetailed Swift)**
  Madagascar
**Zoonavena thomensis (Sao Thomé
  Spinetailed Swift)**
  Sao Thomé I
**Zoonavena sylvatica (Indian White-
  rumped Spinetailed Swift)**
  India, Burma

TELACANTHURA
**Telacanthura ussheri (Mottle-throated
  Spinetailed Swift)**
T. u. ussheri
  Senegal to N Nigeria
T. u. sharpei
  S Cameroun to E Zaire
T. u. stictilaema
  SW Kenya to S Malawi
T. u. marwitzi
  C Tanzania
T. u. benguellensis
  Angola
**Telacanthura melanopygia (Ituri Mottle-
  throated Spinetailed Swift)**
  N Zaire

RAPHIDURA
**Raphidura leucopygialis (White-rumped
  Spinetailed Swift)**
  S Burma to Sumatra, Java, Borneo
**Raphidura sabini (Sabine's Spinetailed
  Swift)**
  Sierra Leone to NE Zaire

NEAFRAPUS
**Neafrapus cassini (Cassin's Spinetailed
  Swift)**
  S Cameroun to N Zaire
**Neafrapus boehmi (Boehm's Spinetailed
  Swift)**
  W Angola to Mozambique & Tanzania

HIRUNDAPUS
**Hirundapus caudacuta (White-throated
  Spinetailed Swift)**
H. c. caudacuta
  NE Asia, Japan » E China, Australia

H. c. nudipes
Himalayas » Java
H. c. bourreti
Indochina
H. c. formosanus
Taiwan
Hirundapus cochinchinensis (White-vented Spinetailed Swift)
H. c. rupchandi
Nepal
H. c. cochinchinensis
E Himalayas to Indochina, Malaysia, Java, Sumatra
Hirundapus gigantea (Brown Spinetailed Swift)
H. g. indicus
E India to Indochina, Andaman Is
H. g. gigantea
Malaysia, Sumatra, Java, Borneo, Palawan I
H. g. dubius
Luzon, Mindoro I, Negros I, Mindanao I
H. g. ernsti
W Java
Hirundapus celebensis (Celebes SpinetailedSwift)
N Celebes

CHAETURA
Chaetura spinicauda (Band-rumped Swift)
C. s. fumosa
W Costa Rica, Panama, N Colombia
C. s. aetherodroma
Panama
C. s. latirostris
Amacuro (Venezuela)
C. s. spinicauda
E Venezuela, the Guianas, N Brazil
C. s. aethalea
C Brazil
Chaetura martinica (Lesser Antillian Swift)
Lesser Antilles
Chaetura cinereiventris (Grey-rumped Swift)
C. c. phaeopygos
E Nicaragua to Panama
C. c. lawrencei
Grenada I, Trinidad, Tobago I
C. c. schistacea
E Colombia, W Venezuela
C. c. guianensis
Guyana, E Venezuela
C. c. occidentalis
W Colombia, W Ecuador
C. c. sclateri
Upper Amazonia
C. c. egregia
Bolivia

C. c. cinereiventris
E Brazil
Chaetura pelagica (Chimney Swift)
S Canada to S USA » C South America
Chaetura vauxi (Vaux's Swift)
C. v. vauxi
SW Canada to SW USA » Central Ame
C. v. tamaulipensis
E Mexico
C. v. richmondi
S Mexico to Costa Rica
C. v. ochropygia
E Panama
C. v. gaumeri
Yucatan peninsula, Cozumel I
C. v. aphanes
N Venezuela
Chaetura chapmani (Chapman's Swift)
C. c. chapmani
French Guiana, Trinidad
C. c. viridipennis
C Brazil
Chaetura andrei (Ashy-tailed Swift)
C. a. andrei
C Venezuela
C. a. meridionalis
C South America » Colombia
Chaetura brachyura (Short-tailed Swift)
C. b. praevelox
Grenada I, St Vincent I
C. b. brachyura
Upper Amazonia, the Guianas, S Brazil
C. b. ocypetes
Peru
C. b. cinereocauda
E Brazil
APODINI

AERONAUTES
Aeronautes saxatilis (White-throated Swift)
A. s. saxatilis
SW Canada to SW USA » Mexico
A. s. nigrior
Guatemala, El Salvador
Aeronautes montivagus (White-tipped Swift)
A. m. montivagus
N Venezuela, Peru, Bolivia
A. m. tatei
Mt Duida (Venezuela)
Aeronautes andecolus (Andean Swift)
A. a. parvulus
W Peru, N Chile
A. a. peruvianus
SE Peru
A. a. andecolus
Bolivia, W Argentina

ACHORNIS

***achornis phoenicobia* (Antillean Palm Swift)**
  T. p. iradii
    Cuba, Isle of Pines
  T. p. phoenicobia
    Hispaniola, Jamaica

***achornis furcata* (Pygmy Swift)**
  T. f. furcata
    NE Colombia, NW Venezuela
  T. f. nigrodorsalis
    W Venezuela

***achornis squamata* (Fork-tailed Palm Swift)**
  T. s. semota
    E Peru, S Venezuela
  T. s. squamata
    Trinidad, the Guianas, C & E Brazil

ANYPTILA

***anyptila sanctihieronymi* (Great Swallow-tailed Swift)**
  W Guatemala

***anyptila cayennensis* (Lesser Swallow-tailed Swift)**
  P. c. veraecrucis
    E Mexico
  P. c. cayennensis
    SE Nicaragua to N South America

YPSIURUS

***ypsiurus batasiensis* (Asian Palm Swift)**
  C. b. batasiensis
    India, Sri Lanka
  C. b. infumatus
    Burma to Indochina, Malaysia, Sumatra, Java, Borneo
  C. b. pallidior
    Philippine Is

***ypsiurus parvus* (African Palm Swift)**
  C. p. parvus
    Senegal to N Ethiopia
  C. p. brachypterus
    Sierra Leone to Angola & S Zaire
  C. p. myochrous
    S Ethiopia to S Malawi
  C. p. gracilis
    Madagascar

PUS

***pus melba* (Alpine Swift)**
  A. m. melba
    S Europe to Himalayas » N Africa
  A. m. tuneti
    N Africa, Israel to Iran
  A. m. archeri
    Somalia
  A. m. maximus
    Mt Ruwenzori (Zaire)
  A. m. africanus
    E & S Africa

  A. m. marjoriae
    Namibia
  A. m. willsi
    Madagascar
  A. m. bakeri
    S India, Sri Lanka

***Apus aequatorialis* (Mottled Swift)**
  A. a. aequatorialis
    Ethiopia to Angola & Malawi
  A. a. reichenowi
    S Kenya
  A. a. furensis
    W Sudan
  A. a. bamendae
    E Cameroun
  A. a. schubotzi
    Mt Ruwenzori (Zaire)
  A. a. lowei
    Sierra Leone

***Apus alexandri* (Alexander's Swift)**
  Cape Verde Is

***Apus barbatus* (African Black Swift)**
  A. b. barbatus
    S Malawi to Cape Province
  A. b. hollidayi
    Zambia
  A. b. balstoni
    Madagascar
  A. b. mayottensis
    Mayotte I
  A. b. sladeniae
    Fernando Po I, S Cameroun
  A. b. roehli
    Kivu area (E Zaire)
  A. b. granvillei
    Sierra Leone

***Apus berliozi* (Berlioz' Swift)**
  A. b. berliozi
    Socotra I
  A. b. bensoni
    N Kenya

***Apus bradfieldi* (Bradfield's Swift)**
  Namibia

***Apus niansae* (Nyanza Swift)**
  A. n. niansae
    N Ethiopia to Malawi
  A. n. somalicus
    Somalia

***Apus pallidus* (Pallid Swift)**
  A. p. brehmorum
    Madeira I, Canary Is, SW Europe, C Sahara
  A. p. illyricus
    Yugoslavia, Cyprus
  A. p. pallidus
    Egypt, Israel, to Iran & Pakistan

***Apus apus* (Common Swift)**
  A. a. apus
    W Europe to C Asia » Africa

A. a. pekinensis
Middle East to N China » India
& E & S Africa

A. a. unicolor
Madeira I, W Canary Is

Apus acuticauda (Dark-backed Swift)
Nepal, Assam

**Apus pacificus (Northern White-rumped
Swift)**

A. p. pacificus
NE Asia, China, Japan » SE Asia, Australia

A. p. leuconyx
Himalayas, N India

A. p. cooki
C Burma, Malaysia to S China, N Indochina

A. p. kanoi
Taiwan

Apus affinis (House Swift)

A. a. bannermani
Sao Thomé I, Principé I, Fernando Po I

A. a. abessynicus
Gambia to Somalia & Cape Province

A. a. galilejensis
N Africa, Middle East, Iran

A. a. theresae
NW Cape Province

A. a. affinis
India

A. a. singalensis
S India, Sri Lanka

A. a. nipalensis
Nepal to N Assam

A. a. subfurcatus
S China, Burma to Philippine Is, Borneo,
Java, Sumatra

Apus horus (Horus Swift)
Ethiopia to Rhodesia

Apus caffer (White-rumped Swift)

A. c. streubelii
N Sudan & Ethiopia to S Kenya

A. c. ansorgei
S Zaire, N Angola

A. c. caffer
South Africa

Apus batesi (Bates' Black Swift)
Cameroun to NE Zaire

80 HEMIPROCNIDAE (TREE SWIFTS)

HEMIPROCNE

**Hemiprocne coronata (Indian Crested
Swift)**
India to Indochina

**Hemiprocne longipennis (Crested Tree
Swift)**

H. l. harterti
S Burma, Malaysia, Sumatra, Borneo

H. l. perlonga
Simalur I

H. l. ocyptera
Nias I

H. l. thoa
Batu I, Pagi Is, Enggano I

H. l. longipennis
Java, Bali I

H. l. wallacii
Celebes, Sula Is

**Hemiprocne mystacea (Whiskered Tree
Swift)**

H. m. confirmata
Moluccas, Aru Is

H. m. mystacea
W Papuan islands & New Guinea

H. m. aëroplanes
Bismarck Archipelago

H. m. woodfordiana
Solomon Is

Hemiprocne comata (Lesser Tree Swift)

H. c. comata
Malaysia, Sumatra, Borneo

H. c. stresemanni
Pagi Is

H. c. major
Philippine Is

H. c. nakamurai
Mindanao I, Basilan I

81 TROCHILIDAE (HUMMINGBIRDS)

DORYFERA

Doryfera johannae (Blue-fronted Lancebill)

D. j. johannae
SE Colombia, E Ecuador, NE Peru

D. j. guianensis
SE Venezuela, S Guyana

**Doryfera ludoviciae (Green-fronted
Lancebill)**

D. l. veraguensis
Costa Rica, W Panama

D. l. ludoviciae
C Colombia, W Venezuela, C Peru

D. l. rectirostris
C Ecuador

D. l. grisea
NW Bolivia

ANDRODON

**Androdon aequatorialis (Tooth-billed
Hummingbird)**
E Panama, W Colombia, W Ecuador

RAMPHODON

Ramphodon naevius (Saw-billed Hermit)
SE Brazil

GLAUCIS

Glaucis dohrnii (Hook-billed Hermit)
E Brazil

Glaucis aenea (Bronzy Hermit)
Nicaragua to NW Ecuador

Glaucis hirsuta (Rufous-breasted Hermit)
G. h. affinis
E Panama to W Venezuela & NE Peru
G. h. insularum
Grenada I, Trinidad, Tobago I
G. h. hirsuta
N & E Venezuela, the Guianas, N Brazil, Bolivia

THRENETES
Threnetes niger (Sooty Barbthroat)
French Guiana
Threnetes loehkeni (Bronze-tailed Barbthroat)
N Brazil
Threnetes grzimeki (Grzimek's Barbthroat)
Brazil
Threnetes leucurus (Pale-tailed Barbthroat)
T. l. cervinicauda
E Colombia, E Ecuador, NE Peru
T. l. rufigastra
E Peru
T. l. leucurus
the Guianas, S Venezuela, N & C Brazil
T. l. medianus
NE Brazil
Threnetes ruckeri (Band-tailed Barbthroat)
T. r. ventosus
Nicaragua to W Panama
T. r. darienensis
E Panama, N Colombia
T. r. ruckeri
W Colombia, W Ecuador
T. r. venezuelensis
W Venezuela

PHAETHORNIS
Phaethornis yaruqui (White-whiskered Hermit)
P. y. sanctijohannis
W Colombia
P. y. yaruqui
W Ecuador
Phaethornis guy (Green Hermit)
P. g. coruscus
Costa Rica, Panama, W Colombia
P. g. apicalis
C Colombia, E Ecuador, E Peru
P. g. guy
NE Venezuela, Trinidad
P. g. emiliae
WC Colombia
Phaethornis syrmatophorus (Tawny-bellied Hermit)
P. s. syrmatophorus
W Colombia, W Ecuador
P. s. columbianus
E Colombia, E Ecuador
P. s. huallagae
NE Peru

Phaethornis superciliosus (Long-tailed Hermit)
P. s. mexicanus
SW Mexico
P. s. veraecrucis
SE Mexico
P. s. longirostris
S Mexico to N Honduras
P. s. cephalus
S Honduras to W Panama
P. s. cassinii
E Panama, NW Colombia
P. s. moorei
E Colombia, E Ecuador, E Peru
P. s. baroni
W Ecuador
P. s. bolivianus
Bolivia
P. s. susurrus
N Colombia
P. s. saturatior
E Venezuela, NW Brazil
P. s. superciliosus
the Guianas, NE Brazil
P. s. muelleri
N Brazil
P. s. insignis
N Brazil
P. s. ochraceiventris
W Brazil
Phaethornis malaris (Great-billed Hermit)
P. m. ucayalii
Rio Ucayali (Peru)
P. m. insolitus
Venezuela
P. m. malaris
French Guiana
Phaethornis margarettae (Margaretta Hermit)
Brazil
Phaethornis eurynome (Scale-throated Hermit)
SE Brazil, Paraguay, NE Argentina
Phaethornis nigrirostris (Black-billed Hermit)
Brazil
Phaethornis hispidus (White-bearded Hermit)
Upper Amazonia
Phaethornis anthophilus (Pale-bellied Hermit)
P. a. hyalinus
Pearl Is (Panama)
P. a. anthophilus
N Colombia, W Venezuela
P. a. fuliginosus
S Colombia
Phaethornis koepckeae (Koepcke's Hermit)
Peru

Phaethornis bourcieri (Straight-billed Hermit)
  P. b. whitelyi
    SE Colombia, S Venezuela, the Guianas
  P. b. bourcieri
    E Ecuador, NE Peru, W Brazil
Phaethornis philippii (Needle-billed Hermit)
  W Brazil
Phaethornis squalidus (Dusky-throated Hermit)
  P. s. rupurumii
    E Venezuela, Guyana, NW Brazil
  P. s. amazonicus
    C Brazil
  P. s. squalidus
    SE Brazil
Phaethornis augusti (Sooty-capped Hermit)
  P. a. augusti
    E Colombia, N Venezuela
  P. a. vicarius
    EC Colombia
  P. a. incanescens
    SE Venezuela, S Guyana
Phaethornis pretrei (Planalto Hermit)
  E Bolivia to SE Brazil
Phaethornis subochraceus (Buff-bellied Hermit)
  NE Bolivia
Phaethornis nattereri (Cinnamon-throated Hermit)
  C & E Brazil
Phaethornis maranhaoensis (Maranhao Hermit)
  EC Brazil
Phaethornis gounellei (Broad-tipped Hermit)
  C & E Brazil
Phaethornis ruber (Reddish Hermit)
  P. r. episcopus
    E & S Venezuela, Guyana
  P. r. ruber
    Surinam, French Guiana, N & C Brazil
  P. r. nigricinctus
    E Ecuador, W Brazil, NE Peru, E Bolivia
  P. r. longipennis
    EC Peru
Phaethornis stuarti (White-browed Hermit)
  Bolivia
Phaethornis griseogularis (Grey-chinned Hermit)
  P. g. griseogularis
    Colombia, Ecuador, E Peru
  P. g. zonura
    N Peru
  P. g. porcullae
    W Peru

Phaethornis longuemareus (Little Hermit)
  P. l. adolphi
    SE Mexico
  P. l. saturatus
    Guatemala to C Panama
  P. l. subrufescens
    E Panama, W Colombia, W Ecuador
  P. l. nelsoni
    NW Colombia
  P. l. striigularis
    N & C Colombia
  P. l. atrimentalis
    E Ecuador, E Peru
  P. l. ignobilis
    San Esteban to Santa Lucia, Venezuela
  P. l. imatacae
    Bolivar (Venezuela)
  P. l. longuemareus
    French Guiana, Surinam, Trinidad
  P. l. aethopyga
    C Brazil
Phaethornis idaliae (Minute Hermit)
  SE Brazil

EUTOXERES
Eutoxeres aquila (White-tipped Sicklebill)
  E. a. salvini
    E & SW Costa Rica, W Panama
  E. a. munda
    E Panama, W Colombia
  E. a. aquila
    E Colombia, E Ecuador
  E. a. heterura
    SW Colombia, W Ecuador
Eutoxeres condamini (Buff-tailed Sicklebill)
  E. c. condamini
    SE Colombia, E Ecuador
  E. c. gracilis
    E Peru

PHAEOCHROA
Phaeochroa cuvierii (Scaly-breasted Hummingbird)
  P. c. roberti
    E Guatemala to E Nicaragua
  P. c. maculicauda
    Costa Rica, W Panama
  P. c. saturatior
    Coiba Is, (Panama)
  P. c. cuvierii
    E Panama
  P. c. berlepschi
    N Colombia

CAMPYLOPTERUS
Campylopterus curvipennis (Wedge-tailed Sabrewing)
  C. c. curvipennis
    SE Mexico

C. c. yucatanensis
Yucatan peninsula
C. c. excellens
S Vera Cruz (Mexico)
C. c. pampa
E Guatemala
Campylopterus largipennis (Grey-breasted Sabrewing)
C. l. largipennis
E Venezuela, the Guianas, NW Brazil
C. l. obscurus
NE Brazil
C. l. aequatorialis
Northern Upper Amazonia
Campylopterus rufus (Rufous Sabrewing)
S Mexico, W Guatemala, El Salvador
Campylopterus hyperythrus (Rufous-breasted Sabrewing)
S Guyana, SE Venezuela
Campylopterus duidae (Buff-breasted Sabrewing)
C. d. duidae
Mt Duida (Venezuela)
C. d. guayquinimae
S Venezuela
Campylopterus hemileucurus (Violet Sabrewing)
C. h. hemileucurus
S Mexico to Nicaragua
C. h. mellitus
Costa Rica, W Panama
Campylopterus ensipennis (White-tailed Sabrewing)
NE Venezuela, Trinidad, Tobago I
Campylopterus falcatus (Lazuline Sabrewing)
E Ecuador, Colombia, W Venezuela
Campylopterus phainopeplus (Santa Marta Sabrewing)
N Colombia
Campylopterus villaviscensio (Napo Sabrewing)
E Ecuador

EUPETOMENA
Eupetomena macroura (Swallow-tailed Hummingbird)
E. m. macroura
the Guianas, Brazil, Paraguay
E. m. simoni
NE Brazil
E. m. hirundo
E Peru, NE Bolivia
E. m. boliviana
Beni (Bolivia)

FLORISUGA
Florisuga mellivora (White-necked Jacobin)

F. m. mellivora   207
C America, N South America, Trinidad
F. m. flabellifera
Tobago I

MELANOTROCHILUS
Melanotrochilus fuscus (Black Jacobin)
E Brazil

COLIBRI
Colibri delphinae (Brown Violetear)
Guatemala to Panama, N & W South America
Colibri thalassinus (Green Violetear)
C. t. thalassinus
C Mexico to Guatemala
C. t. minor
Honduras
C. t. cabanidis
Costa Rica, W Panama
C. t. cyanotus
Venezuela, Colombia to Peru
C. t. crissalis
Bolivia
Colibri coruscans (Sparkling Violetear)
C. c. coruscans
Venezuela, Colombia to NW Argentina
C. c. germanus
SE Venezuela, S Guyana
C. c. rostratus
S Venezuela
Colibri serrirostris (White-vented Violetear)
E Bolivia, S Brazil, N Argentina

ANTHRACOTHORAX
Anthracothorax viridigula (Green-throated Mango)
NE Venezuela, the Guianas, NE Brazil
Anthracothorax prevostii (Green-breasted Mango)
A. p. prevostii
C Mexico to Guatemala & Belize
A. p. gracilirostris
El Salvador to Costa Rica
A. p. hendersoni
Old Providence I
A. p. pinchoti
St Andrews I
A. p. viridicordatus
NW Venezuela
Anthracothorax nigricollis (Black-throated Mango)
A. n. nigricollis
E Panama tropical South America
A. n. iridescens
W Colombia, W Ecuador
Anthracothorax veraguensis (Veraguan Mango)
W Panama

Anthracothorax dominicus (Antillean Mango)
  A. d. dominicus
    Hispaniola
  A. d. aurulentus
    Puerto Rico, St Thomas I
Anthracothorax viridis (Green Mango)
    Puerto Rico
Anthracothorax mango (Jamaican Mango)
    Jamaica

AVOCETTULA
Avocettula recurvirostris (Fiery-throated Awlbill)
    Guyana, French Guiana, NE Brazil, E Ecuador

EULAMPIS
Eulampis jugularis (Purple-throated Carib)
    Lesser Antilles Is

SERICOTES
Sericotes holosericeus (Green-throated Carib)
  S. h. holosericeus
    E Puerto Rico, Virgin Is, Lesser Antilles
  S. h. chlorolaemus
    Grenada I

CHRYSOLAMPIS
Chrysolampis mosquitus (Ruby-Topaz Hummingbird)
    N & E South America

ORTHORHYNCUS
Orthorhyncus cristatus (Antillean Crested Hummingbird)
  O. c. exilis
    Virgin Is & Lesser Antilles to St Lucia I
  O. c. ornatus
    St Vincent I
  O. c. cristatus
    Barbados I
  O. c. emigrans
    Union I to Grenada I

KLAIS
Klais guimeti (Violet-headed Hummingbird)
  K. g. guimeti
    Nicaragua to W Venezuela & E Ecuador
  K. g. pallidiventris
    E Peru, C Bolivia

ABEILLIA
Abeillia abeillei (Emerald-chinned Hummingbird)
  A. a. abeillei
    SE Mexico to N Honduras
  A. a. aurea
    S Honduras, N Nicaragua

STEPHANOXIS
Stephanoxis lalandi (Black-breasted Plovercrest)

  S. l. lalandi
    SE Brazil
  S. l. loddigesii
    S Brazil, Paraguay, NE Argentina

LOPHORNIS
Lophornis ornata (Tufted Coquette)
    E Venezuela, the Guianas, Trinidad
Lophornis gouldii (Dot-eared Coquette)
    N & C Brazil
Lophornis magnifica (Frilled Coquette)
    C & S Brazil
Lophornis delattrei (Rufous-crested Coquette)
  L. d. brachylopha
    SW Mexico
  L. d. lessoni
    W Costa Rica, Panama, C Colombia
  L. d. delattrei
    NE & C Peru, Bolivia
Lophornis stictolopha (Spangled Coquette
    W Venezuela, E Colombia, E Ecuador
Lophornis chalybea (Festive Coquette)
  L. c. verreauxii
    C Colombia to C Bolivia
  L. c. klagesi
    E Venezuela
  L. c. chalybea
    SE Brazil
Lophornis pavonina (Peacock Coquette)
  L. p. punctigula
    Venezuela
  L. p. pavonina
    SE Venezuela, S Guyana
  L. p. duidae
    Mt Duida (Venezuela)
Lophornis insignibarbis (Bearded Coquette
    Colombia

PAPHOSIA
Paphosia helenae (Black-crested Coquette
    C Mexico to E Costa Rica
Paphosia adorabilis (White-crested Coquette)
    SW Costa Rica

POPELAIRIA
Popelairia popelairii (Wire-crested Thorntail)
    E Colombia, E Ecuador, NE Peru
Popelairia langsdorfi (Black-bellied) Thorntail)
  P. l. melanosternon
    E Ecuador, E Peru, W Brazil
  P. l. langsdorffi
    E Brazil
Popelairia letitiae (Coppery Thorntail)
    Bolivia
Popelairia conversii (Green Thorntail)
    Costa Rica to W Ecuador

DISCOSURA
Discosura longicauda (Racquet-tailed Coquette)
  E Venezuela, Guyana, French Guiana,
    E Brazil

CHLORESTES
Chlorestes notatus (Blue-chinned Sapphire)
  C. n. obsoletus
    SE Colombia
  C. n. notatus
    Ecuador & W Brazil to Trinidad & Surinam
  C. n. cyanogenys
    C & E Brazil

CHLOROSTILBON
Chlorostilbon mellisugus (Blue-tailed Emerald)
  C. m. mellisugus
    Surinam, French Guiana, NE Brazil
  C. m. subfurcatus
    E & S Venezuela, Guyana, NW Brazil
  C. m. duidae
    S Venezuela
  C. m. phoeopygus
    Upper Amazonia
  C. m. peruanus
    Peru, E Bolivia
Chlorostilbon vitticeps (Simon's Emerald)
    E Ecuador
Chlorostilbon aureoventris (Glittering-bellied Emerald)
  C. a. pucherani
    E Brazil
  C. a. aureoventris
    Bolivia, Paraguay, W Argentina
  C. a. berlepschi
    Uruguay, E Argentina
Chlorostilbon canivetii (Fork-tailed Emerald)
  C. c. auriceps
    C & W Mexico
  C. c. canivetii
    SE Mexico, Belize, N Guatemala
  C. c. forficatus
    Holbox I, Cozumel I
  C. c. osberti
    C & W Guatemala, El Salvador, Honduras
  C. c. salvini
    W Nicaragua, W Costa Rica
  C. c. assimilis
    SW Costa Rica, SW Panama, Pearl Is
      (Panama)
  C. c. caribaeus
    Netherlands Antilles, Trinidad,
      NE Venezuela
  C. c. nitens
    N Colombia, NW Venezuela

C. c. nanus
  C Venezuela
Chlorostilbon ricordii (Cuban Emerald)
  C. r. bracei
    Bahama Is
  C. r. ricordii
    Cuba, Isle of Pines
Chlorostilbon swainsonii (Hispaniolan Emerald)
    Hispaniola, Gonave I
Chlorostilbon maugaeus (Puerto Rican Emerald)
    Puerto Rico
Chlorostilbon gibsoni (Red-billed Emerald)
  C. g. gibsoni
    C Colombia
  C. g. chrysogaster
    N Colombia
  C. g. pumilus
    W Colombia, W Ecuador
  C. g. melanorhynchus
    SC Colombia, NE Ecuador
Chlorostilbon russatus (Coppery Emerald)
    N Colombia, NW Venezuela
Chlorostilbon stenura (Narrow-tailed Emerald)
  C. s. stenura
    Colombia, Venezuela
  C. s. ignota
    N Venezuela
Chlorostilbon alice (Green-tailed Emerald)
    N Venezuela
Chlorostilbon poortmani (Short-tailed Emerald)
  C. p. poortmani
    Colombia, NW Venezuela
  C. p. euchloris
    Colombia

CYNANTHUS
Cynanthus sordidus (Dusky Hummingbird)
    W & S Mexico
Cynanthus latirostris (Broad-billed Hummingbird)
  C. l. magicus
    SW USA, NW Mexico
  C. l. latirostris
    EC Mexico
  C. l. propinquus
    C Mexico
  C. l. toroi
    W Mexico
  C. l. doubledayi
    W Mexico (S of *C. l. toroi*)
  C. l. lawrencei
    Tres Marias Is
  C. l. nitida
    SW Mexico

CYANOPHAIA
Cyanophaia bicolor (Blue-headed Hummingbird)
Guadelupe I, Dominica I, Martinique I
THALURANIA
Thalurania furcata (Fork-tailed Woodnymph)
T. f. ridgwayi
W Jalisco (Mexico)
T. f. townsendi
E Guatemala to SE Honduras
T. f. venusta
Nicaragua to W Panama
T. f. subtropicalis
E Panama, W Colombia
T. f. fannyi
W Colombia
T. f. colombica
N Colombia, W Venezuela
T. f. viridipectus
SC Colombia
T. f. verticeps
S Colombia, N Ecuador
T. f. hypochlora
W Ecuador
T. f. nigrofasciata
S Colombia, Ecuador, NW Brazil
T. f. taczanowskii
NE Peru
T. f. jelskii
E Peru
T. f. boliviana
NE Bolivia
T. f. simoni
W Brazil
T. f. rostrifera
W Venezuela
T. f. orenocensis
E Venezuela
T. f. fissilis
E Venezuela
T. f. refulgens
NE Venezuela
T. f. furcata
the Guianas, NE Brazil
T. f. furcatoides
NE Brazil
T. f. balzani
W Brazil, E Bolivia
T. f. baeri
NE C Brazil to SE Bolivia
T. f. eriphile
E & SE Brazil, Paraguay
Thalurania watertonii (Long-tailed Woodnymph)
Guyana, E Brazil
Thalurania glaucopis (Violet-capped Woodnymph)
E & S Brazil, Uruguay, Paraguay

Thalurania lerchi (Lerch's Woodnymph)
NC Colombia
NEOLESBIA
Neolesbia nehrkorni (Blue-tailed Sylph)
C Colombia
PANTERPE
Panterpe insignis (Fiery-throated Hummingbird)
Costa Rica, W Panama
DAMOPHILA
Damophila julie (Violet-bellied Hummingbird)
D. j. panamensis
Panama
D. j. julie
N Colombia
D. j. feliciana
W Ecuador
LEPIDOPYGA
Lepidopyga coeruleogularis (Sapphire-throated Hummingbird)
L. c. coeruleogularis
W Panama
L. c. confinis
NE Panama, NW Colombia
L. c. coelina
NE Colombia
Lepidopyga lilliae (Sapphire-bellied Hummingbird)
N Colombia
Lepidopyga goudoti (Shining Green Hummingbird)
L. g. goudoti
NC Colombia
L. g. zuliae
NW Venezuela
L. g. luminosa
N Colombia
L. g. phaeochroa
N Venezuela
HYLOCHARIS
Hylocharis xantusii (Black-fronted Hummingbird)
S Baja (California)
Hylocharis leucotis (White-eared Hummingbird)
H. l. borealis
SE Arizona, N Mexico
H. l. leucotis
C & S Mexico, Guatemala
H. l. pygmaea
El Salvador, Honduras, Nicaragua
Hylocharis eliciae (Blue-throated Goldentail)
S Mexico to W Panama

Hylocharis sapphirina (Rufous-throated Sapphire)
   E Venezuela and the Guianas to
   N Argentina
Hylocharis cyanus (White-chinned Sapphire)
   H. c. viridiventris
     N Colombia to the Guianas, N Brazil
   H. c. cyanus
     E Brazil
   H. c. rostrata
     E Peru, NE Bolivia, W Brazil
   H. c. conversa
     Bolivia
Hylocharis pyropygia (Flame-rumped Sapphire)
   NE Brazil
Hylocharis chrysura (Gilded Hummingbird)
   E Bolivia, S Brazil, Uruguay,
   N Argentina
Hylocharis grayi (Blue-headed Sapphire)
   H. g. grayi
     C Colombia to N Ecuador
   H. g. humboldtii
     W Colombia to NW Ecuador

CHRYSURONIA
Chrysuronia oenone (Golden-tailed Sapphire)
   C. o. oenone
     N & E Venezuela, C Ecuador
   C. o. longirostris
     C Colombia
   C. o. azurea
     Ecuador
   C. o. intermedia
     Upper Amazon River
   C. o. josephinae
     E Peru, NE Bolivia

GOLDMANIA
Goldmania violiceps (Violet-capped Hummingbird)
   E Panama

GOETHALSIA
Goethalsia bella (Pirre Hummingbird)
   E Panama

TROCHILUS
Trochilus polytmus (Streamertail)
   T. p. polytmus
     Jamaica
   T. p. scitulus
     NE Jamaica

EUCOCHLORIS
Leucochloris albicollis (White-throated Hummingbird)
   SE Brazil, Paraguay, N Argentina

Polytmus guainumbi (White-tailed Goldenthroat)
   P. g. doctus
     Colombia
   P. g. guainumbi
     Venezuela, the Guianas, Trinidad
   P. g. thaumantias
     E & C Brazil, Paraguay, Bolivia
Polytmus milleri (Tepui Goldenthroat)
   SE Venezuela
Polytmus theresiae (Green-tailed Goldenthroat)
   P. t. theresiae
     the Guianas, N Brazil
   P. t. leucorrhous
     N Peru, NW Brazil

LEUCIPPUS
Leucippus fallax (Buffy Hummingbird)
   L. f. cervina
     NE Colombia, NW Venezuela
   L. f. richmondi
     N Venezuela, Margarita I
   L. f. fallax
     N Venezuela
Leucippus baeri (Tumbes Hummingbird)
   W Peru
Leucippus taczanowskii (Spot-throated Hummingbird)
   L. t. fractus
     N Peru
   L. t. taczanowskii
     C Peru
Leucippus chlorocercus (Olive-spotted Hummingbird)
   E Peru

TAPHROSPILUS
Taphrospilus hypostictus (Many-spotted Hummingbird)
   T. h. hypostictus
     E Ecuador
   T. h. peruvianus
     E Peru, N Bolivia

AMAZILIA
Amazilia chionogaster (White-bellied Hummingbird)
   A. c. chionogaster
     N & C Peru
   A. c. hypoleucus
     Bolivia, NW Argentina
Amazilia viridicauda (Green and White Hummingbird)
   Peru
Amazilia candida (White-bellied Emerald)
   A. c. genini
     EC Mexico
   A. c. candida
     SE Mexico to Nicaragua

A. c. pacifica
W Guatemala
Amazilia chionopectus (White-chested Emerald)
A. c. chionopectus
E Venezuela to Surinam, Trinidad
A. c. whitelyi
Guyana
A. c. orienticola
French Guiana
Amazilia versicolor (Versicoloured Emerald)
A. v. millerii
E Colombia, Venezuela, W Brazil
A. v. hollandi
E Venezuela
A. v. nitidifrons
NE Brazil
A. v. versicolor
E Bolivia, Paraguay
Amazilia luciae (Honduras Emerald)
Honduras
Amazilia fimbriata (Glittering-throated Emerald)
A. f. elegantissima
N Venezuela
A. f. obscuricauda
Venezuela
A. f. maculicauda
E Venezuela to Surinam
A. f. fimbriata
French Guiana, E Brazil
A. f. apicalis
E Colombia, W Venezuela
A. f. fluviatilis
S Colombia, E Ecuador
A. f. laeta
NE Peru, W Brazil
A. f. alia
C Brazil
A. f. nigricauda
Bolivia to E Brazil
A. f. tephrocephala
SE Brazil
Amazilia distans (Tachira Emerald)
W Venezuela
Amazilia lactea (Sapphire-spangled Emerald)
A. l. bartletti
E & SE Peru, N Bolivia
A. l. zimmeri
SE Venezuela
A. l. lactea
E Brazil
Amazilia amabilis (Blue-chested Hummingbird)
A. a costaricensis
E Nicaragua to C Panama

A. a. decora
SW Costa Rica, W Panama
A. a. amabilis
E Panama, W Colombia, W Ecuador
Amazilia rosenbergi (Purple-chested Hummingbird)
W Colombia, NW Ecuador
Amazilia boucardi (Mangrove Hummingbird)
W Costa Rica
Amazilia franciae (Andean Emerald)
A. f. franciae
C Colombia
A. f. viridiceps
SW Colombia, W Ecuador
A. f. cyanocollis
N Peru
A. f. veneta
Colombia?
Amazilia leucogaster (Plain-bellied Emerald)
A. l. leucogaster
the Guianas, N Brazil
A. l. bahiae
E Brazil
Amazilia cyanocephala (Red-billed Azurecrown)
A. c. cyanocephala
SE Mexico, NW Guatemala
A. c. guatemalensis
Guatemala to N Nicaragua
Amazilia microrhyncha (Small-billed Azurecrown)
Honduras?
Amazilia cyanifrons (Indigo-capped Hummingbird)
A. c. alfaroana
Costa Rica
A. c. cyanifrons
N Colombia
Amazilia beryllina (Berylline Hummingbird)
A. b. viola
N & W Mexico
A. b. beryllina
E & C Mexico
A. b. lichtensteinei
S Mexico
A. b. devillei
S Mexico to Belize, El Salvador
Amazilia cyanura (Blue-tailed Hummingbird)
A. c. guatemalae
S Mexico, Guatemala
A. c. cyanura
El Salvador to W Nicaragua
Amazilia saucerrottei (Steely-vented Hummingbird)

A. s. hoffmanni
  W & S Nicaragua, Costa Rica
A. s. saucerrottei
  C Colombia
A. s. australis
  S Colombia
A. s. warscewiczi
  N & E Colombia
A. s. braccata
  W Venezuela
Amazilia tobaci (Copper-rumped
Hummingbird)
A. t. feliciae
  N Venezuela
A. t. monticola
  NW Venezuela
A. t. caudata
  NE Venezuela
A. t. caurensis
  E & SE Venezuela
A. t. aliciae
  NE Venezuela, Margarita I
A. t. erythronotos
  Trinidad
A. t. tobaci
  Tobago I
Amazilia viridigaster (Green-bellied
Hummingbird)
A. v. viridigaster
  E Colombia, W Venezuela
A. v. duidae
  Mt Duida (Venezuela
A. v. cupreicauda
  S Venezuela, S Guyana
Amazilia edward (Snowy-breasted
Hummingbird)
A. e. niveoventer
  SW Costa Rica, W Panama
A. e. edward
  C Panama
A. e. margaritarum
  Pearl Is (Panama)
A. e. crosbyi
  SE Panama
Amazilia rutila (Cinnamon Humming-
bird)
A. r. diluta
  NW Mexico
A. r. rutila
  W & S Mexico to W Costa Rica
A. r. corallirostris
  SW Mexico to El Salvador
A. r. graysoni
  Maria Madre I
Amazilia yucatanensis (Buff-bellied
Hummingbird)
A. y. chalconota
  S Texas, NE Mexico

A. y. cerviniventris
  S Mexico
A. y. yucatanensis
  SE Mexico, N Guatemala, Belize
Amazilia tzacatl (Rufous-tailed Humming-
bird)
A. t. tzacatl
  E Mexico to W Venezuela
A. t. jucunda
  SW Colombia, W Ecuador
Amazilia castaneiventris (Chestnut-bellied
Hummingbird)
  NC Colombia
Amazilia amazilia (Amazilia Humming-
bird)
A. a. dumerilii
  W Ecuador, NW Peru
A. a. alticola
  S Ecuador, N Peru
A. a. amazilia
  W Peru
A. a. caeruleigularis
  W Peru
A. a. leucophoea
  E & S Peru
Amazilia viridifrons (Green-fronted
Hummingbird)
  SW & S Mexico
Amazilia violiceps (Violet-crowned
Hummingbird)
A. v. ellioti
  W Mexico
A. v. violiceps
  SC Mexico

EUPHERUSA
Eupherusa poliocerca (White-tailed
Hummingbird)
  SW Mexico
Eupherusa eximia (Stripe-tailed Humming-
bird)
E. e. nelsoni
  SE Mexico
E. e. eximia
  S Mexico to N Nicaragua
E. e. egregia
  Costa Rica, W Panama
Eupherusa cyanophrys (Black-fronted
Hummingbird)
  Oaxaca (Mexico)
Eupherusa nigriventris (Black-bellied
Hummingbird)
  E Costa Rica

ELVIRA
Elvira chionura (White-tailed Emerald)
  SW Costa Rica
Elvira cupreiceps (Coppery-headed
Emerald)
  E Costa Rica

Microchera albocoronata (Snowcap)
M. a. parvirostris
E Nicaragua, E Costa Rica
M. a. albocoronata
NW Panama

CHALYBURA
Chalybura buffonii (White-veined Plumeleteer)
C. b. micans
E Panama, NW Colombia
C. b. buffonii
NC Colombia, W Venezuela
C. b. aeneicauda
NE Colombia, N Venezuela
C. b. caeruleogaster
E Colombia
C. b. intermedia
SW Ecuador
Chalybura urochrysia (Bronze-tailed Plumeleteer)
C. u. melanorrhoa
E Nicaragua, E Costa Rica
C. u. isaurae
NW Panama
C. u. incognita
E Panama
C. u. urochrysia
W Colombia, NW Ecuador

APHANTOCHROA
Aphantochroa cirrochloris (Sombre Hummingbird)
C & E Brazil

LAMPORNIS
Lampornis clemenciae (Blue-throated Hummingbird)
L. c. bessophilus
SW USA, NW Mexico
L. c. clemenciae
S USA, N & C Mexico
Lampornis amethystinus (Amethyst-throated Hummingbird)
L. a. amethystinus
E Mexico
L. a. brevirostris
W Mexico
L. a. margaritae
SW Mexico
L. a. salvini
S Mexico, C Guatemala
L. a. nobilis
Honduras
Lampornis viridipallens (Green-throated Mountain Gem)
L. v. ovandensis
S Mexico
L. v. viridipallens
S Mexico, Guatemala

L. v. nubivagus
El Salvador, W Honduras
L. v. connectens
El Salvador
L. v. sybillae
C Honduras, N Nicaragua
Lampornis hemileucus (White-bellied Mountain Gem)
NE Costa Rica
Lampornis castaneoventris (White-throated Mountain Gem)
L. c. pectoralis
W Nicaragua, NW Costa Rica
L. c. calolaema
N & C Costa Rica, W Panama
L. c. castaneoventris
W Panama
Lampornis cinereicauda (Grey-tailed Mountain Gem)
SW Costa Rica

LAMPROLAIMA
Lamprolaima rhami (Garnet-throated Hummingbird)
L. r. rhami
S Mexico
L. r. saturatior
Honduras & N El Salvador

ADELOMYIA
Adelomyia melanogenys (Speckled Hummingbird)
A. m. cervina
W & C Colombia
A. m. connectens
Colombia
A. m. melanogenys
E Colombia, W Venezuela
A. m. aeneosticta
C & N Venezuela
A. m. maculata
C Ecuador, N Peru
A. m. chlorospila
SE Peru
A. m. inornata
Bolivia, NW Argentina

ANTHOCEPHALA
Anthocephala floriceps (Blossomcrown)
A. f. berlepschi
C Colombia
A. f. floriceps
N Colombia

UROSTICTE
Urosticte benjamini (Whitetip)
U. b. rostrata
W Colombia
U. b. benjamini
W Ecuador, SW Colombia
U. b. ruficrissa
E Ecuador

U. b. intermedia
NE Peru

PHLOGOPHILUS
Phlogophilus hemileucurus (Ecuadorean Piedtail)
E Ecuador
Phlogophilus harterti (Peruvian Piedtail)
S Peru

CLYTOLAEMA
Clytolaema rubricauda (Brazilian Ruby)
SE Brazil

POLYPLANCTA
Polyplancta aurescens (Gould's Jewel-front)
E Ecuador, E Peru, S Venezuela, N Brazil

HELIODOXA
Heliodoxa rubinoides (Fawn-breasted Brilliant)
H. r. rubinoides
E Colombia
H. r. aequatorialis
W Colombia, W Ecuador
H. r. cervinigularis
E Ecuador, E Peru
Heliodoxa leadbeateri (Violet-fronted Brilliant)
H. l. leadbeateri
Upper Amazonia
H. l. sagitta
SC Colombia
H. l. parvula
W Venezuela
Heliodoxa jacula (Green-crowned Brilliant)
H. j. henryi
Costa Rica, W Panama
H. j. jacula
E Panama, E Colombia
H. j. jamesoni
W Ecuador
Heliodoxa xanthogonys (Velvet-browed Brilliant)
SE Venezuela, S Guyana
Heliodoxa schreibersii (Black-throated Brilliant)
H. s. schreibersii
E Ecuador, NE Peru, NW Brazil
H. s. whitelyana
E Peru
Heliodoxa gularis (Pink-throated Brilliant)
E Ecuador, NE Peru
Heliodoxa branickii (Rufous-webbed Brilliant)
C Peru
Heliodoxa imperatrix (Empress Brilliant)
W Ecuador

Eugenes fulgens (Rivoli's Hummingbird)
E. f. fulgens
SW USA, N & C Mexico
E. f. viridiceps
S Mexico to Nicaragua
E. f. spectabilis
Costa Rica, W Panama

HYLONYMPHA
Hylonympha macrocerca (Scissor-tailed Hummingbird)
Venezuela

STERNOCLYTA
Sternoclyta cyanopectus (Violet-chested Hummingbird)
NW Venezuela

TOPAZA
Topaza pella (Crimson Topaz)
T. p. pella
N Brazil, S Venezuela, Guyana, Surinam
T. p. smaragdula
French Guiana
T. p. microrhyncha
NE Brazil
T. p. pamprepta
E Ecuador
Topaza pyra (Fiery Topaz)
SE Colombia, E Ecuador, W Brazil

OREOTROCHILUS
Oreotrochilus melanogaster (Black-breasted Hillstar)
C Peru
Oreotrochilus estella (Andean Hillstar)
O. e. jamesonii
N Ecuador
O. e. söderströmi
Mt Quillotoa (Ecuador)
O. e. chimborazo
Mt Chimborazo (Ecuador)
O. e. stolzmanni
N Peru
O. e. estella
S Peru to N Chile & NW Argentina
O. e. boliviana
C Bolivia
Oreotrochilus leucopleurus (White-sided Hillstar)
S Bolivia, Chile, W Argentina
Oreotrochilus adela (Wedgetailed Hillstar)
C Bolivia

UROCHROA
Urochroa bougueri (White-tailed Hillstar)
U. b. bougueri
SW Colombia, NW Ecuador
U. b. eulcura
SW Colombia
U. b. leucura
E Ecuador

PATAGONA
Patagona gigas (Giant Hummingbird)
  P. g. peruviana
    Ecuador to N Chile, NW Argentina
  P. g. gigas
    C Chile, W Argentina

AGLAEACTIS
Aglaeactis cupripennis (Shining Sunbeam)
  A. c. cupripennis
    Colombia, N & C Ecuador
  A. c. parvulus
    S Ecuador, N Peru
  A. c. ruficauda
    C Peru
  A. c. caumatonotus
    SC Peru
Aglaeactis aliciae (Purple-backed Sunbeam)
    N Peru
Aglaeactis castelnaudii (White-tufted Sunbeam)
    C Peru
Aglaeactis pamela (Black-hooded Sunbeam)
    Bolivia

LAFRESNAYA
Lafresnaya lafresnayi (Mountain Velvetbreast)
  L. l. liriope
    N Colombia, W Venezuela
  L. l. lafresnayi
    C Colombia
  L. l. greenewalti
    W Venezuela
  L. l. saül
    W Colombia, Ecuador, N Peru
  L. l. rectirostris
    C Peru

PTEROPHANES
Pterophanes cyanopterus (Great Sapphire-wing)
  P. c. cyanopterus
    Colombia, Ecuador
  P. c. caeruleus
    S Colombia
  P. c. peruvianus
    Peru, N Bolivia

COELIGENA
Coeligena coeligena (Bronzy Inca)
  C. c. ferruginea
    W Colombia
  C. c. columbiana
    C Colombia to C Ecuador & W Venezuela
  C. c. zuloagae
    NW Venezuela
  C. c. boliviana
    C Peru, C Bolivia

  C. c. coeligena
    N Venezuela
  C. c. zuliana
    W Venezuela, NE Colombia
Coeligena wilsoni (Brown Inca)
    SW Colombia, W Ecuador
Coeligena prunellei (Black Inca)
    E Colombia
Coeligena torquata (Collared Inca)
  C. t. torquata
    Colombia, E Ecuador
  C. t. fuligidigula
    W Ecuador
  C. t. margaretae
    N Peru
  C. t. insectivora
    NC Peru
  C. t. omissa
    S Peru
  C. t. conradii
    NE Colombia, NW Venezuela
  C. t. inca
    S Peru, N Bolivia
Coeligena phalerata (White-tailed Starfrontlet)
    N Colombia
Coeligena bonapartei (Golden-bellied Starfrontlet)
  C. b. consita
    NE Colombia, NW Venezuela
  C. b. bonapartei
    E Colombia
  C. b. eos
    NW Venezuela
Coeligena orina (Dusky Starfrontlet)
    Colombia
Coeligena helianthea (Blue-throated Starfrontlet)
  C. h. tamae
    NE Colombia
  C. h. helianthea
    E Colombia
Coeligena lutetiae (Buff-winged Starfrontlet)
    C Colombia, Ecuador
Coeligena violifer (Violet-throated Starfrontlet)
  C. v. dichroura
    N & C Peru
  C. v. osculans
    S Peru
  C. v. violifer
    NW Bolivia
Coeligena iris (Rainbow Starfrontlet)
  C. i. iris
    S Ecuador
  C. i. aurora
    S Ecuador, N Peru

C. i. fulgidiceps
N Peru
C. i. flagrans
N Peru
C. i. hypocrita
N Peru
C. i. eva
N Peru
C. i. hesperus
SC Ecuador

ENSIFERA
Ensifera ensifera (Sword-billed Humming-bird)
Venezuela, Colombia to N Bolivia

SEPHANOIDES
Sephanoides sephaniodes (Green-Backed) Firecrown)
Chile, SW Argentina
Sephanoides ferandensis (Fernandez Firecrown)
S. f. fernandensis
Masatierra I
S. f. leyboldi
Masafuera I

BOISSONNEAUA
Boissonneaua flavescens (Buff-tailed Coronet)
B. f. flavescens
Colombia, W Venezuela
B. f. tinochlora
W Ecuador
Boissonneaua matthewsii (Chestnut-breasted Coronet)
Ecuador, Peru
Boissonneaua jardini (Velvet-Purple Coronet)
W Colombia, W Ecuador

HELIANGELUS
Heliangelus mavors (Orange-throated Sunangel)
NE Colombia, W Venezuela
Heliangelus spencei (Merida Sunangel)
W Venezuela
Heliangelus amethysticollis (Amethyst-throated Sunangel)
H. a. clarisse
N Colombia, W Venezuela
H. a. violiceps
NE Colombia
H. a. viridiscutatus
NE Colombia
H. a. laticlavius
S Ecuador to C Peru
H. a. amethysticollis
S Peru, Bolivia

Heliangelus strophianus (Gorgeted Sunangel)
W Ecuador
Heliangelus exortis (Tourmaline Sunangel)
Colombia, E Ecuador
Heliangelus viola (Purple-throated Sunangel)
W Ecuador, NW Peru
Heliangelus micraster (Little Sunangel)
H. m. micraster
S Ecuador
H. m. cutervensis
N Peru
Heliangelus squamigularis (Olive-throated Sunangel)
Colombia

ERIOCNEMIS
Eriocnemis nigrivestris (Black-breasted Puffleg)
NW Ecuador
Eriocnemis söderströmi (Söderström's Puffleg)
Ecuador
Eriocnemis vestitus (Glowing Puffleg)
E. v. vestitus
E Colombia, W Venezuela
E. v. paramillo
NW Colombia
E. v. smaragdinipectus
SC Colombia, E Ecuador
Eriocnemis godini (Turquoise-throated Puffleg)
Ecuador
Eriocnemis cupreoventris (Coppery-bellied Puffleg)
E Colombia, W Venezuela
Eriocnemis luciani (Sapphire-vented Puffleg)
E. l. luciani
W Ecuador
E. l. catharina
N Peru
E. l. sapphiropygia
C Peru
Eriocnemis isaacsonii (Isaacson's Puffleg)
Colombia
Eriocnemis mosquera (Golden-breasted Puffleg)
Colombia, N Ecuador
Eriocnemis glaucopoides (Blue-capped Puffleg)
Bolivia, N Argentina
Eriocnemis mirabilis (Colourful Puffleg)
N Peru
Eriocnemis alinae (Emerald-bellied Puffleg)
E. a. alinae
Colombia, N Ecuador

E. a. dybowskii
N & C Peru

Eriocnemis derbyi (Black-thighed Puffleg)
E. d. longirostris
NC Colombia
E. d. derbyi
S Colombia, N Ecuador

HAPLOPHAEDIA
Haplophaedia aureliae (Greenish Puffleg)
H. a. caucensis
E Panama, W Colombia
H. a. aureliae
C & E Colombia
H. a. russata
E Ecuador
H. a. affinis
N Peru
H. a. assimilis
SE Peru
Haplophaedia lugens (Hoary Puffleg)
WC Colombia, C Ecuador

OCREATUS
Ocreatus underwoodii (Booted Racquet-tail)
O. u. polystictus
N Venezuela
O. u. underwoodii
Colombia, W Venezuela
O. u. ambiguus
S Colombia
O. u. discifer
W Venezuela
O. u. melanantherus
W Ecuador
O. u. peruanus
E Ecuador, NE Peru
O. u. annae
C Peru
O. u. addae
Bolivia

LESBIA
Lesbia victoriae (Black-tailed Trainbearer)
L. v. victoriae
S & E Colombia
L. v. eucharis
Colombia
L. v. aequatorialis
W Ecuador
L. v. juliae
N & C Peru
L. v. berlepschi
SW Peru
Lesbia nana (Green-tailed Trainbearer)
L. n. gouldii
Colombia, W Venezuela
L. n. gracilis
Ecuador

L. n. pallidiventris
N Peru
L. n. chlorura
C Peru
L. n. nuna
SW Peru
L. n. boliviana
N Bolivia

SAPPHO
Sappho sparganura (Red-tailed Comet)
S. s. sparganura
N & C Bolivia
S. s. sappho
S Bolivia, N & W Argentina

POLYONYMUS
Polyonymus caroli (Bronze-tailed Comet)
Peru

ZODALIA
Zodalia glyceria (Purple-tailed Comet)
Colombia, Ecuador

RAMPHOMICRON
Ramphomicron microrhynchum (Purple-backed Thornbill)
R. m. andicolum
W Venezuela
R. m. microrhynchum
Colombia, Ecuador
R. m. albiventre
Peru
Ramphomicron dorsale (Black-backed Thornbill)
N Colombia

METALLURA
Metallura phoebe (Black Metaltail)
Peru, Bolivia, N Chile
Metallura theresiae (Coppery Metaltail)
N Peru
Metallura purpureicauda (Purple-tailed Thornbill)
Ecuador
Metallura aeneocauda (Scaled Metaltail)
M. a. aeneocauda
S Peru, Bolivia
M. a. malagae
Bolivia
Metallura baroni (Violet-throated Metal-tail)
SW Ecuador
Metallura eupogon (Fire-throated Metal-tail)
N & C Peru
Metallura williami (Viridian Metaltail)
M. w. williami
C Colombia
M. w. primolina
NE Ecuador

M. w. atrigularis
  S Ecuador
Metallura tyrianthina (Tyrian Metaltail)
  M. t. chloropogon
    N Venezuela
  M. t. oreopola
    W Venezuela
  M. t. districta
    N Colombia
  M. t. tyrianthina
    Colombia, E & S Ecuador
  M. t. quitensis
    NW Ecuador
  M. t. septentrionalis
    N Peru
  M. t. peruviana
    C Peru
  M. t. smaragdinicollis
    S Peru, Bolivia
Metallura iracunda (Perija Metaltail)
  E Colombia, W Venezuela

CHALCOSTIGMA
Chalcostigma ruficeps (Rufous-capped Thornbill)
  C. r. aureofastigata
    S Ecuador
  C. r. ruficeps
    Peru, N Bolivia
Chalcostigma olivaceum (Olivaceous Thornbill)
  C. o. olivaceum
    N & C Peru, Bolivia
  C. o. pallens
    WC Peru
Chalcostigma stanleyi (Blue-mantled Thornbill)
  C. s. stanleyi
    Ecuador
  C. s. versigularis
    C Peru
  C. s. vulcani
    SE Peru, Bolivia
Chalcostigma heteropogon (Bronze-tailed Thornbill)
  E Colombia, W Venezuela
Chalcostigma herrani (Rainbow-bearded Thornbill)
  C. h. tolimae
    W Colombia
  C. h. herrani
    S Colombia, N Ecuador

OXYPOGON
Oxypogon guerinii (Bearded Helmetcrest)
  O. g. stübelii
    C Colombia
  O. g. guerinii
    E Colombia

O. g. cyanolaemus
  N Colombia
O. g. lindenii
  W Venezuela

OPISTHOPRORA
Opisthoprora euryptera (Mountain Avocetbill)
  S Colombia, NE Ecuador

TAPHROLESBIA
Taphrolesbia griseiventris (Grey-bellied Comet)
  Peru

AGLAIOCERCUS
Aglaiocercus kingi (Long-tailed Sylph)
  A. k. berlepschi
    Venezuela
  A. k. margarethae
    Venezuela
  A. k. kingi
    E Colombia
  A. k. mocoa
    C Colombia to N Peru
  A. k. smaragdinus
    C Peru, N Bolivia
  A. k. emmae
    NC Colombia
  A. k. caudata
    Colombia, W Venezuela
Aglaiocercus coelestis (Violet-tailed Sylph)
  A. c. coelestis
    W Colombia, NW Ecuador
  A. c. pseudocoelestis
    SW Colombia
  A. c. aethereus
    SW Ecuador

OREONYMPHA
Oreonympha nobilis (Bearded Mountaineer)
  O. n. albolimbata
    WC Peru
  O. n. nobilis
    S Peru

AUGASTES
Augastes scutatus (Hyacinth Visor-bearer)
  Brazil
Augastes lumachellus (Hooded Visor-bearer)
  E Brazil

SCHISTES
Schistes geoffroyi (Wedge-billed Hummingbird)
  S. g. albogularis
    WC Colombia, W Ecuador
  S. g. geoffroyi
    N Venezuela, E Colombia to E Peru

HELIOTHRYX
Heliothryx barroti (Purple-crowned Fairy)
Guatemala to W Ecuador
Heliothryx aurita (Black-eared Fairy)
H. a. aurita
N Colombia to the Guianas, N Brazil
H. a. major
W Ecuador
H. a. phainolaema
NE Brazil
H. a. auriculata
E Peru, Bolivia, C & S Brazil

HELIACTIN
Heliactin cornuta (Horned Sungem)
C & E Brazil

LODDIGESIA
Loddigesia mirabilis (Marvellous Spatule-tail)
N Peru

HELIOMASTER
Heliomaster constantii (Plain-capped Starthroat)
H. c. surdus
NW Mexico
H. c. pinicola
W Mexico
H. c. leocadiae
W Mexico, W Guatemala
H. c. constantii
El Salvador to Costa Rica
Heliomaster longirostris (Long-billed Starthroat)
H. l. pallidiceps
S Mexico to Nicaragua
H. l. longirostris
E Costa Rica to N & NW South America
H. l. stuartae
Colombia
H. l. albicrissa
W Ecuador, NW Peru
Heliomaster squamosus (Stripe-breasted Starthroat)
EC Brazil
Heliomaster furcifer (Blue-tufted Starthroat)
C Brazil to Bolivia & N Argentina

RHODOPIS
Rhodopis vesper (Oasis Hummingbird)
R. v. tertia
N Peru
R. v. koepckeae
Peru
R. v. vesper
SW Peru, N Chile
R. v. atacamensis
N Chile

THAUMASTURA
Thaumastura cora (Peruvian Sheartail)
W Peru

PHILODICE
Philodice evelynae (Bahama Woodstar)
P. e. evelynae
Bahama Is
P. e. lyrura
Gt Inagua I
P. e. salita
Caicos Is
Philodice bryantae (Magenta-throated Woodstar)
Costa Rica, W Panama
Philodice mitchellii (Purple-throated Woodstar)
W Colombia, W Ecuador

DORICHA
Doricha enicura (Slender Sheartail)
S Mexico, Guatemala, El Salvador
Doricha eliza (Mexican Sheartail)
SE Mexico, Holbox I

TILMATURA
Tilmatura dupontii (Dupont's Hummingbird)
S Mexico to N Nicaragua

MICROSTILBON
Microstilbon burmeisteri (Slender-tailed Woodstar)
C & S Bolivia, N Argentina

CALOTHORAX
Calothorax lucifer (Lucifer Hummingbird)
SW USA to SC Mexico
Calothorax pulcher (Beautiful Hummingbird)
S Mexico

ARCHILOCHUS
Archilochus colubris (Ruby-throated Hummingbird)
S Canada, E USA to Panama
Archilochus alexandri (Black-chinned Hummingbird)
SW Canada, W USA to W Mexico

CALLIPHLOX
Calliphlox amethystina (Amethyst Woodstar)
Ecuador & Bolivia to the Guianas, NE Argentina

MELLISUGA
Mellisuga minima (Vervain Hummingbird)
M. m. minima
Jamaica
M. m. vieilloti
Gonave I, Hispaniola

CALYPTE
Calypte anna (Anna's Hummingbird)
C California, NW Baja, California
Calypte costae (Costa's Hummingbird)
SW USA, NW Mexico
Calypte helenae (Bee Hummingbird)
Cuba, Isle of Pines

STELLULA
Stellula calliope (Calliope Hummingbird)
S. c. calliope
W USA to SC Mexico
S. c. lowei
Guerrero, (Mexico)

ATTHIS
Atthis heloisa (Bumblebee Hummingbird)
A. h. margarethae
NW Mexico
A. h. heloisa
C & S Mexico

Atthis ellioti (Wine-throated Hummingbird)
A. e. ellioti
S Mexico, Guatemala
A. e. selasphoroides
Honduras

MYRTIS
Myrtis fanny (Purple-collared Woodstar)
Ecuador, W Peru

EULIDIA
Eulidia yarrellii (Chilean Woodstar)
N Chile

MYRMIA
Myrmia micrura (Short-tailed Woodstar)
W Ecuador, W Peru

ACESTRURA
**Acestrura mulsant (White-bellied
Woodstar)**
Colombia

Acestrura bombus (Little Woodstar)
Ecuador, N Peru
Acestrura heliodor (Gorgeted Woodstar)
A. h. astreans
N Colombia
A. h. heliodor
W Ecuador to W Venezuela
A. h. cleavesi
NE Ecuador
A. h. meridae
Venezuela
**Acestrura berlepschi (Esmeralda's
Woodstar)**
W Ecuador
Acestrura harterti (Hartert's Woodstar)
Ecuador

CHAETOCERCUS
**Chaetocercus jourdanii (Rufous-shafted
Woodstar)**
C. j. andinus
W Venezuela, NE Colombia
C. j. jourdanii
NE Venezuela, Trinidad
C. j. rosae
E Colombia, N & W Venezuela

SELASPHORUS
**Selasphorus playcercus (Broad-tailed
Hummingbird)**
S. p. platycercus
W USA to WC Mexico
S. p. guatemalae
W Guatemala
Selasphorus rufus (Rufous Hummingbird)
SE Alaska to WC Mexico
Selasphorus sasin (Allen's Hummingbird)
S. s. sasin
SW California, NW Mexico
S. s. sedentarius
Santa Barbara I (California)
**Selasphorus flammula (Rose-throated
Hummingbird)**
Costa Rica
**Selasphorus torridus (Heliotrope-throated
Hummingbird)**
Costa Rica, W Panama
**Selasphorus simoni (Cerise-throated
Hummingbird)**
Costa Rica
**Selasphorus ardens (Glow-throated
Hummingbird)**
W Panama
**Selasphorus scintilla (Scintillant
Hummingbird)**
Costa Rica, W Panama

Coliiformes

82 COLIIDAE (MOUSEBIRDS)

COLIUS
Colius striatus (Speckled Mousebird)
C. s. nigricollis
N Nigeria to W Zaire
C. s. leucophthalmus
S Sudan, NE Zaire
C. s. leucotis
W Sudan, Ethiopia
C. s. hilgerti
E Ethiopia, Somalia
C. s. erlangeri
W Ethiopia

C. s. jebelensis
SW Sudan, NE Zaire
C. s. ugandensis
Uganda, NW Tanzania
C. s. kikuyensis
W & C Kenya
C. s. marangu
N Tanzania
C. s. cinerascens
NW Tanzania
C. s. affinis
S Somalia, E Kenya, E Tanzania
C. s. berlepschi
S Tanzania, Malawi, NW Mozambique
C. s. kiwuensis
Kivu (Rwanda)
C. s. congicus
S Zaire
C. s. lungae
W Zambia
C. s. rhodesiae
E Rhodesia
C. s. minor
Mozambique to E Cape Province
C. s. striatus
S Cape Province

Colius castanotus (Red-backed Mousebird)
Angola

Colius colius (White-backed Mousebird)
W South Africa

Colius leucocephalus (White-headed Mousebird)
C. l. turneri
N & NE Kenya
C. l. leucocephalus
SE Kenya to NE Tanzania

Colius indicus (Red-faced Mousebird)
C. i. lualabae
S Zaire
C. i. angolensis
S Angola
C. i. lacteifrons
S Angola, N Namibia
C. i. pallidus
S Tanzania, N Malawi
C. i. transvaalensis
Rhodesia, Transvaal, Natal
C. i. indicus
Cape Province

Colius macrourus (Blue-naped Mousebird)
C. m. macrourus
Senegal to Somalia
C. m. laeneni
Niger to Aïr Mountains
C. m. pulcher
W Uganda, S Ethiopia to N Tanzania

C.m. griseogularis
Sudan to E Zaire

Trogoniformes

83 TROGONIDAE (TROGONS)

PHAROMACHRUS
Pharomachrus mocinno (Resplendent Quetzal)
P. m. mocinno
S Mexico to N Nicaragua
P. m. costaricensis
Costa Rica to W Panama
Pharomachrus antisianus (Crested Quetzal)
W Venezuela, Colombia to Brazil
Pharomachrus fulgidus (White-tipped Quetzal)
P. f. festatus
N Colombia
P. f. fulgidus
NE & NC Venezuela
Pharomachrus auriceps (Golden-headed Trogon)
Venezuela, Colombia to N Bolivia
Pharomachrus pavoninus (Pavonine Quetzal)
P. p. hargitti
E Colombia, W Venezuela
P. p. heliactin
W Ecuador
P. p. pavoninus
Upper Amazonia
P. p. viridiceps
NE Brazil

EUPTILOTIS
Euptilotis neoxenus (Eared Trogon)
C Mexico

PRIOTELUS
Priotelus temnurus (Cuban Trogon)
P. t. temnurus
Cuba
P. t. vescus
Isle of Pines

TEMNOTROGON
Temnotrogon roseigaster (Hispaniolan Trogon)
Hispaniola

TROGON
Trogon massena (Slaty-tailed Trogon)
T. m. massena
S Mexico to Nicaragua
T. m. hoffmanni
Costa Rica, Panama

T. m. australis
W Colombia
Trogon clathratus (Lattice-tailed Trogon)
E Costa Rica, W Panama
Trogon melanurus (Black-tailed Trogon)
T. m. macroura
E Panama, N Colombia
T. m. mesurus
W Ecuador, NW Peru
T. m. eumorphus
Peru
T. m. occidentalis
Brazil
T. m. melanurus
Colombia to Bolivia & N Brazil
Trogon comptus (Blue-tailed Trogon)
Colombia
Trogon viridis (White-tailed Trogon)
T. v. bairdii
SW Costa Rica, W Panama
T. v. chionurus
E Panama, W Colombia, W Ecuador
T. v. viridis
Colombia to Peru, Brazil & Trinidad
T. v. melanopterus
SE Brazil
Trogon citreolus (Citreoline Trogon)
T. c. citreolus
W Mexico
T. c. sumichrasti
S Mexico
T. c. melanocephala
E Mexico to NE Costa Rica
T. c. illaetabilis
W Costa Rica
Trogon mexicanus (Mountain Trogon)
T. m. clarus
NW Mexico
T. m. mexicanus
C Mexico to W Guatemala
T. m. lutescens
Honduras
Trogon elegans (Coppery-tailed Trogon)
T. e. canescens
S Arizona, NW Mexico
T. e. ambiguus
S Texas, E & C Mexico
T. e. elegans
Guatemala
T. e. lubricus
Nicaragua, Costa Rica
T. e. goldmani
Tres Marias Is
Trogon collaris (Collared Trogon)
T. c. puella
C Mexico to W Panama
T. c. extimus
E Panama

223

T. c. virginalis
W Colombia, W Ecuador, NW Peru
T. c. subtropicalis
C Colombia
T. c. exoptatus
N Venezuela
T. c. collaris
Colombia to Bolivia, Trinidad, S Brazil
T. c. castaneus
SE Colombia, NW Brazil
Trogon aurantiiventris (Orange-bellied Trogon)
T. a. underwoodi
NW Costa Rica
T. a. aurantiiventris
C Costa Rica to W Panama
T. a. flavidior
E Panama
Trogon personatus (Masked Trogon)
T. p. sanctaemartae
N Colombia
T. p. ptaritepui
Venezuela
T. p. personatus
W Venezuela, E Colombia, E Peru
T. p. assimilis
W Ecuador
T. p. temperatus
C Colombia, Ecuador
T. p. submontanus
Bolivia
T. p. duidae
Mt Duida (Venezuela)
T. p. roraimae
SE Venezuela, S Guyana
Trogon rufus (Black-throated Trogon)
T. r. tenellus
SE Honduras to NW Colombia
T. r. cupreicauda
W Colombia, W Ecuador
T. r. rufus
E Venezuela, the Guianas, N Brazil
T. r. sulphureus
E Peru, W Brazil
T. r. amazonicus
NE Brazil
T. r. chrysochloros
S Brazil, Paraguay, NE Argentina
Trogon surracura (Surucua Trogon)
T. s. aurantius
E Brazil
T. s. surracura
S Brazil, Paraguay, Uruguay, N Argentina
Trogon curucui (Blue-crowned Trogon)
T. c. bolivianus
S Colombia to Bolivia, W Brazil
T. c. peruvianus
SC Colombia

T. c. curucui
E Brazil
T. c. behni
E Bolivia, S Brazil, Paraguay, N Argentina
Trogon violaceus (Violaceous Trogon)
T. v. braccatus
C Mexico to Nicaragua
T. v. concinnus
Costa Rica to W Ecuador
T. v. caligatus
N Colombia, W Venezuela
T. v. violaceus
Venezuela, the Guianas, N Brazil, Trinidad
T. v. ramonianus
Upper Amazonia
T. v. crissalis
E Brazil

APALODERMA
Apaloderma narina (Narina's Trogon)
A. n. constantia
Liberia to Ghana
A. n. brachyurum
S Cameroun to Uganda, Zaire
A. n. narina
Sudan & Ethiopia to Cape Province
A. n. littoralis
E Kenya, E Tanzania, Zanzibar I
Apaloderma aequatoriale (Bare-cheeked Trogon)
Cameroun to S Zaire

HETEROTROGON
Heterotrogon vittatus (Bartailed Trogon)
H. v. camerunensis
Cameroun, Angola, Zaire
H. v. vittatus
Kenya, Tanzania

HARPACTES
Harpactes reinwardtii (Reinwardt's Blue-tailed Trogon)
H. r. mackloti
Sumatra
H. r. reinwardtii
Java
Harpactes fasciatus (Malabar Trogon)
H. f. malabaricus
W & S India
H. f. fasciatus
Sri Lanka
H. f. parvus
Sri Lanka
Harpactes kasumba (Red-naped Trogon)
H. k. kasumba
Malaysia, Sumatra
H. k. impavidus
Borneo

Harpactes diardii (Diard's Trogon)
H. d. sumatranus
Malaysia, Sumatra
H. d. diardii
Borneo, Bangka I
Harpactes ardens (Philippine Trogon)
H. a. ardens
Philippine Is
H. a. luzoniensis
Luzon, Bataan I
Harpactes whiteheadi (White-head's Trogon)
Mt Kinabalu (N Borneo)
Harpactes orrhophaeus (Cinnamon-rumped Trogon)
H. o. orrhophaeus
Malaysia, Sumatra
H. o. vidua
NW Borneo
Harpactes duvaucelii (Scarlet-rumped Trogon)
S Burma, Malaysia, Sumatra
Harpactes oreskios (Orange-breasted Trogon)
H. o. stellae
S Burma, S Indochina
H. o. uniformis
S Burma, Malaysia, Sumatra
H. o. oreskios
Java
H. o. dulitensis
NW Borneo
H. o. nias
Nias I
Harpactes erythrocephalus (Red-headed Trogon)
H. e. erythrocephalus
Himalayas, Burma, NW Thailand
H. e. helenae
W Yunnan, N Burma
H. e. yamakanensis
SE China
H. e. rosa
SC China
H. e. intermedius
N Laos, N Vietnam
H. e. annamensis
NE Thailand, S Indochina
H. e. klossi
W Cambodia
H. e. chaseni
Malaysia
H. e. hainanus
Hainan I
H. e. flagrans
Sumatra
Harpactes wardi (Ward's Trogon)
N Burma, NE Vietnam

Coraciiformes

84 ALCEDINIDAE (KINGFISHERS)

CERYLINAE

CERYLE

Ceryle lugubris (Greater Pied Kingfisher)
  C. l. guttulata
    Himalayas, China, Burma, Thailand
  C. l. pallida
    Hokkaido I
  C. l. lugubris
    Japan, Korea
Ceryle maxima (Giant Kingfisher)
  C. m. maxima
    Senegal to Nigeria, Ethiopia to Cape
    Province
  C. m. gigantea
    S Nigeria to Zaire, Tanzania
Ceryle torquata (Ringed Kingfisher)
  C. t. torquata
    Mexico to N Argentina, Peru
  C. t. stictipennis
    Guadeloupe I, Dominica I
  C. t. stellata
    Chile, Argentina
Ceryle alcyon (Belted Kingfisher)
  C. a. caurina
    Alaska to W Mexico
  C. a. alcyon
    C & E Canada to N South America
    & West Indies
Ceryle rudis (Lesser Pied Kingfisher)
  C. r. rudis
    Asia Minor, Iran, Africa
  C. r. leucomelanura
    Pakistan to Burma, Indochina
  C. r. travancoreensis
    SW India
  C. r. insignis
    SE China, Hainan I

CHLOROCERYLE
**Chloroceryle amazona (Amazon
  Kingfisher)**
  C. a. mexicana
    S Mexico to E Panama
  C. a. amazona
    N South America
Chloroceryle americana (Green Kingfisher)
  C. a. hachisukai
    W Texas, NW Mexico
  C. a. septentrionalis
    SE Texas, E Mexico, Guatemala
  C. a. isthmica
    Honduras to N Colombia, Pearl Is
    (Panama)

  C. a. americana
    N South America (East of Andes)
  C. a. hellmayri
    W Colombia
  C. a. ecuadorensis
    W Ecuador
  C. a. cabanisii
    W Peru
  C. a. croteta
    Trinidad, Tobago I
  C. a. mathewsii
    C & SC South America
**Chloroceryle inda (Green and Rufous
  Kingfisher)**
  C. i. inda
    Panama & tropical South America
  C. i. chocoensis
    W Colombia, W Ecuador
Chloroceryle aenea (Pygmy Kingfisher)
  C. a. stictoptera
    S Mexico to Nicaragua
  C. a. aenea
    Costa Rica, Panama, N South America,
    Trinidad

ALCEDININAE

ALCEDO
Alcedo hercules (Blyth's Kingfisher)
    E Himalayas to N Vietnam
Alcedo atthis (Common Kingfisher)
  A. a. ispida
    Europe
  A. a. atthis
    Mediterranean, Syria, Arabia
  A. a. bengalensis
    N India to Philippine Is & Gtr Sunda Is
  A. a. taprobana
    S India, Sri Lanka
  A. a. japonica
    Sakhalin I, Japan, Taiwan
  A. a. floresiana
    Bali to Timor I
  A. a. hispidoides
    Celebes to Bismarck Archipelago
      & NE New Guinea
  A. a. salomonensis
    Solomon Is
**Alcedo semitorquata (Half-collared
  Kingfisher)**
    Ethiopia to Angola & Cape Province
Alcedo meninting (Blue-eared Kingfisher)
  A. m. coltarti
    Sikkim to S Burma & Laos
  A. m. laubmanni
    E India
  A. m. phillipsi
    SW India, Sri Lanka

A. m. scintillans
S Burma, S Thailand
A. m. rufigaster
Andaman Is
A. m. verreauxii
Malaysia, Sumatra, Borneo
A. m. proxima
Pagi Is
A. m. subviridis
Banjak Is, Nias I
A. m. callima
Batu Is
A. m. meninting
Java to Lombok I & Sula Is
Alcedo quadribrachys (Shining-blue Kingfisher)
A. q. quadribrachys
Gambia to N Nigeria
A. q. guentheri
S Nigeria to Uganda, S Zaire & Angola
Alcedo euryzona (Broad-zoned Kingfisher)
A. e. peninsulae
Malaysia, Sumatra
A. e. euryzona
Java, Borneo
Alcedo coerulescens (Small Blue Kingfisher)
Java to Sumbawa I
Alcedo cristata (Malachite Kingfisher)
A. c. cristata
Senegal to Ethiopia & Cape Province
A. c. robertsi
Botswana
A. c. johannae
Comoro Is
A. c. vintsioides
Madagascar
Alcedo leucogaster (White-bellied Kingfisher)
A. l. leucogaster
S Nigeria to N Angola, Fernando Po I
A. l. bowdleri
Guinea to Ghana
A. l. thomensis
Sao Tomé I
A. l. nais
Principé I
A. l. leopoldi
WC Zaire

MYIOCEYX
Myioceyx lecontei (African Dwarf Kingfisher)
M. l. lecontei
Sierra Leone to Angola & E Zaire
M. l. ugandae
W Uganda

ISPIDINA
Ispidina picta (African Pygmy Kingfisher)
I. p. picta
Senegal to Angola, Kenya & Ethiopia
I. p. jubaensis
S Somalia
I. p. natalensis
S Zaire & Tanzania to Natal
Ispidina madagascariensis (Madagascar Pygmy Kingfisher
I. m. madagascariensis
Madagascar
I. m. diluta
Sakaraha, Madagascar

CEYX
Ceyx cyanopectus (Dwarf River Kingfishe
C. c. cyanopectus
Luzon I, Mindoro I, Masbate I, Ticao I
C. c. nigrirostris
Panay I, Negros I, Cebu I
Ceyx argentatus (Silvery Kingfisher)
C. a. argentatus
Panay I, Negros I, Cebu I, Mindanao I
C. a. flumenicolus
Samar I, Leyte I
Ceyx goodfellowi (Goodfellow's Kingfisher)
C. g. goodfellowi
Mindanao I
C. g. virgicapitus
Tawitawi Is
Ceyx lepidus (Dwarf Kingfisher)
C. l. margarethae
S Philippine Is
C. l. wallacii
Sula Is
C. l. lepidus
Moluccas
C. l. cajeli
Buru I
C. l. solitarius
New Guinea & islands, Aru Is
C. l. dispar
Admiralty Is
C. l. mulcatus
New Hanover, New Ireland
C. l. sacerdotis
New Britain, Rook I
C. l. pallidus
Bougainville I, Buka I
C. l. collectoris
Choiseul I, Vella Lavella I, New Georgia I
Rendova I
C. l. meeki
Choiseul I, Ysabel I
C. l. malaitae
Malaita I

C. l. nigromaxilla
  Guadalcanal I
C. l. gentianus
  San Cristobal I
Ceyx azureus (Azure Kingfisher)
  C. a. affinis
    N Moluccas
  C. a. yamdenae
    Tenimber Is
  C. a. wallaceanus
    Aru Is
  C. a. lessonii
    W Papuan Is, New Guinea lowlands
  C. a. ochrogaster
    N New Guinea & Geelvinck Bay Is
  C. a. ruficollaris
    Northern Australia
  C. a. mixtus
    NE Queensland
  C. a. azureus
    E & S Australia, Tasmania
Ceyx websteri (Bismarck Pygmy Kingfisher)
    Bismarck Archipelago
Ceyx pusillus (Mangrove Kingfisher)
  C. p. halmaherae
    Halmahera I, Obi I
  C. p. pusillus
    W Papuan Is, New Guinea, Kei Is
  C. p, laetior
    N New Guinea
  C. p. ramsayi
    N Territory (Australia)
  C. p. halli
    N Queensland
  C. p. masauji
    Bismarck Archipelago
  C. p. bougainvillei
    Bougainville I, Choiseul I, Ysabel I
  C. p. richardsi
    Vella Lavella I, Kolambangaa I,
      New Georgia I
  C. p. aolae
    Guadalcanal I
Ceyx erithacus (Three-toed Kingfisher)
  C. e. erithacus
    India to SE China, Indochina, Sumatra
  C. e. macrocarus
    Andaman Is, Nicobar Is
  C. e. motleyi
    N Bornean Is, Borneo
  C. e. captus
    Nias I
  C. e. vargasi
    Mindoro I

Ceyx rufidorsum (Malay Forest Kingfisher) 227
  C. r. rufidorsum
    Malaysia to W Philippine Is, Borneo &
    Flores I
  C. r. jungei
    Batu Is, Simalur I
Ceyx melanurus (Philippine Forest Kingfisher)
  C. m. melanurus
    Luzon I
  C. m. samarensis
    Samar I, Leyte I
  C. m. mindanensis
    Mindanao I, Basilan I
Ceyx fallax (Celebes Pygmy Kingfisher)
  C. f. sangirensis
    Sanghir Is
  C. f. fallax
    Celebes

DACELONINAE

PELARGOPSIS
Pelargopsis amauroptera (Brown-winged Kingfisher)
    NE India to Malaysia
Pelargopsis capensis (Stork-billed Kingfisher)
  P. c. capensis
    Nepal, India, Sri Lanka
  P. c. burmanica
    Burma to Indochina & N Malaysia
  P. c. intermedia
    Nicobar Is
  P. c. malaccensis
    S Malaysia
  P. c. cyanopteryx
    Sumatra, Bangka I, Billiton I
  P. c. simalurensis
    Simalur I
  P. c. sodalis
    Banjak Is
  P. c. nesoeca
    Nias I, Batu Is
  P. c. isoptera
    Pagi Is, Siberut I, Sipora I
  P. c. fraseri
    Java
  P. c. floresiana
    Bali I to Flores I
  P. c. javana
    Borneo
  P. c. gouldi
    N & W Philippine Is
  P. c. smithi
    SE Luzon, Masbate I, Panay I, Negros I
  P. c. gigantea
    S Philippine Is

Pelargopsis melanorhyncha (Black-bellied Kingfisher)
P. m. melanorhyncha
N, NC & SE Celebes
P. m. dicrorhyncha
Peleng I, Banggai Is
P. m. eutreptorhyncha
Sula Is

LACEDO
Lacedo pulchella (Banded Kingfisher)
L. p. amabilis
S Burma, Thailand, S Vietnam
L. p. deignani
S Thailand
L. p. pulchella
Malaysia, Sumatra, Java
L. p. melanops
Borneo, Bangka I

DACELO
Dacelo novaeguineae (Laughing Kookaburra)
D. n. minor
N Queensland
D. n. novaeguineae
Australia, Tasmania
Dacelo leachii (Blue-winged Kookaburra)
D. l. superflua
S New Guinea
D. l. intermedia
SE New Guinea
D. l. cliftoni
NW Australia
D. l. kempi
N Queensland
D. l. cervina
Melville I, N Northern Territory
D. l. leachii
C Northern Territory, S Queensland
Dacelo tyro (Aru Giant Kingfisher)
D. t. archboldi
S New Guinea
D. t. tyro
Aru Is
Dacelo gaudichaud (Rufous-bellied Giant Kingfisher)
New Guinea, New Guinea Is, Aru Is

CLYTOCEYX
Clytoceyx rex (Shovel-billed Kingfisher)
C. r. rex
E New Guinea
C. r. imperator
C New Guinea

MELIDORA
Melidora macrorrhina (Hook-billed Kingfisher)
M. m. waigiuensis
Waigeu I

M. m. macrorrhina
Misoöl I, Batanta I, New Guinea
M. m. jobiensis
Japen I, N New Guinea

CITTURA
Cittura cyanotis (Celebes Blue-eared Kingfisher)
C. c. sanghirensis
Sanghir Is
C. c. cyanotis
N Celebes
C. c. modesta
E & SE Celebes

HALCYON
Halcyon coromanda (Ruddy Kingfisher)
H. c. major
Korea, Japan to S China & Celebes
H. c. coromanda
Nepal to Malaysia & Indochina
H. c. mizorhina
Andaman & Nicobar Is
H. c. minor
S Malaysia, Borneo, Sumatra, Java
H. c. bangsi
Riukiu Is, Taiwan, N & W Philippine Is
H. c. ochrothorectis
S Philippine Is
H. c. pelingensis
Celebes, Peling Is
H. c. rufa
Sula Is
Halcyon badia (Chocolate-backed Kingfisher)
H. b. lopezi
Fernando Po I
H. b. badia
Liberia to Gabon & E Zaire
H. b. budongensis
W & C Uganda
Halcyon smyrnensis (White-Breasted Kingfisher)
H. s. smyrnensis
Asia Minor to S Yemen & India
H. s. fusca
W India, Sri Lanka
H. s. saturatior
Andaman Is
H. s. perpulchra
Burma, Malaysia to Indochina
H. s. fokiensis
S & E China, Taiwan
H. s. gularis
Philippine Is
Halcyon pileata (Black-capped Kingfisher)
India to China, Philippine Is, Celebes
Halcyon cyanoventris (Java Kingfisher)
Java, Bali I

Halcyon leucocephala (Grey-headed Kingfisher)
H. l. acteon
　Cape Verde Is
H. l. leucocephala
　Senegal to N Zaire & Ethiopia
H. l. semicaerulea
　Yemen & S Yemen
H. l. centralis
　Kenya, N Tanzania
H. l. hyacinthina
　E Kenya to Mozambique
H. l. pallidiventris
　S Zaire to Namibia & Rhodesia
Halcyon senegalensis (Woodland Kingfisher)
H. s. fuscopilea
　Sierra Leone to Angola & S Zaire
H. s. senegalensis
　Senegal to Ethiopia & Kenya
H. s. cyanoleuca
　S Angola to Malawi & Transvaal
Halcyon senegaloides (African Mangrove Kingfisher)
H. s. ranivora
　coast of E Africa
H. s. senegaloides
　coast of SE Africa
Halcyon malimbica (Blue-breasted Kingfisher)
H. m. fortis
　Senegal
H. m. torquata
　Gambia, Guinea
H. m. forbesi
　Sierra Leone to S Cameroun
H. m. dryas
　Principé I
H. m. malimbica
　S Cameroun to Angola & Zaire
H. m. prenticei
　Sudan, E Zaire, Uganda
Halcyon albiventris (Brown-hooded Kingfisher)
H. a. erlangeri
　S Somalia, NE Kenya
H. a. orientalis
　S Gabon & Angola to N Kenya & Mozambique
H. a. albiventris
　Rhodesia to E Cape Province
H. a. vociferans
　NE South Africa
Halcyon chelicuti (Striped Kingfisher)
H. c. eremogiton
　S Niger to E Sudan

H. c. chelicuti
　Senegal to Ethiopia & Zambia
H. c. damarensis
　S Angola to Transvaal & Mozambique
Halycon nigrocyanea (Blue-black Kingfisher)
H. n. nigrocyanea
　W New Guinea
H. n. quadricolour
　Japen I, N New Guinea
H. n. stictolaema
　S New Guinea
Halcyon winchelli (Winchell's Kingfisher)
H. w. nigrorum
　Negros I
H. w. winchelli
　S Philippine Is
Halcyon diops (Moluccan Kingfisher)
　N Moluccas
Halcyon lazuli (South Moluccan Kingfisher)
　S Moluccas
Halcyon macleayii (Forest Kingfisher)
H. m. elizabeth
　E New Guinea
H. m. insularis
　Aru Is
H. m. macleayii
　N & E Australia to New Guinea
H. m. incincta
　E Queensland » E New Guinea
Halcyon albonotata (White-backed Kingfisher)
　New Britain
Halcyon leucopygia (Ultramarine Kingfisher)
　Solomon Is
Halcyon farquhari (Chestnut-bellied Kingfisher)
　C New Hebrides
Halcyon pyrrhopygia (Red-backed Kingfisher)
　dry areas of Australia
Halcyon tototoro (Lesser Yellow-billed Kingfisher)
H. t. torotoro
　W Papuan Is & W New Guinea
H. t. tentelare
　Aru Is
H. t. pseustes
　S New Guinea
H. t. brevirostris
　S New Guinea
H. t. meeki
　SE New Guinea
H. t. flavirostris
　N Queensland
H. t. ochracea
　D'Entrecasteaux Archipelago

Halcyon megarhyncha (Mountain Yellow-billed Kingfisher)
H. m. wellsi
C New Guinea
H. m. sellamontis
E New Guinea
H. m. megarhyncha
SE New Guinea
Halcyon australasia (Timor Kingfisher)
H. a. australasia
Lombok I, Sumba I, Timor I, Wetar I
H. a. tringorum
Roma I
H. a. dammeriana
Damar I, Babar I
H. a. interposita
Leti I, Moa I
H. a. odites
Timorlaut
Halcyon sancta (Sacred Kingfisher)
H. s. sancta
Australia to Sumatra, Borneo, Philippine Is
H. s. vagans
New Zealand, Kermadec Is
H. s. norfolkiensis
Norfolk I
H. s. adamsi
Lord Howe I
H. s. canacorum
New Caledonia I
H. s. macmillani
Loyalty Is
Halcyon cinnamomina (Micronesian Kingfisher)
H. c. pelewensis
Palau Is
H. c. reichenbachii
Ponapé I
H. c. cinnamomina
Guam I
Halcyon funebris (Sombre Kingfisher)
Halmahera I, Ternate I
Halcyon chloris (White-collared Kingfisher)
H. c. abyssinica
Red Sea
H. c. vidali
W India
H. c. davisoni
Andaman Is
H. c. occipitalis
Nicobar Is
H. c. humii
Burma, Malaysia, NE Sumatra
H. c. armstrongi
S Thailand, S Vietnam
H. c. chloroptera
W Sumatran Is

H. c. azela
Enggano I
H. c. palmeri
Java, Bali I
H. c. laubmanniana
Borneo & Bornean Is, S Sumatra
H. c. collaris
Philippine Is
H. c. enigma
Talaut I
H. c. chloris
Celebes to NW New Guinea, E Lesser Sunda Is
H. c. sordida
SE New Guinea, Louisiade Archipelago
H. c. colona
SE New Guinea, Louisiade Arch
H. c. teraokai
Palau Is
H. c. owstoni
Ascuncion I, Pagan I, Alamagan Is (Mariana Is)
H. c. albicilla
Saipan I, Tinan I (Mariana Is)
H. c. orii
Rota I
H. c. matthiae
St Matthias Is
H. c. stresemanni
French I, Rook I
H. c. nusae
Bismarck Archipelago
H. c. novaehiberniae
SW New Ireland
H. c. bennetti
Nissan I
H. c. tristrami
New Britain
H. c. alberti
N & C Solomon Is
H. c. mala
Malaita I
H. c. pavuvu
Pavuvu I
H. c. solomonis
Ugi I, San Cristobal I, St Anna I
H. c. amoena
Rennell I
H. c. brachyura
Reef I
H. c. vicina
Duff I
H. c. ornata
Santa Cruz Is, Tinakula I
H. c. utupuae
Utupua I
H. c. melanodera
Vanikoro I

H. c. torresiana
Torres I
H. c. santoensis
Espiritu Santo I, Banks Is
H. c. erromangae
Erromanga I
H. c. tannensis
Tanna I
H. c. juliae
Aneitum I, Efate I
H. c. vitiensis
Viti Levu I, Vanua Levu I, Taviuni I
H. c. eximia
Kandavu I, Ono I, Vanua Kula I
H. c. marina
Lau Archipelago
H. c. sacra
Tonga I
H. c. regina
Futuna I
H. c. pealei
Tutuila I, Samoa
H. c. manuae
Ofu I, Olosinga I, Tau I
Halcyon saurophaga (White-headed Kingfisher)
H. s. saurophaga
N Moluccas to Solomon Is
H. s. anachoreta
Hermit I, Ninigo I
H. s. admiralitatis
Admiralty Is
Halcyon recurvirostris (Flat-billed Kingfisher)
Samoa
Halcyon venerata (Tahitian Kingfisher)
H. v. venerata
Tahiti I
H. v. youngi
Moorea I
Halcyon tuta (Borabora Kingfisher)
H. t. tuta
Borabora I
H. t. atiu
Atiu I (Cook Is)
H. t. mauke
Mauke I (Cook Is)
Halcyon ruficollaris (Mangaia Kingfisher)
Mangaia I (Cook Is)
Halcyon gambieri (Tuamotu Kingfisher)
H. g. gambieri
Mangareva I
H. g. gertrudae
Niau I
Halcyon godeffroyi (Marquesas Kingfisher)
Marquesas Is

Halcyon bougainvillei (Moustached Kingfisher)
H. b. bougainvillei
Bougainville I
H. b. excelsa
Guadalcanal I
Halcyon concreta (Chestnut-collared Kingfisher)
H. c. concreta
S Burma, Malaysia, Sumatra, Bangka I
H. c. peristephes
S Thailand
H. c. borneana
Borneo
Halcyon lindsayi (Spotted Wood Kingfisher)
H. l. lindsayi
Luzon I
H. l. moseleyi
Negros I
H. l. hombroni
Mindanao I
Halcyon fulgida (Glittering Kingfisher)
H. f. fulgida
Lombok I, Sumbawa I
H. f. gracilirostris
Flores I
Halcyon monacha (Lonely Kingfisher)
H. m. monacha
N Celebes
H. m. intermedia
NC Celebes
H. m. capucina
E, S & SE Celebes
Halcyon princeps (Princely Kingfisher)
H. p. princeps
NE Celebes
H. p. erythrorhamphus
NW & C Celebes
H. p. regalis
SE Celebes

TANYSIPTERA
Tanysiptera hydrocharis (Aru Paradise Kingfisher)
S New Guinea, Aru Is
Tanysiptera galatea (Common Paradise Kingfisher)
T. g. emiliae
Rau I, Moluccas
T. g. doris
Morotai I
T. g. margarethae
Halmahera I, Batjan I
T. g. sabrina
Kayoa I, Moluccas
T. g. obiensis
Obi I, Oblilatu I

T. g. actis
Buru I
T. g. nais
S Moluccas Is
T. g. galatea
NW New Guinea & W Papuan Is
T. g. meyeri
N New Guinea
T. g. minor
S & SE New Guinea
T. g. vulcani
Vulcan I
T. g. rosseliana
Rossel I
Tanysiptera riedelii (Biak Paradise Kingfisher)
Biak I
Tanysiptera carolinae (Numfor Paradise Kingfisher)
Numfor I
Tanysiptera ellioti (Kofiau Paradise Kingfisher)
Kofiau I
Tanysiptera nympha (Pink-breasted Paradise Kingfisher)
New Guinea
Tanysiptera danae (Brown-backed Paradise Kingfisher)
SE New Guinea
Tanysiptera sylvia (White-tailed Kingfisher)
T. s. leucura
Rook I
T. s. nigriceps
New Britain, Duke of York I
T. s. salvadoriana
SE New Guinea
T. s. sylvia
N Queensland to S New Guinea

85 TODIDAE (TODIES)

TODUS
Todus multicolor (Cuban Tody)
Cuba, Isle of Pines
Todus angustirostris (Narrow-billed Tody)
Hispaniola
Todus todus (Jamaican Tody)
Jamaica
Todus mexicanus (Puerto Rican Tody)
Puerto Rico
Todus subulatus (Broad-billed Tody)
Hispaniola, Gonave I

86 MOMOTIDAE (MOTMOTS)

HYLOMANES
Hylomanes momotula (Tody-Motmot)
H. m. chiapensis
(Pacific) S Mexico

H. m. momotula
(Carribean) S Mexico to Honduras
H. m. obscurus
NW Costa Rica to NW Colombia

ASPATHA
Aspatha gularis (Blue-throated Motmot)
S Mexico to Honduras, El Salvador

ELECTRON
Electron platyrhynchum (Broad-billed Motmot)
E. p. minor
E Honduras to C Colombia
E. p. platyrhynchum
W Colombia, W Ecuador
E. p. pyrrholaemum
E Colombia, E Ecuador, Peru, N Bolivia
E. p. orienticola
W Brazil
E. p. chlorophrys
SW & C Brazil
E. p. colombianum
Colombia
Electron carinatum (Keel-billed Motmot)
S Mexico to NW Costa Rica

EUMOMOTA
Eumomota superciliosa (Turquoise-browed Motmot)
E. s. bipartita
S Mexico, W Guatemala
E. s. superciliosa
SE Mexico
E. s. vanrossemi
C Guatemala
E. s. sylvestris
E Guatemala
E. s. apiaster
El Salvador, W Honduras, NW Nicaragua
E. s. euroaustris
N Honduras
E. s. australis
NW Costa Rica

BARYPHTHENGUS
Baryphthengus ruficapillus (Rufous Motmot)
B. r. semirufus
Panama to W Ecuador
B. r. costaricensis
E Nicaragua, E Costa Rica
B. r. ruficapillus
S & E Brazil, Paraguay, NE Argentina
Baryphthengus martii (Martin's Rufous Motmot)
Upper Amazonia

Momotus mexicanus (Russet-crowned Motmot)
  M. m. vanrossemi
    NW Mexico
  M. m. mexicanus
    NC & C Mexico
  M. m. saturatus
    SW Mexico
  M. m. castaneiceps
    C Guatemala
Momotus momota (Blue-crowned Motmot)
  M. m. coeruliceps
    NE & C Mexico
  M. m. goldmani
    SE Mexico, N Guatemala
  M. m. exiguus
    S Mexico
  M. m. lessonii
    S Mexico to W Panama
  M. m. conexus
    S Panama, NW Colombia
  M. m. reconditus
    E Panama, N Colombia
  M. m. spatha
    Colombia
  M. m. subrufescens
    N Colombia, N Venezuela
  M. m. osgoodi
    W Venezuela
  M. m. bahamensis
    Trinidad, Tobago I
  M. m. aequatorialis
    WC Colombia, E Ecuador
  M. m. chlorolaemus
    E Peru
  M. m. microstephanus
    SE Colombia, E Ecuador, NW Brazil
  M. m. momota
    E Venezuela, the Guianas, N Brazil
  M. m. argenticinctus
    W Ecuador, NW Peru
  M. m. ignobilis
    E Peru, W Brazil
  M. m. nattereri
    NE Bolivia
  M. m. simplex
    W Brazil
  M. m. cametensis
    NC Brazil
  M. m. parensis
    NE Brazil
  M. m. pilcomajensis
    S Bolivia, S Brazil, NW Argentina

NYCTYORNIS
Nyctyornis amicta (Red-bearded Bee Eater)
  Malaysia, Sumatra, Borneo
Nyctyornis athertoni (Blue-bearded Bee Eater)
  N. a. athertoni
    SW India & S Himalayas to Indochina
  N. a. brevicaudata
    Hainan I

MEROPOGON
Meropogon forsteni (Celebes Bearded Bee Eater)
  Celebes

MEROPS
Merops gularis (Black Bee Eater)
  M. g. gularis
    Sierra Leone to Niger river
  M. g. australis
    Cameroun to Uganda & Angola
Merops muelleri (Blue-headed Bee Eater)
  M. m. mentalis
    Sierra Leone to Cameroun
  M. m. muelleri
    S Cameroun to E Zaire
  M. m. yalensis
    Uganda, W Kenya
Merons bulocki (Red-throated Bee Eater)
  M. b. bulocki
    Senegal to Central African Republic
  M. b. frenatus
    E Sudan to N Zaire & N Uganda
Merops bullockoides (White-fronted Bee Eater)
  Gabon to Angola, Kenya & Natal
Merops pusillus (Little Bee Eater)
  M. p. pusillus
    Senegal to N Zaire
  M. p. ocularis
    Sudan, W Ethiopia
  M. p. cyanostictus
    Ethiopia & Somalia to Tanzania
  M. p. meridionalis
    S Zaire & Tanzania to Namibia & Natal
Merops variegatus (Blue-breasted Bee Eater)
  M. v. loringi
    Cameroun to Uganda
  M. v. variegatus
    Gabon to Zaire & Angola
  M. v. bangweoloensis
    S Zaire & Zambia
  M. v. lafresnayii
    Ethiopia
Merops oreobates (Cinnamon-chested Bee Eater)
  S Sudan, E Zaire, N Tanzania

***Merops hirundineus* (Swallow-tailed Bee Eater)**
M. h. chrysolaimus
Senegal to Ghana & Central African Republic
M. h. heuglini
N Zaire, Uganda to Tanzania
M. h. hirundineus
SE Kenya to Angola & Natal
***Merops breweri* (Black-headed Bee Eater)**
Cameroun, Gabon, W Zaire
***Merops revoilii* (Somali Bee Eater)**
SE Ethiopia, Somalia, NE Kenya
***Merops albicollis* (White-throated Bee Eater)**
Senegal to Ethiopia & Tanzania
***Merops orientalis* (Little Green Bee Eater)**
M. o. viridissimus
Senegal to Aïr & N Ethiopia
M. o. cleopatra
Nile valley, Egypt
M. o. cyanophrys
W Saudi Arabia
M. o. muscatensis
Oman
M. o. najdanus
C Saudi Arabia
M. o. beludschicus
SE Iran to NW India
M. o. orientalis
India
M. o. ceylonicus
Sri Lanka
M. o. birmanus
Assam, Burma, W China, Indochina
***Merops boehmi* (Boehm's Bee Eater)**
Tanzania, E Zambia, Malawi
***Merops viridis* (Chestnut-headed Bee Eater)**
M. v. viridis
SE China to Sumatra, Java, Borneo
M. v. americanus
Philippine Is
***Merops superciliosus* (Blue-cheeked Bee Eater)**
M. s. persicus
Israel to C Asia » NW India & Africa
M. s. chrysocercus
N Africa to W Africa
M. s. superciliosus
Madagascar to S, C & E Africa
***Merops philippinus* (Blue-tailed Bee Eater)**
M. p. philippinus
India to SE China, Borneo & Lesser Sunda Is
M. p. celebensis
S Celebes

M. p. salvadorii
E New Guinea, New Britain
***Merops ornatus* (Australian Bee Eater)**
Australia to Lesser Sunda Is
***Merops apiaster* (European Bee Eater)**
S Europe & C Asia » N India & Africa
***Merops leschenaulti* (Bay-headed Bee Eater)**
M. l. leschenaulti
W India to Malaysia & Indochina
M. l. quinticolor
Java, Bali I
M. l. andamanensis
S Andaman Is
***Merops malimbicus* (Rosy Bee Eater)**
Ghana to N & W Zaire
***Merops nubicus* (Carmine Bee Eater)**
M. n. nubicus
Senegal to Zaire & Ethiopia
M. n. nubicoides
Angola to Natal » S Zaire & Tanzania

88 CORACIIDAE (ROLLERS)

CORACIAS
***Coracias garrulus* (Common Roller)**
C. g. garrulus
S Europe & C Asia » Africa & India
C. g. semenowi
Transcaspia to NW India
***Coracias abyssinica* (Abyssinian Roller)**
Senegal to S Yemen & Kenya
***Coracias caudata* (Lilac-breasted Roller)**
C. c. lorti
S Ethiopia, Somalia, N Kenya
C. c. caudata
Uganda to Angola & N & E South Africa
***Coracias spatulata* (Racquet-tailed Roller)**
Angola to Tanzania & Mozambique
***Coracias naevia* (Rufous-crowned Roller)**
C. n. naevia
Senegal to Ethiopia & N Tanzania
C. n. mosambica
Angola & S Zaire to E Cape Province
***Coracias benghalensis* (Indian Roller)**
C. b. benghalensis
E Saudi Arabia to NE India
C. b. indica
S India, Sri Lanka
C. b. affinis
Bhutan to Malaysia & Indochina
***Coracias temminckii* (Celebes Roller)**
Celebes
***Coracias cyanogaster* (Blue-bellied Roller)**
Senegal to N Zaire & Sudan

EURYSTOMUS
Eurystomus glaucurus (Broad-billed Roller)
  E. g. afer
    Senegal to NE Zaire & E Ethiopia
  E. g. aethiopicus
    Sudan, W Ethiopia
  E. g. rufobuccalis
    C & S Uganda
  E. g. suahelicus
    Somalia to C Zaire & NE Zambia
  E. g. pulcherrimus
    Angola to Mozambique & Natal
  E. g. glaucurus
    Madagascar to C Africa
Eurystomus gularis (Blue-throated Roller)
  E. g. gularis
    Senegal to Mali & Togo
  E. g. neglectus
    Cameroun to Angola & E Zaire
Eurystomus orientalis (Eastern Broad-billed Roller)
  E. o. abundus
    N Himalayas to Korea, Indochina, Malaysia
  E. o. deignani
    N Thailand to Sumatra, Java, Borneo
  E. o. orientalis
    S Himalayas to Sumatra & N Celebes
  E. o. gigas
    S Andaman Is
  E. o. oberholseri
    Simalur I
  E. o. latouchei
    NE China
  E. o. connectens
    S Celebes, Lombok I to Damar I
  E. o. azureus
    N Moluccas
  E. o. waigiouensis
    New Guinea & islands
  E. o. pacificus
    Australia to New Guinea & Kei Is
  E. o. crassirostris
    Bismarck Archipelago
  E. o. solomonensis
    Feni I, Solomon Is

89 BRACHYPTERACIIDAE (GROUND ROLLERS)

BRACHYPTERACIAS
Brachypteracias leptosomus (Short-legged Ground Roller)
  NE Madagascar
Brachypteracias squamigera (Scaly Ground Roller)
  NE Madagascar

ATELORNIS
Atelornis pittoides (Pitta-like Ground Roller)
  Madagascar
Atelornis crossleyi (Crossley's Ground Roller)
  NE Madagascar

URATELORNIS
Uratelornis chimaera (Long-tailed Ground Roller)
  SW Madagascar

90 LEPTOSOMATIDAE (COUROLS)

LEPTOSOMUS
Leptosomus discolor (Courol)
  L. d. gracilis
    Gd Comoro I
  L. d. intermedius
    Anjouan I
  L. d. discolor
    Mayotte I, Madagascar

91 UPUPIDAE (HOOPOES)

UPUPA
Upupa epops (Hoopoe)
  U. e. epops
    Europe & W Asia to W & C Africa & India
  U. e. major
    Egypt
  U. e. senegalensis
    Senegal to Ethiopia & NE Tanzania
  U. e. orientalis
    NW India
  U. e. ceylonensis
    C & S India, Sri Lanka
  U. e. saturata
    E Siberia to N & E China
  U. e. longirostris
    Assam to Indochina, Malaysia, Sumatra
  U. e. marginata
    Madagascar
  U. e. africana
    S Zaire to Uganda, Kenya & Cape Province
  U. e. waibeli
    Cameroun to N Kenya

92 PHOENICULIDAE (WOOD HOOPOES)

PHOENICULUS
Phoeniculus purpureus (Green Wood Hoopoe)
  P. p. senegalensis
    Senegal to Ghana
  P. p. guineensis
    Mali to N Ivory Coast & Central African Republic

P. *p. niloticus*
N Sudan to E Zaire
P. p. abyssinicus
N Ethiopia
P. p. somaliensis
Somalia
P. p. neglectus
S Ethiopia
P. p. marwitzi
E Uganda, E Zaire to Natal, Zanzibar
P. p. angolensis
Angola
P. p. purpureus
C & SW South Africa
Phoeniculus damarensis (Violet Wood Hoopoe)
N & C Namibia
Phoeniculus granti (Grant's Wood Hoopoe)
S Ethiopia, W Kenya
Phoeniculus bollei (White-headed Wood Hoopoe)
P. b. bollei
Ghana to Cameroun
P. b. jacksoni
E Zaire, W Kenya
P. b. okuensis
S Cameroun
Phoeniculus castaneiceps (Forest Wood Hoopoe)
P. c. castaneiceps
Ghana, SW Nigeria
P. c. brunneiceps
S Cameroun, N Zaire
P. c. adolfifriederici
E Zaire, Uganda, W Kenya
Phoeniculus aterrimus (Black Wood Hoopoe)
P. a. aterrimus
Senegal to N Zaire, S Sahara
P. a. emini
S Sudan, NE Zaire
P. a. notatus
N Ethiopia
P. a. anchietae
SW Zaire, N Angola

RHINOPOMASTUS
Rhinopomastus minor (Abyssinian Scimitar-bill)
R. m. minor
Ethiopia to C Somalia
R. m. somalicus
S Somalia, E Kenya
R. m. cabanisi
Uganda, N Kenya
R. m. extimus
S Kenya to C Tanzania

Rhinopomastus cyanomelas (Scimitar-bi
R. c. schalowi
N Kenya to E Zaire, NE Transvaal & Mozambique
R. c. cyanomelas
Angola to Namibia, Botswana & Natal

93 BUCEROTIDAE (HORNBILLS)

TOCKUS
Tockus birostris (Indian Grey Hornbill)
N & C India
Tockus fasciatus (Pied Hornbill)
T. f. semifasciatus
Senegal to Ghana
T. f. fasciatus
Cameroun to SW Sudan, Zaire, Angola
Tockus alboterminatus (Crowned Hornbi
T. a. geloensis
Ethiopia to Zambia & Malawi
T. a. stegmanni
Uganda to E Zaire, W Kenya, W Tanzani
T. a. alboterminatus
Mozambique to Angola » Somalia
T. a. australis
E South Africa
Tockus bradfieldi (Bradfield's Hornbill)
T. b. bradfieldi
S Angola, N Namibia
T. b. williaminae
Botswana, W Rhodesia
Tockus pallidirostris (Pale-billed Hornbill
T. p. pallidirostris
Angola to SW Tanzania
T. p. neumanni
S Kenya, E Tanzania, Malawi
Tockus nasutus (African Grey Hornbill)
T. n. nasutus
Senegal to Ethiopia & N Kenya
T. n. forskalii
NE Ethiopia, W & S Saudi Arabia
T. n. epirhinus
S Kenya to Angola, Botswana & Natal
T. n. dorsalis
S Angola, Namibia
Tockus hemprichii (Hemprich's Hornbill)
T. h. hemprichii
Ethiopia, Somalia
T. h. exsul
NW Kenya
Tockus monteiri (Monteiro's Hornbill)
S Angola, N Namibia
Tockus griseus (Malabar Grey Hornbill)
T. g. griseus
W India
T. g. gingalensis
Sri Lanka

***Tockus hartlaubi* (Black Dwarf Hornbill)**
  T. h. hartlaubi
    Guinea to S Cameroun
  T. h. granti
    WC to NE Zaire
***Tockus camurus* (Red-billed Dwarf Hornbill)**
  T. c. pulchrirostris
    Liberia to S Nigeria
  T. c. camurus
    Cameroun & Gabon to NE Zaire
***Tockus erythrorhynchus* (Red-billed Hornbill)**
  T. e. erythrorhynchus
    Senegal to Somalia & Tanzania
  T. e. rufirostris
    Angola to Malawi & Transvaal
  T. e. damarensis
    N Namibia
***Tockus flavirostris* (Yellow-billed Hornbill)**
  T. f. flavirostris
    Ethiopia & W Somalia to S Kenya
  T. f. somaliensis
    E Somalia
  T. f. elegans
    Angola
  T. f. leucomelas
    Namibia to Mozambique & Natal
***Tockus deckeni* (Von der Decken's Hornbill)**
  C Ethiopia to C Tanzania
***Tockus jacksoni* (Jackson's Hornbill)**
  C Ethiopia to C Tanzania

BERENICORNIS
***Berenicornis comatus* (Long-crested Hornbill)**
  S Vietnam, Malaysia, Sumatra, Borneo
***Berenicornis albocristatus* (African White-crested Hornbill)**
  B. a. albocristatus
    Sierra Leone to Ivory Coast
  B. a. macrourus
    Ghana & Togo
  B. a. cassini
    W Nigeria to Gabon & Uganda

PTILOLAEMUS
***Ptilolaemus tickelli* (Tickell's Hornbill)**
  P. t. austeni
    S Assam
  P. t. tickelli
    S Burma
  P. t. indochinensis
    Indochina

ANORRHINUS
***Anorrhinus galeritus* (Bushy-crested Hornbill)**
  A. g. carinatus
    S Burma, S Thailand, Malaysia

237

  A. g. galeritus
    Sumatra, N Borneo
  A. g. minor
    S Borneo

PENELOPIDES
***Penelopides panini* (Rufous-tailed Hornbill)**
  P. p. manilloe
    Luzon I, Marinduque I
  P. p. subnigra
    Polillo Is
  P. p. mindorensis
    Mindoro I
  P. p. ticaensis
    Ticao I
  P. p. panini
    Masbate I, Panay I, Negros I
  P. p. samarensis
    Samar I, Leyte I, Bohol I
  P. p. affinis
    Dinagat I, Mindanao I
  P. p. basilanica
    Basilan I
***Penelopides exarhatus* (Temminck's Hornbill)**
  P. e. exarhatus
    N Celebes
  P. e. sanfordi
    C, SE & S Celebes

ACEROS
***Aceros nipalensis* (Rufous-necked Hornbill)**
  Nepal to N Indochina
***Aceros corrugatus* (Wrinkled Hornbill)**
  A. c. corrugatus
    Malaysia, Borneo
  A. c. megistus
    Sumatra, Batu Is
***Aceros leucocephalus* (White-headed Hornbill)**
  A. l. waldeni
    Panay I, Guimaras I, Negros I
  A. l. leucocephalus
    Mindanao I, Camiguin (South I)
***Aceros cassidix* (Celebes Hornbill)**
  Celebes
***Aceros undulatus* (Wreathed Hornbill)**
  A. u. ticehursti
    S Assam to Indochina & N Malaysia
  A. u. undulatus
    S Malaysia, Sumatra, Java, Bali I, Borneo
***Aceros plicatus* (Blyth's Hornbill)**
  A. p. subruficollis
    S Burma, S Thailand, Malaysia, Sumatra, Borneo
  A. p. plicatus
    S Moluccas
  A. p. ruficollis
    N Moluccas, W & N New Guinea & Is

A. p. jungei
E New Guinea, Fergusson I, Goodenough I
A. p. dampieri
Bismarck Archipelago
A. p. harterti
Buka I, Bougainville I, Shortland I
A. p. mendanae
Choiseul I, Ysabel I, Guadalcanal I, Malaita I
Aceros everetti (Everett's Hornbill)
Sumba I
Aceros narcondami (Narcondam Hornbill)
Narcondam I

ANTHRACOCEROS
Anthracoceros malayanus (Black Hornbill)
S Malaysia, Sumatra, Borneo
**Anthracoceros malabaricus (Indian Pied
Hornbill)**
A. m. malabaricus
S Himalayas, N Burma
A. m. leucogaster
Burma to Malaysia, Indochina, SE China
**Anthracoceros coronatus (Malabar Pied
Hornbill)**
A. c. coronatus
S India, Sri Lanka
A. c. convexus
Malaysia, Sumatra, Java, Borneo
Anthracoceros montani (Sulu Hornbill)
Jolo I, Tawitawi Is
Anthracoceros marchei (Palawan Hornbill)
Calamian I, Palawan I, Balabac I

BYCANISTES
Bycanistes bucinator (Trumpeter Hornbill)
B. b. fistulator
Senegal to W Nigeria
B. b. sharpii
SE Nigeria to C Zaire & N Angola
B. b. duboisi
Cameroun to W Uganda
B. b. bucinator
Angola to N Kenya & E Cape Province
**Bycanistes cylindricus (Brown-cheeked
Hornbill)**
B. c. cylindricus
Sierra Leone to Benin
B. c. albotibialis
Nigeria & Cameroun to Uganda
**Bycanistes subcylindricus (Black and
White Casqued Hornbill)**
B. s. subcylindricus
Ghana to S Nigeria
B. s. subquadratus
Kenya & E Zaire to Cameroun » Angola
**Bycanistes brevis (Silvery-cheeked
Hornbill)**
B. b. brevis
S Kenya to Malawi & Rhodesia

B. b. omissus
Ethiopia to C Kenya

CERATOGYMNA
**Ceratogymna atrata (Black-casqued
Hornbill)**
Liberia to Sudan & Angola
**Ceratogymna elata (Yellow-casqued
Hornbill)**
Guinea to W Cameroun

BUCEROS
Buceros rhinoceros (Rhinoceros Hornbill)
B. r. rhinoceros
Malaysia
B. r. sumatranus
Sumatra, Billiton I
B. r. silvestris
Java
B. r. borneoensis
Borneo
Buceros bicornis (Great Indian Hornbill)
B. b. bicornis
W India, Himalayas to Indochina, Malays
B. b. cavatus
SW India
Buceros hydrocorax (Rufous Hornbill)
B. h. hydrocorax
Luzon I, Marinduque I
B. h. semigaleatus
Samar I, Leyte I, Bohol I
B. h. mindanensis
Mindanao I
B. h. basilanicus
Basilan I

RHINOPLAX
Rhinoplax vigil (Helmeted Hornbill)
Malaysia, Sumatra, Borneo

BUCORVUS
**Bucorvus abyssinicus (Abyssinian Grour
Hornbill)**
Gambia to C Kenya
**Bucorvus leadbeateri (Southern Ground
Hornbill)**
N Angola to Kenya & E Cape Province

Piciformes

94 GALBULIDAE (JACAMARS)

GALBALCYRHYNCHUS
**Galbalcyrhynchus leucotis (White-eared
Jacamar)**
N Upper Amazonia
**Galbalcyrhynchus purusianus (Chestnut
Jacamar)**
E & S Peru, W Brazil, N Bolivia

BRACHYGALBA
Brachygalba albogularis (White-throated Jacamar)
E Peru
Brachygalba lugubris (Black-billed Jacamar)
B. l. fulviventris
E Colombia
B. l. caquetae
SE Colombia to E Peru
B. l. lugubris
E & S Venezuela, the Guianas, N Brazil
B. l. obscuriceps
S Venezuela, NW Brazil
B. l. naumbergi
NE Brazil
B. l. melanosterna
E Bolivia, C & SW Brazil
B. l. phaeonota
C Brazil
Brachygalba goeringi (Pale-headed Jacamar)
E Colombia, N Venezuela
Brachygalba salmoni (Dusky-backed Jacamar)
E Panama, NW Colombia

JACAMARALCYON
Jacamaralcyon tridactyla (Three-toed Jacamar)
SE Brazil

GALBULA
Galbula albirostris (Yellow-billed Jacamar)
G. a. chalcocephala
S Colombia, Ecuador, NW Peru, W Brazil
G. a. albirostris
E Venezuela, the Guianas, N Brazil
Galbula cyanicollis (Blue-necked Jacamar)
C Brazil
Galbula galbula (Green-tailed Jacamar)
E & S Venezuela, the Guianas, N & C Brazil
Galbula ruficauda (Rufous-tailed Jacamar)
G. r. melanogenis
S Mexico to W Ecuador
G. r. ruficauda
C Colombia, Venezuela, the Guianas, N Brazil
G. r. pallens
N Colombia
G. r. brevirostris
NW Venezuela
G. r. rufoviridis
S Brazil, N Bolivia, Paraguay, N Argentina
G. r. heterogyna
E Bolivia, SW Brazil
Galbula tombacea (White-chinned Jacamar)
G. t. tombacea
S Colombia, Ecuador, Peru, W Brazil

G. t. mentalis
C & WC Brazil
Galbula cyanescens (Bluish-fronted Jacamar)
W Brazil, E Peru
Galbula pastazae (Coppery-chested Jacamar)
W Brazil, E Ecuador
Galbula leucogastra (Bronzy Jacamar)
G. l. chalcothorax
W Brazil, E Ecuador, E Peru
G. l. leucogastra
S Venezuela, the Guianas, W Brazil
G. l. viridissima
C Brazil
Galbula dea (Paradise Jacamar)
G. d. dea
Venezuela, the Guianas, N Brazil
G. d. amazonum
N Bolivia, SW Brazil
G. d. brunneiceps
E Colombia, E Peru, W Brazil
G. d. phainopepla
WC Brazil

JACAMEROPS
Jacamerops aurea (Great Jacamar)
J. a. penardi
Costa Rica to W Colombia
J. a. aurea
E Colombia, the Guianas, Venezuela
J. a. ridgwayi
NE & C Brazil
J. a. isidori
E Ecuador, E Peru, N Bolivia, W Brazil

95 BUCCONIDAE (PUFFBIRDS)

NOTHARCHUS
Notharchus macrorhynchos (White-necked Puffbird)
N. m. cryptoleucus
El Salvador, NW Nicaragua
N. m. hyperrhynchus
S Mexico to NW South America
N. m. macrorhynchos
the Guianas, N Brazil
N. m. paraensis
E Brazil
N. m. swainsoni
SE Brazil, E Paraguay, NE Argentina
Notharchus pectoralis (Black-breasted Puffbird)
E Panama to NW Ecuador
Notharchus ordii (Brown-banded Puffbird)
S Venezuela, NW Brazil
Notharchus tectus (Pied Puffbird)
N. t. subtectus
E Panama to C Colombia & SW Ecuador

240

N. t. picatus
    E Ecuador, E Peru
N. t. tectus
    S Venezuela, the Guianas, N Brazil

BUCCO
Bucco macrodactylus (Chestnut-capped Puffbird)
B. m. macrodactylus
    N & W Amazonia
B. m. caurensis
    S Venezuela
Bucco tamatia (Spotted Puffbird)
B. t. pulmentum
    S Colombia, E Ecuador, E Peru, W Brazil
B. t. tamatia
    E Colombia, Venezuela, the Guianas,
    N Brazil
B. t. inexpectatus
    NC Brazil
B. t. punctuliger
    C Brazil
B. t. hypneleus
    EC Brazil
B. t. interior
    SW Brazil
Bucco noanamae (Sooty-capped Puffbird)
    W Colombia
Bucco capensis (Collared Puffbird)
B. c. dugandi
    SE Colombia, Ecuador, C Peru
B. c. capensis
    the Guianas, Brazil, E Peru

NYSTALUS
Nystalus radiatus (Barred Puffbird)
    W Panama to W Ecuador
Nystalus chacuru (White-eared Puffbird)
N. c. uncirostris
    E Peru, E Bolivia
N. c. chacuru
    S Brazil, Paraguay, NE Argentina
Nystalus striolatus (Striolated Puffbird)
N. s. striolatus
    W Amazonia
N. s. torridus
    S Brazil
Nystalus maculatus (Spot-backed Puffbird)
N. m. maculatus
    E Brazil
N. m. parvirostris
    C Brazil
N. m. pallidigula
    SW Brazil
N. m. striatipectus
    E & S Bolivia, N Argentina

HYPNELUS
Hypnelus ruficollis (Russet-throated Puffbird)
H. r. ruficollis
    N Colombia, W Venezuela
H. r. decolor
    NE Colombia, NW Venezuela
H. r. striaticollis
    NW Venezuela
H. r. coloratus
    W Venezuela
H. r. bicinctus
    N Venezuela
H. r. stoicus
    Margarita I

MALACOPTILA
Malacoptila striata (Crescent-chested Puffbird)
M. s. minor
    E Brazil
M. s. striata
    SE Brazil
Malacoptila fusca (White-chested Puffbird)
M. f. fusca
    N & NW Amazonia
M. f. venezuelae
    S Venezuela
Malacoptila semicincta (Semicollared Puffbird)
    S Peru, N Bolivia, W Brazil
Malacoptila fulvogularis (Black-streaked Puffbird)
M. f. substriata
    Colombia
M. f. huilae
    N Colombia
M. f. fulvogularis
    E Ecuador to Bolivia
Malacoptila rufa (Rufous-necked Puffbird)
M. r. rufa
    E Ecuador, E Peru, W Brazil
M. r. brunnescens
    C Brazil
Malacoptila panamensis (White-whiskered Puffbird)
M. p. inornata
    S Mexico to N Nicaragua
M. p. fuliginosa
    SE Nicaragua to W Panama
M. p. panamensis
    SW Costa Rica to W Colombia
M. p. poliopis
    SW Colombia, W Ecuador
M. p. magdalenae
    N Colombia
Malacoptila mystacalis (Moustached Puffbird)
    Colombia, NW Venezuela

Micromonacha lanceolata (Lanceolated Monklet)
M. l. austinsmithi
E Costa Rica, W Panama
M. l. lanceolata
W Colombia, E Ecuador, E Peru, W Brazil

NONNULA
Nonnula rubecula (Rusty-breasted Nunlet)
N. r. duidae
S Venezuela
N. r. interfluvialis
S Venezuela, N Brazil
N. r. cineracea
W Brazil, NE Peru
N. r. simplex
NE Brazil
N. r. rubecula
SE Brazil, Paraguay, NE Argentina
Nonnula sclateri (Fulvous-chinned Nunlet)
W Brazil
Nonnula brunnea (Brown Nunlet)
S Colombia, E Ecuador, E Peru
Nonnula ruficapilla (Grey-cheeked Nunlet)
N. r. frontalis
E Panama, N Colombia
N. r. pallescens
NE Colombia
N. r. rufipectus
NE Peru
N. r. ruficapilla
E Peru, W Brazil
N. r. nattereri
SW Brazil
Nonnula amaurocephala (Chestnut-headed Nunlet)
W Brazil

HAPALOPTILA
Hapaloptila castanea (White-faced Nunbird)
W Colombia, W Ecuador

MONASA
Monasa atra (Black Nunbird)
S Venezuela, the Guianas, N Brazil
Monasa nigrifrons (Black-fronted Nunbird)
M. n. nigrifrons
W & NW Amazonia
M. n. canescens
E Bolivia
Monasa morphoeus (White-fronted Nunbird)
M. m. grandior
Nicaragua to NW Panama
M. m. fidelis
E Panama
M. m. pallescens
E Panama, NW Colombia

M. m. sclateri
N Colombia
M. m. peruana
SE Colombia, E Peru, NW Brazil
M. m. morphoeus
S & E Brazil
M. m. boliviana
NE Bolivia
Monasa flavirostris (Yellow-billed Nunbird)
E Colombia, E Ecuador, E Peru, W Brazil

CHELIDOPTERA
Chelidoptera tenebrosa (Swallow-wing Puffbird)
C. t. tenebrosa
NE & NC South America
C. t. brasiliensis
E & SE Brazil
C. t. pallida
W Venezuela

96 CAPITONIDAE (BARBETS)

CAPITO
Capito aurovirens (Scarlet-crowned Barbet)
Upper Amazonia
Capito maculicoronatus (Spot-crowned Barbet)
C. m. maculicoronatus
W Panama
C. m. pirrensis
E Panama (Pacific), NW Colombia
C. m. melas
E Panama (Caribbean)
C. m. rubrilateralis
W Colombia
Capito squamatus (Orange-fronted Barbet)
SW Colombia, W Ecuador
Capito hypoleucus (White-mantled Barbet)
N Colombia
Capito dayi (Black-girdled Barbet)
W Brazil
Capito quinticolor (Five-coloured Barbet)
W Colombia
Capito niger (Black-spotted Barbet)
C. n. niger
the Guianas, NE Brazil
C. n. punctatus
E Colombia to E Peru
C. n. intermedius
WC Venezuela
C. n. aurantiicinctus
S Venezuela
C. n. auratus
NW Peru
C. n. orosae
NW Peru, NW Brazil

C. n. amazonicus
NW Brazil
C. n. transilens
NW Brazil
C. n. nitidior
NW Brazil
C. n. hypochondriacus
NC Brazil
C. n. novaolindae
NW Brazil
C. n. arimae
NW Brazil
C. n. insperatus
SE Peru, N Bolivia, W Brazil
C. n. bolivianus
W Bolivia
C. n. brunneipectus
NC Brazil

EUBUCCO
Eubucco richardsoni (Lemon-throated Barbet)
E. r. richardsoni
SE Colombia, E Ecuador, E Peru
E. r. nigriceps
NW Peru
E. r. aurantiicollis
E Peru, W Brazil
E. r. coccineus
C Peru
Eubucco bourcierii (Red-headed Barbet)
E. b. salvini
Costa Rica, W Panama
E. b. anomalus
E Panama
E. b. occidentalis
W Colombia
E. b. bourcierii
C & E Colombia
E. b. aequatorialis
W Ecuador
E. b. orientalis
E Ecuador
Eubucco tucinkae (Scarlet-hooded Barbet)
SE Peru
Eubucco versicolor (Versicoloured Barbet)
E. v. steerii
N Peru
E. v. glaucogularis
C Peru
E. v. versicolor
S Peru, NW Bolivia

SEMNORNIS
Semnornis frantzii (Prong-billed Barbet)
Costa Rica, W Panama
Semnornis ramphastinus (Toucan Barbet)
S. r. caucae
W Colombia

S. r. ramphastinus
C Ecuador

PSILOPOGON
Psilopogon pyrolophus (Fire-tufted Barbet)
Malaysia, Sumatra

MEGALAIMA
Megalaima virens (Great Barbet)
M. v. marshallorum
NW Himalayas
M. v. magnifica
Assam, N Burma
M. v. clamator
C Burma
M. v. virens
E & S China to S Burma, Thailand,
N Indochina
Megalaima lagrandieri (Red-vented Barbet)
M. l. rothschildi
N Laos, N Vietnam
M. l. lagrandieri
S Laos, S Vietnam
Megalaima zeylanica (Oriental Green Barbet)
M. z. kangrae
W Himalayas
M. z. inornata
W India
M. z. caniceps
C & E India
M. z. zeylanica
S India, Sri Lanka
Megalaima lineata (Lineated Barbet)
M. l. hodgsoni
W Himalayas to Malaysia & Indochina
M. l. lineata
Java, Bali I
Megalaima viridis (Small Green Barbet)
S India
Megalaima faiostricta (Green-eared Barbet)
M. f. praetermissa
S China, N Vietnam
M. f. faiostricta
Thailand, Laos, S Vietnam
Megalaima corvina (Brown-throated Barbet)
Java
Megalaima chrysopogon (Gold-whiskered Barbet)
M. c. laeta
S Thailand, Malaysia
M. c. chrysopogon
Sumatra
M. c. chrysopsis
Borneo

Megalaima rafflesii (Many-coloured Barbet)
  M. r. malayensis
    S Burma, Malaysia
  M. r. rafflesii
    Sumatra, Bangka I
  M. r. billitonis
    Billiton I, Mendanau I
  M. r. borneensis
    Borneo
Megalaima mystacophanos (Gaudy Barbet)
  M. m. mystacophanos
    S Burma, Malaysia, Sumatra
  M. m. humii
    Borneo
  M. m. ampala
    Batu Is
Megalaima javensis (Black-banded Barbet)
  Java
Megalaima flavifrons (Yellow-fronted Barbet)
  Sri Lanka
Megalaima franklinii (Golden-throated Barbet)
  M. f. franklinii
    E Himalayas to S China & N Vietnam
  M. f. ramsayi
    S Burma, N & W Thailand
  M. f. auricularis
    S Laos, S Vietnam
  M. f. trangensis
    S Thailand
  M. f. minor
    Malaysia
Megalaima oorti (Muller's Barbet)
  M. o. oorti
    Malaysia, Sumatra
  M. o. annamensis
    S Indochina
  M. o. nuchalis
    Taiwan
  M. o. faber
    Hainan I
  M. o. sini
    SE China
Megalaima asiatica (Blue-throated Barbet)
  M. a. asiatica
    N India, Assam, N & C Burma
  M. a. rubescens
    S Assam, NW Burma
  M. a. davisoni
    S Burma to S China, N Indochina
  M. a. chersonesus
    S Thailand
  M. a. monticola
    N Borneo

Megalaima incognita (Hume's Blue-throated Barbet)
  M. i. incognita
    S Burma
  M. i. elbeli
    S Thailand
  M. i. euroa
    S Thailand, Indochina
Megalaima henricii (Yellow-crowned Barbet)
  M. h. henricii
    S Thailand, Malaysia, Sumatra
  M. h. brachyrhyncha
    Borneo
Megalaima armillaris (Blue-crowned Barbet)
  M. a. armillaris
    W & C Java
  M. a. baliensis
    E Java, Bali I
Megalaima pulcherrima (Golden-naped Barbet)
  NW Borneo
Megalaima australis (Blue-eared Barbet)
  M. a. cyanotis
    Himalayas to Indochina
  M. a. stuarti
    S Burma, S Thailand
  M. a. duvaucelii
    Malaysia, Sumatra, Borneo
  M. a. gigantorhinus
    Nias I
  M. a. tanamassae
    Batu Is
  M. a. australis
    Java
  M. a. herbereri
    Bali I
Megalaima eximia (Black-throated Barbet)
  M. e. eximia
    N Borneo
  M. e. cyanea
    NE Borneo
Megalaima rubricapilla (Crimson-throated Barbet)
  M. r. malabarica
    SW India
  M. r. rubricapilla
    Sri Lanka
Megalaima haemacephala (Crimson-breasted Barbet)
  M. h. indica
    NW India to Malaysia & Indonesia
  M. h. delica
    Sumatra
  M. h. rosea
    Java, Bali I

M. h. haemacephala
Luzon I, Mindoro I, Samar I, Leyte I
Mindanao I
M. h. intermedia
Tablas I, Romblon I, Masbate I, Negros I,
Cebu I

CALORHAMPHUS ·
Calorhamphus fuliginosus (Brown Barbet)
C. f. hayii
S Burma, Malaysia, Sumatra
C. f. fuliginosus
Borneo (except North)
C. f. tertius
N Borneo

GYMNOBUCCO
Gymnobucco calvus (Naked-faced Barbet)
G. c. calvus
Sierra Leone to S Nigeria
G. c. major
S Cameroun, Gabon
G. c. congicus
SW Zaire, N Angola
G. c. vernayi
S Angola
Gymnobucco peli (Bristle-nosed Barbet)
Ghana to Gabon
Gymnobucco sladeni (Sladen's Barbet)
N & E Zaire
Gymnobucco bonapartei (Grey-throated Barbet)
G. b. bonapartei
W Cameroun to E Zaire
G. b. intermedius
S Sudan, Uganda to NW Tanzania
G. b. cinereiceps
W Kenya

SMILORHIS
Smilorhis leucotis (White-eared Barbet)
S. l. kenyae
C & S Kenya
S. l. kilimensis
S Kenya, N Tanzania
S. l. leucogrammicus
Tanzania
S. l. leucotis
Malawi to Natal

STACTOLAEMA
Stactolaema olivacea (Green Barbet)
S. o. olivacea
E Kenya, Tanzania
S. o. woodwardi
SE Tanzania
S. o. rungweensis
SW Tanzania, N Malawi
S. o. belcheri
Malawi, N Mozambique

Stactolaema anchietae (Yellow-headed Barbet)
S. a. rex
Angola
S. a. anchietae
Angola, S Zaire
S. a. katangae
S Zaire, N Zambia
Stactolaema whytii (Whyte's Barbet)
S. w. stresemanni
S Tanzania
S. w. whytii
S Malawi
S. w. terminatum
Iringa (E Tanzania)
S. w. sowerbyi
S Malawi, Rhodesia
S. w. buttoni
N Zambia
S. w. irwini
E Rhodesia
S. w. eurorum
S Tanzania
S. w. angoniensis
W Malawi, NE Zambia

POGONIULUS
Pogoniulus duchaillui (Yellow-spotted Barbet)
P. d. duchaillui
Sierra Leone & Gabon to Uganda
P. d. gabriellae
W Zaire
P. d. bannermani
W Cameroun
Pogoniulus scolopaceus (Speckled Tinkerbird)
P. s. scolopaceus
Sierra Leone & E Nigeria
P. s. stellatus
Fernando Po I
P. s. flavisquamatus
Cameroun to NE & S Zaire
P. s. aloysii
Uganda, W Kenya
P. s. flavior
N Angola
Pogoniulus leucomystax (Moustached Green Tinkerbird)
P. l. leucomystax
W Kenya to W Malawi
P. l. chyulu
WC Kenya
Pogoniulus simplex (Green Tinkerbird)
S Kenya, Tanzania to S Malawi
Pogoniulus coryphaeus (Western Green Tinkerbird)
P. c. coryphaeus
N & W Cameroun

P. c. hildamariae
E Zaire, W Uganda
P. c. angolensis
W Angola
Pogoniulus pusillus (Red-fronted Tinkerbird)
P. p. uropygialis
Ethiopia, N Somalia
P. p. affinis
Kenya, S Somalia, N Tanzania
P. p. eupterus
SE Uganda, SW Kenya, NW Tanzania
P. p. pusillus
SE South Africa
Pogoniulus chrysoconus (Yellow-fronted Tinkerbird)
P. c. chrysoconus
Senegal to EC Nigeria
P. c. schubotzi
Niger, Chad, W Sudan
P. c. centralis
N & NE Zaire, Uganda
P. c. zedlitzi
E Sudan
P. c. schoanus
Ethiopia
P. c. xanthostictus
C & S Ethiopia
P. c. rhodesiae
E Zaire to NE Rhodesia & N Malawi
P. c. extoni
S Angola & Namibia to SE Malawi & N Transvaal
P. c. mayri
S Zaire to NE Angola
Pogoniulus bilineatus (Golden-rumped Tinkerbird)
P. b. sharpei
Gambia to S Nigeria
P. b. leucolaima
Cameroun to Uganda & N Angola
P. b. poensis
Fernando Po I
P. b. mfumbiri
S Uganda, E Zaire, Rwanda
P. b. urungensis
SE Zaire, SW Tanzania, NE Zambia
P. b. jacksoni
W Kenya
P. b. alius
C Kenya
P. b. fischeri
E Kenya, Tanzania, Zanzibar I
P. b. conciliator
EC Tanzania
P. b. bilineatus
Malawi, Mozambique, E South Africa

Pogoniulus makawai (Black-chinned Tinkerbird)
NW Zambia
Pogoniulus subsulphureus (Yellow-throated Tinkerbird)
P. s. chrysopygus
Guinea to Ghana
P. s. flavimentum
S Nigeria to Uganda & SW Zaire
P. s. subsulphureus
Fernando Po I
Pogoniulus atroflavus (Red-rumped Tinkerbird)
Guinea to NE Zaire

TRICHOLAEMA
Tricholaema lacrymosum (Spotted-flanked Barbet)
T. l. lacrymosum
N Uganda & S Ethiopia to C Tanzania
T. l. narokense
SW Kenya
T. l. radcliffei
E Zaire, Rwanda, W Tanzania
T. l. ruahae
C Tanzania
Tricholaema leucomelan (Pied Barbet)
T. l. namaqua
W Cape Province
T. l. nkatiense
N Botswana
T. l. centrale
Transvaal
T. l. zuluense
E Rhodesia, E Transvaal, N Natal
T. l. leucomelan
Orange Free State, S Cape Province
T. l. affine
Natal
Tricholaema diadematum (Red-fronted Barbet)
T. d. diadematum
S Sudan, Ethiopia, N Somalia
T. d. mustum
NE Uganda to C Kenya
T. d. massaicum
S Kenya, N Tanzania
T. d. frontatum
Angola, S Zaire, N Zambia, Malawi
Tricholaema melanocephalum (African Black-throated Barbet)
T. m. melanocephalum
N Ethiopia, NW Somalia
T. m. stigmatothorax
S Ethiopia, S Somalia to C Tanzania
T. m. blandi
C & E Somalia, SE Ethiopia

Tricholaema flavibuccale (Yellow-cheeked Barbet)
C Tanzania

Tricholaema hirsutum (Hairy-breasted Barbet)
T. h. hirsutum
Sierra Leone to Togo
T. h. hybridum
S Nigeria
T. h. flavipunctatum
Cameroun, Gabon, Cabinda
T. h. chapini
SE Cameroun to N & C Zaire
T. h. angolense
S Zaire, N Angola
T. h. ansorgii
E Zaire, Uganda

LYBIUS
Lybius undatus (Banded Barbet)
L. u. thiogaster
N Ethiopia
L. u. undatus
C Ethiopia
L. u. leucogenys
W & SW Ethiopia
L. u. squamatus
E Ethiopia

Lybius vieilloti (Vieillot's Barbet)
L. v. buchanani
S Sahara
L. v. rubescens
Senegal to N Cameroun
L. v. vieilloti
Ethiopia, S Sudan, N Zaire

Lybius torquatus (Black collared Barbet)
L. t. albigularis
S Tanzania
L. t. zombae
S Malawi
L. t. pumilio
E Zaire, Burundi
L. t. irroratus
E Kenya, NE Tanzania
L. t. congicus
SE Zaire, N Angola, N Zambia,
SW Tanzania
L. t. bocagei
SW Angola
L. t. torquatus
S Angola, Rhodesia, South Africa

Lybius guifsobalito (Black-billed Barbet)
L. g. guifsobalito
Ethiopia, E Sudan
L. g. ugandae
S Sudan, NE Zaire, Uganda

Lybius rubrifacies (Red-faced Barbet)
S Uganda, NW Tanzania

Lybius chaplini (Chaplin's Barbet)
S Zambia

Lybius leucocephalus (White-headed Barbet)
L. l. leucocephalus
S Sudan, Uganda, NE Zaire
L. l. adamauae
N Nigeria to N Zaire
L. l. usukumae
NW Tanzania
L. l. albicauda
S Kenya, N Tanzania
L. l. senex
C Kenya
L. l. leucogaster
SW Angola

Lybius minor (Black-backed Barbet)
L. m. minor
SW Zaire, NW Angola
L. m. intercedens
C & S Zaire, N Angola
L. m. macclounii
C & SE Zaire, Zambia, N Malawi

Lybius melanopterus (Brown-breasted Barbet)
S Somalia to Malawi, Mozambique

Lybius bidentatus (Double-toothed Barbet)
L. b. bidentatus
Guinea to S Nigeria
L. b. friedmanni
S Cameroun to N Angola
L. b. aequatorialis
N Zaire, W Kenya, NW Tanzania
L. b. aethiops
SW Sudan, S Ethiopia

Lybius dubius (Bearded Barbet)
Senegal to S Chad

Lybius rolleti (Black-breasted Barbet)
Central African Republic to
W & SW Sudan

TRACHYPHONUS
Trachyphonus purpuratus (Yellow-billed Barbet)
T. p. goffinii
Sierra Leone to Ghana
T. p. togoensis
Togo, SW Nigeria
T. p. purpuratus
Cameroun to N Zaire & N Angola
T. p. elgonensis
NE Zaire & Uganda

Trachyphonus vaillantii (Levaillant's Barbet)
T. v. suahelicus
N Angola to Tanzania
T. v. nobilis
Botswana

T. v. vaillantii
  Southern Africa
Trachyphonus erythrocephalus (Red and Yellow Barbet)
  T. e. gallarum
    SC Ethiopia
  T. e. shelleyi
    E Ethiopia, N Somalia
  T. e. jacksoni
    S Ethiopia, N & C Kenya
  T. e. versicolor
    N Uganda, W Kenya
  T. e. erythrocephalus
    S Kenya, N Tanzania
Trachyphonus darnaudii (d'Arnaud's Barbet)
  T. d. darnaudii
    E Sudan, W Ethiopia, N Uganda, W Kenya
  T. d. zedlitzi
    WC Kenya
  T. d. böhmi
    S Somalia, E Kenya, NE Tanzania
  T. d. emini
    C & SW Tanzania
Trachyphonus usambiro (Usambiro Barbet)
    C Kenya to NW Tanzania
Trachyphonus margaritatus (Yellow-breasted Barbet)
  T. m. kingi
    NE Sudan
  T. m. berberensis
    N Sudan
  T. m. margaritatus
    Niger & N Nigeria to W Ethiopia
  T. m. somalicus
    C Ethiopia, N Somalia

97 INDICATORIDAE (HONEYGUIDES)

PRODOTISCUS
Prodotiscus insignis (Cassin's Honeybird)
  P. i. flavodorsalis
    Sierra Leone to Togo
  P. i. insignis
    S Cameroun & W Zaire to Uganda
  P. i. ellenbecki
    S Ethiopia to C Tanzania
  P. i. zambesiae
    SE Zaire, N Angola to Rhodesia & Mozambique
  P. i. lathburyi
    C Angola
Prodotiscus regulus (Wahlberg's Honeybird)
  P. r. camerunensis
    Cameroun

P. r. regulus
  Ethiopia to N Angola and Natal

MELIGNOMON
Melignomon zenkeri (Zenker's Honeyguide)
    S Cameroun to Uganda

INDICATOR
Indicator maculatus (Spotted Honeyguide)
  I. m. maculatus
    Gambia to Ghana
  I. m. stictithorax
    Cameroun to NE Zaire ⸳
Indicator variegatus (Scaly-throated Honeyguide)
  I. v. jubaensis
    S Somalia to N Tanzania
  I. v. variegatus
    S Ethiopia to Cape Province
Indicator indicator (Black-throated Honeyguide)
    Senegal to Ethiopia & Cape Province
Indicator minor (Lesser Honeyguide)
  I. m. senegalensis
    Senegal
  I. m. alexanderi
    N Ghana, N Nigeria to W Sudan
  I. m. riggenbachi
    W Cameroun to N Zaire
  I. m. diadematus
    E Sudan, Ethiopia, Somalia
  I. m. erlangeri
    S Somalia, E Kenya
  I. m. teitensis
    Uganda, Kenya to Malawi
  I. m. minor
    N Angola to Natal & Cape Province
  I. m. albigularis
    Transvaal
  I. m. damarensis
    Namibia
  I. m. ussheri
    Ghana
  I. m. conirostris
    N Nigeria to W Uganda
  I. m. pallidus
    S Nigeria
Indicator exilis (Least Honeyguide)
  I. e. poensis
    Fernando Po I
  I. e. exilis
    S Nigeria to E Zaire
  I. e. pachyrhynchus
    Sudan, Uganda to W Tanzania
  I. e. angolensis
    N Angola

Indicator willcocksi (Willcocks' Honeyguide)
I. w. ansorgei
Guinea
I. w. willcocksi
Ghana
I. w hutsoni
Nigeria, N Cameroun
Indicator meliphilus (Eastern Least Honeyguide)
Kenya to Malawi, Rhodesia
Indicator pumilio (Pygmy Honeyguide)
E Zaire, Rwanda
Indicator xanthonotus (Indian Honeyguide)
I. x. xanthonotus
W Himalayas to E Assam
I. x. fulvus
Naga Hills (E Assam)
Indicator archipelagus (Malay Honeyguide)
Malaysia, Sumatra, Borneo

MELICHNEUTES
Melichneutes robustus (Lyre-tailed Honeyguide)
Cameroun to C Zaire

98 RAMPHASTIDAE (TOUCANS)

AULACORHYNCHUS
Aulacorhynchus prasinus (Emerald Toucanet)
A. p. wagleri
SW Mexico
A. p. prasinus
SE Mexico
A. p. stenorhabdus
S Mexico, W Guatemala, El Salvador
A. p. virescens
N Guatemala, Belize to N Nicaragua
A. p. volcanius
E El Salvador
A. p. maxillaris
Costa Rica, W Panama
A. p. caeruleogularis
EC Panama
A. p. cognatus
E Panama
A. p. griseigularis
NW Colombia
A. p. phaeolaemus
W Colombia
A. p. lautus
N Colombia
A. p. albivitta
E Colombia, E Ecuador, W Venezuela
A. p. cyanolaemus
SE Ecuador, N Peru

A. p. dimidiatus
N Peru
A. p. atrogularis
E Peru
Aulacorhynchus sulcatus (Groove-billed Toucanet)
A. s. sulcatus
N Venezuela
A. s. erythrognathus
NE Venezuela
A. s. calorhynchus
N Colombia, NW Venezuela
Aulacorhynchus derbianus (Chestnut-tipped Toucanet)
A. d. derbianus
E Ecuador, E Peru, NE Bolivia
A. d. nigrirostris
C Peru
A. d. duidae
S Venezuela
A. d. whitelianus
S Venezuela, S Guyana
A. d. osgoodi
S Guyana
Aulacorhynchus haematopygus (Crimson-rumped Toucanet)
A. h. sexnotatus
SW Colombia, W Ecuador
A. h. haematopygus
N Colombia, W Venezuela
Aulacorhynchus huallagae (Yellow-browed Toucanet)
NC Peru
Aulacorhynchus coeruleicinctis (Blue-banded Toucanet)
S Peru, N Bolivia

PTEROGLOSSUS
Pteroglossus viridis (Green Aracari)
P. v. humboldti
SE Colombia to N Bolivia, W Brazil
P. v. didymus
?
P. v. viridis
E Venezuela, the Guianas, N Brazil
Pteroglossus inscriptus (Lettered Aracari)
C & S Brazil
Pteroglossus bitorquatus (Red-necked Aracari)
P. b. sturmii
WC Brazil
P. b. reichenowi
NC Brazil
P. b. bitorquatus
NE Brazil
Pteroglossus flavirostris (Ivory-billed Aracari)
P. f. flavirostris
N Upper Amazonia

P. f. azara
NW Brazil
P. f. mariae
NE Peru, W Brazil, N Bolivia
Pteroglossus aracari (Black-necked Aracari)
P. a. roraimae
S & E Venezuela, Guyana, Surinam
P. a. atricollis
French Guiana, N Brazil
P. a. aracari
C & E Brazil
P. a. vergens
S & SE Brazil
Pteroglossus castanotis (Chestnut-eared Aracari)
P. c. castanotis
E Colombia, E Ecuador, E Peru, NW Brazil
P. c. australis
E Bolivia, W Brazil, NE Argentina
Pteroglossus pluricinctus (Many-banded Aracari)
E Peru & E Colombia to E Venezuela
Pteroglossus torquatus (Collared Aracari)
P. t. torquatus
S Mexico to W Panama
P. t. erythrozonus
SE Mexico, N Guatemala, Belize
P. t. frantzii
Costa Rica, W Panama
P. t. nuchalis
N Colombia, N Venezuela
P. t. pectoralis
NW Venezuela
P. t. sanguineus
W Colombia, NW Ecuador
P. t. erythropygius
W Ecuador
Pteroglossus beauharnaesii (Curl-crested Aracari)
E Peru, N Bolivia, W Brazil

SELENIDERA
Selenidera maculirostris (Spot-billed Toucanet)
S. m. hellmayri
NC Brazil
S. m. maculirostris
SE Brazil
Selenidera gouldii (Gould's Toucanet)
NE Brazil
Selenidera reinwardtii (Golden-collared Toucanet)
S. r. reinwardtii
S Colombia, E Ecuador, NE Peru
S. r. langsdorffii
E Peru, W Brazil

Selenidera nattereri (Tawny-tufted Toucanet) 249
E Venezuela, NW Brazil
Selenidera culik (Guianan Toucanet)
the Guianas, N Brazil
Selenidera spectabilis (Yellow-eared Toucanet)
Honduras to Panama, NC & NW Colombia

BAILLONIUS
Baillonius bailloni (Saffron Toucanet)
SE Brazil

ANDIGENA
Andigena hypoglauca (Grey-breasted Mountain Toucan)
A. h. hypoglauca
C Colombia
A. h. lateralis
E Ecuador, E Peru
Andigena laminirostris (Plate-billed Mountain Toucan)
SW Colombia, W Ecuador
Andigena cucullata (Hooded Mountain Toucan)
S Peru, W Bolivia
Andigena nigrirostris (Black-billed Mountain Toucan)
A. n. occidentalis
W Colombia
A. n. spilorhynchus
S Colombia, NE Ecuador
A. n. nigrirostris
E Colombia

RAMPHASTOS
Ramphastos dicolorus (Red-breasted Toucan)
SE Brazil, Paraguay, NE Argentina
Ramphastos vitellinus (Channel-billed Toucan)
R. v. culminatus
Upper Amazonia
R. v. citreolaemus
C Colombia
R. v. vitellinus
Trinidad, Venezuela, the Guianas, N Brazil
R. v. ariel
C & S Brazil
R. v. pintoi
SE Brazil
R. v. theresae
NE Brazil
Ramphastos brevis (Choco Toucan)
E Panama, W Colombia, W Ecuador
Ramphastos sulfuratus (Keel-billed Toucan)
R. s. sulfuratus
S Mexico, N Guatemala, Belize

R. s. brevicarinatus
  SE Guatemala to N Colombia,
    NW Venezuela
Ramphastos toco (Toco Toucan)
  R. t. toco
    the Guianas, N & E Brazil
  R. t. albogularis
    E & S Brazil, Paraguay, Bolivia, ·.
      N Argentina
Ramphastos tucanus (Cuvier's Toucan)
  R. t. tucanus
    SE Venezuela, the Guianas, N Brazil
  R. t. cuvieri
    Upper Amazonia
  R. t. oblitus
    NC Brazil
  R. t. inca
    E Bolivia
Ramphastos ambiguus (Black-mandibled Toucan)
  R. a. swainsonii
    SE Honduras to W Ecuador
  R. a. ambiguus
    N Upper Amazonia
  R. a. abbreviatus
    W Venezuela, NE Colombia

99 PICIDAE (WOODPECKERS)

JYNGINAE

JYNX
Jynx torquilla (Wryneck)
  J. t. torquilla
    Europe, W Asia
  J. t. tschusii
    Italy, Sardinia, Corsica
  J. t. mauretanica
    N Algeria
  J. t. chinensis
    C & SE Asia, India
  J. t. japonica
    Sakhalin I, Japan
Jynx ruficollis (Red-breasted Wryneck)
  J. r. thorbeckei
    C Cameroun
  J. r. rougeoti
    Gabon
  J. r. pulchricollis
    W Zaire to SW Sudan, W Uganda
  J. r. aequatorialis
    Ethiopia
  J. r. cosensi
    Kenya, Tanzania
  J. r. ruficollis
    Southern Africa

PICUMNINAE

PICUMNUS
Picumnus cinnamomeus (Chestnut Piculet)
  P. c. cinnamomeus
    N Colombia, NW Venezuela
  P. c. perijanus
    NW Venezuela
  P. c. venezuelensis
    W Venezuela
Picumnus rufiventris (Rufous-breasted Piculet)
  P. r. rufiventris
    E Ecuador, NE Peru, W Brazil
  P. r. grandis
    C Peru, N Bolivia
Picumnus fulvescens (Tawny Piculet)
  NE Brazil
Picumnus fuscus (Rusty-necked Piculet)
  S Brazil
Picumnus castelnau (Plain-breasted Piculet)
  E Ecuador, NE Peru
Picumnus spilogaster (White-bellied Piculet)
  P. s. leucogaster
    C Venezuela, N Brazil
  P. s. orinocensis
    E Venezuela
  P. s. spilogaster
    Guyana
Picumnus minutissimus (Arrowhead Piculet)
  P. m. minutissimus
    Surinam, French Guiana
  P. m. pallidus
    NE Brazil
  P. m. guttifer
    C Brazil
  P. m. corumbanus
    SW Brazil
  P. m. albosquamatus
    Bolivia
Picumnus squamulatus (Scaled Piculet)
  P. s. squamulatus
    N & E Colombia
  P. s. röhli
    N Venezuela
  P. s. obsoletus
    NE Venezuela
Picumnus limae (Ochraceous Piculet)
  E Brazil
Picumnus olivaceus (Olivaceous Piculet)
  P. o. dimotus
    Honduras, Nicaragua
  P. o. flavotinctus
    Costa Rica, W Panama

P. o. olivaceus
E Panama, N Colombia
P. o. antioquensis
N Colombia
P. o. eisenmanni
NE Colombia, NW Venezuela
P. o. tachirensis
C Colombia, NE Venezuela
P. o. harterti
SW Colombia, W Ecuador
Picumnus granadensis (Greyish Piculet)
NC Colombia
Picumnus nebulosus (Mottled Piculet)
S Brazil
Picumnus nigropunctatus (Black-dotted Piculet)
NE Venezuela
Picumnus exilis (Golden-spangled Piculet)
P. e. salvini
?
P. e. clarus
EC Venezuela
P. e. undulatus
SE Venezuela, S Guyana, N Brazil
P. e. buffoni
Surinam, French Guiana, NE Brazil
P. e. pernambucensis
E Brazil
P. e. alegriae
NE Brazil
P. e. exilis
E Brazil
Picumnus borbae (Bar-breasted Piculet)
P. b. juruanus
E Peru, W Brazil
P. b. borbae
C Brazil
Picumnus aurifrons (Gold-fronted Piculet)
P. a. lafresnayei
S Colombia, E Ecuador, N Peru
P. a. taczanowskii
NE Peru
P. a. punctifrons
C Peru
P. a. flavifrons
E Peru, W Brazil
P. a. purusianus
W Brazil
P. a. pusillus
W Brazil
P. a. wallacei
WC Brazil
P. a. aurifrons
C Brazil
P. a. transfasciatus
EC Brazil

Picumnus temminckii (Ochre-collared Piculet)
SE Brazil, Paraguay, NE Argentina
Picumnus cirratus (White-barred Piculet)
P. c. confusus
Guyana
P. c. macconnelli
N Brazil
P. c. cirratus
SE Brazil
P. c. pilcomayensis
SW Brazil, Paraguay, N Argentina
P. c. tucumanus
N Argentina
P. c. thamnophiloides
S Bolivia, NW Argentina
Picumnus d'orbignianus (Ocellated Piculet)
P. d. jelskii
C Peru
P. d. d'orbignianus
N & C Bolivia
Picumnus sclateri (Ecuadorean Piculet)
P. s. parvistriatus
W Ecuador
P. s. sclateri
SW Ecuador, NW Peru
Picumnus subtilis (Spot-crowned Piculet)
Cuzco (SE Peru)
Picumnus steindachneri (Speckle-chested Piculet)
NE Peru
Picumnus varzeae (Varzea Piculet)
central Amazon Is
Picumnus pygmaeus (Spotted Piculet)
P. p. pygmaeus
NE Brazil
P. p. distinctus
NE Brazil
Picumnus asterias (Blackish Piculet)
Brazil
Picumnus pumilus (Orinoco Piculet)
Colombia?
Picumnus innominatus (Speckled Piculet)
P. i. simlaensis
NW Himalayas
P. i. innominatus
Assam, E Himalayas
P. i. avunculorum
S India
P. i. malayorum
E India to Indochina, Sumatra, Borneo
P. i. chinensis
W & S China

SASIA
Sasia africana (African Piculet)
Nigeria to C Zaire

Sasia ochracea (White-browed Rufous Piculet)
  S. o. ochracea
    Himalayas
  S. o. kinneari
    S China, N Vietnam
  S. o. querulivox
    NE India, NW Burma
  S. o. reichenowi
    Burma, Thailand, Indochina
  S. o. hasbroucki
    S Burma
Sasia abnormis (Rufous Piculet)
  S. a. abnormis
    S Burma, Malaysia, Sumatra, Java, Borneo
  S. a. magnirostris
    Nias I

NESOCTITES
Nesoctites micromegas (Antillean Piculet)
  N. m. micromegas
    Hispaniola
  N. m. abbotti
    Gonave I

PICINAE

MELANERPES
Melanerpes candidus (White Woodpecker)
  N & E Brazil to C Argentina
Melanerpes lewis (Lewis's Woodpecker)
  W Canada to NW Mexico
Melanerpes herminieri (Guadeloupe Woodpecker)
  Guadeloupe I
Melanerpes portoricensis (Puerto Rican Woodpecker)
  Puerto Rico
Melanerpes erythrocephalus (Red-headed Woodpecker)
  M. e. caurinus
    WC USA
  M. e. erythrocephalus
    SC Canada, E USA
Melanerpes formicivorus (Acorn Woodpecker)
  M. f. bairdi
    coast of SW USA
  M. f. martirensis
    W Baja California
  M. f. angustifrons
    S Baja California
  M. f. formicivorus
    SW USA, NW Mexico
  M. f. lineatus
    S Mexico to N Nicaragua
  M. f. albeolus
    coast of Belize
  M. f. striatipectus
    Costa Rica, W Panama

  M. f. flavigula
    Colombia
Melanerpes cruentatus (Yellow-tufted Woodpecker)
  M. c. extensus
    Upper Amazonia
  M. c. cruentatus
    E Venezuela, the Guianas, NE Brazil
Melanerpes flavifrons (Yellow-fronted Woodpecker)
  M. f. flavifrons
    SC Brazil
  M. f. rubriventris
    SE Brazil, Paraguay, NE Argentina
Melanerpes chrysauchen (Golden-naped Woodpecker)
  M. c. chrysauchen
    SW Costa Rica, W Panama
  M. c. pulcher
    N Colombia
Melanerpes pucherani (Black-cheeked Woodpecker)
  M. p. perileucus
    S Mexico to N Honduras
  M. p. pucherani
    SE Honduras to C Colombia & W Ecuador
Melanerpes cactorum (White-fronted Woodpecker)
  S Peru to C Argentina
Melanerpes chrysogenys (Golden-cheeked Woodpecker)
  M. c. chrysogenys
    NW Mexico
  M. c. flavinuchus
    SW Mexico
  M. c. morelensis
    Morelos (C Mexico)
Melanerpes striatus (Hispaniolan Woodpecker)
  Hispaniola
Melanerpes hypopolius (Grey-breasted Woodpecker)
  M. h. albescens
    California, S Nevada to S Sonora
  M. h. cardonensis
    C Baja California
  M. h. brewsteri
    S Baja California
  M. h. fuscescens
    NW Mexico
  M. h. tiburonensis
    Tiburon I
  M. h. sulfuriventer
    W Mexico
  M. h. hypopolius
    C & SW Mexico

Melanerpes radiolatus (Jamaican Woodpecker)
  Jamaica
Melanerpes rubricapillus (Red-crowned Woodpecker)
  M. r. rubricomus
    N Yucatan
  M. r. pygmaeus
    Cozumel I
  M. r. tysoni
    Bonacca I
  M. r. costaricensis
    SW Costa Rica
  M. r. rubricapillus
    Panama, N Colombia, W Venezuela
  M. r. seductus
    Pearl Is (Panama)
  M. r. paraguanae
    NW Venezuela
  M. r. terricolor
    N Venezuela, Margarita I, Trinidad, Tobago I
Melanerpes hoffmannii (Hoffmann's Woodpecker)
  Nicaragua, W Costa Rica
Melanerpes uropygialis (Gila Woodpecker)
  S Arizona, New Mexico, N Sonora
Melanerpes aurifrons (Golden-fronted Woodpecker)
  M. a. polygrammus
    SW Mexico
  M. a. frontalis
    S Mexico, NW Guatemala
  M. a. aurifrons
    Texas to SC Mexico
  M. a. incanescens
    Big Bend (W Texas)
  M. a. grateloupensis
    E Mexico
  M. a. veraecrucis
    S Mexico, N Guatemala
  M. a. dubius
    SE Mexico, Belize
  M. a. leei
    Mecos, Cozumel I
  M. a. santacruzi
    S Chiapas to N Nicaragua
  M. a. pauper
    E Honduras
  M. a. insulans
    Utilla I
  M. a. canescens
    Ruatan I, Barburat I
Melanerpes carolinus (Red-bellied Woodpecker)
  M. c. zebra
    C & S USA

  M. c. carolinus
    E USA
  M. c. perplexus
    S Florida
Melanerpes superciliaris (West Indian Red-bellied Woodpecker)
  M. s. bahamensis
    Gt Bahama I
  M. s. nyeanus
    Watling's I
  M. s. blakei
    Abaco I
  M. s. superciliaris
    Cuba
  M. s. sanfelipensis
    Cuba
  M. s. murceus
    Isle of Pines
  M. s. caymanensis
    Gd Cayman I

SPHYRAPICUS
Sphyrapicus varius (Yellow-bellied Sapsucker)
  S Canada, E USA to C America
Sphyrapicus nuchalis (Red-naped Sapsucker)
  W Canada, W USA, W Mexico
Sphyrapicus ruber (Red-breasted Sapsucker)
  S. r. ruber
    SE Alaska to W Oregon
  S. r. daggetti
    S Oregon to SC California
Sphyrapicus thyroideus (Williamson's Sapsucker)
  S. t. thyroideus
    S British Columbia to S California
  S. t. nataliae
    SE British Columbia, WC USA, C Mexico

XIPHIDIOPICUS
Xiphidiopicus percussus (Cuban Green Woodpecker)
  X. p. percussus
    Cuba
  X. p. insulae-pinorum
    Isle of Pines

CAMPETHERA
Campethera nubica (Nubian Woodpecker)
  C. n. nubica
    Sudan, Ethiopia to SC Tanzania
  C. n. pallida
    coast of S Somalia, Kenya, Tanzania
Campethera bennettii (Bennett's Woodpecker)
  C. b. uniamwesica
    N Angola to C Tanzania

C. b. scriptoricauda
C Tanzania to N Mozambique
C. b. vincenti
Malawi
C. b. bennettii
Rhodesia, Transvaal, Natal
C. b. capricorni
S Angola, N Namibia

Campethera punctuligera (Fine-spotted Woodpecker)
C. p. punctuligera
Senegal to Niger & Central African Republic
C. p. batesi
E Cameroun
C. p. balia
S Chad, S Sudan, N Zaire

Campethera abingoni (Golden-tailed Woodpecker)
C. a. chrysura
Senegal to N Zaire & S Sudan
C. a. tessmanni
E Cameroun
C. a. annectens
Gabon to N Angola, E Zaire, Malawi
C. a. kavirondensis
SW Kenya to SC Tanzania
C. a. mombassica
coast from S Somalia to NE Tanzania
C. a. suahelica
C Tanzania
C. a. abingoni
Malawi, Mozambique to E Transvaal & Natal
C. a. smithii
W Rhodesia, W Transvaal, Botswana
C. a. anderssoni
Namibia

Campethera notata (Knysna Woodpecker)
S Natal, S & E Cape Province

Campethera cailliautii (Little Spotted Woodpecker)
C. c. togoensis
Ghana to S Nigeria
C. c. permista
Cameroun to E Zaire & N Angola
C. c. kaffensis
SW Ethiopia
C. c. nyansae
Rwanda, NW Tanzania
C. c. cailliautii
coast of Kenya, N Tanzania
C. c. fülleborni
S Zaire to Zambia & Mozambique

Campethera maculosa (Western Golden-backed Woodpecker)
Guinea to Ghana

Campethera tullbergi (Tullberg's Woodpecker)
C. t. tullbergi
Cameroun
C. t. bansoensis
Banso Mountains
C. t. wellsi
Oku district, Cameroun
C. t. taeniolaema
W Kenya, W Uganda, E Zaire
C. t. barakae
SE Zaire
C. t. hausburgi
E & C Kenya

Campethera nivosa (Buff-spotted Woodpecker)
C. n. nivosa
Guinea to Ghana
C. n. poensis
Fernando Po I
C. n. efulenensis
Cameroun to N Angola
C. n. herberti
N Zaire to Uganda
C. n. yalensis
W Kenya

Campethera caroli (Brown-eared Woodpecker)
C. c. arizela
Liberia
C. c. caroli
Guinea to C Zaire & Angola
C. c. budongoensis
Uganda & W Kenya

GEOCOLAPTES
Geocolaptes olivaceus (Ground Woodpecker)
G. o. theresae
NW Cape Province
G. o. olivaceus
S Cape Province to S Transvaal & Natal
G. o. prometheus
Natal, E Cape Province

DENDROPICOS
Dendropicos elachus (Little Grey Woodpecker)
Senegal to W Sudan
Dendropicos abyssinicus (Golden-backed Woodpecker)
Ethiopia
Dendropicos poecilolaemus (Uganda Spotted Woodpecker)
N Cameroun to Uganda, Kenya
Dendropicos fuscescens (Cardinal Woodpecker)
D. f. cosensi
Senegal

D. f. lafresnayei
Gambia to Nigeria
D. f. camerunensis
W Cameroun to N Zaire
D. f. sharpei
Gabon to C Zaire
D. f. loandae
N Angola, S Zaire
D. f. camacupae
W Angola to SE Zaire & Malawi
D. f. stresemanni
N Namibia
D. f. harei
S Namibia, W Botswana
D. f. capriviensis
SW Zambia, N Botswana
D. f. transvaalensis
NE Transvaal, S Rhodesia
D. f. orangensis
S Transvaal, Orange Free State
D. f. intermedius
SE Transvaal, W Natal
D. f. fuscescens
S & E Cape Province
D. f. natalensis
E Transvaal, N Natal
D. f. noomei
NE Natal, S Mozambique
D. f. hartlaubii
coast from N Kenya to S Mozambique
D. f. massaicus
C Kenya to C Tanzania
D. f. chyulu
SC Kenya
D. f. lepidus
W Ethiopia, Uganda, W Kenya, E Zaire
D. f. hemprichii
Ethiopia, Somalia
Dendropicos gabonensis (Gabon Woodpecker)
D. g. lugubris
Guinea to Ghana
D. g. reichenowi
NW Cameroun
D. g. gabonensis
Cameroun & Gabon to NE & C Zaire
Dendropicos stierlingi (Stierling's Woodpecker)
S Tanzania, N Mozambique
Dendropicos namaquus (Bearded Woodpecker)
D. n. schoënsis
W Sudan, S Ethiopia, N Kenya
D. n. saturatus
Central African Republic
D. n. decipiens
SW Uganda & N Kenya to C Tanzania

D. n. namaquus
N Angola to Malawi & Cape Province
D. n. coalescens
E Cape Province to S Mozambique
Dendropicos xantholophus (Yellow-crested Woodpecker)
Cameroun to S Angola & W Kenya
Dendropicos pyrrhogaster (Fire-bellied Woodpecker)
Sierra Leone to SE Nigeria
Dendropicos elliotii (Elliot's Woodpecker)
D. e. schultzei
Fernando Po I
D. e. johnstoni
Cameroun Mt
D. e. sordidatus
Oku district, W Cameroun
D. e. elliotii
Cameroun to N Angola & W Kenya
D. e. kupeensis
Mt. Kupé (Cameroun)
D. e. gabela
NW Angola
Dendropicos goertae (Grey Woodpecker)
D. g. königi
Mali to N Sudan
D. g. goertae
Senegal to N Nigeria
D. g. agmen
Gambia to S Sudan
D. g. centralis
Cameroun to NW Kenya, NE Zaire
D. g. oreites
C Cameroun
D. g. abessinicus
E Sudan, N & C Ethiopia
D. g. spodocephalus
S Ethiopia
D. g. rhodeogaster
C Kenya, N Tanzania
Dendropicos griseocephalus (African Grey-headed Woodpecker)
D. g. ruwenzori
E Zaire, Rwanda, NW Tanzania
D. g. persimilis
W Angola to N Malawi
D. g. kilimensis
N Tanzania
D. g. griseocephalus
N Transvaal to Natal & Cape Province

PICOIDES
Picoides temminckii (Celebean Pied Woodpecker)
Celebes, Togian Is
Picoides moluccensis (Brown-capped Pied Woodpecker)
P. m. nanus
N & C India

P. m. cinereigula
SW India
P. m. hardwickii
SE India
P. m. gymnophthalmus
Sri Lanka
P. m. moluccensis
Malaysia, Sumatra, Java, Borneo
P. m. grandis
Lombok I, Sumbawa I, Flores I, Lomblen I
P. m. excelsior
Alor I
Picoides maculatus (Philippine Pygmy Woodpecker)
P. m. validirostris
Luzon, Catanduanes I, Mindoro I
P. m. menagei
Sibuyan I
P. m. maculatus
Panay I, Cebu I, Negros I
P. m. leytensis
Samar I, Leyte I, Bohol I
P. m. fulvifasciatus
Mindanao I, Basilan I
P. m. apo
Mt Apo (Mindanao I)
P. m. ramsayi
Jolo I, Tawitawi Is, Bongao I
P. m. siasiensis
Siasi I
Picoides obsoletus (Brown-backed Woodpecker)
P. o. obsoletus
Gambia to NE Zaire
P. o. heuglini
N Sudan, NE Ethiopia
P. o. nigricans
S Ethiopia, N Uganda
P. o. ingens
W Kenya
P. o. crateri
N Tanzania
Picoides kizuki (Japanese Pygmy Woodpecker)
P. k. wilderi
NE Hopeh (NE China)
P. k. permutatus
NE Asia
P. k. acutirostris
E Korea
P. k. kurilensis
Kurile Is
P. k. shikokuensis
S Honshu I, Shikoku I
P. k. kizuki
Kyushu I
P. k. matsudairai
Takushima I

P. k. seebohmi
Sakhalin I, Hokkaido I
P. k. nippon
N & C Honshu I, Korea
P. k. kotataki
Oki Is, Tsushima I
P. k. amamii
N Riukiu Is
P. k. nigrescens
C Riukiu Is
P. k. orii
S Riukiu Is
Picoides canicapillus (Grey-headed Pygmy Woodpecker)
P. c. doerriesi
NE Asia
P. c. scintilliceps
N & E China
P. c. nagamichii
S & W China
P. c. kaleënsis
Taiwan
P. c. swinhoei
Hainan I
P. c. omissus
SE Sikang, Szechwan, NW Yunnan
P. c. obscurus
SE Yunnan
P. c. tonkinensis
N Indochina
P. c. semicoronatus
Bhutan, Sikkim, E Assam
P. c. mitchellii
Nepal
P. c. canicapillus
Burma, Thailand, S Vietnam
P. c. delacouri
E Thailand
P. c. auritus
Malaysia
P. c. volzi
NW Sumatra
P. c. aurantiiventris
N & E Borneo
Picoides minor (Lesser Spotted Woodpecker)
P. m. comminutus
C & S England
P. m. hortorum
NC Europe
P. m. jordansi
C Europe
P. m. wagneri
Romania
P. m. hispaniae
Spain
P. m. ledouci
N Algeria, N Tunisia

P. m. buturlini
SE France, Switzerland, Italy
P. m. serbicus
Yugoslavia, Greece
P. m. danfordi
Asia Minor
P. m. colchicus
Caucasus
P. m. quadrifasciatus
S Caucasus
P. m. hyrcanus
N Iran
P. m. morgani
SW Iran
P. m. minor
Scandinavia, N & C Russia
P. m. mongolicus
W Siberia, NW Mongolia
P. m. kamtschatkensis
E Siberia, Altai
P. m. immaculatus
Anadyr, Kamchatka
P. m. amurensis
N & C Manchuria, Sakhalin I, Hokkaido I
P. m. nojidoensis
NE Korea
Picoides macei (Fulvous-breasted Woodpecker)
P. m. westermanni
W Himalayas
P. m. macei
E Himalayas, N Burma
P. m. longipennis
C & S Burma to S Vietnam
P. m. andamanensis
Andaman Is
P. m. montis
W Java
P. m. analis
Sumatra, E Java, Bali I
Picoides atratus (Stripe-breasted Woodpecker)
Burma, N Thailand, Laos
Picoides auriceps (Brown-fronted Pied Woodpecker)
NW Himalayas
Picoides mahrattensis (Yellow-crowned Woodpecker)
P. m. pallescens
NW India
P. m. aurocristatus
N India
P. m. mahrattensis
S & SW India
P. m. koelzi
SE Madras, Sri Lanka
P. m. blanfordi
Burma

Picoides dorae (Arabian Woodpecker)
C Arabia
Picoides hyperythrus (Rufous-bellied Pied Woodpecker)
P. h. marshalli
NW Himalayas, W Tibet
P. h. hyperythrus
E Himalayas to N Thailand
P. h. subrufinus
C Manchuria to C China
P. h. annamensis
S Laos, S Vietnam
Picoides cathpharius (Lesser Pied Woodpecker)
P. c. cathpharius
E Himalayas
P. c. pyrrothorax
S Assam
P. c. tenebrosus
W Yunnan, C Burma to N Indochina
P. c. pernyii
W China
P. c. innixus
C Hupeh
Picoides darjellensis (Darjeeling Pied Woodpecker)
P. d. darjellensis
Nepal to N Burma, N Vietnam
P. d. desmursi
W China
Picoides leucotos (White-backed Woodpecker)
P. l. leucotos
Scandinavia, E Europe, N Russia
P. l. lilfordi
Greece, Asia Minor
P. l. uralensis
S Urals, W Siberia
P. l. voznesenskii
E Siberia, Kamchatka
P. l. saghalinensis
Sakhalin I
P. l. ussuriensis
Amurland, N Manchuria, NE Korea
P. l. sinicus
NE China, Korea
P. l. tangi
W China
P. l. quelpartensis
Quelpart I
P. l. subcirrus
S Kurile Is, Hokkaido I
P. l. stejnegeri
N & C Honshu I
P. l. namiyei
SW Honshu I, Shikoku I, Kyushu I
P. l. takahashii
Dagelet Is

P. l. fohkiensis
SE China
P. l. owstoni
N Riukiu Is
P. l. insularis
Taiwan
Picoides medius (Middle Spotted Woodpecker)
P. l. medius
S Sweden, C Europe
P. l. lilianae
NW Spain
P. l. splendidior
SE Europe
P. l. anatoliae
Asia Minor
P. l. caucasicus
N Caucasia
P. m. laubmanni
Transcaucasia, N Iran
P. m. sancti-johannis
SW Iran
Picoides himalayensis (Himalayan Pied Woodpecker)
P. h. albescens
W Himalayas
P. h. himalayensis
C Himalayas
Picoides assimilis (Sind Pied Woodpecker)
SE Iran to W Punjab
Picoides syriacus (Syrian Woodpecker)
P. s. balcanicus
E Yugoslavia, Bulgaria, Romania
P. s. syriacus
Asia Minor, Israel, W Iran
P. s. transcaucasicus
Transcaucasia
P. s. milleri
SE Iran
Picoides leucopterus (White-winged Pied Woodpecker)
P. l. albipennis
S & E Transcaspia
P. l. jaxartensis
S Kazakhstan
P. l. leptorhynchus
Turkestan
P. l. korejevi
SE Kazakhstan
P. l. leucopterus
N Sinkiang
Picoides major (Great Spotted Woodpecker)
P. m. major
Scandinavia, N Russia
P. m. pinetorum
C & S Europe

P. m. anglicus
England & Scotland
P. m. italiae
S France, Switzerland, Italy
P. m. alpestris
S Switzerland
P. m. parroti
Corsica
P. m. harterti
Sardinia
P. m. hispanus
Portugal, S Spain
P. m. canariensis
Tenerife I
P. m. thanneri
Gran Canaria I
P. m. mauritanus
N Morocco
P. m. lynesi
C Morocco
P. m. numidus
Algeria, Tunisia
P. m. candidus
Romania, Bulgaria, S Russia
P. m. tenuirostris
Caucasus, Transcaucasia
P. m. paphlagoniae
N Turkey
P. m. poelzami
N Iran
P. m. brevirostris
Siberia, S Altai, N Mongolia
P. m. tianshanicus
Tien Shan
P. m. kamtschaticus
Kamchatka
P. m. tscherskii
Ussuriland, Sakhalin I
P. m. japonicus
S Kurile Is, Hokkaido I, NE Korea
P. m. hondoensis
N & C Hoshu I, S Korea
P. m. cabanisi
S Manchuria, NE China
P. m. mandarinus
S & SE China, N Indochina
P. m. biecki
W China
P. m. stresemanni
SW China, N Burma
P. m. hainanus
Hainan I
Picoides mixtus (Checkered Woodpecker
P. m. cancellatus
SE Brazil
P. m. mixtus
E Paraguay, Uruguay, E Argentina

P. m. malleator
W Paraguay, SE Bolivia, N & W Argentina
P. m. berlepschi
W & S Argentina
Picoides lignarius (Striped Woodpecker)
Bolivia, Chile, W & S Argentina
Picoides scalaris (Ladder-backed Woodpecker)
P. s. cactophilus
SW USA, NW Mexico
P. s. eremicus
N Baja California
P. s. lucasanus
S Baja California
P. s. graysoni
Tres Marias Is
P. s. sinaloensis
S Sonora, Sinaloa
P. s. centrophilus
W Mexico
P. s. azelus
SW Mexico
P. s. symplectus
SC USA to E Mexico
P. s. giraudi
C & E Mexico
P. s. scalaris
NE Vera Cruz
P. s. ridgwayi
SE Vera Cruz
P. s. parvus
N Yucatan, Cozumel I
P. s. percus
S Mexico
P. s. leucoptilurus
Belize
Picoides nuttallii (Nuttall's Woodpecker)
W California, NW Baja California
Picoides pubescens (Downy Woodpecker)
P. p. glacialis
E Alaska
P. p. gairdnerii
S British Columbia to N California
P. p. turati
SW Oregon, W California
P. p. leucurus
WC USA
P. p. nelsoni
W & C Canada
P. p. microleucus
Newfoundland, Anticosti I
P. p. medianus
S Canada to EC USA
P. p. pubescens
SE USA

Picoides borealis (Red-cockaded Woodpecker)
P. b. borealis
SC & SE USA
P. b. hylonomus
C & S Florida
Picoides stricklandi (Brown-backed Woodpecker)
P. s. arizonae
Arizona, NW Mexico
P. s. fraterculus
W Mexico
P. s. aztecus
C Mexico
P. s. stricklandi
E Mexico
Picoides villosus (Hairy Woodpecker)
P. v. septentrionalis
SC Alaska, S Canada
P. v. terraenovae
Newfoundland
P. v. villosus
SE Canada, NC & E USA
P. v. audubonii
SE USA
P. v. piger
Grand Bahama I, Mores I, Abaco I
P. v. maynardi
New Providence I, Andros I
P. v. picoideus
Queen Charlotte Is
P. v. sitkensis
SE Alaska, N British Columbia
P. v. harrisi
S British Columbia to N California
P. v. hyloscopus
W California
P. v. scrippsae
N Baja California
P. v. orius
SC Washington to NW Nevada
P. v. monticola
WC USA
P. v. leucothorectis
E California to W Texas
P. v. icastus
SE Arizona, NW Mexico
P. v. intermedius
E Mexico
P. v. jardinii
S Mexico
P. v. sanctorum
Chiapas, Guatemala
P. v. parvulus
El Salvador, N & W Honduras
P. v. fumeus
S Honduras, N Nicaragua

P. v. extimus
Costa Rica, W Panama
Picoides albolarvatus (White-headed Woodpecker)
P. a. albolarvatus
W USA
P. a. gravirostris
S California
Picoides tridactylus (Three-toed Woodpecker)
P. t. tridactylus
Scandinavia to NE Asia
P. t. alpinus
Alps to Romania
P. t. crissoleucus
N Siberia, N Mongolia
P. t. tianschanicus
Tien Shan, N Sikang
P. t. albidior
Kamchatka
P. t. sakhalinensis
Sakhalin I
P. t. inouyei
EC Hokkaido I
P. t. funebris
W China
P. t. fasciatus
N Alaska, W Canada, NW USA
P. t. dorsalis
N Montana to New Mexico
P. t. bacatus
C & E Canada, NE USA
Picoides arcticus (Black-backed Woodpecker)
Canada, W & N USA

VENILIORNIS
Veniliornis callonotus (Scarlet-backed Woodpecker)
V. c. callonotus
W Ecuador
V. c. major
SW Ecuador, N Peru
Veniliornis dignus (Yellow-fronted Woodpecker)
V. d. dignus
W Colombia
V. d. abdominalis
SW Venezuela
V. d. baezae
E Ecuador
V. d. valdizani
C Peru
Veniliornis nigriceps (Bar-bellied Woodpecker)
V. n. equifasciatus
WC Colombia, N Ecuador
V. n. pectoralis
C Peru

V. n. nigriceps
W Bolivia
Veniliornis fumigatus (Smoky-brown Woodpecker)
V. f. oleagineus
E Mexico
V. f. sanguinolentus
C & S Mexico to W Panama
V. f. exsul
N Colombia
V. f. reichenbachi
N Venezuela
V. f. tectricialis
NE Venezuela
V. f. fumigatus
Upper Amazonia
V. f. obscuratus
NW Peru
Veniliornis passerinus (Little Woodpecker)
V. p. fidelis
E Colombia, W Venezuela
V. p. modestus
NE Venezuela
V. p. diversus
N Brazil
V. p. agilis
E Ecuador to N Bolivia, W Brazil
V. p. insignis
WC Brazil
V. p. tapajozensis
C Brazil
V. p. saturatus
W French Guiana
V. p. passerinus
the Guianas, NE Brazil
V. p. taenionotus
E Brazil
V. p. transfluvialis
EC Brazil
V. p. olivinus
S Bolivia, S Brazil, Paraguay,
N Argentina
Veniliornis frontalis (Dot-fronted Woodpecker)
NW Argentina
Veniliornis spilogaster (White-spotted Woodpecker)
S Brazil, Paraguay, NE Argentina
Veniliornis sanguineus (Blood-coloured Woodpecker)
the Guianas
Veniliornis maculifrons (Yellow-eared Woodpecker)
SE Brazil
Veniliornis affinis (Red-stained Woodpecker)
V. a. chocoensis
W Colombia

V. a. orenocensis
E Colombia, E Venezuela, N Brazil
V. a. hilaris
E Ecuador, E Peru, N Bolivia, W Brazil
V. a. ruficeps
C & E Brazil
V. a. affinis
E Brazil
Veniliornis cassini (Golden-collared Woodpecker)
V. c. caquetanus
S Colombia
V. c. cassini
Venezuela, the Guianas, N Brazil
Veniliornis kirkii (Red-rumped Woodpecker)
V. k. neglectus
SW Costa Rica, Panama
V. k. cecilii
E Panama, W Colombia, W Ecuador
V. k. continentalis
N & W Venezuela
V. k. monticola
Mt Roraima (S Venezuela)
V. k. kirkii
Trinidad, Tobago I

PICULUS
Piculus leucolaemus (White-throated Woodpecker)
P. l. allophyeus
Honduras
P. l. simplex
Nicaragua to W Panama
P. l. callopterus
E Panama
P. l. litae
W Colombia, NW Ecuador
P. l. leucolaemus
E Colombia to Bolivia, W Brazil
Piculus flavigula (Yellow-throated Woodpecker)
P. f. flavigula
Northern Amazonia
P. f. magnus
SE Colombia, NW Brazil
P. f. erythropis
E & SE Brazil
Piculus chrysochloros (Golden-green Woodpecker)
P. c. aurosus
Panama
P. c. xanthochlorus
NE Colombia, NW Venezuela
P. c. capistratus
C Colombia to Guyana, NW Brazil
P. c. guianensis
French Guiana

261

P. c. laemostictus
W Brazil
P. c. hypochryseus
W Brazil, N Bolivia
P. c. paraensis
NE Brazil
P. c. polyzonus
SE Brazil
P. c. chrysochlorus
C & S Brazil, Bolivia, N Argentina
Piculus aurulentus (White-browed Woodpecker)
SE Brazil, N Argentina
Piculus rubiginosus (Golden-olive Woodpecker)
P. r. aeruginosus
NE Mexico
P. r. yucatanensis
C & S Mexico to Nicaragua
P. r. differens
W Guatemala
P. r. maximus
E & C Guatemala
P. r. uropygialis
Costa Rica, W Panama
P. r. alleni
N Colombia
P. r. buenavistae
E Colombia, E Ecuador
P. r. meridensis
W Venezuela
P. r. rubiginosus
N Venezuela
P. r. deltanus
NE Venezuela
P. r. paraquensis
E Venezuela
P. r. guianae
SE Venezuela, S Guyana
P. r. viridissimus
S Venezuela
P. r. nigriceps
S Guyana
P. r. trinitatis
Trinidad
P. r. tobagensis
Tobago I
P. r. fortirostris
Nassau Gebergte (Surinam)
P. r. poliocephalus
Brownsberg (Surinam)
P. r. gularis
C Colombia
P. r. pacificus
SW Colombia
P. r. michaelis
C Colombia

P. r. palmitae
NC Colombia
P. r. rubripileus
SW Colombia, NW Peru
P. r. coloratus
NC Peru
P. r. chrysogaster
C Peru
P. r. canipileus
N Bolivia
P. r. tucumanus
C Bolivia to NW Argentina
Piculus auricularis (Grey-crowned Woodpecker)
P. a. sonoriensis
NW Mexico
P. a. auricularis
W Mexico
Piculus rivolii (Crimson-mantled Woodpecker)
P. r. quindiuna
NC Colombia
P. r. rivolii
W Venezuela, EC Colombia
P. r. meridae
W Venezuela
P. r. brevirostris
SW Colombia to C Peru
P. r. atriceps
SE Peru, Bolivia

COLAPTES
Colaptes atricollis (Black-necked Woodpecker)
C. a. atricollis
W Peru
C. a. peruvianus
E Peru
Colaptes punctigula (Spot-breasted Woodpecker)
C. p. lutescens
E Panama
C. p. ujhelyii
N Colombia
C. p. striatigularis
WC Colombia
C. p. punctipectus
E Colombia, Venezuela
C. p. notatus
? Colombia
C. p. zuliae
NW Venezuela
C. p. speciosus
Upper Amazonia
C. p. punctigula
Surinam, French Guiana
C. p. rubidipectus
NE Brazil

C. p. guttatus
NC Brazil
Colaptes melanochloros (Green-barred Woodpecker)
C. m. mariae
Marajo I
C. m. flavilumbis
E Brazil
C. m. nattereri
E Bolivia, S Brazil
C. m. melanochloros
C Brazil
C. m. cristatus
E Paraguay, Uruguay, NE Argentina
C. m. melanolaimus
Bolivia, W Argentina
C. m. nigroviridis
S Bolivia, Paraguay
C. m. perplexus
E Argentina
C. m. patagonicus
W Argentina
Colaptes auratus (Common Flicker)
C. a. cafer
S Alaska to N California
C. a. collaris
SE British Colombia to NW Mexico
C. a. sedentarius
Santa Cruz Is
C. a. martirensis
W Baja California
C. a. nanus
NE Mexico
C. a. mexicanus
C Mexico
C. a. mexicanoïdes
S Mexico, Guatemala
C. a. pinicolus
El Salvador, Honduras, N Nicaragua
C. a. borealis
Canada, C USA
C. a. luteus
S Canada, WC & S USA
C. a. auratus
SE USA
C. a. chrysocaulosus
Cuba
C. a. gundlachi
Gd Cayman I
C. a. mearnsi
SE California, NW Baja California
C. a. tenebrosus
NW Mexico
C. a. brunnescens
C Baja California
C. a. chrysoïdes
S Baja California

Colaptes fernandinae (Fernandina's Flicker)
Cuba
Colaptes pitius (Chilean Flicker)
  C. p. pitius
    C & S Chile
  C. p. cachinnans
    S Argentina
Colaptes rupicola (Andean Flicker)
  C. r. cinereicapilla
    N Peru
  C. r. puna
    C & S Peru
  C. r. rupicola
    Bolivia, N Chile, NW Argentina
Colaptes campestris (Campo Flicker)
  C. c. chrysosternus
    NE Brazil
  C. c. campestris
    E Bolivia, C & SE Brazil
  C. c. campestroïdes
    S Brazil, Paraguay, Uruguay,
      N & C Argentina

CELEUS
Celeus loricatus (Cinnamon Woodpecker)
  C. l. diversus
    SE Costa Rica, W Panama
  C. l. mentalis
    E Panama, NW Colombia
  C. l. innotatus
    N Colombia
  C. l. degener
    NC Colombia
  C. l. loricatus
    W Colombia, W Ecuador
Celeus undatus (Waved Woodpecker)
  C. u. amarcurensis
    NE Venezuela
  C. u. undatus
    the Guianas, N Brazil
  C. u. multifasciatus
    NE Brazil
Celeus grammicus (Scale-breasted Woodpecker)
  C. g. verreauxii
    SE Colombia, E Ecuador
  C. g. grammicus
    S Venezuela, NE Peru, W Brazil
  C. g. undulatus
    SC Venezuela
  C. g. subcervinus
    NC Brazil
  C. g. latifasciatus
    SE Peru, NE Bolivia
Celeus brachyurus (Rufous Woodpecker)
  C. b. humei
    NW Himalayas
  C. b. phaioceps
    E Himalayas, NE India

  C. b. jerdonii
    W India, Sri Lanka
  C. b. kanarae
    W India
  C. b. annamensis
    Laos, Cambodia, S Vietnam
  C. b. fokiensis
    SE China, N Vietnam
  C. b. holroydi
    Hainan I
  C. b. squamigularis
    Malaysia
  C. b. badius
    Sumatra, Bangka I, Billiton I
  C. b. celaenephis
    Nias I
  C. b. brachyurus
    Java
  C. b. badiosus
    Borneo, N Natuna Is
Celeus castaneus (Chestnut-coloured Woodpecker)
    SE Mexico to C Panama
Celeus elegans (Chestnut Woodpecker)
  C. e. hellmayri
    E Venezuela, Guyana, Surinam
  C. e. deltanus
    NE Venezuela
  C. e. leotaudi
    Trinidad
  C. e. approximans
    NE Brazil, S Guyana
  C. e. elegans
    NE Brazil, French Guiana
  C. e. citreopygius
    SE Colombia, E Ecuador, Peru
  C. e. jumana
    E Colombia, S Venezuela, N Brazil
  C. e. saturatus
    N Bolivia
Celeus lugubris (Pale-crested Woodpecker)
    Bolivia
Celeus flavescens (Blond-crested Woodpecker)
  C. f. ochraceus
    E Brazil
  C. f. intercedens
    NE Brazil
  C. f. flavescens
    SE Brazil, E Paraguay
  C. f. roosevelti
    SE Bolivia, SW Brazil
  C. f. kerri
    W Paraguay, N Argentina

***Celeus flavus* (Cream-coloured Woodpecker)**
C. f. semicinnamomeus
N Venezuela
C. f. flavus
C Colombia to the Guianas, N Brazil
C. f. peruvianus
W Brazil, E Peru
C. f. inornatus
C Brazil
C. f. tectricialis
NE Brazil
C. f. subflavus
E Brazil

***Celeus spectabilis* (Rufous-headed Woodpecker)**
C. s. spectabilis
E Ecuador
C. s. obrieni
Piauhy, (Brazil)
C. s. exsul
C Bolivia

***Celeus torquatus* (Ringed Woodpecker)**
C. t. torquatus
E Venezuela, the Guianas, N Brazil
C. t. occidentalis
E Peru, W Brazil
C. t. angustus
C Brazil
C. t. tinnunculus
E Brazil

DRYOCOPUS
***Dryocopus galeatus* (Helmeted Woodpecker)**
S Brazil, Paraguay, NE Argentina
***Dryocopus schulzi* (Black-bodied Woodpecker)**
N Argentina
***Dryocopus lineatus* (Lineated Woodpecker)**
D. l. obsoletus
NW Mexico
D. l. scapularis
W Mexico
D. l. petersi
NE Mexico
D. l. similis
S Mexico to NW Costa Rica
D. l. mesorhynchus
E & S Costa Rica, W Panama
D. l. nuperus
E Panama, N & W Colombia
D. l. lineatus
Trinidad, N & W Amazonia
D. l. fuscipennis
W Ecuador, NW Peru
D. l. improcerus
E Brazil

D. l. erythrops
SE & S Brazil
D. l. fulcitus
N Argentina
***Dryocopus pileatus* (Pileated Woodpecke**
D. p. picinus
SW Canada, W USA
D. p. abieticola
C & E Canada, NE USA
D. p. pileatus
C & E USA
D. p. floridanus
SE USA
***Dryocopus javensis* (White-bellied Black Woodpecker)**
D. j. hodgei
Andaman Is
D. j. hodgsonii
W India
D. j. richardsi
C & S Korea
D. j. forresti
SE Sikang, W Yunnan, N Vietnam
D. j. feddeni
Burma, N Thailand, S Indochina
D. j. javensis
Malaysia, Sumatra, Java, Borneo
D. j. parvus
Simalur I
D. j. buttikoferi
Nias I
D. j. hargitti
Palawan I
D. j. confusus
Luzon I
D. j. mindorensis
Mindoro I
D. j. philippensis
Masbate I, Panay I, Negros I
D. j. pectoralis
Leyte I
D. j. samarensis
Samar I, Bohol I
D. j. multilunatus
Mindanao I, Basilan I
D. j. suluënsis
Sulu Archipelago
***Dryocopus martius* (Black Woodpecker)**
D. m. pinetorum
C & S Europe to N Iran
D. m. martius
Scandinavia to NE Asia, Japan
D. m. khamensis
W China

Campephilus guatemalensis (Pale-bellied Woodpecker)
  C. g. regius
    E & C Mexico
  C. g. dorsofasciatus
    NW Mexico
  C. g. nelsoni
    W Mexico
  C. g. guatemalensis
    S Mexico to W Panama

Campephilus melanoleucos (Crimson-crested Woodpecker)
  C. m. malherbii
    E Panama to W Venezuela
  C. m. melanoleucos
    N & W Amazonia
  C. m. albirostris
    S Brazil, Paraguay, NW Argentina
  C. m. cearae
    NE Brazil

Campephilus gayaquilensis (Guayaquil Woodpecker)
  W Ecuador, NW Peru

Campephilus pollens (Powerful Woodpecker)
  C. p. pollens
    Colombia, Ecuador
  C. p. peruvianus
    E Peru

Campephilus haematogaster (Crimson-bellied Woodpecker)
  C. h. splendens
    Panama to NW Ecuador
  C. h. haematogaster
    N Colombia to S Peru

Campephilus robustus (Robust Woodpecker)
  SE Brazil, Paraguay, NE Argentina

Campephilus rubricollis (Red-necked Woodpecker)
  C. r. rubricollis
    C Colombia to the Guianas, N Brazil
  C. r. trachelopyrus
    E Peru, N Bolivia, W Brazil
  C. r. olallae
    W Bolivia to C & E Brazil

Campephilus leucopogon (Cream-backed Woodpecker)
  Bolivia to Uruguay & NE Argentina

Campephilus magellanicus (Magellanic Woodpecker)
  S South America

Campephilus principalis (Ivory-billed Woodpecker)
  C. p. principalis
    N Louisiana

  C. p. bairdii
    Cuba

Campephilus imperialis (Imperial Woodpecker)
  NW & W Mexico

Picus miniaceus (Banded Red Woodpecker)
  P. m. perlutus
    S Burma, SW Thailand
  P. m. malaccensis
    Malaysia, Sumatra, NW Borneo
  P. m. niasensis
    Nias I
  P. m. miniaceus
    W & C Java
  P. m. dayak
    Borneo

Picus puniceus (Crimson-winged Woodpecker)
  P. p. continentis
    S Burma, Malaysia
  P. p. observandus
    Sumatra, Borneo
  P. p. soligae
    Nias I
  P. p. puniceus
    Java

Picus chlorolophus (Lesser Yellow-naped Woodpecker)
  P. c. simlae
    NW Himalayas
  P. c. chlorolophus
    E Himalayas, N India, N Burma
  P. c. chlorigaster
    C & S India
  P. c. wellsi
    Sri Lanka
  P. c. chlorolophoides
    S Burma, N Thailand
  P. c. citrinocristatus
    SE China, N Indochina
  P. c. longipennis
    Hainan I
  P. c. laotianus
    NE Thailand, N Laos
  P. c. annamensis
    S Indochina
  P. c. krempfi
    S Vietnam
  P. c. rodgeri
    NW Malaysia
  P. c. vanheysti
    Sumatra

Picus mentalis (Checker-throated Woodpecker)
  P. m. humii
    S Burma, Malaysia, Sumatra, W Borneo

P. m. mentalis
Java

P. m. saba
S & E Borneo

Picus flavinucha (Greater Yellow-naped Woodpecker)

P. f. flavinucha
E Himalayas, Nepal to N Assam

P. f. archon
NE Thailand, N Vietnam

P. f. kumaonensis
W Himalayas

P. f. marianae
S Assam

P. f. styani
SE China, NE Vietnam, Hainan I

P. f. lylei
NW & SW Thailand

P. f. pierrei
C, E & SE Thailand, S Indochina

P. f. ricketti
C Fukien

P. f. mystacalis
N Sumatra

P. f. korinchi
S Sumatra

Picus vittatus (Laced Green Woodpecker)

P. v. viridanus
Burma, SW Thailand

P. v. weberi
S Thailand, N Malaysia

P. v. eisenhoferi
E Burma, N Indochina

P. v. eurous
SE Thailand, W Cambodia

P. v. connectens
Langkawi Is

P. v. vittatus
S Malaysia, Sumatra, W Java

P. v. limitans
E Java, Bali I, Kangean I

Picus xanthopygaeus (Little Scaly-bellied Green Woodpecker)
Himalayas, India to Indochina

Picus squamatus (Scaly-bellied Green Woodpecker)

P. s. flavirostris
Caspian Sea to Afghanistan

P. s. squamatus
W & C Himalayas

Picus awokera (Japanese Green Woodpecker)

P. a. awokera
Honshu I

P. a. horii
Shikoku I, Kyushu I

P. a. takatsukasae
Tanegashima I, Yakushima I

Picus canus (Grey-headed Green Woodpecker)

P. c. canus
Norway to Alps & E Europe

P. c. perspicuus
Bulgaria, SE Yugoslavia

P. c. biedermanni
Altai, C Asia, N Mongolia

P. c. jessoensis
Manchuria, Korea, Hokkaido I

P. c. zimmermanni
NE China

P. c. kogo
W China

P. c. setschuanus
SW China

P. c. brunneatus
Szechwan

P. c. guerini
E China

P. c. sobrinus
SE China, N Vietnam

P. c. tancolo
Taiwan, Hainan I

P. c. sordidior
NW Yunnan

P. c. sanguiniceps
NW Himalayas

P. c. gyldenstolpei
E Nepal, Assam, N Burma

P. c. hessei
S Burma, Thailand, Indochina

P. c. robinsoni
Malaysia

P. c. dedemi
Sumatra

Picus erythropygius (Red-rumped Green Woodpecker)

P. e. nigrigenis
Burma, S Thailand

P. e. erythropygius
SE Thailand, S Indochina

Picus rabieri (Red-collared Woodpecker)
Indochina

Picus viridis (Green Woodpecker)

P. v. pluvius
England, Wales

P. v. viridis
Scandinavia, W Russia

P. v. frondium
C Europe

P. v. pronus
S Switzerland, Italy

P. v. dofleini
SE Europe

P. v. romaniae
Romania

P. v. sharpei
  Iberia
P. v. saundersi
  Caucasus
P. v. karelini
  N Turkey, N Iran
P. v. innominatus
  W & SW Iran
P. v. bampurensis
  Baluchistan
Picus vaillantii (Algerian Green Woodpecker)
  Morocco to Tunisia

DINOPIUM
Dinopium rafflesii (Olive-backed Three-toed Woodpecker)
D. r. peninsulare
  S Burma, S Thailand, Malaysia
D. r. rafflesii
  Sumatra, Bangka I
D. r. dulitense
  Borneo
Dinopium shorii (Himalayan Three-toed Woodpecker)
  Himalayas, N Burma
Dinopium javanense (Golden-backed Three-toed Woodpecker)
D. j. malabaricum
  SW India
D. j. intermedium
  NE India to Indochina
D. j. javanense
  Malaysia, Sumatra, W & C Java
D. j. exsul
  E Java, Bali I
D. j. borneonense
  Borneo
D. j. raveni
  NE Borneo
D. j. everetti
  SW Philippine Is
Dinopium benghalense (Lesser Golden-backed Woodpecker)
D. b. benghalense
  E & C India
D. b. dilutum
  Baluchistan, Pakistan
D. b. puncticolle
  S India
D. b. tehminae
  W India
D. b. jaffnense
  N Sri Lanka
D. b. erithronothon
  S Sri Lanka

CHRYSOCOLAPTES
Chrysocolaptes lucidus (Crimson-backed Woodpecker)
C. l. sultaneus
  NW Himalayas
C. l. guttacristatus
  E India, Burma, Thailand, S Indochina
C. l. chersonesus
  S India, S Malaysia, Sumatra, Java
C. l. stricklandi
  Sri Lanka
C. l. strictus
  E Java, Bali I, Kangean I
C. l. andrewsi
  Sebattick Is, Borneo
C. l. erythrocephalus
  Palawan I, Balabac I
C. l. haematribon
  N Luzon, Marinduque I
C. l. grandis
  Polillo Is
C. l. ramosi
  S Luzon
C. l. xanthocephalus
  Masbate I, Panay I, Negros I
C. l. rufopunctatus
  Samar I, Leyte I, Bohol I
C. l. lucidus
  Mindanao I
C. l. maculiceps
  Basilan I
Chrysocolaptes festivus (Black-backed Woodpecker)
C. f. festivus
  C & S India
C. f. tantus
  Sri Lanka

GECINULUS
Gecinulus grantia (Pale-headed Woodpecker)
G. g. grantia
  Nepal to E Assam, N Burma
G. g. indochinensis
  N & C Indochina
G. g. poilanei
  SE Indochina
G. g. viridanus
  S China
Gecinulus viridis (Bamboo Woodpecker)
G. v. viridis
  C Burma to E Thailand
G. v. robinsoni
  SE Thailand, Malaysia

SAPHEOPIPO
Sapheopipo noguchii (Pryer's Woodpecker)
  Okinawa I

Blythipicus rubiginosus (Lesser Bay Woodpecker)
B. r. parvus
Sumatra, Borneo
B. r. rubiginosus
S Burma, S Thailand, Malaysia
Blythipicus pyrrhotis (Bay Woodpecker)
B. p. pyrrhotis
NE Himalayas, NE India to Indochina
B. p. cameroni
Malaysia
B. p. annamensis
S Indochina
B. p. sinensis
SE China
B. p. hainanus
Hainan I

REINWARDTIPICUS
Reinwardtipicus validus (Orange-backed Woodpecker)
R. v. xanthopygius
Malaysia, Sumatra, Borneo
R. v. validus
W & C Java

MEIGLYPTES
Meiglyptes tristis (Fulvous-rumped Barred Woodpecker)
M. t. grammithorax
S Burma, S Thailand, Malaysia
M. t. micropterus
Sumatra, Borneo
M. t. microterus
Nias I
M. t. tristis
Java
Meiglyptes jugularis (Black and Buff Woodpecker)
Burma to S Indochina
Meiglyptes tukki (Buff-necked Barred Woodpecker)
M. t. tukki
Malaysia, Sumatra, Borneo
M. t. azaleus
N Natuna Is
M. t. pulonis
Banggai I
M. t. percnerpes
S Borneo
M. t. calceuticus
Banjak Is
M. t. infuscatus
Nias I
M. t. batu
Batu Is

HEMICIRCUS
Hemicircus concretus (Malaysian Grey-breasted Woodpecker)
H. c. sordidus
S Burma, S Thailand, Malaysia
H. c. coccometopus
Sumatra, Borneo
H. c. concretus
W & C Java
Hemicircus canente (Heart-spotted Woodpecker)
H. c. canente
NE India to S Indochina
H. c. cordatus
W India

MULLERIPICUS
Mulleripicus fulvus (Fulvous Woodpecker)
M. f. fulvus
N Celebes, Togian Is
M. f. wallacei
C & S Celebes
Mulleripicus funebris (Sooty Woodpecker)
M. f. funebris
Luzon I, Marinduque I
M. f. fuliginosus
Samar I, Leyte I, Mindanao I
Mulleripicus pulverulentus (Great Slaty Woodpecker)
M. p. harterti
N India to C & S Indochina
M. p. pulverulentus
Malaysia, Sumatra, Java, Borneo, Palawan I

Passeriformes

100 EURYLAIMIDAE (BROADBILLS)

EURYLAIMINAE

SMITHORNIS
Smithornis capensis (African Broadbill)
S. c. delacouri
Liberia, Ghana, Ivory Coast
S. c. camerunensis
S Cameroun, Gabon
S. c. albigularis
N Angola, S Zaire
S. c. medianus
E Zaire, Uganda, Kenya
S. c. capensis
S Kenya, Tanzania, Zambia, Rhodesia, Malaysia, Mozambique, Natal

***Smithornis rufolateralis* (Red-sided Broadbill)**
S. r. rufolateralis
West Africa, Cameroun, Central African Republic
S. r. budongoensis
NE Zaire, W Uganda
***Smithornis sharpei* (Grey-headed Broadbill)**
S. s. sharpei
Fernando Po I
S. s. zenkeri
Cameroun
S. s. eurylaemus
E Zaire

PSEUDOCALYPTOMENA
***Pseudocalyptomena graueri* (Grauer's Broadbill)**
E Zaire

CORYDON
***Corydon sumatranus* (Dusky Broadbill)**
C. s. laoensis
S Burma, Thailand Laos, N Vietnam
C. s. morator
S Thailand
C. s. pallescens
Malaysia
C. s. ardescens
SE Thailand
C. s. sumatranus
Sumatra
C. s. brunnescens
N Borneo, N Natuna Is
C. s. orientalis
S Borneo

CYMBIRHYNCHUS
***Cymbirhynchus macrorhynchos* (Black and Red Broadbill)**
C. m. affinis
SE Burma
C. m. siamensis
S Burma, S Thailand, Cambodia, S Vietnam
C. m. malaccensis
S Malaysia
C. m. lemniscatus
Sumatra, Bangka I, Billiton I
C. m. tenebrosus
SE Sumatra
C. m. macrorhynchos
Borneo

EURYLAIMUS
***Eurylaimus javanicus* (Banded Broadbill)**
E. j. pallidus
S Burma, Malaysia, Thailand, Laos, S Vietnam
E. j. harterti
Sumatra
E. j. javanicus
Java
E. j. billitonis
Billiton I
E. j. brookei
Borneo
***Eurylaimus ochromalus* (Black and Yellow Broadbill)**
E. o. ochromalus
S Burma, Malaysia, Sumatra
E. o. mecistus
Banjak Is
E. o. kalamantan
Borneo
***Eurylaimus steerii* (Wattled Broadbill)**
E. s. samarensis
Samar I, Leyte I, Philippine Is
E. s. steerii
Mindanao I, Basilan I
E. s. mayri
Mindanao I

SERILOPHUS
***Serilophus lunatus* (Silver-breasted Broadbill)**
S. l. rubropygius
Nepal, N Burma
S. l. atrestus
E Burma, E Thailand, N Laos, N Vietnam
S. l. polionotus
Hainan I
S. l. impavidus
S Laos
S. l. lunatus
S Burma
S. l. intrepidus
NW Thailand
S. l. stolidus
S Burma, S Thailand
S. l. rothschildi
Malaysia
S. l. moderatus
N Sumatra
S. l. intensus
S Sumatra

PSARISOMUS
***Psarisomus dalhousiae* (Long-tailed Broadbill)**
P. d. dalhousiae
Himalayas, Burma, N & W Thailand, Laos, N Vietnam
P. d. cyanicauda
SE Thailand
P. d. divinus
Cambodia, S Vietnam
P. d. psittacinus
Malaysia, Sumatra
P. d. borneensis
mountains of NW Borneo

CALYPTOMENA
Calyptomena viridis (Lesser Green Broadbill)
C. v. continentis
S Burma, S Thailand, Malaysia
C. v. viridis
Nias I, N Natuna Is, Sumatra, Borneo
C. v. siberu
Siberut I, S Pagi Is
Calyptomena hosii (Magnificent Green Broadbill)
mountains of N Borneo
Calyptomena whiteheadi (Black-throated Green Broadbill)
Mt Kinabalu (N Borneo)

101 DENDROCOLAPTIDAE (WOOD-CREEPERS)

DENDROCINCLA
Dendrocincla tyrannina (Tyrannine Woodcreeper)
D. t. tyrannina
Colombia
D. t. hellmayri
E Colombia, W Venezuela
Dendrocincla macrorhyncha (Large Tyrannine Woodcreeper)
E Ecuador
Dendrocincla fuliginosa (Plain-brown Woodcreeper)
D. f. ridgwayi
E C America, W Colombia, W Ecuador
D. f. lafresnayei
N & E Colombia, NW Venezuela
D. f. meruloides
coast of N Venezuela, Trinidad
D. f. deltana
delta of R Orinoco
D. f. barinensis
C Venezuela
D. f. phaeochroa
S Colombia, E Ecuador, E Peru
D. f. neglecta
W Brazil
D. f. atrirostris
NE Bolivia, SW Brazil
D. f. fuliginosa
E Venezuela, the Guianas, N Brazil
D. f. rufoolivacea
EC Brazil
D. f. taunayi
NE Brazil
D. f. turdina
E & S Brazil, E Paraguay, NE Argentina
D. f. brumaii
C Brazil

Dendrocincla anabatina (Tawny-winged Woodcreeper)
D. a. anabatina
S Mexico to Costa Rica
D. a. typhla
SE Mexico
Dendrocincla merula (White-chinned Woodcreeper)
D. m. bartletti
S Venezuela, W Brazil, NE Paraguay
D. m. merula
the Guianas, N Brazil
D. m. obidensis
Brazil
D. m. remota
EC Bolivia
D. m. olivascens
Brazil
D. m. castanoptera
C Brazil
D. m. badia
C Brazil
Dendrocincla homochroa (Ruddy Woodcreeper)
D. h. homochroa
S Mexico to Honduras
D. h. acedesta
SW Nicaragua, W Costa Rica
D. h. ruficeps
Panama, W Venezuela
D. h. meridionalis
NE Colombia

DECONYCHURA
Deconychura longicauda (Long-tailed Woodcreeper)
D. l. typica
SW Costa Rica, W Panama
D. l. darienensis
E Panama
D. l. minor
N Colombia
D. l. longicauda
the Guianas, N Brazil
D. l. connectens
NW Amazonia
D. l. pallida
SE Peru, N Bolivia, W Brazil
D. l. zimmeri
Pará, Brazil
Deconychura stictolaema (Spot-throated Woodcreeper)
D. s. clarior
French Guiana, NE Brazil
D. s. secunda
E Ecuador, NE Peru, W Brazil, S Venezuela
D. s. stictolaema
C Brazil

SITTASOMUS
Sittasomus griseicapillus (Olivaceous Woodcreeper)
S. g. jaliscensis
SW Mexico
S. g. sylvioides
SE Mexico to Costa Rica
S. g. gracileus
E Mexico
S. g. levis
W Panama, N Colombia
S. g. veraguensis
E Panama
S. g. aequatorialis
W Ecuador, NW Peru
S. g. perijanus
NW Venezuela
S. g. tachiranus
W Venezuela
S. g. griseus
coast of N Venezuela, Tobago I
S. g. enochrus
Colombia
S. g. amazonus
SE Colombia, S Venezuela, E Ecuador, W Brazil
S. g. axillaris
E Venezuela, N Brazil
S. g. viridis
N & E Bolivia
S. g. viridior
E Bolivia
S. g. transitivus
C Brazil
S. g. griseicapillus
S Bolivia, W Brazil, W Paraguay, NW Argentina
S. g. reiseri
NE Brazil
S. g. olivaceus
E Brazil
S. g. sylviellus
SE Brazil, NE Argentina

GLYPHORHYNCHUS
Glyphorhynchus spirurus (Wedge-billed Woodcreeper)
G. s. pectoralis
S Mexico to Nicaragua
G. s. sublestus
Costa Rica to W Ecuador, W Venezuela
G. s. subrufescens
W Colombia
G. s. integratus
NE Colombia
G. s. rufigularis
E Colombia, S Venezuela, N Ecuador
G. s. amacurensis
NE Venezuela

G. s. coronobscurus
S Venezuela
G. s. spirurus
E Venezuela, the Guianas, N Brazil
G. s. pallidulus
Panama
G. s. castelnaudii
E Ecuador, N Peru
G. s. albigularis
SE Peru, N Bolivia
G. s. inornatus
C Brazil
G. s. cuneatus
EC Brazil
G. s. paraensis
Belem (Brazil)

DRYMORNIS
Drymornis bridgesii (Bridge's Woodhewer)
Paraguay, Uruguay, Argentina

NASICA
Nasica longirostris (Long-billed Woodcreeper)
W Amazonia to French Guiana

DENDREXETASTES
Dendrexetastes rufigula (Cinnamon-throated Woodcreeper)
D. r. devillei
W Amazonia
D. r. rufigula
the Guianas, N Brazil
D. r. moniliger
W Brazil
D. r. paraensis
NE Brazil

HYLEXETASTES
Hylexetastes perrotii (Red-billed Woodcreeper)
H. p. perrotii
E Venezuela, Guyana, French Guiana, N Brazil
H. p. uniformis
N Brazil
Hylexetastes stresemanni (Bar-bellied Woodcreeper)
H. s. insignis
NW Brazil
H. s. stresemanni
NW Brazil
H. s. undulatus
E Peru, W Brazil

XIPHOCOLAPTES
Xiphocolaptes promeropirhynchus (Strong-billed Woodcreeper)
X. p. omiltemensis
SW Mexico
X. p. sclateri
S Mexico

X. p. emigrans
S Mexico to N Nicaragua
X. p. costaricensis
Costa Rica
X. p. panamensis
S Panama
X. p. rostratus
N Colombia
X. p. sanctaemartae
N Colombia, W Venezuela
X. p. virgatus
C Colombia
X. p. macarenae
WC Colombia
X. p. promeropirhynchus
EC Colombia, W Venezuela
X. p. procerus
N Venezuela
X. p. tenebrosus
E Venezuela
X. p. neblinae
S Venezuela
X. p. ignotus
W Ecuador
X. p. crassirostris
SW Ecuador, NW Peru
X. p. compressirostris
N Peru
X. p. phaeopygus
E Peru
X. p. solivagus
E Peru
X. p. lineatuscephalus
SE Peru, N & W Bolivia
X. p. orenocensis
Venezuela, E Ecuador, E Peru, W Brazil
X. p. berlepschi
E Peru, W Brazil
X. p. paraensis
C Brazil
X. p. obsoletus
N & E Bolivia
Xiphocolaptes albicollis (White-throated Woodcreeper)
X. a. bahiae
NE Brazil
X. a. albicollis
SE Brazil, E Paraguay, NE Argentina
Xiphocolaptes villanovae (Vila Nova Woodcreeper)
E Brazil
Xiphocolaptes falcirostris (Moustached Woodcreeper)
NE Brazil
Xiphocolaptes franciscanus (Snethlage's Woodcreeper)
C Brazil

Xiphocolaptes major (Great Rufous Woodcreeper)
X. m. remoratus
C Brazil
X. m. castaneus
S Brazil, E & S Bolivia, NW Argentina
X. m. major
Paraguay, N Argentina

DENDROCOLAPTES
Dendrocolaptes certhia (Barred Woodcreeper)
D. c. sanctithomae
S Mexico to Nicaragua
D. c. scheffleri
Oaxaca (Mexico)
D. c. nigrirostris
Costa Rica, Panama
D. c. hesperius
SW Costa Rica
D. c. colombianus
W Colombia, NW Ecuador
D. c. hyleorus
NE Colombia
D. c. radiolatus
SE Colombia, E Ecuador, NE Peru, NW Brazil
D. c. punctipectus
NW Venezuela
D. c. certhia
S Venezuela, the Guianas, N Brazil
D. c. juruanus
E Peru, E Bolivia, W Brazil
D. c. polyzonus
N Bolivia
D. c. ridgwayi
N Brazil
D. c. medius
NE Brazil
Dendrocolaptes concolor (Concolor Woodcreeper)
N Brazil
Dendrocolaptes hoffmannsi (Hoffmann's Woodcreeper)
C Brazil
Dendrocolaptes picumnus (Black-banded Woodcreeper)
D. p. puncticollis
Guatemala, Honduras
D. p. costaricensis
Costa Rica, W Panama
D. p. veraguensis
S Panama
D. p. multistrigatus
E Colombia, W Venezuela
D. p. seilerni
N Colombia, N Venezuela
D. p. picumnus
E Venezuela, the Guianas, N Brazil

D. p. validus
W Amazonia
D. p. transfasciatus
C Brazil
D. p. olivaceus
C Bolivia
D. p. pallescens
S Brazil, S Bolivia, Paraguay
D. p. extimus
E Paraguay
D. p. casaresi
NW Argentina
Dendrocolaptes platyrostris (Planalto Woodcreeper)
D. p. intermedius
NE Brazil, N Paraguay
D. p. platyrostris
SE Brazil, Paraguay, N Argentina

XIPHORHYNCHUS
Xiphorhynchus picus (Straight-billed Woodcreeper)
X. p. extimus
S Panama
X. p. dugandi
N Colombia
X. p. picirostris
NW Colombia, W Venezuela
X. p. saturatior
E Colombia, W Venezuela
X. p. borreroi
SW Colombia
X. p. choicus
N Venezuela
X. p. paraguanae
NW Venezuela
X. p. longirostris
Margarita I
X. p. altirostris
Trinidad
X. p. phalera
S Venezuela
X. p. deltans
NE Venezuela
X. p. picus
E Colombia to the Guianas, N Brazil
X. p. duidae
S Venezuela, NW Brazil
X. p. peruvianus
E Peru, W Brazil, N Bolivia
X. p. kienerii
W Brazil
X. p. rufescens
C Brazil
X. p. bahiae
NE Brazil
Xiphorhynchus necopinus (Zimmer's Woodcreeper)
C & NE Brazil

Xiphorhynchus obsoletus (Striped Woodcreeper) 273
X. o. palliatus
W Amazonia
X. o. notatus
E Colombia, SW Venezuela, NW Brazil
X. o. obsoletus
E Venezuela to French Guiana, N Brazil
X. o. caicarae
NE Venezuela
Xiphorhynchus ocellatus (Ocellated Woodcreeper)
X. o. napensis
SE Colombia, E Ecuador, NE Peru
X. o. lineatocapillus
E Venezuela
X. o. ocellatus
E Colombia, S Venezuela, NE Peru, NW Brazil
X. o. perplexus
NE Peru, W Brazil
X. o. chunchotambo
E Peru
X. o. brevirostris
SE Peru, NE Bolivia
Xiphorhynchus spixii (Spix's Woodcreeper)
X. s. buenavistae
W Colombia
X. s. insignis
EC Peru
X. s. juruanus
SE Peru, NE Bolivia, W Brazil
X. s. spixii
S Brazil
Xiphorhynchus elegans (Elegant Woodcreeper)
X. e. ornatus
SE Colombia, E Ecuador, NE Peru, W Brazil.
X. e. elegans
S Brazil
Xiphorhynchus pardalotus (Chestnut-rumped Woodcreeper)
X. p. caurensis
SE Venezuela, W Guyana
X. p. pardalotus
the Guianas, N Brazil
Xiphorhynchus guttatus (Buff-throated Woodcreeper)
X. g. confinis
E Guatemala, N Honduras
X. g. costaricensis
SW Honduras to W Panama
X. g. marginatus
E Panama
X. g. nanus
E Panama, N Colombia, W Venezuela

X. g. rosenbergi
W Colombia

X. g. demonstratus
E Colombia, NW Venezuela

X. g. susurrans
NE Venezuela, Trinidad, Tobago I

X. g. jardinei
NE Venezuela

X. g. margaritae
Margarita I

X. g. polystictus
E Colombia to the Guianas, N Brazil

X. g. connectens
N Brazil

X. g. guttatoides
W Amazonia

X. g. vicinalis
S Brazil

X. g. dorbignyanus
NE Bolivia, SW Brazil

X. g. guttatus
coast of E Brazil

Xiphorhynchus eytoni (Dusky-billed Woodcreeper)
E & S Brazil

Xiphorhynchus flavigaster (Ivory-billed Woodcreeper)

X. f. tardus
NW Mexico

X. f. mentalis
W Mexico

X. f. flavigaster
SW Mexico

X. f. saltuarius
NE Mexico

X. f. yucatanensis
Yucatan peninsula, Meco I

X. f. ascensor
S Mexico

X. f. eburneirostris
SE Mexico to NW Costa Rica

X. f. ultimus
NW Costa Rica

Xiphorhynchus striatigularis (Stripe-throated Woodcreeper)
NE Mexico

Xiphorhynchus lachrymosus (Black-striped Woodcreeper)

X. l. lachrymosus
E Nicaragua to W Ecuador

X. l. alarum
N Colombia

Xiphorhynchus erythropygius (Spotted Woodcreeper)

X. e. erythropygius
S Mexico

X. e. parvus
S Mexico to N Nicaragua

X. e. punctigula
S Nicaragua to W Panama

X. e. insolitus
E Panama, NW Colombia

X. e. aequatorialis
W Colombia, W Ecuador

Xiphorhynchus triangularis (Olive-backed Woodcreeper)

X. t. triangularis
Colombia, W Venezuela, E Ecuador, N Peru

X. t. hylodromus
N Venezuela

X. t. intermedius
C & S Peru

X. t. bangsi
Bolivia

LEPIDOCOLAPTES

Lepidocolaptes leucogaster (White-striped Woodcreeper)

L. l. umbrosus
NW Mexico

L. l. leucogaster
C & S Mexico

Lepidocolaptes souleyetii (Streak-headed Woodcreeper)

L. s. guerrerensis
W Mexico

L. s. insignis
SE Mexico to N Honduras

L. s. compressus
S Mexico to W Panama

L. s. lineaticeps
E Panama, N Colombia, W Venezuela

L. s. littoralis
N Colombia to Guyana, Trinidad, N Brazil

L. s. uaireni
SE Venezuela

L. s. esmeraldae
SW Colombia, W Ecuador

L. s. souleyetii
SW Ecuador, NW Peru

Lepidocolaptes angustirostris (Narrow-billed Woodcreeper)

L. a. griseiceps
Sipaliwini (Surinam)

L. a. coronatus
N Brazil

L. a. bahiae
NE Brazil

L. a. bivittatus
E Bolivia, C & E Brazil

L. a. hellmayri
WC Bolivia

L. a. certhiolus
C Bolivia to Paraguay, NW Argentina

L. a. dabbenei
SW Paraguay, N Argentina

L. a. angustirostris
E Paraguay, SW Brazil, N Argentina
L. a. praedatus
W Uruguay, E & S Argentina
Lepidocolaptes affinis (Spot-crowned Woodcreeper)
L. a. lignicida
NE Mexico
L. a. affinis
S Mexico to N Nicaragua
L. a. neglectus
Costa Rica, W Panama
L. a. sanctaemartae
N Colombia
L. a. sneiderni
W Colombia
L. a. lacrymiger
E Colombia, W Venezuela
L. a. lafresnayi
N Venezuela
L. a. aequatorialis
SW Colombia, Ecuador
L. a. frigidus
SW Colombia
L. a. warscewiczi
N & C Peru
L. a. carabayae
SE Peru
L. a. bolivianus
Bolivia
Lepidocolaptes squamatus (Scaled Woodcreeper)
L. s. wagleri
NE Brazil
L. s. squamatus
E Brazil
L. s. falcinellus
SE Brazil, Paraguay
Lepidocolaptes fuscus (Lesser Woodcreeper)
L. f. atlanticus
E Brazil
L. f. brevirostris
NE Brazil
L. f. tenuirostris
E Brazil
L. f. fuscus
SE Brazil, E Paraguay, NE Argentina
Lepidocolaptes albolineatus (Lineated Woodcreeper)
L. a. albolineatus
E Venezuela, the Guianas, N Brazil
L. a. duidae
S Venezuela, NW Brazil
L. a. fuscicapillus
SW Amazonia
L. a. madeirae
C Brazil

L. a. layardi
C Brazil

275

CAMPYLORHAMPHUS
Campylorhamphus pucheranii (Greater Scythebill)
S Colombia, E Ecuador
Campylorhamphus trochilirostris (Red-billed Scythebill)
C. t. brevipennis
E Panama, W Colombia
C. t. venezuelensis
N Colombia, N Venezuela
C. t. thoracicus
SW Colombia, W Ecuador
C. t. zarumillanus
NW Peru
C. t. napensis
E Ecuador, E Peru
C. t. notabilis
W Brazil
C. t. snethlageae
C Brazil
C. t. devius
N Bolivia
C. t. lafresnayanus
E Bolivia, N Paraguay
C. t. major
NE Brazil
C. t. omissus
NE Brazil
C. t. trochilirostris
NE Brazil
C. t. hellmayri
N Argentina
Campylorhamphus falcularius (Black-billed Scythebill)
SE Brazil, Paraguay, NE Argentina
Campylorhamphus pusillus (Brown-billed Scythebill)
C. p. borealis
Costa Rica, W Panama
C. p. olivaceus
C Panama
C. p. tachirensis
NE Colombia
C. p. pusillus
Colombia, W Ecuador
Campylorhamphus procurvoides (Curve-billed Scythebill)
C. p. sanus
E Colombia, Venezuela, W Guyana, N Brazil
C. p. procurvoides
French Guiana, N Brazil
C. p. probatus
C Brazil
C. p. multistriatus
C Brazil

FURNARIINAE

GEOSITTA
Geositta poeciloptera (Campo Miner)
Brazil
Geositta cunicularia (Common Miner)
G. c. juninensis
C Peru
G. c. titicacae
S Peru to N Chile, NW Argentina
G. c. georgei
Peru
G. c. frobeni
S Peru
G. c. deserticolor
SW Peru, N Chile
G. c. fissirostris
C Chile
G. c. hellmayri
W Argentina
G. c. cunicularia
S Brazil, Uruguay, Argentina
Geositta maritima (Greyish Miner)
Peru, N Chile
Geositta peruviana (Coastal Miner)
G. p. paytae
N Peru
G. p. peruviana
C Peru
G. p. rostrata
SC Peru
Geositta punensis (Puna Miner)
Bolivia, Peru, Chile, N Argentina
Geositta saxicolina (Dark-winged Miner)
C Peru
Geositta isabellina (Creamy-rumped Miner)
C Chile, W Argentina
Geositta antarctica (Short-billed Miner)
S Chile, S Argentina
Geositta rufipennis (Rufous-banded Miner)
G. r. fasciata
W Bolivia, C Chile, W Argentina
G. r. hellmayri
N Chile
G. r. rufipennis
W Argentina
G. r. ottowi
Cordoba, Argentina
Geositta crassirostris (Thick-billed Miner)
central coast of Peru
Geositta excelsior (Stout-billed Miner)
G. e. colombiana
C Colombia
G. e. excelsior
SW Colombia, Ecuador
G. e. aricomae
N Peru
Geositta tenuirostris (Slender-billed Miner)
S Peru, W Bolivia, NW Argentina

UPUCERTHIA
Upucerthia certhioides (Chaco Earthcreeper)
U. c. harterti
S Bolivia
U. c. luscinia
W Argentina
U. c. estebani
S Paraguay, N Argentina
U. c. certhioides
N & C Argentina
Upucerthia ruficauda (Straight-billed Earthcreeper)
U. r. montana
S Peru
U. r. ruficauda
W Bolivia, N Chile, NW Argentina
Upucerthia andaecola (Rock Earthcree
W Bolivia, NW Argentina
Upucerthia albigula (White-throated Earthcreeper
S Peru, N Chile
Upucerthia serrana (Striated Earthcreeper)
U. s. serrana
N Peru
U. s. huancavelicae
SW Peru
Upucerthia dumetaria (Scale-throated Earthcreeper)
U. d. hypoleuca
SW Bolivia, N Chile, W Argentina
U. d. hallinani
N Chile, NW Argentina
U. d. saturatior
C Chile
U. d. dumetaria
Tierra del Fuego, C & S Argentina
Upucerthia validirostris (Buff-breasted Earthcreeper)
U. v. saturata
W Peru
U. v. pallida
S Peru, Bolivia, N Chile, NW Argentin
U. v. validirostris
W Argentina
Upucerthia jelskii (Plain-breasted Earthcreeper)
C Peru

CINCLODES
Cinclodes fuscus (Bar-winged Cinclod
C. f. heterurus
W Venezuela

C. f. oreobates
  N Colombia
C. f. paramo
  SW Colombia
C. f. albidiventris
  Ecuador
C. f. longipennis
  N Peru
C. f. rivularis
  C & S Peru
C. f. albiventris
  S Peru, Bolivia, N Chile, NW Argentina
C. f. fuscus
  S Brazil, Uruguay, S Chile, S Argentina
**Cinclodes comechingonus
(Comechingones Cinclodes)**
  C Argentina
**Cinclodes pabsti (Long-tailed
Cinclodes)**
  S Brazil
**Cinclodes atacamensis (White-winged
Cinclodes)**
  C. a. atacamensis
    S Peru, W Bolivia, N Chile, N Argentina
  C. a. schocolatinus
    C Argentina
**Cinclodes palliatus (White-bellied
Cinclodes)**
  C Peru
**Cinclodes oustaleti (Grey-flanked
Cinclodes)**
  C. o. oustaleti
    S Chile
  C. o. hornensis
    Cape Horn Is, Tierra del Fuego
  C. o. baeckstroemii
    Juan Fernandez I
**Cinclodes patagonicus (Dark-bellied
Cinclodes)**
  C. p. chilensis
    C Chile, W Argentina
  C. p. patagonicus
    S Chile, S Argentina
**Cinclodes nigrofumosus (Seaside
Cinclodes)**
  coast of N Chile
**Cinclodes taczanowskii (Taczanowski's
Cinclodes)**
  central coast of Peru
Cinclodes antarcticus (Blackish Cinclodes)
  C. a. maculirostris
    Cape Horn Is
  C. a. antarcticus
    Falkland Is

CHILIA
Chilia melanura (Crag Chilia)
  C. m. atacamae
    N Chile

C. m. melanura
  C Chile

FURNARIUS
Furnarius minor (Lesser Hornero)
  NE Peru, W Brazil
Furnarius figulus (White-banded Hornero)
  F. f. pileatus
    C Brazil
  F. f. figulus
    E Brazil
Furnarius tricolor (Tricolour Hornero)
  E Peru, W Brazil, N Bolivia
Furnarius leucopus (Pale-legged Hornero)
  F. l. longirostris
    N Colombia, NW Venezuela
  F. l. endoecus
    C Colombia, W Venezuela
  F. l. leucopus
    Guyana, N Brazil
  F. l. cinnamomeus
    SW Ecuador, NW Peru
  F. l. assimilis
    E & S Brazil, SE Bolivia
  F. l. torridus
    NE Peru, W Brazil
Furnarius rufus (Rufous Hornero)
  F. r. albogularis
    SE Brazil
  F. r. commersoni
    Bolivia, W Brazil
  F. r. schuhmacheri
    S Bolivia
  F. r. paraguayae
    Paraguay, N Argentina
  F. r. rufus
    S Brazil, Uruguay, C & E Argentina
Furnarius cristatus (Crested Hornero)
  Paraguay, N Argentina

SYNALLAXINAE

SYLVIORTHORHYNCHUS

**Sylviorthorhynchus desmursii (Des Murs'
Wiretail)**
  S Chile, W Argentina

APHRASTURA
**Aphrastura spinicauda (Thorn-tailed
Rayadito)**
  A. s. spinicauda
    Tierra del Fuego, S Chile, W Argentina
  A. s. bullocki
    Moncha I, (Chile)
  A. s. fulva
    Chiloé I, (Chile)
**Aphrastura masafuerae (Masafuera
Rayadito)**
  Mas Afuera Is

LEPTASTHENURA

Leptasthenura fuliginiceps (Brown-capped Tit-Spinetail)
  L. f. fuliginiceps
    W Bolivia
  L. f. paranensis
    W Argentina
Leptasthenura yanacensis (Tawny Tit-Spinetail)
  W Peru, W Bolivia
Leptasthenura platensis (Tufted Tit-Spinetail)
  S Brazil, Uruguay, Argentina
Leptasthenura aegithaloides (Plain-mantled Tit-Spinetail)
  L. a. grisescens
    S Peru, N Chile
  L. a. berlepschi
    S Peru, Bolivia, N Chile, W Argentina
  L. a. aegithaloides
    C Chile
  L. a. pallida
    W & S Argentina
Leptasthenura setaria (Araucaria Tit-Spinetail)
  S Brazil
Leptasthenura striata (Streaked Tit-Spinetail)
  L. s. superciliaris
    C Peru
  L. s. albigularis
    W Peru
  L. s. striata
    SW Peru, N Chile
Leptasthenura striolata (Striolated Tit-Spinetail)
  SE Brazil
Leptasthenura pileata (Rusty-crowned Tit-Spinetail)
  L. p. latistriata
    W Peru
  L. p. cajabambae
    C Peru
  L. p. pileata
    central coast of Peru
  L. p. xenothorax
    S Peru
Leptasthenura andicola (Andean Tit-Spinetail)
  L. a. certhia
    W Venezuela
  L. a. extima
    N Colombia
  L. a. exterior
    E Colombia
  L. a. andicola
    C Colombia, Ecuador

  L. a. peruviana
    C Peru, N Bolivia

SCHIZOEACA
Schizoeaca fuliginosa (White-chinned Spinetail)
  S. f. fumigata
    Colombia
  S. f. coryi
    Venezuela
  S. f. fuliginosa
    W Venezuela, E Colombia, N Ecuador
  S. f. griseomurina
    S Ecuador
  S. f. peruviana
    N Peru
  S. f. avacuchensis
    Ayacucho (Peru)
  S. f. vilcabambae
    Cuzco (Peru)
  S. f. plengei
    C Peru
  S. f. palpebralis
    C Peru
  S. f. helleri
    SE Peru
  S. f. harterti
    N Bolivia
Schizoeaca moreirae (Itatiaya Spinetail)
  Rio de Janeiro

SCHOENIOPHYLAX
Schoeniophylax phryganophila (Chotoy Spinetail)
  S. p. phryganophila
    E Bolivia, S Brazil, N Argentina
  S. p. petersi
    E Brazil

SYNALLAXIS
Synallaxis ruficapilla (Rufous-capped Spinetail)
  SE Brazil to N Argentina
Synallaxis superciliosa (Buff-browed Spinetail)
  S. s. samaipatae
    S Bolivia
  S. s. superciliosa
    NW Argentina
Synallaxis poliophrys (Grey-browed Spinetail)
  French Guiana
Synallaxis frontalis (Sooty-fronted Spinetail)
  S. f. fuscipennis
    Bolivia, NW Argentina
  S. f. frontalis
    Brazil, Paraguay, Uruguay, N Argentina

***Synallaxis azarae* (Azara's Spinetail)**
  S. a. media
    W Colombia, N Ecuador
  S. a. ochracea
    S Ecuador, NW Peru
  S. a. fruticicola
    N Peru
  S. a. infumata
    NC Peru
  S. a. urubambae
    SE Peru
  S. a. carabayae
    SE Peru, N Bolivia
  S. a. azarae
    N Bolivia
***Synallaxis elegantior* (Elegant Spinetail)**
  E Colombia, W Venezuela
***Synallaxis albigularis* (Dark-breasted Spinetail)**
  S. a. rodolphei
    S Colombia
  S. a. albigularis
    S Colombia, E Ecuador, E Peru
***Synallaxis albescens* (Pale-breasted Spinetail)**
  S. a. latitabunda
    SW Costa Rica
  S. a. hypoleuca
    S Panama, NW Colombia
  S. a. insignis
    C Colombia
  S. a. occipitalis
    E Colombia, NW Venezuela
  S. a. littoralis
    coast of N Colombia
  S. a. perpallida
    NE Colombia, NW Venezuela
  S. a. nesiotis
    N Colombia, N Venezuela, Margarita I
  S. a. trinitatis
    E Venezuela, Trinidad
  S. a. josephinae
    S Venezuela, Guyana, Surinam, N Brazil
  S. a. inaequalis
    French Guiana
  S. a. griseonota
    C Brazil
  S. a. albescens
    E Brazil, Paraguay, NE Argentina
  S. a. australis
    E Bolivia, W Paraguay, NW Argentina
***Synallaxis spixi* (Chicli Spinetail)**
  S Brazil to N Argentina
***Synallaxis hypospodia* (Cinereous-breasted Spinetail)**
  E Peru, N Bolivia, W Brazil
***Synallaxis infuscata* (Plain Spinetail)**
  E Brazil

  S. b. nigrofumosa
    E Honduras to Panama
  S. b. chapmani
    SW Costa Rica to W Ecuador
  S. b. caucae
    C Colombia
  S. b. brachyura
    E Colombia
  S. b. jaraguana
    N Brazil
***Synallaxis courseni* (Blake's Spinetail)**
  Apurimac, Peru
***Synallaxis moesta* (Dusky Spinetail)**
  S. m. moesta
    E Colombia
  S. m. obscura
    SE Colombia
  S. m. brunneicaudalis
    E Ecuador, NE Peru
***Synallaxis cabanisi* (Cabanis' Spinetail)**
  S. c. yavii
    Venezuela·
  S. c. obscurior
    French Guiana
  S. c. cabanisi
    Peru
  S. c. fulviventris
    Bolivia
***Synallaxis macconnelli* (McConnell's Spinetail)**
  Mt Roraima (Venezuela)
***Synallaxis subpudica* (Silvery-throated Spinetail)**
  E Colombia, Ecuador
***Synallaxis tithys* (Blackish-headed Spinetail)**
  SW Ecuador, NW Peru
***Synallaxis cinerascens* (Grey-bellied Spinetail)**
  SE Brazil, Paraguay, NE Argentina
***Synallaxis maranonica* (Maranon Spinetail)**
  N Peru
***Synallaxis propinqua* (White-bellied Spinetail)**
  N & W Amazonia
***Synallaxis hellmayri* (Reiser's Spinetail)**
  NE Brazil
***Synallaxis gujanensis* (Plain-crowned Spinetail)**
  S. g. colombiana
    E Colombia
  S. g. gujanensis
    Venezuela, the Guianas, N Brazil
  S. g. huallagae
    NE Peru
  S. g. canipileus
    SE Peru

S. g. inornata
W Bolivia, W & C Brazil
S. g. certhiola
N Bolivia
S. g. simoni
C Brazil
Synallaxis albilora (Ochre-breasted Spinetail)
SE Brazil, N Paraguay
Synallaxis rutilans (Ruddy Spinetail)
S. r. caquetensis
SE Colombia, E Ecuador, NE Peru
S. r. confinis
NW Brazil
S. r. dissors
E Colombia to the Guianas, N Brazil
S. r. amazonica
E Peru, N Bolivia, W & C Brazil
S. r. rutilans
C & S Brazil
S. r. omissa
EC Brazil
S. r. tertia
NE Bolivia, SW Brazil
Synallaxis cherriei (Chestnut-throated Spinetail)
S. c. napoensis
E Ecuador, N Peru
S. c. cherriei
S Brazil
Synallaxis unirufa (Rufous Spinetail)
S. u. unirufa
N Colombia, E Ecuador
S. u. munotztebari
NE Colombia
S. u. meridana
E Colombia, W Venezuela
S. u. ochrogaster
Peru
Synallaxis castanea (Black-throated Spinetail)
N Venezuela
Synallaxis fuscorufa (Santa Marta Spinetail)
N Colombia
Synallaxis zimmeri (Russet-bellied Spinetail)
C Peru
Synallaxis erythrothorax (Rufous-breasted Spinetail)
S. e. furtiva
SE Mexico
S. e. erythrothorax
SE Mexico to NW Honduras
S. e. pacifica
S Mexico to El Salvador

Synallaxis cinnamomea (Stripe-breasted Spinetail)
S. c. carri
Trinidad
S. c. terrestris
Tobago I
S. c. cinnamomea
E Colombia, NW Venezuela
S. c. aveledoi
W Venezuela
S. c. bolivari
N Venezuela
S. c. striatipectus
NE Venezuela
S. c. pariae
Paria peninsula (Venezuela)
Synallaxis stictothorax (Necklaced Spinetail)
S. s. stictothorax
NW Ecuador, Puna Is
S. s. maculata
NW Peru
S. c. chinchipensis
N Peru
Synallaxis candei (White-whiskered Spinetail)
S. c. candei
N Colombia, W Venezuela
S. c. atrigularis
NC Colombia
S. c. venezuelensis
NE Colombia, NW Venezuela
Synallaxis kollari (Hoary-throated Spinetail)
N Brazil
Synallaxis scutatus (Ochre-cheeked Spinetail)
S. s. scutatus
E & C Brazil
S. s. whitei
E Bolivia, S Brazil, NW Argentina
Synallaxis gularis (Lafresnaye's White-browed Spinetail)
S. g. gularis
Colombia, N Ecuador, W Venezuela
S. g. brunneidorsalis
NE Colombia
S. g. cinereiventris
W Venezuela
S. g. rufiventris
C Peru

CERTHIAXIS
Certhiaxis erythrops (Red-faced Spinetail)
C. e. rufigenis
Costa Rica
C. e. griseigularis
W Colombia

C. e. erythrops
W Ecuador
Certhiaxis demissa (Tepui Spinetail)
S Venezuela
Certhiaxis antisiensis (Fraser's Spinetail)
C. a. antisiensis
S Ecuador
C. a. palamblae
N Peru
C. a. furcata
N Peru
Certhiaxis pallida (Pallid Spinetail)
SE Brazil
Certhiaxis curtata (Ash-browed Spinetail)
C. c. curtata
E Colombia
C. c. cisandina
C Colombia, E Ecuador, N Peru
C. c. debilis
C Peru
Certhiaxis obsoleta (Olive Spinetail)
SE Brazil, E Paraguay, N Argentina
Certhiaxis hellmayri (Streak-capped Spinetail)
N Colombia
Certhiaxis subcristata (Crested Spinetail)
C. s. fuscivertex
NE Colombia
C. s. subcristata
E Colombia, N Venezuela
Certhiaxis pyrrhophia (Stripe-crowned Spinetail)
C. p. rufipennis
C Bolivia
C. p. striaticeps
E Bolivia
C. p. pyrrhophia
S Bolivia to Uruguay, N Argentina
Certhiaxis marcapatae (Marcapata Spinetail)
Cuzco (SE Peru)
Certhiaxis albiceps (Light-crowned Spinetail)
C. a. albiceps
La Paz (Bolivia)
C. a. discolor
Cochabamba (Bolivia)
Certhiaxis semicinerea (Grey-headed Spinetail)
C. s. semicinerea
Ceara (Brazil), Baia (Brazil)
C. s. goyana
Goiaz, N Brazil
Certhiaxis albicapilla (Creamy-chested Spinetail)
C. a. albicapilla
C Peru

C. a. albigula
SE Peru
Certhiaxis vulpina (Rusty-backed Spinetail)
C. v. apurensis
SW Venezuela
C. v. alopecias
E Colombia, W Venezuela, N Brazil
C. v. vulpecula
NE Peru, W Brazil, NE Bolivia
C. v. vulpina
W & C Brazil
C. v. foxi
W Bolivia
C. v. reiseri
NE Brazil
Certhiaxis muelleri (Scaled Spinetail)
N Brazil
Certhiaxis gutturata (Speckled Spinetail)
C. g. peruviana
S Colombia to N Bolivia
C. g. hyposticta
S Venezuela to Surinam, N Brazil
C. g. gutturata
S Venezuela to French Guiana, N Brazil
Certhiaxis sulphurifera (Sulphur-throated Spinetail)
E Argentina, Uruguay
Certhiaxis cinnamomea (Yellow-throated Spinetail)
C. c. fuscifrons
N Colombia
C. c. marabina
NW Venezuela
C. c. valenciana
Venezuela
C. c. orenocensis
Orinoco valley (Venezuela)
C. c. cinnamomea
Trinidad, NE Venezuela, the Guianas, NE Brazil
C. c. pallida
N Brazil
C. c. cearensis
E Brazil
C. c. russeola
W Bolivia, S Brazil, Paraguay, NW Argentina
Certhiaxis mustelina (Red and White Spinetail)
NE Peru

THRIPOPHAGA
Thripophaga pyrrholeuca (Lesser Canastero)
T. p. affinis
S Bolivia, W Argentina
T. p. pyrrholeuca
Paraguay, NW Argentina

T. p. sordida
Chile, W Argentina

T. p. flavogularis
E & S Argentina

Thripophaga baeri (Short-billed Canastero)

T. b. chacoensis
NW Paraguay

T. b. baeri
S Brazil, NE & C Argentina

Thripophaga pudibunda (Canyon Canastero)

T. p. neglecta
W Peru

T. p. pudibunda
SC Peru

Thripophaga ottonis (Rusty-fronted Canastero)
SE Peru

Thripophaga heterura (Iquico Canastero)
Bolivia

Thripophaga modesta (Cordillera Canastero)

T. m. cactorum
Peru

T. m. lachayensis
central coast of Peru

T. m. monticola
W Peru

T. m. proxima
C & S Peru

T. m. modesta
S Peru to N Chile, W Argentina

T. m. rostrata
N Bolivia

T. m. australis
Chile, C Argentina

Thripophaga dorbignyi (Creamy-breasted Canastero)

T. d. huancavelicae
C Peru

T. d. usheri
SC Peru

T. d. arequipae
S Peru, N Chile, W Bolivia

T. d. consobrina
NW Bolivia

T. d. dorbignyi
E Bolivia, NW Argentina

Thripophaga berlepschi (Berlepsch's Canastero)
N Bolivia

Thripophaga steinbachi (Chestnut Canastero)
W Argentina

Thripophaga humicola (Dusky-tailed Canastero)

T. h. humicola
N & C Chile

T. h. polysticta
S Chile

Thripophaga patagonica (Patagonian Canastero)
S Argentina

Thripophaga humilis (Streak-throated Canastero)

T. h. cajamarcae
W Peru

T. h. humilis
C Peru

T. h. robusta
SE Peru, W Bolivia

Thripophaga anthoides (Austral Canastero)
S Chile, S Argentina

Thripophaga wyatti (Streak-backed Canastero)

T. w. wyatti
NC Colombia

T. w. sanctaemartae
N Colombia

T. w. mucuchiesi
NW Venezuela

T. w. perijanus
W Venezuela

T. w. aequatorialis
C Ecuador

T. w. azuay
S Ecuador

T. w. graminicola
Peru

T. w. cuchacanchae
Bolivia

T. w. lilloi
NW Argentina

Thripophaga punensis (Puna Canastero)
SE Peru, W Bolivia

Thripophaga sclateri (Cordoba Canastero)
C Argentina

Thripophaga urubambensis (Line-fronted Canastero)

T. u. huallagae
N Peru

T. u. urubambensis
SE Peru, N Bolivia

Thripophaga virgata (Junin Canastero)
C Peru

Thripophaga maculicauda (Scribble-tailed Canastero)
Peru, Bolivia, NW Argentina

Thripophaga flammulata (Many-striped Canastero)

T. f. multostriata
E Colombia

T. f. quindiana
C Colombia

T. f. flammulata
S Colombia, Ecuador

T. f. pallida
NE Peru
T. f. taczanowskii
NC Peru
Thripophaga cherriei (Orinoco Softtail)
Venezuela
Thripophaga macroura (Striated Softtail)
E Brazil
Thripophaga hudsoni (Hudson's Canastero)
Uruguay, NE Argentina
Thripophaga hypochondriacus (Great Spinetail)
N Peru

PHACELLODOMUS
Phacellodomus rufifrons (Rufous-fronted Thornbird)
P. r. inornatus
N Venezuela
P. r. peruvianus
N Peru
P. r. specularis
NE Brazil
P. r. rufifrons
E Brazil
P. r. fargoi
S Brazil, Paraguay
P. r. sincipitalis
Bolivia, W Argentina
Phacellodomus sibilatrix (Little Thornbird)
Paraguay, Argentina
Phacellodomus striaticeps (Streak-fronted Thornbird)
P. s. griseipectus
SE Peru
P. s. striaticeps
Bolivia, N Argentina
Phacellodomus erythrophthalmus (Red-eyed Thornbird)
P. e. erythrophthalmus
coast of E Brazil
P. e. ferrugineigula
SE Brazil
Phacellodomus striaticollis (Freckle-breasted Thornbird)
P. s. maculipectus
E Bolivia, NW Argentina
P. s. striaticollis
SE Brazil, Uruguay, E Argentina
Phacellodomus dorsalis (Chestnut-backed Thornbird)
N Peru
Phacellodomus ruber (Greater Thornbird)
Bolivia, C Brazil to Argentina
Phacellodomus fusciceps (Plain Softtail)
P. f. dimorpha
Ecuador, E Peru

P. f. obidensis
N Brazil
P. f. fusciceps
Bolivia
Phacellodomus berlepschi (Russet-mantled Softtail)
N Peru
Phacellodomus dendrocolaptoides (Canebrake Groundcreeper)
SE Brazil, Paraguay, NE Argentina

SPARTONOICA
Spartonoica maluroides (Bay-capped Wren Spinetail)
S Brazil, Uruguay, Argentina

PHLEOCRYPTES
Phleocryptes melanops (Wren-like Rushbird)
P. m. brunnescens
S Peru
P. m. juninensis
C Peru
P. m. schoenobaenus
S Peru, W Bolivia, NW Argentina
P. m. loaensis
N Chile
P. m. melanops
S Brazil to C Chile, C Argentina

LIMNORNIS
Limnornis curvirostris (Curve-billed Reedhaunter)
S Brazil, E Argentina
Limnornis rectirostris (Straight-billed Reedhaunter)
SE Uruguay, NE Argentina

ANUMBIUS
Anumbius annumbi (Firewood Gatherer)
SE Brazil to N Argentina

CORYPHISTERA
Coryphistera alaudina (Lark-like Brushrunner)
C. a. campicola
E Bolivia, W Paraguay
C. a. alaudina
S Bolivia, NW Argentina

EREMOBIUS
Eremobius phoenicurus (Band-tailed Earthcreeper)
W & S Argentina

SIPTORNIS
Siptornis striaticollis (Spectacled Prickletail)
Colombia, E Ecuador

METOPOTHRIX
Metopothrix aurantiacus (Orange-fronted Plushcrown)
  W Amazonia

XENERPESTES
Xenerpestes minlosi (Double-banded Greytail)
  X. m. minlosi
    E Panama, Colombia
  X. m. umbraticus
    W Colombia
  X. m. singularis
    C Ecuador

PHILYDORINAE

MARGARORNIS
Margarornis adustus (Roraima Barbtail)
  M. a. obscurodorsalis
    SE Venezuela
  M. a. duidae
    Mt Duida (S Venezuela)
  M. a. adustus
    E Venezuela, W Guyana
Margarornis guttuligera (Rusty-winged Barbtail)
  M. g. guttuligera
    Colombia, Ecuador, Peru
  M. g. venezuelana
    NW Venezuela
Margarornis brunnescens (Spotted Barbtail)
  M. b. brunneicauda
    Costa Rica, W Panama
  M. b. distinctus
    C Panama
  M. b. mnionophilus
    Panama
  M. b. albescens
    E Panama
  M. b. coloratus
    N Colombia
  M. b. brunnescens
    Venezuela, Colombia, Ecuador, N Peru
  M. b. stictonotus
    SE Peru, W Bolivia
  M. b. rostratus
    N Venezuela
Margarornis tatei (White-throated Barbtail)
  M. t. tatei
    NE Venezuela
  M. t. pariae
    NE Venezuela
Margarornis rubiginosus (Ruddy Treerunner)
  M. r. rubiginosus
    Costa Rica, W Panama
  M. r. boultoni
    C Panama

Margarornis stellatus (Fulvous-dotted Tree Runner)
  W Colombia, NW Ecuador
Margarornis bellulus (Beautiful Tree Runner)
  E Panama
Margarornis squamiger (Pearled Tree Runner)
  M. s. perlatus
    Venezuela, Colombia, Ecuador, N Peru
  M. s. peruvianus
    C Peru
  M. s. squamiger
    SE Peru, W Bolivia

LOCHMIAS
Lochmias nematura (Sharp-tailed Streamcreeper)
  L. n. nelsoni
    E Panama
  L. n. sororia
    Venezuela, Colombia, E Ecuador, NE Peru
  L. n. chimantae
    SE Venezuela
  L. n. castanonota
    E Venezuela
  L. n. obscurata
    Peru, Bolivia
  L. n. nematura
    Brazil, Paraguay, Uruguay, NE Argentina

PSEUDOSEISURA
Pseudoseisura cristata (Rufous Cachalote)
  P. c. cristata
    E Brazil
  P. c. unirufa
    E Bolivia, S Brazil
Pseudoseisura lophotes (Brown Cachalote)
  Paraguay, Uruguay, N Argentina
Pseudoseisura gutturalis (White-throated Cachalote)
  W Argentina

PSEUDOCOLAPTES
Pseudocolaptes lawrencii (Buffy Tuftedcheek)
  P. l. lawrencii
    Costa Rica, W Panama
  P. l. panamensis
    C Panama
  P. l. johnsoni
    W Colombia, W Ecuador
Pseudocolaptes boissonneautii (Streaked Tuftedcheek)
  P. b. striaticeps
    N Venezuela
  P. b. meridae
    W Venezuela
  P. b. boissonneautii
    C Colombia, NW Ecuador

P. b. oberholseri
S Colombia

P. b. orientalis
S Ecuador

P. b. intermedius
NW Peru

P. b. pallidus
NW Peru

P. b. medianus
N Peru

P. b. auritus
C Peru

P. b. carabayae
SE Peru, W Bolivia

BERLEPSCHIA
Berlepschia rikeri (Point-tailed Palmcreeper)
S Venezuela, Guyana, N Brazil

PHILYDOR
Philydor strigilatus (Chestnut-winged Hookbill)
P. s. strigilatus
NW Amazonia

P. s. cognitus
NC Brazil

Philydor subulatus (Striped Woodhaunter)
P. s. nicaraguae
E Nicaragua

P. s. virgatus
Costa Rica, W Panama

P. s. assimilis
E Panama, W Colombia, W Ecuador

P. s. cordobae
NW Colombia

P. s. lemae
SE Venezuela

P. s. subulatus
N & W Amazonia

Philydor guttulatus (Guttulated Foliage-gleaner)
P. g. guttulatus
N Venezuela

P. g. pallidus
NE Venezuela

P. g. mirandae
C Brazil

Philydor subalaris (Striped-bellied Foliage-gleaner)
P. s. lineata
Costa Rica, W Panama

P. s. tacarcunae
E Panama

P. s. subalaris
W Colombia, W Ecuador

P. s. striolatus
N Colombia, W Venezuela

P. s. mentalis
E Ecuador

P. s. colligatus
NW Peru

P. s. ruficrissus
C Peru

Philydor rufosuperciliatus (Buff-browed Foliage-gleaner)
P. r. similis
N Peru

P. r. cabanisi
W Peru, W Bolivia

P. r. oleagineus
SE Bolivia, NW Argentina

P. r. rufosuperciliatus
SE Brazil

P. r. acritus
S Brazil, Paraguay, Uruguay, N Argentina

Philydor striaticollis (Montane Foliage-gleaner)
P. s. striaticollis
Colombia, Venezuela

P. s. anxius
N Colombia

P. s. perijanus
NW Venezuela

P. s. venezuelanus
N Venezuela

P. s. montanus
E Ecuador, C Peru

P. s. yungae
SE Peru, NW Bolivia

Philydor amaurotis (White-browed Foliage-gleaner)
SE Brazil

Philydor variegaticeps (Scaly-throated Foliage-gleaner)
P. v. variegaticeps
S Mexico to W Panama

P. v. temporalis
W Colombia, Ecuador

Philydor ruficaudatus (Rufous-tailed Foliage-gleaner)
P. e. ruficaudatus
N & W Amazonia

P. e. flavipectus
S Venezuela, N Brazil

Philydor erythrocercus (Rufous-rumped Foliage-gleaner)
P. e. fuscipennis
W Panama

P. e. subfulvus
SE Colombia, E Ecuador, N Peru

P. e. ochrogaster
C & SE Peru, Bolivia

P. e. lyra
E Peru, NE Bolivia, S Brazil

P. e. suboles
W Brazil
P. e. erythrocercus
Guyana, French Guiana, N Brazil
Philydor erythropterus (Chestnut-winged Foliage-gleaner)
P. e. erythropterus
W Amazonia
P. e. diluvialis
NC Brazil
Philydor lichtensteini (Lichtenstein's Foliage-gleaner)
SE Brazil, Paraguay, NE Argentina
Philydor erythronotus (Rufous-backed Foliage-gleaner)
E Panama to NW Ecuador
Philydor atricapillus (Black-capped Foliage-gleaner)
SE Brazil, E Paraguay, NE Argentina
Philydor rufus (Buff-fronted Foliage-gleaner)
P. r. panerythrus
Costa Rica to E Colombia
P. r. riveti
W Colombia, NW Ecuador
P. r. colombianus
N Venezuela
P. r. cuchiverus
Venezuela
P. r. bolivianus
E Peru, Bolivia
P. r. chapadensis
S Brazil
P. r. rufus
C & S Brazil, E Paraguay, NE Argentina
Philydor pyrrhodes (Cinnamon-rumped Foliage-gleaner)
N & C South America
Philydor dimidiatus (Russet-mantled Foliage-gleaner)
P. d. dimidiatus
SC Brazil
P. d. baeri
S & SE Brazil, N Paraguay
Philydor fuscus (White-collared Foliage-gleaner)
SE Brazil
Philydor ucayalae (Recurvebill)
P. u. ucayalae
Peru
P. u. striatus
N Bolivia

CICHLOCOLAPTES
Cichlocolaptes leucophrus (Pale-browed Treehunter)
SE Brazil

THRIPADECTES
Thripadectes ignobilis (Uniform Treehunter)
W Colombia, NW Ecuador
Thripadectes rufobrunneus (Streak-breasted Treehunter)
Costa Rica, W Panama
Thripadectes melanorhynchus (Black-billed Treehunter)
T. m. melanorhynchus
E Ecuador, E Peru
T. m. striaticeps
Colombia
Thripadectes holostictus (Striped Treehunter)
T. h. striatidorsus
SW Colombia, W Ecuador
T. h. holostictus
Colombia, E Ecuador, N Peru
T. h. moderatus
E Peru, N Bolivia
Thripadectes virgaticeps (Streak-capped Treehunter)
T. v. sclateri
W Colombia
T. v. magdelenae
N Colombia
T. v. virgaticeps
NW Ecuador
T. v. sumaco
E Ecuador
T. v. klagesi
N Venezuela
T. v. tachirensis
NW Venezuela
Thripadectes scrutator (Buff-throated Treehunter)
C Peru
Thripadectus flammulatus (Flammulated Treehunter)
T. f. flammulatus
Colombia, Ecuador
T. f. bricenoi
Venezuela

AUTOMOLUS
Automolus ruficollis (Rufous-necked Foliage-gleaner)
A. r. celicae
SW Ecuador
A. r. ruficollis
NW Peru
Automolus ochrolaemus (Buff-throated Foliage-gleaner)
A. o. cervinigularis
S Mexico to Nicaragua
A. o. amusos
SE Guatemala to Honduras

A. o. hypophaeus
E Nicaragua to NW Panama
A. o. exsertus
SW Costa Rica, W Panama
A. o. pallidigularis
E Panama, Colombia, NW Ecuador
A. o. turdinus
N & W Amazonia
A. o. ochrolaemus
E Peru, N Bolivia, W Brazil
A. o. auricularis
NE Bolivia, W Brazil

Automolus infuscatus (Olive-backed Foliage-gleaner)
A. i. infuscatus
SE Colombia, E Ecuador, E Peru
A. i. badius
S Venezuela, E Colombia, NW Brazil
A. i. cervicalis
E Venezuela, Guyana, Surinam, N Brazil
A. i. perusianus
W Brazil
A. i. paraensis
C Brazil

Automolus dorsalis (Crested Foliage-gleaner)
SE Colombia, E Ecuador, Peru

Automolus leucophthalmus (White-eyed Foliage-gleaner)
A. l. lammi
E Brazil
A. l. leucophthalmus
EC Brazil
A. l. sulphurascens
S Brazil, NE Paraguay, NE Argentina

Automolus melanopezus (Brown-rumped Foliage-gleaner)
SE Colombia, E Ecuador, W Brazil

Automolus albigularis (White-throated Foliage-gleaner)
A. a. paraquensis
S Venezuela
A. a. duidae
Mt Duida (S Venezuela)
A. a. albigularis
SE Venezuela
A. a. roraimae
Mt Roraima (SE Venezuela)

Automolus rubiginosus (Ruddy Foliage-gleaner)
A. r. guerrerensis
SW Mexico
A. r. rubiginosus
E Mexico
A. r. veraepacis
N Guatemala
A. r. umbrinus
S Mexico to N Nicaragua

A. r. fumosus
W Panama
A. r. saturatus
E Panama, NW Colombia
A. r. sasaimae
N Colombia
A. r. nigricauda
W Colombia, W Ecuador
A. r. rufipectus
N Colombia
A. r. cinnamomeigula
E Colombia
A. r. caquetae
SE Colombia
A. r. venezuelanus
S Venezuela
A. r. obscurus
French Guiana
A. r. brunnescens
E Ecuador, NE Peru
A. r. moderatus
N Peru
A. r. watkinsi
SE Peru, N Bolivia

Automolus rufipileatus (Chestnut-crowned Foliage-gleaner)
A. r. consobrinus
N & W Amazonia
A. r. rufipileatus
C Brazil

Automolus rectirostris (Chestnut-capped Foliage-gleaner)
C Brazil

Automolus erythrocephalus (Henna-hooded Foliage-gleaner)
A. e. erythrocephalus
SW Ecuador, N Peru
A. e. palamblae
W Peru

SCLERURUS

Sclerurus mexicanus (Tawny-throated Leafscraper)
S. m. mexicanus
SE Mexico to Honduras
S. m. pullus
Costa Rica to W Panama
S. m. andinus
E Panama, Colombia, to Guyana
S. m. obscurior
W Colombia, W Ecuador
S. m. peruvianus
W Amazonia
S. m. macconnelli
N Brazil, Guyana, French Guiana
S. m. bahiae
E Brazil

Sclerurus rufigularis (Short-billed Leafscraper)
S. r. fulvigularis
E & S Venezuela to French Guiana, N Brazil
S. r. brunnescens
N Brazil
S. r. furfurosus
C Brazil
S. r. rufigularis
N Bolivia, SW Brazil
Sclerurus albigularis (Grey-throated Leafscraper)
S. a. canigularis
Costa Rica, W Panama
S. a. propinquus
N Colombia
S. a. albigularis
E Colombia, Venezuela, Trinidad, Tobago l
S. a. kunanensis
Venezuela
S. a. zamorae
SE Ecuador, N Peru
S. a. albicollis
N Bolivia
Sclerurus caudacutus (Black-tailed Leafscraper)
S. c. caudacutus
Guyana, French Guiana
S. c. insignis
S Venezuela, N Brazil
S. c. brunneus
W Amazonia
S. c. olivascens
Peru, Bolivia
S. c. pallidus
N Brazil
S. c. umbretta
coast of E Brazil
Sclerurus scansor (Rufous-breasted Leafscraper)
S. s. cearensis
NE Brazil
S. s. scansor
C & E Brazil, Paraguay, NE Argentina
Sclerurus guatemalensis (Guatemala Leafscraper)
S. g. guatemalensis
S Mexico to Panama
S. g. salvini
W Colombia, W Ecuador
S. g. ennosiphyllus
C Colombia

XENOPS
Xenops contaminatus (Sharp-billed Treehunter)
SE Brazil, Paraguay, NE Argentina

Xenops milleri (Rufous-tailed Xenops)
N Amazonia
Xenops tenuirostris (Slender-billed Xenops)
X. t. acutirostris
SE Colombia, S Venezuela, E Ecuador, NE Peru
X. t. hellmayri
French Guiana, Surinam
X. t. tenuirostris
S Venezuela, E Peru, N Bolivia, N & W Brazil
Xenops minutus (Plain Xenops)
X. m. mexicanus
S Mexico to Honduras
X. m. ridgwayi
Nicaragua to W Panama
X. m. littoralis
E Panama to W Ecuador
X. m. neglectus
N Colombia, N Venezuela
X. m. remoratus
E Colombia, Venezuela, N Brazil
X. m. ruficaudus
E Colombia, Venezuela, the Guianas, N Brazil
X. m. olivaceus
NE Colombia
X. m. obsoletus
E Ecuador, E Peru, N Bolivia, W Brazil
X. m. genibarbis
N Brazil
X. m. minutus
E & SE Brazil, E Paraguay
Xenops rutilans (Streaked Xenops)
X. r. septentrionalis
Costa Rica, W Panama
X. r. heterurus
E Panama to NE Ecuador, Venezuela
X. r. incomptus
Darien (Panama)
X. r. perijanus
NE Colombia
X. r. phelpsi
N Colombia
X. r. guayae
W Ecuador, NW Peru
X. r. peruvianus
E Ecuador, E Peru
X. r. purusianus
C Brazil
X. r. connectens
E Bolivia, NW Argentina
X. r. chapadensis
SW Brazil, N Bolivia
X. r. rutilans
SE Brazil, Paraguay, NE Argentina

MEGAXENOPS
Megaxenops parnaguae (Reiser's Recurvebill)
NE Brazil

PYGARRHICHAS
Pygarrhichas albogularis (White-throated Treerunner)
S Chile, SW Argentina, Tierra del Fuego

103 FORMICARIIDAE (ANTBIRDS)

CYMBILAIMUS
Cymbilaimus lineatus (Fasciated Antshrike)
C. l. fasciatus
Nicaragua to NW Ecuador
C. l. intermedius
Upper Amazonia
C. l. lineatus
SE Venezuela, the Guianas, NE Brazil
C. l. sanctaemariae
NE Bolivia

HYPOEDALEUS
Hypoedaleus guttatus (Spot-backed Antshrike)
H. g. leucogaster
E Brazil
H. g. guttatus
S Brazil, Paraguay, NE Argentina

BATARA
Batara cinerea (Giant Antshrike)
B. c. excubitor
E Bolivia
B. c. argentina
S Bolivia, NW Argentina
B. c. cinerea
SE Brazil, NE Argentina

MACKENZIAENA
Mackenziaena leachii (Large-tailed Antshrike)
SE Brazil, NE Argentina
Mackenziaena severa (Tufted Antshrike)
SE Brazil, NE Argentina

FREDERICKENA
Frederickena viridis (Black-throated Antshrike)
E Venezuela, Guyana
Frederickena unduligera (Undulated Antshrike)
F. u. fulva
SE Colombia, E Ecuador
F. u. diversa
E & SE Peru
F. u. unduligera
NW Brazil
F. u. pallida
Brazil

TARABA
Taraba major (Great Antshrike)
T. m. melanocrissa
SE Mexico to W Panama
T. m. obscura
SW Costa Rica to NW Colombia
T. m. transandeana
SW Colombia, W Ecuador, NW Peru
T. m. granadensis
E Colombia, Venezuela
T. m. semifasciata
E Colombia to the Guianas, N & E Brazil
T. m. duidae
SE Venezuela
T. m. melanura
Upper Amazonia
T. m. borbae
C Brazil
T. m. stagura
E & NE Brazil
T. m. major
E Bolivia, S Brazil, Paraguay, N Argentina

SAKESPHORUS
Sakesphorus canadensis (Black-crested Antshrike)
S. c. pulchellus
N Colombia, W Venezuela
S. c. paraguanae
NE Colombia, NW Venezuela
S. c. intermedius
S Venezuela, N Brazil
S. c. fumosus
S Venezuela
S. c. trinitatis
NE Venezuela, Guyana, Trinidad
S. c. canadensis
Surinam, French Guiana
S. c. loretoyacuensis
SE Colombia, NW Brazil
Sakesphorus cristatus (Silvery-cheeked Antshrike)
E Brazil
Sakesphorus bernardi (White-naped Antshrike)
S. b. bernardi
W Ecuador
S. b. piurae
SW Ecuador, N Peru
S. b. cajamarcae
W Peru
S. b. shumbae
N Peru
Sakesphorus melanonotus (Black-backed Antshrike)
NE Colombia, W Venezuela
Sakesphorus melanothorax (Black-throated Antshrike)
French Guiana

Sakesphorus luctuosus (Glossy Antshrike)
S. l. luctuosus
NE Brazil
S. l. araguayae
C Brazil
BIATAS
Biatas nigropectus (White-bearded Antshrike)
SE Brazil
THAMNOPHILUS
Thamnophilus doliatus (Barred Antshrike)
T. d. intermedius
E Mexico to E Costa Rica
T. d. yucatanensis
S Mexico, N Guatemala
T. d. pacificus
W Honduras to W Costa Rica
T. d. nigricristatus
E Panama, N Colombia
T. d. albicans
N Colombia
T. d. zarumae
SW Ecuador, NW Peru
T. d. palamblae
NW Peru
T. d. nigrescens
NE Colombia, NW Venezuela
T. d. tobagensis
Tobago I
T. d. nesiotes
Isla del Rey
T. d. fraterculus
E Colombia, N Venezuela, Trinidad
T. d. doliatus
E Venezuela, the Guianas, N Brazil
T. d. subradiatus
E Peru, W Brazil
T. d. signatus
NE Bolivia, SW Brazil
T. d. difficilis
E Brazil
T. d. capistratus
E Brazil
T. d. radiatus
E Bolivia, S Brazil, N Argentina
T. d. cadwaladeri
S Bolivia
Thamnophilus multistriatus (Bar-crested Antshrike)
T. m. brachyurus
W Colombia
T. m. selvae
W Colombia
T. m. multistriatus
C Colombia
T. m. oecotonophilus
NE Colombia

Thamnophilus palliatus (Lined Antshrike)
T. p. tenuepunctatus
E Colombia
T. p. tenuifasciatus
SE Colombia, E Ecuador
T. p. berlepschi
SE Ecuador, N Peru
T. p. similis
C Peru
T. p. puncticeps
SE Peru, Bolivia, W Brazil
T. p. palliatus
C & E Brazil
Thamnophilus bridgesi (Black-hooded Antshrike)
SW Costa Rica, W Panama
Thamnophilus nigriceps (Black Antshrike)
T. n. nigriceps
E Panama, NW Colombia
T. n. magdalenae
N Colombia
Thamnophilus praecox (Cocha Antshrike)
S Ecuador
Thamnophilus nigrocinereus (Blackish-grey Antshrike)
T. n. cinereoniger
Colombia, Venezuela, NW Brazil
T. n. kulczynskii
French Guiana
T. n. nigrocinereus
NE Brazil
T. n. cryptoleucus
NE Peru, W Brazil
T. n. tschudii
W Brazil
T. n. huberi
N Brazil
Thamnophilus aethiops (White-shouldered Antshrike)
T. a. aethiops
E Ecuador, NE Peru
T. a. wetmorei
SE Colombia
T. a. polionotus
S & E Venezuela, NW Brazil
T. a. kapouni
E & SE Peru, N Bolivia, W Brazil
T. a. juruanus
W Brazil
T. a. injunctus
NE Brazil
T. a. punctuliger
C Brazil
T. a. atriceps
C Brazil
T. a. incertus
NE Brazil

Thamnophilus unicolor (Uniform Antshrike)
  T. u. unicolor
    W Ecuador
  T. u. grandior
    Colombia, E Ecuador, N Peru
  T. u. caudatus
    N Peru

Thamnophilus schistaceus (Black-capped Antshrike)
  T. s. capitalis
    Upper Amazonia
  T. s. dubius
    S Ecuador, N Peru
  T. s. schistaceus
    SE Peru, N Bolivia, W Brazil
  T. s. heterogynus
    W Brazil
  T. s. inornatus
    C Brazil

Thamnophilus murinus (Mouse-coloured Antshrike)
  T. m. murinus
    E Ecuador, E Colombia to Surinam
  T. m. cayennensis
    French Guiana, N Brazil
  T. m. canipennis
    NE Peru, W Brazil

Thamnophilus aroyae (Upland Antshrike)
  SE Peru, NW Bolivia

Thamnophilus punctatus (Slaty Antshrike)
  T. p. atrinucha
    Honduras to Ecuador & Venezuela
  T. p. gorgonae
    Gorgona I
  T. p. subcinereus
    N Colombia, NW Venezuela
  T. p. interpositus
    E Colombia
  T. p. punctatus
    E Venezuela, the Guianas, N Brazil
  T. p. leucogaster
    N Peru
  T. p. saturatus
    C Brazil
  T. p. zimmeri
    C Brazil
  T. p. stictocephalus
    C Brazil
  T. p. sticturus
    Bolivia, S Brazil
  T. p. pelzelni
    C & E Brazil
  T. p. ambiguus
    coastal SE Brazil

Thamnophilus amazonicus (Amazonian Antshrike)
  T. a. cinereiceps
    Venezuela, Colombia
  T. a. huallagae
    Peru
  T. a. amazonicus
    S Colombia to N Bolivia
  T. a. obscurus
    C Brazil
  T. a. paraensis
    E Venezuela, the Guianas, N Brazil

Thamnophilus insignis (Streak-backed Antshrike)
  T. i. insignis
    S Venezuela
  T. i. nigrofrontalis
    S Venezuela

Thamnophilus caerulescens (Variable Antshrike)
  T. c. subandinus
    N Peru
  T. c. melanochrous
    C & S Peru
  T. c. aspersiventer
    N Bolivia
  T. c. connectens
    E Bolivia
  T. c. dinellii
    C & S Bolivia, NW Argentina
  T. c. paraguayensis
    S Brazil, N Paraguay
  T. c. gilvigaster
    SE Brazil, NE Argentina
  T. c. caerulescens
    S Brazil, E Paraguay, NE Argentina
  T. c. albonotatus
    EC Brazil
  T. c. ochraceiventer
    SC Brazil
  T. c. pernambucensis
    E Brazil
  T. c. cearensis
    E Brazil

Thamnophilus torquatus (Rufous-winged Antshrike)
  Brazil

Thamnophilus ruficapillus (Rufous-capped Antshrike)
  T. r. jaczewskii
    N Peru
  T. r. marcapatae
    SE Peru
  T. r. subfasciatus
    W Bolivia
  T. r. cochabambae
    W Bolivia, NW Argentina

T. r. ruficapillus
  S & E Brazil, NE Argentina

PYGIPTILA
Pygiptila stellaris (Spot-winged Antshrike)
  P. s. maculipennis
    SE Colombia to NE Peru
  P. s. occipitalis
    S Colombia to the Guianas, N Brazil
  P. s. purusiana
    W Brazil
  P. s. stellaris
    C Brazil

MEGASTICTUS
**Megastictus margaritatus (Pearly
Antshrike)**
  N Upper Amazonia

NEOCTANTES
Neoctantes niger (Black Bushbird)
  E Ecuador, N Peru, W Brazil

CLYTOCTANTES
Clytoctantes alixii (Recurvebill Bushbird)
  Colombia

XENORNIS
**Xenornis setifrons (Speckle-breasted
Antshrike)**
  E Panama, NW Colombia

THAMNISTES
Thamnistes anabatinus (Russet Antshrike)
  T. a. anabatinus
    SE Mexico to Honduras
  T. a. saturatus
    Nicaragua to W Panama
  T. a. coronatus
    C & E Panama
  T. a. intermedius
    W Colombia, W Ecuador
  T. a. gularis
    C Colombia
  T. a. aequatorialis
    SE Colombia, E Ecuador
  T. a. rufescens
    C & SE Peru, N Bolivia

DYSITHAMNUS
**Dysithamnus stictothorax (Spot-breasted
Antvireo)**
  SE Brazil
Dysithamnus mentalis (Plain Antvireo)
  D. m. septentrionalis
    S Mexico to W Panama
  D. m. suffusus
    E Panama, NW Colombia
  D. m. extremus
    C Colombia
  D. m. semicinereus
    NE Colombia

D. m. viridis
  NE Colombia, NW Venezuela
D. m. cumbreanus
  N Venezuela
D. m. andrei
  E Venezuela, Trinidad
D. m. oberi
  Tobago
D. m. ptaritepui
  S Venezuela
D. m. spodionotus
  S & E Venezuela
D. m. aequatorialis
  W Ecuador, NW Peru
D. m. napensis
  E Ecuador
D. m. tambillanus
  N Peru
D. m. olivaceus
  C Peru
D. m. tavarae
  SE Peru, Bolivia
D. m. emiliae
  E Brazil
D. m. affinis
  C Brazil
D. m. mentalis
  S & SE Brazil, E Paraguay, NE Argentina
**Dysithamnus striaticeps (Streak-crowned
Antvireo)**
  E Nicaragua, E Costa Rica
**Dysithamnus puncticeps (Spot-crowned
Antvireo)**
  D. p. puncticeps
    E Costa Rica, Panama, N Colombia
  D. p. intensus
    S Panama, W Colombia
  D. p. flemmingi
    SW Colombia, W Ecuador
**Dysithamnus xanthopterus
(Rufous-backed Antvireo)**
  SE Brazil
**Dysithamnus ardesiacus (Grey-throated
Antvireo)**
  D. a. ardesiacus
    SE Colombia, E Ecuador, N & C Peru
  D. a. obidensis
    S Venezuela, the Guinas, N Brazil

THAMNOMANES
**Thamnomanes saturninus (Saturnine
Antshrike)**
  T. s. huallagae
    E Peru, W Brazil
  T. s. saturninus
    WC Brazil

Thamnomanes occidentalis (Chapman's Antshrike)
T. o. occidentalis
  S Colombia
T. o. punctitectus
  S Ecuador

Thamnomanes plumbeus (Plumbeous Antshrike)
T. p. tucuyensis
  NW Venezuela
T. p. leucostictus
  E Colombia, E Ecuador
T. p. plumbeus
  SE Brazil

Thamnomanes caesius (Cinereous Antshrike)
T. c. glaucus
  N & W Amazonia
T. c. intermedius
  C Peru
T. c. persimilis
  C Brazil
T. c. hoffmannsi
  SC Brazil
T. c. caesius
  E Brazil

Thamnomanes schistogynus (Bluish-slate Antshrike)
  SE Peru, W Brazil

MYRMOTHERULA

Myrmotherula brachyura (Pygmy Antwren)
M. b. ignota
  C & E Panama, NW Colombia
M. b. brachyura
  N & W Amazonia

Myrmotherula obscura (Short-billed Antwren)
  SE Colombia, NE Peru, W Brazil

Myrmotherula sclateri (Sclater's Antwren)
  C Brazil

Myrmotherula klagesi (Klages' Antwren)
  NE Brazil

Myrmotherula surinamensis (Streaked Antwren)
M. s. pacifica
  E Panama to E Ecuador
M. s. surinamensis
  S Venezuela, the Guianas, N Brazil
M. s. multostriata
  W Amazonia

Myrmotherula ambigua (Yellow-throated Antwren)
  E Colombia, S Venezuela, NW Brazil

Myrmotherula cherriei (Cherrie's Antwren)
  E Colombia, W Venezuela, N Brazil

Myrmotherula guttata (Rufous-bellied Antwren)
  N Amazonia

Myrmotherula longicuada (Stripe-chested Antwren)
M. l. söderströmi
  E Ecuador
M. l. pseudoaustralis
  E Ecuador, N Peru
M. l. longicuada
  E Peru
M. l. australis
  SE Peru, N Bolivia

Myrmotherula hauxwelli (Plain-throated Antwren)
M. h. suffusa
  SE Colombia, E Ecuador, NE Peru
M. h. hauxwelli
  E Peru, W Brazil
M. h. clarior
  C Brazil
M. h. hellmayri
  NE Brazil

Myrmotherula gularis (Star-throated Antwren)
  SE Brazil

Myrmotherula gutturalis (Brown-bellied Antwren)
  the Guianas, Venezuela, N Brazil

Myrmotherula fulviventris (Checker-throated Antwren)
M. f. costaricensis
  S Honduras to W Panama
M. f. fulviventris
  E Panama to W Ecuador
M. f. salmoni
  C Colombia

Myrmotherula leucophthalma (White-eyed Antwren)
M. l. dissita
  SE Peru, N Bolivia
M. l. leucophthalma
  WC Brazil
M. l. phaeonota
  NC Brazil
M. l. sordida
  NE Brazil

Myrmotherula haematonota (Stipple-throated Antwren)
M. h. pyrrhonota
  SE Colombia, S Venezuela, NW Brazil
M. h. spodionota
  E Ecuador
M. h. haematonota
  NE Peru
M. h. sororia
  N & C Peru

M. h. amazonica
W Brazil
Myrmotherula ornata (Ornate Antwren)
M. o. ornata
E Colombia
M. o. saturata
SE Colombia, E Ecuador, NE Peru
M. o. atrogularis
N & C Peru
M. o. meridionalis
SE Peru, N Bolivia
M. o. hoffmannsi
C Brazil
Myrmotherula erythrura (Rufous-tailed Antwren)
M. e. erythrura
NW Amazonia
M. e. septentrionalis
E Peru, W Brazil
Myrmotherula erythronotos (Black-hooded Antwren)
SE Brazil
Myrmotherula axillaris (White-flanked Antwren)
M. a. albigula
Central America, W Colombia, Ecuador
M. a. melaena
NW Amazonia
M. a. heterozyga
E Peru, W Brazil
M. a. axillaris
Trinidad, Venezuela, the Guianas, N Brazil
M. a. fresnayana
SE Peru, Bolivia
M. a. luctuosa
E Brazil
Myrmotherula schisticolor (Slaty Antwren)
M. s. schisticolor
Mexico to W Ecuador
M. s. sanctaemartae
N Colombia, N Venezuela
M. s. interior
E Colombia, E Ecuador, N Peru
Myrmotherula sunensis (Rio Suno Antwren)
M. s. sunensis
E Ecuador, NE Peru
M. s. yessupi
W Peru
Myrmotherula longipennis (Long-winged Antwren)
M. l. longipennis
N & W Amazonia
M. l. zimmeri
E Ecuador, NE Peru
M. l. garbei
NE Peru, W Brazil

M. l. transitiva
WC Brazil
M. l. ochrogyna
C Brazil
M. l. paraensis
EC Brazil
Myrmotherula minor (Salvadori's Antwren)
NE Peru, W Brazil
Myrmotherula iheringi (Ihering's Antwren)
M. i. heteroptera
SC Brazil
M. i. iheringi
C Brazil
Myrmotherula grisea (Ashy Antwren)
W Bolivia
Myrmotherula unicolor (Unicoloured Antwren)
SE Brazil
Myrmotherula behni (Plain-winged Antwren)
M. b. behni
E Colombia
M. b. yavii
S Venezuela
M. b. inornata
SE Venezuela, Guyana
M. b. camanii
S Venezuela
Myrmotherula urosticta (Band-tailed Antwren)
SE Brazil
Myrmotherula menetriesii (Menetries' Antwren)
M. m. pallida
NW & W Amazonia
M. m. cinereiventris
E Venezuela, the Guianas, N Brazil
M. m. menetriesii
E Peru, N Bolivia, W Brazil
M. m. berlepschi
WC Brazil
M. m. omissa
NE Brazil
Myrmotherula assimilis (White-backed Antwren)
NE Peru, W Brazil

DICHROZONA
Dichrozona cincta (Banded Antcatcher)
D. c. cincta
E Colombia, S Venezuela, NW Brazil
D. c. stellata
E Ecuador, W Brazil
D. c. zononota
C Brazil, N Bolivia

MYRMURCHILUS
Myrmorchilus strigilatus (Stripe-backed Antbird)
  M. s. strigilatus
    E Brazil
  M. s. suspicax
    S Bolivia, S Brazil, W Paraguay,
      N Argentina

HERPSILOCHMUS
Herpsilochmus pileatus (Black-capped Antwren)
  H. p. pileatus
    E Brazil
  H. p. atricapillus
    C & S Brazil, Bolivia, Paraguay,
      N Argentina
  H. p. motacilloides
    C Peru
Herpsilochmus sticturus (Spot-tailed Antwren)
  H. s. dugandi
    Colombia
  H. s. sticturus
    S Venezuela, the Guianas, N Brazil
Herpsilochmus stictocephalus (Todd's Antwren)
    E Venezuela, the Guianas
Herpsilochmus dorsimaculatus (Spot-backed Antwren)
    S Venezuela, NW Brazil
Herpsilochmus roraimae (Roraiman Antwren)
    SE Venezuela, SW Guyana
Herpsilochmus pectoralis (Pectoral Antwren)
    E Brazil
Herpsilochmus longirostris (Large-billed Antwren)
    SC Brazil
Herpsilochmus axillaris (Yellow-breasted Antwren)
  H. a. senex
    SW Colombia
  H. a. aequatorialis
    E Ecuador
  H. a. puncticeps
    N Peru
  H. a. axillaris
    S Peru
Herpsilochmus rufimarginatus (Rufous-winged Antwren)
  H. r. exiguus
    E Panama
  H. r. frater
    N & W Amazonia
  H. r. scapularis
    E Brazil

  H. r. rufimarginatus
    SE Brazil, E Paraguay, NE Argentina

MICRORHPIAS
Microrhopias quixensis (Dot-winged Antwren)
  M. q. boucardi
    S Mexico to SW Honduras
  M. q. virgata
    Nicaragua to W Panama
  M. q. consobrina
    E Panama to W Ecuador
  M. q. quixensis
    E Ecuador, NE Peru
  M. q. intercedens
    N Peru
  M. q. nigriventris
    C Peru
  M. q. albicauda
    SE Peru
  M. q. microsticta
    French Guiana
  M. q. bicolor
    N Bolivia, C Brazil
  M. q. emiliae
    C Brazil

FORMICIVORA
Formicivora iheringi (Narrow-billed Antwren)
    E Brazil
Formicivora grisea (White-fringed Antwren)
  F. g. alticincta
    Pearl Is (Panama)
  F. g. hondae
    N Colombia
  F. g. fumosa
    E Colombia, W Venezuela
  F. g. intermedia
    NE Colombia, NW Venezuela, Margarita I
  F. g. tobagensis
    Tobago I
  F. g. orenocensis
    S Venezuela
  F. g. rufiventris
    E Colombia, S Venezuela
  F. g. grisea
    the Guianas, NE Brazil
  F. g. deluzae
    SE Brazil
Formicivora serrana (Serra Antwren)
    SE Brazil
Formicivora melanogaster (Black-bellied Antwren)
  F. m. melanogaster
    E Bolivia, W & C Brazil
  F. m. bahiae
    E Brazil

Formicivora rufa (Rusty-backed Antwren)
  F. r. urubambae
    E Peru
  F. r. chapmani
    E Brazil
  F. r. rufa
    E Bolivia, E Paraguay, C & S Brazil

DRYMOPHILA
Drymophila ferruginea (Ferruginous Antbird)
    SE Brazil to NE Argentina
Drymophila genei (Rufous-tailed Antbird)
    SE Brazil
Drymophila ochropyga (Ochre-rumped Antbird)
    SE Brazil
Drymophila devillei (Striated Antbird)
  D. d. devillei
    E Ecuador, E Peru, N Bolivia
  D. d. subochracea
    C Brazil
Drymophila caudata (Long-tailed Antbird)
  D. c. hellmayri
    NE Colombia
  D. c. klagesi
    N Venezuela
  D. c. caudata
    Colombia to N Bolivia
Drymophila malura (Dusky-tailed Antbird)
    SE Brazil, N Argentina
Drymophila squamata (Scaled Antbird)
    C & SE Brazil

TERENURA
Terenura maculata (Streak-capped Antwren)
    SE Brazil, NE Argentina
Terenura callinota (Rufous-rumped Antwren)
  T. c. callinota
    Panama to N Peru
  T. c. peruviana
    C Peru
  T. c. guianensis
    Guyana
Terenura humeralis (Chestnut-shouldered Antwren)
  T. h. humeralis
    E Ecuador, NE Peru, W Brazil
  T. h. transfluvialis
    C Brazil
Terenura sharpei (Yellow-rumped Antwren)
    SE Peru
Terenura spodioptila (Ash-winged Antwren)
  T. s. signata
    SE Colombia, NW Brazil

T. s. spodioptila
    S Venezuela, Guyana, NW Brazil
T. s. elaopteryx
    French Guiana, NE Brazil
T. s. meridionalis
    C Brazil

CERCOMACRA
Cercomacra cinerascens (Grey Antbird)
  C. c. cinerascens
    Upper Amazonia
  C. c. immaculata
    E Venezuela, the Guianas, N Brazil
  C. c. sclateri
    SW Amazonia
  C. c. iterata
    C Brazil
Cercomacra brasiliana (Rio de Janeiro Antbird)
    SE Brazil
Cercomacra tyrannina (Dusky Antbird)
  C. t. crepera
    S Mexico to W Panama
  C. t. rufiventris
    E Panama to W Ecuador
  C. t. tyrannina
    E Colombia, S Venezuela, NW Brazil
  C. t. vicina
    NE Colombia, W Venezuela
  C. t. saturatior
    E Venezuela, Guyana, Surinam
  C. t. laeta
    N & C Brazil
  C. t. sabinoi
    NE Brazil
Cercomacra nigrescens (Blackish Antbird)
  C. n. nigrescens
    Surinam, French Guiana
  C. n. aequatorialis
    E Ecuador, N Peru
  C. n. notata
    C Peru
  C. n. fuscicauda
    E Peru, W Brazil, N Bolivia
  C. n. approximans
    C Brazil
  C. n. ochrogyna
    C Brazil
Cercomacra serva (Black Antbird)
  C. s. serva
    E Ecuador, NE Peru
  C. s. hypomelaena
    E & SE Peru, N Bolivia, W Brazil
Cercomacra nigricans (Jet Antbird)
  C. n. nigricans
    E Panama to N Brazil
  C. n. atrata
    NW Colombia

Cercomacra carbonaria (Rio Branco Antbird)
Rio Branco, Brazil
Cercomacra melanaria (Matto Grosso Antbird)
N Bolivia, C & S Brazil
Cercomacra ferdinandi (Bananal Antbird)
SE Brazil

SIPIA
Sipia berlepschi (Stub-tailed Antbird)
W Colombia, NW Ecuador
Sipia rosenbergi (Esmeralda's Antbird)
W Colombia, NW Ecuador

PYRIGLENA
Pyriglena leuconota (White-backed Fire-eye)
P. l. pacifica
W Ecuador
P. l. castanoptera
E Ecuador, N Peru
P. l. picea
N & C Peru
P. l. similis
C Brazil
P. l. marcapatensis
SE Peru
P. l. hellmayri
W Bolivia
P. l. maura
SE Bolivia, SE Brazil
P. l. interposita
EC Brazil
P. l. leuconota
S Brazil
P. l. pernambucensis
E Brazil
Pyriglena atra (Swainson's Fire-eye)
E Brazil
Pyriglena leuceptera (White-shouldered Fire-eye)
E Paraguay, SE Brazil

RHOPORNIS
Rhopornis ardesiaca (Slender Antbird)
SE Brazil

MYRMOBORUS
Myrmoborus leucophrys (White-browed Antcreeper)
M. l. erythrophrys
E Colombia
M. l. leucophrys
N & W Amazonia
M. l. griseigula
C Brazil, N Bolivia
M. l. angustirostris
N Amazonia

Myrmoborus lugubris (Ash-breasted Antcreeper)   297
M. l. berlepschi
NE Peru, W Brazil
M. l. stictopterus
C Brazil
M. l. femininus
C Brazil
M. l. lugubris
C Brazil
Myrmoborus myotherinus (Black-faced Antcreeper)
M. m. elegans
E Colombia, S Venezuela, NW Brazil
M. m. napensis
E Ecuador, NE Peru
M. m. myotherinus
S Peru, NE Bolivia, S & W Brazil
M. m. incanus
WC Brazil
M. m. ardesiacus
W Brazil
M. m. proximus
W Brazil
M. m. ochrolaema
C Brazil
M. m. sororius
C & S Brazil
Myrmoborus melanurus (Black-tailed Antcreeper)
NE Peru

HYPOCNEMIS
Hypocnemis cantator (Warbling Antbird)
H. c. flavescens
S Venezuela, E Colombia, NW Brazil
H. c. notaea
SE Venezuela, Guyana, N Brazil
H. c. cantator
Surinam, French Guiana, N Brazil
H. c. saturata
SE Colombia, E Ecuador, NE Peru
H. c. peruviana
E Peru, W Brazil
H. c. implicata
C Brazil
H. c. striata
EC Brazil
H. c. affinis
EC Brazil
H. c. subflava
C Peru
H. c. collinsi
SE Peru, N Bolivia
H. c. ochrogyna
NE Bolivia, S Brazil

Hypocnemis hypoxantha (Yellow-browed Antbird)
H. h. hypoxantha
SE Colombia, E Ecuador, NE Peru
H. h. ochraceiventris
E Brazil

HYPOCNEMOIDES
Hypocnemoides melanopogon (Black-chinned Antcreeper)
H. m. occidentalis
E & S Colombia, Venezuela, NW Brazil
H. m. melanopogon
the Guianas, N Brazil
H. m. minor
C Brazil
Hypocnemoides maculicauda (Band-tailed Antcreeper)
H. m. maculicauda
Peru, N Bolivia, N Paraguay, W & S Brazil
H. m. orientalis
C & SE Brazil

MYRMOCHANES
Myrmochanes hemileucus (Black & White Antcatcher)
Peru, N Bolivia, W Brazil

GYMNOCICHLA
Gymnocichla nudiceps (Bare-crowned Antcatcher)
G. n. chiroleuca
E Guatemala to Costa Rica
G. n. erratilis
SW Costa Rica, W Panama
G. n. nudiceps
E Panama, NW Colombia
G. n. sanctaemartae
N Colombia

SCLATERIA
Sclateria naevia (Silvered Antcatcher)
S. n. naevia
NE Venezuela, the Guianas, N Brazil, Trinidad
S. n. diaphora
Venezuela
S. n. argentata
Upper Amazonia
S. n. toddi
C Brazil

PERCNOSTOLA
Percnostola rufifrons (Black-headed Antbird)
P. r. rufifrons
the Guianas, NE Brazil
P. r. subcristata
N Brazil
P. r. minor
NW Amazonia

Percnostola macrolopha (White-lined Antbird)
Peru
Percnostola schistacea (Slate-coloured Antbird)
SE Colombia, NE Peru, W Brazil
Percnostola leucostigma (Spot-winged Antbird)
P. l. subplumbea
E Colombia, E Ecuador, NE Peru
P. l. obscura
C Venezuela
P. l. saturata
SE Venezuela
P. l. leucostigma
S Venezuela, the Guianas, N Brazil
P. l. intensa
C Peru
P. l. brunneiceps
SE Peru
P. l. infuscata
S Venezuela, N & W Brazil
P. l. humaythae
C Brazil
P. l. rufifacies
C Brazil
Percnostola caurensis (Caura Antbird)
P. c. caurensis
C Venezuela
P. c. australis
S Venezuela, N Brazil
Percnostola lophotes (Rufous-crested Antbird)
Peru

MYRMECIZA
Myrmeciza longipes (Swainson's Antcatcher)
M. l. panamensis
E Panama, N Colombia
M. l. longipes
E Colombia, N Venezuela, Trinidad
M. l. boucardi
NC Colombia
M. l. griseipectus
SE Colombia, S Venezuela, Guyana, NE Brazil
Myrmeciza exsul (Chestnut-backed Antbird)
M. e. exsul
E Nicaragua to W Panama
M. e. occidentalis
W Costa Rica, S Panama
M. e. cassini
E Panama, N Colombia
M. e. niglarus
NW Colombia
M. e. maculifer
W Colombia, W Ecuador

Myrmeciza ferruginea (Ferruginous-backed Antbird)
   M. f. ferruginea
     the Guianas, N Brazil
   M. f. eluta
     C Brazil
Myrmeciza ruficauda (Rufous-tailed Antbird)
   M. r. soror
     NE Brazil
   M. r. ruficauda
     SE Brazil
Myrmeciza loricata (White-bibbed Antbird)
   SE Brazil
Myrmeciza squamosa (Squamate Antbird)
   SE Brazil
Myrmeciza laemosticta (Dull-mantled Antbird)
   M. l. laemosticta
     E Costa Rica
   M. l. palliata
     E Panama, NW Colombia
   M. l. bolivari
     C Colombia
   M. l. nigricauda
     SW Colombia, NW Ecuador
   M. l. venezuelae
     W Venezuela
Myrmeciza disjuncta (Yapacana Antbird)
   Venezuela
Myrmeciza pelzelni (Grey-bellied Antbird)
   E Colombia, Venezuela, N Brazil
Myrmeciza hemimelaena (Chestnut-tailed Antbird)
   M. h. hemimelaena
     W Amazonia
   M. h. pallens
     C Brazil
Myrmeciza hyperythra (Plumbeous Antbird)
   W Amazonia
Myrmeciza goeldii (Goeldi's Antbird)
   W Brazil
Myrmeciza melanoceps (White-shouldered Antbird)
   W Amazonia
Myrmeciza fortis (Sooty Antbird)
   M. f. fortis
     SE Colombia, Peru, W Brazil
   M. f. incanescens
     C Brazil
Myrmeciza immaculata (Immaculate Antbird)
   M. i. zeledoni
     E Costa Rica, W Panama
   M. i. berlepschi
     E Panama to W Ecuador

   M. i. immaculata
     E Colombia, W Venezuela
   M. i. brunnea
     NW Venezuela
Myrmeciza griseiceps (Grey-headed Antbird)
   SW Ecuador, NW Peru
Myrmeciza atrothorax (Black-throated Antbird)
   M. a. metae
     E Colombia
   M. a. atrothorax
     S Venezuela, the Guianas, N Brazil
   M. a. tenebrosa
     NE Peru, W Brazil
   M. a. maynana
     N Peru
   M. a. obscurata
     E Peru, W Brazil
   M. a. griseiventris
     W Bolivia
   M. a. melanura
     E Bolivia, SW Brazil
Myrmeciza stictothorax (Spot-breasted Antbird)
   C Brazil

PITHYS
Pithys albifrons (White-faced Antcatcher)
   P. a. albifrons
     S Venezuela, the Guianas, N Brazil
   P. a. brevibarba
     NW Amazonia
   P. a. peruviana
     N & E Peru
Pithys castanea (White-masked Antcatcher)
   W Ecuador

GYMNOPITHYS
Gymnopithys rufigula (Rufous-throated Antcatcher)
   G. r. pallida
     S Venezuela
   G. r. pallidigula
     S Venezuela
   G. r. rufigula
     E Venezuela, the Guianas, N Brazil
Gymnopithys salvini (White-throated Antcatcher)
   G. s. maculata
     E Peru, W Brazil
   G. s. salvini
     Bolivia, SW Brazil
Gymnopithys lunulata (Lunulated Antcatcher)
   E Peru

Gymnopithys leucaspis (Bicoloured Antcatcher)
G. l. olivascens
  Honduras to W Panama
G. l. bicolor
  E Panama, NW Colombia
G. l. daguae
  W Colombia
G. l. aequatorialis
  SW Colombia, W Ecuador
G. l. ruficeps
  C Colombia
G. l. leucaspis
  E Colombia
G. l. castanea
  E Ecuador, NE Peru
G. l. peruana
  N Peru
G. l. lateralis
  W Brazil

RHEGMATORHINA
Rhegmatorhina gymnops (Bare-eyed Antcatcher)
  N Brazil
Rhegmatorhina berlepschi (Harlequin Antcatcher)
  N Brazil
Rhegmatorhina cristata (Chestnut-crested Antcatcher)
  NW Brazil
Rhegmatorhina hoffmannsi (White-breasted Antcatcher)
  W Brazil
Rhegmatorhina melanosticta (Hairy-crested Antcatcher)
R. m. melanosticta
  E Ecuador
R. m. brunneiceps
  N Peru
R. m. purusiana
  E Peru, W Brazil
R. m. badia
  SE Peru, N Bolivia, W Brazil

HYLOPHYLAX
Hylophylax naevioïdes (Spotted Antbird)
H. n. capnitis
  E Nicaragua to W Panama
H. n. naevioïdes
  E Panama to W Ecuador
H. n. subsimilis
  WC Colombia
Hylophylax naevia (Spot-backed Antbird)
H. n. theresae
  W Amazonia
H. n. peruviana
  N Peru

H. n. consobrina
  S Venezuela, NW Brazil
H. n. naevia
  S Venezuela, the Guianas
H. n. obscura
  N Brazil
H. n. ochracea
  N Brazil
Hylophylax punctulata (Des Murs' Spotted Antbird)
H. p. punctulata
  S & E Venezuela, NE Peru, Brazil
H. p. subochracea
  C Brazil
Hylophylax poecilonota (Scale-backed Antbird)
H. p. poecilonota
  SE Venezuela, the Guianas, N Brazil
H. p. duidae
  E Colombia, S Venezuela, NW Brazil
H. p. lepidonota
  SE Colombia, E Ecuador, NE Peru
H. p. griseiventris
  SE Peru, N Bolivia, SW Brazil
H. p. gutturalis
  W Brazil
H. p. nigrigula
  C Brazil
H. p. vidua
  EC Brazil

PHLEGOPSIS
Phlegopsis nigromaculata (Black-spotted Bare-eye)
P. n. nigromaculata
  E Peru, N Bolivia, W & SW Brazil
P. n. bowmani
  N Brazil
P. n. confinis
  N Brazil
P. n. paraensis
  N Brazil
Phlegopsis barringeri (Argus Bare-eye)
  Colombia
Phlegopsis erythroptera (Reddish-winged Bare-eye)
P. e. erythroptera
  N & W Amazonia
P. e. ustulata
  E Peru, W Brazil

SKUTCHIA
Skutchia borbae (Pale-faced Bare-eye)
  C Brazil

PHAENOSTICTUS
Phaenostictus mcleannani (Ocellated Antbird)
P. m. saturatus
  SE Nicaragua to W Panama

P. m. mcleannani
  EC Panama
P. m. chocoanus
  E Panama, NW Colombia
P. m. pacificus
  SW Colombia, NW Ecuador

FORMICARIUS
Formicarius colma (Rufous-capped Ant-thrush)
F. c. colma
  E Colombia, S Venezuela, the Guianas, N Brazil
F. c. nigrifrons
  E Ecuador, E Peru, NW Brazil
F. c. amazonicus
  C Brazil
F. c. ruficeps
  E & SE Brazil
Formicarius analis (Rufous-necked Ant-thrush)
F. a. moniliger
  S Mexico, E Guatemala
F. a. pallidus
  SE Mexico
F. a. intermedius
  Belize, Honduras
F. a. umbrosus
  E Nicaragua to W Panama
F. a. hoffmanni
  S Costa Rica, SW Panama
F. a. panamensis
  E Panama, NW Colombia
F. a. virescens
  N Colombia
F. a. saturatus
  NC Colombia, NW Venezuela, Trinidad
F. a. griseoventris
  NE Colombia
F. a. connectens
  E Colombia
F. a. zamorae
  E Ecuador, NE Peru, W Brazil
F. a. olivaceus
  N Peru
F. a. crissalis
  SE Venezuela, the Guianas, N Brazil
F. a. analis
  Peru, W Brazil, N & E Bolivia
Formicarius rufifrons (Rufous-fronted Ant-thrush)
  E Peru
Formicarius nigricapillus (Black-headed Ant-thrush)
F. n. nigricapillus
  E Costa Rica, W Panama
F. n. destructus
  W Colombia, W Ecuador

Formicarius rufipectus (Rufous-breasted Ant-thrush)
F. r. rufipectus
  E Costa Rica, Panama
F. r. carrikeri
  W Colombia, W Ecuador
F. r. lasallei
  NW Venezuela
F. r. thoracicus
  E Ecuador, E Peru

CHAMAEZA
Chamaeza campanisona (Short-tailed Ant-thrush)
C. c. colombiana
  E Colombia
C. c. punctigula
  E Ecuador, N Peru
C. c. olivacea
  C Peru
C. c. huachamacarii
  C Peru
C. c. berlepschi
  SE Peru
C. c. venezuelana
  N Venezuela
C. c. yavii
  SC Venezuela
C. c. obscura
  E Venezuela
C. c. fulvescens
  SE Venezuela, Guyana
C. c. boliviana
  W Bolivia
C. c. campanisona
  SE Brazil, E Paraguay
Chamaeza nobilis (Striated Ant-thrush)
C. n. rubida
  SE Colombia, E Ecuador, NE Peru
C. n. nobilis
  NE Peru, W Brazil
C. n. fulvipectus
  C Brazil
Chamaeza ruficauda (Rufous-tailed Ant-thrush)
C. r. turdina
  C Colombia
C. r. chionogaster
  N Venezuela
C. r. ruficauda
  SE Brazil
Chamaeza mollissima (Barred Ant-thrush)
C. m. mollissima
  Colombia, Ecuador
C. m. yungae
  N Brazil

MYRMORNIS
Myrmornis torquata (Wing-banded Antthrush)
M. t. stictoptera
SE Nicaragua, Panama, NW Colombia
M. t. torquata
N & E Amazonia

PITTASOMA
Pittasoma michleri (Black-crowned Antpitta)
P. m. zeledoni
Costa Rica, W Panama
P. m. michleri
E Panama, NW Colombia
Pittasoma rufopileatum (Rufous-crowned Antpitta)
P. r. rosenbergi
W Colombia
P. r. harterti
SW Colombia
P. r. rufopileatum
NW Ecuador

GRALLARIA
Grallaria squamigera (Undulated Antpitta)
G. s. squamigera
Colombia, Venezuela, Ecuador
G. s. canicauda
Peru, NW Bolivia
Grallaria gigantea (Giant Antpitta)
G. g. lehmanni
C Colombia
G. g. hylodroma
W Ecuador
G. g. gigantea
E Ecuador
Grallaria excelsa (Great Antpitta)
G. e. excelsa
W Venezuela
G. e. phelpsi
N Venezuela
Grallaria varia (Variegated Antpitta)
G. v. cinereiceps
S Venezuela, NW Brazil
G. v. varia
the Guianas, NW Brazil
G. v. distincta
NC Brazil
G. v. intercedens
E Brazil
G. v. imperator
SE Brazil, Paraguay, NE Argentina
Grallaria alleni (Moustached Antpitta)
C Colombia
Grallaria guatimalensis (Scaled Antpitta)
G. g. ochraceiventris
SW Mexico

G. g. guatimalensis
S Mexico to N Nicaragua
G. g. princeps
Costa Rica, W Panama
G. g. chocoensis
mountains of E Panama, NW Colombia
G. g. regulus
Ecuador, Peru
G. g. carmelitae
NE Colombia, NW Venezuela
G. g. aripoensis
N Trinidad
G. g. roraimae
S Venezuela, N Brazil
Grallaria chthonia (Tachira Antpitta)
Venezuela
Grallaria haplonota (Plain-backed Antpitta)
G. h. haplonota
N Venezuela
G. h. pariae
NE Venezuela
G. h. parambae
NW Ecuador
Grallaria dignissima (Stripe-sided Antpitta)
E Ecuador, NE Peru
Grallaria eludens (Elusive Antpitta)
E Peru
Grallaria ruficapilla (Chestnut-crowned Antpitta)
G. r. ruficapilla
C Colombia, N Ecuador
G. r. perijana
NW Venezuela
G. r. avilae
N Venezuela
G. r. nigrolineata
W Venezuela
G. r. connectens
SW Ecuador
G. r. albiloris
S Ecuador, NW Peru
G. r. interior
N Peru
Grallaria watkinsi (Watkins' Antpitta)
SW Ecuador, NW Peru
Grallaria bangsi (Santa Marta Antpitta)
NE Colombia
Grallaria andicola (Stripe-headed Antpitta)
C Peru
Grallaria punensis (Puno Antpitta)
SE Peru
Grallaria rufocinerea (Bicoloured Antpitta)
C Colombia
Grallaria nuchalis (Chestnut-naped Antpitta)
G. n. ruficeps
C Colombia

G. n. obsoleta
NW Ecuador
G. n. nuchalis
E Ecuador
Grallaria albigula (White-throated Antpitta)
SE Peru, E Bolivia
Grallaria erythroleuca (Chestnut-brown Antpitta)
SE Peru
Grallaria hypoleuca (Bay-backed Antpitta)
G. h. flavotincta
WC Colombia
G. h. castanea
C Colombia, E Ecuador
G. h. hypoleuca
W Colombia
Grallaria griseonucha (Grey-naped Antpitta)
G. g. tachirae
Venezuela
G. g. griseonucha
W Venezuela
Grallaria rufula (Rufous Antpitta)
G. r. spatiator
NE Colombia
G. r. saltuensis
NE Colombia
G. r. rufula
Colombia, W Venezuela, Ecuador
G. r. cajamarcae
N Peru
G. r. obscura
C Peru
G. r. occabambae
SE Peru
G. r. cochabambae
N Bolivia
Grallaria erythrotis (Rufous-faced Antpitta)
Yungas of N Bolivia
Grallaria quitensis (Tawny Antpitta)
G. q. quitensis
C Colombia, Ecuador
G. q. alticola
E Colombia
G. q. atuensis
N Peru
Grallaria milleri (Brown-banded Antpitta)
C Colombia

HYLOPEZUS
Hylopezus perspicillatus (Streak-chested Antpitta)
H. p. intermedius
Caribbean slope from E Costa Rica to W Panama

303

H. p. lizanoi
W Costa Rica, W Panama
H. p. perspicillatus
E Panama, NW Colombia
H. p. periophthalmicus
Pacific coast of W Colombia, W Ecuador
H. p. pallidior
C Colombia
Hylopezus macularius (Spotted Antpitta)
H. m. diversus
SE Colombia, NE Peru, S Venezuela
H. m. macularius
E Venezuela, the Guianas, N Brazil
H. m. paraensis
Brazil
H. m. auricularis
Bolivia
Hylopezus fulviventris (Fulvous-bellied Antpitta)
H. f. dives
Caribbean slope of Nicaragua, Costa Rica
H. f. flammulatus
Caribbean slope of W Panama
H. f. barbacoae
E Panama, W Colombia
H. f. caquetae
Colombia
H. f. fulviventris
E Ecuador
Hylopezus berlepschi (Amazonian Antpitta)
H. b. yessupi
Peru
H. b. berlepschi
N Bolivia, C & S Brazil
Hylopezus ochroleucus (Speckle-breasted Antpitta)
H. o. ochroleucus
E Brazil
H. o. nattereri
SE Brazil, E Paraguay, NE Argentina

MYRMOTHERA
Myrmothera campanisona (Thrush-like Antpitta)
M. c. modesta
SE Colombia
M. c. dissors
E Colombia, S Venezuela, NW Brazil
M. c. campanisona
SE Venezuela, the Guianas, N Brazil
M. c. signata
E Ecuador, NE Peru
M. c. minor
E Peru, W Brazil
M. c. subcanescens
N & NC Brazil

304 ***Myrmothera simplex* (Brown-breasted Antpitta)**
  M. s. guaiquinimae
    SE Venezuela
  M. s. duidae
    S Venezuela
  M. s. simplex
    SE Venezuela

GRALLARICULA
***Grallaricula flavirostris* (Ochre-breasted Antpitta)**
  G. f. costaricensis
    Costa Rica, Panama
  G. f. brevis
    Mt Pirri (E Panama)
  G. f. ochraceiventris
    W Colombia
  G. f. mindoensis
    N Ecuador
  G. f. zarumae
    SW Ecuador
  G. f. flavirostris
    E Colombia, E Ecuador
  G. f. similis
    N Peru
  G. f. boliviana
    N Bolivia
***Grallaricula ferrugineipectus* (Rusty-breasted Antpitta)**
  G. f. rara
    E Colombia, NW Venezuela
  G. f. ferrugineipectus
    NE Colombia, N Venezuela
  G. f. leymebambae
    N Peru
***Grallaricula nana* (Slate-crowned Antpitta)**
  G. n. occidentalis
    W Colombia
  G. n. nana
    E Colombia, W Venezuela
  G. n. olivascens
    N Venezuela
  G. n. cumanensis
    N Venezuela
  G. n. pariae
    NE Venezuela
  G. n. kukenamensis
    SE Venezuela
***Grallaricula loricata* (Scallop-breasted Antpitta)**
    N Venezuela
***Grallaricula peruviana* (Peruvian Antpitta)**
    NW Peru
***Grallaricula lineifrons* (Crescent-faced Antpitta)**
    N Ecuador

***Grallaricula cucullata* (Hooded Antpitta)**
  G. c. cucullata
    W Colombia
  G. c. venezuelana
    NW Venezuela

104 CONOPOPHAGIDAE (GNATEATERS)

CONOPOPHAGA
***Conopophaga lineata* (Silvery-tufted Gnateater)**
  C. l. lineata
    E & SE Brazil
  C. l. vulgaris
    SE Brazil, E Paraguay, NE Argentina
  C. l. cearae
    E Brazil
***Conopophaga aurita* (Chestnut-belted Gnateater)**
  C. a. inexpectata
    SE Colombia, NW Brazil
  C. a. aurita
    the Guianas, N Brazil
  C. a. occidentalis
    E Ecuador, NE Peru
  C. a. australis
    E Peru, W Brazil
  C. a. snethlageae
    C Brazil
  C. a. pallida
    Brazil
***Conopophaga roberti* (Hooded Gnateater)**
    NE Brazil
***Conopophaga peruviana* (Ash-throated Gnateater)**
    E Ecuador, E Peru, W Brazil
***Conopophaga ardesiaca* (Slaty Gnateater)**
  C. a. saturata
    SE Peru
  C. a. ardesiaca
    Bolivia
***Conopophaga castaneiceps* (Chestnut-crowned Gnateater)**
  C. c. chocoensis
    W Colombia
  C. c. castaneiceps
    E Colombia, NE Ecuador
  C. c. chapmani
    SE Ecuador, NE Peru
  C. c. brunneinucha
    C Peru
***Conopophaga melanops* (Black-cheeked Gnateater)**
  C. m. perspicillata
    E Brazil
  C. m. melanops
    SE Brazil

Conopophaga melanogaster (Black-bellied
  Gnateater)
   N Bolivia, Brazil

105 RHINOCRYPTIDAE (TAPACULOS)

PTEROPTOCHOS
**Pteroptochos castaneus (Chestnut-
  breasted Huet-huet)**
   C Chile
Pteroptochos tarnii (Huet-huet)
   S Chile, W Argentina
**Pteroptochos megapodius (Moustached
  Turco)**
   P. m. atacamae
    N Chile
   P. m. megapodius
    C Chile

SCELORCHILUS
**Scelorchilus albicollis (White-throated
  Tapaculo)**
   S. a. atacamae
    N Chile
   S. a. albicollis
    C Chile
Scelorchilus rubecula (Chucao Tapaculo)
   S. r. rubecula
    Chile, W Argentina
   S. r. mochae
    Mocha !

RHINOCRYPTA
Rhinocrypta lanceolata (Grey Gallito)
   R. l. saturata
    Paraguay
   R. l. lanceolata
    Argentina

TELEDROMAS
Teledromas fuscus (Sandy Gallito)
   Argentina

LIOSCELES
**Liosceles thoracicus (Rusty-belted
  Tapaculo)**
   L. t. dugandi
    SE Colombia, W Brazil
   L. t. erithacus
    E Ecuador, E Peru
   L. t. thoracicus
    SE Peru, C Brazil

MELANOPAREIA
**Melanopareia torquata (Collared
  Crescentchest)**
   M. t. torquata
    E Brazil
   M. t. rufescens
    C Brazil

**Melanopareia maximiliani (Olive-crowned
  Crescentchest)**
   M. m. maximiliani
    W Bolivia
   M. m. argentina
    W Bolivia, Paraguay, N Argentina
**Melanopareia maranonica (Maranon
  Crescentchest)**
   N Peru
**Melanopareia elegans (Elegant
  Crescentchest)**
   M. e. elegans
    W Ecuador
   M. e. paucalensis
    E Peru

PSILORHAMPHUS
**Psilorhamphus guttatus (Spotted
  Bamboowren)**
   SE Brazil, NE Argentina

MERULAXIS
Merulaxis ater (Slaty Bristlefront)
   SE Brazil
**Merulaxis stresemanni (Stresemann's
  Bristlefront)**
   Brazil

EUGRALLA
**Eugralla paradoxa (Ochre-flanked
  Tapaculo)**
   Chile, S Argentina

MYORNIS
Myornis senilis (Ash-coloured Tapaculo)
   C Colombia, N Ecuador

SCYTALOPUS
**Scytalopus unicolor (Unicoloured
  Tapaculo)**
   S. u. latrans
    Colombia, W Venezuela, E Ecuador,
     N Peru
   S. u. subcinereus
    SW Ecuador, W Peru
   S. u. intermedius
    N Peru
   S. u. unicolor
    N Peru
   S. u. parvirostris
    C & S Peru, N Bolivia
**Scytalopus speluncae (Mouse-coloured
  Tapaculo)**
   SE Brazil, NE Argentina
**Scytalopus macropus (Large-footed
  Tapaculo)**
   Peru
**Scytalopus femoralis (Rufous-vented
  Tapaculo)**
   S. f. sanctaemartae
    NE Colombia

S. f. atratus
E Colombia
S. f. confusus
C Colombia
S. f. micropterus
E Ecuador, N Peru
S. f. nigricans
NE Colombia
S. f. femoralis
C Peru
S. f. bolivianus
SE Peru, N Bolivia
Scytalopus argentifrons (Silvery-fronted Tapaculo)
S. a. argentifrons
Costa Rica, W Panama
S. a. chiriquensis
W Panama
Scytalopus panamensis (Pale-throated Tapaculo)
Mt Tacarcuna (Panama)
Scytalopus vicinior (Narino Tapaculo)
E Panama, W Colombia
Scytalopus latebricola (Brown-rumped Tapaculo)
S. l. latebricola
NE Colombia
S. l. meridanus
C & E Colombia, W Venezuela
S. l. caracae
N Venezuela
S. l. spillmanni
W Ecuador
Scytalopus novacapitalis (Brasilia Tapaculo)
SE Brazil
Scytalopus indigoticus (White-breasted Tapaculo)
SE Brazil
Scytalopus magellanicus (Andean Tapaculo)
S. m. griseicollis
E Colombia
S. m. fuscicauda
Venezuela
S. m. canus
W Colombia
S. m. opacus
E Ecuador
S. m. altirostris
N Peru
S. m. affinis
W Peru
S. m. acutirostris
C & SE Peru
S. m. urubambae
S Peru

S. m. simonsi
N Bolivia
S. m. zimmeri
C Bolivia
S. m. fuscus
N Chile, W Argentina
S. m. magellanicus
S Chile, S Argentina
Scytalopus superciliaris (White-browed Tapaculo)
NW Argentina

ACROPTERNIS
Acropternis orthonyx (Ocellated Tapaculo)
A. o. orthonyx
E Colombia, W Venezuela
A. o. infuscata
E Ecuador

106 COTINGIDAE (COTINGAS)

PHOENICERCUS
Phoenicercus carnifex (Guianian Red-Cotinga)
the Guianas, E Venezuela, Brazil
Phoenicercus nigricollis (Black-necked Red-Cotinga)
NW South America

LANIISOMA
Laniisoma elegans (Shrike-like Cotinga)
L. e. venezuelensis
NE Colombia, NW Venezuela
L. e. buckleyi
E Peru, E Ecuador
L. e. elegans
SE Brazil
L. e. cadwaladeri
Bolivia

PHIBALURA
Phibalura flavirostris (Swallow-tailed Cotinga)
Paraguay, SE Brazil, NW Bolivia, NE Argentina

TIJUCA
Tijuca atra (Black & Gold Cotinga)
SE Brazil

CARPORNIS
Carpornis cucullatus (Hooded Berryeater)
SE Brazil
Carpornis melanocephalus (Black-headed Berryeater)
SE Brazil

AMPELION
Ampelion rubrocristata (Red-crested Cotinga)
Venezuela, Colombia to NW Bolivia

Ampelion rufaxilla (Chestnut-crested Cotinga)
A. r. antioquiae
W Colombia
A. r. rufaxilla
Peru
Ampelion sclateri (Bay-vented Cotinga)
C Peru
Ampelion stresemanni (White-cheeked Cotinga)
W Peru

PIPREOLA
Pipreola riefferii (Green & Black Fruiteater)
P. r. occidentalis
W Colombia, W Ecuador
P. r. riefferii
E Colombia, E Ecuador
P. r. melanolaema
NW Venezuela
P. r. confusa
Peru, N Bolivia
P. r. chachapoyas
N Peru
Pipreola intermedia (Band-tailed Fruiteater)
P. i. intermedia
N & C Peru
P. i. signata
SE Peru, Bolivia
Pipreola arcuata (Barred Fruiteater)
P. a. arcuata
Colombia, W Venezuela
P. a. viridicauda
N Bolivia, C Peru
Pipreola aureopectus (Golden-breasted Fruiteater)
P. a. decora
N Colombia
P. a. festiva
N Venezuela
P. a. aureopectus
E Colombia, W Venezuela
P. a. jucunda
W Colombia, W Ecuador
P. a. lubomirskii
S Colombia, E Ecuador, E Peru
P. a. pulchra
E Peru
Pipreola frontalis (Scarlet-breasted Fruiteater)
P. f. squamipectus
SE Ecuador, N Peru
P. f. frontalis
S Peru, Bolivia
Pipreola chlorolepidota (Fiery-throated Fruiteater)
E Ecuador, E Peru

Pipreola formosa (Handsome Fruiteater) 307
P. f. formosa
N Venezuela
P. f. rubidior
NE Venezuela
P. f. pariae
NE Venezuela
Pipreola whitelyi (Red-banded Fruiteater)
P. w. kathleenae
SE Venezuela
P. w. whiteleyei
Guyana

AMPELIOIDES
Ampelioides tschudii (Scaled Fruiteater)
NW Venezuela to N Peru

IODOPLEURA
Iodopleura fusca (Dusky Purpletuft)
the Guianas, Venezuela
Iodopleura isabellae (White-browed Purpletuft)
Colombia, E Ecuador, E Peru, N Brazil
Iodopleura pipra (Buff-throated Purpletuft)
I. p. leucopygia
Guyana
I. p. pipra
E Brazil

CALYPTURA
Calyptura cristata (Kinglet Calyptura)
S Brazil

LIPAUGUS
Lipaugus subalaris (Grey-tailed Piha)
E Ecuador, E Peru
Lipaugus cryptolophus (Olivaceus Piha)
L. c. mindoensis
W Ecuador, SW Colombia
L. c. cryptolophus
E Colombia, E Ecuador, E Peru
Lipaugus fuscocinereus (Dusky Piha)
Colombia, E Ecuador
Lipaugus vociferans (Screaming Piha)
the Guianas, N & W Amazonia
Lipaugus unirufus (Rufous Piha)
L. u. unirufus
SE Mexico to N Colombia
L. u. castaneotinctus
SW Colombia to NW Ecuador
Lipaugus lanioides (Cinnamon-vented Piha)
SE Brazil
Lipaugus streptophorus (Rose-collared Piha)
NW Guyana, Venezuela, N Brazil

CHIROCYLLA
Chirocylla uropygialis (Scimitar-winged Piha)
N Bolivia

Xenopsaris albinucha (White-naped Xenopsaris)
X. a. albinucha
Brazil, Paraguay, Argentina
X. a. minor
Venezuela, the Guianas

PACHYRAMPHUS
Pachyramphus viridis (Green-backed Becard)
P. v. griseigularis
Guyana
P. v. xanthogenys
E Ecuador
P. v. peruanus
C Peru
P. v. viridis
E & S Brazil, Bolivia, Paraguay, N Argentina
Pachyramphus versicolor (Barred Becard)
P. v. costaricensis
Costa Rica
P. v. versicolor
W Venezuela, Colombia, Ecuador, Peru
P. v. meridionalis
Peru, N Bolivia
Pachyramphus spodiurus (Slaty Becard)
W Ecuador, NW Peru
Pachyramphus rufus (Cinereous Becard)
P. r. rufus
Panama, N South America
P. r. juruanus
E Peru, W Brazil
Pachyramphus castaneus (Chestnut-crowned Becard)
P. c. saturatus
SE Colombia, E Ecuador, N Peru, NW Brazil
P. c. intermedius
N Venezuela
P. c. parui
S Venezuela
P. c. amazonus
NE Brazil
P. c. castaneus
E Brazil, Paraguay, Argentina
Pachyramphus cinnamomeus (Cinnamon Becard)
P. c. cinnamomeus
E Panama, Colombia, Ecuador
P. c. fulvidior
SE Mexico to W Panama
P. c. magdalenae
N & E Colombia, W Venezuela
P. c. badius
W Venezuela

Pachyramphus polychopterus (White-winged Becard)
P. p. similis
Guatemala to Panama
P. p. cinereiventris
N Colombia
P. p. dorsalis
W Colombia, NW Ecuador
P. p. tenebrosus
S Colombia
P. p. tristis
N & NE South America
P. p. nigriventris
W Amazonia
P. p. polychopterus
E Brazil
P. p. spixii
S Brazil, E Bolivia to N Argentina
Pachyramphus marginatus (Black-capped Becard)
P. m. nanus
N South America
P. m. marginatus
E Brazil
Pachyramphus albogriseus (Black & White Becard)
P. a. ornatus
W Nicaragua to W Panama
P. a. coronatus
N Colombia, NW Venezuela
P. a. albogriseus
E Colombia, N Venezuela
P. a. guayaquilensis
E Ecuador
P. a. salvini
N Peru, E Ecuador
Pachyramphus major (Mexican Becard)
P. m. uropygialis
W Mexico
P. m. major
E Mexico
P. m. matudai
S Mexico, N Guatemala
P. m. itzensis
SE Mexico, Belize
P. m. australis
Guatemala to E Nicaragua
Pachyramphus surinamus (Glossy-backed Becard)
Surinam, E Brazil, French Guiana
Pachyramphus aglaiae (Rose-throated Becard)
P. a. albiventris
S Arizona, W Mexico
P. a. richmondi
NW Mexico
P. a. gravis
NE Mexico

P. a. yucatanensis
E Mexico
P. a. insularis
Tres Marias Is
P. a. aglaiae
NE Mexico
P. a. sumichrasti
SE Mexico to El Salvador
P. a. hypophaeus
Honduras to NE Costa Rica
P. a. latirostris
W Nicaragua, W Costa Rica
P. a. homochrous
E Panama to NW Peru
P. a. quimarinus
NW Colombia
P. a. canescens
N Colombia, NW Venezuela
Pachyramphus minor (Pink-throated Becard)
N South America
Pachyramphus validus (Plain Becard)
P. v. audax
S Peru, C Bolivia, NW Argentina
P. v. validus
E Bolivia to C Brazil, N Argentina
Pachyramphus niger (Jamaican Becard)
Jamaica

TITYRA
Tityra cayana (Black-tailed Tityra)
T. c. candida
C & SW Colombia
T. c. cayana
N South America, Trinidad
T. c. braziliensis
E & S Brazil, Paraguay, NE Argentina
Tityra semifasciata (Masked Tityra)
T. s. hannumi
NW Mexico
T. s. griseiceps
W Mexico
T. s. deses
Yucatan peninsula
T. s. personata
E Mexico to El Salvador
T. s. costaricensis
S Honduras to W Panama
T. s. columbiana
E Panama, Colombia, W Venezuela
T. s. nigriceps
SW Colombia, W Ecuador
T. s. semifasciata
N & NW Amazonia
T. s. fortis
C & SE Peru, N & E Bolivia, C Brazil
Tityra inquisitor (Black-crowned Tityra)
T. i. fraserii
SE Mexico to W Panama

T. i. albitorques
E Panama to Peru, N Brazil
T. i. buckleyi
SE Colombia, E Ecuador
T. i. erythrogenys
E Colombia, Venezuela, the Guianas
T. i. pelzelni
E Bolivia, W Brazil
T. i. inquisitor
E Brazil, Paraguay, N Argentina

PORPHYROLAEMA
Porphyrolaema porphyrolaema (Purple-throated Cotinga)
W Amazonia

COTINGA
Cotinga amabilis (Lovely Cotinga)
SE Mexico to Costa Rica
Cotinga ridgwayi (Ridgway's Cotinga)
SW Costa Rica, Panama
Cotinga nattererii (Blue Cotinga)
NW Venezuela to N & E Peru
Cotinga maynana (Plum-throated Cotinga)
W Amazonia
Cotinga cotinga (Purple-breasted Cotinga)
E Colombia, to the Guianas, N Brazil
Cotinga maculata (Banded Cotinga)
SE Brazil
Cotinga cayana (Spangled Cotinga)
N & W South America

XIPHOLENA
Xipholena punicea (Pompadour Cotinga)
N & NW Amazonia
Xipholena lamellipennis (White-tailed Cotinga)
E Brazil
Xipholena atropurpurea (White-winged Cotinga)
SE Brazil

CARPODECTES
Carpodectes hopkei (White Cotinga)
E Panama to NW Ecuador
Carpodectes nitidus (Snowy Cotinga)
E Honduras to E Panama
Carpodectes antoniae (Yellow-billed Cotinga)
W Costa Rica, W Panama

CONIOPTILON
Conioptilon mcilhennyi (Black-faced Cotinga)
SE Peru

GYMNODERUS
Gymnoderus foetidus (Bare-necked Fruitcrow)
N South America

HAEMATODERUS
Haematoderus militaris (Crimson Fruit-crow)
  the Guianas, Brazil

QUERULA
Querula purpurata (Purple-throated Fruitcrow)
  Costa Rica, Panama, N South America

PYRODERUS
Pyroderus scutatus (Red-ruffed Fruitcrow)
  P. s. occidentalis
    W Colombia
  P. s. granadensis
    E Colombia, W Venezuela
  P. s. orenocensis
    N Venezuela, Guyana
  P. s. masoni
    E Peru
  P. s. scutatus
    SE Brazil, Paraguay, N Argentina

CEPHALOPTERUS
Cephalopterus glabricollis (Bare-necked Umbrellabird)
  Costa Rica, W Panama
Cephalopterus ornatus (Amazonian Umbrellabird)
  N & W South America
Cephalopterus penduliger (Long-wattled Umbrellabird)
  Colombia, Ecuador

PERISSOCEPHALUS
Perissocephalus tricolor (Capuchin Bird)
  the Guianas, Venezuela, N Brazil

PROCNIAS
Procnias tricarunculata (Three-wattled Bellbird)
  Nicaragua to Panama
Procnias alba (White Bellbird)
  Venezuela to Surinam, N Brazil
Procnias averano (Bearded Bellbird)
  P. a. carnobarba
    N Venezuela, Trinidad, W Guyana
  P. a. averano
    NE Brazil
Procnias nudicollis (Bare-throated Bellbird)
  S Brazil, Paraguay, NE Argentina

RUPICOLA
Rupicola rupicola (Guianan Cock of the Rock)
  E Colombia to the Guianas, N Brazil
Rupicola peruviana (Andean Cock of the Rock)
  R. p. sanguinolenta
    W Colombia, W Ecuador

R. p. aequatorialis
  W Venezuela, Colombia, E Ecuador, N Peru
R. p. peruviana
  C Peru
R. p. saturata
  SE Peru, N Bolivia

107 PIPRIDAE (MANAKINS)

SCHIFFORNIS
Schiffornis major (Greater Manakin)
  S. m. major
    N Brazil, E Peru
  S. m. duidae
    SE Venezuela
Schiffornis virescens (Greenish Manakin)
  SE Brazil to NE Argentina
Schiffornis turdinus (Thrush-like Manakin)
  S. t. veraepacis
    SE Mexico to W Panama
  S. t. dumicola
    W & C Panama
  S. t. panamensis
    E Panama, NW Colombia
  S. t. acrolophites
    E Panama, NW Colombia
  S. t. rosenbergi
    W Ecuador, W Colombia
  S. t. stenorhynchus
    N Venezuela, E Colombia
  S. t. aeneus
    E Ecuador, N Peru
  S. t. amazonus
    S Venezuela to E Peru, W Brazil
  S. t. olivaceus
    E Venezuela, Guyana
  S. t. wallacei
    N Brazil, French Guiana, Surinam
  S. t. steinbachi
    N Bolivia, SE Peru
  S. t. intermedius
    E Brazil
  S. t. turdinus
    E Brazil

SAPAYOA
Sapayoa aenigma (Broad-billed Manakin)
  E Panama to NW Ecuador

PIPRITES
Piprites griseiceps (Grey-hooded Manakin)
  Costa Rica, Nicaragua
Piprites chloris (Wing-barred Manakin)
  P. c. antioquiae
    NC Colombia
  P. c. perijanus
    N Colombia, W Venezuela
  P. c. tschudii
    S Colombia to C Peru, NW Brazil

P. c. chlorion
  the Guianas, N Brazil
P. c. grisescens
  Para (Brazil)
P. c. bolivianus
  N Bolivia, C Brazil
P. c. chloris
  SE Brazil, Paraguay, NE Argentina
Piprites pileatus (Black-capped Manakin)
  SE Brazil

NEOPIPO
Neopipo cinnamomea (Cinnamon Manakin)
  N. c. helenae
    Guyana, French Guiana, N Brazil
  N. c. cinnamomea
    E Ecuador, E Peru, W Brazil

CHLOROPIPO
Chloropipo flavicapilla (Yellow-headed Manakin)
  Colombia
Chloropipo holochlora (Green Manakin)
  C. h. suffusa
    E Panama
  C. h. litae
    E Panama to NW Ecuador
  C. h. holochlora
    E Colombia, E Ecuador, N Peru
  C. h. viridior
    SE Peru
Chloropipo uniformis (Olive Manakin)
  C. u. duidae
    S Venezuela
  C. u. uniformis
    Guyana, N Brazil
Chloropipo unicolor (Jet Manakin)
  Peru

XENOPIPO
Xenopipo atronitens (Black Manakin)
  N & NW Amazonia

ANTILOPHIA
Antilophia galeata (Helmeted Manakin)
  Brazil, Paraguay

TYRANNEUTES
Tyranneutes stolzmanni (Dwarf Tyrant Manakin)
  N & W Amazonia
Tyranneutes virescens (Tiny Tyrant Manakin)
  Venezuela to Surinam, N Brazil

NEOPELMA
Neopelma pallescens (Pale-bellied Tyrant Manakin)
  WC Brazil

Neopelma chrysocephalum (Saffron-crested Tyrant Manakin)
  the Guianas, N Brazil, S Venezuela, E Colombia
Neopelma sulphureiventer (Sulphur-bellied Tyrant Manakin)
  E Peru, N Bolivia, W Brazil
Neopelma aurifrons (Wied's Tyrant Manakin)
  N. a. aurifrons
    SE Brazil
  N. a. chrysolophum
    E Brazil

HETEROCERCUS
Heterocercus aurantiivertex (Orange-crowned Manakin)
  E Ecuador, NE Peru
Heterocercus flavivertex (Yellow-crowned Manakin)
  E Colombia, Venezuela, N Brazil
Heterocercus linteatus (Flame-crowned Manakin)
  NE Peru, WC Brazil

MACHAEROPTERUS
Machaeropterus deliciosus (Club-winged Manakin)
  W Colombia, NW Ecuador
Machaeropterus regulus (Striped Manakin)
  M. r. antioquiae
    W & C Colombia
  M. r. striolatus
    E Colombia, E Ecuador, NE Peru
  M. r. obscurostriatus
    W Venezuela
  M. r. zulianus
    W Venezuela
  M. r. aureopectus
    SE Venezuela
  M. r. regulus
    SE Brazil
Machaeropterus pyrocephalus (Fiery-capped Manakin)
  M. p. pallidiceps
    E Venezuela
  M. p. pyrocephalus
    N Brazil, E Peru

MANACUS
Manacus candei (Cande's Manakin)
  SE Mexico to Costa Rica
Manacus vitellinus (Golden-collared Manakin)
  M. v. vitellinus
    E Panama
  M. v. milleri
    N Colombia
  M. v. viridiventris
    W Colombia

Manacus cerritus **(Almirante Manakin)**
NW Panama
Manacus aurantiacus **(Salvin's Manakin)**
SW Costa Rica, W Panama
Manacus manacus **(White-bearded Manakin)**
M. m. trinitatis
Trinidad, NE Venezuela
M. m. abditivus
N Colombia
M. m. flaveolus
E Colombia
M. m. bangsi
SW Colombia
M. m. interior
S Colombia, E Ecuador, N Peru,
NW Brazil
M. m. umbrosus
S Venezuela
M. m. manacus
the Guianas, N Brazil
M. m. leucochlamys
W Ecuador
M. m. gutturosus
SE Brazil, E Paraguay, NE Argentina
M. m. purus
N Brazil
M. m. subpurus
C Brazil

CORAPIPO
Corapipo leucorrhoa **(White-ruffed**
Manakin)
C. l. altera
E Nicaragua, NW Costa Rica, Panama
C. l. heteroleuca
SW Costa Rica, W Panama
C. l. leucorrhoa
Colombia
Corapipo gutturalis **(White-throated**
Manakin)
Guyana, Brazil, Venezuela

ILICURA
Ilicura militaris **(Pin-tailed Manakin)**
SE Brazil

MASIUS
Masius chrysopterus **(Golden-winged**
Manakin)
M. c. bellus
W Colombia
M. c. pax
SE Colombia
M. c. coronulatus
SW Colombia, W Ecuador
M. c. chrysopterus
E Colombia, NW Venezuela, E Ecuador
M. c. peruvianus
N Peru

CHIROXIPHIA
Chiroxiphia caudata **(Swallow-tailed**
Manakin)
Brazil, Paraguay, N Argentina
Chiroxiphia pareola **(Blue-backed Manakin)**
C. p. atlantica
Tobago I
C. p. pareola
the Guianas, N & E Brazil
C. p. regina
N Brazil
C. p. napensis
SE Colombia, E Ecuador, NE Peru
C. p. boliviana
SE Peru, Bolivia
Chiroxiphia lanceolata **(Lance-tailed**
Manakin)
Panama to NW Venezuela
Chiroxiphia linearis **(Long-tailed Manakin)**
S Mexico to Costa Rica

PIPRA
Pipra filicauda **(Wire-tailed Manakin)**
Venezuela, Colombia, Peru, Brazil
Pipra vilasboasi **(Golden-crowned Manakin)**
Brazil
Pipra nattereri **(Snow-capped Manakin)**
Brazil
Pipra iris **(Opal-crowned Manakin)**
P. i. iris
EC Brazil
P. i. eucephala
C Brazil
Pipra serena **(White-fronted Manakin)**
P. s. suavissima
Guyana, SE Venezuela
P. s. serena
French Guiana, N Brazil
Pipra coronata **(Blue-crowned Manakin)**
P. c. velutina
SW Costa Rica, W Panama
P. c. minuscula
E Panama to NW Ecuador
P. c. caquetae
C Colombia
P. c. carbonata
SE Colombia, NE Ecuador, NW Brazil
P. c. coronata
NW Brazil
P. c. caelestipileata
W Brazil, SE Peru
P. c. exquisita
C Peru
P. c. regalis
NC Bolivia

Pipra caeruleocapilla (Caerulean-capped Manakin)
  C & SE Peru
Pipra isidorei (Blue-rumped Manakin)
  P. i. isidorei
    E Colombia, E Ecuador
  P. i. leucopygia
    N Peru
Pipra pipra (White-crowned Manakin)
  P. p. anthracina
    Costa Rica, W Panama
  P. p. bolivari
    NW Colombia
  P. p. coracina
    E Colombia, E Ecuador, NW Peru
  P. p. discolor
    NE Peru
  P. p. minima
    W Colombia
  P. p. unica
    NC Colombia
  P. p. pipra
    the Guianas, E Venezuela, N Brazil
  P. p. occulta
    NC Peru
  P. p. pygmaea
    NC Peru
  P. p. microlopha
    E Peru, W Brazil
  P. p. comata
    Peru
  P. p. separabilis
    EC Brazil
  P. p. cephaleucos
    E Brazil
Pipra cornuta (Scarlet-horned Manakin)
  Guyana, Venezuela, Brazil
Pipra chloromeros (Round-tailed Manakin)
  Peru, Bolivia
Pipra mentalis (Red-capped Manakin)
  P. m. mentalis
    SE Mexico to E Costa Rica
  P. m. ignifera
    W Costa Rica, W Panama
  P. m. minor
    E Panama to W Ecuador
Pipra rubrocapilla (Red-headed Manakin)
  NE Peru, W Brazil
Pipra erythrocephala (Golden-headed Manakin)
  P. e. erythrocephala
    Panama, N South America
  P. e. berlepschi
    W Amazonia
  P. e. flammiceps
    E Colombia

Pipra fasciicauda (Band-tailed Manakin)
  P. f. calamae
    C & W Brazil
  P. f. satura
    N Peru
  P. f. purusiana
    W Brazil, E Peru
  P. f. fasciicauda
    E Bolivia, SE Peru
  P. f. scarlatina
    Paraguay, S Brazil
Pipra aureola (Crimson-hooded Manakin)
  P. a. aureola
    the Guianas, NE Venezuela, NE Brazil
  P. a. aurantiicollis
    N Brazil
  P. a. flavicollis
    N Brazil
  P. a. borbae
    C Brazil

108 TYRANNIDAE (TYRANT FLY-CATCHERS)

FLUVICOLINAE

AGRIORNIS
Agriornis livida (Great Shrike Tyrant)
  A. l. livida
    SC Chile
  A. l. fortis
    S Chile, S Argentina
Agriornis microptera (Grey-bellied Shrike Tyrant)
  A. m. andecola
    Bolivia, S Peru, N Chile, NW Argentina
  A. m. microptera
    Uruguay, Argentina
Agriornis montana (Black-billed Shrike Tyrant)
  A. m. solitaria
    Ecuador, Colombia
  A. m. insolens
    Peru
  A. m. intermedia
    W Bolivia, N Chile
  A. m. montana
    E Bolivia, NW Argentina
  A. m. maritima
    NC Chile
  A. m. leucura
    C Chile, C Argentina
Agriornis albicauda (White-tailed Shrike Tyrant)
  Ecuador, Peru, W Bolivia, N Chile, N Argentina

NEOXOLMIS
Neoxolmis rufiventris (Chocolate-vented Tyrant)
Uruguay, Chile, Argentina

XOLMIS
Xolmis cinerea (Grey Monjita)
X. c. cinerea
S Brazil, Uruguay, N Argentina
X. c. pepoaza
E Bolivia, Paraguay, N Argentina
Xolmis velata (White-rumped Monjita)
E Bolivia, S Brazil, Paraguay
Xolmis dominicana (Black & White Monjita)
S Brazil, Uruguay, Paraguay, E Argentina
Xolmis coronata (Black-crowned Monjita)
E Bolivia, Uruguay, Paraguay, N Argentina
Xolmis irupero (White Monjita)
X. i. nivea
E Brazil
X. i. irupero
E Bolivia, S Brazil, Uruguay, Paraguay, N Argentina
Xolmis murina (Mouse-brown Monjita)
E Bolivia, Paraguay, N Argentina
Xolmis rubetra (Rusty-backed Monjita)
W Argentina
Xolmis rufipennis (Rufous-webbed Monjita)
Peru, Bolivia

PYROPE
Pyrope pyrope (Fire-eyed Diucon)
S Chile, S Argentina

MUSCISAXICOLA
Muscisaxicola rufivertex (Rufous-naped Ground-Tyrant)
M. r. occipitalis
Peru, NW Bolivia
M. r. pallidiceps
SW Bolivia, NW Argentina, N Chile
M. r. rufivertex
S Chile, SW Argentina
Muscisaxicola albilora (White-browed Ground-Tyrant)
Ecuador, Peru, Bolivia, Chile
Muscisaxicola juninensis (Puna Ground-Tyrant)
S Peru, N Chile, N Argentina
Muscisaxicola flavinucha (Ochre-naped Ground-Tyrant)
M. f. flavinucha
Peru, Bolivia, N Argentina, N Chile
M. f. brevirostris
S Argentina, S Chile
Muscisaxicola capistrata (Cinnamon-bellied Ground-Tyrant)
Bolivia, S Peru, Argentina, Chile

Muscisaxicola frontalis (Black-fronted Ground-Tyrant)
Bolivia, Peru, Argentina, Chile
Muscisaxicola albifrons (White-fronted Ground-Tyrant)
S Peru, W Bolivia, N Chile
Muscisaxicola alpina (Plain-capped Ground-Tyrant)
M. a. columbiana
WC Colombia
M. a. quesadae
C Colombia
M. a. alpina
N Ecuador
M. a. grisea
Peru, W Bolivia
M. a. cinerea
N & C Chile
M. a. argentina
NW Argentina
Muscisaxicola macloviana (Dark-faced Ground-Tyrant)
M. m. mentalis
Peru, Bolivia, Chile, Argentina
M. m. macloviana
Falkland Is
Muscisaxicola maculirostris (Spot-billed Ground-Tyrant)
M. m. niceforoi
C Colombia
M. m. rufescens
Ecuador
M. m. maculirostris
Peru, Bolivia, Chile, W Argentina
Muscisaxicola fluviatilis (Little Ground-Tyrant)
E Peru, N Bolivia, W Brazil, N Argentina

MUSCIGRALLA
Muscigralla brevicauda (Short-tailed Field-Tyrant)
SW Ecuador, W Peru, N Chile

LESSONIA
Lessonia rufa (Rufous-backed Negrito)
L. r. oreas
Peru, W Bolivia, N Chile, NW Argentina
L. r. rufa
S Brazil, Uruguay, E Chile, W Argentina

MYIOTHERETES
Myiotheretes striaticollis (Streak-throated Bush-Tyrant)
M. s. striaticollis
Venezuela, Colombia, Ecuador, Peru, W Bolivia
M. s. pallidus
NW Argentina, E Peru, Bolivia

Myiotheretes pernix (Santa Marta Bush-Tyrant)
NW Argentina, E Peru, Bolivia

Myiotheretes fumigatus (Smoky Bush-Tyrant)
M. f. olivaceus
N Colombia, W Venezuela
M. f. fumigatus
Colombia, Ecuador, Peru
M. f. lugubris
W Venezuela
M. f. cajamarcae
S Ecuador, N Peru

Myiotheretes fuscorufus (Rufous-bellied Bush-Tyrant)
Bolivia, SE Peru

Myiotheretes signatus (Jelski's Bush-Tyrant)
C Peru

Miotheretes erythropygius (Red-rumped Bush-Tyrant)
M. e. orinomus
N Colombia
M. e. erythropygius
C Colombia to Ecuador, Peru, N Bolivia

OCHTHOECA

Ochthoeca oenanthoides (D'Orbigny's Chat-Tyrant)
O. o. polionota
Peru
O. o. oenanthoides
Bolivia, N Chile, NW Argentina

Ochthoeca fumicolor (Brown-backed Chat-Tyrant) .
O. f. superciliosa
W Venezuela
O. f. ferruginea
C Colombia
O. f. fumicolor
E Colombia, W Venezuela
O. f. brunneifrons
Peru, Ecuador, W Colombia
O. f. berlepschi
SE Peru, W Bolivia

Ochthoeca leucophrys (White-browed Chat-Tyrant)
O. l. dissors
N Peru
O. l. interior
C Peru
O. l. urubambae
C & S Peru
O. l. leucometopa
W Peru, NW Chile
O. l. leucophrys
Bolivia
O. l. tucumana
W Argentina

Ochthoeca piurae (Piura Chat-Tyrant)
NW Peru

Ochthoeca rufipectoralis (Rufous-breasted Chat-Tyrant)
O. r. poliogastra
N Colombia
O. r. rubicundulus
NE Colombia, NW Venezuela
O. r. obfuscata
SW & W Colombia to Peru
O. r. rufopectus
C Colombia, Ecuador, NW Peru
O. r. centralis
N Peru
O. r. tectricialis
S Peru
O. r. rufipectoralis
Bolivia, SE Peru

Ochthoeca cinnamomeiventris (Slaty-backed Chat-Tyrant)
O. c. nigrita
W Venezuela
O. c. cinnamomeiventris
Colombia, E Ecuador
O. c. angustifasciata
N Peru
O. c. thoracica
Peru, Bolivia

Ochthoeca frontalis (Crowned Chat-Tyrant)
O. f. albidiadema
E Colombia
O. f. frontalis
W Ecuador, W Colombia
O. f. orientalis
E Ecuador, N Peru
O. f. boliviana
C & S Peru, E Bolivia
O. f. spodionota
C & SE Peru

Ochthoeca pulchella (Golden-browed Chat-Tyrant)
O. p. jelskii
NW Peru, SW Ecuador
O. p. similis
C Peru
O. p. pulchella
W Bolivia, SE Peru

Ochthoeca diadema (Yellow-bellied Chat-Tyrant)
O. d. rubellula
NE Colombia, NW Venezuela
O. d. jesupi
N Colombia
O. d. tovarensis
N Venezuela
O. d. diadema
Colombia, W Venezuela

O. d. meridana
NW Venezuela
O. d. gratiosa
NW Peru, W Ecuador, W Colombia

SAYORNIS
Sayornis phoebe (Eastern Phoebe)
C & SE Canada, E USA, E Mexico
Sayornis nigricans (Black Phoebe)
S. n. nigricans
SW USA, Mexico
S. n. salictaria
N Mexico
S. n. brunnescens
Baja California
S. n. semiatra
W Mexico, W USA
S. n. aquatica
Guatemala, Nicaragua
S. n. amnicola
Costa Rica, W Panama
S. n. angustirostris
C & N Colombia, E Panama, W Venezuela
to Peru
S. n. latirostris
Bolivia, NW Argentina
NW Argentina
Sayornis saya (Say's Phoebe)
S. s. yukonensis
SE Alaska, W Canada, California
S. s. saya
WC Canada, W USA, N Mexico
S. s. quiescens
NW Baja California

COLONIA
Colonia colonus (Long-tailed Tyrant)
C. c. leuconotus
S Honduras to Panama, W Colombia,
Ecuador
C. c. fuscicapillus
Colombia, E Ecuador, E Peru, W Brazil,
Bolivia
C. c. poecilonotus
the Guianas, SE Venezuela
C. c. niveiceps
S Peru, N Bolivia
C. c. colonus
S Brazil, Paraguay, N Argentina

GUBERNETES
**Gubernetes yetapa (Streamer-tailed
Tyrant)**
S Brazil, Paraguay, E Bolivia, N Argentina

ALECTRURUS
Alectrurus tricolor (Cock-tailed Tyrant)
S Brazil, Paraguay, E Bolivia, N Argentina

YETAPA
Yetapa risoria (Strange-tailed Tyrant)
S Brazil, Paraguay, Uruguay, N Argentina

KNIPOLEGUS
Knipolegus lophotes (Crested Black Tyrant)
S Brazil, Uruguay
**Knipolegus nigerrimus (Velvety Black
Tyrant)**
SE Brazil
**Knipolegus aterrimus (White-winged
Black Tyrant)**
K. a. heterogyna
N Peru
K. a. anthracinus
S Peru, W Bolivia
K. a. aterrimus
E Bolivia, W Argentina
K. a. franciscanus
CE Brazil
Knipolegus orenocensis (Riverside Tyrant)
K. o. orenocensis
Venezuela
K. o. xinguensis
N Brazil
K. o. sclateri
N Peru, C Brazil
**Knipolegus poecilurus (Rufous-tailed
Tyrant)**
K. p. poecilurus
Colombia
K. p. peruanus
Peru, Bolivia
K. p. venezuelanus
Trinidad, Venezuela, NW Brazil
K. p. salvini
Guyana
K. p. paraquensis
S Venezuela
**Knipolegus cyanirostris (Blue-billed
Black Tyrant)**
SE Brazil, Uruguay, Paraguay, E Argentina
Knipolegus cabanisi (Plumbeous Tyrant)
SE Peru, NW Argentina
**Knipolegus subflammulatus (Berlioz
Tyrant)**
Bolivia

PHAEOTRICCUS
**Phaeotriccus poecilocercus (Amazonian
Black Tyrant)**
Venezuela, Guyana, N Brazil, NE Peru
**Phaeotriccus hudsoni (Hudson's Black
Tyrant)**
S Brazil, E Bolivia, Argentina

ENTOTRICCUS
Entotriccus striaticeps (Cinereous Tyrant)
E Bolivia, SW Brazil, Paraguay,
N Argentina

HYMENOPS
Hymenops perspicillata (Spectacled Tyrant)
　H. p. perspicillata
　　Argentina, Paraguay, Uruguay
　H. p. andina
　　C Chile, NW Argentina, S Bolivia

MUSCIPIPRA
Muscipipra vetula (Shear-tailed Grey Tyrant)
　　SE Brazil, Paraguay, Argentina

FLUVICOLA
Fluvicola pica (Pied Water-Tyrant)
　F. p. pica
　　Trinidad, Venezuela, the Guianas, Colombia, N Brazil
　F. p. albiventer
　　S Brazil, E Bolivia, Paraguay, N Argentina
Fluvicola nengeta (Masked Water-Tyrant)
　F. n. atripennis
　　SW Ecuador, NW Peru
　F. n. nengeta
　　E Brazil

ARUNDINICOLA
Arundinicola leucocephala (White-headed Marsh-Tyrant)
　　NE South America

PYROCEPHALUS
Pyrocephalus rubinus (Vermilion Flycatcher)
　P. r. mexicanus
　　SW USA, Mexico
　P. r. flammeus
　　N Mexico
　P. r. blatteus
　　S Mexico to Honduras
　P. r. pinicola
　　Nicaragua
　P. r. piurae
　　W Colombia to NW Peru
　P. r. saturatus
　　N Colombia to Surinam, N Brazil
　P. r. ardens
　　NC Peru
　P. r. cocachacrae
　　SW Peru, N Chile
　P. r. obscurus
　　W Peru
　P. r. rubinus
　　W & C Amazonia
　P. r. major
　　SE Peru
　P. r. nanus
　　Galapagos Is
　P. r. dubius
　　Chatham I (Galapagos)

OCHTHORNIS
Ochthornis littoralis (Drab Water-Tyrant)
　　Guyana, French Guiana, N Brazil, S Venezuela, Colombia, Ecuador, Peru

TUMBEZIA
Tumbezia salvini (Tumbes Tyrant)
　　NW Peru

SATRAPA
Satrapa icterophrys (Yellow-browed Tyrant)
　　Bolivia, Brazil, Paraguay, Uruguay, N Argentina

MACHETORNIS
Machetornis rixosus (Cattle Tyrant)
　M. r. flavigularis
　　N Colombia, N Venezuela
　M. r. obscurodorsalis
　　SW Venezuela, E Colombia
　M. r. rixosus
　　E Bolivia, S Brazil, Paraguay, Uruguay, N Argentina

SIRYSTES
Sirystes sibilator (Sirystes)
　S. s. albogriseus
　　E Panama, NW Colombia
　S. s. albocinereus
　　S Colombia, E Ecuador, E Peru, W Brazil
　S. s. subcanescens
　　NE Brazil, S Surinam
　S. s. sibilator
　　E Brazil, Paraguay, NE Argentina
　S. s. atimastus
　　SW Brazil

TYRANNINAE

MUSCIVORA
Muscivora forficata (Scissor-tailed Flycatcher)
　　SC USA, Mexico, Central America
Muscivora tyrannus (Fork-tailed Flycatcher)
　M. t. tyrannus
　　C & S South America
　M. t. sanctaemartae
　　N Colombia, W Venezuela
　M. t. monachus
　　S Mexico to C Brazil
　M. t. circumdatus
　　EC Brazil

TYRANNUS
Tyrannus tyrannus (Eastern Kingbird)
　　S Canada, C & E USA, Central America, N South America
Tyrannus cubensis (Giant Kingbird)
　　Cuba, Gtr Antilles Is

***Tyrannus melancholicus* (Tropical Kingbird)**
T. m. occidentalis
W Mexico
T. m. chloronotus
S Mexico to Panama, N Colombia
T. m. despotes
N Venezuela, the Guianas, N Brazil,
Trinidad
T. m. melancholicus
S Colombia & S Venezuela to Paraguay
& Argentina
***Tyrannus couchii* (Couch's Kingbird)**
S USA, E Mexico
***Tyrannus dominicensis* (Grey Kingbird)**
T. d. fugax
SE USA, Bahama Is
T. d. sequax
Cuba, Cayman Is, S Bahama Is
T. d. dominicensis
Gtr Antilles Is, N Lesser Antilles Is
T. d. tenax
Margarita I, Curacao I, Bonaire I
T. d. vorax
Trinidad, S Lesser Antilles Is
***Tyrannus caudifasciatus* (Loggerhead
Kingbird)**
T. c. bahamensis
Bahama Is
T. c. caudifasciatus
Cuba
T. c. flavescens
Isle of Pines, Gtr Antilles
T. c. caymanensis
Cayman Is
T. c. jamaicensis
Jamaica
T. c. taylori
Puerto Rico
T. c. gabbii
Haiti
***Tyrannus verticalis* (Western Kingbird)**
SW Canada, W USA, W Mexico,
Guatemala
***Tyrannus niveigularis* (Snowy-throated
Kingbird)**
SW Colombia, Ecuador, NW Peru
***Tyrannus albogularis* (White-throated
Kingbird)**
Brazil, Venezuela to E Peru, N Bolivia
***Tyrannus apolites* (Heine's Kingbird)**
SE Brazil
***Tyrannus vociferans* (Cassin's Kingbird)**
T. c. vociferans
SW USA, W Mexico, Guatemala
T. c. xenopterus
SW Mexico

***Tyrannus crassirostris* (Thick-billed
Kingbird)**
T. c. sequestratus
N Mexico
T. c. pompalis
C Mexico
T. c. crassirostris
S Mexico, W Guatemala

TYRANNOPSIS
***Tyrannopsis sulphurea* (Sulphury Flycatcher)**
Trinidad, the Guianas, Venezuela, Brazil,
Peru, Ecuador
***Tyrannopsis luteiventris* (Dusky-chested
Flycatcher)**
T. l. luteiventris
Colombia, Ecuador, Peru, Brazil
T. l. septentrionalis
Surinam

EMPIDONOMUS
***Empidonomus varius* (Variegated
Flycatcher)**
E. v. varius
E Bolivia, SE Brazil, Paraguay, N Argentina
E. v. rufinus
N & E Brazil, E Peru, E Venezuela, Guyana,
French Guiana
E. v. septentrionalis
N Venezuela, E Colombia
***Empidonomus aurantioatrocristatus*
(Crowned Slaty Flycatcher)**
E. a. aurantioatrocristatus
E Peru, E Bolivia, S Brazil, Uruguay
Paraguay, N Argentina
E. a. pallidiventris
NE Brazil

LEGATUS
***Legatus leucophaius* (Piratic Flycatcher)**
L. l. variegatus
SE Mexico, Guatemala, Honduras
L. l. leucophaius
Nicaragua to Panama, Trinidad,
N & C South America

CONOPIAS
***Conopias trivirgata* (Three-striped
Flycatcher)**
C. t. berlepschi
N Brazil, SW Venezuela
C. t. trivirgata
SE Brazil, Paraguay, NE Argentina
***Conopias cinchoneti* (Lemon-browed
Flycatcher)**
C. c. icterophrys
C Colombia, W Venezuela
C. c. cinchoneti
E Ecuador, Peru

Conopias parva (White-ringed Flycatcher)
  C. p. distincta
    E Costa Rica
  C. p. albovittata
    E Panama, W Colombia, NW Ecuador
  C. p. parva
    Guyana, French Guiana, N Brazil

MEGARHYNCHUS

Megarhynchus pitangua (Boat-billed Flycatcher)
  M. p. mexicanus
    SE Mexico to NW Colombia
  M. p. tardiusculus
    NW Mexico
  M. p. caniceps
    W Mexico
  M. p. deserticola
    C Guatemala
  M. p. pitangua
    Trinidad, North & Central South America
  M. p. chrysogaster
    W Ecuador, NW Peru

MYIODYNASTES

Myiodynastes luteiventris (Sulphur-bellied Flycatcher)
  M. l. swarthi
    S USA, N Mexico
  M. l. luteiventris
    S Mexico to NW South America

Myiodynastes maculatus (Streaked Flycatcher)
  M. m. insolens
    SE Mexico to Honduras » N South America
  M. m. nobilis
    NE Colombia
  M. m. difficilis
    W Costa Rica to Venezuela
  M. m. chapmani
    SW Colombia to W Peru
  M. m. maculatus
    N Peru, Venezuela, the Guianas, N Brazil
  M. m. tobagensis
    Guyana, Trinidad, Tobago I
  M. m. solitarius
    S Peru to Uruguay, N Argentina

Myiodynastes bairdi (Baird's Flycatcher)
  SW Ecuador, W Peru

Myiodynastes chrysocephalus (Golden-crowned Flycatcher)
  M. c. cinerascens
    NW Venezuela
  M. c. intermedius
    N Venezuela, N Colombia
  M. c. minor
    Colombia, Ecuador
  M. c. chrysocephalus
    Peru, Bolivia

Myiodynastes hemichrysus (Golden-bellied Flycatcher)
  Costa Rica, W Panama

MYIOZETETES

Myiozetetes cayanensis (Rusty-margined Flycatcher)
  M. c. harterti
    E Panama
  M. c. rufipennis
    N Venezuela, E Colombia
  M. c. hellmayri
    Columbia, E Ecuador, NW Venezuela
  M. c. cayanensis
    the Guianas, N Brazil, E Bolivia,
     S Venezuela
  M. c. erythropterus
    SE Brazil

Myiozetetes granadensis (Grey-capped Flycatcher)
  M. g. granadensis
    E Honduras to CE Panama
  M. g. occidentalis
    E Panama to NW Peru
  M. g. obscurior
    S Venezuela, S Colombia, E Ecuador,
     W Brazil, SE Peru

Myiozetetes similis (Vermilion-crowned Flycatcher)
  M. s. primulus
    N Mexico
  M. s. hesperis
    W Mexico
  M. s. texensis
    S Mexico to N Costa Rica
  M. s. colombianus
    SW Costa Rica, Panama, N Colombia,
     N Venezuela
  M. s. connivens
    Colombia, SE Peru, Venezuela, N Brazil
  M. s. grandis
    W Ecuador, NW Peru
  M. s. pallidventris
    E Brazil, E Paraguay, NE Argentina
  M. s. similis
    E Brazil, Paraguay, NE Argentina

Myiozetetes inornatus (White-bearded Flycatcher)
  Venezuela

PITANGUS

Pitangus sulphuratus (Great Kiskadee)
  P. s. derbianus
    S Texas, C Mexico
  P. s. palliatus
    W Mexico
  P. s. texanus
    E Mexico, S Texas

P. s. guatimalensis
S Mexico, Guatemala to Pará
P. s. pallidus
Honduras to Costa Rica
P. s. trinitatis
C Colombia, Trinidad, Venezuela
P. s. caucensis
W Colombia
P. s. rufipennis
N Venezuela, Colombia
P. s. sulphuratus
S Colombia, the Guianas, N Brazil,
NE Peru, E Ecuador
P. s. maximiliani
E & C Brazil, E Bolivia
P. s. bolivianus
E Bolivia
P. s. argentinus
Paraguay, Bolivia, N Argentina
Pitangus lictor (Lesser Kiskadee)
P. l. panamensis
E Panama, N Colombia
P. l. lictor
Venezuela, the Guianas, N Brazil, E Peru,
E Ecuador, E Colombia

MYIARCHINAE

MYIARCHUS
Myiarchus semirufus (Rufous Flycatcher)
Peru
**Myiarchus validus (Rufous-tailed
Flycatcher)**
Jamaica
Myiarchus ferox (Short-crested Flycatcher)
M. f. brunnescens
Venezuela
M. f. ferox
S Colombia to E Peru, N Brazil, the Guianas
M. f. australis
E Bolivia to S Brazil, N Argentina
**Myiarchus venezuelensis (Venezuelan
Flycatcher)**
M. v. venezuelensis
NE Colombia, NW Venezuela
M. v. insulicola
Tobago I
Myiarchus panamensis (Panama Flycatcher)
M. p. actiosus
Costa Rica
M. p. panamensis
Panama, N Colombia, NW Venezuela
Myiarchus apicalis (Apical Flycatcher)
SW Colombia
**Myiarchus cephalotes (Pale-edged
Flycatcher)**
M. c. caucae
N Colombia

M. c. caribbaeus
Venezuela
M. c. cephalotes
Bolivia, Peru, Ecuador, W Colombia
**Myiarchus phaeocephalus (Sooty-crowned
Flycatcher)**
M. p. phaeocephalus
W Ecuador, NW Peru
M. p. interior
NW Peru
**Myiarchus tyrannulus (Brown Crested
Flycatcher)**
M. t. magister
SW USA, W Mexico, Tres Marias I
M. t. cooperi
SW USA, W Mexico to Honduras
M. t. tyrannulus
Trinidad, Venezuela, the Guianas, N Brazil,
N Colombia
M. t. brevipennis
North Venezuelan Islands
M. t. tobagensis
Tobago I
M. t. bahiae
N & E Brazil
M. t. chlorepiscius
S Brazil, Bolivia, Peru, Paraguay,
N Argentina
**Myiarchus nuttingi (Pale-throated
Flycatcher)**
M. n. inquietus
W & C Mexico
M. n. nuttingi
mountains of Central America
M. n. flavidior
Pacific coast of Central America
Myiarchus oberi (Wied's Crested Flycatcher)
M. o. oberi
Domenica I, Guadelupe I
M. o. sanctaeluciae
St Lucia I
M. o. berlepschii
Nevis I, St Kitts I
M. o. sclateri
Martinique I
Myiarchus nugator (Grenada Flycatcher)
Lesser Antilles Is
**Myiarchus yucatanensis (Yucatan
Flycatcher)**
M. y. yucatanensis
Yucatan peninsula, Guatemala, Belize
M. y. lanyoni
Cozumel I
Myiarchus stolidus (Stolid Flycatcher)
M. s. dominicensis
Hispaniola
M. s. stolidus
Jamaica

Myiarchus antillarum (Peurto Rican Flycatcher)
Puerto Rico
Myiarchus sagrae (La Sagra's Flycatcher)
M. s. sagrae
Cuba, Grand Cayman Is
M. s. lucaysiensis
Bahama Is
Myiarchus swainsoni (Swainson's Flycatcher)
M. s. swainsoni
E Paraguay, NE Argentina » E Colombia, N Venezuela
M. s. phaeonotus
S Guyana, S Venezuela
M. s. amazonus
NE Brazil
M. s. pelzelni
E Peru, SE Brazil, N Bolivia
M. s. ferocior
SE Bolivia, N Argentina » SE Colombia
Myiarchus crinitus (Great Crested Flycatcher)
E Canada, E USA » Mexico, Central America
Myiarchus cinerascens (Ash-throated Flycatcher)
M. c. cinerascens
W USA, W Mexico » Guatemala, NW Costa Rica
M. c. pertinax
Baja California
Myiarchus tuberculifer (Olivaceous Flycatcher)
M. t. olivascens
SW USA, W Mexico
M. t. tresmariae
Tres Marias Is
M. t. lawrencei
E & S Mexico
M. t. querulus
SW Mexico
M. t. platyrhynchus
SE Mexico
M. t. connectens
Guatemala to N Nicaragua
M. t. littoralis
Pacific coast from SE Honduras to Costa Rica
M. t. nigricapillus
SE Nicaragua, Costa Rica
M. t. bangsi
SW Costa Rica, W Panama
M. t. brunneiceps
E Panama, W Colombia
M. t. pallidus
N Colombia, W Venezuela

M. t. tuberculifer
Colombia and Surinam to Bolivia and S Brazil
M. t. tricolor
French Guiana, E Brazil
M. t. nigriceps
W Ecuador, W Colombia
M. t. atriceps
C Peru, C Bolivia, NW Argentina
Myiarchus barbirostris (Dusky-capped Flycatcher)
Jamaica
Myiarchus magnirostris (Galapagos Flycatcher)
Galapagos Is

ATTILA
Attila spadiceus (Bright-rumped Attila)
A. s. pacificus
NW Mexico
A. s. cozumelae
Cozumel I
A. s. gaumeri
SE Mexico
A. s. flammulatus
SE Mexico to El Salvador
A. s. citreopygus
Nicaragua to W Panama
A. s. sclateri
E Panama, NW Colombia
A. s. caniceps
N Colombia
A. s. parvirostris
NE Colombia, NW Venezuela
A. s. parambae
W Ecuador, W Colombia
A. s. spadiceus
the Guianas, Trinidad, N Venezuela N Brazil, NE Peru, N Bolivia
A. s. uropygiatus
SE Brazil
Attila bolivianus (Dull-capped Attila)
A. b. nattereri
N Brazil
A. b. bolivianus
SW Brazil, E Bolivia, E Peru
Attila rufus (Grey-hooded Attila)
SE Brazil
Attila citriniventris (Citron-bellied Attila)
Venezuela, Ecuador, N Peru, NW Brazil
Attila cinnamomeus (Cinnamon Attila)
South America
Attila torridus (Ochraceous Attila)
W Ecuador, SW Colombia

PSEUDATTILA
Pseudattila phoenicurus (Rufous-tailed Attila)
Venezuela, Brazil, Paraguay, N Argentina

RHYTIPTERNA

Rhytipterna simplex (Greyish Mourner)
R. s. frederici
N South America
R. s. simplex
SE Brazil
Rhytipterna immunda (Pale-bellied Mourner)
Surinam, French Guiana, SE Colombia,
N Brazil
Rhytipterna holerythra (Rufous Mourner)
R. h. holerythra
Guatemala to Panama, N Colombia
R. h. rosenbergi
W Colombia, NW Ecuador

CASIORNIS
Casiornis rufa (Rufous Casiornis)
E Bolivia, C Brazil, Paraguay, N Argentina
Casiornis fusca (Ash-throated Casiornis)
NE Brazil

LANIOCERA
Laniocera hypopyrra (Cinereous Mourner)
the Guianas, Venezuela, Colombia,
Bolivia, N & W Brazil
Laniocera rufescens (Speckled Mourner)
L. r. rufescens
Guatemala to Panama, W Colombia
L. r. tertia
NW Ecuador, SW Colombia
L. r. griseigula
NC Colombia

NESOTRICCUS
Nesotriccus ridgwayi (Cocos I Flycatcher)
Cocos I, Panama

DELTARHYNCHUS
Deltarhynchus flammulatus (Flammulated Flycatcher)
SW & S Mexico

NUTTALLORNIS
Nuttallornis borealis (Olive-sided Flycatcher)
W Canada, W USA, W Mexico,
Central America, N South America

CONTOPUS
Contopus virens (Eastern Wood Pewee)
E Canada, E USA » Central America,
N South America
Contopus sordidulus (Western Wood Pewee)
C. s. sordidulus
S Mexico » Colombia, Ecuador
C. s. siccicola
NW USA
C. s. veliei
W Mexico, SW USA » Panama

C. s. saturatus
W North America » N South America
C. s. peninsulae
S Baja California, SE Mexico
C. s. griscomi
Mexico
C. s. amplus
WC North America » N South America
Contopus cinereus (Tropical Pewee)
C. c. cinereus
SE Brazil, N Argentina, Paraguay
C. c. pallescens
S Brazil, N Paraguay
C. c. surinamensis
the Guianas, S Venezuela, N Brazil
C. c. bogotensis
Trinidad, N Venezuela, N Colombia
C. c. punensis
SW Ecuador, Peru
C. c. rhizophorus
W Costa Rica
C. c. brachytarsus
SE Mexico to Panama
C. c. aithalodes
Coiba I, Panama
Contopus albogularis (White-throated Pewee)
French Guiana, Surinam
Contopus nigrescens (Blackish Pewee)
C. n. nigrescens
E Ecuador
C. n. canescens
NE Peru
Contopus fumigatus (Smoke-coloured Pewee)
C. f. lugubris
Costa Rica, W Panama
C. f. cineraceus
N Venezuela
C. f. duidae
SE Venezuela
C. f. roraimae
SE Venezuela
C. f. ardosiacus
NE Peru, E Ecuador, Colombia,
NW Venezuela
C. f. zarumae
W Ecuador, NW Peru
C. f. fumigatus
SE Peru, Bolivia
C. f. brachyrhynchus
NW Argentina
Contopus pertinax (Greater Pewee)
C. p. pertinax
C & S Mexico, Guatemala, Belize

C. p. pallidiventris
S Arizona, N Mexico » Guatemala
C. p. minor
Nicaragua, Honduras, Belize
Contopus caribaeus (Greater Antillean Pewee)
C. c. caribaeus
Cuba
C. c. morenoi
S Cuba
C. c. nerlyi
islands off SC Cuba
C. c. tacitus
Gonave I
C. c. bahamensis
Bahama Is
C. c. hispaniolensis
Hispaniola
C. c. pallidus
Jamaica
Contopus latirostris (Lesser Antillean Pewee)
C. l. latirostris
St Lucia I
C. l. brunneicapillus
Domenica I, Guadelupe I, Martinique I
C. l. blancoi
Puerto Rico
Contopus ochraceus (Ochraceous Pewee)
Costa Rica, W Panama

EMPIDONAX
Empidonax flaviventris (Yellow-bellied Flycatcher)
S Canada, N USA » S Mexico,
Central America
Empidonax virescens (Acadian Flycatcher)
E USA, E Mexico » Central America,
Colombia, W Ecuador
Empidonax traillii (Traill's Flycatcher)
Canada, USA » Mexico, Central America,
N South America
Empidonax alnorum (Alder Flycatcher)
E Canada, E USA » Central America
& South America
Empidonax minimus (Least Flycatcher)
E Canada, E USA » S Mexico,
Central America, NW South America
Empidonax hammondii (Hammond's Flycatcher)
W Canada, W USA » Mexico, Guatemala
Empidonax oberholseri (Wright's Flycatcher)
W USA, Mexico
Empidonax wrightii (Grey Flycatcher)
W USA, California » Mexico

Empidonax affinis (Pine Flycatcher)
E. a. pulverius
NW Mexico
E. a. trepidus
NE Mexico, Guatemala
E. a. affinis
C Mexico
E. a. bairdi
C & S Mexico
E. a. vigensis
E Mexico
Empidonax difficilis (Western Flycatcher)
E. d. difficilis
W Canada, W USA, NW Mexico
E. d. cineritus
Baja (California)
E. d. insulicola
Channel Is, S California
E. d. hellmayri
N Mexico
E. d. occidentalis
S & C Mexico
Empidonax flavescens (Yellowish Flycatcher)
E. f. dwighti
S Mexico
E. f. imperturbatus
S Mexico
E. f. salvini
SE Mexico to Nicaragua
E. f. flavescens
Costa Rica, W Panama
Empidonax euleri (Euler's Flycatcher)
E. a. euleri
N Peru, Brazil, Uruguay, Paraguay,
NE Argentina
E. e. argentinus
S Peru, W Paraguay, NW Argentina
E. e. bolivianus
NW & E Bolivia
Empidonax lawrencei (Lawrence's Flycatcher)
E. l. lawrencei
Trinidad, Venezuela, Surinam, N Brazil,
N Peru
E. l. johnstonei
Grenada I
Empidonax griseipectus (Grey-breasted Flycatcher)
SW Ecuador, NW Peru
Empidonax albigularis (White-throated Flycatcher)
E. a. timidus
NW Mexico
E. a. albigularis
C & S Mexico, Guatemala, Honduras

E. a. australis
Nicaragua to Panama
Empidonax atriceps (Black-capped Flycatcher)
Costa Rica, W Panama
Empidonax fulvifrons (Buff-breasted Flycatcher)
E. f. pygmaeus
SW USA, W Mexico
E. f. fulvifrons
NE Mexico
E. f. rubicundus
C & S Mexico
E. f. fusciceps
SE Mexico, Guatemala
E. f. brodkorbi
S Oaxaca
E. f. inexpectatus
SC Honduras

CNEMOTRICCUS
Cnemotriccus fuscatus (Fuscous Flycatcher)
C. f. cabanisi
Trinidad, Tobago I, Venezuela, Colombia,
C. f. fuscatior
SW Venezuela, N Brazil, E Peru
C. f. duidae
SE Venezuela
C. f. fumosus
the Guianas, N Brazil
C. f. bimaculatus
W & C Brazil, E Bolivia, Paraguay, N Argentina
C. f. beniensis
N Bolivia
C. f. fuscatus
SE Brazil, N Argentina

MITREPHANES
Mitrephanes phaeocercus (Tufted Flycatcher)
M. p. tenuirostris
W Mexico
M. p. phaeocercus
S & E Mexico to Honduras
M. p. hidalgensis
C Mexico
M. p. burleighi
Guerrero, SW Oaxaca
M. p. nicaraguae
S Mexico to Nicaragua
M. p. aurantiiventris
Costa Rica, W Panama
M. p. vividus
C Panama

M. p. eminulus
E Panama, W Colombia
M. p. berlepschi
S Colombia, NW Ecuador
M. p. olivaceus
E Peru, Bolivia

XENOTRICCUS
Xenotriccus callizonus (Belted Flycatcher)
Mexico

AECHMOLOPHUS
Aechmolophus mexicanus (Pileated Flycatcher)
S Mexico

TERENOTRICCUS
Terenotriccus erythrurus (Ruddy-tailed Flycatcher)
T. e. fulvigularis
Guatemala to Panama, Colombia, Venezuela
T. e. signatus
C & S Colombia to NE Peru
T. e. venezuelensis
E Colombia, W Venezuela, NW Brazil
T. e. brunneifrons
SW Brail, E Peru, N Bolivia
T. e. erythrurus
the Guianas, S Venezuela, N Brazil
T. e. amazonus
C Brazil
T. e. hellmayri
N Brazil

APHANOTRICCUS
Aphanotriccus capitalis (Tawny-chested Flycatcher)
Nicaragua, Costa Rica
Aphanotriccus audax (Black-billed Flycatcher)
Panama, NW Colombia

MYIOBIUS
Myiobius villosus (Tawny-breasted Flycatcher)
M. v. villosus
E Panama, Colombia, W Ecuador
M. v. schaeferi
NW Venezuela, NE Colombia
M. v. clarus
E Ecuador
M. v. peruvianus
SE Peru, W Bolivia

Myiobius barbatus (Whiskered Flycatcher)
the Guianas, E Venezuela, SE Colombia, E Ecuador, N Brazil

Myiobius sulphureipygius (Sulphur-rumped Flycatcher)
  M. s. sulphureipygius
    S Mexico to Honduras
  M. s. aureatus
    S Honduras to Panama, W Colombia,
      W Ecuador
  M. s. amazonicus
    W Brazil, E Peru
  M. s. insignis
    NE Brazil
  M. s. mastacalis
    E Brazil
  M. s. semiflavus
    E Colombia
Myiobius atricaudus (Black-tailed Flycatcher)
  M. a. atricaudus
    SW Costa Rica, Panama, W Colombia
  M. a. portovelae
    W Ecuador, N Peru
  M. a. modestus
    E Venezuela
  M. a. adjacens
    S Colombia, E Ecuador, E Peru, W Brazil
  M. a. connectens
    NE Brazil
  M. a. snethlagei
    NE Brazil
  M. a. ridgwayi
    SE Brazil

MYIOTRICCUS
Myiotriccus ornatus (Ornate Flycatcher)
  M. o. ornatus
    C Colombia
  M. o. stellatus
    W Colombia, W Ecuador
  M. o. phoenicurus
    SE Colombia, E Ecuador, N Peru
  M. o. aureiventris
    S Peru

PYRRHOMYIAS
Pyrrhomyias cinnamomea (Cinnamon Flycatcher)
  P. c. assimilis
    NW Colombia
  P. c. pyrrhoptera
    Colombia, Venezuela, Ecuador, N Peru
  P. c. vieillotioides
    Venezuela
  P. c. spadix
    NE Venezuela
  P.c. pariae
    NE Venezuela
  P. c. cinnamomea
    Bolivia, Peru, NW Argentina

Myiophobus flavicans (Flavescent Flycatcher)
  M. f. flavicans
    Colombia, Ecuador, N Peru
  M. f. perijanus
    NW Venezuela
  M. f. venezuelanus
    N Venezuela
  M. f. caripensis
    NE Venezuela
  M. f. superciliosus
    Peru
Myiophobus phoenicomitra (Orange-crested Flycatcher)
  M. p. litae
    NW Ecuador, W Colombia
  M. p. phoenicomitra
    E Ecuador, N Peru
Myiophobus cryptoxanthus (Olive-crested Flycatcher)
    E Ecuador, E Peru
Myiophobus inornatus (Unadorned Flycatcher)
    Peru, Bolivia
Myiophobus pulcher (Handsome Flycatcher)
  M. p. pulcher
    W Colombia, W Ecuador
  M. p. bellus
    E Colombia, E Ecuador
  M. p. oblitus
    SE Peru
Myiophobus lintoni (Orange-banded Flycatcher)
    SE Ecuador
Myiophobus ochraceiventris (Ochraceous-breasted Flycatcher)
    C Peru, NW Bolivia
Myiophobus fasciatus (Bran-coloured Flycatcher)
  M. f. furfurosus
    SW Costa Rica, Panama
  M. f. fasciatus
    the Guianas, Trinidad, N Venezuela
      Colombia
  M. f. crypterythrus
    S Colombia, W Ecuador, N Peru
  M. f. saturatus
    E Peru
  M. f. rufescens
    W Peru, N Chile
  M. f. auriceps
    SE Peru, N & E Bolivia, N Argentina,
      W Paraguay
  M. f. flammiceps
    Brazil, Bolivia, Uruguay, Paraguay,
      N Argentina

Myiophobus roraimae (Roraiman Flycatcher)
Guyana

HIRUNDINEA
Hirundinea ferruginea (Cliff Flycatcher)
H. f. ferruginea
Guyana, French Guiana, N Brazil
H. f. sclateri
E Colombia, Peru
H. f. bellicosa
S Brazil, Paraguay, NE Argentina
H. f. pallidior
Bolivia, NW Argentina

ONYCHORHYNCHUS
Onychorhynchus coronatus (Amazonian Royal Flycatcher)
O. c. castelnaudi
Western Amazonia
O. c. coronatus
E Venezuela, the Guianas, N Brazil
O. c. occidentalis
W Ecuador
O. c. swainsoni
SE Brazil
Onychorhynchus mexicanus (Northern Royal Flycatcher)
O. m. mexicanus
S Mexico to E Panama
O. m. fraterculus
N Colombia, W Venezuela

PLATYRINCHINAE

PLATYRINCHUS
Platyrinchus platyrhynchos (White crested Spadebill)
P. p. platyrhynchos
S Venezuela, the Guianas, N Brazil
P. p. senex
E Ecuador, E Peru, NW Bolivia
P. p. nattereri
W Brazil
P. p. amazonicus
E Brazil
Platyrinchus leucoryphus (Russet-winged Spadebill)
SE Brazil, E Paraguay
Platyrinchus mystaceus (White-throated Spadebill)
P. m. neglectus
E Costa Rica to E Colombia
P. m. perijanus
NW Venezuela
P. m. insularis
Trinidad, N Venezuela
P. m. imatacae
E Venezuela

P. m. ventralis
S Venezuela
P. m. duidae
SE Venezuela, N Brazil
P. m. ptaritepui
SE Venezuela
P. m. albogularis
W Ecuador, W Colombia
P. m. zamorae
E Ecuador, N Peru
P. m. mystaceus
E Brazil, Paraguay, N Argentina
P. m. partridgei
C Bolivia
P. m. bifasciatus
SW Brazil
P. m. cancromus
E Brazil
P. m. niveigularis
NE Brazil
Platyrinchus cancrominus (Mexican Spadebill)
P. c. cancrominus
S Mexico to E Nicaragua
P. c. timothei
SE Mexico to N Guatemala
P. c. dilutus
El Salvador to NW Costa Rica
Platyrinchus coronatus (Golden-crowned Spadebill)
P. c. superciliaris
Nicaragua to W Ecuador
P. c. gumia
the Guianas, N Brazil
P. c. coronatus
W Amazonia
Platyrinchus saturatus (Cinnamon-crested Spadebill)
P. s. saturatus
S Venezuela, the Guianas, N Brazil
P. s. pallidiventris
C Brazil
Platyrinchus flavigularis (Yellow-throated Spadebill)
P. f. flavigularis
Colombia, Peru
P. f. vividus
W Venezuela

CNIPODECTES
Cnipodectes subbrunneus (Brownish Flycatcher)
C. s. subbrunneus
W Ecuador, W Colombia
C. s. panamensis
E Panama, N Colombia

C. s. minor
SE Colombia, E Peru, W Brazil

Tolmomyias sulphurescens (Yellow-olive Flycatcher)

T. s. cinereiceps
S Mexico to Costa Rica

T. s. flavoolivaceus
Panama

T. s. berlepschi
Trinidad

T. s. exortivus
N Venezuela, N Colombia

T. s. asemus
Colombia

T. s. confusus
C Colombia, SW Venezuela, NE Ecuador

T. s. duidae
SE Venezuela, NW Brazil

T. s. cherriei
E Colombia to the Guianas, N Brazil

T. s. peruvianus
SE Ecuador, N Peru

T. s. insignis
NE Peru, W Brazil

T. s. mixtus
NE Brazil

T. s. inornatus
SE Peru

T. s. pallescens
C Brazil to N Argentina

T. s. grisescens
C Paraguay, N Argentina

T. s. sulphurescens
S Brazil, N Argentina

Tolmomyias assimilis (Yellow-margined Flycatcher)

T. a. flavotectus
Costa Rica to NW Ecuador

T. a. neglectus
E Colombia, S Venezuela, NE Brazil

T. a. obscuriceps
S Colombia to NE Peru

T. a. examinatus
SE Venezuela, the Guianas, N Brazil

T. a. assimilis
C Brazil

T. a. clarus
C Peru

T. a. paraensis
NE Brazil

T. a. calamae
N Bolivia, SW Brazil

Tolmomyias poliocephalus (Grey-crowned Flycatcher)

T. p. poliocephalus
W Amazonia

T. p. klagesi
S Venezuela

T. p. sclateri
the Guianas, N Brazil

Tolmomyias flaviventris (Yellow-breasted Flycatcher)

T. f. aurulentus
N Colombia, N Venezuela

T. f. collingwoodi
C & E Colombia to Guyana, N Brazil, Trinidad

T. f. dissors
NE Brazil, SE Venezuela

T. f. viridiceps
SE Colombia, E Ecuador, E Peru

T. f. borbae
W Brazil

T. f. zimmeri
NC Peru

T. f. subsimilis
SE Peru, NW Bolivia, SW Brazil

T. f. flaviventris
E Brazil

Rhynchocyclus olivaceus (Olivaceus Flatbill)

R. o. bardus
E Panama, N Colombia

R. o. mirus
NW Colombia

R. o. tamborensis
Colombia

R. o. flavus
NW Colombia, N Venezuela

R. o. aequinoctialis
S Colombia, E Ecuador, E Peru, NC Bolivia

R. o. guianensis
N & NW Amazonia

R. o. sordidus
C Brazil

R. o. olivaceus
SE Brazil

Rhynchocyclus brevirostris (Eye-ringed Flatbill)

R. b. brevirostris
S Mexico to W Panama

R. b. pallidus
S Mexico

R. b. hellmayri
E Panama, N Colombia

R. b. pacificus
NW Ecuador, W Colombia

Rhynchocyclus fulvipectus (Fulvous-breasted Flatbill)
Colombia, E Ecuador, SE Peru

Ramphotrigon ruficauda (Rufous-tailed Flatbill)
N Amazonia

Ramphotrigon fuscicauda (Dusky-tailed Flatbill)
E Ecuador, S Colombia, E Peru

Ramphotrigon megacephala (Large-headed Flatbill)

R. m. pectoralis
S Colombia, S Venezuela

R. m. venezuelensis
W Venezuela

R. m. boliviana
SE Peru, W Brazil, N Bolivia

R. m. megacephala
SE Brazil, Paraguay, N Argentina

EUSCARTHMINAE

TODIROSTRUM

Todirostrum nigriceps (Black-headed Tody Tyrant)
Costa Rica, Panama, N Colombia, W Ecuador

Todirostrum chrysocrotaphum (Painted Tody Tyrant)

T. c. guttatum
SW Venezuela, Colombia, NW Brazil, N Peru

T. c. pictum
The Guianas, N Brazil

T. c. neglectum
E Peru, N Bolivia, SW Brazil

T. c. similis
NE Brazil

T. c. illigeri
NE Brazil

T. c. chrysocrotaphum
E Peru, N Bolivia, W Brazil

Todirostrum calopterum (Golden-winged Tody Tyrant)

T. c. calopterum
S Colombia, E Ecuador

T. c. pulchellum
SE Peru

Todirostrum poliocephalum (Grey-headed Tody Tyrant)
SE Brazil

Todirostrum cinereum (Common Tody Tyrant)

T. c. virididorsale
SC Mexico

T. c. finitimum
S Mexico to Panama

T. c. wetmorei
C & E Costa Rica, Panama

T. c. sclateri
SW Colombia, W Ecuador, NW Peru

T. c. viridanum
NW Venezuela

T. c. cinereum
the Guianas, N Brazil, S Venezuela, S Colombia

T. c. peruanum
E Ecuador, N & E Peru

T. c. coloreum
C Brazil, E Bolivia

T. c. cearae
E Brazil

Todirostrum maculatum (Spotted Tody Tyrant)

T. m. amacurense
NE Venezuela, Guyana, Trinidad

T. m. maculatum
E Venezuela, the Guianas, N Brazil

T. m. signatum
E Ecuador, E Peru, W Brazil

T. m. diversum
WC Brazil

T. m. annectens
C Brazil

Todirostrum fumifrons (Smoky-fronted Tody Tyrant)

T. f. fumifrons
NE Brazil

T. f. penardi
French Guiana, Surinam

Todirostrum senex (Plumbeous-crowned Tody Tyrant)
C Brazil

Todirostrum capitale (Black and White Tody Tyrant)

T. c. capitale
SE Colombia, E Ecuador, NE Peru

T. c. tricolor
C Brazil, SE Peru

Todirostrum russatum (Ruddy Tody Tyrant)
SE Venezuela, NE Brazil

Todirostrum plumbeiceps (Ochre-faced Tody Tyrant)

T. p. obscurum
SE Peru, N Bolivia

T. p. viridiceps
Bolivia, NW Argentina

T. p. plumbeiceps
SE Brazil, Paraguay, NE Argentina

T. p. cinereipectum
SC Brazil

Todirostrum latirostre (Rusty-fronted Tody Tyrant)

T. l. mituense
Colombia

T. l. caniceps
SE Colombia, E Ecuador, E Peru

T. l. latirostre
C Brazil
T. l. mixtum
SE Peru
T. l. ochropterum
S Brazil, SE Bolivia
T. l. austroriparium
Santarem, Brazil
T. l. senectum
Lower Amazon, Brazil
Todirostrum sylvia (Slate-headed Tody Tyrant)
T. s. schistaceiceps
S Mexico to Panama
T. s. superciliare
N Colombia
T. s. griseolum
N Venezuela
T. s. sylvia
Guyana, French Guiana, N Brazil
T. s. schulzi
NE Brazil

CERATOTRICCUS
Ceratotriccus furcatus (Fork-tailed Pygmy Tyrant)
SE Brazil

ONCOSTOMA
Oncostoma olivaceum (Southern Bentbill)
E Panama, N Colombia
Oncostoma cinereigulare (Northern Bentbill)
O. c. pacifica
W Mexico
O. c. cinereigulare
S Mexico to W Panama

IDIOPTILON
Idioptilon nidipendulum (Hangnest Tody Tyrant)
I. n. nidipendulum
E Brazil
I. n. paulistus
SE Brazil
Idioptilon rufigulare (Buff-throated Tody Tyrant)
C & SE Peru, NW Bolivia
Idioptilon striaticolle (Stripe-necked Tody Tyrant)
I. s. griseiceps
N Brazil
I. s. iohannis
W Amazonia
I. s. striaticolle
C & E Brazil, N Bolivia, N Peru, E Colombia
Idioptilon spodiops (Yungas Tody Tyrant)
NW Bolivia

Idioptilon aenigma (Zimmer's Tody Tyrant)
Brazil
Idioptilon inornatum (Pelzeln's Tody Tyrant)
NW Brazil
Idioptilon mirandae (Buff-breasted Tody Tyrant)
I. m. mirandae
NE Brazil
I. m. kaempferi
Santa Caterina (Brazil)
Idioptilon margaritaceiventer (Pearly-vented Tody Tyrant)
I. m. impiger
N Venezuela, N Colombia
I. m. septentrionalis
E Colombia, W Venezuela
I. m. duidae
SE Venezuela
I. m. breweri
Cerro Jaua (S Venezuela)
I. m. wuchereri
NE Brazil
I. m. margaritaceiventer
S Peru, E Bolivia, SW Brazil, Paraguay, N Argentina
I. m. auyantepui
SE Venezuela
Idioptilon granadense (Black-throated Tody Tyrant)
I. g. granadense
Colombia, NE Ecuador
I. g. intense
NW Venezuela
I. g. pyrrhops
S Ecuador, N Peru
I. g. andinum
E & C Colombia, W Venezuela
I. g. lehmanni
NW Colombia
I. g. federalis
N Venezuela
I. g. caesius
SE Peru
Idioptilon zosterops (White-eyed Tody Tyrant)
I. z. zosterops
NW Brazil, Venezuela, E Ecuador, SE Colombia
I. z. flaviviridis
N Peru
I. z. griseipectus
SE Peru, N Brazil
I. z. naumburgae
E Brazil

Idioptilon orbitatum (Olivaceous Tody Tyrant)
SE Brazil

MICROCOCHLEARIUS
Microcochlearius josephinae (Boat-billed Tody Tyrant)
Guyana, NE Brazil

SNETHLAGEA
Snethlagea minor (Snethlage's Tody Tyrant)
S. m. minor
N Brazil
S. m. pallens
W Brazil
S. m. minima
C Brazil

POECILOTRICCUS
Poecilotriccus ruficeps (Rufous-crowned Tody Tyrant)
P. r. melanomystax
C Colombia
P. r. ruficeps
E Ecuador, S Colombia, SW Venezeula
P. r. rufigenis
W Ecuador, W Colombia
P. r. peruvianus
NW Peru

TAENIOTRICCUS
Taeniotriccus andrei (Black-chested Tyrant)
T. a. andrei
SE Venezuela, N Brazil
T. a. klagesi
Rio Tapajoz (Brazil)

LOPHOTRICCUS
Lophotriccus pileatus (Scale-crested Pygmy Tyrant)
L. p. luteiventris
Costa Rica, W Panama
L. p. hesperius
W Andes of Colombia
L. p. sanctaeluciae
NE Colombia, N coast of Venezuela
L. p. squamaecrista
S & C Colombia, W Ecuador, W Venezuela
L. p. pileatus
Peru, E Ecuador
L. p. hypochlorus
SE Peru
Lophotriccus vitiosus (Double-banded Pygmy Tyrant)
L. v. affinis
SW Colombia to NE Peru, NW Brazil
L. v. guianensis
SC Colombia, the Guianas, NE Brazil

L. v. vitiosus
E Peru
L. v. congener
NW Brazil
Lophotriccus eulophotes (Long-crested Pygmy Tyrant)
W Brazil, Peru

COLOPTERYX
Colopteryx galeatus (Helmeted Pygmy Tyrant)
the Guianas, N Brazil, Venezuela

ATALOTRICCUS
Atalotriccus pilaris (Pale-eyed Pygmy Tyrant)
A. p. wilcoxi
W Panama
A. p. pilaris
W Venezuela, N & E Colombia
A. p. venezuelensis
N Venezuela
A. p. griseiceps
S Venezuela, W Guyana

MYIORNIS
Myiornis auricularis (Eared Pygmy Tyran)
SE Brazil, N Argentina
Myiornis ecaudatus (Short-tailed Pygmy Tyrant)
M. e. miserabilis
C Colombia, Trinidad, Guyana, Venezue Surinam
M. e. ecaudatus
E Peru & Bolivia
M. e. atricapillus
E Costa Rica to NW Ecuador
Myiornis albiventris (White-bellied Pygmy Tyrant)
C Peru

PSEUDOTRICCUS
Pseudotriccus pelzelni (Bronze-olive Pygmy Tyrant)
P. p. berlepschi
E Panama
P. p. annectens
W Colombia, W Ecuador
P. p. pelzelni
E Colombia, E Ecuador
P. p. peruvianus
E Peru
Pseudotriccus simplex (Hazel-fronted Pygmy Tyrant)
Bolivia, SE Peru
Pseudotriccus ruficeps (Rufous-headed Pygmy Tyrant)
Colombia to NW Bolivia

EMITRICCUS
Hemitriccus diops (Drab-breasted Pygmy Tyrant)
  SE Brazil, Paraguay
Hemitriccus obsoletus (Brown-breasted Pygmy Tyrant)
  H. o. obsoletus
    SE Brazil
  H. o. zimmeri
    SE Brazil
Hemitriccus flammulatus (Flammulated Pygmy Tyrant)
  H. f. flammulatus
    Peru, Bolivia, W Brazil
  H. f. olivascens
    E Bolivia

OGONOTRICCUS
Pogonotriccus eximius (Southern Bristle Tyrant)
  SE Brazil, Paraguay, N Argentina
Pogonotriccus ophthalmicus (Marble-faced Bristle Tyrant)
  P. o. ophthalmicus
    NW Venezuela, Colombia, Ecuador, Peru
  P. o. ottonis
    SE Peru, W Bolivia
  P. o. purus
    coast of Venezuela
Pogonotriccus gualaquizae (Ecuadorean Bristle Tyrant)
  E Ecuador, N Peru
Pogonotriccus poecilotis (Variegated Bristle Tyrant)
  P. p. poecilotis
    N Colombia to Ecuador
  P. p. pifanoi
    NE Colombia, NW Venezuela
Pogonotriccus orbitalis (Spectacled Bristle Tyrant)
  E Ecuador, Peru, S Colombia
Pogonotriccus venezuelanus (Venezuelan Bristle Tyrant)
  NW Venezuela
Pogonotriccus flaviventris (Yellow-bellied Bristle Tyrant)
  NW Venezuela

EPTOTRICCUS
Leptotriccus sylviolus (Bay-ringed Tyrannulet)
  SE Brazil, Paraguay

HYLLOSCARTES
Phylloscartes flavovirens (Yellow-green Tyrannulet)
  Panama
Phylloscartes virescens (Olive-green Tyrannulet)
  the Guianas

Phylloscartes ventralis (Mottle-cheeked Tyrannulet)
  P. v. angustirostris
    Peru, Bolivia, NW Argentina
  P. v. tucumanus
    NW Argentina
  P. v. ventralis
    SE Brazil, Uruguay, Paraguay, NE Argentina
Phylloscartes chapmani (Chapman's Tyrannulet)
  P. c. chapmani
    S Venezuela
  P. c. duidae
    SE Venezuela
Phylloscartes nigrifrons (Black-fronted Tyrannulet)
  S Venezuela
Phylloscartes oustaleti (Oustalet's Tyrannulet)
  SE Brazil, Uruguay, Paraguay, NE Argentina
Phylloscartes difficilis (Ihering's Tyrannulet)
  SE Brazil
Phylloscartes paulistus (Sao Paulo Tryrannulet)
  SE Brazil, Paraguay
Phylloscartes superciliaris (Rufous-browed Tyrannulet)
  P. s. superciliaris
    Costa Rica to W Panama
  P. s. griseocapillus
    NW Venezuela
  P. s. palloris
    E Panama
Phylloscartes roquettei (Minas Geraes Tyrannulet)
  Brazil

CAPSIEMPIS
Capsiempis flaveola (Yellow Tyrannulet)
  C. f. semiflava
    Nicaragua to Panama
  C. f. cerula
    Venezuela, Colombia, Ecuador
  C. f. amazona
    French Guiana, N Brazil
  C. f. leucophrys
    Colombia, W Venezuela
  C. f. magnirostris
    SW Ecuador
  C. f. flaveola
    S Colombia, SE Brazil, E Bolivia, Paraguay

Euscarthmus meloryphus (Tawny-crowned Pygmy Tyrant)
E. m. padulus
Venezuela, Colombia
E. m. fulviceps
W Ecuador, W Peru
E. m. meloryphus
Brazil, E Bolivia, Paraguay, N Argentina
Euscarthmus rufomarginatus (Rufous-sided Pygmy Tyrant)
E. r. rufomarginatus
Brazil
E. r. savannophilus
Surinam

PSEUDOCOLOPTERYX
Pseudocolopteryx dinellianus (Dinelli's Doradito)
NW Argentina, SE Bolivia, W Paraguay
Pseudocolopteryx sclateri (Crested Doradito)
Trinidad, Guyana, Brazil, Paraguay, E Argentina
Pseudocolopteryx acutipennis (Subtropical Doradito)
Colombia, Ecuador, Peru, Bolivia, W Argentina
Pseudocolopteryx flaviventris (Warbling Doradito)
Uruguay, C Chile, N Argentina, S Brazil

POLYSTICTUS
Polystictus pectoralis (Bearded Tachuri)
P. p. bogotensis
Colombia
P. p. brevipennis
Guyana, S Venezuela, N Brazil
P. p. pectoralis
E Bolivia, SW Brazil, Uruguay, Paraguay, N Argentina
Polystictus superciliaris (Grey-backed Tachuri)
SE Brazil

CULICIVORA
Culicivora caudacuta (Sharp-tailed Tyrant)
S Brazil, E Bolivia, Paraguay, NE Argentina

SERPOPHAGINAE

TACHURIS
Tachuris rubigastra (Many-coloured Rush Tyrant)
T. r. libertatis
W Peru
T. r. alticola
Peru, W Bolivia, NW Argentina
T. r. rubigastra
SE Brazil, Paraguay, Uruguay, Chile, N Argentina

T. r. loaensis
N Chile

ANAIRETES
Anairetes parulus (Tufted Tit Tyrant)
A. p. aequatorialis
S Colombia, Ecuador, Peru, Bolivia, NW Argentina
A. p. patagonicus
C Argentina
A. p. parulus
SC Chile, W Argentina
A. p. lippus
S Chile
Anairetes fernandezianus (Juan Fernande Tit Tyrant)
Masatierra I
Anairetes flavirostris (Yellow-billed Tit Tyrant)
A. f. huancabambae
NW Peru
A. f. arequipae
SW Peru, NW Chile
A. f. cuzcoensis
SE Peru
A. f. flavirostris
W Peru, Bolivia, N Chile, W Argentina
Anairetes reguloides (Pied-crested Tit Tyrant)
A. r. nigrocristatus
N Peru
A. r. albiventris
W Peru
A. r. reguloides
SW Peru, NW Chile
Anairetes alpinus (Ash-breasted Tit Tyrant)
Peru, NW Bolivia

UROMYIAS
Uromyias agilis (Agile Tit Tyrant)
Colombia, Ecuador
Uromyias agraphia (Unstreaked Tit Tyran
U. a. agraphia
SE Peru
U. a. squamigera
E Peru

STIGMATURA
Stigmatura napensis (Lesser Wagtail Tyrant)
S. n. napensis
SE Colombia, NE Peru, W Brazil
S. n. bahiae
NE Brazil
Stigmatura budytoides (Greater Wagtail Tyrant)
S. b. budytoides
NC Bolivia

S. b. inzonata
SE Bolivia, N Argentina
S. b. flavocinerea
C Argentina
S. b. gracilis
Brazil

SERPOPHAGA

Serpophaga hypoleuca (River Tyrannulet)
S. h. venezuelana
N Venezuela
S. h. hypoleuca
SE Colombia, E Peru, Venezuela
S. h. pallida
EC Brazil
Serpophaga cinerea (Torrent Tyrannulet)
S. c. grisea
Costa Rica, W Panama
S. c. cana
Colombia, W Venezuela
S. c. cinerea
W Ecuador, W Peru, W Bolivia
**Serpophaga subcristata (White-crested
Tyrannulet)**
S. s. straminea
SC Brazil, Uruguay
S. s. subcristata
Bolivia to E Brazil, Argentina
**Serpophaga munda (White-bellied
Tyrannulet)**
E Bolivia, N Argentina
Serpophaga nigricans (Sooty Tyrannulet)
SE Brazil, Uruguay, Paraguay, N Argentina
**Serpophaga araguayae (Bananal
Tyrannulet)**
Brazil

INEZIA

Inezia subflava (Pale-tipped Tyrannulet)
I. s. intermedia
NW Venezuela, N Colombia
I. s. caudata
the Guianas, Venezuela
I. s. subflava
EC N Brazil
I. s. saturatior
Maracaibo, Venezuela
I. s. obscura
NE Venezuela, NW Brazil
**Inezia tenuirostris (Slender-billed
Tyrannulet)**
N Colombia, NW Venezuela
Inezia inornata (Plain Tyrannulet)
SW Brazil, E Bolivia, W Paraguay, S Peru

MECOCERCULUS

**Mecocerculus leucophrys (White-throated
Tyrannulet)**
M. l. montensis
N Colombia

M. l. nigriceps
N Venezuela
M. l. notatus
W Colombia
M. l. setophagoides
E Colombia
M. l. palliditergum
coast of N Venezuela
M. l. gularis
W Venezuela
M. l. parui
S Venezuela
M. l. rufomarginatus
S Colombia, Ecuador, NW Peru
M. l. roraimae
C Venezuela
M. l. brunneomarginatus
C Peru
M. l. pallidor
W Peru
M. l. leucophrys
SE Peru, NW Argentina
**Mecocerculus poecilocercus (White-
tailed Tyrannulet)**
Colombia, Ecuador, Peru
**Mecocerculus hellmayri (Buff-banded
Tyrannulet)**
SE Peru, Bolivia, Argentina
**Mecocerculus calopterus (Rufous-winged
Tyrannulet)**
W Ecuador, NW Peru
**Mecocerculus minor (Sulphur-bellied
Tyrannulet)**
E Colombia, Venezuela, NW Peru
**Mecocerculus stictopterus (White-banded
Tyrannulet)**
M. s. stictopterus
Colombia, Ecuador, N Peru
M. s. taeniopterus
SE Peru, W Bolivia
M. s. albocaudatus
NW Venezuela

COLORAMPHUS

**Coloramphus parvirostris (Patagonian
Tyrannulet)**
C & S Chile

ELAENIINAE

ELAENIA

**Elaenia flavogaster (Yellow-bellied
Elaenia)**
E. f. subpagana
Pacific coast of S Mexico to Panama
E. f. flavogaster
Trinidad, N South America
E. f. semipagana
W Ecuador, NW Peru

E. f. pallididorsalis
Pearl Is (Panama)
Elaenia martinica (Caribbean Elaenia)
E. m. martinica
Lesser Antilles Is
E. m. chinchorrensis
Great Key I, E Mexico
E. m. barbadensis
Barbados
E. m. riisii
Virgin Is, Antigua I, Curaçao I
E. m. caymanensis
Cayman Is
E. m. cinerescens
St Andrew I, Old Providence I
E. m. remota
Yucatan coast islands
Elaenia spectabilis (Large Elaenia)
E. s. spectabilis
NE Peru, N & C Brazil, W Bolivia,
N Argentina
E. s. ridleyana
Fernando de Noronha I
Elaenia albiceps (White-crested Elaenia)
E. a. griseigularis
Ecuador
E. a. diversa
NC Peru
E. a. urubambae
SE Peru
E. a. albiceps
Bolivia, Brazil
E. a. modesta
Peru, NW Chile
E. a. chilensis
S Chile, SW Argentina
Elaenia parvirostris (Small-billed Elaenia)
C & E South America
Elaenia mesoleuca (Olivaceous Elaenia)
SE Brazil, Paraguay, NE Argentina
Elaenia strepera (Slaty Elaenia)
Colombia, Venezuela, Peru, Bolivia,
NW Argentina
Elaenia gigas (Mottle-backed Elaenia)
C Colombia, E Ecuador, E Peru, NE Bolivia
Elaenia pelzelni (Brownish Elaenia)
W Brazil, NE Peru
Elaenia cristata (Plain-crested Elaenia)
E. c. alticola
S Venezuela, N Brazil
E. c. cristata
French Guiana to E Peru, Venezuela
Elaenia chiriquensis (Lesser Elaenia)
E. c. chiriquensis
SW Costa Rica, Panama
E. c. brachyptera
SW Colombia, NW Ecuador

E. c. albivertex
Trinidad, C & W Northern South America
Elaenia ruficeps (Rufous-crowned Elaenia)
the Guianas, N Brazil, S Venezuela
Elaenia frantzii (Mountain Elaenia)
E. f. browni
N Colombia, N Venezuela
E. f. pudica
E Colombia, W Venezuela
E. f. ultima
Guatemala to Nicaragua
E. f. frantzii
Nicaragua to Panama
Elaenia obscura (Highland Elaenia)
E. o. sordida
SE Brazil, E Paraguay, NE Argentina
E. o. obscura
S Brazil, Peru, Bolivia, Paraguay,
N Argentina
Elaenia dayi (Great Elaenia)
E. d. dayi
Mt Roraima (S Venezuela)
E. d. auyantepui
SE Venezuela
E. d. tyleri
S Venezuela
Elaenia pallatangae (Sierran Elaenia)
E. p. pallatangae
W Colombia, Ecuador
E. p. olivina
S Guyana, S Venezuela
E. p. exsul
Bolivian Andes
E. p. intensa
Peru
Elaenia fallax (Greater Antillean Elaenia)
E. f. fallax
Jamaica
E. f. cherriei
Hispaniola

MYIOPAGIS
Myiopagis gaimardii (Forest Elaenia)
M. g. macilvainii
E Panama, N Colombia
M. g. trinitatis
Trinidad
M. g. bogotensis
E Colombia, N Venezuela
M. g. guianensis
the Guianas, N Brazil
M. g. gaimardii
S Venezuela, Brazil, E Peru, N Bolivia
M. g. subcinereus
EC Brazil
Myiopagis caniceps (Grey Elaenia)
M. c. parambae
W Colombia, NW Ecuador

M. c. cinerea
S Venezuela, E Colombia, E Ecuador,
Peru, NW Brazil
M. c. caniceps
E & S Brazil, Paraguay, N Argentina
M. c. absita
Panama
Myiopagis subplacens (Pacific Elaenia)
SW Ecuador, NW Peru
Myiopagis flavivertex (Yellow-crowned Elaenia)
French Guiana, Surinam, S Venezuela,
N Peru, N Brazil
Myiopagis viridicata (Greenish Elaenia)
M. v. jaliscensis
SW Mexico
M. v. minima
Tres Marias Is
M. v. placens
S Mexico to Honduras
M. v. pacifica
SE Chiapas, Mexico
M. v. accola
Nicaragua to Panama, NW Colombia
M. v. pallens
NW Colombia, N Venezuela
M. v. restricta
N coast of Venezuela
M. v. zuliae
N Venezuela
M. v. implacens
S Colombia, W Ecuador
M. v. viridicata
SE Peru, E Bolivia, Brazil, Paraguay,
N Argentina
Myiopagis cotta (Yellow Elaenia)
Jamaica

SUIRIRI
Suiriri suiriri (Suiriri Flycatcher)
S. s. affinis
C Brazil, Surinam, NW Bolivia
S. s. bahiae
E Brazil
S. s. suiriri
E Bolivia, Brazil, Uruguay, Paraguay,
N Argentina

SUBLEGATUS
Sublegatus modestus (Short-billed Flycatcher)
S. m. atrirostris
Panama to NE Colombia
S. m. obscurior
W Amazonia
S. m. modestus
E Peru to E Brazil, N Argentina

Sublegatus arenarum (Scrub Flycatcher) 335
S. a. arenarum
SW Costa Rica
S. a. pallens
Arub I, Curaçao I, Bonaire I
S. a. tortugensis
Tortuga
S. a. orinocensis
C Venezuela
S. a. glaber
N Venezuela, Trinidad

PHAIOMYIAS
Phaiomyias murina (Mouse-coloured Tyrannulet)
P. m. incomta
Trinidad, the Guianas, Colombia
Venezuela, N Brazil
P. m. tumbezana
SW Ecuador, N Peru
P. m. inflava
W Peru
P. m. maranonica
NC Peru
P. m. wagae
E Peru, W Bolivia
P. m. ignobilis
S Bolivia, Paraguay, NW Argentina
P. m. murina
S Brazil
P. m. eremonoma
Panama
Phaiomyias leucospodia (Grey and White Tyrannulet)
P. l. cinereifrons
SW Ecuador
P. l. leucospodia
NW Peru

CAMPTOSTOMA
Camptostoma obsoletum (Southern Beardless Tyrannulet)
C. o. flaviventre
W Costa Rica, Panama
C. o. orphnum
Coiba I, Afuerita I
C. o. major
Pearl Is (Panama)
C. o. caucae
W Colombia
C. o. bogotensis
C Colombia
C. o. pusillum
N Colombia, NW Venezuela
C. o. napaeum
N Venezuela, the Guianas
N Brazil
C. o. venezuelae
N & C Venezuela, Trinidad

C. o. maranonicum
N Peru

C. o. olivaceum
S Colombia, E Ecuador, NE Peru, W Brazil

C. o. sclateri
W Ecuador, W Peru

C. o. griseum
W Peru

C. o. bolivianum
C Bolivia, NW Argentina

C. o. cinerascens
E Bolivia, E & C Brazil

C. o. obsoletum
SE Brazil, Uruguay, N Argentina

**Camptostoma imberbe (Northern Beard-
less Tyrannulet)**
SW USA, Mexico to NW Costa Rica

XANTHOMYIAS

**Xanthomyias virescens (Greenish
Tyrannulet)**
X. v. urichi
NE Venezuela

X. v. virescens
SE Brazil, Paraguay, NE Argentina

Xanthomyias reiseri (Reiser's Tyrannulet)
NE Brazil

Xanthomyias sclateri (Sclater's Tyrannulet)
X. s. subtropicalis
SE Peru

X. s. sclateri
Bolivia, NW Argentina

PHYLLOMYIAS

**Phyllomyias fasciatus (Planalto
Tyrannulet)**
P. f. cearae
NE Brazil

P. f. virescens
C Brazil

P. f. fasciatus
E Brazil

P. f. brevirostris
S Brazil, Paraguay, NE Argentina

**Phyllomyias griseiceps (Sooty-headed
Tyrannulet)**
P. g. cristatus
E Panama, N Colombia, N Venezuela

P. g. caucae
WC Colombia

P. g. griseiceps
Ecuador

P. g. pallidiceps
NE Brazil, Peru, SE Venezuela

TYRANNISCUS

**Tyranniscus nigrocapillus (Black-capped
Tyrannulet)**
T. n. flavimentum
N Colombia

T. n. nigrocapillus
W Colombia, Ecuador, N Peru

T. n. aureus
W Venezuela

**Tyranniscus uropygialis (Tawny-rumped
Tyrannulet)**
Colombia, Ecuador, Peru, W Bolivia,
Venezuela

**Tyranniscus cinereiceps (Ashy-headed
Tyrannulet)**
Colombia, Ecuador, Peru

Tyranniscus vilissimus (Paltry Tyrannulet
T. v. vilissimus
S Mexico, Guatemala, Honduras

T. v. parvus
Nicaragua to Panama

T. v. tamae
N Colombia

T. v. improbus
N Colombia, W Venezuela

T. v. petersi
N Venezuela

**Tyranniscus bolivianus (Bolivian
Tyrannulet)**
T. b. bolivianus
N Bolivia

T. b. viridissimus
SE Peru

**Tyranniscus cinereicapillus (Red-billed
Tyrannulet)**
C Peru, NE Ecuador

**Tyranniscus gracilipes (Slender-footed
Tyrannulet)**
T. g. acer
S Venezuela, the Guianas, N Brazil

T. g. gracilipes
S Venezuela, S Guyana, N Brazil,
N Bolivia, E Peru

T. g. gilvus
W Brazil, NW Bolivia

**Tyranniscus viridiflavus (Golden-faced
Tyrannulet)**
T. v. minimus
N Colombia

T. v. cumanensis
NE Venezuela

T. v. albigularis
W Ecuador, SW Colombia

T. v. flavidifrons
SW Ecuador

T. v. chrysops
N Peru, Ecuador, S Colombia,
W Venezuela

T. v. viridiflavus
C Peru

OREOTRICCUS
Oreotriccus plumbeiceps (Plumbeous-crowned Tyrannulet)
Colombia, Ecuador, Peru
Oreotriccus griseocapillus (Grey-capped Tyrannulet)
SE Brazil

TYRANNULUS
Tyrannulus elatus (Yellow-crowned Tyrannulet)
T. e. panamensis
Panama, W Ecuador, Colombia, W Venezuela
T. e. elatus
E Venezuela, the Guianas, N Brazil, S Colombia, N Peru

ACROCHORDOPUS
Acrochordopus burmeisteri (Rough-legged Tyrannulet)
A. b. zeledoni
Costa Rica, W Panama
A. b. viridiceps
N Venezuela
A. b. wetmorei
NW Venezuela
A. b. bunites
SC Venezuela
A. b. leucogonys
Colombia, Ecuador, Peru
A. b. burmeisteri
SE Brazil, E Bolivia, Paraguay, N Argentina

ORNITHION
Ornithion inerme (White-lored Tyrannulet)
S Venezuela, the Guianas, Ecuador, N Brazil
Ornithion semiflavum (Yellow-bellied Tyrannulet)
S Mexico to Costa Rica
Ornithion brunneicapillum (Brown-capped Tyrannulet)
O. b. brunneicapillum
Costa Rica, Panama, W Colombia, NW Ecuador
O. b. dilutum
NW Venezuela, N Colombia

EPTOPOGON
Leptopogon superciliaris (White-bellied Leptopogon)
L. s. superciliaris
SE Colombia, N Peru
L. s. poliocephalus
N & C Colombia
L. s. hellmayri
Costa Rica to W Panama
L. s. venezuelensis
N Venezuela, N Brazil

L. s. pariae
NE Venezuela, Trinidad
L. s. transandinus
SW Colombia, W Ecuador
L. s. albidiventer
Bolivia, SE Peru
Leptopogon amaurocephalus (Sepia-capped Leptopogon)
L. a. pileatus
S Mexico, Guatemala, Honduras
L. a. faustus
Costa Rica, Panama
L. a. idius
Coiba I
L. a. diversus
N Colombia
L. a. orinocensis
W & SW Venezuela
L. a. obscuritergum
S Venezuela
L. a. peruvianus
N & W Amazonia
L. a. amaurocephalus
SE Brazil, E Bolivia, N Argentina, Paraguay
Leptopogon rufipectus (Rufous-breasted Leptopogon)
L. r. rufipectus
E Ecuador, E Colombia, Peru
L. r. venezuelanus
NE Colombia, NW Venezuela
Leptopogon taczanowskii (Inca Leptopogon)
E Peru

MIONECTES
Mionectes striaticollis (Streak-necked Flycatcher)
M. s. colombianus
Colombia, E Ecuador
M. s. viridiceps
W Ecuador
M. s. palamblae
N Peru
M. s. poliocephalus
N & C Peru
M. s. striaticollis
Bolivia, SE Peru
M. s. selvae
WC Colombia
Mionectes olivaceus (Olive-striped Flycatcher)
M. o. olivaceus
Costa Rica, W Panama
M. o. hederaceus
E Panama, W Colombia, W Ecuador
M. o. galbinus
N Colombia

M. o. pallidus
E Colombia
M. o. venezuelanus
N Venezuela, Trinidad
M. o. fasciaticollis
E Ecuador, E Peru
M. o. meridae
NW Venezuela, NE Colombia

PIPROMORPHA
Pipromorpha oleaginea (Ochre-billed Flycatcher)
P. o. assimilis
S Mexico to Costa Rica
P. o. obscura
El Salvador
P. o. dyscola
W Costa Rica, W Panama
P. o. lutescens
W Panama
P. o. parca
E Panama, N Colombia, NW Venezuela
P. o. chloronota
W Amazonia
P. o. abdominalis
N Venezuela
P. o. pallidiventris
NE Venezuela, Trinidad
P. o. intensa
E Venezuela, Guyana
P. o. dorsalis
SE Venezuela
P. o. pacifica
W Colombia, W Ecuador
P. o. hauxwelli
E Ecuador, NE Peru
P. o. wallacei
N Brazil, the Guianas
P. o. maynana
E Peru
P. o. oleaginea
SE Brazil
Pipromorpha macconnelli (McConnell's Flycatcher)
P. m. macconnelli
Guyana, French Guiana, N Brazil, E Venezuela
P. m. roraimae
S Guyana, S Venezuela
P. m. peruana
C Peru
P. m. amazona
C Brazil, E Bolivia
Pipromorpha rufiventris (Grey-hooded Flycatcher)
SE Brazil, Paraguay, N Argentina

CORYTHOPIS
Corythopis delalandi (Delalande's Antpipit)
E Bolivia, S Brazil, E Paraguay, NE Argentir
Corythopis torquata (Ringed Antpipit)
C. t. sarayacuensis
SE Colombia, E Ecuador, NE Peru
C. t. torquata
C Peru, W Brazil
C. t. anthoides
S Venezuela, Guianas, N & E Brazil
C. t. subtorquata
NE Bolivia

109 OXYRUNCIDAE (SHARPBILL)

OXYRUNCUS
Oxyruncus cristatus (Sharpbill)
O. c. frater
Costa Rica, W Panama
O. c. brooksi
E Panama
O. c. hypoglaucus
Guyana, SE Venezuela
O. c. tocantinsi
C Brazil
O. c. cristatus
SE Brazil, Paraguay

110 PHYTOTOMIDAE (PLANTCUTTERS)

PHYTOTOMA
Phytotoma rara (Chilean Plantcutter)
S Chile, S Argentina, Falkland Is
Phytotoma rutila (Red-breasted Plant-cutter)
P. r. angustirostris
NW Argentina, Bolivia
P. r. rutila
N Argentina, Uruguay, Paraguay
Phytotoma raimondii (Peruvian Plantcutter
NW Peru

111 PITTIDAE (PITTAS)

PITTA
Pitta phayrei (Phayre's Pitta)
P. p. phayrei
Burma, Thailand
P. p. obscura
N Indochina
Pitta nipalensis (Blue-naped Pitta)
P. n. nipalensis
Himalayas to Burma, S China
P. n. hendeei
N Vietnam
Pitta soror (Blue-backed Pitta)
P. s. soror
C Indochina

P. s. tonkinensis
  C China to N Vietnam
P. s. douglasi
  Hainan I
P. s. petersi
  C Vietnam
Pitta oatesi (Fulvous Pitta)
P. o. oatesi
  Burma, Thailand, NW Laos
P. o. castaneiceps
  N Laos, N Vietnam
P. o. bolovenensis
  S Laos
P. o. deborah
  Malaysia
Pitta schneideri (Schneider's Pitta)
  N Sumatra
Pitta caerulea (Giant Pitta)
P. c. caerulea
  Malaysia, Sumatra, S Thailand
P. c. hosei
  Borneo
Pitta kochi (Koch's Pitta)
  N Luzon I
Pitta erythrogaster (Red-breasted Pitta)
P. e. erythrogaster
  Philippine Is
P. e. thompsoni
  Culion I
P. e. propinqua
  Balabac I, Palawan I
P. e. inspeculata
  Taulaut Is
P. e. caeruleitorques
  Gr. Sanghir I
P. e. palliceps
  Sanghir Is
P. e. cyanonota
  Ternate I
P. e. rubrinucha
  Buru I
P. e. celebensis
  N Celebes
P. e. dohertyi
  Sula Is
P. e. piroensis
  Ceram I
P. e. rufiventris
  Obi I to Morotai I, Damar I
P. e. novaehibernicae
  New Ireland
P. e. gazellae
  New Britain
P. e. extima
  New Hanover
P. e. splendida
  Tabar I

P. e. mackloti
  W & S New Guinea, N Queensland
P. e. habenichti
  N New Guinea
P. e. oblita
  SE New Guinea
P. e. loriae
  SE New Guinea
P. e. aruensis
  Aru Is
P. e. finschii
  D'Entrecasteaux Archipelago
P. e. meeki
  Rossel I
P. e. kuehni
  Kei Is
Pitta arcuata (Blue-banded Pitta)
  Borneo
Pitta granatina (Garnet Pitta)
P. g. coccinea
  Malaysia, E Sumatra
P. g. venusta
  W Sumatra
P. g. ussheri
  N Borneo
P. g. granatina
  S Borneo
Pitta cyanea (Blue Pitta)
P. c. cyanea
  Himalayas, Burma, N Thailand
P. c. aurantiaca
  SE Thailand
P. c. willoughbyi
  S Vietnam, S Laos
Pitta ellioti (Elliot's Pitta)
  S Indochina
Pitta guajana (Blue-tailed Pitta)
P. g. irena
  Malaysia, Sumatra
P. g. ripleyi
  S Thailand
P. g bangkae
  Bangka I
P. g. affinis
  W Java
P. g. guajana
  E Java, Bali
P. g. schwaneri
  Borneo
Pitta gurneyi (Gurney's Pitta)
  S Burma, S Thailand
Pitta baudi (Blue-headed Pitta)
  Borneo
Pitta sordida (Hooded Pitta)
P. s. cucullata
  Himalayas to Malaysia, Indochina

P. s. mulleri
  Sumatra, Java, Borneo, S Thailand,
    Malaysia
P. s. abbotti
  Nicobar Is
P. s. bangkana
  Bangka I, Billiton I
P. s. novaeguineae
  New Guinea
P. s. hebetior
  Dampier I
P. s. sanghirana
  Sanghir Is
P. s. forsteni
  Celebes
P. s. goodfellowi
  Aru Is
P. s. mafoorana
  Numfor I
P. s. rosenbergii
  Biak I
P. s. palawanensis
  Balabac I, Palawan I
P. s. sordida
  Philippine Is

Pitta brachyura (Blue-winged Pitta)
P. b. brachyura
  Himalayas, India
P. b. nympha
  E China, NE Asia » Indochina, Borneo

Pitta angolensis (African Pitta)
P. a. pulih
  Sierra Leone to S Cameroun
P. a. angolensis
  Cameroun to N Angola
P. a. longipennis
  Uganda, E Zaire to Transvaal

Pitta reichenowi (Green-breasted Pitta)
  Cameroun to Uganda

Pitta superba (Superb Pitta)
  Admiralty Is

Pitta maxima (Great Pitta)
P. m. maxima
  Batjan I, Halmahera I
P. m. morotaiensis
  Morotai I

Pitta steerei (Steere's Pitta)
P. s. steerei
  Mindanao I
P. s. coelstis
  Bohol I, Leyte I, Samar I

Pitta moluccensis (Moluccan Pitta)
P. m. moluccensis
  S China, Burma » Borneo, Moluccas
P. m. megarhyncha
  coast of Burma, Thailand, Malaysia,
    Sumatra

Pitta versicolor (Noisy Pitta)
P. v. virginalis
  Djampea I
P. v. plesseni
  Kalao tua I
P. v. kalaoensis
  Kalao I
P. v. vigorsii
  Tukangbesi, Tenimber I
P. v. hutzi
  S Nasa Penida I
P. v. concinna
  Lombok I, Sumbawa I, Flores
P. v. everetti
  Alor I
P. v. maria
  Sumba I
P. v. elegans
  Timor I, S Moluccas
P. v. intermedia
  N Queensland
P. v. simillima
  S New Guinea, N Queensland
P. v. versicolor
  S Queensland, New South Wales

Pitta iris (Rainbow Pitta)
  N Northern Territory

Pitta anerythra (Black-faced Pitta)
P. a. anerythra
  Ysabel I
P. a. pallida
  Bougainville I
P. a. nigrifrons
  Choiseul I

112 XENICIDAE (NEW ZEALAND WRENS)

ACANTHISITTA
Acanthisitta chloris (Rifleman)
A. c. granti
  North Island, New Zealand
A. c. chloris
  South Island, New Zealand
A. c. citrina
  SW South I, New Zealand

XENICUS
Xenicus longipes (Bush Wren)
X. l. stokesi
  North Island, New Zealand **e?**
X. l. longipes
  South Island, New Zealand
X. l. variabilis
  SW of Stewart I, New Zealand
Xenicus gilviventris (Rock Wren)
  South Island, New Zealand

113 PHILEPITTIDAE (ASITIES)

PHILEPITTA
Philepitta castanea (Velvet Asity)
  E Madagascar
Philepitta schlegeli (Schlegel's Asity)
  W Madagascar

NEODREPANIS
Neodrepanis coruscans (Wattled False Sunbird)
  E Madagascar
Neodrepanis hypoxantha (Small-billed False Sunbird)
  E Madagascar **e?**

114 MENURIDAE (LYREBIRDS)

MENURA
Menura superba (Superb Lyrebird)
  M. s. edwardi
    E Queensland
  M. s. superba
    New South Wales, Victoria
Menura alberti (Prince Albert's Lyrebird)
  E Queensland, New South Wales

115 ATRICHORNITHIDAE (SCRUBBIRDS)

ATRICHORNIS
Atrichornis clamosus (Western Scrubbird)
  SW Australia
Atrichornis rufescens (Rufous Scrubbird)
  A. r. jacksoni
    SE Queensland
  A. r. rufescens
    NE New South Wales

116 ALAUDIDAE (LARKS)

MIRAFA
Mirafa javanica (Singing Bush Lark)
  M. j. marginata
    Somalia, Uganda, Kenya, Tanzania
  M. j. chadensis
    Senegal to Sudan
  M. j. simplex
    W Arabia
  M. j. cantillans
    N India
  M. j. williamsoni
    C Burma, Thailand, Indochina
  M. j. beaulieui
    S Vietnam
  M. j. philippinensis
    Luzon I, Mindoro I
  M. j. mindanensis
    Mindanao I
  M. j. javanica
    S Borneo, Java, Bali I

  M. j. parva
    Lombok I, Sumbawa I, Sumba I, Flores I
  M. j. timorensis
    Savu Is, Timor I
  M. j. sepikiana
    N New Guinea
  M. j. aliena
    NE New Guinea
  M. j. woodwardi
    WC Australia
  M. j. halli
    NW Australia
  M. j. subrufescens
    NW Australia
  M. j. soderbergi
    W Northern Territory
  M. j. melvillensis
    Melville I
  M. j. rufescens
    E Northern Territory, N Queensland
  M. j. horsfieldii
    C & S Queensland, New South Wales, Victoria
  M. j. secunda
    South Australia
Mirafa hova (Hova Lark)
  Madagascar
Mirafa cordofanica (Kordofan Bush Lark)
  Niger, Chad, W Sudan
Mirafa williamsi (Williams' Lark)
  Kenya
Mirafa cheniana (Southern Singing Bush Lark)
  Rhodesia, Transvaal, Orange Free State, N & E Cape Province
Mirafa albicauda (Northern White-tailed Bush Lark)
  M. a. albicauda
    Chad to Ethiopia and Tanzania
  M. a. rukwensis
    S Tanzania
Mirafa passerina (White-tailed Bush Lark)
  Namibia, Botswana
Mirafa candida (Nyiro Bush Lark)
  Nyiro river, Kenya
Mirafa pulpa (Sagon Bush Lark)
  Sagon river, Ethiopia
Mirafa hypermetra (Red-winged Bush Lark)
  M. h. kathangorensis
    Sudan
  M. h. kidepoensis
    S Sudan, N Uganda
  M. h. gallarum
    S Ethiopia
  M. h. hypermetra
    S Somalia, Kenya, N Tanzania

Mirafa somalica (Somali Long-billed Lark)
N Somalia

Mirafa africana (Rufous-naped Bush Lark)
M. a. henrici
Guinea, Liberia
M. a. batesi
Niger, N Nigeria
M. a. stresemanni
N Cameroun
M. a. bamendae
Cameroun
M. a. kurrae
E Chad
M. a. tropicalis
E Zaire, Uganda, Kenya, Tanzania
M. a. sharpii
Somalia
M. a. ruwenzoria
W Uganda
M. a. athi
Kenya
M. a. harterti
S Kenya
M. a. malbranti
SC Zaire
M. a. nyikae
E Zambia, N Malawi
M. a. chapini
SE Zaire, NW Zambia
M. a. occidentalis
Gabon, W & S Angola
M. a. irwini
Cuando, Angola
M. a. kabalii
NE Angola
M. a. anchietae
Huila, Angola
M. a. gomesi
E Angola
M. a. grisescens
W Zambia, Rhodesia
M. a. pallida
Namibia, Botswana
M. a. ghansiensis
SW Botswana
M. a. nigrescens
SW Tanzania
M. a. zuluensis
SW Tanzania, N Natal, Mozambique
M. a. transvaalensis
Transvaal, Natal, Rhodesia, Zambia, Malawi
M. a. africana
S Natal, E Cape Province

Mirafa chuana (Short-clawed Lark)
W Transvaal, S Botswana

Mirafa angolensis (Angolan Lark)
M. a. marungensis
SE Zaire
M. a. angolensis
W Angola
M. a. niethammeri
Cuando District (Angola)
M. a. antonii
E Angola
M. a. minyanyae
NW Zambia

Mirafa rufocinnamomea (Cinnamon Bush Lark)
M. r. buckleyi
Gambia & Mali to Nigeria & Cameroun
M. r. serlei
E Nigeria
M. r. tigrina
NE Cameroun
M. r. furensis
W Sudan
M. r. sobatensis
E Sudan
M. r. rufocinnamomea
Ethiopia
M. r. omoensis
SW Ethiopia
M. r. kawirondensis
Uganda, Kenya, Tanzania
M. r. fischeri
SE Zaire & Zambia to Kenya & Mozambique
M. r. torrida
C Tanzania
M. r. pintoi
S Mozambique, NE Transvaal
M. r. mababiensis
SW Zambia, N Botswana

Mirafa apiata (Clapper Lark)
M. a. reynoldsi
W Zambia
M. a. adendorffi
NW Cape Province
M. a. apiata
SW Cape Province
M. a. marjoriae
Cape Town
M. a. algoensis
SE Cape Province
M. a. jappi
W Barotseland

Mirafa damarensis (Damara Clapper Lark)
M. d. damarensis
N Namibia
M. d. hewetti
NE Cape Province, Transvaal

M. d. deserti
   C Namibia
M. d. kalaharica
   SW Botswana
M. d. nata
   E Botswana
**Mirafa africanoides (Fawn-coloured
   Bush Lark)**
M. a. intercedens
   Ethiopia, Somalia, Kenya, NE Tanzania
M. a. alopex
   S Somalia, Ethiopia
M. a. macdonaldi
   S Ethiopia
M. a. longonotensis
   E Uganda, W Kenya
M. a. omaruru
   NW Namibia
M. a. trapnelli
   W Zambia
M. a. harei
   C Namibia
M. a. gobabisensis
   E Namibia
M. a. rubidior
   N Namibia
M. a. makarikari
   S Zambia, NE Botswana
M. a. sarwensis
   N Namibia, C Botswana, Mozambique
M. a. vincenti
   Rhodesia, S Mozambique
M. a. austenrobertsi
   SE Botswana, W Transvaal
M. a. africanoides
   S Namibia, N Cape Province
Mirafa collaris (Collared Lark)
   Somalia, N Kenya
**Mirafa assamica (Rufous-winged Bush
   Lark)**
M. a. assamica
   N India, Nepal, Assam
M. a. affinis
   S India, Sri Lanka
M. a. microptera
   C Burma
M. a. subsessor
   N Thailand
M. a. marionae
   S Burma, S Thailand, S Indochina
Mirafa rufa (Rusty Bush Lark)
M. r. nigriticola
   Mali
M. r. rufa
   W Sudan
M. r. lynesi
   C Sudan

Mirafa gilletti (Gillett's Bush Lark)   343
   Ethiopia, Somalia
Mirafa poecilosterna (Pink-breasted Lark)
M. p. australoabyssinica
   N Sudan, Ethiopia
M. p. poecilosterna
   N & E Kenya
M. p. massaica
   N Uganda, Kenya, Tanzania
Mirafa sabota (Sabota Lark)
M. s. sabotoides
   W Botswana
M. s. veseyfitzgeraldi
   NW Botswana
M. s. plebeja
   SW Zaire
M. s. ansorgei
   W Angola
M. s. sabota
   S Mozambique, Transvaal, Natal, Cape
   Province
M. s. fradei
   S Mozambique
**Mirafa naevia (Large-billed Sabota
   Lark)**
M. n. herero
   SW Namibia
M. n. bradfieldi
   E Cape Province
M. n. naevia
   C Namibia
M. n. waibeli
   N Namibia, NW Botswana
**Mirafa erythroptera (Red-winged Bush
   Lark)**
M. e. sindiana
   NW India
M. e. furva
   Kathiawar (NW India)
M. e. erythroptera
   S & C India

PINAROCORYS
**Pinarocorys nigricans (Dusky Bush
   Lark)**
   S Zaire & Angola to Natal & Mozambique
**Pinarocorys erythropygia (Red-tailed
   Bush Lark)**
   Gambia to Sudan & Uganda

HETEROMIRAFA
Heteromirafa ruddi (Long-clawed Lark)
H. r. archeri
   W Somalia
H. r. ruddi
   SE Transvaal, N Orange Free State

Certhilauda curvirostris (Long-billed Lark)

C. c. damarensis
   WC Namibia
C. c bradshawi
   S Namibia, N Cape Province
C. c. subcoronata
   E Cape Province
C. c. curvirostris
   S & W Cape Province
C. c. semitorquata
   S Transvaal, Natal, E Cape Province
C. c. benguelensis
   W Angola
C. c. falcirostris
   NW Cape Province
C. c. kaokoensis
   W Namibia
C. c. algida
   E Cape Province

Certhilauda albescens (Karroo Lark)

C. a. erythrochlamys
   W Namibia
C. a. barlowi
   S Namibia
C. a. cavei
   S Namibia
C. a. patae
   NW Cape Province
C. a. saldanhae
   W Cape Province
C. a. albescens
   SW Cape Province
C. a. guttata
   C & W Cape Province

Certhilauda albofasciata (Spike-heeled Lark)

C. a. beesleyi
   N Tanzania
C. a. obscurata
   C Angola
C. a. longispina
   W Huila, Angola
C. a. erikssoni
   N Namibia
C. a. kalahariae
   S Botswana
C. a. boweni
   W Namibia
C. a. arenaria
   C Namibia
C. a. bathoeni
   SE Botswana
C. a. subpallida
   NE Transvaal
C. a. robertsi
   SC Transvaal

C. a. alticola
   N Orange Free State, S Transvaal
C. a. baddeleyi
   S Orange Free State, N Cape Province
C. a. albofasciata
   Natal, S Orange Free State, C & E Cape Province
C. a. meinertzhageni
   NW Cape Province
C. a. bradfieldi
   N Cape Province
C. a. garrula
   W Cape Province
C. a. macdonaldi
   S Karoo, Cape Province
C. a. latimerae
   Transkei

EREMOPTERIX

Eremopterix australis (Black-eared Finch Lark)
   S Namibia, Botswana, W Transvaal, N Cape Province

Eremopterix leucotis (Chestnut-backed Finch Lark)

E. l. melanocephala
   Senegal to Nile valley
E. l. leucotis
   Ethiopia
E. l. madaraszi
   Kenya, Tanzania, Mozambique
E. l. smithi
   S & SE Africa

Eremopterix signata (Chestnut-headed Finch Lark)

E. s. harrisoni
   SE Sudan, N Kenya
E. s. signata
   Ethiopia, Somalia, Kenya

Eremopterix verticalis (Grey-backed Finch Lark)

E. v. verticalis
   Botswana, W Rhodesia, Transvaal, W Cape Province
E. v. damarensis
   Angola, Namibia, NW Cape Province
E. v. khama
   NE Botswana

Eremopterix nigriceps (Black-crowned Finch Lark)

E. n. nigriceps
   Cape Verde Is
E. n. albifrons
   Mauretania to Nile valley
E. n. melanauchen
   Egypt, Ethiopia, Sudan, Socotra I, Arabia, Iraq
E. n. affinis
   Pakistan, NW India

Eremopterix grisea (Ashy-crowned Finch Lark)
    Pakistan, India, Sri Lanka
Eremopterix leucopareia (Fischer's Finch Lark)
    Uganda, Kenya, Malawi

AMMOMANES
Ammomanes cincturus (Bar-tailed Desert Lark)
A. c. cincturus
    Cape Verde Is
A. c. pallens
    Mali to Sudan
A. c. arenicolor
    N Africa, Sinai, Arabia
A. c. zarudnyi
    E Iran, Afghanistan, NW India
Ammomanes phoenicurus (Rufous-tailed Desert Lark)
A. p. phoenicurus
    N India
A. p. testaceus
    C India
Ammomanes deserti (Desert Lark)
A. d. payni
    Morocco
A. d. algeriensis
    Algeria, Tunisia
A. d. whitakeri
    NW Libya
A. d. mya
    S Algeria, Niger
A. d. janeti
    S Algeria
A. d. geyri
    S Algeria, Mauretania, N Nigeria
A. d. monodi
    C Mauretania
A. d. mirei
    Tibesti Mountains
A. d. kollmanspergeri
    NE Chad
A. d. deserti
    E Libya, Egypt
A. d. erythrochrous
    Sudan
A. d. isabellinus
    Egypt, Arabia, Israel, Syria
A. d. samharensis
    E Sudan, S Arabia
A. d. taimuri
    Oman
A. d. assabensis
    Eritrea, N Somalia
A. d. akeleyi
    Somalia
A. d. azizi
    EC Arabia

A. d. saturatus
    S Arabia
A. d. annae
    Transjordan
A. d. insularis
    Bahrain I
A. d. cheesmani
    E Iraq, W Iran
A. d. parvirostris
    Transcaspia
A. d. orientalis
    N Afghanistan
A. d. iranicus
    S Iran, S Afghanistan
A. d. phoenicuroides
    NW India
Ammomanes dunni (Dunn's Lark)
A. d. dunni
    S Sahara, W Sudan
A. d. eremodites
    SW Arabia
Ammomanes grayi (Gray's Lark)
A. g. grayi
    W & S Namibia
A. g. hoeschi
    NW Namibia
Ammomanes burra (Ferruginous Lark)
    S Namibia, W Cape Province

ALAEMON
Alaemon alaudipes (Hoopoe Lark)
A. a. boavistae
    Cape Verde Is
A. a. alaudipes
    N Africa, Sahara
A. a. doriae
    E Arabia, Iraq to NW India
A. a. desertorum
    Red Sea
Alaemon hamertoni (Lesser Hoopoe Lark)
A. h. altera
    NE Somalia
A. h. tertia
    EC Somalia
A. h. hamertoni
    SE Somalia

RAMPHOCORIS
Ramphocoris clotbey (Thick-billed Lark)
    N Africa, N Arabia, Syria

MELANOCORYPHA
Melanocorypha calandra (Calandra Lark)
M. c. calandra
    S Europe, N Africa, Iran
M. c. psammochroa
    Transcaspia, Iran, Afghanistan
M. c. gaza
    Jordan

M. c. dathei
Turkey
Melanocorypha bimaculata (Bimaculated Lark)
M. b. bimaculata
SW Asia, Iran, NE Africa
M. b. torquata
E Iran, Afghanistan, NW India
M. b. rufescens
Asia Minor, Jordan, NE Africa
Melanocorypha mongolica (Mongolian Lark)
C Asia, Mongolia, Tsinghai
Melanocorypha maxima (Long-billed Calandra Lark)
M. m. maxima
Sikkim, S Tibet, W China
M. m. holdereri
NE Tibet, N Kashmir
Melanocorypha leucoptera (White-winged Lark)
S Russia, C Asia, Iran
Melanocorypha yeltoniensis (Black Lark)
S Russia, C Asia, Caucasus

CALANDRELLA
Calandrella razae (Raza Island Lark)
Raza I, Cape Verde Is
Calandrella cinerea (Short-toed Lark)
C. c. woltersi
Turkey
C. c. dukhunensis
N India, Burma, Mongolia, W China, Tibet
C. c. longipennis
C Asia, Afghanistan, N India
C. c. orientalis
C Asia, Mongolia, Manchuria
C. c. artemisiana
Caucasus, W Siberia, Asia Minor, Iran
C. c. brachydactyla
S Europe, Russia, N Africa
C. c. rubiginosa
S Morocco, S Algeria, S Tunisia
C. c. hermonensis
Lebanon, Israel, Red Sea
C. c. eremica
SW Arabia
C. c. erlangeri
Ethiopia
C. c. saturatior
Uganda to Botswana & Natal
C. c. williamsi
W Kenya
C. c. alluvia
S Mozambique
C. c. anderssoni
N Namibia
C. c. ongumaensis
N Namibia

C. c. witputzi
S Namibia
C. c. millardi
SW Kalahari
C. c. niveni
SW Transvaal, Orange Free State, Natal
C. c. spleniata
S Angola, W Namibia
C. c. cinerea
S Cape Province
Calandrella blanfordi (Blanford's Lark)
N Ethiopia, Somalia
Calandrella acutirostris (Hume's Short-toed Lark)
C. a. acutirostris
N Afghanistan, CS Asia, N & C India
C. a. tibetana
C Asia, S Tibet, N India
Calandrella raytal (Indian Sand Lark)
C. r. raytal
N India, N Burma
C. r. krishnarkumarsinhji
Kathiawar (NW India)
C. r. adamsi
NW India
Calandrella rufescens (Lesser Short-toed Lark)
C. r. rufescens
Tenerife I
C. r. polatzeki
Gran Canaria I, Lanzarote I
C. r. apetzii
S Spain
C. r. minor
N Sahara, Sinai
C. r. nicolli
N Egypt
C. r. aharonii
Asia Minor, Jordan
C. r. pseudobaetica
W Caspian Sea
C. r. persica
Iraq to Afghanistan
C. r. heinei
SE Russia, W Siberia
C. r. somalica
Somalia
C. r. vulpecula
Somalia
C. r. megaensis
S Ethiopia
C. r. athensis
S Kenya, NE Tanzania
Calandrella cheleënsis (Mongolian Short-toed Lark)
C. c. cheleënsis
N China, Manchuria

C. c. leucophaea
Turkestan
C. c. kukunoorensis
Kuku Nor
C. c. seebohmi
C Asia
C. c. biecki
N Kansu
C. c. tangutica
NE Tibet

SPIZOCORYS
**Spizocorys conirostris (Pink-billed
Lark)**
S. c. damerensis
Namibia
S. c. crypta
NE Botswana
S. c. makawai
W Barotseland
S. c. griseovinacea
W Transvaal
S. c. conirostris
S Botswana, S Transvaal, N Cape Province
**Spizocorys starki (Stark's Short-toed
Lark)**
Angola to W Transvaal
**Spizocorys sclateri (Sclater's Short-toed
Lark)**
S. c. sclateri
Namibia, Cape Province
S. c. theresae
NW Cape Province
S. c. capensis
C & E Cape Province
Spizocorys obbiensis (Obbia Lark)
Somalia
Spizocorys personata (Masked Lark)
S. p. personata
E Ethiopia
S. p. yavelloensis
S Ethiopia
S. p. mechesneyi
N Kenya
S. p. intensa
C Kenya

BOTHA
Botha fringillaris (Botha's Lark)
S Transvaal, N Orange Free State

CHERSOPHILUS
Chersophilus duponti (DuPont's Lark)
C. d. duponti
S Spain, N Algeria, N Tunisia
C. d. margaritae
S Algeria, S Tunisia, Libya, NW Egypt

PSEUDALAEMON
**Pseudalaemon fremantlii (Short-tailed
Lark)**
P. f. fremantlii
Somalia
P. f. megaensis
S Ethiopia
P. f. delamerei
SE Kenya, NE Tanzania

GALERIDA
Galerida cristata (Crested Lark)
G. c. pallida
Portugal, Spain
G. c. cristata
C Europe, Crimea, N Morocco
G. c. meridionalis
S Italy, SE Europe
G. c. subtaurica
C & S Asia Minor
G. c. caucasica
Caucasus, W Asia Minor, Cyprus,
Crete
G. c. riggenbachi
W Morocco
G. c. macrorhyncha
S Algeria
G. c. randoni
C Algeria
G. c. carthaginis
N Algeria, N Tunisia
G. c. arenicola
SE Algeria, S Tunisia
G. c. balsaci
W Mauretania
G. c. festae
Libya
G. c. senegallensis
Senegal & Gambia to Sierra Leone &
Mali
G. c. jordonsi
Aïr Mts (Niger)
G. c. alexanderi
N Cameroun, Mali, S Niger, Chad
G. c. zalingei
W Sudan
G. c. isabellina
N Chad C Sudan
G. c. somaliensis
Somalia
G. c. altirostris
Egypt, Arabia
G. s. maculata
C Egypt, SW Arabia
G. c. nigricans
N Egypt
G. c. cinnamomina
Lebanon

G. c. zion
  Turkey, Syria
G. c. magna
  C & S Asia, NW China, N India
G. c. leautungensis
  Manchuria, N China
G. c. coreensis
  Korea
G. c. lynesi
  Kashmir
G. c. chendoola
  N & NW India

Galerida theklae (Thekla Lark)
  G. t. theklae
    Portugal, Spain, Balearic Is
  G. t. erlangeri
    N Morocco
  G. t. ruficolor
    C Morocco, N Algeria, N Tunisia
  G. t. superflua
    E Morocco, C Algeria, S Tunisia,
    Libya
  G. t. deichleri
    S Algeria, S Tunisia
  G. t. harrarensis
    Harar (Ethiopia)
  G. t. huei
    Bale (Ethiopia)
  G. t. praetermissa
    Ethiopia
  G. t. ellioti
    Somalia
  G. t. huriensis
    Kenya

Galerida malabarica (Malabar Crested Lark)
  W India

Galerida deva (Sykes' Crested Lark)
  WC & SC India

Galerida modesta (Sun Lark)
  G. m. giffardi
    Ghana to Sudan
  G. m. modesta
    S Sudan
  G. m. nigrita
    Guinea, Sierra Leone
  G. m. strümpelli
    W Cameroun
  G. m. bucolica
    Central African Republic, N Zaire,
    SW Sudan

CALENDULA
Calendula magnirostris (Thick-billed Lark)
  C. m. magnirostris
    W & SW Cape Province

C. m. harei
  SW Transvaal, Orange Free State, Cape
    Province
C. m. montivaga
  Lesotho

LULLULA
Lullula arborea (Wood Lark)
  L. a. arborea
    N & W Europe, N Africa
  L. a. pallida
    S Europe, N Africa, Caucasus, Iran

ALAUDA
Alauda arvensis (Sky Lark)
  A. a. arvensis
    N & W Europe
  A. a. sierrae
    N Portugal, Spain
  A. a. harterti
    W North Africa
  A. a. cantarella
    SE Europe, Iran, E North Africa
  A. a. dulcivox
    SE Russia, C Asia, N India
  A. a. kiborti
    EC Asia, Manchuria, E China
  A. a. intermedia
    NE Manchuria, E China
  A. a. pekinensis
    NC & NE Asia, Japan, N China
  A. a. lönnbergi
    Sakhalin I, Korea, NE China, Japan
  A. a. japonica
    Japan, Riukiu Is

Alauda gulgula (Oriental Skylark)
  A. g. inconspicua
    SW Asia, Afghanistan, NW India
  A. g. lhamarum
    W Himalayas
  A. g. inopinata
    SE Tibet, W China, N Burma, Nepal
  A. g. sala
    Hainan I
  A. g. herberti
    C & S Thailand, S Indochina
  A. g. wattersi
    Taiwan
  A. g. wolfei
    Philippine Is
  A. g. vernayi
    E Bhutan, SE Tibet, N Burma
  A. g. weigoldi
    C China
  A. g. coelivox
    SE China, N Vietnam
  A. g. gulgula
    S India, Sri Lanka, S Burma
  A. g. australis
    S India, Sri Lanka

EREMOPHILA
Eremophila alpestris (Shore (Horned) Lark)
  E. a. flava
    N Europe, N Asia
  E. a. balcanica
    SE Europe
  E. a. penicillata
    Asia Minor, W Iran
  E. a. albigula
    N Iran, Afghanistan, C Asia
  E. a. brandti
    EC Asia, N China
  E. a. longirostris
    Baluchistan, NW Himalayas
  E. a. teleschowi
    C Siking
  E. a. przewalskii
    NW Tsinghai
  E. a. argalea
    NW India
  E. a. elwesi
    N India, Sikkim, Nepal, S Tibet
  E. a. nigrifrons
    E Tsinghai, NW China
  E. a. khamensis
    C Sikang
  E. a. atlas
    C Morocco
  E. a. bicornis
    S Asia Minor, Lebanon
  E. a. arcticola
    N Alaska, W Canada, NW USA
  E. a. alpina
    W Washington State
  E. a. hoyti
    N Canada, N USA
  E. a. alpestris
    NE Canada, NE USA
  E. a. leucolaema
    S Canada, C & S USA, N Mexico
  E. a. enthymia
    C Canada, C USA
  E. a. praticola
    SE Canada, C & EC USA
  E. a. strigata
    NW USA
  E. a. merrilli
    W Canada, W USA
  E. a. lamprochroma
    W & SW USA
  E. a. utahensis
    WC USA
  E. a. sierrae
    NE California
  E. a. rubea
    C California
  E. a. actia
    S California, N Baja California
  E. a. insularis
    S California islands
  E. a. ammophila
    SW USA, NE Baja California
    NW Mexico
  E. a. leucansiptila
    SW USA, NE Baja California, NW Mexico
  E. a. occidentalis
    S USA, N Mexico
  E. a. adusta
    S USA
  E. a. giraudi
    S Texas, NC Mexico
  E. a. enertera
    WC Baja California
  E. a. aphrasta
    NC Mexico
  E. a. diaphora
    E Mexico
  E. a. lactea
    Coalhuila (Mexico)
  E. a. chrysolaema
    SC Mexico
  E. a. oaxacae
    S Mexico
  E. a. peregrina
    Colombia
Eremophila bilopha (Temminck's Horned Lark)
    N Africa, N Arabia, Iraq

117 HIRUNDINIDAE (SWALLOWS, MARTINS)

PSEUDOCHELIDONINAE

PSEUDOCHELIDON
Pseudochelidon eurystomina (African River Martin)
    Zaire
Pseudochelidon sirintarae (White-eyed River Martin)
    C Thailand

HIRUNDININAE

TACHYCINETA
Tachycineta bicolor (Tree Swallow)
    W Canada, W USA, Central America, Cuba
Tachycineta albilinea (Mangrove Swallow)
  T. a. rhizophorae
    NW Mexico
  T. a. albilinea
    E & S Mexico, Central America
  T. a. stolzmanni
    W Peru

Tachycineta albiventer (White-winged Swallow)
NE South America, Trinidad
Tachycineta leucorrhoa (White-rumped Swallow)
SC South America
Tachycineta leucopyga (Chilean Swallow)
S South America
Tachycineta thalassina (Violet-green Swallow)
T. t. lepida
NW Canada, W & SW USA, NW Mexico, Central America
T. t. brachyptera
C & S Baja California, NW Mexico
T. t. thalassina
C Mexico
Tachycineta cyaneoviridis (Bahama Swallow)
E Cuba, Bahama Is
Tachycineta euchrysea (Golden Swallow)
T. e. euchrysea
Jamaica
T. e. sclateri
Hispaniola

PHAEOPROGNE
Phaeoprogne tapera (Brown-chested Martin)
P. t. tapera
Colombia, Venezuela, the Guianas, Ecuador, Peru, Brazil
P. t. fusca
Central South America

PROGNE
Progne subis (Purple Martin)
P. s. subis
S Canada, W USA, E Mexico to Panama, N South America
P. s. hesperia
Arizona, Baja California, W Mexico to Nicaragua
P. s. arboricola
Utah
Progne dominicensis (Caribbean Martin)
P. d. cryptoleuca
Cuba, Isle of Pines
P. d. dominicensis
Jamaica, Hispaniola, Lesser Antilles
P. d. sinaloae
NW Mexico
Progne chalybea (Grey-breasted Martin)
P. c. chalybea
S USA, Central America, N South America
P. c. macroramphus
C South America
Progne modesta (Southern Martin)
P. m. modesta
C & S Galapagos Is

P. m. elegans
Bolivia, Brazil, Argentina
P. m. murphyi
W Peru, N Chile

NOTIOCHELIDON
Notiochelidon murina (Brown-bellied Swallow)
N. m. murina
Colombia, Ecuador, Peru
N. m. meridensis
W Venezuela
N. m. cyanodorsalis
W Bolivia
Notiochelidon cyanoleuca (Blue and White Swallow)
N. c. cyanoleuca
Costa Rica, Panama, N & C South America
N. c. peruviana
W Peru
N. c. patagonica
S South America
Notiochelidon flavipes (Pale-footed Swallow)
Peru, Colombia
Notiochelidon pileata (Black-capped Swallow)
S Mexico, Guatemala

ATTICORA
Atticora fasciata (White-banded Swallow)
N & W Amazonia
Atticora melanoleuca (Black-collared Swallow)
N Amazonia

NEOCHELIDON
Neochelidon tibialis (White-thighed Swallow)
N. t. minimus
E Panama, Colombia, W Ecuador
N. t. griseiventris
S Colombia, SE Venezuela, E Ecuador, E Peru, W Brazil
N. t. tibialis
SE Brazil

ALOPOCHELIDON
Alopochelidon fucata (Tawny-headed Swallow)
Venezuela to C Argentina

STELGIDOPTERYX
Stelgidopteryx ruficollis (Rough-winged Swallow)
S. r. serripennis
S Canada, USA, Mexico, Central America
S. r. psammochroa
SW USA, Baja California, S Mexico
S. r. fulvipennis
C & S Mexico to Costa Rica

S. r. ridgwayi
  Yucatan
S. r. stuarti
  SE Mexico, E Guatemala
S. r. decolor
  W Costa Rica, W Panama
S. r. uropygialis
  W Colombia, Ecuador, NW Peru
S. r. aequalis
  N Colombia, W Venezuela, Trinidad
S. r. cacabata
  E Venezuela, the Guianas
S. r. ruficollis
  SE Colombia, E Ecuador, E Peru,
    Bolivia, N Argentina

IERAMOECA
**heramoeca leucosterna (White-backed
Swallow)**
  W, S & C Australia

PARIA
iparia paludicola (African Sand Martin)
R. p. mauretanica
  W Morocco
R. p. minor
  Niger, Mali, Chad, Sudan, Ethiopia
R. p. newtoni
  SE Nigeria
R. p. ducis
  Uganda, E Zaire, Kenya, Tanzania
R. p. paludicola
  Zambia, South Africa
R. p. cowani
  Madagascar
R. p. chinensis
  N India, South East Asia
R. p. tantilla
  Luzon I
iparia congica (Congo Sand Martin)
  C Zaire
iparia riparia (Sand Martin)
R. r. riparia
  North America, N South America, Europe,
    Asia, N & E Africa
R. r. ijimae
  NE Asia, Burma, Thailand, Philippine Is
R. r. tibetana
  C Asia
R. r. diluta
  NW India, Nepal
R. r. fokienensis
  C & S China
R. r. indica
  Afghanistan, NW India
R. r. shelleyi
  Egypt, Sudan

Riparia cincta (Banded Sand Martin)
R. c. erlangeri
  Ethiopia
R. c. suahelica
  Uganda, Kenya, N Tanzania
R. c. parvula
  S Zaire
R. c. cincta
  W & S Africa
R. c. xerica
  W Angola

PHEDINA
Phedina borbonica (Mascarene Martin)
P. b. borbonica
  Mauritius I, Reunion I
P. b. madagascariensis
  Malawi, Madagascar

PHEDINOPSIS
Phedinopsis brazzae (Brazza's Martin)
  S Zaire, N Angola

HIRUNDO
**Hirundo griseopyga (Grey-rumped
Swallow)**
H. g. liberiae
  Liberia
H. g. gertrudis
  NE Nigeria
H. g. melbina
  Gabon
H. g. griseopyga
  Ethiopia to Natal
Hirundo rupestris (Crag Martin)
H. r. rupestris
  S Europe, C & SW Asia, NE Africa, India
H. r. theresae
  S Morocco
Hirundo obsoleta (Pale Crag Martin)
H. o. spatzi
  SC Algeria
H. o. presaharica
  NC Algeria
H. o. buchanani
  N Niger
H. o. obsoleta
  Egypt, Sudan, Sinai, Iran
H. o. arabica
  E Sudan, W Arabia, Somalia, Socotra I
H. o. perpallida
  E Arabia
H. o. pallida
  E Iran, Afghanistan, NW India
Hirundo fuligula (African Rock Martin)
H. f. pusilla
  S Sudan, Ethiopia
H. f. rufigula
  N Nigeria, Chad, S Sudan, Ethiopia,
    Zaire, Uganda, N Tanzania

H. f. birwae
Sierra Leone, Guinea
H. f. bansoensis
SE Nigeria
H. f. fusciventris
S Tanzania, Malawi, N Mozambique
H. f. anderssoni
S Angola, Namibia, Botswana, W Cape
Province
H. f. fuligula
E Cape Province
H. f. pretoriae
E Transvaal, Natal
Hirundo concolor (Dusky Crag Martin)
H. c. concolor
India
H. c. sintaungensis
Burma, N Thailand, N Laos, N Vietnam
Hirundo rustica ((Barn) Swallow)
H. r. rustica
Europe, W Asia, Africa, India
H. r. transitiva
Asia Minor, Egypt, Kenya, Uganda
H. r. savignii
Egypt
H. r. gutteralis
NE Asia, India, S China, SE Asia, New
Guinea
H. r. tytleri
Bhutan, Siberia, W Mongolia, W China,
Burma
H. r. mandschurica
Manchuria, E China
H. r. saturata
E Siberia
H. r. erythrogaster
N & S America, West Indies
Hirundo lucida (Red-chested Swallow)
H. l. lucida
Senegal to Ghana
H. l. clara
Mali, Upper Volta
H. l. subalaris
E Zaire
H. l. rothschildi
Ethiopia
Hirundo angolensis (Angola Swallow)
H. a. arcticincta
Uganda, W Kenya, NW Tanzania
H. a. angolensis
SE Zaire, Tanzania, Angola, Malawi,
Zambia
Hirundo tahitica (Pacific Swallow)
H. t. domicola
S India, Sri Lanka
H. t. abbotti
Malaysia, Sumatra, Borneo, Philippine Is

H. t. nameyei
Riukiu Is
H. t. mallopega
Andaman Is, E Sumatra, Java
H. t. frontalis
Lesser Sunda Is, New Guinea, Celebes
Moluccas
H. t. ambiens
New Britain
H. t. subfusca
Polynesia, Melanesia, Fiji Is, Tonga I
H. t. tahitica
Society Is
H. t. carteri
W Australia
H. t. parsonsi
NE Queensland
H. t. neoxena
S Queensland, New South Wales,
Victoria, South Australia
**Hirundo albigularis (White-throated
Swallow)**
H. a. ambigua
N & E Angola, NW Zambia
H. a. albigularis
Southern Africa
Hirundo aethiopica (Ethiopian Swallow)
H. a. fulvipectus
Nigeria, Cameroun, Sudan
H. a. aethiopica
Ethiopia, Somalia, E Kenya, Tanzania
Hirundo smithii (Wire-tailed Swallow)
H. s. smithii
W, C, E & SE Africa
H. s. filifera
SW Asia, India, Burma, Thailand, Laos,
N Vietnam
Hirundo atrocaerulea (Blue Swallow)
Tanzania to Natal
**Hirundo nigrita (White-throated Blue
Swallow)**
W & C Africa
**Hirundo leucosoma (Pied-winged
Swallow)**
Senegal to Nigeria
**Hirundo megaensis (White-tailed
Swallow)**
S Ethiopia
**Hirundo nigrorufa (Black and Rufous
Swallow)**
Angola, S Zaire, Zambia
**Hirundo dimidiata (Pearl-breasted
Swallow)**
H. d. marwitzi
Angola, Zambia, SW Tanzania, Malawi
H. d. dimidiata
South Africa, Rhodesia

Hirundo cucullata (Greater Striped Swallow)
  Southern Africa
Hirundo abyssinica (Lesser Striped Swallow)
  H. a. puella
    Sierra Leone to Nigeria
  H. a. maxima
    S Nigeria, Cameroun
  H. a. bannermani
    S Sudan
  H. a. abyssinica
    Ethiopia, Uganda, Kenya, Tanzania
  H. a. unitatis
    W Uganda, E Zaire, SE Africa
  H. a. ampliformis
    Caprivi Strip to NE Zambia
Hirundo semirufa (Red-breasted Swallow)
  H. s. gordoni
    W & C Africa
  H. s. semirufa
    SE Africa
Hirundo senegalensis (Mosque Swallow)
  H. s. senegalensis
    W & NC Africa
  H. c. saturatior
    C & E Africa
  H. s. monteiri
    SC Africa
Hirundo daurica (Red-rumped Swallow)
  H. d. daurica
    C Asia
  H. d. japonica
    E Asia, Japan, China, N India
  H. d. gephyra
    W China
  H. d. nipalensis
    Himalayas, India, N Burma
  H. d. erythropygia
    S India, Sri Lanka
  H. d. hyperythra
    Sri Lanka
  H. d. rufula
    S Europe, Iran, Afghanistan, NW India
  H. d. domicella
    NW Africa
  H. d. disjuncta
    Sierra Leone
  H. d. kumboensis
    Cameroun
  H. d. emini
    E Africa
  H. d. melanocrissa
    N Ethiopia

Hirundo striolata (Greater Striated Swallow)
  H. s. striolata
    Taiwan, Philippine Is, Borneo, Sumatra, Lesser Sunda Is
  H. s. mayri
    Assam, N Burma, NW Thailand
  H. s. stanfordi
    Burma, N Thailand, N Laos
  H. s. vernayi
    S Thailand
  H. s. badia
    C Malaysia

PETROCHELIDON
Petrochelidon rufigula (Red-throated Cliff Swallow)
    Angola, S Zaire, Zambia
Petrochelidon preussi (Preuss' Cliff Swallow)
    W Africa, N Zaire
Petrochelidon andecola (Andean Swallow)
  P. a. oroyae
    C Peru
  P. a. andecola
    S Peru, N Bolivia, N Chile
Petrochelidon nigricans (Tree Martin)
  P. n. timoriensis
    Timor I, Lesser Sunda Is
  P. n. neglecta
    W & N Australia
  P. n. nigricans
    E & S Australia, New Guinea, Solomon Is
Petrochelidon spilodera (South African Cliff Swallow)
    Southern Africa
Petrochelidon pyrrhonota (American Cliff Swallow)
  P. p. pyrrhonota
    North America, Central America, N South America
  P. p. tachina
    SW USA, W Central America
  P. p. minima
    SW USA, N Mexico
  P. p. melanogaster
    S Mexico, S Brazil, N Argentina
Petrochelidon fulva (Cave Swallow)
  P. f. pelodoma
    S USA, Mexico, Guatemala
  P. f. citata
    SE Mexico
  P. f. fulva
    Puerto Rico, Cuba, Hispaniola, Jamaica
  P. f. chapmani
    SW Ecuador
  P. f. rufocollaris
    W Peru

***Petrochelidon fluvicola* (Indian Cliff Swallow)**
Afghanistan, Himalayas, N India
***Petrochelidon ariel* (Fairy Martin)**
Australia, Tasmania
***Petrochelidon fuliginosa* (Dusky Cliff Swallow)**
S Cameroun

DELICHON
***Delichon urbica* (House Martin)**
D. u. urbica
Europe, C & W Asia, W & SE Africa
D. u. meridionalis
Mediterranean, N Africa, Iran, N India
D. u. lagopoda
E Asia, S China, Burma, Thailand
***Delichon dasypus* (Asian House Martin)**
D. d. cashmiriensis
Himalayas, India, W China
D. d. nigrimentalis
S China, Taiwan
D. d. dasypus
NE Asia, N China, Malaysia, Borneo, Philippine Is
***Delichon nipalensis* (Nepal House Martin)**
D. n. nipalensis
Himalayas, Assam
D. n. cuttingi
NE Burma

PSALIDOPROCNE
***Psalidoprocne nitens* (Square-tailed Saw-wing)**
P. n. nitens
W Africa, N Zaire
P. n. centralis
NE Zaire
***Psalidoprocne fuliginosa* (Cameroun Saw-wing)**
Cameroun, Fernando Po I
***Psalidoprocne albiceps* (White-headed Saw-wing)**
P. a. albiceps
EC Africa
P. a. suffusa
Angola
***Psalidoprocne pristoptera* (African Blue Saw-wing)**
P. p. pristoptera
Somalia, N Ethiopia
P. p. blanfordi
S Ethiopia
P. p. mangbettorum
NE Zaire
***Psalidoprocne oleaginea* (Kaffa Saw-wing)**
SW Ethiopia
***Psalidoprocne antinorii* (Brown Saw-wing)**
S Ethiopia

***Psalidoprocne petiti* (Petit's Saw-wing)**
P. p. petiti
Gabon, Cameroun, Central African Republic
P. p. chalybea
N Cameroun, NE Zaire
P. p. reichenowi
Angola, SW Zaire, Zambia
P. p. orientalis
Tanzania, Malawi, E Zambia, Mozambiqu
***Psalidoprocne holomelaena* (Black Saw-wing)**
P. h. ruwenzori
E Zaire, W Uganda
P. h. massaica
Kenya
P. h. holomelaena
Mozambique, Malawi, Transvaal, Natal, E Cape Province
***Psalidoprocne obscura* (Fantee Saw-win**
Port Guinea to Cameroun

118 MOTACILLIDAE (WAGTAILS, PIPITS

DENDRONANTHUS
***Dendronanthus indicus* (Forest Wagtail)**
NE Asia, China, India, Thailand, Malaysia Sumatra, Java, Borneo

MOTACILLA
***Motacilla flava* (Yellow Wagtail)**
M. f. flavissima
NW Europe, Spain, N Africa
M. f. flava
N Europe, S Africa
M. f. iberiae
S France, Spain, NW Africa
M. f. cinereocapilla
Italy, Sardinia, Arabia, NE Africa
M. f. pygmaea
Egypt
M. f. beema
SE Russia, C Asia, India, NE Africa
M. f. leucocephala
Mongolia, C Asia, NW India
M. f. lutea
SE Russia, S Africa, India
M. f. zaissanensis
C Asia, India
M. f. thunbergi
NE Europe, C & S Africa
M. f. plexa
N Siberia, N Asia, India
M. f. angarensis
N & C Asia, E Mongolia, E China, Burma
M. f. macronyx
C Asia, E China, Burma, Malaysia, Sumatra
M. f. simillima
N Siberia, E China, Philippine Is

M. f. tschutschensis
NE Asia, Alaska, E China, Java
M. f. taivana
E Siberia, China, Philippine Is
M. f. feldegg
Balkans, Asia Minor, Iraq, Iran, E Africa
M. f. melanogrisea
SW Asia, NW & C India
Motacilla citreola (Citrine Wagtail)
M. c. citreola
Russia, C Asia, Manchuria, India, SE China
M. c. werae
Siberia, Iran, SW Asia, India
M. c. calcarata
E Iran, Himalayas, Tibet, Burma
Afghanistan
Motacilla cinerea (Grey Wagtail)
M. c. patriciae
Azores Is
M. c. schmitzi
Madeira I
M. c. canariensis
Canary Is
M. c. cinerea
Europe, N Africa, Iran, India, SE Asia
C & S Africa
M. c. robusta
NE Asia, Japan, E China, Philippine Is
Motacilla alba (Pied Wagtail)
M. a. yarrelli
British Isles, Spain, Morocco
M. a. alba
Europe, Russia, N & E Africa, Iran, Arabia
M. a. subpersonata
Morocco
M. a. dukhunensis
S Russia, SW Asia, Afghanistan, India
M. a. personata
Siberia, W Asia, Afghanistan, Iran, N India
M. a. persica
Iran
M. a. baicalensis
C Asia, Iran, India, Thailand, SW China
M. a. ocularis
E Siberia, E India, China, Thailand,
Philippine Is
M. a. lugens
NE Asia, NE China, Japan, Taiwan
M. a. leucopsis
E Asia, China, Thailand, Himalayas
M. a. alboides
S China, E Himalayas, Burma
Motacilla grandis (Japanese Pied Wagtail)
Japan, Korea, E China, Taiwan
Motacilla maderaspatensis (Large Pied Wagtail)
Pakistan, India

Motacilla aguimp (African Pied Wagtail)
M. a. vidua
W, C & E Africa, S Africa
M. a. aguimp
Orange River, NW Cape Province
Motacilla clara (Mountain Wagtail)
M. c. chapini
Guinea to E Zaire
M. c. clara
Ethiopia
M. c. torrentium
Uganda and E Zaire, to W Angola and
Natal
Motacilla capensis (Cape Wagtail)
M. c. simplicissima
Angola, S Zaira, Zambia
M. c. capensis
Southern Africa
M. c. wellsi
E Zaire, Uganda, Kenya
**Motacilla flaviventris (Madagascar
Wagtail)**
Madagascar

TMETOTHYLACUS
Tmetothylacus tenellus (Golden Pipit)
Somalia, Kenya, Tanzania

MACRONYX
Macronyx capensis (Cape Longclaw)
M. c. capensis
W Cape Province
M. c. colletti
Botswana, Transvaal, C Cape Province,
Natal
M. c. stabilior
Rhodesia
**Macronyx croceus (Yellow-throated
Longclaw)**
W, E & Southern Africa
**Macronyx fuelleborni (Fülleborn's
Longclaw)**
M. f. fuelleborni
C Tanzania
M. f. ascensi
Angola, Zaire, Zambia, SW Tanzania
Macronyx sharpei (Sharpe's Longclaw)
Kenya
**Macronyx flavicollis (Abyssinian
Longclaw)**
Ethiopia
Macronyx aurantiigula (Pangani Longclaw)
Somalia, Kenya
**Macronyx ameliae (Rosy-breasted
Longclaw)**
Zaira, Kenya to Natal

Macronyx grimwoodi (Grimwood's Longclaw)
M. g. grimwoodi
  E Angola, NW Zambia
M. g. cuandocubangensis
  Cuando, Angola

ANTHUS
Anthus novaeseelandiae (Richard's Pipit)
A. n. cameroonensis
  Cameroun
A. n. lynesi
  E Cameroun, Sudan
A. n. cinnamomeus
  Ethiopia, East Africa, Zambia
A. n. lacuum
  E Africa
A. n. lwenarum
  NW Zambia
A. n. bocagei
  Angola, Namibia, Botswana
A. n. rufuloides
  South Africa
A. n. editus
  Lesotho, W Natal
A. n. richardi
  C Asia, Pakistan, India, Thailand, Siberia,
  N Vietnam
A. n. dauricus
  N Mongolia
A. n. centralasiae
  C Asia
A. n. sinensis
  E Siberia, E China, Malaysia, Sumatra
A. n. rufulus
  Nepal, Burma, Thailand, Laos, Vietnam
A. n. waitei
  Pakistan, NW India
A. n. malayensis
  S India, Sri Lanka, Malaysia, Sumatra, Java
  Borneo
A. n. lugubris
  Palawan, Philippine Is
A. n. albidus
  Lesser Sunda Is
A. n. medius
  Savu Is, Timor I
A. n. exiguus
  C New Guinea
A. n. rogersi
  N Australia
A. n. subaustralis
  C & W Australia
A. n. bilbali
  SW Australia
A. n. australis
  SE Australia
A. n. bistriatus
  Tasmania

A. n. reischeki
  North I, New Zealand
A. n. novaeseelandiae
  South I, New Zealand
A. n. chathamensis
  Chatham I
A. n. aucklandicus
  Auckland Is
A. n. steindachneri
  Antipodes Is
Anthus godlewskii (Blyth's Pipit)
  EC Asia, Tibet, India, Burma, Sri Lanka
Anthus campestris (Tawny Pipit)
A. c. campestris
  Europe, N Africa, Iran, Arabia, SW Asia
A. c. griseus
  C Asia, Afghanistan, W India
A. c. kastschenkoi
  W Siberia, N India
Anthus similis (Long-billed Pipit)
A. s. nicholsoni
  Rhodesia, South Africa
A. s. leucocraspedon
  Namibia
A. s. bannermani
  Sierra Leone, Guinea
A. s. josensis
  C Nigeria
A. s. asbenaicus
  S Sahara
A. s. jebelmarrae
  W Sudan
A. s. hararensis
  Ethiopia, Kenya, N Tanzania
A. s. nivescens
  NE Sudan, Red Sea
A. s. sokotrae
  Socotra I
A. s. dewittei
  C Zaire
A. s. hellae
  E Zaire, W Uganda
A. s. nyassae
  Angola, Zambia, Malawi, S Tanzania
A. s. moco
  C Angola
A. s. petricola
  Lesotho
A. s. schoutedeni
  S Angola, S Zaire, Zambia, SW Tanzania
A. s. captus
  Lebanon, Syria, Israel
A. s. arabicus
  SW Arabia
A. s. decaptus
  Afghanistan, Pakistan, NW India
A. s. jerdoni
  E Afghanistan, Himalayas, Burma

A. s. yamethini
C Burma
A. s. similis
C & S India
A. s. travancoriensis
SW India
Anthus vaalensis (Sandy Plain-backed Pipit)
A. v. saphiroi
E Ethiopia, Somalia
A. v. goodsoni
Kenya
A. v. neumanni
Angola, S Zaire, Zambia
A. v. chobiensis
W Zambia, Botswana, Rhodesia
A. v. vaalensis
Namibia, W Rhodesia, Cape Province
A. v. daviesii
E Cape Province
Anthus leucophrys (Dark Plain-backed Pipit)
A. l. ansorgei
Senegal to N Nigeria
A. l. gouldii
Sierra Leone, Ivory Coast
A. l. zenkeri
S Nigeria to N Uganda & Kenya
A. l. omoensis
Ethiopia, Uganda, W Kenya
A. l. bohndorffi
Angola, S Zaire, Zambia, Malawi
A. l. leucophrys
S Angola, Botswana, South Africa
A. l. tephridorsus
NW Rhodesia
Anthus pallidiventris (Long-legged Pipit)
A. p. pallidiventris
Gabon, NW Angola
A. p. esobe
C Zaire
Anthus pratensis (Meadow Pipit)
A. p. theresae
W Ireland
A. p. pratensis
Greenland, Europe, N Africa, Asia Minor, Iran
Anthus trivialis (Tree Pipit)
A. t. trivialis
Europe, Asia, India, Africa
A. t. haringtoni
EC Asia, Himalayas, N India
Anthus hodgsoni (Indian Tree Pipit)
A. h. yunnanensis
N & E Asia, India, SE China, Borneo
A. h. hodgsoni
Himalayas, NW China, Japan, India

Anthus roseatus (Hodgson's Pipit)
C & E Asia, N India, Tibet, W China
Anthus cervinus (Red-throated Pipit)
E Europe, E Asia, W & E Africa, India
Anthus gustavi (Petchora Pipit)
A. g. gustavi
NE Asia, China, Philippine Is, Borneo
Celebes
A. g. commanderensis
Commander Is
A. g. menzbieri
S Ussuriland
Anthus spinoletta (Rock Pipit)
A. s. rubescens
N & NE Asia, North America, Mexico, Guatemala
A. s. pacificus
W Canada, W USA, W Mexico
A. s. alticola
SW USA, NW Mexico
A. s. japonicus
E Asia, Japan, E China, N India, Burma
A. s. coutellii
C Asia, Tibet, China, N India, Iran
A. s. spinoletta
S & E Europe
A. s. kleinschmidti
Faroe Is
A. s. petrosus
British Isles
A. s. littoralis
NW Europe
Anthus nilghiriensis (Nilgiri Pipit)
S India
Anthus sylvanus (Upland Pipit)
Afghanistan, Himalayas, W China
Anthus berthelotii (Canarian Pipit)
A. b. berthelotii
Canary Is
A. b. madeirensis
Madeira I
Anthus lineiventris (Large-striped Pipit)
Angola, Tanzania to Natal
Anthus brachyurus (Short-tailed Pipit)
A. b. brachyurus
Natal
A. b. leggei
Angola, Zaire, Uganda, Tanzania, Zambia
Anthus caffer (Bushveld Pipit)
A. c. australoabyssinicus
S Ethiopia
A. c. blayneyi
S Kenya, Tanzania
A. c. mzimbaensis
Malawi
A. c. caffer
Botswana, Angola, Rhodesia, Mozambique, Transvaal, Natal

Anthus sokokensis (Sokoke Pipit)
SE Kenya, NE Tanzania
Anthus melindae (Malindi Pipit)
S Somalia, Kenya
Anthus chloris (Yellow-breasted Pipit)
S & E South Africa
Anthus crenatus (Large Yellow-tufted Pipit)
E Transvaal, Cape Province
Anthus gutturalis (New Guinea Pipit)
A. g. gutturalis
SE New Guinea
A. g. rhododendri
EC New Guinea
A. g. wollastoni
WC New Guinea
Anthus spragueii (Sprague's Pipit)
NC & S USA, S Mexico
Anthus furcatus (Short-billed Pipit)
A. f. brevirostris
Peru, Bolivia
A. f. furcatus
Brazil, Paraguay, Uruguay, Argentina
Anthus lutescens (Yellowish Pipit)
A. l. parvus
W Panama
A. l. peruvianus
Peru, N Chile
A. l. lutescens
Colombia, Venezula, the Guianas, Brazil, Argentina
Anthus chacoensis (Chaco Pipit)
Paraguay, Argentina
Anthus correndera (Correndera Pipit)
A. c. calcaratus
Peru
A. c. catamarcae
Bolivia, N Chile, NW Argentina
A. c. chilensis
S Chile, S Argentina
A. c. grayi
Falkland Is
A. c. correndera
S Brazil, Uruguay, Paraguay, N Argentina
Anthus antarcticus (South Georgia Pipit)
S Georgia I
Anthus nattereri (Ochre-breasted Pipit)
SE Brazil, Paraguay
Anthus hellmayri (Hellmayr's Pipit)
A. h. hellmayri
Peru, Bolivia, NW Argentina
A. h. dabbenei
Chile, W Argentina
A. h. brasilianus
SE Brazil, Uruguay, N Argentina
Anthus bogotensis (Paramo Pipit)
A. b. bogotensis
Colombia, Ecuador

A. b. immaculatus
Bolivia, Peru
A. b. shiptoni
Bolivia, NW Argentina
A. b. meridae
NW Venezuela

119 CAMPEPHAGIDAE (CUCKOO SHRIKES)

PTEROPODOCYS
Pteropodocys maxima (Ground Cuckoo Shrike)
P. m. pallida
N Australia
P. m. maxima
S Australia

CORACINA
Coracina novaehollandiae (Large Cuckoo Shrike)
C. n. macei
India
C. n. nipalensis
Assam, Himalayas
C. n. lushaiensis
S Assam
C. n. rexpineti
SE China, Taiwan, N Laos
C. n. layardi
Sri Lanka
C. n. andamani
Andaman Is
C. n. siamensis
Burma, Thailand, S Indochina
C. n. larutensis
N Malaysia
C. n. larvivorus
Hainan I
C. n. javensis
Java, Bali I
C. n. floris
Lesser Sunda Is, Sumbawa I
C. n. sumbensis
Sumba I
C. n. alfrediana
Lomblen I, Alor I
C. n. personata
Timor I, Wetar I
C. n. lettiensis
Sumba Is, Leti I, Moa I
C. n. subpallida
Kei Is, C Western Australia
C. n. didimus
N Australia, S Moluccas, W New Guinea
C. n. melanops
E New Guinea, Bismarck Archipelago, S & E Australia

C. n. novaehollandiae
  Tasmania, Flinders I
Coracina fortis (Buru Is Cuckoo Shrike)
  S Moluccas
Coracina atriceps (Moluccan Cuckoo Shrike)
  C. a. magnirostris
    N Moluccas
  C. a. atriceps
    S Moluccas
Coracina pollens (Kei Is Cuckoo Shrike)
  C. p. pollens
    Kei Is
  C. p. unimoda
    Tenimber Is
Coracina schistacea (Sula Is Cuckoo Shrike)
  C. s. petersi
    Peleng Is
  C. s. schistacea
    Sula Is
Coracina caledonica (Melanesian Greybird)
  C. c. bougainvillei
    Bougainville I
  C. c. kulambangrae
    Kulambangra I
  C. c. welchmani
    Ysabel I
  C. c. amadonis
    Guadalcanal I
  C. c. thilenii
    Espiritu Santo I, Malekula I
  C. c. seiuncta
    Erromango I
  C. c. lifuensis
    Lifu I, Loyalty Is
  C. c. caledonica
    New Caledonia I
Coracina caeruleogrisea (Stout-billed Greybird)
  C. c. strenua
    Japan, W & C New Guinea
  C. c. caeruleogrisea
    Aru Is, S New Guinea
  C. c. adamsoni
    SE New Guinea
Coracina temminckii (Temminck's Cuckoo Shrike)
  C. c. temminckii
    N Celebes
  C. c. rileyi
    C & SE Celebes
  C. c. tonkeana
    E Celebes
Coracina larvata (Black-faced Greybird)
  C. l. melanocephala
    Sumatra

C. l. larvata
  Java
C. l. normani
  Borneo
Coracina striata (Barred Cuckoo Shrike)
  C. s. dobsoni
    Andaman Is
  C. s. sumatrensis
    Thailand, Malaysia, Sumatra, Borneo
  C. s. bungurensis
    Anamba Is, Natuna Is
  C. s. simalurensis
    Simalur I, Sumatra
  C. s. babiensis
    Babi I, Sumatra
  C. s. kannegieteri
    Nias I
  C. s. enganensis
    Enggano I
  C. s. vordermani
    Kangean I
  C. s. difficilis
    Palawan I, Balabac I
  C. s. striata
    Luzon I, Lubang I
  C. s. mindorensis
    Mindoro I
  C. s. panayensis
    Masbate I, Panay I, Negros I
  C. s. boholensis
    Bohol I, Leyte I, Samar I
  C. s. kochii
    Mindanao I, Basilan I
  C. s. guillemardi
    Sulu Archipelago
Coracina bicolor (Muna Greybird)
  Muna I, Celebes
Coracina lineata (Lineated Cuckoo Shrike)
  C. l. axillaris
    Waigeu I, C New Guinea
  C. l. maforensis
    Numfor I
  C. l. sublineata
    New Ireland, New Britain
  C. l. nigrifrons
    Bougainville I, Ysabel I
  C. l. ombriosa
    Kulambangra I, New Georgia I, Rendova I
  C. l. pusilla
    Guadalcanal I
  C. l. malaitae
    Malaita I
  C. l. makirae
    San Cristobal I
  C. l. gracilis
    Rennell I
  C. l. lineata
    E Queensland, E New South Wales

***Coracina boyeri* (White-lored Cuckoo Shrike)**
C. b. boyeri
Japen I, W New Guinea
C. b. subalaris
S New Guinea
***Coracina leucopygia* (White-rumped Cuckoo Shrike)**
Muna I, Celebes
***Coracina papuensis* (Papuan Cuckoo Shrike)**
C. p. melanolora
Misol I, Moluccas
C. p. papuensis
Japen I, W New Guinea
C. p. intermedia
S New Guinea
C. p. oriomo
SE New Guinea, N Queensland
C. p. angustifrons
SE New Guinea
C. p. louisiadensis
Louisiade Archipelago
C. p. ingens
Admiralty Is
C. p. sclateri
Bismarck Archipelago
C. p. perpallida
Bougainville I, Choiseul I, Ysabel I
C. p. elegans
New Georgia I, Rendova I, Guadalcanal I
C. p. eyerdami
Malaita I
C. p. timorlaoensis
Tenimber Is
C. p. hypoleuca
Aru Is, Melville I, N Australia
C. p. stalkeri
N & C Queensland
***Coracina robusta* (Little Cuckoo Shrike)**
E Australia
***Coracina longicauda* (Black-hooded Greybird)**
C. l. grisea
WC New Guinea
C. l. longicauda
C & SE New Guinea
***Coracina parvula* (Halmahera Greybird)**
Halmahera I
***Coracina abbotti* (Celebes Mountain Greybird)**
C Celebes
***Coracina analis* (Caledonian Greybird)**
New Caledonia
***Coracina caesia* (African Grey Cuckoo Shrike)**
C. c. preussi
E Nigeria, Fernando Po I

C. c. pura
Ethiopia and Sudan to Malawi
C. c. caesia
Rhodesia, South Africa
***Coracina pectoralis* (White-breasted Cuckoo Shrike)**
W, C, E & SC Africa
***Coracina graueri* (Grauer's Cuckoo Shrike)**
E Zaire
***Coracina cinerea* (Madagascar Cuckoo Shrike)**
C. c. cucullata
Great Comoro I
C. c. cinerea
N & E Madagascar
C. c. pallida
C, W & SW Madagascar
***Coracina azurea* (African Blue Cuckoo Shrike)**
W & WC Africa
***Coracina typica* (Mauritius Greybird)**
Mauritius I
***Coracina newtoni* (Reunion Greybird)**
Réunion I
***Coracina coerulescens* (Philippine Black Greybird)**
C. c. coerulescens
Luzon I
C. c. deschauenseei
Marinduque I
***Coracina dohertyi* (Black-barred Cuckoo Shrike)**
Sumba I
***Coracina tenuirostris* (Slender-billed Greybird)**
C. t. timoriensis
Timor I, Lomblen I
C. t. kalaotuae
Kalaotua I
C. t. emancipata
Djampea I
C. t. pererrata
Tukangbesi I
C. t. edithae
S Celebes
C. t. amboinensis
Ambon I, Ceram I
C. t. obiensis
Obi I, Bisa I
C. t. pelingi
Peleng Is
C. t. dispar
Banda I, Kei Is
C. t. tenuirostris
Queensland, New South Wales, Victoria
C. t. melvillensis
N Queensland, Northern Territory, NW Australia

C. t. aruensis
Aru Is, S New Guinea
C. t. muelleri
Kofiau I, Misol I, New Guinea, D'Entre-
casteaux Archipelago
C. t. nehrkorni
Waigeu I
C. t. grayi
N Moluccas
C. t. talautensis
Talaut Is
C. t. salvadorii
Sangir Is
C. t. numforana
Numfor I
C. t. meyeri
Biak I
C. t. tagulana
Tagula I, Louisiade Archipelago
C. t. rostrata
Rossel I
C. t. admiralitatis
Admiralty Is
C. t. matthiae
Storm I, St Matthias I
C. t. remota
New Ireland, New Hanover
C. t. heinrothi
New Britain
C. t. rooki
Rook I
C. t. monacha
Palau Is
C. t. nesiotis
Yap I
C. t. saturatior
N & C Solomon Is
C. t. nisoria
Russell I
C. t. erythropygia
Guadalcanal I, Malaita I
C. t. salomonis
San Cristobal I
C. t. insperata
Ponapé I
C. t. ultima
Lihir Is, Tanga I

Coracina morio (Moluccan Greybird)
C. m. morio
N & C Celebes
C. m. wiglesworthi
S & SE Celebes
C. m. sula
Sula Is
C. m. marginata
Buru I
C. m. ceramensis
Ceram I

C. m. hoogerwerfi
Obi I
C. m. incerta
Waigeu I, Japen I, New Guinea
C. m. everetti
Sulu Is
C. m. mindanensis
Mindanao I, Basilan I
C. m. elusa
Mindoro I
C. m. lecroyae
Luzon I
C. m. ripleyi
Bohol I, Samar I, Leyte I
**Coracina schisticeps (New Guinea
Greybird)**
C. s. schisticeps
Misol I, NW New Guinea
C. s. reichenowi
N New Guinea
C. s. poliopsa
S New Guinea
C. s. vittata
D'Entrecasteaux Archipelago
Coracina melaena (Black Greybird)
C. m. waigeuense
Waigeu I
C. m. tommasonis
Japen I
C. m. melaena
W New Guinea
C. m. meeki
E New Guinea
C. m. goodsoni
Aru Is
C. m. batantae
Batanta I
Coracina montana (Black-bellied Greybird)
C. m. montana
New Guinea
C. m. bicinia
Sepik district, New Guinea
**Coracina holopolia (Black-bellied Cuckoo
Shrike)**
C. h. holopolia
Bougainville I, Choiseul I, Guadalcanal I
C. h. pygmaea
Kulambangra I, Vangunu I
C. h. tricolor
Malaita I
**Coracina mcgregori (Sharp-tailed
Greybird)**
N Mindanao
Coracina panayensis (Philippines Greybird)
Negros I, Panay I

Coracina polioptera (Indochinese Cuckoo Shrike)
  C. p. jabouillei
    N Vietnam
  C. p. indochinensis
    Burma, C Thailand, C Laos, S Vietnam
  C. p. polioptera
    S Burma, S Thailand, S Laos
Coracina melaschistos (Dark-grey Cuckoo Shrike)
  C. m. melaschistos
    N India, Himalayas
  C. m. avensis
    W China, Burma, N Thailand, N Vietnam
  C. m. intermedia
    C & S China, Burma, S Thailand, S Vietnam
  C. m. saturata
    N Vietnam, Hainan I
Coracina fimbriata (Lesser Cuckoo Shrike)
  C. f. neglecta
    S-Burma, S Thailand
  C. f. culminata
    S Malaysia
  C. f. schierbrandi
    Sumatra, Borneo
  C. f. compta
    W Sumatran Islands
  C. f. fimbriata
    Java, Bali I
Coracina melanoptera (Black-headed Cuckoo Shrike)
  C. m. melanoptera
    N India
  C. m. sykesi
    S India, Sri Lanka

CAMPOCHAERA
Campochaera sloetii (Orange Cuckoo Shrike)
  C. s. sloetii
    NW New Guinea
  C. s. flaviceps
    SE New Guinea

CHLAMYDOCHAERA
Chlamydochaera jefferyi (Black-breasted Triller)
  Borneo

LALAGE
Lalage melanoleuca (Black and White Triller)
  L. m. melanoleuca
    Luzon I, Mindoro I
  L. m. minor
    Samar I, Leyte I, Mindanao I
Lalage nigra (Pied Triller)
  L. n. davisoni
    Nicobar Is

  L. n. nigra
    Malaysia, Sumatra, Java
  L. n. chilensis
    Borneo, Philippine Is
  L. n. leucopygialis
    Sula Is, Celebes
Lalage sueurii (White-winged Triller)
  L. s. sueruii
    E Java, Lesser Sunda Is, S Celebes
  L. s. tricolor
    N & C Australia, SE New Guinea
Lalage aurea (Red-bellied Triller)
  N Moluccas
Lalage atrovirens (Black-browed Triller)
  L. a. moesta
    Tenimber Is
  L. a. atrovirens
    Misol I, Waigeu I, N New Guinea
  L. a. leucoptera
    Biak I
Lalage leucomela (White-browed Triller)
  L. l. keyensis
    Kei Is
  L. l. rufiventer
    Melville I, Northern Territory
  L. l. leucomela
    E Queensland, NE New South Wales
  L. l. yorki
    N Queensland
  L. l. polygrammica
    Aru Is, E New Guinea
  L. l. obscurior
    D'Entrecasteaux Archipelago
  L. l. trobriandi
    Trobriand Is
  L. l. pallescens
    Louisiade Archipelago
  L. l. falsa
    New Britain, Rook I
  L. l. karu
    New Ireland
  L. l. albidior
    New Hanover
  L. l. ottomeyeri
    Lihir Is
  L. l. tabarensis
    Tabar I
  L. l. conjuncta
    St Matthias Is
  L. l. sumunae
    Dyaul I
Lalage maculosa (Spotted Triller)
  L. m. ultima
    Efate I
  L. m. modesta
    N & C New Hebrides
  L. m. melanopygia
    Santa Cruz I

L. m. vanikorensis
Vanikoro I
L. m. soror
Kandavu I
L. m. pumila
Viti Levu I
L. m. mixta
C & NW Fiji Is
L. m. woodi
Vanua Levu I
L. m. rotumae
Rotuma I
L. m. nesophila
Lau Archipelago
L. m. tabuensis
Tonga I
L. m. vauana
Vavau group, Fiji Is
L. m. keppeli
Keppel I, Boscawen I
L. m. futunae
Futuna I, Horne I
L. m. whitmeei
Niue I, Savage I
L. m. maculosa
Upolu I, Savaii I, Samoa Is

Lalage sharpei (Samoan Triller)
L. s. sharpei
Upolu I, Samoa Is
L. s. tenebrosa
Savaii I, Samoa Is

Lalage leucopyga (Long-tailed Triller)
L. l. affinis
San Cristobal I
L. l. deficiens
Torres I, Banks Is
L. l. albiloris
C & N New Hebrides
L. l. simillima
S New Hebrides, Loyalty Is
L. l. montrosieri
New Caledonia I
L. l. leucopyga
Norfolk I

CAMPEPHAGA
Campephega sulphurata (African Black Cuckoo Shrike)
Uganda, Somalia to Angola & South Africa
Campephega phoenicea (Red-shouldered Cuckoo Shrike)
Gambia to Ethiopia, N Zaire, Uganda
Campephaga petiti (Petit's Cuckoo Shrike)
S Cameroun to Kenya
Campephaga quiscalina (Purple-throated Cuckoo Shrike)
C. q. quiscalina
Sierra Leone to Cameroun & N Angola

C. q. martini
E Zaire, Uganda, Kenya
C. q. munzneri
Tanzania
Campephaga lobata (Wattled Cuckoo Shrike)
C. l. lobata
Liberia, Ghana
C. l. oriolina
S Cameroun, Gabon to E Zaire

PERICROCOTUS
Pericrocotus roseus (Rosy Minivet)
P. r. cantonensis
E China, Thailand, Laos
P. r. stanfordi
S China, S Thailand, S Laos
P. r. roseus
˙ SW China, Burma, Himalayas, N India
Pericrocotus divaricatus (Ashy Minivet)
P. d. divaricatus
NE Asia, Japan, E China, SE Asia, Philippine Is
P. d. tegimae
Riukiu Is
Pericrocotus cinnamomeus (Small Minivet)
P. c. malabaricus
W India
P. c. cinnamomeus
S India, Sri Lanka
P. c. pallidus
Pakistan
P. c. peregrinus
N India, Himalayas
P. c. vividus
Andaman Is
P. c. thai
Bhutan, Burma, N Thailand, Laos
P. c. sacerdos
Cambodia, S Vietnam
P. c. seperatus
S Burma, S Thailand
P. c. saturatus
Java, Bali I
P. c. igneus
Malaysia, Sumatra, Borneo, Palawan I
P. c. trophis
Simalur I
Pericrocotus lansbergei (Flores Minivet)
Sumbawa I, Flores I
Pericrocotus erythropygius (Jerdon's Minivet)
P. e. erythropygius
W Pakistan, C India
P. e. albifrons
C Burma

Pericrocotus solaris **(Yellow-throated Minivet)**

P. s. solaris
E Himalayas, NW Burma

P. s. rubrolimbatus
S Burma, N Thailand

P. s. montpellieri
SW China

P. s. griseogularis
SE China, Taiwan, N Indochina

P. s. deignani
S Vietnam

P. s. nassovicus
SE Thailand, Cambodia

P. s. montanus
Malaysia, W Sumatra

P. s. cinereigula
N Borneo

Pericrocotus ethologus **(Flame-coloured Minivet)**

P. e. favillaceus
Afghanistan, W Himalayas, W India

P. e. laetus
E Nepal, W Assam

P. e. ethologus
W China, N Thailand, N Indochina

P. e. yvettae
NE Burma

P. e. mariae
SE Assam, W Burma

P. e. ripponi
E Burma, NW Thailand

P. e. annamensis
S Vietnam

Pericrocotus brevirostris **(Short-billed Minivet)**

P. b. brevirostris
Himalayas, Nepal, W Assam

P. b. affinis
E Assam, NW Burma

P. b. neglectus
N Thailand, N Laos

P. b. anthoides
S China, N Vietnam

Pericrocotus miniatus **(Sunda Minivet)**
W Sumatra, Java

Pericrocotus flammeus **(Scarlet Minivet)**

P. f. flammeus
S India, Sri Lanka

P. f. siebersi
Java, Bali I

P. f. exul
Lombok I

P. f. andamanensis
Andaman Is

P. f. minythomelas
Simalur I

P. f. modiglianii
Enggano I

P. f. speciosus
Himalayas, N India

P. f. elegans
S Assam, N Burma, N Thailand,
N Indochina

P. f. fohkiensis
Fukien

P. f. semiruber
E India, S Burma, Thailand

P. f. flammifer
S Thailand, N & C Malaysia

P. f. xanthogaster
S Malaysia, Sumatra

P. f. insulanus
Borneo

P. f. novus
Luzon I, Negros I

P. f. leytensis
Samar I, Leyte I

P. f. johnstoniae
Mt Apo (Mindanao I)

P. f. marchesae
Jolo I

P. f. gonzalesi
Mt Katanglad (Mindanao I)

P. f. neglectus
Mindanao I

P. f. fraterculus
Assam

HEMIPUS

Hemipus picatus **(Bar-winged Flycatcher Shrike)**

H. p. capitalis
Himalayas, N Burma, N Thailand,
N Indochina

H. p. picatus
India, S Burma, S Thailand, S Indochina

H. p. intermedius
S Thailand, Malaysia, Sumatra, N Borneo

H. p. leggei
Sri Lanka

Hemipus hirundinaceus **(Black-winged Flycatcher Shrike)**
Malaysia, Sumatra, Java, Bali I, Borneo

TEPHRODORNIS

Tephrodornis gularis **(Brown-tailed Woo⌀ Shrike)**

T. g. sylvicola
W India

T. g. pelvica
E Himalayas, N Burma

T. g. jugans
S Burma, N Thailand

T. g. vernayi
SW Thailand

T. g. annectens
  S Thailand, N Malaysia
T. g. fretensis
  S Malaysia, Sumatra
T. g. gularis
  SW Sumatra, Java
T. g. frenata
  Borneo
T. g. mekongensis
  E Thailand, Cambodia, S Indochina
T. g. hainana
  N Indochina, Hainan I
T. g. latouchei
  Fukien

ephrodornis pondicerianus (Common Wood Shrike)
T. p. affinis
  Sri Lanka
T. p. pondicerianus
  E India, Burma, N Thailand, S Laos
T. p. pallidus
  Pakistan, NW India
T. p. orientis
  Cambodia, S Vietnam

20 PYCNONOTIDAE (BULBULS)

IZIXOS

oizixos canifrons (Crested Finchbill)
S. c. canifrons
  S Assam, W Burma
S. c. ingrami
  E Burma to S China, N Indochina

oizixos semitorques (Collared Finchbill)
S. s. semitorques
  S China
S. s. cinereicapillus
  Taiwan

CNONOTUS

ycnonotus zeylanicus (Straw-crowned Bulbul)
  Malaysia to Java, Borneo

ycnonotus striatus (Striated Green Bulbul)
P. s. striatus
  E Himalayas, W Burma
P. s. arctus
  NE Assam
P. s. paulus
  Burma to N Indochina, S China

ycnonotus leucogrammicus (Striated Bulbul)
  W Sumatra

ycnonotus tympanistrigus (Olive-crowned Bulbul)
  W Sumatra

ycnonotus melanoleucos (Black & White Bulbul)
  Malaysia, Sumatra, Borneo

Pycnonotus priocephalus (Grey-headed Bulbul)
  SW India

Pycnonotus atriceps (Black-headed Bulbul)
P. a. fuscoflavescens
  Andaman Is
P. a. atriceps
  NE India to Bali I, Borneo, Palawan I
P. a. hyperemnus
  W Sumatra Is
P. a. baweanus
  Bawean I
P. a. hodiernus
  Maratua I

Pycnonotus melanicterus (Black-crested Bulbul)
P. m. melanicterus
  Sri Lanka
P. m. gularis
  SW India
P. m. flaviventris
  Himalayas, NE India, N Burma
P. m. vantynei
  S Burma to N Indochina
P. m. xanthops
  SE Burma, N Thailand
P. m. auratus
  NE Thailand, W Laos
P. m. johnsoni
  SE Thailand, S Indochina
P. m. elbeli
  SE Thailand islands
P. m. negatus
  SW Thailand
P. m. caecilii
  N Malaysia
P. m. dispar
  Sumatra, Java
P. m. montis
  N Borneo

Pycnonotus squamatus (Scaly-breasted Bulbul)
P. s. weberi
  Malaysia, Sumatra
P. s. squamatus
  W & C Java
P. s. borneensis
  Borneo

Pycnonotus cyaniventris (Grey-bellied Bulbul)
P. c. cyaniventris
  Malaysia, Sumatra
P. c. paroticalis
  Borneo

Pycnonotus jocusus (Red-whiskered Bulbul)
P. j. fuscicaudatus
  W India

P. j. abuensis
N Bombay, SW Rajasthan

P. j. pyrrhotis
Nepal, N India

P. j. emeria
E India, Burma, SW Thailand

P. j. whistleri
Andaman Is

P. j. monticola
E Himalayas to SW China

P. j. pattani
Thailand, N Malaysia, S Indochina

P. j. hainanensis
N Vietnam, SE China

P. j. jocosus
S China

**Pycnonotus xanthorrhous (Anderson's
Bulbul)**

P. x. xanthorrhous
NE Burma to N Vietnam

P. x. andersoni
S China

Pycnonotus sinensis (Chinese Bulbul)

P. s. hoyi
C China

P. s. sinensis
E China

P. s. hainanus
Hainan I, SE China, N Vietnam

P. s. formosae
Taiwan

P. s. orii
S Riukiu Is

Pycnonotus taivanus (Formosan Bulbul)
Taiwan

**Pycnonotus leucogenys (White-cheeked
Bulbul)**

P. l. mesopotamiae
Iraq

P. l. dactylus
E Saudi Arabia

P. l. leucotis
S Iran to NW India

P. l. humii
NW Pakistan

P. l. leucogenys
Himalayas

Pycnonotus cafer (Red-vented Bulbul)

P. c. cafer
Sri Lanka

P. c. pusillus
S India

P. c. humayuni
Pakistan, NW India

P. c. wetmorei
NE India

P. c. intermedius
W Himalayas

P. c. bengalensis
E Himalayas, NE India

P. c. primrosei
S Assam

P. c. stanfordi
N Burma, W Yunnan

P. c. melanchimus
SC Burma

**Pycnonotus aurigaster (White-eared
Bulbul)**

P. a. chrysorrhoides
S China

P. a. resurrectus
SE China, N Vietnam

P. a. dolichurus
C Vietnam

P. a. latouchei
Burma to SW China, N Vietnam

P. a. klossi
SE Burma, N Thailand

P. a. schauenseei
S Burma, SW Thailand

P. a. thais
S Thailand

P. a. germani
SE Thailand, S Indochina

P. a. aurigaster
Sumatra, Java

**Pycnonotus xanthopygos (Black-capped
Bulbul)**
Syria to Aden

Pycnonotus nigricans (Red-eyed Bulbul)

P. n. nigricans
Namibia, S Botswana, N Cape Province

P. n. grisescentior
E & N Botswana, S Angola to Rhodesia

P. n. superior
NE Cape Province, S Transvaal

Pycnonotus capensis (Cape Bulbul)
S & SW Cape Province

Pycnonotus barbatus (Common Bulbul)

P. b. barbatus
North Africa

P. b. inornatus
Senegal to Ghana

P. b. goodi
S Sahara, N Cameroun

P. b. arsinoe
Nile valley, Sudan

P. b. schoanus
E Ethiopia

P. b. somaliensis
SE Ethiopia, Somalia

P. b. nigeriae
C & S Nigeria to Gabon

P. b. gabonensis
W Gabon

P. b. tricolor
  N Namibia to S Uganda, S Tanzania
P. b. minor
  N Zaire, S Sudan
P. b. spurius
  S Ethiopia
P. b. fayi
  Kenya, C Tanzania
P. b. ngamii
  S Zambia, Botswana
P. b. layardi
  SE Africa
P. b. tenebrior
  E Cape Province, S Lesotho
P. b. micrus
  SE Kenya, E Tanzania
P. b. peasei
  S Ethiopia, E Kenya
P. b. dodsoni
  N Kenya, S Somalia, E Ethiopia
Pycnonotus eutilotus (Puff-backed Bulbul)
  Malaysia, Sumatra, Borneo
Pycnonotus nieuwenhuisii (Blue-wattled Bulbul)
P. n. inexpectatus
  Lesten (Sumatra)
P. n. nieuwenhuisii
  Kayan river (Borneo)
Pycnonotus urostictus (Yellow-wattled Bulbul)
P. u. ilokensis
  N Luzon I
P. u. urostictus
  C Luzon I
P. u. otricaudatus
  Bohol I, Samar I, Leyte I
P. u. philippensis
  Mindanao I
P. u. basilanicus
  Basilan I
Pycnonotus bimaculatus (Orange-spotted Bulbul)
P. b. snouckaerti
  NW Sumatra
P. b. barat
  SW Sumatra, W & C Java
P. b. bimaculatus
  E Java, Bali I
Pycnonotus finlaysoni (Stripe-throated Bulbul)
P. f. davisoni
  S Burma
P. f. eous
  Thailand, C & S Indochina
P. f. finlaysoni
  Malaysia

Pycnonotus xantholaemus (Yellow-throated Bulbul)
  S India
Pycnonotus penicillatus (Yellow-tufted Bulbul)
  Sri Lanka
Pycnonotus flavescens (Flavescent Bulbul)
P. f. flavescens
  S Assam, W Burma
P. f. vividus
  Burma, Thailand, N Indochina
P. f. sordidus
  S Indochina
P. f. leucops
  N Borneo
Pycnonotus goiavier (Yellow-vented Bulbul)
P. g. jambu
  SE Thailand, S Indochina
P. g. personatus
  Malaysia, Sumatra
P. g. analis
  Java, Bali I, Lombok I
P. g. gourdini
  Borneo
P. g. goiavier
  N & C Philippine Is
P. g. suluensis
  S Philippine Is
Pycnonotus luteolus (White-browed Bulbul)
P. l. luteolus
  C & S India
P. l. insulae
  Sri Lanka
Pycnonotus plumosus (Olive-brown Bulbul)
P. p. plumosus
  Malaysia, E Sumatra, Java
P. p. porphyreus
  W Sumatra and islands
P. p. billitonis
  Billiton I, W & S Borneo
P. p. hutzi
  N & E Borneo
P. p. chiroplethis
  Anamba Is
P. p. hachisukae
  N Borneo Is
P. p. cinereifrons
  Palawan I
P. p. sibergi
  Bawean I, Java Sea
Pycnonotus blanfordi (Blanford's Olive Bulbul)
P. b. blanfordi
  C & S Burma

P. b. conradi
Thailand, N Malaysia, S Indochina
P. b. robinsoni
C Malaysia
Pycnonotus simplex (White-eyed Brown Bulbul)
P. s. simplex
S Thailand, Malaysia, Sumatra
P. s. prillwitzi
Java
P. s. oblitus
Bangka I, Billiton I, S & W Borneo
P. s. halizonus
Anamba Is, N Natuna Is
P. s. perplexus
N & E Borneo
Pycnonotus brunneus (Red-eyed Brown Bulbul)
P. b. brunneus
Malaysia, Sumatra, Borneo
P. b. zapolius
Anamba Is
Pycnonotus erythrophthalmus (Lesser Brown Bulbul)
P. e. erythrophthalmus
Malaysia, Billiton I, Sumatra
P. e. salvadorii
Borneo
Pycnonotus masukuensis (Shelley's Greenbul)
P. m. kakamegae
E Zaire, W Kenya, W Tanzania
P. m. roehli
C Tanzania
P. m. masukuensis
SW Tanzania, N Malawi
Pycnonotus montanus (Mountain Little Greenbul)
Togo, Ghana, Cameroun
Pycnonotus virens (Little Greenbul)
P. v. erythropterus
Gambia to S Nigeria
P. v. virens
Gabon to Sudan, Uganda, Angola
P. v. holochlorus
W Uganda
P. v. zombensis
E Angola, SE Zaire to E Kenya, Mozambique
P. v. marwitzi
SE Kenya
P. v. zanzibaricus
Zanzibar I
Pycnonotus hallae (Hall's Greenbul)
E Zaire
Pycnonotus gracilis (Little Grey Greenbul)
P. g. extremus
Sierra Leone to S Nigeria

P. g. gracilis
Cameroun to Uganda & N Angola
P. g. ugandae
E Zaire, Uganda
Pycnonotus ansorgei (Ansorge's Greenbu
P. a. ansorgei
Sierra Leone to S Nigeria
P. a. muniensis
Cameroun, Gabon, N Zaire
P. a. kavirondensis
Kenya
Pycnonotus curvirostris (Cameroun Sombre Greenbul)
P. c. leoninus
Sierra Leone to Ghana
P. c. curvirostris
S Ghana to W Kenya, N Angola
Pycnonotus importunus (Sombre Greenbul)
P. i. fricki
WC Kenya
P. i. somaliensis
S Somalia
P. i. subalaris
S Kenya
P. i. insularis
E Tanzania, Zanzibar I
P. i. hypoxanthus
S Tanzania, Malawi, Mozambique
P. i. oleaginus
S Mozambique, N Natal
P. i. noomei
E Rhodesia to Natal, C Cape Province
P. i. importunus
S & E Cape Province
Pycnonotus latirostris (Yellow-whiskerec Greenbul)
P. l. congener
Sierra Leone to S Nigeria
P. l. latirostris
SE Nigeria to W Zaire, N Angola
P. l. eugenius
S Sudan, E Zaire to NW Tanzania
P. l. saturatus
E Kenya, N Tanzania
Pycnonotus gracilirostris (Slender-billed Greenbul)
P. g. gracilirostris
Senegal to Nigeria
P. g. congensis
S Cameroun to W Zaire, N Angola
P. g. chagwensis
N Zaire to W Kenya, NW Tanzania
P. g. percivali
C Kenya

Pycnonotus tephrolaemus (Olive-breasted Mountain Greenbul)
P. t. tephrolaemus
    Cameroun Mt, Fernando Po I
P. t. bamendae
    SE Nigeria, Cameroun
P. t. kikuyuensis
    E Zaire to Uganda, W Kenya
P. t. kungwensis
    W Tanzania
P. t. nigriceps
    SW Kenya, N Tanzania
P. t. usambarae
    NE Tanzania
P. t. neumanni
    E Tanzania
P. t. fusciceps
    SW Tanzania, Malawi, NW Mozambique
P. t. chlorigula
    C Tanzania

Pycnonotus milanjensis (Stripe-cheeked Greenbul)
P. m. striifacies
    SE Kenya, N Tanzania
P. m. olivaceiceps
    SW Tanzania, N Malawi, N Mozambique
P. m. milanjensis
    Malawi, Rhodesia, W Mozambique
P. m. disjuncta
    E Rhodesia

CALYPTOCICHLA
Calyptocichla serina (Serine Greenbul)
    Sierra Leone to N Zaire, Gabon

BAEOPOGON
Baeopogon indicator (Honeyguide Greenbul)
B. i. leucurus
    Sierra Leone, Liberia
B. i. togoensis
    Ghana, Togo
B. i. indicator
    Cameroun to N Angola, W Zaire
B. i. chlorosaturata
    E Zaire to Sudan, Uganda

Baeopogon clamans (Sjostedt's Honeyguide Greenbul)
    Cameroun to NE Zaire, Gabon

IXONOTUS
Ixonotus guttatus (Spotted Greenbul)
I. g. guttatus
    Ghana, Gabon to C Zaire
I. g. bugoma
    E Zaire, W Uganda

CHLOROCICHLA
Chlorocichla falkensteini (Yellow-necked Greenbul)
C. f. viridescentior
    River Ja, Cameroun
C. f. falkensteini
    SW Zaire, N Angola

Chlorocichla simplex (Simple Greenbul)
    Guinea to Zaire, N Angola

Chlorocichla flavicollis (Yellow-throated Leaf-Love)
C. f. flavicollis
    Senegal to Cameroun
C. f. adamauae
    N Cameroun
C. f. simplicicolor
    E Cameroun
C. f. soror
    Cameroun to Zaire, S Sudan
C. f. flavigula
    Angola to NW Tanzania, Zambia
C. f. pallidigula
    Uganda, W Kenya

Chlorocichla flaviventris (Yellow-bellied Greenbul)
C. f. centralis
    Kenya, Tanzania, N Mozambique
C. f. occidentalis
    N Namibia, S Angola to S Mozambique
C. f. flaviventris
    Natal

Chlorocichla laetissima (Joyful Greenbul)
C. l. laetissima
    E Zaire to S Sudan, W Kenya
C. l. schoutedeni
    SE Zaire, SW Tanzania, NE Zambia

Chlorocichla prigoginei (Prigogine's Greenbul)
    Lake Edward, E Zaire

THESCELOCICHLA
Thescelocichla leucopleura (Swamp Bulbul)
    Senegal to Gabon, W Uganda

PHYLLASTREPHUS
Phyllastrephus scandens (Leaf-Love)
P. s. scandens
    Senegal to Cameroun
P. s. acedis
    S Cameroun, Gabon, SW Zaire
P. s. orientalis
    Central African Republic to Sudan & Tanzania
P. s. upembae
    S Zaire, W Tanzania

***Phyllastrephus terrestris* (Bristle-necked Brownbul)**
P. t. bensoni
C Kenya
P. t. katangae
Katanga, Zaire
P. t. suahelicus
SE Kenya, E Tanzania, N Mozambique
P. t. intermedius
S Angola to Mozambique, N Natal
P. t. terrestris
Transvaal, S Natal, Cape Province
***Phyllastrephus strepitans* (Northern Brownbul)**
S Sudan to E Tanzania
***Phyllastrephus cerviniventris* (Grey Olive Greenbul)**
P. c. cerviniventris
C Kenya to Zambia & Mozambique
P. c. schoutedeni
Katanga, Zaire
***Phyllastrephus fulviventris* (Pale Olive Greenbul)**
Central African Republic to Angola
***Phyllastrephus poensis* (Cameroun Olive Greenbul)**
S Nigeria, Cameroun Mt
***Phyllastrephus hypochloris* (Toro Olive Greenbul)**
S Sudan to E Zaire
***Phyllastrephus baumanni* (Baumann's Greenbul)**
Sierra Leone to S Nigeria
***Phyllastrephus poliocephalus* (Grey-headed Greenbul)**
SE Nigeria, Cameroun Mt
***Phyllastrephus flavostriatus* (Yellow-streaked Greenbul)**
P. f. graueri
E Zaire
P. f. olivaceogriseus
E Zaire, SW Uganda
P. f. kungwensis
W Tanzania
P. f. tenuirostris
SE Kenya to NE Mozambique
P. f. alfredi
SW Tanzania, E Zambia, N Malawi
P. f. vincenti
S Malawi, W Mozambique
P. f. flavostriatus
E South Africa
***Phyllastrephus debilis* (Slender Greenbul)**
P. d. rabai
E Kenya, E Tanzania
P. d. albigula
N Tanzania

P. d. debilis
S Tanzania, Mozambique
***Phyllastrephus lorenzi* (Sassi's Olive Greenbul)**
E Zaire
***Phyllastrephus albigularis* (White-throated Greenbul)**
P. a. albigularis
Sierra Leone to Sudan, Uganda
P. a. viridiceps
N Angola
***Phyllastrephus fischeri* (Fischer's Greenbul)**
P. f. sucosus
S Sudan to E Zaire, W Tanzania
P. f. cabanisi
Angola to S Zaire & Zambia
P. f. placidus
SE Kenya to Malawi, Mozambique
P. f. fischeri
E Tanzania, E Mozambique
***Phyllastrephus orostruthus* (Dappled Mountain Greenbul)**
P. o. amani
N Tanzania
P. o. orostruthus
N Mozambique
***Phyllastrephus icterinus* (Icterine Greenbul)**
P. i. icterinus
Sierra Leone to Nigeria
P. i. tricolor
Cameroun to W Uganda, C Zaire
***Phyllastrephus xavieri* (Xavier's Greenbul)**
P. x. serlei
Cameroun Mt
P. x. xavieri
Cameroun to S Central African Republic, N Zaire
P. x. sethsmithi
E Zaire, Uganda
***Phyllastrephus madagascariensis* (Madagascar Tetraka)**
P. m. madagascariensis
E Madagascar
P. m. inceleber
N & W Madagascar
***Phyllastrephus zosterops* (Short-billed Tetraka)**
P. z. fulvescens
N Madagascar
P. z. andapae
NE Madagascar
P. z. zosterops
E Madagascar
P. z. ankafanae
SE Madagascar

Phyllastrephus apperti (Appert's Tetraka)
  SW Madagascar
Phyllastrephus tenebrosus (Dusky Tetraka)
  E Madagascar
**Phyllastrephus xanthophrys
  (Yellow-browed Foditany)**
  E Madagascar
**Phyllastrephus cinereiceps (Grey-crowned
  Foditany)**
  E Madagascar

BLEDA
Bleda syndactyla (Common Bristle-Bill)
  B. s. syndactyla
    Senegal to S Nigeria
  B. s. multicolor
    S Nigeria to Zambia
  B. s. woosnami
    Sudan, Uganda, NW Kenya
Bleda eximia (Green-tailed Bristle-Bill)
  B. e. eximia
    Sierra Leone to Ghana
  B. e. notata
    S Nigeria to Central African Republic
  B. e. ugandae
    Sudan, Uganda, N Zaire
**Bleda canicapilla (Grey-headed Bristle-
  Bill)**
    Gambia to S Nigeria

CRINIGER
Criniger barbatus (Bearded Greenbul)
  C. b. barbatus
    Sierra Leone to Togo
  C. b. ansorgeanus
    S Nigeria
  C. b. chloronotus
    Cameroun to Central African Republic
  C. b. weileri
    E Zaire
Criniger calurus (White-bearded Greenbul)
  C. c. verreauxi
    Guinea to Nigeria
  C. c. calurus
    S Nigeria to Central African Republic
  C. c. emini
    Zaire, Uganda
**Criniger ndussumensis (White-bearded
  Bulbul)**
    Cameroun to N Zaire
**Criniger olivaceus (Yellow-throated Olive
  Bulbul)**
    Senegal to Ghana
Criniger finschii (Finsch's Bearded Bulbul)
    Malaysia, Sumatra, Borneo
**Criniger flaveolus (Ashy-fronted Bearded
  Bulbul)**
  C. f. flaveolus
    Himalayas to NE Burma

  C. f. burmanicus
    SE Burma, W Thailand
**Criniger pallidus (Olivaceus Bearded
  Bulbul)**
  C. p. griseiceps
    S Burma
  C. p. robinsoni
    Tenasserim, S Burma
  C. p. henrici
    N Thailand, N Indochina
  C. p. pallidus
    Hainan I
  C. p. isani
    NE Thailand
  C. p. annamensis
    C Indochina
  C. p. khmerensis
    S Indochina
**Criniger ochraceus (Ochraceous Bearded
  Bulbul)**
  C. o. hallae
    S Vietnam
  C. o. cambodianus
    SE Thailand, SW Cambodia
  C. o. ochraceus
    S Burma, SW Thailand
  C. o. sordidus
    C Malaysia
  C. o. sacculatus
    S Malaysia
  C. o. sumatranus
    W Sumatra
  C. o. fowleri
    N Borneo
  C. o. ruficrissus
    NE Borneo
**Criniger bres (Grey-cheeked Bearded
  Bulbul)**
  C. b. tephrogenys
    Malaysia, E Sumatra
  C. b. bres
    W & C Java
  C. b. balicus
    E Java, Bali I
  C. b. gutteralis
    Borneo
  C. b. frater
    Palawan I
**Criniger phaeocephalus (Grey-headed
  Bearded Bulbul)**
  C. p. phaeocephalus
    Malaysia, Sumatra, Bangka I, Billiton I
  C. p. connectens
    NE Borneo
  C. p. sulphuratus
    C Borneo
  C. p. diardi
    W Borneo

Setornis criniger (Long-billed Bulbul)
E Sumatra, Bangka I, Borneo

HYPSIPETES

Hypsipetes viridescens (Blyth's Olive Bulbul)
H. v. cacharensis
S Assam
H. v. myitkyinensis
NE Burma
H. v. viridescens
S Burma, SW Thailand

Hypsipetes propinquus (Grey-eyed Bulbul)
H. p. aquilonis
N Vietnam
H. p. propinquus
E Burma, N Thailand, N Laos
H. p. simulator
SE Thailand, S Indochina
H. p. innectens
S Vietnam
H. p. lekhakuni
S Burma, SW Thailand
H. p. cinnamomeoventris
N Malaysia

Hypsipetes charlottae (Crested Olive Bulbul)
H. c. cryptus
Malaysia, Sumatra & islands
H. c. charlottae
S & W Borneo
H. c. perplexus
N & E Borneo

Hypsipetes palawanensis (Golden-eyed Bulbul)
Palawan I

Hypsipetes criniger (Hairy-backed Bulbul)
H. c. criniger
Malaysia, E Sumatra
H. c. sericeus
W Sumatra
H. c. viridis
Borneo

Hypsipetes philippinus (Rufous-breasted Bulbul)
H. p. philippinus
Luzon I, Samar I, Leyte I, Bohol I
H. p. guimarasensis
Masbate I, Panay I, Negros I
H. p. saturatior
E Mindanao I
H. p. mindorensis
Mindoro I
H. p. rufigularis
W Mindanao I, Basilan I

Hypsipetes siquijorensis (Slaty-crowned Bulbul)
H. s. cinereiceps
Tablas I, Romblon I
H. s. monticola
Cebu I
H. s. siquijorensis
Siquijor I

Hypsipetes everetti (Yellow-washed Bulbul)
H. e. everetti
Dinagat I, E & C Mindanao I
H. e. haynaldi
Sulu Archipelago
H. e. samarensis
Samar I, Leyte I
H. e. catarmanensis
Camiguin (South I)

Hypsipetes affinis (Golden Bulbul)
H. a. platenae
Sanghir Is
H. a. aureus
Togian I
H. a. harterti
Peleng Is, Banggai I
H. a. longirostris
Sula Is
H. a. chloris
Morotai I, Halmahera I, Batjan I
H. a. lucasi
Obi I
H. a. mystacalis
Buru I
H. a. affinis
Ceram I
H. a. flavicaudus
Ambon I

Hypsipetes indicus (Golden-browed Bulbul)
H. i. ictericus
W India
H. i. indicus
SW India, Sri Lanka
H. i. guglielmi
SW Sri Lanka

Hypsipetes mcclellandii (Mountain Streaked Bulbul)
H. m. mcclellandii
E Himalayas, Assam
H. m. ventralis
SW Burma
H. m. tickelli
E Burma, NW Thailand
H. m. similis
NE Burma to N Indochina
H. m. holtii
S China

H. m. loquax
N & E Thailand, S Laos
H. m. griseiventer
S Vietnam
H. m. canescens
SE Thailand
H. m. peracensis
S Thailand, N Malaysia
Hypsipetes malaccensis (Green-backed Bulbul)
S Vietnam, Malaysia, Sumatra, Borneo
Hypsipetes virescens (Sumatran Bulbul)
H. v. sumatranus
W Sumatra
H. v. virescens
Java
Hypsipetes flavalus (Ashy Bulbul)
H. f. flavalus
E Himalayas, NW Burma
H. f. cannipennis
S China, NE Vietnam
H. f. castanotus
Hainan I
H. f. bourdellei
E Thailand, N Laos
H. f. remotus
S Indochina
H. f. hildebrandi
S Burma, NW Thailand
H. f. davisoni
S Burma, SW Thailand
H. f. cinereus
Malaysia, Sumatra
H. f. connectens
N Borneo
Hypsipetes amaurotis (Chestnut-eared Bulbul)
H. a. hensoni
N Japan, S Korea, NE China
H. a. amaurotis
C Japan, Riukiu Is
H. a. matchiae
S Kyushu Is
H. a. squamiceps
Bonin Is
H. a. magnirostris
Volcano Is
H. a. borodinonis
Borodino Is
H. a. ogawae
N Riukiu Is
H. a. pryeri
C Riukiu Is
H. a. insignis
Miyakojima Is (S Riukiu Is)
H. a. stejnegeri
S Riukiu Is

H. a. nagamichii
S Taiwan
H. a. batanensis
Batjan I
H. a. fugensis
Calayan I, Fuga I
H. a. camiguinensis
Camiguin Is
Hypsipetes crassirostris (Thick-billed Bulbul)
Seychelles Is
Hypsipetes borbonicus (Reunion Bulbul)
H. b. borbonicus
Réunion I
H. b. olivaceus
Mauritius I
Hypsipetes madagascariensis (Black Bulbul)
H. m. madagascariensis
Madagascar
H. m. grotei
Glorioso I
H. m. parvirostris
Comoro Is
H. m. rostratus
Aldabra I
H. m. humii
Sri Lanka
H. m. ganeesa
SW India
H. m. psaroides
Himalayas
H. m. nigrescens
E Assam, W Burma
H. m. concolor
E Burma, SW China to S Vietnam
H. m. ambiens
NE Burma
H. m. sinensis
SW China, Thailand, Laos
H. m. stresemanni
SW China, Thailand, Laos
H. m. leucothorax
W China to N Vietnam
H. m. leucocephalus
SE China
H. m. nigerrimus
Taiwan
H. m. perniger
Hainan I
Hypsipetes nicobariensis (Nicobar Bulbul)
Nicobar Is
Hypsipetes thompsoni (Bingham's Bulbul)
S Burma, NW Thailand

NEOLESTES
Neolestes torquatus (Black-collared Bulbul)
Gabon, Zaire, Angola

Tylas eduardi (Kinkimavo)
　T. e. eduardi
　　E Madagascar
　T. e. albigularis
　　WC Madagascar

121 IRENIDAE (LEAFBIRDS, IORAS)

AEGITHINA
Aegithina tiphia (Common Iora)
　A. t. multicolor
　　S India, Sri Lanka
　A. t. deignani
　　SC India, N & C Burma
　A. t. humei
　　C India
　A. t. tiphia
　　NE India
　A. t. septentrionalis
　　Pakistan, NW India
　A. t. philipi
　　SW China, C Burma, N Thailand, Laos,
　　　N Vietnam
　A. t. cambodiana
　　Cambodia, SE Thailand, S Vietnam
　A. t. horizoptera
　　S Burma, S Thailand, Malaysia, Sumatra
　A. t. micromelaena
　　N Malaysia
　A. t. singapurensis
　　S Malaysia
　A. t. scapularis
　　Java, Bali I
　A. t. viridus
　　S Borneo
　A. t. aequanimis
　　N Borneo, Palawan I
　A. t. trudiae
　　Brunei Bay
Aegithina nigrolutea (Marshall's Iora)
　Pakistan, NC India
Aegithina viridissima (Green Iora)
　A. v. viridissima
　　S Thailand, Malaysia, Sumatra, Borneo
　A. v. thapsina
　　Anamba Is
Aegithina lafresnayei (Great Iora)
　A. l. lafresnayei
　　S Thailand, Malaysia
　A. l. innotata
　　S Burma, N Thailand, N Indochina
　A. l. xanthotis
　　Cambodia, S Indochina

CHLOROPSIS
Chloropsis flavipennis (Yellow-quilled Leafbird)
　Cebu I, Mindanao I

Chloropsis palawanensis (Palawan Leafbird)
　Palawan I
Chloropsis sonnerati (Greater Green Leafbird)
　C. s. sonnerati
　　Java
　C. s. zosterops
　　S Thailand, Malaysia, Sumatra, Borneo
　C. s. parvirostris
　　Nias I
Chloropsis cyanopogon (Lesser Green Leafbird)
　C. c. cyanopogon
　　S Burma, Thailand, Malaysia, Sumatra,
　　　Borneo
　C. c. septentrionalis
　　S Thailand
Chloropsis cochinchinensis (Blue-winged Leafbird)
　C. c. cochinchinensis
　　Burma, SE Thailand, Cambodia,
　　　S Indochina
　C. c. kinneari
　　E Thailand, N Indochina
　C. c. serithai
　　S Thailand
　C. c. moluccensis
　　S Thailand, Malaysia
　C. c. icterocephala
　　S Malaysia, Sumatra
　C. c. natunensis
　　Natuna Is
　C. c. billitonis
　　Billiton I
　C. c. viridinucha
　　Borneo
　C. c. nigricollis
　　Java
　C. c. jerdoni
　　S India, Sri Lanka
Chloropsis aurifrons (Golden-fronted Leafbird)
　C. a. aurifrons
　　Himalayas, Burma, NE India
　C. a. frontalis
　　C & S India
　C. a. insularis
　　SW India, Sri Lanka
　C. a. pridii
　　S Burma, N Thailand, N Laos
　C. a. inornata
　　C & S Thailand, Cambodia, S Vietnam
　C. a. incompta
　　SW Thailand, S Indochina
　C. a. media
　　Sumatra

Chloropsis hardwickei (Orange-bellied Leafbird)
  C. h. hardwickei
    Burma, E Himalayas, N Thailand, N Vietnam
  C. h. malayana
    Malaysia
  C. h. melliana
    S China, N Vietnam
  C. h. lazulina
    Hainan I
Chloropsis venusta (Blue-masked Leafbird)
  Sumatra

IRENA
Irena puella (Blue-backed Fairy Bluebird)
  I. p. puella
    S India
  I. p. sikkimensis
    Sikkim, Assam, N India, Burma, Thailand
  I. p. malayensis
    Malaysia
  I. p. criniger
    Sumatra, Borneo
  I. p. turcosa
    Java
  I. p. tweeddalei
    Palawan I
Irena cyanogaster (Black-mantled Fairy Bluebird)
  I. c. cyanogaster
    Luzon I
  I. c. ellae
    Samar I, Leyte I
  I. c. melanochlamys
    Basilan I
  I. c. hoogstraali
    Mindanao I

122 LANIIDAE (SHRIKES)

PRIONOPINAE

EUROCEPHALUS
Eurocephalus rüppelli (Rüppells White-crowned Shrike)
  S Sudan to Tanzania
Eurocephalus anguitimens (White-crowned Shrike)
  E. a. anguitimens
    Namibia to E Transvaal
  E. a. niveus
    E Transvaal

PRIONOPS
Prionops plumata (Long-crested Helmet Shrike)
  P. p. plumata
    Senegal to Nigeria

  P. p. adamauae
    N Cameroun
  P. p. concinnata
    Cameroun to Sudan & Uganda
  P. p. cristata
    E & S Ethiopia, SE Sudan
  P. p. melanoptera
    Somalia, E Ethiopia
  P. p. vinaceigularis
    E & C Ethiopia, N & E Kenya
  P. p. angolica
    Namibia to E Zaire, S Kenya
  P. p. poliocephala
    E Tanzania to Transvaal, Natal
Prionops poliolopha (Grey-crested Helmet Shrike)
  SW Kenya, W Tanzania
Prionops caniceps (Red-billed Shrike)
  P. c. caniceps
    Sierra Leone to Togo
  P. c. harterti
    S Nigeria
  P. c. rufiventris
    Cameroun, Central African Republic, N Zaire
  P. c. mentalis
    E & S Zaire, W Uganda
Prionops alberti (Yellow-crested Helmet Shrike)
  E Zaire
Prionops retzii (Retz's Red-billed Helmet Shrike)
  P. r. neumanni
    S Somalia
  P. r. graculina
    E Kenya, NE Tanzania
  P. r. tricolor
    Tanzania, Zambia to Mozambique
  P. r. intermedia
    NW Tanzania
  P. r. nigricans
    W Tanzania, S Zaire to Angola
  P. r. retzii
    Namibia to NE Transvaal
Prionops gabela (Rand's Red-billed Helmet Shrike)
  Gabela (Angola)
Prionops scopifrons (Chestnut-fronted Helmet Shrike)
  P. s. keniensis
    C Kenya
  P. s. kirki
    E Kenya, NE Tanzania
  P. s. scopifrons
    SE Tanzania, Mozambique

LANIOTURDUS
Lanioturdus torquatus (Chat-Shrike)
  L. t. torquatus
    S Angola, Namibia
  L. t. mesicus
    Huila, Angola

NILAUS
Nilaus afer (Brubru Shrike)
  N. a. afer
    Senegal to Ethiopia
  N. a. camerunensis
    Cameroun, Central African Republic
  N. a. hilgerti
    C Ethiopia
  N. a. minor
    E Eritrea to E Kenya
  N. a. massaicus
    SW Kenya to Rwanda, E Zaire
  N. a. nigritemporalis
    SC Zaire to Tanzania & Natal
  N. a. brubru
    S Angola to N Cape Province
  N. a. solivagus
    Natal
  N. a. affinis
    N Angola
  N. a. miombensis
    Sul do Save, Mozambique

DRYOSCOPUS
Dryoscopus pringlii (Pringle's Puffback)
  Somalia to NE Tanzania
Dryoscopus gambensis (Puffback)
  D. g. gambensis
    Senegal to Cameroun & Chad
  D. g. congicus
    Gabon to SW Zaire
  D. g. malzacii
    Central African Republic to Sudan &
      Kenya
  D. g. erythreae
    E Sudan, Ethiopia
  D. g. erwini
    E Zaire to N Tanzania
Dryoscopus cubla (Black-backed Puffback)
  D. c. affinis
    E Kenya, Zanzibar
  D. c. nairobiensis
    S Kenya, N Tanzania
  D. c. hamatus
    S Kenya to Mozambique & Angola
  D. c. chapini
    S Mozambique to N Transvaal
  D. c. okavangensis
    N Botswana to S Angola, Namibia
  D. c. cubla
    Natal, Cape Province
Dryoscopus senegalensis (Red-eyed Puffback)
  S Nigeria to Uganda
Dryoscopus angolensis (Pink-footed Puffback)
  D. a. boydi
    Cameroun
  D. a. angolensis
    SW Zaire, N Angola
  D. a. nandensis
    E Zaire to Sudan & W Kenya
  D. a. kungwensis
    W Tanzania
Dryoscopus sabini (Sabine's Puffback)
  D. s. sabini
    Sierra Leone to S Nigeria
  D. s. melanoleucus
    Cameroun to C Zaire

TCHAGRA
Tchagra minuta (Lesser Bush Shrike)
  T. m. minuta
    Sierra Leone to Ethiopia & Kenya
  T. m. reichenowi
    E Kenya, NE Tanzania
  T. m. anchietae
    Angola to Tanzania, Malawi
  T. m. remota
    S Rhodesia
Tchagra senegala (Black-headed Bush Shrike)
  T. s. cucullata
    N Africa
  T. s. percivali
    S Arabia
  T. s. remigialis
    Sudan
  T. s. notha
    Mali to Chad
  T. s. senegala
    Senegal to Sierra Leone
  T. s. pallida
    Upper Volta, Ivory Coast to N Central
      African Republic
  T. s. camerunensis
    Cameroun to S Sudan, Uganda
  T. s. habessinica
    E Sudan to Somalia
  T. s. armena
    S Uganda to SE Zaire, Zambia
  T. s. orientalis
    S Somalia to E Tanzania
  T. s. confusa
    E Transvaal, Natal, E Cape Province
  T. s. kalahari
    Rhodesia to S Angola, Namibia

T. s. rufofusca
SW Zaire, N Angola
Tchagra tchagra (Levaillant's Bush Shrike)
T. t. tchagra
S Cape Province
T. t. natalensis
E Cape Province to Natal
T. t. caffrariae
E Cape Province
Tchagra australis (Brown-headed Bush Shrike)
T. a. ussheri
Sierra Leone to Nigeria
T. a. emini
E Zaire to S Sudan, W Kenya
T. a. frater
Nigeria to Gabon, W Zaire
T. a. minor
Kenya, NW Tanzania
T. a. littoralis
E Kenya to Rhodesia, Natal
T. a. congener
S Tanzania, Malawi, Zambia
T. a. ansorgei
W Angola
T. a. bocagei
Cuando, Angola
T. a. souzae
SE Zaire to Angola
T. a. australis
E Botswana, Transvaal, Rhodesia
T. a. damarensis
Namibia, W Botswana
Tchagra jamesi (Three-streaked Bush Shrike)
T. j. jamesi
Uganda to Somalia, N Kenya
T. j. mandana
E Kenya, Manda I, Lamu I
Tchagra cruenta (Rosy-patched Shrike)
T. c. cruenta
Sudan, N Ethiopia
T. c. hilgerti
Somalia, E Ethiopia, N Kenya
T. c. cathemagmena
S Kenya, E Tanzania

LANIARIUS
Laniarius ruficeps (Red-crowned Bush Shrike)
L. r. ruficeps
Somalia
L. r. rufinuchalis
Ethiopia to SE Kenya
L. r. kismayensis
S Somalia
Laniarius lühderi (Lüdher's Bush Shrike)
L. l. lühderi
Cameroun to Sudan, Kenya

L. l. castaneiceps
S Uganda, W Kenya
L. l. brauni
NW Angola
L. l. amboimensis
W Angola
Laniarius turatii (Turati's Boubou)
Senegal to Sierra Leone
Laniarius aethiopicus (Tropical Boubou)
L. a. major
Sierra Leone to Sudan & Malawi
L. a. aethiopicus
Ethiopia, Somalia, N Kenya
L. a. ambiguus
Kenya, N Tanzania
L. a. erlangeri
S Somalia
L. a. sublacteus
E Kenya, Zanzibar I
L. a. mossambicus
S Zaire, E Zambia, Mozambique
Laniarius bicolor (Gabon Boubou)
L. b. bicolor
Cameroun, Gabon
L. b. guttatus
W Zaire, Angola
L. b. sticturus
S Angola, N Botswana, W Zambia
Laniarius ferrugineus (Southern Boubou)
L. f. limpopoensis
SE Rhodesia, N Transvaal
L. f. transvaalensis
S & E Transvaal
L. f. tongensis
S Mozambique, N Natal
L. f. natalensis
W Natal
L. f. pondoensis
E Cape Province
L. f. savensis
S Mozambique
L. f. ferrugineus
W Cape Province
Laniarius barbarus (Common Gonolek)
L. b. helenae
Sierra Leone
L. b. barbarus
Senegal to N Cameroun
Laniarius erythrogaster (Black-headed Gonolek)
N Cameroun to Tanzania
Laniarius mufumbiri (Mufumbiri Shrike)
Uganda, Rwanda
Laniarius atrococcineus (Burchell's Gonolek)
S Angola to Transvaal

Laniarius atroflavus (Yellow-breasted Boubou)
L. a. atroflavus
Cameroun Mt
L. a. craterum
highlands of Cameroun
Laniarius fülleborni (Fülleborn's Black Boubou)
L. f. camerunensis
W Cameroun
L. f. poensis
E Nigeria, Cameroun
L. f. holomelas
E Zaire, Uganda
L. f. usambaricus
W Tanzania
L. f. ulugurensis
Tanzania
L. f. fulleborni
SW Tanzania, N Malawi, E Zambia
Laniarius funebris (Slate-coloured Boubou)
L. f. funebris
S Sudan & Somalia to Tanzania
L. f. degener
S Ethiopia, S Somalia, E Kenya
Laniarius leucorhynchus (Sooty Boubou)
Sierra Leone to Sudan, W Kenya

TELOPHORUS
Telophorus bocagei (Grey-green Bush Shrike)
T. b. bocagei
C Cameroun to N Angola
T. b. jacksoni
C Zaire, Uganda, W Kenya
T. b. ansorgei
SW Zaire, N Angola
Telophorus sulfureopectus (Sulphur-breasted Bush Shrike)
T. s. sulfureopectus
Senegal to NE Zaire
T. s. similis
Ethiopia to Angola & Cape Province
Telophorus olivaceus (Olive Bush Shrike)
T. o. makawa
C & S Malawi, E Rhodesia
T. l. bertrandi
S Malawi
T. o. vitorum
Sol do Save, Mozambique
T. o. interfluvius
Mozambique
T. o. olivaceus
S Mozambique, E Transvaal, E Cape Province

Telophorus nigrifrons (Black-fronted Bush Shrike)
T. n. nigrifrons
C Kenya, Tanzania, N Malawi
T. n. manningi
SE Zaire, N Namibia
T. n. sandgroundi
Mozambique, Rhodesia, NE Transvaal
Telophorus multicolor (Many-coloured Bush Shrike)
T. m. multicolor
Sierra Leone to Cameroun Mt
T. m. batesi
Cameroun to W Uganda, N Angola
T. m. graueri
E Zaire
Telophorus kupeensis (Serle's Bush Shrike)
Kupé Mt (Cameroun)
Telophorus zeylonus (Bokmakierie Shrike)
T. z. restrictus
Rhodesia
T. z. phanus
S Angola, Namibia
T. z. zeylonus
Transvaal, Cape Province
Telophorus viridis (Perrin's Bush Shrike)
S Zaire, N Angola, NW Zambia
Telophorus quadricolor (Four-coloured Bush Shrike)
T. q. nigricauda
SE Kenya, E Tanzania
T. q. quadricolor
Mozambique & S Malawi to Natal
Telophorus dohertyi (Doherty's Bush Shrike)
W Kenya, W Uganda, E Zaire

MALACONOTUS
Malaconotus cruentus (Fiery-breasted Bush Shrike)
M. c. cruentus
Sierra Leone to Cameroun
M. c. gabonensis
Cameroun, Gabon
M. c. adolfi-friederici
E Zaire
Malaconotus lagdeni (Lagden's Bush Shrike)
M. l. lagdeni
Liberia to Ghana
M. l. centralis
E Zaire
Malaconotus gladiator (Green-breasted Bush Shrike)
Cameroun Mt
Malaconotus blanchoti (Grey-headed Bush Shrike)
M. b. blanchoti
Senegal to N Cameroun

M. b. catharoxanthus
N Zaire to Ethiopia, W Kenya
M. b. approximans
S Ethiopia to N Tanzania
M. b. hypopyrrhus
Rwanda, Tanzania to Natal
M. b. extremus
E Cape Province
M. b. interpositus
SE Zaire, W Zambia
M. b. monteiri
Angola, S Zaire
M. b. citrinifuetus
SW Angola
Malaconotus alius (Black-cap Bush Shrike)
Tanzania

Nicator chloris (Western Nicator)
Senegal to Sudan, Zaire, Uganda
Nicator gularis (Eastern Nicator)
Kenya & Zambia to Natal
Nicator vireo (Yellow-throated Nicator)
Cameroun to N Angola, Uganda

LANIINAE

Corvinella corvina (Western Long-tailed Shrike)
C. c. corvina
Senegal & Gambia to Mali
C. c. affinis
Guinea to Uganda
C. c. chapini
NE Zaire, W Kenya
C. c. caliginosa
SW Sudan
Corvinella melanoleuca (Eastern Long-tailed Shrike)
C. m. aequatorialis
S Kenya, Tanzania
C. m. melanoleuca
S Angola, Southern Africa

Lanius tigrinus (Tiger Shrike)
E Asia, Sumatra to Philippine Is
& Celebes
Lanius souzae (Souza's Shrike)
L. s. souzae
Zaire, Angola, Zambia
L. s. tacitus
E Zambia
L. s. burigi
SE Zaire to Tanzania, Mozambique
Lanius bucephalus (Bull-headed Shrike)
L. b. bucephalus
E Asia, Japan, China

L. b. sicarius
NW China
Lanius cristatus (Brown Shrike)
L. c. cristatus
E Asia, India, China
L. c. confusus
NE Asia » Thailand, Malaysia
L. c. superciliosus
Japan, E China » Sunda Is
L. c. lucionensis
China, Philippine Is, N Borneo
Lanius collurio (Red-backed Shrike)
L. c. juxtus
S Britain » W Europe
L. c. collurio
Europe, Siberia, W Asia, » S Africa
L. c. pallidifrons
W Siberia, WC Asia
L. c. kobylini
Iran, Arabia, E Africa
L. c. phoenicuroides
S Russia, NW India, NE Africa
L. c. speculigerus
Iran, C Asia
L. c. isabellinus
E Turkistan, NW India » NE Africa
L. c. tsaidamensis
W China
Lanius collurioides (Burmese Shrike)
L. c. collurioides
E India to N Vietnam
L. c. nigricapillus
S Vietnam
Lanius gubernator (Emin's Shrike)
Ghana to Sudan
Lanius vittatus (Bay-backed Shrike)
L. v. nargianus
Iran, Afghanistan, Pakistan
L. v. vittatus
N & C India
Lanius schach (Black-headed Shrike)
L. s. stresemanni
E New Guinea
L. s. bentet
Malaysia, Sumatra to Timor I
L. s. suluensis
Sulu Archipelago
L. s. nasutus
Philippine Is, N Borneo
L. s. schach
E & S China, N Vietnam
L. s. longicaudatus
C Thailand
L. s. tricolor
Himalayas, Burma, N Indochina
L. s. nigriceps
E India

L. s. caniceps
S & W India, Sri Lanka

L. s. erythronotus
C Asia, W India

L. s. lahulensis
NW India

L. s. tephronotus
Himalayas, S & W China

Lanius validirostris (Strong-billed Shrike)

L. v. validirostris
Luzon I

L. v. tertius
Mindoro I

L. v. hachisuka
SE Mindanao I

L. v. quartus
W Mindanao I

Lanius mackinnoni (Mackinnon's Shrike)
Cameroun to Angola and Tanzania

Lanius minor (Lesser Grey Shrike)

L. m. minor
S & E Europe » E & S Africa

L. m. turanicus
C Asia, Iran » E Africa

Lanius ludovicianus (Loggerhead Shrike)

L. l. gambeli
W North America » W Mexico

L. l. excubitorides
C Canada, C USA » E Mexico

L. l. migrans
E North America » NE Mexico

L. l. ludovicianus
SE USA

L. l. miamensis
S Florida

L. l. mexicanus
C Mexico

L. l. sonoriensis
SW USA, NW Mexico

L. l. grinnelli
N Baja California

L. l. nelsoni
S Baja California

L. l. anthonyi
Santa Barbara I

L. l. mearnsi
San Clemente I

Lanius excubitor (Great Grey Shrike)

L. e. borealis
E Canada, E USA

L. e. invictus
W Canada, W USA

L. e. sibiricus
E Siberia, NE Asia, Mongolia

L. e. excubitor
Europe, Asia Minor, W Siberia

L. e. bianchii
Sakhalin I, N Japan

L. e. mollis
C Asia

L. e. funereus
Chinese Turkistan

L. e. homeyeri
SE Europe, WC Asia

L. e. leucopterus
W Siberia, Russian Turkistan

L. e. meridionalis
S France, Iberia

L. e. koenigi
Canary Is

L. e. algeriensis
NW Africa

L. e. elegans
Sahara, S Egypt

L. e. leucopygus
S Sahara, Chad, W Sudan

L. e. aucheri
NE Africa, Arabia, S Iran

L. e. buryi
SW Arabia

L. e. uncinatus
Socotra I

L. e. lahtora
NW India

L. e. pallidirostris
SC Asia, Iraq, Arabia, NE Africa

Lanius excubitoroides (Grey-backed Fiscal)

L. e. excubitoroides
Sudan to E Zaire, W Kenya

L. e. intercedens
C Ethiopia, W Kenya

L. e. bohmi
Ethiopia to Tanzania

Lanius sphenocercus (Chinese Great Grey Shrike)

L. s. sphenocercus
NE Asia, Korea, N & E China

L. s. giganteus
NW China

Lanius cabanisi (Long-tailed Fiscal)
Somalia, Kenya, Tanzania

Lanius dorsalis (Taita Fiscal)
Ethiopia, E Uganda, NE Tanzania

Lanius somalicus (Somali Fiscal)
Somalia, E & S Ethiopia, N Kenya

Lanius collaris (Fiscal Shrike)

L. c. smithii
Sierra Leone to W Tanzania

L. c. humeralis
Ethiopia to Zambia, N Mozambique

L. c. marwitzi
SW Tanzania

L. c. capelli
W Uganda to Angola
L. c. pyrrhostictus
E Botswana to Rhodesia, Natal
L. c. collaris
Orange Free State, Cape Province
L. c. subcoronatus
SW Angola, Namibia, W Botswana
Lanius newtoni (Newton's Fiscal)
Sao Thomé I
Lanius senator (Woodchat Shrike)
L. s. senator
Europe, N Africa
L. s. badius
W Mediterranean Is, NW Africa
L. s. niloticus
Syria, Iran, NE Africa
Lanius nubicus (Masked Shrike)
SE Europe to Iraq, NE Africa

PITYRIASINAE

PITYRIASIS
Pityriasis gymnocephala (Bornean Bristlehead)
Borneo

123 VANGIDAE (VANGA SHRIKES)

CALICALICUS
Calicalicus madagascariensis (Red-tailed Vanga)
E Madagascar

SCHETBA
Schetba rufa (Rufous Vanga)
S. r. rufa
E Madagascar
S. r. occidentalis
WC Madagascar

VANGA
Vanga curvirostris (Hook-billed Vanga)
V. c. curvirostris
E & N Madagascar
V. c. cetera
SW Madagascar

XENOPIROSTRIS
Xenopirostris xenopirostris (Lafresnaye's Vanga)
SW Madagascar
Xenopirostris damii (Van Dam's Vanga)
NW Madagascar
Xenopirostris polleni (Pollen's Vanga)
NW & E Madagascar

FALCULEA
Falculea palliata (Sicklebill)
N & W Madagascar

ARTAMELLA
Artamella viridis (White-headed Vanga)
A. v. viridis
E Madagascar
A. v. annae
W Madagascar

LEPTOPTERUS
Leptopterus chabert (Chabert Vanga)
L. c. chabert
N & E Madagascar
L. c. schistocercus
SW Madagascar
Leptopterus madagascarinus (Blue Vanga)
L. m. madagascarinus
N & C Madagascar
L. m. comorensis
Great Comoro I

ORIOLIA
Oriolia bernieri (Bernier's Vanga)
E Madagascar

EURYCEROS
Euryceros prevostii (Helmet Bird)
E Madagascar

HYPOSITTA
Hypositta corallirostris (Coral-billed Nuthatch)
Madagascar

124 BOMBYCILLIDAE (WAXWINGS)

BOMBYCILLINAE

BOMBYCILLA
Bombycilla garrulus (Bohemian Waxwing)
B. g. garrulus
N Europe
B. g. centralasiae
N, C & E Asia, China, Japan
B. g. pallidiceps
W Canada, N & W USA
Bombycilla japonica (Japanese Waxwing)
NE Asia, Japan
Bombycilla cedrorum (Cedar Waxwing)
Canada, USA, Mexico, Central America, Colombia, Venezuela

PTILOGONATINAE

PTILOGONYS
Ptilogonys cinereus (Grey Silky Flycatcher)
P. c. otofuscus
NW Mexico
P. c. cinereus
C & E Mexico
P. c. pallescens
SW Mexico
P. c. molybdophanes
S Mexico, W Guatemala

P. c. schistaceus
S Mexico
Ptilogonys caudatus (Long-tailed Silky Flycatcher)
Costa Rica, W Panama

PHAINOPEPLA
Phainopepla nitens (Phainopepla)
P. n. lepida
SW USA, NW Mexico
P. n. nitens
S Texas, NC Mexico

PHAINOPTILA
Phainoptila melanoxantha (Black & Yellow Silky Flycatcher)
Costa Rica, W Panama

HYPOCOLIINAE

HYPOCOLIUS
Hypocolius ampelinus (Grey Hypocolius)
Iraq, SW Arabia

125 DULIDAE (PALMCHAT)

DULUS
Dulus dominicus (Palm Chat)
Gonave I, Hispaniola

126 CINCLIDAE (DIPPERS)

CINCLUS
Cinclus cinclus (Dipper)
C. c. hibernicus
Ireland, W Scotland
C. c. gularis
Scotland, W & C England
C. c. cinclus
N Europe, Turkey, W Spain, Corsica
C. c. aquaticus
W Europe, Balkans
C. c. minor
NW Africa
C. c. caucasicus
Caucasus, Iraq, Iran
C. c. rufiventris
W Syria
C. c. persicus
SW Iran
C. c. leucogaster
C Asia
C. c. cashmeriensis
Himalayas
C. c. przewalskii
S Tibet, W China
Cinclus pallasii (Brown Dipper)
C. p. tenuirostris
C Asia, Himalayas
C. p. dorjei
S Assam, N Burma, N Thailand

C. p. pallasii
NE Asia, Japan, W China, N Thailand, N Vietnam
C. p. marila
Khasia hills, India
Cinclus mexicanus (Mexican Dipper)
C.m. unicolor
W Canada, W USA
C. m. mexicanus
N & C Mexico
C. m. anthonyi
S Mexico, Guatemala
C. m. dickermani
S Mexico
C. m. ardesiacus
Costa Rica, W Panama
Cinclus leucocephalus (White-capped Dipper)
C. l. rivularis
N Colombia
C. l. leuconotus
W Venezuela, S Colombia, Ecuador
C. l. leucocephalus
Peru, Bolivia
Cinclus schulzi (Rufous-throated Dipper)
NW Argentina

127 TROGLODYTIDAE (WRENS)

CAMPYLORHYNCHUS
Campylorhynchus jocosus (Spotted Wren)
SC Mexico
Campylorhynchus gularis (Spotted Cactus Wren)
NW & W Mexico
Campylorhynchus yucatanicus (Yucatan Cactus-Wren)
SE Mexico
Campylorhynchus brunneicapillus (Cactus Wren)
C. b. couesi
SW USA, N Baja California, NW Mexico
C. b. bryanti
W Baja California
C. b. purus
C Baja California
C. b. seri
Tiburon I
C. b. affinis
S Baja California
C. b. brunneicapillus
NW Mexico
C. b. guttatus
C Mexico
Campylorhynchus chiapensis (Giant Wren)
Chiapas

***Campylorhynchus griseus* (Bicoloured Wren)**
C. g. albicilius
N Colombia, NW Venezuela
C. g. bicolor
Colombia
C. g. minor
E Colombia, N Venezuela
C. g. pallidus
S Venezuela
C. g. griseus
E Venezuela, Guyana, N Brazil
***Campylorhynchus rufinucha* (Rufous-naped Wren)**
C. r. humilis
SW Mexico
C. r. rufinucha
E Mexico
C. r. nigricaudatus
S Mexico, W Guatemala
C. r. castaneus
Guatemala to Nicaragua
C. r. capistratus
El Salvador to NW Costa Rica
***Campylorhynchus turdinus* (Thrush-like Wren)**
C. t. albobrunneus
C Panama
C. t. harterti
E Panama, W Colombia
C. t. aenigmaticus
SW Colombia
C. t. hypostictus
NW & W Amazonia
C. t. turdinus
EC Brazil
C. t. unicolor
E Bolivia, W Brazil
***Campylorhynchus nuchalis* (Stripe-backed Wren)**
C. n. pardus
N Colombia
C. n. brevipennis
N Venezuela
C. n. nuchalis
C Venezuela
***Campylorhynchus fasciatus* (Fasciated Wren)**
C. f. pallescens
SW Ecuador, NW Peru
C. f. fasciatus
W Peru
***Campylorhynchus zonatus* (Banded-backed Wren)**
C. z. vanblockeri
Oaxaca (Mexico)
C. z. zonatus
EC Mexico

C. z. restrictus
S Mexico, Guatemala
C. z. vulcanius
S Mexico to Nicaragua
C. z. costaricensis
E Costa Rica, W Panama
C. z. curvirostris
N Colombia
C. z. brevirostris
N Colombia, NW Ecuador
***Campylorhynchus megalopterus* (Grey-barred Wren)**
C. m. megalopterus
C Mexico
C. m. nelsoni
SC Mexico

ODONTORCHILUS
***Odontorchilus cinereus* (Tooth-billed Wren)**
N Brazil
***Odontorchilus branickii* (Grey-mantled Wren)**
O. b. branickii
Colombia, Ecuador, Peru
O. b. minor
N Ecuador

SALPINCTES
***Salpinctes obsoletus* (Rock Wren)**
S. o. obsoletus
SW Canada, W USA, N & C Mexico
S. o. guadeloupensis
Guadeloupe I
S. o. tenuirostris
San Benito I
S. o. exsul
San Benedicto I
S. o. neglectus
SE Mexico to Honduras
S. o. guttatus
El Salvador to Costa Rica

CATHERPES
***Catherpes mexicanus* (Canyon Wren)**
C. m. conspersus
W USA, NW Mexico
C. m. albifrons
SW USA, N Mexico
C. m. mexicanus
N, C & S Mexico
C. m. meliphonus
NW Mexico
C. m. cantator
S Mexico

HYLORCHILUS
***Hylorchilus sumichrasti* (Slender-billed Wren)**
H. s. sumichrasti
Vera Cruz

H. s. navai
Chiapas

CINNYCERTHIA
Cinnycerthia unirufa (Rufous Wren)
C. u. unirufa
NE Colombia
C. u. chakei
NW Venezuela
C. u. unibrunnea
S & C Colombia, Ecuador
Cinnycerthia peruana (Sepia-brown Wren)
C. p. bogotensis
W Colombia
C. p. olivascens
SW Colombia, W Ecuador
C. p. peruana
Peru
C. p. fulva
S Peru, N Bolivia

CISTOTHORUS
Cistothorus platensis (Short-billed Marsh Wren)
C. p. stellaris
E Canada, E USA, NE Mexico
C. p. tinnulus
W Mexico
C. p. potosinus
San Luis Potosi
C. p. jalapensis
Vera Cruz
C. p. warneri
W Chiapas
C. p. russelli
Belize
C. p. graberi
SE Honduras, NE Nicaragua
C. p. elegans
S Mexico, Guatemala
C. p. lucidus
S Costa Rica, W Panama
C. p. alticola
N Colombia, N Venezuela, N Guyana
C. p. tamae
Colombia, Venezuela
C. p. tolimae
C Colombia
C. p. aequatorialis
S Colombia, Ecuador, Peru
C. p. graminicola
C Peru
C. p. minimus
S Peru
C. p. boliviae
NW Bolivia
C. p. polyglottus
SE Brazil to NE Argentina

C. p. tucumanus
NW Argentina
C. p. platensis
C & E Argentina
C. p. hornensis
S Chile, S Argentina
C. p. falklandicus
Falkland Is
Cistothorus meridae (Paramo Wren)
NW Venezuela
Cistothorus apolinari (Apolinar's Marsh Wren)
C Colombia
Cistothorus palustris (Long-billed Marsh Wren)
C. p. palustris
E USA
C. p. waynei
CE USA
C. p. griseus
SE USA
C. p. marianae
SE USA
C. p. thryophilus
S USA
C. p. iliacus
C Canada, NC to SE USA
C. p. laingi
WC Canada, WC USA » N Mexico
C. p. plesius
SW Canada, W USA » NW Mexico
C. p. paludicola
W USA, N Baja California
C. p. aestuarinus
SW USA, NW Mexico
C. p. tolucensis
C Mexico

THRYOMANES
Thryomanes bewickii (Bewick's Wren)
T. b. bewickii
C & S USA
T. b. altus
EC & SC USA
T. b. cryptus
SC USA, NE Mexico
T. b. eremophilus
WC & SW USA, NW Mexico
T. b. calophonus
SW Canada, NW USA
T. b. drymoecus
W USA
T. b. marinensis
SW USA
T. b. atrestus
W USA
T. b. spilurus
SW USA

T. b. correctus
SW USA

T. b. nesophilus
Santa Cruz I (S California)

T. b. catalinae
Santa Catalina I, (California)

T. b. leucophrys
San Clemente I, (California)

T. b. charienturus
NW Baja California

T. b. cerroensis
WC Baja California

T. b. magdalenensis
SW Baja California

T. b. murinus
C Mexico

T. b. mexicanus
SC Mexico

Thryomanes sissonii (Revillagigedo Wren)
Socorro I, Revillagigedo Group

FERMINIA

Ferminia cerverai (Zapata Wren)
Cuba

THRYOTHORUS

Thryothorus atrogularis (Black-throated Wren)

T. a. atrogularis
Nicaragua, Costa Rica, W Panama

T. a. xerampelinus
E Panama

T. a. spadix
W Colombia

Thryothorus fasciatoventris (Black-bellied Wren)

T. f. melanogaster
SW Costa Rica, W Panama

T. f. albigularis
E Panama, W Colombia

T. f. fasciatoventris
N Colombia

Thryothorus euophrys (Plain-tailed Wren)

T. e. euophrys
Ecuador

T. e. longipes
Ecuador

T. e. atriceps
NW Peru

Thryothorus genibarbis (Moustached Wren)

T. g. macrurus
Colombia

T. g. amaurogaster
E Colombia

T. g. saltuensis
W Colombia

T. g. yananchae
SW Colombia

T. g. consobrinus
NW Venezuela

T. g. ruficaudatus
N Venezuela

T. g. tachirensis
NW Venezuela

T. g. mystacalis
Ecuador

T. g. genibarbis
NC Brazil

T. g. juruanus
W Brazil, NE Bolivia

T. g. intercedens
C Brazil

T. g. bolivianus
C Bolivia

Thryothorus coraya (Coraya Wren)

T. c. obscurus
E Venezuela

T. c. caurensis
E Colombia, S Venezuela, N Brazil

T. c. ridgwayi
E Venezuela, W Guyana

T. c. coraya
the Guianas, N Brazil

T. c. herberti
N Brazil

T. c. griseipectus
Colombia, Ecuador, W Brazil, N Peru

T. c. amazonicus
E Peru

T. c. albiventris
N Peru

T. c. cantator
C Peru

Thryothorus felix (Happy Wren)

T. f. sonorae
NW Mexico

T. f. pallidus
W Mexico

T. f. lawrencii
Maria Madre I, (Mexico)

T. f. magdalenae
Maria Magdalena I, (Mexico)

T. f. felix
C & S Mexico

T. f. grandis
C Mexico

Thryothorus maculipectus (Spot-breasted Wren)

T. m. microstictus
NE Mexico

T. m. maculipectus
E Mexico

T. m. umbrinus
Guatemala, Honduras, El Salvador, E Nicaragua, S Mexico

T. m. canobrunneus
SE Mexico, Guatemala

Thryothorus rutilus (Rufous-breasted Wren)

T. r. hyperythrus
W Costa Rica, W Panama

T. r. tobagensis
Tobago I

T. r. rutilus
Trinidad, N Venezuela

T. r. intensus
NW Venezuela

T. r. laetus
NW Venezuela, N Colombia

T. r. interior
C Colombia

T. r. hypospodius
NC Colombia

T. r. columbianus
W Colombia

T. r. paucimaculatus
W Ecuador, NW Peru

T. r. sclateri
N Peru

Thryothorus nigricapillus (Bay Wren)

T. n. costaricensis
E Nicaragua, Costa Rica, NW Panama

T. n. semibadius
SW Costa Rica, SW Panama

T. n. castaneus
C Panama

T. n. schottii
E Panama, NW Colombia

T. n. reditus
NE Panama

T. n. connectens
SW Colombia

T. n. nigricapillus
W Ecuador

Thryothorus thoracicus (Stripe-throated Wren)

T. t. thoracicus
E Nicaragua, Costa Rica, W Panama

T. t. grisescens
E Panama

T. t. leucopogon
SE Panama, W Colombia, NW Ecuador

Thryothorus pleurostictus (Banded Wren)

T. p. nisorius
W & C Mexico

T. p. oaxacae
SW Mexico

T. p. acaciarum
S Mexico

T. p. oblitus
S Mexico, Guatemala, W El Salvador

T. p. pleurostictus
Guatemala

T. p. lateralis
El Salvador, W Honduras

T. p. ravus
Nicaragua, NW Costa Rica

Thryothorus ludovicianus (Carolina Wren)

T. l. ludovicianus
C, S, SE USA

T. l. miamensis
Florida

T. l. nesophilus
Florida

T. l. burleighi
Cat I

T. l. lomitensis
S USA, NE Mexico

T. l. berlandieri
NC & NE Mexico

T. l. tropicalis
NC Mexico

T. l. albinucha
SE Mexico, N Guatemala

T. l. subfulvus
Guatemala, Nicaragua

Thryothorus rufalbus (Rufous and White Wren)

T. r. transfinis
S Mexico

T. r. rufalbus
Guatemala, El Salvador

T. r. castanonotus
W Honduras to W Panama

T. r. cumanensis
N Colombia, N Venezuela

T. r. minlosi
EC Colombia, NW Venezuela

Thryothorus nicefori (Nicefori's Wren)
N Colombia

Thryothorus sinaloa (Bar-vented Wren)

T. s. cinereus
NW Mexico

T. s. sinaloa
WC Mexico

T. s. russeus
SW Mexico

Thryothorus modestus (Plain Wren)

T. m. modestus
S Mexico, Guatemala, Honduras, El Salvador, Nicaragua

T. m. zeledoni
E Nicaragua, E Costa Rica, NW Panama

T. m. elutus
W Panama

Thryothorus leucotis (Buff-breasted Wren)

T. l. galbraithii
E Panama, NW Colombia

T. l. conditus
Islas San Miguel, Panama

T. l. leucotis
  N Colombia
T. l. collinus
  NE Colombia
T. l. venezuelanus
  NE Colombia, NW Venezuela
T. l. zuliensis
  Colombia, Venezuela
T. l. hypoleucus
  NC Venezuela
T. l. bogotensis
  E Colombia, C Venezuela
T. l. albipectus
  NE Venezuela, the Guianas, NE Brazil
T. l. peruanus
  E Peru, W Brazil, SE Colombia,
  E Ecuador
T. l. rufiventris
  C Brazil

Thryothorus superciliaris (Superciliated Wren)
T. s. superciliaris
  Ecuador
T. s. baroni
  S Ecuador, N Peru

Thryothorus guarayanus (Fawn-breasted Wren)
  Bolivia, SW Brazil

Thryothorus longirostris (Long-billed Wren)
T. l. bahiae
  NE Brazil
T. l. longirostris
  C Brazil

Thryothorus griseus (Grey Wren)
  W Brazil

TROGLODYTES

Troglodytes troglodytes ((Winter) Wren)
T. t. hiemalis
  C & S Canada, C & E USA
T. t. pullus
  SE USA
T. t. pacificus
  W Canada, W USA
T. t. helleri
  Kodiak I, Alaska
T. t. semidiensis
  Semidi I, Alaska
T. t. kiskensis
  Aleutian Is, Alaska
T. t. meligerus
  Attu I, Agatta I, Aleutian Is
T. t. alascensis
  Pribilof Is, Alaska
T. t. pallescens
  Kamchatka, Commander Is
T. t. kurilensis
  N Kurile Is

T. t. fumigatus
  S Kurile Is, Japan, Izu Is
T. t. mosukei
  Iku Is, Borodino Is
T. t. ogawae
  Tanegashima I, Yakushima I
T. t. taivanus
  Taiwan
T. t. dauricus
  NE Asia, Korea
T. t. idius
  N China
T. t. szetschuanus
  W China
T. t. talifuensis
  Sikang, NE Burma
T. t. subpallidus
  Afghanistan
T. t. nipalensis
  C & E Himalayas
T. t. neglectus
  W Himalayas
T. t. magrathi
  NW India
T. t. zagrossiensis
  Iran
T. t. tianschanicus
  NE Iran, C Asia
T. t. hyrcanus
  Caucasus, NW Iran
T. t. cypriotes
  Crete, Rhodes, Cyprus
T. t. juniperi
  NW Libya
T. t. kabylorum
  NW Africa, Balearic Is
T. t. koenigi
  Corsica, Sardinia
T. t. troglodytes
  Europe, Asia Minor
T. t. indigenus
  Ireland, Scotland, England
T. t. hirtensis
  St Kilda I, Scotland
T. t. hebridensis
  Outer Hebrides, Scotland
T. t. fridariensis
  Fair Isle, Scotland
T. t. zetlandicus
  Shetland Is, Scotland
T. t. borealis
  Faroe Is
T. t. islandicus
  Iceland

Troglodytes aëdon (House Wren)
T. a. aëdon
  SE Canada, E USA

T. a. parkmanii
SW Canada, C & W USA, N Mexico
T. a. cahooni
SW USA, NW Mexico
T. a. compositus
C & NE Mexico
T. a. brunneicollis
C & S Mexico
T. a. intermedius
S Mexico, Guatemala, Honduras, El
Salvador, Nicaragua, Costa Rica
T. a. tanneri
Isla Clarion, Revillagigedo
T. a. beani
Cozumel I, SE Mexico
T. a. inquietus
Panama
T. a. carychrous
Coiba I, Panama
T. a. rufescens
Dominica I
T. a. mesoleucus
St Lucia I
T. a. musicus
St Vincent I
T. a. atopus
N Colombia
T. a. striatulus
Colombia, Venezuela
T. a. columbae
E Colombia
T. a. effutitus
NW & W Venezuela
T. a. albicans
Trinidad, Colombia, Venezuela
W Ecuador, N Peru, the Guianas, Brazil
T. a. tobagensis
Tobago I
T. a. audax
W Peru
T. a. puna
W Bolivia, Peru
T. a. carabayae
Peru
T. a. tecellatus
Peru, N Chile
T. a. rex
Bolivia, Paraguay, Argentina
T. a. atacamensis
N & C Chile
T. a. musculus
C & S Brazil, E Paraguay, N Argentina
T. a. bonariae
S Brazil, Uruguay, NE Argentina
T. a. chilensis
S Chile, S Argentina
T. a. cobbi
Falkland Is

Troglodytes solstitialis (Mountain Wren)
T. s. chiapensis
S Mexico
T. s. rufociliatus
E Guatemala, N El Salvador
T. s. nannoides
W El Salvador
T. s. rehni
Honduras
T. s. ochraceus
Costa Rica
T. s. ligea
W Panama
T. s. festinus
E Panama
T. s. monticola
N Colombia
T. s. solitarius
Colombia, Venezuela
T. s. solstitialis
S Colombia, Ecuador, N Peru
T. s. macrourus
EC Peru
T. s. frater
SE Peru, Bolivia
T. s. auricularis
N Argentina
Troglodytes rufulus (Tepui Wren)
T. r. rufulus
SE Venezuela
T. r. fulvigularis
SE Venezuela
T. r. yavii
S Venezuela
T. r. duidae
S Venezuela
T. r. wetmorei
S Venezuela
Troglodytes browni (Timberline Wren)
T. b. ridgwayi
Costa Rica
T. b. basultoi
Costa Rica
T. b. browni
W Panama

UROPSILA
**Uropsila leucogastra (White-bellied
Wren)**
U. l. leucogastra
EC & E Mexico
U. l. pacifica
SW Mexico
U. l. musica
S Mexico
U. l. brachyura
SE Mexico, Guatemala

HENICORHINA
Henicorhina leucosticta (Lowland Wood Wren)
H. l. prostheleuca
S & E Mexico, Guatemala
H. l. tropaea
Guatemala, Honduras, Nicaragua, Costa Rica, NW Panama
H. l. smithei
Peten, Guatemala
H. l. costaricensis
Cartago, Costa Rica
H. l. pittieri
SW Costa Rica, W Panama
H. l. dariensis
E Panama, NW Colombia
H. l. albilateralis
C Colombia
H. l. leucosticta
S Venezuela, Guyana, Surinam, N Brazil
H. l. eucharis
Colombia
H. l. inornata
S Colombia, Ecuador
H. l. hauxwelli
S Colombia, E Ecuador, Peru
Henicorhina leucophrys (Highland Wood Wren)
H. l. mexicana
E Mexico
H. l. festiva
W Mexico
H. l. castanea
Honduras, S Mexico, N Guatemala
H. l. capitalis
S Mexico, W Guatemala, El Slavador
H. l. minuscula
S Mexico
H. l. collina
Costa Rica, W Panama
H. l. anachoreta
N Colombia
H. l. bangsi
N Colombia
H. l. manastarae
NW Venezuela
H. l. sanluisensis
NW Venezuela
H. l. venezuelensis
N Venezuela
H. l. meridana
W Venezuela
H. l. tamae
E Colombia, NW Venezuela
H. l. leucophrys
W Colombia, Ecuador, Peru
H. l. brunneiceps
SW Colombia, N Ecuador

H. l. hilaris
SW Ecuador
H. l. boliviana
W Bolivia

MICROCERCULUS
Microcerculus marginatus (Nightingale Wren)
M. m. philomela
S Mexico, Guatemala, Honduras, Costa Rica, Panama, NW Colombia
M. m. taeniatus
S Colombia, Ecuador
M. m. corrasus
N Colombia
M. m. squamulatus
NE Colombia, N Venezuela
M. m. marginatus
W Venezuela, E Colombia, E Ecuador, Peru, N Bolivia, W Brazil
Microcerculus ustulatus (Flutist Wren)
M. u. duidae
S Venezuela
M. u. lunatipectus
S Venezuela
M. u. obscurus
SE Venezuela
M. u. ustulatus
SE Venezuela, W Guyana
Microcerculus bambla (Wing-banded Wren)
M. b. albigularis
E Ecuador, W Brazil
M. b. caurensis
S Venezuela
M. b. bambla
SE Venezuela, the Guianas, NE Brazil

CYPHROHINUS
Cyphorinus thoracicus (Chestnut-breasted Wren)
C. t. dichrous
S Colombia, Ecuador, Peru
C. t. thoracicus
E Peru
Cyphorhinus aradus (Quadrille Wren)
C. a. richardsoni
Nicaragua, SE Honduras
C. a. infuscatus
Costa Rica, NW Panama
C. a. laurencii
Panama, NW Colombia
C. a. propinquus
N Colombia
C. a. chocoanus
W Colombia
C. a. phaeocephalus
SW Colombia, Ecuador

C. a. urbanoi
S Venezuela
C. a. aradus
S Venezuela, the Guianas, NE Brazil
C. a. faroensis
N Brazil
C. a. griseolateralis
N Brazil
C. a. interpositus
S Brazil
C. a. transfluvialis
N Brazil, SE Colombia
C. a. salvini
SE Colombia, E Ecuador, NE Peru
C. a. modulator
E Peru, W Brazil

128 MIMIDAE (MOCKING-BIRDS, THRASHERS)

DUMETELLA
Dumetella carolinensis (Catbird)
S Canada, C, S & SE USA, Central America, West Indies

MELANOPTILA
Melanoptila glabrirostris (Black Catbird)
SE Mexico, N Guatemala, N Honduras

MELANOTIS
Melanotis caerulescens (Blue Mockingbird)
M. c. longirostris
Tres Marias Is
M. c. caerulescens
C & S Mexico
Melanotis hypoleucus (Blue & White Mockingbird)
SE Mexico, Guatemala, Honduras, El Salvador

MIMUS
Mimus polyglottos (Northern Mockingbird)
M. p. polyglottos
C, E & SE USA
M. p. leucopterus
SW USA, NW Mexico
M. p. orpheus
Bahama Is, Greater Antilles
Mimus gilvus (Tropical Mockingbird)
M. g. gracilis
S Mexico, Guatemala, Honduras, El Salvador
M. g. leucophaeus
SE Mexico, Belize
M. g. antillarum
Martinique I, Windward Is
M. g. tobagensis
Trinidad, Tobago I
M. g. rostratus
N Venezuela Is

M. g. magnirostris
St Andrews I
M. g. tolimensis
W & C Colombia
M. g. melanopterus
N & E Colombia, Venezuela, Guyana, N Brazil
M. g. gilvus
French Guiana, Surinam
M. g. antelius
N & E Brazil
Mimus gundlachii (Bahama Mockingbird)
M. g. gundlachii
N Cuba, Inagua I, Caicos I
M. g. hillii
Jamaica
Mimus thenca (Chilean Mockingbird)
C Chile
Mimus longicaudatus (Long-tailed Mockingbird)
M. l. platensis
La Plata I, W Ecuador
M. l. albogriseus
SW Ecuador, N Peru
M. l. longicaudatus
W Peru
M. l. maranonicus
NE Peru
Mimus saturninus (Chalk-browed Mockingbird)
M. s. saturninus
N Brazil
M. s. arenaceus
NE Brazil
M. s. frater
N Bolivia, SW Brazil
M. s. modulator
SE Bolivia, S Brazil, Uruguay, N Argentina
Mimus patagonicus (Patagonian Mockingbird)
W & S Argentina, S Chile
Mimus triurus (White-banded Mockingbird)
E Bolivia, S Brazil, Paraguay, Uruguay, Argentina
Mimus dorsalis (Brown-backed Mockingbird)
Bolivia, NW Argentina

NESOMIMUS
Nesomimus trifasciatus (Galapagos Mockingbird)
N. t. trifasciatus
Gardner I, Champion I, Galapagos Is
N. t. macdonaldi
Hood I, Gardner I
N. t. melanotis
Chatham I

N. t. parvulus
  Narboro' I, Albemarle I, Daphne I,
  Seymour I, Indefatigable I
N. t. barringtoni
  Barrington I
N. t. personatus
  Abingdon I, Bindloe I, James I, Jervis I
N. t. wenmani
  Wenman I
N. t. hulli
  Culpeper I
N. t. bauri
  Tower I

MIMODES
Mimodes graysoni (Socorro Thrasher)
  Socorro I, Revillagigedo Is

OREOSCOPTES
Oreoscoptes montanus (Sage Thrasher)
  W & SW USA, Baja California

TOXOSTOMA
Toxostoma rufum (Brown Thrasher)
T. r. rufum
  SE Canada, NC, E & SE USA
T. r. longicauda
  SC Canada, C & S USA
Toxostoma longirostre (Long-billed Thrasher)
T. l. sennetti
  S Texas, NE Mexico
T. l. longirostre
  E Mexico
Toxostoma guttatum (Cozumel Thrasher)
  Cozumel I
Toxostoma cinereum (Grey Thrasher)
T. c. mearnsi
  W Baja California
T. c. cinereum
  S Baja California
Toxostoma bendirei (Bendire Thrasher)
T. b. bendirei
  SW USA, NW Mexico
T. b. candida
  CW Sonora, Mexico
T. b. rubricatum
  SE Sonora, Mexico
Toxostoma ocellatum (Ocellated Thrasher)
  SC Mexico
Toxostoma curvirostre (Curve-billed Thrasher)
T. c. palmeri
  S Arizona, N Sonora, Mexico
T. c. insularum
  San Esteban I, Tiburon I
T. c. maculatum
  NW Mexico
T. c. occidentale
  WC Mexico

T. c. celsum
  S USA, NC Mexico
T. c. curvirostre
  C & SC Mexico
T. c. oberholseri
  S Texas, NE Mexico
Toxostoma lecontei (Le Conte Thrasher)
T. l. lecontei
  SW USA, NW Mexico, N Baja California
T. l. macmillanorum
  S California
T. l. arenicola
  W Baja California
Toxostoma redivivum (California Thrasher)
T. r. sonomae
  N California
T. r. redivivum
  S California, NW Baja California
Toxostoma dorsale (Crissal Thrasher)
T. d. coloradense
  SW USA, NW Mexico, Baja California
T. d. dorsale
  SW USA, N Mexico
T. d. trinitatis
  N Baja California
T. d. dumosum
  NC Mexico

CINCLOCERTHIA
Cinclocerthia ruficauda (Brown Trembler)
C. r. pavida
  NW Leeward Is
C. r. tremula
  Guadeloupe I
C. r. ruficauda
  Dominica I
C. r. gutteralis
  Martinique I
C. r. macrorhyncha
  St Lucia I
C. r. tenebrosa
  St Vincent I

RAMPHOCINCLUS
Ramphocinclus brachyurus (White-breasted Trembler)
R. b. brachyurus
  Martinique I
R. b. sanctaeluciae
  St Lucia I

DONACOBIUS
Donacobius atricapillus (Black-capped Mockingthrush)
D. a. brachypterus
  E Panama, N Colombia
D. a. nigrodorsalis
  SE Colombia, E Ecuador, E Peru

D. a. atricapillus
Venezuela, the Guianas, Brazil, Paraguay'
NE Argentina
D. a. albovittatus
E Bolivia

ALLENIA
Allenia fusca (Scaly-breasted Thrasher)
Lesser Antilles

MARGAROPS
Margarops fuscatus (Pearly-eyed Thrasher)
M. f. fuscatus
S Bahama Is, Hispaniola, Puerto Rico,
N Leeward Is
M. f. densirostris
S Leeward Is
M. f. bonairensis
Bonaire I, Los Hermanos Is, N Venezuela

129 PRUNELLIDAE (ACCENTORS)

PRUNELLA
Prunella collaris (Alpine Accentor)
P. c. collaris
SW Europe, N Africa, W Mediterranean Is
P. c. subalpina
SE Europe, Crete, W Turkey
P. c. montana
Caucasus, S Iran, N Iraq
P. c. rufilata
Tadzhikistan, W Sinkiang, N Afghanistan
P. c. whymperi
NW India, W Himalayas
P. c. nipalensis
E Sinkiang, E Himalayas, SE Tibet,
SW China
P. c. tibetana
E Tibet, NW China
P. c. erythropygia
Altai, N China, Korea, Japan
P. c. fennelli
Taiwan
Prunella himalayana (Himalayan Accentor)
C Asia, Pakistan, N India, Himalayas
Prunella rubeculoides (Robin Accentor)
P. r. rubeculoides
N India, Pakistan, Himalayas, SE Tibet
P. r. fusca
E Tibet, W China
**Prunella strophiata (Rufous-breasted
Accentor)**
P. s. jerdoni
NW Himalayas
P. s. strophiata
E Himalayas, N Burma, W China
Prunella montanella (Mountain Accentor)
Siberia, Mongolia, Korea
Prunella fulvescens (Brown Accentor)
P. f. fulvescens
Tien Shan, Afghanistan, Pakistan

P. f. dahurica
Altai, Mongolia
P. f. dresseri
SW Sinkiang, N Tibet
P. f. nanschanica
Nan Shan Mountains
P. f. khamensis
NE Tibet, W China
P. f. suinkini
S & SE Tibet
Prunella ocularis (Radde's Accentor)
P. o. ocularis
Iran, S Russia, NE Turkey
P. o. fagani
Yemen
**Prunella atrogularis (Black-throated
Accentor)**
P. a. atrogularis
Ural Mts, Iran
P. a. huttoni
Altai, Sinkiang, Pakistan, W Himalayas
Prunella koslowi (Koslov's Accentor)
Mongolia, Ningsia
Prunella modularis (Dunnock)
P. m. hebridium
Ireland, W Scotland
P. m. occidentalis
E Scotland, England, W France
P. m. modularis
Scandinavia, E & C Europe, N Africa,
Turkey
P. m. mabbotti
Iberian peninsula, SW France
P. m. obscura
E Caucasus, N Iran, Lebanon
P. m. euxina
N Turkey, W Caucasus
Prunella rubida (Japanese Hedge Sparrow)
P. r. rubida
S Kurile Is, N Hokkaido I
P. r. fervida
Honshu I, Kyushu I, Japan
**Prunella immaculata (Maroon-backed
Accentor)**
SE Tibet, N Burma, W China

Muscicapidae

130 TURDINAE (THRUSHES, CHATS)

BRACHYPTERYX
Brachypteryx stellata (Gould's Shortwing)
B. s. stellata
E Himalayas, SE Tibet, NE Burma
B. s. fusca
N Vietnam

Brachypteryx hyperythra (Rusty-bellied Shortwing)
  E Himalayas, Assam
Brachypteryx major (White-bellied Shortwing)
  B. m. major
  Mysore, W Madras
  B. m. albiventris
  Kerala, SW Madras
Brachypteryx calligyna (Celebes Shortwing)
  B. c. simplex
  N Celebes
  B. c. calligyna
  SC Celebes
  B. c. picta
  SE Celebes
Brachypteryx leucophrys (Lesser Shortwing)
  B. l. nipalensis
  Himalayas, Burma, W Yunnan
  B. l. carolinae
  S China, N Thailand, N Indochina
  B. l. langbianensis
  S Indochina
  B. l. wrayi
  Malaysia
  B. l. leucophrys
  Sumatra, Java, Lesser Sunda Is, Timor I
Brachypteryx montana (Blue Shortwing)
  B. m. cruralis
  E Himalayas, N Burma, W China »
  N Indochina
  B. m. sinensis
  NW Fukien
  B. m. goodfellowi
  Taiwan
  B. m. sillimani
  S Palawan I
  B. m. poliogyna
  Luzon I, Mindoro I
  B. m. andersoni
  Mt Isarog (S Luzon)
  B. m. brunneiceps
  Negros I
  B. m. malindangensis
  Mt Malindang (Mindanao I)
  B. m. mindanensis
  Mt Apo (Mindanao I)
  B. m. erythrogyna
  N Borneo
  B. m. saturata
  Sumatra
  B. m. montana
  Java
  B. m. floris
  Flores I

Erythropygia coryphaeus (Karroo Scrub Robin)
  E. c. coryphaeus
  Namibia, Botswana, W Cape Province
  E. c. cinerea
  SE Namibia, SW Cape Province
  E. c. curina
  Orange Free State
Erythropygia leucoptera (White-winged Scrub Robin)
  S Sudan to Somalia, N Kenya, N Uganda
Erythropygia leucophrys (White-browed Scrub Robin)
  E. l. eluta
  S Somalia
  E. l. brunneiceps
  C Kenya, N Tanzania
  E. l. vulpina
  SC Kenya
  E. l. zambesiana
  E Kenya to S Mozambique, E Zambia
  E. l. munda
  N Angola, S Zaire, W Zambia
  E. l. ovamboensis
  S Angola, SW Zambia, N Namibia
  E. l. makalaka
  E Botswana, W Rhodesia
  E. l. limpopoensis
  NE Transvaal, SE Rhodesia,
    S Mozambique
  E. l. pectoralis
  SW Rhodesia, Transvaal, Swaziland
  E. l. leucophrys
  Natal, S & E Cape Province
Erythropygia hartlaubi (Brown-backed Scrub Robin)
  E. h. hartlaubi
  Cameroun to W Kenya, N Angola
  E. h. kenia
  C Kenya
Erythropygia galactotes (Rufous Bushchat)
  E. g. galactotes
  W Mediterranean, N Africa » S Sahara
  E. g. syriaca
  E Mediterranean, Middle East » E Africa
  E. g. familiaris
  S Saudi Arabia, Iran to NW India
  E. g. minor
  Senegal to Sudan & Ethiopia
  E. g. hamertoni
  N Somalia
Erythropygia paena (Kalahari Sandy Scrub Robin)
  E. p. benguellensis
  S Angola

E. p. paena
Rhodesia, Botswana, W Transvaal,
N Cape Province

E. p. damarensis
Namibia

E. p. oriens
S Transvaal to N Cape Province

Erythropygia leucosticta (Western Bearded Scrub Robin)

E. l. leucosticta
Sierra Leone to Ghana

E. l. collsi
NE Zaire

E. l. reichenowi
N Angola

Erythropygia quadrivirgata (Eastern Bearded Scrub Robin)

E. q. erlangeri
Juba river, Somalia

E. q. quadrivirgata
E Kenya to Transvaal, C Mozambique

E. q. interna
SE Zambia, Rhodesia

E. q. wilsoni
SE Transvaal, Natal, S Mozambique

E. q. brunnea
NC Tanzania

E. q. greenwayi
Mafia I, Zanzibar

Erythropygia barbata (Central Bearded Scrub Robin)

E. b. thamnodytes
NE Angola, S Zaire, N Zambia

E. b. barbata
Angola, NW Zambia

Erythropygia signata (Brown Scrub Robin)

E. s. oatleyi
N Transvaal

E. s. tongensis
N Natal

E. s. reclusa
W Natal

E. s. signata
E Cape Province, S Natal

NAMIBORNIS
Namibornis herero (Herero Chat)
Namibia

CERCOTRICHAS
Cercotrichas podobe (Black Bush Robin)

C. p. podobe
Senegal to N Somalia

C. p. melanoptera
W Saudi Arabia, Yemen, Aden

PINARORNIS
Pinarornis plumosus (Boulder Chat)
E Zambia, Rhodesia, Mozambique

CHAETOPS
Chaetops frenatus (Rufous Rockjumper)

C. f. frenatus
W Cape Province

C. f. aurantius
Natal, E Cape Province

DRYMODES
Drymodes brunneopygia (Southern Scrub Robin

D. b. brunneopygia
Interior of New South Wales, Victoria,
E South Australia

D. b. pallidus
S & W South Australia

Drymodes superciliaris (Northern Scrub Robin)

D. s. beccarii
NW New Guinea

D. s. nigriceps
WC New Guinea

D. s. brevirostris
Aru Is, S New Guinea

D. s. colcloughi
Northern Territory

D. s. superciliaris
N Queensland

POGONOCICHLA
Pogonocichla stellata (Starred Robin)

P. s. ruwenzorii
Kivu area, NE Zaire

P. s. elgonensis
Mt Elgon (Kenya)

P. s. friedmanni
Kigezi, Uganda

P. s. guttifer
S Sudan, Kenya, NE Tanzania

P. s. macarthuri
Chyulu Mts (SE Kenya)

P. s. orientalis
Malawi, Zambia, Tanzania, Mozambique

P. s. hygrica
SC Mozambique

P. s. transvaalensis
NE Transvaal, SW Mozambique

P. s. lebombo
Swaziland

P. s. margaritata
C Natal

P. s. stellata
S Natal, Cape Province

Pogonocichla swynnertoni (Swynnerton's Bush Robin)

P. s. swynnertoni
E Rhodesia

P. s. umbratica
W Mozambique

Erithacus gabela (Gabela Akelat)
Angola
Erithacus cyornithopsis (Common Akelat)
  E. c. houghtoni
  Sierra Leone, Liberia
  E. c. cyornithopsis
  S Cameroun
  E. c. lopezi
  NE Zaire, Uganda
  E. c. acholiensis
  S Sudan
Erithacus aequatorialis (Jackson's Akelat)
  E Zaire, S Uganda, W Kenya
Erithacus erythrothorax (Forest Robin)
  E. e. erythrothorax
  Sierra Leone to S Nigeria
  E. e. gabonensis
  Fernando Po I, W Gabon
  E. e. xanthogaster
  S Cameroun, N Zaire
  E. e. mabirae
  E Zaire, Uganda
Erithacus sharpei (Sharpe's Akelat)
  E. s. usambarae
  C Tanzania
  E. s. sharpei
  SW Tanzania, N Malawi
Erithacus gunningi (East Coast Akelat)
  E. g. sokokensis
  E Kenya, E Tanzania
  E. g. bensoni
  NW Malawi
  E. g. gunningi
  C Mozambique
Erithacus rubecula (European Robin)
  E. r. melophilus
  British Isles
  E. r. rubecula
  W Europe, NW Morocco » NE Africa
  E. r. superbus
  Teneriffe I, Gd Canary I
  E. r. witherbyi
  E Algeria, Tunisia
  E. r. sardus
  Corsica, Sardinia
  E. r. balcanicus
  Balkans, Turkey
  E. r. hyrcanus
  E Turkey, S Russia » Iran, Iraq
  E. r. tataricus
  W Siberia » Iran
Erithacus akahige (Japanese Robin)
  E. a. akahige
  Sakhalin I, N Japan » S China
  E. a. rishirensis
  Rishiri Is

  E. a. tanensis
  S Japan & Is
Erithacus komadori (Riukiu Robin)
  E. k. komadori
  Tanegashima I, N Riukiu Is
  E. k. namiyei
  Okinawa I
  E. k. subrufus
  S Riukiu Is
Erithacus sibilans (Swinhoe's Robin)
  SE Siberia, N China » S China
Erithacus luscinia (Thrush Nightingale)
  Europe, W Asia » SC Africa
Erithacus megarhynchos (Nightingale)
  E. m. megarhynchos
  W Europe, N Africa » W & C Africa
  E. m. africanus
  Syria, SW Iran » E Africa
  E. m. hafizi
  C Asia » E Africa
Erithacus calliope (Siberian Rubythroat)
  Siberia » S China, India
Erithacus svecicus (Bluethroat)
  E. s. svecicus
  N Europe, N Asia » India, China
  E. s. cyaneculus
  C Europe » N Africa
  E. s. volgae
  SW Russia
  E. s. luristanicus
  Iran » Iraq, Sudan
  E. s. pallidogularis
  Turkistan, W Siberia » India
  E. s. abbotti
  Pakistan, NW India
  E. s. saturatior
  C Asia to E Tibet, Afghanistan
Erithacus pectoralis (Himalayan Rubythroat)
  E. p. pectoralis
  S Russia, W Himalayas » NW India
  E. p. confusus
  E Himalayas » NE India
  E. p. tschebaiewi
  Tibet, NW China » Assam, Burma
Erithacus ruficeps (Rufous-headed Robin)
  SW Shensi
Erithacus obscurus (Black-throated Blue Robin)
  SW Shensi, SE Kansu
Erithacus pectardens (David's Rubythroat)
  SE Tibet, SW China
Erithacus brunneus (Indian Bluechat)
  E. b. brunneus
  Pakistan, N India, » S India
  E. b. wickhami
  Chin hills, Burma

Erithacus cyane **(Siberian Blue Robin)**
E. c. cyane
C Siberia » SE Asia
E. c. bochaiensis
E Siberia, Japan » Malaysia, Borneo
Erithacus cyanurus **(Red-flanked Bluetail)**
E. c. cyanurus
N Russia, N Japan » S China
E. c. pallidior
Pakistan, NW India
E. c. rufilatus
Himalayas, W China » Burma, Indochina
Erithacus chrysaeus **(Golden Bush Robin)**
E. c. whistleri
Pakistan, NW India
E. c. chrysaeus
Nepal, NE India, W China » N Vietnam
Erithacus indicus **(White-browed Bush Robin)**
E. i. indicus
E Himalayas, NE India
E. i. yunnanensis
W China » N Burma, N Indochina
E. i. formosanus
Taiwan
Erithacus hyperythrus **(Rufous-breasted Bush Robin)**
Himalayas, N Burma, SE Tibet
Erithacus johnstoniae **(Collared Bush Robin)**
Taiwan

COSSYPHA

Cossypha roberti **(White-bellied Robin Chat)**
C. r. roberti
S Cameroun, Fernando Po I
C. r. rufescentior
E Zaire
Cossypha natalensis **(Red-capped Robin Chat)**
C. n. intensa
S Sudan & Ethiopia to Zambia & Mozambique
C. n. larischi
N Angola
C. n. garguensis
Mt Gargues (Kenya)
C. n. tennenti
Mt Endau (Kenya)
C. n. natalensis
Natal, Cape Province
C. n. egregior
S Mozambique
C. n. hylophona
Malawi
Cossypha dichroa **(Chorister Robin Chat)**
E Transvaal, Natal, S Cape Province

Cossypha semirufa **(Black-tailed Robin Chat)**
C. s. semirufa
S & W Ethiopia, SE Sudan, N Kenya
C. s. donaldsoni
E & SE Ethiopia
C. s. intercedens
C & S Kenya, N Tanzania
Cossypha heuglini **(White-browed Robin Chat)**
C. h. pallidior
Chad
C. h. heuglini
S Sudan, Ethiopia to Zambia, Malawi
C. h. subrufescens
Gabon, W Zaire
C. h. intermedia
E Somalia, E Kenya, E Tanzania
C. h. euronota
N Natal, E Transvaal, Rhodesia, Mozambique
Cossypha cyanocampter **(Blue-shouldered Robin Chat)**
C. c. cyanocampter
Sierra Leone to Cameroun, Gabon
C. c. bartteloti
NE Zaire, Uganda, Kenya
Cossypha caffra **(Cape Robin Chat)**
C. c. iolaema
S Sudan to Zambia & Mozambique
C. c. kivuensis
Kivu area (E Zaire)
C. c. drakensbergi
E Transvaal
C. c. vespera
E Rhodesia
C. c. namaquensis
S Namibia, W Transvaal
C. c. caffra
Natal, Swaziland, Cape Province
Cossypha anomala **(Olive-flanked Robin Chat)**
C. a. mbuluensis
Mbulu dis (N Tanzania)
C. a. albigularis
S Tanzania
C. a. macclounii
N Malawi, SW Tanzania
C. a. anomala
Milanje, Malawi
C. a. gurue
N Mozambique
Cossypha humeralis **(White-throated Robin Chat)**
C. h. humeralis
Rhodesia
C. h. crepuscula
E Transvaal, Natal, S Mozambique

Cossypha ansorgei (Ansorge's Robin Chat)
W Angola
Cossypha niveicapilla (Snowy-headed Robin Chat)
C. n. niveicapilla
Senegal to Sudan & SW Ethiopia
C. n. melanonota
NW Cameroun, Gabon, Zaire
Cossypha heinrichi (Rand's Robin Chat)
N Angola, W Zaire
Cossypha albicapilla (White-crowned Robin Chat)
C. a. albicapilla
Senegal to Guinea
C. a. giffardi
Ghana to N Cameroun
C. a. omoensis
SE Sudan, SW Ethiopia

DRYOCICHLOIDES
Dryocichloides bocagei (Rufous-cheeked Robin Chat)
D. b. insulana
Fernando Po I
D. b. granti
Mt Kupé (Cameroun)
D. b. kaboboensis
Kivu area (E Zaire)
D. b. kungwensis
W Tanzania
D. b. schoutedeni
E Zaire
D. b. chapini
NW Zambia
D. b. bocagei
SW Zaire, W Angola
D. b. hallae
SE Zaire
Dryocichloides polioptera (Grey-winged Robin Chat)
D. p. polioptera
S Sudan, Uganda, N Angola
D. p. nigriceps
Sierra Leone to W Cameroun
D. p. tessmanni
E Cameroun
D. p. grimwoodi
NW Zambia
Dryocichloides archeri (Archer's Robin Chat)
D. a. archeri
NE Zaire, W Uganda
D. a. albimentalis
Kivu area (E Zaire)
D. a. kimbutui
Mt Kabobo (SE Zaire)

Dryocichloides isabellae (Mountain Robin
Chat)
D. i. batesi
E Nigeria
D. i. isabellae
Cameroun Mt
Dryocichloides montana (Usambara Robin Chat)
Usambara Mts, NE Tanzania
Dryocichloides lowei (Iringa Robin Chat)
S Tanzania, N Malawi

MODULATRIX
Modulatrix stictigula (Spot Throat)
M. s. stictigula
N Tanzania
M. s. pressa
N Malawi, SW Tanzania

CICHLADUSA
Cichladusa guttata (Spotted Morning Warbler)
C. g. guttata
S Sudan to SE Kenya, N Tanzania
C. g. rufipennis
SE Ethiopia, E Kenya, E Tanzania
Cichladusa arquata (Collared Morning Warbler)
SE Zaire, S Kenya to Zambia & Mozambique
Cichladusa ruficauda (Red-tailed Morning Warbler)
Gabon to N Angola

ALETHE
Alethe diademata (White-tailed Alethe)
Guinea to Togo
Alethe castanea (Fire-crested Alethe)
A. c. castanea
Nigeria to Zaire
A. c. woosnami
E Zaire, Uganda
Alethe poliophrys (Red-throated Alethe)
A. p. poliophrys
NE Zaire
A. p. kaboboensis
E Zaire
Alethe fuelleborni (White-chested Alethe)
A. f. usambarae
E. Tanzania
A. f. fuelleborni
SW Tanzania, N Malawi
A. f. xuthera
S Mozambique
Alethe poliocephala (Brown-chested Alethe)
A. p. castanonota
Sierra Leone to Ghana
A. p. poliocephala
Fernando Po I, S Cameroun to N Angola

A. p. hallae
Gabela, Angola
A. p. carruthersi
S Sudan, NE Zaire, Uganda
A. p. akeleyae
C Kenya
A. p. kungwensis
W Tanzania
A. p. ufipae
SW Tanzania

Alethe choloensis (Cholo Mountain Alethe)
A. c. choloensis
E & S Malawi
A. c. namuli
Namuli Mt (Mozambique)

COPSYCHUS
Copsychus saularis (Magpie Robin)
C. s. saularis
Pakistan, N & W India
C. s. ceylonensis
SE India, Sri Lanka
C. s. erimelas
NE India to Thailand & Indochina
C. s. andamanensis
Andaman Is
C. s. prosthopellus
S & E China, Hainan I
C. s. musicus
S Thailand, Malaysia, Sumatra, Billiton I
C. s. nesiotes
Bangka I, SE Sumatra
C. s. zacnecus
Simalur I
C. s. nesiarchus
Nias I
C. s. masculus
Batu Is
C. s. pagiensis
Mentawei Is, Siberut I, Sipora I
C. s. javensis
W Java
C. s. amoenus
E Java, Bali I
C. s. problematicus
S & W Borneo
C. s. adamsi
N Borneo, Banguey I
C. s. pluto
Maratua I, E & SE Borneo
C. s. deuteronymus
Luzon I
C. s. mindanensis
S Philippine Is
Copsychus sechellarum (Seychelles Magpie Robin)
Seychelles Is

Copsychus albospecularis (Madagascar Magpie Robin)
C. a. albospecularis
N Madagascar
C. a. inexpectatus
E Madagascar
C. a. pica
W Madagascar
C. a. winterbottomi
SW Madagascar
Copsychus malabaricus (White-rumped Sh|
C. m. malabaricus
S India
C. m. leggei
Sri Lanka
C. m. indicus
Nepal, Assam, NE India
C. m. albiventris
Andaman Is
C. m. interpositus
Burma, Thailand, Indochina
C. m. minor
Hainan I
C. m. mallopercnus
Malaysia
C. m. tricolor
Sumatra, W Java
C. m. mirabilis
Prinsen I
C. m. melanurus
N West Sumatra Is
C. m. opisthopelus
S West Sumatra Is
C. m. javanus
WC & C Java
C. m. omissus
E Java
C. m. ochroptilus
Anamba Is
C. m. abbotti
Bangka I, Billiton I
C. m. eumesus
Natuna Is
C. m. suavis
Borneo
C. m. nigricauda
Kangean I
Copsychus stricklandii (Strickland's Shar|
C. s. stricklandii
Banguey I, N Borneo
C. s. barbouri
Maratua I, E Borneo
Copsychus luzoniensis (White-browed Sh|
C. l. luzoniensis
Cantaduanes I, Marinduque I, Luzon I
C. l. parvimaculatus
Polillo Is

C. l. superciliaris
Ticao I, Masbate I, Panay I, Negros I

Copsychus niger (Black Shama)
C. n. niger
Calamianes I, Balabac I, Palawan I
C. n. cebuensis
Cebu I

Copsychus pyrrhopygus (Orange-tailed Shama)
Malaysia, Sumatra, Borneo

IRANIA
Irania gutteralis (White-throated Robin)
Asia Minor, S Asia » E Africa

PHOENICURUS
Phoenicurus alaschanicus (Przewalski's Redstart)
W China
Phoenicurus erythronotus (Eversmann's Redstart)
C Asia » Iran, N India
Phoenicurus caeruleocephalus (Blue-headed Redstart)
C Asia, Himalayas
Phoenicurus ochruros (Black Redstart)
P. o. gibraltariensis
Europe, N Africa » Israel, Egypt
P. o. ochruros
Asia Minor, N Iran » Israel, Iraq
P. o. semirufus
Syria, Lebanon » Israel
P. o. phoenicuroides
C Asia » NE Africa, N India
P. o. rufiventris
Himalayas, Tibet, NW China » India, N Burma
Phoenicurus phoenicurus (Redstart)
P. p. phoenicurus
Europe, N Africa, C Asia » W & E Africa
P. p. samamisicus
Iran, S Russia » NE Africa
P. p. algeriensis
SW Iberian peninsula, NW Africa
Phoenicurus hodgsoni (Hodgson's Redstart)
W China » Burma, NE India
Phoenicurus frontalis (Blue-fronted Redstart)
N India, Tibet, W China » N Vietnam
Phoenicurus fuliginosus (Plumbeous Water Redstart)
P. f. fuliginosus
Tibet, Himalayas to N Thailand, W China
P. f. affinis
Taiwan
Phoenicurus leucocephalus (White-capped Redstart)
C Asia » India, E China, Indochina

Phoenicurus schisticeps (White-throated Redstart)
Tibet, W China » Assam, N Burma
Phoenicurus auroreus (Daurian Redstart)
P. a. leucopterus
W China, Tibet » NE India, N Indochina
P. a. auroreus
Siberia, N China » Japan & S China
Phoenicurus moussieri (Moussier's Redstart)
Tunisia, Algeria, Morocco
Phoenicurus erythrogaster (Güldenstadt's Redstart)
P. e. erythrogaster
Caucasus, Iran
P. e. grandis
C Asia, Tibet, Pakistan, N India » NE China

RHYACORNIS
Rhyacornis bicolor (Philippine Water Redstart)
N Luzon I

HODGSONIUS
Hodgsonius phaenicuroides (White-bellied Redstart)
H. p. phaenicuroides
Himalayas, N India, Tibet, N Burma
H. p. ichangensis
W China » N Indochina

CINCLIDIUM
Cinclidium leucurum (White-tailed Blue Robin)
C. l. leucurum
India, Indochina, Malaysia, Burma
C. l. cambodianum
Cambodia
Cinclidium diana (Sunda Blue Robin)
C. d. sumatranum
N & WC Sumatra
C. d. diana
Java
Cinclidium frontale (Blue-fronted Callene)
C. f. frontale
Nepal, Sikkim
C. f. orientale
N Indochina

GRANDALA
Grandala coelicolor (Hodgson's Grandala)
N India, Burma, W China

SIALIA
Sialia sialis (Eastern Bluebird)
S. s. sialis
E USA » N Mexico
S. s. grata
S Florida
S. s. fulva
Arizona, N Mexico » Guatemala

S. s. guatemalae
SE Mexico, Guatemala
S. s. meridionalis
El Salvador, Nicaragua
S. s. caribaea
Nicaragua

Sialia mexicana (Western Bluebird)
S. m. occidentalis
W Canada, W USA
S. m. bairdi
SW USA, NW Mexico
S. m. anabelae
N Baja California
S. m. amabilis
C Mexico
S. m. mexicana
NE Mexico
S. m. australis
SC Mexico

Sialia currucoides (Mountain Bluebird)
W Canada, W USA » SW USA, W Mexico

ENICURUS

Enicurus scouleri (Little Forktail)
E. s. scouleri
SE Russia, Himalayas, N India, W China
E. s. fortis
Taiwan

Enicurus velatus (Lesser Forktail)
E. v. sumatranus
Sumatra
E. v. velatus
Java

Enicurus ruficapillus (Chestnut-backed Forktail)
Malaysia, Borneo, Sumatra, S Thailand

Enicurus immaculatus (Black-backed Forktail)
Himalayas, Burma, Thailand

Enicurus schistaceus (Slaty-backed Forktail)
Himalayas, Burma, Thailand, Indochina

Enicurus leschenaulti (White-crowned Forktail)
E. l. indicus
NE India, Burma, Thailand, Indochina
E. l. sinensis
W & S China, Hainan I
E. l. frontalis
Malaysia, Sumatra, Nias I, Borneo
E. l. chaseni
Batu Is, W Sumatra
E. l. leschenaulti
Java, Bali I
E. l. borneensis
W Borneo

Enicurus maculatus (Spotted Forktail)
E. m. maculatus
W & C Himalayas

E. m. guttatus
E Himalayas, SW China
E. m. bacatus
S China, N Indochina
E. m. robinsoni
Dalat, S Vietnam

COCHOA

Cochoa purpurea (Purple Cochoa)
N India to N Vietnam

Cochoa viridis (Green Cochoa)
N India to S China, Indochina

Cochoa azurea (Malaysian Cochoa)
C. a. azurea
W & C Java
C. a. beccarii
W Sumatra

MYADESTES

Myadestes townsendi (Townsend's Solitaire)
M. t. townsendi
W Canada, W USA, W Mexico
M. t. calophonus
N Mexico

Myadestes obscurus (Brown-backed Solitaire)
M. o. obscurus
E Mexico
M. o. cinereus
C Mexico
M. o. occidentalis
N & W Mexico
M. o. insularis
Tres Marias Is
M. o. deignani
Oaxaca, S Chiapas
M. o. oberholseri
S Mexico, Guatemala, El Salvador

Myadestes elisabeth (Cuban Solitaire)
M. e. elisabeth
E & W Cuba
M. e. retrusus
Isle of Pines

Myadestes genibarbis (Rufous-throated Solitaire)
M. g. solitarius
Jamaica
M. g. montanus
Hispaniola
M. g. dominicanus
Dominica I
M. g. genibarbis
Martinique I
M. g. sanctaeluciae
St Lucia I
M. g. sibilans
St Vincent I

Myadestes ralloides (Andean Solitaire)
  M. r. melanops
    Costa Rica, W Panama
  M. r. coloratus
    E Panama
  M. r. plumbeiceps
    W Colombia, W Ecuador
  M. r. candelae
    NC Colombia
  M. r. venezuelensis
    N Venezuela, E Colombia to N Peru
  M. r. ralloides
    C & S Peru, W Bolivia
Myadestes unicolor (Slate-coloured Solitaire)
  M. u. unicolor
    S Mexico, Guatemala, N Honduras
  M. u. pallens
    Nicaragua
Myadestes leucogenys (Rufous-brown Solitaire)
  M. l. gularis
    Guyana
  M. l. chubbi
    W Ecuador
  M. l. peruvianus
    C Peru
  M. l. leucogenys
    SE Brazil

ENTOMODESTES
Entomodestes leucotis (White-eared Solitaire)
  Peru, Bolivia
Entomodestes coracinus (Black Solitaire)
  W Colombia, W Ecuador

STIZORHINA
Stizorhina fraseri (Rufous Broad-billed Ant-thrush)
  S. f. fraseri
    Fernando Po I
  S. f. rubicunda
    Cameroun to W Zaire & Angola
  S. f. vulpina
    N & E Zaire
Stizorhina finschii (Finsch's Broad-billed Ant-thrush)
  Sierra Leone to Nigeria

NEOCOSSYPHUS
Neocossyphus rufus (Red-tailed Ant-thrush)
  N. r. rufus
    Tanzania, N Kenya, Zanzibar
  N. r. gabunensis
    S Cameroun to Uganda

Neocossyphus poensis (White-tailed Ant-thrush)
  N. p. poensis
    Sierra Leone to Gabon, Fernando Po I
  N. p. praepectoralis
    N & E Zaire, W Uganda
  N. p. pallidigularis
    N Angola

CERCOMELA
Cercomela sinuata (Sicklewing Chat)
  C. s. hypernephela
    Lesotho
  C. s. ensifera
    E Transvaal, Orange Free State, N Cape Province
  C. s. sinuata
    S Cape Province
Cercomela familiaris (Familiar Chat)
  C. f. falkensteini
    Ghana to SW Sudan, N Ethiopia
  C. f. omoensis
    SE Sudan, SW Ethiopia
  C. f. modesta
    Uganda to Angola & Mozambique
  C. f. angolensis
    N Angola, N Namibia
  C. f. hoeschi
    NW Namibia
  C. f. galtoni
    E Namibia, W Botswana, N Cape Province
  C. f. hellmayri
    E Botswana, Rhodesia, Transvaal
  C. f. actuosa
    W Natal
  C. f. familiaris
    S Mozambique, Natal to S Cape Province
  C. f. richardi
    NW Cape Province
  C. f. dodsoni
    E Cape Province
Cercomela tractrac (Layard's Chat)
  C. t. hoeschi
    S Angola, N Namibia
  C. t. albicans
    N coastal Namibia
  C. t. barlowi
    Gt Namaqualand
  C. t. nebulosa
    S coastal Namibia
  C. t. tractrac
    Little Namaqualand
Cercomela schlegelii (Karoo Chat)
  C. s. benguellensis
    S Angola
  C. s. schlegelii
    coastal Namibia

C. s. namaquensis
Little Namaqualand
C. s. kobosensis
C Great Namaqualand
C. s. pollux
Orange Free State, Cape Province
Cercomela fusca (Brown Rockchat)
Pakistan, N & C India
Cercomela dubia (Sombre Rockchat)
Somalia, C Ethiopia
Cercomela melanura (Blackstart)
C. m. melanura
Israel to Saudi Arabia
C. m. neumanni
W Saudi Arabia, Yemen, Aden
C. m. lypura
W Red Sea coast
C. m. aussae
E Ethiopia
C. m. airensis
E Niger, Chad, Sudan
C. m. ultima
E Mali, W Niger
Cercomela scotocerca (Brown-tailed Rockchat)
C. s. furensis
W Sudan
C. m. scotocerca
Sudan coast
C. s. turkana
SW Ethiopia, NW Kenya
C. s. spectatrix
Somalia
C. s. validior
Run, Somalia
Cercomela sordida (Hill Chat)
C. s. sordida
Ethiopia
C. s. rudolfi
Mt Elgon (Kenya)
C. s. ernesti
Aberdare Mts, Mt Kenya
C. s. olimotiensis
N Tanzania
C. s. hypospodia
Mt Kilimanjaro (Tanzania)

SAXICOLA
Saxicola rubetra (Whinchat)
Europe, Asia, N Africa » W & C Africa
Saxicola macrorhyncha (Stoliczka's Bushchat)
S Afghanistan, N India
Saxicola insignis (Hodgson's Bushchat)
Russia, W China, Tibet » N India
Saxicola dacotiae (Canary Islands Chat)
S. d. dacotiae
Fuerteventura I

S. d. murielae
Allegranza I
Saxicola torquata (Stonechat)
S. t. hibernans
British Isles, W France
S. t. rubicola
W Europe, N Africa » Middle East
S. t. variegata
Asia Minor, NE Africa, Iraq
S. t. armenica
Iran, N Iraq, NE Africa, Saudi Arabia
S. t. maura
E Russia, C Asia » Iran, Iraq, N India
S. t. indica
Himalayas » C India
S. t. przewalskii
W China » Burma, N India
S. t. stejnergeri
E Siberia, Japan » S China, Burma, Indochina
S. t. felix
SW Saudi Arabia, Yemen
S. t. albofasciata
Ethiopia
S. t. jebelmarrae
W Sudan
S. t. moptana
S Mali
S. t. nebularum
Sierra Leone, Ivory Coast
S. t. adamauae
N & W Cameroun
S. t. pallidigula
Cameroun Mt, Fernando Po I
S. t. axillaris
E Zaire, Uganda, Kenya, N Tanzania
S. t. promiscua
C Tanzania
S. t. salax
Cameroun to N Angola & Rhodesia
S. t. stonei
Angola to Mozambique, N South Africa
S. t. clanceyi
W Namibia, NW Cape Province
S. t. torquata
SW Cape Province to Natal, Transvaal
S. t. oreobates
S Rhodesia, W Natal, Orange Free State
S. t. sibilla
Madagascar
S. t. voeltzkowi
Gt Comoro I
S. t. tectes
Réunion I
Saxicola leucura (White-tailed Stonechat)
Pakistan, N India

Saxicola caprata (Pied Stonechat)
S. c. rossorum
SW Asia » Iran & Pakistan
S. c. bicolor
Pakistan » N & C India
S. c. burmanica
C India, Burma, N Thailand, Indochina
S. c. nilgiriensis
S India
S. c. atrata
Sri Lanka
S. c. caprata
Luzon I, Mindoro I, Cebu I
S. c. randi
Negros I, Bohol I, Siquijor I
S. c. anderseni
C Mindanao I
S. c. fruticola
Java I to Flores I & Alor I
S. c. pyrrhonota
Kisser I, Wetar I, Savu Is, Timor I
S. c. francki
Sumba I
S. c. albonotata
Saleyer I, Celebes
S. c. cognata
Babar I
S. c. aethiops
New Britain, N New Guinea
S. c. belensis
WC New Guinea
S. c. wahgiensis
EC & E New Guinea
Saxicola jerdoni (Jerdon's Bushchat)
E India, Burma, N Indochina
Saxicola ferrea (Grey Bushchat)
Himalayas to S China »
S Indochina
Saxicola gutturalis (Timor Bushchat)
S. g. gutturalis
Timor I
S. g. luctuosa
Semau I

MYRMECOCICHLA
Myrmecocichla tholloni (Congo Moorchat)
Gabon, N Angola
Myrmecocichla aethiops (Anteater Chat)
M. a. aethiops
Senegal to Chad, N Nigeria, N Cameroun
M. a. sudanensis
W Sudan
M. a. cryptoleuca
C Kenya, N Tanzania
Myrmecocichla formicivora (Southern Anteater Chat)
M. f. formicivora
E Botswana, Natal, C & E Cape Province

M. f. minor
W Botswana, Namibia
Myrmecocichla nigra (Sooty Chat)
Nigeria to Sudan, Angola, Tanzania
Myrmecocichla arnotti (White-headed Black Chat)
M. a. leucolaema
SE Zaire, W Tanzania
M. a. harterti
SW Zaire, Angola
M. a. arnotti
E Angola & Namibia to Malawi,
N Transvaal
Myrmecocichla albifrons (White-fronted Black Chat)
M. a. frontalis
Senegal to Nigeria & Chad
M. a. limbata
N & E Cameroun, Central African Republic
M. a. albifrons
N Ethiopia
M. a. pachyrhyncha
SW Ethiopia
M. a. clericalis
S Sudan, NE Zaire, N Uganda
Myrmecocichla melaena (Ruppells Chat)
Ethiopia

THAMNOLAEA
Thamnolaea cinnamomeiventris (Cliffchat)
T. c. cavernicola
Fiko, Mali
T. c. bambarae
Kulikoro, Mali
T. c. albiscapulata
E & S Ethiopia, E Sudan
T. c. subrufipennis
Sudan & Ethiopia to Zambia & Malawi
T. c. odica
E Botswana, Transvaal, Rhodesia,
Mozambique
T. c. cinnamomeiventris
E Transvaal, Natal, E Cape Province
T. c. autochthones
N Natal, S Mozambique
Thamnolaea coronata (White-crowned Cliffchat)
T. c. coronata
Togo to N Cameroun, W Sudan
T. c. kordofanensis
C Sudan
Thamnolaea semirufa (White-winged Cliffchat)
Ethiopia

OENANTHE
Oenanthe bifasciata (Buff-streaked Chat)
S Transvaal, Natal, Cape Province
Oenanthe isabellina (Isabelline Wheatear)
E Europe, W China » India, C Africa

Oenanthe bottae (Red-breasted Wheatear)
  O. b. bottae
    Yemen
  O. b. frenata
    Ethiopia
  O. b. heuglini
    Mali, Central African Republic, Sudan
Oenanthe xanthoprymna (Red-tailed Wheatear)
  O. x. xanthoprymna
    SW Iran » NE Africa
  O. x. chrysopygia
    E Turkey, N Iran » Iraq, Saudi Arabia
  O. x. kingi
    Afghanistan » Pakistan, NW India
Oenanthe oenanthe (Common Wheatear)
  O. o. leucorhoa
    Greenland, NE Canada » W Europe, W Africa
  O. o. oenanthe
    N & C Europe, N Asia » N & C Africa
  O. o. nivea
    Balearic Is, S Spain
  O. o. virago
    E Mediterranean Is » Israel, Egypt
  O. o. seebohmi
    Morocco, Algeria
  O. o. libanotica
    S Europe, NW Africa
  O. o. phillipsi
    Somalia
Oenanthe deserti (Desert Wheatear)
  O. d. homochroa
    N Africa
  O. d. deserti
    W & C Asia » Pakistan, N India, NE Africa
  O. d. oreophila
    Tibet & Sinkiang » Pakistan, Saudi Arabia
Oenanthe hispanica (Black-eared Wheatear)
  O. h. hispanica
    S Europe, N Africa » W Africa
  O. h. melanoleuca
    E Europe, Asia Minor » NE & W Africa
Oenanthe finschii (Finsch's Wheatear)
  O. f. finschii
    Turkey, Saudi Arabia » Iran, Pakistan
  O. f. barnesi
    NE Iran, C Asia » S Iran, Pakistan
Oenanthe picata (Eastern Pied Wheatear)
  Iran, Pakistan » N India
Oenanthe lugens (Mourning Wheatear)
  O. l. halophila
    N Africa
  O. l. lugens
    N Egypt, Israel, Iraq

  O. l. persica
    S Egypt, S Israel, S Iran, N Sudan
  O. l. lugentoides
    SW Saudi Arabia, Yemen
  O. l. boscaweni
    S Saudi Arabia
  O. l. vauriei
    NE Somalia
  O. l. lugubris
    N & C Ethiopia
  O. l. schalowi
    S Kenya, NE Tanzania
Oenanthe monacha (Hooded Wheatear)
  Egypt to Pakistan
Oenanthe alboniger (Hume's Wheatear)
  S Iran, Afghanistan, Pakistan
Oenanthe pleschanka (Pied Wheatear)
  O. p. pleschanka
    E Europe to W China » E Africa
  O. p. cypriaca
    Cyprus » E & N Africa
Oenanthe leucopyga (White-crowned Black Wheatear)
  O. l. aegra
    Algeria, Tunisia
  O. l. ernesti
    Egypt, Saudi Arabia, Iraq
  O. l. leucopyga
    Mali to Ethiopia
Oenanthe leucura (Black Wheatear)
  O. l. leucura
    W Mediterranean
  O. l. syenitica
    NW Africa
Oenanthe monticola (Mountain Chat)
  O. m. albipileata
    Benguella, Angola
  O. m. nigricauda
    Huambo, Angola
  O. m. atmorii
    W Namibia
  O. m. monticola
    E Namibia, Cape Province
  O. m. griseiceps
    S Botswana, Natal, Transvaal
Oenanthe moesta (Red-rumped Wheatear)
  O. m. moesta
    N Africa
  O. m. brooksbanki
    E Egypt, Jordan, Iraq
Oenanthe pileata (Capped Wheatear)
  Angola to Kenya & Cape Province

SAXICOLOIDES
Saxicoloides fulicata (Black-backed Robin)
  S. f. cambaiensis
    Pakistan, N & W India

S. f. erythrura
  NE India
S. f. intermedia
  C India
S. f. fulicata
  S India
S. f. leucoptera
  Sri Lanka

PSEUDOCOSSYPHUS

Pseudocossyphus imerinus (Madagascar Robin Chat)
P. i. erythronotus
  N Madagascar
P. i. sharpei
  C Madagascar
P. i. imerinus
  SE Madagascar
P. i. salomonseni
  E Madagascar

Pseudocossyphus bensoni (Farkas' Robin Chat)
  SW Madagascar

MONTICOLA

Monticola rupestris (Cape Rock Thrush)
  South Africa

Monticola explorator (Sentinel Rock Thrush)
M. e. explorator
  Transvaal, Natal, Cape Province
M. e. tenebriformis
  Lesotho » N Natal, S Mozambique

Monticola brevipes (Short-toed Rock Thrush)
M. b. niveiceps
  Huila, Angola
M. b. brevipes
  S Angola, Namibia, N Cape Province
M. b. leucocapilla
  S Botswana, W Transvaal, Orange Free State

Monticola rufocinereus (Little Rock Thrush)
M. r. rufocinereus
  Ethiopia, Sudan to NE Tanzania
M. r. sclateri
  W Saudi Arabia

Monticola angolensis (Miombo Rock Thrush)
M. a. angolensis
  S Zaire, Angola to Tanzania, Mozambique
M. a. hylophila
  NW Rhodesia

Monticola saxatilis (Rock Thrush)
M. s. saxatilis
  C & S Europe to W China » N India & E Africa

M. s. coloratus
  E Europe

Monticola cinclorhynchus (Blue-capped Rock Thrush)
  Himalayas » W Burma, S India

Monticola gularis (White-throated Rock Thrush)
  NE Asia » Burma, Thailand, Indochina

Monticola rufiventris (Chestnut-bellied Rock Thrush)
  Himalayas, W China » Indochina

Monticola solitarius (Blue Rock Thrush)
M. s. solitarius
  S Europe, Middle East » W & C Africa
M. s. longirostris
  N Iraq, Iran, Pakistan » N India & NE Africa
M. s. pandoo
  Himalayas, C Asia » India, SE Asia, Indonesia
M. s. philippensis
  NE Russia, China, Japan » Philippine Is, Indonesia
M. s. madoci
  Malaysia

MYIOPHONEUS

Myiophoneus blighi (Ceylon Whistling Thrush)
  Sri Lanka

Myiophoneus melanurus (Shiny Whistling Thrush)
  Sumatra

Myiophoneus glaucinus (Sunda Whistling Thrush)
M. g. glaucinus
  Java, Bali I
M. g. castaneus
  Sumatra
M. g. borneensis
  Borneo

Myiophoneus robinsoni (Malayan Whistling Thrush)
  Malaysia

Myiophoneus horsfieldii (Malabar Whistling Thrush)
  S India

Myiophoneus insularis (Formosan Whistling Thrush)
  Taiwan

Myiophoneus caeruleus (Himalayan Whistling Thrush)
M. c. temminckii
  C Asia, Pakistan, N India, Burma
M. c. eugenei
  S Burma, Thailand, W China, Indochina
M. c. caeruleus
  W China » C & S China, N Indochina

M. c. crassirostris
SE Thailand, N Malaysia
M. c. dichrorhynchus
C & S Malaysia, W Sumatra
M. c. flavirostris
Java

GEOMALIA
Geomalia heinrichi (Celebes Mountain Thrush)
G. h. heinrichi
SC Celebes
G. h. matinangensis
N & SE Celebes

ZOOTHERA
Zoothera schistacea (White-eared Ground Thrush)
Tenimber Is
Zoothera dumasi (Buru Ground Thrush)
Z. d. dumasi
Buru I
Z. d. joiceyi
Ceram I
Zoothera interpres (Kuhl's Ground Thrush)
Z. i. interpres
S Thailand, Sumatra to Flores I,
Borneo, Basilan I
Z. i. leucolaema
Enggano I
Zoothera erythronota (Celebes Ground Thrush)
Z. e. erythronota
Celebes
Z. e. dohertyi
Lombok I to Timor I
Z. e. mendeni
Peling Is
Zoothera wardii (Pied Ground Thrush)
N India» S India, Sri Lanka
Zoothera cinerea (Ashy Ground Thrush)
Mindoro I, N Luzon I
Zoothera peronii (Peroni's Ground Thrush)
Z. p. peronii
W Timor I
Z. p. audacis
N Timor I, Damar I
Zoothera citrina (Orange-headed Ground Thrush)
Z. c. citrina
Pakistan to N Burma » S India, Sri
Lanka
Z. c. cyanotus
S India
Z. c. innotata
Burma, S China, Indochina » Malaysia

Z. c. melli
SE China
Z. c. courtoisi
Anhwei
Z. c. aurimacula
S Vietnam, Hainan I
Z. c. andamanensis
Andaman Is
Z. c. albogularis
Nicobar Is
Z. c. gibsonhilli
S Burma, S Thailand
Z. c. aurata
N Borneo
Z. c. rubecula
W Java
Z. c. orientis
E Java, Bali I
Zoothera everetti (Everett's Ground Thrush)
N Borneo
Zoothera sibirica (Siberian Ground Thrush)
Z. s. sibirica
NE Asia » SE Asia, Java
Z. s. davisoni
Japan » S China, Thailand, Malaysia
Zoothera naevia (Varied Thrush)
Z. n. naevia
SE Alaska, W Canada, NW USA » SW USA
Z. n. meruloides
N Alaska, NW Canada » to WC USA
Zoothera pinicola (Aztec Thrush)
C Mexico
Zoothera piaggiae (Abyssinian Ground Thrush)
Z. p. piaggiae
Ethiopia, Sudan, E Zaire, N Kenya
Z. p. hadii
SE Sudan
Z. p. kilimensis
C & S Kenya, N Tanzania
Z. p. rowei
N Tanzania
Zoothera tanganjicae (Western Orange Ground Thrush)
SW Uganda
Zoothera oberlaenderi (Forest Ground Thrush)
NE Zaire, Uganda
Zoothera gurneyi (Orange Ground Thrush)
Z. g. chuka
Mt Kenya
Z. g. chyulu
SE Kenya
Z. g. otomitra
S Kenya to Angola, N Malawi

Z. g. gurneyi
Natal, E Cape Province
Z. g. disruptans
C & S Malawi, E Rhodesia, N Transvaal
Mozambique
Zoothera cameronensis (Black-eared Ground Thrush)
Z. c. cameronensis
Cameroun
Z. c. prigoginei
W Zaire
Zoothera princei (Grey Ground Thrush)
Z. p. princei
Sierra Leone to Ghana
Z. p. batesi
S Cameroun, N Zaire
Z. p. graueri
NE Zaire
Zoothera crossleyi (Crossley's Ground Thrush)
Z. c. crossleyi
Mt Kupé, Cameroun Mt
Z. c. pilettei
NE Zaire
Zoothera guttata (Spotted Ground Thrush)
Z. g. guttata
S Malawi, Natal, Cape Province
Z. g. fischeri
coast of Kenya & Tanzania
Zoothera spiloptera (Spotted-winged Thrush)
Sri Lanka
Zoothera andromedae (Sunda Ground Thrush)
Sumatra to Timor I, Mindoro I, Mindanao I
Zoothera mollissima (Plain-backed Mountain Thrush)
Z. m. whiteheadi
N Pakistan, W Himalayas
Z. m. mollissima
E Himalayas, SE Tibet » Burma, Indochina
Z. m. griseiceps
SW China, N Vietnam
Zoothera dixoni (Long-tailed Mountain Thrush)
E Himalayas, Tibet » Burma, Thailand, N Vietnam
Zoothera dauma (White's Thrush)
Z. d. aurea
N & NE Asia » S China, Indochina
Z. d. dauma
Himalayas, Burma, China, Thailand » S India
Z. d. neilgherriensis
S India
Z. d. imbricata
Sri Lanka

Z. d. toratugumi
Manchuria, Japan » Taiwan
Z. d. major
N Riukiu Is
Z. d. hancii
S Riukiu Is, S Thailand, S Vietnam, Taiwan
Z. d. horsfieldi
Sumatra, Java, Lombok I
Z. d. machiki
Tenimber Is
Z. d. papuensis
SE New Guinea
Z. d. eichhorni
St Matthias Is
Z. d. choiseuli
Choiseul I
Z. d. cuneata
N Queensland
Z. d. heinei
S Queensland
Z. d. lunulata
New South Wales, Victoria, South Australia
Z. d. macrorhyncha
Tasmania
Zoothera talaseae (New Britain Ground Thrush)
New Britain
Zoothera margaretae (San Cristobal Ground Thrush)
Z. m. turipavae
Guadalcanal I
Z. m. margaretae
San Cristobal I
Zoothera monticola (Greater Long-billed Thrush)
Z. m. monticola
Himalayas, Assam, NE Burma
Z. m. atrata
N Vietnam
Zoothera marginata (Lesser Long-billed Thrush)
N India to Indochina

AMALOCICHLA
Amalocichla sclateriana (Greater New Guinea Thrush)
A. s. occidentalis
W New Guinea
A. s. sclateriana
SE New Guinea
Amalocichla incerta (Lesser New Guinea Thrush)
A. i. incerta
Arfak Mts (W New Guinea)
A. i. olivascentior
WC New Guinea

A. i. brevicauda
E & SE New Guinea

CATAPONERA
Cataponera turdoides (Cataponera Thrush)
  C. t. abditiva
    NC Celebes
  C. t. tenebrosa
    S Celebes
  C. t. turdoides
    SW Celebes
  C. t. heinrichi
    SE Celebes

NESOCICHLA
Nesocichla eremita (Tristan Thrush)
  N. e. eremita
    Tristan da Cunha I
  N. e. gordoni
    Inaccessible I
  N. e. procax
    Nightingale I

CICHLHERMINIA
Cichlherminia lherminieri (Forest Thrush)
  C. l. lherminieri
    Guadeloupe I
  C. l. lawrencii
    Montserrat I
  C. l. dominicensis
    Dominica I
  C. l. sanctaelucae
    St Lucia I

PHAEORNIS
Phaeornis obscurus (Hawaiian Thrush)
  P. o. myadestinus
    Kauai I
  P. o. rutha
    Molokai I **e?**
  P. o. lanaiensis
    Lanai I **e?**
  P. o. obscurus
    Hawaii I
Phaeornis palmeri (Small Kauai Thrush)
    Kauai I

CATHARUS
Catharus gracilirostris (Slender-billed Nightingale Thrush)
  C. g. gracilirostris
    Costa Rica
  C. g. accentor
    W Panama
Catharus aurantiirostris (Orange-billed Nightingale Thrush)
  C. a. aenopennis
    NW Mexico
  C. a. clarus
    NC Mexico
  C. a. melpomene
    C Mexico to Costa Rica

C. a. russatus
  SW Costa Rica, W Panama
C. a. griseiceps
  W Panama
C. a. phaeoplurus
  C Colombia
C. a. aurantiirostris
  NE Colombia, NW Venezuela
C. a. birchalli
  NE Venezuela, Trinidad
C. a. barbaritoi
  C Venezuela
C. a. sierrae
  Santa Marta Mts (Colombia)
C. a. inornatus
  EC Colombia
C. a. insignis
  N Colombia
Catharus fuscater (Slaty-backed Nightingale Thrush)
  C. f. hellmayri
    Costa Rica, W Panama
  C. f. mirabilis
    E Panama
  C. f. sanctaemartae
    N Colombia
  C. f. fuscater
    Ecuador, Colombia, W Venezuela
  C. f. opertaneus
    W Colombia
  C. f. caniceps
    N & C Peru
  C. f. mentalis
    SE Peru, N Bolivia
Catharus occidentalis (Russet Nightingale Thrush)
  C. o. olivascens
    N Mexico
  C. o. durangensis
    Durango
  C. o. lambi
    N Puebla
  C. o. fulvescens
    C Mexico
  C. o. occidentalis
    SE Mexico
Catharus frantzii (Frantzius' Nightingale Thrush)
  C. f. chiapensis
    C Chiapas
  C. f. confusus
    NE Puebla
  C. f. nelsoni
    E Oaxaca
  C. f. waldroni
    N Nicaragua
  C. f. wetmorei
    Chiriqui, Panama

C. f. juancitonis
  S Mexico to Honduras
C. f. frantzii
  Costa Rica, W Panama
Catharus mexicanus (Black-headed Nightingale Thrush)

C. m. mexicanus
  EC Mexico
C. m. cantator
  S Mexico, E Guatemala, Honduras
C. m. fumosus
  Nicaragua, Costa Rica, W Panama
Catharus dryas (Spotted Nightingale Thrush)

C. d. harrisoni
  Oaxaca
C. d. ovandensis
  Chiapas
C. d. dryas
  W Guatemala, Honduras, W Ecuador
C. d. maculatus
  E Colombia, E Ecuador, Peru, Bolivia
C. d. ecuadoreanus
  W Ecuador
C. d. blakei
  Jujuy, Argentina
Catharus fuscescens (Veery)

C. f. fuscescens
  E Canada, E USA » E Mexico, Panama
  NE South America
C. f. fuliginosa
  SE Canada » E USA
C. f. salicicola
  W Canada, W USA » Mexico & N South
  America
C. f. subpallidus
  NW USA » SW USA
Catharus minimus (Grey-cheeked Thrush)

C. m. minimus
  E Siberia, Canada » E USA, N South
  America
C. m. aliciae
  SE Canada » E USA, West Indies
Catharus ustulatus (Swainson's Thrush)

C. u. almae
  S Alaska, W Canada » S USA
C. u. ustulatus
  SE Alaska, W Canada » W USA, Mexico
C. u. oedicus
  W USA » Mexico
C. u. swainsoni
  C & E Canada, E USA » S Mexico, West
  Indies, E South America
Catharus guttatus (Hermit Thrush)

C. g. guttatus
  Alaska, W Canada » W USA, N & C Mexico

C. g. nanus
  SE Alaska, W Canada » W USA, Baja
  California
C. g. slevini
  W USA » NW Mexico
C. g. sequoiensis
  W USA » N Mexico
C. g. polionotus
  W USA » S Mexico
C. g. auduboni
  W & SW USA » Mexico, Guatemala
C. g. faxoni
  Canada, E USA » SE USA
C. g. crymophilus
  Newfoundland » SE USA

HYLOCICHLA
Hylocichla mustelina (Wood Thrush)
  SE Canada, E USA » E Mexico, Cuba,
  Central America

PLATYCICHLA
Platycichla flavipes (Yellow-legged Thrush)

P. f. venezuelensis
  Colombia, N & W Venezuela
P. f. melanopleura
  NE Venezuela, Trinidad
P. f. xanthoscelus
  Tobago I
P. f. polionota
  S Venezuela, Guyana
P. f. flavipes
  SE Brazil, Argentina, NE Paraguay
Platycichla leucops (Pale-eyed Thrush)
  N South America

TURDUS
Turdus bewsheri (Comoro Thrush)

T. b. comorensis
  Great Comoro I
T. b. moheliensis
  Moheli I
T. b. bewsheri
  Anjouan I
Turdus olivaceofuscus (Sao Thomé Thrush)

T. o. olivaceofuscus
  Sao Thomé I
T. o. xanthorhynchus
  Principé I
Turdus olivaceus (Olive Thrush)

T. o. chiguancoides
  Senegal to W Ghana
T. o. saturatus
  W Ghana to N Zaire
T. o. adamauae
  N Cameroun
T. o. nigrilorum
  Cameroun Mt

T. o. poensis
Fernando Po I
T. o. bocagei
S Zaire, N Angola, NW Tanzania
T. o. centralis
N Zaire, Uganda, Central African Republic
T. o. pelios
Sudan, Ethiopia
T. o. graueri
S Uganda, NW Tanzania
T. o. stormsi
SE Zaire, NE Angola, NW Zambia
T. o. williami
Zambia
T. o. swynnertoni
E Rhodesia
T. o. transvaalensis
N Transvaal
T. o. smithi
N Cape Province, Orange Free State,
Transvaal
T. o. olivaceus
SW Cape Province
T. o. pondoensis
Transkei, Natal, Swaziland
Turdus abyssinicus (Mountain Thrush)
T. a. abyssinicus
Ethiopia, W Kenya, NE Tanzania
T. a. baraka
E Zaire, W & S Uganda
T. a. deckeni
NE Tanzania
T. a. oldeani
NE Tanzania
T. a. bambusicola
Ruanda, Kivu (E Zaire)
T. a. roehli
NE Tanzania
T. a. nyikae
C Tanzania, Malawi, NE Zambia
T. a. milanjensis
S Malawi, Mozambique
Turdus helleri (Taita Olive Thrush)
SE Kenya
Turdus libonyanus (Kurrichane Thrush)
T. l. verreauxi
S Zaire, Angola, N Namibia
T. l. chobiensis
E Namibia, Zambia, NW Rhodesia
T. l. libonyanus
E Botswana, Transvaal, N Natal
T. l. peripheris
C Natal
T. l. tropicalis
SE Zaire, Mozambique, Malawi, Tanzania
Turdus tephronotus (African Bare-eyed Thrush)
Ethiopia, Somalia, Kenya, E Tanzania

Turdus menachensis (Yemen Thrush)
S Saudi Arabia, Yemen
Turdus ludoviciae (Somali Blackbird)
N Somalia
Turdus litsipsirupa (Groundscraper Thrush)
T. l. simensis
Ethiopia
T. l. litsipsirupa
Botswana, Rhodesia, Zambia, S Africa
T. l. pauciguttatus
NW Botswana, Namibia
T. l. stierlingi
N Angola to W & S Tanzania
Turdus dissimilis (Black-breasted Thrush)
T. d. dissimilis
NE India to SW China, N Indochina
T. d. hortulorum
Siberia, Manchuria » SE China,
Vietnam
Turdus unicolor (Tickell's Thrush)
Pakistan, Nepal, N India
Turdus cardis (Japanese Grey Thrush)
Japan, China » Indochina
Turdus albocinctus (White-collared Blackbird)
Himalayas, SE Tibet, SW Sikang »
N Burma
Turdus torquatus (Ring Ousel)
T. t. torquatus
N Europe » S Europe, NW Africa
T. t. alpestris
S & E Europe » Asia Minor, N Africa
T. t. amicorum
Turkey, Caucasus, N Iran » S Iran
Turdus boulboul (Grey-winged Blackbird)
Himalayas, S China, N Indochina »
N Burma
Turdus merula (Blackbird)
T. m. merula
W Europe
T. m. azorensis
Azores Is
T. m. cabrerae
Madeira I, W Canary Is
T. m. mauretanicus
Morocco to Tunisia
T. m. aterrimus
SE Europe, Caucasus » Med Is
T. m. insularum
Crete, Rhodes, Mytilene I
T. m. syriacus
S Turkey, Middle East, Iran
T. m. intermedius
C Asia, Afghanistan » S Iraq
T. m. maximus
Pakistan, India, SE Tibet

T. m. sowerbyi
  Szechwan
T. m. mandarinus
  Kweichow
T. m. nigropileus
  SC India
T. m. spencei
  E India
T. m. simillimus
  SE India
T. m. bourdilloni
  S India
T. m. kinnisii
  Sri Lanka

Turdus poliocephalus (Island Thrush)
T. p. erythropleurus
  Christmas Is
T. p. loeseri
  N Sumatra
T. p. indrapurae
  C Sumatra
T. p. biesenbachi
  Mt Papandajan (W Java)
T. p. fumidus
  Mt Gedeh (W Java)
T. p. stresemanni
  Mt Lawoe (C Java)
T. p. javanicus
  C Java
T. p. whiteheadi
  E Java
T. p. seebohmi
  N Borneo
T. p. niveiceps
  Taiwan
T. p. thomassoni
  N Luzon I
T. p. mayonensis
  S Luzon I
T. p. mindorensis
  Mindoro I
T. p. nigrorum
  Negros I
T. p. malindangensis
  Mt Malindang (NW Mindanao I)
T. p. katanglad
  Mt Katanglad (C Mindanao I)
T. p. kelleri
  Mt Apo (SE Mindanao I)
T. p. hygroscopus
  S Celebes
T. p. celebensis
  SW Celebes
T. p. schlegelii
  W Timor I
T. p. sterlingi
  E Timor I

T. p. deningeri
  Ceram I
T. p. versteegi
  W New Guinea
T. p. carbonarius
  Bismarck Mts, (New Guinea)
T. p. keysseri
  Huon, SE New Guinea
T. p. papuensis
  SE New Guinea
T. p. canescens
  Goodenough I
T. p. heinrothi
  St Matthias Is
T. p. bougainvillei
  Bougainville I
T. p. kulambangrae
  Kulambangra I
T. p. sladeni
  Guadalcanal I
T. p. rennellianus
  Rennell I
T. p. vanikorensis
  Vanikoro I, Santa Cruz I, Espiritu
    Santo I
T. p. placens
  Ureparapara I, Vanue Lava I
T. p. whitneyi
  Gaua I, Banks Is
T. p. malekulae
  Pentecost I, Malekula I, Ambrim I
T. p. becki
  Paema I, Lopevi I, Epi I, Mai I
T. p. efatensis
  Efate I, Nguna I
T. p. albifrons
  Erromanga I
T. p. pritzbueri
  Tana I, Lifu I
T. p. mareensis
  Maré I **e?**
T. p. xanthopus
  New Caledonia I
T. p. poliocephalus
  Norfolk I
T. p. layardi
  Viti Levu I, Ovalau I, Yasawa I, Koro I
T. p. ruficeps
  Kandavu I
T. p. vitiensis
  Vanua Levu I
T. p. hades
  Ngau I
T. p. tempesti
  Taveuni I
T. p. samoensis
  Savaii I, Upolu I

Turdus chrysolaus (Red-bellied Thrush)
T. c. orii
N & C Kurile Is » Japan, Riukiu Is
T. c. chrysolaus
N Japan » SE China, N Philippine Is
Turdus celaenops (Seven Islands Thrush)
Izu I, Yakushima I
Turdus rubrocanus (Grey-headed Thrush)
T. r. rubrocanus
Pakistan, Himalayas
T. r. gouldi
SE Tibet, W China
Turdus kessleri (Kessler's Thrush)
W China » E Tibet, SW Sikang
Turdus feae (Fea's Thrush)
N China » Burma, Assam
Turdus pallidus (Pale Thrush)
NE Siberia » China, Japan, Taiwan
Turdus obscurus (Eye-browed Thrush)
NE Asia » China, Indonesia
Turdus ruficollis (Black-throated Thrush)
T. r. atrogularis
W Siberia, C Asia » N India, China
T. r. ruficollis
E Siberia » W China, Burma, NE India
Turdus naumanni (Dusky Thrush)
T. n. eunomus
N Siberia » Japan, S China, Burma
T. n. naumanni
C Siberia, C Asia » N China
Turdus pilaris (Fieldfare)
N Europe, N Asia » S Europe, Caucasus
Turdus iliacus (Redwing)
T. i. coburni
Iceland, Faroe Is » NW Europe
T. i. iliacus
N Europe, C Asia » N Africa, Caucasus
Turdus philomelos (Song Thrush)
T. p. hebridensis
Outer Hebrides, Isle of Skye
T. p. clarkei
British Isles, W Europe
T. p. philomelos
C Asia, C & E Europe » N Africa, S Europe,
Iran
T. p. nataliae
C Asia, Iran
**Turdus mupinensis (Mongolian Song
Thrush)**
W China
Turdus viscivorus (Mistle Thrush)
T. v. viscivorus
Europe, Asia Minor, S Russia
T. v. bonapartei
Siberia, C Asia, Himalayas » N India
Turdus aurantius (White-chinned Thrush)
Jamaica

Turdus ravidus (Grand Cayman Thrush)
Grand Cayman I
Turdus plumbeus (Red-legged Thrush)
T. p. plumbeus
N Bahama Is
T. p. schistaceus
E Cuba
T. p. rubripes
C & W Cuba, Isle of Pines
T. p. coryi
Cayman Brac I
T. p. ardosiaceus
Hispaniola, Puerto Rico, Gonave I
T. p. albiventris
Dominica I
Turdus chiguanco (Chiguanco Thrush)
T. c. chiguanco
coastal Peru, NW Bolivia
T. c. conradi
S Ecuador, C Peru
T. c. anthracinus
S Bolivia, NE Chile, W Argentina
Turdus nigrescens (Sooty Robin)
Costa Rica, W Panama
Turdus fuscater (Great Thrush)
T. f. opertaneus
NW Colombia
T. f. cacozelus
N Colombia
T. f. clarus
E Colombia, W Venezuela
T. f. quindio
S & W Colombia, N Ecuador
T. f. gigas
E Colombia, W Venezuela
T. f. gigantodes
S Ecuador, N Peru
T. f. ockendeni
SE Peru
T. f. fuscater
W Bolivia
Turdus serranus (Glossy-black Thrush)
T. s. infuscatus
SE Mexico, Guatemala, El Salvador,
Honduras
T. s. cumanensis
NE Venezuela
T. s. atrosericeus
NE Colombia, N Venezuela
T. s. fuscobrunneus
C & S Colombia, Ecuador
T. s. serranus
Peru, Bolivia
Turdus nigriceps (Slaty Thrush)
T. n. nigriceps
SE Ecuador, E Peru, E Bolivia, W Argentin
T. n. subalaris
S Brazil, Paraguay, N Argentina

Turdus reevei (Plumbeous-backed Thrush)
  W Ecuador, NW Peru
Turdus olivater (Black-hooded Thrush)
  T. o. sanctaemartae
    N Colombia
  T. o. olivater
    E Colombia, Venezuela
  T. o. paraquensis
    S Venezuela
  T. o. kemptoni
    C Venezuela
  T. o. duidae
    Mt Duida (S Venezuela)
  T. o. roraimae
    S Venezuela, S Guyana
  T. o. caucae
    C Colombia
  T. o. ptaritepui
    SE Venezuela
Turdus maranonicus (Maranon Thrush)
  N Peru
Turdus fulviventris (Chestnut-bellied Thrush)
  E Colombia, Venezuela, E Ecuador
Turdus rufiventris (Rufous-bellied Thrush)
  T. r. juensis
    NE Brazil
  T. r. rufiventris
    S Brazil, Uruguay, Paraguay, N Argentina
Turdus falcklandii (Austral Thrush)
  T. f. falcklandii
    Falkland Is
  T. f. magellanicus
    S Chile, S Argentina
  T. f. pembertoni
    SC Argentina
Turdus leucomelas (Pale-breasted Thrush)
  T. l. leucomelas
    S Brazil, E Peru, Paraguay
  T. l. albiventer
    N Colombia, Venezuela, NE Brazil, the Guianas
  T. l. cautor
    N Colombia
Turdus amaurochalinus (Creamy-bellied Thrush)
  Central South America
Turdus plebejus (Mountain Robin)
  T. p. differens
    SE Mexico, Guatemala
  T. p. rafaelensis
    Nicaragua, El Salvador
  T. p. plebejus
    Costa Rica, W Panama
Turdus ignobilis (Black-billed Thrush)
  T. i. ignobilis
    E Colombia

  T. i. goodfellowi
    W Colombia
  T. i. debilis
    SE Colombia, Venezuela, W Amazonia
  T. i. murinus
    SE Venezuela, Guyana
  T. i. arthuri
    SE Venezuela, Guyana, French Guiana
Turdus lawrencii (Lawrence's Thrush)
  Upper Amazonia
Turdus fumigatus (Cocoa Thrush)
  T. f. aquilonalis
    NE Colombia, N Venezuela, Trinidad
  T. f. orinocensis
    E Colombia, W Venezuela
  T. f. fumigatus
    N & E Brazil, the Guianas
Turdus personus (Lesser Antillean Thrush)
  T. p. bondi
    St Vincent I
  T. p. personus
    Grenada I
Turdus obsoletus (Pale-vented Thrush)
  T. o. obsoletus
    Costa Rica, Panama, NW Colombia
  T. o. parambanus
    W Colombia, W Ecuador
  T. o. colombianus
    C Colombia
  T. o. hauxwelli
    Upper Amazonia
Turdus haplochrous (Unicoloured Thrush)
  E Bolivia
Turdus grayi (Clay-coloured Thrush)
  T. g. tamaulipensis
    E Mexico
  T. g. microrhynchus
    San Luis Potosi
  T. g. umbrinus
    S Mexico, W Guatemala
  T. g. linnaei
    S Mexico
  T. g. grayi
    S Mexico to Nicaragua
  T. g. casius
    Costa Rica to NW Colombia
  T. g. incomptus
    N Colombia
Turdus nudigenis (Bare-eyed Thrush)
  T. n. nudigenis
    Lesser Antilles, Trinidad, NE South America
  T. n. extimus
    N Brazil
  T. n. maculirostris
    W Ecuador, NW Peru
Turdus jamaicensis (White-eyed Thrush)
  Jamaica

Turdus albicollis (White-necked Thrush)
T. a. calliphthongus
  NW Mexico
T. a. lygrus
  C & S Mexico
T. a. assimilis
  C Mexico
T. a. renominatus
  SC Mexico
T. a. oaxacae
  Oaxaca
T. a. leucauchen
  S Mexico to Honduras
T. a. rubicundus
  W Guatemala, El Salvador
T. a. atrotinctus
  E Nicaragua
T. a. oblitus
  Costa Rica
T. a. cnephosus
  SW Costa Rica, W Panama
T. a. coibensis
  Coiba I
T. a. daguae
  E Panama to NW Ecuador
T. a. minusculus
  NE Colombia
T. a. phaeopygoides
  NE Colombia, N Venezuela, Trinidad
T. a. phaeopygus
  E Colombia to the Guianas, N Brazil
T. a. berlepschi
  C & S Colombia
T. a. spodiolaemus
  E Ecuador to N Bolivia, W Brazil
T. a. contemptus
  S Bolivia
T. a. crotopezus
  E Brazil
T. a. albicollis
  SE Brazil
T. a. paraguayensis
  SW Brazil, Paraguay, N Argentina
Turdus rufopalliatus (Rufous-backed Robin)
T. r. griseor
  NW Mexico
T. r. rufopalliatus
  W Mexico
T. r. graysoni
  Tres Marias Is
Turdus swalesi (La Selle Thrush)
  Haiti
Turdus rufitorques (Rufous-collared Robin)
  SE Mexico, Guatemala, El Salvador

Turdus migratorius (American Robin)
T. m. migratorius
  Canada, C USA » E USA, E Mexico
T. m. nigrideus
  E Canada, EC USA
T. m. achrusterus
  S USA » SE Mexico
T. m. caurinus
  SE Alaska, W Canada » SW USA
T. m. propinquus
  W Canada, W USA, SW Mexico
    » Guatemala
T. m. phillipsi
  C Mexico
T. m. confinis
  S Baja California
T. m. permixtus
  SW Mexico

MUSCICAPIDAE

131 ORTHONYCHINAE (LOGRUNNERS)

ORTHONYX
Orthonyx temminckii (Spine-tailed Logrunner)
O. t. novaeguineae
  W New Guinea
O. t. dorsalis
  W New Guinea
O. t. victoriana
  SE New Guinea
O. t. temminckii
  SE Queensland, E New South Wales
Orthonyx spaldingii (Spalding's Logrunner
  N Queensland

ANDROPHOBUS
Androphobus viridis (Green-backed Babbler)
  W New Guinea

PSOPHODES
Psophodes olivaceus (Eastern Whipbird)
P. o. lateralis
  N Queensland
P. o. magnirostris
  C Queensland
P. o. olivaceus
  S Queensland, E New South Wales, Victoria
Psophodes nigrogularis (Western Whipbir
P. n. leucogaster
  NW Victoria, SE South Australia
P. n. nigrogularis
  SW Western Australia
P. n. pondalowiensis
  S South Australia

SPHENOSTOMA
Sphenostoma cristatum (Wedgebill)
  C & W Australia

CINCLOSOMA
Cinclosoma punctatum (Spotted Quail Thrush)
  C. p. punctatum
    Eastern Australia
  C. p. dovei
    Tasmania
Cinclosoma castanotum (Chestnut Quail Thrush)
  C. c. castanotum
    SE Australia
  C. c. mayri
    New South Wales
  C. c. morgani
    South Australia
  C. c. clarum
    C Australia
  C. c. dundasi
    SW Western Australia
Cinclosoma alisteri (Nullarbor Quail Thrush)
    Nullarbor Plain
Cinclosoma cinnamomeum (Cinnamon Quail Thrush)
  C. c. castaneothorax
    S Queensland, N New South Wales
  C. c. cinnamomeum
    EC Australia
  C. c. samueli
    South Australia
  C. c. marginatum
    SW Australia
Cinclosoma ajax (Ajax Quail Thrush)
  C. a. ajax
    W New Guinea
  C. a. muscale
    S New Guinea
  C. a. alare
    SC New Guinea
  C. a. goldiei
    SE New Guinea
PTILORRHOA
Ptilorrhoa leucosticta (High Mountain Rail Babbler)
  P. l. leucosticta
    W New Guinea
  P. l. mayri
    W New Guinea
  P. l. centralis
    W New Guinea
  P. l. sibilans
    N New Guinea
  P. l. amabilis
    E New Guinea
  P. l. loriae
    SE New Guinea
  P. l. menawa
    N coast of New Guinea

Ptilorrhoa caerulescens (Lowland Rail Babbler)
  P. c. caerulescens
    W New Guinea
  P. c. neumanni
    N New Guinea
  P. c. nigricrissa
    S New Guinea
  P. c. geislerorum
    E New Guinea
Ptilorrhoa castanonota (Mid-mountain Rail Babbler)
  P. c. castanonota
    W New Guinea
  P. c. saturata
    W New Guinea
  P. c. uropygialis
    W New Guinea
  P. c. buergersi
    C New Guinea
  P. c. par
    E New Guinea
  P. c. pulcher
    SE New Guinea
  P. c. gilliardi
    Batanta I

EUPETES
Eupetes macrocerus (Malay Rail Babbler)
  E. m. macrocerus
    Malaysia, Thailand, Sumatra
  E. m. borneensis
    N Borneo

MELAMPITTA
Melampitta lugubris (Lesser Melampitta)
  M. l. lugubris
    W New Guinea
  M. l. rostrata
    W New Guinea
  M. l. longicauda
    NC & E New Guinea
Melampitta gigantea (Greater Melampitta)
    W New Guinea

IFRITA
Ifrita kowaldi (Blue-capped Babbler)
  I. k. kowaldi
    E & C New Guinea
  I. k. brunnea
    WC New Guinea

MUSCICAPIDAE

132 TIMALIINAE (BABBLERS)

PELLORNEUM
Pellorneum ruficeps (Spotted Babbler)
  P. r. olivaceum
    SW India

P. r. ruficeps
W & C India

P. r. punctatum
W Himalayas

P. r. mandellii
Sikkim, Bhutan, Nepal, NE India

P. r. chamelum
S Assam

P. r. pectorale
Mishmi Hills, NE Assam

P. r. ripleyi
Lakhimpur, NE Assam

P. r. vocale
C Manipur

P. r. stageri
NE Burma

P. r. shanense
SW Yunnan, C Burma

P. r. hilarum
C Burma

P. r. victoriae
Chin hills, N Burma

P. r. minus
S Burma

P. r. subochraceum
S Burma, SW Thailand

P. r. insularum
Mergui Archipelago

P. r. acrum
C Thailand, N Malaysia

P. r. chthonium
N Thailand

P. r. indistinctum
N Thailand

P. r. oreum
S China, N Indochina

P. r. vividum
N Vietnam

P. r. elbeli
E Thailand

P. r. ubonense
E Thailand, S Laos

P. r. deignani
S Vietnam

P. r. dilloni
S Indochina

P. r. euroum
W Cambodia, C & SE Thailand

P. r. smithi
coastal islands of SE Thailand &
Cambodia

Pellorneum palustre (Marsh Spotted Babbler)
C & E Assam

Pellorneum fuscocapillum (Brown-capped Jungle Babbler)
P. f. babaulti
N & E Sri Lanka

P. f. fuscocapillum
SW Sri Lanka

P. f. scortillum
SW Sri Lanka

Pellorneum albiventre (Plain Brown Babbler)
P. a. ignotum
Mishmi hills, NE Assam

P. a. albiventre
Bhutan, Assam, W Burma

P. a. nagaense
Burma

P. a. cinnamomeum
C Burma, NW Thailand, S Indochina

P. a. pusillum
NW Vietnam, N Laos

Pellorneum capistratum (Black-capped Babbler)
P. c. nigrocapitatum
Malaysia, N Natuna Is, Billiton I

P. c. nyctilampis
Sumatra, Bangka I

P. c. capistratoides
W & S Borneo

P. c. morrelli
Banggai I, N & E Borneo

P. c. capistratum
Java

TRICHASTOMA

Trichastoma tickelli (Tickell's Jungle Babbler)
T. t. assamense
Assam, NW Burma

T. t. grisescens
Arakan Yoma, SW Burma

T. t. fulvum
SW Yunnan, NE Burma, N Thailand, Indochina

T. t. annamense
S & C Vietnam, S Laos

T. t. tickelli
N Malaysia, E Burma, W Thailand

T. t. ochracea
S China

T. t. australis
N Malaysia

Trichastoma pyrrogenys (Temminck's Jungle Babbler)
T. p. buettikoferi
Sumatra

T. p. pyrrogenys
W Java

T. p. besuki
E Java

T. p. erythrote
W Sarawak, N Borneo

T. p. longstaffi
Sarawak, N Borneo

T. p. canicapillum
N Borneo

Trichastoma malaccense (Short-tailed Jungle Babbler)
T. m. malaccense
N Natuna Is, Malaysia, Sumatra, Anamba Is
T. m. saturatum
Bangka I, Billiton I, W Borneo
T. m. poliogene
E Borneo
T. m. feriatum
Sarawak, N Borneo

Trichastoma cinereiceps (Ashy-headed Jungle Babbler)
Balabac I, Palawan I

Trichastoma rostratum (White-chested Jungle Babbler)
T. r. rostratum
Malaysia, Sumatra, Billiton I
T. r. macropterum
Banggai I, Borneo

Trichastoma bicolor (Ferruginous Jungle Babbler)
Malaysia, E Sumatra, Bangka I, Borneo

Trichastoma sepiarium (Horsfield's Jungle Babbler)
T. s. tardinatum
Malaysia
T. s. liberale
NW Sumatra
T. s. barussanum
SW Sumatra
T. s. sepiarium
W & C Java
T. s. minus
E Java, Bali I
T. s. rufiventre
W & S Borneo
T. s. harterti
N & E Borneo

Trichastoma celebense (Celebes Jungle Babbler)
T. c. celebense
N Celebes
T. c. connectens
NC Celebes
T. c. rufofuscum
C Celebes
T. c. finschi
SW Celebes
T. c. improbatum
Pulau Is, E & S Celebes
T. c. togianense
Togian I

Trichastoma abbotti (Abbott's Jungle Babbler)
T. a. abbotti
Himalayas, Burma, Thailand, NW Malaysia

T. a. williamsoni
E Thailand, NW Cambodia
T. a. obscurius
SE Thailand
T. a. rufescentior
Thailand
T. c. alterum
C Laos, C Vietnam
T. a. olivaceum
Thailand, Malaysia, E Sumatra
T. a. sirense
Pulau Mata Siri I, Billiton I
T. a. baweanum
Bawean I
T. a. finschi
Borneo

Trichastoma perspicillatum (Black-browed Jungle Babbler)
Borneo

Trichastoma vanderbilti (Vanderbilt's Jungle Babbler)
N Sumatra

Trichastoma pyrrhopterum (Mountain Thrush Babbler)
T. p. pyrrhopterum
East Africa, Malawi
T. p. kivuense
E Zaire, W Uganda, W Tanzania

Trichastoma cleaveri (Blackcap Thrush Babbler)
T. c. johnsoni
Sierra Leone, Liberia
T. c. cleaveri
Ghana
T. c. marchanti
S Nigeria
T. c. batesi
SE Nigeria, Gabon, Cameroun
T. c. poense
Fernando Po I

Trichastoma albipectus (Scaly-breasted Thrush Babbler)
T. a. barakae
N Zaire, Uganda, S Sudan, SW Kenya
T. a. albipectus
N Angola, W Zaire

Trichastoma rufescens (Rufous-winged Thrush Babbler)
Sierra Leone to Ghana

Trichastoma rufipenne (Pale-breasted Thrush Babbler)
T. r. bocagei
Fernando Po I
T. r. extremum
Sierra Leone to Ghana
T. r. rufipenne
S Nigeria to Uganda, Kenya

T. r. distans
NE Tanzania, Zanzibar I

Trichastoma fulvescens (Brown Thrush Babbler)

T. f. gulare
Sierra Leone to Ghana

T. f. moloneyanum
E Ghana, Togo

T. f. iboense
S Nigeria

T. f. fulvescens
Cameroun, W Zaire

T. f. ugandae
N Zaire, Uganda

T. f. dilutius
N Angola

Trichastoma puveli (Puvel's Thrush Babbler)

T. p. puveli
Guinea to Sierra Leone

T. p. strenuipes
S Nigeria to NE Zaire

KAKAMEGA

Kakamega poliothraox (Grey-chested Thrush Babbler)
S Cameroun, Fernando Po I, E Zaire, SW Kenya

LEONARDINA

Leonardina woodi (Bagobo Babbler)
Mindanao I

PTYRTICUS

Ptyrticus turdinus (African Thrush Babbler)

P. t. harterti
C Cameroun

P. t. turdinus
SW Sudan, NE Zaire

P. t. upembae
SE Zaire, N Zambia

MALACOPTERON

Malacopteron magnirostre (Moustached Tree Babbler)

M. m. magnirostre
S Burma, Thailand, Malaysia, Sumatra

M. m. cinereocapillum
Borneo

M. m. flavum
Anamba Is

Malacopteron affine (Sooty-capped Babbler)

M. a. affine
S Thailand, Malaysia, Sumatra

M. a. notatum
Banyak I

M. a. phoeniceum
Borneo

Malacopteron cinereum (Scaly-crowned Babbler)

M. c. indochinense
SE Thailand, S Indochina

M. c. rufifrons
Java

M. c. cinereum
Malaysia, Sumatra, Bangka I, Borneo

M. c. niasense
Nias I

M. c. bungurense
N Natuna Is

Malacopteron magnum (Rufous-crowned Tree Babbler)

M. m. magnum
S Burma, Malaysia, Sumatra, Borneo, Natuna Is

M. m. saba
NE Borneo

Malacopteron palawanense (Palawan Tree Babbler)
Balabac I, Palawan I

Malacopteron albogulare (Grey-breasted Babbler)

M. a. albogulare
Malaysia, NE Sumatra

M. a. moultoni
NW Borneo

POMATORHINUS

Pomatorhinus hypoleucos (Long-billed Scimitar Babbler)

P. h. hypoleucos
Assam, Bangladesh, W Burma

P. h. tickelli
Thailand, N Indochina

P. h. brevirostris
S Indochina

P. h. wrayi
Malaysia

P. h. hainanus
Hainan I

Pomatorhinus erythrogenys (Rusty-cheeked Scimitar Babbler)

P. e. erythrogenys
W Himalayas

P. e. ferrugilatus
W & C Nepal

P. e. haringtoni
W Himalayas

P. e. mcclellandi
S Assam, W Burma

P. e. imberbis
Karenni, Burma

P. e. celatus
C Burma, NW Thailand

P. e. odicus
NE Burma, N Laos, SW China

P. e. decarlei
S Szechwan, N Yunnan

P. e. dedekeni
  E & S Sikang, NW Yunnan
P. e. gravivox
  NW Szechwan, S Kansu
P. e. sowerbyi
  N Shensi
P. e. cowensae
  SW Hupeh, E Szechwan
P. e. swinhoei
  Anhwei, Kiangsi, Kwangsi, Hunan,
  Fukien
P. e. erythrocnemis
  Taiwan

Pomatorhinus horsfieldii (Travencore Scimitar Babbler)
P. h. melanurus
  Sri Lanka
P. h. travancoreensis
  SW India
P. h. horsfieldii
  W India
P. h. obscurus
  NW India
P. h. maderaspatensis
  EC India

Pomatorhinus schisticeps (Slaty-headed Scimitar Babbler)
P. s. leucogaster
  NW Himalayas
P. s. schisticeps
  E Himalayas, NE India, NW Burma
P. s. salimalii
  Mishmi hills, NE Assam
P. s. cryptanthus
  Lakhimpur, NE Assam
P. s. mearsi
  W Burma
P. s. ripponi
  E Burma, N Thailand, N Laos
P. s. nuchalis
  E Burma
P. s. difficilis
  S Burma, SW Thailand
P. s. olivaceus
  S Burma, SW Thailand
P. s. fastidiosus
  Malaysia
P. s. humilis
  E Thailand, S Laos, C Vietnam
P. s. annamensis
  S Vietnam
P. s. klossi
  SE Thailand, SW Cambodia

Pomatorhinus montanus (Chestnut-backed Scimitar Babbler)
P. m. occidentalis
  S Malaysia, Sumatra

P. m. montanus
  W & C Java
P. m. ottolanderi
  E Java, Bali I
P. m. bornensis
  Borneo

Pomatorhinus ruficollis (Streak-breasted Scimitar Babbler)
P. r. ruficollis
  W & C Nepal
P. r. godwini
  E Himalyas, N Assam
P. r. bakeri
  SE Assam, W Burma
P. r. bhamoensis
  N Burma
P. r. similis
  NE Burma, NW Yunnan
P. r. albipectus
  SW Yunnan, N Laos
P. r. beaulieui
  N Laos
P. r. laurentei
  S Yunnan
P. r. reconditus
  SE Yunnan, N Vietnam
P. r. stridulus
  SE China
P. r. hunonensis
  C China
P. r. eidos
  S Szechwan
P. r. musicus
  Taiwan
P. r. nigrostellatus
  Hainan I

Pomatorhinus ochraceiceps (Red-billed Scimitar Babbler)
P. o. stenorhynchus
  NE Assam, N Burma
P. o. austeni
  Manipur, E Assam
P. o. ochraceiceps
  Burma, N Thailand, N Indochina
P. o. alius
  E Thailand, S Indochina

Pomatorhinus ferruginosus (Coral-billed Scimitar Babbler)
P. f. ferruginosus
  E Himalayas
P. f. formosus
  S Assam
P. f. phayrei
  Arakan Yoma, SW Burma
P. f. stanfordi
  NE Burma
P. f. mariae
  C Burma

P. f. albogularis
E Burma, NW Thailand
P. f. orientalis
N Indochina

GARRITORNIS
Garritornis isidorei (Isidor's Rufous Babbler)
G. i. isidorei
C & S New Guinea, Misol I
G. i. calidus
N New Guinea

POMATOSTOMUS
Pomatostomus temporalis (Grey-crowned Babbler)
P. t. tregellasi
SE South Australia, Victoria, SE New South Wales
P. t. trivirgatus
E New South Wales, S Queensland
P. t. temporalis
coastal C Queensland
P. t. cornwalli
coastal N Queensland
P. t. strepitans
S New Guinea
P. t. intermedius
C Australia
P. t. mountfordae
N Northern Territory
P. t. browni
NW Northern Territory
P. t. rubeculus
C Northern Territory
P. t. bamba
Melville I
P. t. nigrescens
Western Australia
Pomatostomus superciliosus (White-browed Babbler)
P. s. gilgandra
W New South Wales, Victoria, South Australia
P. s. superciliosus
SE South Australia, Victoria
P. s. ashbyi
SW Western Australia
P. s. gwendolenae
Gascoyne valley, Western Australia
Pomatostomus halli (Hall Babbler)
SW Queensland
Pomatostomus ruficeps (Chestnut-crowned Babbler)
SW Queensland, W New South Wales, NW Victoria, NE South Australia

XIPHIRHYNCHUS
Xiphirhynchus superciliaris (Slender-billed Scimitar Babbler)
X. s. superciliaris
E Himalayas
X. s. intextus
S Assam, W Burma
X. s. forresti
NE Burma, NW Yunnan
X. s. rothschildi
N Vietnam

JABOUILLEIA
Jabouilleia danjoui (Danjou's Babbler)
J. d. danjoui
C Vietnam
J. d. parvirostris
C Vietnam

RIMATOR
Rimator malacoptilus (Long-billed Wren Babbler)
R. m. malacoptilus
E Himalayas, Assam, NE Burma
R. m. pasquieri
N Vietnam
R. m. albostriatus
W Sumatra

PTILOCICHLA
Ptilocichla leucogrammica (Bornean Wren Babbler)
Borneo
Ptilocichla mindanensis (Streaked Ground Babbler)
P. m. minuta
Leyte I, Samar I
P. m. fortichi
Bohol I
P. m. mindanensis
Mindanao I
P. m. basilanica
Basilan I
Ptilocichla falcata (Palawan Wren Babbler)
Balabac I, Palawan I

KENOPIA
Kenopia striata (Striped Wren Babbler)
Malaysia, E Sumatra, Borneo

NAPOTHERA
Napothera rufipectus (Sumatran Wren Babbler)
W Sumatra
Napothera atrigularus (Black-throated Wren Babbler)
Borneo
Napothera macrodactyla (Large Wren Babbler)
N. m. macrodactyla
Malaysia

N. m. beauforti
NE Sumatra
N. m. lepidopleura
Java
**Napothera marmorata (Marbled Wren
Babbler)**
N. m. grandior
C Malaysia
N. m. marmorata
W Sumatra
**Napothera crispifrons (Limestone Wren
Babbler)**
N. c. annamensis
N Indochina
N. c. calcicola
NE Thailand
N. c. crispifrons
N Thailand, S Burma
**Napothera brevicaudata (Streaked
Wren Babbler)**
N. b. striata
S Assam, SW Burma
N. b. venningi
W Yunnan, NE Burma
N. b. brevicaudata
N Thailand
N. b. stevensi
N Indochina
N. b. proxima
C Vietnam, S Laos
N. b. rufiventer
S Vietnam
N. b. griseigularis
SE Thailand, SW Cambodia
N. b. leucosticta
N Malaysia
**Napothera crassa (Mountain Wren
Babbler)**
N Borneo
Napothera rabori (Luzon Wren Babbler)
N. r. rabori
Ilocos Norte, Luzon I
N. r. mesoluzonica
Laguna, Luzon I
N. r. sorsogonensis
Sorsogon, Luzon I
**Napothera epilepidota (Lesser Wren
Babbler)**
N. e. guttaticollis
N Assam
N. e. roberti
S Assam, NW Burma
N. e. bakeri
C Burma
N. e. davisoni
N Thailand
N. e. amyae
N Indochina

N. e. delacouri
Kwangsi
N. e. hainana
Hainan I
N. e. clara
S Vietnam
N. e. granti
N Malaysia
N. e. lucilleae
N Sumatra
N. e. diluta
W Sumatra
N. e. mendeni
SW Sumatra
N. e. epilepidota
W & C Java
N. e. exsul
N Borneo

PNOEPYGA
**Pnoepyga albiventer (Scaly-breasted
Wren Babbler)**
P. a. pallidior
N & C Himalayas
P. a. albiventer
E Himalayas, Assam, N Burma, S China
Pnoepyga pusilla (Pygmy Wren Babbler)
P. p. pusilla
Himalayas, Assam, N Burma, N Thailand,
S China
P. p. formosana
Taiwan
P. p. annamensis
S Indochina
P. p. harterti
C Malaysia
P. p. lepida
W Sumatra
P. p. rufa
Java
P. p. everetti
Flores I
P. p. timorensis
Timor I

SPELAEORNIS
**Spelaeornis caudatus (Short-tailed Wren
Babbler)**
Nepal, Sikkim, Bhutan
**Spelaeornis badeigularis (Mishmi Wren
Babbler)**
Mishmi hills, NE Assam
**Spelaeornis troglodytoides (Bar-winged
Wren Babbler)**
S. t. sherriffi
E Bhutan
S. t. souliei
NE Burma, NW Yunnan
S. t. rocki
NW Yunnan

S. t. troglodytoides
Sikang, NW Szechwan
S. t. halsueti
Shensi
Spelaeornis formosus (Spotted Wren Babbler)
E Himalayas, W Burma, S China
Spelaeornis chocolatinus (Godwin-Austin's Wren Babbler)
S. c. chocolatinus
S Assam, Manipur
S. c. oatesi
N Burma
S. c. reptatus
NE Burma, SW Yunnan
S. c kinneari
N Vietnam
Spelaeornis longicaudatus (Long-tailed Wren Babbler)
S Assam, Manipur

SPHENOCICLA
Sphenocicla humei (Wedge-billed Wren Babbler)
S. h. humei
Sikkim to N Assam
S. h. roberti
S Assam, NE Burma

NEOMIXIS
Neomixis tenella (Northern Jery)
N. t. tenella
N Madagascar
N. t. decaryi
W Madagascar
N. t. orientalis
C & S Madagascar
N. t. debilis
SW Madagascar
Neomixis viridis (Southern Green Jery)
N. v. delacouri
NE Madagascar
N. v. viridis
SE Madagascar
Neomixis striatigula (Stripe-throated Jery)
N. s. sclateri
NE Madagascar
N. s. striatigula
SE Madagascar
N. s. pallidior
SW Madagascar
Neomixis flavoviridis (Wedge-tailed Jery)
SE Madagascar

STACHYRIS
Stachyris rodolphei (Deignan's Babbler)
Thailand

Stachyris rufifrons (Red-fronted Tree Babbler)
S. r. pallescens
Arakan Yoma, SW Burma
S. r. rufifrons
SE Burma, W Thailand
S. r. obscura
S Thailand
S. r. poliogaster
W Malaysia, Sumatra
S. r. sarawacensis
Borneo
Stachyris ambigua (Buff-chested Babbler)
S. a. ambigua
E Himalayas, Assam
S. a. planicola
NE Burma
S. a. adjuncta
N & E Thailand, N Indochina
S. a. insuspecta
S Laos
Stachyris ruficeps (Red-headed Tree Babbler)
S. r. ruficeps
E Himalayas, N Assam
S. r. rufipectus
NW Burma
S. r. bhamoensis
NE Burma, NW Yunnan
S. r. davidi
C & S China, N Indochina
S. r. praecognita
Taiwan
S. r. goodsoni
Hainan I
S. r. pagana
S Vietnam
Stachyris pyrrhops (Red-billed Tree Babbler)
Pakistan, W Himalayas
Stachyris chrysaea (Golden-headed Tree Babbler)
S. c. chrysaea
E Himalayas, Assam, N Burma
S. c. binghami
SE Assam, SW Burma
S. c. aurata
S Burma, N Indochina
S. c. assimilis
C Burma, NW Thailand
S. c. chrysops
C Malaysia
S. c. frigida
W Sumatra
Stachyris plateni (Pygmy Tree Babbler)
S. p. pygmaea
Samar I, Leyte I

S. p. plateni
Mindanao I

Stachyris capitalis (Rufous-crowned Tree Babbler)
S. c. dennistouni
NE Luzon I
S. c. affinis
S Luzon I
S. c. nigrocapitata
Samar I, N Leyte I
S. c. boholensis
Bohol I
S. c. capitalis
Dinagat I, Mindanao I
S. c. isabelae
Basilan I

Stachyris speciosa (Rough-templed Tree Babbler)
Negros I

Stachyris whiteheadi (Whitehead's Tree Babbler)
N Luzon I

Stachyris striata (Striped Tree Babbler)
N Luzon I

Stachyris nigrorum (Negros Tree Babbler)
Negros I

Stachyris hypogrammica (Palawan Tree Babbler)
Palawan I

Stachyris grammiceps (White-breasted Tree Babbler)
W Java

Stachyris herberti (Sooty Tree Babbler)
Laos

Stachyris nigriceps (Black-throated Tree Babbler)
S. n. nigriceps
E Himalayas
S. n. coei
Mishmi Hills, E Assam
S. n. coltarti
Naga Hills, E Assam, N Burma
S. n. spadix
S Assam, S Burma, NW Thailand
S. n. yunnanensis
N Thailand, E Burma, N Indochina,
SW Yunnan
S. n. rileyi
S Vietnam
S. n. dipora
N Malaysia
S. n. davisoni
C Malaysia
S. n. larvata
Lingga Archipelago, Sumatra
S. n. natunensis
N Natuna Is

S. n. tionis
Tioman I
S. n. hartleyi
W Sarawak
S. n. borneensis
Borneo

Stachyris poliocephala (Grey-headed Tree Babbler)
S. p. poliocephala
Malaysia, Sumatra, Borneo
S. p. pulla
NE Sumatra

Stachyris striolata (Spot-necked Tree Babbler)
S. s. swinhoei
Hainan I
S. s. tonkinensis
Kwansi, N Indochina
S. s. helenae
N Thailand, N Laos
S. s. guttata
W Thailand
S. s. nigrescentior
S Thailand
S. s. umbrosa
NE Sumatra
S. s. striolata
W Sumatra

Stachyris oglei (Austen's Spotted Tree Babbler)
E Assam

Stachyris maculata (Chestnut-rumped Tree Babbler)
S. m. pectoralis
C & S Malaysia
S. m. maculata
Sumatra, Borneo
S. m. banjakensis
Banyak I
S. m. hypopyrrha
Batu I

Stachyris leucotis (White-necked Tree Babbler)
S. l. leucotis
S Malaysia
S. l. sumatrensis
Sumatra
S. l. obscurata
Borneo

Stachyris nigricollis (Black-throated Tree Babbler)
S. n. erythronotus
N Malaysia
S. n. nigricollis
S Malaysia, E Sumatra, Borneo

Stachyris thoracica (White-collared Tree Babbler)
   S. t. thoracica
     S Sumatra, W & C Java
   S. t. orientalis
     E Java

Stachyris erythroptera (Chestnut-winged Tree Babbler)
   S. e. erythroptera
     S Malaysia, N Natuna Is
   S. e. apega
     Bangka I, Billiton I
   S. e. pyrrhophaea
     Sumatra, Batu I
   S. e. fulviventris
     Banyak I
   S. e. bicolor
     Banggai I, N & E Borneo
   S. e. rufa
     SW Borneo

Stachyris melanothorax (Pearl-cheeked Tree Babbler)
   S. m. melanothorax
     W Java
   S. m. albigula
     Java
   S. m. mendeni
     Java
   S. m. intermedia
     E Java
   S. m. baliensis
     Bali I

DUMETIA
Dumetia hyperythra (Rufous-bellied Babbler)
   D. h. hyperythra
     SW Nepal, N & C India
   D. h. albogularis
     S India
   D. h. phillipsi
     Sri Lanka
   D. h. navarroi
     W India

RHOPOCICHLA
Rhopocichla atriceps (Black-headed Babbler)
   R. a. atriceps
     C India
   R. a. bourdilloni
     SW India
   R. a. siccata
     N & E Sri Lanka
   R. a. nigrifrons
     SW Sri Lanka

MACRONOUS
Macronous gularis (Striped Tit-Babbler)
   M. g. rubricapilla
     Nepal, NE India, Assam
   M. g. ticehursti
     W Burma
   M. g. sulphureus
     E Burma, N Thailand
   M. g. lutescens
     SE Yunnan, N & E Thailand, Laos, N Vietnam
   M. g. kinneari
     C Vietnam
   M. g. versuricola
     E Cambodia, S Vietnam
   M. g. saraburiensis
     E Thailand, W Cambodia
   M. g. connectens
     S Thailand
   M. g. inveteratus
     coastal islands of SE Thailand & Cambodia
   M. g. condorensis
     Pulau Kondor, S Vietnam
   M. g. archipelagicus
     Mergui Archipelago
   M. g. chersonesophilus
     N Malaysia
   M. g. gularis
     S Malaysia, Sumatra, Batu I
   M. g. zopherus
     Anamba Is
   M. g. zaperissus
     N Natuna Is
   M. g. everetti
     Bunguran I, N Natuna Is
   M. g. ruficoma
     Bangka I, Billiton I
   M. g. javanicus
     W & C Java
   M. g. flavicollis
     E Java
   M. g. prillwitzi
     Kangean I
   M. g. montanus
     NE Borneo
   M. g. bornensis
     Borneo
   M. g. cagayanensis
     Cagayan Sulu I
   M. g. argenteus
     N Borneo Islands
   M. g. woodi
     Palawan I

Macronous kelleyi (Grey-faced Tit-Babbler)
   S Indochina

Macronous striaticeps (Brown Tit-Babbler)
   M. s. mindanensis
     Samar I, Leyte I, Bohol I, Mindanao I

M. s. alcasidi
Dinagat I
M. s. striaticeps
Basilan I, Malamaui I
M. s. kettlewelli
Sulu Archipelago
Macronous ptilosus (Fluffy-backed Tit-Babbler)
M. p. ptilosus
Malaysia
M. p. trichorrhos
Sumatra, Batu Is
M. p. sordidus
Bangka I, Billiton I
M. p. reclusus
Borneo

MICROMACRONOUS
Micromacronous leytensis (Leyte Tit-Babbler)
M. l. leytensis
Leyte I
M. l. sordidus
Mindanao I

TIMALIA
Timalia pileata (Chestnut-capped Babbler)
T. p. bengalensis
E Himalayas, NW Burma
T. p. smithi
N Burma, S China, N Thailand, N Indochina
T. p. intermedia
C & S Burma, SW Thailand
T. p. patriciae
WC Thailand
T. p. dictator
S & E Thailand, S Indochina
T. p. pileata
Java

CHRYSOMMA
Chrysomma sinense (Oriental Yellow-eyed Babbler)
C. s. nasale
Sri Lanka
C. s. hypoleucum
Pakistan, India, Bangladesh, W Burma
C. s. sinense
S China, E Himalayas, Burma, Thailand, Indochina

MOUPINIA
Moupinia altirostris (Jerdon's Babbler)
M. a. scindica
Pakistan
M. a. griseigularis
N India, S Assam, NE Burma
M. a. altirostris
SC Burma

Moupinia poecilotis (Rufous-crowned Babbler)
W China

CHAMAEA
Chamaea fasciata (Wren-Tit)
C. f. phaea
coast of Oregon
C. f. rufula
coast of N California
C. f. intermedia
San Francisco area
C. f. fasciata
coast of C California
C. f. henshawi
SW Oregon, N & C California
C. f. canicauda
NW Baja California

TURDOIDES
Turdoides nipalensis (Spiny Babbler)
W & C Nepal
Turdoides altirostris (Iraq Babbler)
SE Iraq, SW Iran
Turdoides caudatus (Common Babbler)
T. c. salvadorii
SE Iraq, SW Iran
T. c. huttoni
Afghanistan, E Iran, S Pakistan
T. c. eclipes
N Pakistan
T. c. caudatus
SE Pakistan, India
Turdoides earlei (Striated Babbler)
T. e. sonivius
Pakistan, NW India
T. e. earlei
NE India, Assam, Burma
Turdoides gularis (White-throated Babbler)
C & S Burma
Turdoides longirostris (Slender-billed Babbler)
Nepal, Assam
Turdoides malcolmi (Large Grey Babbler)
C India
Turdoides squamiceps (Arabian Babbler)
T. s. squamiceps
coast of W & S Saudi Arabia
T. s. yemensis
S Yemen, Aden
T. s. muscatensis
coast of Oman
Turdoides fulvus (Fulvous Babbler)
T. f. maroccanus
SW Morocco
T. f. fulvus
N Algeria, Tunisia, NW Libya

T. f. buchanani
C Sahara
T. f. acaciae
S Egypt, N Sudan, NE Ethiopia
Turdoides aylmeri (Scaly Chatterer)
T. a. aylmeri
Somalia, SE Ethiopia
T. a. boranensis
SC Ethiopia
T. a. kenianus
C Kenya
T. a. loveridgei
SE Kenya, NE Tanzania
T. a. mentalis
NC Tanzania
Turdoides rubiginosus (Rufous Chatterer)
T. r. bowdleri
SE Ethiopia
T. r. rubiginosus
E Uganda, W Kenya, C & S Ethiopia,
S Sudan
T. r. heuglini
East African coast from Somalia to
Tanzania
T. r. schnitzeri
NW Tanzania
Turdoides subrufus (Rufous Babbler)
T. s. subrufus
SW India
T. s. hyperythrus
SW Madras
Turdoides striatus (White-headed Jungle Babbler)
T. s. malabaricus
SW India
T. s. somervillei
W coast of India
T. s. sindianus
Pakistan, NW India
T. s. striatus
N India, E Assam
T. s. orientalis
C & S India
Turdoides rufescens (Ceylon Jungle Babbler)
Sri Lanka
Turdoides affinis (White-headed Babbler)
T. a. affinis
S India
T. a. taprobanus
Sri Lanka
Turdoides melanops (Black-lored Babbler)
T. m. vepres
S Kenya
T. m. clamosus
C Kenya
T. m. sharpei
W Kenya, S Uganda, NW Tanzania

T. m. melanops
SW Angola, N Namibia, Botswana
T. m. angolensis
Huila, Angola
Turdoides tenebrosus (Dusky Babbler)
NE Zaire, S Sudan, SW Ethiopia
Turdoides reinwardtii (Blackcap Babbler)
T. r. reinwardtii
Senegal to Sierra Leone
T. r. stictilaemus
Ghana to N Zaire
T. r. houyi
N Cameroun, Central African Republic
Turdoides plebejus (Brown Babbler)
T. p. platycircus
Senegal to Sierra Leone, Togo, Niger
T. p. uamensis
E & C Cameroun
T. p. plebejus
S Cameroun, Nigeria, Central African
Republic
T. p. leucocephalus
E Sudan, Ethiopia
T. p. cinereus
E Nigeria to Ethiopia, Sudan, W Kenya
T. p. gularis
W Cameroun, N Zaire
Turdoides jardineii (Arrow-marked Babbler)
T. j. hypostictus
S Zaire, N Angola
T. j. tanganjicae
SE Zaire, N Zambia
T. j. emini
Uganda, Tanzania
T. j. kikuyuensis
SW Kenya, NW Tanzania
T. j. kirkii
coastal zone from Kenya to Mozambique
Malawi
T. j. tamalakanei
SW Zambia, N Botswana, S Angola
T. j. jardineii
Rhodesia, Mozambique, Transvaal, Natal
Turdoides squamulatus (Scaly Babbler)
T. s. jubaensis
S Somalia
T. s. squamulatus
coast of Kenya
Turdoides leucopygius (White-rumped Babbler)
T. l. leucopygius
coast of E Ethiopia
T. l. limbatus
NW Ethiopia
T. l. smithii
W Somalia, SE Ethiopia

T. l. lacuum
SW Ethiopia
T. l. omoensis
SW Ethiopia, SE Sudan
T. l. ater
SE Zaire, NE Zambia, SW Tanzania
T. l. hartlaubii
W Zambia, S Angola, N Botswana
T. l. griseosquamatus
N Botswana
Turdoides hindei (Hinde's Pied Babbler)
E Kenya
Turdoides hypoleucus (Northern Pied Babbler)
T. h. hypoleucus
C Kenya
T. h. rufuensis
NE Tanzania
Turdoides bicolor (Pied Babbler)
Namibia, Botswana, W Transvaal
Turdoides gymnogenys (Bare-cheeked Babbler)
T. g. gymnogenys
SW Angola
T. g. kaokensis
N Namibia

BABAX
Babax lanceolatus (Chinese Babax)
B. l. lanceolatus
SW China, NE Burma
B. l. woodi
SE Assam, W Burma
B. l. latouchei
SE China
Babax waddelli (Giant Babax)
B. w. waddelli
SE Tibet
B. w. lumsdeni
NE Tibet
B. w. jomo
SE Tibet
Babax koslowi (Koslow's Babax)
N Sikang

GARRULAX
Garrulax cinereifrons (Ashy-headed Laughing Thrush)
SW Sri Lanka
Garrulax palliatus (Grey & Brown Laughing Thrush)
G. p. palliatus
W Sumatra
G. p. schistochlamys
N Borneo
Garrulax rufifrons (Red-fronted Laughing Thrush (Hwamei))
G. r. rufifrons
W Java

G. r. slamatensis
Java
Garrulax perspicillatus (Spectacled Laughing Thrush)
C & S China, N Vietnam
Garrulax albogularis (White-throated Laughing Thrush)
G. a. whistleri
Pakistan, W Himalayas, NW India
G. a. albogularis
E Himalayas, Bhutan
G. a. eous
SE Sikang, SW China, NW Vietnam
G. a. ruficeps
Taiwan
Garrulax leucolophus (White-crested Laughing Thrush)
G. l. leucolophus
Himalayas, N Assam
G. l. patkaicus
S Assam, W Burma
G. l. belangeri
S Burma, SW Thailand
G. l. diardi
SE Burma, Thailand, Yunnan, Indochina
G. l. bicolor
W Sumatra
Garrulax monileger (Lesser Necklaced Laughing Thrush)
G. m. monileger
E Himalayas, NE Burma
G. m. badius
Mishmi hills, NE Assam
G. m. stuarti
SE Burma, NW Thailand
G. m. fuscatus
SW Thailand
G. m. mouhoti
SE Thailand, S Indochina
G. m. pasquieri
C Vietnam
G. m. schauenseei
E Burma, NE Thailand, N Laos
G. m. tonkinensis
Kwangsi, N Vietnam
G. m. melli
Kwangtung to Anhwei, SE China
G. m. schmackeri
Hainan I
Garrulax pectoralis (Greater Necklaced Laughing Thrush)
G. p. pectoralis
Nepal
G. p. melanotis
E Himalayas, Assam, N Burma
G. p. subfusus
SE Burma, W Thailand, NW Laos

G. p. robini
NE Laos, N Vietnam
G. p. picticollis
Kwangtung to Anhwei, SE China
G. p. semitorquatus
Hainan I
Garrulax lugubris (Black Laughing Thrush)
G. l. lugubris
Malaysia, W Sumatra
G. l. calvus
NE Borneo
Garrulax striatus (Striated Laughing Thrush)
G. s. striatus
NW Himalayas
G. s. vibex
C Himalayas
G. s. sikkimensis
Sikkim, E Himalayas
G. s. cranbrooki
Bhutan, Assam, N & W Burma
Garrulax strepitans (Tickell's Laughing Thrush)
G. s. strepitans
E & S Burma, W Thailand, NW Laos
G. s. ferrarius
SE Thailand
Garrulax milleti (Black-hooded Laughing Thrush)
S Vietnam
Garrulax maesi (Maës' Laughing Thrush)
G. m. grahami
SE Sikang, SW China
G. m. maesi
Kwangsi, N Vietnam
G. m. varennei
NE & C Laos
G. m. castanotis
Hainan I
Garrulax nuchalis (Chestnut-backed Laughing Thrush)
NE Assam, N Burma
Garrulax chinensis (Black-throated Laughing Thrush)
G. c. lochmius
SW Yunnan, SE Burma, N Thailand, N Laos
G. c. propinquus
S Burma, SW Thailand
G. c. germaini
S Vietnam
G. c. chinensis
S China, NE Indochina
G. c. monachus
Hainan I
Garrulax vassali (White-cheeked Laughing Thrush)
S Indochina

Garrulax galbanus (Austen's Laughing Thrush)
G. g. galbanus
SE Assam, W Burma
G. g. courtoisi
NE Kiangsi
Garrulax delesserti (Rufous-vented Laughing Thrush)
G. d. delesserti
SW India
G. d. gularis
Bhutan, Assam, N Burma, N Laos
Garrulax variegatus (Variegated Laughing Thrush)
G. v. variegatus
W Himalayas
G. v. similis
Pakistan, NW India
Garrulax davidi (David's Laughing Thrush)
G. d. chinganicus
N Manchuria
G. d. davidi
N China, S Mongolia
G. d. experrectus
N Kansu
G. d. concolor
NW Szechwan
Garrulax sukatschewi (Black-fronted Laughing Thrush)
S Kansu
Garrulax cineraceus (Ashy Laughing Thrush)
G. c. cineraceus
S Assam, W Burma
G. c. strenuus
NE Burma, SW China
G. c. cinereiceps
C & SE China
Garrulax rufogularis (Rufous-chinned Laughing Thrush)
G. r. occidentalis
Pakistan, W Himalayas
G. r. grosvenori
W Nepal
G. r. rufogularis
E Himalayas, N Assam
G. r. assamensis
NE Assam
G. r. rufitinctus
S Assam
G. r. rufiberbis
N Burma
G. r. intensior
N Vietnam
Garrulax lunulatus (Bar-backed Laughing Thrush)
S Kansu, S Shensi
Garrulax bieti (Biet's Laughing Thrush)
SE Sikang, W Szechwan

***Garrulax maximus* (Giant Laughing Thrush)**
   W China, SE Tibet
***Garrulax ocellatus* (White-spotted**
  Laughing Thrush)
  G. o. griseicauda
   W Himalayas
  G. o. ocellatus
   E Himalayas, S Tibet
  G. o. maculipectus
   NW Yunnan, NE Burma
  G. o. artemisiae
   SW Szechwan, E Sikang
***Garrulax caerulatus* (Grey-sided Laughing**
  Thrush)
  G. c. caerulatus
   E Himalayas
  G. c. subcaerulatus
   S Assam
  G. c. livingstoni
   E Assam, NW Burma
  G. c. kaurensis
   N Burma
  G. c. latifrons
   W Yunnan, NE Burma
  G. c. ricinus
   S Yunnan
  G. c. berthemyi
   NW Fukien
***Garrulax poecilorhynchus* (Rufous**
  Laughing Thrush)
   Taiwan
***Garrulax mitratus* (Chestnut-capped**
  Laughing Thrush)
  G. m. mitratus
   W Sumatra
  G. m. major
   C Malaysia
  G. m. damnatus
   E Sarawak
  G. m. griswoldi
   C Borneo
  G. m. treacheri
   N Borneo
***Garrulax ruficollis* (Rufous-necked**
  Laughing Thrush)
   E Himalayas, NE Burma
***Garrulax merulinus* (Spot-breasted**
  Laughing Thrush)
  G. m. merulinus
   W Yunnan, N Burma, S Assam
  G. m. obscurus
   SE Yunnan, N Indochina
  G. m. annamensis
   S Vietnam
***Garrulax canorus* (Melodious Laughing**
  Thrush (Hwamei))
  G. c. canorus
   S China, N Indochina

G. c. owstoni
  Hainan I
G. c. taewanus
  Taiwan
***Garrulax sannio* (White-browed Laughing**
  Thrush)
  G. s. albosuperciliaris
   E Assam
  G. s. comis
   Yunnan, SE Sikang, NE Burma,
    N Indochina
  G. s. sannio
   N Vietnam, S China
  G. s. oblectans
   WC China
***Garrulax cachinnans* (Nilgiri White-**
  breasted Laughing Thrush)
   Nilgiri Hills, W Madras
***Garrulax jerdoni* (White-breasted Laughing**
  Thrush)
  G. j. jerdoni
   Coorg, W Mysore
  G. j. fairbanki
   Palni hills, S India
  G. j. meridionalis
   S Kerala, SW India
***Garrulax lineatus* (Himalayan Streaked**
  Laughing Thrush)
  G. l. bilkevitchi
   Tadzhikistan, NW Pakistan
  G. l. gilgit
   NE Pakistan
  G. l. lineatus
   W Himalayas
  G. l. setafer
   Sikkim, Nepal, W Bengal
  G. l. imbricatus
   Bhutan, SE Tibet
***Garrulax virgatus* (Striped Laughing**
  Thrush)
   S Assam, SW Burma
***Garrulax austeni* (Brown-capped Laughing**
  Thrush)
  G. a. austeni
   S Assam
  G. a. victoriae
   N Burma
***Garrulax squamatus* (Blue-winged**
  Laughing Thrush)
   E Himalayas, Burma, Assam, SW China
***Garrulax subunicolor* (Plain-coloured**
  Laughing Thrush)
  G. s. subunicolor
   E Himalayas, E Assam
  G. s. griseatus
   NE Burma, NW Yunnan
  G. s. fooksi
   NW Vietnam

Garrulax elliotii (Elliot's Laughing Thrush)
  G. e. prjevalskii
    Kansu, E Tsinghai
  G. e. elliotii
    C & SW China
Garrulax henrici (Prince Henry's Laughing
Thrush)
    SE Tibet, SW Sikang
Garrulax affinis (Black-faced Laughing
Thrush)
  G. a. affinis
    W & C Nepal
  G. a. bethelae
    E Himalayas
  G. a. oustaleti
    NE Assam, SW Sikang, N Burma,
    NW Yunnan
  G. a. muliensis
    NW Yunnan, SE Sikang
  G. a. blythii
    SW Szechwan, E Sikang
  G. a. saturatus
    N Vietnam
  G. a. morrisonianus
    Taiwan
Garrulax erythrocephalus (Red-headed
Laughing Thrush)
  G. e. erythrocephalus
    W Himalayas
  G. e. kali
    W & C Nepal
  G. e. nigrimentum
    Sikkim, Bhutan
  G. e. imprudens
    NE Assam
  G. e. chrysopterus
    S Assam
  G. e. godwini
    SE Assam
  G. e. erythrolaema
    E Manipur, SW Burma
  G. e. woodi
    NE Burma, SW Yunnan
  G. e. connectens
    N Indochina
  G. e. subconnectens
    NW Thailand
  G. e. schistaceus
    E Burma, NW Thailand
  G. e. melanostigma
    SE Burma, NW Thailand
  G. e. ramsayi
    S Burma
  G. e. peninsulae
    S Thailand, N Malaysia
Garrulax yersini (Yersin's Laughing Thrush)
    S Vietnam

Garrulax formosus (Crimson-winged
Laughing Thrush)
  G. f. formosus
    SW Szechwan, NE Yunnan
  G. f. greenwayi
    NW Vietnam
Garrulax milnei (Red-tailed Laughing
Thrush)
  G. m. sharpei
    E Burma, Yunnan, NW Thailand,
    N Indochina
  G. m. vitryi
    S Laos
  G. m. sinianus
    Kwangsi
  G. m. milnei
    NW Fukien

LIOCICHLA
Liocichla phoenicea (Red-faced Liocichla)
  L. p. phoenicea
    E Himalayas
  L. p. bakeri
    S Assam, NW Burma
  L. p. ripponi
    E & S Burma, NW Thailand
  L. p. wellsi
    S Yunnan, N Indochina
Liocichla omeiensis (Mount Omei
Liocichla)
    Mt Omei (Szechwan)
Liocichla steerii (Steere's Liocichla)
    S Taiwan

LEIOTHRIX
Leiothrix argentauris (Silver-eared Mesia)
  L. a. argentauris
    Himalayas, N Assam
  L. a. vernayi
    S Assam, Burma, W Yunnan
  L. a. galbana
    E Burma, N Thailand
  L. a. ricketti
    SE Yunnan, N Indochina
  L. a. cunhaci
    S Indochina
  L. a. tahanensis
    S Thailand, N Malaysia
  L. a. rookmakeri
    NW Sumatra
  L. a. laurinae
    W Sumatra
Leiothrix lutea (Pekin Robin)
  L. l. kumaiensis
    W Himalayas
  L. l. calipyga
    E Himalayas
  L. l. luteola
    SW Burma, S Assam

L. l. yunnanensis
  NE Burma, NW Yunnan, SE Sikang
L. l. kwangtungensis
  S China, NE Vietnam
L. l. lutea
  SE & C China

CUTIA
Cutia nipalensis (Nepal Cutia)
  C. n. nipalensis
    E Himalayas, Assam, W Burma
  C. n. melanchima
    E Burma, NW Thailand, N Indochina
  C. n. cervinicrissa
    N Malaysia
  C. n. legalleni
    S Vietnam

PTERUTHIUS
Pteruthius rufiventer (Rufous-bellied Shrike Babbler)
  P. r. rufiventer
    E Himalayas, Assam, N Burma, Yunnan
  P. r. delacouri
    NW Vietnam
Pteruthius flaviscapis (Red-winged Shrike Babbler)
  P. f. validirostris
    Himalayas, Assam, NW Burma
  P. f. ricketti
    NE Burma, S China, N Indochina
  P. f. annamensis
    S Vietnam
  P. f. schauenseei
    S Thailand, E Burma
  P. f. cameranoi
    Malaysia, W Sumatra
  P. f. flaviscapis
    Java
  P. f. robinsoni
    N Borneo
Pteruthius xanthochlorus (Green Shrike Babbler)
  P. x. occidentalis
    W Himalayas
  P. x. xanthochlorus
    E Himalayas
  P. x. hybridus
    Naga hills, Assam, W Burma
  P. x. pallidus
    NE Burma, SE Sikang, W & S China
Pteruthius melanotis (Black-eared Shrike Babbler)
  P. m. melanotis
    E Himalayas, Burma, N Thailand,
      N Indochina
  P. m. tahanensis
    C Malaysia

Pteruthius aenobarbus (Chestnut-fronted 431
Shrike Babbler)
  P. a. aenobarbulus
    Garo hills, Assam
  P. a. intermedius
    E Burma, NW Thailand, N Indochina
  P. a. yaoshanensis
    Kwangsi
  P. a. indochinensis
    S Vietnam
  P. a. aenobarbus
    W Java

GAMPSORHYNCHUS
Gampsorhynchus rufulus (White-headed Shrike Babbler)
  G. r. rufulus
    Sikkim, Assam, Burma
  G. r. torquatus
    SE Burma, Thailand, S Laos, Vietnam
  G. r. saturatior
    C Malaysia

ACTINODURA
Actinodura egertoni (Rusty-fronted Barwing)
  A. e. egertoni
    Nepal, Sikkim, Bhutan, N Assam
  A. e. lewisi
    Mishmi hills, NE Assam
  A. e. khasiana
    S Assam
  A. e. ripponi
    E Assam, SW Burma
Actinodura ramsayi (Spectacled Barwing)
  A. r. yunnanensis
    SE Yunnan, N Vietnam
  A. r. radcliffei
    E Burma, N Laos
  A. r. ramsayi
    E Burma, NW Thailand
Actinodura nipalensis (Hoary Barwing)
  A. n. nipalensis
    W & C Nepal
  A. n. vinctura
    E Nepal, Sikkim, Bhutan
Actinodura waldeni (Austen's Barwing)
  A. w. daflaensis
    N Assam
  A. w. waldeni
    SE Assam, NW Burma
  A. w. poliotis
    Mt Victoria, N Burma
  A. w. saturatior
    NE Burma, NW Yunnan
Actinodura souliei (Streaked Barwing)
  A. s. souliei
    NW Yunnan
  A. s. griseinucha
    NW Vietnam

Actinodura morrisoniana (Formosan
Barwing)
Taiwan

MINLA
Minla cyanouroptera (Blue-winged Minla)
M. c. cyanouroptera
C & E Himalayas, E Assam
M. c. aglae
SE Assam, W Burma
M. c. sordida
E & S Burma, NW Thailand
M. c. wingatei
NE Burma, N Thailand, S China,
N Indochina
M. c. croizati
Szechwan
M. c. rufodorsalis
SE Thailand, SW Cambodia
M. c. orientalis
S Vietnam
M. c. sordidior
S Thailand, N Malaysia
Minla strigula (Chestnut-tailed Minla)
M. s. simlaensis
W Himalayas
M. s. strigula
E Himalayas, N Assam
M. s. cinereigenae
Mt Japvo (E Assam)
M. s. yunnanensis
E Assam, W Burma, N Indochina
M. s. castanicauda
S Burma, NW Thailand
M. s. malayana
C Malaysia
Minla ignotincta (Red-tailed Minla)
M. i. ignotincta
E Nepal, Burma, Assam, NW Yunnan
M. i. mariae
SE Yunnan, N Vietnam
M. i. sini
Kwangsi
M. i. jerdoni
SW Szechwan

ALCIPPE
Alcippe chrysotis (Golden-breasted
Fulvetta)
A. c. chrysotis
E Himalayas, E Assam
A. c. albilineata
S Assam
A. c. forresti
NE Burma, NW Yunnan
A. c. amoena
NW Vietnam
A. c. swinhoii
SE Sikang, S Szechwan

Alcippe variegaticeps (Variegated
Fulvetta)
Kwangsi
Alcippe cinerea (Yellow-throated Fulvetta)
E Himalayas, N Burma, N Laos
Alcippe castaneceps (Chestnut-headed
Fulvetta)
A. c. castaneceps
E Himalayas, Assam, Burma,
NW Thailand
A. c. exul
N Thailand, Laos, NW Vietnam
A. c. soror
C Malaysia
A. c. klossi
S Vietnam
Alcippe vinipectus (White-browed Fulvetta)
A. v. kangrae
W Himalayas
A. v. vinipectus
W & C Nepal
A. v. chumbiensis
E Nepal, SE Tibet, Sikkim, Bhutan
A. v. austeni
S Assam
A. v. ripponi
Chin hills, W Burma
A. v. perstriata
NE Burma
A. v. valentinae
N Vietnam
A. v. bieti
NW Yunnan, SE Sikang
Alcippe striaticollis (Chinese Mountain
Fulvetta)
NW China
Alcippe ruficapilla (Spectacled Fulvetta)
A. r. ruficapilla
S Shensi, Szechwan
A. r. sordidior
NW Yunnan
A. r. danisi
SE Yunnan, N Laos
Alcippe cinereiceps (Streak-throated
Fulvetta)
A. c. ludlowi
E Bhutan, SE Tibet
A. c. manipurensis
E Assam, N Burma, NW Yunnan
A. c. tonkinensis
NE Laos, NW Vietnam
A. c. guttaticollis
Fukien, N Kwangtung
A. c. formosana
Taiwan
A. c. fucata
Hupeh, Hunan

A. c. cinereiceps
W Hupeh, Szechwan, SE Sikang
A. c. fessa
SW Kansu
Alcippe rufogularis (Rufous-throated Fulvetta)
A. r. rufogularis
E Himalayas, N Assam
A. r. collaris
E Assam, Bangladesh
A. r. major
E Burma, N & E Thailand, N Laos
A. r. stevensi
N Indochina
A. r. kelleyi
C Vietnam
A. r. khmerensis
SE Thailand, SW Cambodia
Alcippe brunnea (Gould's Fulvetta)
A. b. mandellii
S Assam, W Burma
A. b. intermedia
E Burma
A. b. dubia
S Burma
A. b. genestieri
SW China, N Indochina
A. b. superciliaris
E & SE China
A. b. brunnea
Taiwan
A. b. arguta
Hainan I
A. b. olivacea
W Hupeh, Szechwan
Alcippe brunneicauda (Brown Fulvetta)
A. b. brunneicauda
Malaysia, Sumatra, NW Borneo, N Natuna Is
A. b. eriphaea
Borneo
Alcippe poioicephala (Brown-cheeked Fulvetta)
A. p. poioicephala
S India
A. p. brucei
C & S India
A. p. fusca
S Assam, NW Burma
A. p. phayrei
SW Burma
A. p. haringtoniae
NE Burma, NW Thailand
A. p. alearis
N & E Thailand, N Indochina
A. p. karenni
SE Burma, SW Thailand

A. p. davisoni
S Thailand, Mergui Archipelago
Alcippe pyrrhoptera (Javanese Fulvetta)
W & C Java
Alcippe peracensis (Mountain Fulvetta)
A. p. grotei
N & C Vietnam, S Laos
A. p. annamensis
S Indochina
A. p. eremita
SE Thailand
A. p. peracensis
N & C Malaysia
Alcippe morrisonia (Grey-cheeked Fulvetta)
A. m. yunnanensis
SE Sikang, NW Yunnan, NE Burma
A. m. fraterculus
SW Yunnan, SE Burma, N Indochina
A. m. schaefferi
SE Yunnan, NW Vietnam
A. m. rufescentior
Hainan I
A. m. morrisonia
Taiwan
A. m. hueti
Kwangtung to Anhwei, SE China
A. m. davidi
W Hupeh, Szechwan
Alcippe nipalensis (Nepal Fulvetta)
A. n. nipalensis
E Himalayas
A. n. commoda
Bangladesh, Assam, N Burma
A. n. stanfordi
SW Burma
Alcippe abyssinica (African Hill Babbler)
A. a. monachus
Cameroun Mt
A. a. claudi
Fernando Po I
A. a. ansorgei
C & W Angola, SE Zaire, W Tanzania
A. a. stierlingi
S & C Tanzania, N Malawi
A. a. abyssinica
W Ethiopia, W Kenya, N Tanzania
A. a. atriceps
Cameroun, NE Zaire, W Uganda
A. a. hildegardae
SW Tanzania

LIOPTILUS
Lioptilus nigricapillus (Bush Blackcap)
E Cape Province, Natal, N Transvaal
Lioptilus gilberti (White-throated Mountain Babbler)
Mt Kupé (Cameroun)

Lioptilus rufocinctus (Red-collared Flycatcher Babbler)
E Zaire

Lioptilus chapini (Chapin's Flycatcher Babbler)
  L. c. chapini
    Ituri river, E Zaire
  L. c. nyombensis
    Mt Nyombe (E Zaire)
  L. c. kalindei
    E Zaire

PAROPHASMA
Parophasma galinieri (Abyssinian Catbird)
C & S Ethiopia

PHYLLANTHUS
Phyllanthus atripennis (Capuchin Babbler)
  P. a. atripennis
    Senegal to Liberia
  P. a. rubiginosus
    Ivory Coast to S Nigeria
  P. a. bohndorffi
    NE Zaire to W Uganda

CROCIAS
Crocias langbianis (Mt Langbian Sibia)
S Vietnam
Crocias albonotatus (Spotted Sibia)
W & C Java

HETEROPHASIA
Heterophasia annectens (Chestnut-backed Sibia)
  H. a. annectens
    E Himalayas, Assam, NW Burma
  H. a. mixta
    SE Burma, N Thailand, N Indochina
  H. a. saturata
    SE Burma, NW Thailand
  H. a. eximia
    Dalat, S Vietnam
Heterophasia capistrata (Black-capped Sibia)
  H. c. capistrata
    W Himalayas
  H. c. nigriceps
    C Himalayas
  H. c. bayleyi
    E Himalayas
Heterophasia gracilis (Grey Sibia)
S Assam, N Burma, W Yunnan
Heterophasia melanoleuca (Black-headed Sibia)
  H. m. desgodinsi
    NE Burma, W China
  H. m. castanoptera
    SE Burma
  H. m. tonkinensis
    N Vietnam

  H. m. melanoleuca
    E Burma, NW Thailand
  H. m. engelbachi
    S Laos
  H. m. robinsoni
    S Vietnam
Heterophasia auricularis (White-eared Sibia)
Taiwan
Heterophasia pulchella (Beautiful Sibia)
SE Tibet, Assam, NE Burma
Heterophasia picaoides (Long-tailed Sibia)
  H. p. picaoides
    E Himalayas, NE Burma
  H. p. cana
    E & S Burma, N Thailand, N Indochina
  H. p. wrayi
    C Malaysia
  H. p. simillima
    W Sumatra

YUHINA
Yuhina castaniceps (Striated Yuhina)
  Y. c. rufigenis
    W Benegal, Sikkim
  Y. c. plumbeiceps
    N Assam, N Burma
  Y. c. castaniceps
    S Assam, SW Burma
  Y. c. striata
    E Burma, NW Thailand
  Y. c. torqueola
    N Thailand, S China, N Indochina
  Y. c. everetti
    N Borneo
Yuhina bakeri (White-naped Yuhina)
E Himalayas, Assam
Yuhina flavicollis (Whiskered Yuhina)
  Y. f. albicollis
    W Himalayas
  Y. f. flavicollis
    E Himalayas
  Y. f. rouxi
    Assam, N Burma, SW China, N Indochina
  Y. f. clarki
    E Burma
  Y. f. humilis
    S Burma
  Y. f. constantiae
    N Laos
  Y. f. rogersi
    Thailand
Yuhina gularis (Striped-throated Yuhina)
  Y. g. vivax
    W Himalayas
  Y. g. gularis
    E Nepal, Burma, Assam, NW Vietnam
  Y. g. omeiensis
    SW China

Yuhina diademata (White-collared Yuhina)
  NE Burma, N Vietnam, SW & S China
Yuhina occipitalis (Rufous-vented Yuhina)
  Y. o. occipitalis
    E Himalayas, SE Tibet, N Assam
  Y. o. obscurior
    NE Burma, NW Yunnan
Yuhina brunneiceps (Formosan Yuhina)
  Taiwan
Yuhina nigrimenta (Black-chinned Yuhina)
  Y. n. nigrimenta
    Himalayas, Assam
  Y. n. intermedia
    NE Burma, SW China, N Indochina
  Y. n. pallida
    Fukien, SE China
Yuhina zantholeuca (White-bellied Yuhina)
  Y. z. zantholeuca
    E Himalayas, Burma, Thailand
  Y. z. tyrannula
    N Thailand, N Indochina, Hainan I
  Y. z. griseiloris
    Kwangtung, Fukien, Taiwan
  Y. z. sordida
    E Thailand, S Indochina
  Y. z. canescens
    SE Thailand, W Cambodia
  Y. z. interposita
    Malaysia
  Y. z. saani
    NW Sumatra
  Y. z. brunnescens
    Borneo

MALIA
Malia grata (Malia Babbler)
  M. g. recondita
    N Celebes
  M. g. stresemanni
    C & SE Celebes
  M. g. grata
    SW Celebes

MYZORNIS
Myzornis pyrrhoura (Fire-tailed Myzornis)
  E Himalayas, SE Tibet, NE Burma

HORIZORHINUS
Horizorhinus dohrni (Dohrn's Thrush-Babbler)
  Principé I

OXYLABES
Oxylabes cinereiceps (Grey-crowned Oxylabes)
  E Madagascar
Oxylabes madagascariensis (White-throated Oxylabes)
  E Madagascar

Oxylabes xanthophrys (Yellow-browed Oxylabes)
  EC Madagascar

MYSTACORNIS
Mystacornis crossleyi (Crossley's Babbler)
  Madagascar

MUSCICAPIDAE

133 PANURINAE (PARROTBILLS)

PANURUS
Panurus biarmicus (Bearded Reedling)
  P. b. biarmicus
    England, S & E Europe
  P. b. occidentalis
    Balkans
  P. b. russicus
    E Europe, Russia, Iran, Manchuria

CONOSTOMA
Conostoma oemodium (Great Parrotbill)
  Himalayas, NE Burma, SE Tibet, SW China

PARADOXORNIS
Paradoxornis paradoxus (Three-toed Parrotbill)
  P. p. paradoxus
    NW China
  P. p. taipaiensis
    Shensi
Paradoxornis unicolor (Brown Parrotbill)
  E Himalayas, N Burma, SE Tibet, SW China
Paradoxornis flavirostris (Gould's Parrotbill)
  E Himalayas, W Burma
Paradoxornis guttaticollis (Spot-breasted Parrotbill)
  Assam to N Indochina
Paradoxornis conspicillatus (Spectacled Parrotbill)
  P. c. conspicillatus
    WC China
  P. c. rocki
    Hupeh
Paradoxornis ricketti (Yunnan Parrotbill)
  NW Yunnan
Paradoxornis webbianus (Vinous-throated Parrotbill)
  P. w. mantschuricus
    E Manchuria
  P. w. suffusus
    NW to SE China
  P. w. fulvicauda
    NE China, S Korea
  P. w. webbianus
    coast of S Kiangsu, N Chekiang
  P. w. bulomachus
    Taiwan

P. w. elisabethae
SE Yunnan
P. w. brunneus
NE Burma, NW Yunnan
Paradoxornis alphonsianus (Ashy-throated Parrotbill)
P. a. alphonsianus
WC China
P. a. yunnanensis
SE Yunnan, NW Vietnam
Paradoxornis zappeyi (Zappey's Parrotbill)
W Szechwan
Paradoxornis przewalskii (Grey-crowned Parrotbill)
S Kansu
Paradoxornis fulvifrons (Fulvous-fronted Parrotbill)
P. f. chayulensis
N Assam, SE Tibet
P. f. fulvifrons
Nepal, Sikkim, Bhutan
P. f. albifacies
NW Yunnan, SE Sikang
P. f. cyanophrys
NW Szechwan, SW Shensi
Paradoxornis nipalensis (Blyth's Parrotbill)
P. n. nipalensis
C Nepal
P. n. humii
E Nepal, Sikkim
P. n. crocotius
SE Tibet, E Bhutan
P. n. poliotis
Assam, NE Burma, NW Yunnan
P. n. patriciae
SE Assam
P. n. ripponi
Mt Victoria, N Burma
P. n. feae
SE Burma, NW Thailand
P. n. verreauxi
E Sikang, SW Szechwan
P. n. pallidus
NW Fukien
P. n. morrisonianus
Taiwan
P. n. beaulieu
N Laos
P. n. craddocki
NW Vietnam
Paradoxornis davidianus (David's Parrotbill)
P. d. davidianus
Fukien
P. d. tonkinensis
N Vietnam
P. d. thompsoni
E Burma, NW Laos, E Thailand

Paradoxornis atrosuperciliaris (Lesser Red-headed Parrotbill)
P. a. oatesi
W Bengal, Sikkim
P. a. atrosuperciliaris
Assam, N Burma, N Laos, W Yunnan
Paradoxornis ruficeps (Greater Red-headed Parrotbill)
P. r. ruficeps
E Himalayas
P. r. bakeri
Assam, N & E Burma
P. r. magnirostris
N Vietnam
Paradoxornis gularis (Grey-headed Parrotbill)
P. g. gularis
E Himalayas, N Assam
P. g. transfluvialis
S Assam, N & E Burma, NW Thailand
P. g. laotianus
E Burma, N Thailand, N Indochina
P. g. fokiensis
Fukien, Anhwei
P. g. hainanus
Hainan I
P. g. rasus
Chin hills, W Burma
P. g. margaritae
S Vietnam
Paradoxornis heudei (Heude's Parrotbill)
P. h. heudei
Kiangsu, C China
P. h. polivanovi
Lake Khanka, USSR

MUSCICAPIDAE

134 PICATHARTINAE (ROCKFOWL)

PICATHARTES
Picathartes gymnocephalus (White-necked Bald Crow)
Sierra Leone to Ghana
Picatharte soreas (Grey-necked Bald Crow)
Cameroun

MUSCICAPIDAE

135 POLIOPTILINAE (GNATWRENS)

MICROBATES
Microbates collaris (Collared Gnatwren)
M. c. paraguensis
Venezuela
M. c. collaris
SE Colombia to French Guiana
M. c. perlatus
N Brazil

Microbates cinereiventris (Half-collared Gnatwren)
M. c. semitorquatus
S Nicaragua to W Panama
M. c. magdalenae
E Panama, N Colombia
M. c. cinereiventris
W Colombia, SW Ecuador
M. c. peruvianus
Colombia, E Ecuador, Peru

RAMPHOCAENUS

Ramphocaenus melanurus (Long-billed Gnatwren)
R. m. rufiventris
SE Mexico, Central America to E Ecuador
R. m. ardeleo
Yucatan, N Guatemala
R. m. sanctaemarthae
N Colombia, NW Venezuela
R. m. griseodorsalis
W Colombia
R. m. pallidus
NE Colombia, N Venezuela
R. m. trinitatis
E Colombia to Trinidad
R. m. duidae
S Venezuela to NE Ecuador
R. m. badius
NE Peru, SE Ecuador
R. m. obscurus
Peru
R. m. amazonum
E Peru, NW Brazil
R. m. sticturus
NW Brazil
R. m. albiventris
E Venezuela, the Guianas, NE Brazil
R. m. austerus
Brazil
R. m. melanurus
N & E Brazil

POLIOPTILA

Polioptila caerula (Blue-grey Gnatcatcher)
P. c. caerulea
C & E USA, E Mexico, West Indies
P. c. amoenissima
SW USA, NW Mexico, N Baja California
P. c. obscura
S Baja California
P. c. gracilis
SE Sonora (Mexico)
P. c. mexicana
SE Mexico
P. c. nelsoni
SW & S Mexico
P. c. deppei
Yucatan

P. c. cozumelae
Cozumel I
Polioptila melanura (Black-tailed Gnatcatcher)
P. m. californica
SW California, NW Baja California
P. m. lucida
SW USA, N Mexico, NE Baja California
P. m. melanura
S USA
P. m. pontilis
C Baja California
P. m. margaritae
S Baja California, Santa Margarita I
P. m. curtata
Tiburon I
Polioptila lembeyei (Cuban Gnatcatcher)
E Cuba
Polioptila albiloris (White-lored Gnatcatcher)
P. a. vanrossemi
S & W Mexico
P. a. albiventris
N Yucatan
P. a. albiloris
Guatemala to Costa Rica
Polioptila nigriceps (Black-capped Gnatcatcher)
P. n. restricta
Sonora (Mexico)
P. n. nigriceps
N Sinaloa (Mexico)
Polioptila plumbea (Tropical Gnatcatcher)
P. p. brodkorbi
SE Mexico to Nicaragua
P. p. superciliaris
SE Mexico to Panama
P. p. cinericia
Coiba I (Panama)
P. p. bilineata
Colombia to W Peru
P. p. plumbiceps
N Colombia, N Venezuela
P. p. anteocularis
Colombia
P. p. daguae
Colombia
P. p. innotata
E Colombia, S Venezuela, N Brazil
P. p. plumbea
the Guianas, NE Brazil
P. p. maior
N Peru
P. p. parvirostris
E Peru
P. p. atricapilla
NE Brazil

***Polioptila lactea* (Cream-bellied Gnatcatcher)**
SE Brazil to Argentina
***Polioptila guianensis* (Guianan Gnatcatcher)**
P. g. facilis
Venezuela, NE Brazil
P. g. guianensis
the Guianas
P. g. paraensis
Brazil
***Polioptila schistaceigula* (Slate-throated Gnatcatcher)**
E Panama to W Ecuador
***Polioptila dumicola* (Masked Gnatcatcher)**
P. d. berlepschi
Brazil, E Bolivia
P. d. dumicola
Bolivia to Uruguay, Argentina
P. d. saturata
Bolivia

MUSCICAPIDAE

136 SYLVINAE (OLD WORLD WARBLERS)

TESIA
***Tesia castaneocoronata* (Chestnut-headed Ground Warbler)**
T. c. castaneocoronata
Himalayas, Burma, Thailand, S China
T. c. abadiei
N Vietnam
T. c. ripleyi
SW China
***Tesia cyaniventer* (Grey-bellied Ground Warbler)**
Himalayas, Burma, Thailand, Laos, S China
***Tesia olivea* (Slaty-bellied Ground Warbler)**
Burma, Thailand, Laos, SW China, N Vietnam
***Tesia superciliaris* (Java Ground Warbler)**
Java

PSAMATHIA
***Psamathia annae* (Palau Bush Warbler)**
Palau Is

CETTIA
***Cettia subulata* (Timor Bush Warbler)**
Timor I
***Cettia whiteheadi* (Bornean Short-tailed Bush Warbler)**
Borneo
***Cettia squameiceps* (Short-tailed Bush Warbler)**
E Siberia, Japan, S China
***Cettia pallidipes* (Pale-footed Bush Warbler)**
C. p. pallidipes
Sikkim

C. p. laurentei
W China
C. p. osmastoni
S Andaman Is
***Cettia diphone* (Japanese Bush Warbler)**
C. d. borealis
Manchuria, Korea, S China
C. d. canturians
N China
C. d. sakhalinensis
Sakhalin I, N Japan
C. d. cantans
C & S Japan
C. d. takahashii
Quelpart I
C. d. ijimae
Tanegashima I
C. d. panafidinica
Panafidin I
C. d. riukiuensis
Riukiu Is
C. d. restricta
Borodino I
C. d. diphone
Bonin Is
C. d. iwootoensis
Iwo Jima I
C. d. seebohmi
N Luzon
***Cettia fortipes* (Strong-footed Bush Warbler)**
C. f. pallida
Pakistan, NW India
C. f. fortipes
Nepal
C. f. davidiana
WS China
C. f. sinensis
SE China
C. f. oreophila
NE Borneo
C. f. banksi
Borneo
C. f. sepiaria
N Sumatra
C. f. sumatrana
C Sumatra
C. f. montana
E Sumatra, Java, Bali I, Lombok I
C. f. everetti
Timor I
C. f. palawanae
Palawan I
***Cettia major* (Large Bush Warbler)**
C. m. major
Nepal, Burma, W China
C. m. vafer
Assam

Cettia flavolivacea (Aberrant Bush Warbler)
  C. f. flavolivacea
    Nepal, S Tibet
  C. f. intricata
    S China
  C. f. weberi
    Chin hills, Burma
  C. f. alexanderi
    Burma
  C. f. oblita
    W China, N Vietnam
  C. f. stresemanni
    Assam
Cettia acanthizoides (Verreaux's Bush Warbler)
  C. a. brunnescens
    SE Assam, Nepal, SE Tibet
  C. a. acanthizoides
    E Burma, W China
  C. a. robustipes
    S China, Taiwan
Cettia brunnifrons (Rufous-capped Bush Warbler)
  C. b. whistleri
    NW Himalayas
  C. b. brunnifrons
    E Himalayas, Nepal
  C. b. muroides
    Assam
  C. b. umbratica
    Burma
Cettia cetti (Cetti's Warbler)
  C. c. cetti
    S Europe, Asia Minor, N Africa
  C. c. orientalis
    Middle East, N Iran
  C. c. cettioides
    WC Asia, SE Iran, Turkistan
  C. c. interpositus
    Iran
  C. c. albiventris
    W Pakistan

RADYPTERUS

Bradypterus baboecala (African Sedge Warbler)
  B. b. centralis
    S Nigeria, Cameroun to E Zaire
  B. b. chadensis
    Lake Chad
  B. b. elgonensis
    E Chad, Uganda, N Kenya
  B. b. tongensis
    Sudan
  B. b. sudanensis
    S Sudan
  B. b. abyssinicus
    Ethiopia

  B. b. moreaui
    SE Kenya, Tanzania, Malawi, Mozambique
  B. b. msiri
    Angola, S Zaire, Botswana
  B. b. benguellensis
    S Angola
  B. b. baboecalus
    Rhodesia, Transvaal, Natal, Cape Province
Bradypterus graueri (Grauer's Warbler)
    E Zaire
Bradypterus grandis (Ja River Warbler)
    Cameroun, Gabon
Bradypterus carpalis (White-winged Warbler)
    NE Zaire, Uganda
Bradypterus cinnamomeus (Cinnamon Bracken Warbler)
  B. c. bangwaensis
    E Nigeria, Cameroun
  B. c. cavei
    S Sudan
  B. c. macdonaldi
    W Ethiopia
  B. c. cinnamomeus
    S Ethiopia, Kenya, NE Zaire
  B. c. mildbreadi
    E Zaire
  B. c. rufoflavidus
    SE Kenya, N Tanzania
  B. c. ufipae
    S Tanzania, Zambia
  B. c. nyassae
    E Tanzania, Malawi
Bradypterus victorini (Victorin's Scrub Warbler)
    S Cape Province
Bradypterus barratti (Scrub Warbler)
  B. b. lopezi
    Fernando Po I
  B. b. camerunensis
    Cameroun Mt
  B. b. manengubae
    Manenguba Mt (Cameroun)
  B. b. barakae
    E Zaire, W Uganda
  B. b. mariae
    SE Kenya, NE Tanzania
  B. b. usambarae
    S Kenya, W Tanzania, E Zambia, N Malawi
  B. b. boultoni
    C Angola
  B. b. granti
    W & S Malawi
  B. b. priesti
    Rhodesia
  B. b. barratti
    E Transvaal, Natal

B. b. godfreyi
Lesotho, E Cape Province

Bradypterus sylvaticus (Knysna Scrub Warbler)
S Natal, SE Cape Province

Bradypterus alfredi (Bamboo Warbler)

B. a. kungwensis
N Zambia, SW Tanzania

B. a. alfredi
E Zaire

B. a. albicrissalis
W Uganda

Bradypterus thoracicus (Spotted Bush Warbler)

B. t. davidi
NE Asia, S China

B. t. suschkini
C Asia, N Vietnam

B. t. przewalskii
W Himalayas, S & W China

B. t. thoracicus
Bangladesh, E Himalayas, Nepal

B. t. shanensis
Burma

Bradypterus major (Large-billed Bush Warbler)

B. b. major
W Himalayas, Turkistan, Sinkiang

B. b. netrix
W China

Bradypterus tacsanowskius (Chinese Bush Warbler)

B. t. tacsanowskius
SE Siberia, N China, Burma, N Indochina

B. t. chui
S China

Bradypterus luteoventris (Brown Bush Warbler)

B. l. luteoventris
Assam, Nepal, SE Tibet

B. l. ticehursti
Burma

Bradypterus seebohmi (Mountain Scrub Warbler)

B. s. idoneus
Taiwan, N Thailand, S Indochina

B. s. melanorhynchus
NW Fukien

B. s. seebohmi
N Luzon I

B. s. montis
E Java

B. s. timorensis
Timor I

Bradypterus caudatus (Long-tailed Ground Warbler)

B. c. caudatus
N Luzon I

B. c. unicolor
Mindanao I

B. c. malindangensis
S Mindanao I

Bradypterus accentor (Kinabalu Scrub Warbler)
Borneo

Bradypterus castaneus (East Indies Bush Warbler)

B. c. disturbans
Buru I

B. c. musculus
Ceram I

B. c. castaneus
C Moluccas

Bradypterus palliseri (Palliser's Warbler)
Sri Lanka

LOCUSTELLA

Locustella fasciolata (Gray's Grasshopper Warbler)
NE Asia, Sakhalin, Japan » Philippine Is, Celebes, New Guinea

Locustella amnicola (Stepanyan's Grasshopper Warbler)
Sakhalin I, Kurile Is

Locustella luscinioides (Savi's Warbler)

L. l. luscinioides
C & E Europe, Iberia, N Africa

L. l. sarmatica
S Russia

L. l. fusca
WC Asia

Locustella fluviatilis (River Warbler)
NE Europe, NW Asia, » SE Africa

Locustella certhiola (Pallas's Grasshopper Warbler)

L. c. certhiola
NC Asia » NW India

L. c. centralasiae
C Asia, Himalayas » Burma

L. c. rubescens
E Siberia » C & S India, Sri Lanka

L. c. minor
E China, Indochina

Locustella ochotensis (Middendorff's Grasshopper Warbler)
NE Asia, Kurile I, Sakhalin I » Philippine Borneo

Locustella pleskei (Styan's Grasshopper Warbler)
Japan, Korea » SE China & Sunda Is

Locustella naevia (Grasshopper Warbler)

L. n. naevia
Europe, N Africa, Russia

L. n. obscurior
Caucasus

L. n. straminea
Iran, N India, W Siberia, C Asia

L. n. mongolica
Afghanistan, W Mongolia
Locustella lanceolata (Lanceolated Warbler)
NC & NE Asia, Sakhalin I » Philippine Is, SE Asia

ACROCEPHALUS
Acrocephalus paludicola (Aquatic Warbler)
CS & E Europe, W Russia, Asia Minor, Egypt
Acrocephalus schoenobaenus (Sedge Warbler)
Europe & W & C Asia » EC & SE Africa
Acrocephalus agricola (Paddyfield Warbler)
A. a. agricola
WC Asia, N India
A. a. brevipennis
S Turkistan, Pakistan, N & C China
A. a. tangorum
Manchuria
Acrocephalus concinens (Blunt-winged Paddyfield Warbler)
A. c. harringtoni
Afghanistan, NW India, Pakistan
A. c. stevensi
Bangladesh, Assam, Burma
A. c. concinens
N & C China » S Burma, S Thailand
Acrocephalus bistrigiceps (Schrenk's Reed Warbler)
NE Asia » Burma, S China, N Vietnam
Acrocephalus sorghophilus (Speckled Reed Warbler)
N & E China » Philippine Is
Acrocephalus orinus (Large-billed Reed Warbler)
N India
Acrocephalus baeticatus (African Reed Warbler)
A. b. hopsoni
Lake Chad
A. b. cinnamomeus
S Sudan, S & E Zaire, Uganda, Angola
A. b. suahelicus
Kenya, Tanzania, Malawi
A. b. hallae
Namibia
A. b. baeticatus
Rhodesia, South Africa
A. b. dumetorum
E Europe, W & C Asia, N Iran, Himalayas, India, Burma
Acrocephalus scirpaceus (Reed Warbler)
A. s. scirpaceus
Europe, W Russia » WC & E Africa
A. s. fuscus
Asia Minor, C Asia » E Africa

Acrocephalus palustris (Marsh Warbler)
N Europe, Russia » NW & SE Africa
Acrocephalus melanopogon (Moustached Warbler)
A. m. melanopogon
Europe, N Africa
A. m. mimica
C Asia, S Russia, Iraq, Iran, Afghanistan
A. m. albiventris
Krasnodor (USSR)
Acrocephalus arundinaceus (Great Reed Warbler)
A. a. arundinaceus
Europe, Asia Minor » NW, W & SC Africa
A. a. zarudnyi
S Russia C Asia » C Africa
A. a. griseldis
S Iran » E Africa
Acrocephalus orientalis (Oriental Great Reed Warbler)
SE Siberia, N China, » Philippine Is
Acrocephalus stentoreus (Clamorous Reed Warbler)
A. s. stentoreus
Egypt, Sinai
A. s. brunnescens
Iran, Afghanistan, NW India
A. s. amyae
N India, Thailand, Indochina
A. s. meridionalis
Sri Lanka
A. s. siebirsi
W Java
A. s. lentecaptus
Lombok I, Sumbawa I
A. s. sumbae
Moluccas, Sumba I
A. s. celebensis
Celebes
A. s. toxopei
Buru I
A. s. harterti
Philippine Is
A. s. meyeri
Bismarck Archipelago, Solomon Is
A. s. cervinus
N Queensland, New Guinea
A. s. gouldi
Western Australia
A. s. australis
SE Australia, Tasmania
Acrocephalus luscinia (Nightingale Reed Warbler)
A. l. luscinia
Guam I, Saipan I, Almagan I
A. l. syrinx
Caroline Is

A. l. yamashinae
Pagan I
A. l. nijoi
Agiguan I
A. l. astrolabii
unknown **e?**

Acrocephalus aedon (Thick-billed Reed Warbler)
A. a. aedon
NC Asia, Burma, Thailand, Indonesia
A. a. rufescens
NE Asia, Korea, Japan, Malaysia

Acrocephalus rehsei (Finsch's Reed Warbler)
Gilbert Is

Acrocephalus kingii (Hawaiian Reed Warbler)
Nihoa (Hawaii)

Acrocephalus aequinoctialis (Polynesian Reed Warbler)
A. a. aequinoctialis
Christmas I
A. a. pistor
Fanning I

Acrocephalus caffra (Long-billed Reed Warbler)
A. c. caffra
Tahiti I, Society Is
A. c. longirostris
Moorea I
A. c. garretti
Huatrine I **e?**

Acrocephalus atypha (Tuamotu Warbler)
A. a. atypha
NW Tuamotu Is
A. a. rava
SE Tuamotu Is
A. a. palmarum
Anaa I
A. a. niauensis
Niau I
A. a. erema
Makatea I
A. a. flavida
Napuka I

Acrocephalus mendanae (Marquesas Warbler)
A. m. mendanae
Takuata I
A. m. percernis
Nukuhiva I
A. m. consobrina
Motane I
A. m. fatuhivae
Fatuhiva I
A. m. idae
Ua Huka I

A. m. dido
Ua Pou I
A. m. aquilonis
Eiao I
A. m. postrema
Hatutu I

Acrocephalus vaughanii (Pitcairn Warbler)
A. v. vaughanii
Pitcairn I
A. v. rimitarae
Rimitara I
A. v. taiti
Henderson I
A. v. kerearako
Mangaia I (Cook Is)
A. v. kaoko
Mitiaro I (Cook Is)

Acrocephalus gracilirostris (Swamp Warbler)
A. g. neglecta
Lake Chad
A. g. tsanae
N Ethiopia
A. g. nilotica
Sudan, Uganda, W Kenya, E Zaire, N Zambia
A. g. jacksoni
NE Zaire, Uganda, S Sudan
A. g. parva
S Kenya
A. g. leptorhyncha
Tanzania, S Zaire, Angola to Mozambique
A. g. winterbottomi
E Angola, W Zambia
A. g. cunenensis
S Angola
A. g. gracilirostris
Namibia, Botswana, South Africa

Acrocephalus rufescens (Rufous Swamp Warbler)
A. r. rufescens
W & WC Africa
A. r. chadensis
Chad
A. r. nilotica
S Sudan to Zambia
A. r. foxi
E Zaire, SW Uganda
A. r. ansorgei
N Angola

Acrocephalus brevipennis (Cape Verde Swamp Warbler)
Cape Verde Is

Acrocephalus newtoni (Madagascar Swamp Warbler)
Madagascar

BEBRORNIS
Bebrornis rodericanus (Rodriguez Brush Warbler)
Rodriguez I
Bebrornis sechellensis (Seychelles Brush Warbler)
Cousin I

NESILLAS
Nesillas typica (Tsikirity Warbler)
N. t. ellisii
NW Madagascar
N. t. typica
C & E Madagascar
N. t. lentzii
S & W Madagascar
N. t. longicaudata
Anjouan I
N. t. brevicaudata
Great Comoro I
Nesillas mariae (Comoro Warbler)
Moheli I (Comores)
Nesillas aldabranus (Aldabra Warbler)
Aldabra I

THAMNORNIS
Thamnornis chloropetoides (Kiritika)
S Madagascar

CHLOROPETA
Chloropeta natalensis (Yellow Warbler)
C. n. batesi
E Nigeria, Cameroun, Gabon, E Zaire
C. n. massaica
Zaire to Ethiopia & Tanzania
C. n. major
Angola, S Zaire, Zambia
C. n. natalensis
S Tanzania, Malawi, Rhodesia, N South Africa
Chloropeta similis (Mountain Yellow Warbler)
Zaire to Sudan, Malawi, Tanzania
Chloropeta gracilirostris (Yellow Swamp Warbler)
C. g. gracilirostris
E Zaire, W Uganda
C. g. bensoni
Lake Mweru, NE Zambia

HIPPOLAIS
Hippolais icterina (Icterine Warbler)
H. i. icterina
C & E Europe, W Siberia » South Africa
H. i. alaria
Asia Minor, Iran
Hippolais polyglotta (Melodious Warbler)
SW Europe » NW & W Africa
Hippolais olivetorum (Olive-tree Warbler)
SE Europe, Asia Minor, N Africa

Hippolais languida (Upcher's Warbler)
Egypt, Syria to Afghanistan
Hippolais pallida (Olivaceous Warbler)
H. p. opaca
S Spain, NW Africa
H. p. elaeica
SE Europe, Iran, SE Asia » Ethiopia
H. p. reiseri
S Algeria, S Tunisia
H. p. pallida
Egypt, Sudan
H. p. laeneni
Lake Chad
Hippolais caligata (Booted Warbler)
H. c. caligata
C & E Russia » S & W India
H. c. annectens
Altai, NW Mongolia » N India
H. c. rama
E Iran to Pakistan

SYLVIA
Sylvia nisoria (Barred Warbler)
S. n. nisoria
C & E Europe, W Russia, E Africa
S. n. merzbacheri
N Iran, Afghanistan, C Asia
Sylvia hortensis (Orphean Warbler)
S. h. hortensis
S Europe, N & W Africa
S. h. crassirostris
Asia Minor, Iran, Afghanistan, Arabia
S. h. jerdoni
Pakistan, N India
S. h. balchanica
Iraq, W Iran
Sylvia leucomelaena (Red Sea Warbler)
S. l. leucomelaena
Saudi Arabia
S. l. blanfordi
Eritrea
S. l. somaliensis
NE Somalia
Sylvia borin (Garden Warbler)
S. b. borin
Europe, W Russia » WC Africa
S. b. pallida
C Asia, W Siberia » E Africa
S. b. woodwardi
N Iran
Sylvia atricapilla (Blackcap)
S. a. atricapilla
W Europe, W Russia » N & E Africa
S. a. dammholzi
Caucasus, Asia Minor, W Iran » E Africa
S. a. heineken
Madeira I
S. a. riphaea
W Siberia

S. a. pauluccii
Sardinia, Balearic Is
Sylvia communis (Whitethroat)
S. c. communis
Europe, N Africa, Russia » C & S Africa
S. c. icterops
Iran, Asia Minor » NW India
S. c. volgensis
Altai, W Siberia
Sylvia curruca (Lesser Whitethroat)
S. c. curruca
Europe, W Russia » N & C Africa
S. c. blythi
Siberia » Pakistan, India
S. c. talengitica
SW Altai, C Asia » N India
S. c. halimodendri
Kazakhstan, SC Asia » N India
S. c. minula
W Mongolia, Tibet, Pakistan, NW India
S. c. caucasica
Caucasus, Iran
S. c. margelanica
NE Tsinghai, Gobi, NW China
S. c. althaea
Transcaspia, Iran
S. c. monticola
S Russia, Turkistan
S. c. zagrossiensis
Iraqi, SW Iran
Sylvia nana (Desert Whitethroat)
S. n. nana
Iran, Afghanistan, Tibet, N India
S. n. deserti
N & NE Africa
S. n. theresae
NW India
Sylvia rüppelli (Rüppell's Warbler)
SE Europe, NE Africa
Sylvia melanocephala (Sardinian Warbler)
S. m. melanocephala
S Europe, N Africa
S. m. muricolor
Portugal
S. m. carmichael-lowi
SE Italy
S. m. leucogastra
Canary Is
S. m. pasiphaë
Rhodes, Crete
S. m. norrisae
Egypt
S. m. momus
Syria, Israel, Sinai
Sylvia melanothorax (Cyprus Warbler)
Cyprus

Sylvia mystacea (Ménétries' Warbler)
NE Africa, Iran, Afghanistan
Sylvia cantillans (Subalpine Warbler)
S. c. cantillans
SW Europe, NW Africa
S. c. albistriata
SE Europe, Asia Minor, NE Africa
S. c. inornata
N Africa
Sylvia conspicillata (Spectacled Warbler)
S. c. conspicillata
S Europe, N Africa
S. c. orbitalis
Canary Is, Cape Verde Is
Sylvia deserticola (Tristram's Warbler)
S. d. deserticola
Algeria, Tunisia
S. d. maroccana
W Morocco
Sylvia ticehursti (Meinertzhagen's Warbler)
Morocco
Sylvia undata (Dartford Warbler)
S. u. dartfordiensis
S England
S. u. tingitana
Morocco
S. u. undata
SW Europe
S. u. toni
Portugal, S Spain, N Africa
S. u. corsa
Corsica, Sardinia
Sylvia sarda (Marmora's Warbler)
S. s. balearica
Balearic Is
S. s. sarda
Corsica, Sardinia, S France, N Africa

PHYLLOSCOPUS
Phylloscopus trochilus (Willow Warbler)
P. t. trochilus
Britain, W Europe » W & WC Africa
P. t. acredula
Scandinavia, C & E Europe, W Siberia »
C Africa
P. t. yakutensis
N & NE Asia » E Africa
Phylloscopus collybitus (Chiff-chaff)
P. c. abietinus
N & E Europe » Asia Minor, Arabia,
Somalia
P. c. collybitus
W & S Europe » N Africa
P. c. canariensis
Canary Is

P. c. exsul
  Lanzarote I
P. c. lorenzii
  Caucasus
P. c. ibericus
  Iberia, Algeria
P. c. tristis
  C Asia, N India, Bangladesh
P. c. sindianus
  Pamir, W Himalayas
Phylloscopus neglectus (Plain Willow Warbler)
  NE Iran, N Afghanistan
Phylloscopus bonelli (Bonelli's Warbler)
P. b. bonelli
  S Europe, N Africa
P. b. orientalis
  Balkans, Asia Minor
Phylloscopus tytleri (Tytler's Willow Warbler)
  Pakistan, India
Phylloscopus sibilatrix (Wood Warbler)
  WC & NE Europe » C Africa
Phylloscopus affinis (Tickell's Willow Warbler)
  S Tibet, India, Burma, W China
Phylloscopus subaffinis (Grant's Leaf Warbler)
P. s. arcanus
  W Nepal
P. s. subaffinis
  W China, N Burma, N Indochina
Phylloscopus griseolus (Jerdon's Willow Warbler)
  C Asia, W Himalayas » N India
Phylloscopus fuligiventer (Smoky Warbler)
P. f. fuligiventer
  Bhutan, Sikkim, Himalayas
P. f. tibetanus
  SE Tibet, SW Sikiang
Phylloscopus fuscatus (Dusky Warbler)
P. f. fuscatus
  C & NE Asia » India, China, Burma, Thailand
P. f. weigoldi
  S Tibet, E Himalayas, W China
Phylloscopus armandii (Milne-Edwards' Willow Warbler)
P. a. armandii
  Mongolia, E China
P. a. perplexus
  Sikiang, W China
Phylloscopus schwarzi (Radde's Bush Warbler)
  NC & NE Asia » Burma, Thailand, Indochina

Phylloscopus pulcher (Orange-barred Willow Warbler)
P. p. kangrae
  NW Himalayas
P. p. pulcher
  N Burma, E Nepal, S Tibet
Phylloscopus inornatus (Yellow-browed Warbler)
P. i. inornatus
  N India, Assam, Bangladesh
P. i. humei
  C Asia, Himalayas, Altai
P. i. mandellii
  Burma, Sikkim, S Tibet, W China
Pylloscopus subviridis (Brooks's Willow Warbler)
  Afghanistan, Pakistan, N India
Phylloscopus proregulus (Pallas's Leaf Warbler)
P. p. proregulus
  NE & C Asia, Sakhalin I, N China
P. p. simlaensis
  Afghanistan, NW India, W Himalayas
P. p. chloronotus
  E Himalayas, W China » Thailand, Malaysia
P. p. kansuensis
  NW China
Phylloscopus maculipennis (Grey-faced Willow Warbler)
P. m. virens
  NW Himalayas
P. m. centralis
  W & C Nepal
P. m. maculipennis
  E Himalayas, SW China, N Burma, N Indochina
P. m. debilis
  SW China
Phylloscopus borealis (Arctic Warbler)
P. b. borealis
  NE Europe, N & NE Asia » SE China, Philippine Is
P. b. hylebata
  C Asia, Mongolia, Sakhalin I » Indochina
P. b. xanthodryas
  Kamchatka, N Kurile Is » Philippine Is, Indochina
P. b. examinandus
  S Kurile Is, Japan » Borneo, Sumatra
P. b. kennikotti
  Alaska
P. b. talovka
  N Russia, N Siberia, NW Mongolia
P. b. transbaicalicus
  E Siberia, N Mongolia

Phylloscopus magnirostris (Large-billed Willow Warbler)
Himalayas, India, W China, E Tibet

Phylloscopus trochiloides (Greenish Warbler)
P. t. viridanus
NE Europe, W & C Asia » Pakistan, W India
P. t. trochiloides
Himalayas, Tibet, W China, Burma
P. t. ludlowi
Ladakh, NW Himalayas
P. t. obscuratus
NW China
P. t. plumbeitarsus
E Asia, Manchuria » Thailand, Indochina

Phylloscopus nitidus (Green Willow Warbler)
Caucasus, Iran, W India

Phylloscopus tenellipes (Pale-legged Willow Warbler)
P. t. tenellipes
E Manchuria, Korea, Sakhalin I » Burma, Indochina
P. t. borealoides
Japan » N Vietnam

Phylloscopus occipitalis (Large Crowned Willow Warbler)
C Asia, Afghanistan » W India

Phylloscopus coronatus (Temminck's Crowned Willow Warbler)
NE Asia, Korea, Japan » Indochina, Malaysia

Phylloscopus ijimae (Ijima's Willow Warbler)
Izu Is

Phylloscopus reguloides (Blyth's Crowned Willow Warbler)
P. r. kashmirensis
NW India
P. r. reguloides
NE India, Nepal, Bangladesh
P. r. assamensis
Assam, N Burma, SE Tibet
P. r. claudiae
W China
P. r. fokiensis
S China
P. r. ticehursti
S Vietnam

Phylloscopus davisoni (White-tailed Willow Warbler)
P. d. davisoni
E & S Sikang » Burma, N Indochina
P. d. disturbans
SW China
P. d. ogilviegranti
SE China, N Vietnam

P. d. klossi
S Indochina

Phylloscopus presbytes (Timor Leaf Warbler)
P. p. presbytes
Timor I
P. p. floris
Flores I

Phylloscopus cantator (Yellow-faced Leaf Warbler)
N India

Phylloscopus ricketti (Rickett's Willow Warbler)
P. r. ricketti
S China, N Vietnam
P. r. goodsoni
S Hainan I

Phylloscopus trivirgatus (Island Leaf Warbler)
P. t. parvirostris
Malaysia
P. t. trivirgatus
Sumatra, Java, Bali I, NW Borneo
P. t. kinabaluensis
NE Borneo
P. t. sarawacensis
W Borneo
P. t. nesophilus
SC Celebes
P. t. sarasinorum
S Celebes
P. t. capitalis
SE Celebes
P. t. waterstradti
Moluccas
P. t. everetti
Buru I
P. t. matthiae
St Matthias Is
P. t. avicola
Great Kei Is
P. t. ceramensis
Ceram I
P. t. maforensis
Numfor I
P. t. misoriensis
Biak I
P. t. poliocephala
NW New Guinea
P. t. albigularis
WC New Guinea
P. t. paniaiae
W New Guinea
P. t. cyclopum
N New Guinea
P. t. henrietta
N Halmahera I

P. t. giulianettii
C & SE New Guinea

P. t. hamlini
Goodenough I

P. t. becki
Gualdalcanal I, Malaita I

P. t. bougainvillei
Bougainville I

P. t. pallescens
Kulambangra I

P. t. makirensis
San Cristobal I

P. t. crookshanki
D'Entrecasteaux Archipelago

P. t. nigrorum
Luzon I, Negros I, Mindoro I

P. t. diuttae
NE Mindanao I

P. t. mindanensis
Mindanao I

P. t. malindangensis
Mt Malindang (Mindanao I)

P. t. flavostriatus
Mindanao I

P. t. petersoni
Palawan I

P. t. moorhousei
New Britain

P. t. leletensis
New Ireland

Phylloscopus amoenus (Kulambangra Warbler)
Kulambangra I

Phylloscopus olivaceus (Philippine Leaf Warbler)
Philippine Is

Phylloscopus cebuensis (Dubois' Leaf Warbler)

P. c. cebuensis
Cebu I, Negros I

P. c. luzonensis
N Luzon I

P. c. sorsogonensis
S Luzon I

Phylloscopus ruficapilla (Yellow-throated Woodland Warbler)

P. r. ochrogularis
W Tanzania

P. r. minullus
SE Kenya, E Tanzania

P. r. johnstonei
SW Tanzania, Malawi, Rhodesia

P. r. quelimanensis
N Mozambique

P. r. alacris
Manica e Sofala (Mozambique)

P. r. ruficapilla
E Transvaal, Natal, S Cape Province

Phylloscopus laurae (Mrs Boulton's Woodland Warbler)

P. l. eustacei
SE Zaire, NE Zambia

P. l. laurae
Angola, W Zambia

Phylloscopus laetus (Red-faced Woodland Warbler)

P. l. schoutedeni
E Zaire

P. l. laetus
Rwanda, W Uganda

Phylloscopus budongoensis (Uganda Woodland Warbler)
E Zaire, Uganda, W Kenya

Phylloscopus herberti (Black-capped Woodland Warbler)

P. h. herberti
Fernando Po I

P. h. camerunensis
S Nigeria, Cameroun Mt

Phylloscopus umbrovirens (Brown Woodland Warbler)

P. u. umbrovirens
N & C Ethiopia, Somalia

P. u. mackenzianus
S Sudan, Uganda, Kenya

P. u. omoensis
W & S Ethiopia

P. u. wilhelmi
E Zaire

P. u. alpinus
W Uganda

P. u. dorchadichrous
NE Tanzania

P. u. fugglescouchmani
E Tanzania

SEICERCUS

Seicercus burkii (Yellow-eyed Flycatcher Warbler)

S. b. whistleri
Himalayas

S. b. burkii
Assam, SE Tibet, Nepal

S. b. tephrocephala
N Thailand, Burma

S. b. distincta
NW Thailand, W China

S. b. latouchei
SW China

S. b. valentini
S China

S. b. intermedia
S China, Indochina

S. b. cognita
NW Fukien

***Seicercus poliogenys* (Grey-cheeked Flycatcher Warbler)**
N India, N Burma

***Seicercus affinis* (Allied Flycatcher Warbler)**
Himalayas, S China, Burma, Indonesia

***Seicercus montis* (Yellow-breasted Flycatcher Warbler)**
S. m. davisoni
Malaysia
S. m. montis
Borneo
S. m. xanthopygius
Palawan I
S. m. floris
S Flores I
S. m. paulinae
Timor I
S. m. neglecta
Waigeu I, Misol I

***Seicercus castaneiceps* (Chestnut Flycatcher Warbler)**
S. c. castaneiceps
Assam, Nepal
S. c. collinsi
N Thailand
S. c. butleri
Malaysia
S. c. muelleri
Sumatra
S. c. stresemanni
S Laos
S. c. sinensis
N Indochina, S & W China
S. c. joungi
S Thailand
S. c. annamensis
S Vietnam

***Seicercus xanthoschista* (Grey-headed Flycatcher Warbler)**
S. x. albosuperciliaris
Pakistan, NW India
S. x. xanthoschista
Sikkim, Bhutan, Nepal
S. x. tephrodiras
E Assam, Burma
S. x. flavogularis
Assam, Burma

***Seicercus grammiceps* (Sunda Flycatcher Warbler)**
S. g. sumatrana
Sumatra
S. g. grammiceps
Java, Bali I

***Abroscopus hodgsoni* (Broad-billed Flycatcher Warbler)**
A. h. hodgsoni
Himalayas, Burma
A. h. tonkinensis
N Vietnam

***Abroscopus albogularis* (White-throated Flycatcher Warbler)**
A. a. albogularis
Assam, Nepal
A. a. hugonis
N Thailand
A. a. fulvifacies
S China

***Abroscopus superciliaris* (Yellow-bellied Flycatcher Warbler**
A. s. albigularis
E Himalayas
A. s. superciliaris
N India, Burma, W Thailand
A. s. drasticus
N India, SW Thailand
A. s. smythiesi
Burma
A. s. sakaiorum
Malaysia, Sumatra
A. s. schwaneri
Borneo
A. s. vordermani
Java
A. s. bambusarum
S Thailand

***Abroscopus schisticeps* (Black-faced Flycatcher Warbler)**
A. s. schisticeps
Nepal
A. s. flavimentalis
SE Tibet, Burma
A. s. ripponi
W China

***Regulus calendula* (Ruby-crowned Kinglet**
R. c. calendula
N & E Canada, E USA » Central America
R. c. arizonensis
Arizona
R. c. cineraceus
SW USA, W Mexico
R. c. obscurus
Guadelupe I (Mexico)

***Regulus regulus* (Goldcrest)**
R. r. anglorum
British Isles
R. r. regulus
Europe, Asia Minor, Russia, WC Asia
R. r. azoricus
San Miguel (Azores)

R. r. sanctaemariae
  Santa Maria (Azores)
R. r. inermis
  Azores Is
R. r. interni
  Corsica, Sardinia
R. r. buturlini
  Crimea, Caucasus
R. r. hyrcanus
  N Iran
R. r. coatsi
  W Siberia, Altai
R. r. tristis
  C Asia
R. r. himalayensis
  W Himalayas
R. r. sikkimensis
  Nepal, E Himalayas, NW China
R. r. japonensis
  NE Asia, Japan, N China, Manchuria
R. r. yunnanensis
  SE Tibet, SW China

Regulus ignicapillus (Firecrest)
R. i. ignicapillus
  C & S Europe, Asia Minor
R. i. madeirensis
  Madeira I
R. i. balearicus
  Balearic Is, N Africa
R. i. teneriffae
  Canary Is

Regulus goodfellowi (Taiwan Firecrest)
  Taiwan

Regulus satrapa (Golden-crowned Kinglet)
R. s. amoensis
  W Canada, W USA » W Mexico,
    Guatemala
R. s. satrapa
  SE Canada, E USA » NE Mexico
R. s. clarus
  S Mexico, Central America

Leptopoecile sophiae (Severtzov's Tit Warbler)
L. s. sophiae
  Pakistan, NW India, C Asia
L. s. stoliczkae
  SC Asia, W Gobi Desert
L. s. major
  E Tien Shan
L. s. obscura
  NW China, Tibet, E Himalayas

Leptopoecile elegans (Crested Tit Warbler)
L. e. meissneri
  SE Tibet
L. e. elegans
  S China

Scotocerca inquieta (Streaked Scrub Warbler)
S. i. theresae
  S Morocco
S. i. saharae
  SE Morocco, Algeria
S. i. harterti
  Cyrenaica
S. i. grisea
  W Arabia
S. i. buryi
  S Arabia
S. i. inquieta
  E Egypt, N Arabia
S. i. platyura
  Transcaspia, Afghanistan
S. i. striata
  Iran, Baluchistan, Pakistan, NW India
S. i. montana
  Turgak, USSR

Rhopophilus pekinensis (White-browed Chinese Warbler)
R. p. albosuperciliaris
  Tarim Basin to Lop Nor
R. p. leptorhynchus
  Kansu, NE Tsinghai
R. p. pekinensis
  S Manchuria, Korea, Shansi, Ningsia

Cisticola textrix (Tink-tink Cisticola)
C. t. bulubulu
  W & C Angola, W Zambia
C. t. anselli
  E Angola, NW Zambia
C. t. major
  Transvaal, E Cape Province
C. t. marleyi
  N Natal
C. t. textrix
  SW Cape Province

Cisticola brunnescens (Pectoral-patch Cisticola)
C. b. mbangensis
  Cameroun
C. b. lynesi
  Cameroun
C. b. wambera
  W Ethiopia
C. b. brunnescens
  E Ethiopia, Somalia
C. b. midcongo
  W Zaire
C. b. cinnamomea
  E Zaire, Tanzania, Zambia, Rhodesia

C. b. hindii
W Kenya, N Tanzania
C. b. nakuruensis
Kenya, Tanzania
C. b. egregia
S Rhodesia, E Transvaal, Natal
Cisticola ayresii (Wing-snapping Cisticola)
C. a. gabun
Gabon
C. a. imatong
S Sudan
C. a. entebbe
E Zaire, Uganda, NW Tanzania
C. a. itombwensis
E Zaire
C. a. mauensis
Kenya
C. a. ayresii
C, E & SE Africa
Cisticola eximia (Black-necked Cisticola)
C. e. occidens
Guinea to Nigeria
C. e. winneba
S Ghana
C. e. eximia
NE Zaire to Sudan, Ethiopia
Cisticola dambo (Cloud-scraping Cisticola)
C. d. kasai
C Zaire
C. d. dambo
Angola, S Zaire, Zambia
Cisticola exilis (Gold-capped Cisticola)
C. e. tytleri
Bangladesh, Assam, Nepal, N India, China
C. e. erythrocaphala
S India
C. e. equicaudata
Thailand
C. e. lineocapilla
Java, Bali I, Northern Territory (Australia)
C. e. rustica
Celebes, Moluccas, Philippine Is
C. e. exilis
Australia
C. e. diminuta
Solomon Is, N Queensland, New Guinea
C. e. alexandrae
NW Australia, W Queensland
C. e. mixta
S Queensland
C. e. volitans
Taiwan, SW China
C. e. courtoisi
Kiangsi, Fukien
C. e. semirufa
Philippine Is
C. e. polionota
Bismarck Archipelago

Cisticola juncidis (Zitting Cisticola)
(Fan-tailed Warbler)
C. j. juncidis
S Europe, Asia Minor, Egypt
C. j. intermedia
Balearic Is
C. j. cisticola
Iberian peninsula, NW Africa
C. j. annae
Cyprus
C. j. neurotica
Syria, Iraq
C. j. uropygialis
W & NC Africa
C. j. perennia
E Africa
C. j. terrestris
S Africa
C. j. cursitans
Pakistan, India, Sri Lanka
C. j. salimalii
SW India
C. j. omalura
Sri Lanka
C. j. malaya
Malaysia
C. j. brunneiceps
Japan, Batjan I
C. j. tinnabulans
E China, Philippine Is
C. j. nigrostriatus
Palawan I
C. j. fuscicapilla
Lesser Sunda Is, Moluccas, Celebes
C. j. leanyeri
Northern Territory (Australia)
C. j. normani
W Queensland
Cisticola haesitata (Socotra Cisticola)
Socotra I
Cisticola cherina (Madagascar Cisticola)
Madagascar
Cisticola aridula (Desert Cisticola)
C. a. aridula
Niger, Chad, Sudan
C. a. lavendulae
Ethiopia, Somalia
C. a. tanganyika
Kenya, Tanzania
C. a. lobito
S Angola
C. a. perplexa
E Angola, S Zambia
C. a. kalahari
Namibia
C. a. traylori
NE Angola, W Zambia

***Cisticola natalensis* (Croaking Cisticola)**
  C. n. strangei
    Senegal to W & C Zaire
  C. n. inexpectata
    Ethiopia
  C. n. argentea
    S Ethiopia, N Kenya
  C. n. tonga
    Sudan
  C. n. valida
    E Zaire, W Sudan, NW Kenya,
    NW Tanzania
  C. n. kapitensis
    C Kenya
  C. n. littoralis
    E Kenya, E Tanzania
  C. n. katanga
    NE Angola, S Zaire, Zambia
  C. n. huambo
    N & C Angola
  C. n. natalensis
    SE Africa
  C. n. willi
    W Angola
  C. n. holubi
    NE Botswana, SW Rhodesia
***Cisticola robusta* (Stout Cisticola)**
  C. r. schraderi
    S Eritrea
  C. r. robusta
    Ethiopia
  C. r. omo
    SW Ethiopia
  C. r. santae
    Cameroun
  C. r. nuchalis
    NE Zaire, S Sudan, N Kenya, NW Tanzania
  C. r. ambigua
    C & S Kenya, NE Tanzania
  C. r. angolensis
    N & C Angola, NW Zambia
  C. r. awemba
    SW Tanzania, NE Zambia
***Cisticola aberdare* (Aberdare Mountain
Cisticola)**
    C Kenya
***Cisticola subruficapilla* (Red-headed
Cisticola)**
  C. s. newtoni
    Mossamedes, Angola
  C. s. karaensis
    Namibia
  C. s. namacua
    NW Cape Province
  C. s. subruficapilla
    SW Cape Province
  C. s. jamesi
    E Cape Province

***Cisticola lais* (Wailing Cisticola)**
  C. l. distincta
    E Uganda, N Kenya
  C. l. mashona
    E Rhodesia, N Transvaal
  C. l. namba
    C Angola
  C. l. semifasciata
    S Tanzania, Malawi, N Mozambique
  C. l. lais
    SE Southern Africa
  C. l. monticola
    S Transvaal
  C. l. maculata
    SW & S Cape Province
  C. l. oreobates
    Mozambique
***Cisticola rufilata* (Grey Cisticola)**
  C. r. ansorgei
    Angola to Malawi
  C. r. rufilata
    N Namibia to W Transvaal
  C. r. vicinior
    Rhodesia
***Cisticola cinereola* (Ashy Cisticola)**
  C. c. cinerola
    E & S Ethiopia
  C. c. schillingsi
    N & E Kenya
***Cisticola restricta* (Tana River Cisticola)**
    Tana river, Kenya
***Cisticola chiniana* (Rattling Cisticola)**
  C. c. simplex
    S Sudan, N Kenya
  C. c. victoria
    W Kenya, N Tanzania
  C. c. fricki
    Ethiopia, N Kenya
  C. c. humilis
    C Kenya
  C. c. fischeri
    E Zaire, Tanzania
  C. c. ukamba
    SW Kenya, Tanzania
  C. c. heterophrys
    E Kenya, E Tanzania
  C. c. fortis
    S Zaire, Angola, N Zambia
  C. c. emendata
    S Tanzania, N Malawi, N Mozambique
  C. c. procera
    C Malawi, C Mozambique
  C. c. frater
    Namibia, N Botswana, W Zambia,
    S Angola

C. c. huilensis
Huila, Angola
C. c. smithers
NE Botswana, S Zambia
C. c. campestris
S Mozambique, Natal
C. c. chiniana
E Botswana, Rhodesia, Transvaal
Cisticola bodessa (Boran Cisticola)
C. b. bodessa
E Sudan, S Ethiopia, N Kenya
C. b. kaffensis
Kaffa (S Ethiopia)
Cisticola njombe (Churring Cisticola)
C. n. njombe
S Tanzania
C. n. mariae
W Malawi
Cisticola ruficeps (Red-pate Cisticola)
C. r. guinea
Gambia to N Nigeria
C. r. ruficeps
Central African Republic to Sudan
C. r. scotoptera
E Sudan, N Ethiopia
C. r. mongalla
S Sudan, N Uganda
Cisticola nana (Tiny Cisticola)
S Ethiopia, E Kenya, N Tanzania
Cisticola brachyptera (Siffling Cisticola)
C. b. brachyptera
Senegal to Sudan, Uganda
C. b. zedlitzi
Ethiopia
C. b. hypoxantha
SE Sudan, N Uganda
C. b. reichenowi
N Kenya
C. b. ankole
SW Uganda, NW Tanzania
C. b. kericho
C & S Kenya
C. b. katonae
S Kenya, N Tanzania
C. b. loanda
C Angola, S Zaire, Zambia
C. b. isabellina
S Tanzania, Malawi, Rhodesia,
Mozambique
Cisticola rufa (Rufous Cisticola)
Gambia to N Cameroun
Cisticola troglodytes (Foxy Cisticola)
C. t. troglodytes
Niger to Sudan, Kenya
C. t. ferruginea
E Sudan, W Ethiopia

Cisticola fulvicapilla (Piping Cisticola)
C. f. dispar
Angola
C. f. muelleri
Zambia to Mozambique
C. f. hallae
S Angola, NE Namibia, NW Botswana
C. f. nigricapilla
N Namibia, N Botswana, Rhodesia,
Transvaal
C. f. lebombo
N Natal
C. f. fulvicapilla
S Natal, Cape Province
C. f. silberbaueri
SW Cape Province
C. f. dexter
Botswana, S Zambia
Cisticola angusticauda (Tabora Cisticola)
SW Kenya to Zambia
Cisticola aberrans (Lazy Cisticola)
C. a. petrophila
N Nigeria to Sudan & NE Zaire
C. a. admiralis
Mali & Sierra Leone to Ghana
C. a. emini
E Zaire, NW Tanzania
C. a. nyika
NE Zambia, Botswana to Mozambique
C. a. aberrans
Transvaal, Natal
C. a. minor
E Cape Province, S Natal
Cisticola lateralis (Whistling Cisticola)
C. l. lateralis
Gambia to Cameroun
C. l. modesta
N Angola to Gabon, W Zaire
C. l. antinorii
NE Zaire, Sudan, Uganda
C. l. vincenti
Angola, S Zaire
Cisticola woosnami (Trilling Cisticola)
C. w. woosnami
E Zaire, Uganda to N Malawi
C. w. lufira
SE Zaire, Zambia, W Tanzania
C. w. schusteri
N & E Tanzania
Cisticola anonyma (Chattering Cisticola)
Ghana to Zaire, Angola
Cisticola bulliens (Bubbling Cisticola)
N & C Angola
Cisticola erythrops (Red-faced Cisticola)
C. e. erythrops
Gambia to Zaire
C. e. pyrrhomitra
Ethiopia, S Sudan

C. e. nilotica
SW Sudan

C. e. sylvia
E Zaire, Sudan to Tanzania

C. e. lepe
N & S Angola

C. e. nyasa
SE Africa

Cisticola cantans (Singing Cisticola)

C. c. swanzii
Gambia to S Nigeria

C. c. concolor
Niger to Sudan

C. c. adamauae
Cameroun, NW Zaire

C. c. cantans
N Ethiopia

C. c. belli
E Zaire & S Sudan to Tanzania

C. c. pictipennis
Kenya, N Tanzania

C. c. munzneri
Zambia to Mozambique

Cisticola hunteri (Hunter's Cisticola)

C. h. masaba
NW Kenya

C. h. prinioides
N Kenya

C. h. hunteri
C Kenya

C. h. hypernephala
NE Tanzania

Cisticola chubbi (Chubb's Cisticola)

C. c. discolor
Cameroun Mt

C. c. adametzi
highlands of Cameroun

C. c. chubbi
NE Zaire, Kenya, Tanzania

C. c. marungensis
Marungu highland (E Zaire)

C. c. nigriloris
S Tanzania, Malawi

Cisticola galactotes (Winding Cisticola)

C. g. amphilecta
Senegal to Cameroun, N Zaire

C. g. zalingei
N Cameroun to W Sudan

C. g. grisea
Gabon

C. g. lugubris
Ethiopia

C. g. marginata
S Sudan, N Uganda

C. g. haematocephala
S Somalia, E Kenya, E Tanzania

C. g. nyansae
S Uganda, Kenya, NW Tanzania

C. g. suahelica
E Zaire, Zambia

C. g. schoutedeni
NW Zambia

C. g. luapula
Angola, Namibia to Mozambique

C. g. galactotes
Malawi, Rhodesia, Natal

C. g. stagnans
N Botswana

Cisticola carruthersi (Carruthers' Cisticola)
NE Zaire, Kenya

Cisticola pipiens (Chirping Cisticola)

C. p. congo
E Angola, S Zaire, Zambia, N Botswana

C. p. pipiens
S Angola

Cisticola tinniens (Levaillant's Cisticola)

C. t. dyleffi
E Zaire

C. t. oreophila
C Kenya

C. t. shiwae
NE Zambia, SE Zaire

C. t. perpulla
Angola

C. t. tinniens
SE Africa

PRINIA

Prinia subflava (Tawny-flanked Prinia)

P. s. subflava
Senegal to Ethiopia

P. s. melanorhyncha
Sierra Leone to Gabon

P. s. pallescens
Mali, Niger, Sudan

P. s. tenella
C Uganda, Kenya, Tanzania

P. s. affinis
SE Zaire, Zambia to Mozambique

P. s. kasokae
N Angola

P. s. graueri
C Angola, S Zaire, W Zambia

P. s. bechuanae
N Botswana, S Angola, N Namibia

P. s. pondoensis
E Cape Province, Natal

P. s. terricolor
Pakistan, N India

P. s. inornata
SE & C India

P. s. franklinii
SW India

P. s. insularis
Sri Lanka

P. s. fusca
Nepal, Assam, Bangladesh

P. s. blanfordi
Burma
P. s. blythi
Java
P. s. herberti
S Thailand, C Indochina
P. s. extensicauda
W & S China, N Indochina
P. s. formosa
Taiwan
Prinia flavicans (Black-chested Prinia)
P. f. bihe
E Angola, W Zambia
P. f. ansorgei
S Angola
P. f. flavicans
Namibia, Botswana
P. f. ortleppi
N Cape Province, Transvaal, Rhodesia
Prinia maculosa (Karroo Prinia)
P. m. maculosa
Namibia, Botswana, W Cape Province
P. m. hypoxantha
E Cape Province, Natal, E Transvaal
Prinia somalica (Pale Prinia)
P. s. somalica
N Somalia
P. s. erlangeri
S Ethiopia, S Somalia, SE Sudan, N Kenya
Prinia leucopogon (White-chinned Prina)
P. l. leucopogon
Gabon to Zambia
P. l. reichenowi
NE Zaire, S Sudan, Kenya, Tanzania
Prinia leontica (Sierra Leone Prinia)
Sierra Leone to Ghana
Prinia robertsi (Roberts' Prinia)
E Rhodesia
Prinia substriata (White-breasted Prinia)
W & C Cape Province
Prinia molleri (Sao Thomé Prinia)
Sao Thomé I
Prinia bairdii (Banded Prinia)
P. b. bairdii
Cameroun, Gabon
P. b. melanops
E Zaire, W Kenya
P. b. obscura
Kivu, Ruwenzori
P. b. heinrichi
N Angola
Prinia pectoralis (Rufous-eared Prinia)
P. p. ocularia
N Namibia, Botswana, N Cape Province
P. p. pectoralis
S Namibia, Cape Province, W Transvaal

Prinia gracilis (Graceful Prinia)
P. g. carlo
NE Sudan, Somalia
P. g. gracilis
Nile valley
P. g. deltae
Nile delta
P. g. natronensis
lower Egypt
P. g. palestinae
Suez to Syria
P. g. irakensis
Iraq to SW Iran
P. g. lepida
S Iran to NW India
P. g. hufufae
Bahrein I, Hasa, E Arabia
P. g. yemensis
S Arabia
P. g. carpenteri
Oman
Prinia socialis (Ashy Prinia)
P. s. stewarti
Pakistan, N India
P. s. inglisi
NE India, Nepal, Bhutan, Assam, Bangladesh
P. s. socialis
S India
P. s. brevicauda
Sri Lanka
Prinia rufescens (Lesser Brown Prinia)
P. r. rufescens
Bhutan, Nepal to Burma
P. r. extrema
Malaysia
P. r. peninsularis
S Thailand
P. r. objurgans
S China, N Vietnam
P. r. dalatensis
S Vietnam
Prinia hodgsoni (Franklin's Prinia)
P. h. rufula
Pakistan, Himalayas to Burma
P. h. albogularis
SW India
P. h. pectoralis
Sri Lanka
P. h. hodgsoni
N & C India, S Bangladesh, Burma
P. h. stevensi
NE India
P. h. confusa
N Bangladesh, Assam
P. h. erro
Thailand

Prinia flaviventris (Yellow-bellied Prinia)
P. f. sindiana
NW India, Pakistan
P. f. flaviventris
Bhutan, Himalayas, Bangladesh
P. f. delacouri
Thailand
P. f. sonitans
SE China, Taiwan, Hainan I
P. f. rafflesi
Malaysia, Sumatra, Java
P. f. halistona
Nias I
P. f. chaseni
Borneo
Prinia familiaris (Bar-winged Prinia)
P. f. olivacea
Sumatra, W Java
P. f. familiaris
E Java, Bali I
Prinia polychroa (Brown Hill Prinia)
P. p. cooki
S Burma
P. p. catharia
W China
P. p. striata
C China
P. p. parumstriata
SE China
P. p. polychroa
. Java
Prinia criniger (Hill Prinia)
P. c. striatula
W Pakistan
P. c. criniger
Himalayas, Assam
P. c. yunnanensis
N Burma, SW China
Prinia sylvatica (Jungle Prinia)
P. s. gangetica
Nepal, N India, Bangladesh
P. s. mahendrae
Orissa
P. s. sylvatica
S India
P. s. valida
Sri Lanka
Prinia atrogularis (White-browed Prinia)
P. a. atrogularis
Nepal, N India, SE Tibet
P. a. khasiana
Assam, Burma
P. a. erythropleura
Burma
P. a. superciliaris
SE China, Burma
P. a. waterstradti
Malaysia

P. a. albogularis
Sumatra
P. a. klossi
N Indochina
Prinia burnesi (Long-tailed Grass Warbler)
Pakistan, N India
Prinia cinerascens (Assam Prinia)
Assam, Bangladesh
Prinia buchanani (Rufous-fronted Prinia)
Pakistan, India
**Prinia cinereocapilla (Hodgson's
Long-tailed Warbler)**
N India

APALIS
Apalis flavida (Yellow-chested Apalis)
A. f. caniceps
Cameroun to Sudan, NW Kenya
A. f. viridiceps
NE Ethiopia
A. f. abyssinica
Illubabor, Ethiopia
A. f. malensis
SW Ethiopia, E Uganda, N Kenya
A. f. flavocincta
SW Uganda, Kenya
A. f. pugnax
Mt Kenya
A. f. tenerrima
E Kenya, Tanzania
A. f. golzi
SE Kenya, N Tanzania
A. f. neglecta
Angola to Mozambique
A. f. flavida
S Angola, Namibia, Botswana
A. f. florisuga
E Cape Province, Natal
A. f. renata
Sol do Save, Mozambique
Apalis binotata (Masked Apalis)
A. b. binotata
Cameroun to W Uganda
A. b. personata
SW Uganda, E Zaire
A. b. marungensis
SE Zaire
Apalis ruddi (Rudd's Apalis)
A. r. ruddi
S Mozambique, N Natal
A. r. caniviridis
S Malawi
Apalis jacksoni (Black-throated Apalis)
A. j. bambuluensis
N Cameroun
A. j. minor
S Cameroun, Central African Republic
A. j. jacksoni
SE Sudan, Uganda, Kenya, Angola

Apalis chariessa **(White-winged Apalis)**
Kenya to Mozambique

Apalis nigriceps **(Black-capped Apalis)**
A. n. nigriceps
Sierra Leone to Cameroun
A. n. collaris
NE Zaire, W Uganda

Apalis thoracica **(Bar-throated Apalis)**
A. t. fuscigularis
SE Kenya
A. t. griseiceps
SE Kenya, NE Tanzania
A. t. uluguru
E Tanzania
A. t. lynesi
N Mozambique
A. t. quarta
Mozambique
A. t. pareensis
NE Tanzania
A. t. iringae
S Tanzania
A. t. youngi
SW Tanzania, N Malawi
A. t. murina
NE Zambia, N Malawi
A. t. whitei
Zambia, Tanzania, Malawi
A. t. flavigularis
Malawi
A. t. rhodesiae
W Rhodesia
A. t. arnoldi
E Rhodesia
A. t. drakensbergensis
E Transvaal, N Natal
A. t. flaviventris
W & C Transvaal
A. t. spelonkensis
E Transvaal
A. t. lebomboensis
NE Natal
A. t. capensis
W Cape Province
A. t. venusta
E Cape Province, Natal
A. t. thoracica
S Cape Province

Apalis cinerea **(Grey Apalis)**
A. c. cinerea
Cameroun to N Tanzania
A. c. sclateri
Fernando Po I
A. c. grandis
Angola

Apalis alticola **(Brown-headed Apalis)**
A. a. marungensis
NE Zaire

A. a. alticola
S Tanzania, NE Zambia
A. a. brunneiceps
S Tanzania, Zambia, Malawi

Apalis karamojae **(Karamoja Apalis)**
E Uganda

Apalis rufogularis **(Buff-throated Apalis)**
A. r. rufogularis
Fernando Po I, S Nigeria to Gabon
A. r. sanderi
SW Nigeria
A. r. nigrescens
S Sudan to Zambia
A. r. angolensis
N Angola
A. r. brauni
C & S Angola

Apalis argentea **(Kungwe Apalis)**
A. a. argentea
W Tanzania
A. a. eidos
Idjwi Is, Kivu Lake

Apalis porphyrolaema **(Chestnut-throated Apalis)**
A. p. porphyrolaema
Uganda, Kenya, NE Tanzania
A. p. kaboboensis
E Zaire

Apalis sharpii **(Sharpe's Apalis)**
A. s. sharpii
Sierra Leone, Ivory Coast
A. s. bamendae
Cameroun
A. s. goslingi
Cameroun to N Zaire
A. s. strausae
SW Tanzania, Zambia, Malawi
A. s. chapini
SE Tanzania

Apalis melanocephala **(Black-headed Apalis)**
A. m. ellinorae
C Kenya
A. m. nigrodorsalis
C Kenya
A. m. moschi
SE Kenya, NE Tanzania
A. m. muhuluensis
S Tanzania
A. m. melanocephala
E Tanzania
A. m. lightoni
Malawi, Mozambique
A. m. fuliginosa
S Malawi
A. m. tenebricosa
Mozambique

A. m. adjacens
  N Mozambique
A. m. addenda
  Sol do Save, Mozambique
Apalis chirindensis (Chirinda Apalis)
  E Rhodesia
Apalis pulchra (Black-collared Apalis)
  A. p. pulchra
    Cameroun to S Sudan, Kenya
  A. p. murpheyi
    SE Zaire
Apalis ruwenzori (Collared Apalis)
  A. r. catiodes
    SW Lake Kivu (E Zaire)
  A. r. ruwenzori
    NW Lake Kivu
Apalis moreaui (Long-billed Apalis)
  A. m. moreaui
    NE Tanzania
  A. m. sousae
    N Mozambique
Apalis melanura (Angolan Slender-tailed Apalis)
  Angola, S Zaire

GRAMINICOLA
Graminicola bengalensis (Large Grass Warbler)
  G. b. bengalensis
    Himalayas, N India, Bangladesh
  G. b. sinica
    S China
  G. b. striata
    N Vietnam

SPHENOEACUS
Sphenoeacus mentalis (Moustached Grass Warbler)
  S. m. mentalis
    Guinea to Central African Republic &
      C Zaire
  S. m. granviki
    W Ethiopia
  S. m. amauroura
    S Sudan to N Zambia
  S. m. orientalis
    Tanzania
  S. m. grandis
    Angola to N Mozambique
  S. m. luangwae
    S Zambia
Sphenoeacus afer (Cape Grassbird)
  S. a. transvaalensis
    E Rhodesia, NE Transvaal
  S. a. excisus
    Rhodesia
  S. a. natalensis
    Transvaal, Natal
  S. a. intermedius
    E Cape Province

S. a. afer
  S Cape Province
Sphenoeacus pycnopygius (Damaraland Rock Jumper)
  S. p. pycnopygius
    S Angola, N Namibia
  S. p. spadix
    Huila, Angola

DROMAEOCERCUS
Dromaeocercus brunneus (Brown Feather-tailed Warbler)
  EC Madagascar
Dromaeocercus seebohmi (Seebohm's Feather-tailed Warbler)
  SC Madagascar

INCANA
Incana incana (Socotra Grass Warbler)
  Socotra I

SPILOPTILA
Spiloptila clamans (Cricket Warbler)
  Mali to N Ethiopia
Spiloptila rufifrons (Red-faced Warbler)
  S. r. rufifrons
    Sudan, Ethiopia, Somalia
  S. r. smithi
    SE Ethiopia to N Tanzania
  S. r. rufidorsalis
    SE Kenya

UROLAIS
Urolais epichlora (Green Longtail)
  U. e. epichlora
    N Cameroun
  U. e. mariae
    Fernando Po I
  U. e. cinderella
    W Cameroun

HELIOLAIS
Heliolais erythroptera (Red-winged Warbler)
  H. e. erythroptera
    Guinea to Nigeria
  H. e. jodoptera
    Cameroun to Sudan
  H. e. major
    Ethiopia
  H. e. rhodoptera
    W Kenya, Zambia to Mozambique

PHYLLOLAIS
Phyllolais pulchella (Buff-bellied Warbler)
  Chad, Ethiopia to Tanzania

DRYMOCICHLA
Drymocichla incana (Red-winged Grey Warbler)
  Cameroun to Uganda

Poliolais lopezi (White-tailed Warbler)

   P. l. lopezi
     Fernando Po I
   P. l. alexanderi
     Cameroun Mt
   P. l. manengubae
     Manenguba, Kupé Mt (Cameroun)

ORTHOTOMUS

Orthotomus sutorius (Long-tailed Tailor Bird)

   O. s. guzuratus
     NW Himalayas, N India
   O. s. patia
     Nepal, NE India, Burma
   O. s. sutorius
     Sri Lanka
   O. s. fernandonis
     Sri Lanka
   O. s. luteus
     NE Assam, N Burma
   O. s. inexpectatus
     W China
   O. s. longicauda
     S China
   O. s. maculicollis
     Malaysia
   O. s. edela
     Java

Orthotomus atrogularis (Black-necked Tailor Bird)

   O. a. nitidus
     Assam, Burma
   O. a. atrogularis
     Borneo, Malaysia, Sumatra
   O. a. humphreysi
     N Borneo
   O. a. major
     Anamba Is
   O. a. davao
     SE Mindanao I
   O. a. mearnsi
     Basilan I
   O. a. rabori
     Negros I
   O. a. chloronotus
     N Luzon I
   O. a. castaneiceps
     Masbate I, Panay I, Ticao I
   O. a. frontalis
     Bohol I, Leyte I, Mindanao I, Samar I

Orthotomus derbianus (Luzon Tailor Bird)

     S Catanduanes I, C Luzon I

Orthotomus ruficeps (Ashy Tailor Bird)

   O. r. ruficeps
     Sumatra, Malaysia, Java

   O. r. sepium
     Java
   O. r. borneonensis
     Borneo
   O. r. palliolatus
     Karimon Is
   O. r. concinnus
     Siberut I, Sipora I
   O. r. cagayanensis
     Cagayan Sulu I

Orthotomus sericeus (Red-headed Tailor Bird)

   O. s. hesperius
     Burma, Malaysia, Sumatra
   O. s. sericeus
     Borneo, Palawan I
   O. s. rubicundulus
     Sirhassen I, Natuna Is
   O. s. nuntius
     Balabac I, Cagayan Sulu I

Orthotomus cucullatus (Mountain Tailor Bird)

   O. c. coronatus
     E Himalayas, Assam
   O. c. malayensis
     Malaysia
   O. c. cucullatus
     Sumatra, Java, Bali I
   O. c. riedeli
     Celebes
   O. c. cinereicollis
     Borneo
   O. c. thais
     Thailand
   O. c. everetti
     Flores I
   O. c. dumasi
     Buru I
   O. c. batjanensis
     Batjan I
   O. c. viridicollis
     Palawan I
   O. c. philippinus
     Luzon I
   O. c. heterolaemus
     Mindanao I

Orthotomus cinereiceps (White-eared Tailor Bird)

     Basilan I, Mindanao I

Orthotomus samarensis (Samar Tailor Bird)

     Samar I, Bohol I, Leyte I

Orthotomus nigriceps (Black-headed Tailor Bird)

     Mindanao I

Orthotomus metopias (Red-capped Forest Warbler)

     Tanzania, N Mozambique

BATHMOCERCUS
Bathmocercus cerviniventris (Black-capped Rufous Warbler)
Sierra Leone, Ghana
Bathmocercus rufus (Black-faced Rufous Warbler)
B. r. rufus
Cameroun, Gabon
B. r. vulpinus
E Cameroun to Sudan, N Kenya

SCEPOMYCTER
Scepomycter winifredae (Mrs Moreau's Warbler)
E Tanzania

CAMAROPTERA
Camaroptera brachyura (Green-backed Camaroptera)
C. b. bororensis
SE Zaire to Mozambique
C. b. pileata
E Kenya, E Tanzania, Zanzibar
C. b. fugglescouchmani
S Tanzania, N Malawi
C. b. transitiva
Sabi river, Rhodesia
C. b. constans
S Mozambique, E Transvaal, N Natal
C. b. brachyura
SE Transvaal, S Cape Province, Natal
Camaroptera brevicaudata (Grey-backed Camaroptera)
C. b. brevicaudata
Senegal to Ethiopia
C. b tincta
Sierra Leone to Tanzania, S Zaire
C. b. abessinica
NE Sudan to Kenya
C. b. erlangeri
E Somalia, E Kenya, E Tanzania
C. b. griseigula
S Kenya, N Tanzania
C. b. aschani
E Zaire
C. b. harterti
W Angola
C. b. intercalata
S Zaire, Angola, S Zambia
C. b. sharpei
Southern Africa
Camaroptera fasciolata (Barred Camaroptera)
C. f. pallidior
S Angola
C. f. fasciolata
SW Africa
C. f. aurophila
W Transvaal

Camaroptera stierlingi (Stierling's Wren Warbler) 459
C. s. buttoni
N Malawi, NW Zambia
C. s. stierlingi
S Malawi, Tanzania, Mozambique
C. s. irwini
W Malawi, Zambia, S Rhodesia
C. s. pintoi
S Mozambique, E Transvaal
C. s. olivascens
Mozambique
Camaroptera simplex (Grey Wren Warbler)
C. s. simplex
Ethiopia, Somalia, N Kenya
C. s. undosus
S Kenya, Tanzania, Zambia
C. s. cinerea
S Zaire, N Angola
G. s. katangae
SE Zaire, W Zambia
C. s. huilae
S Angola
Camaroptera superciliaris (Yellow-browed Camaroptera)
C. s. willoughbyi
Sierra Leone to Ghana
C. s. flavigularis
S Nigeria to C Zaire
C. s. superciliaris
Fernando Po I
C. s. pulchra
N Angola, S Zaire
C. s. ugandae
E Zaire, Uganda
Camaroptera chloronota (Olive-green Camaroptera)
C. c. kelsalli
Senegal to Ghana
C. c. chloronota
Togo to Cameroun, W Zaire
C. c. kamitugaensis
E Zaire
C. c. toroensis
S Uganda, E Zaire

EURYPTILA
Euryptila subcinnamomea (Kopje Warbler)
W Namibia, NW Cape Province

HYPERGERUS
Hypergerus atriceps (Oriole Warbler)
Senegal to Central African Republic
Hypergerus lepida (Grey-capped Warbler)
Uganda, Kenya, Tanzania

Eremomela icteropygialis (Yellow-bellied Eremomela)

E. i. alexanderi
Niger, Chad, Sudan

E. i. griseoflava
Somalia, Ethiopia, N Kenya

E. i. abdominalis
C Tanzania

E. i. belli
SE Tanzania

E. i. polioxantha
E Angola to Mozambique

E. i. luandae
N Angola

E. i. puellula
S Angola

E. i. icteropygialis
Namibia, NW Cape Province

E. i. perimacha
NW Cape Province to W Transvaal

E. i. viriditincta
Lesotho

E. i. saturatior
C & E Cape Province

Eremomela salvadorii (Salvadori Eremomela)
Angola, S Zaire, W Zambia

Eremomela flavocrissalis Yellow-vented Eremomela)
Somalia, NE Kenya

Eremomela scotops (Green-cap Eremomela)

E. s. congensis
W & C Zaire

E. s. mentalis
E Zaire

E. s. citriniceps
E Zaire, Uganda, Tanzania

E. s. occipitalis
E Kenya, E Tanzania

E. s. angolensis
N Angola

E. s. pulchra
E Angola to Malawi

E. s. scotops
Botswana to Tanzania, Mozambique

E. s. chlorochlamys
Rhodesia

Eremomela canescens (Green-backed Eremomela)

E. c. elegans
Cameroun, Chad, W Sudan

E. c. abyssinica
Ethiopia, E Sudan

E. c. canescens
S Sudan, Uganda, W Kenya

Eremomela pusilla (Smaller Green-backed Eremomela)
Senegal to N Cameroun

Eremomela gregalis (Yellow-rumped Eremomela)

E. g. damarensis
N & C Namibia

E. g. gregalis
S Namibia, NW Cape Province

Eremomela badiceps (Brown-crowned Eremomela)

E. b. fantiensis
Sierra Leone to Ghana

E. b. badiceps
Fernando Po I, Cameroun to N Angola

E. b. latukae
S Sudan

Eremomela turneri (Turner's Eremomela)

E. t. kalindei
E & C Zaire

E. t. turneri
Uganda, W Kenya

Eremomela atricollis (Black-necked Eremomela)

E. a. venustula
NW Zambia, SW Zaire

E. a. atricollis
W Angola, SE Zaire, Zambia

Eremomela usticollis (Burnt-neck Eremomela)

E. u. usticollis
C Southern Africa

E. u. rensi
Mozambique, Malawi

SYLVIETTA

Sylvietta ruficapilla (Red-capped Crombec)

S. r. schoutedeni
W Tanzania

S. r. rufigenis
W & S Zaire

S. r. chubbi
E Zaire to Mozambique

S. r. mackayi
N Angola

S. r. ruficapilla
S Angola, W Zambia

S. r. gephyra
SE Zaire, SW Zambia

Sylvietta leucophrys (White-browed Crombec)

S. l. leucophrys
Uganda, N Kenya

S. l. chloronata
E Zaire, SW Uganda, W Tanzania

S. l. chapini
E Zaire

Sylvietta virens (Green Crombec)
  S. v. flaviventris
    Sierra Leone to Ghana
  S. v. nigeriae
    S Nigeria
  S. v. virens
    SE Nigeria to W Zaire
  S. v. baraka
    S Sudan, Uganda
  S. v. tando
    W Angola
  S. v. meridionalis
    C Angola
Sylvietta denti (Lemon-bellied Crombec)
  S. d. hardyi
    Sierra Leone to Ghana
  S. d. denti
    S Cameroun
Sylvietta whytii (Red-faced Crombec)
  S. w. abayensis
    SE Sudan, S Ethiopia, NW Kenya
  S. w. jacksoni
    S & E Uganda, Kenya, Tanzania
  S. w. minima
    E Kenya, E Tanzania
  S. w. whytii
    S Malawi, Rhodesia, Mozambique
Sylvietta brachyura (Northern Crombec)
  S. b. brachyura
    Senegal to Ethiopia
  S. b. carnapi
    N Cameroun, Central African Republic
  S. b. leucopsis
    Ethiopia, Sudan to N Tanzania
  S. b. dilutior
    SE Sudan, Uganda, W Kenya
Sylvietta philippae (Somali Short-billed Crombec)
  Somalia
Sylvietta rufescens (Long-billed Crombec)
  S. r. flecki
    N Angola
  S. r. adelphe
    E & SE Zaire
  S. r. ansorgei
    S Angola
  S. r. pallida
    Zambia, Botswana to Mozambique
  S. r. transvaalensis
    Rhodesia, E Botswana, Transvaal
  S. r. mossamedes
    S Angola
  S. r. rufescens
    Namibia, S Botswana, W Cape Province
  S. r. diverga
    E Cape Province

  S. r. resurga
    Natal
Sylvietta isabellina (Somali Long-billed Crombec)
  Ethiopia, Somalia, N Kenya

HEMITESIA
Hemitesia neumanni (Neumann's Short-tailed Warbler)
  E Zaire

GRAUERIA
Graueria vittata (Grauer's Warbler)
  E Zaire

PARISOMA
Parisoma subcaeruleum (Southern Tit Warbler)
  P. s. ansorgei
    S Angola
  P. s. cinerascens
    Namibia to W Rhodesia
  P. s. orpheanum
    C Natal
  P. s. subcaeruleum
    Transvaal, S Natal, E Cape Province
Parisoma layardi (Layard's Tit Warbler)
  P. l. aridicola
    Namibia, S Botswana, N & C Cape Province
  P. l. barnesi
    Lesotho
  P. l. layardi
    SW Cape Province
Parisoma lugens (Brown Tit Warbler)
  P. l. lugens
    N Ethiopia
  P. l. jacksoni
    E Zaire, Tanzania, Zambia, Malawi
  P. l. prigoginei
    SE Zaire
Parisoma bohmi (Banded Tit Warbler)
  P. b. somalicum
    Ethiopia, N Somalia
  P. b. marsabit
    N Kenya
  P. b. bohmi
    E & S Kenya, N Tanzania
Parisoma buryi (Yemen Tit Warbler)
  S Arabia

MACROSPHENUS
Macrosphenus concolor (Grey Longbill)
  M. c. concolor
    Sierra Leone to Uganda
  M. c. griscens
    Kamituga, Zaire
Macrosphenus pulitzeri (Pulitzer's Longbill)
  Angola

Macrosphenus kretschmeri (Kretschmer's
 Longbill)
   Tanzania, Mozambique
Macrosphenus flavicans (Yellow
 Longbill)
   M. f. flavicans
     Cameroun, Gabon
   M. f. leoninus
     Fernando Po I
   M. f. hypochondriacus
     E Zaire, W Uganda
   M. f. angolensis
     N Angola
Macrosphenus kempi (Kemp's Longbill)
   M. k. kempi
     Sierra Leone
   M. k. flammeus
     S Nigeria

RANDIA
Randia pseudozosterops (Marvantsetra
 Warbler)
   Madagascar

AMAUROCICHLA
Amaurocichla bocagei (Bocage's Longbill)
   Sao Thomé I

CHAETORNIS
Chaetornis striatus (Bristled Grass
 Warbler)
   Pakistan, N India

SCHOENICOLA
Schoenicola platyura (Broad-tailed
 Warbler)
   S. p. alexinae
     Sierra Leone to Angola, Tanzania
   S. p. brevirostris
     Southern Africa
   S. p. platyura
     SW India, Sri Lanka

MEGALURUS
Megalurus pryeri (Japanese Marsh
 Warbler)
   M. p. sinensis
     China
   M. p. pryeri
     Japan
Megalurus timoriensis (Tawny Marshbird)
   M. t. timoriensis
     Timor I
   M. t. stresemanni
     NW New Guinea
   M. t. mayri
     N New Guinea
   M. t. wahgiensis
     C New Guinea
   M. t. montanus
     C New Guinea

M. t. macrurus
   C & S E New Guinea
M. t. harterti
   E New Guinea
M. t. alpinus
   SE New Guinea
M. t. muscalis
   S New Guinea
M. t. celebensis
   Celebes
M. t. amboinensis
   Ambon I
M. t. interscapularis
   New Britain
M. t. alisteri
   N Western Australia, Northern Territory,
    N Queensland
M. t. oweni
   S Queensland, New South Wales
M. t. tweeddalei
   Luzon I, Panay I, Tablas I
M. t. mindorensis
   Mindoro I
M. t. alopex
   Bohol I, Cebu I, Leyte I
M. t. crex
   Mindanao I
Megalurus albolimbatus (Fly River Grass
 Warbler)
   SE New Guinea
Megalurus palustris (Striated Canegrass
 Warbler)
   M. p. toklao
     NE India to Indochina, S China
   M. p. palustris
     Java
   M. p. forbesi
     Luzon I Mindanao I
Megalurus gramineus (Little Marshbird)
   M. g. papuensis
     New Guinea
   M. g. milligani
     WC Australia
   M. g. goulburni
     New South Wales
   M. g. thomasi
     S Western Australia
   M. g. wilsoni
     South Australia, Victoria
   M. g. halmaturinus
     Kangaroo I
   M. g. flindersi
     Flinders I
   M. g. gramineus
     Tasmania

BOWDLERIA
Bowdleria punctata (Fernbird)
　B. p. vealeae
　　North I (New Zealand)
　B. p. punctata
　　South I (New Zealand)
　B. p. stewartiana
　　Stewart I
　B. p. caudata
　　Snares I
　B. p. wilsoni
　　Codfish I

CINCLORHAMPHUS
Cinclorhamphus mathewsi (Rufous Songlark)
　Australia
Cinclorhamphus cruralis (Brown Songlark)
　Australia

EREMIORNIS
Eremiornis carteri (Spinifex Bird)
　E. c. rogersi
　　N Western Australia
　E. c. carteri
　　WC Australia, Barrow I
　E. c. queenslandicus
　　W Queensland

MEGALURULUS
Megalurulus mariei (New Caledonian Grass Warbler)
　New Caledonia

CICHLORNIS
Cichlornis whitneyi (Thicket Warbler)
　C. w. whitneyi
　　Espiritu Santo I
　C. w. turipavae
　　Guadalcanal I
Cichlornis grosvenori (Whiteman Mountains Warbler)
　New Britain

ORTYGOCICHLA
Ortygocichla rubiginosa (Rufous-faced Thicket Warbler)
　New Britain

TRICHOCICHLA
Trichocichla rufa (Long legged Warbler)
　T. r. rufa
　　Viti Levu I, Fiji Is
　T. r. cluniei
　　Vanua Levu I

BUETTIKOFERELLA
Buettikoferella bivittata (Buettikofer's Warbler)
　Timor I

VITIA
Vitia ruficapilla (Fiji Warbler)
　V. r. ruficapilla
　　Kandavu I
　V. r. badiceps
　　Viti Levu I
　V. r. castaneoptera
　　Vanua Levu I
　V. r. funebris
　　Taviuni I
Vitia parens (Shade Warbler)
　San Cristobal I

STENOSTIRA
Stenostira scita (Fairy Flycatcher)
　S Transvaal, Natal, Cape Province

HYLIOTA
Hyliota flavigaster (Yellow-bellied Flycatcher)
　H. f. flavigaster
　　Senegal to Ethiopia, Kenya
　H. f. barbozae
　　Angola to Tanzania, Mozambique
Hyliota australis (Southern Yellow-bellied Flycatcher)
　H. a. australis
　　W Uganda, W Kenya
　H. a. usambarae
　　E Tanzania
　H. a. inornata
　　Angola to Mozambique
　H. a. slatini
　　E Zaire to Zambia, Malawi
　H. a. pallidipectus
　　W Zambia, E Angola
Hyliota violacea (Violet-backed Flycatcher)
　H. v. nehrkorni
　　Liberia to Ghana
　H. v. violacea
　　Togo to S Cameroun, W Zaire

HYLIA
Hylia prasina (Green Hylia)
　H. p. prasina
　　Cameroun, Angola to W Kenya
　H. p. superciliaris
　　Guinea to S Nigeria
　H. p. poensis
　　Fernando Po I

MUSCICAPIDAE

137 MALURINAE (AUSTRALIAN WRENS)
MALURINI

CLYTOMIAS
Clytomias insignis (Rufous Wren Warbler)
　C. i. insignis
　　NW New Guinea

C. i. oorti
C and SE New Guinea

Chenorhamphus grayi (Broad-billed Wren Warbler)
C. g. grayi
NW New Guinea
C. g. pileatus
N New Guinea

Todopsis wallacei (Wallace's Wren Warbler)
T. w. wallacei
Misol I
T. w. coronata
Aru Is
Todopsis cyanocephala (Blue Wren Warbler)
T. c. cyanocephala
W New Guinea
T. c. dohertyi
N New Guinea
T. c. bonapartii
S New Guinea, Aru Is
T. c. mysorensis
Biak I

Malurus coronatus (Purple-crowned Wren)
M. c. rogersiana
NW Australia
M. c. coronatus
Northern Territory
M. c. caeruleus
NW Queensland
Malurus cyaneus (Blue Wren)
M. c. cyanochlamys
S Queensland, NE New South Wales
M. c. australis
New South Wales. Victoria
M. c. ashbyi
Kangaroo I
M. c. elizabethae
King I
M. c. cyaneus
Tasmania
Malurus splendens (Banded Wren)
M. s. perthi
SW Western Australia
M. s. splendens
S Western Australia
M. s. aridus
EC Western Australia
M. s. riordani
E Western Australia
M. s. callainus
S Northern Territory, N South Australia

M. s. whitei
S Queensland
M. s. musgravi
W New South Wales
M. s. melanotus
SE South Australia, NW Victoria
Malurus lamberti (Variegated Wren)
M. l. dulcis
NW Western Australia, Northern Territory
M. l. bernieri
Bernier I
M. l. mastersi
Western & C Australia, Northern Territory
M. l. assimilis
SW Queensland, W New South Wales, South Australia, NW Victoria
M. l. amabilis
N Queensland
M. l. lamberti
E Queensland, E New South Wales
Malurus pulcherrimus (Blue-breasted Wren)
Western & South Australia
Malurus elegans (Red-winged Wren)
SW Western Australia
Malurus leucopterus (White-winged Wren)
M. l. leucopterus
Barrow I, Dirk Hartog I
M. l. leuconotus
S W, S & EC Australia
Malurus melanocephalus (Red-backed Wren)
M. m. boweri
N Western Australia
M. m. cruentatus
N Northern Territory
M. m. pyrrhonotus
N Queensland
M. m. melanocephalus
S Queensland, N New South Wales
Malurus alboscapulatus (Black & White Wren)
M. a. alboscapulatus
NW New Guinea
M. a. aida
NW New Guinea
M. a. tappenbecki
NE New Guinea
M. a. randi
W New Guinea
M. a. balim
WC New Guinea
M. a. lorentzi
SW New Guinea
M. a. dogwa
S New Guinea

M. a. mortoni
  SE New Guinea
M. a. naimii
  SE New Guinea
M. a. mafulu
  SE New Guinea
M. a. kutubu
  S New Guinea

AMYTORNIS
Amytornis textilis (Thick-billed Grass Wren)
  A. t. textilis
    Western Australia, W South Australia
  A. t. macrourus
    S Western Australia
  A. t. myalli
    Eyre Peninsula
  A. t. everardi
    C South Australia
  A. t. modestus
    W New South Wales
  A. t. inexpectatus
    NE South Australia
Amytornis goyderi (Eyrean Grass Wren)
  South Australia
Amytornis striatus (Striped Grass Wren)
  A. s. whitei
    NW Western Australia, S Northern Territory
  A. s. merrotsyi
    N South Australia
  A. s. striatus
    NW New South Wales
  A. s. owensi
    NW Victoria
Amytornis barbatus (Grey Grass Wren)
  New South Wales
Amytornis dorotheae (Red-winged Grass Wren)
  Northern Territory
Amytornis woodwardi (White-throated Grass Wren)
  Northern Territory
Amytornis housei (Black Grass Wren)
  N Western Australia
Amytornis purnelli (Dusky Grass Wren)
  A. p. purnelli
    Northern Territory
  A. p. ballarae
    NW Queensland

STIPITURUS
Stipiturus malachurus (Southern Emu Wren)
  S. m. hartogi
    Dirk Hartog I

S. m. westernensis
  S Western Australia
S. m. malachurus
  SE South Australia, E New South Wales, Victoria
S. m. tregellasi
  S Victoria
S. m. littleri
  Tasmania
Stipiturus ruficeps (Rufous-crowned Emu Wren)
  S. r. ruficeps
    Western & C Australia
  S. r. mallee
    SE South Australia, NW Victoria

ACANTHIZINI

DASYORNIS
Dasyornis brachypterus (Eastern Bristlebird)
  D. b. brachypterus
    E New South Wales
  D. b. victoriae
    NE Victoria
Dasyornis longirostris (Western Bristlebird)
  SW Western Australia
Dasyornis broadbenti (Rufous Bristlebird)
  D. b. litoralis
    SW Western Australia
  D. b. broadbenti
    South Australia, Victoria
  D. b. whitei
    South Australia

GERYGONE
Gerygone olivacea (White-throated Flyeater)
  G. o. cinerascens
    SE New Guinea
  G. o. rogersi
    NW Australia
  G. o. flavigaster
    NW Queensland
  G. o. olivacea
    S Queensland, New South Wales, Victoria
Gerygone hypoxantha (Biak Flyeater)
  Biak I
Gerygone mouki (Brown Flyeater)
  G. m. mouki
    N Queensland
  G. m. amalia
    S Queensland
  G. m. richmondi
    N New South Wales
Gerygone palpebrosa (Black-headed Flyeater)
  G. p. palpebrosa
    Aru Is, NW New Guinea

G. p. wahnesi
Japen I, NW New Guinea

G. p. inconspicua
SE New Guinea

G. p. tarara
S New Guinea

G. p. personata
N Queensland

G. p. johnstoni
NE Queensland

Gerygone flavida (Fairy Flyeater)
N Queensland

**Gerygone magnirostris (Large-billed
Flyeater)**

G. m. mimikae
S & SE New Guinea

G. m. conspicillata
NW New Guinea

G. m. affinis
Japen I, Dampier I, N New Guinea

G. m. brunneipectus
Aru Is

G. m. cobana
Waigeu I, Batanta I

G. m. occasa
Kofiau I

G. m. proxima
D'Entrecasteaux Archipelago

G. m. onerosa
Misima I

G. m. tagulana
Tagula I

G. m. rosseliana
Sudest I

G. m. magnirostris
N Queensland

Gerygone tenebrosa (Dusky Flyeater)
coast of N Western Australia

**Gerygone chloronota (Green-backed
Flyeater)**

G. c. cinereiceps
New Guinea

G. c. aruensis
Waigeu I, Aru Is

G. c. chloronota
N Western Australia, N Northern
Territory

Gerygone levigaster (Mangrove Flyeater)

G. l. broomei
N Western Australia

G. l. levigaster
Northern Territory

G. l. mastersi
N Queensland

G. l. cantator
E Queensland

Gerygone fusca (White-tailed Flyeater)

G. f. simplex
Philippine Is

G. f. pallida
S New Guinea

G. f. dendyi
N Western Australia

G. f. wayensis
WC Australia

G. f. fusca
S Western Australia

G. f. musgravei
C Australia

G. f. exsul
S Queensland to Victoria

G. f. keyensis
Kei Is

Gerygone cinerea (Grey Flyeater)
New Guinea

**Gerygone chrysogaster (Yellow-bellied
Flyeater)**

G. c. leucothorax
NW New Guinea

G. c. notata
NW New Guinea, Misol I, Batanta I

G. c. neglecta
Waigeu I

G. c. dohertyi
SW New Guinea

G. c. chrysogaster
S & E New Guinea, Japen I, Aru Is

**Gerygone ruficollis (Treefern
Flyeater)**

G. r. ruficollis
NW New Guinea

G. r. insperata
C & SE New Guinea

**Gerygone flavolateralis (Fan-tailed
Flyeater)**

G. f. flavolateralis
New Caledonia

G. f. lifuensis
Loyalty Is

G. f. correiae
Banks Is

G. f. citrina
Rennell I

**Gerygone igata (New Zealand Grey
Flyeater)**

G. i. flaviventris
North I (New Zealand)

G. i. macleani
North I (New Zealand)

G. i. igata
South I (New Zealand)

G. i. sylvestris
South I (New Zealand)

Gerygone albofrontata (Chatham Is Flyeater)
  Chatham I
Gerygone inornata (Plain Flyeater)
  G. i. inornata
    Timor I
  G. i. everetti
    Savu I
  G. i. keyensis
    Kei Is
  G. i. kuhni
    Dammer I
Gerygone sulphurea (Yellow-breasted Flyeater)
  Malaysia

SMICRORNIS
Smicrornis brevirostris (Weebill)
  S. b. cairns
    NE Queensland
  S. b. flavescens
    W Northern Territory
  S. b. pallescens
    C Queensland
  S. b. stirlingi
    S Western Australia
  S. b. mathewsi
    South Australia
  S. b. brevirostris
    New South Wales
  S. b. mallee
    Victoria

APHELOCEPHALA
Aphelocephala leucopsis (Southern White-face)
  A. l. castaneiventris
    Western Australia
  A. l. whitei
    C Australia
  A. l. leucopsis
    South Australia, New South Wales, Victoria
Aphelocephala pectoralis (Chestnut-breasted Whiteface)
  C South Australia
Aphelocephala nigricincta (Banded Whiteface)
  A. n. tanami
    C Northern Territory
  A. n. nigricincta
    C South Australia

ACANTHIZA
Acanthiza nana (Little Thornbill)
  A. n. flava
    N Queensland
  A. n. modesta
    C Queensland

A. n. nana
  S Queensland, New South Wales
A. n. burtoni
  SE Queensland
A. n. mathewsi
  South Australia, Victoria
A. n. laetior
  Mt Lofty Range
Acanthiza lineata (Striated Thornbill)
  A. l. alberti
    S Queensland
  A. l. lineata
    New South Wales
  A. l. clelandi
    South Australia
  A. l. chandleri
    Victoria
Acanthiza pusilla (Brown Thornbill)
  A. p. bunya
    S Queensland
  A. p. pusilla
    S Queensland, E New South Wales
  A. p. maculata
    Victoria
  A. p. zietzi
    Kangaroo I
  A. p. diemenensis
    Tasmania
Acanthiza apicalis (Broad-tailed Thornbill)
  A. a. whitlocki
    S Northern Territory, N Western Australia
  A. a. apicalis
    S Western Australia
  A. a. leeuwinensis
    S Western Australia
  A. a. tanami
    C Australia
  A. a. albiventris
    SW New South Wales
Acanthiza katharina (Mountain Thornbill)
  Queensland
Acanthiza murina (De Vis' Tree Warbler)
  C & SE New Guinea
Acanthiza ewingi (Tasmanian Thornbill)
  Tasmania
Acanthiza robustirostris (Robust Thornbill)
  A. r. robustirostris
    Western Australia
  A. r. marianae
    C Australia

Acanthiza inornata (Western Thornbill)
  A. i. mastersi
    SW Western Australia
  A. i. inornata
    SC Western Australia

Acanthiza iredalei (Samphire Thornbill)
  A. i. iredalei
    Western Australia
  A. i. hedleyi
    South Australia
  A. i. rosinae
    S South Australia
Acanthiza reguloides (Buff-tailed Thornbill)
  A. r. squamata
    Queensland
  A. r. reguloides
    New South Wales
  A. r. australis
    South Australia
  A. r. nesa
    N New South Wales
Acanthiza chrysorrhoa (Yellow-tailed Thornbill)
  A. c. multi
    S Western Australia
  A. c. alexanderi
    W C Australia
  A. c. ferdinandi
    C Australia
  A. c. addenda
    E C Australia
  A. c. normantoni
    N Queensland
  A. c. chrysorrhoa
    S Queensland, New South Wales
  A. c. sandlandi
    South Australia, Victoria, Tasmania
Acanthiza uropygialis (Chestnut-tailed Thornbill)
  A. u. augusta
    W C Australia, W New South Wales
  A. u. uropygialis
    C & South Australia

SERICORNIS
Sericornis magnus (Scrub Tit)
    Tasmania
Sericornis spilodera (Pale-billed Sericornis)
  S. s. spilodera
    Japen I, NW New Guinea
  S. s. granti
    WC New Guinea
  S. s. wuroi
    S New Guinea
  S. s. guttatus
    SE New Guinea
  S. s. ferrugineus
    Waigeu I
  S. s. aruensis
    Aru Is
  S. s. intermedia
    Batanta I

Sericornis virgatus (Perplexing Sericornis)
  S. v. cantans
    NW New Guinea
  S. v. imitator
    NW New Guinea
  S. v. jobiensis
    Japen I
  S. v. boreonesioticus
    coast of N New Guinea
  S. v. idenburgi
    Snowy Mountains
  S. v. pontifex
    NC New Guinea
Sericornis beccarii (Little Sericornis)
  S. b. wondiwoi
    NW New Guinea
  S. b. cyclopum
    coast of N New Guinea
  S. b. weylandi
    Weyland mountains
  S. b. randi
    S New Guinea
  S. b. beccarii
    Aru Is
  S. b. minimus
    Cape York
  S. b. dubius
    N Queensland
Sericornis nouhuysi (Large Mountain Sericornis)
  S. n. nouhuysi
    Weyland & Snowy mountains
  S. n. stresemanni
    Schrader Mountains
  S. n. oorti
    Huon peninsula
  S. n. monticola
    SE New Guinea
Sericornis frontalis (White-browed Sericornis)
  S. f. geraldtoni
    W Western Australia
  S. f. maculatus
    S Western Australia
  S. f. mellori
    W South Australia
  S. f. balstoni
    W New South Wales, W Victoria
  S. f. laevigaster
    NW Queensland
  S. f. herbertoni
    NE Queensland
  S. f. frontalis
    S Queensland, New South Wales
  S. f. rosinae
    NE South Australia

S. f. harterti
Victoria
S. f. archboldi
N Tasmania
S. f. humilis
Tasmania
S. f. gularis
Kent I
S. f. insularis
Forsyth I
S. f. flindersi
Flinders I
S. f. tregellasi
King I

Sericornis perspicillatus (Buff-faced Sericornis)
C & SE New Guinea

Sericornis magnirostris (Large-billed Sericornis)
S. m. viridior
Queensland
S. m. magnirostris
New South Wales, Victoria

Sericornis rufescens (Arfak Buff-faced Sericornis)
NW New Guinea

Sericornis nigroviridis (Morobe Sericornis)
Morobe district, New Guinea

Sericornis papuensis (Papuan Sericornis)
S. p. meeki
W New Guinea
S. p. burgersi
C New Guinea
S. p. papuensis
SE New Guinea

Sericornis arfakianus (Grey-green Sericornis)
S. a. arfakianus
NW New Guinea
S. a. olivaceus
C & E New Guinea

Sericornis citreogularis (Yellow-throated Sericornis)
S. c. cairnsi
N Queensland
S. c. citreogularis
NE Australia

Sericornis keri (Atherton Sericornis)
NE Queensland

Sericornis fuliginosus (Striated Field Wren)
S. f. hartogi
Dirk Hartog I
S. f. dorrie
Dorrie I
S. f. perone
Western Australia

S. f. rubiginosus
Western Australia
S. f. campestris
SW Western Australia
S. f. montanellus
S Western Australia
S. f. carteri
S Western Australia
S. f. wayensis
WC Australia
S. f. isabellinus
C Australia
S. f. macgillivrayi
N South Australia, W New South Wales
S. f. ethelae
South Australia
S. f. obscurior
E New South Wales
S. f. albiloris
Victoria
S. f. howei
S Victoria
S. f. fuliginosus
Tasmania

Sericornis pyrrhopygia (Chestnut-rumped Heath Wren)
S. p. pyrrhopygia
New South Wales
S. p. belcheri
South Australia, Victoria

Sericornis cautus (Shy Heath Wren)
S. c. whitlocki
S Western Australia
S. c. cautus
South Australia, Victoria

Sericornis brunneus (Redthroat)
Western C & South Australia

Sericornis sagittata (Little Field Wren)
S. s. sagittata
Queensland, New South Wales
S. s. inexpectata
South Australia, Victoria

CRATEROSCELIS

Crateroscelis gutturalis (Fern Wren)
NE Queensland

Crateroscelis murina (Lowland Mouse Warbler)
C. m. murina
Japen I, New Guinea
C. m. monacha
Aru Is
C. m. pallida
SE New Guinea
C. m. capitalis
Waigeu I
C. m. fumosa
Misol I

Crateroscelis nigrorufa (Mid-mountain Mouse Warbler)
C. n. blissi
N New Guinea
C. n. nigrorufa
SE New Guinea
Crateroscelis robusta (Mountain Mouse Warbler)
C. r. peninsularis
NW New Guinea
C. r. ripleyi
NW New Guinea
C. r. bastille
coast of N New Guinea
C. r. deficiens
N New Guinea
C. r. sanfordi
C New Guinea
C. r. robusta
SE New Guinea

ORIGMA
Origma solitaria (Rock Warbler)
New South Wales

PYCNOPTILUS
Pycnoptilus floccosus (Pilot Bird)
P. f. floccosus
New South Wales
P. f. sandlandi
Victoria

MOHOUINI

MOHOUA
Mohoua albicilla (Whitehead)
North I (New Zealand)
Mohoua ochrocephala (Yellowhead)
South I (New Zealand)

FINSCHIA
Finschia novaeseelandiae (New Zealand Creeper)
South I (New Zealand)

EPHTHIANURINI

EPHTHIANURA
Ephthianura albifrons (White-faced Chat)
E. a. albifrons
S Western to Victoria, New South Wales
E. a. tasmanica
Tasmania
Ephthianura tricolor (Crimson Chat)
C & E Australia
Ephthianura aurifrons (Orange Chat)
all Australia except SW
Ephthianura crocea (Yellow Chat)
E. c. boweri
Fitzroy river (NW Australia)
E. c. tunneyi
Aligator river (Northern Territory)
E. c. crocea
Norman river (W Queensland)
E. c. macgregori
Fitzroy river (Queensland)

ASHBYIA
Ashbyia lovensis (Desert Chat)
N South Australia

LAMPROLIA
Lamprolia victoriae (Silktail)
L. v. victoriae
Taviuni I
L. v. kleinschmidti
Vanua Levu I

MUSCICAPIDAE

138 MUSCICAPINAE (OLD WORLD FLYCATCHERS)

BRADORNIS
Bradornis microrhynchus (Grey Flycatcher)
B. m. microrhynchus
Ethiopia, Somalia to Tanzania
B. m. pumilis
S Sudan, Uganda, W Kenya
B. m. burae
Tana river (Kenya)
Bradornis mariquensis (Mariqua Flycatcher)
B. m. acaciae
SW Angola, Namibia, NW Cape Province
B. m. mariquensis
SW Zambia, S Botswana, NE Cape Province
Bradornis pallidus (Pale Flycatcher)
B. p. nigeriae
Gambia to N Central African Republic
B. p. modestus
Guinea to Cameroun
B. p. murinus
Gabon to Angola & Natal
B. p. bowdleri
NE Ethiopia
B. p. duyerali
NE Ethiopia
B. p. neumanni
S Ethiopia
B. p. pallidus
Sudan, NW Uganda
B. p. griseus
NE Zaire to Kenya, Tanzania
B. p. bafirawari
E Kenya
B. p. subalaris
Zambia to Cape Province
B. p. sibilans
E Natal

Bradornis infuscatus (African Brown Flycatcher)
  B. i. benguellensis
    S Angola
  B. i. namaquensis
    Namibia, W Botswana
  B. i. seimundi
    S Botswana, W Transvaal, N Cape Province
  B. i. infuscatus
    W Cape Province

EMPIDORNIS
Empidornis semipartitus (Silver Bird)
  E. s. semipartitus
    N Ethiopia
  E. s. orleansi
    S Sudan, W Ethiopia
  E. s. kavirondensis
    SE Sudan to N Tanzania

MELAENORNIS
Melaenornis chocolatina (Abyssinian Slaty Flycatcher)
  M. c. chocolatina
    N Ethiopia
  M. c. reichenowi
    W Ethiopia
Melaenornis ardesiaca (Berlioz' Black Flycatcher)
    E Zaire
Melaenornis annamarulae (Mrs Forbes-Watson's Black Flycatcher)
    Liberia
Melaenornis edolioides (Black Flycatcher)
  M. e. edolioides
    Senegal to Cameroun
  M. e. lugubris
    Ethiopia, Sudan to N Tanzania
  M. e. schistacea
    E Ethiopia, N Kenya
Melaenornis pammelaina (South African Black Flycatcher)
  M. p. tropicalis
    Kenya, Tanzania
  M. p. pammalaina
    Angola to Mozambique & Natal
Melaenornis silens (Fiscal Flycatcher)
    SE South Africa

DIOPTRORNIS
Dioptrornis fischeri (White-eyed Slaty Flycatcher)
  D. f. toruensis
    E Zaire, W Uganda
  D. f. semicinctus
    E Zaire
  D. f. nyikensis
    N Tanzania, N Malawi

D. f. fischeri
    Tanzania
Dioptrornis brunneus (Angolan Flycatcher)
  D. b. brunneus
    N Angola
  D. b. bailundensis
    S Angola

FRASERIA
Fraseria ocreata (Forest Flycatcher)
  F. o. kelsalli
    Sierra Leone
  F. o. prosphora
    Liberia to Ghana
  F. o. ocreata
    Cameroun to Zaire, Uganda
Fraseria cinerascens (White-browed Forest Flycatcher)
  F. c. guineae
    Guinea to Ivory Coast
  F. c. cinerascens
    Liberia to Gabon, N Zaire

RHINOMYIAS
Rhinomyias addita (Buru Jungle Flycatcher)
    Buru I
Rhinomyias oscillans (Flores Jungle Flycatcher)
    Flores I
Rhinomyias olivacea (Olive-backed Jungle Flycatcher)
  R. o. olivacea
    Malaysia, Burma
  R. o. nicobarica
    Nicobar Is
  R. o. perolivacea
    Banguey I
Rhinomyias brunneata (White-gorgetted Jungle Flycatcher)
    S China
Rhinomyias umbratilis (White-throated Jungle Flycatcher)
    Malaysia
Rhinomyias ruficauda (Rufous-tailed Jungle Flycatcher)
  R. r. isola
    Sarawak
  R. r. ruficrissa
    Kinabalu
  R. r. ocularis
    Sulu Is, Pangamican I, Tawitawi Is
  R. r. ruficauda
    Basilan I
  R. r. zamboanga
    W Mindanao I
  R. r. boholensis
    Bohol I
  R. r. samarensis
    Leyte I, Samar I, E Mindanao I

Rhinomyias colonus **(Sula Jungle Flycatcher)**
Sula I
Rhinomyias gularis **(White-browed Jungle Flycatcher)**
R. g. gularis
Borneo
R. g. albigularis
Negros I
R. g. insignis
N Luzon I
R. g. goodfellowi
Mindanao I

FICEDULA

Ficedula hypoleuca **(Pied Flycatcher)**
F. h. hypoleuca
N Europe, W Siberia » NC Africa
F. h. iberiae
Spain, Portugal
F. h. speculigera
N Africa
F. h. semitorquata
Asia Minor, Syria, Iraq
F. h. tomensis
SW Asia » C Africa
Ficedula albicollis **(Collared Flycatcher)**
C & E Europe » SC Africa
Ficedula zanthopygia **(Yellow-rumped Flycatcher)**
NE Asia » Malaysia
Ficedula narcissina **(Narcissus Flycatcher)**
F. n. narcissina
Sakhalin, Japan » Philippine Is,
N Borneo
F. n. jakuschimae
Yakushima I
F. n. shonis
N Riukiu Is
F. n. owstoni
S Riukiu Is
Ficedula mugimaki **(Mugimaki Flycatcher)**
C & E Asia » Philippine Is
Ficedula parva **(Red-breasted Flycatcher)**
F. p. parva
C & E Europe, W Himalayas » N India
F. p. albicilla
C & NE Asia » Burma, S China
F. p. subrubra
NW Himalayas » Sri Lanka
Ficedula strophiata **(Orange-gorgetted Flycatcher)**
F. s. strophiata
Himalayas to N Thailand, S China
F. s. fuscogularis
Vietnam

Ficedula monileger **(White-gorgetted Flycatcher)**
F. m. monileger
C Nepal
F. m. submonileger
Burma
F. m. arakanensis
Burma
F. m. leucops
NE India to NW Thailand
F. m. malayana
Malaysia
Ficedula solitaria **(Rufous-browed Flycatcher)**
Malaysia, Indochina, Sumatra
Ficedula hyperythra **(Thicket Flycatcher)**
F. h. hyperythra
Himalayas, Burma, Thailand
F. h. annamensis
C Vietnam
F. h. sumatrana
Malaysia, Sumatra, Borneo
F. h. mjobergi
W Borneo
F. h. vulcani
Java, Bali I
F. h. trinitatis
Luzon I, Mindoro I
F. h. calayensis
Calayan I
F. h. nigrorum
Negros I
F. h. montigena
Mindanao I
F. h. daggayana
N Mindanao I
F. h. malindangensis
SE Mindanao I
F. h. jugosae
Celebes
F. h. negroides
Ceram I
F. h. pallidipectus
Batjan I, Buru I
F. h. alifurus
Buru I
F. h. luzoniensis
Luzon I, Mindoro I
Ficedula rufigula **(White-vented Flycatcher)**
Celebes
Ficedula dumetoria **(Orange-breasted Flycatcher)**
F. d. muelleri
Malaysia, Sumatra, Borneo
F. d. dumetoria
Java, Lombok I

F. d. riedeli
  Tenimber Is
**Ficedula basilanica (Little Slaty
  Flycatcher)**
  F. b. basilanica
    Basilan I, Mindanao I
  F. b. samarensis
    Leyte I, Samar I
Ficedula buruensis (Buru Flycatcher)
  F. b. buruensis
    Buru I
  F. b. ceramensis
    Ceram I
  F. b. siebersi
    Kei Is
Ficedula henrici (Damar Flycatcher)
  Damar I
**Ficedula hodgsonii (Rusty-breasted
  Blue Flycatcher)**
  Nepal to W China
Ficedula platenae (Palawan Flycatcher)
  Palawan I
Ficedula crypta (Vaurie's Flycatcher)
  F. c. crypta
    Mindanao I
  F. c. disposita
    Luzon I
Ficedula bonthaina (Mountain Flycatcher)
  Celebes
Ficedula harterti (Hartert's Flycatcher)
  Sumba I
**Ficedula nigrorufa (Black and Orange
  Flycatcher)**
  SW India
**Ficedula timorensis (White-throated
  Flycatcher)**
  Timor I
**Ficedula westermanni (Little Pied
  Flycatcher)**
  F. w. collini
    Himalayas
  F. w. australorientis
    S China, Indochina, Indonesia
  F. w. langbianus
    S Vietnam
  F. w. hasselti
    Sumatra, Java, Bali I
  F. w. palawanensis
    Palawan I
  F. w. westermanni
    Luzon I, Negros I, Mindanao I
  F. w. rabori
    Culion I
**Ficedula superciliaris (White-browed
  Blue Flycatcher)**
  F. s. superciliaris
    W Himalayas, C India

F. s. aestigma
  E Himalayas, Tibet, W China
**Ficedula tricolor (Slaty Blue
  Flycatcher)**
  F. t. tricolor
    W Himalayas
  F. t. minuta
    E Himalayas, SE Tibet, S China
  F. t. cerviniventris
    Assam, Burma
  F. t. notata
    NE India, Nepal
**Ficedula sapphira (Sapphire-headed
  Flycatcher)**
  F. s. sapphira
    E Himalayas, N Laos, S China
  F. s. laotiana
    S Laos

CYANOPTILA
**Cyanoptila cyanomelaena (Blue and
  White Flycatcher)**
  C. c. intermedia
    N Asia
  C. c. cumatilis
    NE Asia » S Burma, S Thailand
  C. c. cyanomelaena
    Japan » Philippine Is, Borneo

NILTAVA
Niltava grandis (Large Niltava)
  N. g. grandis
    E Himalayas to Malaysia, Vietnam
  N. g. decipiens
    Sumatra
Niltava macgregoriae (Small Niltava)
  N. m. macgregoriae
    W & C Himalayas
  N. m. signata
    E Himalayas, Assam
Niltava davidi (Fukien Niltava)
  S China
**Niltava sundara (Rufous-bellied
  Niltava)**
  N. s. whistleri
    W Himalayas
  N. s. sundara
    E Himalayas, SW China, N Laos
  N. s. denotata
    S China, Thailand
Niltava sumatrana (Sumatran Niltava)
  Malaysia, Sumatra
Niltava vivida (Vivid Niltava)
  N. v. oatesi
    NE India to N Vietnam
  N. v. vivida
    Taiwan
**Niltava hyacinthina (Blue-backed
  Niltava)**

N. h. hyacinthina
Timor I
N. h. kuhni
Wetar I
Niltava hoevelli (Celebes Niltava)
C Celebes
Niltava sanfordi (Sanford's Niltava)
N Celebes
Niltava concreta (White-tailed Niltava)
N. c. cyanea
NE India, Burma
N. c. leucoprocta
Burma
N. c. concreta
Malaysia, Sumatra
N. c. everetti
Borneo
Niltava ruecki (Rueck's Niltava)
Malaysia
Niltava herioti (Blue-breasted Niltava)
N. b. herioti
N & C Luzon I
N. h. comorinensis
S Luzon I
Niltava hainana (Grant's Niltava)
S China
Niltava pallipes (White-bellied Niltava)
SW India
Niltava poliogenys (Brooks' Niltava)
N. p. poliogenys
C Himalayas, NE India
N. p. vernayi
EC India
N. p. cachariensis
E Himalayas, NW Burma
Niltava unicolor (Pale Niltava)
N. u. unicolour
Himalayas, Burma, N Laos
N. u. infuscata
Malaysia, Sumatra, Java
N. u. harterti
Borneo
Niltava rubeculoides (Blue-throated Niltava)
N. r. rubeculoides
Himalayas, Burma, India
N. r. dialilaema
Burma
N. r. rogersi
Burma
N. r. glaucicomans
S Thailand, S & C China
N. r. klossi
S Vietnam
Niltava banyumas (Hill Blue Niltava)
N. b. magnirostris
E Himalayas, Assam, Burma
N. b. whitei
Burma

N. b. caerulifrons
Thailand, Malaysia
N. b. deignani
C Thailand
N. b. cantatrix
W Java
N. b. banyumas
C & E Java
N. b. montana
Borneo
N. b. lemprieri
Palawan I, Balabac I
Niltava superba (Bornean Niltava)
Borneo
Niltava caerulata (Large-billed Niltava)
N. c. albiventer
Sumatra
N. c. rufifrons
W Borneo
N. c. caerulata
Borneo
Niltava turcosa (Malaysian Niltava)
N. t. rupatensis
Malaysia, Sumatra, W Borneo
N. t. turcosa
C & E Borneo
Niltava tickelliae (Tickell's Niltava)
N. t. tickelliae
NE, C & S India
N. t. jerdoni
Sri Lanka
N. t. sumatrensis
Malaysia, Sumatra
N. t. indochina
Indochina
Niltava rufigastra (Mangrove Niltava)
N. r. rufigastra
Malaysia, Sumatra, Borneo
N. r. indochina
S Vietnam
N. r. sumatrensis
NE Sumatra
N. r. rhizophorae
W Java
N. r. lampra
Anamba Is
N. r. longipennis
Karimon-Java I
N. r. karimatensis
Karimata I
N. r. omissa
Celebes
N. r. simplex
Luzon I
N. r. marinduquensis
Marinduque I
N. r. mindorensis
Mindoro I

N. r. litoralis
    Palawan I
N. r. philippinensis
    Philippine Is

MUSCICAPELLA
Muscicapella hodgsoni (Pygmy Blue Flycatcher)
M. h. hodgsoni
    C Himalayas to Thailand, SW China
M. h. sondaica
    Malaysia, Sumatra, Borneo

MUSCICAPA
Muscicapa striata (Spotted Flycatcher)
M. s. striata
    Europe, Asia Minor » S Africa
M. s. neumanni
    W & S Asia » E Africa
M. s. tyrrhenica
    Corsica, Sardinia
M. s. balearicae
    Balearic Is » W & S Africa
M. s. sarudnyi
    N Iran, Caucasus, Afghanistan
Muscicapa sibirica (Siberian Flycatcher)
M. s. sibirica
    E Asia, Japan
M. s. gulmergi
    Pakistan, W Himalayas
M. s. cacabata
    E Himalayas, Tibet
M. s. rothschildi
    SW China
Muscicapa griseisticta (Spot-breasted Flycatcher)
    NE Asia » New Guinea, Philippine Is
Muscicapa latirostris (Brown Flycatcher)
M. l. daurica
    NE Asia, Japan
M. l. poonensis
    E India, Burma, SW China
M. l. randi
    Philippine Is
M. l. latirostris
    Sumatra
Muscicapa williamsoni (Brown-streaked Flycatcher)
    Burma, Thailand, Malaysia, Sumatra
Muscicapa segregata (Sumba Flycatcher)
    Sumba I
Muscicapa muttui (Brown-breasted Flycatcher)
    NE & SW India
Muscicapa ruficauda (Rufous-tailed Flycatcher)
    W Himalayas, W India

Muscicapa ferruginea (Ferruginous Flycatcher)   475
    Mindoro I, Palawan I
Muscicapa gambagae (Gambaga Spotted Flycatcher)
    Ghana to Somalia, Arabia
Muscicapa adusta (Dusky Flycatcher)
M. a. albiventris
    Cameroun
M. a. sjostedti
    Cameroun Mt, Fernando Po I
M. a. grotei
    Central African Republic
M. a. pumilis
    NE Zaire, S Sudan, Uganda
M. a. minima
    NE Ethiopia
M. a. interposita
    S Sudan, N Kenya
M. a. subtilis
    E Zaire
M. a. subadusta
    S Zaire to Rhodesia,Mozambique
M. a. angolensis
    Angola, SW Zaire
M. a. marsabit
    N Kenya
M. a. murina
    SE Kenya
M. a. chyulu
    NE Tanzania
M. a. fuelleborni
    Tanzania
M. a. roehli
    E Tanzania
M. a. adusta
    S E Africa
Muscicapa aquatica (Swamp Flycatcher)
M. a. aquatica
    Senegal to Sudan
M. a. infulatus
    S Sudan, NE Zaire, W Kenya
M. a. ruandae
    Rwanda, S Uganda
M. a. lualabae
    SE Zaire
M. a. grimwoodi
    C Zambia
Muscicapa olivascens (Olivaceous Flycatcher)
M. o. olivascens
    Liberia to Gabon, E Zaire
M. o. itombwensis
    Itombwe (E Zaire)
Muscicapa lendu (Chapin's Flycatcher)
    Lake Albert (NE Zaire)

476 ***Muscicapa cassini*** **(Cassin's Grey Flycatcher)**
Sierra Leone to Uganda, Zambia
Muscicapa epulata **(Little Grey Flycatcher)**
Liberia to Gabon, E Zaire
Muscicapa sethsmithi **(Yellow-footed Flycatcher)**
Cameroun, Gabon to Uganda
Muscicapa coerulescens **(Ashy Flycatcher)**
M. c. nigrorum
Guinea to Togo
M. c. brevicauda
S Nigeria to Gabon, Sudan
M. c. cinereolus
S Angola to Kenya, Mozambique
M. c. impavida
N Namibia to N Mozambique
M. c. coerulescens
E Transvaal, Natal, E Cape Province
Muscicapa comitata **(Dusky Blue Flycatcher)**
M. c. aximensis
Sierra Leone to S Nigeria
M. c. camerunensis
Cameroun
M. c. comitata
Gabon to Uganda, Angola
Muscicapa tessmanni **(Tessman's Flycatcher)**
Ivory Coast to N Zaire
Muscicapa infuscata **(African Sooty Flycatcher)**
M. i. chapini
S Nigeria
M. i. in fuscata
Cameroun to Angola
M. i. minuscula
NE Zaire to Sudan, Uganda
Muscicapa ussheri **(Ussher's Dusky Flycatcher)**
Sierra Leone to Ghana

MYIOPORNIS
Myiopornis böhmi **(Böhm's Flycatcher)**
M. b. sharpei
Angola, Zambia
M. b. bohmi
SE Zambia, Tanzania, Malawi

EUMYIAS
Eumyias sordida **(Sri Lanka Dusky Blue Flycatcher)**
Sri Lanka
Eumyias thalassina **(Indian Verditer Flycatcher)**
E. t. thalassina
Himalayas to N Laos
E. t. thalassoides
Malaysia, Sumatra, Borneo

Eumyias panayensis **(Philippine Verditer Flycatcher)**
E. p. septentrionalis
N Celebes
E. p. meridionalis
S Celebes
E. p. obiensis
Obi I, Moluccas
E. p. harterti
Ceram I
E. p. panayensis
Negros I, Panay I
E. p. nigrimentalis
Luzon I, Mindoro I
E. p. nigriloris
Mindanao I
Eumyias albicaudata **(Nilgiri Verditer Flycatcher)**
SW India
Eumyias indigo **(Indigo Flycatcher)**
E. i. ruficrissa
Sumatra
E. i. indigo
Java
E. i. cerviniventris
Borneo

MYIOPARUS
Myioparus plumbeus **(Grey Tit Flycatcher)**
M. p. plumbeus
Senegal to Ethiopia, Uganda
M. p. orientalis
Kenya to Angola, Natal
M. p. grandior
C Tanzania to Natal
Myioparus griseigularis **(Grey-throated Flycatcher)**
M. g. parelii
Ivory Coast
M. g. holospodius
E Nigeria to Gabon
M. g. griseigularis
E Zaire, Uganda

HUMBLOTIA
Humblotia flavirostris **(Humblot's Flycatcher)**
Comoro Is

NEWTONIA
Newtonia amphichroa **(Tulear Newtonia)**
NE Madagascar
Newtonia brunneicauda **(Common Newtonia)**
N. b. brunneicauda
Madagascar
N. b. monticola
Mt Ankarata
Newtonia archboldi **(Tabity Newtonia)**
SW Madagascar

***Newtonia fanovanae* (Fanovana Newtonia)**
   E Madagascar

MICROECA
***Microeca leucophaea* (Australian Brown Flycatcher)**
  M. l. zimmeri
   New Guinea
  M. l. pallida
   Northern Territory, N Queensland
  M. l. leucophaea
   S Queensland, New South Wales
  M. l. barcoo
   C Australia
  M. l. assimilis
   S Western Australia
***Microeca tormenti* (Brown-tailed Flycatcher)**
   N Western Australia
***Microeca flavigaster* (Lemon-breasted Flycatcher)**
  M. f. tarara
   New Guinea
  M. f. laeta
   New Guinea
  M. f. terraereginae
   N Queensland
  M. f. flavigaster
   Northern Territory
***Microeca hemixantha* (Tenimber Microeca Flycatcher)**
   Tenimber Is
***Microeca griseoceps* (Yellow-footed Flycatcher)**
  M. g. occidentalis
   NW New Guinea
  M. g. poliocephala
   NE New Guinea
  M. g. bartoni
   S New Guinea
  M. g. griseoceps
   SE New Guinea, S Queensland
***Microeca flavovirescens* (Olive Microeca Flycatcher)**
  M. f. flavovirescens
   Aru Is, New Guinea
  M. f. cuicui
   New Guinea
***Microeca papuana* (Papuan Microeca Flycatcher)**
  M. p. papuana
   NW New Guinea
  M. p. punctata
   Arfak mountains, New Guinea

CULICICAPA
***Culicicapa ceylonensis* (Grey-headed Canary Flycatcher)**
  C. c. calochrysea
   N India, Burma

  C. c. ceylonensis
   S India, Sri Lanka
  C. c. antioxantha
   Thailand
  C. c. percnocara
   Malaysia
  C. c. connectens
   Celebes
  C. c. sejuncta
   Flores I
***Culicicapa helianthea* (Citrine Canary Flycatcher)**
  C. h. helianthea
   Banggai I, Celebes
  C. h. panayensis
   Leyte I, Mindanao I, Palawan I
  C. h. mayri
   Bongao I, Tawitawi Is
  C. h. septentrionalis
   NW Luzon I
  C. h. zimmeri
   C & S Luzon I

PELTOPS
***Peltops blainvillii* (Lowland Peltops Flycatcher)**
   New Guinea
***Peltops montanus* (Mountain Peltops Flycatcher)**
   New Guinea

MONACHELLA
***Monachella muelleriana* (River Flycatcher)**
  M. m. saxicolina
   NW New Guinea
  M. m. muelleriana
   SW New Guinea
  M. m. albofrontata
   SE New Guinea
  M. m. coultasi
   New Britain

EUGERYGONE
***Eugerygone rubra* (Red-backed Warbler)**
  E. r. rubra
   NW New Guinea
  E. r. saturatior
   C New Guinea

PETROICA
***Petroica multicolor* (Scarlet Robin)**
  P. m. kleinschmidti
   Fiji Is
  P. m. pusilla
   Samoa Is
  P. m. feminina
   Efate I, Mai I
  P. m. soror
   Vanua Levu I
  P. m. similis
   Tanna I

P. m. ambrynensis
 New Hebrides, Banks Is
P. m. cognata
 Erromanga I
P. m. becki
 Kandavu I
P. m. polymorpha
 San Cristobal I
P. m. septentrionalis
 Bougainville I
P. m. kulambangrae
 Kulambangra I
P. m. campbelli
 S Western Australia
P. m. boodang
 E Australia, Tasmania
P. m. multicolor
 Norfolk I
P. m. dennisi
 Guadalcanal I
Petroica goodenovii (Red-capped Robin)
 W, C & E Australia
Petroica phoenicea (Flame Robin)
 New South Wales, SE Australia
 Tasmania
Petroica archboldi (Rock Robin)
 C New Guinea
Petroica rodinogastor (Pink Robin)
 SE Australia, Tasmania
Petroica rosea (Rose Robin)
 coastal S Queensland to Victoria
Petroica bivittata (Forest Robin)
P. b. caudata
 C New Guinea
P. b. bivittata
 SE New Guinea
Petroica cucullata (Hooded Robin)
P. c. picata
 Western Australia
P. c. cucullata
 S Queensland, New South Wales, Victoria
Petroica macrocephala (New Zealand Tit)
P. m. toitoi
 North I (New Zealand)
P. m. macrocephala
 South I (New Zealand)
P. m. marrineri
 Auckland Is
P. m. chathamensis
 Chatham I
P. m. dannefaerdi
 Snares I
Petroica vittata (Dusky Robin)
P. v. kingi
 King I
P. v. vittata
 Tasmania

Petroica australis (New Zealand Robin)
P. a. longipes
 North I (New Zealand)
P. a. australis
 South I (New Zealand)
P. a. rakiura
 Stewart I
Petroica traversi (Chatham I Robin)
 Chatham I

TREGELLASIA
Tregellasia leucops (White-faced Robin)
T. l. leucops
 NW New Guinea
T. l. mayri
 WC New Guinea
T. l. nigroorbitalis
 NC New Guinea
T. l. heurni
 C New Guinea
T. l. nigriceps
 EC New Guinea
T. l. melanogenys
 N New Guinea
T. l. wahgiensis
 C & E New Guinea
T. l. albifacies
 SE New Guinea
T. l. auricularis
 S New Guinea
T. l. albigularis
 N Queensland
Tregellasia capito (Pale Yellow Robin)
T. c. nana
 N Queensland
T. c. capito
 S Queensland, New South Wales

EOPSALTRIA
Eopsaltria australis (Eastern Yellow Robin)
E. a. magnirostris
 N Queensland
E. a. chrysorrhoa
 C Queensland
E. a. coomooboolaroo
 EC Queensland
E. a. australis
 S Queensland, New South Wales
E. a. austina
 C & N New South Wales
E. a. viridior
 Victoria
Eopsaltria griseogularis (Western Yellow Robin)
E. g. griseogularis
 S Western Australia
E. g. rosinae
 South Australia

Eopsaltria georgiana **(White-breasted Robin)**
    coastal S Western Australia
Eopsaltria flaviventris **(Yellow-bellied Robin)**
    New Caledonia

PENEOENANTHE
Peneoenanthe pulverulenta **(Mangrove Robin)**
    P. p. pulverulenta
        S New Guinea
    P. p. leucura
        Aru Is, N Queensland
    P. p. cinereiceps
        N Western Australia
    P. p. alligator
        NC Australia

PHILENTOMA
Philentoma pyrrhoptera **(Chestnut-winged Monarch Flycatcher)**
    P. p. pyrrhoptera
        S Vietnam, Malaysia, Sumatra, Borneo
    P. p. dubia
        Natuna Is
Philentoma velata **(Maroon-breasted Monarch Flycatcher)**
    P. v. caesia
        Malaysia, Borneo, Sumatra
    P. v. velata
        Java

POECILODRYAS
Poecilodryas brachyura **(White-breasted Robin)**
    P. b. brachyura
        NW New Guinea
    P. b. albotaeniata
        Japen I, New Guinea
    P. b. dumasi
        N New Guinea
Poecilodryas hypoleuca **(Black and White Robin)**
    P. h. hypoleuca
        NW New Guinea
    P. h. steini
        Misol I, W New Guinea
    P. h. hermani
        N New Guinea
Poecilodryas superciliosa **(White-browed Robin)**
    P. s. superciliosa
        N Queensland
    P. s. cerviniventris
        N Western Australia, Northern Territory
Poecilodryas placens **(Olive-yellow Robin)**
    SE New Guinea

Poecilodryas albonotata **(Black-throated Robin)**   479
    P. a. albonotata
        NW New Guinea
    P.a. griseiventris
        SW New Guinea
    P. a. correcta
        SE New Guinea

PENEOTHELLO
Peneothello sigillatus **(White-winged Thicket Flycatcher)**
    P. s. saruwagedi
        NE New Guinea
    P. s. quadrimaculatus
        W New Guinea
    P. s. hagenensis
        EC New Guinea
    P. s. sigillatus
        SE New Guinea
Peneothello cryptoleucus **(Grey Thicket Flycatcher)**
    P. c. cryptoleucus
        NW New Guinea
    P. c. albidior
        WC New Guinea
Peneothello cyanus **(Slaty Thicket Flycatcher)**
    P. c. cyanus
        NW New Guinea
    P. c. atricapillus
        NE New Guinea
    P. c. subcyanus
        SE & C New Guinea
Peneothello bimaculatus **(White rumped Thicket Flycatcher)**
    P. b. bimaculatus
        NW New Guinea
    P. b. vicarius
        SE New Guinea

HETEROMYIAS
Heteromyias albispecularis **(Ground Thicket Robin)**
    H. a. albispecularis
        NW New Guinea
    H. a. atricapillus
        NW New Guinea
    H. a. rothschildi
        WC New Guinea
    H. a. centralis
        C New Guinea
    H. a. armiti
        SE New Guinea
Heteromyias cinereifrons **(Grey-headed Thicket Robin)**
    N Queensland

Pachycephalopsis hattamensis (Green Thicket Flycatcher)

P. h. hattamensis
NW New Guinea
P. h. ernesti
NW New Guinea
P. h. axillaris
WC New Guinea

Pachycephalopsis poliosoma (White-throated Thicket Flycatcher)

P. p. idenburgi
N New Guinea
P. p. hypopolia
NE New Guinea
P. p. albigularis
WC New Guinea
P. p. balim
WC New Guinea
P. p. approximans
C New Guinea
P. p. hunsteini
EC New Guinea
P. p. poliosoma
SE New Guinea

MUSCICAPIDAE

139 PLATYSTEIRINAE (PUFFBACK & WATTLED ·FLYCATCHERS)

MEGABYAS

Megabyas flammulatus (African Shrike Flycatcher)

M. f. flammulatus
Sierra Leone to Gabon, Fernando Po I
M. f. carolathi
N Angola
M. f. aequatorialis
NE Angola to S Sudan, Uganda

BIAS

Bias musicus (Black & White Flycatcher)

B. m. musicus
Sierra Leone to C Zaire
B. m. femininus
C Zaire to SW Sudan, Uganda
B. m. pallidiventris
N Angola, S Zaire
B. m. changamwensis
E Kenya to Rhodesia, Mozambique
B. m. clarens
S Mozambique

PSEUDOBIAS

Pseudobias wardi (Ward's Flycatcher)
Madagascar

Batis capensis (Cape Puff-back Flycatcher)

B. c. dimorpha
Zambia, S Malawi, Mozambique
B. c. reichenowi
SE Tanzania
B. c. kennedyi
W Rhodesia
B. c. capensis
E Rhodesia, South Africa
B. c. erythrophthalma
S Rhodesia, W Mozambique

Batis mixta (Short-tailed Puff-back Flycatcher)
SE Kenya, Tanzania, N Malawi

Batis margaritae (Boulton's Puff-back Flycatcher)

B. m. margaritae
S Angola
B. m. kathleenae
NW Zambia

Batis diops (Ruwenzori Puff-back Flycatcher)
E Zaire, S Uganda

Batis fratrum (Zululand Puff-back Flycatcher)

B. f. ultima
SE Kenya
B. f. fratrum
Mozambique, N Natal

Batis molitor (Chin Spot Puff-back Flycatcher)

B. m. molitor
Sudan & Kenya to S Africa
B. m. pintoi
Angola

Batis soror (Paler Chin-spot Puff-back Flycatcher)
E Kenya to Mozambique

Batis pirit (Pirit Puff-back Flycatcher)
S Angola to Cape Province

Batis senegalensis (Senegal Puff-back Flycatcher)
Senegal to Nigeria

Batis orientalis (Grey-headed Puff-back Flycatcher)

B. o. chadensis
Niger to W Sudan
B. o. lynesi
N Sudan
B. o. orientalis
Ethiopia, E Sudan, N Kenya

Batis perkeo (Pygmy Puff-back Flycatcher)
S Ethiopia, Kenya, Somalia

Batis minor (Black-headed Puff-back Flycatcher)
 B. m. batesi
  Cameroun
 B. m. erlangeri
  Cameroun & Angola to Somalia
 B. m. minor
  Somalia
 B. m. suahelica
  E Kenya, E Tanzania
Batis minulla (Angola Puff-back Flycatcher)
  Cameroun to Angola
Batis minima (Verreaux's Puff-back Flycatcher)
 B. m. minima
  Gabon
 B. m. ituriensis
  NE Zaire

Batis poensis (Fernando Po Puff-back Flycatcher)
  Liberia to Cameroun

PLATYSTEIRA
Platysteira cyanea (Brown-throated Wattle-eye)
 P. c. cyanea
  Senegal to Gabon, Central African Republic
 P. c. nyanzae
  N Zaire, Uganda, S Sudan, Kenya
 P. c. aethiopica
  E Ethiopia
Platysteira albifrons (White-fronted Wattle-eye)
  N Angola, SW Zaire
Platysteira peltata (Black-throated Wattle-eye)
 P. p. laticincta
  Cameroun
 P. p. mentalis
  Angola to Zambia & Uganda
 P. p. peltata
  S E Africa
Platysteira concreta (Yellow-bellied Wattle-eye)
 P. c. concreta
  Sierra Leone to Ghana
 P. c. harterti
  Cameroun, Gabon
 P. c. kumbaensis
  SW Cameroun
 P. c. ansorgei
  Angola
 P. c. graueri
  E Zaire, Uganda
 P. c. silvae
  W Kenya

 P. c. kungwensis
  W Tanzania
Platysteira blissetti (Red-cheeked Wattle-eye)
 P. b. blissetti
  Sierra Leone to Cameroun
 P. b. chalybea
  Cameroun to N Angola
 P. b. jamesoni
  C Zaire to S Sudan & N Kenya
Platysteira castanea (Chestnut Wattle-eye)
 P. c. castanea
  Sierra Leone to Togo
 P. c. hormophora
  S Nigeria to Angola & W Kenya
Platysteira tonsa (White-spotted Wattle-eye)
  S Nigeria to N Zaire

MUSCICAPIDAE

140 MONARCHINAE (MONARCH FLYCATCHERS)

ERYTHROCERCUS
Erythrocercus holochlorus (Little Yellow Flycatcher)
  Kenya, Tanzania
Erythrocercus mccallii (Chestnut-capped Flycatcher)
 E. m. nigeriae
  Guinea to Nigeria
 E. m. mccallii
  Cameroun, Gabon
 E. m. congicus
  E Zaire, Uganda
Erythrocercus livingstonei (Livingstone's Flycatcher)
 E. l. thomsoni
  S Tanzania, N Mozambique
 E. l. livingstonei
  S Zambia, S Malawi, C Mozambique
 E. l. francisci
  N Malawi

ERANNORNIS
Erannornis longicauda (Blue Flycatcher)
 E. l. longicauda
  Sierra Leone to Central African Republic
 E. l. teresita
  Cameroun to S Sudan & Kenya
 E. l. loandae
  N & C Angola
Erannornis albicauda (White-tailed Blue Flycatcher)
  Angola to Tanzania

Trochocercus albonotatus (White-tailed Crested Flycatcher)

T. a. albonotatus
Uganda to Tanzania & Malawi

T. a. swynnertoni
E Rhodesia

T. a. subcaeruleus
N Tanzania, NE Zambia, N Mozambique

Trochocercus albiventris (White-bellied Crested Flycatcher)

T. a. albiventris
Cameroun, Fernando Po I

T. a. toroensis
NE Zaire, Uganda

Trochocercus nigromitratus (Dusky Crested Flycatcher)
Liberia to Uganda

Trochocercus cyanomelas (Cape Crested Flycatcher)

T. c. vivax
Uganda to S Zaire, Zambia

T. c. kikuyuensis
C Kenya

T. c. bivittatus
E Kenya to Mozambique, Malawi

T. c. cyanomelas
E South Africa

Trochocercus nitens (Blue-headed Crested Flycatcher)

T. n. reichenowi
Sierra Leone to Togo

T. n. nitens
Nigeria to E Zaire & Angola

Terpsiphone viridis (African Paradise Flycatcher)

T. v. viridis
Senegal to N Nigeria & Central African Republic

T. v. speciosa
S Ivory Coast to Gabon & W Sudan

T. v. violacea
Cameroun to Botswana & Kenya

T. v. ferretti
Ethiopia to Tanzania

T. v. restricta
N Kenya

T. v. ruwenzoriae
E Zaire, W Uganda, NW Tanzania

T. v. kivuensis
Rwanda, Kivu, NW Tanzania

T. v. suahelica
E Tanzania

T. v. ungujaensis
E Tanzania, Zambia

T. v. plumbeiceps
Angola, W Zaire, Namibia

T. v. granti
E South Africa

Terpsiphone rufocinerea (Rufous-vented Paradise Flycatcher)

T. r. bates
Cameroun to C Zaire

T. r. rufocinerea
Gabon to N Angola

T. r. bannermani
N Angola

Terpsiphone atrochalybea (Sao Thomé Paradise Flycatcher)
Sao Thomé I

Terpsiphone mutata (Madagascar Paradise Flycatcher)
Madagascar

Terpsiphone corvina (Seychelles Paradise Flycatcher)
Seychelles

Terpsiphone bourbonnensis (Mascarene Paradise Flycatcher)
Mauritius I

Terpsiphone paradisi (Asiatic Paradise Flycatcher)

T. p. harterti
Arabia

T. p. turkestanica
Turkistan

T. p. leucogaster
Afghanistan, Pakistan, W India

T. p. paradisi
C & S India, Sri Lanka

T. p. ceylonensis
Sri Lanka

T. p. incei
China, Manchuria, Korea

T. p. saturatior
E Himalayas, Assam, Bangladesh

T. p. burmae
Burma

T. p. affinis
S Burma, Thailand, Laos, Malaysia

T. p. nicobarica
Nicobar Is, Andaman Is

T. p. indochinensis
S Thailand, Cambodia

T. p. borneensis
Borneo

T. p. matzoedi
N Sumatra

T. p. australis
Java, S Sumatra

T. p. procera
Simalur I

T. p. insularis
Nias I

T. p. sumbaensis
Sumba I

T. p. floris
 Sumbawa I, Alor I, Flores I
Terpsiphone atrocaudata (Black Paradise Flycatcher)
 T. a. atrocaudata
  Japan, SE Asia
 T. a. illex
  S Japan, Riukiu Is
 T. a. periophthalmica
  Mindoro I, Botel Tobago I
Terpsiphone rufiventer (Red-bellied Paradise Flycatcher)
 T. r. rufiventer
  Senegal to Guinea
 T. r. nigriceps
  Guinea to Togo
 T. r. fagani
  S Nigeria
 T. r. tricolor
  Fernando Po I
 T. r. smithii
  Annobon I
 T. r. neumanni
  Cameroun, Gabon
 T. r. schubotzi
  Central African Republic
 T. r. bedfordi
  N Zaire
 T. r. mayombe
  W Zaire
 T. r. somereni
  W Uganda
 T. r. emini
  SW Uganda, NW Tanzania
 T. r. ignea
  S Zaire, N Angola, Zambia
Terpsiphone unirufa (Luzon Paradise Flycatcher)
 Luzon I, Mindoro I, Negros I
Terpsiphone cinnamomea (Rufous Paradise Flycatcher)
 T. c. cinnamomea
  Mindanao I, Basilan I, Sulu Archipelago
 T. c. talautensis
  Talaut I
Terpsiphone cyanescens (Blue Paradise Flycatcher)
 Palawan I

EUTRICHOMYIAS
Eutrichomyias rowleyi (Rowley's Flycatcher)
 Gt Sangai I, Peleng I, Banggai I

HYPOTHYMIS
Hypothymis helenae (Short-crested Blue Monarch)
 H. h. helenae
  Luzon I, Samar I

483

H. h. agusanae
 NE Mindanao I
H. h. personata
 Camiguin I, (North)
Hypothymis coelestis (Celestial Blue Monarch)
 H. c. coelestis
  Luzon I, Mindanao I, Basilan I, Samar I
 H. c. rabori
  Negros I
Hypothymis azurea (Black-naped Blue Monarch)
 H. a. styani
  India to S China & Vietnam
 H. a. forrestia
  Burma
 H. a. ceylonensis
  Sri Lanka
 H. a. prophata
  Malaysia, Sumatra, Borneo
 H. a. tytleri
  Andaman Is, Cocos Is
 H. a. idiochroa
  Car Nicobar I
 H. a. nicobarica
  S Nicobar Is
 H. a. javana
  Java
 H. a. karimatensis
  Karimata I
 H. a. opisthocyanea
  Anamba Is
 H. a. gigantoptera
  Bunguran I, Natuna Is
 H. a. aeria
  Maratua I
 H. a. consobrina
  Simalur I
 H. a. leucophila
  Siberut I
 H. a. richmondi
  Enggano I
 H. a. abbotti
  Babi I, Masia I
 H. a. symmixta
  Lesser Sunda Is
 H. a. azurea
  Philippine Is
 H. a. catarmanensis
  Camiguin I (South)
Hypothymis puella (Small Monarch)
 H. p. puella
  Celebes
 H. p. blasii
  Sula Is

Seisura inquieta (Restless Flycatcher)
S. i. nana
 N Western Australia, Northern Territory
S. i. westralensis
 S Western Australia
S. i. inquieta
 E Australia

MACHAERIRHYNCHUS
Machaerirhynchus flaviventer (Yellow-breasted Flatbill Flycatcher)
M. f. albifrons
 Waigeu I, Misol I, N New Guinea
M. f. albigula
 NW New Guinea
M. f. novus
 NE New Guinea
M. f. xanthogenys
 S New Guinea, Aru Is
M. f. secundus
 N Queensland
M. f. flaviventer
 Queensland
Machaerirhynchus nigripectus (Black-breasted Flatbill Flycatcher)
M. n. nigripectus
 NW New Guinea
M. n. saturatus
 C New Guinea
M. n. harterti
 SE New Guinea

CHASIEMPIS
Chasiempis sandwichensis (Elepaio)
C. s. sandwichensis
 Hawaii I
C. s. sclateri
 Kauai I
C. s. gayi
 Oahu I

POMAREA
Pomarea dimidiata (Raratonga Flycatcher)
 Raratonga I
Pomarea nigra (Society Is Flycatcher)
P. n. nigra
 Tahiti Is
P. n. pomarea
 Maupiti I
Pomarea mendozae (Marquesas Flycatcher)
P. m. mendozae
 Tahuata I, Hivaoa I
P. m. motanensis
 Motane I
P. m. mira
 Huapu I
P. m. nukuhivae
 Nukuhiva I

Pomarea iphis (Allied Flycatcher)
P. i. iphis
 Huahuna I
P. i. fluxa
 Eioa I
Pomarea whitneyi (Large Flycatcher)
 Fatuhiva I

MAYRORNIS
Mayrornis schistaceus (Small Slaty Flycatcher)
 Vanikoro I
Mayrornis versicolor (Versicolored Flycatcher)
 Ongea Levu I
Mayrornis lessoni (Slaty Flycatcher)
M. l. lessoni
 NW Fiji Is
M. l. orientalis
 S Fiji Is

NEOLALAGE
Neolalage banksiana (Buff-bellied Flycatcher)
 Banks Is, New Hebrides

CLYTORHYNCHUS
Clytorhynchus pachycephaloides (Southern Shrikebill)
C. p. pachycephaloides
 New Caledonia
C. p. grisescens
 Banks Is, New Hebrides
Clytorhynchus vitiensis (Fiji Shrikebill)
C. v. powelli
 Manua I
C. v. compressirostris
 Kandavu I
C. v. vitiensis
 Viti Levu I, Ovalau I
C. v. buensis
 Vanua Levu I
C. v. layardi
 Taviuni I
C. v. pontifex
 Ngambia I, Rambi I
C. v. vatuana
 N Lau Archipelago
C. v. heinei
 Tonga I
C. v. wiglesworthi
 Rotuma I
C. v. nesiotes
 S Lau Archipelago
C. v. fotunae
 Fotuna I, Alofa I
C. v. keppeli
 Keppel I, Boscawen I

Clytorhynchus nigrogularis (Black-throated Shrikebill)
  C. n. nigrogularis
    Fiji Is
  C. n. sanctaecrucis
    Santa Cruz I
Cytorhynchus hamlini (Rennell Shrikebill)
    Rennell I

METABOLUS
Metabolus rugiensis (Truk Monarch)
    Truk I

MONARCHA
Monarcha axillaris (Black Monarch)
  M. a. axillaris
    NW New Guinea
  M. a. fallax
    EC New Guinea
  M. a. reichenowi
    N New Guinea
Monarcha rubiensis (Rufous Monarch)
  M. r. rubiensis
    Rubi I, NW New Guinea
  M. r. rufum
    NE New Guinea
Monarcha alecto (Shining Monarch)
  M. a. alecto
    Ternate I, Moluccas
  M. a. chalybeocephalus
    New Ireland
  M. a. lucidus
    Woodlark I
  M. a. manumudari
    Vulcan I
  M. a. rufolateralis
    Aru Is
  M. a. longirostris
    Timor I
  M. a. nitens
    Batjan I
  M. a. novaeguineensis
    W New Guinea
  M. a. tormenti
    N Western Australia
  M. a. nitida
    Northern Territory
  M. a. wardelli
    N Queensland
Monarcha hebetior (Dull Monarch)
  M. h. hebetior
    St Matthias Is
  M. h. eichhorni
    New Hanover
  M. h. cervinicolor
    Dyaul I
Monarcha sericeus (New Hebrides Monarch)
    New Hebrides

Monarcha pileatus (Moluccan Monarch)
  M. p. pileatus
    Halmahera I
  M. p. buruensis
    Buru I
  M. p. castus
    Tenimber Is
Monarcha cinerascens (Island Grey-headed Monarch)
  M. c. cinerascens
    Gt Banda I, Sulu Is, Timor I
  M. c. disjuncta
    Kalao I, Djampea I
  M. c. perpallidus
    St Matthias Is, Emirau I, New Hanover
  M. c. inornatus
    NW New Guinea
  M. c. steini
    New Guinea
  M. c. geelvinkianus
    Misol I, Japen I
  M. c. fuscescens
    Jamna I
  M. c. nigrirostris
    New Guinea
  M. c. rosselianus
    Rossel I
  M. c. impediens
    Lihir Is, Feni I
  M. c. fulviventris
    Ninigo I, Echiquier I
  M. c. kisserensis
    Kei Is, Kisser I, Tenimber Is
  M. c. commutator
    Sangi Is
  M. c. harterti
    Halmahera I, Ternate I, Buru I
  M. c. tenchi
    Tench I (St Matthias)
  M. c. intercedens
    Tukangbesi I
Monarcha melanopsis (Pearly-winged Monarch)
  M. m. melanopsis
    S New Guinea, Queensland, New South Wales
  M. m. pallida
    N Queensland
Monarcha frater (Black-winged Monarch)
  M. f. everetti
    Djampea I
  M. f. frater
    NW New Guinea
  M. f. kunupi
    C New Guinea
  M. f. periophthalmicus
    SE New Guinea

M. f. canescens
N Queensland

Monarcha erythrosticta (Bougainville Monarch)
Bougainville I

Monarcha castaneiventris (Chestnut-bellied Monarch)
M. c. castaneiventris
Guadalcanal I, Malaita I, Choiseul I
M. c. obscurior
Rossel I
M. c. megarhyncha
San Cristobal I
M. c. ugiensis
Ugi Is
M. c. florenciae
Rubiana I

Monarcha richardsii (Richard's Monarch)
C Solomon Is

Monarcha leucotis (White-eared Monarch)
Queensland

Monarcha guttula (Spot-winged Monarch)
E New Guinea, Aru Is

Monarcha julienae (Kofiau Monarch)
Kofiau I

Monarcha mundus (Tenimber Monarch)
Tenimber Is

Monarcha trivirgatus (Spectacled Monarch)
M. t. trivirgatus
Timor I, Flores I, Alor I
M. t. bernsteini
NW New Guinea
M. t. melanopterus
Louisiade Archipelago
M. t. diadematus
Obi I
M. t. wellsi
Goram I
M. t. bimaculatus
Halmahera I, Batjan I
M. t. morotensis
Morotai I
M. t. nigrimentum
Ceram I, Ambon I
M. t. albiventris
N Queensland
M. t. gouldi
S Queensland, New South Wales
M. t. boanensis
Boano I
M. t. loricata
Buru I

Monarcha sacerdotum (Mees' Monarch)
Flores I

Monarcha leucurus (Kei Monarch)
Kei Is

Monarcha barbatus (Pied Monarch)
M. b. barbatus
Bougainville I, Guadalcanal I
M. b. floridanus
Florida I
M. b. squamulatus
Ugi I
M. b. meeki
Rendova I
M. b. malaitae
Malaita I

Monarcha infelix (Unhappy Monarch)
M. i. infelix
Manus I
M. i. coultasi
Rambutyo I

Monarcha menckei (St Matthias Monarch)
St Matthias Is

Monarcha viduus (San Cristobal Monarch)
San Cristobal I

Monarcha browni (Kulambangra Monarch)
M. b. browni
Kulambangra I
M. b. ganongae
Ganonga I
M. b. nigrotectus
Vella Lavella I

Monarcha verticalis (New Britain Pied Monarch)
Bismarck Archipelago

Monarcha ateralba (Bismarck Monarch)
Dyaul I

Monarcha godeffroyi (Yap Monarch)
Yap I

Monarcha brehmii (Biak Monarch)
Biak I, Misol I

Monarcha manadensis (Black & White Monarch)
New Guinea

Monarcha chrysomela (Black & Yellow Monarch)
M. c. chrysomela
New Hanover, New Ireland
M. c. kordensis
Biak I, Misol I
M. c. melanonotus
New Guinea
M. c. aurantiacus
NE New Guinea
M. c. praerepta
D'Entrecasteaux Archipelago, New Guinea
M. c. aruensis
Aru Is, S New Guinea
M. c. pulcherrima
Dyaul I

M. c. whitneyorum
  Lihir Is
M. c. tabarensis
  Tabar I
Monarcha takatsukasae (Tinian Monarch)
  Tinian I

Arses kaupi (Pied Flycatcher)
  N Queensland
**Arses telescophthalmus (Frilled
  Flycatcher)**
  A. t. telescophthalmus
    Misol I, NW New Guinea
  A. t. insularis
    Japen I, N New Guinea
  A. t. batantae
    Batanta I, Waigeu I
  A. t. aruensis
    Aru Is
  A. t. lauterbachi
    NE New Guinea
  A. t. harterti
    SW & S New Guinea
  A. t. henkei
    SE New Guinea
  A. t. orientalis
    SE New Guinea
  A. t. lorealis
    N Queensland

**Myiagra pluto (Ponapé Myiagra
  Flycatcher)**
  Ponapé I
**Myiagra oceanica (Truk Myiagra
  Flycatcher)**
  Truk I
**Myiagra freycineti (Guam Myiagra
  Flycatcher)**
  Guam I
**Myiagra erythrops (Palau Myiagra
  Flycatcher)**
  Palau Is
Myiagra galeata (Helmet Flycatcher)
  M. g. galeata
    Batjan I
  M. g. goramensis
    Goram I
  M. g. seranensis
    Ceram I
  M. g. buruensis
    Buru I
Myiagra rubecula (Leaden Flycatcher)
  M. r. papuana
    New Guinea
  M. r. sciurorum
    Louisiade Archipelago

M. r. concinna
  N Western Australia, Northern Territory,
  N Queensland
M. r. yorki
  NE Queensland
M. r. rubecula
  S Queensland to South Australia &
  Victoria
Myiagra atra (Black Myiagra Flycatcher)
  Misol Is
**Myiagra ferrocyanea (Steel-blue
  Flycatcher)**
  M. f. ferrocyanea
    Ysabel I, Choiseul I, Guadalcanal I
  M. f. feminina
    Kulambangra I
  M. f. pallida
    Vella Lavella I
  M. f. cinerea
    Bougainville I
  M. f. malaitae
    Malaita I
  M. f. cervinicauda
    Ugi I, San Cristobal I
**Myiagra caledonica (New Caledonian
  Myiagra Flycatcher)**
  M. c. caledonica
    New Caledonia
  M. c. melanura
    Tanna I, Erromanga I, Maré I
  M. c. marina
    N & C New Hebrides
  M. c. perspicillata
    Nu I (New Caledonia)
  M. c. viridinitens
    Lifu I, Urea I
  M. c. occidentalis
    Rennell I
**Myiagra vanikorensis (Red-bellied
  Flycatcher)**
  M. v. vanikorensis
    Santa Cruz I, Vanikoro I
  M. v. castaneiventris
    Samoa Is
  M. v. rufiventris
    Navigator I, NW Fiji Is
  M. v. townsendi
    S Lau Is
  M. v. kandavensis
    Kandavu I
  M. v. dorsalis
    SC Fiji Is, N Lau Is
**Myiagra albiventris (White-vented
  Flycatcher)**
  Samoa Is
Myiagra cyanoleuca (Satin Flycatcher)
  M. c. novaepomeraniae
    New Britain

M. c. nupta
Louisiade Archipelago
M. c. robinsoni
N Queensland
M. c. cyanoleuca
E Australia, Tasmania
Myiagra ruficollis (Broad-billed Flycatcher)
M. r. ruficollis
Alor I, Timor I
M. r. rufigula
Timor I
M. r. mimikae
New Guinea, N Queensland
M. r. fulviventris
Tenimber Is
M. r. colonus
Kalao I, Djampea I
Myiagra azureocapilla (Blue-headed Flycatcher)
M. a. azureocapilla
Taviuni I
M. a. castaneigularis
Vanua Levu I, Kambara I
M. a. whitneyi
Viti Levu I

MUSCICAPIDAE

141 RHIPIDURINAE (FANTAIL FLY-CATCHERS)

RHIPIDURA
Rhipidura hypoxantha (Yellow-bellied Fantail)
Himalayas, S China
Rhipidura threnothorax (Sooty Thicket Fantail)
R. t. threnothorax
E New Guinea
R. t. novaeguineensis
New Guinea
R. t. fumosa
Japen I
R. t. rosenbergi
Aru Is
Rhipidura maculipectus (Black Thicket Fantail)
R. m. maculipectus
Ambon I, Aru Is
R. m. mimika
New Guinea
R. m. saturata
Salawati I (New Guinea)
Rhipidura clamosa (Karimui Thicket Fantail)
E Highlands, New Guinea

Rhipidura leucothorax (White-breasted Fantail)
R. l. leucothorax
NW New Guinea
R. l. episcopalis
SE New Guinea
Rhipidura superciliaris (Blue Fantail)
R. s. superciliaris
Basilan I, N Mindanao
R. s. apo
SE Mindanao
R. s. samarensis
Bohol I, Samar I, Leyte I
Rhipidura cyaniceps (Blue-headed Fantail)
R. c. cyaniceps
Luzon I
R. c. pinicola
NW Luzon I
R. c. albiventris
Masbate I, Negros I, Panay I
R. c. sauli
Tablas I
Rhipidura phoenicura (Red-tailed Fantail)
Java
Rhipidura nigrocinnamomea (Black and Cinnamon Fantail)
R. n. hutchinsoni
N Mindanao I
R. n. nigrocinnamomea
SE Mindanao I
Rhipidura opistherythra (Tenimber Rufous Fantail)
Tenimber Is
Rhipidura lepida (Palau Fantail)
Palau Is
Rhipidura dedemi (Ceram Rufous Fantail)
Ceram I
Rhipidura superflua (Moluccan Fantail)
Buru I
Rhipidura sulaensis (Sula Fantail)
Sula Is
Rhipidura teijsmanni (Celebes Rufous Fantail)
R. t. teijsmanni
S & C Celebes
R. t. toradja
mountains of Celebes
Rhipidura rufifrons (Rufous Fantail)
R. r. uraniae
Mariana Is, Guam I
R. r. saipanensis
Saipan I, Tinian I
R. r. mariae
Rota I

R. r. kubaryi
Ponapé I
R. r. versicolor
Yap I
R. r. griseicauda
Waigeu I
R. r. torrida
Halmahera I, Ternate I
R. r. semicollaris
Timor I
R. r. sumbensis
Sumba I
R. r. agilis
Santa Cruz I
R. r. melaenolaema
Vanikoro I
R. r. utupuae
Utupua I
R. r. commoda
Bougainville I
R. r. rufofronta
Guadalcanal I
R. r. granti
Rendova I
R. r. russata
San Cristobal I
R. r. semirubra
Admiralty Is
R. r. hamadryas
Tenimber Is
R. r. astrolabi
Santa Cruz I
R. r. brunnea
Malaita I
R. r. kuperi
Santa Anna I
R. r. ugiensis
Ugi I
R. r. streptophora
SW New Guinea
R. r. mimosae
Kalao I
R. r. celebensis
Djampea I
R. r. elegantula
Roma I, Leti I, Moa I, Damar I
R. r. reichenowi
Babar I
R. r. squamata
Banda I
R. r. henrici
Ceram I, Kei Is
R. r. louisiadensis
Louisiade Archipelago
R. r. dryas
N Western Australia, Northern Territory
R. r. rufifrons
Queensland to Victoria

Rhipidura dahli (Island Rufous Fantail)
R. d. dahli
New Britain
R. d. antonii
New Ireland
Rhipidura matthiae (St Matthias Rufous Fantail)
St Matthias Is
Rhipidura personata (Kandavu Fantail)
Kandavu I (Fiji Is)
Rhipidura rufidorsa (Grey-breasted Rufous Fantail)
R. r. rufidorsa
Misol I, Japen I, NW New Guinea
R. r. kumusi
SE New Guinea
R. r. kubuna
S New Guinea
R. r. nova
E New Guinea
R. r. montana
SE New Guinea
Rhipidura brachyrhyncha (Dimorphic Rufous Fantail)
R. b. brachyrhyncha
NW New Guinea
R. b. devisi
SE New Guinea
Rhipidura spilodera (Spotted Fantail)
R. s. sancta
New Hebrides
R. s. spilodera
N & C New Hebrides, Banks Is
R. s. layardi
Ovalau I, Viti Levu I
R. s. erythronota
Yanganga I, Vanua Levu I
R. s. rufilateralis
Taviuni I
R. s. verreauxi
Lifu I, Meré I, New Caledonia
Rhipidura rennelliana (Rennell Fantail)
Rennell I
Rhipidura drownei (Mountain Fantail)
R. d. drownei
Bougainville I
R. d. ocularis
Guadalcanal I
Rhipidura tenebrosa (Dusky Fantail)
San Cristobal I
Rhipidura fuliginosa (Collared Grey Fantail)
R. f. bulgeri
Lifu I, New Caledonia
R. f. erromangae
Erromanga I

R. f. phasiana
New Guinea
R. f. brenchleyi
New Hebrides, Banks Is
R. f. preissi
S Western Australia
R. f. subphasiana
N Western Australia
R. f. buchanani
Melville I, Northern Territory
R. f. albicauda
C Australia
R. f. harterti
N Queensland
R. f. frerei
C Queensland
R. f. alisteri
S Queensland to Victoria
R. f. albiscapa
King I, Tasmania
R. f. placabilis
North I (New Zealand)
R. f. fuliginosa
South I (New Zealand)
R. f. penitus
Chatham I
R. f. pelzelni
Norfolk I
R. f. cervina
Lord Howe I
Rhipidura nebulosa (Samoan Fantail)
R. n. nebulosa
Upolu I
R. n. altera
Savaii I
**Rhipidura malaitae (Malaita Rufous
Fantail)**
Malaita I
Rhipidura atra (Black Fantail)
R. a. atra
NW New Guinea
R. a. vulpes
N New Guinea
**Rhipidura hyperythra (Chestnut-bellied
Fantail)**
R. h. hyperythra
Aru Is
R. h. mulleri
SW New Guinea
R. h. castaneothorax
SE New Guinea
R. h. manayoensis
SE New Guinea
Rhipidura euryura (White-bellied Fantail)
Java
Rhipidura albolimbata (Friendly Fantail)
R. a. albolimbata
NW New Guinea

R. a. lorentzi
SW New Guinea
R. a. auricularis
SE New Guinea
**Rhipidura albicollis (White-throated
Fantail)**
R. a. canescens
W Himalayas
R. a. albicollis
N India, Nepal
R. a. orissae
NE India
R. a. stanleyi
E Himalayas, Assam, Burma
R. a. robinsoni
Malaysia
R. a. atrata
Sumatra
R. a. sarawacensis
N Borneo
R. a. kinabalu
Borneo
R. a. cinerescens
S Indochina
**Rhipidura albogularis (White-spotted
Fantail)**
R. a. albogularis
SW India
R. a. vernayi
SE India
Rhipidura aureola (White-browed Fantail)
R. a. aureola
N India
R. a. compressirostris
S India, Sri Lanka
R. a. burmanica
Assam, Burma
Rhipidura javanica (Pied Fantail)
R. j. longicauda
Sumatra
R. j. javanica
Java
R. j. nigritorquis
Philippine Is
**Rhipidura rufiventris (Red-vented
Fantail)**
R. r. rufiventris
Timor I
R. r. perneglecta
Tiandu I
R. r. finitima
Watubela I
R. r. assimilis
Kei Is
R. r. buruensis
Buru I
R. r. obiensis
Obi I

R. r. pallidiceps
Wetar I
R. r. gigantea
Lihir Is, Tabar I
R. r. tangensis
Boang I, Tanga I
R. r. cinerea
Ceram I
R. r. lenzi
Ambon I
R. r. buttikkoferi
Damar I
R. r. hoedti
Leti I
R. r. diluta
Flores I
R. r. sumbawensis
Sumbawa I
R. r. tenkatei
Rotti I
R. r. niveiventris
Admiralty Is
R. r. mussaui
St Matthias Is
R. r. setosa
New Ireland
R. r. finschii
New Britain
R. r. vidua
New Guinea
R. r. gularis
Waigeu I, Japen I
R. r. nigromentalis
Sudest I
R. r. kordensis
Misol I
R. r. superciliosa
N Australia
R. r. isura
coast of N Western Australia
Rhipidura perlata (Pearlated Fantail)
Malaysia
Rhipidura cockerelli (Cockerell's Fantail)
R. c. cockerelli
Guadalcanal I
R. c. coultasi
N Solomon Is
R. c. septentrionalis
Bougainville I
R. c. interposita
Ysabel I
R. c. floridana
Florida I, Tulagi I
R. c. lavellae
Vella Lavella I
R. c. albina
Kulambangra I, Rendova I

Rhipidura leucophrys (Black & White Fantail) (Willie Wagtail)
R. l. amboinensis
Ambon I, Ceram I, Buru I
R. l. melanoleuca
Solomon Is, New Guinea
R. l. atripennis
Aru Is, SW New Guinea
R. l. picata
N Western Australia, Northern Territory
R. l. leucophrys
S Australia
R. l. melaleuca
Bismarck Archipelago

MUSCICAPIDAE

142 PACHYCEPHALINAE (WHISTLERS)

EULACESTOMA
Eulacestoma nigropectus (Wattled Shrike Tit)
E. n. clara
C New Guinea
E. n. nigropectus
SE New Guinea

FALCUNCULUS
Falcunculus frontatus (Crested Shrike Tit)
F. f. leucogaster
S Western Australia
F. f. whitei
Northern Territory, NW Western Australia
F. f. frontatus
E Australia

OREOICA
Oreoica gutturalis (Crested Bellbird)
O. g. pallescens
N Western Australia
O. g. gutturalis
WC & E Australia

PACHYCARE
Pachycare flavogrisea (Golden-faced Pachycare)
P. f. flavogrisea
W New Guinea
P. f. subaurantia
C New Guinea
P. f. randi
N New Guinea
P. f. subpallida
SE New Guinea

RHAGOLOGUS
Rhagologus leucostigma (Mottled Whistler)
R. l. leucostigma
NW New Guinea
R. l. novus
N New Guinea

R. l. obscurus
C & SE New Guinea

HYLOCITREA
Hylocitrea bonensis (Buff-throated Thickhead)
H. b. bonensis
NC & SE Celebes
H. b. bonthaina
S Celebes

PACHYCEPHALA
Pachycephala raveni (Raven's Whistler)
C & SE Celebes
Pachycephala rufinucha (Rufous-naped Whistler)
P. r. rufinucha
NW New Guinea
P. r. niveifrons
C New Guinea
P. r. lochmia
E New Guinea
P. r. gamblei
SE New Guinea
P. r. prasinonota
SE New Guinea
Pachycephala tenebrosa (Sooty Whistler)
P. t. atra
N New Guinea
P. t. tenebrosa
S New Guinea
Pachycephala olivacea (Olive Whistler)
P. o. macphersoniana
New South Wales, S Queensland
P. o. olivacea
S Victoria, SE South Australia, Tasmania
Pachycephala rufogularis (Red-lored Whistler)
NW Victoria, E South Australia
Pachycephala inornata (Gilbert Whistler)
P. i. gilbertii
S Western Australia
P. i. inornata
SE Australia
Pachycephala hypoxantha (Bornean Mountain Whistler)
P. h. hypoxantha
N Borneo
P. h. sarawacensis
Poi mountains, NW Borneo
Pachycephala cinerea (Mangrove Whistler)
P. c. cinerea
W Malaysia, Bangladesh, Burma, Thailand, Mergui Archipelago
P. c. vandepolli
E Malaysia, S Indochina
P. c. butaloides
Bangka I, Billiton I, S Borneo, Java, Bali I, Lombok I

P. c. secedens
N Borneo, Natuna Is
P. c. homeyeri
Sulu Is
P. c. plateni
Palawan I
P. c. winchelli
C Philippine Is
P. c. mindorensis
Mindoro I
P. c. crissalis
SC Luzon I
P. c. albiventris
N Luzon I
Pachycephala phaionota (Island Whistler)
P. p. phaionota
Aru Is, N Moluccas, NW New Guinea islands
P. p. stresemanni
Majau I (N Moluccas)
Pachycephala hyperythra (Rufous-breasted Whistler)
P. h. hyperythra
W New Guinea
P. h. sepikiana
C New Guinea
P. h. reichenowi
NE New Guinea
P. h. salvadorii
SE New Guinea
Pachycephala modesta (Brown-backed Whistler)
P. m. modesta
SE New Guinea
P. m. hypoleuca
NE New Guinea
P. m. telefolminensis
C New Guinea
Pachycephala philippinensis (Yellow-bellied Whistler)
P. p. fallax
Calayan I
P. p. illex
Camiguin I (North)
P. p. philippinensis
Luzon I
P. p. siquijorensis
Siquijor I
P. p. apoensis
Samar I, Leyte I, Mindanao I
P. p. basilanica
Basilan I
P. p. boholensis
Bohol I
Pachycephala sulfuriventer (Yellow-vented Whistler)
P. s. sulfuriventer
N, C & SE Celebes

P. s. meridionalis
  S Celebes
Pachycephala meyeri (Vogelkop Whistler)
  NW New Guinea
Pachycephala soror (Sclater's Whistler)
  P. s. soror
    W New Guinea
  P. s. klossi
    C & E New Guinea
  P. s. bartoni
    SE New Guinea & Goodenough I
Pachycephala simplex (Brown Whistler)
  P. s. simplex
    Northern Territory, Melville I
  P. s. rufipennis
    Kei Is
  P. s. gagiensis
    Gagi I
  P. s. waigeunensis
    Waigeu I
  P. s. griseiceps
    Aru Is, NE New Guinea
  P. s. miosnomensis
    Meos Num I
  P. s. jobiensis
    Japen I, N New Guinea
  P. s. perneglecta
    S New Guinea
  P. s. peninsulae
    N Queensland
  P. s. dubia
    SE New Guinea, D'Entrecasteaux
      Archipelago
  P. s. sudestensis
    Tagula I, Louisiade Archipelago
Pachycephala orpheus (Timor Whistler)
  P. o. orpheus
    Timor I
  P. o. wetterensis
    Wetar I
Pachycephala pectoralis (Golden Whistler)
  P. p. teysmanni
    Saleyer I
  P. p. everetti
    Djampea I, Kalao Tua I, Madu I
  P. p. javana
    E Java, Bali I
  P. p. fulvotincta
    Sumbawa I, Flores I
  P. p. jubilarii
    Lomblen I, Pantar I, Alor I
  P. p. fulviventris
    Sumba I
  P. p. calliope
    Timor I, Semau I
  P. p. arthuri
    Wetar I

P. p. sharpei
  Babar I
P. p. dammeriana
  Damar I
P. p. par
  Roma I
P. p. compar
  Leti I, Moa I
P. p. fuscoflava
  Larat I (Tenimber Is)
P. p. macrorhynchus
  Ambon I
P. p. alfurorum
  Ceram I
P. p. buruensis
  Buru I
P. p. clio
  Sula Is
P. p. pelengensis
  Banggai I, Peleng I
P. p. obiensis
  Obi I
P. p. tidorensis
  Tidore I, Ternate I
P. p. mentalis
  Batjan I, Halmahera I, Morotai I
P. p. occidentalis
  S Western Australia
P. p. fuliginosa
  South Australia, W Victoria
P. p. glaucura
  Tasmania, King I
P. p. youngi
  E Victoria
P. p. pectoralis
  New South Wales
P. p. ashbyi
  N New South Wales, S Queensland
P. p. queenslandica
  N Queensland
P. p. contempta
  Lord Howe I
P. p. xanthoprocta
  Norfolk I
P. p. collaris
  Louisiade Archipelago
P. p. rosseliana
  Rossel I
P. p. fergussonis
  Fergusson I
P. p. misimae
  Misima I
P. p. citreogaster
  New Hanover, New Britain, New Ireland
P. p. sexuvaria
  St Matthias Is
P. p. goodsoni
  Admiralty Is

P. p. tabarensis
Tabar I
P. p. ottomeyeri
Lihir I
P. p. whitneyi
Whitney I
P. p. bougainvillei
Buka I, Bougainville I
P. p. orioloides
Choiseul I, Ysabel I, Florida I
P. p. cinnamomea
Beagle I, Guadalcanal I
P. p. sanfordi
Malaita I
P. p. pavuvu
Pavuvu Is
P. p. centralis
E New Georgia Is
P. p. feminina
Rennell I
P. p. melanoptera
S New Georgia Is
P. p. melanonota
Ganonga I, Vella Lavella I
P. p. christophori
Santa Ana I, San Cristobal I
P. p. littayei
Loyalty Is
P. p. cucullata
Aneiteum I
P. p. chlorura
Erromango I
P. p. intacta
Banks Is, N & C New Hebrides
P. p. vanikorensis
Vanikoro I, Santa Cruz I
P. p. utupuae
Utupua I
P. p. ornata
N Santa Cruz I
P. p. kandavensis
Kandavu Is
P. p. lauana
S Lau Archipelago
P. p. vitiensis
Ngau I
P. p. bella
Vatu Vara I
P. p. koroana
Karo I
P. p. torquata
Taviuni I
P. p. ambigua
Rambi I, Kio I
P. p. optata
Ovalau I, SE Viti Levu I
P. p. graeffii
Waia I, Viti Levu I

P. p. aurantiiventris
Yanganga I, Vanua Levu I
Pachycephala melanops (Tonga Whistler)
Vavau I, Tonga I
Pachycephala melanura (Mangrove Golden Whistler)
P. m. balim
N New Guinea
P. m. dahli
islands off S New Guinea
P. m. bynoei
Western Australia
P. m. hilli
N Western Australia
P. m. melanura
N Western Australia
P. m. violatae
Northern Territory, Melville I
P. m. spinicauda
N Queensland, Torres Straits islands
Pachycephala flavifrons (Yellow-fronted Whistler)
Samoa Is
Pachycephala caledonica (New Caledonian Whistler)
New Caledonia
Pachycephala implicata (Mountain Whistler)
P. i. implicata
Guadalcanal I
P. i. richardsi
Bougainville I
Pachycephala lorentzi (Lorentz's Whistler)
C & E New Guinea
Pachycephala nudigula (Bare-throated Whistler)
P. n. nudigula
Sumbawa I
P. n. ilsa
Flores I
Pachycephala schlegelii (Schlegel's Whistler)
P. s. schlegelii
W New Guinea
P. s. obscurior
C & E New Guinea
P. s. cyclopum
WC New Guinea
Pachycephala aurea (Yellow-backed Whistler)
SE New Guinea
Pachycephala rufiventris (Rufous Whistler)
P. r. kebirensis
Moa I, Roma I, Damar I, Wetar I
P. r. arctitorquis
Tenimber Is
P. r. tianduana
Tiandou I, (W Kei Is)

P. r. falcata
Melville I, Northern Territory
P. r. colletti
N Western Australia
P. r. pallida
NW Queensland
P. r. dulcior
N Queensland
P. r. rufiventris
South Australia
P. r. maudeae
C Australia
P. r. xanthetraea
New Caledonia
P. r. cinerascens
N Moluccas, Ternate I
P. r. johni
Obi Major I
P. r. lineolata
Sula Is
P. r. examinata
Buru I
P. r. griseonota
Ceram I
P. r. kuehni
Kei Is
P. r. monarcha
Aru Is
P. r. dorsalis
C & E New Guinea
P. r. leucogaster
SE New Guinea
P. r. meeki
Rossel I

Pachycephala lanioides (White-bellied Whistler)
P. l. carnarvoni
Shark Bay (Western Australia)
P. l. bulleri
coast of Western Australia
P. l. lanioides
N Western Australia
P. l. fretorum
Northern Territory, NW Queensland

COLLURICINCLA
***Colluricincla megarhyncha* (Rufous Shrike Thrush)**
C. m. sanghirensis
Sanghir Is
C. m. affinis
Waigeu I
C. m. batantae
Batanta I
C. m. misoliensis
Misol I
C. m. megarhyncha
W New Guinea

C. m. ferruginea
NW New Guinea
C. m. aruensis
Aru Is
C. m. goodsoni
S New Guinea
C. m. wuroi
S New Guinea
C. m. palmeri
S New Guinea
C. m. despecta
SE New Guinea
C. m. superflua
SE New Guinea
C. m. nea
E New Guinea
C. m. madaraszi
E New Guinea
C. m. tappenbecki
NE New Guinea
C. m. maeandrina
NE New Guinea
C. m. idenburgi
N New Guinea
C. m. hybrida
N New Guinea
C. m. obscura
Japen I
C. m. melanorhyncha
Biak I
C. m. fortis
D'Entrecasteaux Archipelago
C. m. trobriandi
Trobriand Is
C. m. discolor
Tagula I
C. m. parvula
Northern Territory, Melville I
C. m. conigravi
N Western Australia
C. m. griseata
Cape York islands
C. m. normani
N Queensland
C. m. parvissima
N Queensland
C. m. gouldii
C & S Queensland
C. m. rufogaster
N New South Wales
***Collurincincla boweri* (Stripe-breasted Shrike-Thrush)**
N Queensland
***Collurincincla harmonica* (Grey Shrike-Thrush)**
C. h. roebucki
Roebuck Bay, N Western Australia

C. h. parryi
Kimberley, Western Australia
C. h. julietae
N Western Australia
C. h. brunnea
Northern Territory, Melville I
C. h. superciliosa
N Queensland
C. h. tachycrypta
SE New Guinea
C. h. pallescens
NC Queensland
C. h. harmonica
S Queensland to E Victoria
C. h. strigata
Tasmania, Bass Strait islands
C. h. halmaturina
SW New South Wales, NW Victoria,
SE South Australia
C. h. anda
NE South Australia
C. h. whitei
C South Australia
C. h. rufiventris
W & C Australia

Colluricincla woodwardi (Sandstone Shrike-Thrush)
C. w. woodwardi
Northern Territory
C. w. assimilis
N Western Australia

PITOHUI
Pitohui kirhocephalus (Variable Pitohui)
P. k. kirhocephalus
NW New Guinea
P. k. salvadorii
NW New Guinea
P. k. dohertyi
NW New Guinea
P. k. rubiensis
NW New Guinea
P. k. stramineipectus
SW New Guinea
P. k. decipiens
SW New Guinea
P. k. adiensis
Adi I
P. k. carolinae
SW New Guinea
P. k. brunneivertex
W New Guinea
P. k. jobiensis
Kurudu I, Japen I
P. k. meyeri
N New Guinea
P. k. senex
N New Guinea

P. k. brunneicaudus
N New Guinea
P. k. meridionalis
SE New Guinea
P. k. brunneiceps
S New Guinea
P. k. nigripectus
S New Guinea
P. k. aruensis
Aru Is
P. k. uropygialis
Salawati I, Misol I
P. k. tibialis
NW New Guinea
P. k. pallidus
Sagewin I, Batanta I
P. k. cerviniventris
Waigeu I

Pitohui dichrous (Black-headed Pitohui)
P. d. dichrous
N New Guinea
P. d. monticola
C New Guinea

Pitohui incertus (Mottle breasted Pitohui)
S New Guinea

Pitohui ferrugineus (Rusty Pitohui)
P. f. leucorhynchus
Waigeu I
P. f. fuscus
Batanta I
P. f. brevipennis
Aru Is
P. f. ferrugineus
Misol I, NW New Guinea
P. f. holerythrus
Japen I, N New Guinea
P. f. clarus
SE New Guinea

Pitohui cristatus (Crested Pitohui)
P. c. cristatus
W New Guinea
P. c. arthuri
N & S New Guinea
P. c. kodonophonos
SE New Guinea

Pitohui nigrescens (Black Pitohui)
P. n. nigrescens
NW New Guinea
P. n. wandamensis
N New Guinea
P. n. meeki
C New Guinea
P. n. burgersi
N & C New Guinea
P. n. schistaceus
SE New Guinea
P. n. harterti
E New Guinea

***Pitohui tenebrosus* (Morning Bird)**
Palau Is

TURNAGRA
Turnagra capensis* (New Zealand Thrush)
T. c. turnagra
North I,(New Zealand)
T. c. capensis
South I,(New Zealand)

143 AEGITHALIDAE (LONG-TAILED TITS)

AEGITHALOS
Aegithalos caudatus* (Long-tailed Tit)
A. c. caudatus
N Europe, N Asia, N Korea
A. c. rosaceus
British Isles
A. c. europaeus
C Europe
A. c. aremoricus
NW & C France
A. c. taiti
N Iberia, S France
A. c. irbii
S Iberia, Corsica
A. c. italiae
Italy
A. c. siculus
Sicily
A. c. macedonicus
Albania, Greece
A. c. tauricus
S Russia
A. c. major
Caucasus
A. c. tephronotus
Asia Minor
A. c. alpinus
N Iran
A. c. passekii
SW Iran
A. c. vinaceus
N & W China
A. c. glaucogularis
C China
A. c. trivirgatus
Honshu I
A. c. kiusiuensis
S Japan
A. c. magnus
S Korea
Aegithalos leucogenys* (White-cheeked Tit)
Afghanistan to NW India
Aegithalos concinnus* (Red-headed Tit)
A. c. iredalei
Pakistan, W Himalayas
A. c. rubricapillus
E Himalayas, Assam

A. c. manipurensis
S Assam, NE India, W Burma
A. c. talifuensis
NE Burma, W China, N Vietnam
A. c. pulchellus
E Burma
A. c. concinnus
C & E China, Taiwan
A. c. annamensis
S Indochina
Aegithalos iouschistos* (Blyth's Long-tailed Tit)
A. i. niveogularis
Pakistan, W Himalayas
A. i. iouschistos
E Himalayas, SE Tibet
A. i. bonvaloti
NE Burma, SW China
A. i. obscuratus
W Szechwan
A. i. sharpei
E Burma
Aegithalos fuliginosus* (Sooty Long-tailed Tit)
W & C China

PSALTRIA
Psaltria exilis* (Pygmy Tit)
W & C Java

PSALTRIPARUS
Psaltriparus minimus* (Common Bushtit)
P. m. minimus
W USA
P. m. californicus
S Oregon, California
P. m. sociabilis
S California
P. m. melanurus
NW Baja California
P. m. grindae
S Baja California
P. m. plumbeus
WC & S USA, N Mexico
P. m. providentialis
SE California, S Nevada
P. m. cecaumenorum
NW Mexico
Psaltriparus melanotis* (Black-eared Bushtit)
P. m. lloydi
S USA, N Mexico
P. m. dimorphicus
N Mexico
P. m. iulus
W & C Mexico
P. m. melanotis
S Mexico, Guatemala

REMIZ
Remiz pendulinus (Penduline Tit)
  R. p. pendulinus
    S & E Europe, Asia Minor, W Siberia
  R. p. caspius
    N & W Caspian Sea
  R. p. coronatus
    C Asia, NW India
  R. p. macronyx
    WC Asia, N Iran
  R. p. nigricans
    E Iran
  R. p. stoliczkae
    N Mongolia
  R. p. consobrinus
    Manchuria, N China, Korea

ANTHOSCOPUS
Anthoscopus punctifrons (Sennar Kapok Tit)
    S Sahara
Anthoscopus parvulus (Yellow Penduline Tit)
    Senegal to Sudan
Anthoscopus musculus (Mouse-coloured Tit)
    NE & E Africa
Anthoscopus flavifrons (Yellow-fronted Tit)
  A. f. waldroni
    Ghana
  A. f. flavifrons
    Gabon, Cameroun, N Zaire
  A. f. ruthae
    E Zaire
Anthoscopus caroli (African Penduline Tit)
  A. c. roccattii
    S Uganda
  A. c. taruensis
    S Kenya, N Tanzania
  A. c. pallescens
    Tanzania
  A. c. ansorgei
    Angola, Zaire
  A. c. rhodesiae
    SE Zaire, NE Zambia, S Tanzania
  A. c. robertsi
    NE Zambia to Mozambique
  A. c. caroli
    Namibia to S Mozambique
  A. c. winterbottomi
    NW Zambia
  A. c. rankinei
    Zambia

Anthoscopus sylviella (Rungwe Penduline Tit)
    S Kenya, Tanzania
Anthoscopus minutus (Southern Kapok Tit)
  A. m. damarensis
    Namibia, Rhodesia, W Transvaal
  A. m. minutus
    W Cape Province

AURIPARUS
Auriparus flaviceps (Verdin)
  A. f. flaviceps
    Baja California, NW Mexico
  A. f. acaciarum
    SW USA, NW Mexico
  A. f. ornatus
    SW USA, N Mexico
  A. f. fraterculus
    N Mexico

CEPHALOPYRUS
Cephalopyrus flammiceps (Fire-capped Tit Warbler)
  C. f. flammiceps
    Pakistan, W Himalayas, N India
  C. f. olivaceus
    E Himalayas, W China

145 PARIDAE (TITS, CHICKADEES)

PARUS
Parus palustris (Marsh Tit)
  P. p. palustris
    Italy, NW Europe
  P. p. brandtii
    N Caucasus
  P. p. brevirostris
    C Asia, Manchuria, N China
  P. p. hensoni
    S Kurile Is, N Japan
  P. p. hellmayri
    S Korea, China
  P. p. hypermelaena
    W China, E Burma
Parus lugubris (Sombre Tit)
  P. l. lugubris
    Hungary, N Greece
  P. l. lugens
    C & S Greece
  P. l. anatoliae
    Asia Minor
  P. l. hyrcanus
    N Iran
  P. l. dubius
    W Iran
  P. l. kirmanensis
    SE Iran
  P. l. talischensis
    Azerbaidjan (USSR)

Parus montanus (Willow Tit)
  P. m. loennbergi
    Lapland, N Russia
  P. m. borealis
    NE & EC Europe, Siberia
  P. m. montanus
    SE Europe
  P. m. salicarius
    NW Europe
  P. m. kamtschatkensis
    N Kurile Is, Kamchatka
  P. m. sachalinensis
    S Kurile Is, Sakhalin I
  P. m. restrictus
    N Japan
  P. m. songarus
    C Asia
  P. m. affinis
    NW China
  P. m. stoetzneri
    N China, SW Manchuria
  P. m. weigoldicus
    W China
Parus atricapillus (Black-capped Chickadee)
  P. a. turneri
    NW Canada
  P. a. occidentalis
    W Canada, W USA
  P. a. septentrionalis
    WC Canada, C USA
  P. a. nevadensis
    WC USA
  P. a. atricapillus
    E Canada, NE USA
  P. a. bartletti
    Newfoundland
  P. a. practicus
    NE USA
Parus carolinensis (Carolina Chickadee)
  P. c. atricapilloides
    SC USA
  P. c. agilis
    S USA
  P. c. carolinensis
    SE USA
  P. c. extimus
    E USA
  P. c. impiger
    Florida
Parus sclateri (Mexican Chickadee)
  P. s. eidos
    S USA, N Mexico
  P. s. sclateri
    SC Mexico
  P. s. rayi
    S Mexico

Parus gambeli (Mountain Chickadee)
  P. g. abbreviatus
    W Canada, NW USA
  P. g. inyoensis
    W USA
  P. g. gambeli
    SW USA
  P. g. baileyae
    SW California
  P. g. atratus
    N Baja California
Parus superciliosus (White-browed Tit)
    W China
Parus davidi (Père David's Tit)
    W China
Parus cinctus (Siberian Tit)
  P. c. lapponicus
    Lapland
  P. c. cinctus
    Siberia
  P. c. sayanus
    C Asia
  P. c. lathami
    NW Alaska
Parus hudsonicus (Boreal Chickadee)
  P. h. columbianus
    W Canada
  P. h. cascadensis
    NW USA
  P. h. hudsonicus
    Canada
  P. h. littoralis
    SE Canada, NE USA
Parus rufescens (Chestnut-backed Chickadee)
  P. r. rufescens
    W Canada, W USA
  P. r. neglectus
    California
  P. r. barlowi
    S California
Parus wollweberi (Bridled Titmouse)
  P. w. phillipsi
    SW USA, NW Mexico
  P. w. wollweberi
    C & S Mexico
  P. w. caliginosus
    SW Mexico
Parus rubidiventris (Black-crested Tit)
  P. r. rubidiventris
    C Himalayas
  P. r. beavani
    E Himalayas, W China, NE Burma
  P. r. saramatii
    NW Burma
Parus rufonuchalis (Rufous-naped Tit)
    W & C Asia, N India

Parus melanolophus (Vigors Crested Tit)
Pakistan, W Himalayas
Parus ater (Coal Tit)
P. a. ater
Europe, Siberia
P. a. britannicus
Great Britain
P. a. hibernicus
Ireland
P. a. vieirae
Spain, Portugal
P. a. sardus
Corsica, Sardinia
P. a. atlas
N Morocco
P. a. ledouci
N Africa
P. a. cypriotes
Cyprus
P. a. moltchanovi
S Russia
P. a. michaelowskii
Caucasus
P. a. derjugini
N Armenia
P. a. gaddi
Iran
P. a. chorassanicus
NE Iran
P. a. phaeonotus
SW Iran
P. a. rufipectus
C Asia
P. a. aemodius
E Himalayas, W China, N Burma
P. a. pekinensis
N China
P. a. insularis
Japan
P. a. kuatunensis
SE China
P. a. ptilosus
Taiwan
Parus venustulus (Yellow-bellied Tit)
S & W China
Parus elegans (Elegant Tit)
P. e. edithae
Babuyan I
P. e. montigenus
N Luzon I
P. e. gilliardi
Batjan I (Luzon)
P. e. elegans
S Luzon I, Panay I, Mindoro I
P. e. visayanus
Cebu I
P. e. albescens
Guimares I, Masbate I, Negros I

P. e. mindanensis
Mindanao I
P. e. suluensis
Tawitawi Is, Sulu I
P. e. bongaoensis
Bongao I
Parus amabilis (Palawan Tit)
Balabac I, Palawan I
Parus cristatus (Crested Tit)
P. c. cristatus
N & E Europe, Alps
P. c. scoticus
NC Scotland
P. c. abadiei
NW France
P. c. weigoldi
S & W Iberia
P. c. mitratus
C & W Europe
P. c. baschkirikus
C Russia
Parus dichrous (Brown Crested Tit)
P. d. kangrae
Pakistan, NW Himalayas
P. d. dichrous
C & E Himalayas
P. d. dichroides
NW China
P. d. wellsi
SW China, NE Burma
Parus afer (Acacia Grey Tit)
P. a. thruppi
Ethiopia, Somalia
P. a. barakae
Uganda, Kenya, Tanzania
P. a. benguelae
SW Angola
P. a. cinerascens
Namibia, Rhodesia, South Africa
P. a. afer
W Cape Province
Parus griseiventris (Miombo Grey Tit)
Zambia, Rhodesia, Tanzania
Parus niger (Southern Black Tit)
P. n. ravidus
S Rhodesia, Transvaal, E Zambia
P. n. niger
Southern Africa
P. n. xanthostomus
S Zambia
Parus leucomelas (White-winged Black Tit
P. l. guineensis
W & WC Africa
P. l. leucomelas
Ethiopia
P. l. insignis
C & SC Africa

P. l. carpi
 S Angola, N Namibia
***arus albiventris* (White-breasted Tit)**
 Nigeria to Sudan, Tanzania
***arus leuconotus* (White-backed Black Tit)**
 Ethiopia
***arus funereus* (Dusky Tit)**
 P. f. funereus
  Cameroun to Kenya
 P. f. gabela
  Angola
***arus fasciiventer* (Stripe-breasted Tit)**
 P. f. fasciiventer
  Rwanda (E Zaire)
 P. f. tanganjicae
  S Kivu (E Zaire)
 P. f. kaboboensis
  Mt Kabobo (SE Zaire)
***arus fringillinus* (Red-throated Tit)**
 S Kenya, N & C Tanzania
***arus rufiventris* (Rufous-bellied Tit)**
 P. r. rufiventris
  WC Africa
 P. r. masukuensis
  Zambia, Malawi
 P. r. pallidiventris
  Tanzania, Malawi, Mozambique
   Rhodesia
***arus major* (Great Tit)**
 P. m. newtoni
  British Isles
 P. m. major
  Europe, Asia Minor, C Asia
 P. m. excelsus
  NW Africa
 P. m. corsus
  Corsica, Sardinia
 P. m. aphrodite
  S Greece, Mediterranean islands
 P. m. terraesanctae
  Lebanon, Israel, Jordan, Syria
 P. m. blanfordi
  Iran
 P. m. karelini
  NW Iran
 P. m. intermedius
  W Iran
 P. m. kapustini
  C Asia
 P. m. caschmirensis
  NW India, Pakistan
 P. m. decolorans
  E Afghanistan
 P. m. ziaratensis
  N Baluchistan, S Afghanistan
 P. m. mahrattarum
  S India, Sri Lanka

P. m. stupae
 C & W India
P. m. nipalensis
 Nepal, N India, W Burma
P. m. vauriei
 E Assam
P. m. templorum
 W Thailand, S Indochina
P. m. cinereus
 Java, Lesser Sunda Is
P. m. ambiguus
 SE Burma, Malaysia, Sumatra
P. m. sarawacensis
 W Sarawak
P. m. hainanus
 Hainan I
P. m. nigriloris
 S Riukiu Is
P. m. commixtus
 S China, N Vietnam
P. m. okinawae
 C Riukiu Is
P. m. amamiensis
 N Riukiu Is
P. m. kagoshimae
 S Kyushu I, Goto I
P. m. dageletensis
 Dagelet I (Japan)
P. m. minor
 Japan, E Asia, N China, E Tibet
P. m. tibetanus
 Tibet, SW China, N Burma
P. m. nubicolus
 E Burma, N Thailand, W Indochina
***Parus bokharensis* (Turkistan Tit)**
 P. b. bokharensis
  Russia, C Asia
 P. b. turkestanicus
  W Mongolia
***Parus monticolus* (Green-backed Tit)**
 P. m. monticolus
  W Himalayas
 P. m. yunnanensis
  E Himalayas, Burma, W China
 P. m. legendrei
  S Vietnam
 P. m. insperatus
  Taiwan
***Parus nuchalis* (White-naped Tit)**
 NW India
***Parus xanthogenys* (Black-spotted Yellow Tit)**
 P. x. xanthogenys
  W Himalayas
 P. x. aplonotus
  C India
 P. x. travancoreensis
  S India

Parus spilonotus (Chinese Yellow Tit)
  P. s. spilonotus
    E Himalayas
  P. s. subviridis
    Burma, Thailand, Assam
  P. s. rex
    S China, N Vietnam
  P. s. basileus
    S Indochina
Parus holsti (Formosan Yellow Tit)
  Taiwan
Parus caeruleus (Blue Tit)
  P. c. obscurus
    British Isles
  P. c. caeruleus
    N & E Europe
  P. c. ogliastrae
    S Iberia, Corsica, Sardinia
  P. c. balearicus
    Majorca I
  P. c. orientalis
    E & C Russia
  P. c. satunini
    Caucasus, NW Iran
  P. c. raddei
    N Iran
  P. c. persicus
    SW Iran
  P. c. ultramarinus
    NW Africa
  P. c. cyrenaicae
    Libya
  P. c. ombriosus
    Hierro I (Canary Is)
  P. c. palmensis
    Palma I
  P. c. teneriffae
    Grand Canary I, Tenerife I
  P. c. degener
    Fuerteventura I, Lanzarote I
Parus cyanus (Azure Tit)
  P. c. cyanus
    W Russia, WC Asia
  P. c. yenisseensis
    C Asia
  P. c. tianschanicus
    C & E Asia, Manchuria
  P. c. kotkalensis
    S Russia
  P. c. flavipectus
    WC Asia
  P. c. carruthersi
    N Iran
  P. c. berezowskii
    NW China
Parus varius (Varied Tit)
  P. v. varius
    Japan, Korea

  P. v. sunsunpi
    S Japanese Is
  P. v. amamii
    Amami I
  P. v. orii
    C Riukiu Is
  P. v. olivaceus
    S Riukiu Is
  P. v. castaneoventris
    Taiwan
  P. v. namiyei
    N Izu Is
  P. v. owstoni
    S Izu Is
Parus semilarvatus (White-fronted Tit)
  P. s. snowi
    N Luzon I
  P. s. semilarvatus
    C & S Luzon I, Negros I
  P. s. nehrkorni
    Mindanao I
Parus inornatus (Plain Titmouse)
  P. i. sequestratus
    SW Oregon, NW California
  P. i. zaleptus
    SE Oregon, E California, W Nevada
  P. i. inornatus
    WC California
  P. i. kernensis
    SC California
  P. i. mohavensis
    SE California
  P. i. transpositus
    SW California
  P. i. affabilis
    N Baja California
  P. i. cineraceus
    S Baja California
  P. i. ridgwayi
    WC USA
  P. i. plumbescens
    SW New Mexico, SW Arizona
Parus bicolor (Tufted Titmouse)
  P. b. bicolor
    E, C & SE USA
  P. b. sennetti
    C & S Texas
  P. b. paloduro
    N Texas
  P. b. dysleptus
    W Texas, N Mexico
  P. b. atricristatus
    S Texas, NE Mexico

MELANOCHLORA
Melanochlora sultanea (Sultan Tit)
  M. s. sultanea
    E Himalayas, Assam, Burma, N Thailand

M. s. flavocristata
  S Burma, Malaysia, Sumatra
M. s. seorsa
  S China, Hainan I, N Indochina
M. s. gayeti
  C Vietnam

SYLVIPARUS

Sylviparus modestus (Yellow-browed Tit)
  S. m. simlaensis
    NW Himalayas
  S. m. modestus
    C & E Himalayas, N Burma, SW China,
    N Laos
  S. m. klossi
    S Vietnam

46 SITTIDAE (NUTHATCHES)

SITTINAE

CITTA

Sitta europaea (European Nuthatch)
  S. e. europaea
    NW Europe
  S. e. asiatica
    Russia, N Asia, N Japan
  S. e. seorsa
    W Sinkiang
  S. e. amurensis
    Manchuria, Korea, C Japan
  S. e. arctica
    N Siberia
  S. e. albifrons
    Kamchatka
  S. e. roseilia
    S Japan
  S. e. bedfordi
    Quelpart I
  S. e. caesia
    WC Europe, N Mediterranean
  S. e. hispaniensis
    Spain, NW Africa
  S. e. levantina
    Israel, Lebanon, Turkey
  S. e. persica
    W Iran
  S. e. caucasica
    Caucasus
  S. e. rubiginosa
    N Iran, SE Russia
  S. e. sinensis
    W & S China, Taiwan
  S. e. montium
    SE Tibet
  S. e. nagaensis
    N India, Assam, N Burma, N Thailand,
    SW China
  S. e. griseiventris
    S Burma, S Vietnam

S. e. nebulosa
  C China
S. e. whistleri
  S Thailand
Sitta castanea (Chestnut-bellied Nuthatch)
  S. c. cashmirensis
    Pakistan, NW India
  S. c. almorae
    W Himalayas
  S. c. cinnamoventris
    E Himalayas, Bangladesh
  S. c. koelzi
    E Assam, N Burma
  S. c. neglecta
    Burma, S Thailand, S Laos, S Vietnam
  S. c. castanea
    C India
  S. c. prateri
    EC India
  S. c. tonkinensis
    N Thailand, N Laos, N Vietnam
Sitta himalayensis (White-tailed Nuthutch)
  S. h. himalayensis
    Himalayas, Assam, Nepal
  S. h. australis
    S Assam, Burma, N Vietnam
Sitta victoriae (White-browed Nuthatch)
  W Burma
Sitta pygmaea (Pygmy Nuthatch)
  S. p. pygmaea
    W California
  S. p. melanotis
    SW Canada, W USA, NW Mexico
  S. p. canescens
    Nevada
  S. p. leuconucha
    S California, Baja California
  S. p. chihuahuae
    NW Mexico
  S. p. brunnescens
    W Mexico
  S. p. flavinucha
    E Mexico
Sitta pusilla (Brown-headed Nuthatch)
  S. p. pusilla
    S USA
  S. p. caniceps
    Florida
  S. p. insularis
    Gd Bahama I
Sitta whiteheadi (Corsican Nuthatch)
  Corsica
Sitta yunnanensis (Yunnan Nuthatch)
  W China
Sitta canadensis (Red-breasted Nuthatch)
  Canada, USA

***Sitta villosa* (Chinese Nuthatch)**
  S. v. bangsi
    W China
  S. v. villosa
    NE China
***Sitta leucopsis* (White-cheeked Nuthatch)**
  S. l. leucopsis
    Pakistan, W Himalayas
  S. l. przewalskii
    SE Tibet, NW China
***Sitta carolinensis* (White-breasted Nuthatch)**
  S. c. aculeata
    W USA
  S. c. tenuissima
    SW Canada, NW & W USA
  S. c. atkinsi
    Florida
  S. c. lagunae
    S Baja California
  S. c. nelsoni
    C & S USA, N Mexico
  S. c. alexandrae
    N Mexico
  S. c. umbrosa
    N Mexico
  S. c. mexicana
    C Mexico
  S. c. oberholseri
    C Mexico
  S. c. kinneari
    SW Mexico
  S. c. carolinensis
    E Canada, E USA
***Sitta krüperi* (Kruper's Nuthatch)**
  Turkey, Caucasus
***Sitta ledanti* (Kabylie Nuthatch)**
  N Algeria
***Sitta neumayer* (Rock Nuthatch)**
  S. n. neumayer
    SE Europe
  S. n. syriaca
    Turkey, N Israel
  S. n. rupicola
    Caucasus, Iran
  S. n. tschitscherini
    Iraq, Iran
  S. n. plumbea
    SE Iran
***Sitta tephronota* (Eastern Rock Nuthatch)**
  S. t. tephronota
    C Asia, N Iran, Afghanistan, Pakistan
  S. t. obscura
    N & E Iran
  S. t. dresseri
    SW Asia

***Sitta frontalis* (Velvet-fronted Nuthatch)**
  S. f. frontalis
    India, Burma, N Thailand, N Vietnam,
    S Sumatra, Java
  S. f. saturatior
    Malaysia, N Sumatra
  S. f. corallipes
    Borneo
  S. f. palawana
    Palawan I
  S. f. isarog
    NE, E & S Luzon I
  S. f. mesoleuca
    N Luzon I
  S. f. oenochlamys
    Cebu I, Panay I, Negros I
  S. f. lilacea
    Samar I, Leyte I
  S. f. apo
    SE Mindanao I
  S. f. zamboanga
    Mindanao I, Basilan I
***Sitta solangiae* (Lilac Nuthatch)**
  S. s. solangiae
    N Vietnam
  S. s. fortior
    C & S Vietnam
***Sitta azurea* (Azure Nuthatch)**
  S. a. expectata
    Malaysia, Sumatra
  S. a. nigriventer
    W Java
  S. a. azurea
    E Java
***Sitta magna* (Giant Nuthatch)**
  S. m. ligea
    SW China
  S. m. magna
    C Burma, N Thailand
***Sitta formosa* (Beautiful Nuthatch)**
  E Himalayas to N Laos

TICHADROMADINAE

TICHADROMA
***Tichadroma muraria* (Wallcreeper)**
  T. m. muraria
    S & E Europe, Turkey, NW Iran
  T. m. nepalensis
    C Asia, Pakistan, Himalayas, China

DAPHOENOSITTINAE

NEOSITTA
***Neositta chrysoptera* (Varied Sitella)**
  N. c. pilesta
    C Australia
  N. c. lathami
    E Victoria

N. c. chrysoptera
  E New South Wales
N. c. leucocephala
  C & SE Queensland
N. c. lumholzi
  E Queensland
N. c. albata
  Bowen, E Queensland
N. c. magnirostris
  NE Queensland
N. c. rothschildi
  N Queensland
N. c. striata
  N & NW Queensland
N. c. leucoptera
  Northern Territory, NC Australia
Neositta papuensis (Papuan Sitella)
N. p. toxopeusi
  NW New Guinea
N. p. intermedia
  NW New Guinea
N. p. wahgiensis
  W New Guinea
N. p. papuensis
  W New Guinea
N. p. alba
  C New Guinea
N. p. albifrons
  SE New Guinea

DAPHOENOSITTA
Daphoenositta miranda (Pink-faced Nuthatch)
D. m. miranda
  SE New Guinea
D. m. kuboriensis
  NE New Guinea
D. m. frontalis
  NW New Guinea

147 CERTHIIDAE (TREECREEPERS)

CERTHIINAE

CERTHIA
Certhia familiaris (Treecreeper)
C. f. britannica
  Britain, Ireland
C. f. macrodactyla
  C & S Europe
C. f. pyrenaica
  Pyrenees
C. f. familiaris
  N & E Europe, W Siberia
C. f. corsa
  Corsica
C. f. persica
  Caucasus, N Iran
C. f. tianschanica
  Russian & Chinese Turkistan

C. f. hodgsoni
  Pakistan, W Himalayas
C. f. mandellii
  E Himalayas
C. f. bianchii
  W China
C. f. khamensis
  SE Tibet, SW China, N Burma
C. f. daurica
  E Siberia, N Mongolia, N Korea, N Japan
C. f. montana
  W Canada, W USA
C. f. occidentalis
  NW Canada, W USA
C. f. zelotes
  S California
C. f. leucosticta
  S Nevada, Utah
C. f. albescens
  SW USA, NW Mexico
C. f. molinensis
  C Mexico
C. f. jaliscensis
  SW Mexico
C. f. guerrerensis
  SW Mexico
C. f. alticola
  SE Mexico
C. f. pernigra
  S Mexico, Guatemala
C. f. extima
  Nicaragua
C. f. americana
  C & E Canada, CE & SE USA
C. f. nigrescens
  EC USA
Certhia brachydactyla (Short-toed Treecreeper)
  C & E Europe, Caucasus
Certhia himalayana (Himalayan Treecreeper)
C. h. taeniura
  SW Asia, Afghanistan
C. h. himalayana
  N Pakistan, W Himalayas
C. h. limes
  Pakistan, NW India
C. h. infima
  W Nepal
C. h. yunnanensis
  W China
C. h. ripponi
  N Burma
Certhia nipalensis (Stoliczka's Treecreeper)
  SE Tibet, C Nepal, NE Burma

Certhia discolor **(Brown-throated Tree-
creeper)**
C. d. discolor
  E Himalayas, Nepal, Assam
C. d. manipurensis
  E Assam, W Burma
C. d. shanensis
  N Burma, N Thailand
C. d. laotiana
  Laos
C. d. meridionalis
  S Vietnam

SALPORNITHINAE

SALPORNIS
**Salpornis spilonotus (Spotted Grey
Creeper)**
S. s. emini
  Portuguese Guinea to Sudan, Uganda
S. s. erlangeri
  SW Ethiopia
S. s. salvadori
  Angola to Tanzania & Mozambique
S. s. rajputanae
  NW India
S. s. spilonotus
  N & C India
S. s. xylodromus
  E Rhodesia, W Mozambique

**148 RHABDORNITHIDAE (PHILIPPINE
CREEPERS)**

RHABDORNIS
**Rhabdornis mystacalis (Stripe-headed
Creeper)**
R. m. mystacalis
  Luzon I, Masbate I, Negros I, Panay I
R. m. minor
  Samay I, Leyte I, Mindanao I
**Rhabdornis inornatus (Plain-headed
Creeper)**
R. i. grandis
  N Luzon I
R. i. inornatus
  Samar I
R. i. rabori
  Negros I
R. i. alaris
  Mindanao I
R. i. zamboanga
  Mt Malindang (Mindanao I)
R. i. leytensis
  Leyte I

**149 CLIMACTERIDAE (AUSTRALIAN
CREEPERS)**

CLIMACTERIS
**Climacteris erythrops (Red-browed
Treecreeper)**
C. e. erythrops
  E New South Wales, E & S Victoria
C. e. olinda
  S Victoria
**Climacteris affinis (White-browed
Treecreeper)**
C. a. superciliosus
  WC Australia
C. a. affinis
  C Australia
Climacteris picumnus (Brown Treecreeper)
C. p. melanota
  N Queensland
C. p. picumnus
  S & E Australia
Climacteris rufa (Rufous Treecreeper)
  SW Western Australia
**Climacteris melanura (Black-tailed
Treecreeper)**
C. m. melanura
  N Western Australia, Northern Territory,
  NW Queensland
C. m. wellsi
  NW Western Australia
**Climacteris leucophaea (White-throated
Treecreeper)**
C. l. minor
  N Queensland
C. l. leucophaea
  E Australia
C. l. grisescens
  S South Australia
Climacteris placens (Papuan Treecreeper)
C. p. placens
  NW New Guinea
C. p. steini
  W New Guinea
C. p. inexpectata
  N New Guinea
C. p. meridionalis
  SE New Guinea

150 DICAEIDAE (FLOWERPECKERS)

MELANOCHARIS
**Melanocharis arfakiana (Obscure
Berrypecker)**
  New Guinea
Melanocharis nigra (Black Berrypecker)
M. n. pallida
  Waigeu I
M. n. nigra
  Misol I, W New Guinea

M. n. unicolor
Japen I, N & E New Guinea
M. n. chloroptera
Aru Is, S New Guinea
Melanocharis longicauda (Mid-mountain Berrypecker)
M. l. longicauda
NW New Guinea
M. l. chloris
NW New Guinea
M. l. umbrosa
NW New Guinea
M. l. captata
C & E New Guinea
M. l. orientalis
SE New Guinea
Melanocharis versteri (Fan-tailed Berrypecker)
M. v. versteri
NW New Guinea
M. v. meeki
NW New Guinea
M. v. virago
N & NE New Guinea
M. v. maculiceps
SE New Guinea
Melanocharis striativentris (Streaked Berrypacker)
M. s. axillaris
NW New Guinea
M. s. striativentris
C & SE New Guinea
M. s. prasina
SE New Guinea
M. s. chrysocome
E New Guinea

RHAMPHOCHARIS
Rhamphocharis crassirostris (Spotted Berrypecker)
R. c. crassirostris
NW & C New Guinea
R. c. piperata
SE New Guinea
R. c. viridescens
SE New Guinea

PRIONOCHILUS
Prionochilus olivaceus (Olive-backed Flowerpecker)
P. o. parsonsi
NE Luzon I
P. o. olivaceus
Basilan I, Mindanao I, Bohol I
P. o. samarensis
Samar I, Leyte I
Prionochilus maculatus (Yellow-throated Flowerpecker)
P. m. septentrionalis
S Burma, S Thailand

507

P. m. oblitus
Malaysia
P. m. maculatus
Sumatra, Billiton I, Nias I, Borneo
P. m. natunensis
Great Natuna I
Prionochilus percussus (Crimson-breasted Flowerpecker)
P. p. ignicapilla
S Burma to Sumatra & Borneo
P. p. regulus
Batu I
P. p. percussus
Java
Prionochilus plateni (Palawan Yellow-rumped Flowerpecker)
Palawan I, Culion I
Prionochilus xanthopygius (Borneo Yellow-rumped Flowerpecker)
Borneo
Prionochilus thoracicus (Scarlet-breasted Flowerpecker)
Malaysia, Billiton I, Borneo

DICAEUM
Dicaeum annae (Sunda Flowerpecker)
D. a. sumbavense
Sumbawa I
D. a. annae
Flores I
Dicaeum agile (Thick-billed Flowerpecker)
D. a. agile
N India
D. a. zeylonicum
Sri Lanka
D. a. deignani
Assam, N Burma
D. a. modestum
Bangladesh, S Burma, Thailand, N Vietnam
D. a. remotum
S Burma, S Thailand, Malaysia
D. a. atjehense
N Sumatra
D. a. finschi
W Java
D. a. tinctum
Sumba I, Flores I, Alor I
D. a. obsoletum
Timor I
Dicaeum everetti (Everett's Flowerpecker)
D. e. sordidum
Bintan I, Malaysia
D. e. everetti
Labuan I, Borneo
D. e. bungurense
Great Natuna I

**Dicaeum aeruginosum (Striped Flower-
pecker)**
D. a. striatissimum
Sibuyan I, Luzon I
D. a. aeruginosum
Cebu I, Negros I, Mindoro I, Mindanao I
D. a. affine
Palawan I
**Dicaeum proprium (Grey-breasted
Flowerpecker)**
Mt Mayo (Mindanao)
**Dicaeum chrysorrheum (Yellow-vented
Flowerpecker)**
D. c. chrysoclore
E Himalayas to SW China, Indochina
D. c. chrysorrheum
S Thailand to Sumatra, Borneo, Java
**Dicaeum melanoxanthum (Yellow-bellied
Flowerpecker)**
E Himalayas to SW China
Dicaeum vincens (Legge's Flowerpecker)
Sri Lanka
**Diceaum aureolimbatum (Celebean
Flowerpecker)**
D. a. aureolimbatum
Muna I, Buton I, Celebes
D. a. laterale
Great Sanghir I
**Dicaeum nigrilore (Olive-capped Flower-
pecker)**
Mindanao I
**Dicaeum anthonyi (Yellow-crowned
Flowerpecker)**
D. a. anthonyi
Cagayan I, Luzon I,
D. a. masawan
NW Mindanao I
D. a. kampalili I
SE Mindanao I
Dicaeum bicolor (Bicoloured Flowerpecker)
D. b. inexpectatum
Luzon I, Mindanao I, Leyte I, Samar I
D. b. bicolor
Mindanao I
D. b. viridissimum
Negros I
**Dicaeum australe (Philippine Flower-
pecker)**
D. a. australe
Philippine Is
D. a. haematostictum
Panay I, Negros I
**Diceaum retrocinctum (Mindoro Flower-
pecker)**
Mindoro I

**Diceaum trigonostigma (Orange-bellied
Flowerpecker)**
D. t. rubropygium
Assam, S Burma, S Thailand
D. t. trigonostigma
S Thailand
D. t. melanostigma
Bangka I, Billiton I, Malaysia, Sumatra
D. t. antioproctum
Simalur I
D. t. megastoma
Great Natuna I
D. t. flaviclunis
Java, Bali I
D. t. dayakanum
Borneo, N Borneo islands
D. t. sibutuense
Sibutu I
D. t. assimile
Tawitawi Is, Jolo I, Siasi I
D. t. cinereigulare
Mindanao I, Samar I, Leyte I, Bohol I
D. t. besti
Siquijor I
D. t. dorsale
Masbate I, Panay I, Negros I
D. t. intermedium
Romblon I, Tablas I
D. t. sibuyanicum
Sibuyan I
D. t. isidroi
Camiguin I (South)
D. t. xanthopygium
Marinduque I, Mindoro I, Luzon I
**Dicaeum hypoleucum (White-bellied
Flowerpecker)**
D. h. lagunae
N & C Luzon I
D. h. pontifex
Bohol I, Samar I, Leyte I, Mindanao I
D. h. hypoleucum
W Mindanao I, Basilan I, Sulu Is
D. h. cagayanensis
NE Luzon I
**Dicaeum erythrorhynchos (Tickell's
Flowerpecker)**
D. e. erythrorhynchos
W Burma, Bangladesh, India
D. e. ceylonense
Sri Lanka
Dicaeum concolor (Plain Flowerpecker)
D. c. olivaceum
Himalayas to S China, N Indochina
D. c. concolor
SW India
D. c. virescens
S Andaman Is

D. c. minullum
   Hainan I
D. c. uchidai
   Taiwan
D. c. borneanum
   Malaysia, Sumatra, Borneo
D. c. sollicitans
   Java, Bali I
Dicaeum pygmaeum (Palawan Flower-pecker)
D. p. salomonseni
   N Luzon I
D. p. pygmaeum
   S Luzon I, Mindoro I, Negros I, Leyte I,
   Cebu I
D. p. davao
   Mindanao I
D. p. palawanorum
   Balabac I, Palawan I
Dicaeum nehrkorni (Red-headed Flower-pecker)
   Celebes
Dicaeum vulneratum (Ashy-fronted Flowerpecker)
   S Moluccas
Dicaeum erythrothorax (White-throated Flowerpecker)
D. e. schistaceiceps
   Halmahera I
D. e. erythrothorax
   Buru I
Dicaeum pectorale (Olive-crowned Flowerpecker)
D. p. ignotum
   Gebe I
D. p. pectorale
   Misol I, Waigeu I, NW New Guinea
Dicaeum geelvinkianum (Red-capped Flowerpecker)
D. g. maforense
   Numfor I
D. g. misoriense
   Biak I
D. g. geelvinkianum
   Japen I
D. g. obscurifrons
   W New Guinea
D. g. setekwa
   SW New Guinea
D. g. diversum
   N New Guinea
D. g. centrale
   C New Guinea
D. g. albopunctatum
   SC New Guinea
D. g. rubrigulare
   S New Guinea

D. g. rubrocoronatum
   SE New Guinea
D. g. violaceum
   D'Entrecasteaux Archipelago
Dicaeum nitidum (Louisiade Flowerpecker)
D. n. nitidum
   Tagula I, Misima I
D. n. rosseli
   Rossel I
Dicaeum eximium (New Ireland Flower-pecker)
D. e. layardorum
   New Britain
D. e. eximium
   New Ireland, New Hanover
D. e. phaeopygium
   Dyaul I
Dicaeum aeneum (Solomon Is Flower-pecker)
D. a. aeneum
   N Solomon Is
D. a. becki
   Guadalcanal I
D. a. malaitae
   Malaita I
Dicaeum tristrami (San Cristobal Flower-pecker)
   San Cristobal I
Dicaeum igniferum (Black-banded Flowerpecker)
D. i. igniferum
   Sumbawa I, Flores I
D. i. cretum
   Pantar I, Alor I
Dicaeum maugei (Blue-cheeked Flower-pecker)
D. m. maugei
   Semau I, Timor I, Sawu I
D. m. romae
   Roma I, Damar I
D. m. salvadorii
   Babar I, Moa I
D. m. splendidum
   Saleyer I, Djampea I
D. m. neglectum
   Lombok I
Dicaeum hirundinaceum (Mistletoe Flowerpecker)
D. h. hirundinaceum
   Australia
D. h. ignicolle
   Aru Is
D. h. keiense
   Kei Is
D. h. fulgidum
   Tenimber Is

510 ***Dicaeum celebicum*** (Black-sided Flower-pecker)
   D. c. kuehni
     Tukangbesi I
   D. c. sulaense
     Sula Is, Banguey I
   D. c. celebicum
     Muna I, Buton I, Celebes
   D. c. sanghirense
     Sanghir Is
   D. c. talautense
     Talaut I
Dicaeum monticolum (Bornean Fire-breasted Flowerpecker)
   Borneo
Dicaeum ignipectus (Green-backed Flowerpecker)
   D. i. ignipectus
     Himalayas to S China, Indochina
   D. i. dolichorhynchum
     S Thailand, Malaysia
   D. i. cambodianum
     Cambodia, SE Thailand
   D. i. formosum
     Taiwan
   D. i. luzoniense
     N Luzon I
   D. i. apo
     Negros I, Mindanao I
   D. i. bonga
     Samar I
   D. i. beccarii
     N Sumatra
   D. i. sanguinolentum
     Java, Bali I
   D. i. rhodopygiale
     Flores I
   D. i. wilhelminae
     Sumba I
   D. i. hanieli
     Timor I
Dicaeum cruentatum (Scarlet-backed Flowerpecker)
   D. c. cruentatum
     NE India to S China, Indochina
   D. c. siamense
     E Thailand
   D. c. ignitum
     Malaysia
   D. c. sumatranum
     Sumatra
   D. c. batuense
     Mentawai Is
   D. c. simalurense
     Simalur I
   D. c. nigrimentum
     Borneo

   D. c. niasense
     Nias I
Dicaeum trochileum (Scarlet-headed Flowerpecker)
   D. t. trochileum
     Java, Bali I, SE Borneo, Kangean Is
   D. t. stresemanni
     Lombok I

OREOCHARIS
Oreocharis arfaki (Tit Berrypecker)
   New Guinea

PARAMYTHIA
Paramythia montium (Crested Berrypecker)
   P. m. olivaceum
     C New Guinea
   P. m. montium
     C & SE New Guinea
   P. m. brevicauda
     SE New Guinea

PARDALOTUS
Pardalotus quadragintus (Forty-spotted Pardalote)
   Tasmania
Pardalotus punctatus (Spotted Pardalote)
   W Western Australia, E Australia, Tasmania
Pardalotus xanthopygus (Yellow-tailed Pardalote)
   Western Australia to NW Victoria
Pardalotus rubricatus (Red-browed Pardalote)
   P. r. parryi
     N Australia
   P. r. rubricatus
     C Australia
   P. r. carpenteriae
     NW Queensland
   P. r. yorki
     NE Queensland
Pardalotus striatus (Yellow-tipped Pardalote)
   E Australia, Tasmania
Pardalotus ornatus (Red-tipped Pardalote)
   S Queensland to S Victoria
Pardalotus substriatus (Striated Pardalote)
   Southern Australia
Pardalotus melanocephalus (Black-headed Pardalote)
   P. m. uropygialis
     N Western Australia to NW Queensland
   P. m. melvillensis
     Melville I
   P. m. restrictus
     N Queensland
   P. m. barroni
     NC Queensland
   P. m. bowensis
     E Queensland

P. m. melanocephalus
SE Queensland, NE New South Wales

151 NECTARINIIDAE (SUNBIRDS)

ANTHREPTES
Anthreptes gabonicus (Brown Sunbird)
Gambia to Gabon
Anthreptes fraseri (Scarlet-tufted Sunbird)
A. f. cameroonensis
S Nigeria, Cameroun, Central African
Republic, N Angola
A. f. idius
Sierra Leone to Ghana
A. f. fraseri
Fernando Po I
A. f. axillaris
NE Zaire, Uganda
**Anthreptes reichenowi (Plain-backed
Sunbird)**
A. r. yokanae
S Kenya, NE Tanzania
A. r. reichenowi
SE Rhodesia, Mozambique
Anthreptes anchietae (Anchieta's Sunbird)
Angola, N Zambia, SW Tanzania, Malawi,
W Mozambique
**Anthreptes simplex (Plain-coloured
Sunbird)**
S Burma, S Thailand, Malaysia, Sumatra,
Borneo
**Anthreptes malacensis (Plain-throated
Sunbird)**
A. m. malacensis
S Burma to Indochina, Sumatra, S Borneo
A. m. mjobergi
Maratua Is
A. m. borneensis
N Borneo
A. m. birgitae
Luzon I
A. m. chlorigaster
WC Philippine Is, SW Mindanao I
A. m. griseigularis
Samar I, Leyte I, NE Mindanao I
A. m. heliolusius
W Mindanao I, Basilan I
A. m. cagayanensis
Cagayan I
A. m. paraguae
Palawan I
A. m. wiglesworthi
Sulu Archipelago (except Sibutu)
A. m. iris
Sibutu I
A. m. heliocalus
Sangi Is
A. m. celebensis
S & C Celebes

A. m. citrinus
SE Celebes
A. m. extremus
Sula Is
A. m. convergens
Lesser Sunda Is
A. m. rubrigena
Sumba I
**Anthreptes rhodolaema (Shelley's
Sunbird)**
S Burma, S Thailand, Malaysia, Sumatra,
Borneo
**Anthreptes singalensis (Ruby-cheeked
Sunbird)**
A. s. assamensis
E Nepal, Bangladesh, N Burma, N Thailand
A. s. internotus
S Burma, S Thailand
A. s. koratensis
E Thailand, Laos, Vietnam
A. s. interpositus
S Thailand
A. s. singalensis
Malaysia
A. s. panopsius
W Sumatra Is, Nias I
A. s. sumatranus
Sumatra, Billiton I
A. s. pallidus
N Natuna Is
A. s. borneanus
Banguey I, Borneo
A. s. phoenicotis
E & C Java
A. s. bantenensis
W Java
**Anthreptes longuemarei (Violet-backed
Sunbird)**
A. l. longuemarei
Senegal to Guinea
A. l. haussarum
Liberia to Cameroun, N Zaire, Sudan,
Uganda
A. l. angolensis
S Zaire, Angola, Zambia, Malawi,
W Tanzania
A. l. nyassae
SE Tanzania, N Mozambique, E Rhodesia
**Anthreptes orientalis (Kenya Violet-backed
Sunbird)**
A. o. orientalis
S Sudan, Ethiopia, N Uganda, Kenya,
E Tanzania
A. o. neumanni
NE Kenya, Somalia
**Anthreptes neglectus (Uluguru Violet-
backed Sunbird)**
SE Kenya, NE Tanzania, N Mozambique

512   **Anthreptes aurantium (Violet-tailed Sunbird)**
   S Nigeria, Gabon, Central African
   Republic, NE Angola
Anthreptes pallidigaster (Amani Sunbird)
   E Kenya, NE Tanzania
Anthreptes rectirostris (Green Sunbird)
  A. r. rectirostris
   Sierra Leone to Ghana
  A. r. tephrolaema
   Fernando Po I, S Nigeria to Angola
   & Uganda
Anthreptes rubritorques (Banded Green Sunbird)
   NE Tanzania
Anthreptes collaris (Collared Sunbird)
  A. c. subcollaris
   Guinea to Nigeria
  A. c. hypodilus
   Fernando Po I
  A. c. somereni
   SE Nigeria, N & W Zaire, N Angola,
   SW Sudan
  A. c. jubaensis
   S Ethiopia, Somalia, N Kenya
  A. c. djamdjamensis
   SW Ethiopia
  A. c. garguensis
   C & E Zaire, Uganda
  A. c. elachior
   E Kenya, NE Tanzania, Zanzibar I
  A. c. philipsi
   E Angola, SE Zaire, N Zambia
  A. c. zambesianus
   S Tanzania, SE Zambia, Botswana
  A. c. patersonae
   E Rhodesia, W Mozambique
  A. c. zuluensis
   Rhodesia, N Natal, Mozambique,
   Transvaal
  A. c. collaris
   E Cape Province, S Natal, Swaziland
Anthreptes platurus (Pygmy Sunbird)
  A. p. platurus
   Senegal to NW Kenya
  A. p. metallicus
   NE Africa, SW Arabia

HYPOGRAMMA
Hypogramma hypogrammicum (Blue-naped Sunbird)
  H. h. lisettae
   N Burma, N Thailand, N & C Indochina
  H. h. mariae
   Cambodia, S Indochina
  H. h. nuchale
   S Burma, S Thailand, Malaysia
  H. h. hypogrammicum
   Sumatra, Borneo

  H. h. natunense
   N Natuna Is
NECTARINIA
Nectarinia seimundi (Little Green Sunbird)
  N. s. kruensis
   Sierra Leone to Ghana
  N. s. seimundi
   Fernando Po I
  N. s. traylori
   Nigeria to Zaire, Uganda, N Angola
Nectarinia batesi (Bates's Olive Sunbird)
   Fernando Po I, S Nigeria to Zaire,
   Zambia
Nectarinia olivacea (Olive Sunbird)
  N. o. guineensis
   Guinea to W Ghana
  N. o. cephaëlis
   E Ghana to Zaire, N Angola
  N. o. obscura
   Principé I, Fernando Po I
  N. o. vincenti
   S Sudan, NW Kenya, Uganda
  N. o. ragazzii
   Sudan, Ethiopia to N Zambia, N Malawi
  N. o. neglecta
   C Kenya, N Tanzania
  N. o. changamwensis
   E Kenya, E Tanzania
  N. o. granti
   Pemba I, Zanzibar I
  N. o. lowei
   W Tanzania, N Zambia
  N. o. alfredi
   S Tanzania, Malawi, Zambia
  N. o. sclateri
   E Rhodesia
  N. o. olivacina
   E Mozambique, N Natal
  N. o. olivacea
   C Natal
Nectarinia ursulae (Fernando Po Sunbird)
   Fernando Po I, Cameroun Mt
Nectarinia veroxii (Mouse-coloured Sunbird)
  N. v. fischeri
   Somalia, E Kenya, E Tanzania,
   Mozambique, E Natal
  N. v. zanzibarica
   Zanzibar I
  N. v. veroxii
   E Natal, E Cape Province
Nectarinia balfouri (Socotra Sunbird)
   Socotra I
Nectarinia reichenbachii (Reichenbach's Sunbird)
   Ghana to N Zaire
Nectarinia hartlaubii (Principé Sunbird)
   Principé I

Nectarinia newtonii (Newton's Yellow-breasted Sunbird)
Sao Thomé I
Nectarinia thomensis (Sao Thomé Giant Sunbird)
Sao Thomé I
Nectarinia oritis (Cameroun Blue-headed Sunbird)
N. o. poensis
mountains of Fernando Po I
N. o. oritis
Cameroun Mt
N. o. bansoensis
W Cameroun
Nectarinia alinae (Blue-headed Sunbird)
N. a. alinae
E Zaire, SW Uganda
N. a. tanganjicae
SE Zaire
Nectarinia bannermani (Bannerman's Sunbird)
Angola, S Zaire, NW Zambia
Nectarinia verticalis (Green-headed Sunbird)
N. v. verticalis
Senegal to Nigeria
N. v. bohndorffi
Cameroun to Zaire, Angola
N. v. cyanocephala
W Gabon
N. v. viridisplendens
S Sudan, E Zaire, W Kenya to NE Zambia
Nectarinia cyanolaema (Blue-throated Brown Sunbird)
N. c. magnirostrata
Sierra Leone to Ghana
N. c. cyanolaema
Fernando Po I
N. c. octaviae
Ghana to Uganda & N Angola
Nectarinia fuliginosa (Carmelite Sunbird)
N. f. aurea
Liberia to Gabon
N. f. fuliginosa
Zaire, Angola
Nectarinia rubescens (Green-throated Sunbird)
N. r. stangerii
Fernando Po I
N. r. crossensis
Cameroun
N. r. rubescens
Cameroun to Sudan, Angola, Zambia, Kenya
Nectarinia amethystina (Amethyst Sunbird)
N. a. kalckreuthi
Somalia, E Kenya, NE Tanzania

N. a. doggetti
W Kenya, Uganda, NW Tanzania
N. a. kirkii
SW Tanzania, SE Zaire, Rhodesia, E Zambia
N. a. deminuta
S Zaire, W Zambia, Angola, W Botswana
N. a. adjuncta
E Transvaal, N Natal, S Mozambique
N. a. amethystina
S Natal, S Transvaal, Cape Province
Nectarinia senegalensis (Scarlet-chested Sunbird)
N. s. senegalensis
Senegal to N Nigeria
N. s. adamauae
NE Cameroun
N. s. acik
Cameroun to S Sudan, Uganda
N. s. cruentata
SE Sudan, Ethiopia
N. s. lamperti
E Zaire, Kenya, Tanzania
N. s. saturatior
Angola, W Zambia, Namibia
N. s. gutteralis
SE Africa
Nectarinia hunteri (Hunter's Sunbird)
Somalia, Kenya, Tanzania
Nectarinia adelberti (Buff-throated Sunbird)
N. a. adelberti
Sierra Leone to Ghana
N. a. eboensis
Togo to SE Nigeria
Nectarinia zeylonica (Purple-rumped Sunbird)
N. z. flaviventris
Bangladesh, India
N. z. sola
S India
N. z. zeylonica
Sri Lanka
Nectarinia minima (Small Sunbird)
W & S India
Nectarinia sperata (Van Hasselt's Sunbird)
N. s. phayrei
Burma
N. s. brasiliana
Assam, Bangladesh, Thailand, Malaysia, Borneo, Java, Sumatra
N. s. emmae
Cambodia, S Laos, S Vietnam
N. s. mecynorhyncha
Simalur I
N. s. eumecis
Anamba Is

N. s. axantha
Natuna Is
N. s. henkei
N Luzon I
N. s. theresae
C Luzon I
N. s. davoensis
SE Mindanao I
N. s. juliae
W & S Mindanao I, Basilan I
N. s. marinduquensis
Marinduque I
N. s. sperata
Maratua Is, Palawan I, C Philippine Is
Nectarinia sericea (Black Sunbird)
N. s. talautensis
Talaut I
N. s. sangirensis
Sanghir Is
N. s. grayi
N Celebes
N. s. porphyrolaema
C & S Celebes
N. s. auriceps
Peleng I, N Moluccas
N. s. auricapilla
Kajoa I (W Moluccas)
N. s. proserpina
Buru I
N. s. aspasioides
S Moluccas
N. s. chlorolaema
Kei Is
N. s. sericea
New Guinea, except SE
N. s. vicina
SE New Guinea
N. s. mariae
Kofiau I
N. s. cochrani
Misol I, Waigeu I
N. s. maforensis
Numfor I
N. s. salvadorii
W Japen I
N. s. chlorocephala
Aru Is
N. s. nigriscapularis
Meos Num I, Rani I
N. s. mysorensis
Biak I
N. s. veronica
Liki I
N. s. cornelia
Tarawai I
N. s. christianae
D'Entrecasteaux & Louisiade Archipelagos

N. s. caeruleogula
New Britain, Rook I
N. s. corinna
Bismarck Archipelago
N. s. eichhorni
Feni I (Bismarck Archipelago)
Nectarinia calcostetha (Macklot's Sunbird)
Burma to Malaysia, Indochina, Sumatra,
Borneo, Java, Philippine Is
Nectarinia dussumieri (Seychelles Sunbird)
Seychelles Is
Nectarinia lotenia (Loten's Sunbird)
N. l. hindustanica
S India
N. l. lotenia
Sri Lanka
Nectarinia jugularis (Yellow-bellied Sunbird)
N. j. andamanica
Andaman Is
N. j. klossi
N Nicobar Is
N. j. proselia
Car Nicobar I
N. j. flammaxillaris
Burma, Thailand, Cambodia, N Malaysia
N. j. pectoralis
C Malaysia
N. j. microleuca
S Malaysia, Singapore
N. j. rhizophorae
N Vietnam, Hainan I
N. j. ornata
Sumatra, Java, Borneo, Lesser Sunda Is
N. j. polyclysta
Enggano
N. j. obscurior
N Luzon I
N. j. jugularis
S Luzon I & C & S Philippine Is
N. j. aurora
Palawan I
N. j. woodi
Sulu Archipelago
N. j. meyeri
N & SE Celebes
N. j. plateni
S Celebes
N. j. saleyerensis
Saleyer I
N. j. infrenata
Tukangbesi I
N. j. robustirostris
Sula Is
N. j. teijsmanni
Djampea I, Kalao I
N. j. buruensis
Buru I

N. j. clementiae
S Moluccas
N. j. keiensis
Kei Is
N. j. idenburgi
N New Guinea
N. j. frenata
N Moluccas, Aru Is, New Guinea,
N Queensland
N. j. flavigaster
Solomon Is, Bismarck Archipelago
Nectarinia buettikoferi (Sumba I Sunbird)
Sumba I
Nectarinia solaris (Timor
Sunbird)
N. s. degener
Sumbawa I, Flores I, Lomblen I, Alor I
N. s. solaris
Timor I, Samau I
N. s. exquisita
Wetar I
Nectarinia asiatica (Purple Sunbird)
N. a. brevirostris
SE Arabia, SE Iran, Afghanistan, Pakistan,
N India
N. a. asiatica
S India, Sri Lanka
N. a. intermedia
Bangladesh, Assam, Burma, Thailand,
N Vietnam
Nectarinia souimanga (Souimanga
Sunbird)
N. s. souimanga
Glorioso I, Madagascar
N. s. apolis
SW Madagascar
N. s. aldabrensis
Aldabra I
N. s. abbotti
Assumption I (Aldabra)
N. s. buchenorum
Cosmoledo I (Aldabra)
Nectarinia humbloti (Humblot's Sunbird)
N. h. humbloti
Great Comoro I
N. h. mohelica
Moheli I (Comoro Is)
Nectarinia comorensis (Anjouan Sunbird)
Anjouan I (Comoro Is)
Nectarinia coquerellii (Mayotte Sunbird)
Mayotte I (Comoro Is)
Nectarinia venusta (Variable Sunbird)
N. v. venusta
Senegal to Cameroun
N. v. falkensteini
Gabon, Angola, Zaire, Zambia, Rhodesia,
Tanzania

515

N. v. igneiventris
Uganda, E Zaire
N. v. fazoqlensis
Sudan, Ethiopia
N. v. albiventris
Somalia, E Ethiopia, N Kenya
N. v. blicki
S Ethiopia, S Sudan, NW Kenya
Nectarinia talatala (Southern White-
bellied Sunbird)
Angola, Namibia, Zambia, Tanzania,
Mozambique, Natal
Nectarinia oustaleti (Oustalet's White-
bellied Sunbird)
N. o. oustaleti
C Angola
N. o. rhodesiae
N Zambia
Nectarinia fusca (Dusky Sunbird)
N. f. fusca
S Angola to W Cape Province
N. f. indusa
Mossamedes, Angola
Nectarinia chalybea (Lesser Double-
collared Sunbird)
N. c. pintoi
Angola, S Zaire, W Zambia
N. c. gertrudis
Tanzania, Malawi
N. c. manoensis
SW Tanzania, S Malawi, S Zambia,
Rhodesia
N. c. subalaris
Transvaal, Natal, E Cape Province
N. c. chalybea
S Cape Province
N. c. albilateralis
W Cape Province
Nectarinia afra (Greater Double-collared
Sunbird)
N. a. stuhlmanni
W Uganda
N. a. graueri
Rwanda, SW Uganda
N. a. chapini
E Zaire, S Burundi
N. a. prigoginei
SE Zaire
N. a. whytei
Zambia, Malawi
N. a. afra
South Africa
N. a. amicorum
S Mozambique
Nectarinia preussi (Northern Double-
collared Sunbird)
N. p. preussi
Fernando Po I, Cameroun Mt

N. p. eriksoni
S Sudan, Uganda, W Kenya, NE Zaire

N. p. ludovicensis
Angola

Nectarinia mediocris (Eastern Double-collared Sunbird)

N. m. mediocris
Kenya, Zambia

N. m. usambarica
SE Kenya, NE Tanzania

N. m. fuelleborni
Tanzania, N Malawi, NE Zambia

N. m. bensoni
Malawi, Zambia, Mozambique

Nectarinia neergaardi (Neergaard's Sunbird)
S Mozambique, N Natal

Nectarinia chloropygia (Olive-bellied Sunbird)

N. c. kempi
Sierra Leone to Ivory Coast

N. c. chloropygia
Ghana to Nigeria

N. c. insularis
Fernando Po I

N. c. luhderi
Cameroun, Zaire, Angola

N. c. bineschensis
SW Ethiopia

N. c. orphogaster
NE Angola, E Zaire, S Sudan, Uganda, W Tanzania

Nectarinia minulla (Tiny Sunbird)

N. m. amadoni
Fernando Po I

N. m. minulla
Ghana to W Uganda

Nectarinia regia (Regal Sunbird)

N. r. regia
Uganda

N. r. kivuensis
E Zaire, SW Uganda

N. r. anderseni
W Tanzania

Nectarinia loveridgei (Loveridge's Sunbird)
E Tanzania

Nectarinia moreaui (Moreau's Sunbird)
NE Tanzania

Nectarinia rockefelleri (Rockefeller's Sunbird)
E Zaire

Nectarinia violacea (Orange-breasted Sunbird)
Cape Province

Nectarinia habessinica (Shining Sunbird)

N. h. kinneari
W Saudi Arabia

N. h. hellmayri
S Arabia

N. h. habessinica
NE Sudan, W Ethiopia

N. h. altera
E Ethiopia, N Somalia

N. h. turkanae
S Ethiopia, S Sudan, S Somalia, N Kenya, Uganda

Nectarinia bouvieri (Orange-tufted Sunbird)
Cameroun to W Kenya & N Angola

Nectarinia osea (Palestine Sunbird)

N. o. osea
Syria, Israel, Arabia

N. o. decorsei
Mali to S Sudan

Nectarinia cuprea (Coppery Sunbird)

N. c. cuprea
Senegal to Zaire, Uganda, Tanzania

N. c. chalcea
Malawi, Rhodesia, Angola, W Zambia

Nectarinia tacazze (Tacazze Sunbird)

N. t. tacazze
Ethiopia

N. t. jacksoni
S Sudan, Uganda, W Kenya, N Tanzania

Nectarinia bocagii (Bocage's Sunbird)
Angola, Zaire

Nectarinia purpureiventris (Purple-breasted Sunbird)
Uganda, E Zaire

Nectarinia shelleyi (Shelley's Sunbird)

N. s. hofmanni
E Tanzania

N. s. shelleyi
SE Zaire, E Zambia to N Mozambique

Nectarinia mariquensis (Mariqua Sunbird)

N. m. osiris
Ethiopia, S Sudan, N Kenya, N Uganda

N. m. suahelica
S Uganda, E Zaire to NE Zambia

N. m. mariquensis
S Angola to Rhodesia

N. m. lucens
E Rhodesia, S Mozambique, Natal

Nectarinia pembae (Violet-breasted Sunbird)

N. p. chalcomelas
Somalia, E Kenya

N. p. pembae
Pemba I

Nectarinia bifasciata (Purple-banded Sunbird)

N. b. bifasciata
Gabon to C Angola

N. b. microrhyncha
Uganda to Angola, N Malawi,
Mozambique
N. b. tsavoensis
E Kenya, NE Tanzania
N. b. strophium
SE Zambia, S Mozambique, N Natal
**Nectarinia coccinigastra (Splendid
Sunbird)**
Senegal to NE Zaire
**Nectarinia erythrocerca (Red-chested
Sunbird)**
Sudan, Uganda, NW Tanzania
**Nectarinia congensis (Congo Black-
bellied Sunbird)**
Zaire
Nectarinia pulchella (Beautiful Sunbird)
N. p. pulchella
Senegal, Mali, Niger, W Sudan
N. p. aegra
S Niger, Aïr Massif
N. p. lucidipectus
S Sudan, Ethiopia, NE Zaire, Uganda,
NW Kenya
N. p. melanogastra
S Kenya, Tanzania
**Nectarinia nectarinioides (Smaller
Black-bellied Sunbird)**
N. n. erlangeri
S Somalia
N. n. nectarinioides
E Kenya, NE Tanzania
**Nectarinia famosa (Yellow-tufted
Malachite Sunbird)**
N. f. cupreonitens
Ethiopia, SE Sudan
N. f. aeneigularis
Kenya, Uganda, E Zaire, N Malawi
N. f. famosa
Rhodesia, South Africa
**Nectarinia johnstoni (Red-tufted
Malachite Sunbird)**
N. j. johnstoni
W Kenya, N Tanzania
N. j. dartmouthi
E Zaire, W Uganda
N. j. nyikensis
S Tanzania, Zambia, Malawi
Nectarinia notata (Noted Sunbird)
N. n. notata
Madagascar
N. n. moebii
Gt Comoro I
N. n. voeltzkowi
Moheli I (Comoro)

**Nectarinia johannae (Madame Verreaux's
Sunbird)**
N. j. fasciata
Sierra Leone to Benin
N. j. johannae
Cameroun, Zaire
Nectarinia superba (Superb Sunbird)
N. s. ashantiensis
Sierra Leone to Ghana
N. s. nigeriae
S Nigeria
N. s. superba
S Cameroun, W Zaire, Angola
N. s. buvuma
E Zaire, Uganda
Nectarinia kilimensis (Bronze Sunbird)
N. k. kilimensis
E Zaire, Uganda, W Kenya, Tanzania
N. k. arturi
S Tanzania, Malawi, NE Zambia,
E Rhodesia
N. k. gadowi
C Angola
**Nectarinia reichenowi (Golden-winged
Sunbird)**
N. r. shelleyae
E Zaire
N. r. lathburyi
N Kenya
N. r. reichenowi
C & S Kenya, NE Tanzania, Mozambique

AETHOPYGA
**Aethopyga primigenius (Hachisuka's
Sunbird)**
A. p. diuatae
NE Mindanao
A. p. primigenius
C & E Mindanao
Aethopyga boltoni (Apo Sunbird)
A. b. malindangensis
C & W Mindanao
A. b. boltoni
E Mindanao
Aethopyga flagrans (Flaming Sunbird)
A. f. decolor
NE Luzon I
A. f. flagrans
W & S Luzon I
A. f. guimarasensis
Panay I, Guimaras I
A. f. daphoenonota
Negros I
**Aethopyga pulcherrima (Mountain
Sunbird)**
A. p. jeffreyi
Luzon I
A. p. pulcherrima
Basilan I, Samar I, Leyte I, Mindanao I

A. p. decorosa
Bohol I

Aethopyga duyvenbodei (Sanghir Yellow-backed Sunbird)
Sanghir Is

Aethopyga shelleyi (Palawan Sunbird)
A. s. flavipectus
Luzon I, Mindoro I
A. s. rubrinota
Lubang Is
A. s. bella
Samar I, Leyte I, Mindanao I
A. s. bonita
Ticao I, Masbate I, Panay I, Negros I, Cebu I
A. s. arolasi
Sulu Archipelago
A. s. shelleyi
Balabac I, Palawan I

Aethopyga gouldiae (Mrs Gould's Sunbird)
A. g. gouldiae
N Assam, Himalayas, SE Tibet
A. g. isolata
S Assam, Bangladesh, Burma
A. g. dabryii
E Sikang, SW China, N Vietnam
A. g. annamensis
S Laos, S Vietnam

Aethopyga nipalensis (Green-tailed Sunbird)
A. n. horsfieldii
W Himalayas
A. n. nipalensis
C Nepal, Sikkim
A. n. koelzi
E Himalayas, NE Burma, S Assam, N Vietnam
A. n. victoriae
W Burma
A. n. karenensis
SE Burma
A. n. angkanensis
N Thailand
A. n. australis
S Thailand
A. n. blanci
Laos
A. n. ezrai
S Vietnam

Aethopyga eximia (Kuhl's Sunbird)
Java

Aethopyga christinae (Fork-tailed Sunbird)
A. c. latouchii
SE China, N Vietnam
A. c. christinae
Hainan I

Aethopyga saturata (Black-throated Sunbird)
A. s. saturata
W Himalayas
A. s. assamensis
Bangladesh, Assam, N Burma, W China
A. s. galenae
NW Thailand
A. s. petersi
E Burma, Laos, N Vietnam, SE Yunnan
A. s. sanguinipectus
SE Burma
A. s. anomala
S Thailand
A. s. wrayi
Malaysia
A. s. ochra
S Laos, C Vietnam
A. s. cambodiana
SW Cambodia
A. s. johnsi
S Vietnam

Aethopyga siparaja (Yellow-backed Sunbird)
A. s. vigorsii
N India
A. s. seheriae
Nepal, Assam, Bangladesh, NE India, Burma, N Thailand
A. s. labecula
NE India, S Bangladesh
A. s. owstoni
Nauchow I (Hainan)
A. s. tonkinensis
NE Vietnam
A. s. mangini
SE Thailand, C & S Indochina
A. s. insularis
Phuquoc I (Cambodia)
A. s. cara
S Burma, Thailand
A. s. trangensis
S Thailand
A. s. siparaja
Malaysia, Sumatra, Borneo
A. s. nicobarica
Nicobar Is
A. s. heliogona
Java
A. s. natunae
N Natuna Is
A. s. magnifica
WC Philippine Is
A. s. flavostriata
N Celebes
A. s. beccarii
S Celebes

Aethopyga mystacalis (Scarlet Sunbird)
  A. m. temminckii
    Malaysia, Sumatra, Borneo
  A. m. mystacalis
    Java
Aethopyga ignicauda (Fire-tailed Sunbird)
  A. i. ignicauda
    Himalayas, Sikang, N Burma, Yunnan
  A. i. flavescens
    NW Burma

ARACHNOTHERA
Arachnothera longirostra (Little Spider-hunter)
  A. l. longirostra
    SW India, Nepal, Assam, Burma, W Thailand
  A. l. sordida
    S Yunnan, NE Thailand, N Indochina
  A. l. pallida
    SE Thailand, C Indochina
  A. l. cinereicollis
    S Thailand, Malaysia, Sumatra
  A. l. niasensis
    Nias I
  A. l. prillwitzi
    Java
  A. l. buettikoferi
    Borneo
  A. l. atita
    S Natuna Is
  A. l. rothschildi
    N Natuna Is
  A. l. dilutior
    Palawan
  A. l. flammifera
    Samar I, Leyte I, Bohol I, Mindanao I
  A. l. randi
    Basilan I
Arachnothera crassirostris (Thick-billed Spiderhunter)
    S Thailand, Malaysia, Sumatra, Borneo
Arachnothera robusta (Long-billed Spiderhunter)
  A. r. robusta
    Malaysia, Sumatra, Borneo
  A. r. armata
    Java
Arachnothera flavigaster (Greater Yellow-eared Spiderhunter)
    S Thailand, Malaysia, Sumatra, Borneo
Arachnothera chrysogenys (Lesser Yellow-eared Spiderhunter)
  A. c. chrysogenys
    S Burma, S Thailand, Malaysia, Sumatra, Java, W Borneo
  A. c. harrissoni
    E Borneo

Arachnothera clarae (Naked-faced Spiderhunter)
  A. c. philippinensis
    Samar I, Leyte I
  A. c. clarae
    E Mindanao I
  A. c. malindangensis
    C & W Mindanao I
  A. c. luzonensis
    C Luzon I, Laguna I
Arachnothera affinis (Grey-breasted Spiderhunter)
  A. a. caena
    S Burma, Thailand
  A. a. modesta
    S Thailand, Malaysia, W Borneo
  A. a. pars
    E Borneo
  A. a. affinis
    Java, Bali I
  A. a. concolor
    Sumatra
Arachnothera magna (Streaked Spider-hunter)
  A. m. magna
    Himalayas, N Burma, Yunnan
  A. m. aurata
    EC Burma
  A. m. musarum
    SE Burma, N Thailand, N Laos
  A. m. pagodarum
    S Burma, SW Thailand
  A. m. remota
    S Vietnam
Arachnothera everetti (Everett's Spiderhunter)
    N & C Borneo
Arachnothera juliae (Whitehead's Spiderhunter)
    N Borneo

152 ZOSTEROPIDAE (WHITE EYES)

ZOSTEROPS
Zosterops erythropleura (Chestnut-flanked White eye)
    Manchuria, Amur, N Korea, China
Zosterops japonica (Japanese White eye)
  Z. j. yesoensis
    Hokkaido I
  Z. j. japonica
    Honshu I, S Japan
  Z. j. stejnegeri
    Bonin Is, Izu Is
  Z. j. alani
    Iwo Jima I
  Z. j. insularis
    Tanegashima I, Yakushima I

Z. j. loochooensis
Riukiu Is
Z. j. daitoensis
Borodino Is
Z. j. simplex
Sikang, China, Burma, N Vietnam, Taiwan
Z. j. hainana
Hainan I

Zosterops meyeni (Philippine White eye)
Z. m. batanis
Botel Tobago I, Kashoto I, Batan I
Z. m. meyeni
Luzon I, Calayan I, Lubang I

Zosterops palpebrosa (Oriental White eye)
Z. p. occidentis
NW India
Z. p. palpebrosa
C India, Sri Lanka, Bangladesh, W Assam,
Nepal, Bhutan
Z. p. nilgiriensis
SW India
Z. p. salimalii
SE India
Z. p. siamensis
SE Tibet, Burma, N Thailand, SW China,
Indochina
Z. p. nicobarica
Andaman Is, Nicobar Is
Z. p. williamsoni
S Thailand, Malaysia
Z. p. joannae
W China
Z. p. auriventer
S Burma, Malaysia, Bangka I, W Borneo
Z. p. sumatrana
W Sumatra
Z. p. buxtoni
E Sumatra, W Java
Z. p. melanura
E & C Java, Bali I
Z. p. unica
Sumbawa I, Flores I

Zosterops ceylonensis (Large Sri Lanka White eye)
Sri Lanka

Zosterops conspicillata (Bridled White eye)
Z. c. saypani
Tinian I, Saipan I
Z. c. conspicillata
Guam I
Z. c. rotensis
Rota I
Z. c. semperi
Palau Is
Z. c. owstoni
Truk I

Z. c. takatsukasai
Ponapé I
Z. c. hypolais
Yap I

Zosterops salvadorii (Enggano White eye)
Enggano I

Zosterops atricapilla (Black-capped White eye)
Z. a. viridicata
N Sumatra
Z. a. atricapilla
C & S Sumatra, N Borneo

Zosterops everetti (Everett's White eye)
Z. e. everetti
Cebu I
Z. e. basilanica
Samar I, Leyte I, Mindanao I, Basilan I
Z. e. boholensis
Bohol I
Z. e. siquijorensis
Siquijor I
Z. e. mandibularis
Sulu Archipelago
Z. e. babelo
Talaut I
Z. e. tahanensis
N Borneo, Malaysia, S Thailand
Z. e. wetmorei
S Thailand

Zosterops nigrorum (Philippine Yellow White eye)
Z. n. meyleri
Camiguin Is
Z. n. aureiloris
N Luzon I
Z. n. sierramadrensis
Cagayan Province, Luzon I
Z. n. luzonica
SE Luzon I
Z. n. nigrorum
Masbate I, Negros I, Panay I
Z. n. richmondi
Cagayancillo I (Sulu Sea)
Z. n. mindorensis
Mindoro I
Z. n. catarmanensis
Camiguin I (South)

Zosterops montana (Mountain White eye)
Z. m. ternatana
Ternate I
Z. m. obstinata
Batjan I
Z. m. seranensis
Ceram I
Z. m. whiteheadi
N Luzon I

Z. m. halconensis
Mindoro I
Z. m. gilli
Marinduque I
Z. m. parkesi
Palawan I
Z. m. diuatae
N Mindanao
Z. m. vulcani
Mt Apo & Mt Katanglad (Mindanao)
Z. m. pectoralis
N Negros I
Z. m. steini
Timor I
Z. m. montana
Sumatra, Java, Bali I, Lesser Sunda Is,
Celebes, Buru I
Z. m. difficilis
S Sumatra
Zosterops wallacei (Wallace's White eye)
Sumbawa I, Sumba I, Flores I
Zosterops flava (Javan White eye)
NW Java, S Borneo
Zosterops chloris (Moluccan White eye)
Z. c. maxi
Lombok I
Z. c. intermedia
Sumbawa I, Flores I, SW Celebes
Z. c. mentoris
NC Celebes
Z. c. flavissima
Tukangbesi I
Z. c. solombensis
Solombo Besar I
Z. c. zachlora
Kalambau I
Z. c. chloris
Aru Is, Kei Is, Ceram I, Misol I, Halmahera I
Z. c. albiventris
S Moluccan Is, Tenimber Is, Torres Straits Is
Z. c. citrinella
Timor I, Sumba I
Z. c. harterti
Alor I
**Zosterops consobrinorum (Peninsular
White eye)**
SE Celebes
Zosterops grayi (Gt Kei I White eye)
Gt Kei I
**Zosterops uropygialis (Little Kei I White
eye)**
Little Kei I
Zosterops anomala (Celebean White eye)
S Celebes
Zosterops atriceps (Batjan White eye)
Z. a. dehaani
Morotai I

Z. a. fuscifrons
Halmahera I
Z. a. atriceps
Batjan I
**Zosterops atrifrons (Moluccan Black-
fronted White eye)**
Z. a. nehrkorni
Gt Sanghir Is, Celebes
Z. a. atrifrons
Banggai I, N Celebes
Z. a. surda
NC Celebes
Z. a. sulaensis
Sula Is
Z. a. stalkeri
Ceram I
**Zosterops minor (New Guinea Black-
fronted White eye)**
Z. m. minor
Japen I, New Guinea
Z. m. chrysolaema
NW New Guinea
Z. m. rothschildi
C New Guinea
Z. m. gregaria
E New Guinea
Z. m. tenuifrons
SE New Guinea
Z. m. delicatula
SE New Guinea
Z. m. pallidogularis
Fergusson I, Goodenough I
**Zosterops meeki (White throated White
eye)**
Z. m. meeki
Tagula I, Louisiade Archipelago
Z. m. hypoxantha
New Britain
Z. m. ultima
New Hanover, New Ireland
Z. m. admiralitatus
Manus I (Admiralty Is)
Zosterops mysorensis (Biak White eye)
Biak I, New Guinea
**Zosterops fuscicapilla (Yellow-bellied
Mountain White eye)**
Z. f. fuscicapilla
C & W New Guinea
Z. f. crookshanki
Goodenough I
Zosterops buruensis (Buru I White eye)
Buru I
Zosterops kuehni (Ambon white eye)
Ambon I
**Zosterops novaeguineae (New Guinea
Mountain White eye)**
Z. n. novaeguineae
NW New Guinea

Z. n. aruensis
Aru Is
Z. n. wuroi
S New Guinea
Z. n. wahgiensis
C New Guinea
Z. n. crissalis
SE New Guinea
Z. n. oreophila
E New Guinea
Z. n. magnirostris
NW New Guinea
Zosterops metcalfii (Yellow-throated White eye)
Z. m. exigua
Buka I, Bougainville I, Choiseul I
Z. m. metcalfii
Ysabel I, St George I
Z. m. floridana
Florida I
Zosterops natalis (Christmas Island White eye)
Christmas I
Zosterops lutea (Yellow Silver eye)
Z. l. balstoni
NW Western Australia
Z. l. lutea
Nothern Territory, N Queensland
Zosterops griseotincta (Louisiades White eye)
Z. g. pallidipes
Rossel I (Louisiade Archipelago)
Z. g. aignani
Louisiade Archipelago
Z. g. griseotincta
Louisiade Archipelago
Z. g. longirostris
Bonvouloir I (Louisiade Archipelago)
Z. g. eichhorni
Nauna I, Nissan I, Long I (New Britain)
Zosterops rennelliana (Rennell Is White eye)
Rennell I
Zosterops rendovae (Solomon Is White eye)
Z. r. vellalavella
Bagga I, Vella Lavella I
Z. r. luteirostris
Gizo I
Z. r. splendida
Ganonga I
Z. r. kulambangrae
Kulambangra I, Vangunu I, New Georgia I
Z. r. rendovae
Rendova I
Z. r. tetiparia
Tetipari I

Zosterops murphyi (Kulambangra Mountain White eye)
Kulambangra I
Zosterops ugiensis (Grey-throated White eye)
Z. u. ugiensis
San Cristobal I
Z. u. oblita
Guadalcanal I
Z. u. hamlini
Bougainville I
Zosterops stresemanni (Malaita White eye)
Malaita I
Zosterops sanctaecrucis (Santa Cruz White eye)
Santa Cruz I
Zosterops samoensis (Savaii White eye)
Savaii I (Samoa Is)
Zosterops explorator (Layard's White eye)
Fiji Is
Zosterops flavifrons (Yellow-fronted White eye)
Z. f. gauensis
Gaua I (Banks Is)
Z. f. perplexa
N New Hebrides, Vanua Levu I
Z. f. brevicauda
Malo I, Espiritu Santo I
Z. f. macgillivrayi
Malekula I
Z. f. efatensis
Nguna I, Efate I, Erromanga I
Z. f. flavifrons
Tanna I
Z. f. majuscula
Aneitum I
Zosterops minuta (Small Lifu White eye)
Lifu I, Loyalty Is
Zosterops xanthochroa (New Caledonia White eye)
New Caledonia
Zosterops gouldi (Western Silvereye)
S Western Australia
Zosterops lateralis (Grey-backed White eye)
Z. l. halmaturina
Tasmania, W Victoria, SE South Australia
Z. l. lateralis
Victoria, E New South Wales, SE Queensland, New Zealand
Z. l. familiaris
E New South Wales
Z. l. ramsayi
E Queensland
Z. l. tephropleura
Lord Howe I **e?**

Z. l. chlorocephala
Capricorn I
Z. l. griseonota
New Caledonia
Z. l. nigrescens
Maré I, Uvea I (Loyalty Is)
Z. l. melanops
Lifu I (Loyalty Is)
Z. l. macmillani
Tanna I, Aniwa I (New Hebrides)
Z. l. tropica
Espiritu Santo I
Z. l. vatensis
N New Hebrides, Banks Is, Torres Is
Z. l. valuensis
Valua I (Banks Is)
Z. l. flaviceps
Fiji Archipelago

Zosterops tenuirostris (Slender-billed White eye)
Norfolk I

Zosterops albogularis (White-chested White eye)
Norfolk I

Zosterops inornata (Large Lifu White eye)
Lifu I

Zosterops cinerea (Grey-brown White eye)
Z. c. finschii
Palau Is
Z. c. ponapensis
Ponapé I
Z. c. cinerea
Kusaie I

Zosterops abyssinica (White-breasted White eye)
Z. a. abyssinica
E Ethiopia, SE Sudan
Z. a. socotrana
Socotra I, N Somalia
Z. a. arabs
Yemen, Aden
Z. a. omoensis
SW Ethiopia
Z. a. jubaensis
SE Ethiopia, Somalia, N Kenya
Z. a. flavilateralis
E Kenya, E Tanzania

Zosterops pallida (Pale White eye)
Z. p. pallida
Namibia, SW Transvaal, NW Cape Province
Z. p. sundevalli
N Cape Province
Z. p. caniviridis
W Transvaal, E Botswana

Zosterops senegalensis (African Yellow White eye)
Z. s. senegalensis
Senegal to Ethiopia, Uganda
Z. s. demeryi
Sierra Leone, Liberia, Ivory Coast
Z. s. stenocricota
Fernando Po I, SE Nigeria to Gabon
Z. s. stuhlmanni
E Zaire, Uganda
Z. s. reichenowi
E Zaire
Z. s. toroensis
NE Zaire
Z. s. jacksoni
W Kenya, N Tanzania
Z. s. kasaica
SW Zaire, NE Angola
Z. s. heinrichi
N Angola
Z. s. quanzae
C Angola
Z. s. anderssoni
S Angola to Mozambique, Natal
Z. s. stierlingi
S Tanzania, Zambia, Malawi
Z. s. kirki
Gt Comoro I
Z. s. poliogastra
C Ethiopia
Z. s. kaffensis
W Ethiopia
Z. s. kulalensis
N Kenya
Z. s. kikuyuensis
W Kenya
Z. s. silvana
SE Kenya
Z. s. eurycricota
N Tanzania
Z. s. mbuluensis
N Tanzania
Z. s. winifredae
NE Tanzania

Zosterops virens (Green White eye)
Z. v. capensis
W Cape Province
Z. v. virens
S Mozambique to C & E Cape Province
Z. v. atmorii
W Natal, Lesotho

Zosterops borbonica (Bourbon White eye)
Z. b. mauritiana
Mauritius I
Z. b. borbonica
Reunion I
Z. b. alopekion
Cilaos I, Reunion I

Z. b. xerophila
  Etang les Bains, Reunion I
Zosterops ficedulina (Principé White eye)
  Z. f. ficedulina
    Principé I
  Z. f. feae
    Sao Thomé I
Zosterops griseovirescens (Annobon White eye)
  Annobon I
Zosterops hovarum (Hova Grey-backed White eye)
  Madagascar
Zosterops maderaspatana (Madagascar White eye)
  Z. m. aldabransis
    Aldabra I
  Z. m. maderaspatana
    Madagascar, Glorioso I
  Z. m. anjouanensis
    Anjouan I
  Z. m. comorensis
    Moheli I
  Z. m. voeltzkowi
    Europa I
  Z. m. menaiensis
    Cosmoledo Atoll
Zosterops mayottensis (Chestnut-sided White eye)
  Mayotte I
Zosterops modesta (Seychelles Brown White eye)
  Mahé I
Zosterops mouroniensis (Grand Comoro White eye)
  Gt Comoro I
Zosterops olivacea (Olive White eye)
  Reunion I
Zosterops chloronothos (Mauritius Olive White eye)
  Mauritius I
Zosterops vaughani (Pemba White eye)
  Pemba I

WOODFORDIA
Woodfordia superciliosa (Woodford's White eye)
  Rennell I
Woodfordia lacertosa (Sanford's White eye)
  Santa Cruz I

RUKIA
Rukia palauensis (Palau White eye)
  Palau Is
Rukia oleaginea (Yap White eye)
  Yap I
Rukia ruki (Truk White eye)
  Truk I

Rukia longirostra (Ponapé White eye)
  Ponapé I

TEPHROZOSTEROPS
Tephrozosterops stalkeri (Ceram White eye)
  Ceram I

MADANGA
Madanga ruficollis (Madanga White eye)
  NW Buru I

LOPHOZOSTEROPS
Lophozosterops pinaiae (Brown-breasted White eye)
  C Ceram I
Lophozosterops goodfellowi (Goodfellow's White eye)
  L. g. goodfellowi
    Mt Apo (Mindano I)
  L. g. malindangensis
    Mt Malindang (NW Mindanao I)
  L. g. gracilis
    NE Mindanao I

  L. s. stresemanni
    N Celebes
  L. s. heinrichi
    N Celebes
  L. s. striaticeps
    NC Celebes
  L. s. stachyrina
    SC Celebes
  L. s. squamiceps
    S Celebes
  L. s. analoga
    SE Celebes
Lophozosterops javanica (Javan Grey-throated White eye)
  L. j. frontalis
    W Java
  L. j. javanica
    C & E Java
  L. j. elongata
    E Java, Bali I
Lophozosterops superciliaris (White-browed White eye)
  L. s. hartertiana
    W Sumbawa I
  L. s. superciliaris
    Flores I
Lophozosterops dohertyi (Crested White eye)
  L. d. dohertyi
    Sumbawa I
  L. d. subcristata
    Flores I

OCULOCINCTA
Oculocincta squamifrons (Pygmy White eye)
N & W Borneo

HELEIA
Heleia muelleri (Timor White eye)
W Timor I
Heleia crassirostris (Stripe-headed White eye)
H. c. crassirostris
Flores I
H. c. junior
Sumbawa I

CHLOROCHARIS
Chlorocharis emiliae (Olive Black eye)
C. e. emiliae
Mt Kinabalu (N Borneo)
C. e. trinitae
Mt Trus Madi (N Borneo)
C. e. fusciceps
NE Sarawak
C. e. moultoni
Sarawak

HYPOCRYPTADIUS
Hypocryptadius cinnamomeus (Cinnamon White eye)
Mindanao I

SPEIROPS
Speirops brunnea (Fernando Po Speirops)
Fernando Po I
Speirops leucophaea (Prince's I Speirops)
Principé I
Speirops lugubris (Black-capped Speirops)
S. l. melanocephala
Mt Cameroun
S. l. lugubris
Sao Thomé I

153 MELIPHAGIDAE (HONEY EATERS)

TIMELIOPSIS
Timeliopsis fulvigula (Mountain Straight-billed Honeyeater)
T. f. fulvigula
NW New Guinea
T. f. meyeri
C & SE New Guinea
T. f. fuscicapilla
E New Guinea
Timeliopsis griseigula (Lowland Straight-billed Honeyeater)
T. g. griseigula
W New Guinea
T. g. fulviventris
SE New Guinea

MELILESTES
Melilestes megarhynchus (Long-billed Honeyeater)
M. m. vagans
Batana I, Waigeu I
M. m. brunneus
NW New Guinea
M. m. megarhynchus
Aru Is, S & SE New Guinea
M. m. stresemanni
N New Guinea, Japen I
Melilestes bougainvillei (Bougainville Honeyeater)
Bougainville I

TOXORHAMPHUS
Toxorhamphus novaeguineae (Yellow-bellied Longbill)
T. n. novaeguineae
W New Guinea & islands
T. n. flaviventris
Aru Is, S New Guinea
Toxorhamphus poliopterus (Slaty-chinned Longbill)
T. p. maximus
NC New Guinea
T. p. poliopterus
C & SE New Guinea

OEDISTOMA
Oedistoma iliolophum (Grey-bellied Honeyeater)
O. i. cinerascens
Waigeu I
O. i. affine
NW New Guinea
O. i. iliolophum
Japen I, N New Guinea
O. i. flavum
S & SE New Guinea
O. i. fergussonis
D'Entrecasteaux Archipelago
Oedistoma pygmaeum (Pygmy Honeyeater)
O. p. waigeuense
Waigeu I
O. p. pygmaeum
Misol I, W New Guinea
O. p. flavipectus
S New Guinea
O. p. olivascens
SE New Guinea
O. p. meeki
D'Entrecasteaux Archipelago

GLYCICHAERA
Glycichaera fallax (White-eyed Honeyeater)
G. f. pallida
Batanta I, Waigeu I
G. f. poliocephala
Misol I, Aru Is, NW New Guinea

G. f. fallax
Japen I, E & S New Guinea
G. f. sylvia
N New Guinea
G. f. claudi
N Queensland

LICHMERA
Lichmera lombokia (Lombok Honeyeater)
L. l. lombokia
Lombok I
L. l. fumidigula
Flores I, Sumbawa I
Lichmera argentauris (Plain Olive Honey-eater)
L. a. argentauris
Waigeu I, W New Guinea islands
L. a. chloris
Halmahera I
L. a. patasiwa
Lusaolate I (Ceram)
Lichmera indistincta (Brown Honeyeater)
L. i. limbata
Bali I, Lombok I, Timor I, Lesser Sunda Is
L. i. indistincta
Western Australia, Northern Territory
L. i. ocularis
NE Australia, S New Guinea
L. i. melvillensis
Melville I
L. i. nupta
Aru Is
Lichmera incana (Silver-eared Honey-eater)
L. i. incana
New Caledonia
L. i. poliotis
Loyalty Is
L. i. mareensis
Maré Is (Loyalty Is)
L. i. griseoviridis
C New Hebrides
L. i. flavotincta
Erromanga I (New Hebrides)
Lichmera alboauricularis (White-eared Honeyeater)
L. a. alboauricularis
SE New Guinea
L. a. olivacea
N New Guinea
Lichmera squamata (Tenimber Honey-eater)
L. s. squamata
Kei Is
L. s. salvadorii
Tenimber Is
L. s. kebirensis
S Banda Sea Islands

Lichmera deningeri (Buru Honeyeater)
Buru I
Lichmera monticola (Ceram Honeyeater)
Ceram I
Lichmera flavicans (Timor Honeyeater)
Timor I
Lichmera notabilis (Wetar Honeyeater)
Wetar I
Lichmera cockerelli (White-streaked Honeyeater)
N Queensland

MYZOMELA
Myzomela blasii (Ambon Honeyeater)
Ceram I, Ambon I
Myzomela albigula (White-chinned Honeyeater)
M. a. albigula
Rossel I
M. a. pallidior
W Louisiade Archipelago
Myzomela cineracea (Sclater's Honeyeater
M. c. cineracea
New Britain
M. c. rooki
Umboi I (Bismarck Archipelago)
Myzomela eques (Red-spot Honeyeater)
M. e. eques
NW New Guinea & islands
M. e. primitiva
N New Guinea
M. e. nymani
S & E New Guinea
M. e. karimuiensis
E New Guinea
Myzomela obscura (Dusky Honeyeater)
M. o. harterti
E Queensland
M. o. munna
N Queensland, Torres Strait
M. o. obscura
Northern Territory, Melville I
M. o. fumata
S New Guinea
M. o. aruensis
Aru Is
M. o. simplex
Damar I, Ternate I, Batjan I, Halmahera I
M. o. rubrotincta
Obi Is
M. o. mortyana
Morotai I
M. o. rubrobrunnea
Biak I
Myzomela cruentata (Red Honeyeater
M. c. cruentata
Japen I, New Guinea
M. c. coccinea
New Britain, Duke of York Is

M. c. erythrina
New Ireland
M. c. lavongai
New Hanover
M. c. cantans
Tabar I (Bismarck Archipelago)
M. c. vinacea
Dyaul I (Bismarck Archipelago)

Myzomela nigrita (Black Honeyeater)
M. n. steini
Waigeu I
M. n. nigrita
Aru Is, S New Guinea
M. n. meyeri
Japen I, N New Guinea
M. n. pluto
Meos Num I
M. n. forbesi
D'Entrecasteaux Archipelago
M. n. louisiadensis
Louisiade Archipelago
M. n. hades
St Matthias Is (Bismarck Archipelago)
M. n. ramsayi
Tingwon I (Bismarck Archipelago)
M. n. pammelaena
Admiralty Is
M. n. ernstmayri
Manus I, Admiralty Is
M. n. nigerrima
Long I (NE New Guinea)

Myzomela pulchella (New Ireland Honey-eater)
New Ireland

Myzomela kuehni (Wetar Honeyeater)
Wetar I

Myzomela erythrocephala (Mangrove Red-headed Honeyeater)
M. e. erythrocephala
coast of N Western Australia
M. e. infuscata
NE Australia, Aru Is, S New Guinea
M. e. dammermanni
Sumba I

Myzomela adolphinae (Mountain Red-headed Honeyeater)
New Guinea

Myzomela sanguinolenta (Scarlet Honeyeater)
M. s. chloroptera
N Celebes
M. s. charlottae
C & SE Celebes
M. s. juga
SW Celebes
M. s. eva
Djampea I, Saleyer I (Flores Sea)

M. s. batjanensis
Batjan I
M. s. elisabethae
Ceram I
M. s. wakoloensis
Buru I
M. s. annabellae
Babar I, Tenimber Is
M. s. boiei
Banda I
M. s. caledonica
New Caledonia
M. s. sanguinolenta
coast of E Queensland, New South Wales

Myzomela cardinalis (Cardinal Honeyeater)
M. c. lifuensis
Loyalty Is
M. c. cardinalis
S New Hebrides
M. c. tenuis
N New Hebrides
M. c. tucopiae
Tikopia I
M. c. nigriventris
Samoa Is
M. c. sanctaecrucis
Torres Is, Santa Cruz I
M. c. sanfordi
Rennell I
M. c. pulcherrima
San Cristobal I, Ugi I
M. c. kobayashii
Palau Is
M. c. kurodai
Yap I
M. c. saffordi
S Marianas Is
M. c. asuncionis
N Marianas Is
M. c. major
Truk I
M. c. dichromata
Ponapé I
M. c. rubratra
Kusaie I (Caroline Is)
M. c. chermesina
Rotuma Is

Myzomela sclateri (Sclater's Honeyeater)
N New Guinea islands & New Britain

Myzomela lafargei (Small Bougainville Honeyeater)
Bougainville Group, Solomon Is

Myzomela melanocephala (Black-headed Honeyeater)
Guadalcanal Group, Solomon Is

Myzomela eichhorni (Yellow-vented Honeyeater)
M. e. eichhorni
Solomon Is
M. e. ganongae
Ganonga I
M. e. atrata
Vella Lavella I, Baga I
Myzomela malaitae (Malaita Honeyeater)
Malaita I
Myzomela tristrami (Tristram's Honey-eater)
San Cristobal I, Santa Ana I
Myzomela jugularis (Orange-breasted Honeyeater)
Fiji Is
Myzomela erythromelas (Black-bellied Honeyeater)
New Britain
Myzomela vulnerata (Sunda Honeyeater)
Timor I
Myzomela rosenbergii (Black & Red Honeyeater)
M. r. rosenbergii
NW New Guinea
M. r. longirostris
Goodenough I (D' Entrecasteaux Archipelago)
M. r. wahgiensis
W & C New Guinea

CERTHIONYX
Certhionyx niger (Black Honey-eater)
C Australia
Certhionyx variegatus (Pied Honeyeater)
C Australia

MELIPHAGA
Meliphaga mimikae (Large Spot-breasted Honeyeater)
M. m. rara
N New Guinea
M. m. mimikae
C New Guinea
M. m. bastille
E New Guinea
M. m. granti
SE New Guinea
Meliphaga auga (Southern White-eared Mountain Honeyeater)
M. a. gretae
SC New Guinea
M. a. setekwa
SC New Guinea
M. a. auga
SE New Guinea

Meliphaga montana (White-eared Mountai Honeyeater)
M. m. montana
NW New Guinea
M. m. margaretae
Batanta I
M. m. sepik
C New Guinea
M. m. steini
Japen I
M. m. germanorum
N New Guinea
M. m. huonensis
NE New Guinea
M. m. aicora
SE New Guinea
Meliphaga orientalis (Small Spot-breasted Honeyeater)
M. o. facialis
E, N & E New Guinea, Waigeu I,
M. o. becki
NE New Guinea
M. o. orientalis
SE New Guinea
M. o. citreola
N New Guinea
Meliphaga albonotata (White-marked Honeyeater)
New Guinea
Meliphaga aruensis (Puff-backed Honey-eater)
M. a. sharpei
W, N & E New Guinea, Waigeu I,
D'Entrecasteaux Archipelago
M. a. aruensis
S New Guinea, Aru Is
Meliphaga analoga (Mimic Meliphaga)
M. a. papuae
S New Guinea
M. a. analoga
S New Guinea, W Papuan islands
M. a. longirostris
Aru Is
M. a. flavida
N New Guinea, Japen I
M. a. connectens
N New Guinea
Meliphaga vicina (Louisiades Honey-eater)
Tagula I
Meliphaga gracilis (Graceful Honeyeater)
M. g. stevensi
SE New Guinea
M. g. cinereifrons
SE New Guinea
M. g. gracilis
S New Guinea, Aru Is, N Queensland
M. g. imitatrix
NE Queensland

Meliphaga notata (Lesser Lewin Honey-eater)
 M. n. notata
  Torres Strait (N Queensland)
 M. n. mixta
  NE Queensland
Meliphaga flavirictus (Yellow-gaped Honeyeater)
 M. f. flavirictus
  SE New Guinea
 M. f. crockettorum
  N & W New Guinea
Meliphaga lewinii (Lewin Honeyeater)
 M. l. lewinii
  E Queensland, E New South Wales
 M. l. nea
  E Victoria
Meliphaga flava (Yellow Honeyeater)
 E Queensland
Meliphaga albilineata (White-striped Honeyeater)
 Northern Territory
Meliphaga virescens (Singing Honeyeater)
 M. v. virescens
  SC, S & Western Australia,
   S & W Australia islands
 M. v. insularis
  Rottnest I (Western Australia)
 M. v. westwoodia
  S Queensland
 M. v. forresti
  NW & C Australia
 M. v. cooperi
  N Northern Territory, Melville I
Meliphaga versicolor (Varied Honeyeater)
 M. v. sonoroides
  W Papuan Is, NW New Guinea
 M. v. vulgaris
  Japen I, N New Guinea, Fergusson I
 M. v. intermedia
  Samarai I (E New Guinea)
 M. v. versicolor
  S New Guinea, Torres Strait,
   NE Queensland
Meliphaga fasciogularis (Mangrove Honeyeater)
 E Queensland, N New South Wales
Meliphaga inexpectata (Guadalcanal Honeyeater)
 Guadalcanal I
Meliphaga fusca (Fuscous Honeyeater)
 M. f. fusca
  SE South Australia, Victoria, E New
   South Wales
 M. f. dawsoni
  SE Queensland
 M. f. subgermana
  E Queensland

 M. f. zanda
  NW Queensland, E Northern Territory
 M. f. flavescens
  N Western Australia, N Northern Territory
 M. f. deserticola
  N Western Australia
 M. f. melvillensis
  Melville I
 M. f. germana
  SE New Guinea
Meliphaga plumula (Yellow-fronted Honeyeater)
 M. p. planasi
  N Western Australia
 M. p. plumula
  C Australia
 M. p. ethelae
  E South Australia, NW Victoria, W New
   South Wales
Meliphaga chrysops (Yellow-faced Honeyeater)
 M. c. samueli
  SE South Australia
 M. c. chrysops
  E Victoria, E New South Wales,
   E Queensland
Meliphaga cratitia (Purple-gaped Honeyeater)
 M. c. cratitia
  W Victoria, SE South Australia,
   SW Western Australia
 M. c. halmaturina
  Kangaroo I
Meliphaga keartlandi (Grey-headed Honeyeater)
 C Australia
Meliphaga penicillata (White-plumed Honeyeater)
 M. p. carteri
  NW Western Australia
 M. p. geraldtonensis
  W Western Australia
 M. p. ladasi
  C Western Australia
 M. p. centralia
  C Australia
 M. p. leilavalensis
  W Queensland, NE South Australia
 M. p. interioris
  NW New South Wales, SC Queensland
 M. p. penicillata
  E & N Victoria, E South Australia,
   W New South Wales, SE Queensland
 M. p. mellori
  SW Victoria, SE South Australia
Meliphaga ornata (Mallee Honeyeater)
 S & Western Australia

***Meliphaga reticulata* (Reticulated Honeyeater)**
Timor I
***Meliphaga leucotis* (White-eared Honeyeater)**
M. l. novaenorciae
S Western Australia
M. l. leucotis
SE South Australia, Victoria, New South Wales, Kangaroo I
***Meliphaga flavicollis* (Yellow-throated Honeyeater)**
Tasmania, King I
***Meliphaga melanops* (Yellow-tufted Honeyeater)**
M. m. melanops
E New South Wales, E & C Victoria, SE Queensland
M. m. cassidix
S Victoria
***Meliphaga unicolor* (White-gaped Honeyeater)**
Northern Australia
***Meliphaga flaviventer* (Tawny-breasted Honeyeater)**
M. f. fusciventris
Waigeu I, Batanta I
M. f. flaviventer
W Papuan Is, NW New Guinea
M. f. rubiensis
WC New Guinea
M. f. saturatior
Aru Is, S New Guinea
M. f. tararae
S New Guinea
M. f. giulianettii
SE New Guinea
M. f. visi
SE New Guinea
M. f. kumusii
SE New Guinea
M. f. madaraszi
NE New Guinea
M. f. philemon
N New Guinea
M. f. meyeri
Japen I
M. f. spilogaster
Trobriand Is (D'Entrecasteaux Archipelago)
M. f. filigera
N Queensland
***Meliphaga polygramma* (Spotted Honeyeater)**
M. p. polygramma
Waigeu I
M. p. kuehni
Misol I
M. p. poikilosternos
Salawati I, NW & C New Guinea

M. p. septentrionalis
N New Guinea
M. p. lophotis
SE New Guinea
M. p. candidior
S New Guinea
***Meliphaga macleayana* (Yellow-streaked Honeyeater)**
NE Queensland
***Meliphaga frenata* (Bridled Honeyeater)**
NE Queensland
***Meliphaga subfrenata* (Black-throated Honeyeater)**
M. s. subfrenata
NW New Guinea
M. s. melanolaema
C New Guinea
M. s. utakwensis
SC New Guinea
M. s. salvadorii
SE New Guinea
***Meliphaga obscura* (Obscure Honeyeater)**
M. o. viridifrons
NW New Guinea
M. o. obscura
C & SE New Guinea

OREORNIS
***Oreornis chrysogenys* (Orange-cheeked Honeyeater)**
C New Guinea

FOULEHAIO
***Foulehaio carunculata* (Carunculated Honeyeater)**
F. c. carunculata
Samoan Islands, Tonga, E Fiji Is
F. c. taviunensis
Taveuni I, Vanua Levu I
F. c. procerior
W Fiji Is
***Foulehaio provocator* (Yellow-faced Honeyeater)**
Kandavu I

CLEPTORNIS
***Cleptornis marchei* (Golden Honeyeater)**
Saipan I (Mariana Is)

APALOPTERON
***Apalopteron familiare* (Bonin Island Honeyeater)**
A. f. familiare
N Bonin Is
A. f. hahasima
S Bonin Is

MELITHREPTUS

Melithreptus brevirostris (Brown-headed Honeyeater)
M. b. augustus
S Western Australia, S South Australia, NW Victoria
M. b. brevirostris
SE Queensland, E New South Wales, Victoria
M. b. magnirostris
Kangaroo I
Melithreptus lunatus (White-naped Honeyeater)
M. l. lunatus
E Queensland, SE New South Wales, SE South Australia
M. l. chloropsis
SW Western Australia
Melithreptus albogularis (White-throated Honeyeater)
M. a. subalbogularis
N Western Australia
M. a. albogularis
Northern Territory, N Queensland, NE New South Wales, S New Guinea
Melithreptus affinis (Black-headed Honeyeater)
M. a. alisteri
King I, Furneaux Group
M. a. affinis
Tasmania
Melithreptus gularis (Black-chinned Honeyeater)
SE Queensland, New South Wales, Victoria, SE South Australia
Melithreptus laetior (Golden-backed Honeyeater)
M. l. normantoniensis
N Queensland
M. l. carpentarianus
C Queensland
M. l. laetior
N Western Australia, S Northern Territory NW South Australia
M. l. parus
WC Western Australia
Melithreptus validirostris (Strong-billed Honeyeater)
M. v. kingi
King I, Furneaux Group
M. v. validirostris
Tasmania

ENTOMYZON

Entomyzon cyanotis (Blue-faced Honeyeater)
E. c. albipennis
N Western Australia, Northern Territory
E. c. apsleyi
Melville I

531

E. c. cyanotis
E South Australia, Victoria, New South Wales, E & C Queensland
E. c. harterti
S New Guinea, N Queensland

NOTIOMYSTIS

Notiomystis cincta (Stitch-bird)
N. c. hautura
Little Barrier I (New Zealand)
(N. c. cincta — extinct)

PYCNOPYGIUS

Pycnopygius ixoides (New Guinea Brown Honeyeater)
P. i. simplex
N New Guinea
P. i. proximus
N New Guinea
P. i. unicus
NE New Guinea
P. i. ixoides
NW New Guinea
P. i. cinereifrons
S New Guinea
P. i. finschi
SE New Guinea
Pycnopygius cinereus (Grey-fronted Honeyeater)
P. c. cinereus
NW New Guinea
P. c. dorsalis
WC New Guinea
P. c. marmoratus
SE New Guinea
Pycnopygius stictocephalus (Streak-capped Honeyeater)
Aru Is, New Guinea

PHILEMON

Philemon meyeri (Meyer's Friarbird)
E New Guinea
Philemon brassi (Brass's Friarbird)
NW New Guinea
Philemon citreogularis (Little Friarbird)
P. c. papuanus
S New Guinea
P. c. kisserensis
S Banda Sea islands
P. c. occidentalis
N Western Australia
P. c. breda
Melville I
P. c. sordidus
N Northern Territory
P. c. carpentariae
NW Queensland
P. c. johnstoni
NE Queensland

P. c. citreogularis
SE South Australia, Victoria, New South Wales, E & C Queensland
Philemon inornatus (Plain Friarbird)
P. i. inornatus
W Timor I
P. i. robustus
E Timor I
Philemon gilolensis (Striated Friarbird)
N Moluccas
Philemon fuscicapillus (Morotai I Friarbird)
N Moluccas
Philemon subcorniculatus (Ceram Friarbird)
Ceram I
Philemon moluccensis (Moluccas Friarbird)
P. m. moluccensis
Buru I
P. m. timorlaoensis
Tenimber Is
P. m. plumigenis
Kei Is
Philemon buceroides (Timor Helmeted Friarbird)
P. b. neglectus
Lombok I, Sumbawa I, Flores I
P. b. sumbanus
Sumba I
P. b. plesseni
Lomblen I, Pantar I, Alor I
P. b. pallidiceps
Wetar I
P. b. buceroides
N Western Australia, Timor I, Savu Is
Philemon gordoni (Melville I Friarbird)
Melville I, N Northern Territory
Philemon novaeguineae (New Guinea Friarbird)
P. n. novaeguineae
NW & S New Guinea, West Papuan islands
P. n. aruensis
Aru Is
P. n. jobiensis
Japen I, N New Guinea
P. n. brevipennis
S New Guinea
P. n. trivialis
SE New Guinea
P. n. subtuberosus
Trobriand Is (D'Entrecasteaux Archipelago)
P. n. tagulanus
Tagula I
P. n. yorki
Torres Strait, N Queensland
P. n. confusus
NE Queensland

Philemon cockerelli (New Britain Friarbird)
P. c. umboi
Rook I
P. c. cockerelli
New Britain
Philemon eichhorni (New Ireland Friarbird)
New Ireland
Philemon albitorques (White-naped Friarbird)
Manus I
Philemon argenticeps (Silver-crowned Friarbird)
P. a. argenticeps
N Western Australia
P. a. melvillensis
Melville I
P. a. alexis
N Northern Territory
P. a. kempi
N Queensland
Philemon corniculatus (Noisy Friarbird)
P. c. ellioti
S New Guinea, NE Queensland
P. c. clamans
SE Queensland
P. c. corniculatus
NE Victoria, E New South Wales
Philemon diemenensis (New Caledonian Friarbird)
Loyalty Is, New Caledonia

PTILOPRORA
Ptiloprora plumbea (Leaden Honeyeater)
P. p. granti
C New Guinea
P. p. plumbea
SE New Guinea
Ptiloprora meekiana (Meek's Streaked Honeyeater)
P. m. occidentalis
C New Guinea
P. m. meekiana
SE New Guinea
Ptiloprora erythropleura (Red-sided Streaked Honeyeater)
P. e. erythropleura
NW New Guinea
P. e. dammermani
C New Guinea
Ptiloprora guisei (Red-backed Honeyeater)
P. g. acrophila
N coast of New Guinea
P. g. umbrosa
N New Guinea
P. g. mayri
N New Guinea
P. g. guisei
SE New Guinea

Ptiloprora perstriata (Black-backed Streaked Honeyeater)
 P. p. praedicta
  NW New Guinea
 P. p. incerta
  WC New Guinea
 P. p. perstriata
  C & E New Guinea

MELIDECTES
Melidectes fuscus (Sooty Honeyeater)
 M. f. occidentalis
  C New Guinea
 M. f. gilliardi
  E New Guinea
 M. f. fuscus
  E & SE New Guinea
Melidectes whitemanensis (Gilliard's Honeyeater)
 New Britain
Melidectes princeps (Long-bearded Honeyeater)
 EC New Guinea
Melidectes nouhuysi (Short-bearded Honeyeater)
 WC New Guinea
Melidectes ochromelas (Mid-mountain Honeyeater)
 M. o. ochromelas
  W New Guinea
 M. o. batesi
  C & SE New Guinea
 M. o. lucifer
  NE New Guinea
Melidectes leucostephes (White-fronted Melidectes)
 NW New Guinea
Melidectes belfordi (Belford's Melidectes)
 M. b. brassi
  NW New Guinea
 M. b. joiceyi
  W New Guinea
 M. b. kinneari
  S New Guinea
 M. b. belfordi
  SE New Guinea
 M. b. schraderensis
  Schrader mountains, New Guinea
Melidectes rufocrissalis (Reichenow's Melidectes)
 M. r. rufocrissalis
  C New Guinea
 M. r. thomasi
  E New Guinea
 M. r. gilliardi
  EC New Guinea
Melidectes foersteri (Foerster's Melidectes)
 NE New Guinea

Melidectes torquatus (Cinnamon-breasted Wattle Bird)
 M. t. torquatus
  NW New Guinea
 M. t. nuchalis
  C New Guinea
 M. t. mixtus
  C New Guinea
 M. t. cahni
  NE New Guinea
 M. t. polyphonus
  NE New Guinea
 M. t. emilii
  SE New Guinea

MELIPOTES
Melipotes gymnops (Arfak Melipotes)
 NW New Guinea
Melipotes ater (Huon Melipotes)
 NE New Guinea
Melipotes fumigatus (Common Melipotes)
 M. f. goliathi
  C New Guinea
 M. f. fumigatus
  SE New Guinea

MYZA
Myza celebensis (Brown Honeysucker)
 M. c. celebensis
  N & C Celebes
 M. c. parvirostris
  SE Celebes
 M. c. meridionalis
  S Celebes
Myza sarasinorum (Spot-headed Honey-Sucker)
 M. s. sarasinorum
  N Celebes
 M. s. chionogenys
  SC Celebes
 M. s. pholidota
  SE Celebes

MELIARCHUS
Meliarchus sclateri (San Cristobal Honeyeater)
 San Cristobal I

GYMNOMYZA
Gymnomyza viridis (Green Honeyeater)
 G. v. viridis
  Taveuni I, Vanua Levu I
 G. v. brunneirostris
  Viti Levu I
Gymnomyza samoensis (Black-breasted Honeyeater)
 Samoa Is
Gymnomyza aubryana (Red-faced Honeyeater)
 New Caledonia

MOHO
Moho braccatus (Kauai O-o)
Kauai I (Hawaii)

PHYLIDONYRIS
Phylidonyris pyrrhoptera (Crescent Honeyeater)
P. p. pyrrhoptera
E New South Wales, S Victoria
P. p. indistincta
SE South Australia
P. p. halmaturina
Kangaroo I
P. p. rex
King I, Furneaux Group
P. p. inornata
Tasmania
Phylidonyris novaehollandiae (Yellow-winged Honeyeater)
P. n. longirostris
SW Western Australia
P. n. novaehollandiae
SE Australian coast, S Queensland to South Australia
P. n. campbelli
Kangaroo I
P. n. caudata
King I, Furneaux Group
P. n. canescens
Tasmania
Phylidonyris nigra (White-cheeked Honeyeater)
P. n. nigra
E Queensland, E New South Wales
P. n. gouldii
SW Western Australia
Phylidonyris albifrons (White-fronted Honeyeater)
C Australia
Phylidonyris melanops (Tawny-crowned Honeyeater)
P. m. melanops
New South Wales, Victoria, South Australia, SW Western Australia
P. m. braba
Kangaroo I
P. m. crassirostris
King I (Tasmania)
Phylidonyris undulata (Barred Honeyeater)
New Caledonia
Phylidonyris notabilis (White-bellied Honeyeater)
P. n. notabilis
Banks Is, NW New Hebrides
P. n. superciliaris
N New Hebrides

RAMSAYORNIS
Ramsayornis fasciatus (Bar-breasted Honeyeater)
R. f. fasciatus
N Northern Territory, N Queensland
R. f. apsleyi
Melville I
R. f. broomei
N Western Australia
Ramsayornis modestus (Brown-backed Honeyeater)
New Guinea, N Queensland

PLECTORHYNCHA
Plectorhyncha lanceolata (Striped Honeyeater)
E Queensland, New South Wales, Victoria, SE South Australia

CONOPOPHILA
Conopophila whitei (Grey Honeyeater)
C Western Australia, S Northern Territory
Conopophila albogularis (Rufous-banded Honeyeater)
C. a. mimikae
NW & S New Guinea, Aru Is
C. a. albogularis
N Queensland, N Northern Territory
Conopophila rufogularis (Red-throated Honeyeater)
C. r. rufogularis
N Western Australia, N Northern Territory
C. r. queenslandica
N Queensland
Conopophila picta (Painted Honeyeater)
E Australia

XANTHOMYZA
Xanthomyza phrygia (Regent Honeyeater)
S Queensland, New South Wales, Victoria, SE South Australia

CISSOMELA
Cissomela pectoralis (Banded Honeyeater)
N Australia

ACANTHORHYNCHUS
Acanthorhynchus tenuirostris (Eastern Spinebill)
A. t. cairnsensis
E Queensland
A. t. trochiloides
SE Queensland
A. t. tenuirostris
E New South Wales, E & S Victoria, SE South Australia
A. t. loftyi
S South Australia
A. t. halmaturinus
Kangaroo I

A. t. regius
King I, Furneaux Group
A. t. dubius
Tasmania
Acanthorhynchus superciliosus (Western Spinebill)
SW Western Australia

MANORINA
Manorina melanophrys (Bell Miner)
SE Australia
Manorina melanocephala (Noisy Miner)
M. m. melanocephala
New South Wales, Victoria, Tasmania
M. m. crassirostris
E Queensland
Manorina obscura (Dusky Miner)
M. o. obscura
S Western Australia
M. o. clelandi
SW Western Australia
Manorina flavigula (Yellow-throated Miner)
M. f. casuarina
N Western Australia
M. f. lutea
C Western Australia
M. f. alligator
Northern Territory
M. f. melvillensis
Melville I
M. f. pallida
C Australia
M. f. flavigula
W Queensland, New South Wales, Victoria, E & S South Australia, SE Western Australia
Manorina melanotis (Black-eared Miner)
NW Victoria, E South Australia

ANTHORNIS
Anthornis melanura (New Zealand Bell Bird)
A. m. obscura
Three Kings I
A. m. dumerilii
North I (New Zealand)
A. m. melanura
South I (New Zealand) Stewart I
A. m. incoronata
Auckland Is

ANTHOCHAERA
Anthochaera rufogularis (Spiny-cheeked Honeyeater)
C Australia
Anthochaera chrysoptera (Little Wattle Bird)
A. c. chrysoptera
S Queensland, New South Wales, Victoria, SE South Australia

A. c. halmaturina
Kangaroo I
A. c. tasmanica
Tasmania
A. c. lunulata
SW Western Australia
Anthochaera carunculata (Red Wattle Bird)
A. c. carunculata
S & SE coast of Australia
A. c. woodwardi
SW Western Australia
Anthochaera paradoxa (Yellow Wattle Bird)
Tasmania, King I

PROSTHEMADURA
Prosthemadura novaeseelandiae (Parson Bird) (Tui)
P. n. novaeseelandiae
New Zealand, Auckland Is, Stewart I
P. n. kermadecensis
Kermadec Is
P. n. chathamensis
Chatham I

PROMEROPS
Promerops cafer (Cape Sugarbird)
Cape Province, South Africa
Promerops gurneyi (Gurney's Sugarbird)
P. g. gurneyi
Cape Province, Natal, E Transvaal
P. g. ardens
E Rhodesia

EMBERIZIDAE

154 EMBERIZINAE (BUNTINGS)

MELOPHUS
Melophus lathami (Crested Bunting)
Pakistan to S China, Indochina

LATOUCHEORNIS
Latoucheornis siemsseni (Fokien Blue Bunting)
C China

EMBERIZA
Emberiza calandra (Corn Bunting)
Europe to Sinkiang » S Iran
Emberiza citrinella (Yellow Hammer)
E. c. caliginosa
N & W British Isles
E. c. citrinella
NW Europe, C Russia » N Africa
E. c. erythrogenys
E Europe to Siberia » Mongolia & Iraq
Emberiza leucocephala (Pine Bunting)
E. l. leucocephala
Tibet, Siberia » Iraq, India, China

E. l. fronto
NE China
Emberiza cia (Rock Bunting)
E. c. cia
S Europe, Asia Minor
A. c. africana
N Africa
E. c. prageri
Caucasus, NW Iran
E. c. par
C Asia, Pakistan, N India
E. c. stracheyi
W Himalayas
E. c. decolorata
Sinkiang
E. c. godlewskii
Mongolia, NW China
E. c. khamensis
NE Tibet, W China
E. c. yunnanensis
SE Tibet, SW China
E. c. omissa
NE China
E. c. flemingorum
Nepal
Emberiza cioides (Siberian Meadow Bunting)
E. c. tarbagataica
C Asia » N Mongolia
E. c. cioides
NC Asia
E. c. weigoldi
NE Asia » Shensi, C Korea
E. c. castaneiceps
S Korea, E China
E. c. ciopsis
N Japan » S Japan
Emberiza jankowskii (Jankowski's Bunting)
NE Manchuria
Emberiza buchanani (Grey-necked Bunting)
E. b. cerrutii
E Turkey, SW Russia, Iran
E. b. buchanani
Afghanistan, W Pakistan » SE India
E. b. neobscura
C Asia, W Mongolia
Emberiza stewarti (White-capped Bunting)
S Russia, Afghanistan » Pakistan, NW India
Emberiza cineracea (Cinereous Bunting)
E. c. cineracea
SW Turkey » Eritrea
E. c. semenowi
Yemen, SW Iran » NE Africa

Emberiza hortulana (Ortolan Bunting)
Europe, N Africa, C Asia » Senegal, Sudan, Iran
Emberiza caesia (Cretzschmar's Bunting)
E Europe, NE Africa » Iran, Sudan
Emberiza cirlus (Cirl Bunting)
E. c. cirlus
S British Isles, S Europe, N Africa
E. c. nigrostriata
Corsica, Sardinia
Emberiza striolata (Striped Bunting)
E. s. sahari
NW Africa
E. s. sanghae
S Mali
E. s. saturatior
W Sudan, Ethiopia, NW Kenya
E. s. jebelmarrae
Darfur, Kordofan
E. s. striolata
NE Africa, Iran, Pakistan, N & C India
Emberiza impetuani (Larklike Bunting)
E. s. impetuani
Angola, Namibia, Botswana, W Cape Province
E. s. sloggetti
C Cape Province
Emberiza tahapisi (Cinnamon-breasted Rock Bunting)
E. t. arabica
S Arabia
E. t. insularis
Socotra I
E. t. septemstriata
E Sudan, NW Ethiopia
E. t. tahapisi
Gabon, Zaire, E & S Africa
E. t. goslingi
Sierra Leone to Sudan, N Zaire
Emberiza socotrana (Socotra Mountain Bunting)
Socotra I
Emberiza capensis (Cape Bunting)
E. c. vincenti
C Malawi, E Zambia
E. c. smithersii
E Rhodesia, Mozambique
E. c. plowesi
Rhodesia, NE Botswana
E. c. reidi
S Transvaal, Natal, Orange, Free State, N Lesotho
E. c. limpopoensis
C & SW Transvaal
E. c. basutoensis
Lesotho, W Natal
E. c. vinacea
N Cape Province

E. c. media
S Transvaal, C Cape Province
E. c. capensis
S Namibia, W Cape Province
E. c. nebularum
SW Angola
E. c. bradfieldi
N Namibia
Emberiza yessoensis (Japanese Reed Bunting)
E. y. yessoensis
N Japan » S Japan
E. y. continentalis
E Manchuria » S Korea, E China
Emberiza tristrami (Tristam's Bunting)
Ussuri region » SW China, Burma
Emberiza fucata (Grey-hooded Bunting)
E. f. arcuata
Pakistan, W Himalayas » N Burma, S China
E. f. fucata
E Asia, N Japan, SE China » Indochina
E. f. kuatunensis
S China
Emberiza pusilla (Little Bunting)
N Asia » N India, Burma, S China
Emberiza chrysophrys (Yellow-browed Bunting)
Siberia, NE Asia » SE China
Emberiza rustica (Rustic Bunting)
E. r. rustica
N Europe, N Asia » E China, Japan
E. r. latifascia
NE Siberia » E China & Japan
Emberiza elegans (Yellow-headed Bunting)
E. e. elegans
Manchuria » S Japan, E China
E. e. ticehursti
E Amur » S Manchuria
E. e. elegantula
SW China
Emberiza aureola (Yellow-breasted Bunting)
E. a. aureola
N Asia » India, Malaysia, Indochina
E. a. ornata
NE Asia
Emberiza poliopleura (Somali Golden-breasted Bunting)
EC Africa
Emberiza flaviventris (Golden-breasted Bunting)
E. f. flavigaster
Mali to Ethiopia
E. f. flaviventris
C,E & Southern Africa
E. f. carychroa
Nairobi, Kenya

E. f. princeps
S Angola, N Namibia
Emberiza affinis (Brown-rumped Bunting)
E. a. affinis
S Sudan, SW Ethiopia, N Uganda, NE Zaire
E. a. vulpecula
Cameroun, Central African Republic
E. a. nigeriae
Gambia to W Cameroun
Emberiza cabanisi (Cabanis's Yellow Bunting)
E. c. cabanisi
W & NC Africa
E. c. cognominata
SW Zaire, N Angola
E. c. orientalis
Zambia, Tanzania, Rhodesia, Mozambique
Emberiza rutila (Chestnut Bunting)
NE Asia » SE China, Burma, Indochina
Emberiza koslowi (Koslow's Bunting)
Tibet, Tsinghai
Emberiza melanocephala (Black-headed Bunting)
SE Europe, Iran, Caucasus » N & C India
Emberiza bruniceps (Red-headed Bunting)
C Asia, Altai » S India
Emberiza sulphurata (Japanese Yellow Bunting)
C Japan » S Japan, SE China, N Philippine Is
Emberiza spodocephala (Black-faced Bunting)
E. s. spodocephala
C & E Asia » E China, Taiwan
E. s. personata
Sakhalin I, N Japan » S Japan
E. s. sordida
W China » E India, N Burma
Emberiza variabilis (Japanese Grey Bunting)
Sakhalin I, N Japan
Emberiza pallasi (Pallas' Reed Bunting)
E. p. pallasi
C & E Asia » Sinkiang & Mongolia
E. p. polaris
NE Asia » Manchuria & E China
E. p. lydiae
C Mongolia
Emberiza schoeniclus (Reed Bunting)
E. s. schoeniclus
NW Europe, C Russia » Turkey, N Africa
E. s. passerina
NW Siberia » Mongolia, N Iran
E. s. parvirostris
C Siberia » Mongolia
E. s. pyrrhulina
NE Asia » Japan

E. s. minor
SE Siberia, Manchuria
E. s. pallidior
SW Siberia » NW India, Mongolia
E. s. ukrainae
S Russia » N Caucasus
E. s. incognita
C Russia » Sinkiang
E. s. pyrrhuloides
W & C Asia, W Mongolia, Sinkiang
E. s. zaidamensis
N Tsinghai
E. s. witherbyi
W Spain, Sardinia, Balearic Is
E. s. canetti
SE Europe, N Turkey
E. s. reiseri
S Yugoslavia, N Greece
E. s. caspia
E Caucasus, W & S Iran
E. s. korejewi
E Iran

CALCARIUS
Calcarius mccownii (McCown's Longspur)
SC Canada, WC USA » S USA, N Mexico
Calcarius lapponicus (Lapland Bunting)
C. l. lapponicus
N Canada, S Greenland » N Europe,
E USA, N Asia
C. l. coloratus
E Siberia » N China
C. l. alascensis
Alaska, W Canada » W USA
Calcarius pictus (Smith's Longspur)
N Canada » SC USA
Calcarius ornatus (Chestnut-coloured Longspur)
S Canada » S USA, N Mexico

PLECTROPHENAX
Plectrophenax nivalis (Snow Bunting)
P. n. nivalis
N North America, N Europe » S USA,
S Europe
P. n. insulae
Iceland » N Scotland
P. n. vlasowae
NE Asia » C Asia, Manchuria
P. n. townsendi
W Aleutian Is, Commander Is
Plectrophenax hyperboreus (McKay's Bunting)
Bering Sea Is » W Alaska

CALAMOSPIZA
Calamospiza melanocorys (Lark Bunting)
S Canada » C & S USA, N Mexico

PASSERELLA
Passerella iliaca (Fox Sparrow)
P. i. iliaca
E Canada » E USA
P. i. zaboria
W Canada » C & S USA
P. i. altivagans
SW Canada » California
P. i. unalaschensis
Aleutian Is » S California
P. i. ridgwayi
Alaska » S California
P. i. sinuosa
Alaska » S Califorina
P. i. annectens
Alaska » S California
P. i. townsendi
SE Alaska » C California
P. i. fuliginosa
W Canada » S California
P. i. olivacea
SW Canada » NW Mexico
P. i. schistacea
NW USA » SW USA
P. i. swarthi
NW Utah, SE Idaho
P. i. fulva
C Oregon, California » NW Mexico
P. i. megarhyncha
SW Oregon » NW Mexico
P. i. brevicauda
N California » S California
P. i. monoensis
C California » S California
P. i. canescens
E California, Nevada » S California
P. i. stephensi
S California

MELOSPIZA
Melospiza melodia (Song Sparrow)
M. m. melodia
S Canada » SE USA
M. m. atlantica
NE USA » E USA
M. m. euphonia
NC USA » S USA
M. m. juddi
WC Canada » WC USA
M. m. montana
WC USA » SW USA, N Mexico
M. m. fallax
SE Nevada, SW Utah, Arizona,
New Mexico
M. m. saltonis
S Nevada, SE California
M. m. inexpectata
SE Alaska » S Oregon

M. m. rufina
SE Alaska » W Washington
M. m. merrilli
SW Canada » S California
M. m. morphna
SW Canada » N California
M. m. fisherella
Oregon » S California, W Nevada
M. m. maxima
Aleutian Is
M. m. sanaka
Seguam I, Sanak I, Unimak I
M. m. amaka
Amak I
M. m. insignis
Kodiak I
M. m. kenaiensis
S Alaska
M. m. caurina
SE Alaska » N California
M. m. cleonensis
NW California
M. m. gouldii
WC California
M. m. mailliardi
C California
M. m. samuelis
NW California
M. m. maxillaris
NW California
M. m. pusillula
NW California
M. m. heermani
C California
M. m. cooperi
SW California, N Baja California
M. m. micronyx
San Miguel I
M. m. clementae
Santa Roza I, Santa Cruz I
M. m. graminea
Santa Barbara I
M. m. coronatorum
Coronados I
M. m. rivularis
SC Baja California
M. m. goldmani
WC Mexico
M. m. niceae
EC Mexico
M. m. mexicana
SC Mexico
M. m. azteca
SC Mexico
M. m. villai
W Mexico
M. m. yuriria
C Mexico

M. m. adusta
SW Mexico
M. m. zacapu
W Mexico
Melospiza lincolnii (Lincoln's Sparrow)
M. l. lincolnii
Canada » SW USA, S Mexico, Guatemala
M. l. gracilis
S Alaska, W Canada » California
M. l. alticola
NW USA » Mexico, Guatemala
Melospiza georgiana (Swamp Sparrow)
M. g. ericrypta
W & C Canada » SW USA, NW Mexico
M. g. georgiana
NE USA » SE USA

ZONOTRICHIA
Zonotrichia capensis (Rufous-collared Sparrow)
Z. c. septentrionalis
S Mexico, Guatemala, El Salvador, Honduras
Z. c. antillarum
Dominica I
Z. c. costraricensis
Costa Rica, Panama, Venezuela, Colombia
Z. c. orestera
W Panama
Z. c. insularis
Curaçao I, Aruba I
Z. c. venezuelae
N Venezuela
Z. c. inaccessibilis
C Venezuela
Z. c. roraimae
S Colombia, E Venezuela, Guyana, N Brazil
Z. c. macconelli
Venezuela
Z. c. capensis
French Guiana
Z. c. tocantinsi
E Brazil
Z. c. matutina
NE Brazil, E Bolivia
Z. c. subtorquata
E & C Brazil, Paraguay, Uruguay
Z. c. mellea
C Paraguay, N Argentina
Z. c. hypoleuca
E & S Bolivia, NE Argentina
Z. c. choraules
W Argentina
Z. c. australis
S Chile, S Argentina » N Bolivia
Z. c. chilensis
Chile, S Argentina

Z. c. sanborni
Chile, W Argentina

Z. c. antofagastae
Chile

Z. c. pulacayensis
Peru, W Bolivia, N Argentina

Z. c. peruviensis
W Peru

Z. c. carabayae
Peru, Bolivia

Z. c. huancabambae
N Peru

Z. c. illescasensis
N Peru

Zonotrichia querula (Harris' Sparrow)
W Canada » W USA

Zonotrichia leucophrys (White-crowned Sparrow)

Z. l. leucophrys
C & E Canada » SE USA, Cuba

Z. l. gambelii
NW & W Canada » W USA, N Mexico

Z. l. oriantha
SW Canada » WC USA, N Mexico

Z. l. pugetensis
SW Canada » SW California

Z. l. nuttalli
WC California

Zonotrichia albicollis (White-throated Sparrow)
Canada, N & E USA » S USA, E Mexico

Zonotrichia atricapilla (Golden-crowned Sparrow)
Alaska, W Canada » W USA, NW Mexico

JUNCO

Junco vulcani (Volcano Junco)
Costa Rica, W Panama

Junco hyemalis (Slate-coloured Junco)

J. h. hyemalis
N Canada, NC USA » S USA, N Mexico

J. h. carolinensis
EC USA

J. h. aikeni
WC USA » S USA

J. h. oreganus
S Alaska, W Canada » C California

J. h. cismontanus
W Canada » W USA

J. h. shufeldti
NW USA » S California

J. h. montanus
W Canada, W USA » NW Mexico

J. h. mearnsi
SW Canada » WC USA, NW Mexico

J. h. thurberi
S Oregon » California, N Baja California

J. h. pinosus
C & S California

J. h. pontilus
N Baja California

J. h. townsendi
N Baja California

J. h. insularis
Guadeloupe I

Junco caniceps (Grey-headed Junco)

J. c. caniceps
C & SC USA » S USA & N Mexico

J. c. dorsalis
New Mexico, N Arizona

J. c. mutabilis
S Nevada, SE California

Junco phaeonotus (Mexican Junco)

J. p. palliatus
SW USA, N Mexico

J. p. phaeonotus
C & S Mexico

J. p. bairdi
S Baja California

J. p. fulvescens
S Mexico

J. p. alticola
S Mexico, W Guatemala

PASSERCULUS

Passerculus sandwichensis (Savannah Sparrow)

P. s. labradorius
E Canada » SE USA

P. s. savanna
SE Canada » SE USA, SE Mexico

P. s. princeps
Sable I » SE USA

P. s. mediogriseus
SE Canada, NE USA » SE USA

P. s. oblitus
C Canada, C USA, NE Mexico

P. s. nevadensis
SW Canada, WC USA » SC USA, N Mexico

P. s. brooksi
SW Canada » California, Baja California

P. s. athinus
Alaska, W Canada, W USA » SW USA, W Mexico

P. s. sandwichensis
Alaska » W USA

P. s. crassus
Aleutian Is, W Alaska » C California

P. s. alaudinus
N & C California

P. s. beldingi
S California, N Baja California

P. s. anulus
WC Baja California

P. s. sanctorum
San Benito I, Baja California

P. s. guttatus
  W & S Baja California
P. s. magdalenae
  S Baja California
P. s. rostratus
  S California, Baja California, W Mexico
P. s. rufofuscus
  Arizona, New Mexico, N Mexico
P. s. atratus
  NW Mexico
P. s. brunnescens
  NC Mexico
P. s. wetmorei
  SW Guatemala

AMMODRAMUS
**Ammodramus maritimus (Seaside
Sparrow)**
A. m. maritimus
  NE USA » SE USA
A. m. macgillivrayi
  SE USA
A. m. pelonota
  SE USA
A. m. mirabilis
  SE USA
A. m. peninsulae
  SE USA
A. m. junicola
  SE USA
A. m. fisheri
  SW & S USA
A. m. sennetti
  S USA
**Ammodramus caudacutus (Sharp-tailed
Sparrow)**
A. c. nelsoni
  WC Canada » SE USA
A. c. alterus
  E Canada » SE USA
A. c. subvirgatus
  E Canada » SE USA
A. c. caudacutus
  NE USA » SE USA
A. c. diversus
  NE USA » SE USA
**Ammodramus leconteii (Le Conte's
Sparrow)**
  WC Canada » C & SE USA
Ammodramus bairdii (Baird's Sparrow)
  WC Canada, W USA » N Mexico
**Ammodramus henslowii (Henslow's
Sparrow)**
A. h. susurrans
  NE » SE USA
A. h. henslowii
  C USA » SE USA

Ammodramus savannarum (Grasshopper 541
Sparrow)
A. s. pratensis
  S Canada, E USA » SE Mexico, West Indies
A. s. floridanus
  Florida
A. s. perpallidus
  SW Canada, C & SW USA » Mexico,
  Guatemala
A. s. ammolegus
  S Arizona, NW Mexico » Guatemala
A. s. bimaculatus
  S Mexico, Honduras, Nicaragua,
  NW Costa Rica, W Panama
A. s. cracens
  Guatemala, E Honduras, NE Nicaragua
A. s. caucae
  Colombia
A. s. savannarum
  Jamaica
A. s. intricatus
  Hispaniola
A. s. borinquensis
  Puerto Rico
A. s. caribaeus
  Bonaire I, Curaçao I

XENOSPIZA
Xenospiza baileyi (Sierra Madre Sparrow)
  N & C Mexico

MYOSPIZA
Myospiza humeralis (Grassland Sparrow)
M. h. humeralis
  Colombia, Venezuela, Guyana, French
  Guiana, Brazil
M. h. pallidulus
  Colombia, Venezuela
M. h. xanthornus
  Bolivia, Brazil, Paraguay, Uruguay,
  Argentina
M. h. tarijensis
  E Bolivia
**Myospiza aurifrons (Yellow-browed
Sparrow)**
M. a. apurensis
  NE Colombia, W Venezuela
M. a. cherriei
  E Colombia
M. a. tenebrosus
  Venezuela, Colombia
M. a. aurifrons
  SE Colombia, E Ecuador, Peru, Bolivia,
  Brazil

SPIZELLA
Spizella arborea (Tree Sparrow)
S. a. arborea
  N Canada, N USA » C USA

S. a. ochracae
NW & W Canada » W USA

Spizella passerina (Chipping Sparrow)
S. p. passerina
SE Canada, C USA » S USA
S. p. arizonae
W Canada » SW USA, W Mexico
S. p. atremaeus
NC Mexico
S. p. mexicana
C & S Mexico, Guatemala
S. p. repetens
Guerrero, Oaxaca
S. p. comparanda
Nayarit to Vera Cruz
S. p. pinetorum
S Guatemala to NE Nicaragua

Spizella pusilla (Field Sparrow)
S. p. pusilla
SE Canada » C & SE USA
S. p. arenacea
C USA » SE USA, NE Mexico
S. p. wortheni
NE & E Mexico

Spizella atrogularis (Black-chinned Sparrow)
S. a. evura
SW USA » NW Mexico
S. a. caurina
C California
S. a. cana
SW California » S Baja California
S. a. atrogularis
NC Mexico

Spizella pallida (Clay-coloured Sparrow)
SC Canada, C & SC USA » W Mexico

Spizella breweri (Brewer's Sparrow)
S. b. taverneri
SW Canada » SW USA
S. b. breweri
SW Canada, W & SW USA » NW Mexico

POOECETES
Pooecetes gramineus (Vesper Sparrow)
P. g. gramineus
SE Canada, E USA » S Mexico
P. g. confinis
SW Canada, WC USA » SW USA,
W Mexico
P. g. affinis
W USA » NW Baja California

CHONDESTES
Chondestes grammacus (Lark Sparrow)
C. g. grammacus
N & C USA » SE USA, E & S Mexico
C. g. strigatus
SW Canada, W USA » Mexico, Guatemala

AMPHISPIZA
Amphispiza bilineata (Black-throated Sparrow)
A. b. bilineata
NC Texas, NE Mexico
A. b. opuntia
SC USA, N Mexico
A. b. deserticola
WC USA » NW Mexico, Baja California
A. b. bangsi
S Baja California
A. b. tortugae
Tortuga I
A. b. belvederei
Cerralvo I
A. b. pacifica
NW Mexico
A. b. cana
San Esteban I
A. b. grisea
C Mexico

Amphispiza belli (Sage Sparrow)
A. b. nevadensis
W USA » SW USA, N Baja California,
NW Mexico
A. b. canescens
SW California, W Nevada, NE Baja
California
A. b. belli
S California, NW Baja California
A. b. clementeae
San Clemente I
A. b. cinerea
C Baja California

AIMOPHILA
Aimophila mystacalis (Bridled Sparrow)
SC Mexico
Aimophila humeralis (Black-chested Sparrow)
WC Mexico
Aimophila ruficauda (Stripe-headed Sparrow)
A. r. acuminata
WC Mexico
A. r. lawrencii
S Mexico
A. r. connectens
E Guatemala
A. r. ruficauda
SE Guatemala, El Salvador, Honduras,
Nicaragua
Aimophila sumichrasti (Cinnamon-tailed Sparrow)
S Mexico
Aimophila strigiceps (Stripe-capped Sparrow)
A. s. strigiceps
E Argentina

A. s. dabbenei
NW Argentina

Aimophila aestivalis (Bachman's Sparrow)
A. a. bachmani
SC USA » SE USA
A. a. illinoensis
NC USA » S USA
A. a. aestivalis
S California, Georgia, Florida

Aimophila botterii (Botteri's Sparrow)
A. b. arizonae
SE Arizona, NW Mexico
A. b. texana
S Texas, NE Mexico
A. b. mexicana
NC Mexico
A. b. goldmani
W Mexico
A. b. botterii
SC & S Mexico
A. b. petenica
SE Mexico, Guatemala, Honduras
A. b. tabascensis
E coast of Mexico
A. b. spadiconigrescens
N Honduras, NE Nicaragua
A. b. vantynei
C Guatemala
A. b. vulcanica
Nicaragua, N Costa Rica

Aimophila cassinii (Cassin's Sparrow)
SC USA » C Mexico

Aimophila quinquestriata (Five-striped Sparrow)
A. q. septentrionalis
NW Mexico
A. q. quinquestriata
W Mexico

Aimophila carpalis (Rufous-winged Sparrow)
A. c. carpalis
SC Arizona, NW Mexico
A. c. distinguenda
NW Mexico
A. c. cohaerens
NW Mexico

Aimophila ruficeps (Rufous-crowned Sparrow)
A. r. eremoeca
SC USA » E Mexico
A. r. scottii
Arizona, New Mexico
A. r. ruficeps
C California
A. r. canescens
SW California, NE Baja California
A. r. pallidissima
S Nuevo Leon

A. r. extima
S Oaxaca
A. r. obscura
Santa Catalina I
A. r. sanctorum
Todos Santos I
A. r. soraria
S Baja California
A. r. rupicola
SW Arizona
A. r. simulans
NW Mexico
A. r. fusca
W Mexico
A. r. boucardi
E Mexico
A. r. australis
S Mexico

Aimophila notosticta (Oaxaca Sparrow)
S Mexico

Aimophila rufescens (Rusty Sparrow)
A. r. antonensis
NW Mexico
A. r. mcleodii
NW Mexico
A. r. disjuncta
Guerrero
A. r. rufescens
W & SW Mexico
A. r. pyrgitoides
Guatemala, Honduras, El Salvador,
E & SE Mexico
A. r. discolor
N Honduras, NE Nicaragua
A. r. pectoralis
SE Mexico, Guatemala, El Salvador
A. r. hypaethrus
NW Costa Rica
A. r. brodkorbi
SW Chiapas
A. r. newmani
NE Puebla

RHYNCHOSPIZA
Rhynchospiza stolzmanni (Tumbes Sparrow)
SW Ecuador, N Peru

TORREORNIS
Torreornis inexpectata (Zapata Sparrow)
T. i. inexpectata
SW Cuba
T. i. sigmani
S Cuba

ORITURUS
Orriturus superciliosus (Striped Sparrow)
O. s. palliatus
NW & W Mexico

O. s. superciliosus
C & SW Mexico

PHRYGILUS
Phrygilus atriceps (Black-hooded Sierra Finch)
   P. a. chloronotus
   Peru
   P. a. punensis
   Peru, Bolivia
   P. a. atriceps
   Peru, Bolivia, Chile, Argentina
Phrygilus gayi (Grey-hooded Sierra Finch)
   P. g. gayi
   N Chile
   P. g. minor
   C Chile
   P. g. caniceps
   S Chile, Argentina
Phrygilus patagonicus (Patagonian Sierra Finch)
   Chile, Argentina
Phrygilus fruticeti (Mourning Sierra Finch)
   P. f. peruvianus
   Peru, Bolivia
   P. f. fruticeti
   SW Bolivia, Chile, Argentina
Phrygilus unicolor (Plumbeous Sierra Finch)
   P. u. nivarius
   N Colombia, NW Venezuela
   P. u. geospizopsis
   S Colombia, Ecuador
   P. u. inca
   Peru, Bolivia
   P. u. unicolor
   SW Peru, Chile, W Argentina
   P. u. tucumanus
   Bolivia, NW Argentina
   P. u. ultimus
   Argentina
Phrygilus dorsalis (Red-backed Sierra Finch)
   Bolivia, Chile, Argentina
Phrygilus erythronotus (White-throated Sierra Finch)
   Peru, Bolivia, Chile
Phrygilus plebejus (Ash-breasted Sierra Finch)
   P. p. ocularis
   Ecuador, N Peru
   P. p. plebejus
   Peru, Chile, Bolivia, Argentina
Phrygilus carbonarius (Carbonated Sierra Finch)
   C Argentina

Phrygilus alaudinus (Band-tailed Sierra Finch)
   P. a. bipartitus
   W Ecuador, Peru
   P. a. humboldti
   S Ecuador, N Peru
   P. a. excelsus
   S Peru, Bolivia
   P. a. alaudinus
   C Chile
   P. a. venturii
   Argentina

MELANODERA
Melanodera melanodera (Black-throated Finch)
   M. m. princetoniana
   Chile, Argentina
   M. m. melanodera
   Falkland Islands
Melanodera xanthogramma (Yellow-bridled Finch)
   M. x. barrosi
   Chile, W Argentina
   M. x. xanthogramma
   S Argentina

HAPLOSPIZA
Haplospiza rustica (Slaty Finch)
   H. r. uniformis
   S Mexico
   H. r. barrilesensis
   Honduras, Costa Rica, W Panama
   H. r. arcana
   Venezuela
   H. r. rustica
   N Venezuela, Colombia, Ecuador,
   Peru, Bolivia
Haplospiza unicolor (Uniform Finch)
   SE Brazil, E Paraguay, NE Argentina

ACANTHIDOPS
Acanthidops bairdii (Peg-billed Sparrow)
   Costa Rica

LOPHOSPINGUS
Lophospingus pusillus (Black-crested Finch)
   S Bolivia, Paraguay, Argentina
Lophospingus griseocristatus (Grey-crested Finch)
   Bolivia, N Argentina

DONACOSPIZA
Donacospiza albifrons (Long-tailed Reed Finch)
   Brazil, Paraguay, Uruguay, Argentina

ROWETTIA
Rowettia goughensis (Gough I Finch)
   Gough I

NESOSPIZA
Nesospiza acunhae (Nightingale Finch)
  N. a. acunhae
    Inaccessible I
  N. a. questi
    Nightingale I, Tristan de Cunha I
Nesospiza wilkinsi (Wilkins's Finch)
  N. w. wilkinsi
    Nightingale I, Tristan de Cunha I
  N. w. dunnei
    Inaccessible I

DIUCA
Diuca speculifera (White-winged Diuca Finch)
  D. s. magnirostris
    Peru
  D. s. speculifera
    SE Peru, N Chile, N Bolivia
Diuca diuca (Common Diuca Finch)
  D. d. crassirostris
    N Chile, Argentina
  D. d. diuca
    NC Chile, Argentina
  D. d. chiloensis
    SC Chile
  D. d. minor
    Argentina

IDIOPSAR
Idiopsar brachyurus (Short-tailed Finch)
  Peru, Bolivia, Argentina

PIEZORHINA
Piezorhina cinerea (Cinereous Finch)
  NW Peru

XENOSPINGUS
Xenospingus concolor (Slender-billed Finch)
  S Peru, N Chile

INCASPIZA
Incaspiza pulchra (Great Inca Finch)
  Peru
Incaspiza personata (Rufous-backed Inca Finch)
  Peru
Incaspiza ortizi (Grey-winged Inca Finch)
  Peru
Incaspiza laeta (Buff-bridled Inca Finch)
  Peru
Incaspiza watkinsi (Little Inca Finch)
  Peru

POOSPIZA
Poospiza thoracica (Bay-chested Warbling Finch)
  SE Brazil
Poospiza boliviana (Bolivian Warbling Finch)
  C Bolivia

Poospiza alticola (Plain-tailed Warbling Finch)
  N Peru
Poospiza hypochondria (Rufous-sided Warbling Finch)
  P. h. hypochondria
    Bolivia
  P. h. affinis
    Argentina
Poospiza erythrophrys (Rusty-browed Warbling Finch)
  P. e. cochabambae
    Bolivia
  P. e. erythrophrys
    Bolivia, NW Argentina
Poospiza ornata (Cinnamon Warbling Finch)
  NW Argentina
Poospiza nigrorufa (Black & Rufous Warbling Finch)
  P. n. nigrorufa
    S Brazil, Uruguay, Paraguay
  P. n. whitii
    Bolivia, NW Argentina
  P. n. wagneri
    Bolivia
Poospiza lateralis (Red-rumped Warbling Finch)
  P. l. lateralis
    SE Brazil
  P. l. cabanisi
    SE Brazil, Uruguay, Paraguay, NE Argentina
Poospiza rubecula (Rufous-breasted Warbling Finch)
  N Peru
Poospiza caesar (Chestnut-breasted Mountain Finch)
  SE Peru
Poospiza hispaniolensis (Collared Warbling Finch)
  SW Ecuador, Peru
Poospiza torquata (Ringed Warbling Finch)
  P. t. torquata
    Bolivia
  P. t. pectoralis
    SE Bolivia, W Paraguay, N & C Argentina
Poospiza melanoleuca (Black-capped Warbling Finch)
  Bolivia, Paraguay, Uruguay, SW Brazil, N Argentina
Poospiza cinerea (Cinereous Warbling Finch)
  C Brazil

SICALIS
Sicalis citrina (Stripe-tailed Yellow Finch)
  S. c. browni
    Colombia, Venezuela, Guyana, NE Brazil

S. c. citrina
E Brazil
S. c. occidentalis
Peru
Sicalis lutea (Puna Yellow Finch)
Peru, Bolivia, Argentina
Sicalis uropygialis (Bright-rumped Yellow Finch)
S. u. sharpei
N Peru
S. u. connectens
Peru
S. u. uropygialis
S Peru, Bolivia, N Chile, NW Argentina
Sicalis luteocephala (Citron-headed Yellow Finch)
C Bolivia
Sicalis auriventris (Greater Yellow Finch)
Chile, Argentina
Sicalis olivascens (Greenish Yellow Finch)
S. o. salvini
N Peru
S. o. chloris
C Peru, N Chile
S. o. olivascens
SE Peru, W Bolivia, NW Argentina
S. o. mendozae
W Argentina
Sicalis lebruni (Patagonian Yellow Finch)
S Argentina, S Chile
Sicalis colombiana (Orange-fronted Yellow Finch)
S. c. colombiana
Venezuela, E Colombia
S. c. leopoldinae
E Brazil
S. c. goeldii
E Peru, E Brazil
Sicalis flaveola (Saffron Finch)
S. f. flaveola
Colombia, Venezuela, the Guianas, Trinidad
S. f. valida
Ecuador, NW Peru
S. f. brasiliensis
NE Brazil
S. f. pelzelni
SE Brazil, E Bolivia, Paraguay, Uruguay, N Argentina
Sicalis luteola (Grassland Yellow Finch)
S. l. chrysops
S Mexico, Guatemala, E Honduras, Nicaragua
S. l. mexicana
S Mexico
S. l. eisenmanni
Panama

S. l. bogotensis
Colombia, Ecuador, Peru, Venezuela
S. l. luteola
Colombia, Venezuela, Guyana, Brazil
S. l. flavissima
N Brazilian islands
S. l. chapmani
NE Brazil
S. l. luteiventris
C & SC South America
Sicalis raimondii (Raimondi's Yellow Finch)
Peru
Sicalis taczanowskii (Sulphur-breasted Finch)
SW Ecuador, N Peru

COMPOSPIZA
Compospiza garleppi (Cochabamba Mountain Finch)
Bolivia
Compospiza baeri (Tucuman Mountain Finch)
NW Argentina

EMBERIZOIDES
Emberizoides herbicola (Wedge-tailed Grass Finch)
E. h. lucaris
SW Costa Rica
E. h. hypochondriacus
W & C Panama
E. h. floresae
Panama
E. h. apurensis
E Colombia, W Venezuela
E. h. sphenurus
N Colombia to the Guianas, N Brazil
E. h. herbicola
E & S Brazil, E Bolivia, NE Argentina
Emberizoides ypirangus (Lesser Grass Finch)
S Venezuela
Emberizoides duidae (Mt Duida Grass Finch)
SE Venezuela

EMBERNAGRA
Embernagra platensis (Great Pampa Finch)
E. p. platensis
SE Brazil, Paraguay, Uruguay, E Argentina
E. p. olivascens
SE Bolivia, W Paraguay, NW Argentina
Embernagra longicauda (Buff-throated Pampa Finch)
Brazil

VOLATINIA
Volatinia jacarina (Blue-black Grassquit)
V. j. splendens
Central America, N South America, Trinidad

V. j. jacarina
  E & C Brazil, SE Peru, E Bolivia,
  N Argentina
V. j. peruviensis
  Ecuador, Peru, N Chile

SPOROPHILA

**Sporophila frontalis (Buffy-throated
Seedeater)**
  SE Brazil, Paraguay, N Argentina
**Sporophila falcirostris (Temminck's
Seedeater)**
  SE Brazil
**Sporophila schistacea (Slate-coloured
Seedeater)**
  S. s. subconcolor
    S Mexico
  S. s. schistacea
    Costa Rica, Panama, N Colombia
  S. s. incerta
    W Colombia, Ecuador
  S. s. longipennis
    Venezuela, E Colombia, N Brazil
Sporophila intermedia (Grey Seedeater)
  S. i. intermedia
    Colombia, N Venezuela, Guyana, Trinidad
  S. i. bogotensis
    W Colombia
  S. i. agustini
    N Colombia
  S. i. anchicayae
    Colombia
**Sporophila plumbea (Plumbeous
Seedeater)**
  S. p. colombiana
    N Colombia
  S. p. whiteleyana
    E Colombia, S Venezuela, the Guianas,
    N Brazil
  S. p. plumbea
    C & S Brazil, Paraguay, NW Bolivia,
    N Argentina
Sporophila aurita (Variable Seedeater)
  S. a. corvina
    Central America from E Mexico to Panama
  S. a. aurita
    Costa Rica, Panama
  S. a. chocoana
    Panama, W Colombia
**Sporophila americana (Wing-barred
Seedeater)**
  S. a. ophthalmica
    SW Colombia, Ecuador, Peru
  S. a. murallae
    SE Colombia
  S. a. americana
    NE Venezuela, the Guianas, Brazil,
    Tobago I

S. a. dispar
  Brazil
**Sporophila torqueola (White-collared
Seedeater)**
  S. t. sharpei
    S Texas, NE Mexico
  S. t. torqueola
    C & SW Mexico
  S. t. morelleti
    Atlantic slopes of Central America,
    S Mexico to Panama
  S. t. mutanda
    Pacific slopes from SW Mexico to
    El Salvador
**Sporophila collaris (Rusty-collared
Seedeater)**
  S. c. ochrascens
    N Bolivia, W Brazil
  S. c. collaris
    E Brazil
  S. c. melanocephala
    Brazil, Paraguay, N Argentina
Sporophila lineola (Lined Seedeater)
  S. l. bouvronides
    Trinidad, Tobago I
  S. l. restricta
    Colombia
  S. l. lineola
    NW and C South America to Argentina
**Sporophila luctuosa (Black & White
Seedeater)**
  NW South America
**Sporophila nigricollis (Yellow-bellied
Seedeater)**
  S. n. nigricollis
    Costa Rica, Panama & N South America
    to Bolivia
  S. n. vivida
    SW Colombia, W Ecuador
  S. n. inconspicua
    W Peru
Sporophila ardesiaca (Dubois' Seedeater)
  Brazil
Sporophila melanops (Hooded Seedeater)
  Brazil
**Sporophila obscura (Dull-coloured
Seedeater)**
  S. o. haplochroma
    N Colombia, NW Venezuela
  S. o. pauper
    S Colombia, Ecuador, NW Peru
  S. o. obscura
    C Peru, Bolivia, Argentina
  S. o. pacifica
    W Peru

Sporophila caerulescens (Double-collared Seedeater)
　S. c. caerulescens
　　Brazil, Bolivia, Paraguay, Uruguay,
　　Argentina
　S. c. hellmayri
　　Brazil
　S. c. yungae
　　N Bolivia
Sporophila albogularis (White-throated Seedeater)
　NE Brazil
Sporophila leucoptera (White-bellied Seedeater)
　S. l. mexianae
　　Mexiana I, Brazil
　S. l. cinereola
　　E Brazil
　S. l. leucoptera
　　C & SW Brazil, Paraguay, N Argentina
　S. l. bicolor
　　E Bolivia
Sporophila peruviana (Parrot-billed Seedeater)
　S. p. devronis
　　C Ecuador, N Peru
　S. p. peruviana
　　Peru
Sporophila simplex (Drab Seedeater)
　Peru
Sporophila nigrorufa (Black & Tawny Seedeater)
　Brazil, E Bolivia
Sporophila bouvreuil (Capped Seedeater)
　S. b. bouvreuil
　　E Brazil
　S. b. crypta
　　Rio de Janeiro, Brazil
　S. b. pileata
　　S Brazil, Paraguay, N Argentina
　S. b. saturata
　　Brazil
Sporophila insulata (Tumaco Seedeater)
　SW Colombia
Sporophila minuta (Ruddy-breasted Seedeater)
　S. m. parva
　　Central America from SW Mexico
　　to Nicaragua
　S. m. centralis
　　SW Costa Rica, W Panama
　S. m. minuta
　　Trinidad and N South America
　　to S Brazil
　S. m. hypoxantha
　　Paraguay, E & C Brazil, Uruguay

Sporophila hypochroma (Rufous-naped Seedeater)
　E Bolivia
Sporophila ruficollis (Dark-throated Seedeater)
　S Brazil, Bolivia, Uruguay, Argentina
Sporophila palustris (Marsh Seedeater)
　SE Brazil, Paraguay, Uruguay, N Argentina
Sporophila castaneiventris (Chestnut-bellied Seedeater)
　N South America
Sporophila cinnamomea (Chestnut Seedeater)
　Brazil, E Paraguay
Sporophila melanogaster (Black-bellied Seedeater)
　SE Brazil
Sporophila telasco (Chestnut-throated Seedeater)
　W Ecuador, Peru, N Chile

ORYZOBORUS
Oryzoborus crassirostris (Large-billed Seed Finch)
　O. c. nuttingi
　　Nicaragua, N Costa Rica, Panama
　O. c. crassirostris
　　Colombia, Venezuela, the Guianas,
　　N Brazil
　O. c. magnirostris
　　Trinidad, E Venezuela
　O. c. maximiliani
　　Brazil
　O. c. occidentalis
　　Colombia, NW Ecuador
　O. c. atrirostris
　　N Peru
　O. c. gigantirostris
　　N Bolivia
Oryzoborus angolensis (Lesser Seed Finch)
　O. a. funereus
　　S Mexico, Central America, Colombia,
　　Ecuador
　O. a. torridus
　　Trinidad, Peru, Ecuador, S Colombia,
　　Venezuela, the Guianas, Brazil
　O. a. angolensis
　　S Brazil, Bolivia, Paraguay, N Argentina

AMAUROSPIZA
Amaurospiza concolor (Blue Seedeater)
　A. c. relicta
　　S Mexico
　A. c. concolor
　　Honduras, Nicaragua, Costa Rica, Panama
　A. c. aequatorialis
　　SW Colombia, Ecuador

Amaurospiza moesta (Blackish-blue Seedeater)
  E Brazil, N Argentina

MELOPYRRHA
Melopyrrha nigra (Cuban Bullfinch)
  M. n. nigra
    Cuba, Isle of Pines
  M. n. taylori
    Grand Cayman I

DOLOSPINGUS
Dolospingus fringilloides (White-naped Seedeater)
  Venezuela, Brazil

CATAMENIA
Catamenia analis (Band-tailed Seedeater)
  C. a. alpica
    N Colombia
  C. a. schistaceifrons
    C Colombia
  C. a. soederstromi
    N Ecuador
  C. a. insignis
    Peru
  C. a. analoides
    W Peru
  C. a. griseiventris
    SE Peru
  C. a. analis
    N Chile, Bolivia, NW Argentina
Catamenia inornata (Plain-coloured Seedeater)
  C. i. mucuchiesi
    Venezuela
  C. i. minor
    W Venezuela, Colombia, Ecuador, Peru
  C. i. inornata
    SE Peru, Bolivia, NW Argentina
Catamenia homochroa (Paramo Seedeater)
  C. h. homochroa
    W Venezuela, Colombia, Ecuador, Peru, Bolivia
  C. h. duncani
    Venezuela, NE Brazil
Catamenia oreophila (Colombian Seedeater)
  N Colombia

TIARIS
Tiaris canora (Cuban Grassquit)
  Cuba
Tiaris olivacea (Yellow-faced Grassquit)
  T. o. pusilla
    E Mexico, Central America, Colombia, Venezuela
  T. o. intermedia
    Cozumel I, Holbox I, E Mexico
  T. o. ravida
    Panama

  T. o. olivacea
    Cuba, Jamaica, Cayman Is
  T. o. bryanti
    Puerto Rico
Tiaris bicolor (Black-faced Grassquit)
  T. b. bicolor
    Bahama Is, Cuba
  T. b. marchii
    Jamaica, Hispaniola
  T. b. omissa
    Puerto Rico, Tobago I, Colombia, Venezuela
  T. b. huilae
    Colombia
  T. b. grandior
    Old Providence I, St Andrew I
  T. b. johnstonei
    La Blanquilla I
  T. b. sharpei
    Aruba I, Curaçao I
  T. b. tortugensis
    La Tortuga I
Tiaris fuliginosa (Sooty Grassquit)
  T. f. fumosa
    Trinidad, Venezuela
  T. f. zuliae
    Venezuela
  T. f. fuliginosa
    NE & C Brazil

LOXIPASSER
Loxipasser anoxanthus (Yellow-shouldered Grassquit)
  Jamaica

LOXIGILLA
Loxigilla portoricensis (Puerto Rican Bullfinch)
  Puerto Rico
Loxigilla violacea (Greater Antillean Bullfinch)
  L. v. violacea
    Bahama Is
  L. v. maurella
    Tortue I, Gonave I, Saona I
  L. v. affinis
    Hispaniola
  L. v. parishi
    Ile-à-vache, Beata I
  L. v. ruficollis
    Jamaica
Loxigilla noctis (Lesser Antillean Bullfinch)
  L. n. coryi
    St Kitts I, Monserrat I
  L. n. ridgwayi
    Anguilla I, Antigua I, Barbuda I
  L. n. desiradensis
    Desirade I

L. n. dominicana
  Guadeloupe I, Dominica I
L. n. noctis
  Martinique I
L. n. sclateri
  St Lucia I
L. n. crissalis
  St Vincent I
L. n. grenadensis
  Grenada I
L. n. barbadensis
  Barbados I

MELANOSPIZA
Melanospiza richardsoni (St Lucia Black Finch)
  St Lucia I

GEOSPIZA
Geospiza magnirostris (Large Ground Finch)
  Galapagos Is
Geospiza fortis (Medium Ground Finch)
  Galapagos Is
Geospiza fuliginosa (Small Ground Finch)
  Galapagos Is
Geospiza difficilis (Sharp-beaked Ground Finch)
G. d. difficilis
  Tower I, Abingdon I
G. d. debilirostris
  James I, Albemarle I, Narborough I
G. d. septentrionalis
  Culpepper I, Wenman I
Geospiza scandens (Cactus Ground Finch)
G. s. scandens
  James I, Jervis I
G. s. intermedia
  Barrington I, Charles I, Duncan I,
  Indefatigable I, Albemarle I
G. s. abingdoni
  Abingdon I
G. s. rothschildi
  Bindloe I
Geospiza conirostris (Large Cactus Ground Finch)
G. c. conirostris
  Hood I
G. c. propinqua
  Tower I
G. c. darwini
  Culpepper I

CAMARHYNCHUS
Camarhynchus crassirostris (Vegetarian Tree Finch)
  Galapagos Is

Camarhynchus psittacula (Large Insectivorous Tree Finch)
C. p. habeli
  Abingdon I, Bindloe I
C. p. affinis
  Albemarle I, Narborough I
C. p. psittacula
  Seymour I, Barrington I, Indefatigable I,
  Charles I, Duncan I, Jervis I, James I
Camarhynchus pauper (Charles Insectivorous Tree Finch)
  Charles I
Camarhynchus parvulus (Small Insectivorous Tree Finch)
C. p. parvulus
  James I, Jervis I, Indefatigable I,
  Seymour I, Barrington I, Albemarle I,
  Duncan I, Charles I, Narborough I
C. p. salvini
  Chatham I
Camarhynchus pallidus (Woodpecker Finch)
C. p. pallidus
  James I, Jervis I, Seymour I, Duncan I,
  Indefatigable I, Charles I
C. p. productus
  Albemarle I, Narborough I
C. p. striatipectus
  Chatham I
Camarhynchus heliobates (Mangrove Finch)
  Albemarle I, Narborough I

CERTHIDEA
Certhidea olivacea (Warbler Finch)
C. o. becki
  Culpepper I, Wenman I
C. o. mentalis
  Tower I
C. o. fusca
  Abingdon I, Bindloe I
C. o. olivacea
  James I, Jervis I, Seymour I, Duncan I,
  Albemarle I, Narborough I
C. o. bifasciata
  Barrington I
C. o. luteola
  Chatham I
C. o. cinerascens
  Hood I
C. o. ridgwayi
  Charles I

PINAROLOXIAS
Pinaroloxias inornata (Cocos Finch)
  Cocos Is

Pipilo ocai (Collared Towhee)
  P. o. alticola
    W Mexico
  P. o. nigrescens
    W Mexico
  P. o. guerrerensis
    SW Mexico
  P. o. brunnescens
    S Mexico
  P. o. ocai
    EC Mexico
Pipilo erythrophthalmus (Rufous-sided Towhee)
  P. e. erythrophthalmus
    S Canada, E USA » S USA
  P. e. rileyi
    SE USA
  P. e. alleni
    Florida
  P. e. canaster
    SC USA » SE USA
  P. e. arcticus
    S Canada, NC, C & SC USA » N Mexico
  P. e. montanus
    SW USA » N Mexico
  P. e. gaigei
    Texas
  P. e. curtatus
    SW Canada, W USA » SE California
  P. e. oregonus
    W USA » S California
  P. e. falcinellus
    W USA
  P. e. falcifer
    SW USA
  P. e. megalonyx
    SW USA, NW Baja California
  P. e. clementae
    San Clemente I
  P. e. umbraticola
    NW Baja California
  P. e. magnirostris
    S Baja California
  P. e. griseipygius
    W Mexico
  P. e. orientalis
    EC Mexico
  P. e. maculatus
    E Mexico
  P. e. macronyx
    SC Mexico
  P. e. vulcanorum
    SC Mexico
  P. e. oaxacae
    S Mexico
  P. e. repetens
    S Mexico, W Guatemala

  P. e. chiapensis
    S Mexico
  P. e. socorroensis
    Socorro I, Revillagigedo Group
  P. e. sympatricus
    Vera Cruz
Pipilo fuscus (Brown Towhee)
  P. f. bullatus
    SW Oregon, NC California
  P. f. carolae
    SC California
  P. f. petulans
    NC California
  P. f. crissalis
    WC California
  P. f. eremophilus
    EC California
  P. f. senicula
    S California, NW Baja California
  P. f. aripolius
    C Baja California
  P. f. albigula
    S Baja California
  P. f. mesoleucus
    SW USA, N Mexico
  P. f. intermedius
    N Mexico
  P. f. jamesi
    Tiburon I
  P. f. mesatus
    SW USA
  P. f. texanus
    W & C Texas, N Mexico
  P. f. perpallidus
    N & C Mexico
  P. f. fuscus
    E & C Mexico
  P. f. potosinus
    N & C Mexico
  P. f. campoi
    EC Mexico
  P. f. toroi
    SC Mexico
Pipilo aberti (Abert's Towhee)
  P. a. aberti
    SW USA
  P. a. vorhiesi
    Arizona
  P. a. dumeticolus
    NE Baja California, NW Mexico
Pipilo albicollis (White-throated Towhee)
  P. a. albicollis
    SC Mexico
  P. a. marshalli
    Puebla, Mexico

CHLORURUS
Chlorurus chlorurus (Green-tailed Towhee)
    W USA » C Mexico

Melozone kieneri (Rusty-crowned Ground Sparrow)

M. k. grisior
NW Mexico

M. k. kieneri
W Mexico

M. k. rubricatum
C & SW Mexico

M. k. obscurior
SW Oaxaca

Melozone biarcuatum (Prévost's Ground Sparrow)

M. b. biarcuatum
S Mexico to W Honduras

M. b. cabanisi
C Costa Rica

Melozone leucotis (White-eared Ground Sparrow)

M. l. occipitalis
S Mexico, Guatemala, El Salvador

M. l. nigrior
Nicaragua

M. l. leucotis
Costa Rica

ARREMON

Arremon taciturnus (Pectoral Sparrow)

A. t. axillaris
Colombia, W Venezuela

A. t. taciturnus
SE Venezuela, the Guianas, Brazil, Bolivia

A. t. semitorquatus
EC Brazil

A. t. nigrirostris
SE Peru, N Bolivia

Arremon flavirostris (Saffron-billed Sparrow)

A. f. flavirostris
EC Brazil

A. f. dorbignii
E Bolivia, NW Argentina

A. f. devillii
Brazil, E Bolivia

A. f. polionotus
Brazil, Paraguay, Argentina

Arremon aurantiirostris (Orange-billed Sparrow)

A. a. saturatus
SE Mexico, Guatemala, Belize

A. a. rufidorsalis
Honduras, Nicaragua, Costa Rica

A. a. aurantiirostris
W Costa Rica, Panama

A. a. strictocollaris
E Panama, NW Colombia

A. a. occidentalis
W Colombia, NW Ecuador

A. a. erythrorhynchus
N Colombia

A. a. spectabilis
SE Colombia, E Ecuador, Peru

A. a. santarosae
SW Ecuador

Arremon schlegeli (Golden-winged Sparrow)

A. s. fratruelis
N Colombia

A. s. canidorsum
Colombia

A. s. schegeli
E Colombia, Venezuela

Arremon abeillei (Black-capped Sparrow)

A. a. abeillei
NW Peru, SW Ecuador

A. a. nigriceps
NW Peru

ARREMONOPS

Arremonops rufivirgatus (Olive Sparrow)

A. r. rufivirgatus
S Texas, NE Mexico

A. r. ridgwayi
E Mexico

A. r. crassirostris
SE Mexico

A. r. verticalis
SE Mexico, Guatemala, Belize

A. r. sinaloae
W Mexico

A. r. sumichrasti
SW Mexico

A. r. rhyptothorax
Yucatan, Mexico

A. r. chiapensis
S Mexico

A. r. superciliosus
W Costa Rica

Arremonops tocuyensis (Tocuyo Sparrow)
NE Colombia, NW Venezuela

Arremonops chloronotus (Green-backed Sparrow)

A. c. chloronotus
SE Mexico, Guatemala, NW Honduras

A. c. twomeyi
NC Honduras

Arremonops conirostris (Black-striped Sparrow)

A. c. richmondi
E Honduras, Nicaragua, Costa Rica, Panama

A. c. striaticeps
C & E Panama, Colombia, W Ecuador

A. c. inexpectatus
Colombia

A. c. conirostris
E Colombia, N Venezuela, N Brazil

A. c. umbrinus
E Colombia, W Venezuela

Atlapetes albinucha (White-naped Brush Finch)
E Mexico

Atlapetes gutturalis (Yellow-throated Brush Finch)

A. g. griseipectus
S Mexico, W Guatemala, El Salvador

A. g. fuscipygius
Honduras, El Salvador, NW Nicaragua

A. g. parvirostris
Costa Rica

A. g. brunnescens
Panama

A. g. coloratus
Panama

A. g. azuerensis
S Panama

A. g. gutturalis
N Colombia

Atlapetes pallidinucha (Pale-naped Brush Finch)

A. p. pallidinucha
E Colombia, SW Venezuela

A. p. papallactae
Colombia, Ecuador

Atlapetes rufinucha (Rufous-naped Brush Finch)

A. r. phelpsi
Venezuela, Colombia

A. r. elaeoprorus
Colombia

A. r. simplex
Colombia

A. r. caucae
Colombia

A. r. spodionotus
S Colombia, N Ecuador

A. r. comptus
SW Ecuador, Peru

A. r. latinuchus
SE Ecuador, NE Peru

A. r. chugurensis
NW Peru

A. r. baroni
N Peru

A. r. melanolaemus
SE Peru

A. r. rufinucha
Bolivia

A. r. carrikeri
E Bolivia

Atlapetes leucopis (White-rimmed Brush Finch)
S Colombia, N Ecuador

Atlapetes melanocephalus (Santa Marta Brush Finch)
N Colombia

Atlapetes pileatus (Rufous-capped Brush Finch)

A. p. dilutus
N & C Mexico

A. p. pileatus
S Mexico

Atlapetes flaviceps (Olive-headed Brush Finch)
Colombia

Atlapetes fuscoolivaceus (Dusky-headed Brush Finch)
Colombia

Atlapetes tricolor (Tricoloured Brush Finch)

A. t. crassus
Colombia, Ecuador

A. t. tricolor
C Peru

Atlapetes albofrenatus (Moustached Brush Finch)

A. a. meridae
Venezuela

A. a. albofrenatus
Colombia

Atlapetes schistaceus (Slaty Brush Finch)

A. s. castaneifrons
Venezuela

A. s. tamae
Venezuela, Colombia

A. s. fumidus
Venezuela, Colombia

A. s. schistaceus
Colombia, Ecuador

A. s. taczanowskii
C Peru

A. s. canigenis
EC Peru

Atlapetes nationi (Rusty-bellied Brush Finch)

A. n. celicae
S Ecuador

A. n. nationi
W Peru

A. n. brunneiceps
SW Peru

Atlapetes seebohmi (Bay-crowned Brush Finch)

A. s. simonsi
S Ecuador

A. s. seebohmi
NW Peru

Atlapetes leucopterus (White-winged Brush Finch)
A. l. leucopterus
Ecuador
A. l. dresseri
SW Ecuador, NW Peru
Atlapetes albiceps (White-headed Brush Finch)
SE Ecuador, NW Peru
Atlapetes pallidiceps (Pale-headed Brush Finch)
S Ecuador
Atlapetes rufigenis (Rufous-eared Brush Finch)
A. r. rufigenis
NW Peru
A. r. forbesi
SC Peru
Atlapetes semirufus (Ochre-breasted Brush Finch)
A. s. denisei
Venezuela
A. s. benedettii
Venezuela
A. s. albigula
Venezuela
A. s. zimmeri
Venezuela, NE Colombia
A. s. majusculus
Colombia
A. s. semirufus
Colombia
Atlapetes personatus (Tepui Brush Finch)
A. p. personatus
Venezuela
A. p. collaris
Venezuela
A. p. duidae
Venezuela
A. p. parui
Venezuela
A. p. paraquensis
Venezuela
A. p. jugularis
Venezuela, N Brazil
Atlapetes fulviceps (Fulvous-headed Brush Finch)
Bolivia, NW Argentina
Atlapetes citrinellus (Yellow-striped Brush Finch)
Argentina
Atlapetes apertus (Plain-breasted Brush Finch)
E Mexico
Atlapetes brunneinucha (Chestnut-capped Brush Finch)
A. b. brunneinucha
E Mexico

A. b. suttoni
S Mexico
A. b. nigrilatera
Oaxaca (Mexico)
A. b. parkesi
S Vera Cruz
A. b. macrourus
S Mexico, SW Guatemala
A. b. alleni
El Salvador, Honduras, W Nicaragua
A. b. elsae
Costa Rica, W & C Panama
A. b. frontalis
E Panama, Colombia Venezuela, Ecuad
Peru
A. b. allinornatus
NW Venezuela
A. b. inornatus
WC Ecuador
Atlapetes torquatus (Stripe-headed Brush Finch)
A. t. colimae
W Mexico
A. t. verecundus
NW Mexico
A. t. virenticeps
C Mexico
A. t. basilicus
N Colombia
A. t. perijanus
E Colombia, W Venezuela
A. t. larensis
Venezuela
A. t. phaeopleurus
N Venezuela
A. t. phygas
NE Venezuela
A. t. assimilis
Venezuela, Ecuador, Colombia, Peru
A. t. nigrifrons
SW Ecuador, NW Peru
A. t. poliophrys
C & SE Peru
A. t. torquatus
NW Bolivia
A. t. fimbriatus
Bolivia
A. t. borelli
Bolivia, Argentina
Atlapetes atricapillus (Black-headed Brush Finch)
A. a. atricapillus
N Colombia
A. a. costaricensis
SW Costa Rica, W Panama
A. a. tacarcunae
E Panama

PEZOPETES
Pezopetes capitalis (Big-footed Sparrow)
Costa Rica, W Panama

OREOTHRAUPIS
Oreothraupis arremonops (Tanager Finch)
SW Colombia, NW Ecuador

PSELLIOPHORUS
Pselliophorus tibialis (Yellow-thighed Sparrow)
Costa Rica, W Panama
Pselliophorus luteoviridis (Yellow-green Sparrow)
E Panama

LYSURUS
Lysurus castaneiceps (Olive Finch)
L. c. crassirostris
Costa Rica, Panama
L. c. castaneiceps
Colombia, Ecuador, SE Peru

UROTHRAUPIS
Urothraupis stolzmanni (Black-backed Bush Tanager)
C Colombia to C Ecuador

CHARITOSPIZA
Charitospiza eucosma (Coal-crested Finch)
C & E Brazil, NE Argentina

SALTATRICULA
Saltatricula multicolor (Many-coloured Chaco Finch)
Bolivia, Paraguay, Uruguay, N Argentina

CORYPHASPIZA
Coryphaspiza melanotis (Black-masked Finch)
C. m. marajoara
Marajoara I, Brazil
C. m. melanotis
Brazil, Bolivia, Paraguay, NE Argentina

CORYPHOSPINGUS
Coryphospingus pileatus (Pileated Finch)
C. p. rostratus
Colombia
C. p. brevicaudus
N Colombia, N Venezuela
C. p. pileatus
EC Brazil
Coryphospingus cucullatus (Red-crested Finch)
C. c. cucullatus
the Guianas, Brazil
C. c. rubescens
S Brazil, E Paraguay, Uruguay, Argentina
C. c. fargoi
Peru, Bolivia, N Argentina, W Paraguay

RHODOSPINGUS
Rhodospingus cruentus (Crimson Finch)
Ecuador, Peru

EMBERIZIDAE

155 CATAMBLYRHYNCHINAE (PLUSH-CAPPED FINCH)

CATAMBLYRHYNCHUS
Catamblyrhynchus diadema (Plush-capped Finch)
C. d. federalis
N Venezuela
C. d. diadema
NW Venezuela, Colombia, Ecuador
C. d. citrinifrons
Peru, Bolivia, NW Argentina

EMBERIZIDAE

156 CARDINALINAE (CARDINAL-GROSBEAKS)

GUBERNATRIX
Gubernatrix cristata (Yellow Cardinal)
Uruguay, N & E Argentina

PAROARIA
Paroaria coronata (Red-crested Cardinal)
Bolivia, Paraguay, Uruguay, Argentina
Paroaria dominicana (Red-cowled Cardinal)
NE Brazil
Paroaria gularis (Red-capped Cardinal)
P. g. nigrogenis
Trinidad, E Colombia, Venezuela
P. g. gularis
Colombia, Venezuela, the Guianas, Ecuador, Peru, W Brazil
P. g. cervicalis
E Bolivia, Brazil
Paroaria baeri (Crimson-fronted Cardinal)
P. b. baeri
Brazil
P. b. xinguensis
Brazil
Paroaria capitata (Yellow-billed Cardinal)
P. c. capitata
Brazil, Paraguay, N Argentina
P. c. fuscipes
SE Bolivia

SPIZA
Spiza americana (Dickcissel)
E North America » Central America, Trinidad, Colombia, Venezuela

PHEUCTICUS
Pheucticus chrysopeplus (Yellow Grosbreak)
P. c. dilutus
NW Mexico

P. c. chrysopeplus
W Mexico
P. c. rarissimus
SC Mexico
P. c. aurantiacus
S Mexico, Guatemala
P. c. laubmanni
N Colombia, N Venezuela
Pheucticus tibialis (Black-thighed Grosbeak)
C Costa Rica, W Panama
Pheucticus chrysogaster (Yellow-bellied Grosbeak)
SW Colombia, Ecuador, Peru
Pheucticus aureoventris (Black-backed Grosbeak)
P. a. meridensis
Venezuela
P. a. uropygialis
Colombia
P. a. crissalis
SW Colombia, Ecuador
P. a. terminalis
Peru
P. a. aureoventris
S Peru, Bolivia, Brazil, Paraguay, NW Argentina
Pheucticus ludovicianus (Rose-breasted Grosbeak)
S Canada, C & SE USA » Mexico, Central America, N South America
Pheucticus melanocephalus (Black-headed Grosbeak)
P. m. melanocephalus
S Canada, WC USA, Mexico
P. m. maculatus
SW Canada, W USA, Mexico, Baja California

CARDINALIS
Cardinalis cardinalis (Common Cardinal)
C. c. cardinalis
E USA
C. c. floridanus
SE Georgia, Florida
C. c. magnirostris
SE Texas, Louisiana
C. c. canicaudus
SC USA, C & E Mexico
C. c. coccineus
E Mexico
C. c. littoralis
E Mexico
C. c. yucatanicus
SE Mexico
C. c. flammigerus
SE Mexico, Guatemala, Belize
C. c. sinaloensis
W Mexico

C. c. saturatus
Cozumel I, SE Mexico
C. c. superbus
SW USA, NW Mexico
C. c. townsendi
Tiburon I, NW Mexico
C. c. affinis
WC Mexico
C. c. mariae
Tres Marias Is
C. c. carneus
W & S Mexico
C. c. seftoni
C Baja California
C. c. igneus
S Baja California
C. c. dintoni
Cerralvo I

PYRRHULOXIA
Pyrrhuloxia phoeniceus (Vermilion Cardinal)
Colombia, Venezuela
Pyrrhuloxia sinuatus (Pyrrhuloxia)
P. s. sinuatus
S USA, N & C Mexico
P. s. fulvescens
S Arizona, NW Mexico
P. s. peninsulae
Baja California

CARYOTHRAUSTES
Caryothraustes canadensis (Yellow-green Grosbeak)
C. c. canadensis
Colombia, Venezuela, the Guianas, Brazil
C. c. frontalis
NE Brazil
C. c. brasiliensis
EC Brazil
Caryothraustes poliogaster (Black-faced Grosbeak)
C. p. poliogaster
SE Mexico, Guatemala, Honduras
C. p. scapularis
Nicaragua, Costa Rica, W Panama
C. p. simulans
E Panama
Caryothraustes humeralis (Yellow-shouldered Grosbeak)
Colombia, Ecuador, Brazil

RHODOTHRAUPIS
Rhodothraupis celaeno (Crimson-collared Grosbeak)
NE Mexico

PERIPORPHYRUS
Periporphyrus erythromelas (Red & Black Grosbeak)
    Venezuela, Guyana, French Guiana, Brazil

PITYLUS
Pitylus grossus (Slate-coloured Grosbeak)
  P. g. saturatus
    Nicaragua to Ecuador
  P. g. grossus
    Venezuela, Guyana, Brazil, W Colombia, W Ecuador, Peru, Bolivia
Pitylus fuliginosus (Black-throated Grosbeak)
    Brazil, Paraguay, N Argentina

SALTATOR
Saltator atriceps (Black-headed Saltator)
  S. a. atriceps
    E Mexico, Guatemala, Honduras, Costa Rica
  S. a. suffuscus
    SE Vera Cruz, Mexico
  S. a. flavicrissus
    Guerrero, Mexico
  S. a. peeti
    S Mexico
  S. a. raptor
    SE Mexico
  S. a. lacertosus
    W Costa Rica, Panama
Saltator maximus (Buff-throated Saltator)
  S. m. gigantodes
    E & S Mexico
  S. m. magnoides
    S Mexico to Panama
  S. m. intermedius
    SW Costa Rica, NW Panama
  S. m. iungens
    E Panama, NW Colombia
  S. m. maximus
    Colombia, Venezuela, the Guianas, Ecuador, Peru, Bolivia, Paraguay
Saltator atripennis (Black-winged Saltator)
  S. a. atripennis
    Colombia, NW Ecuador
  S. a. caniceps
    Colombia, W Ecuador
Saltator similis (Green-winged Saltator)
  S. s. similis
    Brazil, Bolivia, Paraguay, Uruguay, Argentina
  S. s. ochraceiventris
    SE Brazil
Saltator coerulescens (Greyish Saltator)
  S. c. vigorsii
    NW Mexico

S. c. richardsoni
    WC Mexico
S. c. grandis
    E Mexico, Guatemala, Honduras Nicaragua, Costa Rica
S. c. yucatanensis
    SE Mexico
S. c. hesperis
    Guatemala, El Salvador, Honduras, Nicaragua
S. c. brevicaudus
    W Costa Rica
S. c. plumbeus
    N Colombia
S. c. brewsteri
    NE Colombia, Venezuela, Trinidad
S. c. olivascens
    Venezuela, the Guianas, N Brazil
S. c. azarae
    E Colombia, Ecuador, E Peru, Bolivia, Brazil
S. c. mutus
    N Brazil
S. c. superciliaris
    NE Brazil
S. c. coerulescens
    E Bolivia, SW Brazil, Paraguay, N Argentina
Saltator orenocensis (Orinocan Saltator)
  S. o. rufescens
    NE Colombia, NW Venezuela
  S. o. orenocensis
    Venezuela
Saltator maxillosus (Thick-billed Saltator)
    SE Brazil, Paraguay, N Argentina
Saltator aurantiirostris (Golden-billed Saltator)
  S. a. iteratus
    N Peru
  S. a. albociliaris
    Peru, N Chile
  S. a. hellmayri
    Bolivia
  S. a. aurantiirostris
    Bolivia, N Argentina, Paraguay, Uruguay, S Brazil
  S. a. nasica
    W Argentina
Saltator cinctus (Masked Saltator)
    E Ecuador
Saltator atricollis (Black-throated) Saltator)
    E Bolivia, Paraguay, S Brazil
Saltator rufiventris (Rufous-bellied Saltator)
    Bolivia,

Saltator albicollis (Streaked Saltator)
  S. a. albicollis
   Martinique I, St Lucia I
  S. a. guadelupensis
   Guadeloupe I, Dominica I
  S. a. furax
   SW Costa Rica, Panama
  S. a. isthmicus
   W Panama
  S. a. scotinus
   Coiba I (Panama)
  S. a. melicus
   Taboga I (Panama)
  S. a. speratus
   Pearl I (Panama)
  S. a. striatipectus
   E Panama, W Colombia
  S. a. perstriatus
   NE Colombia, Venezuela, Trinidad
  S. a. flavidicollis
   SW Colombia, Ecuador, NW Peru
  S. a. immaculatus
   W Peru
  S. a. peruvianus
   N Peru

CYANOLOXIA
Cyanoloxia glaucocaerulea (Indigo Grosbeak)
   S Brazil, Uruguay, N Argentina

CYANOCOMPSA
Cyanocompsa cyanoides (Blue-black Grosbeak)
  C. c. concreta
   SE Mexico, Guatemala, Honduras
  C. c. toddi
   Nicaragua, Costa Rica, W Panama
  C. c. cyanoides
   E Panama, Colombia, W Venezuela, Ecuador
  C. c. rothschildii
   Upper Amazonia, W Brazil
Cyanocompsa brissonii (Ultramarine Grosbeak)
  C. b. caucae
   W Colombia
  C. b. minor
   N Venezuela
  C. b. brissonii
   NE Brazil
  C. b. sterea
   E & S Brazil, NE Argentina, W Paraguay
  C. b. argentina
   W Brazil, E Bolivia, Paraguay, N Argentina
Cyanocompsa parellina (Blue Bunting)
  C. p. beneplacita
   NE Mexico

  C. p. indigotica
   W & SW Mexico
  C. p. lucida
   NE Mexico
  C. p. parellina
   E & S Mexico to Nicaragua

GUIRACA
Guiraca caerulea (Blue Grosbeak)
  G. c. caerulea
   SE USA » E Mexico & Central America
  G. c. interfusa
   SW USA » W Mexico, Guatemala, Honduras
  G. c. salicaria
   SW USA » W Mexico, Baja California
  G. c. eurhyncha
   C & S Mexico
  G. c. chiapensis
   S Mexico
  G. c. deltarhyncha
   W coast of Mexico
  G. c. lazula
   Honduras, Nicaragua, Costa Rica

PASSERINA
Passerina cyanea (Indigo Bunting)
   S Canada, E USA » Central America, Cuba Jamaica, Colombia, Venezuela
Passerina amoena (Lazuli Bunting)
   W USA » W Mexico, Baja California
Passerina versicolor (Varied Bunting)
  P. v. versicolor
   S USA, C & S Mexico
  P. v. dickeyae
   S Arizona, W Mexico
  P. v. pulchra
   S Baja California, NW Mexico
  P. v. purpurascens
   S Mexico, Guatemala
Passerina ciris (Painted Bunting)
  P. c. ciris
   SE USA » SE Mexico, Bahama Is
  P. c. pallidior
   S USA » Mexico, Central America
Passerina rositae (Rose-bellied Bunting)
   S Mexico
Passerina leclancherii (Orange-breasted Bunting)
  P. l. grandior
   Oaxaca (Mexico)
  P. l. leclancherii
   SW Mexico

PORPHYROSPIZA
Porphyrospiza caerulescens (Blue Finch)
   Brazil, SE Bolivia

EMBERIZIDAE
157 THRAUPINAE (TANAGERS)

ORCHESTICUS
Orchesticus abeillei (Brown Tanager)
  SE Brazil

SCHISTOCLAMYS
Schistoclamys ruficapillus (Cinnamon Tanager)
  S. r. capistrata
    NE Brazil
  S. r. sicki
    E Mato Grosso (Brazil)
  S. r. ruficapillus
    SE Brazil

Schistoclamys melanopis (Black-faced Tanager)
  S. m. aterrima
    NE Colombia, Venezuela, W Guyana
  S. m. melanopis
    the Guianas, NE Brazil
  S. m. grisea
    EC Peru
  S. m. olivina
    E Bolivia, SC Brazil
  S. m. amazonica
    SE Brazil

NEOTHRAUPIS
Neothraupis fasciata (White-banded Tanager)
  E & S Brazil, E Bolivia, NE Paraguay

CYPSNAGRA
Cypsnagra hirundinacea (White-rumped Tanager)
  C. h. pallidigula
    C Brazil, NE Bolivia
  C. h. hirundinacea
    S Brazil, E Bolivia, NE Paraguay

CONOTHRAUPIS
Conothraupis speculigera (Black & White Tanager)
  S Ecuador, N & E Peru
Conothraupis mesoleuca (Cone-billed Tanager)
  Mato Grosso (Brazil)

LAMPROSPIZA
Lamprospiza melanoleuca (Red-billed Pied Tanager)
  the Guianas, N Brazil, SE Peru, N Bolivia

CISSOPIS
Cissopis leveriana (MagpieTanager)
  C. l. leveriana
    Upper Amazonia
  C. l. major
    Paraguay, SE Brazil, N Argentina

CHLORORNIS
Chlorornis riefferii (Grass-green Tanager)
  C. r. riefferii
    Colombia, Ecuador
  C. r. diluta
    N Peru
  C. r. elegans
    C Peru
  C. r. celata
    SE Peru
  C. r. boliviana
    W Bolivia

COMPSOTHRAUPIS
Compsothraupis loricata (Scarlet-throated Tanager)
  E Brazil

SERICOSSYPHA
Sericossypha albocristata (White-capped Tanager)
  SW Venezuela, Colombia, Ecuador, E Peru

NESOSPINGUS
Nesospingus speculiferus (Puerto Rican Tanager)
  Puerto Rica

CHLOROSPINGUS
Chlorospingus ophthalmicus (Common Bush Tanager)
  C. o. albifrons
    SW Mexico
  C. o. wetmorei
    E Mexico
  C. o. persimilis
    S Oaxaca
  C. o. ophthalmicus
    SE Mexico
  C. o. dwighti
    S Mexico, E Guatemala
  C. o. postocularis
    S Mexico, W Guatemala
  C. o. honduratius
    El Salvador, Honduras
  C. o. regionalis
    Nicaragua, E Costa Rica
  C. o. novicius
    SW Costa Rica, W Panama
  C. o. jaqueti
    NE Colombia, N Venezuela
  C. o. falconensis
    NW Venezuela
  C. o. venezuelanus
    SW Venezuela
  C. o. ponsi
    W Venezuela
  C. o. eminens
    NE Colombia

C. o. flavopectus
C Colombia
C. o. macarenae
E Colombia
C. o. nigriceps
C Colombia
C. o. phaeocephalus
Ecuador
C. o. cinereocephalus
C Peru
C. o. peruvianus
S Peru
C. o. bolivianus
WC Bolivia
C. o. fulvigularis
C Bolivia
C. o. argentinus
C Bolivia, N Argentina
Chlorospingus tacarcunae (Tacarcuna Bush Tanager)
E Panama
Chlorospingus inornatus (Pirre Bush Tanager)
E Panama
Chlorospingus punctulatus (Dotted Bush Tanager)
W Panama
Chlorospingus semifuscus (Dusky-bellied Bush Tanager)
C. s. livingstoni
W Colombia
C. s. semifuscus
SW Colombia, W Ecuador
Chlorospingus zeledoni (Zeledon's Bush Tanager)
Costa Rica
Chlorospingus pileatus (Pileated Bush Tanager)
C. p. pileatus
Costa Rica, W Panama
C. p. diversus
W Panama
Chlorospingus parvirostris (Short-billed Bush Tanager)
C. p. huallagae
S Colombia, Peru
C. p. medianus
EC Peru
C. p. parvirostris
SE Peru, W Bolivia
Chlorospingus flavigularis (Yellow-throated Bush Tanager)
C. f. hypophaeus
W Panama
C. f. marginatus
SW Colombia, W Ecuador
C. f. flavigularis
S Colombia, E Ecuador, E Peru

Chlorospingus flavovirens (Yellow-green Bush Tanager)
W Ecuador
Chlorospingus canigularis (Ash-throated Bush Tanager)
C. c. olivaceiceps
W Costa Rica
C. c. canigularis
C Colombia, SW Venezuela
C. c. conspicillatus
W Colombia
C. c. paulus
SW Ecuador
C. c. signatus
E Ecuador, NW Peru

CNEMOSCOPUS
Cnemoscopus rubrirostris (Grey-hooded Bush Tanager)
C. r. rubrirostris
SW Venezuela, Colombia, E Ecuador
C. r. chrysogaster
N & C Peru

HEMISPINGUS
Hemispingus atropileus (Black-capped Hemispingus)
H. a. atropileus
SW Venezuela, Colombia, Ecuador
H. a. auricularis
E Peru
Hemispingus calophrys (Yungas Hemispingus)
W Bolivia
Hemispingus parodii (Parodi's Tanager)
Cuzco, Peru
Hemispingus superciliaris (Superciliaried Hemispingus)
H. s. chrysophrys
SW Venezuela
H. s. superciliaris
C Colombia
H. s. nigrifrons
Colombia, Ecuador
H. s. maculifrons
SW Ecuador, NW Peru
H. s. insignis
N Peru
H. s. leucogaster
C Peru
H. s. urubambae
S Peru, W Bolivia
Hemispingus reyi (Grey-capped Hemispingus)
SW Venezuela
Hemispingus frontalis (Oleaginous Hemispingus)
H. f. frontalis
Colombia, E Ecuador, E Peru

H. f. ignobilis
  W Venezuela
H. f. flavidorsalis
  W Venezuela
H. f. hanieli
  N Venezuela
H. f. iteratus
  NE Venezuela
Hemispingus melanotis (Black-eared Hemispingus)
H. m. melanotis
  SW Venezuela, C & E Colombia,
  E Ecuador
H. m. ochraceus
  SW Colombia, W Ecuador
H. m. piurae
  NW Peru
H. m. macrophrys
  W Peru
H. m. berlepschi
  C Peru
H. m. castaneicollis
  SE Peru, W Bolivia
Hemispingus goeringi (Slaty-backed Hemispingus)
  SW Venezuela
Hemispingus rufosuperciliaris (Rufous-browed Hemispingus)
  C Peru
Hemispingus verticalis (Black-headed Hemispingus)
  S & C Colombia, E Ecuador
Hemispingus xanthophthalmus (Drab Hemispingus)
  C Peru
Hemispingus trifasciatus (Three-striped Hemispingus)
  SE Peru, W Bolivia

PYRRHOCOMA
Pyrrhocoma ruficeps (Chestnut-headed Tanager)
  SE Brazil, E Paraguay, N Argentina

THLYPOPSIS
Thlypopsis fulviceps (Fulvous-headed Tanager)
T. f. fulviceps
  NE Colombia, NW Venezuela
T. f. obscuriceps
  W Venezuela
T. f. meridensis
  W Venezuela
T. f. intensa
  NE Colombia
Thlypopsis ornata (Rufous-chested Tanager)
T. o. ornata
  SW Colombia, W Ecuador

561

T. o. media
  S Ecuador, N & C Peru
T. o. macropteryx
  C & S Peru
Thlypopsis pectoralis (Brown-flanked Tanager)
  C Peru
Thlypopsis sordida (Orange-headed Tanager)
T. s. orinocensis
  EC Venezuela
T. s. chrysopis
  E Ecuador, E Peru, W Brazil
T. s. sordida
  E & S Brazil, E Bolivia, Paraguay,
  N Argentina
Thlypopsis inornata (Buff-bellied Tanager)
  N Peru
Thlypopsis ruficeps (Rust and Yellow Tanager)
  SE Peru, NW Argentina

HEMITHRAUPIS
Hemithraupis guira (Guira Tanager)
H. g. nigrigula
  NC Colombia to NE Brazil
H. g. roraimae
  SE Venezuela, Guyana
H. g. guirina
  W Colombia to NW Peru
H. g. huambina
  SE Colombia to NE Peru, W Brazil
H. g. boliviana
  NE Bolivia, NW Argentina
H. g. amazonica
  C Brazil
H. g. guira
  E Brazil
H. g. fosteri
  SE Brazil, Paraguay, NE Argentina
Hemithraupis ruficapilla (Rufous-headed Tanager)
H. r. ruficapilla
  SE Brazil
H. r. bahiae
  E Brazil
Hemithraupis flavicollis (Yellow-backed Tanager)
H. f. ornata
  E Panama, NW Colombia
H. f. albigularis
  Colombia
H. f. peruana
  SC Colombia to NE Peru
H. f. sororia
  N Peru
H. f. centralis
  SE Peru, N Bolivia, C Brazil

H. f. aurigularis
SE Colombia, S Venezuela, N Brazil
H. f. hellmayri
SE Venezuela, W Guyana
H. f. flavicollis
Surinam, French Guiana, NE Brazil
H. f. obidensis
N Brazil
H. f. melanoxantha
E Brazil
H. f. insignis
SE Brazil

CHRYSOTHLYPIS
**Chrysothlypis chrysomelas (Black &
Yellow Tanager)**
C. c. chrysomelas
E Costa Rica, W Panama
C. c. ocularis
E Panama
**Chrysothlypis salmoni (Scarlet &
White Tanager)**
W Colombia, NW Ecuador

NEMOSIA
Nemosia pileata (Hooded Tanager)
N. p. hypoleuca
N Colombia, N Venezuela
N. p. surinamensis
Guyana, Surinam
N. p. pileata
French Guiana, Brazil, N Bolivia
N. p. interna
N Brazil
N. p. nana
NE Peru, W Brazil
N. p. caerulea
S & E Brazil, E Bolivia, Paraguay,
N Argentina
**Nemosia rourei (Cherry-throated
Tanager)**
SE Brazil

PHAENICOPHILUS
**Phaenicophilus palmarum (Black-
crowned Palm Tanager)**
Hispaniola, Saona I
**Phaenicophilus poliocephalus (Grey-
crowned Palm Tanager)**
P. p. poliocephalus
S Haiti
P. p. coryi
Gonave I

CALYPTOPHILUS
Calyptophilus frugivorus (Chat-Tanager)
C. f. frugivorus
Dominica I
C. f. tertius
S Haiti

C. f. abbotti
Gonave I

RHODINOCICHLA
**Rhodinocichla rosea (Rose-breasted
Thrush Tanager)**
R. r. schistacea
W Mexico
R. r. eximia
SW Costa Rica, W Panama
R. r. harterti
C Colombia
R. r. beebei
NE Colombia, NW Venezuela
R. r. rosea
NW Venezuela

MITROSPINGUS
**Mitrospingus cassinii (Dusky-faced
Tanager)**
M. c. costaricensis
E Costa Rica, W Panama
M. c. cassinii
E Panama, W Colombia, W Ecuador
**Mitrospingus oleagineus (Olive-
backed Tanager)**
M. o. obscuripectus
SE Venezuela, N Brazil
M. o. oleagineus
SE Venezuela, Guyana

CHLOROTHRAUPIS
**Chlorothraupis carmioli (Carmiol's
Tanager)**
C. c. carmioli
Nicaragua to NW Panama
C. c. magnirostris
W Panama
C. c. lutescens
E Panama, NW Colombia
C. c. frenata
S Colombia, SE Peru
**Chlorothraupis olivacea (Lemon-
browed Tanager)**
E Panama to NW Ecuador
**Chlorothraupis stolzmanni (Ochre-
breasted Tanager)**
C. s. dugandi
SW Colombia
C. s. stolzmanni
W Ecuador

ORTHOGONYS
**Orthogonys chloricterus (Olive-green
Tanager)**
SE Brazil

EUCOMETIS
**Eucometis penicillata (Grey-headed
Tanager)**
E. p. pallida
SE Mexico to E Guatemala

E. p. spodocephala
  Nicaragua, W Costa Rica
E. p. stictothorax
  SW Costa Rica, W Panama
E. p. cristata
  E Panama to W Venezuela
E. p. affinis
  N Venezuela
E. p. penicillata
  SE Colombia, E Ecuador, E Peru, the
  Guianas, N Brazil
E. p. albicollis
  E Bolivia, SC Brazil, N Paraguay

LANIO

Lanio fulvus (Fulvous Shrike-Tanager)
  L. f. peruvianus
    S Colombia to NE Peru
  L. f. fulvus
    S Venezuela, the Guianas, N Brazil
Lanio versicolor (White-winged Shrike-Tanager)
  L. v. versicolor
    E Peru, N Bolivia, W Brazil
  L. v. parvus
    S Brazil
Lanio aurantius (Black-throated Shrike-Tanager)
  SE Mexico to Honduras
Lanio leucothorax (White-throated Shrike-Tanager)
  L. l. leucothorax
    E Honduras to E Costa Rica
  L. l. reversus
    NW Costa Rica
  L. l. melanopygius
    SW Costa Rica, W Panama
  L. l. ictus
    NW Panama

CREURGOPS

Creurgops verticalis (Rufous-crested Tanager)
  SW Venezuela to Peru
Creurgops dentata (Slaty Tanager)
  SE Peru, N Bolivia

HETEROSPINGUS

Hererospingus xanthopygius (Scarlet-browed Tanager)
  H. x. rubrifrons
    E Costa Rica, Panama
  H. x. xanthopygius
    E Panama, N Colombia
  H. x. berliozi
    W Colombia, NW Ecuador

Tachyphonus cristatus (Flame-crested Tanager)
  T. c. cristatus
    French Guiana, NE Brazil
  T. c. intercedens
    E Venezuela, Guyana, Surinam
  T. c. orinocensis
    E Colombia, S Venezuela
  T. c. cristatellus
    S Venezuela to N Peru
  T. c. fallax
    S Colombia to NE Peru
  T. c. huarandosae
    N Peru
  T. c. madeirae
    C Brazil
  T. c. pallidigula
    NE Brazil
  T. c. brunneus
    E Brazil
  T. c. nattereri
    SW Brazil
Tachyphonus rufiventer (Yellow-crested Tanager)
  E Peru, N Bolivia, W Brazil
Tachyphonus surinamus (Fulvous-crested Tanager)
  T. s. surinamus
    E & S Venezuela, the Guianas, N Brazil
  T. s. brevipes
    S Venezuela to NE Peru
  T. s. napensis
    E Peru, NW Brazil
  T. s. insignis
    N Brazil
Tachyphonus luctuosus (White-shouldered Tanager)
  T. l. axillaris
    E Honduras to W Panama
  T. l. nitidissimus
    SW Costa Rica, W Panama
  T. l. panamensis
    E Panama to W Ecuador, W Venezuela
  T. l. luctuosus
    tropical South America
  T. l. flaviventris
    NE Venezuela, Trinidad
Tachyphonus delatrii (Tawny-crested Tanager)
  Nicaragua to W Ecuador
Tachyphonus coronatus (Ruby-crowned Tanager)
  SE Brazil to NW Argentina
Tachyphonus rufus (White-lined Tanager)
  Costa Rica, Panama, N South America

Tachyphonus phoenicius (Red-shouldered Tanager)
N South America

TRICHOTHRAUPIS
Trichothraupis melanops (Black-goggled Tanager)
SW Amazonia

HABIA
Habia rubica (Red-crowned Ant-Tanager)
H. r. holobrunnea
E Mexico
H. r. rosea
SW Mexico
H. r. affinis
S Mexico
H. r. nelsoni
SE Mexico
H. r. rubicoides
S Mexico to El Salvador
H. r. vinacea
W Costa Rica, W Panama
H. r. alfaroana
NW Costa Rica
H. r. rubra
Trinidad
H. r. crissalis
NE Venezuela
H. r. mesopotamia
E Bolivar (Venezuela)
H. r. perijana
NE Colombia, NW Venezuela
H. r. coccinea
NC Colombia, W Venezuela
H. r. rhodinolaema
SE Colombia to NE Peru, NW Brazil
H. r. peruviana
E Peru, NC Bolivia
H. r. hesterna
C Brazil
H. r. bahiae
E Brazil
H. r. rubica
SE Brazil, Paraguay, N Argentina
Habia fuscicauda (Red-throated Ant-Tanager)
H. f. salvini
SE Mexico to El Salvador
H. f. insularis
SE Mexico, N Guatemala
H. f. discolor
Nicaragua
H. f. fuscicauda
S Nicaragua to W Panama
H. f. willisi
C Panama
H. f. erythrolaema
N Colombia

Habia atrimaxillaris (Black-cheeked Ant-Tanager)
SW Costa Rica
Habia gutturalis (Sooty Ant-Tanager)
NW Colombia
Habia cristata (Crested Ant-Tanager)
W Colombia

PIRANGA
Piranga bidentata (Flame-coloured Tanager)
P. b. bidentata
W Mexico
P. b. alvarezi
S Mexico
P. b. flammea
Tres Marias Is
P. b. sanguinolenta
E Mexico to El Salvador
P. b. citrea
Costa Rica, W Panama
Piranga flava (Hepatic Tanager)
P. f. hepatica
SW USA, W Mexico
P. f. intensa
SW Oaxaca
P. f. dextra
SW USA, E Mexico » W Guatemala
P. f. figlina
E Guatemala, Belize
P. f. savannarum
Honduras, NE Nicaragua
P. f. albifacies
W Guatemala to N Nicaragua
P. f. testacea
Costa Rica, Panama
P. f. desidiosa
SW Colombia
P. f. lutea
W Ecuador to NW Bolivia
P. f. haemalea
S Venezuela, W Guyana, N Brazil
P. f. faceta
N Colombia, N Venezuela, Trinidad
P. f. toddi
Magdelena (Colombia)
P. f. macconnelli
S Guyana, N Brazil
P. f. saira
E Brazil
P. f. rosacea
E Bolivia
P. f. flava
S Bolivia to Uruguay, N Argentina
Piranga rubra (Summer Tanager)
P. r. cooperi
SW USA » C Mexico
P. r. rubra
SE USA » Central & South America

P. r. ochracea
  Arizona & W Mexico
Piranga roseogularis (Rose-throated Tanager)
P. r. roseogularis
  SE Mexico
P. r. tincta
  SE Mexico, N Guatemala
P. r. cozumelae
  Cozumel I
Piranga olivacea (Scarlet Tanager)
  SE Canada, NE USA » NW South America
Piranga ludoviciana (Western Tanager)
  W North America » W Mexico, W Central America
Piranga leucoptera (White-winged Tanager)
P. l. leucoptera
  E Mexico to Nicaragua
P. l. latifasciata
  Costa Rica, W Panama
P. l. venezuelae
  Colombia, Venezuela, N Brazil
P. l. ardens
  SW Colombia to Bolivia
Piranga erythrocephala (Red-headed Tanager)
P. e. candida
  NW Mexico
P. e. erythrocephala
  SC & S Mexico
Piranga rubriceps (Red-hooded Tanager)
  W Colombia to N Peru

CALOCHAETES
Calochaetes coccineus (Vermilion Tanager)
  S Colombia to E Peru

RAMPHOCELUS
Ramphocelus sanguinolentus (Crimson-collared Tanager)
R. s. sanguinolentus
  SE Mexico to Honduras
R. s. apricus
  E Honduras to NW Panama
Ramphocelus nigrogularis (Masked Crimson Tanager)
  SE Colombia to E Peru, N Brazil
Ramphocelus dimidiatus (Crimson-backed Tanager)
R. d. isthmicus
  W & C Panama
R. d. arestus
  Coiba I
R. d. limatus
  Pearl Archipelago
R. d. dimidiatus
  E Panama, N Colombia, W Venezuela

R. d. molochinus
  N Colombia
Ramphocelus melanogaster (Black-bellied Tanager)
R. m. melanogaster
  N Peru
R. m. transitus
  EC Peru
Ramphocelus carbo (Silver-beaked Tanager)
R. c. unicolor
  E Colombia
R. c. capitalis
  NE Venezuela
R. c. magnirostris
  Trinidad
R. c. carbo
  E Peru to Surinam
R. c. venezuelensis
  E Colombia, W Venezuela
R. c. connectens
  SE Peru, NW Bolivia
R. c. atrosericeus
  N & E Bolivia
R. c. centralis
  EC Brazil, N Paraguay
Ramphocelus bresilius (Brazilian Tanager)
R. b. bresilius
  NE Brazil
R. b. dorsalis
  SE Brazil
Ramphocelus passerinii (Scarlet-rumped Tanager)
R. p. passerinii
  SE Mexico to W Panama
R. p. costaricensis
  W Costa Rica
Ramphocelus flammigerus (Flame-rumped Tanager)
R. f. icteronotus
  Panama to W Ecuador
R. f. flammigerus
  W Colombia

SPINDALIS
Spindalis zena (Stripe-headed Tanager)
S. z. townsendi
  N Bahama Is
S. z. zena
  C Bahama Is
S. z. pretrei
  Cuba, Isle of Pines
S. z. salvini
  Grand Cayman I
S. z. benedicti
  Cozumel I
S. z. dominicensis
  Hispaniola

S. z. portoricensis
Puerto Rico
S. z. nigricephala
Jamaica

THRAUPIS
Thraupis episcopus (Blue-grey Tanager)
T. e. cana
SE Mexico to N Venezuela
T. e. caesitia
W Panama
T. e. cumatilis
Coiba I
T. e. nesophilus
E Colombia to Trinidad
T. e. berlepschi
Tobago I
T. e. mediana
SE Colombia, NW Brazil, N Bolivia
T. e. episcopus
the Guianas, N Brazil
T. e. leucoptera
C Colombia
T. e. quaesita
SW Colombia, W Ecuador, NW Peru
T. e. caerulea
SE Ecuador, N Peru
T. e. major
C Peru
T. e. urubambae
SE Peru
T. e. coelestis
SE Colombia to C Peru, W Brazil
Thraupis sayaca (Sayaca Tanager)
T. s. boliviana
NW Bolivia
T. s. obscura
C & S Bolivia, W Argentina
T. s. sayaca
E & S Brazil, Paraguay to Uruguay
T. s. glaucocolpa
N Colombia, Venezuela
Thraupis cyanoptera (Azure-shouldered Tanager)
E Paraguay, SE Brazil
Thraupis ornata (Golden-chevroned Tanager)
SE Brazil
Thraupis abbas (Yellow-winged Tanager)
E Mexico to Nicaragua
Thraupis palmarum (Palm Tanager)
T. p. atripennis
E Nicaragua to NW Venezuela
T. p. violilavata
SW Colombia, W Ecuador
T. p. melanoptera
Amazonia, Trinidad
T. p. palmarum
E Bolivia, Paraguay, E & S Brazil

Thraupis cyanocephala (Blue-capped Tanager)
T. c. cyanocephala
W Ecuador to N Bolivia
T. c. annectens
C Colombia
T. c. auricrissa
NC Colombia, W Venezuela
T. c. margaritae
N Colombia
T. c. hypophaea
NW Venezuela
T. c. olivicynanea
N Venezuela
T. c. subcinerea
NE Venezuela
T. c. buesingi
NE Venezuela, Trinidad
Thraupis bonariensis (Blue & Yellow Tanager)
T. b. darwinii
Ecuador to N Chile
T. b. composita
E & C Bolivia
T. b. schulzei
Paraguay, NW Argentina
T. b. bonariensis
S Brazil to EC Argentina

CYANICTERUS
Cyanicterus cyanicterus (Blue-backed Tanager)
E Venezuela, the Guianas

BUTHRAUPIS
Buthraupis arcaei (Arce's Tanager)
B. a. caeruleigularis
E Costa Rica
B. a. arcaei
W Panama
Buthraupis melanochlamys (Black & Gold Tanager)
W Colombia
Buthraupis rothschildi (Golden-chested Tanager)
SW Colombia, NW Ecuador
Buthraupis edwardsi (Moss-backed Tanager)
SW Colombia, NW Ecuador
Buthraupis aureocincta (Gold-ringed Tanager)
W Colombia
Buthraupis montana (Hooded Mountain Tanager)
B. m. gigas
NC Colombia, Venezuela
B. m. cucullata
W Colombia, Ecuador

B. m. cyanonota
N & C Peru

B. m. saturata
SE Peru

B. m. montana
N Bolivia

Buthraupis eximia (Black-chested Mountain Tanager)

B. e. eximia
NC Colombia, SW Venezuela

B. e. zimmeri
WC Colombia

B. e. chloronota
SE Colombia, NW Ecuador

B. e. cyanocalyptra
SC Ecuador

Buthraupis aureodorsalis (Golden-backed Mountain Tanager)
C Peru

Buthraupis wetmorei (Masked Mountain Tanager)
SW Colombia, SC Ecuador

WETMORETHRAUPIS

Wetmorethraupis sterrhopteron (Orange-throated Tanager)
N Peru

ANISOGNATHUS

Anisognathus lacrymosus (Lacrimose Mountain Tanager)

A. l. melanogenys
N Colombia

A. l. pallididorsalis
E Colombia, Venezuela

A. l. melanops
W Venezuela

A. l. tamae
NC Colombia, SW Venezuela

A. l. intensus
SW Colombia

A. l. oliveiceps
W Colombia

A. l. palpebrosus
SW Colombia, E Ecuador

A. l. caerulescens
S Ecuador, N Peru

A. l. lacrymosus
C Peru

Anisognathus igniventris (Scarlet-bellied Mountain Tanager)

A. i. lunulatus
NC Colombia, W Venezuela

A. i. erythrotus
S Colombia, Ecuador

A. i. ignicrissus
NC Peru

A. i. igniventris
SE Peru, Bolivia

Anisognathus flavinuchus (Blue-winged Mountain Tanager) 567

A. f. venezuelanus
N Venezuela

A. f. virididorsalis
Venezuela

A. f. antioquiae
Colombia

A. f. victorini
C Colombia, SW Venezuela

A. f. cyanopterus
SW Colombia, W Ecuador

A. f. baezae
S Colombia, E Ecuador

A. f. alamoris
SW Ecuador

A. f. somptuosus
SE Ecuador, E Peru

A. f. flavinuchus
SE Peru, Bolivia

Anisognathus notabilis (Black-chinned Mountain Tanager)
SW Colombia, NW Ecuador

STEPHANOPHORUS

Stephanophorus diadematus (Diademed Tanager)
SE Brazil, N Argentina

IRIDOSORNIS

Iridosornis porphyrocephala (Purplish-mantled Tanager)
W Colombia, W Ecuador

Iridosornis analis (Yellow-throated Tanager)
E Ecuador, E Peru

Iridosornis jelskii (Golden-collared Tanager)

I. j. jelskii
Peru

I. j. bolivianus
SE Peru, W Bolivia

Iridosornis rufivertex (Golden-crowned Tanager)

I. r. rufivertex
W Venezuela to E Ecuador

I. r. caeruleoventris
NW Colombia

I. r. ignicapillus
SW Colombia

I. r. subsimilis
W Ecuador

Iridosornis reinhardti (Yellow-scarfed Tanager)
E Peru

DUBUSIA

Dubusia taeniata (Buff-breasted Mountain Tanager)
D. t. carrikeri
N Colombia
D. t. taeniata
W Venezuela to Ecuador
D. t. stictocephala
SE Peru

DELOTHRAUPIS
Delothraupis castaneoventris (Chestnut-bellied Mountain Tanager)
D. c. peruviana
E Peru
D. c. castaneoventris
W Bolivia

PIPRAEIDEA
Pipraeidea melanonota (Fawn-breasted Tanager)
P. m. venezuelensis
Venezuela to W Bolivia, N Argentina
P. m. melanonota
Paraguay, SE Brazil to NE Argentina

EUPHONIA
Euphonia jamaica (Jamaican Euphonia)
Jamaica
Euphonia plumbea (Plumbeous Euphonia)
S Venezuela to Surinam, N Brazil
Euphonia affinis (Scrub Euphonia)
E. a. godmani
W Mexico
E. a. affinis
E Mexico to Costa Rica
Euphonia luteicapilla (Yellow-crowned Euphonia)
E Nicaragua to Panama
Euphonia chlorotica (Purple-throated Euphonia)
E. c. cynophora
E Colombia, S Venezuela, N Brazil
E. c. chlorotica
the Guianas, N & NE Brazil
E. c. serrirostris
SE Bolivia to Uruguay, S Brazil
E. c. taczanowskii
E Peru, N Bolivia
E. c. amazonica
C Brazil
Euphonia trinitatis (Trinidad Euphonia)
N Colombia to Trinidad
Euphonia concinna (Velvet-fronted Euphonia)
C Colombia
Euphonia saturata (Orange-crowned Euphonia)
W Colombia to NW Peru

Euphonia finschi (Finsch's Euphonia)
E Venezuela, the Guianas
Euphonia violacea (Violaceous Euphonia)
E. v. rodwayi
E Venezuela, Trinidad
E. v. violacea
the Guianas, N Brazil
E. v. aurantiicollis
SE Brazil, Paraguay
Euphonia laniirostris (Thick-billed Euphonia)
E. l. crassirostris
Costa Rica to N Venezuela
E. l. melanura
Colombia to N Peru, W Brazil
E. l. hypoxantha
E Ecuador, NW Peru
E. l. zopholega
EC Peru
E. l. laniirostris
E Bolivia, SW Brazil
Euphonia hirundinacea (Yellow-throated Euphonia)
E. h. suttoni
E Mexico
E. h. russelli
SE Mexico
E. h. caribbaea
SE Mexico
E. h. hirundinacea
E Mexico to E Nicaragua
E. h. gnatho
NW Nicaragua to W Panama
Euphonia chalybea (Green-throated Euphonia)
SE Brazil, Paraguay
Euphonia musica (Blue-hooded Euphonia)
E. m. rileyi
NW Mexico
E. m. elegantissima
C & S Mexico to Honduras
E. m. vincens
SE Guatemala to Panama
E. m. pelzelni
S Colombia, W Ecuador
E. m. insignis
S Ecuador
E. m. aureata
N South America
E. m. musica
Hispaniola
E. m. sclateri
Puerto Rico
E. m. flavifrons
Lesser Antilles

***Euphonia fulvicrissa* (Fulvous-vented Euphonia)**
E. f. fulvicrissa
Panama, NW Colombia
E. f. omissa
C Colombia
E. f. purpurascens
SW Colombia, NW Ecuador
***Euphonia imitans* (Tawny-billed Euphonia)**
W Costa Rica, W Panama
***Euphonia gouldi* (Olive-backed Euphonia)**
E. g. loetscheri
E Mexico
E. g. gouldi
SE Mexico to Honduras
E. g. praetermissa
E Honduras to Panama
***Euphonia chrysopasta* (Golden-bellied Euphonia)**
E. c. chrysopasta
Western Amazonia
E. c. nitida
E Colombia to French Guiana, N Brazil
***Euphonia mesochrysa* (Bronze-green Euphonia)**
E. m. mesochrysa
C Colombia, E Ecuador
E. m. media
N Peru
E. m. tavarae
SE Peru, C Bolivia
***Euphonia minuta* (White-vented Euphonia)**
E. m. humilis
S Mexico to W Ecuador
E. m. minuta
the Guianas to C Bolivia, W Brazil
***Euphonia anneae* (Tawny-capped Euphonia)**
E. a. anneae
W Costa Rica, W Panama
E. a. rufivertex
W Panama, NW Colombia
***Euphonia xanthogaster* (Orange-bellied Euphonia)**
E. x. chocoensis
E Panama to NW Ecuador
E. x. quitensis
W Ecuador
E. x. dilutior
S Colombia, NE Peru
E. x. cyanonota
W Brazil
E. x. brunneifrons
SE Peru
E. x. ruficeps
W Bolivia
E. x. brevirostris
N & W Amazonia

E. x. exsul
NE Colombia, N Venezuela
E. x. xanthogaster
S & E Brazil
***Euphonia rufiventris* (Rufous-bellied Euphonia)**
Western Amazonia
***Euphonia pectoralis* (Chestnut-bellied Euphonia)**
SE Brazil, Paraguay
***Euphonia cayennensis* (Golden-sided Euphonia)**
SE Venezuela, the Guianas, N Brazil

CHLOROPHONIA
***Chlorophonia flavirostris* (Yellow-collared Chlorophonia)**
C. f. minima
SW Colombia
C. f. flavirostris
Ecuador
***Chlorophonia cyanea* (Blue-naped Chlorophonia)**
C. c. psittacina
N Colombia
C. c. frontalis
N Venezuela
C. c. minuscula
NE Venezuela
C. c. roraimae
S Venezuela, Guyana
C. c. intensa
W Colombia
C. c. longipennis
W Venezuela to W Bolivia
C. c. cyanea
SE Brazil, Paraguay, NE Argentina
***Chlorophonia pyrrhophrys* (Chestnut-breasted Chlorophonia)**
W Venezuela to E Ecuador
***Chlorophonia occipitalis* (Blue-crowned Chlorophonia)**
C. o. occipitalis
SE Mexico to Nicaragua
C. o. callophrys
Costa Rica, W Panama

CHLOROCHRYSA
***Chlorochrysa phoenicotis* (Glistening-green Tanager)**
W Colombia, W Ecuador
***Chlorochrysa calliparaea* (Orange-eared Tanager)**
C. c. bourcierci
Colombia to NE Peru
C. c. calliparaea
EC Peru
C. c. fulgentissima
SE Peru, N Bolivia

***Chlorochrysa nitidissima* (Multicoloured Tanager)**
W Colombia

TANGARA

***Tangara inornata* (Plain-coloured Tanager)**
T. i. rava
Costa Rica, W Panama
T. i. languens
Panama, NW Colombia
T. i. inornata
N Colombia

***Tangara cabanisi* (Azure rumped Tanager)**
S Mexico, SW Guatemala

***Tangara palmeri* (Grey and Gold Tanager)**
E Panama to W Ecuador

***Tangara mexicana* (Turquoise Tanager)**
T. m. vieilloti
Trinidad
T. m. media
S & E Venezuela, NW Brazil
T. m. mexicana
the Guianas
T. m. boliviana
Western Amazonia
T. m. brasiliensis
SE Brazil

***Tangara chilensis* (Paradise Tanager)**
T. c. paradisea
the Guianas, N Brazil
T. c. coelicolor
E Colombia, S Venezuela
NW Brazil
T. c. chlorocorys
NC Peru
T. c. chilensis
Western Amazonia

***Tangara fastuosa* (Seven-coloured Tanager)**
E Brazil

***Tangara seledon* (Green-headed Tanager)**
SE Brazil, Paraguay, N Argentina

***Tangara cyanocephala* (Red-necked Tanager)**
T. c. cearensis
NE Brazil
T. c. corallina
E Brazil
T. c. cyanocephala
SE Brazil, E Paraguay, N Argentina

***Tangara desmaresti* (Brassy-breasted Tanager)**
SE Brazil

***Tangara cyanoventris* (Gilt-edged Tanager)**
SE Brazil

***Tangara johannae* (Blue-whiskered Tanager)**
W Colombia, NW Ecuador

***Tangara schrankii* (Green and Gold Tanager)**
T. s. venezuelana
S Venezuela
T. s. anchicayae
W Colombia
T. s. schrankii
Upper Amazonia

***Tangara florida* (Emerald Tanager)**
T. f. florida
Costa Rica, W Panama
T. f. auriceps
W Colombia, E Panama

***Tangara arthus* (Golden Tanager)**
T. a. arthus
N & E Venezuela
T. a. palmitae
Magdalena (E Colombia)
T. a. sclateri
E Colombia
T. a. aurulenta
C Colombia, NW Venezuela
T. a. occidentalis
W Colombia
T. a. goodsoni
W Ecuador
T. a. aequatorialis
E Ecuador, N Peru
T. a. pulchra
C Peru
T. a. sophiae
SE Peru, W Bolivia

***Tangara icterocephala* (Silver-throated Tanager)**
T. i. frantzii
Costa Rica, W Panama
T. i. oresbia
WC Panama
T. i. icterocephala
E Panama, W Colombia, W Ecuador

***Tangara xanthocephala* (Saffron-crowned Tanager)**
T. x. venusta
W Venezuela to N & C Peru
T. x. xanthocephala
C Peru
T. x. lamprotis
SE Peru

***Tangara chrysotis* (Golden-eared Tanager)**
S Colombia to N Bolivia

***Tangara parzudakii* (Flame-faced Tanager)**
T. p. parzudakii
SW Venezuela to Peru
T. p. urubambae
S Peru
T. p. lunigera
W Colombia, W Ecuador

Tangara xanthogastra (Yellow-bellied
Tanager)
  T. x. xanthogastra
    S Venezuela to N Bolivia
  T. x. phelpsi
    S Venezuela, N Brazil
Tangara punctata (Spotted Tanager)
  T. p. punctata
    S Venezuela, the Guianas, N Brazil
  T. p. zamorae
    E Ecuador, N Peru
  T. p. perenensis
    E Peru
  T. p. annectens
    SE Peru
  T. p. punctulata
    N Bolivia
Tangara guttata (Speckled Tanager)
  T. g. eusticta
    Costa Rica, W Panama
  T. g. tolimae
    Tolima (Colombia)
  T. g. bogotensis
    E Colombia, W Venezuela
  T. g. chrysophrys
    Venezuela, NW Brazil
  T. g. guttata
    SE Venezuela, N Brazil
  T. g. trinitatis
    N Trinidad
Tangara varia (Dotted Tanager)
  S Venezuela, the Guianas, N Brazil
Tangara rufigula (Rufous-throated
Tanager)
  W Colombia, NW Ecuador
Tangara gyrola (Bay-headed Tanager)
  T. g. bangsi
    Costa Rica, W Panama
  T. g. deleticia
    E Panama, W Colombia
  T. g. nupera
    SW Colombia, W Ecuador
  T. g. toddi
    N Colombia, NW Venezuela
  T. g. viridissima
    Trinidad, NE Venezuela
  T. g. catharinae
    E Colombia, to C Bolivia
  T. g. parva
    S Venezuela to NE Peru, NW Brazil
  T. g. gyrola
    S Venezuela, the Guianas, N Brazil
  T. g. albertinae
    C Brazil
Tangara lavinia (Rufous-winged
Tanager)
  T. l. cara
    E Guatemala to Costa Rica

  T. l. dalmasi
    W Panama
  T. l. lavinia
    E Panama to NW Ecuador
Tangara cayana (Burnished Buff Tanager)
  T. c. fulvescens
    C Colombia
  T. c. cayana
    the Guianas to E Peru, N Brazil
  T. c. huberi
    NE Brazil
  T. c. flava
    NE Brazil
  T. c. sincipitalis
    C Brazil
  T. c. chloroptera
    SE Brazil, Paraguay
  T. c. margaritae
    C Brazil
Tangara cucullata (Hooded Tanager)
  T. c. versicolor
    St Vincent I
  T. c. cucullata
    Grenada I
Tangara peruviana (Black-backed Tanager)
  SE Brazil
Tangara preciosa (Chestnut-backed
Tanager)
  Paraguay to Uruguay, SE Brazil
Tangara vitriolina (Scrub Tanager)
  W Colombia, NW Ecuador
Tangara rufigenis (Rufous-cheeked
Tanager)
  N Venezuela
Tangara ruficervix (Golden-naped Tanager)
  T. r. ruficervix
    Colombia
  T. r. leucotis
    W Ecuador
  T. r. taylori
    SE Colombia, E Ecuador
  T. r. amabilis
    N Peru
  T. r. inca
    S Peru
  T. r. fulvicervix
    N Bolivia
Tangara labradorides (Metallic-green
Tanager)
  T. l. labradorides
    W Colombia, W Ecuador
  T. l. chaupensis
    NW Peru
Tangara cyanotis (Blue-browed Tanager)
  T. c. lutleyi
    S Colombia, Ecuador, E Peru
  T. c. cyanotis
    NW Bolivia

Tangara cyanicollis (Blue-necked Tanager)
 T. c. granadensis
  W Colombia
 T. c. caeruleocephala
  C Colombia to N Peru
 T. c. cyanicollis
  E Peru, E Bolivia
 T. c. cyanopygia
  W Ecuador
 T. c. hannahiae
  E Colombia, W Venezuela
 T. c. melanogaster
  C Brazil
 T. c. albotibialis
  Goias (Brazil)

Tangara larvata (Golden-masked Tanager)
 T. l. larvata
  S Mexico to N Costa Rica
 T. l. centralis
  E Costa Rica, W Panama
 T. l. franciscae
  W Costa Rica, W Panama
 T. l. fanny
  E Panama to NW Ecuador

Tangara nigrocincta (Masked Tanager)
 N & W Amazonia

Tangara dowii (Dow Tanager)
 T. d. dowii
  Costa Rica, W Panama
 T. d. fucosa
  E Panama

Tangara nigroviridis (Beryl-spangled Tanager)
 T. n. cyanescens
  NW Venezuela to W Ecuador
 T. n. consobrina
  C Colombia
 T. n. nigroviridis
  E Colombia, E Ecuador
 T. n. berlepschi
  E Peru, Bolivia

Tangara vassorii (Blue and Black Tanager)
 T. v. vassorii
  NW Venezuela to NW Peru
 T. v. branickii
  N Peru
 T. v. atrocoerulea
  S Peru, Bolivia

Tangara heinei (Black-capped Tanager)
 NW Venezuela to E Ecuador

Tangara viridicollis (Silvery Tanager)
 T. v. fulvigula
  S Ecuador, N Peru
 T. v. viridicollis
  C & S Peru

Tangara argyrofenges (Green-throated Tanager)
 T. a. caeruleigularis
  N Peru
 T. a. argyrofenges
  WC Bolivia

Tangara cyanoptera (Black-headed Tanager)
 T. c. whitelyi
  S Venezuela, Guyana
 T. c. cyanoptera
  N Colombia, N & W Venezuela

Tangara pulcherrima (Yellow-collared Tanager)
 T. p. pulcherrima
  Colombia to E Peru
 T. p. aureinucha
  W Ecuador

Tangara velia (Opal-rumped Tanager)
 T. v. velia
  the Guianas, N Brazil
 T. v. iridina
  NW Amazonia
 T. v. signata
  NE Brazil
 T. v. cyanomelaena
  SE Brazil

Tangara callophrys (Opal-crowned Tanager)
 SE Colombia to E Peru, W Brazil

DACNIS

Dacnis albiventris (White-bellied Dacnis)
 S Venezuela to NE Peru

Dacnis lineata (Black-faced Dacnis)
 D. l. egregia
  C Colombia
 D. l. aequatorialis
  W Ecuador
 D. l. lineata
  N & W Amazonia

Dacnis flaviventer (Yellow-bellied Dacnis)
 N & W Amazonia

Dacnis hartlaubi (Turquoise Dacnis)
 W Colombia

Dacnis nigripes (Black-legged Dacnis)
 SE Brazil

Dacnis venusta (Scarlet-thighed Dacnis)
 D. v. venusta
  Costa Rica, W Panama
 D. v. fuliginata
  E Panama to NW Ecuador

Dacnis cayana (Blue Dacnis)
 D. c. callaina
  W Costa Rica, W Panama
 D. c. ultramarina
  E Nicaragua to NW Colombia

D. c. napaea
N Colombia
D. c. baudoana
SW Colombia, W Ecuador
D. c. coerebicolor
C Colombia
D. c. cayana
E Colombia to French Guiana, N & C Brazil
D. c. glaucogularis
S Colombia to N & E Bolivia
D. c. paraguayensis
S & E Brazil, Paraguay, NE Argentina
Dacnis viguieri (Viridian Dacnis)
E Panama, NW Colombia
Dacnis berlepschi (Scarlet-breasted Dacnis)
SW Colombia, NW Ecuador

CHLOROPHANES
Chlorophanes spiza (Green Honeycreeper)
C. s. guatemalensis
S Mexico to Honduras
C. s. arguta
E Honduras to NW Colombia
C. s. exsul
SW Colombia, W Ecuador
C. s. subtropicalis
Colombia, W Venezuela
C. s. spiza
Venezuela, Trinidad, the Guianas, N Brazil
C. s. caerulescens
SE Colombia to Bolivia
C. s. axillaris
E Brazil

CYANERPES
Cyanerpes nitidus (Short-billed Honey-creeper)
C. n. nitidus
NW Amazonia
C. n. caquetae
SW Colombia
Cyanerpes lucidus (Shining Honeycreeper)
C. l. lucidus
S Mexico to N Nicaragua
C. l. isthmicus
Costa Rica to NW Colombia
Cyanerpes caeruleus (Purple Honey-creeper)
C. c. chocoanus
W Colombia, W Ecuador
C. c. caeruleus
Colombia to the Guianas, NE Brazil
C. c. hellmayri
Guyana
C. c. longirostris
Trinidad
C. c. microrhynchus
W & C Amazonia

Cyanerpes cyaneus (Red-legged Honey-creeper) 573
C. c. carneipes
E & S Mexico to N Colombia
C. c. striatipectus
W Chiapas (Mexico)
C. c. gemmeus
N Colombia
C. c. eximius
N Colombia, N Venezuela
C. c. tobagensis
Tobago I
C. c. cyaneus
SE Venezuela, Trinidad, the Guianas, N Brazil
C. c. brevipes
C Brazil
C. c. dispar
S Venezuela to NE Peru, W Brazil
C. c. holti
E Brazil
C. c. violaceus
C Bolivia, W Brazil
C. c. pacificus
W Colombia, W Ecuador
C. c. gigas
Gorgona I (W Colombia)

XENODACNIS
Xenodacnis parina (Tit-like Dacnis)
X. p. bella
N Peru
X. p. petersi
WC Peru
X. p. parina
SC Peru

OREOMANES
Oreomanes fraseri (Giant Conebill)
O. f. fraseri
SW Colombia, Ecuador
O. f. binghami
Peru
O. f. sturninus
W Bolivia

DIGLOSSA
Diglossa baritula (Slaty Flower-piercer)
D. b. baritula
C Mexico
D. b. montana
S Mexico to El Salvador
D. b. parva
E Guatemala, Honduras
D. b. plumbea
Costa Rica, W Panama
D. b. veraguensis
W Panama
D. b. hyperythra
NE Colombia, N Venezuela

D. b. mandeli
NE Venezuela
D. b. coelestis
W Venezuela
D. b. dorbignyi
E Colombia, W Venezuela
D. b. decorata
Ecuador, Peru
D. b. sittoides
Bolivia, NW Argentina
Diglossa lafresnayii (Glossy Flower-piercer)
D. l. gloriosissima
W Colombia
D. l. lafresnayii
W Venezuela to Ecuador, N Peru
D. l. unicincta
N Peru
D. l. pectoralis
C Peru
D. l. albilinea
SE Peru
D. l. mystacalis
W Bolivia
Diglossa carbonaria Coal-black Flower-piercer)
D. c. gloriosa
W Venezuela
D. c. nocticolor
N Colombia, W Venezuela
D. c. humeralis
C Colombia, SW Venezuela
D. c. aterrima
W Colombia, Ecuador, NW Peru
D. c. brunneiventris
NW Colombia to N Chile
D. c. carbonaria
Bolivia
Diglossa venezuelensis (Venezuelan Flowerpiercer)
NE Venezuela
Diglossa albilatera (White-sided Flower-piercer)
D. a. federalis
N Venezuela
D. a. albilatera
W Venezuela to Ecuador
D. a. schistacea
SW Ecuador to NW Peru
D. a. affinis
NC Peru
Diglossa duidae (Scaled Flowerpiercer)
D. d. hitchcocki
S Venezuela
D. d. duidae
S Venezuela, N Brazil

Diglossa major (Greater Flowerpiercer)
D. m. gilliardi
SE Venezuela
D. m. disjuncta
SE Venezuela
D. m. chimantae
SE Venezuela
D. m. major
SE Venezuela, N Brazil
Diglossa indigotica (Indigo Flower-piercer)
SW Colombia, W Ecuador
Diglossa glauca (Deep-blue Flower-piercer)
D. g. tyrianthina
S Colombia, E Ecuador
D. g. glauca
SE Peru, NW Bolivia
Diglossa caerulescens (Bluish Flower-piercer)
D. c. caerulescens
N Venezuela
D. c. ginesi
NW Venezuela
D. c. saturata
SW Venezuela, Colombia
D. c. media
S Ecuador, NW Peru
D. c. pallida
C Peru
D. c. mentalis
SE Peru, NW Bolivia
Diglossa cyanea (Masked Flowerpiercer)
D. c. tovarensis
N Venezuela
D. c. obscura
NW Venezuela
D. c. cyanea
W Venezuela, to Ecuador
D. c. dispar
SW Ecuador, NW Peru
D. c. melanopis
Peru, NW Bolivia

EUNEORNIS
Euneornis campestris (Orangequit)
Jamaica

EMBERIZIDAE

158 TERSININAE (SWALLOW TANAGER)

TERSINA
Tersina viridis (Swallow Tanager)
T. v. grisescens
N Colombia

T. v. occidentalis
  E Panama, Colombia, Venezuela,
    the Guianas, Ecuador, NE Peru,
    N Bolivia, N Brazil
T. v. viridis
  E & S Brazil, E Bolivia, Paraguay,
    NE Argentina

159 PARULIDAE (NEW WORLD WARBLERS)

MNIOTILTA
Mniotilta varia (Black & White Warbler)
  NW, C & SE Canada, C & E USA » Central
    America, West Indies, Venezuela,
    Colombia

VERMIVORA
Vermivora bachmanii (Bachman's Warbler)
  C & SE USA » Cuba
Vermivora chrysoptera (Golden-winged Warbler)
  E USA » Central America, Colombia,
    Venezuela
Vermivora pinus (Blue-winged Warbler)
  E USA » E Mexico, Central America
Vermivora peregrina (Tennessee Warbler)
  NW, C & SE Canada, E USA » S Mexico,
    Colombia, Venezuela
Vermivora celata (Orange-crowned Warbler)
  V. c. celata
    N & NW Canada, S USA » Mexico,
      Guatemala
  V. c. lutescens
    W Canada, W USA » W Mexico
  V. c. orestera
    WC Canada, WC USA » C Mexico
  V. c. sordida
    S California, N Baja California and islands
Vermivora ruficapilla (Nashville Warbler)
  V. r. ridgwayi
    W USA » W Mexico, Guatemala
  V. r. ruficapilla
    S Canada, C & E, USA » Mexico,
      Guatemala
Vermivora virginiae (Virginia's Warbler)
  SW USA » W Mexico
Vermivora crissalis (Colima Warbler)
  S USA » EC Mexico
Vermivora luciae (Lucy's Warbler)
  SW USA » W Mexico
Vermivora gutteralis (Irazu Warbler)
  Costa Rica, W Panama
Vermivora superciliosa (Crescent-chested Warbler)
  V. s. sodalis
    NC Mexico

V. s. mexicana
  E Mexico
V. s. palliata
  SW Mexico
V. s. superciliosa
  S Mexico, Guatemala, W Honduras
V. s. parva
  E Honduras, Nicaragua

PARULA
Parula americana (Parula Warbler)
  SE Canada, E USA, E Mexico » Central
    America, West Indies
Parula pitiayumi (Olive-backed Warbler) (Tropical Parula)
  P. p. graysoni
    Socorro I, Revillagigedo Is
  P. p. insularis
    Tres Marias Is
  P. p. pulchra
    NW Mexico
  P. p. nigrilora
    S Texas, NE Mexico
  P. p. inornata
    S Mexico, E Guatemala, N Honduras
  P. p. speciosa
    S Honduras, Nicaragua, Costa Rica,
      W Panama
  P. p. cirrha
    Coiba I (Panama)
  P. p. nana
    E Panama, NW Colombia
  P. p. elegans
    Colombia, N Venezuela, N Brazil, Trinidad
  P. p. roraimae
    S Venezuela, N Brazil
  P. p. alarum
    E Ecuador, N Peru
  P. p. pacifica
    SW Colombia, W Ecuador, NW Peru
  P. p. melanogenys
    S Peru, W Bolivia
  P. p. pitiayumi
    E Bolivia, C & S Brazil, Uruguay, Paraguay,
      N Argentina

DENDROICA
Dendroica petechia (Yellow Warbler)
  D. p. amnicola
    Canada » Mexico, Central America,
      N South America
  D. p. rubiginosa
    W Canada » Mexico, Central America
  D. p. aestiva
    S Canada, C USA » Central America,
      N South America
  D. p. morcomi
    W USA » Central America, N South
      America

D. p. sonorana
  SW USA » Central America, Colombia,
  Ecuador
D. p. brewsteri
  Baja California
D. p. hueyi
  C Baja, California
D. p. inedita
  NE Mexico
D. p. dugesi
  C Mexico
D. p. rufivertex
  Cozumel I
D. p. flavida
  St Andrew I
D. p. armouri
  Old Providence I
D. p. eoa
  Jamaica, Cayman Is
D. p. gundlachi
  Cuba, Bahama Is
D. p. albicollis
  Hispaniola
D. p. cruciana
  Puerto Rica, Virgin Is
D. p. bartholemica
  N Lesser Antilles
D. p. melanoptera
  C Lesser Antilles
D. p. ruficapilla
  Martinique I
D. p. babad
  St Lucia I
D. p. petechia
  Barbados I
D. p. alsiosa
  Grenadine Is
D. p. rufopileata
  Curaçao I, Bonaire I
D. p. obscura
  Los Roques I
D. p. chrysendeta
  NE Colombia, NW Venezuela
D. p. paraguanae
  NW Venezuela
D. p. cienagae
  NC Venezuela
D. p. aurifrons
  NC Venezuela and islands
D. p. castaneiceps
  S Baja California
D. p. rhizophorae
  NW Mexico
D. p. oraria
  E Mexico
D. p. bryanti
  Caribbean, SE Mexico to Costa Rica

D. p. xanthotera
  Pacific, W Guatemala to Costa Rica
D. p. aureola
  Cocos Is, Galapagos Is
D. p. aequatorialis
  Pearl Archipelago (Panama)
D. p. erithachorides
  E Panama, N Colombia
D. p. peruviana
  SW Colombia, W Ecuador, N Peru
Dendroica pensylvanica (Chestnut-sided Warbler)
  S Canada, E USA » Central America
Dendroica cerulea (Cerulean Warbler)
  Venezuela, Ecuador, Peru, Bolivia
  E USA » Colombia
Dendroica caerulescens (Black-throated Blue Warbler)
D. c. caerulescens
  SE Canada, NE USA » Bahama Is,
  Gtr Antilles
D. c. cairnsi
  EC USA » Gtr Antilles
Dendroica plumbea (Plumbeous Warbler)
  Dominica I, Guadeloupe I
Dendroica pharetra (Arrow-headed Warbler)
  Jamaica
Dendroica angelae (Puerto Rico Warbler)
  Puerto Rico
Dendroica pinus (Pine Warbler)
D. p. pinus
  SE Canada » SE USA
D. p. florida
  S Florida
D. p. achrustera
  Bahama Is
D. p. chrysoleuca
  Hispaniola
Dendroica graciae (Grace's Warbler)
D. g. graciae
  SW USA » W Mexico
D. g. yaegeri
  W Mexico
D. g. remota
  S Mexico, Guatemala, El Salvador,
  W Honduras
D. g. decora
  Belize, E Honduras, Nicaragua
Dendroica adelaidae (Adelaide's Warbler)
D. a. adelaidae
  Puerto Rico
D. a. subita
  Barbuda I
D. a. delicata
  St Lucia I

Dendroica pityophila (Olive-capped Warbler)
Cuba, Bahama Is
Dendroica dominica (Yellow-throated Warbler)
D. d. albilora
EC & SE USA » E Mexico, Central America, Cuba, Jamaica
D. d. dominica
E & SE USA » Gtr Antilles
D. d. stoddardi
SE USA
D. d. flavescens
Bahama Is
Dendroica nigrescens (Black-throated Grey Warbler)
D. n. nigrescens
SW Canada, W USA » N Mexico, Guatemala
D. n. halseii
SW USA, NW Mexico, N Baja California
Dendroica townsendi (Townsend's Warbler)
W Canada, W USA » Mexico, Guatemala, Honduras, Nicaragua
Dendroica occidentalis (Hermit Warbler)
SW USA » W Mexico, Guatemala, Honduras, Nicaragua
Dendroica chrysopareia (Golden-cheeked Warbler)
S USA » Mexico, Guatemala, Honduras, Nicaragua
Dendroica virens (Black-throated Green Warbler)
C & SE Canada, E USA » Mexico, Central America, West Indies
Dendroica discolor (Prairie Warbler)
D. d. discolor
E USA, West Indies
D. d. paludicola
SE USA » Gtr Antilles
Dendroica vitellina (Vitelline Warbler)
D. v. crawfordi
Little Cayman I
D. v. vitellina
Grand Cayman I
D. v. nelsoni
Swan I
Dendroica tigrina (Cape May Warbler)
C & SE Canada, NC & E USA » West Indies, E Central America
Dendroica fusca (Blackburnian Warbler)
SE Canada, E USA » Central America, Venezuela, Colombia, Ecuador, Peru
Dendroica magnolia (Magnolia Warbler)
S Canada, E USA » Mexico, Central America, Gtr Antilles

Dendroica coronata (Yellow-rumped Warbler)
D. c. coronata
Canada, C & E USA » Central America, West Indies
D. c. auduboni
SW Canada, W USA » Mexico, Guatemala, W Honduras
D. c. nigrifrons
NC Mexico
D. c. goldmani
W Guatemala
D. c. hooveri
SW USA, NW Mexico
Dendroica palmarum (Palm Warbler)
D. p. palmarum
C & E Canada, E USA » Gtr Antilles, Central America
D. p. hypochrysea
SE Canada, NE USA » SE USA
Dendroica kirtlandii (Kirtland's Warbler)
C Michigan » Bahama Is
Dendroica striata (Blackpoll Warbler)
Canada, C & E USA » West Indies, N & C South America
Dendroica castanea (Bay-breasted Warbler)
C & SE Canada, E USA » Central America, Colombia, Venezuela

CATHAROPEZA
Catharopeza bishopi (Whistling Warbler)
St Vincent I

SETOPHAGA
Setophaga ruticilla (American Redstart)
S Canada, C & E USA » Mexico, Central America, West Indies, N South America

SEIURUS
Seiurus aurocapillus (Ovenbird)
S. a. aurocapillus
C & SE Canada, E USA » W Indies, Mexico to Colombia and Venezuela
S. a. cinereus
WC USA » S Mexico, El Salvador, Honduras, Costa Rica
S. a. furvior
Newfoundland » Bahamas, Cuba, E Central America
Seiurus noveboracensis (Northern Water-thrush)
S. n. noveboracensis
Canada, E USA » West Indies, Central America, N South America
S. n. limnaeus
W USA, NW Mexico
S. n. notabilis
SW USA, W Mexico

Seiurus motacilla **(Louisiana Water-
thrush)**
 E USA » Mexico, West Indies, Central
 America, Colombia, Venezuela

LIMNOTHLYPIS
Limnothlypis swainsonii **(Swainson's
Warbler)**
 SE USA » E Mexico, West Indies

HELMITHEROS
Helmitheros vermivorus **(Worm-eating
Warbler)**
 E USA » E Central America, West Indies

PROTONOTARIA
Protonotaria citrea **(Prothonotary
Warbler)**
 E USA » Central America, West Indies,
 N South America

GEOTHLYPIS
Geothlypis trichas **(Yellowthroat)**
 G. t. trichas
  SE Canada, EC USA » Mexico, West
  Indies, Central America, Colombia,
  Venezuela
 G. t. typhicola
  SC USA, NE Mexico
 G. t. ignota
  SE USA
 G. t. insperata
  S Texas
 G. t. campicola
  W Canada, NW USA, SW USA » N Mexico
 G. t. arizela
  W Canada, W USA & NW Mexico
 G. t. occidentalis
  WC USA » Mexico to Honduras
 G. t. sinuosa
  N California
 G. t. scirpicola
  S California, N Baja California
 G. t. chryseola
  W Texas, NW Mexico
 G. t. modesta
  W Sonora, Mexico
 G. t. melanops
  C Mexico
 G. t. chapalensis
  Jalisco
 G. t. riparia
  S Sonora
 G. t. brachydactyla
  E USA, E & S Mexico
Geothlypis beldingi **(Peninsular Yellow-
throat)**
 G. b. goldmani
  C Baja California
 G. b. beldingi
  S Baja California

Geothlypis flavovelata **(Yellow-crowned
Yellowthroat)**
 E Mexico
Geothlypis rostrata **(Bahama
Yellowthroat)**
 G. r. tanneri
  N Bahama Is
 G. r. rostrata
  W Bahama Is
 G. r. coryi
  Eleuthera I, Cat I
Geothlypis semiflava **(Olive-crowned
Yellowthroat)**
 G. s. bairdi
  S Honduras, Nicaragua, Costa Rica,
  NW Panama
 G. s. semiflava
  W Colombia, W Ecuador
Geothlypis speciosa **(Black-polled
Yellowthroat)**
 G. s. speciosa
  C Mexico
 G. s. limnatis
  Guanajuata (Mexico)
Geothlypis nelsoni **(Hooded Yellowthroat)**
 G. n. nelsoni
  E Mexico
 G. n. karlenae
  SW Mexico
Geothlypis chiriquensis **(Chiriqui
Yellowthroat)**
 W Panama
Geothlypis aequinoctialis **(Masked
Yellowthroat)**
 G. a. aequinoctialis
  NE Colombia, Venezuela, the Guianas,
  Surinam, N Brazil
 G. a. auricularis
  W Ecuador, W Peru
 G. a. peruviana
  N Peru
 G. a. velata
  S Peru, Bolivia, Brazil, Paraguay, Uruguay,
  N Argentina
Geothlypis poliocephala **(Grey-crowned
Yellowthroat)**
 G. p. poliocephala
  N & W Mexico
 G. p. ralphi
  NE Mexico
 G. p. palpebralis
  E & S Mexico, Guatemala, Honduras,
  Nicaragua, Costa Rica
 G. p. caninucha
  SW Mexico, W Guatemala, S Honduras,
  El Salvador
 G. p. icterotis
  W Nicaragua, W Costa Rica

G. p. pontilis
W Mexico
G. p. ridgwayi
SW Costa Rica, W Panama
Geothlypis formosa (Kentucky Warbler)
SE USA » E Mexico, Central America,
Colombia, Venezuela
Geothlypis agilis (Connecticut Warbler)
EC Canada, NC USA » Venezuela,
NE Brazil, Colombia
**Geothlypis philadelphia (Mourning
Warbler)**
C & E Canada, NE USA » Nicaragua, Costa
Rica, Colombia, Venezuela
Geothlypis tolmei (MacGillivray's Warbler)
SW Canada, W USA » Central America

MICROLIGEA
**Microligea palustris (Green-tailed Ground
Warbler)**
M. p. palustris
Hispaniola
M. p. vasta
SW Dominica I

XENOLIGEA
**Xenoligea montana (White-winged Ground
Warbler)**
Hispaniola

TERETISTRIS
**Teretistris fernandinae (Yellow-headed
Warbler)**
W Cuba
Teretistris fornsi (Oriente Warbler)
E Cuba

LEUCOPEZA
Leucopeza semperi (Semper's Warbler)
St Lucia I

WILSONIA
Wilsonia citrina (Hooded Warbler)
E USA » E Mexico, Central America
Wilsonia pusilla (Wilson's Warbler)
W. p. pileolata
W Canada, WC USA » C Mexico,
Central America
W. p. chryseola
SW USA » W & S Mexico, Guatemala,
W. p. pusilla
S & E Canada, NE USA » E Mexico,
Central America
Wilsonia canadensis (Canada Warbler)
SE Canada, NE USA » Central America,
N South America

CARDELLINA
Cardellina rubifrons (Red-faced Warbler)
SW USA » W & S Mexico, Guatemala,
W Honduras

ERGATICUS
Ergaticus ruber (Red Warbler)
E. r. melanauris
NW Mexico
E. r. ruber
W & S Mexico
E. r. rowleyi
Oaxaca (Mexico)
**Ergaticus versicolor (Pink-headed
Warbler)**
S Mexico, W Guatemala

MYIOBORUS
Myioborus pictus (Painted Redstart)
M. p. pictus
SW USA, N Mexico
M. p. guatemalae
S Mexico to N Nicaragua
**Myioborus miniatus (Slate-throated
Redstart)**
M. m. miniatus
W & SW Mexico
M. m. molochinus
E Mexico
M. m. intermedius
S Mexico, E Guatemala
M. m. hellmayri
W Guatemala, El Salvador
M. m. connectens
El Salvador, Honduras
M. m. comptus
W Costa Rica
M. m. aurantiacus
E Costa Rica, W Panama
M. m. ballux
E Panama, Colombia, W Venezuela,
NW Ecuador
M. m. sanctaemartae
N Colombia
M. m. pallidiventris
N Venezuela
M. m. subsimilis
SW Ecuador, NW Peru
M. m. verticalis
SE Ecuador, Peru, Bolivia,
SE Venezuela, Guyana, NW Brazil
**Myioborus brunniceps (Brown-capped
Redstart)**
M. b. castaneocapillus
SE Venezuela, W Guyana, N Brazil
M. b. duidae
SE Venezuela
M. b. maguirei
SE Venezuela
M. b. brunniceps
Bolivia, N Argentina
**Myioborus pariae (Yellow-faced
Redstart)**
NE Venezuela

Myioborus cardonai (Saffron-breasted Redstart)
SE Venezuela
Myioborus torquatus (Collared Redstart)
Costa Rica, W Panama
Myioborus ornatus (Golden-fronted Redstart)
M. o. ornatus
E Colombia, SW Venezuela
M. o. chrysops
W Colombia
Myioborus melanocephalus (Spectacled Redstart)
M. m. ruficoronatus
SW Colombia, S Ecuador
M. m. griseonuchus
NW Peru
M. m. malaris
N Peru
M. m. melanocephalus
E Peru
M. m. bolivianus
S Peru, W Bolivia
Myioborus albifrons (White-fronted Redstart)
W Venezuela
Myioborus flavivertex (Yellow-crowned Redstart)
N Colombia
Myioborus albifacies (White-faced Redstart)
S Venezuela

EUTHLYPIS
Euthlypis lachrymosa (Fan-tailed Warbler)
E. l. tephra
W Mexico
E. l. schistacea
W Chiapas
E. l. lachrymosa
S Mexico to N Nicaragua

BASILEUTERUS
Basileuterus fraseri (Grey & Gold Warbler)
B. f. ochraceicrista
W Ecuador
B. f. fraseri
C Ecuador, NW Peru
Basileuterus bivittatus (Two-banded Warbler)
B. b. roraimae
Guyana, SE Venezuela, N Brazil
B. b. bivittatus
SE Peru, W Bolivia
B. b. argentinae
SE Bolivia, NW Argentina

Basileuterus chrysogaster (Golden-bellied Warbler)
B. c. chlorophrys
SW Colombia, NW Ecuador
B. c. chrysogaster
E Peru
Basileuterus flaveolus (Flavescent Warbler)
Colombia, Venezuela, Brazil, Peru, Bolivia
Basileuterus luteoviridis (Citrine Warbler)
E. l. luteoviridis
SW Venezuela, E Colombia, E Ecuador
B. l. quindianus
C Colombia
B. l. richardsoni
W Colombia
B. l. striaticeps
N Peru
B. l. euophrys
SW Peru, W Bolivia
Basileuterus signatus (Pale-legged Warbler)
B. s. signatus
C Peru
B. s. flavovirens
SE Peru, W Bolivia, NW Argentina
Basileuterus nigrocristatus (Black-crested Warbler)
Venezuela, Colombia, Ecuador
Basileuterus griseiceps (Grey-headed Warbler)
NE Venezuela
Basileuterus basilicus (Santa Marta Warbler)
NE Colombia
Basileuterus cinereicollis (Grey-throated Warbler)
B. c. pallidulus
W Venezuela, NE Colombia
B. c. cinereicollis
E Colombia
Basileuterus coronatus (Russet-crowned Warbler)
B. c. conspicillatus
N Colombia
B. c. regulus
Venezuela, Colombia
B. c. elatus
SW Colombia, W Ecuador
B. c. orientalis
E Ecuador
B. c. castaneiceps
SW Ecuador, NW Peru
B. c. chapmani
NW Peru
B. c. inaequalis
N Peru
B. c. coronatus
SE Peru, W Bolivia

B. c. notius
C Bolivia

Basileuterus culicivorus (Golden-crowned Warbler)

B. c. flavescens
W Mexico

B. c. brasherii
E Mexico

B. c. culicivorus
S Mexico to Costa Rica

B. c. godmani
S Costa Rica, W Panama

B. c. occultus
W Colombia

B. c. austerus
C Colombia

B. c. indignus
N Colombia

B. c. cabanisi
NW Venezuela, NE Colombia

B. c. olivascens
Venezuela, Colombia, Trinidad

B. c. segrex
SE Venezuela, W Guyana, N Brazil

B. c. auricapillus
C Brazil

B. c. azarae
S Brazil, Paraguay, Uruguay, NE Argentina

B. c. viridescens
E Bolivia

Basileuterus rufifrons (Rufous-capped Warbler)

B. r. caudatus
NW Mexico

B. r. dugesi
W & C Mexico

B. r. jouyi
E Mexico

B. r. rufifrons
S Mexico, N Guatemala

B. r. salvini
SW Mexico, N Guatemala

B. r. delattrii
W Guatemala to N Costa Rica

B. r. mesochrysus
S Costa Rica, Panama, N Colombia, W Venezuela

B. r. actuosus
Coiba I (Panama)

Basileuterus belli (Golden-browed Warbler)

B. b. bateli
W Mexico

B. b. belli
C & E Mexico

B. b. clarus
SW Mexico

B. b. scitulus
SE Mexico, Guatemala, W Honduras

B. b. subobscurus
C Honduras

Basileuterus melanogenys (Black-cheeked Warbler)

B. m. melanogenys
Costa Rica

B. m. eximus
Panama

B. m. bensoni
Panama

B. m. ignotus
Panama

Basileuterus tristriatus (Three-striped Warbler)

B. t. chitrensis
W Panama

B. t. tacarcunae
E Panama, NW Colombia

B. t. daedalus
W Colombia, W Ecuador

B. t. auricularis
E Colombia, SW Venezuela

B. t. meridanus
W Venezuela

B. t. bessereri
N Venezuela

B. t. pariae
NE Venezuela

B. t. baezae
E Ecuador

B. t. tristriatus
SE Ecuador, C Peru

B. t. inconspicuus
SE Peru, NW Bolivia

B. t. punctipectus
C Bolivia

B. t. canens
E Bolivia

Basileuterus trifasciatus (Three-banded Warbler)

B. t. nitidior
SW Ecuador, NW Peru

B. t. trifasciatus
NW Peru

Basileuterus hypoleucus (White-bellied Warbler)
C Brazil, E Paraguay

Basileuterus leucoblepharus (White-browed Warbler)

B. l. leucoblepharus
S Brazil to NE Argentina

B. l. lemurum
Uruguay

Basileuterus leucophrys (White-striped Warbler)
SC Brazil

Basileuterus rivularis (River Warbler)
  B. r. leucopygia
    Honduras to W Panama
  B. r. veraguensis
    SW Costa Rica, C Panama
  B. r. semicervina
    E Panama to NW Peru
  B. r. motacilla
    N Colombia
  B. r. fulvicauda
    E Colombia, E Ecuador, NE Peru, W Brazil
  B. r. significans
    SE Peru
  B. r. mesoleuca
    E Venezuela, the Guianas, N Brazil
  B. r. rivularis
    SE Brazil, E Paraguay, NE Argentina
  B. r. boliviana
    E Bolivia

ZELEDONIA
Zeledonia coronata (Wren-Thrush)
  Costa Rica, W Panama

PEUCEDRAMUS
Peucedramus taeniatus (Olive Warbler)
  P. t. arizonae
    SW USA, N Mexico
  P. t. jaliscensis
    NW Mexico
  P. t. giraudi
    C Mexico
  P. t. aurantiacus
    Chiapas (S Mexico)
  P. t. taeniatus
    S Mexico, W Guatemala
  P. t. micrus
    El Salvador, Honduras, N Nicaragua

GRANATELLUS
Granatellus venustus (Red-breasted Chat)
  G. v. francescae
    Tres Marias Is
  G. v. venustus
    W & SW Mexico
  G. v. melanotis
    W coast of Mexico
Granatellus sallaei (Grey-throated Chat)
  G. s. sallaei
    E Mexico
  G. s. boucardi
    SE Mexico, E Guatemala, Belize
Granatellus pelzelni (Rose-breasted Chat)
  G. p. pelzelni
    SE Venezuela, Guyana, Surinam,
     NW Brazil
  G. p. paraensis
    N Brazil

ICTERIA
Icteria virens (Yellow-breasted Chat)
  I. v. auricollis
    SW Canada, W USA » W Mexico,
     Guatemala
  I. v. virens
    E USA » E Mexico, Central America
  I. v. tropicalis
    S Sonora (Mexico)

CONIROSTRUM
Conirostrum speciosum (Chestnut-vented Conebill)
  C. s. guaricola
    C Venezuela
  C. s. amazonum
    the Guianas to Ecuador » N Peru
  C. s. speciosum
    SE Peru & Bolivia to N Argentina
Conirostrum leucogenys (White-eared Conebill)
  C. l. panamense
    E Panama, NW Colombia
  C. l. leucogenys
    N Colombia, NE Venezuela
  C. l. cyanochrous
    W Venezuela
Conirostrum bicolor (Bicoloured Conebill)
  C. b. bicolor
    N Colombia to the Guianas, N Brazil
  C. b. minor
    W Brazil, E Ecuador, E Peru
Conirostrum margaritae (Pearly-breasted Conebill)
  N Brazil, NE Peru
Conirostrum cinereum (Cinereous Conebill)
  C. c. fraseri
    SW Colombia, E Ecuador
  C. c. littorale
    W Peru, N Chile
  C. c. cinereum
    SE Peru, W Bolivia
Conirostrum tamarugensis (Tamarugo Conebill)
  SC Peru, N Bolivia
Conirostrum ferrugineiventre (White-browed Conebill)
  S Peru, W Bolivia
Conirostrum rufum (Rufous-browed Conebill)
  N Colombia
Conirostrum sitticolor (Blue-backed Conebill)
  C. s. intermedium
    W Venezuela
  C. s. sitticolor
    S Colombia, Ecuador, NW Peru

C. s. cyaneum
    Peru, W Bolivia
Conirostrum albifrons (Capped Conebill)
  C. a. cyanonotum
    N Venezuela
  C. a. albifrons
    W Venezuela, E Colombia
  C. a. centralandium
    C Colombia
  C. a. atrocyaneum
    SW Colombia, Ecuador, N Peru
  C. a. sordidum
    S Peru, W Bolivia
  C. a. lugens
    E Bolivia

COEREBA
Coereba flaveola (Bananaquit)
  C. f. mexicana
    SE Mexico, Central America
  C. f. cerinoclunis
    Pearl Archipelago (Panama)
  C. f. columbiana
    E Panama, C Colombia, SC Venezuela
  C. f. gorgonae
    Gorgona I, W Colombia
  C. f. caucae
    W Colombia
  C. f. intermedia
    SW Venezuela to Ecuador, W Brazil
  C. f. magnirostris
    N Peru
  C. f. pacifica
    NW Peru
  C. f. dispar
    SE Peru, NW Bolivia
  C. f. caboti
    Cozumel I, Holbox I
  C. f. tricolor
    Old Providence I
  C. f. oblita
    St Andrew I
  C. f. sharpei
    Cayman Is
  C. f. bahamensis
    Bahama Is
  C. f. flaveola
    Jamaica
  C. f. bananivora
    Hispaniola
  C. f. nectarea
    Tortue I, Haiti
  C. f. portoricensis
    Puerto Rico
  C. f. sanctithomae
    Virgin Is
  C. f. newtoni
    St Croix I

C. f. bartholemica
    N Lesser Antilles
C. f. martinicana
    Martinique I, St Lucia I
C. f. barbadensis
    Barbados I
C. f. atrata
    St Vincent I
C. f. aterrima
    Grenada I
C. f. uropygialis
    Aruba I, Curaçao I
C. f. bonairensis
    Bonaire I
C. f. melanornis
    Cayo Sal I
C. f. lowii
    Los Roques I
C. f. ferryi
    La Tortuga I
C. f. frailensis
    Los Frailes I, Los Hermanos I
C. f. laurae
    Los Testigos I
C. f. luteola
    N Colombia to Trinidad & Tobago I
C. f. obscura
    NE Colombia, W Venezuela
C. f. montana
    W Venezuela
C. f. bolivari
    E Venezuela
C. f. guianensis
    E Venezuela, Guyana
C. f. roraimae
    SE Venezuela, NW Brazil, SW Guyana
C. f. minima
    N Brazil, French Guiana, Surinam
C. f. chloropyga
    S Peru, Bolivia to NE Argentina
C. f. alleni
    C Brazil, E Bolivia

160 DREPANIDIDAE (HAWAIIAN HONEY-CREEPERS)

PSITTIROSTRINAE

LOXOPS
Loxops virens (Amakihi)
  L. v. stejnegeri
    Kauai I
  L. v. chloris
    Oahu I
  L. v. wilsoni
    Maui I, Molokai I
  L. v. virens
    Hawaii I

***Loxops parva* (Lesser Amakihi)**
Kauai I
***Loxops maculata* (Hawaiian Creeper)**
L. m. bairdi
Kauai I
L. m. maculata
Oahu I
L. m. flammea
Molokai I **e?**
L. m. montana
Lanai I **e?**
L. m. newtoni
Maui I
L. m. mana
Hawaii I
***Loxops coccinea* (Akepa)**
L. c. coccinea
Hawaii I
L. c. caerulirostris
Kauai I
L. c. ochracea
Maui I

MELAMPROSOPS
***Melamprosops phaeosoma* (Po'o uli)**
Maui I

HEMIGNATHUS
***Hemignathus obscurus* (Akialoa) e?**
Hawaii I
***Hemignathus procerus* (Kauai Akialoa)**
Kauai I
***Hemignathus lucidus* (Nukupuu) e?**
H. l. affinis
Maui I
H. l. hanepepe
Kauai I
***Hemignathus wilsoni* (Akiapolaau)**
Hawaii I

PSEUDONESTOR
***Pseudonestor xanthoprys* (Maui Parrotbill)**
Maui I

PSITTIROSTRA
***Psittirostra psittacea* (Ou)**
Maui I, Hawaii I
***Psittirostra cantans* (Yellow Laysan Finch)**
P. c. cantans
Laysan I
P. c. ultima
Nihoa I
***Psittirostra bailleui* (Palila)**
Hawaii I

DREPANIDINAE

HIMATIONE
***Himatione sanguinea* (Apapane)**
All main Hawaiian Is

PALMERIA
***Palmeria dolei* (Crested Honeycreeper)**
Maui I

VESTIARIA
***Vestiaria coccinea* (Iiwi)**
Molokai I, Oahu I, Kauai I, Maui I, Hawaii I

161 VIREONIDAE (VIREOS)

CYCLARHINAE

CYCLARHIS
***Cyclarhis gujanensis* (Rufous-browed Pepper Shrike)**
C. g. flaviventris
C Mexico, E Guatemala, N Honduras
C. g. yucatanensis
SE Mexico
C. g. insularis
Cozumel I
C. g. nicaraguae
S Mexico, Guatemala, El Salvador, Honduras, Nicaragua
C. g. subflavescens
Costa Rica, W Panama
C. g. perrygoi
WC Panama
C. g. flavens
E Panama
C. g. coibae
Coiba I (Panama)
C. g. canticus
N & E Colombia
C. g. flavipectus
NE Venezuela, Trinidad
C. g. parvus
E Colombia, N Venezuela
C. g. gujanensis
E Colombia, S Venezuela, the Guianas Brazil, E Peru, NW Bolivia
C. g. cearensis
E Brazil
C. g. ochrocephala
SE Brazil, Paraguay, Uruguay, NE Argentina
C. g. viridis
Paraguay, N Argentina
C. g. virenticeps
Ecuador, NW Peru
C. g. contrerasi
N Peru
C. g. saturatus
C Peru
C. g. pax
EC Bolivia
C. g. dorsalis
C Bolivia
C. g. tarijae
SE Bolivia, NW Argentina

Cyclarhis nigrirostris (Black-billed Pepper Shrike)
  C. n. nigrirostris
    C Colombia, E Ecuador
  C. n. atrirostris
    SW Colombia, W Ecuador

VIREOLANIINAE

VIREOLANIUS
Vireolanius melitophrys (Chestnut-sided Shrike Vireo)
  V. m. goldmani
    SC Mexico
  V. m. melitophrys
    S Mexico, W Guatemala
Vireolanius pulchellus (Green Shrike Vireo)
  V. p. pulchellus
    SE Mexico to Honduras
  V. p. verticalis
    Nicaragua, Costa Rica
  V. p. viridiceps
    W Costa Rica, W Panama
  V. p. mutabilis
    E Panama, NW Colombia
  V. p. eximius
    N Colombia, NW Venezuela
Vireolanius leucotis (Slaty-capped Shrike Vireo)
  V. l. mikettae
    W Colombia, NW Ecuador
  V. l. leucotis
    N & W Amazonia
  V. l. simplex
    N Brazil, S Peru
  V. l. bolivianus
    SE Peru, N Bolivia

VIREONINAE

VIREO
Vireo brevipennis (Slaty Vireo)
  V. b. browni
    Guerrero
  V. b. brevipennis
    S Mexico
Vireo huttoni (Hutton's Vireo)
  V. h. insularis
    Vancouver I
  V. h. huttoni
    SW Canada, W USA, N Baja California
  V. h. cognatus
    S Baja California
  V. h. stephensi
    SW USA, NW Mexico
  V. h. carolinae
    S USA, NE Mexico
  V. h. pacificus
    W & SW Mexico

  V. h. mexicanus
    C & S Mexico
  V. h. vulcani
    S Mexico, W Guatemala
Vireo atricapillus (Black-capped Vireo)
  C & S USA » N & W Mexico
Vireo griseus (White-eyed Vireo)
  V. g. noveboracensis
    C & E USA » E Mexico, Guatemala, Cuba
  V. g. griseus
    SE USA » E Mexico, N Honduras, W Cuba
  V. g. maynardi
    S Florida
  V. g. bermudianus
    Bermuda I
  V. g. micrus
    S Texas, E Mexico
  V. g. perquisitor
    EC Mexico
Vireo pallens (Pale Vireo)
  V. p. paluster
    NW Mexico
  V. p. ochraceus
    W Guatemala, W El Salvador
  V. p. pallens
    W Honduras, W Nicaragua, W Costa Rica
  V. p. semiflavus
    E Mexico, E Guatemala, E Honduras, Nicaragua
Vireo caribaeus (St Andrew Vireo)
  St Andrew I
Vireo bairdi (Cozumel Vireo)
  Cozumel I
Vireo gundlachii (Cuban Vireo)
  V. g. magnus
    W Cuba
  V. g. sanfelipensis
    W Cuba
  V. g. gundlachii
    C & E Cuba
Vireo crassirostris (Thick-billed Vireo)
  V. c. crassirostris
    Bahama Is
  V. c. tortugae
    Tortue I, Haiti
  V. c. approximans
    Old Providence I, St Catalina I
Vireo vicinior (Grey Vireo)
  SW USA » NW Mexico
Vireo bellii (Bell's Vireo)
  V. b. pusillus
    S California » S Baja California
  V. b. arizonae
    SW USA » NW Mexico
  V. b. medius
    S USA » NC Mexico

V. b. bellii
C & S USA » Mexico, Guatemala,
El Salvador, Honduras, N Nicaragua
Vireo nelsoni (Dwarf Vireo)
S Mexico
Vireo hypochryseus (Golden Vireo)
V. h. nitidus
S Sonora, Mexico
V. h. hypochryseus
W & SW Mexico
V. h. sordidus
Tres Marias Is
**Vireo modestus (Jamaican White-eyed
Vireo)**
Jamaica
Vireo nanus (Flat-billed Vireo)
Hispaniola
Vireo latimeri (Puerto Rican Vireo)
W Puerto Rico
Vireo osburni (Blue Mountain Vireo)
Jamaica
Vireo carmioli (Carmiol's Vireo)
Costa Rica, W Panama
Vireo solitarius (Solitary Vireo)
V. s. solitarius
Canada, NC & E USA » E Mexico, Central
America, W Cuba
V. s. alticola
EC USA » SE USA
V. s. plumbeus
WC USA » NW Mexico
V. s. cassinii
W USA » Mexico, Guatemala
V. s. lucasanus
S Baja California
V. s. pinicolus
N Mexico
V. s. repetens
C Mexico
V. s. notius
Belize
V. s. montanus
S Mexico, Guatemala, Honduras,
El Salvador
Vireo flavifrons (Yellow-throated Vireo)
S Canada, E & C USA » Colombia,
Venezuela, Central America
Vireo philadelphicus (Philadelphia Vireo)
W Canada, N USA » Mexico, Central
America, Colombia
Vireo olivaceus (Red-eyed Vireo)
V. o. olivaceus
Canada, WC & E USA » Cuba, C South
America
V. o. forreri
Tres Marias Is, N Mexico » Upper
Amazonia

V. o. hypoleucus
NW Mexico
V. o. flavoviridis
S Mexico, Central America » Upper
Amazonia
V. o. insulanus
Pearl Is (Panama)
V. o. caucae
W Colombia
V. o. griseobarbatus
W Ecuador, NW Peru
V. o. pectoralis
N Peru
V. o. solimoensis
E Ecuador, NE Peru
V. o. vividior
Colombia, Venezuela, the Guianas,
N Brazil, Trinidad
V. o. tobagensis
Tobago I
V. o. agilis
NE Brazil
V. o. gracilirostris
Fernando de Noronha I
V. o. diversus
SE Brazil, E Paraguay
V. o. chivi
W & SW Amazonia
Vireo magister (Yucatan Vireo)
V. m. magister
SE Mexico, Belize
V. m. caymanensis
Grand Cayman I
Vireo altiloquus (Black-whiskered Vireo)
V. a. barbatulus
S Florida, Cuba, Haiti » Colombia,
Venezuela, Brazil, Peru
V. a. altiloquus
Gtr Antilles » N South America
V. a. barbadensis
St Croix I, Barbados I
V. a. bonairensis
Aruba I, Curaçao I, Bonaire I
V. a. grandior
Old Providence I, St Catalina I
V. a. canescens
St Andrew I
Vireo gilvus (Warbling Vireo)
V. g. swainsonii
W Canada, W USA » W Mexico,
Guatemala, Honduras, Nicaragua
V. g. victoriae
S Baja California
V. g. leucopolius
WC USA » N Mexico
V. g. gilvus
SW Canada, C, S & NE USA » S Mexico,
El Salvador

V. g. brewsteri
NW Mexico
V. g. eleanorae
NE Mexico
V. g. bulli
Oaxaca
V. g. amauronotus
EC Mexico
V. g. connectens
SC Mexico
V. g. strenuus
S Mexico, Guatemala, Honduras
V. g. chiriquensis
Costa Rica, W Panama
V. g. disjunctus
NC Colombia
V. g. mirandae
N Colombia, NW Venezuela
V. g. leucophrys
C Colombia, Ecuador, N Peru
V. g. dissors
W Colombia
V. g. josephae
SW Colombia, W Ecuador
V. g. maranonicus
N Peru
V. g. laetissimus
SE Peru, N Bolivia

HYLOPHILUS
**Hylophilus poicilotis (Rufous-crowned
Greenlet)**
H. p. amaurocephalus
E Brazil
H. p. poicilotis
SE Brazil, Paraguay, NE Argentina
**Hylophilus thoracicus (Lemon-chested
Greenlet)**
H. t. aemulus
Colombia, Ecuador, Peru,
N Bolivia
H. t. griseiventris
E Venezuela, the Guianas, N Brazil
H. t. thoracicus
SE Brazil
**Hylophilus semicinereus (Grey-chested
Greenlet)**
H. s. viridiceps
S Venezuela, the Guianas, N Brazil
H. s. semicinereus
N Brazil
H. s. juruanus
NW Brazil
**Hylophilus pectoralis (Ashy-headed
Greenlet)**
the Guianas, N Brazil
Hylophilus sclateri (Tepui Greenlet)
S Venezuela, Guyana, NC Brazil

Hylophilus muscicapinus (Buff-chested 587
Greenlet)
H. m. muscicapinus
S Venezuela, the Guianas, N Brazil
H. m. griseifrons
N Brazil
**Hylophilus brunneiceps (Brown-headed
Greenlet)**
H. b. brunneiceps
E Colombia, S Venezuela, NW Brazil
H. b. inornatus
N Brazil
**Hylophilus semibrunneus (Rufous-naped
Greenlet)**
N Colombia, NW Venezuela, E Ecuador
**Hylophilus aurantiifrons (Golden-fronted
Greenlet)**
H. a. aurantiifrons
E Panama, N Colombia
H. a. helvinus
NW Venezuela
H. a. saturatus
E Colombia, N Venezuela, Trinidad
**Hylophilus hypoxanthus (Dusky-capped
Greenlet)**
H. h. hypoxanthus
SE Colombia
H. h. fuscicapillus
E Ecuador, N Peru
H. h. flaviventris
C Peru
H. h. ictericus
W Brazil, NE Peru, N Bolivia
H. h. albigula
N Brazil
Hylophilus flavipes (Scrub Greenlet)
H. f. viridiflavus
SW Costa Rica, W Panama
H. f. xuthus
Coiba I (Panama)
H. f. flavipes
C & N Colombia
H. f. melleus
N Colombia
H. f. galbanus
NE Colombia, NW Venezuela
H. f. acuticauda
N Venezuela
H. f. insularis
Tobago I
H. f. olivaceus
E Ecuador, N Peru
**Hylophilus ochraceiceps (Tawny-crowned
Greenlet)**
H. o. ochraceiceps
S Mexico, Guatemala

H. o. pallidipectus
Honduras, El Salvador, Nicaragua,
Costa Rica
H. o. nelsoni
E Panama
H. o. bulunensis
E Panama, W Colombia, W Ecuador
H. o. ferrugineifrons
SE Colombia, S Venezuela, Guyana,
Ecuador, Peru, NW Brazil
H. o. viridior
S Peru, N Bolivia
H. o. luteifrons
E Venezuela, the Guianas, N Brazil
H. o. lutescens
N Brazil
H. o. rubrifrons
NE Brazil
***Hylophilus decurtatus* (Grey-headed
Greenlet)**
H. d. decurtatus
E Mexico, Central America
H. d. darienensis
E Panama, N Colombia
H. d. minor
SW Colombia, W Ecuador
***Hylophilus puellus* (Tafelberg Greenlet)**
Surinam

**162 ICTERIDAE (NEW WORLD
BLACKBIRDS)**

ICTERINAE

PSAROCOLIUS
***Psarocolius oseryi* (Casqued Oropendola)**
E Ecuador, E Peru
***Psarocolius latirostris* (Band-tailed
Oropendola)**
E Ecuador, N Peru, W Brazil
***Psarocolius decumanus* (Crested
Oropendola)**
P. d. melanterus
Panama, N Colombia
P. d. insularis
Trinidad, Tobago I
P. d. decumanus
N South America
P. d. maculosus
E Peru to Paraguay, N Argentina
***Psarocolius viridis* (Green Oropendola)**
N Amazonia
***Psarocolius atrovirens* (Dusky-green
Oropendola)**
SE Peru, E Bolivia
***Psarocolius angustifrons* (Russet-backed
Oropendola)**
P. a. salmoni
C Colombia

P. a. atrocastaneus
W Ecuador
P. a. sincipitalis
NC Colombia
P. a. neglectus
E Colombia, NW Venezuela
P. a. oleagineus
NC Venezuela
P. a. angustifrons
W Amazonia
P. a. alfredi
SE Ecuador, E Peru, E Bolivia
***Psarocolius wagleri* (Chestnut-headed
Oropendola)**
P. w. wagleri
SE Mexico to NE Nicaragua
P. w. ridgwayi
S Nicaragua to Panama, W Ecuador
***Psarocolius montezuma* (Montezuma
Oropendola)**
S Mexico to Panama
***Psarocolius cassini* (Chestnut-mantled
Oropendola)**
NW Colombia
***Psarocolius bifasciatus* (Para Oropendola)**
N Brazil
***Psarocolius guatimozinus* (Black
Oropendola)**
E Panama, NW Colombia
***Psarocolius yuracares* (Olive Oropendola)**
P. y. yuracares
W Amazonia
P. y. neivae
N Brazil

CACICUS
***Cacicus cela* (Yellow-rumped Cacique)**
C. c. vitellinus
Panama, N Colombia
C. c. flavicrissus
W Ecuador, NW Peru
C. c. cela
N South America, Trinidad
***Cacicus haemorrhous* (Red-rumped
Cacique)**
C. h. haemorrhous
SE Colombia, E Ecuador, N Brazil
C. h. affinis
E & S Brazil, Paraguay, NE Argentina
***Cacicus uropygialis* (Scarlet-rumped
Cacique)**
C. u. microrhynchus
S Honduras to Panama
C. u. pacificus
E Panama, Colombia, E Ecuador
C. u. uropygialis
S Venezuela to N Peru

Cacicus chrysopterus (Golden-winged Cacique)
  E Bolivia to Uruguay
Cacicus koepckeae (Selva Cacique)
  Peru
Cacicus leucoramphus (Mountain Cacique)
  C. l. leucoramphus
    NW Venzuela to E Ecuador
  C. l. peruvianus
    N Peru
  C. l. chrysonotus
    S Peru, Bolivia
Cacicus sclateri (Ecuadorian Black Cacique)
  E Ecuador, N Peru
Cacicus solitarius (Solitary Cacique)
  Central & Northern South America
Cacicus melanicterus (Yellow-winged Cacique)
  W & SW Mexico
Cacicus holosericeus (Yellow-billed Cacique)
  C. h. holosericeus
    SE Mexico to Colombia
  C. h. flavirostris
    W Colombia to NW Peru
  C. h. australis
    Western Amazonia

ICTERUS
Icterus cayanensis (Epaulet Oriole)
  I. c. cayanensis
    Surinam, French Guiana
  I. c. chrysocephalus
    N Peru to S Surinam
  I. c. tibialis
    E Brazil
  I. c. valenciobuenoi
    SE Brazil
  I. c. periporphyrus
    NE Bolivia, W Brazil
  I. c. pyrrhopterus
    SE Bolivia to Uruguay
Icterus chrysater (Yellow-backed Oriole)
  I. c. chrysater
    S Mexico to Nicaragua
  I. c. mayensis
    SE Mexico
  I. c. hondae
    Panama, N Colombia
  I. c. giraudii
    C Colombia, N Venezuela
Icterus nigrogularis (Yellow Oriole)
  I. n. nigrogularis
    NE South America
  I. n. curasoensis
    Aruba, Curaçao I, Bonaire I
  I. n. helioeides
    Margarita I

  I. n. trinitatis
    NE Venezuela, Trinidad
Icterus leucopteryx (Jamaican Oriole)
  I. l. bairdi
    Grand Cayman I
  I. l. leucopteryx
    Jamaica
  I. l. lawrencii
    St Andrew I
Icterus auratus (Orange Oriole)
  SE Mexico
Icterus mesomelas (Yellow-tailed Oriole)
  I. m. mesomelas
    SE Mexico to Honduras
  I. m. salvinii
    Nicaragua to Panama
  I. m. carrikeri
    N & W Colombia, NW Venezuela
  I. m. taczanowskii
    W Ecuador, NW Peru
Icterus auricapillus (Orange-crowned Oriole)
  E Panama to N Venezuela
Icterus graceannae (White-edged Oriole)
  SW Ecuador, NW Peru
Icterus xantholaemus (Yellow-throated Oriole)
  Ecuador
Icterus pectoralis (Spotted-breasted Oriole)
  I. p. pectoralis
    S Mexico to N Nicaragua
  I. p. espinachi
    S Nicaragua to NW Costa Rica
Icterus gularis (Lichtenstein's Oriole)
  I. g. tamaulipensis
    S Texas, E Mexico
  I. g. yucatanensis
    SE Mexico
  I. g. flavescens
    SW Mexico
  I. g. gularis
    S Mexico
  I. g. troglodytes
    S Mexico, W Guatemala
  I. g. gigas
    S Guatemala, Honduras
Icterus pustulatus (Streak-backed Oriole)
  I. p. microstictus
    W Mexico
  I. p. graysonii
    Tres Marias Is
  I. p. pustulatus
    SW & C Mexico
  I. p. formosus
    S Mexico, NW Guatemala

I. p. alticola
Guatemala, E Honduras

I. p. sclateri
El Salvador to NW Costa Rica

Icterus cucullatus (Hooded Oriole)

I. c. nelsoni
SW USA, NW Mexico

I. c. sennetti
S Texas, E Mexico

I. c. cucullatus
SW Texas, NC & C Mexico

I. c. californicus
N Baja California

I. c. trochiloides
S Baja California

I. c. restrictus
S Sonora

I. c. igneus
SE Mexico, Belize

I. c. cozumelae
Cozumel I

I. c. duplexus
Mujeres I, Holbox I

I. c. masoni
SE Quintana Roo

Icterus icterus (Troupial)

I. i. ridgwayi
N Colombia, NW Venezuela, Aruba I,
Curaçao I

I. i. icterus
E Colombia, NW Venezuela

I. i. metae
SW Venezuela

I. i. croconotus
SW Guyana, N Brazil, E Ecuador, E Peru

I. i. jamaicaii
E Brazil

I. i. strictifrons
N & E Bolivia, SW Brazil

Icterus galbula (Northern Oriole)

I. g. galbula
Canada, E USA » Colombia

I. g. bullockii
SW Canada, W USA » W Mexico to
Nicaragua

I. g. parvus
SW USA » NW Mexico

I. g. abeillei
SC Mexico

Icterus spurius (Orchard Oriole)

I. s. spurius
C Canada, E USA » Colombia, Cuba

I. s. phillipsi
C Mexico

I. s. fuertesi
E Mexico

**Icterus dominicensis (Black-cowled
Oriole)**

I. d. prosthemelas
SE Mexico to Nicaragua

I. d. praecox
E Costa Rica, W Panama

I. d. northropi
Andros I (Bahamas)

I. d. melanopsis
Cuba

I. d. dominicensis
Hispaniola

I. d. portoricensis
Puerto Rico

Icterus wagleri (Black-vented Oriole)

I. w. castaneopectus
NW Mexico

I. w. wagleri
W & S Mexico to Nicaragua

Icterus laudabilis (St Lucia Oriole)
St Lucia I

Icterus bonana (Martinique Oriole)
Martinique I

Icterus oberi (Monserrat Oriole)
Monserrat I

Icterus graduacauda (Black-headed Oriole)

I. g. audubonii
N Mexico

I. g. nayaritensis
WC Mexico

I. g. richardsoni
Oaxaca

I. g. dickeyae
Guerrero

I. g. graduacauda
C & S Mexico

Icterus maculialatus (Bar-winged Oriole)
S Mexico to El Salvador

Icterus parisorum (Scott's Oriole)
SC USA, C & W Mexico

NESOPSAR

Nesopsar nigerrimus (Jamaican Blackbird)
Jamaica

XANTHOPSAR

**Xanthopsar flavus (Saffron-cowled
Blackbird)**
Paraguay, NE Argentina

GYMNOMYSTAX

**Gymnomystax mexicanus (Oriole
Blackbird)**
N South America

XANTHOCEPHALUS

**Xanthocephalus xanthocephalus (Yellow-
headed Blackbird)**
SW Canada, W USA, W Mexico

AGELAIUS

Agelaius xanthophthalmus (Yellow-eyed Blackbird)
Peru

Agelaius thilius (Yellow-winged Blackbird)
A. t. alticola
SE Peru, NW Bolivia
A. t. thilius
S Chile, SW Argentina
A. t. petersii
SE Brazil, Uruguay, N Argentina

Agelaius phoeniceus (Red-winged Blackbird)
A. p. arctolegus
Canada, E USA » SC USA
A. p. fortis
WC USA
A. p. nevadensis
SW Canada, SW USA
A. p. caurinus
W USA
A. p. mailliardorum
WC California
A. p. californicus
C California
A. p. aciculatus
SC California
A. p. neutralis
S California, NW Baja California
A. p. sonoriensis
SW USA, NW Mexico
A. p. nyaritensis
SW Mexico
A. p. gubernator
NC Mexico
A. p. pallidulus
N Yucatan
A. p. nelsoni
SC Mexico
A. p. arthuralleni
N Guatemala
A. p. grinnelli
W Guatemala to NW Costa Rica
A. p. phoeniceus
SE Canada, E & S USA
A. p. littoralis
SE USA
A. p. mearnsi
SE USA
A. p. floridanus
S Florida
A. p. megapotamus
S Texas, NE Mexico
A. p. richmondi
S & SE Mexico, N Guatemala
A. p. matudae
SE Mexico

A. p. brevirostris
E Honduras, SE Nicaragua
A. p. bryanti
NW Bahama Is
A. p. assimilis
W Cuba
A. p. subniger
Isle of Pines

Agelaius tricolor (Tricoloured Blackbird)
W USA

Agelaius icterocephalus (Yellow-hooded Blackbird)
A. i. bogotensis
E Colombia
A. i. icterocephalus
Surinam to NE Peru

Agelaius humeralis (Tawny-shouldered Blackbird)
A. h. humaralis
Hispaniola
A. h. scopulus
Cuba

Agelaius xanthomus (Yellow-shouldered Blackbird)
A. x. xanthomus
Puerto Rico
A. x. monensis
Mona I (Puerto Rico)

Agelaius cyanopus (Unicoloured Blackbird)
A. c. xenicus
NE Brazil
A. c. atroolivaceus
E Brazil
A. c. beniensis
N Bolivia
A. c. cyanopus
E Bolivia, Paraguay, N Argentina

Agelaius ruficapillus (Chestnut-capped Blackbird)
A. r. frontalis
French Guiana, E Brazil
A. r. ruficapillus
SE Bolivia to Uruguay, N Argentina

STURNELLA

Sturnella superciliaris (Bonaparte's Blackbird)
S Peru to Uruguay

Sturnella militaris (Red-breasted Blackbird)
South America

Sturnella bellicosa (Peruvian Red-breasted Meadowlark)
S. b. bellicosa
Ecuador, N Peru
S. b. albipes
SW Peru, N Chile
S. b. catamarcanus
NW Argentina

Sturnella defilippi (Lesser Red-breasted Meadowlark)
SE Brazil, Uruguay, NE Argentina
Sturnella loyca (Long-tailed Meadowlark)
S. l. loyca
S Chile, S Argentina
S. l. falklandicus
Falkland Is
Sturnella magna (Eastern Meadowlark)
S. m. magna
SE Canada, C & E USA
S. m. argutula
SC & SE USA
S. m. hippocrepis
Cuba
S. m. hoopesi
S Texas, NE Mexico
S. m. lilianae
SW USA, NW Mexico
S. m. auropectoralis
C & SW Mexico
S. m. saundersi
Oaxaca, Mexico
S. m. alticola
S Mexico to Nicaragua
S. m. mexicana
SE Mexico
S. m. griscomi
SE Mexico
S. m. inexpectata
E Guatemala, Honduras
S. m. subulata
W Panama
S. m. meridionalis
N Colombia, NW Venezuela
S. m. paralios
N Colombia, W Venezuela
S. m. praticola
Northern Amazonia
Sturnella neglecta (Western Meadowlark)
SW Canada, W USA » NW Mexico

PSEUDOLEISTES
Pseudoleistes guirahuro (Yellow-rumped Marshbird)
SE Brazil, N Argentina, Paraguay, Uruguay
Pseudoleistes virescens (Brown-yellow Marshbird)
SE Brazil, Uruguay, NE Argentina

AMBLYRAMPHUS
Amblyramphus holosericeus (Scarlet-headed Blackbird)
Bolivia, Brazil, Paraguay, Uruguay, Argentina

HYPOPYRRHUS
Hypopyrrhus pyrohypogaster (Red-bellied Grackle)
Colombia
CURAEUS
Curaeus curaeus (Austral Blackbird)
C. c. curaeus
S Argentina, Chile
C. c. recurvirostris
Magellanes, Chile
C. c. reynoldsi
Tierra del Fuego
Curaeus forbesi (Forbes's Blackbird)
E Brazil

GNORIMOPSAR
Gnorimopsar chopi (Chopi Blackbird)
G. c. sulcirostris
E Bolivia, NW Argentina, E Brazil
G. c. chopi
SE Bolivia to Uruguay
N Argentina

OREOPSAR
Oreopsar bolivianus (Bolivian Blackbird)
Bolivia

LAMPROPSAR
Lampropsar tanagrinus (Velvet-fronted Grackle)
L. t. guianensis
NE Venezuela, NW Guyana
L. t. tanagrinus
Ecuador, N Peru, W Brazil
L. t. macropterus
W Brazil
L. t. boliviensis
N Bolivia
L. t. violaceus
W Brazil

MACROAGELAIUS
Macroagelaius subalaris (Mountain Grackle)
M. s. subalaris
C Colombia
M. s. imthurni
S Venezuela, N Brazil, W Guyana

DIVES
Dives atroviolacea (Cuban Blackbird)
Cuba
Dives dives (Melodious Blackbird)
D. d. dives
E Mexico to Nicaragua
D. d. warszewiczi
SW Ecuador, NW Peru
D. d. kalinowskii
W Peru

Quiscalus mexicanus (Great-tailed Grackle)
Q. m. nelsoni
SW USA, NW Mexico
Q. m. graysoni
NW Mexico
Q. m. obscurus
W Mexico
Q. m. monsoni
S USA, C Mexico
Q. m. prosopidicola
S USA, NE Mexico
Q. m. mexicanus
C & S Mexico to N Nicaragua
Q. m. loweryi
Belize
Q. m. peruvianus
Costa Rica to Peru, Venezuela
Quiscalus major (Boat-tailed Grackle)
Q. m. torreyi
E USA
Q. m. major
SE USA
Quiscalus nicaraguensis (Nicaraguan Grackle)
Nicaragua
Quiscalus quiscula (Common Grackle)
Q. q. versicolor
C & SE Canada, NE & C USA » S USA
Q. q. stonei
NC USA » SE USA
Q. q. quiscula
SE USA
Quiscalus niger (Antillean Grackle)
Q. n. caribaeus
W Cuba
Q. n. gundlachii
C & E Cuba
Q. n. caymanensis
Grand Cayman I
Q. n. bangsi
Little Cayman I
Q. n. crassirostris
Jamaica
Q. n. niger
Hispaniola
Q. n. brachypterus
Puerto Rico
Quiscalus lugubris (Carib Grackle)
Q. l. guadeloupensis
Monserrat I, Guadeloupe I, Martinique I
Q. l. inflexirostris
St Lucia I
Q. l. contusus
St Vincent I
Q. l. luminosus
Grenada I

Q. l. fortirostris
Barbados I, Antigua I
Q. l. orquillensis
Los Hermanos I (Venezuela)
Q. l. insularis
Margarita I
Q. l. lugubris
Trinidad, N Venezuela, the Guianas,
NE Brazil

EUPHAGUS
Euphagus carolinus (Rusty Blackbird)
E. c. carolinus
Canada, NE & C USA » SE USA
E. c. nigrans
Newfoundland » SE USA
Euphagus cyanocephalus (Brewer's Blackbird)
SW Canada, W USA » Mexico

MOLOTHRUS
Molothrus badius (Bay-winged Cowbird)
M. b. fringillarius
NE Brazil
M. b. badius
Bolivia to Uruguay, N Argentina
M. b. bolivianus
S Bolivia
Molothrus rufoaxillaris (Screaming Cowbird)
S Bolivia to Uruguay
Molothrus bonariensis (Common Cowbird)
M. b. cabanisii
E Panama, Colombia
M. b. aequatorialis
SW Colombia, W Ecuador
M. b. occidentalis
SW Ecuador, W Peru
M. b. venezuelensis
E Colombia, N Venezuela
M. b. minimus
S Lesser Antilles, the Guianas,
N Brazil
M. b. riparius
E Peru
M. b. bonariensis
Central South America
Molothus aeneus (Bronzed Cowbird)
M. a. loyei
SW USA, NW Mexico
M. a. assimilis
S & SW Mexico
M. a. aeneus
S Texas, E Mexico to Panama
M. a. armenti
N Colombia
Molothus ater (Brown-headed Cowbird)
M. a. artemisiae
W Canada, W USA » C Mexico

M. a. obscurus
SW USA » S Mexico
M. a. ater
C & S USA » SE USA
M. a. californicus
SW USA, Los Coronados Is

SCAPHIDURA
Scaphidura oryzivora (Giant Cowbird)
S. o. impacifa
S Mexico to W Panama
S. o. oryzivora
E Panama, Trinidad, N South America

DOLICHONYCHINAE

DOLICHONYX
Dolichonyx oryzivorus (Bobolink)
S Canada » N South America, West Indies

163 FRINGILLIDAE (FINCHES)

FRINGILLINAE

FRINGILLA
Fringilla coelebs (Chaffinch)
F. c. moreletti
Azores Is
F. c. maderensis
Madeira I
F. c. canariensis
Gran Canaria I, Tenerife I
F. c. ombriosa
Hierro I
F. c. palmae
Las Palmas I
F. c. africana
NW Africa
F. c. spodiogenys
Tunisia
F. c. coelebs
continent Europe, Siberia, C Asia, N Africa
F. c. gengleri
British Isles
F. c. sarda
Sardinia
F. c. schiebeli
Crete
F. c. solomkoi
Crimea
F. c. alexsandrovi
N Iran
F. c. transcaspica
S Transcaspia
Fringilla teydea (Blue Chaffinch)
F. t. teydea
Tenerife I

F. t. polatzeki
Gran Canaria I
Fringilla montifringilla (Brambling)
Europe to Japan » N Africa, N India, Chi◖

CARDUELINAE

SERINUS
Serinus pusillus (Red-fronted Serin)
Asia Minor to Tibet » Israel
Serinus serinus (Serin)
W & C Europe, Asia Minor, N Africa
Serinus syriacus (Syrian Serin)
Lebanon, Syria » Iraq, Egypt
Serinus canaria (Canary)
Canary Is, Azores Is, Madeira I
Serinus citrinella (Citril Finch)
S. c. citrinella
S Europe
S. c. corsicana
Corsica, Sardinia
Serinus thibetanus (Tibetan Siskin)
Nepal, SE Tibet » NE Burma & W China
Serinus canicollis (Yellow-crowned Canary)
S. c. flavivertex
Ethiopia to N Tanzania
S. c. sassii
S Zaire to N Malawi
S. c. huillensis
C Angola
S. c. griseitergum
E Rhodesia
S. c. thompsonae
Transvaal, N Cape Province
S. c. canicollis
Cape Province
Serinus nigriceps (Black-headed Siskin)
N Ethiopia
Serinus citrinelloides (African Citril Finch)
S. c. citrinelloides
Ethiopia, SE Sudan
S. c. kikuyensis
W Kenya
S. c. brittoni
Kapenguria, Kenya
S. c. frontalis
W Uganda, E Zaire, NW Tanzania
S. c. hypostictus
S Kenya, E Zambia to Mozambique
S. c. martinsi
Mexico, Angola
Serinus capistratus (Black-faced Canary)
S. c. capistratus
Gabon to N Angola, Zambia
S. c. hildegardae
S Angola
Serinus koliensis (Van Someren's Canary
Uganda, W Kenya, Rwanda

Serinus scotops (Forest Canary)
S. s. transvaalensis
    N & E Transvaal
S. s. umbrosus
    SE Transvaal, Natal, S Cape Province
S. s. scotops
    S Natal, E Cape Province
Serinus leucopygius (White-rumped
Seedeater)
S. l. riggenbachi
    Senegal to Chad, Central African Republic
S. l. pallens
    Aïr to N Nigeria
S. l. leucopygius
    E Sudan, N Ethiopia
Serinus atrogularis (Yellow-rumped
Seedeater)
S. a. rothschildi
    E Arabia
S. a. xanthopygius
    N Ethiopia
S. a. reichenowi
    S Sudan to NE Tanzania
S. a. somereni
    E Zaire, W Uganda, W Kenya
S. a. lwenarum
    S Zaire, Angola, Zambia
S. a. atrogularis
    Rhodesia, W Transvaal
S. a. impiger
    SE Transvaal, W Natal, N Cape Province
S. a. semideserti
    S Angola, N Namibia, S Zambia
S. a. deserti
    SW Angola, NW Namibia
Serinus citrinipectus (Lemon-breasted
Seedeater)
    S Malawi, SE Rhodesia, S Mozambique
Serinus mozambicus (Yellow-fronted
Canary)
S. m. caniceps
    Senegal to N Cameroun
S. m. punctigula
    Cameroun
S. m. barbatus
    N Zaire, Sudan to Kenya
S. m. santhome
    Sao Thomé I
S. m. tando
    SW Zaire, N Angola
S. m. samaliyae
    SE Zaire, Zambia
S. m. vansoni
    SE Angola, Namibia, SW Zambia
S. m. mozambicus
    Kenya to Zambia, Mozambique
S. m. granti
    S Mozambique, South Africa

S. m. grotei
    E Sudan, W Ethiopia
S. m. gommaensis
    W Ethiopia
Serinus donaldsoni (Grosbeak Canary)
S. d. donaldsoni
    Ethiopia, N Kenya
S. d. buchanani
    S Kenya, N Tanzania
Serinus flaviventris (Yellow Canary)
S. f. maculicollis
    S Ethiopia, Kenya, Somalia
S. f. dorsostriatus
    N Tanzania
S. f. damarensis
    Namibia, Botswana
S. f. flaviventris
    W Cape Province
S. f. quintoni
    S & C Cape Province
S. f. marshalli
    NW Cape Province, Transvaal
S. f. guillarmodi
    Lesotho
Serinus sulphuratus (Brimstone Canary)
S. s. sharpii
    Angola to Kenya, Mozambique
S. s. wilsoni
    S Mozambique, South Africa
S. s. sulphuratus
    S Cape Province
Serinus albogularis (White-throated
Seedeater)
S. a. crocopygius
    SW Angola, N Namibia
S. a. sordahlae
    S Namibia, NW Cape Province
S. a. albogularis
    W Cape Province
S. a. hewitti
    C Cape Province
S. a. orangensis
    Orange Free State
Serinus gularis (Streaky-headed
Seedeater)
S. g. canicapilla
    Senegal to N Cameroun
S. g. montanorum
    Cameroun
S. g. uamensis
    W Central African Republic
S. g. elgonensis
    N Zaire, S Sudan, W Kenya
S. g. striatipectus
    S Sudan, S Ethiopia, N Kenya
S. g. reichardi
    S Zaire, Zambia to Tanzania

S. g. benguellensis
C Angola, W Zambia
S. g. mendosus
NE Botswana, NW Transvaal
S. g. gularis
Rhodesia to N Cape Province
S. g. endemion
S Mozambique, E South Africa
S. g. humilis
SW Cape Province
Serinus mennelli (Black-eared Seedeater)
E Angola to Mozambique
Serinus tristriatus (Brown-rumped Seedeater)
E Ethiopia
Serinus ankoberensis (Ankober Serin)
C Ethiopia
Serinus menachensis (Menacha Seedeater)
Saudi Arabia
Serinus striolatus (Streaky Seedeater)
S. s. striolatus
Ethiopia, N Kenya
S. s. affinis
Kenya, N Tanzania
S. s. graueri
Uganda, W Kenya, W Tanzania
S. s. whytii
S Tanzania, N Malawi
Serinus burtoni (Thick-billed Seedeater)
S. b. burtoni
Cameroun
S. b. tanganjicae
E Zaire, W Uganda
S. b. kilimensis
N Kenya, N Tanzania
S. b. albifrons
E Kenya
S. b. melanochrous
S Tanzania
Serinus rufobrunneus (Principé Seedeater)
S. r. rufobrunneus
Principé I
S. r. thomensis
Sao Thomé I
Serinus leucopterus (White-winged Seedeater)
SW Cape Province
Serinus totta (Cape Siskin)
S. t. totta
S Cape Province
S. t. symonsi
E Cape Province, W Natal, Lesotho
Serinus alario (Black-headed Canary)
S. a. leucolaema
Namibia, Botswana, W Cape Province
S. a. alario
N & C Cape Province

Serinus estherae (Malay Goldfinch)
S. e. vanderbilti
N Sumatra
S. e. estherae
W Java
S. e. orientalis
E Java
S. e. mindanensis
Mindanao I

NEOSPIZA
Neospiza concolor (Grosbeak-Weaver)
Sao Thomé I **e?**

LINURGUS
Linurgus olivaceus (Oriole-Finch)
L. o. olivaceus
SE Nigeria, Cameroun, Fernando Po I
L. o. prigoginei
E Zaire
L. o. elgonensis
SE Sudan, N Kenya
L. o. kilimensis
Tanzania, N Malawi

RHYNCHOSTRUTHUS
Rhynchostruthus socotranus (Golden-winged Grosbeak)
R. s. louisae
N Somalia
R. s. percivali
SW Arabia
R. s. socotranus
Socotra I

CARDUELIS
Carduelis chloris (Greenfinch)
C. c. chloris
N Europe » S Europe
C. c. aurantiiventris
S Europe, N Africa
C. c. chlorotica
Syria, Lebanon » Egypt
C. c. turkestanica
Caucasas » Iran, Afghanistan & Iraq
Carduelis sinica (Oriental Greenfinch)
C. s. sinica
E & C China
C. s. chabarovi
Manchuria, Mongolia
C. s. ussuriensis
E Manchuria
C. s. kawarahiba
Sakhalin I, NE Asia » Japan
C. s. minor
S Japan
C. s. kittlitzi
Bonin Is

Carduelis spinoides (Black-headed Greenfinch)
 C. s. spinoides
  Pakistan, N India, E Himalayas
 C. s. heinrichi
  S Assam, W Burma
 C. s. monguilloti
  S Vietnam
Carduelis ambigua (Yunnan Greenfinch)
 C. a. taylori
  SE Tibet, Sikang
 C. a. ambigua
  SW China, N Burma
Carduelis spinus (Siskin)
 N Asia, N Europe » Japan, N Africa & China
Carduelis pinus (Pine Siskin)
 C. p. pinus
  Canada, USA » C Mexico
 C. p. macroptera
  N Baja California, NW & C Mexico
 C. p. perplexa
  S Mexico, W Guatemala
Carduelis atriceps (Black-capped Siskin)
 S Mexico, W Guatemala
Carduelis spinescens (Andean Siskin)
 C. s. spinescens
  Colombia, W Venezuela
 C. s. capitanea
  N Colombia
 C. s. nigricauda
  N Colombia
Carduelis yarrellii (Yellow-faced Siskin)
 N Venezuela, N Brazil
Carduelis cucullata (Red Siskin)
 NE Colombia, N Venezuela
Carduelis crassirostris (Thick-billed Siskin)
 C. c. amadoni
  SE Peru
 C. c. crassirostris
  S Bolivia, C Chile, W Argentina
Carduelis magellanica (Hooded Siskin)
 C. m. capitalis
  S Colombia, Ecuador, NW Peru
 C. m. paula
  S Ecuador, W Peru
 C. m. peruana
  C Peru
 C. m. urubambensis
  S Peru, N Chile
 C. m. boliviana
  S Bolivia
 C. m. tucumana
  NW Argentina
 C. m. santaecrucis
  EC Bolivia
 C. m. alleni
  SE Bolivia, Paraguay, NE Argentina

C. m. icterica
 SE Brazil, E & S Paraguay
C. m. magellanica
 Uruguay, E Argentina
C. m. longirostris
 SE Venezuela, Guyana, N Brazil
Carduelis dominicensis (Antillean Siskin)
 Hispaniola
Carduelis siemiradzkii (Saffron Siskin)
 SW Ecuador
Carduelis olivacea (Olivaceous Siskin)
 SE Ecuador, Peru, Bolivia
Carduelis notata (Black-headed Siskin)
 C. n. notata
  E & C Mexico, N Guatemala
 C. n. forreri
  W Mexico
 C. n. oleacea
  Belize to N Nicaragua
Carduelis xanthogastra (Yellow-bellied Siskin)
 C. x. xanthogastra
  Costa Rica to Colombia, Venezuela
 C. x. stejnegeri
  C Bolivia
Carduelis atrata (Black Siskin)
 S Peru to N Chile, W Argentina
Carduelis uropygialis (Yellow-rumped Siskin)
 S Peru to Chile, W Argentina
Carduelis barbata (Black-chinned Siskin)
 S Chile, W Argentina
Carduelis tristis (American Goldfinch)
 C. t. tristis
  C USA » SE USA, E Mexico
 C. t. pallida
  W Canada. WC USA » N Mexico
 C. t. jewetti
  SW Canada, NW USA
 C. t. salicamans
  SW USA, N Baja California
Carduelis psaltria (Dark-backed Greenfinch)
 C. p. hesperophila
  W USA, NW Mexico
 C. p. witti
  Tres Marias Is
 C. p. psaltria
  SC USA, N Mexico
 C. p. jouyi
  SE Mexico
 C. p. colombiana
  S Mexico to Peru, Venezuela
Carduelis lawrencei (Lawrence's Goldfinch)
 SW USA » NW Mexico

Carduelis carduelis (Goldfinch)
  C. c. carduelis
    W & C Europe
  C. c. britannica
    British Isles, Netherlands
  C. c. parva
    W Mediterranean, Azores Is, Canary Is
  C. c. tschusii
    Corsica, Sardinia, Sicily
  C. c. balcanica
    E Mediterranean
  C. c. niediecki
    Cyprus, Asia Minor, Iraq, Iran, Egypt
  C. c. major
    SW Siberia
  C. c. brevirostris
    Caucasus
  C. c. loudoni
    N Iran
  C. c. paropanisi
    Central Asia » S Iran
  C. c. subulata
    NC Asia » Turkistan
  C. c. caniceps
    Pakistan, W Himalayas, Nepal

ACANTHIS
Acanthis flammea (Redpoll)
  A. f. flammea
    N Europe, Asia, North America » S Europe
    & N China
  A. f. rostrata
    NE Canada » NE USA, NW Europe
  A. f. islandica
    Iceland
  A. f. cabaret
    British Is, Switzerland
Acanthis hornemanni (Arctic Redpoll)
  A. h. exilipes
    N Eurasia, N North America » C Europe
  A. h. hornemanni
    Greenland, C & E Canada » British Isles &
    S Canada
Acanthis flavirostris (Twite)
  A. f. flavirostris
    NE & C Europe » S Europe
  A. f. pipilans
    N British Isles, Ireland
  A. f. breverostris
    Caucasus, NW Iran
  A. f. korejevi
    C Asia
  A. f. altaica
    EC Asia
  A. f. montanella
    N Pakistan, Altai, W Sinkiang
  A. f. miniakensis
    E Sinkiang, NW China

  A. f. rufostrigata
    Pakistan, Tibet, Himalayas, N India
Acanthis cannabina (Linnet)
  A. c. cannabina
    Europe, NW Asia » N Africa
  A. c. autochthona
    Scotland
  A. c. nana
    Madeira I
  A. c. meadewaldoi
    W Canary Is
  A. c. harterti
    E Canary Is
  A. c. bella
    Asia Minor, SW Asia » Egypt, N India
Acanthis yemensis (Yemeni Linnet)
    SW Arabia
Acanthis johannis (Warsangli Linnet)
    NE Somalia

LEUCOSTICTE
Leucosticte nemoricola (Hodgson's Ros Finch)
  L. n. altaica
    W Pakistan, W Sinkiang, Altai
  L. n. nemoricola
    Himalayas, W China » N Burma
Leucosticte brandti (Brandt's Rosy Finch
  L. b. margaritacea
    W Mongolia, SE Altai
  L. b. brandti
    W Tien Shan, W Sinkiang
  L. b. pamirensis
    W Tien Shan, NE Afghanistan
  L. b. haematopygia
    N Pakistan, Himalayas, Tibet
  L. b. pallidior
    SW Sinkiang, NE Tsinghai
Leucosticte arctoa (Rosy Finch)
  L. a. arctoa
    Altai
  L. a. cognata
    Tannu Tuva
  L. a. sushkini
    N Mongolia
  L. a. gigliolii
    Transbaicalia
  L. a. brunneonucha
    E Siberia, Kurile Is
  L. a. griseonucha
    Aleutian Is, Kodiak I, Alaska
  L. a. umbrina
    St Matthew I, Pribilof Is
  L. a. irvingi
    N Alaska
  L. a. littoralis
    E Alaska, W Canada » SW USA
  L. a. tephrocotis
    WC Canada » WC USA

L. a. dawsoni
  E California
L. a. wallowa
  NE Oregon » W Nevada
L. a. atrata
  WC USA » SC USA
L. a. australis
  SW USA

CALLACANTHIS
Callacanthis burtoni (Red-browed Rose Finch)
  W Pakistan, Himalayas

RHODOPECHYS
Rhodopechys sanguinea (Crimson-winged Finch)
R. s. aliena
  Morocco
R. s. sanguinea
  Caucasus, Iran, SC Asia
Rhodopechys githaginea (Trumpeter Finch)
R. g. amantum
  Canary Is
R. g. zedlitzi
  N Africa
R. g. githaginea
  S Egypt, N Sudan
R. g. crassirostris
  Arabia, Iran » NW India
Rhodopechys mongolica (Mongolian Trumpeter Finch)
  E Asia, India » E China
Rhodopechys obsoleta (Lichenstein's Desert Finch)
  Asia Minor » N Pakistan

URAGUS
Uragus sibiricus (Long-tailed Rose Finch)
U. s. sibiricus
  S Siberia, N Manchuria » Turkistan
U. s. ussuriensis
  C Manchuria, Korea » NE China
U. s. sanguinolentus
  Sakhalin I, S Kurile Is » S Japan
U. s. lepidus
  NW China
U. s. henrici
  Sikang

UROCYNCHRAMUS
Urocynchramus pylzowi (Przewalski's Rosefinch)
  W China

CARPODACUS
Carpodacus rubescens (Blanford's Rosefinch)
  Himalayas, W China

Carpodacus nipalensis (Dark Rosefinch)   599
C. n. kangrae
  W Himalayas
C. n. nipalensis
  C Himalayas, N Assam
C. n. intensicolor
  Sikang, W China » N Burma
Carpodacus erythrinus (Common Rosefinch)
C. e. erythrinus
  E Europe, W Asia » India, Indochina
C. e. grebnitskii
  E Siberia, Manchuria » SE China
C. e. kubanensis
  Caucasus, Iran, W India
C. e. ferghanensis
  C Asia » NW India
C. e. roseatus
  Himalayas, Tibet, China » S India, Indochina
Carpodacus purpureus (Purple Finch)
C. p. purpureus
  Canada, NE USA » SE USA
C. p. californicus
  SW Canada » SW USA, Baja California
Carpodacus cassinii (Cassin's Finch)
  SW Canada, W USA » N Mexico
Carpodacus mexicanus (House Finch)
C. m. frontalis
  SW Canada, W USA, NW Mexico
C. m. clementis
  San Clemente I, Los Coronados Is
C. m. mcgregori
  San Benito I
C. m. amplus
  Guadeloupe I
C. m. ruberrimus
  S Baja California, NW Mexico
C. m. rhodopnus
  C Sinaloa
C. m. coccineus
  SW Mexico
C. m. potosinus
  NC Mexico
C. m. centralis
  C Mexico
C. m. mexicanus
  SC Mexico
C. m. griscomi
  Guerrero
Carpodacus pulcherrimus (Beautiful Rosefinch)
C. p. pulcherrimus
  Himalayas
C. p. waltoni
  SE Tibet, SW Sikang
C. p. argyrophrys
  E Tsinghai, W China

C. p. davidianus
C Mongolia
Carpodacus eos (Stresemann's Rosefinch)
W China, E Sikang
Carpodacus rhodochrous (Pink-browed Rosefinch)
Himalayas
Carpodacus vinaceus (Vinaceous Rosefinch)
C. v. vinaceus
W China, E Sikang
C. v. formosanus
Taiwan
Carpodacus edwardsii (Large Rosefinch)
C. e. edwardsii
W China, E Sikang
C. e. rubicunda
Himalayas, SE Tibet » N Burma
Carpodacus synoicus (Sinai Rosefinch)
C. s. synoicus
Sinai
C. s. salimalii
NE Afghanistan
C. s. stoliczkae
SW Sinkiang
C. s. beicki
NE Tsinghai, NW China
Carpodacus roseus (Pallas's Rosefinch)
Altai, E Asia » N China, C Japan
Carpodacus trifasciatus (Three-banded Rosefinch)
W China » SE Tibet
Carpodacus rhodopeplus (Spot-winged Rosefinch)
C. r. rhodopeplus
Himalayas
C. r. verreauxii
W China » N Burma
Carpodacus thura (White-browed Rosefinch)
C. t. blythi
NE Afghanistan, Pakistan, W Himalayas
C. t. thura
C Himalayas
C. t. femininus
SE Tibet, W China
C. t. dubius
SE Tsinghai, NW China
C. t. deserticolor
NE Tsinghai
Carpodacus rhodochlamys (Red-mantled Rosefinch)
C. r. rhodochlamys
C Asia
C. r. kotschubeii
SC Asia
C. r. grandis
Pakistan, W Himalayas

Carpodacus rubicilloides (Eastern Great Rosefinch)
C. r. lucifer
Ladakh, Himalayas
C. r. rubicilloides
E Sikang, E Tsinghai » SW China
Carpodacus rubicillia (Caucasian Great Rosefinch)
C. r. rubicilla
Caucasus
C. r. diabolica
NE Afghanistan
C. r. kobdensis
Altai, W Mongolia
C. r. severtzovi
Pakistan to W China
Carpodacus puniceus (Rose-breasted Rosefinch)
C. p. kilianensis
SC Asia
C. p. humii
Pakistan, N India, W Himalayas
C. p. puniceus
C Himalayas, SW Sikang, SE Tibet
C. p. sikangensis
Sikang
C. p. longirostris
E Tsinghai, W China
Carpodacus roborowskii (Tibet Rosefinch)
Tsinghai

PINICOLA
Pinicola enucleator (Pine Grosbeak)
P. e. enucleator
Scandinavia, Russia
P. e. pacatus
Siberia, Altai, Manchuria
P. e. kamschatkensis
NE Asia, Kamchatka
P. e. sakhalinensis
Sakhalin I, Kurile Is
P. e. alascensis
Alaska, W Canada, NW USA
P. e. flammulus
W Canada » NW USA
P. e. carlottae
Queen Charlotte Is, Vancouver I
P. e. montanus
SW Canada, WC USA
P. e. californicus
E California
P. e. leucurus
C & E Canada » NE USA
P. e. eschatosus
SE Canada » NE USA
Pinicola subhimachalus (Red-headed Finch)
Himalayas, S Sikang

HAEMATOSPIZA
Haematospiza sipahi (Scarlet Finch)
  Himalayas to N Vietnam

LOXIA
Loxia pytyopsittacus (Parrot Crossbill)
  NE Europe, W Siberia
Loxia scotica (Scottish Crossbill)
  Scotland
Loxia curvirostra (Red Crossbill)
  L. c. curvirostra
    N Europe, N & NE Asia
  L. c. corsicana
    Corsica
  L. c. balearica
    Balearic Is
  L. c. poliogyna
    Algeria, Tunisia
  L. c. guillemardi
    Cyprus
  L. c. mariae
    SW Crimea
  L. c. altaiensis
    Altai
  L. c. tianschanica
    Sinkiang
  L. c. himalayensis
    Himalayas, W China » N Burma
  L. c. meridionalis
    S Vietnam
  L. c. japonica
    NE Asia » EC China, S Japan
  L. c. luzoniensis
    N Luzon I
  L. c. pusilla
    Newfoundland » NE USA
  L. c. minor
    SE Canada, NE USA » SE USA
  L. c. benti
    WC USA » S USA
  L. c. bendirei
    SW Canada, W USA » S USA
  L. c. sitkensis
    Canada, W & C USA » E USA
  L. c. grinnelli
    SW USA
  L. c. stricklandi
    S USA, Mexico
  L. c. mesamericana
    Guatemala to N Nicaragua
Loxia leucoptera (White-winged Crossbill)
  L. l. bifasciata
    E Europe, N Asia, Japan
  L. l. leucoptera
    Canada, N USA
  L. l. megaplaga
    Hispaniola

PYRRHULA
Pyrrhula nipalensis (Brown Bullfinch)
  P. n. nipalensis
    Pakistan, N India
  P. n. ricketti
    Tibet to N Vietnam
  P. n. victoriae
    Burma
  P. n. waterstradti
    Malaysia
  P. n. uchidai
    Taiwan
Pyrrhula leucogenys (Philippine Bull-finch)
  P. l. leucogenys
    N Luzon I
  P. l. steerei
    W Mindanao I
  P. l. coriaria
    C Mindanao I
  P. l. apo
    SE Mindanao I
Pyrrhula aurantiaca (Orange Bullfinch)
  Pakistan, NW Himalayas
Pyrrhula erythrocephala (Red-headed Bullfinch)
  Himalayas, SE Tibet
Pyrrhula erythaca (Beavan's Bullfinch)
  P. e. erythaca
    Himalayas to W China
  P. e. wilderi
    NE China
  P. e. owstoni
    Taiwan
Pyrrhula pyrrhula (Bullfinch)
  P. p. pyrrhula
    N Europe to W Mongolia » S Europe, Iran
  P. p. pileata
    British Isles
  P. p. europoea
    NW Europe
  P. p. iberiae
    Azores Is, N Iberia
  P. p. murina
    San Miguel I (Azores)
  P. p. rossikowi
    Caucasus, W Turkey
  P. p. caspica
    NE & N Iran
  P. p. cineracea
    N Altai » Amur, Manchuria
  P. p. cassinii
    Kamchatka » Japan, N China
  P. p. griseiventris
    Ussuri, Sakhalin I to Korea, S Japan

Coccothraustes coccothraustes (Hawfinch)

C. c. coccothraustes
N Europe, W Asia » N Africa

C. c. burryi
NW Africa

C. c. nigricans
Ukraine, N Iran » S Iran

C. c. humii
C Russia » NW India

C. c. japonicus
Sakhalin I, Japan » E China & Bonin I

Coccothraustes migratorius (Black-tailed Hawfinch)

C. m. migratorius
S Ussuri » N Korea & E China

C. m. sowerbyi
E China

Coccothraustes personatus (Masked Hawfinch)

C. p. personatus
N Japan » S Japan, E China

C. p. magnirostris
NE Asia

Coccothraustes icterioides (Black and Yellow Grosbeak)

Afghanistan to N India

Coccothraustes affinis (Allied Grosbeak)

Pakistan to W China, N Burma

Coccothraustes melanozanthos (Spotted-wing Grosbeak)

Pakistan to W China, Thailand

Coccothraustes carnipes (White-winged Grosbeak)

C. c. speculigerus
NE Iran to Pakistan

C. c. carnipes
Pakistan to W China

Coccothraustes vespertinus (Evening Grosbeak)

C. v. vespertinus
C & E Canada » NE USA

C. v. brooksi
W Canada » SW USA

C. v. montanus
W & SW Mexico

Coccothraustes abeillei (Hooded Grosbeak)

C. a. pallidus
NW Mexico

C. a. saturatus
W Mexico

C. a. abeillei
C & S Mexico

C. a. cobanensis
S Mexico, Guatemala

Pyrrhoplectes epauletta (Gold-headed Finch)

Himalayas, SE Tibet » N Burma

164 ESTRILDIDAE (WAXBILLS)

Parmoptila woodhousei (Flowerpecker Weaver Finch)

P. w. woodhousei
SE Nigeria, Cameroun, W Zaire

P. w. ansorgei
N Angola

Parmoptila jamesoni (Red-fronted Flowerpecker Weaver Finch)

P. j. rubrifrons
Ghana

P. j. jamesoni
E Zaire, W Uganda

Nigrita fusconota (White-breasted Negro Finch)

N. f. uropygialis
Guinea to S Nigeria

N. f. fusconota
Fernando Po I, Gabon, Cameroun Mt to Angola, Uganda, Kenya

Nigrita bicolor (Chestnut-breasted Negro Finch)

N. b. bicolor
Guinea to Ghana

N. b. brunnescens
S Nigeria to W Uganda & N Angola

Nigrita luteifrons (Pale-fronted Negro Finch)

N. l. luteifrons
S Nigeria to N Zaire & Gabon

N. l. alexanderi
Fernando Po I

Nigrita canicapilla (Grey-crowned Negro Finch)

N. c. emilae
Guinea to Ghana

N. c. canicapilla
S Nigeria to W Zaire & Uganda

N. c. angolensis
SW Zaire, NW Angola

N. c. sparsimguttata
S Sudan, E Zaire, Uganda, NW Tanzania

N. c. schistacea
SE Sudan, Kenya, N Tanzania

N. c. diabolica
C Kenya

N. c. candida
W Tanzania

Nesocharis shelleyi (Fernando Po Olive-back)
N. s. shelleyi
Fernando Po I, Cameroun Mt
N. s. bansoensis
SE Nigeria, Cameroun
Nesocharis ansorgei (White-collared Olive-back)
E Zaire, W Uganda
Nesocharis capistrata (Grey-headed Olive-back)
Gambia to Sudan, Uganda

PYTILIA

Pytilia phoenicoptera (Crimson-winged Pytilia)
P. p. phoenicoptera
Senegal to Cameroun
P. p. emini
Cameroun to Uganda & S Sudan
P. p. lineata
N Ethiopia
Pytilia hypogrammica (Red-faced Pytilia)
Sierra Leone to Cameroun
Pytilia afra (Orange-winged Pytilia)
Sudan to Angola, Zambia
Pytilia melba (Green-winged Pytilia)
P. m. citerior
Senegal to Sudan
P. m. soudanensis
E Sudan, Ethiopia, Kenya
P. m. jessei
E Ethiopia
P. m. percivali
SW Kenya, N Tanzania
P. m. belli
Uganda, E Zaire to Malawi
P. m. melba
Zaire & Tanzania to Namibia & Transvaal
P. m. hygrophila
N Zambia, N Malawi
P. m. thermophila
E Mozambique, E Natal

MANDINGOA

Mandingoa nitidula (Green-backed Twin-spot)
M. n. schlegeli
Sierra Leone to Zaire, Angola
M. n. virginiae
Fernando Po I
M. n. chubbi
S Ethiopia, S Sudan, Kenya, Tanzania, Zanzibar I
M. n. nitidula
Mozambique & Zambia to E Cape Province

Cryptospiza reichenovii (Red-faced Crimson-wing)
C. r. reichenovii
Cameroun to Uganda, N Angola
C. r. australis
S Uganda, Tanzania, Malawi, Rhodesia, Mozambique
C. r. homogenes
E Rhodesia
Cryptospiza salvadorii (Ethiopian Crimson-wing)
C. s. salvadorii
S Ethiopia, N Kenya
C. s. ruwenzori
E Zaire, W Uganda
C. s. kilimensis
SE Sudan, Kenya, N Tanzania
Cryptospiza jacksoni (Dusky Crimson-wing)
E Zaire, W Uganda
Cryptospiza shelleyi (Shelley's Crimson-wing)
E Zaire, W Uganda

PYRENESTES

Pyrenestes sanguineus (Crimson Seed-cracker)
P. s. sanguineus
Senegal to Ivory Coast
P. s. coccineus
Sierra Leone to Gabon
Pyrenestes ostrinus (Black-bellied Seedcracker)
Ghana to Uganda, Angola
Pyrenestes minor (Lesser Seedcracker)
Tanzania, Malawi, Rhodesia

SPERMOPHAGA

Spermophaga poliogenys (Grant's Bluebill)
E Zaire, W Uganda
Spermophaga haematina (Western Bluebill)
S. h. haematina
Gambia to Ghana
S. h. togoensis
Togo to SW Nigeria
S. h. pustulata
S Nigeria, Cameroun to N Zaire, N Angola
Spermophaga ruficapilla (Red-headed Bluebill)
S. r. ruficapilla
Angola to E Zaire, Uganda, S Sudan, W Kenya
S. r. cana
Tanzania

CLYTOSPIZA

Clytospiza monteiri (Brown Twin-spot)
Cameroun to Sudan, Uganda

Hypargos margaritatus (Rosy Twin-spot)
N Natal, Mozambique
Hypargos niveoguttatus (Peters's Twin-spot)
H. n. macrospilotus
E Zaire, Kenya, Tanzania, Malawi
H. n. idius
Zambia
H. n. interior
Rhodesia
H. n. niveoguttatus
Mozambique
H. n. baddeleyi
Nacola, Mozambique

EUSCHISTOSPIZA
Euschistospiza dybowskii (Dybowski's Dusky Twin-spot)
Sierra Leone to Sudan
Euschistospiza cinereovinacea (Dusky Twin-spot)
E. c. cinereovinacea
W Angola
E. c. graueri
E Zaire, W Tanzania

LAGONOSTICTA
Lagonosticta rara (Black-bellied Fire Finch)
L. r. forbesi
Sierra Leone to Nigeria
L. r. rara
N Cameroun to S Sudan, Uganda, Kenya
Lagonosticta rufopicta (Bar-breasted Fire Finch)
L. r. rufopicta
Senegal to N Cameroun, Central African Republic
L. r. lateritia
Sudan, NE Zaire, W Uganda
Lagonosticta nitidula (Brown Fire Finch)
L. n. nitidula
E Angola, S Zaire, N Zambia
L. n. plumbaria
S Zambia, Botswana
Lagonosticta senegala (Red-billed Fire Finch)
L. s. senegala
Senegal to Nigeria
L. s. guineensis
coast of Guinea & Sierra Leone
L. s. rhodopsis
Chad to SW Sudan
L. s. brunneiceps
Ethiopia
L. s. somaliensis
Somalia, Kenya, Tanzania

L. s. kikuyuensis
C Kenya, N Tanzania
L. s. ruberrima
Uganda, SE Zaire, Zambia, W Tanzania
L. s. rendalli
SE Zaire, S Tanzania, South Africa
L. s. pallidicrissa
S Angola, N Namibia
Lagonosticta rubricata (African Fire Finch)
L. r. polionota
Guinea to Nigeria
L. r. virata
Mali
L. r. ugandae
Cameroun to N Tanzania
L. r. congica
Gabon to S Zaire, NW Zambia
L. r. haematocephala
S Tanzania, Mozambique
L. r. rubricata
S Mozambique to Cape Province
Lagonosticta landanae (Pale-billed Fire Finch)
Cabinda, W Angola
Lagonosticta rhodopareia (Jameson's Fire Finch)
L. r. rhodopareia
Ethiopia, N Kenya
L. r. jamesoni
S Kenya to Transvaal, Natal
L. r. ansorgei
Cabinda, W Angola
Lagonosticta larvata (Black-faced Fire Finch)
L. l. vinacea
Senegal to Guinea
L. l. togoensis
Ghana, Togo to N Cameroun, W Sudan
L. l. nigricollis
Central African Republic to Sudan & Uganda
L. l. larvata
W Ethiopia, Sudan

URAEGINTHUS
Uraeginthus angolensis (Cordon-bleu)
U. a. angolensis
SW Zaire, N Angola, NW Zambia
U. a. cyanopleurus
Rhodesia, N Botswana, W Transvaal
U. a. niassensis
E Tanzania, SE Zaire, to Rhodesia, Transvaal
U. a. damarensis
Botswana, N Namibia

Uraeginthus bengalus (Red-cheeked Cordon-bleu)
U. b. bengalus
  W, NC & E Africa
U. b. brunneigularis
  Kenya
U. b. littoralis
  E Kenya, Tanzania
U. b. ugogoensis
  N & W Tanzania
U. b. katangae
  S Zaire, Zambia
Uraeginthus cyanocephala (Blue-capped Cordon-bleu)
  Ethiopia to Tanzania
Uraeginthus granatina (Common Grenadier)
U. g. granatina
  S Angola to Natal
U. g. siccata
  W Angola to N Cape Province
U. g. retusa
  Mozambique
Uraeginthus ianthinogaster (Purple Grenadier)
U. i. ianthinogaster
  Somalia, N Kenya, N Uganda
U. i. roosevelti
  Kenya
U. i. rothschildi
  Kenya

ESTRILDA
Estrilda caerulescens (Lavender Waxbill)
  Senegal to Central African Republic
Estrilda perreini (Black-tailed Waxbill)
E. p. perreini
  Gabon to N Angola & Tanzania
E. p. poliogastra
  S Tanzania to Rhodesia, Mozambique
E. p. torrida
  Sufala, Mozambique
E. p. incana
  Natal
Estrilda thomensis (Sao Thomé Waxbill)
  Sao Thomé I
Estrilda melanotis (Yellow-bellied Waxbill)
E. m. quartinia
  Ethiopia, SE Sudan
E. m. kilimensis
  E Zaire, Uganda to Zambia, Rhodesia
E. m. bocagei
  W Angola
E. m. stuartirwini
  S Mozambique

E. m. melanotis
  South Africa
Estrilda poliopareia (Anambra Waxbill)
  S Nigeria
Estrilda paludicola (Fawn-breasted Waxbill)
E. p. paludicola
  N Zaire, N Uganda, S Sudan
E. p. ochrogaster
  Ethiopia, SE Sudan
E. p. roseicrissa
  S Uganda, NW Tanzania
E. p. marwitzi
  W Tanzania
E. p. benguellensis
  Angola, N Zambia
E. p. ruthae
  C Zaire
Estrilda melpoda (Orange-cheeked Waxbill)
E. m. melpoda
  Gambia to N Zaire, N Angola, Zambia
E. m. tschadensis
  Cameroun, Chad
Estrilda rhodopyga (Crimson-rumped Waxbill)
E. r. rhodopyga
  Sudan, Ethiopia, N Somalia
E. r. centralis
  S Ethiopia, SE Sudan, Uganda to Tanzania, Malawi
Estrilda rufibarba (Arabian Waxbill)
  SW Arabia
Estrilda troglodytes (Black-rumped Waxbill)
  Senegal to Ethiopia
Estrilda astrild (Common Waxbill)
E. a. kempi
  Sierra Leone, Liberia
E. a. occidentalis
  Fernando Po I, Cameroun to N Zaire
E. a. sousae
  Sao Thomé I
E. a. peasei
  Ethiopia
E. a. macmillani
  Sudan
E. a. adesma
  Uganda, NW Tanzania
E. a. massaica
  Kenya, N Tanzania
E. a. minor
  E Kenya, NE Tanzania, Zanzibar
E. a. cavendishi
  S Tanzania to Zambia, Transvaal, Mozambique
E. a. schoutedeni
  S Zaire

E. a. ngamiensis
E Angola, Zambia, Rhodesia

E. a. angolensis
S Zaire, W Angola

E. a. jagoensis
W Angola, Cape Verde Is

E. a. rubriventris
Gabon

E. a. damarensis
Namibia

E. a. astrild
S Botswana, W Transvaal, Orange
Free State, W Cape Province

E. a. tenebridorsa
E Cape Province, SE Transvaal, Natal

**Estrilda nigriloris (Black-faced
Waxbill)**
Zaire

**Estrilda nonnula (Black-crowned
Waxbill)**

E. n. elizae
Fernando Po I

E. n. eisentrauti
Cameroun Mt

E. n. nonnula
E Cameroun to Sudan, Kenya, Tanzania

**Estrilda atricapilla (Black-headed
Waxbill)**

E. a. atricapilla
S Cameroun to NE Zaire

E. a. avakubi
E Zaire, NE Angola

E. a. graueri
SE Zaire, Uganda, Kenya

**Estrilda erythronotos (Black-cheeked
Waxbill)**

E. e. delamerei
Uganda, Kenya, Tanzania

E. e. soligena
Angola, Namibia to N Transvaal,
N Rhodesia

E. e. erythronotos
S Rhodesia, Transvaal, N Cape Province

Estrilda charmosyna (Red-rumped Waxbill)

E. c. charmosyna
Somalia, S Ethiopia, S Sudan, Uganda,
N Kenya

E. c. pallidior
C Kenya

E. c. kiwanukae
S Kenya, N Tanzania

AMANDAVA
Amandava amandava (Red Munia)

A. a. amandava
Pakistan, India

A. a. flavidiventris
SW China, Burma, Lesser Sunda Is

A. a. punicea
Indochina, Java, Bali I

Amandava formosa (Green Munia)
C India

Amandava subflava (Zebra Waxbill)

A. s. subflava
Senegal to Ethiopia, Uganda

A. s. clarkei
Angola to Mozambique, South Africa

ORTYGOSPIZA
**Ortygospiza atricollis (African Quail-
finch)**

O. a. atricollis
Senegal to Chad, N Zaire

O. a. ansorgei
Guinea to Ivory Coast

O. a. ugandae
S Sudan, Uganda, W Kenya

O. a. fuscocrissa
Ethiopia

O. a. muelleri
S Kenya, Tanzania, Malawi

O. a. miniscula
NW Zambia

O. a. smithersi
NE Zambia

O. a. pallida
Botswana, Rhodesia

O. a. digressa
SE Zambia, Transvaal, Natal, Cape
Province

O. a. bradfieldi
N Namibia

**Ortygospiza gabonensis (Red-billed
Quailfinch)**

O. g. gabonensis
Gabon to C Zaire

O. g. fuscata
Angola, S Zaire, Zambia

O. g. dorsostriata
E Zaire, Uganda

Ortygospiza locustella (Locust Finch)

O. l. uelensis
N Zaire

O. l. locustella
S Zaire, Zambia, Malawi, Mozambique,
Rhodesia

O. l. rendalli
Southern Africa

AEGINTHA
Aegintha temporalis (Red-browed Waxbill)

A. t. loftyi
S Australia

A. t. temporalis
Eastern Australia

A. t. minor
N Queensland

EMBLEMA
Emblema picta (Painted Finch)
 C Australia
Emblema bella (Beautiful Firetail Finch)
 SE Australia, Tasmania
Emblema oculata (Red-eared Firetail Finch)
 SW Western Australia
Emblema guttata (Diamond Firetail Finch)
 WC & SC Australia

OREOSTRUTHUS
Oreostruthus fuliginosus (Crimson-sided Mountain Finch)
 O. f. fuliginosus
 SE New Guinea
 O. f. pallidus
 W New Guinea
 O. f. hagenensis
 C New Guinea

NEOCHMIA
Neochmia phaeton (Crimson Finch)
 N. p. evangelinae
 S New Guinea
 N. p. albiventer
 N Queensland
 N. p. phaeton
 N Western Australia, Northern Territory
Neochmia ruficauda (Star Finch)
 N. r. ruficauda
 C Queensland
 N. r. clarescens
 N Queensland, Northern Territory,
  N Western Australia

POEPHILA
Poephila guttata (Spotted-sided Finch)
 P. g. guttata
 Lesser Sunda Is
 P. g. castanotis
 Australia
Poephila bichenovii (Double-barred Finch)
 P. b. annulosa
 Northern Territory, N Western Australia
 P. b. bichenovii
 E Northern Territory, Queensland,
  N New South Wales
Poephila personata (Masked Finch)
 P. p. personata
 Northern Territory, W Queensland
 P. p. leucotis
 N Queensland
Poephila acuticauda (Long-tailed Finch)
 P. a. acuticauda
 Northern Australia
 P. a. hecki
 N Western Australia

Poephila cincta (Black-throated Finch)
 P. c. nigrotecta
 N Queensland
 P. c. atropygialis
 C Queensland
 P. c. cincta
 S Queensland, N New South Wales

ERYTHRURA
Erythrura hyperythra (Bamboo Parrot Finch)
 E. h. brunneiventris
 N Luzon I, Mindoro I
 E. h. borneensis
 Borneo
 E. h. malayana
 N Malaysia
 E. h. hyperythra
 W Java
 E. h. intermedia
 Lombok I
 E. h. obscura
 Lesser Sunda Is
 E. h. microrhyncha
 Celebes
 E. h. ernstmayri
 S Celebes
Erythrura prasina (Pin-tailed Parrot Finch)
 E. p. prasina
 S Burma, S Thailand, Malaysia, Java,
  Sumatra
 E. p. coelica
 Borneo
Erythrura viridifacies (Green-faced Parrot Finch)
 Luzon I
Erythrura tricolor (Three-coloured Parrot Finch)
 Timor I, Wetar I
Erythrura coloria (Mount Katanglad Parrot Finch)
 Mindanao I
Erythrura trichroa (Blue-faced Parrot Finch)
 E. t. sanfordi
 SC Celebes
 E. t. modesta
 N Moluccas
 E. t. pinaiae
 S Moluccas
 E. t. sigillifera
 NE Australia, New Guinea, New
  Britain, New Ireland
 E. t. eichhorni
 St Matthias Is, Bismarck Archipelago
 E. t. pelewensis
 Palau Is
 E. t. clara
 Truk I, Ponapé I

E. t. trichroa
Kusaie I, Caroline Is
E. t. woodfordi
Guadalcanal I
E. t. cyanofrons
New Hebrides, Loyalty Is
Erythrura papuana (Papuan Parrot Finch)
New Guinea
Erythrura psittacea (Red-throated Parrot Finch)
New Caledonia
Erythrura pealii (Fiji Parrot Finch)
Fiji Is
Erythrura cyaneovirens (Red-headed Parrot Finch)
E. c. cyaneovirens
Samoa Is
E. c. regia
N New Hebrides
E. c. serena
S New Hebrides
E. c. efatensis
Efate I
E. c. gaughrani
Savaii I
Erythrura kleinschmidti (Pink-billed Parrot Finch)
Viti Levu I

CHLOEBIA
Chloebia gouldiae (Gouldian Finch)
Northern Australia

AIDEMOSYNE
Aidemosyne modesta (Plum-headed Finch)
W Queensland, W New South Wales

LONCHURA
Lonchura malabarica (Common Silverbill)
L. m. cantans
Senegal to W Sudan
L. m. orientalis
Somalia, Ethiopia to Tanzania, S Yemen
L. m. malabarica
Saudi Arabia to N India, Sri Lanka
Lonchura griseicapilla (Grey-headed Silverbill)
S Ethiopia to Tanzania
Lonchura nana (Bib-Finch)
Madagascar
Lonchura cucullata (Bronze Mannikin)
L. c. cucullata
Senegal to Sudan, Uganda
L. c. scutata
Ethiopia to Angola & Cape Province
Lonchura bicolor (Black & White Mannikin)
L. b. bicolor
Guinea to Cameroun

L. b. poensis
Cameroun to Angola, Ethiopia, Kenya
L. b. stigmatophora
SW Ethiopia, Uganda
L. b. nigriceps
East Africa to Natal
L. b. minor
S Somalia
L. b. woltersi
SE Zaire, NW Zambia
Lonchura fringilloides (Magpie Mannikin)
Senegal to Somalia & Natal
Lonchura striata (White-backed Munia)
L. s. acuticauda
N India, Bangladesh, Nepal, Burma
L. s. striata
S India, Sri Lanka
L. s. fumigata
Andaman Is
L. s. semistriata
Nicobar Is
L. s. subsquamicollis
S Thailand, Malaysia, Sumatra, Indochina
L. s. swinhoei
S China, Taiwan
Lonchura leucogastroides (Javanese Mannikin)
S Sumatra, Java, Bali I, Lombok I
Lonchura fuscans (Dusky Mannikin)
Borneo
Lonchura molucca (Moluccan Mannikin)
L. m. molucca
N Celebes
L. m. vagans
S Celebes
L. m. propinqua
Lesser Sunda Is
Lonchura punctulata (Nutmeg Mannikin)
L. p. punctulata
India, S Nepal
L. p. subundulata
Bhutan, Bangladesh, Assam
W Burma
L. p. yunnanensis
SW China, NE Burma
L. p. topela
S China, Thailand, Indochina
L. p. cabanisi
Luzon I, Mindoro I
L. p. fretensis
Malaysia, Sumatra
L. p. nisoria
Java, Bali I
L. p. fortior
Lombok I, Sumbawa I
L. p. sumbae
Sumba Is

L. p. blasii
Flores I, Timor I, Lesser Sunda Is
L. p. particeps
Celebes
Lonchura kelaarti (Rufous-bellied Mannikin)
L. k. vernayi
E India
L. k. jerdoni
SW India
L. k. kelaarti
Sri Lanka
Lonchura leucogastra (White-headed Munia)
L. l. leucogastra
S Thailand, Malaysia, Sumatra
L. l. everetti
Luzon I, Mindoro I,
L. l. manueli
C & S Philippine Is
L. l. palawana
Palawan I, N & E Borneo
L. l. smythiesi
SW Sarawak
L. l. castanonota
S Borneo
Lonchura tristissima (Streak-headed Mannikin)
L. t. tristissima
NW New Guinea
L. t. hypomelaena
C New Guinea
L. t. calaminoros
S New Guinea
Lonchura leucosticta (White-spotted Mannikin)
S New Guinea
Lonchura quinticolor (Coloured Finch)
Timor I, Lesser Sunda Is
Lonchura malacca (Chestnut Mannikin)
L. m. rubroniger
N India, E Napal
L. m. malacca
S India, Sri Lanka
L. m. atricapilla
NE India, Bangladesh, Assam, Burma
L. m. deignani
N Thailand, Indochina
L. m. sinensis
S Thailand, Malaysia, Sumatra
L. m. batakana
N Sumatra
L. m. formosana
N Luzon I, Taiwan
L. m. jagori
Philippine Is, Palawan I, Borneo, N Celebes

L. m. brunneiceps
S Celebes
L. m. ferruginosa
Java
Lonchura maja (Pale-headed Mannikin)
S Thailand, Malaysia, Sumatra, Java, Bali I
Lonchura pallida (Pallid Finch)
L. p. pallida
Lombok I, Lesser Sunda Is
L. p. subcastanea
W Celebes
Lonchura grandis (Great-billed Mannikin)
L. g. grandis
SE New Guinea
L. g. ernesti
N New Guinea
L. g. destructa
N New Guinea
L. g. heurni
N New Guinea
Lonchura vana (Arfak Mannikin)
NW New Guinea
Lonchura caniceps (Grey-headed Mannikin)
L. c. caniceps
SE New Guinea
L. c. scratchleyana
SE New Guinea
L. c. kumusii
SE New Guinea
Lonchura nevermanni (White-crowned Mannikin)
S New Guinea
Lonchura spectabilis (New Britain Mannikin)
L. s. wahgiensis
E New Guinea
L. s. gajduseki
C New Guinea
L. s. mayri
N New Guinea
L. s. spectabilis
New Britain
Lonchura forbesi (New Ireland Finch)
New Ireland
Lonchura hunsteini (White-headed Finch)
L. h. hunsteini
N New Ireland
L. h. nigerrima
New Hanover
L. h. minor
Ponapé I
Lonchura flaviprymna (Yellow-tailed Mannikin)
N Australia

Lonchura castaneothorax (Chestnut-breasted Mannikin)
L. c. uropygialis
NW New Guinea
L. c. sharpii
N New Guinea
L. c. boschmai
C New Guinea
L. c. ramsayi
SE New Guinea
L. c. assimilis
Northern Territory
L. c. castaneothorax
E Queensland, E New South Wales
Lonchura stygia (Black Mannikin)
S New Guinea
Lonchura teerinki (Grand Valley Mannikin)
L. t. teerinki
NC New Guinea
L. t. mariae
W New Guinea
Lonchura monticola (Alpine Mannikin)
SE New Guinea
Lonchura montana (Snow Mountain Mannikin)
C New Guinea
Lonchura melaena (New Britain Finch)
New Britain
Lonchura pectoralis (Pictorella Finch)
Northern Australia

PADDA
Padda fuscata (Timor Dusky Sparrow)
Timor I
Padda oryzivora (Java Sparrow)
Java, Bali I

AMADINA
Amadina erythrocephala (Paradise Sparrow)
A. e. erythrocephala
Angola, Rhodesia, Southern Africa
A. e. dissita
E Cape Province, S Natal
Amadina fasciata (Cut-throat Weaver)
A. f. fasciata
Senegal & N Nigeria to Sudan, Uganda
A. f. alexanderi
Ethiopia, Somalia, Kenya, Tanzania
A. f. meridionalis
Malawi, Zambia, Rhodesia, Transvaal, Mozambique

PHOLIDORNIS
Pholidornis rushiae (Tit-Hylia)
P. r. ussheri
Sierra Leone to Ghana
P. r. rushiae
S Nigeria to Angola

P. r. bedfordi
Fernando Po I
P. r. denti
E Zaire, Uganda

165 PLOCEIDAE (WEAVERS, SPARROWS)

VIDUINAE

VIDUA
Vidua chalybeata (Village Indigobird)
V. c. chalybeata
Senegal to Sierra Leone
V. c. neumanni
Mali to Sudan
V. c. ultramarina
Ethiopia
V. c. centralis
Kenya, Uganda, W Tanzania
V. c. amauropteryx
Somalia to Zambia, Mozambique
V. c. okavangoensis
W Zambia, Botswana, Angola
Vidua purpurascens (Dusky Indigobird)
Kenya to Angola, Transvaal
Vidua funerea (Variable Indigobird)
V. f. nigerrima
Angola, Zambia, Tanzania
V. f. codringtoni
S Zambia, Malawi, W Rhodesia
V. f. lusituensis
E Rhodesia
V. f. funerea
C & E South Africa
Vidua wilsoni (Pale-winged Indigobird)
"V. f. wilsoni"
N Nigeria to W Sudan
"V. f. camerunensis"
Gambia to Ethiopia
"V. f. nigeriae"
S Nigeria, Cameroun, S Sudan
(These constitute groups rather than true sub-species)
Vidua hypocherina (Steel-blue Whydah)
Ethiopia & Somalia to Tanzania
Vidua fischeri (Fischer's Whydah)
Somalia to Uganda & N Tanzania
Vidua regia (Shaft-tailed Whydah)
S Angola to S Mozambique
Vidua macroura (Pin-tailed Whydah)
Senegal to Ethiopia & Cape Province
Vidua paradisaea (Paradise Whydah)
E Sudan to S Angola & Natal
Vidua orientalis (Broad-tailed Paradise Whydah)
V. o. acupum
Senegal to N Nigeria
V. o. togoensis
Sierra Leone to Togo

V. o. orientalis
  Chad to Ethiopia
V. o. interjecta
  N Cameroun to S Sudan
V. o. obtusa
  Angola to Kenya & Mozambique

BUBALORNITHINAE

BUBALORNIS
Bubalornis albirostris (White-billed Buffalo Weaver)
B. a. albirostris
  Senegal to Ethiopia, N Uganda, Kenya
B. a. intermedius
  S Ethiopia, Somalia, Kenya
  S Tanzania
B. a. niger
  S Angola to Mozambique, Transvaal

DINEMELLIA
Dinemellia dinemelli (White-headed Buffalo Weaver)
D. d. dinemelli
  S Sudan, S Ethiopia, Somalia
  N Kenya
D. d. boehmi
  SE Zaire, Tanzania

PASSERINAE

PLOCEPASSER
Plocepasser mahali (White-browed Sparrow Weaver)
P. m. melanorhynchus
  S Sudan, S Ethiopia, Uganda, Kenya
P. m. propinquatus
  S Somalia
P. m. pectoralis
  Zambia, N Botswana to S Tanzania,
  Mozambique
P. m. ansorgei
  S Angola, N Namibia
P. m. stentor
  Namibia, W Cape Province, S Botswana,
  Transvaal
P. m. mahali
  W Orange Free State, N Cape Province
Plocepasser superciliosus (Chestnut-crowned Sparrow Weaver)
P. s. superciliosus
  Senegal to Sudan
P. s. brunnescens
  Central African Republic to SW Sudan,
  Uganda
Plocepasser donaldsoni (Donaldson-Smith's Sparrow Weaver)
  N Kenya

Plocepasser rufoscapulatus (Chestnut-mantled Sparrow Weaver)
  S Angola, SE Zaire to Malawi

HISTURGOPS
Histurgops ruficauda (Rufous-tailed Weaver)
  Tanzania

PSEUDONIGRITA
Pseudonigrita arnaudi (Grey-headed Social Weaver)
P. a. arnaudi
  SW Sudan, Kenya, Uganda, N Tanzania
P. a. australoabyssinicus
  S Ethiopia
P. a. dorsalis
  C Tanzania
Pseudonigrita cabanisi (Black-capped Social Weaver)
  S Ethiopia, E Kenya, NE Tanzania

PHILETAIRUS
Philetairus socius (Sociable Weaver)
P. s. geminus
  N & C Namibia
P. s. socius
  S Namibia
P. s. lepidus
  S Botswana, W Transvaal, N Cape
  Province
P. s. eremnus
  N Cape Province

PASSER
Passer ammodendri (Saxaul Sparrow)
P. a. korejewi
  Transcaspia, Iran
P. a. ammodendri
  Russian Turkistan
P. a. stoliczkae
  W China
P. a. timidus
  S Mongolia
Passer domesticus (House Sparrow)
P. d. domesticus
  Europe, N Asia, Americas, South
  Africa, Australia
P. d. italiae
  SE France, Italy, Crete
P. d. tingitanus
  NW Africa
P. d. biblicus
  Asia Minor, S Arabia, Caucasus, Iran
P. d. hufufae
  E Arabia
P. d. niloticus
  NE Africa
P. d. rufidorsalis
  Sudan

P. d. indicus
S Afghanistan, Pakistan, India,
Bangladesh, Burma
P. d. hyrcanus
Transcaspia, N Iran
P. d. bactrianus
SC Asia
P. d. parkini
Himalayas
Passer hispaniolensis (Spanish Sparrow)
P. h. hispaniolensis
SW Europe, North Africa, Asia Minor
P. h. transcaspicus
Caucasus, Tien Shan » S Iran, N India
Passer pyrrhonotus (Sind Jungle Sparrow)
SE Iran, Pakistan, NW India
Passer castanopterus (Somali Sparrow)
P. c. fulgens
Ethiopia, N Kenya
P. c. castanopterus
Somalia
Passer rutilans (Cinnamon Sparrow)
P. r. cinnamomeus
NE Afghanistan, Himalayas
SE Tibet
P. r. intensior
Assam, N Burma, Laos, S China
N Vietnam
P. r. rutilans
China, Taiwan, Korea, N Japan
Passer flaveolus (Pegu House Sparrow)
N Burma, Thailand, Laos, S Vietnam
Passer moabiticus (Dead Sea Sparrow)
P. m. moabiticus
Jordan, Iraq, SW Iran
P. m. yatii
E Iran, W Afghanistan
Passer motitensis (Great Sparrow)
P. m. iagoensis
Cape Verde Is
P. m. cordofanicus
NW Sudan
P. m. shelleyi
S Sudan, N Uganda
P. m. hemileucus
Abd el Kuri I
P. m. motitensis
Botswana, Transvaal
P. m. benguellensis
SW Africa, S Angola
Passer melanurus (Cape Sparrow)
P. m. damarensis
SW Angola, Namibia, Botswana
P. m. melanurus
South Africa
Passer insularis (Socotra Sparrow)
Socotra I

Passer rufocinctus (Kenya Rufous Sparrow)
Kenya, N Tanzania
Passer griseus (Grey-headed Sparrow)
P. g. griseus
Niger, Chad, Senegal to Ghana
P. g. ugandae
Ghana to Somalia, N Zaire
P. g. laeneni
E Chad
P. g. luangwae
Zambia
P. g. mosambicus
E Tanzania, Malawi, Mozambique
P. g. diffusus
Angola, N Namibia, Botswana to Natal
P. g. stygiceps
S Natal, E Cape Province
Passer swainsonii (Swainson's Sparrow)
Somalia, E & S Ethiopia
Passer gongonensis (Parrot-billed Sparrow)
Kenya, SE Tanzania
Passer suahelicus (Swahili Sparrow)
Kenya, C Tanzania
Passer simplex (Desert Sparrow)
P. s. zarudnyi
E Iran
P. s. simplex
S Sahara
P. s. saharae
W Sahara
Passer montanus (Tree Sparrow)
P. m. montanus
Europe, W, N & NE Asia, Asia Minor
P. m. transcaucasicus
Transcaucasia, N Iran
P. m. zaissanensis
C Asia, NE Mongolia
P. m. kansuensis
NE Tsinghai, Kansu
P. m. iubilaeus
N, C & E China
P. m. dilutus
NE Iran, Pakistan, Sinkiang, Manchuria,
W China
P. m. tibetanus
N Himalayas, Tibet, NW China
P. m. saturatus
Sakhalin I, S Korea, Japan, Taiwan
P. m. hepaticus
NE Assam, NW Burma
P. m. malaccensis
S Himalayas, Burma, Thailand,
Indochina, Malaysia, Sumatra, Java

AURIPASSER
Auripasser luteus (Sudan Golden Sparrow)
  N Nigeria, Chad, Sudan, N Ethiopia
Auripasser euchlorus (Arabian Golden Sparrow)
  SW Arabia, Somalia

SORELLA
Sorella eminibey (Chestnut Sparrow)
  Sudan to N Tanzania

PETRONIA
Petronia brachydactyla (Pale Rock Sparrow)
  Syria, Iran » NE Africa
Petronia xanthosterna (Yellow-spotted Petronia)
  P. x. pallida
    Senegal, Mauretania to S Sudan
  P. x. pyrgita
    Ethiopia, Somalia to NE Tanzania
  P. x. transfuga
    S Iraq, Iran, Afghanistan, Pakistan,
      NW India
  P. x. xanthosterna
    India
Petronia petronia (Rock Sparrow)
  P. p. petronia
    S Europe, Morocco, W Asia Minor
  P. p. barbara
    N Africa
  P. p. puteicola
    S Syria, Israel
  P. p. exigua
    Caucasus, Iraq, Iran
  P. p. intermedia
    Transcaspia, N Iran, C Asia
      Pakistan
  P. p. brevirostris
    E Siberia, Mongolia, N China
Petronia superciliaris (South African Rock Sparrow)
  Angola to Tanzania, South Africa
Petronia dentata (Lesser Rock Sparrow)
  P. d. dentata
    Senegal to Ethiopia, SW Arabia
  P. d. buchanani
    S Niger

MONTIFRINGILLA
Montifringilla nivalis (Snow Finch)
  M. n. nivalis
    SW Europe
  M. n. alpicola
    Transcaucasus, Iran, C Asia
  M. n. kwenlunensis
    S Sinkiang, W China
  M. n. henrici
    Tibet, W China

Montifringilla adamsi (Adams' Snow Finch)   613
  M. a. xerophila
    NW China
  M. a. adamsi
    Tibet, N Himalayas, Nepal
Montifringilla taczanowskii (Mandelli's Snow Finch)
  Tibet, N Sikang, Tsinghai
Montifringilla davidiana (Père David's Snow Finch)
  M. d. potanini
    Altai, N Mongolia
  M. d. davidiana
    S Mongolia, NW China
Montifringilla ruficollis (Red-necked Snow Finch)
  M. r. isabellina
    NW China, N Tsinghai
  M. r. ruficollis
    Tibet, W China
Montifringilla blanfordi (Blanford's Snow Finch)
  M. b. barbara
    N China
  M. b. ventorum
    NW China, Sinkiang
  M. b. blanfordi
    N Himalayas, Tibet, W China
Montifringilla theresae (Meinertzhagen's Snow Finch)
  Afghanistan

SPOROPIPES
Sporopipes squamifrons (Scaly Weaver)
  S. s. pallidus
    Mossamedes, Angola
  S. s. squamifrons
    SW Angola to Transvaal, Cape Province
Sporopipes frontalis (Speckle-fronted Weaver)
  S. f. frontalis
    Senegal to E Ethiopia
  S. f. pallidior
    S Sahara
  S. f. emini
    S Sudan, NE Uganda, Kenya,
      N Tanzania

PLOCEINAE

AMBLYOSPIZA
Amblyospiza albifrons (Grosbeak Weaver)
  A. a. capitalba
    Sierra Leone to Nigeria
  A. a. saturata
    Cameroun to N Zaire
  A. a. melanota
    NE Zaire, Ethiopia, Uganda,
      NW Kenya

A. a. *montana*
S Kenya, Zambia, Tanzania, Rhodesia
Malawi
A. a. *unicolor*
E Kenya, E Tanzania
A. a. *tandae*
N Angola
A. a. *kasaica*
S Zaire
A. a. *maxima*
N Botswana
A. a. *woltersi*
S Mozambique
A. a. *albifrons*
South Africa

PLOCEUS
***Ploceus baglafecht* (Baglafecht Weaver)**
P. b. *baglafecht*
Ethiopia, S Sudan
P. b. *reichenowi*
Kenya, N Tanzania
P. b. *stuhlmanni*
E Zaire, S Uganda; W Tanzania
P. b. *sharpii*
SW Tanzania
P. b. *nyikae*
Zambia, Malawi
P. b. *neumanni*
Cameroun
P. b. *eremobius*
NE Zaire, SE Sudan
P. b. *emini*
S Sudan, N Uganda
***Ploceus bannermani* (Bannerman's Weaver)**
Cameroun
***Ploceus batesi* (Bates's Weaver)**
Cameroun
***Ploceus nigrimentum* (Black-chinned Weaver)**
W Angola, S Zaire
***Ploceus bertrandi* (Bertrand's Weaver)**
Tanzania, Malawi, Mozambique
***Ploceus pelzelni* (Slender-billed Weaver)**
P. p. *pelzelni*
Uganda, Kenya, Tanzania, E Zaire
P. p. *tuta*
SE Zaire
P. p. *monachus*
Ghana to Gabon & N Angola
***Ploceus subpersonatus* (Loanga Slender-billed Weaver)**
S Gabon
***Ploceus luteolus* (Little Masked Weaver)**
P. l. *luteolus*
Senegal to Ethiopia

P. l. *kavirondensis*
Uganda, W Kenya, NW Tanzania
***Ploceus ocularis* (Spectacled Weaver)**
P. o. *crocatus*
Cameroun to Ethiopia » Tanzania & Angola
P. o. *suahelicus*
E Kenya, E Tanzania, E Zambia,
Mozambique
P. o. *ocularis*
Transvaal, Natal, Cape Province
***Ploceus nigricollis* (Black-necked Weaver)**
P. n. *brachypterus*
Senegal to Nigeria
P. n. *nigricollis*
Cameroun to Sudan, Zaire, Angola,
W Kenya
P. n. *po*
Fernando Po I
P. n. *melanoxanthus*
S Ethiopia, Somalia, E Kenya,
NE Tanzania
***Ploceus alienus* (Strange Weaver)**
E Zaire, W Uganda
***Ploceus melanogaster* (Black-billed Weaver)**
P. m. *melanogaster*
E Nigeria, W Cameroun, Fernando Po I
P. m. *stephanophorus*
S Sudan, E Zaire, SW Uganda, NW Kenya
***Ploceus capensis* (Cape Weaver)**
P. c. *olivaceus*
E Cape Province, Transvaal, Natal
P. c. *capensis*
W Cape Province
***Ploceus temporalis* (Bocage's Weaver)**
S Angola, W Zambia
***Ploceus subaureus* (Golden Weaver)**
P. s. *aureoflavus*
E Kenya, E Tanzania, Malawi,
Mozambique
P. s. *tongensis*
S Mozambique
P. s. *subaureus*
Natal, E Cape Province
***Ploceus xanthops* (Holub's Golden Weaver)**
Zaire & Angola to Kenya & Mozambique
***Ploceus aurantius* (Orange Weaver)**
P. a. *aurantius*
Senegal to Cameroun, Gabon, Zaire
P. a. *rex*
Uganda, NW Tanzania
***Ploceus heuglini* (Heuglin's Masked Weaver)**
Senegal to NW Kenya
***Ploceus bojeri* (Golden Palm Weaver)**
S Somalia, Kenya

Ploceus castaneiceps (Taveta Golden Weaver)
   SE Kenya, NE Tanzania
Ploceus princeps (Principé Golden Weaver)
   Principé I
Ploceus xanthopterus (Brown-throated Golden Weaver)
   P. x. castaneigula
      N Botswana, SW Zambia
   P. x. marleyi
      Natal
   P. x. xanthopterus
      Transvaal, Natal, S Rhodesia, Malawi, Mozambique
Ploceus castanops (Northern Brown-throated Weaver)
   E Zaire, Uganda
Ploceus galbula (Rüppell's Weaver)
   E Sudan, N Ethiopia, SW Arabia
Ploceus taeniopterus (Northern Masked Weaver)
   P. t. furensis
      W Sudan
   P. t. taeniopterus
      SE Sudan, N Uganda
Ploceus intermedius (Lesser Masked Weaver)
   P. i. intermedius
      Sudan, Ethiopia, Somalia to E Zaire, Tanzania
   P. i. cabanisii
      SE Zaire to Botswana & Transvaal
   P. i. beattyi
      W Angola
Ploceus velatus (African Masked Weaver)
   P. v. uluensis
      Sudan & Somalia to Tanzania
   P. v. upembae
      Zaire
   P. v. katangae
      SE Zaire, NW Zambia
   P. v. velatus
      N Cape Province, SW Transvaal
   P. v. tahatali
      E Transvaal, Natal
   P. v. caurinus
      S Angola, N Namibia, Botswana
   P. v. shelleyi
      Malawi, Mozambique, N Natal
   P. v. finschi
      coast of SW Angola
   P. v. nigrifrons
      E Cape Province
Ploceus reichardi (Tanzanian Masked Weaver)
   SW Tanzania

Ploceus vitellinus (Vitelline Masked Weaver)
   P. v. vitellinus
      Senegal to Chad, W Sudan
   P. v. peixotoi
      Sao Thomé I
Ploceus spekei (Speke's Weaver)
   S Ethiopia, Somalia, Kenya, N Tanzania
Ploceus spekeoides (Fox's Weaver)
   Uganda
Ploceus cucullatus (Village Weaver)
   P. c. cucullatus
      Senegal to Cameroun, Chad, Fernando Po I
   P. c. collaris
      Gabon, Zaire, N Angola
   P. c. bohndorffi
      N Zaire, Uganda, Sudan, NW Tanzania
   P. c. abyssinicus
      Ethiopia
   P. c. frobenii
      S Zaire
   P. c. graueri
      E Zaire, W Tanzania
   P. c. spilonotus
      S Mozambique, Natal, Transvaal, E Cape Province
Ploceus nigriceps (Layard's Blackheaded Weaver)
   Somalia, East Africa, N Mozambique
Ploceus grandis (Giant Weaver)
   Sao Thomé I
Ploceus nigerrimus (Vieillot's Black Weaver)
   P. n. castaneofuscus
      Sierra Leone to W Nigeria
   P. n. nigerrimus
      E Nigeria, Cameroun to W Kenya
Ploceus weynsi (Weyns's Weaver)
   N Zaire, S Uganda, NW Tanzania
Ploceus golandi (Clarke's Weaver)
   E Kenya
Ploceus dicrocephalus (Salvadori's Weaver)
   S Ethiopia, Somalia, N Kenya
Ploceus melanocephalus (Black-headed Weaver)
   P. m. melanocephalus
      Senegal to Benin, Niger, Chad
   P. m. capitalis
      Nigeria, S Chad, Central African Republic
   P. m. duboisi
      Zaire, N Zambia
   P. m. dimidiatus
      NE Sudan

P. m. fischeri
Uganda, Kenya, Tanzania
Ploceus jacksoni (Golden-backed Weaver)
S Sudan, Kenya, Uganda
Ploceus badius (Cinnamon Weaver)
P. b. badius
E Sudan
P. b. axillaris
S Sudan
Ploceus rubiginosus (Chestnut Weaver)
P. r. rubiginosus
Ethiopia, Somalia, Uganda, Kenya, N Tanzania
P. r. trothae
SW Angola, N Namibia
Ploceus aureonucha (Gold-naped Weaver)
NE Zaire
Ploceus tricolor (Yellow-mantled Weaver)
P. t. tricolor
Guinea to Cameroun, Gabon, Angola
P. t. interscapularis
Zaire, W Uganda
Ploceus albinucha (Maxwell's Black Weaver)
P. a. albinucha
Sierra Leone to Ghana
P. a. maxwelli
Fernando Po I
P. a. holomelas
E Nigeria to Gabon, Central African Republic, N Zaire
Ploceus nelicourvi (Nelicourvi Weaver)
N & E Madagascar
Ploceus hypoxanthus (Asian Golden Weaver)
P. h. hymenaicus
S Burma, Thailand, S Indochina
P. h. hypoxanthus
Sumatra, Java
Ploceus superciliosus (Compact Weaver)
Sierra Leone to Ethiopia, Uganda, Kenya & Angola
Ploceus benghalensis (Bengal Weaver)
Pakistan, N India, Nepal, Bangladesh
Ploceus manyar (Streaked Weaver)
P. m. flaviceps
Pakistan, W India, Sri Lanka
P. m. peguensis
NE India, Bangladesh, Burma
P. m. williamsoni
Thailand, Vietnam
P. m. manyar
Java, Bali I
Ploceus philippinus (Baya Weaver)
P. p. philippinus
Pakistan, India, Sri Lanka

P. p. travencoreensis
SW India
P. p. burmanicus
NE India, Bangladesh, Burma
P. p. infortunatus
S Vietnam, Malaysia, Sumatra
P. p. angelorum
C Thailand
Ploceus megarhynchus (Finn's Weaver)
P. m. megarhynchus
S Himalayas
P. m. salimalii
NE India
Ploceus bicolor (Forest Weaver)
P. b. tephronotus
E Nigeria, Cameroun, Fernando Po I
P. b. analogus
S Cameroun
P. b. amaurocephalus
N Angola
P. b. mentalis
S Sudan, NE Zaire, Uganda, W Kenya
P. b. kigomaensis
S Zaire, Zambia, W Tanzania
P. b. kersteni
Somalia, E Kenya, E Tanzania
P. b. stictifrons
E Rhodesia, SE Tanzania, Mozambique, Malawi
P. b. bicolor
S Mozambique, South Africa
Ploceus preussi (Golden-backed Weaver)
Sierra Leone to Cameroun, Central African Republic
Ploceus dorsomaculatus (Yellow Capped Weaver)
Cameroun, Central African Republic, Congo, Zaire
Ploceus olivaceiceps (Olive-headed Golden Weaver)
S Tanzania, Malawi, Mozambique
Ploceus nicolli (Usambara Weaver)
Tanzania
Ploceus insignis (Brown-capped Weaver)
P. i. insignis
Cameroun to Sudan, Angola, Zaire, Kenya, Tanzania
P. i. unicus
Fernando Po I
Ploceus angolensis (Bar-winged Weaver)
Angola, N Namibia, S Zaire, Zambia
Ploceus sanctaethomae (Sao Thomé Weaver)
Sao Thomé I

MALIMBUS
Malimbus flavipes (Yellow-legged Malimbe)
NE Zaire
Malimbus coronatus (Red-crowned Malimbe)
Cameroun

Malimbus cassini (Black-throated Malimbe)
S Cameroun, Gabon, Congo
Malimbus racheliae (Rachel's Malimbe)
E Nigeria to Gabon
Malimbus ballmani (Tai Malimbe)
Thailand, Ivory Coast
Malimbus scutatus (Red-vented Malimbe)
M. s. scutatus
Sierra Leone to Ghana
M. s. scutopartitus
S Nigeria, W Cameroun
Malimbus ibadanensis (Ibadan Malimbe)
E Nigeria
Malimbus nitens (Gray's Malimbe)
M. n. nitens
Guinea to S Nigeria
M. n. moreaui
Cameroun, Gabon, NW Zaire
M. n. microrhynchus
NE Zaire, W Uganda
Malimbus rubricollis (Red-headed Malimbe)
M. r. bartletti
Sierra Leone to Ghana
M. r. nigeriae
Benin, W Nigeria
M. r. rubricollis
E Nigeria to Sudan, Chad, Central
African Republic
M. r. rufovelatus
Fernando Po I
M. r. praedi
N Angola
Malimbus erythrogaster (Red-bellied Malimbe)
E Nigeria to E Zaire
Malimbus malimbicus (Crested Malimbe)
M. m. nigrifrons
Sierra Leone to Nigeria
M. m. malimbicus
Cameroun to Uganda, S Zaire, N Angola

ANAPLECTES
Anaplectes melanotis (Red-headed Weaver)
A. m. melanotis
Senegal to Ethiopia, Uganda, W Kenya
A. m. jubaensis
S Somalia, NE Kenya
A. m. rubriceps
S Angola to Tanzania, Mozambique
A. m. gurneyi
N Namibia

QUELEA
Quelea cardinalis (Cardinal Quelea)
Q. c. cardinalis
S Sudan, S Ethiopia, Uganda, Kenya,
NW Tanzania
Q. c. rhodesiae
Tanzania, Zambia
Quelea erythrops (Red-headed Quelea)
Senegal to Ethiopia, Natal &
Cape Province

Quelea quelea (Red-billed Quelea)
Q. q. quelea
Senegal to Chad, Central African
Republic
Q. q. aethiopica
Sudan, Somalia to E Zaire, N Tanzania
Q. q. lathamii
Angola, S Zaire, Zambia, Southern
Africa

FOUDIA
Foudia madagascariensis (Madagascan Red Fody)
Madagascar, Mauritius I, Reunion I
Foudia eminentissima (Mascarene Fody)
F. e. aldabrana
Aldabra I
F. e. consobrina
Great Comoro I
F. e. anjuanensis
Anjouan I
F. e. eminentissima
Moheli I
F. e. algondae
Mayotte I
Foudia omissa (Red Forest Fody)
E Madagascar
Foudia rubra (Mauritius Fody)
Mauritius I
Foudia sechellarum (Seychelles Fody)
Seychelles Is
Foudia flavicans (Rodriguez Fody)
Rodriguez I
Foudia sakalava (Sakalava Fody)
F. s. sakalava
N & NE Madagascar
F. s. minor
W & SW Madagascar

BRACHYCOPE
Brachycope anomala (Bob-tailed Weaver)
SE Cameroun, Congo

EUPLECTES
Euplectes afer (Golden Bishop)
E. a. afer
Senegal to Chad, Central African
Republic
E. a. ladoensis
S Sudan, Uganda, N Kenya, N Tanzania
E. a. strictus
Ethiopia
E. a. taha
Southern Africa
Euplectes diademata (Fire-fronted Bishop)
E Kenya, NE Tanzania
Euplectes gierowii (Gierow's Bishop)
E. g. ansorgei
S Sudan, S Ethiopia, E Zaire, Uganda

E. g. friederichseni
SW Kenya, N Tanzania
E. g. gierowii
N Angola, SW Zaire
Euplectes nigroventris (Zanzibar Red Bishop)
E Kenya, E Tanzania, E Mozambique,
Zanzibar I
Euplectes hordeacea (Red-crowned Bishop)
E. h. hordeacea
Senegal to W Sudan, Angola, Rhodesia
E. h. craspedoptera
S Sudan, SW Ethiopia, Uganda,
NW Kenya
Euplectes orix (Red Bishop)
E. o. franciscana
Senegal to Ethiopia, Uganda, Kenya
E. o. pusilla
SE Ethiopia, Somalia
E. o. nigrifrons
E Zaire, S Kenya, Tanzania,
Mozambique, Malawi
E. o. orix
N Angola to S Mozambique and
Southern Africa
Euplectes aurea (Golden-backed Bishop)
Sao Thomé I, W Angola
Euplectes capensis (Yellow-rumped Bishop)
E. c. phoenicomera
SE Nigeria, Cameroun, Fernando Po I
E. c. xanthomelas
Sudan, Ethiopia, East Africa, Angola
to Transvaal
E. c. approximans
E Transvaal, Natal, E Cape Province
E. c. capensis
W & S Cape Province
E. c. macrorhynchus
NW Cape Province
Euplectes axillaris (Fan-tailed Whydah)
E. a. bocagei
Niger, Cameroun, Angola, S Zaire,
Zambia
E. a. quanzae
C Angola
E. a. traversii
N Ethiopia
E. a. phoeniceus
S Ethiopia, Sudan, Uganda, W Kenya,
W Tanzania
E. a. batesi
Upper Volta to Upper Niger
E. a. zanzibaricus
Somalia, E Kenya, E Tanzania
E. a. axillaris
Zambia to Mozambique & E South Africa
**Euplectes macrourus (Yellow-mantled
Whydah)**
E. m. macrocercus
Uganda, W Kenya

E. m. macrourus
West Africa to Sudan, Zaire, Angola
to Mozambique
E. m. conradsi
NW Tanzania
E. m. intermedius
W Tanzania
Euplectes hartlaubi (Marsh Whydah)
E. h. humeralis
Cameroun to Uganda, W Kenya
E. h. hartlaubi
Angola, S Zaire, Zambia
E. h. psammocromius
SW Tanzania, Malawi
Euplectes albonotatus (White-winged Whyd
E. a. eques
Sudan to Tanzania
E. a. sassii
E Zaire
E. a. asymmetrurus
Gabon to N Namibia
E. a. albonotatus
SE Zaire and Zambia to Tanzania, Natal
Euplectes ardens (Red-collared Whydah)
E. a. concolor
Senegal to S Sudan, Uganda, Chad
E. a. laticauda
SE Sudan, Ethiopia
E. a. suahelicus
Kenya, NE Tanzania
E. a. ardens
EC Southern Africa
Euplectes progne (Long-tailed Whydah)
E. p. delamerei
E Kenya
E. p. ansorgei
E Angola, W Zambia
E. p. progne
E Zambia, S Africa
E. p. definita
W Zambia
Euplectes jacksoni (Jackson's Whydah)
Kenya, N Tanzania

ANOMALOSPIZA
Anomalospiza imberbis (Parasitic Weaver)
Sierra Leone to Ethiopia & Transvaal

166 STURNIDAE (STARLINGS)

STURNINAE

APLONIS
Aplonis zelandica (New Hebrides Starling)
A. z. rufipennis
C & N New Hebrides, Banks Is
A. z. maxwellii
Santa Cruz I
A. z. zelandica
Vanikoro I

Aplonis santovestris (Mountain Starling)
   Espiritu Santo I
Aplonis pelzelni (Ponapé Starling)
   Ponapé I
Aplonis atrifusca (Samoan Starling)
   Samoan Is
Aplonis cinerascens (Raratonga Starling)
   Cook I
Aplonis tabuensis (Striped Starling)
   A. t. pachyramphus
     Santa Cruz I
   A. t. tucopiae
     Tucopia I
   A. t. rotumae
     Rotuma I
   A. t. vitiensis
     Fiji Is
   A. t. manuae
     Manuan I
   A. t. tabuensis
     Tonga I
   A. t. fortunae
     Fotuna I, Alofa I, Uea I
   A. t. tenebrosa
     Keppel I, Boscawen I
   A. t. nesiotes
     Niuafou I
   A. t. brunnescens
     Niué I
   A. t. tutuilae
     Tutuila I
   A. t. brevirostris
     Upolu I, Savaii I
Aplonis striata (Striated Starling)
   A. s. striata
     New Caledonia
   A. s. atronitens
     Loyalty Is
Aplonis fusca (Norfolk I Starling)
   Norfolk I
Aplonis opaca (Micronesian Starling)
   A. o. aeneus
     Takatsukasa I
   A. o. guami
     Guam I
   A. o. orii
     Palau Is
   A. o. kurodai
     Yap I
   A. o. ponapensis
     Ponapé I
   A. o. opaca
     Kusaie I
   A. o. angus
     Truk I
Aplonis cantoroides (Singing Starling)
   New Guinea, Bismarck Archipelago

Aplonis crassa (Tenimber Starling)
   Tenimber Is
Aplonis feadensis (Fead Is Starling)
   A. f. feadensis
     Solomon Is
   A. f. heureka
     Bismarck Archipelago
Aplonis insularis (Rennell I Starling)
   Rennell I
Aplonis dichroa (San Cristobal Starling)
   San Cristobal I
Aplonis grandis (Large Glossy Starling)
   A. g. malaitae
     Malaita I
   A. g. macrura
     Guadalcanal I
   A. g. grandis
     Bougainville I, Choiseul I, Ysabel I
Aplonis mysolensis (Moluccan Starling)
   A. m. mysolensis
     W New Guinea Is
   A. m. forsteni
     Moluccas
   A. m. sulaensis
     Sula Is
   A. m. persimilis
     Banggai I
Aplonis magna (Long-tailed Starling)
   A. m. magna
     Biak I
   A. m. brevicauda
     Numfor I
Aplonis minor (Lesser Glossy Starling)
   A. m. minor
     Lesser Sunda Is
   A. m. montosa
     Celebes
   A. m. todayensis
     Mindanao I
Aplonis panayensis (Philippine Glossy
Starling)
   A. p. affinis
     Assam, W Burma, S Vietnam
   A. p. strigata
     S Thailand, Malaysia, Sumatra, Java
     W Borneo
   A. p. eustathis
     E Borneo
   A. p. heterochlora
     Anamba Is, Natuna Is
   A. p. tytleri
     Andaman Is, Nicobar Is
   A. p. altirostris
     W Sumatran Is
   A. p. leptorrhyncha
     W Sumatran Is
   A. p. pachistorhina
     W Sumatran Is

A. p. enganensis
Enggano I
A. p. gusti
Bali I
A. p. alipodis
Maratua I, E Borneo
A. p. sanghirensis
Sanghir Is, Talaut I
A. p. panayensis
Celebes, Philippine Is
Aplonis metallica (Shining Starling)
A. m. circumscripta
Tenimber Is, Damar I
A. m. metallica
Moluccas, New Guinea, NE Queensland
A. m. nitida
Solomon Is, Bismarck Archipelago
A. m. purpureiceps
Admiralty Is
A. m. inornata
Biak I, Numfor I
Aplonis mystacea (Grant's Starling)
W & S New Guinea
Aplonis brunneicapilla (White-eyed Starling)
Bougainville I, Rendova I

POEOPTERA
Poeoptera kenricki (Kenrick's Starling)
P. k. bensoni
Kenya
P. k. kenricki
S Kenya, N Tanzania
Poeoptera stuhlmanni (Stuhlmann's Starling)
SW Ethiopia, W Kenya, Uganda, E Zaire
Poeoptera lugubris (Narrow-tailed Starling)
P. l. lugubris
Sierra Leone to W Uganda, N Angola
P. l. webbi
Kigezi, Uganda

GRAFISIA
Grafisia torquata (White-collared Starling)
Cameroun, N Zaire, Central African Republic

ONYCHOGNATHUS
Onychognathus walleri (Waller's Red-winged Starling)
O. w. preussi
Cameroun, Fernando Po I
O. w. elgonensis
S Sudan, Uganda, E Zaire, W Kenya
O. w. walleri
S Kenya, Tanzania, N Malawi

Onychognathus nabouroup (Pale-winged Starling)
O. n. benguellensis
E Angola, N Namibia
O. n. nabouroup
S Namibia, Botswana, N Cape Province
Onychognathus morio (African Red-winged Starling)
O. m. modicus
Senegal, Mali, W Niger
O. m. neumanni
N Nigeria to Central African Republic & W Sudan
O. m. rüppellii
Ethiopia & Sudan to Tanzania
O. m. morio
Rhodesia, S Malawi, S Mozambique, Southern Africa
Onychognathus blythii (Somali Chestnut-winged Starling)
Somalia, Socotra I
Onychognathus frater (Socotra Chestnut-winged Starling)
Socotra I
Onychognathus tristramii (Tristram's Grackle)
Israel, Arabia
Onychognathus fulgidus (Chestnut-winged Starling)
O. f. fulgidus
Sao Thomé I
O. f. hartlaubii
Guinea to W Uganda & Angola
Onychognathus tenuirostris (Slender-billed Red-winged Starling)
O. t. tenuirostris
Ethiopia, N Kenya
O. t. theresae
E Zaire to Uganda, Kenya, Tanzania, Malawi
Onychognathus albirostris (White-billed Starling)
Ethiopia
Onychognathus salvadorii (Bristle-crowned Starling)
Somalia, S Ethiopia, N Kenya

LAMPROTORNIS
Lamprotornis iris (Iris Glossy Starling)
Guinea to Ivory Coast
Lamprotornis cupreocauda (Copper-tailed Glossy Starling)
Sierra Leone to Ghana
Lamprotornis purpureiceps (Purple-headed Glossy Starling)
S Nigeria to Gabon & Uganda

Lamprotornis corruscus (Black-bellied Glossy Starling)
L. c. corruscus
E & SE Africa
L. c. vaughani
Pemba I

Lamprotornis purpureus (Purple Glossy Starling)
L. p. purpureus
Senegal to Nigeria, Mali
L. p. amethystinus
Nigeria & Chad to Sudan & N Kenya

Lamprotornis nitens (Red-shouldered Glossy Starling)
L. n. nitens
Gabon to Angola
L. n. phoenicopterus
SW & SC Africa
L. n. culminator
Cape Province, S Natal

Lamprotornis chalcurus (Bronze-tailed Glossy Starling)
L. c. chalcurus
Senegal to Ghana
L. c. emini
Togo to Central African Republic,
NE Zaire, Uganda, Kenya

Lamprotornis chalybaeus (Greater Blue-eared Glossy Starling)
L. c. chalybaeus
Senegal to Somalia, Kenya
L. c. cyaniventris
Ethiopia, W Kenya, Uganda, E Zaire
L. c. sycobius
Tanzania, Zambia, Malawi, Mozambique
L. c. nordmanni
S Angola, Zambia, Botswana, Transvaal

Lamprotornis chloropterus (Lesser Blue-eared Glossy Starling)
L. c. chloropterus
Senegal to Ethiopia, Uganda, Kenya
L. c. cyanogenys
SE Sudan, Ethiopia, N Uganda
L. c. elisabeth
S Uganda, S Kenya, Tanzania, Zambia,
Mozambique

Lamprotornis acuticaudus (Sharp-tailed Glossy Starling)
Angola, Zambia, S Zaire

Lamprotornis splendidus (Splendid Glossy Starling)
L. s. chrysonotis
Senegal to Sierra Leone
L. s. splendidus
Nigeria & Ethiopia to Angola, W Tanzania
L. s. lessoni
Fernando Po I

L. s. bailundensis
S Angola, S Zaire, Zambia, S Tanzania

Lamprotornis ornatus (Principé Glossy Starling)
Principé I

Lamprotornis australis (Burchell's Starling)
L. a. australis
E Angola to Rhodesia
L. a. degener
NW Transvaal to S Mozambique

Lamprotornis mevesii (Long-tailed Purple Starling)
L. m. chalceus
C Angola
L. m. mevesii
S Angola to S Malawi
L. m. violacior
NW Namibia, SW Angola
L. m. benguelensis
SW & W Angola

Lamprotornis purpuropterus (Rüppell's Long-tailed Glossy Starling)
L. p. aeneocephalus
E Sudan, N Ethiopia
L. p. purpuropterus
S Ethiopia, S Sudan, Uganda, Kenya,
W Tanzania

Lamprotornis caudatus (Long-tailed Purple Starling)
Senegal to Sudan

CINNYRICINCLUS
Cinnyricinclus femoralis (Abbott's Starling)
S Kenya, N Tanzania

Cinnyricinclus sharpii (Sharpe's Starling)
E Zaire to Ethiopia & Tanzania

Cinnyricinclus leucogaster (Violet Starling)
C. l. leucogaster
Senegal to Uganda, Kenya, Tanzania
C. l. arabicus
SW Arabia, NE Sudan, Somalia, N Ethiopia
C. l. friedmanni
S Ethiopia
C. l. verreauxi
Angola to Kenya & Cape Province

SPECULIPASTOR
Speculipastor bicolor (Magpie Starling)
S Ethiopia, N Kenya

NEOCICHLA
Neocichla gutturalis (White-winged Starling)
N. g. gutturalis
S Angola, W Zambia
N. g. angusta
E Zambia, Tanzania, Malawi

SPREO

Spreo fischeri (Fischer's Starling)
S Somalia, Kenya, N Tanzania
Spreo bicolor (Pied Starling)
Ethiopia, E & South Africa
Spreo albicapillus (White-crowned Starling)
S Ethiopia, Somalia
Spreo superbus (Superb Starling)
SE Sudan to Somalia & Tanzania
Spreo pulcher (Chestnut-bellied Starling)
S. p. pulcher
Senegal to S Sudan
S. p. rufiventris
Chad, Sudan, Ethiopia
Spreo hildebrandti (Hildebrandt's Starling)
S Kenya, N Tanzania
Spreo shelleyi (Shelley's Starling)
S Ethiopia, S Somalia, Kenya

COSMOPSARUS

Cosmopsarus regius (Golden-breasted Starling)
C. r. regius
S Ethiopia, S Somalia, Kenya
C. r. magnificus
E Kenya
Cosmopsarus unicolor (Ashy Starling)
S Kenya, Tanzania

SAROGLOSSA

Saroglossa aurata (Madagascar Starling)
Madagascar
Saroglossa spiloptera (Spot-winged Starling)
Himalayas, Burma, Thailand

CREATOPHORA

Creatophora cinerea (Wattled Starling)
Ethiopia to Angola & Cape Province

STURNUS

Sturnus senex (Ceylon White-headed Starling)
SW Sri Lanka
Sturnus malabaricus (Ashy-headed Starling)
S. m. blythii
SW India
S. m. malabaricus
C & E India, Assam
S. m. nemoricola
E India, Burma, Thailand, SW China, Indochina
Sturnus erythropygius (White-headed Starling)
S. e. erythropygius
Andaman Is
S. e. andamanensis
Car Nicobar I

S. e. katchalensis
Katchal I
Sturnus pagodarum (Black-headed Starling)
Afghanistan, India, Sri Lanka
Sturnus sericeus (Silky Starling)
S China
Sturnus philippensis (Violet-backed Starling)
Japan, Borneo, Philippine Is
Sturnus sturninus (Daurian Starling)
E & SE Asia
Sturnus roseus (Rose-coloured Starling)
E Europe, W & C Asia » India
Sturnus vulgaris (Common Starling)
S. v. faroensis
Faroe Is
S. v. zetlandicus
Outer Hebrides, Shetland Is
S. v. vulgaris
N & C Europe, N Africa, N America
S. v. tauricus
SE Europe » Iraq, W Iran
S. v. caucasicus
N Iran
S. v. purpurascens
S Russia » Iraq, Egypt
S. v. nobilior
Transcaspia, NE Iran » N India
S. v. poltaratskyi
C Siberia » E Iran & E India
S. v. porphyronotus
Turkistan » Nepal & N India
S. v. humii
W Himalayas » N India
S. v. minor
Sind
Sturnus unicolor (Spotless Starling)
S Europe, N Africa
Sturnus cineraceus (Grey Starling)
C Asia to Japan » S China
Sturnus contra (Asian Pied Starling)
S. c. contra
N & C India
S. c. sordidus
N Assam
S. c. superciliaris
E Assam, Burma
S. c. floweri
S Burma, Thailand, Laos
S. c. jalla
Sumatra, Java, Bali I
Sturnus nigricollis (Black-collared Starling)
S China, Burma, Thailand, Malaysia, Indochina

Sturnus burmannicus **(Jerdon's Starling)**
  S. b. burmannicus
    Burma
  S. b. leucocephalus
    S Thailand, Cambodia, S Indochina
Sturnus melanopterus **(Black-winged Starling)**
  S. m. melanopterus
    W Java
  S. m. tricolor
    E Java
  S. m. tertius
    Bali I, Lombok I
Sturnus sinensis **(Chinese Starling)**
  S China, N Indochina » Malaysia

LEUCOPSAR
Leucopsar rothschildi **(Rothschild's Mynah)**
  Bali I

ACRIDOTHERES
Acridotheres tristis **(Common Mynah)**
  A. t. tristis
    Afghanistan, India, SE Asia
  A. t. melanosturnus
    Sri Lanka
  A. t. tristoides
    C & N Burma, Nepal & South Africa (intro.)
Acridotheres ginginianus **(Bank Mynah)**
  Pakistan, N India
Acridotheres fuscus **(Indian Jungle Mynah)**
  A. f. mahrattensis
    W & S India
  A. f. fuscus
    N India, Burma
  A. f. fumidus
    NE Assam
  A. f. torquatus
    N & C Malaysia
  A. f. javanicus
    Java
  A. f. cinereus
    S Celebes
Acridotheres grandis **(Great Mynah)**
  Assam, Burma, Indochina
Acridotheres albocinctus **(White-collared Mynah)**
  E India to NW Yunnan
Acridotheres cristatellus **(Chinese Jungle Mynah)**
  A. c. cristatellus
    C & S China, E Burma
  A. c. formosanus
    Taiwan
  A. c. brevipennis
    Hainan I, Indochina

AMPELICEPS
Ampeliceps coronatus **(Gold-crested Mynah)**
  Assam, Burma, Thailand, Laos

MINO
Mino anais **(Golden-breasted Mynah)**
  M. a. anais
    NW New Guinea
  M. a. orientalis
    N New Guinea
  M. a. robertsoni
    S New Guinea
Mino dumontii **(Yellow-faced Mynah)**
  M. d. dumontii
    New Guinea, Aru Is
  M. d. kreffti
    Bismarck Archipelago
  M. d. sanfordi
    Guadalcanal I, Malaita I

BASILORNIS
Basilornis celebensis **(Celebes King Starling)**
  Celebes
Basilornis galeatus **(Greater King Starling)**
  Banggai I, Sula Is
Basilornis corythaix **(Ceram King Starling)**
  Ceram I
Basilornis miranda **(Mount Apo King Starling)**
  Mindanao I

STREPTOCITTA
Streptocitta albicollis **(Celebes Magpie)**
  S. a. torquata
    N & E Celebes
  S. a. albicollis
    S & SE Celebes
Streptocitta albertinae **(Sula Magpie)**
  Sula Is

SARCOPS
Sarcops calvus **(Bald Starling)**
  S. c. calvus
    N Philippine Is
  S. c. melanotus
    C & SE Philippine Is
  S. c. lowii
    Sulu Is

GRACULA
Gracula ptilogenys **(Ceylon Grackle)**
  Sri Lanka
Gracula religiosa **(Southern Grackle) (Hill Myna)**
  G. r. indica
    SW India, Sri Lanka
  G. r. peninsularis
    NE India

G. r. intermedia
N India, Burma, Thailand, Indochina
G. r. andamanensis
Andaman Is, Nicobar Is
G. r. religiosa
Malaysia, Sumatra, Java, Bali I, Borneo,
Bangka I
G. r. batuensis
W Sumatran Is
G. r. robusta
Babi I, Nias I
G. r. palawanensis
Palawan I
G. r. venerata
Sumbawa I
G. r. mertensi
Flores I, Pantar I, Alor I

ENODES
Enodes erythrophris (Celebes Enodes Starling)
E. e. erythrophris
N Celebes
E. e. centralis
NC & SE Celebes
E. e. leptorhynchus
SC Celebes

SCISSIROSTRUM
Scissirostrum dubium (Grosbeak Starling)
S. d. dubium
Celebes
S. d. pelingense
Togian I, Peling I

BUPHAGINAE

BUPHAGUS
Buphagus africanus (Yellow-billed Oxpecker)
B. a. africanus
Senegal & SW Ethiopia to Namibia and
Natal
B. a. langi
Gabon, W Congo
Buphagus erythrorhynchus (Red-billed Oxpecker)
B. e. erythrorhynchus
Ethiopia, Sudan
B. e. caffer
Botswana, W Rhodesia, W Transvaal
B. e. angolensis
S Angola to W Zambia
B. e. scotinus
S Kenya to S Mozambique

167 ORIOLIDAE (ORIOLES)

ORIOLUS
Oriolus szalayi (Brown Oriole)
New Guinea

Oriolus phaeochromus (Moluccan Oriole)
Halmahera I
Oriolus forsteni (Ceram Oriole)
Ceram I
Oriolus bouroensis (Buru Oriole)
O. b. bouroensis
Buru I
O. b. decipiens
Tenimber Is
Oriolus viridifuscus (Timor Oriole)
O. v. finschi
Wetar I
O. v. viridifuscus
Timor I
Oriolus sagittatus (Olive-backed Oriole)
O. s. magnirostris
S New Guinea, N Queensland
O. s. affinis
N Western Australia
O. s. sagittatus
E & SE Australia
Oriolus flavocinctus (Yellow Oriole)
O. f. flavocinctus
N Northern Territory, N Queensland
O. f. mülleri
Aru Is, S New Guinea
Oriolus xanthonotus (Dark-throated Oriole)
O. x. xanthonotus
Malaysia, Sumatra, Java, SW Borneo
O. x. consobrinus
N, C & E Borneo
O. x. mentawi
W Sumatran Is, Siberut I
O. x. cinereogenys
Sulu Is
O. x. persuasus
Palawan I
O. x. basilanicus
Basilan I, W Mindanao I
O. x. samarensis
E Mindanao I, Samar I, Leyte I
O. x. steerii
Masbate I, Negros I
O. x. assimilis
Cebu I
Oriolus albiloris (White-lored Oriole)
Bataan I, Luzon I
Oriolus isabellae (Isabella Oriole)
Bataan I, Luzon I
Oriolus oriolus (Golden Oriole)
O. o. oriolus
Europe, W & WC Asia » E & S Africa,
NW India
O. o. kundoo
C Asia, N India

Oriolus auratus (African Golden Oriole)
  O. a. auratus
    W & NC Africa
  O. a. notatus
    Eastern & Southern Africa
Oriolus chinensis (Black-naped Oriole)
  O. c. tenuirostris
    E Nepal, C Burma » S Burma, Thailand
  O. c. invisus
    S Vietnam
  O. c. diffusus
    E Asia » India, Malaysia, Indochina
  O. c. andamanensis
    Andaman Is
  O. c. macrourus
    Nicobar Is
  O. c. chinensis
    Philippine Is
  O. c. suluensis
    Sulu Is
  O. c. melanisticus
    Talaut I
  O. c. sanghirensis
    Sanghir Archipelago
  O. c. formosus
    Siau I
  O. c. frontalis
    Sula Is, Peling I
  O. c. saani
    Moluccas
  O. c. mundus
    Simalur I
  O. c. sipora
    Sipora I
  O. c. richmondi
    Siberut I, Pagi I
  O. c. insularis
    Kangean I
  O. c. broderipii
    Flores I, Lombok I, Sumba I, Sumbawa I
  O. c. lamprochryseus
    Solombo Besar I
  O. c. oscillans
    Tukangbesi I
  O. c. boneratensis
    Flores Sea Is
  O. c. maculatus
    Sumatra, Java, Borneo, Bali I, Nias I
  O. c. celebensis
    N Celebes
  O. c. macassariensis
    S Celebes
Oriolus chlorocephalus (Green-headed Oriole)
  O. c. amani
    Tanzania
  O. c. chlorocephalus
    Malawi, Mozambique

  O. c. speculifer
    S Mozambique
Oriolus crassirostris (Sao Thomé Oriole)
    Sao Thomé I
Oriolus brachyrhynchus (Western Black-headed Oriole)
  O. b. brachyrhynchus
    W Africa
  O. b. laetior
    WC & C Africa
Oriolus monacha (Dark-Headed Oriole)
  O. m. monacha
    N Ethiopia
  O. m. meneliki
    S Ethiopia
Oriolus larvatus (African Black-headed Oriole)
  O. l. percivali
    Zaire, Kenya
  O. l. rolleti
    Angola, Namibia to Tanzania, Natal
  O. l. larvatus
    South Africa
Oriolus nigripennis (Black-winged Oriole)
  O. n. alleni
    W Africa
  O. n. nigripennis
    WC & C Africa
Oriolus xanthornus (Asian Black-headed Oriole)
  O. x. xanthornus
    N India, Thailand, Indochina
  O. x. maderaspatanus
    S India, Andaman Is
  O. x. ceylonensis
    Sri Lanka
  O. x. tanakae
    NE Borneo
  O. x. thaiocous
    S Thailand, N Malaysia
  O. x. andamanensis
    S Andaman Is
Oriolus hosii (Black Oriole)
    Borneo
Oriolus cruentus (Crimson-breasted Oriole)
  O. c. cruentus
    Java
  O. c. malayanus
    C Malaysia
  O. c. consanguineus
    Sumatra
  O. c. vulneratus
    N Borneo
Oriolus traillii (Maroon Oriole)
  O. t. traillii
    Himalayas, Burma, Thailand

O. t. robinsoni
S Indochina
O. t. nigellicauda
N Vietnam, Hainan I
O. t. ardens
Taiwan
Oriolus mellianus (Stresemann's Maroon Oriole)
W China

SPHECOTHERES
Sphecotheres vieilloti (Southern Figbird)
S. v. vieilloti
NE Australia
S. v. salvadorii
NE Queensland, S New Guinea
Sphecotheres flaviventris (Yellow Figbird)
S. f. flaviventris
N & NE Australia
S. f. cucullatus
Kei Is, Arafura Sea
Sphecotheres viridis (Timor Figbird)
Timor I
Sphecotheres hypoleucus (Wetar Figbird)
Wetar I

168 DICRURIDAE (DRONGOS)

CHAETORHYNCHUS
Chaetorhynchus papuensis (Papuan Mountain Drongo)
New Guinea

DICRURUS
Dicrurus ludwigii (Square-tailed Drongo)
D. l. sharpei
W, WC & C Africa
D. l. ludwigii
Eastern & Southern Africa
D. l. tephrogaster
Mozambique, E Rhodesia, S Malawi
Dicrurus atripennis (Shining Drongo)
W Africa
Dicrurus adsimilis (Fork-tailed Drongo)
D. a. adsimilis
EC & Southern Africa
D. a. divaricatus
W Africa, Chad, Sudan, Ethiopia
D. a. coracinus
WC & C Africa
D. a. atactus
Upper Guinea, Nigeria
D. a. modestus
Principé I
Dicrurus fuscipennis (Comoro Drongo)
Great Comoro I
Dicrurus aldabranus (Aldabra Drongo)
Aldabra I

Dicrurus forficatus (Crested Drongo)
D. f. forficatus
Madagascar
D. f. potior
Anjouan I
Dicrurus waldenii (Mayotte Drongo)
Mayotte I
Dicrurus macrocercus (Black Drongo)
D. m. albirictus
SE Iran, Afghanistan, N India
D. m. macrocercus
S India
D. m. minor
Sri Lanka
D. m. cathoecus
China, N Burma, N Thailand, Laos
N Vietnam, Malaysia
D. m. thai
S Burma, S Thailand, S Vietnam
D. m. harterti
Taiwan
D. m. javanus
Java, Bali I
Dicrurus leucophaeus (Pale Ashy Drongo)
D. l. longicaudatus
E Afghanistan » S India, Sri Lanka
D. l. hopwoodi
Sikkim, Bhutan, Assam, Burma, S China
» S Indochina
D. l. mouhoti
S Burma, N Thailand » S Vietnam,
Indochina
D. l. bondi
S Thailand, Cambodia
D. l. nigrescens
S Thailand, Malaysia
D. l. leucogenis
Manchuria, E China » S Indochina
D. l. salangensis
SE China, S Thailand » Hainan I,
Malaysia
D. l. innexus
Hainan I
D. l. stigmatops
N Borneo
D. l. phaedrus
S Sumatra
D. l. batakensis
N Sumatra
D. l. periophthalmicus
Sipora I, Mentawei Group
D. l. siberu
Siberut I
D. l. leucophaeus
Java, Bali I, Lombok I, Palawan I

***Dicrurus caerulescens* (White-bellied Drongo)**
D. c. caerulescens
Peninsular India
D. c. insularis
N Sri Lanka
D. c. leucopygialis
S Sri Lanka
***Dicrurus annectans* (Crow-billed Drongo)**
Himalayas, Burma, Thailand, Malaysia, India
***Dicrurus aeneus* (Bronzed Drongo)**
D. a. aeneus
India, Burma, S China, Thailand, Indochina
D. a. malayensis
S Malaysia, Sumatra, Borneo
D. a. braunianus
Taiwan
***Dicrurus remifer* (Lesser Racquet-tailed Drongo)**
D. r. tectirostris
Himalayas, Burma, S China, Thailand, Indochina
D. r. remifer
Java, Sumatra
D. r. peracensis
W Laos, S Thailand, Malaysia
D. r. lefoli
S Cambodia
***Dicrurus balicassius* (Balicassio Drongo)**
D. b. balicassius
Lubang, C & S Luzon I, Mindoro I
D. b. abraensis
N Luzon I
D. b. mirabilis
Panay I, Cebu I, Negros I, Masbate I
***Dicrurus hottentottus* (Spangled Drongo)**
D. h. samarensis
Samar I, Leyte I, Bohol I
D. h. striatus
Mindanao I, Basilan I
D. h. morotensis
Morotai I
D. h. atrocaeruleus
Kofiau I, Halmahera I
D. h. carbonarius
New Guinea, D'Entrecasteaux Archipelago
D. h. bracteatus
N & E Australia » S New Guinea
D. h. laemostictus
New Britain
D. h. meeki
Guadalcanal I
D. h. longirostris
San Cristobal I

D. h. amboinensis
S Moluccas
D. h. buruensis
Buru I
D. h. densus
Timor I
D. h. kühni
Tenimber Is
D. h. megalornis
Kei Is
D. h. sumbae
Sumba I
D. h. bimaënsis
Lombok I, Flores I, Alor I
D. h. renschi
Sumbawa I
D. h. sumatranus
Sumatra
D. h. guillemardi
Obi Is
D. h. pectoralis
Sula Is
D. h. banggaiensis
Banggai Is
D. h. leucops
Celebes
D. h. jentincki
Bali I, Kangean I
D. h. viridinitens
Mentawei Is
D. h. borneensis
N Borneo
D. h. suluensis
Sibutu I, Sulu Archipelago
D. h. hottentottus
India, Burma, Thailand, S Indochina
D. h. brevirostris
China, N Burma, N Laos, N Vietnam
D. h. palawanensis
Cagayan I, Sulu Is, Palawan I
D. h. cuyensis
Cuyo I, Semirara I, Philippine Is
D. h. menagei
Tablas I
***Dicrurus megarhynchus* (New Ireland Drongo)**
New Ireland
***Dicrurus montanus* (Celebes Mountain Drongo)**
Celebes
***Dicrurus andamanensis* (Andaman Drongo)**
D. a. andamanensis
S Andaman Is
D. a. dicruriformis
Gt Cocos I, Table I

***Dicrurus paradiseus* (Greater Racquet-tailed Drongo)**
  D. p. brachyphorus
    Borneo
  D. p. banguey
    N Borneo Is
  D. p. microlophus
    Tioman I, Anamba Is, N Natuna Is
  D. p. platurus
    S Malaysia, Sumatra, NW Sumatra Is
  D. p. formosus
    Java
  D. p. malayensis
    N Malaysia
  D. p. paradiseus
    S India, S Thailand, Indochina
  D. p. rangoonensis
    S Burma, W Thailand, C Laos
  D. p. grandis
    N India, N Burma, N Vietnam
  D. p. johni
    Hainan I
  D. p. ceylonicus
    Sri Lanka
  D. p. lophorinus
    W Sri Lanka
  D. p. otiosus
    Andaman Is
  D. p. nicobariensis
    Nicobar Is

169 CALLAEIDAE (WATTLEBIRDS)

CALLAEAS
Callaeas cinerea (Kokako)
  C. c. wilsoni
    North I (New Zealand)
  C. c. cinerea
    South I (New Zealand) Stewart I

CREADION
Creadion carunculatus (Saddleback)
  C. c. rufusater
    North Island (New Zealand)
  C. c. carunculatus
    Stewart I

170 GRALLINIDAE (MAGPIE LARKS)

GRALLININAE

GRALLINA
Grallina cyanoleuca (Magpie Lark)
  Australia
Grallina bruijni (Torrent Lark)
  New Guinea

CORCORACINAE

CORCORAX
Corcorax melanorhamphos (White-winged Chough)
  E & SE Australia

STRUTHIDEA
Struthidea cinerea (Apostle Bird)
  S. c. cinerea
    Eastern Australia
  S. c. dalyi
    Northern Territory

171 ARTAMIDAE (WOOD SWALLOWS)

ARTAMUS
Artamus fuscus (Ashy Wood Swallow)
  India to S China, Indochina
Artamus leucorhynchus (White-breasted Wood Swallow)
  A. l. pelewensis
    Palau Is
  A. l. leucorhynchus
    Philippine Is, Palawan I, Borneo
  A. l. amydrus
    Sumatra, Bangka I, Java, Bali I
  A. l. humei
    Andaman Is, Cocos Is
  A. l. celebensis
    Celebes, Lombok I, Sumbawa I, Flores I
  A. l. albiventer
    Alor I, Wetar I, Timor I
  A. l. musschenbroeki
    Tenimber Is
  A. l. leucopygialis
    Moluccas, Aru Is, New Guinea, N Australia
  A. l. melaleucus
    New Caledonia, Loyalty Is
  A. l. tenuis
    New Hebrides
  A. l. mentalis
    N Fiji Is
Artamus monachus (White-backed Wood Swallow)
  A. m. monachus
    Celebes
  A. m. sulaensis
    Sula Is
Artamus maximus (Papuan Wood Swallow)
  New Guinea
Artamus insignis (Bismarck Wood Swallow)
  New Britain, New Ireland
Artamus personatus (Masked Wood Swallow)
  Australia

Artamus superciliosus (White-browed Wood Swallow)
SE Australia
Artamus cinereus (Black-faced Wood Swallow)
A. c. perspicillatus
Timor I
A. c. cinereus
W, C & SE Australia
A. c. hypoleucos
S New Guinea, N Queensland
A. c. normani
N Queensland
A. c. inkermani
C Queensland
Artamus cyanopterus (Dusky Wood Swallow)
A. c. cyanopterus
E & SE Australia, Tasmania
A. c. perthi
S Western Australia
Artamus minor (Little Wood Swallow)
N & C Australia

172 CRACTICIDAE (BUTCHER BIRDS)

CRACTICUS
Cracticus mentalis (Black-backed Butcher Bird)
C. m. mentalis
SE New Guinea
C. m. kempi
N Queensland
Cracticus torquatus (Grey Butcher Bird)
C. t. argenteus
Northern Territory, NW Western Australia
C. t. leucopterus
Central Australia
C. t. torquatus
E Australia
C. t. cinereus
Tasmania
Cracticus nigrogularis (Black-throated Butcher Bird)
C. n. picatus
Northern Territory, NW Western Australia
C. n. kalgoorli
Central Australia, Western Australia
C. n. nigrogularis
E & SE Australia
Cracticus cassicus (Black-headed Butcher Bird)
C. c. cassicus
New Guinea
C. c. hercules
Trobriand Is, D'Entrecasteaux Archipelago

Cracticus louisiadensis (White-rumped Butcher Bird)
Tagula I
Cracticus quoyi (Black Butcher Bird)
C. q. quoyi
New Guinea
C. q. spaldingi
Aru Is, Northern Territory, N Queensland
C. q. rufescens
NC Queensland

GYMNORHINA
Gymnorhina tibicen (Black-backed Magpie)
G. t. papuana
S New Guinea
G. t. eylandtensis
Northern Territory
G. t. longirostris
Western Australia
G. t. finki
Central Australia
G. t. terraereginae
N Northern Territory, C Queensland
G. t. tibicen
New South Wales, Victoria, South Australia
G. t. leuconota
SE South Australia, W Victoria
G. t. dorsalis
S Western Australia
G. t. hypoleuca
E Victoria, Tasmania

STREPERA
Strepera graculina (Pied Currawong)
S. g. robinsoni
Queensland
S. g. graculina
New South Wales
S. g. ashbyi
Victoria
S. g. crissalis
Lord Howe I
Strepera fuliginosa (Black Currawong)
Tasmania
Strepera versicolor (Grey Currawong)
S. v. versicolor
New South Wales, E Victoria
S. v. centralia
N South Australia
S. v. plumbea
S Western Australia
S. v. howei
NW Victoria, E South Australia
S. v. melanoptera
SE South Australia, Kangaroo I
S. v. intermedia
S South Australia

S. v. arguta
Tasmania

173 PTILONORHYNCHIDAE (BOWERBIRDS)

AILUROEDUS
Ailuroedus buccoides (White-eared Catbird)
  A. b. cinnamomeus
    S New Guinea
  A. b. buccoides
    W Papuan Is, NW New Guinea
  A. b. stonii
    SE New Guinea
  A. b. geislerorum
    Japen I, N New Guinea
Ailuroedus crassirostris (Green Catbird)
  SE Queensland to N Victoria
Ailuroedus melanotis (Spotted Catbird)
  A. m. maculosus
    N Queensland
  A. m. melanotis
    Aru Is, S New Guinea
  A. m. melanocephalus
    SE New Guinea
  A. m. facialis
    WC New Guinea
  A. m. guttaticollis
    N New Guinea
  A. m. astigmaticus
    E New Guinea
  A. m. jobiensis
    WC New Guinea
  A. m. arfakianus
    NW New Guinea
  A. m. misoliensis
    Misol I

SCENOPOEETES
Scenopoeetes dentirostris (Tooth-billed Catbird)
  NE Queensland

ARCHBOLDIA
Archboldia papuensis (Archbold's Bowerbird)
  A. p. papuensis
    WC New Guinea
  A. p. sanfordi
    EC New Guinea

AMBLYORNIS
Amblyornis inornatus (Vogelkop Gardener Bowerbird)
  NW New Guinea
Amblyornis macgregoriae (Macgregor's Gardener Bowerbird)
  A. m. mayri
    WC New Guinea
  A. m. macgregoriae
    EC New Guinea
  A. m. germanus
    E New Guinea
  A. m. kombok
    EC New Guinea
  A. m. nubicola
    SE New Guinea
Amblyornis subularis (Striped Gardener Bowerbird)
  SE New Guinea
Amblyornis flavifrons (Yellow-fronted Gardener Bowerbird)
  W New Guinea?

PRIONODURA
Prionodura newtoniana (Newton's Golden Bowerbird)
  NE Queensland

SERICULUS
Sericulus aureus (Flamed Bowerbird)
  S. a. aureus
    N & W New Guinea
  S. a. ardens
    S New Guinea
Sericulus bakeri (Adelbert Bowerbird)
  NE New Guinea
Sericulus chrysocephalus (Regent Bowerbird)
  S. c. chrysocephalus
    NE New South Wales
  S. c. rothschildi
    C & S Queensland

PTILONORHYNCHUS
Ptilonorhynchus violaceus (Satin Bowerbird)
  P. v. violaceus
    SE Queensland to Victoria
  P. v. minor
    NE Queensland

CHLAMYDERA
Chlamydera maculata (Spotted Bowerbird)
  C. m. maculata
    EC Australia
  C. m. guttata
    WC Australia
Chlamydera nuchalis (Great Grey Bowerbird)
  C. n. oweni
    N Western Australia
  C. n. nuchalis
    N Western Australia to NW Queensland
  C. n. yorki
    N Queensland
  C. n. orientalis
    NW Queensland

Chlamydera lauterbachi (Lauterbach's Bowerbird)
  C. l. lauterbachi
    NC New Guinea
  C. l. uniformis
    C New Guinea
Chlamydera cerviniventris (Fawn-breasted Bowerbird)
    E New Guinea, N Queensland

174 PARADISAEIDAE (BIRDS OF PARADISE)

CNEMOPHILINAE

LORIA
Loria loriae (Loria's Bird of Paradise)
  L. l. inexpectata
    WC New Guinea
  L. l. loriae
    SE New Guinea
  L. l. amethystina
    EC New Guinea

LOBOPARADISEA
Loboparadisea sericea (Wattle-billed Bird of Paradise)
  L. s. sericea
    C New Guinea
  L. s. aurora
    E New Guinea

CNEMOPHILUS
Cnemophilus macgregorii (Sickle Crested Bird of Paradise)
  C. m. sanguineus
    EC New Guinea
  C. m. macgregorii
    SE New Guinea

PARADISAEINAE

MACGREGORIA
Macgregoria pulchra (Macgregor's Bird of Paradise)
  M. p. pulchra
    SE New Guinea
  M. p. carolinae
    WC New Guinea

LYCOCORAX
Lycocorax pyrrhopterus (Paradise Crow)
  L. p. obiensis
    Obi Is
  L. p. pyrrhopterus
    Batjan I, Halmahera I
  L. p. morotensis
    Morotai I, Rau I

MANUCODIA
Manucodia ater (Glossy-mantled Manucode)
  M. a. ater
    C & W New Guinea
  M. a. subalter
    Aru Is, SE New Guinea
  M. a. alter
    Tagula I
Manucodia jobiensis (Jobi Manucode)
  M. j. jobiensis
    Japen I
  M. j. rubiensis
    N & W New Guinea
Manucodia chalybatus (Crinkle-collared Manucode)
    Misol I, all New Guinea except mountains
Manucodia comrii (Curl-crested Manucode)
  M. c. comrii
    Ferguson I, Goodenough I, Normanby I
  M. c. trobriandi
    Trobriand Is

PHONYGAMMUS
Phonygammus keraudrenii (Trumpet Bird)
  P. k. keraudrenii
    NW New Guinea
  P. k. adelberti
    N New Guinea
  P. k. neumanni
    NC New Guinea
  P. k. mayri
    NE New Guinea
  P. k. jamesii
    Aru Is, S New Guinea
  P. k. purpureoviolaceus
    SE New Guinea
  P. k. hunsteini
    D'Entrecasteaux Archipelago
  P. k. gouldii
    N Queensland

PTILORIS
Ptiloris paradiseus (Paradise Riflebird)
    SE Queensland, NE New South Wales
Ptiloris victoriae (Queen Victoria Riflebird)
    NE Queensland
Ptiloris magnificus (Magnificent Riflebird)
  P. m. intercedens
    E New Guinea
  P. m. magnificus
    S & W New Guinea
  P. m. alberti
    N Queensland

Semioptera wallacei (Wallace's Standardwing)
  S. w. halmaherae
  Halmahera I
  S. w. wallacei
  Batjan I

SELEUCIDIS

Seleucidis melanoleuca (Twelve-wired Bird of Paradise)
  S. m. melanoleuca
  Salawati I, coast of New Guinea
  S. m. auripennis
  N New Guinea

PARADIGALLA

Paradigalla carunculata (Long-tailed Paradigalla)
  P. c. carunculata
  Arfak mountains, New Guinea
  P. c. intermedia
  WC New Guinea
Paradigalla brevicauda (Short-tailed Paradigalla)
  C New Guinea

DREPANORNIS

Drepanornis albertisii (Black-billed Sicklebill)
  D. a. albertisii
  NW New Guinea
  D. a. cervinicauda
  C New Guinea
  D. a. geisleri
  E New Guinea
Drepanornis bruijnii (Pale-billed Sicklebill)
  NW New Guinea

EPIMACHUS

Epimachus fastosus (Black Sicklebill)
  E. f. fastosus
  NW New Guinea
  E. f. atratus
  WC New Guinea
  E. f. ultimus
  Mt Menawa (N New Guinea)
  E. f. stresemanni
  EC New Guinea
Epimachus meyeri (Brown Sicklebill)
  E. m. megarhynchus
  Weyland mountains, New Guinea
  E. m. albicans
  C New Guinea
  E. m. bloodi
  EC New Guinea
  E. m. meyeri
  SE New Guinea

ASTRAPIA

Astrapia nigra (Arfak Bird of Paradise)
  Arfak mountains, New Guinea
Astrapia splendidissima (Splendid Bird of Paradise)
  A. s. helios
  NW New Guinea
  A. s. splendidissima
  Weyland mountains, New Guinea
  A. s. elliottsmithi
  WC New Guinea
Astrapia mayeri (Ribbon-tailed Bird of Paradise)
  EC New Guinea
Astrapia stephaniae (Princess Stephanie's Bird of Paradise)
  A. s. feminina
  EC New Guinea
  A. s. ducalis
  E New Guinea
  A. s. stephaniae
  SE New Guinea
Astrapia rothschildi (Huon Bird of Paradise)
  E New Guinea

LOPHORINA

Lophorina superba (Superb Bird of Paradise)
  L. s. superba
  Arfak mountains, NW New Guinea
  L. s. niedda
  Mt Wondiwoi (W New Guinea)
  L. s. feminina
  WC New Guinea
  L. s. pseudoparotia
  EC New Guinea
  L. s. latipennis
  E New Guinea
  L. s. connectens
  E New Guinea
  L. s. minor
  SE New Guinea
  L. s. sphinx
  SE New Guinea

PAROTIA

Parotia sefilata (Arfak Parotia)
  Arfak mountains, New Guinea
Parotia carolae (Queen Carola's Parotia)
  P. c. clelandiae
  Victor Emmanuel mountains, N New Guinea
  P. c. meeki
  Nassau, Oranje mountains, W New Guinea
  P. c. carolae
  Weyland mountains, C New Guinea

P. c. chalcothorax
Idenburg river, C New Guinea
P. c. berlepschi
Van Rees mountains, C New Guinea?
P. c. chrysenia
Bismarck mountains, C New Guinea
Parotia lawesii (Lawes' Parotia)
C & SE New Guinea
Parotia helenae (Eastern Parotia)
SE New Guinea
Parotia wahnesi (Wahnes' Parotia)
E New Guinea

PTERIDOPHORA
**Pteridophora alberti (King of Saxony
Bird of Paradise)**
P. a. alberti
C New Guinea
P. a. hallstromi
EC New Guinea
P. a. bürgersi
EC New Guinea

CICINNURUS
**Cicinnurus regius (King Bird of
Paradise)**
C. r. regius
Aru Is
C. r. rex
W New Guinea Is, New Guinea
C. r. coccineifrons
Japen I
C. r. similis
N New Guinea
C. r. cryptorhynchus
NW New Guinea
C. r. gymnorhynchus
NE New Guinea

DIPHYLLODES
**Diphyllodes magnificus (Magnificent
Bird of Paradise)**
D. m. magnificus
NW New Guinea, Salawati I
D. m. intermedius
Weyland mountains, C New Guinea
D. m. chrysopterus
Japen I, N New Guinea
D. m. hunsteini
E New Guinea
**Diphyllodes respublica (Wilson's
Bird of Paradise)**
Waigeu I, Batanta I

PARADISAEA
**Paradisaea apoda (Greater Bird of
Paradise)**
P. a. apoda
Aru Is, Lt Tobago I, West Indies (intro)
P. a. novaeguineae
S New Guinea

Paradisaea raggiana (Raggiana Bird   633
of Paradise)
P. r. augustaevictoriae
NE New Guinea
P. r. intermedia
E New Guinea
P. r. granti
E New Guinea
P. r. salvadorii
S New Guinea
P. r. raggiana
SE New Guinea
**Paradisaea minor (Lesser Bird of
Paradise)**
P. m. minor
NW & W New Guinea
P. m. finschi
NC New Guinea
P. m. jobiensis
Japen I
P. m. pulchra
Misol I
**Paradisaea decora (Goldie's Bird of
Paradise)**
Fergusson I, Normanby I
**Paradisaea rubra (Red Bird of
Paradise)**
Batanta I, Waigeu I, Saonek I
**Paradisaea guilielmi (Emperor of
Germany Bird of Paradise)**
E New Guinea
**Paradisaea rudolphi (Blue Bird
of Paradise)**
P. r. ampla
Hertzog mountains, W New Guinea
P. r. margaritae
WC New Guinea
P. r. rudolphi
E New Guinea

175 CORVIDAE (CROWS, JAYS)

PLATYLOPHUS
**Platylophus galericulatus (Crested
Shrike-Jay)**
P. g. ardesiacus
S Thailand, Malaysia
P. g. coronatus
Borneo, Sumatra
P. g. galericulatus
Java

PLATYSMURUS
**Platysmurus leucopterus (White-winged
Magpie)**
P. l. leucopterus
Malaysia, Sumatra
P. l. aterrimus
Borneo

GYMNORHINUS
Gymnorhinus cyanocephala (Pinyon Jay)
W USA, NW Mexico

CYANOCITTA
Cyanocitta cristata (Blue Jay)
C. c. bromia
S Canada, C USA » SE USA
C. c. cristata
EC & SE USA
C. c. semplei
S Florida
C. c. cyanotephra
SC USA
Cyanocitta stelleri (Steller's Jay)
C. s. stelleri
W Canada, NW USA
C. s. carlottae
Queen Charlotte Is
C. s. annectens
W Canada, WC USA
C. s. frontalis
W USA
C. s. carbonacea
W California
C. s. macrolopha
C & S USA, N Mexico
C. s. diademata
NC Mexico
C. s. coronata
SC Mexico
C. s. purpurea
SW Mexico
C. s. azteca
C Mexico
C. s. teotepecencis
S Mexico
C. s. ridgwayi
S Mexico to El Salvador
C. s. suavis
Honduras, Nicaragua

APHELOCOMA
Aphelocoma coerulescens (Scrub Jay)
A. c. immanis
W Oregon
A. c. caurina
W USA
A. c. oocleptica
W USA
A. c. californica
W California
A. c. cana
California
A. c. obscura
N Baja California
A. c. cactophila
C Baja California

A. c. hypoleuca
C & S Baja California
A. c. insularis
Santa Cruz I
A. c. nevadae
WC USA, N Mexico
A. c. woodhouseii
WC & SC USA
A. c. texana
WC Texas
A. c. grisea
NW Mexico
A. c. cyanotis
EC Mexico
A. c. sumichrasti
SC Mexico
A. c. remota
SW Mexico
A. c. coerulescens
S Florida
Aphelocoma ultramarina (Mexican Jay)
A. u. arizonae
SW USA, NW Mexico
A. u. wollweberi
W Mexico
A. u. gracilis
WC Mexico
A. u. couchii
S Texas, NE Mexico
A. u. potosina
EC Mexico
A. u. ultramarina
SC Mexico
A. u. colimae
SW Mexico
Aphelocoma unicolor (Unicoloured Jay)
A. u. guerrerensis
C Mexico
A. u. oaxacae
S Mexico
A. u. concolor
SE Mexico
A. u. unicolor
SE Mexico
A. u. griscomi
El Salvador, W Honduras

CYANOLYCA
Cyanolyca viridicyana (White-collared Jay)
C. v. joylaea
NC Peru
C. v. cyanolaema
SE Peru
C. v. viridicyana
W Bolivia

Cyanolyca armillata (Collard Jay)
  C. a. meridana
    NW Venezuela
  C. a. armillata
    E Colombia, W Venezuela
  C. a. quindiuna
    S Colombia, N Ecuador
Cyanolyca turcosa (Turquoise Jay)
  S Colombia, N Peru
Cyanolyca pulchra (Beautiful Jay)
  SW Colombia, W Ecuador
Cyanolyca cucullata (Azure-hooded Jay)
  C. c. mitrata
    E & S Mexico, Guatemala
  C. c. guatemalae
    Chiapas, SE Mexico
  C. c. hondurensis
    W Honduras
  C. c. cucullata
    Costa Rica, W Panama
Cyanolyca pumilo (Black-throated Jay)
  S Mexico to Honduras
Cyanolyca nana (Dwarf Jay)
  S Mexico
Cyanolyca mirabilis (White-throated Jay)
  SW Mexico
Cyanolyca argentigula (Silvery-throated Jay)
  C. a. albior
    Costa Rica
  C. a. argentigula
    S Costa Rica

CISSILOPHA
Cissilopha melanocyanea (Bushy-crested Jay)
  C. m. melanocyanea
    Guatemala to Honduras
  C. m. chavezi
    S Honduras, N Nicaragua
Cissilopha sanblasiana (San Blas Jay)
  C. s. nelsoni
    SW Mexico
  C. s. sanblasiana
    SW Mexico
Cissilopha yucatanica (Yucatan Jay)
  C. y. yucatanica
    SE Mexico, Guatemala
  C. y. rivularis
    SE Mexico
Cissilopha beecheii (Purplish-backed Jay)
  NW Mexico

CYANOCORAX
Cyanocorax caeruleus (Azure Jay)
  SE Brazil to N Argentina
Cyanocorax cyanomelas (Purplish Jay)
  SE Peru to N Argentina

Cyanocorax violaceus (Violaceous Jay) 635
  C. v. pallidus
    N Venezuela
  C. v. violaceus
    N South America
Cyanocorax cristatellus (Curl-crested Jay)
  C & E Brazil
Cyanocorax heilprini (Azure-naped Jay)
  S Venezuela, NW Brazil
Cyanocorax cayanus (Cayenne Jay)
  SE Venezuela, the Guianas, N Brazil
Cyanocorax affinis (Black-chested Jay)
  C. a. zeledoni
    S Costa Rica, Panama
  C. a. affinis
    N Colombia, NW Venezuela
Cyanocorax chrysops (Plush-crested Jay)
  C. c. diesingii
    N Brazil
  C. c. chrysops
    E Bolivia to SE Brazil
  C. c. tucumanus
    NW Argentina
Cyanocorax cyanopogon (White-naped Jay)
  E Brazil
Cyanocorax mystacalis (White-tailed Jay)
  SW Ecuador, NW Peru
Cyanocorax dickeyi (Tufted Jay)
  W Mexico
Cyanocorax yncas (Green Jay)
  C. y. glaucescens
    NE Mexico
  C. y. speciosus
    W Mexico
  C. y. vividus
    SW Mexico
  C. y. luxuosus
    E Mexico
  C. y. centralis
    SE Mexico, Guatemala, Honduras
  C. y. maya
    SE Mexico
  C. y. cozumelae
    Cozumel I
  C. y. galeatus
    C Colombia
  C. y. cyanodorsalis
    E Colombia
  C. y. andicolus
    NW Venezuela
  C. y. guatimalensis
    N Venezuela
  C. y. yncas
    SW Colombia, Ecuador, Peru, N Bolivia

C. y. longirostris
N Peru

PSILORHINUS
Psilorhinus morio (Brown Jay)
  P. m. palliatus
    NE & C Mexico
  P. m. morio
    SE Mexico
  P. m. cyanogenys
    SE Mexico, Central America
  P. m. mexicanus
    E Mexico
  P. m. vociferus
    SE Mexico

CALOCITTA
Calocitta formosa (White-throated Magpie-Jay)
  C. f. formosa
    SW Mexico
  C. f. azurea
    SE Mexico, Guatemala
  C. f. pompata
    S Mexico to Costa Rica
Calocitta colliei (Collie's Magpie-Jay)
  W Mexico

GARRULUS
Garrulus glandarius (Jay)
  G. g. rufitergum
    S Scotland, England, N France
  G. g. hibernicus
    N Scotland, Ireland
  G. g. glandarius
    N & C Europe
  G. g. fasciatus
    Iberia
  G. g. ichnusae
    Sardinia
  G. g. corsicanus
    Corsica
  G. g. albipectus
    Italy
  G. g. cretorum
    Greece, Crete
  G. g. glaszneri
    Cyprus
  G. g. hansguentheri
    Istanbul
  G. g. cervicalis
    E Algeria, Tunisia
  G. g. whitakeri
    N Morocco, W Algeria
  G. g. minor
    NW Africa
  G. g. atricapillus
    Iraq, W Iran
  G. g. rhodius
    Rhodes

G. g. krynicki
  Turkey, Caucasus
G. g. iphigenia
  Crimea
G. g. hyrcanus
  N Iran
G. g. suianae
  Kurdistan, NE Iran
G. g. severzowii
  Scandinavia, S Russia
G. g. brandtii
  NE Russia, C & NE Asia
G. g. kansuensis
  W China
G. g. pekingensis
  N China, NW Manchuria
G. g. sinensis
  SW China, NE Burma
G. g. taivanus
  Taiwan
G. g. leucotis
  E Burma, Thailand, Indochina
G. g. oatesi
  C Burma
G. g. haringtoni
  SC Burma
G. g. interstinctus
  E Himalayas, SE Tibet
G. g. persaturatus
  Assam
G. g. bispecularis
  W Himalayas
G. g. japonicus
  N Japan
G. g. tokugawae
  Sado I
G. g. hiugaensis
  S Japan
G. g. orii
  Yakushima Is
G. g. namiyei
  Tsushima I
Garrulus lanceolatus (Lanceolated Jay)
  W Himalayas, N India
Garrulus lidthi (Purple Jay)
  N Riukiu Is

PERISOREUS
Perisoreus canadensis (Grey Jay)
  P. c. pacificus
    NW Alaska
  P. c. canadensis
    C Canada, N USA
  P. c. nigricapillus
    NE Canada
  P. c. arcus
    SW Canada
  P. c. albescens
    W Canada, NW USA

P. c. bicolor
    SW Canada, NW USA
P. c. capitalis
    WC & SC USA
P. c. griseus
    SW Canada, NW USA
P. c. obscurus
    NW USA
Perisoreus infaustus (Siberian Jay)
P. i. infaustus
    Lapland
P. i. ostjakorum
    NW Siberia
P. i. yakutensis
    N & NE Asia
P. i. ruthenus
    C Russia, C Scandinavia
P. i. opicus
    NC Asia
P. i. rogosowi
    C Siberia
P. i. sibericus
    Outer Mongolia
P. i. varnak
    N Manchuria
P. i. sakhalinensis
    N Sakhalin I
P. i. maritimus
    Lower Amur river
Perisoreus internigrans (Szechwan Grey Jay)
    W China

UROCISSA
Urocissa ornata (Ceylon Blue Magpie)
    Sri Lanka
Urocissa caerulea (Formosan Blue Magpie)
    Taiwan
Urocissa flavirostris (Yellow-billed Blue Magpie)
U. f. cucullata
    W Himalayas
U. f. flavirostris
    E Himalayas, N Burma
U. f. schaferi
    W Burma
U. f. robini
    N Vietnam
Urocissa erythrorhyncha (Red-billed Blue Magpie)
U. e. brevivexilla
    N China
U. e. erythrorhyncha
    C & S China, N Vietnam
U. e. alticola
    SW China, NE Burma
U. e. occipitalis
    Himalayas

U. e. magnirostris
    Assam to Indochina
Urocissa whiteheadi (White-winged Magpie)
U. w. whiteheadi
    Hainan I
U. w. xanthomelana
    C Laos, N Vietnam

CISSA
Cissa chinensis (Green Magpie)
C. c. chinensis
    Himalayas, N Indochina
C. c. robinsoni
    Malaysia
C. c. klossi
    C Indochina
C. c. margaritae
    S Vietnam
C. c. minor
    Sumatra, NW Borneo
Cissa hypoleuca (Eastern Green Magpie)
C. h. jini
    SE China
C. h. concolor
    N Vietnam
C. h. chauleti
    C Vietnam
C. h. hypoleuca
    E Thailand, S Indochina
C. h. katsumatae
    Hainan I
Cissa thalassina (Short-tailed Green Magpie)
C. t. thalassina
    Java
C. t. jeffreyi
    NW Borneo

CYANOPICA
Cyanopica cyana (Azure-winged Magpie)
C. c. cooki
    W Spain, Portugal
C. c. cyana
    C & EC Asia
C. c. pallescens
    NE Asia
C. c. koreensis
    Korea
C. c. stegmanni
    Manchuria
C. c. swinhoei
    E China
C. c. interposita
    N China
C. c. kansuensis
    W China
C. c. japonica
    Japan

DENDROCITTA

Dendrocitta vagabunda (Indian Tree Pie)
 D. v. pallida
  W Himalayas, NW India
 D. v. vagabunda
  E Himalayas, NE India
 D. v. parvula
  SW India
 D. v. vernayi
  SE India
 D. v. sclateri
  W Burma
 D. v. kinneari
  S Burma, NW Thailand
 D. v. saturatior
  S Thailand
 D. v. sakeratensis
  E Thailand, Indochina
Dendrocitta occipitalis (Malaysian Tree Pie)
 D. o. occipitalis
  Sumatra
 D. o. cinerascens
  Borneo
Dendrocitta formosae (Himalayan Tree Pie)
 D. f. occidentalis
  W Himalayas
 D. f. himalayensis
  E Himalayas, Burma, N Laos
 D. f. sarkari
  E India
 D. f. assimilis
  S Burma, Thailand, Andaman Is
 D. f. sinica
  E & S China, N Vietnam
 D. f. sapiens
  W China
 D. f. formosae
  Taiwan
 D. f. insulae
  Hainan I
Dendrocitta leucogastra (Southern Tree Pie)
  S India
Dendrocitta frontalis (Black-browed Tree Pie)
  Himalayas to N Vietnam
Dendrocitta bayleyi (Andaman Tree Pie)
  Andaman Is

CRYPSIRINA
Crypsirina temia (Black Racquet-tailed Tree Pie)
  S Burma to Indochina & Java
Crypsirina cucullata (Hooded Racquet-tailed Tree Pie)
  N & C Burma

TEMNURUS
Temnurus temnurus (Notch-tailed Tree Pie)
  N Vietnam, Hainan I

PICA
Pica pica (Magpie)
 P. p. fennorum
  N Scandinavia, W Russia
 P. p. pica
  British Isles, C & E Europe
 P. p. galliae
  W Europe
 P. p. melanotos
  Spain, Portugal
 P. p. mauretanica
  NW Africa
 P. p. asirensis
  SW Arabia
 P. p. bactriana
  C Russia, to N India
 P. p. hemileucoptera
  W & S Siberia, WC Asia
 P. p. leucoptera
  EC Asia
 P. p. camtschatika
  NE Asia
 P. p. sericea
  S China, Burma, Indochina
 P. p. bottanensis
  N Himalayas, Tibet
 P. p. hudsonia
  W Canada, W USA
Pica nuttalli (Yellow-billed Magpie)
  W California

ZAVATTARIORNIS
Zavattariornis stresemanni (Stresemann's Bush Crow)
  S Ethiopia

PODOCES
Podoces hendersoni (Henderson's Ground Jay)
  C Asia, W China
Podoces biddulphi (Biddulph's Ground Jay)
  W Sinkiang
Podoces panderi (Pander's Ground Jay)
  S Russia
Podoces pleskei (Pleske's Ground Jay)
  E Iran

PSEUDOPODOCES
Pseudopodoces humilis (Hume's Ground Chough)
  Tsinghai, W China

NUCIFRAGA

Nucifraga columbiana (Clark's Nutcracker)
SW Canada, W USA

Nucifraga caryocatactes (Nutcracker)
N. c. caryocatactes
N & E Europe » S Russia
N. c. macrorhynchos
N & NE Asia » N Iran & N China
N. c. rothschildi
Russia, Turkistan
N. c. japonica
N Japan
N. c. owstoni
Taiwan
N. c. interdicta
N China
N. c. multipunctata
Pakistan, NW India
N. c. hemispila
W Himalayas
N. c. macella
E Himalayas, Burma, W China
N. c. yunnanensis
SW China

PYRRHOCORAX

Pyrrhocorax pyrrhocorax (Chough)
P. p. pyrrhocorax
England, Ireland
P. p. erythrorhamphus
W Europe
P. p. barbarus
Canary Is, NW Africa
P. p. baileyi
N Ethiopia
P. p. docilis
E Europe to Arabia, Iran
P. p. centralis
C Asia, Pakistan, NW India
P. p. himalayanus
N India, Himalayas, W China
P. p. brachypus
N China, NE Asia

Pyrrhocorax graculus (Alpine Chough)
P. g. graculus
Europe, N Africa, Caucasus
P. g. digitatus
Iran, C Asia, Himalayas

PTILOSTOMUS

Ptilostomus afer (Piapiac)
Senegal to Ethiopia, Uganda

CORVUS

Corvus monedula (Jackdaw)
C. m. monedula
Scandinavia
C. m. spermologus
W & C Europe

C. m. soemmerringii
E Europe, N & C Asia » Iran,
W India
C. m. cirtensis
N Africa

Corvus dauuricus (Daurian Jackdaw)
C & NE Asia » SE China & Japan

Corvus splendens (House Crow)
C. s. zugmayeri
Baluchistan, NW India
C. s. splendens
India
C. s. protegatus
Sri Lanka, Malaysia
C. s. maledivicus
Laccadive Is, Maldive Is
C. s. insolens
S Burma SW Thailand, W Yunnan

Corvus moneduloides (New Caledonian Crow)
New Caledonia, Loyalty Is

Corvus enca (Slender-billed Crow)
C. e. compilator
Malaysia, Sumatra, Borneo
C. e. enca
Java, Bali I, Montawi Is
C. e. celebensis
Celebes
C. e. unicolor
Banggai I
C. e. mangoli
Sula Archipelago
C. e. violaceus
Ceram I
C. e. pusillus
Balabac I, Palawan I, Mindoro I
C. e. sierramadrensis
NE Luzon I
C. e. samarensis
Samar I, Mindanao I

Corvus typicus (Celebean Crow)
C & S Celebes

Corvus florensis (Flores Crow)
Flores I

Corvus kubaryi (Marianas Crow)
Guam I, Rota I

Corvus validus (Moluccan Crow)
N Moluccas

Corvus woodfordi (White-billed Crow)
C. w. meeki
Bougainville I
C. w. woodfordi
Guadalcanal I
C. w. vegetus
Choiseul I, Ysabel I

Corvus fuscicapillus (Brown-headed Crow)
C. f. fuscicapillus
Aru Is, New Guinea
C. f. megarhynchus
Waigeu I, Geimen I
Corvus tristis (Grey Crow)
New Guinea, D'Entrecasteaux Archipelago
Corvus capensis (Black Crow)
Eastern & Southern Africa
Corvus frugilegus (Rook)
C. f. frugilegus
Europe, W & C Asia » N Africa & NW India
C. f. pastinator
E Asia » Japan & SE China
Corvus brachyrhynchos (Common American Crow)
C. b. hesperis
W Canada, W USA
C. b. brachyrhynchos
C & E Canada, C & NE USA » E USA
C. b. paulus
E & SE USA
C. b. pascuus
S Florida
Corvus caurinus (Northwestern Crow)
W Canada, NW USA
Corvus imparatus (Tamaulipas Crow)
N Mexico
Corvus sinaloae (Sinaloa Crow)
NW Mexico
Corvus ossifragus (Fish Crow)
E USA
Corvus palmarum (Palm Crow)
C. p. minutus
Cuba
C. p. palmarum
Hispaniola
Corvus jamaicensis (Jamaican Crow)
Jamaica
Corvus nasicus (Cuban Crow)
Cuba, Grand Caicos I
Corvus leucognaphalus (White-necked Crow)
Hispaniola, Puerto Rico
Corvus corone (Carrion Crow)
C. c. corone
W Europe » N Africa
C. c. cornix
N & E Europe
C. c. sardonius
S & SE Europe, Asia Minor
C. c. sharpii
Siberia, Iraq, Iran to Turkistan, NW India

C. c. capellanus
S Iraq, SW Iran
C. c. orientalis
E Asia, Japan » NW India, S China
Corvus macrorhynchos (Jungle Crow)
C. m. japonensis
Sakhalin I, Japan
C. m. connectens
C & S Riukiu Is
C. m. osai
S Riukiu Is
C. m. mandschuricus
NE Asia
C. m. colonorum
China, N Indochina
C. m. hainanus
Hainan I
C. m. mengtszensis
SW China
C. m. tibetosinensis
E Himalayas, N Burma, W China
C. m. intermedius
W Himalayas, NW India
C. m. culminatus
S India, Sri Lanka
C. m. levaillantii
NE India, Burma, Thailand
C. m. macrorhynchos
Malaysia, S Indochina, Sunda Is
C. m. philippinus
Philippine Is
C. m. timoriensis
Alor I, Timor I
Corvus orru (Australian Crow)
C. o. orru
Moluccas, New Guinea
C. o. insularis
New Britain, New Ireland, New Hanover
C. o. latirostris
Tenimber Is
C. o. ceciliae
Australia
Corvus bennetti (Little Crow)
W & C Australia
Corvus coronoides (Australian Raven)
C. c. coronoides
E, S & SW Australia
C. c. boreus
New South Wales, Victoria
Corvus tasmanicus (Forest Raven)
C. t. novaanglica
NE New South Wales
C. t. tasmanicus
Tasmania, Wilson's Promontory
Corvus mellori (Little Raven)
SE Australia
Corvus torquatus (Collared Crow)
E & C China, N Vietnam

Corvus albus (Pied Crow)
W, C, E & Southern Africa, Madagascar
Corvus tropicus (Hawaiian Crow)
Hawaii Is
Corvus cryptoleucus
(White-necked Raven)
SW USA, N Mexico
Corvus ruficollis (Brown-necked
Raven)
C. r. ruficollis
N Africa to Pakistan
C. r. edithae
Somalia
Corvus corax (Raven)
C. c. principalis
Alaska, Canada, N USA
C. c. sinuatus
WC USA, Central America
C. c. varius
Iceland, Faroe Is
C. c. corax
Europe, W Asia
C. c. subcorax
SE Europe, Asia Minor to Pakistan
C. c. tingitanus
N Africa
C. c. tibetanus
C Asia, Himalayas
C. c. kamtschaticus
NE Asia, N Japan
Corvus rhipidurus (Fan-tailed Raven)
NE Africa to Syria, Arabia
Corvus albicollis (African White-
necked Raven)
E & S Africa
Corvus crassirostris (Thick-billed
Raven)
Ethiopia, E Sudan

Index

aalge, Uria 134
abbas, Thraupis 566
abbotti, Coracina 360
abbotti, Sula 60
abbotti, Trichastoma 417
abdimii, Ciconia 67
abeillei, Abeillia 208
abeillei, Arremon 552
abeillei, Coccothraustes 602
abeillei, Orchesticus 559
Abeillia 208
aberdare, Cisticola 451
aberrans, Cisticola 452
aberti, Pipilo 551
abingoni, Campethera 254
abnormis, Sasia 252
Abrescopus 448
aburri, Aburria 92
Aburria 92
abyssinica, Alcippe 433
abyssinica, Caracias 234
abyssinica, Hirundo 353
abyssinica, Zosterops 523
abyssinicus, Asio 192
abyssinicus, Bucorvus 238
abyssinicus, Dendropicos 254
abyssinicus, Turdus 410
abyssinicus, Turtur 141
acadicus, Aegolius 192
Acanthidops 544
Acanthis 598
Acanthisitta 340
Acanthiza 467
acanthizoides, Cettia 439
Acanthorhynchus 534
accentor, Bradypterus 440
Accipiter 80
accipitrinus, Deroptyus 171
Aceros 237
Acestrura 221
Acridotheres 623
Acrocephalus 441
Acrochordopus 337
Acropternis 306
Acryllium 110
Actinodura 431
Actitis 127
Actophilornis 120
acuminata, Calidris 128
acunhae, Nesospiza 545
acuta, Anas 72
acuticauda, Apus 203
acuticauda, Poephila 607
acuticaudata, Aratinga 165
acuticaudus, Lamprotornis 621
acutipennis, Chordeiles 194
acutipennis, Pseudocolopteryx 332
acutirostris, Calandrella 346
adamsi, Montifringilla 613
adamsii, Gavia 54

adansonii, Excalfactoria 104
addita, Rhinomyias 471
adela, Oreotrochilus 215
adelaidae, Dendroica 576
adelaidae, Platycercus 161
adelaidae, Platycercus 161
adelberti, Nectarinia 513
adeliae, Pygoscelis 53
Adelomyia 214
adolphinae, Myzomela 527
adorabilis, Paphosia 208
adscitus, Platycercus 161
adsimilis, Dicrurus 626
adspersus, Francolinus 101
adusta, Muscicapa 475
adustus, Margarornis 284
Aechmolophus 324
Aechmophorus 55
aedon, Acrocephalus 442
aedon, Troglodytes 387
Aegintha 606
aegithaloides, Leptasthenura 278
Aegithalos 497
Aegithina 374
Aegolius 192
Aegotheles 193
Aegypius 78
aegyptiacus, Alopochen 71
aegyptius, Caprimulgus 197
aegyptius, Pluvianus 122
aenea, Chloroceryle 225
aenea, Ducula 151
aenea, Glaucia 204
aeneocauda, Metallura 218
aeneum, Dicaeum 509
aeneus, Dicrurus 627
aeneus, Molothrus 593
aenigma, Idioptilon 329
aenigma, Sapayoa 310
aenobarbus, Pteruthius 431
Aepypodius 91
aequatoriale, Apaloderma 224
aequatorialis, Andron 204
aequatorialis, Apus 203
aequatorialis, Erithacus 395
aequinoctialis, Acrocephalus 442
aequinoctialis, Buteogallus 84
aequinoctialis, Geothlypis 578
aequinoctialis, Procellaria 57
aereus, Ceuthmochares 176
Aeronautes 202
Aërornis 199
aeruginosum, Dicaeum 508
aeruginosus, Circus 79
aestiva, Amazona 170
aestivalis, Aimophila 543
aethereus, Nyctibius 193
aethereus, Phaethon 59
Aethia 134
aethiopica, Hirundo 352

aethiopicus, Threskiornis 67
aethiopicus, Laniarius 377
aethiops, Myrmecocichla 403
aethiops, Thamnophilus 290
Aethopyga 517
afer, Francolinus 100
afer, Nilaus 376
afer, Parus 500
afer, Ptilostomus 639
afer, Sphenoeacus 457
afer, Turtur 141
affine, Malacopteron 418
affinis, Apus 203
affinis, Arachnothera 519
affinis, Aythya 74
affinis, Batrachostomus 193
affinis, Caprimulgus 198
affinis, Climacteris 506
affinis, Coccothraustes 602
affinis, Coturnicops 115
affinis, Cyanocorax 635
affinis, Emberiza 537
affinis, Empidonax 323
affinis, Euphonia 568
affinis, Garrulax 430
affinis, Hypsipetes 372
affinis, Lepidocolaptes 275
affinis, Melithreptus 531
affinis, Ninox 188
affinis, Phylloscopus 445
affinis, Seicercus 448
affinis, Turdoides 426
affinis, Veniliornis 260
afra, Euplectes 617
afra, Nectarinia 515
afra, Pytilia 603
africana, Actophilornis 120
africana, Mirafra 342
africana, Sasia 251
africanoides, Mirafra 343
africanus, Bubo 185
africanus, Buphagus 624
africanus, Francolinus 102
africanus, Gyps 78
africanus, Haliëtor 62
africanus, Rhinoptilus 123
africanus, Spizaetus 86
Afropavo 109
Afrotis 119
agami, Agamia 66
Agamia 66
Agapornis 163
Agelaius 591
Agelastes 109
agile, Dicaeum 507
agilis, Amazona 170
agilis, Geothlypis 579
agilis, Uromyias 332
Aglaeactis 216
aglaiae, Pachyramphus 308

Aglaiocercus 219
agraphia, Uromyias 332
agricola, Acrocephalus 441
Agriocharis 93
Agriornis 313
aguimp, Motacilla 355
ahantensis, Francolinus 101
Aidemosyne 608
Ailuroedus 630
Aimophila 542
Aix 71
Ajaia 68
ajaja, Ajaia 68
ajax, Cinclosoma 415
akehige, Erithacus 395
akool, Amaurornis 117
Alaemon 345
alario, Serinus 596
alaschanicus, Phoenicurus 399
Alauda 348
alaudina, Coryphistera 283
alaudinus, Phrygilus 544
alaudipes, Alaemon 345
alba, Cacatua 157
alba, Calidris 128
alba, Chionis 129
alba, Egretta 66
alba, Gygis 133
alba, Motacilla 355
alba, Pagophila 129
alba, Platalea 68
alba, Procnias 310
alba, Pterodroma 56
alba, Tyto 180
albatrus, Diomedea 55
albellus, Mergus 74
albeola, Bucephala 74
alberti, Crax 93
alberti, Menura 341
alberti, Prionops 375
alberti, Pteridophora 633
albertinae, Streptocitta 623
albertisi, Aegotheles 194
albertisii, Drepanornis 632
albertisii, Gymnophaps 153
albescens, Certhilauda 344
albescens, Synallaxis 279
albicapilla, Certhiaxis 281
albicapilla, Cossypha 397
albicapillus, Spreo 622
albicauda, Agriornis 313
albicauda, Erannornis 481
albicauda, Mirafa 341
albicaudata, Eumyias 476
albicaudatus, Buteo 85
albiceps, Atlapetes 554
albiceps, Certhiaxis 281
albiceps, Elaenia 334
albiceps, Psaltidoprocne 354
albiceps, Vanellus 123
albicilla, Haliaeetus 77
albicilla, Mohoua 470
albicollis, Corvus 641
albicollis, Ficedula 472
albicollis, Leucochloris 211

albicollis, Leucopternis 83
albicollis, Merops 234
albicollis, Nyctidromus 195
albicollis, Pipilo 551
albicollis, Porzana 116
albicollis, Rhipidura 490
albicollis, Rynchops 133
albicollis, Saltator 558
albicollis, Scelorchilus 305
albicollis, Streptocitta 623
albicollis, Turdus 414
albicollis, Xiphocolaptes 272
albicollis, Zonotrichia 540
albidinuchus, Lorius 155
albifacies, Myioborus 580
albifacies, Sceloglaux 189
albifrons, Amazona 170
albifrons, Amblyospiza 613
albifrons, Anser 70
albifrons, Conirostrum 583
albifrons, Donacospiza 544
albifrons, Ephthianura 470
albifrons, Henicophaps 141
albifrons, Muscisaxicola 314
albifrons, Myioborus 580
albifrons, Myrmecocichla 403
albifrons, Phylidonyris 534
albifrons, Pithys 299
albifrons, Platysteira 481
albifrons, Sterna 132
albigula, Grallaria 303
albigula, Myzomela 526
albigula, Upucerthia 276
albigularis, Automolus 287
albigularis, Empidonax 324
albigularis, Hirundo 352
albigularis, Laterallus 116
albigularis, Phyllastrephus 370
albigularis, Sclerurus 288
albigularis, Synellaxis 279
albilatera, Diglossa 574
albilinea, Tachycineta 349
albilineata, Meliphaga 529
albilora, Muscisaxicola 314
albilora, Synallaxis 280
albiloris, Oriolus 624
albiloris, Polioptila 437
albinucha, Actophilornis 120
albinucha, Atlapetes 553
albinucha, Columba 136
albinucha, Ploceus 616
albinucha, Xenopsaris 308
albipectus, Pyrrhura 167
albipectus, Trichastoma 417
albipennis, Petrophassa 142
albirostris, Bubalornis 611
albirostris, Galbula 239
albirostris, Onychognathus 620
albispecularis, Heteromyias 479
albistriata, Sterna 132
albitarsus, Ciccaba 190
albitorques, Columba 136
albitorques, Philemon 532
albiventer, Phalacrocorax 62
albiventer, Pnoepyga 421

albiventer, Tachycineta 350
albiventre, Pellorneum 416
albiventris, Dacnis 572
albiventris, Halcyon 229
albiventris, Myiagra 487
albiventris, Myiornis 330
albiventris, Parus 501
albiventris, Trochocercus 482
alboauricularis, Lichmera 526
albocinctus, Acridotheres 623
albocinctus, Turdus 410
albocoronata, Microchera 213
albocristata, Sericossypha 559
albocristatus, Berenicornis 237
albofasciata, Certhilauda 344
albofrenatus, Atlapetes 553
albofrontata, Gerygone 467
albogriseus, Pachyramphus 308
albogulare, Malacopteron 418
albogularis, Abroscopus 448
albogularis, Accipiter 82
albogularis, Brachygalba 239
albogularis, Conopophila 534
albogularis, Contopus 322
albogularis, Francolinus 102
albogularis, Garrulax 427
albogularis, Melithreptus 531
albogularis, Otus 184
albogularis, Phalcoboenus 87
albogularis, Pygarrhichas 289
albogularis, Rhipidura 490
albogularis, Serinus 595
albogularis, Sporophila 548
albogularis, Tyrannus 318
albogularis, Zosterops 523
albolarvatus, Picoides 260
albolimbata, Rhipidura 490
albolimbatus, Megalurus 462
albolineatus, Lepidocolaptes 275
alboniger, Oenanthe 404
alboniger, Spizaetus 87
albonotata, Halcyon 229
albonotata, Meliphaga 528
albonotata, Poecilodryas 479
albonotatus, Buteo 85
albonotatus, Crocias 434
albonotatus, Euplectes 618
albonotatus, Trochocercus 482
alboscapulatus, Malurus 464
albosignata, Eudyptula 53
albospecularis, Copsychus 398
alboterminatus, Tockus 236
albus, Corvus 641
albus, Eudocimus 68
Alca 134
Acedo 225
alchata, Pterocles 134
alcinus, Machaerhamphus 76
Alcippe 432
alcyon, Ceryle 225
aldabranus, Dicrurus 626
aldabranus, Nesillas 443
alecto, Monarcha 485
alector, Crax 93
Alectoris 99

Alectroenas 151
Alectrurus 316
Alectura 91
Alethe 397
aleutica, Sterna 132
aleuticus, Ptychoramphus 134
alexandrae, Polytelis 160
alexandri, Apus 203
alexandri, Archilochus 220
alexandri, Psittacula 164
alexandrinus, Charadrius 125
alfredi, Bradypterus 440
alfredi, Otus 181
alice, Chlorostilbon 209
aliciae, Aglaeactis 216
alienus, Ploceus 614
alinae, Eriocnemis 217
alinae, Nectarinia 513
alisteri, Cinclosoma 415
Alisterus 160
alius, Malaconotus 379
alixii, Clytoctantes 292
Alle 133
alle, Alle 133
alleni, Gallinula 188
alleni, Grallaria 302
Allenia 392
alligator, Ptilinopus 148
alnorum, Empidonax 323
alopex, Falco 88
Alopochelidon 350
Alopochen 71
alpestris, Eremophila 349
alphonsianus, Paradoxornis 436
alpina, Calidris 128
alpina, Muscisaxicola 314
alpinus, Anairetes 332
altaicus, Tetraogallus 99
alticola, Apalis 456
alticola, Poospiza 545
altiloquus, Vireo 586
altirostris, Moupinia 425
altirostris, Turdoides 425
aluco, Strix 191
amabilis, Amazilia 212
amabilis, Charmosyna 155
amabilis, Cotinga 309
amabilis, Loriculus 163
amabilis, Lorius 155
amabilis, Parus 500
Amadina 610
Amalocichla 407
Amandava 606
amandava, Amandava 606
amaurocephala, Nonnula 241
amaurocephalus, Leptopogon 337
amaurochalinus, Turdus 413
Amaurocichla 462
amauroptera, Pelargopsis 227
Amaurornis 117
Amaurospiza 548
amaurotis, Hypsipetes 373
amaurotis, Philydor 285
Amazilia 211
amazilia, Amazilia 213

Amazona 170
amazona, Chloroceryle 225
Amazonetta 71
amazonica, Amazona 170
amazonicus, Thamnophilus 291
amazonina, Hapalopsittaca 169
ambigua, Ara 165
ambigua, Carduelis 597
ambigua, Myrmotherula 293
ambigua, Stachyris 422
ambiguus, Ramphastos 250
Amblyornis 630
Amblyospiza 613
Amblyramphus 592
amboinensis, Alisterus 160
amboinensis, Macropygia 139
ameliae, Macronyx 355
americana, Anas 72
americana, Aythya 73
americana, Chloroceryle 225
americana, Fulica 118
americana, Grus 111
americana, Mycteria 67
americana, Parula 575
americana, Recurvirostra 122
americana, Rhea 49
americana, Spiza 555
americana, Sporophila 547
americanus, Coccyzus 175
americanus, Daptrius 87
americanus, Numenius 126
amethysticollis, Heliangelus 217
amethystina, Calliphlox 220
amethystina, Nectarinia 513
amethystina, Phapitreron 146
amethystinus, Lampornis 214
amherstiae, Chrysolophus 108
amicta, Nyctiornis 233
ammodendri, Passer 611
Ammodramus 541
Ammomanes 345
Ammoperdix 98
amnicola, Locustella 440
amoena, Passerina 558
amoenus, Phylloscopus 447
Ampeliceps 623
ampelinus, Hypocolius 382
Ampelioides 307
Ampelion 306
amphichroa, Newtonia 476
Amphispiza 542
Amytornis 465
anabatina, Dendrocincla 270
anabatinus, Thamnistes 292
anaethetus, Sterna 132
Anairetes 332
anais, Mino 623
analis, Catamenia 549
analis, Coracina 360
analis, Formicarius 301
analis, Iridosornis 567
analoga, Meliphaga 528
Anaplectes 617
Anarhynchus 125
Anas 71

Anastomus 167
anchietae, Anthreptes 511
anchietae, Stactolaema 244
andaecola, Upucerthia 276
andecola, Petrochalidon 353
andecolus, Aeronautes 202
andicola, Grallaria 302
andicola, Leptasthenura 278
Andigena 249
andina, Recurvirostra 122
andinus, Phoenicoparrus 69
andrei, Chaetura 202
andrei, Taeniotriccus 330
andrewsi, Fregata 62
Androdon 204
andromedae, Zoothera 407
Androphobus 414
anerythra, Pitta 340
angelae, Dendroica 576
angolensis, Dryoscopus 376
angolensis, Gypohierax 78
angolensis, Hirundo 352
angolensis, Mirafra 342
angolensis, Monticola 405
angolensis, Oryzoborus 548
angolensis, Pitta 340
angolensis, Ploceus 616
angolensis, Uraeginthus 604
anguitimens, Eurocephalus 375
angulata, Gallinula 118
angusticauda, Cisticola 452
angustifrons, Psarocolius 588
angustirostris, Lepidocolaptes 274
angustirostris, Marmaronetta 73
angustirostris, Todus 232
Anhima 69
Anhinga 62
anhinga, Anhinga 62
ani, Crotophaga 177
Anisognathus 567
Anitibyx 124
ankoberensis, Serinus 596
anna, Calypte 221
annae, Dicaeum 507
annae, Psamathia 438
annamarulae, Melaeornis 471
annaea, Euphonia 569
annectans, Dicrurus 627
annectens, Heterophasia 434
annumbi, Anumbius 283
Anodorhynchus 164
anomala, Brachycope 617
anomala, Cossypha 396
anomala, Zosterops 521
Anomalospiza 618
anomalus, Eleothreptus 199
anonyma, Cisticola 452
Anorrhinus 237
Anous 133
anoxanthus, Loxipasser 549
anselli, Centropus 179
Anser 69
anser, Anser 70
Anseranas 69

646   ansorgei, Cossypha 397
ansorgei, Nesocharis 603
ansorgei, Pycnonotus 368
antarctica, Geositta 276
antarcitca, Pygoscelis 53
antarctica, Thalassoica 56
antarcticus, Anthus 358
antarcticus, Cinclodes 277
antarcticus, Lopholaimus 153
Anthocephala 214
Anthochaera 535
anthoides, Thripophaga 282
anthonyi, Dicaeum 508
anthopeplus, Polytelis 160
anthophilus, Phaethornis 205
Anthornis 535
Anthoscopus 498
anthracinus, Buteogallus 83
Anthracoceros 238
Anthracothorax 207
Anthreptes 511
Anthropoides 111
Anthus 356
antigone, Grus 111
antillarum, Myiarchus 321
Antilophia 311
antinorii, Psalidoprocne 354
antipodes, Megadyptes 53
antiquus, Synthliboramphus 134
antisianus, Pharomachrus 222
antisiensis, Certhiaxis 281
antoniae, Carpodectes 309
Anumbius 283
Anurophasis 100
Apalis 455
Apaloderma 224
Apalopteron 530
apertus, Atlapetes 554
Aphanotriccus 324
Aphantochroa 214
Aphelocephala 467
Aphelocoma 634
Aphrastura 277
Aphriza 128
apiaster, Merops 234
apiata, Mirafa 342
apicalis, Acanthiza 467
apicalis, Myiarchus 320
apicauda, Treron 148
apivorus, Pernis 76
Aplonis 618
Aplopelia 139
apoda, Paradisaea 633
apolinari, Cistothorus 384
apolites, Tyrannus 318
apperti, Phyllastrephus 371
apricaria, Pluvialis 124
Aprosmictus 160
Aptenodytes 53
Apteryx 50
Apus 203
apus, Apus 203
aquatica, Muscicapa 475
aquaticus, Rallus 114
Aquila 86

aquila, Eutoxeres 206
aquila, Fregata 62
Ara 164
arabs, Choriotis 119
aracari, Pteroglossus 249
Arachnothera 519
aradus, Cyphorhinus 389
araea, Flaco 89
araguayae, Serpophaga 333
Aramus 112
ararauna, Ara 164
Aratinga 165
araucana, Columba 137
arausica, Amazona 171
arborea, Dendrocygna 69
arborea, Lullula 348
arborea, Spizella 541
Arborophila 104
arcaei, Buthraupis 566
arcanus, Ptilinopus 151
archboldi, Aegotheles 194
archboldi, Eurostopodus 195
archboldi, Newtonia 476
archboldi, Petroica 478
Archboldia 630
archeri, Dryocichloides 397
Archilochus 220
archipelagus, Indicator 248
arctica, Fratercula 134
arctica, Gavia 54
arcticus, Picoides 260
arctoa, Leucosticte 598
arcuata, Dendrocygna 69
arcuata, Pipreola 307
arcuata, Pitta 339
Ardea 66
ardens, Arborophila 105
ardens, Euplectes 618
ardens, Harpactes 224
ardens, Selasphorus 221
Ardeola 64
ardeola, Dromas 121
ardesiaca, Conopophaga 304
ardesiaca, Egretta 65
ardesiaca, Melaeornis 471
ardesiaca, Rhopornis 297
ardesiaca, Sporophila 547
ardesiacus, Dysithamnus 292
ardosiaceus, Falco 89
Arenaria 127
arenarum, Sublegatus 335
arfaki, Oreocharis 510
arfaki, Oreosittacus 156
arfakiana, Melanocharis 506
arfakianus, Aepypodius 91
arfakianus, Sericornis 469
argentatus, Ceyx 226
argentatus, Larus 130
argentauris, Leiothrix 430
argentauris, Lichmera 526
argentea, Apalis 456
argenticeps, Philemon 532
argentifrons, Scytalopus 306
argentigula, Cyanolyca 635
argentina, Columba 136

argoondah, Perdicula 104
argus, Argusianus 109
Argusianus 109
argyrofenges, Tangara 572
argyrotis, Penelope 92
aridula, Cisticola 450
ariel, Fregata 62
ariel, Petrochelidon 354
aristotelis, Phalacrocorax 61
armandii, Phylloscopus 445
armata, Merganetta 71
armatus, Anitibyx 124
armillaris, Megalaima 243
armillata, Cyanolyca 635
armillata, Fulica 118
arminjoniana, Pterodroma 56
arnaudi, Pseudonigrita 611
arnotti, Myrmecocichla 403
aroyae, Thamnophilus 291
arquata, Cichladusa 397
arquata, Numenius 126
arquatrix, Columba 136
Arremon 552
Arremonops 552
arremonops, Oreothraupis 555
Arses 487
Artamella 381
Artamus 628
arthus, Tangara 571
aruensis, Meliphaga 528
arundinaceus, Acrocephalus 441
Arundinicola 317
arvensis, Alauda 348
Ashbyia 470
asiatica, Megalaima 243
asiatica, Nectarinia 515
asiatica, Perdicula 104
asiatica, Zenaida 142
asiaticus, Caprimulgus 197
asiaticus, Charadrius 125
asiaticus, Ephippiorhynchus 67
Asio 191
asio, Otus 183
Aspatha 232
assamica, Mirafa 343
assimilis, Circus 79
assimilis, Myrmotherula 294
assimilis, Picoides 258
assimilis, Puffinus 58
assimilis, Tolmomyias 327
asterias, Picumus 251
Astrapia 632
astrild, Estilda 605
astur, Eutriorchis 79
Asturina 84
atacamensis, Cinclodes 277
Atalotriccus 330
Atelornis 235
ater, Daptrius 87
ater, Haematopus 121
ater, Manucodia 631
ater, Melipotes 533
ater, Merulaxis 305
ater, Molothrus 593
ater, Parus 500

aateralba, Monarcha 486
aateralbus, Centropus 179
aterrima, Pterodroma 56
aterrimus, Knipolegus 316
aterrimus, Phoeniculus 236
aterrimus, Prosboiger 156
Athene 189
athertoni, Nyctiornis 233
Atlantisia 114
Atlapetes 553
atra, Afrotis 119
atra, Chalcopsitta 153
atra, Fulica 118
atra, Monasa 241
atra, Myiagra 487
atra, Porzana 117
atra, Pyriglena 297
atra, Rhipidura 490
atra, Tijuca 306
atrata, Carduelis 597
atrata, Ceratogymna 238
atratus, Coragyps 75
atratus, Cygnus 69
atratus, Picoides 257
atricapilla, Estilda 606
atricapilla, Heteronetta 74
atricapilla, Sylvia 443
atricapilla, Zonotrichia 540
atricapilla, Zosterops 520
atricapillus, Atlapetes 554
atricapillus, Donacobius 391
atricapillus, Otus 184
atricapillus, Parus 499
atricapillus, Philydor 286
atricapillus, Vireo 585
atricaudatus, Myiobius 325
atriceps, Carduelis 597
atriceps, Coracina 359
atriceps, Empidonax 324
atriceps, Hypergerus 459
atriceps, Phalacrocorax 62
atriceps, Phrygilus 544
atriceps, Pycnonotus 365
atriceps, Rhopocichla 424
atriceps, Saltator 557
atriceps, Zosterops 521
Atrichornis 341
atricilla, Larus 130
atricollis, Colaptes 262
atricollis, Eremomela 460
atricollis, Ortygospiza 606
atricollis, Saltator 557
atrifrons, Odontophorus 97
atrifrons, Zosterops 521
atrifusca, Aplonis 619
atrigularis, Napothera 420
atrimaxillaris, Habia 564
atripennis, Dicrurus 626
atripennis, Phyllanthus 434
atripennis, Saltator 557
atrocaerulea, Hirundo 352
atrocapillus, Crypturellus 51
atrocaudata, Terpsiphone 483
atrochalybea, Terpsiphone 482
atrococcineus, Laniarius 377

atroflavus, Laniarius 378
atroflavus, Pogoniulus 245
atrogularis, Arborophila 104
atrogularis, Orthotomus 458
atrogularis, Prinia 455
atrogularis, Prunella 392
atrogularis, Serinus 595
atrogularis, Spizella 542
atrogularis, Thryothorus 385
atronitens, Xenopipo 311
atropileus, Hemispingus 560
atropurpurea, Xipholena 309
atrosuperciliaris, Paradoxomis
  436
atrothorax, Myrmeciza 299
atroviolacea, Dives 592
atrovirens, Lalage 362
atrovirens, Psarocolius 588
Attagis 129
Atthis 221
atthis, Alcedo 225
Atticora 350
Attila 321
atypha, Acrocephalus 442
aubreyana, Gymnomyza 533
aucklandica, Anas 72
aucklandica, Coenocorypha 127
audax, Aphanotriccus 324
audax, Aquila 86
audeberti, Pachycoccyx 172
audouinii, Larus 130
auga, Meliphaga 528
Augastes 219
auguralis, Buteo 85
augusti, Phaethornis 205
Aulacorhynchus 248
aura, Cathartes 75
aurantia, Sterna 131
aurantia, Tyto 181
aurantiaca, Pyrrhula 601
aurantiacus, Manacus 312
aurantiacus, Metopothrix 284
aurantiifrons, Hylophilus 587
aurantiifrons, Loriculus 164
aurantiifrons, Ptilinopus 149
aurantiigula, Macronyx 355
aurantiirostris, Arremon 552
aurantiirostris, Catharus 408
aurantiirostris, Saltator 557
aurantiiventris, Trogon 223
aurantiivertex, Heterocercus 311
aurantioatrocristatus,
  Empidonomus 318
aurantium, Anthreptes 512
aurantius, Lanio 563
aurantius, Ploceus 614
aurantius, Turdus 412
aurata, Saroglossa 622
auratus, Colaptes 262
auratus, Icterus 589
auratus, Oriolus 625
aurea, Aratinga 166
aurea, Euplectes 618
aurea, Jacamerops 239
aurea, Lalage 362

aurea, Pachycephala 494
aureliae, Haplophaedia 218
aureocincta, Buthraupis 566
aureodorsalis, Buthraupis 567
aureola, Emberiza 537
aureola, Pipra 313
aureola, Rhipidura 490
aureolimbatum, Dicaeum 508
aureonucha, Ploceus 616
aureopectus, Pipreola 307
aureoventris, Chlorostilbon 209
aureoventris, Pheucticus 556
aurescens, Polyplancta 215
aureus, Sericulus 630
auricapilla, Aratinga 165
auricapillus, Icterus 589
auriceps, Cyanoramphus 161
auriceps, Pharomachrus 222
auriceps, Picoides 257
auricollis, Ara 165
auricularis, Heterophasia 434
auricularis, Myiornis 330
auricularis, Piculus 262
auricularis, Puffinus 58
auriculata, Zenaida 142
aurifrons, Bolborhynchus 167
aurifrons, Chloropsis 374
aurifrons, Ephthianura 470
aurifrons, Melanerpes 253
aurifrons, Myospiza 541
aurifrons, Neopelma 311
aurifrons, Picumnus 251
aurigaster, Pycnonotus 366
Auriparus 498
Auripasser 613
aurita, Conopophaga 304
aurita, Heliothryx 220
aurita, Sporophila 547
aurita, Zenaida 142
auritum, Crossoptilon 107
auritus, Batrachostomus 192
auritus, Nettapus 71
auritus, Phalacrocorax 61
auritus, Podiceps 55
auriventris, Sicalis 546
aurocapillus, Seiurus 577
aurorae, Ducula 152
auroreus, Phoenicurus 399
aurovirens, Capito 241
aurulentus, Piculus 261
austeni, Garrulax 429
australasia, Halcyon 230
australe, Dicaeum 508
australis, Apteryx 50
australis, Aythya 73
australis, Choriotis 119
australis, Eopsaltria 478
australis, Eremopterix 344
australis, Gallirallus 115
australis, Hyliota 463
australis, Lamprotornis 621
australis, Megalaima 243
australis, Oxyura 75
australis, Peltohyas 126
australis, Petroica 478

648 australis, Phalcoboenus 87
australis, Tchagra 377
australis, Treron 147
australis, Vini 155
Automolus 286
autumnalis, Amazona 170
autumnalis, Dendrocygna 69
averano, Procnias 310
Aviceda 75
Avocettula 207
avosetta, Recurvivostra 122
awokera, Picus 266
axillaris, Eulabeornis 112
axillaris, Euplectes 618
axillaris, Herpsilochmus 295
axillaris, Monarcha 485
axillaris, Myrmotherula 294
axillaris, Pterodroma 56
aylmeri, Turdoides 426
aymara, Bolborhynchus 167
aymara, Metriopelia 143
ayresi, Coturnicops 115
ayresii, Cisticola 450
Aythya 73
azarae, Synallaxis 279
azurea, Cochoa 400
azurea, Coracina 360
azurea, Hypothymis 483
azurea, Sitta 504
azureocapilla, Myiagra 488
azureus, Ceyx 227

Babax 427
baboecalus, Bradypterus 439
bacchus, Ardeola 64
bachmani, Haematopus 121
bachmanii, Vermivora 575
badeigularis, Spelaeornis 421
badia, Ducula 153
badia, Halcyon 228
badiceps, Eremomela 460
badius, Accipiter 82
badius, Caprimulgus 196
badius, Molothrus 593
badius, Phodilus 181
badius, Ploceus 616
Baeopogon 369
baeticatus, Acrocephalus 441
baeri, Aythya 73
baeri, Compospiza 546
baeri, Leucippus 211
baeri, Paroaria 555
baeri, Thripophaga 282
baglafecht, Ploceus 614
bahamensis, Anas 73
baileyi, Xenospiza 541
bailleui, Psittirostra 584
bailloni, Baillonius 249
Baillonius 249
bairdi, Myiodynastes 319
bairdi, Vireo 585
bairdii, Acanthidops 544
bairdii, Ammodramus 541
bairdii, Calidris 8
bairdii, Prinia 454

bakeri, Ducula 152
bakeri, Sericulus 630
bakeri, Yuhina 434
bakkamoena, Otus 183
balaenarum, Sterna 132
Balaeniceps 66
Balearica 111
balfouri, Nectarinia 512
balicassius, Dicrurus 627
balli, Otus 181
balliviani, Odontophorus 98
bambla, Microcerculus 389
Bambusicola 105
bangsi, Grallaria 302
banksiana, Neolalage 484
bannermani, Nectarinia 513
bannermani, Ploceus 614
bannermani, Tauraco 171
banyumas, Niltava 474
baraui, Pterodroma 56
barbadensis, Amazona 170
barbara, Alectoris 99
barbarus, Laniarius 377
barbarus, Otus 183
barbata, Carduelis 579
barbata, Erythropygia 394
barbata, Penelope 92
barbatus, Amytornis 465
barbatus, Apus 203
barbatus, Criniger 371
barbatus, Dendrortyx 96
barbatus, Gypaetus 78
barbatus, Monarcha 486
barbatus, Myiobius 324
barbatus, Pycnonotus 366
barbirostris, Myiarchus 321
baritula, Diglossa 573
barnardi, Barnardius 161
Barnardius 161
baroni, Metallura 218
barrabandi, Pionopsitta 169
barratti, Bradypterus 439
barringeri, Phlegopsis 300
barroti, Heliothryx 220
bartelsi, Spizaetus 86
bartletti, Crypturellus 52
Bartramia 126
Baryphthengus 232
basalis, Chalcites 174
basilanica, Ficedula 473
Basileuterus 580
basilica, Ducula 152
basilicus, Basileuterus 580
Basilornis 623
bassanus, Morus 60
Batara 289
batasiensis, Cypsiurus 203
batavica, Touit 168
batesi, Apus 204
batesi, Caprimulgus 198
batesi, Nectarinia 512
batesi, Ploceus 614
Bathmocercus 459
Batis 480
Batrachostomus 192

baudi, Pitta 339
baumanni, Phyllastrephus 370
bayleyi, Dendrocitta 638
beauharnaesii, Pteroglossus 249
Bebrornis 443
beccarii, Gallicolumba 146
beccarii, Otus 182
beccarii, Sericornis 468
beecheii, Cissilopha 635
behni, Myrmotherula 294
belcheri, Larus 130
belcheri, Pachyptila 57
beldingi, Geothlypis 578
belfordi, Melidectes 533
bella, Emblema 607
bella, Goethalsia 211
belli, Amphispiza 542
belli, Basileuterus 581
bellicosa, Sturnella 591
bellicosus, Polemaetus 87
bellii, Vireo 585
bellulus, Margarornis 284
bendirei, Toxostoma 391
bengalensis, Centropus 179
bengalensis, Graminicola 457
bengalensis, Gyps 78
bengalensis, Houbaropsis 120
bengalensis, Thalasseus 133
bengalus, Uraeginthus 605
benghalense, Dinopium 267
benghalensis, Coracias 234
benghalensis, Ploceus 616
benghalensis, Rostratula 121
benjamini, Urosticte 214
bennetti, Casuarius 49
bennetti, Corvus 640
bennettii, Aegotheles 193
bennettii, Campethera 253
benschi, Monias 110
bensoni, Pseudocossyphus 405
Berenicornis 237
bergii, Thalasseus 132
berigora, Falco 89
berlepschi, Acestrura 221
berlepschi, Dacnis 573
berlepschi, Hylopezus 303
berlepschi, Phacellodomus 283
berlepschi, Rhegmatorhina 300
berlepschi, Sipia 297
berlepschi, Thripophaga 282
Berlepschia 285
berliozi, Apus 203
bernardi, Sakesphorus 289
bernicla, Branta 70
bernieri, Anas 72
bernieri, Oriolia 381
bernsteini, Centropus 179
bernsteini, Thalasseus 133
berthelotii, Anthus 357
bertrandi, Ploceus 614
beryllina, Amazilia 212
beryllinus, Loriculus 163
bewickii, Thryomanes 384
bewsheri, Turdus 409
biarcuatum, Melozone 552

biarmicus, Falco 90
biarmicus, Panurus 435
Bias 480
Biatas 290
bicalcarata, Galloperdix 105
bicalcaratum, Polyplectron 108
bicalcaratus, Francolinus 101
bichenovii, Poephila 607
bicincta, Treron 147
bicinctus, Charadius 125
bicinctus, Pterocles 135
bicolor, Accipiter 83
bicolor, Amaurornis 117
bicolor, Conirostrum 582
bicolor, Coracina 359
bicolor, Cyanophaia 209
bicolor, Dendrocygna 69
bicolor, Dicaeum 508
bicolor, Ducula 153
bicolor, Laniarius 377
bicolor, Lonchura 608
bicolor, Nigrita 602
bicolor, Parus 502
bicolor, Ploceus 614
bicolor, Rhyacornis 399
bicolor, Speculipastor 621
bicolor, Spreo 622
bicolor, Tachycineta 349
bicolor, Tiaris 549
bicolor, Trichastoma 417
bicolor, Turdoides 427
bicornis, Buceros 238
biddulphi, Podoces 638
bidentata, Piranga 564
bidentatus, Harpagus 77
bidentatus, Lybius 246
bieti, Garrulax 428
bifasciata, Nectarinia 516
bifasciata, Oenanthe 403
bifasciatus, Psarocolius 588
bilineata, Amphispiza 542
bilineatus, Pogoniulus 245
bilopha, Eremophila 349
bimaculata, Melanocorypha 346
bimaculatus, Peneothello 479
bimaculatus, Pycnonotus 367
binotata, Apalis 455
binotatus, Veles 195
birostris, Tockus 236
biscutatus, Streptoprocne 199
bishopi, Catharopeza 577
bistriatus, Burhinus 122
bistrigiceps, Acrocephalus 441
bitorquata, Streptopelia 138
bitorquatus, Pteroglossus 248
bitorquatus, Rhinoptilus 123
bivittata, Buettikoferella 463
bivittata, Petroica 478
bivittatus, Basileuterus 580
Biziura 75
blainvillii, Peltops 477
blakistoni, Ketupa 186
blanchoti, Malaconotus 378
blanfordi, Calandrella 346
blanfordi, Montifringilla 613

blanfordi, Pycnonotus 367
blasii, Myzomela 526
Bleda 371
blewitti, Athene 189
blighi, Myiophoneus 405
blissetti, Platysteira 481
blumenbachii, Crax 93
blythii, Tragopan 106
blythii, Onychognathus 620
Blythipicus 268
bocagei, Amaurocichla 462
bocagei, Dryocichloides 397
bocagei, Telophorus 378
bocagii, Nectarinia 516
bodessa, Cisticola 452
boehmi, Coturnicops 115
boehmi, Merops 234
boehmi, Neafrapus 201
bogotensis, Anthus 358
bohmi, Myiopornis 476
bohmi, Parisoma 461
Boissonneaua 217
boissomeautii, Pseudocolaptes 284
bojeri, Ploceus 614
bokharensis, Parus 501
Bolbopsittacus 158
Bolborhynchus 167
boliviana, Poospiza 545
bolivianus, Attila 321
bolivianus, Oreopsar 592
bolivianus, Tyranniscus 336
bollei, Phoeniculus 236
bollii, Columba 136
boltoni, Aethopyga 517
bombus, Acestrura 221
Bombycilla 381
bonana, Icterus 590
bonapartei, Coeligena 216
bonapartei, Gymnobucco 244
bonapartei, Nothocercus 50
bonariensis, Molothrus 593
bonariensis, Thraupis 566
Bonasa 95
bonasia, Bonasa 95
bonelli, Phylloscopus 445
bonensis, Hylocitrea 492
bonthaina, Ficedula 473
boraquira, Nothura 52
borbae, Picumnus 250
borbae, Skutchia 300
borbonica, Phedina 351
borbonica, Zosterops 523
borbonicus, Hypsipetes 373
borealis, Numenius 126
borealis, Nuttallornis 322
borealis, Phylloscopus 445
borealis, Picoides 259
borin, Sylvia 443
bornea, Eos 154
Bostrychia 68
Botaurus 63
Botha 347
bottae, Oenanthe 404
botterii, Aimophila 543

boucardi, Amazilia 212
boucardi, Crypturellus 51
bougainvillei, Halcyon 231
bougainvillei, Melilestes 525
bougainvillei, Phalacrocorax 61
bougueri, Urochroa 215
boulboul, Turdus 410
bourbonnensis, Terpsiphone 482
bourcieri, Phaethornis 205
bourcierii, Eubucco 242
bourkii, Neophema 162
bouroensis, Oriolus 626
bouvieri, Nectarinia 516
bouvieri, Scotopelia 186
bouvreuil, Sporophila 548
Bowdleria 463
boweri, Colluricincla 495
boyeri, Coracina 360
braccatus, Moho 534
Brachycope 617
brachydactyla, Certhia 505
brachydactyla, Petronia 613
Brachygalba 239
brachyptera, Cisticola 452
Brachypteracias 235
brachypterus, Buteo 85
brachypterus, Dasyornis 465
brachypterus, Tachyeres 71
Brachypteryx 392
Brachyramphus 134
brachyrhyncha, Rhipidura 489
brachrhynchos, Corvus 640
brachyrhynchus, Oriolus 625
brachyura, Camaroptera 459
brachyura, Chaetura 202
brachyura, Myrmotherula 293
brachyura, Pitta 340
brachyura, Poecilodryas 479
brachyura, Sylvietta 461
brachyura, Synallaxis 279
brachyurus, Accipiter 81
brachyurus, Anthus 357
brachyurus, Buteo 84
brachyurus, Celeus 263
brachyurus, Graydidascalus 169
brachyurus, Idiopsar 545
brachyurus, Ramphocinclus 391
bracteatus, Nyctibius 193
bradfieldi, Apus 203
bradfieldi, Tockus 236
Bradornis 470
Bradypterus 439
brama, Athene 189
brandti, Leucosticte 598
branickii, Heliodoxa 215
branickii, Leptosittaca 166
branickii, Odontorchilus 383
branickii, Theristicus 68
Branta 70
brasiliana, Cercomacra 296
brasiliana, Hydropsalis 198
brasilianum, Glaucidium 187
brasiliensis, Amazona 170
brasiliensis, Amazonetta 71

650   *brassi, Philemon* 531
brazzae, Phedinopsis 351
brehmeri, Turtur 141
brehmii, Monarcha 486
brehmii, Psittacella 158
brenchleyi, Ducula 152
bres, Criniger 371
bresilius, Ramphocelus 565
brevicauda, Muscigralla 314
brevicauda, Paradigalla 632
brevicaudata, Camaroptera 459
brevicaudata, Napothera 421
brevipennis, Acrocephalus 442
brevipennis, Vireo 585
brevipes, Accipiter 82
brevipes, Heteroscelus 127
brevipes, Monticola 405
brevipes, Pterodroma 56
brevirostris, Brachyramphus 134
brevirostris, Collocalia 200
brevirostris, Crypturellus 52
brevirostris, Melithreptus 531
brevirostris, Pericrocotus 364
brevirostris, Pterodroma 56
brevirostris, Rhynchocyclus 327
brevirostris, Rissa 131
brevirostris, Smicrornis 467
brevis, Bycanistes 238
brevis, Ramphastos 249
breweri, Merops 234
breweri, Spizella 542
brewsteri, Siphonorhis 195
bridgesi, Thamnophilus 290
bridgesii, Drymornis 271
brissonii, Cyanocompsa 558
broadbenti, Dasyornis 465
brodiei, Glaucidium 187
brookii, Otus 182
Brotogeris 168
browni, Monarcha 486
browni, Reinwardtoena 140
browni, Troglodytes 388
brucei, Otus 181
bruijni, Grallina 628
bruijni, Aepypodius 91
bruijnii, Drepanornis 632
bruijnii, Micropsitta 157
bruniceps, Emberiza 537
brunnea, Alcippe 433
brunnea, Nonnula 241
brunnea, Speirops 525
brunneata, Rhinomyias 471
brunneicapilla, Aplonis 620
brunneicapillum, Ornithion 337
*brunneicapillus, Campylorhyn-
    chus* 382
brunneicauda, Alcippe 433
brunneicauda, Newtonia 476
brunneiceps, Hylophilus 587
brunneiceps, Yuhina 435
brunneinucha, Atlapetes 554
brunneopectus, Arborophila 104
brunneopygia, Drymodes 394
brunnescens, Cisticola 449
brunnescens, Margarornis 284

brunneus, Dioptrornis 471
brunneus, Dromaeocercus 457
brunneus, Erithacus 395
brunneus, Pycnonotus 368
brunneus, Sericornis 469
brunnicephalus, Larus 130
brunniceps, Myioborus 579
brunnifrons, Cettia 439
bryantae, Philodice 220
Bubalornis 611
Bubo 184
bubo, Bubo 185
Bubulcus 64
Bucco 240
buccoides, Ailuroedus 630
Bucephala 74
bucephalus, Lanius 379
buceroides, Philemon 532
Buceros 238
buchanani, Emberiza 536
buchanani, Prinia 455
bucinator, Bycanistes 238
buckleyi, Columbina 143
buckleyi, Micrastur 88
Bucorvus 238
budongoensis, Phylloscopus
    447
budytoides, Stigmatura 332
buergersi, Accipiter 80
Buettikoferella 463
buettikoferi, Nectarinia 515
buffoni, Circus 80
buffonii, Chalybura 214
Bugeranus 111
bulleri, Diomedea 55
bulleri, Larus 130
bulleri, Puffinus 57
bulliens, Cisticola 452
bullockoides, Merops 233
bulocki, Merops 233
Bulweria 57
bulweri, Lophura 107
bulwerii, Bulweria 57
Buphagus 624
burchelli, Pterocles 135
burchellii, Neotis 119
Burhinus 122
burkii, Seicercus 447
burmannicus, Sturnus 623
burmeisteri, Acrochordopus 337
burmeisteri, Chunga 119
burmeisteri, Microstilbon 220
burnesi, Prinia 455
burra, Ammomanes 345
burrovianus, Cathartes 75
burtoni, Callacanthis 599
burtoni, Serinus 596
buruensis, Ficedula 473
buruensis, Zosterops 521
buryi, Parisoma 461
Busarellus 84
Butastur 83
Buteo 84
buteo, Buteo 85
Buteogallus 83

Buthraupis 566
butleri, Accipiter 83
butleri, Strix 190
Butoroides 65
Bycanistes 283

cabanisi, Emberiza 537
cabanisi, Knipolegus 316
cabanisi, Lanius 380
cabanisi, Pseudonigrita 611
cabanisi, Synallaxis 279
cabanisi, Tangara 570
caboti, Tragopan 106
Cacatua 156
cachinnans, Garrulax 429
cachinnans, Herpetotheres 87
Cacicus 588
Cacomantis 173
cactorum, Aratinga 166
cactorum, Melanerpes 252
caerulata, Niltava 474
caerulatus, Garrulax 429
caerulea, Coua 178
caerulea, Guiraca 558
caerulea, Halobaena 57
caerulea, Egretta 65
caerulea, Pitta 339
caerulea, Polioptila 437
caerulea, Urocissa 637
caeruleocapilla, Pipra 313
caeruleocephalus, Phoenicurus
    399
caeruleogrisea, Coracina 359
caerulescens, Anser 70
caerulescens, Dendroica 576
caerulescens, Dicrurus 627
caerulescens, Diglossa 574
caerulescens, Estrilda 605
caerulescens, Eupodotis 120
caerulescens, Geranospiza 79
caerulescens, Harpiprion 68
caerulescens, Melanotis 390
caerulescens, Microhierax 88
caerulescens, Porphyrospiza
    558
caerulescens, Ptilorrhoa 415
caerulescens, Rallus 114
caerulescens, Sporophila 548
caerulescens, Thamnophilus
    291
caeruleus, Cyanerpes 573
caeruleus, Cyanocorax 635
caeruleus, Elanus 76
caeruleus, Myiophoneus 405
caeruleus, Parus 502
caesar, Poospiza 545
caesia, Coracina 360
caesia, Emberiza 536
caesius, Thamnomanes 293
cafer, Cuculus 172
cafer, Promerops 535
cafer, Pycnonotus 366
caffer, Anthus 357
caffer, Apus 204
caffra, Acrocephalus 442

caffra, Cossypha 396
cafra, Neotis 119
cahow, Pterodroma 56
caica, Pionopsitta 169
cailliautii, Campethera 254
Cairina 71
cajaneus, Eulabeornis 112
Calamospiza 538
calandra, Emberiza 535
calandra, Melanocorypha 345
Calandrella 346
Calcarius 538
calcostetha, Nectarinia 514
caledonica, Coracina 359
caledonica, Myiagra 487
caledonica, Pachycephala 494
caledonicus, Nycticorax 64
caledonicus, Platycercus 161
Calendula 348
calendula, Regulus 448
Calicalicus 381
Calidris 128
Caliechthrus 174
california, Geococcyx 178
californianus, Gymnogyps 75
californica, Lophortyx 96
californicus, Larus 130
caligata, Hippolais 443
Callacanthis 599
Callaeas 628
calligyna, Brachypteryx 393
callinota, Terenura 296
calliope, Erithacus 395
calliope, Stellula 221
calliparaea, Chlorochrysa 569
Callipepla 96
Calliphlox 220
calliptera, Pyrrhura 167
callizonus, Xenotriccus 324
Callocephalon 156
Callonetta 71
callonotus, Veniliornis 260
callophrys, Tangara 572
Calochaetes 565
Calocitta 636
Caloenas 145
Calonectris 57
Caloperdix 105
calophrys, Hemispingus 560
calopterum, Todirostrum 328
calopterus, Eulabeornis 112
calopterus, Mecocerculus 333
Calorhamphus 244
Calothorax 220
calthorpae, Psittacula 164
calurus, Criniger 371
calva, Treron 147
calvus, Geronticus 67
calvus, Gymnobucco 244
calvus, Sarcogyps 78
calvus, Sarcops 623
calyorhynchus, Ramphococcyx
177
Calypte 221
Calyptocichla 369

Calyptomena 270
Calyptophilus 562
Calyptorhynchus 156
Calyptura 307
Camarhynchus 550
Camaroptera 459
cambodiana, Arborophila 104
camelus, Struthio 49
cameronensis, Zoothera 407
camerunensis, Francolinus 101
campanisona, Chamaeza 301
campanisona, Myrmothera 303
campbelli, Phalacrocorax 61
Campephaga 363
Campephilus 265
campestris, Anthus 356
campestris, Colaptes 263
campestris, Euneornis 574
campestris, Uropelia 144
Campethera 253
Campochaera 362
Camptostoma 335
Campylopterus 206
Campylorhamphus 275
Campylorhynchus 382
camurus, Tockus 237
cana, Agapornis 163
cana, Tadorna 71
canadensis, Branta 70
canadensis, Caryothraustes 556
canadensis, Dendragapus 93
canadensis, Grus 111
canadensis, Perisoreus 636
canadensis, Sakesphorus 289
canadensis, Sitta 503
canadensis, Wilsonia 579
canagicus, Anser 70
canaria, Serinus 594
cancellata, Prosobonia 127
cancrominus, Platyrinchus 326
candei, Manacus 311
candei, Synallaxis 280
candicans, Caprimulgus 196
candida, Amazilia 211
candida, Mirafa 341
candidus, Melanerpes 252
canente, Hemicircus 268
canescens, Eremomela 460
canicapilla, Bleda 371
canicapilla, Nigrita 602
canicapillus, Picoides 256
caniceps, Geotrygon 144
caniceps, Junco 540
caniceps, Lonchura 609
caniceps, Myiopagis 334
caniceps, Prionops 375
caniceps, Psittacula 164
canicollis, Ortalis 91
canicollis, serinus 594
canicularis, Aratinga 165
canifrons, Gallicolumba 146
canifrons, Spizixos 365
canigularis, Chlorospingus 560
caninde, Ara 164
Canirallus 112

canivetii, Chlorostilbon 209
cannabina, Acanthis 598
canningi, Rallina 115
canora, Tiaris 549
canorus, Cuculus 172
canorus, Garrulax 429
canorus, Melierax 80
cantans, Cisticola 453
cantans, Psittirostra 584
cantator, Hypocnemis 297
cantator, Phylloscopus 446
cantillans, Sylvia 444
cantoroides, Aplonis 619
canus, Larus 130
canus, Picus 266
canutus, Calidris 128
capellei, Treron 147
capense, Daption 56
capense, Glaucidium 187
capensis, Anas 72
capensis, Asio 192
capensis, Batis 480
capensis, Bubo 185
capensis, Bucco 240
capensis, Burhinus 122
capensis, Corvus 640
capensis, Emberiza 536
capensis, Euplectes 618
capensis, Francolinus 101
capensis, Macronyx 355
capensis, Micoparra 120
capensis, Morus 60
capensis, Motacilla 355
capensis, Oena 141
capensis, Pelargopsis 227
capensis, Phalacrocorax 61
capensis, Ploceus 614
capensis, Pycnonotus 366
capensis, Smithornis 268
capensis, Turnagra 497
capensis, Tyto 181
capensis, Zonotrichia 539
capicola, Streptopelia 138
capillatus, Phalacrocorax 61
capistrata, Heterophasia 434
capistrata, Muscisaxicola 314
capistrata, Nesocharis 603
capistratum, Pellorneum 416
capistratus, Serinus 594
capitale, Todirostrum 328
capitalis, Aphanotriccus 324
capitalis, Pezopetes 555
capitalis, Stachyris 423
capitata, Paroaria 555
Capito 241
capito, Tregellasia 478
caprata, Saxicola 403
Caprimulgus 195
Capsiempis 331
caprius, Chrysococcyx 174
capueira, Odontophorus 97
carbo, Phalacrocorax 61
carbo, Cepphus 134
carbo, Ramphocelus 565
carbonaria, Cercomacra 297

652   carbonaria, Diglossa 574
carbonarius, Phrygilus 544
Cardellina 579
Cardinalis 556
cardinalis, Cardinalis 556
cardinalis, Chalcopsitta 154
cardinalis, Myzomela 527
cardinalis, Quelea 617
cardis, Turdus 410
cardonai, Myioborus 580
Carduelis 596
carduelis, Carduelis 598
Cariama 119
caribaea, Columba 137
caribaea, Fulica 118
caribaeus, Contopus 323
caribaeus, Vireo 585
carinatum, Electron 232
caripensis, Steatornis 192
carmioli, Chlorothraupis 562
carmioli, Vireo 586
carneipes, Puffinus 57
carnifex, Phoenicircus 306
carnipes, Coccothraustes 602
carola, Ducula 151
carolae, Parotia 632
caroli, Anthoscopus 498
caroli, Campethera 254
caroli, Polyonymus 218
carolina, Porzana 117
carolinae, Tanysiptera 232
carolinensis, Caprimulgus 195
carolinensis, Dumetella 390
carolinensis, Parus 499
carolinensis, Sitta 504
carolinus, Euphagus 593
carolinus, Melanerpes 253
carpalis, Aimophila 543
carpalis, Bradypterus 439
Carphibis 67
Carpococcyx 178
Carpodacus 599
Carpodectes 309
Carpornis 306
carruthersi, Cisticola 453
carteri, Eremiornis 463
carunculata, Anthochaera 535
carunculata, Bostrychia 68
carunculata, Foulehaio 530
carunculata, Paradigalla 632
carunculatus, Bugeranus 111
carunculatus, Creadion 628
carunculatus, Phalacrocorax 61
carunculatus, Phalcoboenus 87
caryocatactes, Nucifraga 639
caryophyllacea, Rhodonessa 73
Caryothraustes 556
Casiornis 322
casiquiare, Crypturellus 52
caspia, Hydroprogne 131
caspius, Tetraogallus 98
cassicus, Cracticus 629
cassidix, Aceros 237
cassini, Leptotila 144
cassini, Malimbus 617

cassini, Muscicapa 476
cassini, Neafrapus 201
cassini, Psarocolius 588
cassini, Veniliornis 261
cassinii, Aimophila 543
cassinii, Carpodacus 599
cassinii, Mitrospingus 562
castanea, Alethe 397
castanea, Anas 72
castanea, Dendroica 577
castanea, Hapaloptila 241
castanea, Philepitta 341
castanea, Pithys 299
castanea, Platysteira 481
castanea, Sitta 503
castanea, Synallaxis 280
castaneceps, Alcippe 432
castaneiceps, Conopophaga 304
castaneiceps, Lysurus 555
castaneiceps, Phoeniculus 236
castaneiceps, Ploceus 615
castaneiceps, Rallina 115
castaneiceps, Seicercus 448
castaneicollis, Francolinus 100
castaneiventris, Amazilia 213
castaneiventris, Cacomantis 173
castaneiventris, Monarcha 486
castaneiventris, Sporophila 548
castaneocoronata, Tesia 438
castaneothorax, Lonchura 610
castaneoventris, Delothraupis 568
castaneoventris, Eulabeornis 112
castaneoventris, Lampornis 214
castaneus, Bradypterus 440
castaneus, Celeus 263
castaneus, Pachyramphus 308
castaneus, Pteroptochos 305
castaniceps, Yuhina 434
castanilus, Accipiter 81
castanonota, Ptilorrhoa 415
castanops, Ploceus 615
castanopterus, Passer 612
castanota, Turnix 111
castanotis, Pteroglossus 249
castanotum, Cinclosoma 415
castanotus, Colius 222
castelnau, Picumnus 250
castelnaudii, Aglaeactis 216
castro, Oceanodroma 59
Casuarius 49
casuarius, Casuarius 49
Catamenia 549
Catamblyrhynchus 555
Cataponera 408
Catharacta 129
Catharopeza 577
Cathartes 75
Catharus 408
Catherpes 383
cathpharius, Picoides 257
Catoptrophorus 126
Catreus 107
caucasicus, Tetraogallus 98

caudacuta, Culicivora 332
caudacuta, Hirundapus 201
caudacutus, Ammodramus 541
caudacutus, Sclerurus 288
caudata, Chiroxiphia 312
caudata, Coracias 234
caudata, Drymophila296
caudatus, Aegithalos 497
caudatus, Bradypterus 440
caudatus, Lamprotornis 621
caudatus, Ptilogonys 382
caudatus, Spelaeornis 421
caudatus, Theristicus 68
caudatus, Turdoides 425
caudifasciatus, Tyrannus 318
caurensis, Percnostola 298
caurinus, Corvus 640
cauta, Diomedea 55
cautus, Sericornis 469
cayana, Cotinga 309
cayana, Dacnis 572
cayana, Piaya 175
cayana, Tangara 571
cayana, Tityra 309
cayanensis, Icterus 589
cayanensis, Leptodon 76
cayanensis, Myiozetetes 319
cayennensis, Caprimulgus 196
cayennensis, Columba 137
cayennensis, Euphonia 569
cayennensis, Mesembrinibis 68
cayennensis, Panyptila 202
cayanus, Cyanocorax 635
cayanus, Vanellus 124
cebuensis, Phylloscopus 447
ceciliae, Metriopelia 143
cedrorum, Bombycilla 381
cela, Cacicus 588
celaeno, Rhodothraupis 556
celaenops, Turdus 412
celata, Vermivora 575
celebense, Trichastoma 417
celebensis, Basilornis 623
celebensis, Centropus 180
celebensis, Hirundapus 202
celebensis, Myza 533
celebensis, Pernis 76
celebensis, Scolopax 127
celebicum, Dicaeum 510
Celeus 263
cenchroides, Falco 89
centralasicus, Caprimulgus 197
Centrocercus 95
Centropus 178
Cephalopterus 310
Cephalopyrus 498
cephalotes, Myiarchus 320
Cepphus 134
Ceratogymna 238
Ceratotriccus 329
Cercibis 68
Cercococcyx 173
Cercomacra 296
Cercomela 401
Cercotrichas 394

Cereopsis 70
Cerorhinca 134
cerritus, Manacus 312
Certhia 505
certhia, Dendrocolaptes 272
Certhiaxis 280
Certhidea 550
Certhilauda 344
certhioides, Upucerthia 276
certhiola, Locustella 440
Certhionyx 528
cerulea, Dendroica 576
cerulea, Procelsterna 133
cerverai, Cyanolimnas 115
cerverai, Ferminia 385
cerviniventris, Bathmocercus 459
cerviniventris, Chlamydera 631
cerviniventris, Phyllastrephus 370
cervinus, Anthus 357
Ceryle 225
Cettia 438
cetti, Cettia 439
Ceuthmochares 176
ceylonensis, Culicicapa 477
ceylonensis, Himantopus 121
ceylonensis, Zosterops 520
Ceyx 226
chabert, Leptopterus 381
chacoensis, Anthus 358
chacoensis, Nothura 53
chacuru, Nystalus 240
Chaetocercus 221
Chaetops 394
Chaetorhynchus 626
Chaetornis 462
Chaetura 201
Chalcites 174
chalconota, Ducula 152
Chalcophaps 141
Chalcopsitta 153
chalcoptera, Phaps 141
chalcopterus, Pionus 169
chalcopterus, Rhinoptilus 123
chalcospilos, Turtur 141
Chalcostigma 219
chalcurum, Polyplectron 108
chalcurus, Lamprotornis 621
chalybaeus, Lamprotornis 621
chalybatus, Manucodia 631
chalybea, Euphonia 568
chalybea, Lophornis 208
chalybea, Nectarinia 515
chalybea, Progne 350
chalybeata, Vidua 610
chalybeus, Centropus 179
Chalybura 214
Chamaea 425
Chamaepetes 93
Chameza 301
chapini, Lioptilus 434
chaplini, Lybius 246
chapmani, Chaetura 202
chapmani, Phylloscartes 331

Charadrius 124
chariessa, Apalis 456
Charitospiza 555
charlottae, Hypsipetes 372
charltonii, Tropicoperdix 105
Charmosyna 155
charmosyna, Estrilda 606
Chasiempis 484
Chauna 69
chavaria, Chauna 69
cheela, Spilornis 78
cheleensis, Calandrella 346
Chelictinia 77
chelicuti, Halcyon 229
Chelidoptera 241
cheniana, Mirafa 341
Chenonetta 71
Chenorhamphus 464
Cheramoeca 351
cherina, Cisticola 450
cherrieri, Cypseloides 199
cherriei, Myrmotherula 293
cherriei, Synallaxis 280
cherriei, Thripophaga 283
cherrug, Falco 90
Chersophilus 347
chiapensis, Campylorhynchus 382
chicquera, Falco 89
chiguanco, Turdus 412
chihi, Plegadis 68
chilensis, Phoenicopterus 69
chilensis, Tangara 570
chilenois, Vanellus 124
Chilia 277
chimachima, Milvago 87
chimaera, Uratelornis 235
chimango, Milvago 87
chinensis, Cissa 637
chinensis, Excalfactoria 104
chinensis, Garrulax 428
chinensis, Oriolus 625
chinensis, Streptopelia 139
chiniana, Cisticola 451
Chionis 129
chionogaster, Amazilia 211
chionopectus, Amazilia 211
chionura, Elvira 213
chirindensis, Apalis 457
chiriquensis, Elaenia 334
chiriquensis, Geothlypis 578
Chirocylla 307
Chiroxiphia 312
chirurgus, Hydrophasianus 120
Chlamydera 630
Chlamydochaera 302
Chlamydotis 119
Chlidonias 131
Chloebia 608
Chloephaga 70
Chlorestes 208
chloricterus, Orthogonys 562
chloris, Acanthisitta 340
chloris, Anthus 358
chloris, Carduelis 596

chloris, Halcyon 230
chloria, Nicator 379
chloris, Piprites 310
chloris, Zosterops 521
chlorocephalus, Oriolus 625
chlorocercus, Leucippus 211
chlorocercus, Lorius 155
Chloroceryle 225
Chlorocharis 525
Chlorochrysa 569
Chlorocichla 369
chlorolepidota, Pipreola 307
chlorolepidotus, Trichoglossus 154
chlorolophus, Picus 265
chloromeros, Pipra 313
chloronota, Camaroptera 459
chloronota, Gerygone 466
chloronothos, Zosterops 524
chloronotus, Arremonops 552
Chloropeta 443
chloropetoides, Thamnornis 443
chlorophaea, Rhinortha 177
Chlorophanes 572
Chlorophonia 569
Chloropipo 311
Chloropsis 374
chloroptera, Ara 165
chloroptera, Aratinga 165
chloropterus, Alisterus 160
chloropterus, Lamprotornis 621
chloropus, Gallinula 117
chloropus, Tropicoperdix 105
chloropygia, Nectarinia 516
chlororhynchos, Diomedea 55
chlororhynchus, Centropus 179
Chlorornis 559
Chlorospingus 559
Chlorostilbon 208
Chlorothraupis 562
chlorotica, Euphonia 568
Chlorurus 551
chlorurus, Chlorurus 551
chocolatina, Melaeornis 471
chocolatinus, Spelaeornis 422
choliba, Otus 184
choloensis, Alethe 398
Chondestes 542
Chondrohierax 76
chopi, Gnorimopsar 592
Chordeiles 194
Choriotis 119
christinae, Aethopyga 518
chrysaea, Stachyris 422
chrysaetos, Aquila 86
chrysaeus, Erithacus 396
chrysater, Icterus 589
chrysauchen, Melanerpes 252
chrysia, Geotrygon 145
chrysocephalum, Neopelma 311
chrysocephalus, Myiodynastes 319
chrysocephalus, Sericulus 630
chrysochloros, Piculus 261
Chrysococcyx 174

654   *Chrysocolaptes* 267
chrysoconus, Pogoniulus 245
chrysocrotaphum, Todirostrum 328
chrysogaster, Basileuterus 580
chrysogaster, Gerygone 466
chrysogaster, Neophema 162
chrysogaster, Pheucticus 556
chrysogenys, Arachnothera 519
chrysogenys, Melanerpes 252
chrysogenys, Oreornis 530
Chrysolampis 208
chrysolaus, Turdus 412
Chrysolophus 108
chrysolophus, Eudyptes 53
chrysomela, Monarcha 486
chrysomelas, Chrysothlypis 562
Chrysomma 425
chrysopareia, Dendroica 577
chrysopasta, Euphonia 569
chrysopeplus, Pheucticus 555
chrysophrys, Emberiza 537
chrysopogon, Megalaima 242
chrysops, Cyanocorax 635
chrysops, Meliphaga 529
chrysoptera, Anthochaera 535
chrysoptera, Neositta 504
chrysoptera, Vermivora 575
chrysopterus, Brotogeris 168
chrysopterus, Cacicus 589
chrysopterus, Masius 312
chrysopterygius, Psephotus 161
chrysorrheum, Dicaeum 508
chrysorrhoa, Acanthiza 468
chrysostoma, Diomedea 55
chrysostoma, Neophema 162
Chrysothlypis 562
chrysotis, Alcippe 432
chrysotis, Tangara 570
chrysura, Hylocharis 211
Chrysuronia 211
chthonia, Grallaria 302
chuana, Mirafa 342
chubbi, Cisticola 453
chukar, Alectoris 99
Chunga 119
cia, Emberiza 536
Ciccaba 190
Cichladusa 397
Cichlherminia 408
Cichlocolaptes 286
Cichlornis 463
Cicinnurus 633
Ciconia 67
ciconia, Ciconia 67
cinchoneti, Conopias1 318
Cinclidium 399
Cinclocerthia 391
Cinclodes 276
Cincloramphus 463
cinclorhynchus, Monticola 405
Cinclosoma 415
Cinclus 382
cinclus, Cinclus 382
cincta, Dichrozona 294

cincta, Notiomystis 531
cincta, Poephila 607
cincta, Ptilinopus 148
cincta, Riparia 351
cincturus, Ammomanes 345
cinctus, Charadrius 125
cinctus, Parus 499
cinctus, Rhinoptilus 123
cinctus, Rhynchortyx 98
cinctus, Saltator 557
cineracea, Ducula 153
cineracea, Emberiza 536
cineracea, Myzomela 526
cineraceus, Garrulax 428
cineraceus, Sturnus 622
cinerascens, Aplonis 619
cinerascens, Cercomacra 296
cinerascens, Circaetus 78
cinerascens, Fraseria 471
cinerascens, Monarcha 485
cinerascens, Myiarchus 3212
cinerascens, Northoprocta 52
cinerascens, Prinia 455
cinerascens, Synallaxis 279
cinerea, Alcippe 432
cinerea, Apalis 456
cinerea, Ardea 66
cinerea, Batara 289
cinerea, Calandrella 346
cinerea, Callaeas 628
cinerea, Coracina 360
cinerea, Creatophora 622
cinerea, Gallicrex 117
cinerea, Gerygone 466
cinerea, Glareola 123
cinerea, Motacilla 355
cinerea, Mycteria 67
cinerea, Pachycephala 492
cinerea, Piezorhina 545
cinerea, Poospiza 545
cinerea, Porzana 116
cinerea, Procellaria 57
cinerea, Serpophaga 333
cinerea, Struthidea 628
cinerea, Xolmis 314
cinerea, Zoothera 406
cinerea, Zosterops 523
cinereicapillus, Tyranniscus 336
cinereicauda, Lampornis 214
cinereiceps, Alcippe 432
cinereiceps, Ortalis 91
cinereiceps, Orthotomus 458
cinereiceps, Oxylabes 435
cinereiceps, Phyllastrephus 371
cinereiceps, Trichastoma 417
cinereiceps, Tyranniscus 336
cinereicollis, Basileuterus 580
cinereifrons, Garrulax 427
cinereifrons, Heteromyias 479
cinereigulare, Oncostoma 329
cinereiventria, Chaetura 202
cinereiventris, Microbates 437
cinereocapilla, Prinia 455
cinereola, Cisticola 451
cinereovinacea, Euschistospiza

604
cinereum, Conirostrum 582
cinereum, Malacopteron 418
cinereum, Todirostrum 328
cinereum, Toxostoma 391
cinereus, Artamus 629
cinereus, Circaetus 78
cinereus, Circus 79
cinereus, Coccyzus 175
cinereus, Contopus 322
cinereus, Crypturellus 50
cinereus, Odontorchilus 383
cinereus, Ptilogonys 381
cinereus, Pycnopygius 531
cinereus, Vanellus 124
cinereus, Xenus 126
cinnamomea, Certhiaxis 281
cinnamomea, Neopipo 311
cinnamomea, Pyrrhomyias 325
cinnamomea, Sporophila 548
cinnamomea, Synallaxis 280
cinnamomea, Terpsiphone 483
cinnamomeiventris, Ochthoeca
315
cinnamomeiventris,
Thamnolaea 403
cinnamomeum, Cinclosoma
415
cinnamomeus, Attila 321
cinnamomeus, Bradypterus
439
cinnamomeus, Crypturellus
51
cinnamomeus, Hypocryp-
tadius 525
cinnamomeus, Ixobrychus
63
cinnamomeus, Pachyram-
phus 308
cinnamomeus, Pericrocotus
363
cinnamomeus, Picumnus
250
cinnamomina, Halcyon 230
Cinnycerthia 384
Cinnyricinclus 621
cioides, Emberiza 536
Circaetus 78
circumcinctus, Spiziapteryx
88
Circus 79
ciris, Passerina 558
cirlus, Emberiza 536
cirratus, Picumnus 251
cirrhata, Lunda 134
cirrhatus, Spizaetus 86
cirrhocephalus, Accipiter 80
cirrhocephalus, Larus 130
cirrhochloris, Aphantochroa
214
Cissa 637
Cissilopha 635
Cissomela 534
Cissopis 559
Cisticola 449

Cistothorus 384
citrea, Protonotaria 578
citreogularis, Philemon 531
citreogularis, Sericornis 469
citreola, Motacilla 355
citreolus, Trogon 223
citrina, Sicalis 545
citrina, Wilsonia 579
citrina, Zoothera 406
citrinella, Serinus 594
citrinella, Emberiza 535
citrinelloides, Serinus 595
citrinellus, Atlapetes 554
citrinipectus, serinus 595
citriniventris, Attila 321
Cittura 228
Cladorhynchus 121
clamans, Baeopogon 369
clamans, Spiloptila 457
Clamator 172
clamator, Rhinoptyn 191
clamosa, Rhipidura 488
clamosus, Atrichornis 341
clanga, Aquila 86
Clangula 74
clangula, Bucephala 74
clappertoni, Francolinus 101
clara, Motacilla 355
clarae, Arachnothera 519
Claravis 143
clarkii, Otus 184
clathratus, Trogon 223
cleaveri, Trichastoma 417
clemenciae, Lampornis 214
Cleptornis 530
climacocerca, Hydropsalis
    198
Climacteris 506
climacurus, Scotornis 198
clotbey, Ramphocoris 345
clypeata, Anas 73
Clytoceyx 228
Clytoctantes 292
Clytolaema 215
Clytomyias 463
Clytorhynchus 484
Clytospiza 603
Cnemophilus 631
Cnemoscopus 560
Cnemotriccus 324
Cnipodectes 326
coccinea, Loxops 584
coccinea, Vestiaria 584
coccineus, Calochaetes 565
coccinigastra, Nectarinia 517
Coccothraustes 602
coccothraustes, Cocco-
    thraustes 602
Coccyzus 175
cochinchinensis, Chloropsis
    374
cochinchinensis, Hirundapus
    202
Cochlearius 64
cochlearius, Cochlearius 64

Cochoa 400
cockerelli, Lichmera 526
cockerelli, Philemon 532
cockerelli, Rhipidura 491
cocoi, Ardea 66
coelebs, Fringilla 594
coelestis, Aglaiocercus 219
coelestis, Forpus 168
coelestis, Hypothymis 483
coelicolor, Grandala 399
Coeligena 216
coeligena, Coeligena 216
Coenocorypha 127
Coereba 583
coeruleicinctis, Aulaco-
    rhynchus 248
coeruleogularis, Lepidopyga
    210
coerulescens, Alcedo 226
coerulescens, Aphelocoma
    634
coerulescens, Coracina 360
coerulescens, Muscicapa
    476
coerulescens, Saltator 557
Colaptes 262
colchicus, Phasianus 108
Colibri 207
Colinus 96
Colius 221
colius, Colius 222
collaria, Amazona 170
collaris, Accipiter 83
collaris, Anthreptes 512
collaris, Aythya 73
collaris, Charadrius 125
collaris, Lanius 380
collaris, Microbates 436
collaris, Mirafa 343
collaris, Prunella 392
collaris, Sporophila 547
collaris, Trogon 223
colliei, Calocitta 636
Collocalia 199
Colluricincla 495
collurio, Lanius 379
collurioides, Lanius 379
collybitus, Phylloscopus 444
colma, Formicarius 301
Colonia 316
colonus, Colonia 316
colonus, Rhinomyias 472
Colopteryx 330
Coloramphus 333
coloria, Erythrura 607
colubris, Archilochus 220
Columba 135
columbarius, Falco 89
columbiana, Nucifraga 368
columbiana, Sicalis 546
columbianus, Cygnus 69
columbianus, Odontophorus
    98
columbiana, Porzana 116

Columbina 142
columboides, Psittacula 164
comata, Hemiprocne 204
comatus, Berenicornis 237
comechingonous, Cinclodes
    277
comitata, Muscicapa 476
communis, Sylvia 444
comorensis, Nectarinia 515
Compospiza 546
Compsothraupis 559
comptus, Trogon 223
comrii, Manucodia 631
concinens, Acrocephalus
    441
concinna, Ducula 152
concinna, Euphonia 568
concinna, Glossopsitta 155
concinnus, Aegithalos 497
concolor, Amaurospiza 548
concolor, Corythaixoides
    171
concolor, Dendrocolaptes
    272
concolor, Dicaeum 508
concolor, Eulabeornis 112
concolor, Falco 89
concolor, Hirundo 352
concolor, Macrosphenus
    461
concolor, Neospiza 596
concolor, Xenospingus 545
concreta, Halcyon 231
concreta, Niltava 474
concreta, Platysteira 481
concretus, Caprimulgus 198
concretus, Hemicircus 268
condamini, Eutoxeres 206
congensis, Afropavo 109
congensis, Nectarinia 517
congica, Riparia 351
Conioptilon 309
conirostris, Arremonops 552
conirostris, Geospiza 550
conirostris, Spizocorys 347
Conirostrum 582
connivens, Ninox 188
Conopias 318
Conopophaga 304
Conopophila 534
Conostoma 435
Conothraupis 559
conoveri, Leptotila 144
consobrinorum, Zosterops
    521
conspicillata, Sylvia 444
conspicillata, Zosterops 520
conspicillatus, Forpus 168
conspicillatus, Paradoxornis
    435
conspicillatus, Pelecanus 60
constantii, Heliomaster 220
contaminatus, Xenops 288
Contopus 322
contra, Sturnus 622

656 conversii, Popelairia 208
cookii, Pterodroma 56
cooperi, Otus 184
cooperii, Accipiter 83
coprotheres, Gyps 78
Copsychus 398
coquereli, Coua 178
coquerellii, Nectarinia 515
coqui, Francolinus 102
cora, Thaumastura 220
Coracias 234
Coracina 358
coracinus, Entomodestes
401
Coracopsis 162
Coragyps 75
corallirostris, Hypositta 381
Corapipo 312
corax, Corvus 641
coraya, Thryothorus 385
Corcorax 628
cordofanica, Mirafa 341
corensis, Columba 137
corniculata, Fratercula 134
corniculatus, Philemon 532
cornuta, Anhima 69
cornuta, Fulica 118
cornuta, Heliactin 220
cornuta, Pipra 313
cornutus, Cyanoramphus
162
coromanda, Halcyon 228
coromandelianus, Nettapus
71
coromandelica, Coturnix 103
coromandelicus, Cursorius
123
coromandus, Bubo 185
coromandus, Clamator 172
coronata, Dendroica 577
coronata, Hemiprocne 204
coronata, Paroaria 555
coronata, Pipra 312
coronata, Thamnolaea 403
coronata, Xolmis 314
coronata, Zeledonia 582
coronatus, Ampeliceps 623
coronatus, Anthracoceros
238
coronatus, Basileuterus 580
coronatus, Harpyhaliaetus
84
coronatus, Malimbus 616
coronatus, Malurus 464
coronatus, Onychorhynchus
326
coronatus, Phylloscopus 446
coronatus, Platyrinchus 326
coronatus, Pterocles 135
coronatus, Stephanoaetus
87
coronatus, Tachyphonus 563
coronatus, Vanellus 124
corone, Corvus 640
coronoides, Corvus 640

coronulatus, Ptilinopus 150
correndera, Anthus 358
corrugatus, Aceros 237
corruscus, Lamprotornis 220
coruscans, Colibri 207
coruscans, Neodrepanis 341
corvina, Corvinella 379
corvina, Megalaima 242
corvina, Terpsiphone 482
Corvinella 379
Corvus 639
Corydon 269
coryphaea, Erythropygia 393
coryphaeus, Pogoniulus 244
Coryphaspiza 555
Coryphistera 283
Coryphospingus 555
Corythaeola 171
corythaix, Basilornis 623
corythaix, Tauraco 171
Corythaixoides 171
Corythopis 338
Coscoroba 69
coscoroba, Coscoroba 69
Cosmopsarus 622
Cossypha 396
costae, Calypte 221
costaricensis, Geotrygon
144
Cotinga 309
cotinga, Cotinga 309
cotta, Myiopagis 335
Coturnicops 115
Coturnix 103
coturnix, Coturnix 103
Coua 178
couchii, Tyrannus 318
couloni, Aru 165
courseni, Synallaxis 279
Cracticus 629
crassa, Aplonis 619
crassa, Napothera 421
crassirostris, Ailuroedus 630
crassirostris, Arachnothera
519
crassirostris, Camarhynchus
550
crassirostris, Carduelis 597
crassirostris, Chalcites 174
crassirostris, Corvus 641
crassirostris, Cuculus 172
crassirostris, Geositta 276
crassirostris, Heleia 525
crassirostris, Hypsipetes
373
crassirostris, Larus 130
crassirostris, Oriolus 625
crassirostris, Oryzoborus
548
crassirostris, Pachyptila 57
crassirostris, Ramphocharis
507
crassirostris, Reinwardtoena
140
crassirostris, Tyrannus 318

crassirostris, Vanellus 123
crassirostris, Vireo 585
crassus, Poicephalus 162
Crateroscelis 469
cratitia, Meliphaga 529
craveri, Brachyramphus
134
Crax 93
Creadion 628
creagra, Macropsalis 199
Creagrus 131
Creatophora 622
creatopus, Puffinus 57
crecca, Anas 72
crenatus, Anthus 358
crepitans, Psophia 112
crestatus, Eudyptes 53
Creurgops 563
Crex 116
crex, Crex 116
Crinifer 171
crinifrons, Aegotheles 193
Criniger 371
criniger, Gallicolomba 145
criniger, Hypsipetes 372
criniger, Prinia 455
criniger, Setornis 372
crinitus, Myiarchus 321
crispifrons, Napothera 421
crispus, Pelecanus 60
crissalis, Vermivora 575
cristata, Alcedo 226
cristata, Calyptura 307
cristata, Cariama 119
cristata, Corythaeola 171
cristata, Coua 178
cristata, Cyanocitta 634
cristata, Elaenia 334
cristata, Fulica 118
cristata, Galerida 347
cristata, Goura 146
cristata, Gubernatrix 555
cristata, Habia 564
cristata, Lophostrix 184
cristata, Lophotibis 68
cristata, Pseudoseisura 284
cristata, Rhegmatorhina 300
cristatella, Aethia 134
cristatellus, Acridotheres
623
cristatellus, Cyanocorax 635
cristatum, Sphenostoma 414
cristatus, Aegotheles 193
cristatus, Colinus 97
cristatus, Furnarius 277
cristatus, Lanius 379
cristatus, Orthorhyncus 208
cristatus, Oxyruncus 338
cristatus, Parus 500
cristatus, Pavo 109
cristatus, Pitohui 496
cristatus, Podiceps 55
cristatus, Sakesphorus 289
cristatus, Tachyphonus 563
crocea, Ephthianura 470

croceus, Macronyx 355
Crocias 434
crossleyi, Atelornis 235
crossleyi, Mystacornis 435
crossleyi, Zoothera 407
Crossoptilon 107
crossoptilon, Crossoptilon 107
Crotophaga 177
crudigularis, Arborophila 104
cruenta, Tchagra 377
cruentata, Myzomela 526
cruentata, Pyrrhura 166
cruentatum, Dicaeum 510
cruentatus, Melanerpes 252
cruentus, Ithaginis 106
cruentus, Malaconotus 378
cruentus, Oriolus 625
cruentus, Rhodospingus 555
crumeniferus, Leptoptilos 67
cruralis, Cincloramphus 463
cruziana, Columbina 143
Crypsirina 638
crypta, Ficedula 473
cryptoleucus, Corvus 641
cryptoleucus, Peneothello 479
cryptolophus, Lipaugus 307
Cryptophaps 153
Cryptospiza 613
cryptoxanthus, Myiophobus 325
cryptoxanthus, Poicephalus 162
Crypturellus 50
cryptus, Cypseloides199
cubanensis, Caprimulgus 195
cubensis, Tyrannus 317
cubla, Dryoscopus 376
cucullata, Andigena 249
cucullata, Carduelis 597
cucullata, Crypsirina 638
cucullata, Cyanolyca 635
cucullata, Grallericula 304
cucullata, Hirundo 353
cucullata, Lonchura 608
cucullata, Petroica 478
cucullata, Tangara 571
cucullatus, Carpornis 306
cucullatus, Coryphospingus 555
cucullatus, Icterus 590
cucullatus, Mergus 74
cucullatus, Orthotomus 458
cucullatus, Ploceus 615
cuculoides, Aviceda 75
cuculoides, Glaucidium 187
Cuculus 172
Culicicapa 477
Culicivora 332
culicivorus, Basileuterus 581
culik, Selenidera 249
cumingi, Lepidogrammus 177

cuneata, Geopelia 142
cunicularia, Geositta 276
cunicularia, Speotyto 189
cupido, Tympanuchus 95
cuprea, Nectarinia 516
cupreiceps, Elvira 213
cupreocauda, Lamprotornis 620
cupreoventris, Eriocnemis 217
cupreus, Chrysococcyx 174
cupripennis, Aglaeactis 216
Curaeus 592
curaeus, Curaeus 592
curraca, Sylvia 444
currucoides, Sialia 400
cursor, Coua 178
cursor, Cursorius 122
Cursorius 122
curtata, Certhiaxis 281
curucui, Trogon 223
curvipennis, Campylopterus 206
curvirostra, Loxia 601
curvirostra, Treron 147
curvirostre, Toxostoma 391
curvirostris, Certhilauda 344
curvirostris, Limnornis 283
curvirostris, Nothoprocta 52
curvirostris, Pycnonotus 368
curvirostris, Ramphococcyx 177
curvirostris, Vanga 381
Cutia 431
cuvieri, Canirallus 112
cuvieri, Talegalla 91
cuvierii, Falco 89
cuvierii, Phaeochroa 206
cyana, Cyanopica 637
cyane, Erithacus 396
cyanea, Chlorophonia 569
cyanea, Diglossa 574
cyanea, Passerina 558
cyanea, Pitta 339
cyanea, Platysteira 481
cyaneovirens, Erythrura 608
cyaneoviridis, Tachycineta 350
Cyanerpes 573
cyanescens, Galbula 239
cyanescens, Terpsiphone 483
cyaneus, Circus 79
cyaneus, Cyanerpes 573
cyaneus, Malurus 464
cyaniceps, Rhipidura 488
cyanicollis, Galbula 239
cyanicollis, Tangara 572
Cyanicterus 566
cyanicterus, Cyanicterus 566
cyanifrons, Amazilia 212
cyanirostris, Knipolegus 316
cyaniventer, Tesia 438
cyaniventris, Pycnonotus 365

cyanocampter, Cossypha 396
cyanocephala, Amazilia 212
cyanocephala, Eudynamys 175
cyanocephala, Gymnorhinus 634
cyanocephala, Psittacula 164
cyanocephala, Starnoenas 145
cyanocephala, Tangara 570
cyanocephala, Thraupis 566
cyanocephala, Todopsis 464
cyanocephala, Uraeginthus 605
cyanocephalus, Euphagus 593
Cyanochen 70
Cyanocitta 634
Cyanocompsa 558
Cyanocorax 635
cyanogaster, Coracias 234
cyanogaster, Irena 375
cyanogenia, Eos 154
cyanoides, Cyanocompsa 558
cyanolaema, Nectarinia 513
cyanoleuca, Grallina 628
cyanoleuca, Myiagra 487
cyanoleuca, Notiochelidon 350
Cyanolimnas 115
Cyanoliseus 166
Cyanoloxia 558
Cyanolyca 634
cyanomelaena, Cyanoptila 473
cyanomelas, Cyanocorax 635
cyanomelas, Rhinopomastus 236
cyanomelas, Trochocercus 482
cyanopectus, Ceyx 226
cyanopectus, Sternoclyta 215
Cyanophaia 209
cyanophrys, Eupherusa 213
Cyanopica 637
cyanopis, Columbina 143
cyanopogon, Chloropsis 374
cyanopogon, Cyanocorax 635
Cyanopsitta 164
cyanoptera, Anas 73
cyanoptera, Brotogeris 168
cyanoptera, Tangara 572
cyanoptera, Thraupis 566
cyanopterus, Artamus 629
cyanopterus, Cyanochen 70
cyanopterus, Pterophanes 216
Cyanoptila 473
cyanopus, Agelaius 591
cyanopygius, Forpus 168
Cyanoramphus 161

658 cyanotis, Cittura 228
cyanotis, Entomyzon 531
cyanotis, Tangara 571
cyanouroptera, Minla 432
cyanoventris, Halcyon 228
cyanoventris, Tangara 570
cyanura, Amazilia 212
cyanurus, Erithacus 396
cyanurus, Psittinus 158
cyanus, Hylocharis 210
cyanus, Parus 502
cyanus, Peneothello 479
Cyclarhis 584
Cyclorrhynchus 134
cygnoides, Anser 69
Cygnus 69
cygnus, Cygnus 69
cylindricus, Bycanistes 238
Cymbilaimus 289
Cymbirhynchus 269
Cynanthus 209
cyornithopsis, Erithacus 395
Cyphorhinus 389
Cypseloides 199
Cypsnagra 559
Cypsiurus 203
Cyrtonyx 98

dabbenei, Penelope 92
Dacelo 228
Dacnis 572
dacotiae, Saxicola 402
dactylatra, Sula 60
Dactylortyx 98
dahli, Rhipidura 489
dalhousiae, Psarisomus 269
damarensis, Mirafa 342
damarensis, Phoeniculus 236
dambo, Cisticola 450
damii, Xenopirostris 381
Damophila 210
danae, Tanysiptera 232
danjoui, Jabouilleia 420
Daphoenositta 505
Daption 56
Daptrius 87
darjellensis, Picoides 257
darnaudii, Trachyphonus 247
darwinii, Nothura 52
Dasylophus 177
Dasyornis 465
dasypus, Delichon 353
daubentoni, Crax 93
dauma, Zoothera 407
daurica, Hirundo 353
dauuricae, Perdix 103
dauuricus, Corvus 639
davidi, Arborophila 104
davidi, Garrulax 428
davidi, Niltava 473
davidi, Parus 499
davidi, Strix 191
davidiana, Montifringilla 612
davidianus, Paradoxornis 436
davisoni, Phylloscopus 446

davisoni, Pseudibis 67
dayi, Capito 241
dayi, Elaenia 334
dea, Galbula 239
debilis, Phyllastrephus 370
decaocto, Streptopelia 138
decipiens, Streptopelia 138
deckeni, Tockus 237
Deconychura 270
decora, Paradisaea 633
decoratus, Pterocles 135
decumanus, Psarocolius 588
decurtatus, Hylophilus 588
dedemi, Rhipidura 488
defilippi, Sturnella 592
deiroleucus, Falco 90
delelandi, Corythopis 338
delatrii, Tachyphonus 563
delattrei, Lophornis 208
delawarensis, Larus 130
delegorguei, Columba 138
delegorguei, Coturnix 103
delesserti, Garrulax 428
Delichon 354
deliciosus, Machaeropterus 311
Delothraupis 568
delphinae, Colibri 207
Deltarhynchus 322
demersus, Spheniscus 53
demisa, Certhiaxis 281
Dendragapus 93
Dendrexetastes 271
Dendrocincla 270
Dendrocitta 638
Dendrocolaptes 272
dendrocolaptoides,
    Phacellodomus 283
Dendrocygna 69
Dendroica 575
Dendronanthus 354
Dendropicos 254
Dendrortyx 96
deningeri, Lichmera 526
dentata, Creurgops 563
dentata, Petronia 613
denti, Sylvietta 461
dentirostris, Scenopoeetes 630
derbiana, Psittacula 164
derbianus, Aulacorhynchus 248
derbianus, Oreophasis 93
derbianus, Orthotomus 458
derbyi, Eriocnemis 218
Deroptyus 171
deserti, Ammomanes 345
deserti, Oenanthe 404
deserticola, Sylvia 444
desmaresti, Tangara 570
desmarestii, Psittaculirostris
    158
desmursii, Sylviorthorhynchus
    277
desolata, Pachyptila 57
deva, Galerida 348
devillei, Drymophila 296
devillei, Pyrrhur 166

diabolicus, Eurostopodus 195
diadema, Catamblyrhynchus 555
diadema, Charmosyna 155
diadema, Ochthoeca 315
diademata, Alethe 397
diademata, Yuhina 435
diademata, Euplectes 617
diadematum, Tricholaema 245
diadematus, Stephanophorus
    1567
dialeucos, Odontophorus 98
diana, Cinclidium 399
diardi, Lophura 107
diardi, Rhopodytes 176
diardii, Harpactes 224
Dicaeum 507
dichroa, Aplonis 619
dichroa, Cossypha 396
dichrous, Parus 500
dichrous, Pitohui 496
Dichrozona 294
dickeyi, Cyanocorax 635
dickinsoni, Falco 89
dicolorus, Ramphastos 249
dicrocephalus, Ploceus 615
Dicrurus 626
Didunculus 146
diemenensis, Philemon 1532
difficilis, Empidonax 323
difficilis, Geospiza 550
difficilis, Phylloscartes 331
Diglossa 573
dignissima, Grallaria 302
dignus, Veniliornis 260
dilectissima, Touit 168
dimidiata, Hirundo 352
dimidiata, Pomarea 484
dimidiatus, Philydor 286
dimidiatus, Ramphocelus 565
dimorpha, Uroglaux 188
dinellianus, Pseudocolopteryx
    332
dinemelli, Dinemellia 611
Dinemellia 611
Dinopium 267
diodon, Harpagus 77
Diomedea 55
diomedea, Calonectris 57
diophthalma, Opopsitta 158
diops, Batis 480
diops, Halcyon 229
diops, Hemitriccus 331
Dioptrornis 471
diphone, Cettia 438
Diphyllodes 633
discolor, Certhia 506
discolor, Dendroica 577
discolor, Lathamus 162
discolor, Leptosomus 235
discolorus, Ramphastos
discors, Anas 73
Discosura 208
discurus, Prioniturus 159
disjuncta, Myrmeciza 299
dissimilis, Turdus 410

distans, Amazilia 212
Diuca 545
diuca, Diuca 545
divaricatus, Pericrocotus 363
Dives 592
dives, Dives 592
dixoni, Zoothera 407
dohertyi, Coracina 360
dohertyi, Lophozosterops 524
dohertyi, Ptilinopus 148
dohertyi, Telophorus 378
dohrni, Horizorhinus 435
dohrnii, Glaucis 204
dolei, Palmeria 584
doliatus, Thamnophilus 290
Dolichonyx 594
Dolospingus 549
domesticus, Passer 611
domicellus, Lorius 155
dominica, Dendroica 577
dominica, Oxyura 74
dominica, Pluvialis 124
dominicana, Paroaria 555
dominicana, Xolmis 314
dominicanus, Larus 130
dominicensis, Carduelis 597
dominicensis, Icterus 590
dominicensis, Progne 350
dominicensis, Tyrannus 318
dominicus, Anthracothorax 207
dominicus, Dulus 382
dominicus, Podiceps 54
Donacobius 391
Donacospiza 544
donaldsoni, Caprimulgus 197
donaldsoni, Plocepasser 611
donaldsoni, Serinus 595
dorae, Picoides 257
dorbignyi, Thripophaga 282
dorbygnianus, Picumnus 251
doriae, Megatriorchis 80
Doricha 220
dorotheae, Amytornis 465
dorsale, Ramphomicron 218
dorsale, Toxostoma 391
dorsalis, Automolus 287
dorsalis, Lanius, 380
dorsalis, Mimus 390
dorsalis, Phacellodomus 283
dorsalis, Phrygilus 544
dorsimaculatus, Herpsilochmus 295
dorsomaculatus, Ploceus 616
Doryfera 204
dougallii, Sterna 131
douglasii, Lophorytx 96
dowii, Tangara 572
Drepanoptila 151
Drepanornis 632
Dromococcyx 177
Dromaeocercus 457
Dromaius 49
Dromas 121
drownei, Rhipidura 489
dryas, Catharus 409

Drymocichla 457
Drymodes 394
Drymophila 296
Drymornis 271
Dryocichloides 397
Dryocopus 264
Dryoscopus 376
Dryotriorchis 79
dubia, Cercomela 402
dubium, Scissirostrum 624
dubius, Charadrius 124
dubius, Hieraaetus 86
dubius, Leptoptilos 67
dubius, Lybius 246
Dubusia 568
duchaillui, Pogoniulus 244
ducorps, Cacatua 157
Ducula 151
dufresniana, Amazona 170
duidae, Campylopterus 206
duidae, Crypturellus 51
duidae, Diglossa 574
duidae, Emberizoides 546
duivenbodei, Chalcopsitta 153
Dulus 382
dumasi, Zoothera 406
dumetaria, Upucerthia 276
Dumatella 390
Dumetia 424
dumetoria, Ficedula 472
dumicola, Polioptila 438
dumontii, Mino 623
dunni, Ammomanes 345
dupetithouarsii, Ptilinopus 150
duponti, Chersophilus 347
dupontii, Tilmatura 220
dussumieru, Nectarinia 514
duvaucelii, Harpactes 224
duvaucelii, Vanellus 123
duyvenbodei, Aethopyga 518
dybowskii, Euschistospiza 604
Dysithamnus 292

earlei, Turdoides 425
ecaudatus, Myiornis 330
ecaudatus, Terathopius 78
echo, Psittacula 164
Eclectus 160
edolioides, Melaeornis 471
edouardi, Guttera 109
eduardi, Tylas 374
edward, Amazilia 213
edwardsi, Buthraupis 566
edwardsi, Lophura 107
edwardsii, Carpodacus 600
edwardii, Psittaculirostris 158
egertoni, Actinodura 431
egregia, Porzana 116
egregia, Pyrrhura 167
Egretta 65
eichhorni, Myzomela 528
eichhorni, Philemon 532
elachus, Dendropicos 254
Elaenia 333
Elanoides 76

Elanus 76
elaphra, Collocalia 199
elata, Ceratogymna 238
elatus, Tyrannulus 337
eleanorae, Falco 89
Electron 232
elegans, Celeus 263
elegans, Coturnicops 115
elegans, Emberiza 537
elegans, Eudromia 53
elegans, Laniisoma 306
elegans, Leptopoecile 449
elegans, Malurus 464
elegans, Melanopareia 305
elegans, Neophema 162
elegans, Parus 500
elegans, Phaps 141
elegans, Platycercus 161
elegans, Thalasseus 133
elegans, Trogon 223
elegans, Xiphorhynchus 273
elegantior, Synallaxis 279
eleonorae, Falco 89
Eleothreptus 199
elgini, Spilornis 79
eliciae, Hylocharis 210
elisabeth, Myadestes 400
eliza, Doricha 220
ellioti, Atthis 221
ellioti, Pitta 339
ellioti, Syrmaticus 107
ellioti, Tanysiptera 232
elliotii, Dendropicos 255
elliotii, Garrulax 430
elphinstonii, Columba 136
eludens, Grallaria 302
Elvira 213
Emberiza 535
Emberizoides 546
Embernagra 546
Emblema 607
emiliae, Chlorocharis 525
eminentissima, Foudia 617
eminibey, Sorella 613
emphanum, Polyplectron 109
Empidonax 323
Empidonomus 318
Empidornis 471
enarratus, Caprimulgus 198
enca, Corvus 639
Enicognathus 167
enicura, Doricha 220
Enicurus 400
Enodes 624
Ensifera 217
ensifera, Ensifera 217
ensipennis, Campylopterus 207
Entomodestes 401
Entomyzon 531
Entotriccus 316
enucleator, Pinicola 600
Eolophus 156
Eopsaltria 478
Eos 154
eos, Carpodacus 600

660

epauletta, Pyrrhoplectes 602
Ephippiorhynchus 67
Ephthianura 470
epichlora, Urolais 457
epilepidota, Napothera 421
Epimachus 632
episcopus, Ciconia 67
episcopus, Thraupis 566
epomidis, Centropus 179
epomophora, Diomedea 55
epops, Upupa 235
epulata, Muscicapa 476
eques, Myzomela 526
Erannornis 481
erckelii, Francolinus 100
Eremiornis 463
eremita, Geronticus 67
eremita, Nesocichla 408
Eremobius 283
Eremomela 460
Eremophila 349
Eremopterix 344
Ergaticus 579
Eriocnemis 217
Erithacus 395
erithacus, Ceyx 227
erithacus, Psittacus 162
erythaca, Pyrrhula 601
erythrauchen, Accipiter 80
erythrinus, Carpodacus 599
erythrocephala, Amadina 610
erythrocephala, Myzomela 527
erythrocephala, Pipra 313
erythrocephala, Piranga 565
erythrocephala, Pyrrhula 601
erythrocephalus, Automolus 287
erythrocephalus, Garrulax 430
erythrocephalus, Harpactes 224
erythrocephalus, Melanerpes
252
erythrocephalus, Trachyphonus
247
erythrocerca, Nectarinia 517
Erythrocercus 481
erythrocercus, Philydor 285
erythrogaster, Laniarius 377
erythrogaster, Malimbus 617
erythrogaster, Phoenicurus 399
erythrogaster, Pitta 339
erythrogenys, Aratinga 165
erythrogenys, Pomatorhinus
418
erythrogonys, Microhierax 88
erythroleuca, Grallaria 303
erythrolophus, Tauraco 171
erythromelas, Myzomela 528
erythromelas, Periporphyrus
557
erythronota, Zoothera 406
erythronotos, Estilda 606
erythronotos, Myrmotherula 294
erythronotus, Philydor 286
erythronotus, Phoenicurus 399
erythronotus, Phrygilus 544
erythrophris, Enodes 624

erythrophrys, Poospiza 545
erythrophthalma, Lophura 107
erythrophthalma, Netta 73
erythrophthalmus, Coccyzus
175
erythrophthalmus,
Phacellodomus 283
erythrophthalmus, Pipilo 551
erythrophthalmus, Pycnonotus
368
erythropleura, Ptiloprora 532
erythropleura, Zosterops 519
erythrops, Certhiaxis 280
erythrops, Cisticola 452
erythrops, Climacteris 506
erythrops, Myiagra 487
erythrops, Odontophorus 97
erythrops, Porzana 116
erythrops, Quelea 617
erythroptera, Gallicolumba 145
erythroptera, Heliolais 457
erythroptera, Mirafa 343.
erythroptera, Ortalis 91
erythroptera, Phlegopsis 300
erythroptera, Stachyris 424
erythropterus, Aprosmictus 160
erythropterus, Philydor 286
erythropus, Accipiter 81
erythropus, Anser 70
erythropus, Crypturellus 51
erythropus, Tringa 126
Erythropygia 393
erythropygia, Pinarocorys 343
erythropygius, Myiotheretes
315
erythropygius, Pericrocotus 363
erythropygius, Picus 266
erythropygius, Sturnus 622
erythropygius, Xiphorhynchus
274
erythropygus, Morococcyx 177
erythrorhyncha, Anas 73
erythrorhyncha, Perdicula 104
erythrorhyncha, Urocissa 637
erythrorhynchos, Dicaeum 508
erythrorhynchos, Pelecanus 60
erythrorhynchus, Buphagus 624
erythrorhynchus, Tockus 237
erythrosticta, Monarcha 486
erythrothorax, Dicaeum 509
erythrothorax, Erithacus 395
erythrothorax, Synallaxis 280
erythrotis, Grallaria 303
Erythrotriorchis 80
Erythrura 607
erythrura, Myrmotherula 294
erythrurus, Terenotriccus 324
Esacus 122
esculenta, Collocalia 200
estella, Oreotrochilus 215
estherae, Serinus 596
Estrilda 605
ethologus, Pericrocotus 364
Eubucco 242
euchlorus, Auripasser 613

euchrysea, Tachycineta 350
Eucometis 562
eucosma, Charitospiza 555
Eudocimus 68
Eudromia 53
Eudromias 126
Eudynamys 175
Eudyptes 53
Eudyptula 53
Eugenes 215
eugeniae, Ptilinopus 150
Eugerygone 477
Eugralla 305
Eulabeornis 112
Eulacestoma 491
Eulampis 207
euleri, Coccyzus 175
euleri, Empidonax 323
Eulidia 221
Eulipoa 91
eulophotes, Lophotriccus 330
eulophotes, Egretta 65
Eumomota 232
Eumyias 476
Euneornis 574
euophrys, Thryothorus 385
euops, Aratinga 165
eupatria, Psittacula 164
Eupetes 415
Eupetomena 207
Euphagus 593
Eupherusa 213
Euphonia 568
Euptilotis 222
Euplectes 617
Eupodotis 120
eupogon, Metallura 218
eurhythmus, Ixobrychus 63
eurizonoides, Rallina 115
Eurocephalus 375
europaea, Sitta 503
europaeus, Caprimulgus 196
Eurostopodus 194
Euryceros 381
eurygnatha, Thalasseus 133
Eurylaimus 269
eurynome, Phaethornis 205
Eurynorhynchus 128
euryptera, Opisthoprora 219
Euryptila 459
Eurypyga 119
eurystomina, Pseudochelidon 349
Eurystomus 235
euryura, Rhipidura 490
euryzona, Alcedo 226
Euscarthmus 332
Euschistospiza 604
euteles, Trichoglossus 154
Euthlypis 580
eutilotus, Pycnonotus 367
Eutoxeres 206
Eutrichomyias 483
Eutriorchis 79
evelynae, Philodice 220
everetti, Aceros 238

everetti, Arachnothera 519
everetti, Dicaeum 507
everetti, Hypsipetes 372
everetti, Zoothera 406
everetti, Zosterops 520
eversmanni, Columba 136
ewingi, Acanthiza 467
exarhatus, Penelopides 237
Excalfactoria 104
excelsa, Grallaria 302
excelsior, Geositta 276
excubitor, Lanius 380
excubitoroides, Lanius 380
exilis, Cisticola 450
exilis, Indicator 247
exilis, Ixobrychus 63
exilis, Laterallus 116
exilis, Loriculus 163
exilis, Picumnus 251
exilis, Psaltria 497
eximia, Aethopyga 518
eximia, Bleda 371
eximia, Buthraupis 567
eximia, Cisticola 450
eximia, Eupherusa 213
eximia, Megalaima 243
eximium, Dicaeum 509
eximius, Caprimulgus 197
eximius, Platycercus 161
eximius, Pogonotriccus 331
exortis, Heliangelus 217
explorator, Monticola 405
explorator, Zosterops 522
exsul, Myrmeciza 298
externa, Pterodroma 56
exulans, Diomedea 55
exustus, Pterocles 135
eytoni, Dendrocygna 69
eytoni, Xiphorhynchus 274

fabalis, Anser 69
faiostricta, Megalaima 242
falcata, Anas 72
falcata, Ptilocichla 420
falcatus, Campylopterus 207
falcinellus, Limicola 128
falcinellus, Plegadis 68
falcipennis, Dendragapus 93
falcirostris, Sporophila 547
falcirostris, Xiphocolaptes 272
falcklandii, Turdus 413
Falco 88
Falculea 381
falcularius, Campylorhamphus 275
Falcunculus 491
falkensteini, Chlorocichla 369
falklandicus, Charadrius 125
fallax, Bulweria 57
fallax, Ceyx 227
fallax, Elaenia 334
fallax, Glycichaera 525
fallax, Leucippus 211
familiare, Apalopteron 530
familiaris, Cercomela 401

familiaris, Certhia 505
familiaris, Prinia 455
famosa, Nectarinia 517
fanny, Myrtis 221
fanovanae, Newtonia 477
farinosa, Amazona 170
farquhari, Halcyon 229
fasciata, Amadina 610
fasciata, Atticora 350
fasciata, Chamaea 425
fasciata, Columba 137
fasciata, Neothraupis 559
fasciata, Rallina 115
fasciatoventris, Thryothorus 385
fasciatum, Tigrisoma 63
fasciatus, Accipiter 81
fasciatus, Campylorhynchus 383
fasciatus, Harpactes 224
fasciatus, Hieraaetus 86
fasciatus, Laterallus 116
fasciatus, Myiophobus 325
fasciatus, Philortyx 96
fasciatus, Phyllomyias 336
fasciatus, Ramsayornis 534
fasciatus, Tockus 236
fasciicauda, Pipra 313
fasciinucha, Falco 90
fasciiventer, Parus 501
fasciogularis, Meliphaga 529
fasciolata, Camaroptera 459
fasciolata, Crax 93
fasciolata, Locustella 440
fasciolatus, Circaetus 78
fastosus, Epimachus 632
fastuosa, Tangara 570
feadensis, Aplonis 619
feae, Turdus 412
featherstoni, Phalacrocorax 61
fedoa, Limosa 126
felix, Thryothorus 385
femoralis, Cinnyricinclus 621
femoralis, Falco 89
femoralis, Scytalopus 305
ferdinandi, Cercomacra 297
fernandensis, Sephanoides 217
fernandezianus, Anairetes 332
fernandinae, Colaptes 263
fernandinae, Teretistris 579
ferina, Aythya 73
Ferminia 385
ferox, Myiarchus 320
ferrea, Saxicola 403
ferrocyanea, Myiagra 487
ferruginea, Calidris 128
ferruginea, Drymophila 296
ferruginea, Hirundinea 326
ferruginea, Muscicapa 475
ferruginea, Myrmeciza 299
ferruginea, Petrophassa 142
ferruginea, Tadorna 71
ferrugineifrons, Bolborhynchus 167
ferrugineipectus, Gallericula 304
ferrugineiventre, Conirostrum 582

ferrugineus, Enicognathus 167
ferrugineus, Laniarius 377
ferrugineus, Pitohui 496
ferruginosus, Pomatorhinus 419
festiva, Amazona 170
festivus, Chrysocolaptes 267
Ficedula 472
ficedulina, Zosterops 524
figulus, Furnarius 277
filicauda, Pipra 312
fimbriata, Amazilia 212
fimbriata, Coracina 362
fimbriatum, Callocephalon 156
finlaysoni, Pycnonotus 367
finschi, Amazona 170
finschi, Aratinga 165
finschi, Euphonia 568
finschi, Francolinus 102
Finschia 470
finschii, Criniger 371
finschii, Ducula 152
finschii, Micropsitta 157
finschii, Oenanthe 404
finschii, Stizorhina 401
fischeri, Agapornis 163
fischeri, Dioptrornis 471
fischeri, Phyllastrephus 370
fischeri, Ptilinopus 149
fischeri, Somateria 74
fischeri, Spreo 622
fischeri, Vidua 610
flagrans, Aethopyga 517
flammea, Acanthis 598
flammeolus, Otus 182
flammeus, Asio 192
flammeus, Pericrocotus 364
flammiceps, Cephalopyrus 498
flammigerus, Ramphocelus 565
flammula, Selasphorus 221
flammulata, Thripophaga 282
flammulatus, Deltarhynchus 322
flammulatus, Hemitriccus 331
flammulatus, Megabyas 480
flammulatus, Thripadectes 286
flava, Meliphaga 529
flava, Motacilla 354
flava, Piranga 564
flava, Zosterops 520
flavalus, Hypsipetes 373
flaveola, Capsiempis 331
flaveola, Coereba 583
flaveola, Sicalis 546
flaveolus, Basileuterus 580
flaveolus, Criniger 371
flaveolus, Passer 612
flaveolus, Platycercus 161
flavescens, Boissonneaua 217
flavescens, Celeus 263
flavescens, Empidonax 323
flavescens, Pycnonotus 367
flavibuccale, Tricholaema 246
flavicans, Foudia 617
flavicans, Lichmera 526
flavicans, Macrosphenus 462
flavicans, Myiophobus 325

662   *flavicans, Prinia* 454
flavicans, Prioniturus 159
flavicapilla, Chloropipo 311
flaviceps, Atlapetes 553
flaviceps, Auriparus 498
flavicollis, Chlorocichla 369
flavicollis, Hemithraupis 561
flavicollis, Ixobrychus 63
flavicollis, Macronyx 355
flavicollis, Meliphaga 530
flavicollis, Yuhina 434
flavida, Apalis 455
flavida, Gerygone 466
flavifrons, Amblyornis 630
flavifrons, Anthoscopus 498
flavifrons, Megalaima 243
flavifrons, Melanerpes 252
flavifrons, Pachycephala 494
flavifrons, Poicephalus 163
flavifrons, Vireo 586
flavifrons, Zosterops 522
flavigaster, Arachnothera 519
flavigaster, Hyliota 463
flavigaster, Microeca 477
flavigaster, Xiphorhynchus 274
flavigula, Manorina 535
flavigula, Piculus 261
flavigularis, Chlorospingus 560
flavigularis, Chrysococcyx 174
flavigularis, Platyrinchus 326
flavinucha, Muscisaxicola 314
flavinucha, Picus 266
flavinuchus, Anisognathus 567
flavipennis, Chloropsis 374
flavipes, Hylophilus 587
flavipes, Ketupa 186
flavipes, Malimbus 616
flavipes, Notiochelidon 350
flavipes, Platibis 68
flavipes, Platycichla 409
flavipes, Tringa 126
flaviprymna, Lonchura 609
flavirictus, Meliphaga 529
flavirostra, Porzana 116
flavirostris, Acanthis 598
flavirostris, Anairetes 332
Flavirostris, Anas 72
flavirostris, Arremon 552
flavirostris, Chlorophonia 569
flavirostris, Columba 137
flavirostris, Gallinula 118
flavirostris, Grallaricula 304
flavirostris, Humblotia 476
flavirostris, Monasa 241
flavirostris, Paradoxornis 435
flavirostris, Phibalura 306
flavirostris, Pteroglossus 248
flavirostris, Rynchops 133
flavirostris, Tockus 237
flavirostris, Urocissa 637
flaviscapis, Pteruthius 431
flaviventer, Dacnis 572
flaviventer, Machaerirhynchus
   484
flaviventer, Meliphaga 530

flaviventer, Porzana 116
flaviventris, Chlorocichla 369
flaviventris, Empidonax 323
flaviventris, Empidonax 323
flaviventris, Eopsaltria 479
flaviventris, Motacilla 355
flaviventris, Pogonotriccus 331
flaviventris, Prinia 455
flaviventris, Pseudocolopteryx
   332
flaviventris, Serinus 595
flaviventris, Sphecotheres 626
flaviventris, Tolmomyias 327
flavivertex, Heterocercus 311
flavivertex, Myioborus 580
flavivertex, Myiopagis 335
flavocinctus, Oriolus 624
flavocrissalis, Eremomela 460
flavogaster, Elaenia 333
flavogrisea, Pachycare 491
flavolateralis, Gerygone 466
flavolivacea, Cettia 439
flavostriatus, Phyllastrephus 370
flavóvelata, Geothlypis 578
flavovirens, Chlorospingus 560
flavovirens, Phylloscartes 331
flavovirescens, Microeca 477
flavoviridis, Neomixis 422
flavoviridis, Trichoglossus 154
flavus, Celleus 264
flavus, Xanthopsar 590
floccosus, Pycnoptilus 470
florensis, Corvus 639
floriceps, Anthocephala 214
florida, Tangara 570
floris, Treron 147
Florisuga 207
flosculus, Loriculus 163
fluminea, Porzana 117
fluviatilis, Locustella 440
fluviatilis, Muscisaxicola 314
Fluvicola 317
fluvicola, Petrochelidon 354
foersteri, Henicophaps 141
foersteri, Melidectes 533
foetidus, Gymnoderus 309
forbesi, Curaeus 592
forbesi, Lonchura 609
forbesi, Rallina 115
forficata, Muscivora 317
forficatus, Dicrurus 624
forficatus, Elanoides 76
Formicarius 301
Formicivora 295
formicivora, Myrmecocichla 403
formicivorus, Melanerpes 252
formosa, Amandava 606
formosa, Anas 72
formosa, Calocitta 636
formosa, Eudromia 53
formosa, Geothlypis 579
formosa, Pipreola 307
formosa, Sitta 504
formosae, Dendrocitta 638
formosae, Treron 148

formosus, Garrulax 430
formosus, Ptilinopus 149
formosus, Spelaeornis 422
fornsi, Teretistris 579
Forpus 168
forsteni, Ducula 151
forsteni, Meropogon 233
forsteri, Oriolus 624
forsteri, Aptenodytes 53
forsteni, Sterna 131
fortipes, Cettia 438
fortis, Coracina 359
fortis, Geospiza 550
fortis, Myrmeciza 299
fossii, Scotornis 198
Foudia 617
Foulehaio 530
francesii, Accipiter 83
franciae, Amazilia 212
francica, Collocalia 199
franciscanus, Xiphocolaptes 272
Francolinus 100
francolinus, Francolinus 100
franklinii, Megalaima 243
frantzii, Catharus 408
frantzii, Elaenia 334
frantzii, Semnornis 242
fraseri, Anthreptes 511
fraseri, Basileuterus 580
fraseri, Oreomanes 573
fraseri, Stizorhina 401
Fraseria 471
frater, Monarcha 485
frater, Onychognathus 620
Fratercula 134
fratrum, Batis 480
Frederickena 289
Fregata 62
Fregetta 58
fremantlii, Pseudalaemon 347
frenata, Geotrygon 145
frenata, Meliphaga 530
frenatus, Chaetops 394
freycinet, Megapodius 90
freycineti, Myiagra 487
Fringilla 594
fringillaris, Botha 347
fringillarius, Microhierax 88
fringillinus, Parus 501
fringilloides, Dolospingus 549
fringilloides, Lonchura 608
frontale, Cinclidium 399
frontalis, Anarhynchus 125
frontalis, Dendrocitta 638
frontalis, Hemispingus 560
frontalis, Muscisaxicola 314
frontalis, Ochthoeca 315
frontalis, Phoenicurus 399
frontalis, Pipreola 307
frontalis, Pyrrhura 166
frontalis, Sericornis 468
frontalis, Sitta 504
frontalis, Sporophila 547
frontalis, Sporopipes 613
frontalis, Synallaxis 278

frontalis, Veniliornis 260
frontatus, Falcunculus 491
frugilegus, Corvus 640
frugivorus, Calyptophilus 562
fruticeti, Phrygilus 544
fucata, Alopochelidon 350
fucata, Emberiza 537
fuciphaga, Collocalia 200
fuelleborni, Alethe 397
fuelleborni, Macronyx 355
fugax, Cuculus 172
fulgens, Eugenes 215
fulgida, Halcyon 231
fulgidus, Onychognathus 620
fulgidus, Pharomachrus 222
fulgidus, Psittrichas 160
Fulica 118
fulica, Heliornis 119
fulicarius, Phalaropus 127
fulicata, Saxicoloides 404
fuliginiceps, Leptasthenura 278
fuliginosa, Dendrocincla 270
fuliginosa, Geospiza 550
fuliginosa, Nectarinia 513
fuliginosa, Nesofregetta 58
fuliginosa, Petrochalidon 354
fuliginosa, Psalidoprocne 354
fuliginosa, Rhipidura 489
fuliginosa, Schizoeaca 278
fuliginosa, Strepera 629
fuliginosa, Tiaris 549
fuliginosus, Aegithalos 497
fuliginosus, Calorhamphus 244
fuliginosus, Haematopus 121
fuliginosus, Larus 129
fuliginosus, Oreostruthus 607
fuliginosus, Phoenicurus 399
fuliginosus, Pitylus 557
fuliginosus, Sericornis 469
fuligiventer, Phylloscopus 445
fuligula, Aythya 73
fuligula, Hirundo 351
fülleborni, Laniarius 378
Fulmarus 55
fulva, Petrochelidon 353
fulvescens, Picumnus 250
fulvescens, Prunella 392
fulvescens, Trichastoma 418
fulvicapilla, Cisticola 452
fulviceps, Atlapetes 554
fulviceps, Thlypopsis 561
fulvicollis, Treron 146
fulvicrissa, Euphonia 569
fulvifrons, Empidonax 324
fulvifrons, Paradoxornis 436
fulvigula, Timeliopsis 525
fulvipectus, Rhynchocyclus 327
fulviventris, Hylopezus 303
fulviventris, Myrmotherula 293
fulviventris, Phyllastrephus 370
fulviventris, Turdus 413
fulvogularis, Malacoptila 240
fulvus, Gyps 78
fulvus, Lanio 563
fulvus, Mulleripicus 268

fulvus, Turdoides 425
fumicolor, Ochthoeca 315
fumifrons, Todirostrum 328
fumigatus, Contopus 322
fumigatus, Cypseloides
fumigatus, Melipotes 533
fumigatus, Myiotheretes 315
fumigatus, Turdus 413
fumigatus, Veniliornis 260
funebris, Halcyon 230
funebris, Laniarius 378
funebris, Mulleripicus 268
funerea, Vidua 610
funereus, Aegolius 192
funereus, Calyptorhynchus 156
funereus, Parus 501
furcata, Oceanodroma 59
furcata, Tachornis 202
furcata, Thalurania 209
furcatis, Anthus 358
furcatus, Ceratotriccus 329
furcatus, Creagrus 131
furcifer, Heliomaster 220
Furnarius 277
fusca, Alleniá 392
fusca, Aplonis 619
fusca, Casiornis 322
fusca, Cercomela 402
fusca, Dendroica 577
fusca, Gerygone 466
fusca, Iodopleura 307
fusca, Malacoptila 240
fusca, Melanitta 74
fusca, Meliphaga 529
fusca, Nectarinia 515
fusca, Phoebetria 55
fusca, Porzana 117
fuscans, Lonchura 608
fuscata, Padda 610
fuscata, Pseudeos 154
fuscata, Sterna 132
fuscater, Catharus 408
fuscater, Turdus 412
fuscatus, Cremotriccus 324
fuscatus, Margarops 392
fuscatus, Phylloscopus 445
fuscescens, Catharus 409
fuscescens, Dendropicos 254
fuscescens, Phalacrocorax 61
fuscicapilla, Zosterops 521
fuscicapillus, Corvus 640
fuscicapillus, Philemon 532
fuscicauda, Habia 564
fuscicauda, Ramphotrigon 328
fusciceps, Phacellodomus 283
fuscicollis, Calidris 128
fuscicollis, Phalacrocorax 61
fuscipennis, Dicrurus 626
fuscirostris, Talegalla 91
fuscocapillum, Pellorneum 416
fuscocinereus, Lipaugus 307
fusconota, Nigrita 602
fuscoolivaceus, Atlapetes 553
fuscorufa, Synallaxis 280
fuscorufus, Myiotheretes 315

fuscus, Acridotheres 623   663
fuscus, Artamus 628
fuscus, Cinclodes 276
fuscus, Larus 130
fuscus, Lapidocolaptes 275
fuscus, Melanotrochilus 207
fuscus, Melidectes 533
fuscus, Philydor 286
fuscus, Picumnus 250
fuscus, Pionus 170
fuscus, Pipilo 551
fuscus, Teledromas 305
fytchii, Bambusicola 105

gabar, Melierax 80
gabela, Erithacus 395
gabela, Prionops 375
Gabianus 129
gabonensis, Dendropicos 255
gabonensis, Ortygospiza 606
gabonicus, Anthroptes 511
gaimardi, Phalacrocorax 62
gaimardii, Myiopagis 334
galactotes, Cisticola 453
galactotes, Erythropygia 393
galapagoensis, Buteo 85
galapagoensis, Zenaida 142
galatea, Tanysiptera 231
Galbalcyrhynchus 238
galbanus, Garrulax 428
Galbula 239
galbula, Galbula 239
galbula, Icterus 590
galbula, Ploceus 615
galeata, Antilophia 311
galeata, Duclaria 152
galeata, Myiagra 487
galeatus, Basilornis 623
galeatus, Colopteryx 330
galeatus, Dryocopus 264
galericulata, Aix 71
galericulatus, Platylophus 633
Galerida 347
galerita, Cacatua 157
galeritus, Anorrhinus 237
galgulus, Loriculus 163
galinieri, Parophasma 434
gallardoi, Podiceps 55
Gallicolumba 145
Gallicrex 117
gallicus, Circaetus 78
gallinacea, Irediparra 120
Gallinago 127
gallinago, Gallinago 127
Gallinula 117
Gallirallus 115
gallopavo, Meleagris 93
Galloperdix 105
Gallus 106
gallus, Gallus 106
gambagae, Muscicapa 475
gambeli, Parus 499
gambelii, Lophortyx 96
gambensis, Dryoscopus 376
gambensis, Plectropterus 71

gambieri, Halcyon 231
Gampsonyx 76
Gampsorhynchus 431
garleppi, Compospiza 546
garnoti, Pelecanoides 59
Garritornis 420
Garrodia 58
garrula, Ortalis 91
Garrulax 427
Garrulus 636
garrulus, Bombycilla 381
garrulus, Coracias 234
garrulus, Lorius 155
garzetta, Egretta 66
gaudichaud, Dacelo 228
Gavia 54
gavia, Puffinus 58
gayaquilensis, Campephilus 265
gayi, Attagis 129
gayi, Phrygilus 544
Gecinulus 267
geelvinkiana, Micropsitta 157
geelvinkianum, Dicaeum 509
Gelochelidon 131
genei, Drymophila 296
genei, Larus 130
genibarbis, Myadestes 400
genibarbis, Thryothorus 385
gentilis, Accipiter 80
Geococcyx 178
Geocolaptes 254
geoffroyi, Geoffroyus 158
geoffroyi, Neomorphus 178
geoffroyi, Schistes 219
Geoffroyus 158
Geomalia 406
Geopelia 142
Geopsittacus 162
georgiana, Eopsaltria 479
georgiana, Melospiza 539
georgianus, Phalacrocorax 62
georgica, Anas 72
georgicus, Pelecanoides 59
Geositta 276
Geospiza 550
Geothlypis 578
Geotrygon 144
Geranoaetus 84
Geranospiza 79
germaini, Polyplectron 108
Geronticus 67
Gerygone 465
gibberifrons, Anas 72
gibsoni, Chlorostilbon 209
gierowii, Euplectes 617
gigantea, Fulica 118
gigantea, Grallaria 302
gigantea, Hirundapus 202
gigantea, Melampitta 415
gigantea, Thaumatibis 67
giganteus, Macronectes 55
gigas, Collocalia 199
gigas, Coua 178
gigas, Elaenia 334
gigas, Patagona 216

gigas, Podilymbus 54
gilberti, Lioptilus 433
gilletti, Mirafa 343
gilolensis, Philemon 532
gilviventris, Xenicus 340
gilvus, Mimus 390
gilvus, Vireo 586
gingica, Arborophila 104
ginginianus, Acridotheres 623
githaginea, Rhodopechys 599
glabricollis, Cephalopterus 310
glabrirostris, Melanoptila 390
glacialis, Fulmarus 55
glacialoides, Fulmarus 55
gladiator, Malaconotus 378
glandarius, Clamator 172
glandarius, Garrulus 636
Glareola 123
glareola, Tringa 126
glauca, Diglossa 574
glaucescens, Larus 130
Glaucidium 186
glaucinus, Myiophoneus 405
Glaucis 204
glaucocaerulae, Cyanoloxia 558
glaudcoides, Larus 130
glaucopis, Thalurania 210
glaucopoides, Eriocnemis 217
glaucurus, Eurystomus 235
glaucus, Anodorhynchus 164
globulosa, Crax 93
Glossopsitta 155
glyceria, Zodalia 218
Glycichaera 525
Glyphorhynchus 271
gnoma, Glaucidium 186
Gnorimopsar 592
godeffroyi, Halcyon 231
godeffroyi, Monarcha 486
godefrida, Claravis 143
godini, Eriocnemis 217
godlewskii, Anthus 356
goeldii, Myrmeciza 299
goeringi, Brachygalba 239
goeringi, Hemispingus 561
goertae, Dendropicos 255
Goethalsia 211
goffini, Cacatua 157
goiavier, Pycnonotus 367
goisagi, Gorsachius 64
golandi, Ploceus 615
goldiei, Trichoglossus 155
goldmani, Geotrygon 144
Goldmania 211
goliath, Ardea 66
goliath, Centropus 178
goliath, Ducula 152
gongonensis, Passer 612
goodenovii, Petroica 478
goodfellowi, Ceyx 226
goodfellowi, Lophozosterops 524
goodfellowi, Regulus 449
goodsoni, Columba 138
gordoni, Philemon 532

Gorsachius 64
goudoti, Lepidopyga 210
goudotii, Chamaepetes 93
goughensis, Rowettia 544
gouldi, Euphonia 569
gouldi, Zosterops 522
gouldiae, Aethopyga 518
gouldiae, Chloebia 608
gouldii, Lophornis 208
gouldii, Selenidera 249
gounellei, Phaethornis 206
Goura 146
goyderi, Amytornis 465
graceannae, Icterus 589
graciae, Dendroica 576
gracilipes, Tyranniscus 336
gracilirostris, Acrocephalus 442
gracilirostris, Catharus 408
gracilirostris, Chloropeta 443
gracilirostris, Pycnonotus 368
gracilis, Heterophasia 434
gracilis, Meliphaga 528
gracilis, Oceanites 58
gracilis, Prinia 454
gracilis, Pycnonotus 368
Gracula 623
graculina, Strepera 629
graculus, Pyrrhocorax 639
graduacauda, Icterus 590
graeca, Alectoris 99
Grafisia 620
Grallaria 302
grallaria, Fregetta 58
Grallaricula 304
Grallina 628
gramineus, Megalurus 462
gramineus, Pooecetes 542
gramineus, Tanygnathus 160
Graminicola 1457
grammacus, Chondestes 542
grammiceps, Seicercus 448
grammiceps, Stachyris 423
grammicus, Celeus 263
grammicus, Pseudoscops 192
granadense, Idioptilon 329
granadensis, Myiozetetes 319
granadensis, Picumnus 251
Granatellus 582
granatina, Pitta 339
granatina, Uraeginthus 605
Grandala 399
grandidieri, Zoonavena 201
grandis, Acridotheres 623
grandis, Aplonis 619
grandis, Bradypterus 439
grandis, Lonchura 609
grandis, Motacilla 355
grandis, Niltava 473
grandis, Nyctibius 193
grandis, Ploceus 615
granti, Phoeniculus 236
grantia, Gecinulus 267
granulifrons, Ptilinopus 151
grata, Malia 435
graueri, Bradypterus 439

graueri, Coracina 360
graueri, Pseudocalyptomena 269
Graueria 461
gravis, Puffinus 57
Graydidascalus 169
grayi, Ammomanes 345
grayi, Chenorhamphus 464
grayi, Hylocharis 211
grayi, Turdus 413
grayi, Zosterops 521
grayii, Ardeola 64
graysoni, Mimodes 391
gregalis, Eremomela 460
gregarius, Vanellus 124
greyii, Ptilinopus 150
grillii, Centropus 179
grimwoodi, Macroryx 356
grisea, Eremopterix 345
grisea, Formicivora 295
grisea, Myrmotherula 294
grisegena, Podiceps 54
griseicapilla, Lonchura 608
griseicapillus, Sittasomus 271
griseicauda, Treron 147
griseiceps, Accipiter 81
griseiceps, Basileuterus 580
griseiceps, Myrmeciza 299
griseiceps, Phyllomyias 336
griseiceps, Piprites 310
griseilgula, Timeliopsis 525
griseigularis, Myioparus 476
griseipectus, Empidonax 323
griseisticta, Muscicapa 475
griseiventris, Parus 500
griseiventris, Taphrolesbia 219
griseocapillus, Oreotriccus 337
griseocephalus, Dendropicos 255
griseoceps, Microeca 477
griseocristatus, Lophospingus 544
griseogularis, Accipiter 82
griseogularis, Ammoperdix 98
griseogularis, Eopsaltria 478
griseogularis, Phaethornis 206
griseolus, Phylloscopus 445
griseonucha, Grallaria 303
griseopyga, Hirundo 351
griseostriatus, Francolinus 101
griseotincta, Zosterops 522
griseovirescens, Zosterops 523
griseus, Campylorhynchus 383
griseus, Limnodromus 128
griseus, Nyctibius 193
griseus, Passer 612
griseus, Puffinus 57
griseus, Thryothorus 387
griseus, Tockus 236
griseus, Vireo 585
grossus, Pitylus 557
grosvenori, Cichlornis 463
Grus 111
grus, Grus 111
grylle, Cepphus 134

gryphus, Vultur 75
grzimeki, Threnetes 204
guainumbi, Polytmus 211
guajana, Pitta 339
gualaquizae, Pogonotriccus 331
guarauna, Aramus 112
guarayanus, Thryothorus 387
guarouba, Aratinga 165
guatamalae, Otus 183
guatamalensis, Campephilus 265
guatamalensis, Grallaria 302
guatamalensis, Sclerurus 288
guatemozinus, Psarocolius 588
gubernator, Lanius 379
Gubernatrix 555
Gubernetes 316
guerinii, Oxypogon 219
guianensis, Morphnus 85
guianensis, Polioptila 438
guifsobalito, Lybius 246
guildingii, Amazona 171
guilielmi, Paradisaea 633
guimeti, Klais 208
guinea, Columba 136
Guira 177
guira, Guira 177
guira, Hemithraupis 561
Guiraca 558
guirahuro, Pseudoleistes 592
guisei, Ptiloprora 532
gujanensis, Cyclarhis 584
gujanensis, Odontophorus 97
gujanensis, Synallaxis 279
gularis, Accipter 80
gularis, Aspatha 232
gularis, Campylorhynchus 382
gularis, Egretta 65
gularis, Eurystomus 235
gularis, Francolinus 103
gularis, Heliodoxa 215
gularis, Icterus 589
gularis, Macronous 424
gularis, Melithreptus 531
gularis, Merops 233
gularis, Monticola 405
gularis, Myrmotherula 293
gularis, Nicator 379
gularis, Paradoxornis 436
gularis, Paroaria 555
gularis, Rhinomyias 472
gularis, Serinus 595
gularis, Synallaxis 280
gularis, Tephrodornis 364
gularis, Turdoides 425
gularis, Yuhina 434
gulgula, Alauda 348
gulielmi, Poicephalus 162
gulielmitertii, Opopsitta 158
gundlachii, Accipiter 83
gundlachii, Mimus 390
gundlachii, Vireo 585
gunningi, Erithacus 395
gurneyi, Aquila 86
gurneyi, Mimizuku 184

gurneyi, Pitta 339
gurneyi, Promerops 535
gurneyi, Zoothera 406
gustavi, Anthus 357
guttata, Cichladusa 397
guttata, Dendrocygna 69
guttata, Emblema 607
guttata, Myrmotherula 293
guttata, Peophila 607
guttata, Tangara 571
guttata, Zoothera 406
guttaticollis, Paradoxornis 435
guttatum, Toxostoma 391
guttatus, Catharus 409
guttatus, Eurostopodus 194
guttatus, Hypoedaleus 289
guttatus, Ixonotus 369
guttatus, Odontophorus 98
guttatus, Psilorhamphus 305
guttatus, Tinamus 50
guttatus, Xiphorhynchus 273
Guttera 109
guttifer, Tringa 126
guttula, Monarcha 486
guttulatus, Philydor 285
guttuligera, Margarornis 284
gutturalis, Anthus 358
gutturalis, Atlapetes 553
gutturalis, Corapipo 312
gutturalis, Crateroscelis 469
gutturalis, Habia 564
gutturalis, Irania 399
gutturalis, Myrmotherula 293
gutturalis, Neocichla 621
gutturalis, Oreoica 491
gutturalis, Pseudoseisura 284
gutturalis, Pterocles 135
gutturalis, Saxicola 403
gutturalis, Vermivora 575
gutturata, Certhiaxis 1281
guy, Phaethornis 205
Gygis 133
gymnocephala, Pityriasis 381
gymnocephalus, Picathartes 436
Gymnobucco 244
Gymnocichla 298
Gymnoderus 309
gymnogenys, Turdoides 427
Gymnoglaux 189
Gymnogyps 75
Gymnomystax 590
Gymnomyza 533
Gymnophaps 153
Gymnopithys 299
gymnops, Melipotes 533
gymnops, Rhegmatorhina 300
Gymnorhina 629
Gymnorhinus 634
Gypaetus 78
Gypohierax 78
Gypopsitta 169
Gyps 78
gyrola, Tangara 571

haastii, Apteryx 50

666 habessinica, Nectarinia 516
Habia 564
habroptilus, Strigops 171
haemacephala, Megalaima 243
haemasticta, Limosa 126
haematina, Spermophaga 603
Haematoderus 310
haematodus, Trichoglossus 154
haematogaster, Campephilus 265
haematogaster, Psephotus 161
haematonota, Myrmotherula 293
haematonotus, Psephotus 161
Haematopus 121
haematopus, Himantornis 112
haematopygus, Aulacorhynchus 248
Haematortyx 105
Haematospiza 601
haematotis, Pionopsitta 169
haematuropygia, Cacatua 157
haemorrhous, Cacicus 588
haesitata, Cisticola 450
hagedash, Hagedashia 68
Hagedashia 68
hainana, Niltava 474
Halcyon 228
Haliaeetus 77
haliaetus, Pandion 75
Haliastur 77
Haliëtor 62
hallae, Pycnonotus 368
halli, Macronectes 55
halli, Pomatostomus 420
Halobaena 57
Halocyptena 59
hamatus, Rostrhamus 77
hamertoni, Alaemon 345
Hamirostra 77
hamiini, Clytorhynchus 485
hammondii, Empidonax 323
Hapalopsittaca 169
Hapaloptila 241
haplochrous, Accipiter 82
haplochrous, Turdus 413
haplonota, Grallaria 302
Haplophaedia 218
Haplospiza 544
hardwickei, Chloropsis 375
hardwickii, Gallinago 127
harmonica, Colluricincla 495
Harpactes 224
Harpagus 77
Harpia 85
Harpiprion 68
Harpyhaliaetus 84
harpyja, Harpia 85
Harpyopsis 85
harrisi, Nannopterum 62
harrisii, Aegolius 192
harterti, Acestrura 221
harterti, Batrachostomus 193
harterti, Ficedula 473
harterti, Phlogophilus 215

hartlaubi, Dacnis 572
hartlaubi, Erythropygia 393
hartlaubi, Euplectes 618
hartlaubi, Francolinus 101
hartlaubi, Otus 184
hartlaubi, Tauraco 171
hartlaubi, Tockus 236
hartlaubii, Lissotis 120
hartlaubii, Nectarinia 512
hartlaubii, Pteronetta 71
harwoodi, Francolinus 101
hasitata, Pterodroma 56
hattamensis, Pachycephalopsis 480
hauxwelli, Myrmotherula 293
hebetior, Monarcha 485
heermanni, Larus 129
heilprini, Cyanocorax 635
heinei, Tangara 572
heinrichi, Cacomantis 173
heinrichi, Cossypha 397
heinrichi, Geomalia 406
heinrothi, Puffinus 58
helenae, Calypte 221
helenae, Hypothymis 483
helenae, Paphosia 208
helenae, Parotia 633
Heleia 525
heliaca, Aquila 86
Heliactin 220
Heliangelus 217
helianthea, Coeligena 216
helianthea, Culicicapa 477
helias, Eurypyga 119
heliobates, Camarhynchus 550
heliodor, Acestrura 221
Heliodoxa 215
Heliolais 457
Heliomaster 220
Heliopais 119
Heliornis 119
heliosylus, Zonerodius 63
Heliothyrx 220
helleri, Turdus 410
hellmayri, Anthus 358
hellmayri, Certhiaxis 281
hellmayri, Mecocerculus 333
hellmayri, Synallaxis 279
Helmitheros 578
heloisa, Atthis 221
hemichrysus, Myiodynastes 319
Hemicircus 268
Hemignathus 584
hemilasius, Buteo 85
hemileucurus, Campylopterus 207
hemileucurus, Phlogophilus 215
hemileucus, Lampornis 214
hemileucus, Myrmochanes 298
hemimelaena, Myrmeciza 299
Hemiphaga 153
Hemiprocne 204
Hemipus 364
Hemispingus 560
Hemitesia 461

Hemithraupis 561
Hemitriccus 331
hemixantha, Microeca 477
hemprichii, Larus 130
hemprichii, Tockus 236
hendersoni, Podoces 638
henicogrammus, Accipiter 82
Henicopernis 76
Henicophaps 141
Henicorhina 1389
henrici, Ficedula 473
henrici, Garrulax 430
henricii, Megalaima 243
henslowii, Ammodramus 541
henstii, Accipiter 80
herberti, Phylloscopus 447
herberti, Stachyris 423
herbicola, Emberizoides 546
hercules, Alcedo 225
herero, Namibornis 394
herioti, Niltava 474
herminieri, Melanerpes 252
herodias, Ardea 66
Herpetotheres 87
Herpsilochmus 295
herrani, Chalcostigma 219
Heterocercus 311
heteroclitus, Geoffroyus 159
Heteromirafa 343
Heteromyias 479
Heteronetta 74
Heterophasia 434
heteropogon, Chalcostigma 219
Heteroscelus 127
Heterospingus 563
Heterotrogon 224
heterura, Thripophaga 282
heterurus, Tanygnathus 160
heudei, Paradoxornis 436
heuglini, Cossypha 396
heuglini, Ploceus 614
heuglini, Neotis 119
heyi, Ammoperdix 98
hiaticula, Charadrius 124
Hieraeetus 86
hildebrandti, Francolinus 101
hildebrandti, Spreo 622
himalayana, Certhia 505
himalayana, Prunella 392
himalayana, Psittacula 164
himalayensis, Gyps 78
himalayensis, Picoides 258
himalayensis, Sitta 503
himalayensis, Tetraogallus 99
Himantopus 121
himantopus, Himantopus 121
himantopus, Micropalama 129
Himantornis 112
Himatione 584
hindei, Turdoides 427
Hippolais 443
hirsuta, Glaucis 204
hirsutum, Tricholaema 246
Hirundapus 201
hirundinacea, Collocalia 200

hirundinacea, Cypsnagra 559
hirundinacea, Euphonia 568
hirundinacea, Sterna 131
hirundinaceum, Dicaeum 509
hirundinaceus, Caprimulgus 196
hirundinaceus, Hemipus 364
Hirundinea 326
hirundineus, Merops 234
Hirundo 351
hirundo, Sterna 131
hispanica, Oenanthe 404
hispaniolensis, Passer 612
hispaniolensis, Poospiza 545
hispidus, Phaethornis 205
histrio, Eos 154
histrionica, Phaps 141
Histrionicus 74
histrionicus, Histrionicus 74
Histurgops 611
hoatzin, Opisthocomus 110
hodgsoni, Abroscopus 448
hodgsoni, Anthus 357
hodgsoni, Batrachostomus 193
hodgsoni, Muscicapella 475
hodgsoni, Phoenicurus 399
hodgsoni, Prinia 454
hodgsoniae, Perdix 103
hodgsonii, Columba 136
hodgsonii, Ficedula 473
Hodgsonius 399
hoedtii, Gallicolumba 146
hoematotis, Pyrrhura 167
hoevelli, Niltava 474
hoffmanni, Pyrrhura 167
hoffmannii, Melanerpes 253
hoffmannsi, Dendrocolaptes
   272
hoffmansi, Rhegmatorhini 300
holerythra, Rhytipterna 322
hollandicus, Nymphicus 157
holochlora, Aratinga 165
holochlora, Chloropipo 311
holochlorus, Erythrocercus 481
holomelaena, Psalidoprocne 354
holopolia, Coracina 361
holosericea, Drepanoptila 151
holosericeus, Amblyramphus
   592
holosericeus, Cacicus 589
holosericeus, Sericotes 207
holospilus, Spilornis 78
holostictus, Thripadectes 286
holsti, Parus 502
homochroa, Catamenia 549
homochroa, Dendrocincla 270
homochroa, Oceanodroma 59
hopkei, Carpodectes 309
hordeacea, Euplectes 618
Horizorhinus 435
hornbyi, Oceanodroma 59
hornemanni, Acanthis 598
horsfieldii, Myiophoneus 405
horsfieldii, Pomatorhinus 419
hortensis, Sylvia 443
hortulana, Emberiza 536

horus, Apus 204
hosii, Calyptomena 270
hosii, Oriolus 625
hottentotta, Turnix 110
hottentottus, Dicrurus 627
Houbaropsis 120
housei, Amytornis 465
hova, Mirafa 341
hovarum, Zosterops 523
huallagae, Aulacorhynchus 248
hudsoni, Phaeotriccus 316
hudsoni, Thripophaga 283
hudsonicus, Parus 499
huetii, Touit 168
huhula, Ciccaba 190
humbloti, Ardea 66
humbloti, Nectarinia 515
Humblotia 476
humboldti, Spheniscus 53
humeralis, Agelaius 591
humeralis, Aimophila 542
humeralis, Caryothraustes 556
humeralis, Cossypha 396
humeralis, Geopelia 142
humeralis, Myospiza 541
humeralis, Terenura 296
humei, Sphenocichla 422
humiae, Syrmaticus 107
humicola, Thripophaga 282
humilis, Eupodotis 120
humilis, Pseudopodoces 638
humilis, Thripophaga 282
hunsteini, Lonchura 609
hunteri, Cisticola 453
hunteri, Nectarinia 513
huttoni, Ptilinopus 150
huttoni, Puffinus 58
huttoni, Vireo 585
hyacinthina, Niltava 473
hyacinthinus, Andorhynchus 164
hybrida, Chlidonias 131
hybrida, Chloephaga 70
Hydrobates 59
hydrocharis, Tanysiptera 231
hydrocorax, Buceros 238
Hydrophasianus 120
Hydroprogne 131
Hydropsalis 198
hyemalis, Clangula 74
hyemalis, Junco 540
Hylexetastes 271
Hylia 463
Hyliota 463
Hylocharis 210
Hylocichla 409
Hylocitrea 492
Hylomanes 232
Hylonympha 215
Hylopezus 303
hylophila, Strix 191
Hylophilus 587
Hylophylax 300
Hylorchilus 383
Hymenolaimus 71
Hymenops 317

hyogastra, Ptilinopus 151
Hypargos 604
hyperboreus, Larus 130
hyperboreus, Plectrophenax 538
Hypergerus 459
hypermetra, Mirafa 341
hyperythra, Arborophila 105
hyperythra, Brachypteryx 393
hyperythra, Dumetia 424
hyperythra, Erythrura 607
hyperythra, Ficedula 472
hyperythra, Myrmeciza 299
hyperythra, Pachycephala 492
hyperythra, Rhipidura 490
hyperythrus, Campylopterus
   206
hyperythrus, Erithacus 396
hyperythrus, Odontophorus 98
hyperythrus, Picoides 257
Hypnelus 240
hypocherina, Vidua 610
hypochloris, Phyllastrephus 370
hypochondria, Poospiza 545
hypochondriacus, Thripophaga
   283
hypochroma, Sporophila 548
hypochryseus, Vireo 586
Hypocnemis 297
Hypocnemoides 298
Hypocolius 382
Hypocryptadius 525
Hypoedaleus 289
hypoglauca, Andigena 249
Hypogramma 512
hypogrammica, Pytilia 603
hypogrammica, Stachyris 423
hypogrammicum, Hypogramma
   512
hypoinochrous, Lorius 155
hypoleuca, Cissa 637
hypoleuca, Ficedula 472
hypoleuca, Grallaria 303
hypoleuca, Poecilodryas 479
hypoleuca, Pterodroma 56
hypoleuca, Serpophaga 333
hypoleucos, Actitis 127
hypoleucos, Falco 89
hypoleucos, Pomatorhinus 418
hypoleucum, Dicaeum 508
hypoleucus, Basileuterus 581
hypoleucus, Brachyramphus 134
hypoleucus, Capito 241
hypoleucus, Melanotis 390
hypoleucus, Sphecotheres 626
hypoleucus, Turdoides 427
hypopolius, Melanerpes 252
hypopyrrha, Laniocera 322
hypopyrrha, Streptopelia 138
Hypopyrrhus 592
Hyposita 381
hypospodia, Synallaxis 279
hypospodium, Todirostrum
hypostictus, Taphrospilus 211
Hypothymis 483
hypoxantha, Gerygone 465

668 hypoxantha, Hypocnemis 298
hypoxantha, Neodrepanis 341
hypoxantha, Pachycephala 492
hypoxantha, Pyrrhura 166
hypoxantha, Rhipidura 488
hypoxanthus, Hylophilus 586
hypoxanthus, Ploceus 616
Hypsipetes 372

ianthinogaster, Uraeginthus 605
ibadanensis, Malimbus 617
Ibidorhyncha 121
ibis, Bubulcus 64
ibis, Mycteria 67
ichthyaetus, Ichthyophaga 78
ichthyaetus, Larus 130
Ichthyophaga 78
Icteria 581
icterina, Hippolais 443
icterinus, Phyllastrephus 370
icterioides, Coccothraustes 602
icterocephala, Tangara 570
icterocephalus, Agelaius 591
icterophrys, Satrapa 317
icteropygialis, Eremomela 460
icterorhynchus, Francolinus 101
icterorhynchus, Otus 181
icterotis, Ognorhynchus 166
icterotis, Platycercus 161
Icterus 589
icterus, Icterus 590
Ictinaetus 86
Ictinia 77
idae, Ardeola 64
idaliae, Phaethornis 206
Idiopsar 545
Idioptilon 329
Ifrita 415
igata, Gerygone 466
ignicapillus, Regulus 449
ignicauda, Aethopyga 519
igniferum, Dicaeum 509
ignipectus, Dicaeum 510
ignita, Lophura 107
igniventris, Anisognathus 567
ignobilis, Thripadectes 286
ignobilis, Turdus 413
ignotincta, Minla 432
iheringi, Formicivora 295
iheringi, Myrmotherula 294
ijimae, Phylloscopus 446
iliaca, Passerella 538
iliacus, Turdus 412
Ilicura 312
iliolophum, Oedistoma 525
imberbe, Camptostoma 336
imberbis, Anomalospiza 618
imerinus, Pseudocossyphus 405
imitans, Euphonia 569
imitator, Accipiter 82
immaculata, Myrmeciza 299
immaculata, Prunella 392
immaculatus, Enicurus 400
immer, Gavia 54
immunda, Rhytipterna 322

immutabilis, Diomedea 55
imperatrix, Heliodoxa 215
imparatus, Corvus 640
imperialis, Amazona 171
imperialis, Ardea 66
imperialis, Campephilus 265
imperialis, Gallinago 128
imperialis, Lophura 107
impetuani, Emberiza 536
impeyanus, Lophophorus 106
implicata, Pachycephala 494
importunus, Pycnonotus 368
inca, Larosterna 133
inca, Scardafella 143
Incana 457
incana, Drymocichla 457
incana, Incana 457
incana, Lichmera 526
incanus, Heteroscelus 127
Incaspiza 545
incerta, Amalocichla 407
incerta, Pterodroma 56
incertus, Pitohui 496
incognita, Megalaima 243
inda, Chloroceryle 225
indica, Chalcophaps 141
indica, Sypheotides 120
Indicator 247
indicator, Baeopogon 369
indicator, Indicator 247
indicus, Anser 70
indicus, Butastur 83
indicus, Caprimulgus 196
indicus, Colius 222
indicus, Dendronanthus 354
indicus, Erithacus 396
indicus, Gyps 78
indicus, Hypsipetes 372
indicus, Metopidius 120
indicus, Pterocles 135
indicus, Vanellus 124
indigo, Eumyias 476
indigotica, Diglossa 574
indigoticus, Scytalopus 306
indistincta, Lichmera 526
indus, Haliastur 77
ineptus, Amaurornis 117
inerme, Ornithion 337
inexpectata, Meliphaga 529
inexpectata, Pterodroma 56
inexpectata, Torreornis 543
inexspectata, Tyto 181
Inezia 333
infaustus, Perisoreus 637
infelix, Monarcha 486
infuscata, Henicopernis 76
infuscata, Muscicapa 476
infuscata, Synallaxis 279
infuscatus, Automolus 287
infuscatus, Bradornis 471
infuscatus, Phimosus 68
ingens, Otus 184
ingoufi, Tinamotis 53
innominatus, Picumnus 251
innotata, Aythya 73

inopinatum, Polyplectron 108
inornata, Acanthiza 467
inornata, Catamenia 549
inornata, Columba 137
inornata, Gerygone 467
inornata, Inezia 333
inornata, Lophura 107
inornata, Pachycephala 492
inornata, Pinaroloxias 550
inornata, Tangara 570
inornata, Thlypopsis 561
inornata, Zosterops 523
inornatum, Idioptilon 329
inornatus, Amblyornis 630
inornatus, Caprimulgus 198
inornatus, Chlorospingus 560
inornatus, Myiophobus 325
inornatus, Myiozetetes 319
inornatus, Parus 502
inornatus, Philemon 532
inornatus, Phylloscopus 445
inornatus, Rhabdornis 506
inquieta, Collocalia 200
inquieta, Scotocerca 449
inquieta, Seisura 484
inquisitor, Tityra 309
inscriptus, Pteroglossus 248
insignibarbis, Lophornis 208
insignis, Aegotheles 193
insignis, Artamus 628
insignis, Clytomias 463
insignis, Panterpe 210
insignis, Ploceus 616
insignis, Polihierax 88
insignis, Prodotiscus 247
insignis, Rallus 113
insignis, Saxicola 402
insignis, Thamnophilus 291
insolitus, Ptilinopus 151
insularis, Aplonis 619
insularis, Coturnicops 115
insularis, Myiophoneus 405
insularis, Otus 183
insularis, Passer 162
insularis, Ptilinopus 150
insulata, Sporophila 548
intermedia, Egretta 66
intermedia, Pipreola 307
intermedia, Psittacula 164
intermedia, Sporophila 547
intermedius, Ploceus 615
internigrans, Perisoreus 637
interpres, Arenaria 127
interpres, Zoothera 406
involucris, Ixobrychus 63
Iodopleura 307
iouschistos, Aegithalos 497
iozonus, Ptilinopus 150
iphis, Pomarea 484
iracunda, Metallura 219
Irania 399
iredalei, Acanthiza 460
Irediparra 120
Irena 375
ireneae, Otus 181

iriditorques, Columba 138
Iridosornis 567
iris, Coeligena 216
iris, Lamprotornis 620
iris, Pipra 312
iris, Pitta 340
iris, Trichoglossus 154
irrorata, Diomedea 55
irupero, Xolmis 314
isaacsonii, Eriocnemis 217
isabella, Stiltia 123
isabellae, Dryocichloides 397
isabellae, Iodopleura 307
isabellae, Oriolus 624
isabellina, Geositta 276
isabellina, Oenanthe 403
isabellina, Sylvietta 461
isabellinus, Amaurornis 117
isidorei, Garritornis 420
isidorei, Pipra 313
isidori, Oroaetus 87
islandica, Bucephala 74
Ispidina 226
isura, Lophoictinia 77
Ithaginis 106
Ixobrychus 63
ixoides, Pycnopygius 531
Ixonotus 369

Jabiru 67
Jabouilleia 420
Jacamaralcyon 239
Jacamerops 239
Jacaná 120
jacana, Jacana 120
jacarina, Volatinia 546
jacksoni, Apalis 455
jacksoni, Cryptospiza 603
jacksoni, Euplectes 618
jacksoni, Francolinus 101
jacksoni, Ploceus 616
jacksoni, Tockus 237
jacobinus, Clamator 172
jacquacu, Penelope 92
jacquinoti, Ninox 189
jacucaca, Penelope 92
jacula, Heliodoxa 215
jacutinga, Aburria 92
jamaica, Euphonia 568
jamaicensis, Buteo 85
jamaicensis, Corvus 640
jamaicensis, Laterallus 116
jamaicensis, Leptotila 144
jamaicensis, Oxyura 74
jamaicensis, Turdus 413
jambu, Ptilinopus 149
jamesi, Phoenicoparus 69
jamesi, Tchagra 377
jamesoni, Gallinago 128
jamesoni, Parmoptila 602
jandaya, Aratinga 165
jankowskii, Emberiza 536
janthina, Columba 136
japonensis, Grus 111
japonica, Bombycilla 381

japonica, Coturnix 103
japonica, Zosterops 519
jardineii, Turdoides 426
jardini, Boissonneaua 217
jardinii, Glaucidium 187
javanense, Dinopium 267
javanica, Arborophila 105
javanica, Dendrocygna 69
javanica, Lophozosterops 524
javanica, Mirafa 341
javanica, Rhipidura 490
javanicus, Eurylaimus 269
javanicus, Leptotilos 67
javanicus, Zanclostomus 177
javensis, Batrachostomus 193
javensis, Dryocopus 264
javensis, Megalaima 243
jefferyi, Chlamydochaera 362
jefferyi, Pithecophaga 85
jelskii, Iridorsornis 567
jelskii, Upucerthia 276
jerdoni, Aviceda 75
jerdoni, Garrulax 429
jerdoni, Saxicola 403
jobiensis, Gallicolumba 145
jobiensis, Manucodia 631
jobiensis, Talegalla 91
jocosus, Campylorhynchus 382
jocosus, Pycnonotus 365
johannae, Doryfera 204
johannae, Nectarinia 517
johannae, Tangara 570
johannis, Acanthis 598
johnstoni, Nectarinia 517
johnstoni, Tauraco 172
johnstoniae, Erithacus 396
johnstoniae, Trichoglossus 154
jonquillaceus, Aprosmictus 160
josefinae, Charmosyna 156
josephinae, Microcochlearius
330
jourdanii, Chaetocercus 221
jouyi, Columba 137
jubata, Chenonetta 71
jubatus, Neochen 70
jubatus, Rhynochetos 119
Jubula 184
jugger, Falco 90
jugularis, Brotogeris 168
jugularis, Eulampis 207
jugularis, Meiglyptes 268
jugularis, Myzomela 528
jugularis, Nectarinia 514
juliae, Arachnothera 519
julie, Damophila 210
julienae, Monarcha 486
julius, Nothocercus 50
juncidis, Cisticola 450
Junco 540
juninensis, Muscisaxicola 314
junoniae, Columba 136
Jynx 250

Kakamega 418
kalinowskii, Nothoprocta 52

kamtschatschensis, Larus 130
karamojae, Apalis 456
kasumba, Harpactes 224
katharina, Acanthiza 467
kaupi, Arses 487
Kaupifalco 83
keartlandi, Meliphaga 529
keayi, Gallicolumba 145
keiensis, Micropsitta 157
kelaarti, Lonchura 609
kelleyi, Macronous 424
kempi, Macrosphenus 462
Kenopia 420
kenricki, Poeoptera 620
keraudrenii, Phonygammus 631
keri, Sericornis 469
kerriae, Crypturellus 52
kessleri, Turdus 412
Ketupa 186
ketupu, Ketupa 186
kieneri, Melozone 552
kienerii, Hieraaetus 86
kilimensis, Nectarinia 517
kingi, Aglaiocercus 219
kingii, Acrocephalus 442
kioloides, Canirallus 112
kirhocephalus, Pitohui 496
kirkii, Veniliornis 261
kirtlandii, Dendroica 577
kizuki, Picoides 256
klaas, Chrysococcyx 174
klagesi, Myrmotherula 293
Klais 208
kleinschmidti, Erythrura 608
klossi, Spilornis 79
Knipolegus 316
knudseni, Himantopus 121
kochi, Pitta 339
koeniswaldiana, Pulsatrix 186
koepckeae, Cacicus 589
koepckeae, Phaethornis 205
kollari, Synallaxis 280
koliensis, Serinus 594
komadori, Erithacus 395
kori, Choriotis 119
koslowi, Babax 427
koslowi, Emberiza 537
koslowi, Prunella 392
kowaldi, Ifrita 415
krameri, Psittacula 164
kretschmeri, Macrosphenus 462
kreyenborgi, Falco 90
kruperi, Sitta 504
kubaryi, Corvus 639
kubaryi, Gallicolumba 145
kuehni, Myzomela 527
kuehni, Zosterops 521
kuhli, Leucopternis 83
kuhlii, Vini 155
kupensis, Telophorus 378

labradorides, Tangara 571
Lacedo 228
lacernulata, Ducula 153
lacernulata, Leucopternis 83

lacertosa, Woodfordia 524
lacrymosa, Euthlypis 580
lacrymosum, Tricholaema 245
lacrymosus, Anisognathus 567
lacrymosus, Xiphorhynchus 274
lactea, Amazilia 212
lactea, Glareola 123
lactea, Polioptila 438
lacteus, Bubo 185
laemosticta, Myrmeciza 299
laeta, Incaspiza 545
laetior, Melithreptus 531
laetissima, Chlorocichla 369
laetus, Phylloscopus 447
lafargei, Myzomela 527
lafayettei, Galus 106
Lafresnaya 216
lafresnayanus, Rallus 113
lafresnayei, Aegithina 374
lafresnayi, Lafresnaya 216
lafresnayii, Diglossa 574
lagdeni, Malaconotus 378
Lagonostica 604
Lagopus 94
lagopus, Buteo 85
lagopus, Lagopus 94
lagrandieri, Megalaima 242
lais, Cisticola 451
Lalage 362
lalandi, Stephanoxis 208
lamberti, Malurus 464
lamelligerus, Anastomus 67
lamellipennis, Xipholena 309
laminirostris, Andigena 249
Lampornis 214
Lampribis 68
Lamprolaima 214
Lamprolia 470
Lampropsar 592
Lamprospiza 559
Lamprotornis 620
lanceolata, Chiroxiphia 312
lanceolata, Locustella 441
lanceolata, Micromonarcha 241
lanceolata, Plectorhyncha 534
lanceolata, Rhinocrypta 305
lanceolatus, Babax 427
lanceolatus, Garrulus 636
lanceolatus, Spizaetus 87
landanae, Lagonostica 604
langbianis, Crocias 434
langsdorffi, Popelairia 208
languida, Hippolais 443
Laniarius 377
laniirostris, Euphonia 568
Laniisoma 306
Lanio 563
Laniocera 322
lanioides, Lipaugus 307
lanioides, Pachycephala 495
Lanioturdus 376
Lanius 379
lansbergei, Pericrocotus 363
lansbergi, Coccyzus 175
laperouse, Megapodius 91

lapponica, Limosa 126
lapponicus, Calcarius 538
largipennis, Campylopterus 206
Larosterna 133
Larus 129
larvata, Aplopelia 139
larvata, Coracina 359
larvata, Lagonosticta 604
larvata, Tangara 572
larvatus, Oriolus 625
latebricola, Scytalopus 306
lateralis, Cisticola 452
lateralis, Poospiza 545
lateralis, Zosterops 522
Laterallus 116
lathami, Alectura 91
lathami, Calyptorhynchus 156
lathami, Francolinus 103
lathami, Melophus 535
Lathamus 162
latifrons, Microhierax 88
latimeri, Vireo 586
latirostre, Todirostrum 328
latirostris, Contopus 323
latirostris, Cynanthus 209
latirostris, Muscicapa 475
latirostris, Psarocolius 588
latirostris, Pycnonotus 368
Latoucheornis 535
latrans, Ducula 152
laudabilis, Icterus 590
laurae, Phylloscopus 447
lauterbachi, Chlamydera 631
lavinia, Tangara 571
lawesii, Parotia 633
lawrencei, Carduelis 597
lawrencei, Empidonax 323
lawrencii, Geotrygon 144
lawrencii, Glymnoglaux 189
lawrencii, Pseudocolaptes 284
lawrencii, Turdus 413
layardi, Parisoma 461
layardi, Ptilinopus 151
lazuli, Halcyon 229
leachii, Dacelo 228
leachii, Mackenziaena 289
leadbeateri, Bucorvus 236
leadbeateri, Cacatua 156
leadbeateri, Heliodoxa 215
leari, Anodorhynchus 164
lebruni, Sicalis 546
leclancheri, Ptilinopus 149
leclancherii, Passerina 558
lecontei, Myioceyx 226
lecontei, Toxostoma 391
leconteii, Ammodramus 541
ledanti, Sitta 504
Legatus 318
Leiothrix 430
Leipoa 91
lembeyei, Polioptilla 437
lemosi, Cypseloides 1199
lendu, Muscicapa 475
lentiginosus, Botaurus 63
Leonardina 418

leontica, Prinia 454
lepida, Hypergerus 459
lepida, Rhipidura 488
Lepidocolaptes 274
Lepidogrammus 177
Lepidopyga 210
lepidus, Ceyx 226
Leptasthenura 278
Leptodon 76
leptogrammica, Strix 190
Leptopoecile 449
Leptopogon 337
Leptopterus 381
Leptoptilos 67
leptorhynchus, Enicognathus
  167
Leptosittaca 166
Leptosomus 235
leptosomus, Brachypteracias
  235
Leptotila 144
Leptotriccus 331
lepturus, Phaethon 60
lerchi, Thalurania 210
Lerwa 98
lerwa, Lerwa 98
Lesbia 218
leschenaulti, Enicurus 400
leschenaulti, Merops 234
leschenaultii, Charadrius 125
leschenaultii, Taccocua 176
lessoni, Mayrornis 484
lessoni, Pterodroma 56
Lessonia 314
letitiae, Popelairia 208
lettii, Jubula 184
leucaspis, Gymnopithys 300
Leucippus 211
leucoblepharus, Basileuterus
  581
leucocephala, Amazona 170
leucocephala, Arundinicola 317
leucocephala, Columba 137
leucocephala, Emberiza 535
leucocephala, Halcyon 229
leucocephala, Mycteria 67
leucocephala, Oxyura 74
leucocephalus, Aceros 237
leucocephalus, Cinclus 382
leucocephalus, Cladorhynchus
  121
leucocephalus, Colius 222
leucocephalus, Haliaeetus 77
leucocephalus, Himantopus 121
leucocephalus, Lybius 246
leucocephalus, Phoenicurs 399
Leucochloris 221
leucogaster, Alcedo 226
leucogaster, Amazilia 212
leucogaster, Centropus 179
leucogaster, Cinnyricinclus 621
leucogaster, Corythaixoides 171
leucogaster, Haliaeetus 77
leucogaster, Lepidocolaptes 274
leucogaster, Pionites 169

leucogaster, Sula 60
leucogastra, Dendrocitta 638
leucogastra, Galbula 239
leucogastra, Lonchura 609
leucogastra, Ortalis 92
leucogastra, Uropsila 388
leucogastroides, Lonchura 608
leucogenys, Aegithalos 497
leucogenys, Conirostrum 582
leucogenys, Myadestes 401
leucogenys, Pycnonotus 366
leucogenys, Pyrrhula 601
leucogeranus, Grus 111
leucognaphalus, Corvus 640
leucogrammica, Ptilocichla 420
leucogrammicus, Pycnonotus 365
leucolaemus, Odontophorus 98
leucolaemus, Piculus 261
leucolophus, Caliechthrus 174
leucolophus, Garrulax 427
leucolophus, Tauraco 172
leucolophus, Tigriornis 63
leucomela, Columba 137
leucomela, Lalage 362
leucomelaena, Sylvia 443
leucomelan, Tricholaema 245
leucomelana, Lophura 106
leucomelas, Calonectris 57
leucomelas, Parus 500
leucomelas, Turdus 413
leucomystax, Pogoniulus 244
leuconota, Colomba 136
leuconota, Pyriglena 297
leuconotos, Thalassornis 75
leuconotus, Gorsachius 64
leuconotus, Parus 501
leucopareia, Eremopterix 345
Leucopeza 579
leucophaea, Climacteris 506
leucophaea, Collocalia 200
leucophaea, Microeca 477
leucophaeus, Dicrurus 626
leucophaius, Legatus 318
leucophaea, Speirops 525
leucophrus, Cichlocolaptes 286
leucophrys, Anthus 357
leucophrys, Basileuterus 581
leucophrys, Brachypteryx 393
leucophrys, Callonetta 71
leucophrys, Dendrortyx 96
leucophrys, Erythropygia 393
leucophrys, Henicorhina 389
leucophrys, Mecocerculus 333
leucophrys, Myrmoborus 297
leucophrys, Ochthoeca 315
leucophrys, Rhipidura 491
leucophrys, Sylvietta 460
leucophrys, Zonotrichia 540
leucophthalma, Myrmotherula 293
leucophthalmus, Aratinga 165
leucophthalmus, Automolus 287
leucophthalmus, Larus 130
leucopis, Atlapetes 553

leucopleura, Thescelocichla 369
leucopleurus, Oreotrochilus 215
leucopodus, Haematopus 121
leucopogon, Campephilus 265
leucopogon, Colinus 97
leucopogon, Prinia 454
leucops, Platycichla 409
leucops, Tregellasia 478
Leucopsar 623
leucopsis, Aphelocephala 467
leucopsis, Branta 70
leucopsis, Sitta 504
leucoptera, Chlidonias 131
leucoptera, Erythropygia 393
leucoptera, Fulica 118
leucoptera, Loxia 601
leucoptera, Melanocorypha 346
leucoptera, Piranga 565
leucoptera, Psophia 112
leucoptera, Pterodroma 56
leucoptera, Pyriglena 297
leucoptera, Sporophila 548
Leucopternis 83
leucopterus, Atlapetes 554
leucopterus, Malurus 464
leucopterus, Nyctibius 193
leucopterus, Picoides 258
leucopterus, Platysmurus 633
leucopterus, Serinus 596
leucopteryx, Icterus 589
leucopus, Furnarius 277
leucopyga, Lalage 363
leucopyga, Nyctiprogne 194
leucopyga, Oenanthe 404
leucopyga, Tachycineta 350
leucopygia, Coracina 360
leucopygia, Halcyon 229
leucopygialis, Raphidura 201
leucopygius, Serinus 595
leucopygius, Turdoides 426
leucopyrrhus, Laterallus 116
leucoramphus, Cacicus 589
leucorhoa, Oceanodroma 59
leucorhynchus, Artamus 628
leucorhynchus, Laniarius 378
leucorodia, Platalea 68
leucorrhoa, Corapipo 312
leucorrhoa, Tachycineta 350
leucorrhous, Buteo 84
leucorhyphus, Haliaeetus 77
leucoryphus, Platyrinchus 326
Leucosarcia 142
leucoscepus, Francolinus 100
leucosoma, Hirundo 352
leucospila, Rallina 115
leucospodia, Phaiomyias 335
leucostephes, Melidectes 533
leucosterna, Cheramoeca 351
leucosticta, Erythropygia 394
leucosticta, Henicorhina 389
leucosticta, Lonchura 609
leucosticta, Ptilorrhoa 415
Leucosticte 598
leucostictus, Bubo 185
leucostigma, Percnostola 298

leucostigma, Rhagologus 491
leucothorax, Lanio 563
leucothorax, Rhipidura 488
leucotis, Entomodestes 401
leucotis, Eremopterix 344
leucotis, Galbalcyrhynchus 238
leucotis, Hylocharis 210
leucotis, Meliphaga 530
leucotis, Melozone 552
leucotis, Monarcha 486
leucotis, Otus 184
leucotis, Phapitreron 146
leucotis, Pyrrhura 166
leucotis, Smilorhis 244
leucotis, Stachyris 423
leucotis, Tauraco 171
leucotis, Throyothorus 386
leucotis, Vireolanius 585
leucotos, Picoides 257
leucura, Oenanthe 404
leucura, Saxicola 402
leucurum, Cinclidium 399
leucurus, Elanus 76
leucurus, Lagopus 94
leucurus, Monarcha 486
leucurus, Threnetes 204
leucurus, Vanellus 124
leuphotes, Aviceda 76
levaillanti, Clamator 172
levaillantii, Francolinus 102
levalliantoides, Francolinus 102
leveriana, Cissopis 559
levigaster, Gerygone 466
levraudi, Laterallus 116
lewinii, Meliphaga 529
lewis, Melanerpes 252
leytensis, Micromacronous 425
Iherminieri, Cichlherminia 408
Iherminieri, Puffinus 58
Ihuysii, Lophophorus 106
libonyanus, Turdus 410
Lichmera 526
lichtensteini, Philydor 286
lichtensteinii, Pterocles 135
lictor, Pitangus 320
lidthi, Garrulus 636
lignarius, Picoides 259
lilianae, Agapornis 163
lilliae, Lepidopyga 210
limae, Picumnus 250
Limicola 128
limicola, Rallus 114
Limnodromus 128
Limnornis 283
Limnothlypis 578
Limosa 126
limosa, Limosa 126
lincolnii, Melospiza 539
lindsayi, Halcyon 231
linearis, Chiroxiphia 312
linearis, Geotrygon 145
lineata, Acanthiza 467
lineata, Conopophaga 304
lineata, Coracina 359
lineata, Dacnis 572

672   lineata, Megalaima 242
lineatum, Tigrisoma 63
lineatus, Buteo 84
lineatus, Cymbilaimus 289
lineatus, Dryocopus 264
lineatus, Garrulax 429
linteatus, Heterocercus 311
lineifrons, Grallericula 304
lineiventris, Anthus 357
lineola, Bolborhynchus 167
lineola, Sporophila 547
lintoni, Myiophobus 325
Linurgus 596
Liocichla 430
Lioptilus 433
Liosceles 305
Lipaugus 307
Lissotis 120
litsipsirupa, Turdus 410
littoralis, Ochthornis 317
liventer, Butastur 83
livia, Columba 135
livida, Agriornis 313
livingstonei, Erythrocercus 481
lobata, Biziura 75
lobata, Campephaga 363
lobatus, Phalaropus 127
Loboparadisea 631
Lochmias 284
Locustella 440
locustella, Ortygospiza 606
Loddigesia 220
loehkeni, Threnetes 204
lombokia, Lichmera 526
lomvia, Uri 134
Lonchura 608
longicauda, Bartramia 126
longicauda, Coracina 360
longicauda, Deconychura 270
longicauda, Discosura 208
longicauda, Embernagra 546
longicauda, Erannornis 481
longicauda, Henicopernis 76
longicauda, Melanocharis 507
longicauda, Myrmotherula 293
longicauda, Psittacula 164
longicaudatus, Mimus 390
longicaudatus, Spelaeornis 422
longicaudus, Stercorarius 129
longimembris, Tyto 181
longipennis, Falco 89
longipennis, Hemiprocne 204
longipennis, Macrodipteryx 198
longipennis, Myrmotherula 294
longipes, Myrmeciza 298
longipes, Xenicus 340
longirostra, Arachnothera 519
longirostra, Rukia 524
longirostre, Toxostoma 391
longirostris, Caprimulgus 196
longirostris, Dasyornis 465
longirostris, Heliomaster 220
longirostris, Herpsilochmus 295
longirostris, Nasica 271
longirostris, Pterodroma 57

longirostris, Rallus 114
longirostris, Rhizothera 103
longirostris, Thryothorus 387
longirostris, Turdoides 425
longuemarei, Anthreptes 511
longuemareus, Phaethornis 206
lopezi, Poliolais 458
Lophaetus 86
Lophoictinia 77
Lopholaimus 153
Lophophorus 106
Lophorina 632
Lophornis 208
Lophortyx 96
Lophospingus 544
Lophostrix 184
lophotes, Knipolegus 316
lophotes, Ocyphaps 141
lophotes, Percnostola 298
lophotes, Pseudoseisura 284
Lophotibis 68
Lophotis 119
Lophotriccus 330
Lophozosterops 524
Lophura 106
lorata, Sterna 132
lorentzi, Pachycephala 494
lorenzi, Phyllastrephus 370
Loria 631
loriae, Loria 631
loricata, Compsothraupis 559
loricata, Grallaricula 304
loricata, Myrmeciza 299
loricatus, Celeus 263
Loriculus 163
Lorius 115
lory, Lorius 155
lotenia, Nectarinia 514
louisiadensis, Cracticus 628
lovensis, Ashbyia 470
loveridgei, Nectarinia 516
lowei, Dryocichloides 397
loweryi, Xenoglaux 188
Loxia 601
Loxigilla 549
Loxipasser 549
Loxops 583
loyca, Sturnella 592
luciae, Amazilia 212
luciae, Vermivora 575
luciani, Eriocnemis 217
lucida, Hirundo 352
lucidus, Chalcites 174
lucidus, Chrysocolaptes 267
lucidus, Cyanerpes 573
lucidus, Hemignathus 584
lucidus, Phalacrocorax 61
lucifer, Calothorax 220
lucionensis, Tanygnathus 159
luconensis, Prioniturus 159
luctuosa, Ducula 153
luctuosa, Sporophila 547
luctuosus, Sakesphorus 290
luctuosus, Tachyphonus 563
ludoviciae, Doryfera 204

ludoviciae, Turdus 410
ludoviciana, Piranga 565
ludovicianus, Caprimulgus 198
ludovicianus, Lanius 380
ludovicianus, Pheucticus 556
ludovicianus, Thryothorus 386
ludwigii, Dicurus 626
ludwigii, Neotis 119
lugens, Coturnicops 115
lugens, Haplophaedia 218
lugens, Oenanthe 404
lugens, Parisoma 461
lugens, Streptopelia 138
lugubris, Brachygalba 239
lugubris, Celeus 263
lugubris, Ceryle 225
lugubris, Garrulax 428
lugubris, Melampitta 415
lugubris, Myrmoborus 297
lugubris, Parus 498
lugubris, Poeoptera 620
lugubris, Quiscalus 593
lugubris, Speirops 525
lugubris, Surniculus 174
lugubris, Vanellus 123
luhderi, Laniarius 377
Lullula 348
lumachellus, Angastes 219
lunata, Sterna 132
lunatus, Melithreptus 531
lunatus, Serilophus 269
Lunda 134
lunulata, Galloperdix 105
lunulata, Gymnopithys 299
lunulatus, Bolbopsittacus 158
lunulatus, Garrulax 428
Lurocalis 194
luscinia, Acrocephalus 441
luscinia, Erithacus 395
lucinioides, Locustella 440
lutea, Leiothrix 430
lutea, Sicalis 546
lutea, Zosterops 522
luteicapilla, Euphonia 568
luteifrons, Nigrita 602
luteiventris, Myiodynastes 319
luteiventris, Tyrannopsis 318
luteocephala, Sicalis 546
luteola, Sicalis 546
luteolus, Ploceus 614
luteolus, Pycnonotus 367
luteoschistaceus, Accipiter 81
luteoventris, Bradypterus 440
luteovirens, Ptilinopus 151
luteoviridis, Basileuterus 580
luteoviridis, Pselliophorus 555
lutescens, Anthus 358
lutetiae, Coeligena 216
luteus, Auripasser 613
luzonica, Anas 72
luzonica, Gallicolumba 145
luzoniensis, Copsychus 398
Lybius 246
Lycocorax 631
Lymnocryptes 128

lyra, Uropsalis
Lysurus 555

macao, Ara 165
maccoa, Oxyura 75
macconnelli, Pipromorpha 338
macconnelli, Synallaxis 279
maccormicki, Catharacta 129
macei, Picoides 257
macgillivrayi, Pterodroma 57
Macgregoria 631
macgregoriae, Amblyornis 630
macgregoriae, Niltava 473
macgregorii, Cnemophilus 631
Machaerhamphus 76
Machaerirhynchus 484
Machaeropterus 311
Machetornis 317
Mackenziaena 289
mackinlayi, Macropygia 140
mackinnoni, Lanius 380
macleayana, Meliphaga 530
macleayii, Halcyon 229
macloviana, Muscisaxicola 314
Macroagelaius 592
macrocephala, Petroica 478
Macrocephalon 91
macrocerca, Hylonympha 215
macrocercus, Dicrurus 626
macrocerus, Eupetes 415
macrodactyla, Gallinago 127
macrodactyla, Napothera 420
macrodactylus, Bucco 240
Macrodipteryx 198
macrolopha, Percnostola 298
macrolopha, Pucrasia 106
Macronectes 55
Macronous 424
Macronyx 355
Macropsalis 199
macroptera, Pterodroma 56
macropterus, Vanellus 124
macropus, Scytalopus 305
Macropygia 139
macrorhyncha, Dendrocincla
  270
macrorhyncha, Saxicola 402
macrorhynchos, Corvus 640
macrorhynchos, Cymbirhynchus
  269
macrorhynchos, Notharchus 239
macrorhynchus, Tauraco 171
macrorhina, Melidora 228
Macrosphenus 461
macrotis, Eurostopodus 195
macroura, Dendrortyx 96
macroura, Eupetomena 207
macroura, Thripophaga 283
macroura, Vidua 610
macroura, Zenaida 142
macrourus, Circus 79
macrourus, Colius 222
macrourus, Euplectes 618
macrourus, Urotriorchis 83
macrurus, Caprimulgus 197

macularia, Actitis 127
macularius, Hylopezus 303
maculata, Chlamydera 630
maculata, Cotinga 309
maculata, Loxops 584
maculata, Stachyris 423
maculata, Terenura 296
maculatum, Todirostrum 328
maculatus, Chalcites 174
maculatus, Enicurus 400
maculatus, Indicator 247
maculatus, Myiodynastes 319
maculatus, Nystalus 240
maculatus, Picoides 256
maculatus, Prionochilus 507
maculatus, Rallus 113
maculialatus, Icterus 590
maculicauda, Hypocnemoides
  298
maculicauda, Thripophaga 282
maculicaudus, Caprimulgus 196
maculicoronatus, Capito 241
maculifrons, Veniliornis 260
maculipectus, Rhipidura 488
maculipectus, Thryothorus 385
maculipennis, Larus 130
maculipennis, Phylloscopus 445
maculirostris, Muscisaxicola 314
maculirostris, Selendera 249
maculosa, Campethera 254
maculosa, Columba 137
maculosa, Lalage 362
maculosa, Nothura 52
maculosa, Prinia 454
maculosus, Caprimulgus 196
mada, Gymnophaps 153
mada, Prioniturus 159
madagarensis, Margaroperdix
  103
madagascariensis, Accipiter 80
madagascariensis, Alectroenas
  151
madagascariensis, Asio 192
madagascariensis, Aviceda 75
madagascariensis, Calicalicus
  381
madagascariensis, Caprimulgus
  197
madagascariensis, Foudia 617
madagascariensis, Hypsipetes
  373
madagascariensis, Ispidina 226
madagascariensis, Numenius
  126
madagascariensis, Oxylabes 435
madagascariensis, Phyllas
  trephus 370
madagascariensis, Rallus 114
madagascarinus, Leptopterus
  381
Madanga 524
maderaspatana, Zosterops 524
maderaspatensis, Motacilla 355
maderaszi, Psittacella 158
maesi, Garrulax 428

magellani, Pelecanoides 59
magellanica, Carduelis 597
magellanicus, Campephilus 265
magellanicus, Phalacrocorax 61
magellanicus, Scytalopus 306
magellanicus, Spheniscus 53
magentae, Pterodroma 56
magister, Vireo 586
magna, Alectoris 99
magna, Aplonis 619
magna, Arachnothera 519
magna, Macropygia 140
magna, Sitta 504
magna, Sturnella 592
magnifica, Lophornis 208
magnificens, Fregata 62
magnificus, Calyptorhynchus
  156
magnificus, Diphyllodes 633
magnificus, Gorsachius 64
magnificus, Ptilinopus 149
magnificus, Ptiloris 631
magnirostre, Malacopteron 418
magnirostris, Burhinus 122
magnirostris, Buteo 84
magnirostris, Calendula 348
magnirostris, Esacus 122
magnirostris, Geospiza 550
magnirostris, Gerygone 466
magnirostris, Myiarchus 321
magnirostris, Phylloscopus 446
magnirostris, Sericornis 469
magnolia, Dendroica 577
magnum, Malacopteron 418
magnus, Sericornis 468
maguari, Ciconia 67
mahali, Plocepasser 611
mahrattensis, Caprimulgus 197
mahrattensis, Picoides 257
maja, Lonchura 609
major, Brachypteryx 393
major, Bradypterus 440
major, Cettia 438
major, Crotophaga 177
major, Cypseloides 199
major, Diglossa 574
major, Pachyramphus 308
major, Parus 501
major, Picoides 258
major, Podiceps 54
major, Quiscalus 593
major, Schiffornis 310
major, Taraba 289
major, Tinamus 50
major, Xiphocolaptes 272
makawai, Pogoniulus 245
malabarica, Galerida 348
malabarica, Lonchura 608
malabaricus, Anthracoceros 238
malabaricus, Copsychus 398
malabaricus, Sturnus 622
malabaricus, Vanellus 123
malacca, Lonchura 609
malaccense, Trichastoma 417
malaccensis, Hypsipetes 373

674   malacense, Polyplectron 108
malacensis, Anthreptes 511
malachitacea, Triclaria 171
malachurus, Stipiturus 465
Malaconotus 378
Malacopteron 418
Malacoptila 240
malacoptilus, Rimator 420
Malacorhynchus 73
malacorhynchus, Hymenolaimus 71
malaitae, Myzomela 528
malaitae, Rhipidura 490
malaris, Phaethornis 205
malayanus, Anthracoceros 238
malayanus, Chalcites 174
malayensis, Ictinaetus 86
malcolmi, Turdoides 425
maldivarus, Glareola 123
maleo, Macrocephalon 91
malherbi, Cyanoramphus 162
malherbii, Columba 138
Malia 435
malimbica, Halcyon 229
malimbicus, Malimbus 617
malimbicus, Merops 234
Malimbus 616
malouinus, Attagis 129
malura, Drymophila 296
maluroides, Spartonoica 283
Malurus 464
Manacus 311
manacus, Manacus 312
manadensis, Monarcha 486
manadensis, Otus 182
manadensis, Turacoena 140
mandellii, Arborophila 104
Mandingoa 603
mangle, Eulabeornis 112
mango, Antracothorax 207
manilata, Ara 165
manipurensis, Perdicula 104
Manorina 535
mantchuricum, Crossoptilon 107
mantelli, Porphyrio 118
Manucodia 631
manyar, Ploceus 616
maracana, Ara 165
marail, Penelope 92
maranhaoensis, Phaethornis 206
maranonica, Melanopareia 305
maranonica, Synallaxis 279
maranonicus, Turdus 413
marcapatae, Certhiaxis 281
marchei, Anthracoceros 238
marchei, Cleptornis 530
marchei, Ptilinopus 148
margaretae, Zoothera 407
margarethae, Charmosyna 156
margarettae, Phaethornis 205
margaritaceiventer, Idioptilon 329
margaritae, Batis 480
margaritae, Conirostrum 582

margaritatus, Hypargos 604
margaritatus, Megastictus 292
margaritatus, Trachyphomus 247
Margaroperdix 103
Margarops 392
Margarornis 284
marginalis, Porzana 116
marginata, Collocalia 201
marginata, Zoothera 407
marginatus, Charadrius 125
marginatus, Microcerculus 389
marginatus, Pachyramphus 308
mariae, Nesillas 443
mariei, Megalurulus 463
marila, Aythya 73
marina, Pelagodroma 58
marinus, Larus 130
mariquensis, Bradornis 470
mariquensis, Nectarinia 516
maritima, Calidris 128
maritima, Geositta 276
maritimus, Ammodramus 541
markhami, Oceanodroma 59
Marmaronetta 73
marmorata, Napothera 421
marmoratus, Brachyramphus 134
martii, Baryphthengus 232
martinica, Chaetura 202
martinica, Elaenia 334
martinica, Gallinula 118
martius, Dryocopus 264
masafuerae, Aphrastura 277
Masius 312
massena, Trogon 222
masukuensis, Pycnonotus 368
mathewsi, Cincloramphus 463
matsudairae, Oceanodroma 59
matthewsii, Boissonneaua 217
matthiae, Rhipidura 489
maugaeus, Chlorostilbon 209
maugei, Dicaeum 509
mauri, Calidris 128
maurus, Circus 79
mavors, Heliangelus 217
maxillosus, Saltator 557
maximiliani, Melanopareia 305
maximiliani, Pionus 169
maxima, Ceryle 225
maxima, Collocalia 200
maxima, Melanocorypha 346
maxima, Pitta 340
maxima, Pteropodocys 358
maximus, Artamus 628
maximus, Garrulax 429
maximus, Saltator 557
maximus, Thalasseus 132
mayeri, Astrapia 632
mayeri, Columba 138
maynana, Cotinga 359
mayottensis, Zosterops 524
mayri, Rallina 115
Mayrornis 484
mccallii, Erythrocercus 481

mcclellandii, Hypsipetes 372
mccownii, Calcarius 538
mcgregorie, Coracina 361
mcilhennyi, Conioptilon 309
mcleannani, Phaenostictus 300
mcleodii, Otophanes 195
Mearnsia 201
mechowi, Cerococcyx 173
Mecocerculus 333
media, Gallinago 127
mediocris, Nectarinia 516
medius, Picoides 258
meeki, Charmosyna 155
meeki, Microgoura 146
meeki, Micropsitta 157
meeki, Ninox 189
meeki, Zosterops 521
meekiana, Ptiloprora 532
Megabyas 480
megacephala, Ramphotrigon 328
Megadyptes 53
megaensis, Hirundo 352
megala, Gallinago 127
Megalaima 242
megalopterus, Campylorhynchus 383
megalopterus, Phalcoboenus 87
megalorhynchos, Tanygnathus 159
megalura, Leptotila 144
Megalurulus 463
Megalurus 462
Megapodius 90
megapodius, Pteroptochos 305
megarhyncha, Colluricincla 495
megarhyncha, Halcyon 230
megarhynchos, Erithacus 395
Megarhynchus 319
megarhynchus, Dicrurus 627
megarhynchus, Melilestes 525
megarhynchus, Ploceus 616
megarhynchus, Ramphomantis 174
Megastictus 292
Megatriorchis 80
Megaxenops 289
meiffrenii, Ortyxelos 111
Meiglyptes 268
melacoryphus, Coccyzus 175
melaena, Coracina 361
melaena, Lonchura 610
melaena, Myrmecocichla 403
Melaenornis 471
melambrotus, Cathartes 75
Melampitta 415
Melamprosops 584
melanaria, Cercomacra 297
melancholicus, Tyrannus 318
Melanerpes 252
melania, Oceanodroma 59
melanicterus, Cacicus 589
melanicterus, Pycnonotus 365
Melanitta 73
melanocephala, Alectoris 99

melanocephala, Apalis 456
melanocephala 66
melanocephala, Arenaria 127
melanocephala, Emberiza 537
melanocephala, Manorina 535
melanocephala, Myzomela 527
melanocephala, Pionites 169
melanocephala, Sylvia 444
melanocephalum, Tricholaema 245
melanocephalus, Atlapetes 553
melanocephalus, Carpornis 306
melanocephalus, Larus 130
melanocephalus, Malurus 464
melanocephalus, Myioborus 580
melanocephalus, Pardalotus 510
melanocephalus, Pheuticus 556
melanocephalus, Ploceus 615
melanocephalus, Threskiornis 67
melanocephalus, Tragopan 106
melanocephalus, Vanellus 124
melanoceps, Myrmeciza 299
Melanocharis 506
melanochlamys, Accipiter 82
melanochlamys, Buthraupis 566
Melanochlora 502
melanochloros, Colaptes 262
melanochroa, Ducula 153
melanocoryphus, Cygnus 69
Melanocorypha 345
melanocorys, Calamospiza 538
melanocyanea, Cissilopha 635
Melanodera 544
melanodera, Melanodera 544
melanogaster, Anhinga 62
melanogaster, Conopophaga 305
melanogaster, Formicivora 295
melanogaster, Lissotis 120
melanogaster, Oreotrochilus 215
melanogaster, Piaya 176
melanogaster, Ploceus 614
melanogaster, Ramphocelus 565
melanogaster, Sporophila 548
melanogaster, Sterna 132
melanogaster, Turnix 111
melanogenya, Adelomyia 214
melanogenys, Basileuterus 581
melanoleuca, Atticora 350
melanoleuca, Corvinella 379
melanoleuca, Heterophasia 434
melanoleuca, Lalage 362
melanoleuca, Lamprospiza 559
melanoleuca, Leucosarcia 142
melanoleuca, Poospiza 545
melanoleuca, Seleucidis 632
melanoleuca, Tringa 126
melanoleucos, Campephilus 265
melanoleucos, Haliëtor 62
melanoleucos, Pycnonotus 365
melanoleucus, Accipiter 80
melanoleucus, Circus 80

melanoleucus, Geranoaetus 84
melanoleucus, Microhierax 88
melanoleucus, Spizastur 86
melanolophus, Gorsachius 64
melanolophus, Parus 500
melanonota, Pipraeidea 568
melanonota, Touit 169
melanonotus, Odontophorus 97
melanonotus, Sakesphorus 289
Melanopareia 305
Melanoperdix 103
melanopezus, Automolus 287
melanophaius, Laterallus 116
melanophrys, Diomedea 55
melanophrys, Manorina 535
melanopis, Schistochlamys 559
melanopis, Theristicus 68
melanopogon, Hypocnemoides 298
melanopogon, Acrocephalus 441
melanops, Centropus 180
melanops, Charadrius 125
melanops, Conopophaga 304
melanops, Gallinula 118
melanops, Leucopternis 83
melanops, Meliphaga 530
melanops, Pachycephala 494
melanops, Phleocryptes 283
melanops, Philydonyris 534
melanops, Sporophila 547
melanops, Trichathraupis 564
melanops, Turdoides 426
melanopsis, Monarcha 485
melanoptera, Chloephaga 70
melanoptera, Coracina 362
melanoptera, Metriopelia 143
melanopterus, Lybius 246
melanopterus, Sturnus 623
melanopterus, Vanellus 123
Melanoptila 390
melanopygia, Telacanthura 201
melanorhamphos, Corocorax 628
melanorhyncha, Pelargopsis 228
melanorhynchus, Thripadectes 286
melanospila, Ptilinopus 151
Melanospiza 550
melanosternon, Hamirostra 77
melanosticta, Rhegmatorhina 300
melanota, Pulsatrix 186
melanothorax, Sakesphorus 289
melanothorax, Stachyris 424
melanothorax, Sylvia 444
Melanotis 390
melanotis, Ailuroedus 630
melanotis, Anaplectes 617
melanotis, Coryphaspiza 555
melanotis, Estrilda 605
melanotis, Hapalopsittaca 169
melanotis, Hemispingus 561
melanotis, Manorina 535
melanotis, Pslatriparus 497

melanotis, Pteruthius 431
melanotos, Calidris 128
melanotos, Sarkidiornis 71
Melanotrochilus 207
melanoxantha, Phainoptila 382
melanoxanthum, Dicaeum 508
melanozanthos, Coccothraustes 602
melanura, Anthornis 535
melanura, Apalis 457
melanura, Cercomela 402
melanura, Chilia 277
melanura, Climacteris 506
melanura, Pachycephala 494
melanura, Polioptila 437
melanura, Pyrrhura 167
melanurus, Ceyx 227
melanurus, Himantopus 121
melanurus, Myiophoneus 405
melanurus, Myrmoborus 297
melanurus, Passer 612
melanurus, Ramphocaenus 437
melanurus, Trogon 223
melaschistos, Coracina 362
melba, Apus 203
melba, Pytilia 603
meleagrides, Agelastes 109
Meleagris 93
meleagris, Numida 109
Meliarchus 533
Melichneutes 248
Melidectes 533
Melidora 228
Melierax 80
Melignomon 247
Melilestes 525
melindae, Anthus 358
Meliphaga 528
meliphilus, Indicator 248
Melipotes 533
Melithreptus 531
melitophrys, Vireolanius 585
melleri, Anas 72
mellianus, Oriolus 626
Mellisuga 220
mellisugus, Chlorostilbon 208
mellivora, Florisuga 207
mellori, Corvus 640
melodia, Melospiza 538
melodus, Charadrius 125
Melophus 535
Melopsittacus 162
Melopyrrha 549
meloryphus, Euscarthmus 332
Melospiza 538
Melozone 552
melpoda, Estrilda 605
membranaceus, Malacorhynchus 73
menachensis, Serinus 596
menachensis, Turdus 410
menagei, Gallicolumba 145
menbecki, Centropus 178
menckei, Monarcha 486
mendanae, Acrocephalus 442

675

676   mendiculus, Spheniscus 53
mendozae, Pomarea 484
menetriesii, Myrmotherula 294
meninting, Alcedo 225
mennelli, Serinus 596
menstruus, Pionus 169
mentalis, Cracticus 629
mentalis, Dysithamnus 292
mentalis, Picus 265
mentalis, Pipra 313
mentalis, Sphenoeacus 457
Menura 341
mercenaria, Amazona 170
mercierii, Ptilinopus 150
Merganetta 71
merganser, Mergus 74
Mergus 74
meridae, Cistothorus 384
meridionalis, Buteogallus 84
meridionalis, Himantopus 121
meridionalis, Nestor 157
merlini, Saurothera 176
merlini, Tropicoperdix 105
Meropogon 233
Merops 233
merrilli, Ptilinopus 148
merula, Dendrocincla 270
merula, Turdus 410
Merulaxis 305
merulinus, Cacomantis 173
merulinus, Garrulax 429
Mesembrinibis 68
Mesitornis 110
mesochrysa, Euphonia 569
mesoleuca, Conothraupis 559
mesoleuca, Elaenia 334
mesomelas, Icterus 589
metabates, Melierax 80
Metabolus 485
metallica, Aplonis 620
Metallura 218
metcalfii, Zosterops 522
metopias, Orthotomus 458
Metopidius 120
Metopothrix 284
Metriopelia 143
mevesii, Lamprotornis 621
mexicana, Sialia 4002
mexicana, Tangara 570
mexicanum, Tigrisoma 63
mexicanus, Aechmolophus 324
mexicanus, Carpodacus 599
mexicanus, Catharus 409
mexicanus, Catherpes 383
mexicanus, Cinclus 382
mexicanus, Falco 90
mexicanus, Gymnomystax 590
mexicanus, Himantopus 121
mexicanus, Momotus 233
mexicanus, Onychorhynchus 326
mexicanus, Quiscalus 593

mexicanus, Sclerurus 287
mexicanus, Todus 232
mexicanus, Trogon 223
meyeni, Zosterops 520
meyeri, Chalcites 174
meyeri, Epimachus 632
meyeri, Pachycephala 493
meyeri, Philemon 531
meyeri, Poicephalus 162
meyerianus, Accipiter 80
michleri, Pittasoma 302
Micrastur 87
micrastur, Heliangelus 217
Micrathene 188
Microbates 436
Microcerculus 389
Microchera 213
Microcochlearius 330
Microdynamis 174
Microeca 477
Microgoura 146
Microhierax 88
Microligea 579
Micromacronous 425
micromegas, Nesoctites 252
Micromonacha 241
Micropalama 129
Microparra 120
Micropsitta 157
microptera, Agriornis 313
micropterum, Rollandia 54
micropterus, Cuculus 172
Microrhopias 295
microrhyncha, Amazilia 212
microrhynchum, Ramphomicron 218
microrhynchus, Bradornis 470
microsoma, Halocyptena 59
Microstilbon 220
micrura, Myrmia 221
migrans, Milvus 77
migratorius Coccothraustes 602
migratorius, Turdus 414
mikado, Syrmaticus 107
milanjensis, Pycnonotus 369
miles, Vanellus 124
militaris, Ara 164
militaris, Haematoderus 310
militaris, Ilicura 312
militaris, Sturnella 591
milleri, Grallaria 303
milleri, Polytmus 211
milleri, Xenops 288
milleti, Garrulax 428
milnei, Garrulax 430
milo, Centropus 178
Milvago 87
Milvus 77
milvus, Milvus 77
mimikae, Meliphaga 528
Mimizuku 184
Mimodes 391
Mimus 390

mindanensis, Ptilocichla 420
mindorensis, Ducula 151
miniaceus, Picus 265
miniatus, Myioborus 579
miniatus, Pericrocotus 364
minima, Batis 481
minima, Lymnocryptes 128
minima, Mellisuga 220
minima, Nectarinia 513
minimus, Catharus 409
minimus, Empidonax 323
minimus, Otus 184
minimus, Psaltriparus 497
Minla 432
minlosi, Xenerpestes 284
Mino 623
minor, Aplonis 619
minor, Artamus 629
minor, Batis 481
minor, Chionis 129
minor, Chordeiles 194
minor, Coccyzus 175
minor, Eudyptula 53
minor, Fregata 62
minor, Furnarius 277
minor, Indicator 247
minor, Lanius 369
minor, Lybius 246
minor, Mecocerculus 333
minor, Myrmotherula 294
minor, Nothura 52
minor, Pachyramphus 309
minor, Paradisaea 633
minor, Phoeniconaias 69
minor, Picoides 256
minor, Platalea 68
minor, Pyrenestes 603
minor, Rhinopomastus 236
minor, Scolopax 127
minor, Snethlagea 330
minor, Zosterops 521
minulla, Batis 481
minulla, Nectarinia 516
minullus, Accipiter 81
minuta, Calidris 128
minuta, Columbina 143
minuta, Euphonia 569
minuta, Piaya 176
minuta, Sporophila 548
minuta, Tchagra 376
minuta, Zosterops 522
minutilla, Calidris 128
minutissimum, Glaucidium 186
minutissimus, Picumnus 250
minutus, Anous 133
minutus, Anthoscopus 498
minutus, Ixobrychus 63
minutus, Larus 131
minutus, Numenius 126
minutus, Kenops 288
Mionectes 337
mira, Scolopax 127
mirabilis, Cyanolyca 635
mirabilis, Eriocnemis 217
mirabilis, Loddigesia 220

Mirafa 341
miranda, Basilornis 623
miranda, Daphoenositta 505
mirandae, Idioptilon 329
mirandollei, Micrastur 87
misisippiensis, Ictinea 77
Misocalius 174
mitchellii, Phegornis 125
mitchellii, Philodice 220
mitrata, Aratinga 165
mitratus, Garrulax 429
Mitrephanes 324
Mitrospingus 562
mitu, Crax 93
mixta, Batis 480
mixtus, Batrachostomus 193
mixtus, Picoides 258
mlokosiewiczi, Tetrao 94
Mniotilta 575
moabiticus, Passer 612
mocinno, Pharomachrus 222
modesta, Aidemosyne 608
modesta, Galerida 348
modesta, Pachycephala 492
modesta, Progne 350
modesta, Psittacella 158
modesta, Thripophaga 282
modesta, Turacoena 141
modesta, Zosterops 524
modestus, Charadrius 125
modestus, Larus 129
modestus, Ramsayornis 534
modestus, Sublegatus 335
modestus, Sylviparus 503
modestus, Thryothorus 386
modestus, Vireo 586
modularis, Prunella 392
Modulatrix 397
moesta, Amaurospiza 549
moesta, Cenanthe 404
moesta, Synallaxis 279
Moho 534
Mohoua 470
molinae, Pyrrhura 166
molitor, Batis 480
molleri, Prinia 454
mollis, Pterodroma 56
mollissima, Chamaeza 301
mollissima, Somateria 74
mollissima, Zoothera 407
Molothrus 593
molucca, Lonchura 608
molucca, Threskiornis 67
moluccensis, Cacatua 157
moluccensis, Falco 89
moluccensis, Philemon 532
moluccensis, Picoides 255
moluccensis, Pitta 340
momota, Momotus 233
momotula, Hylomanes 232
Momotus 233
monacha, Grus 111
monacha, Halcyon 231
monacha, Oenanthe 404
monacha, Oriolus 625

monacha, Ptilinopus 150
Monachella 477
monachus, Aegypius 78
monachus, Artamus 628
monachus, Centropus 179
monachus, Myiopsitta 167
monachus, Necrosyrtes 78
Monarcha 485
Monasa 241
mondetoura, Claravis 143
monedula, Corvus 639
moneduloides, Corvus 639
mongolica, Melanocorypha 346
mongolica, Rhodopechys 599
mongolus, Charadrius 125
Monias 110
monileger, Ficedula 472
monileger, Garrulax 427
moniliger, Batrachostomus 193
monocerata, Cerorhinca 134
monogrammicus, Kaupifalco 83
monorhis, Oceanodroma 59
monorthonyx, Anurophasis 100
montagnii, Penelope 92
montana, Agriornis 313
montana, Brachypteryx 393
montana, Buthraupis 566
montana, Coracina 360
montana, Dryocichloides 397
montana, Geotrygon 145
montana, Lonchura 610
montana, Meliphaga 528
montana, Xenoligea 579
montana, Zosterops 520
montanella, Prunella 392
montani, Anthracoceros 238
montanus, Cercococcyx 173
montanus, Charadrius 125
montanus, Dicrurus 627
montanus, Oreoscoptes 391
montanus, Parus 499
montanus, Passer 612
montanus, Peltops 477
montanus, Pomatorhinus 419
montanus, Prioriturus 159
montanus, Pycnonotus 368
monteiri, Clytospiza 603
monteiri, Tockus 236
montezuma, Psarocolius 588
montezumae, Cyrtonyx 98
Monticola 405
monticola, Lichmera 526
monticola, Lonchura 610
monticola, Cenanthe 404
monticola, Zoothera 407
monticolum, Dicaeum 510
monticolus, Caprimulgus 198
monticolus, Parus 501
Montifringilla 613
montifringilla, Fringilla 594
montis, Seicercus 448
montium, Paramythia 510
montivagus, Aeronautes 202
moquini, Haematopus 121
moreaui, Apalis 457

moreaui, Nectarinia 516
moreirae, Schizoeaca 278
morenoi, Metriopelia 143
morinellus, Eudromias 126
morio, Coracina 361
morio, Onychognathus 620
morio, Psilorhinus 636
Morococcyx 177
morphnoides, Hieraeatus 86
Morphnus 85
morphoeus, Monasa 241
morrisonia, Alcippe 433
morrisoniana, Actinodura 432
mortierii, Gallinula 117
Morus 60
moschata, Cairina 71
mosquera, Eriocnemis 217
mosquitus, Chrysolampis 208
Motacilla 354
motacilla, Seiurus 578
motitensis, Passer 612
motmot, Ortalis 92
mouki, Gerygone 465
Moupinia 425
mouroniensis, Zosterops 524
moussieri, Phoenicurus 399
mozambicus, Serinus 595
muelleri, Certhiaxis 281
muelleri, Heleia 525
muelleri, Merops 233
muelleriana, Monachella 477
mufumbiri, Laniarius 377
mugimaki, Ficedula 472
mullerii, Ducula 153
Mulleripicus 268
mulsant, Acestrura 221
multicolor, Petroica 477
multicolor, Saltatricula 555
multicolor, Telophorus 378
multicolor, Todus 232
multistriata, Charmosyna 155
multistriatus, Thamnophilus 290
munda, Serpophaga 333
mundus, Monarcha 486
mupinensis, Turdus 412
muraria, Tichodroma 504
murina, Acanthiza 467
murina, Crateroscelis 469
murina, Notiochelidon 350
murina, Phaiomyias 335
murina, Xolmis 314
murinus, Thamnophilus 291
murphyi, Zosterops 522
Muscicapa 475
Muscicapella 475
muscicapinus, Hylophilus 587
Muscigralla 314
Muscipipra 317
Muscisaxicola 314
Muscivora 317
musculus, Anthoscopus 498
musica, Euphonia 568
musicus, Bias 480
Musophaga 171
musschenbroekii, Neopsittacus 156

677

mustelina, Certhiaxis 281
mustelina, Hylocichla 409
mutata, Terpsiphone 482
muticus, Pavo 109
muttui, Muscicapa 475
mutus, Lagopus 94
Myadestes 400
Mycteria 67
mycteria, Jabiru 67
Myiagra 487
Myiarchus 320
Myiobius 324
Myioborus 579
Myioceyx 226
Myiodynastes 319
Myiopagis 334
Myioparus 476
Myiophobus 325
Myiophoneus 405
Myiopornis 476
Myiopsitta 167
myioptilus Schoutedenapus 201
Myiornis 330
Myiotheretes 314
Myiotriccus 325
Myiozetetes 319
Myiornis 305
Myospiza 541
myotherinus, Myrmoborus 297
myristicivora, Ducula 152
Myrmeciza 298
Myrmecocichla 403
Myrmia 221
Myrmoborus 297
Myrmochanes 298
Myrmorchilus 295
Myrmornis 302
Myrmothera 303
Myrmotherula 293
Myrtis 221
mysolensis, Aplonis 619
mysorensis, Zosterops 521
mystacalis, Aethopyga 519
mystacalis, Aimophila 542
mystacalis, Cyanocorax 635
mystacalis, Eurostopodus 195
mystacalis, Malacoptila 240
mystacalis, Rhabdornis 506
mystacea, Aplonis 620
mystacea, Geotrygon 145
mystacea, Hemiprocne 204
mystacea, Sylvia 444
mystaceus, Platyrinchus 326
mystacophanos, Megalaima 243
Mystacornis 435
Myza 533
Myzomela 526
Myzornis 435

nabouroup, Onychognathus 620
nacunda, Podager 194
naevia, Coracias 234
naevia, Hylophylax 300
naevia, Locustella 440
naevia, Mirafa 343

naevia, Sclateria 298
naevia, Tapera 177
naevia, Zoothera 406
naevioides, Hylophylax 300
naevius, Ramphodon 204
naevosa, Stictonetta 70
nahani, Francolinus 103
naina, Ptilinopus 151
namaqua, Pterocles 135
namaquus, Dendropicos 255
Namibornis 394
nana, Acanthiza 467
nana, Aratinga 165
nana, Cisticola 452
nana, Cyanolyca 635
nana, Grallaricula 304
nana, Ichthyophaga 78
nana, Lesbia 218
nana, Lonchura 608
nana, Sylvia 444
nana, Turnix 110
Nandayus 166
Nannopsittaca 168
Nannopterum 62
nanus, Accipiter 80
nanus, Spizaetus 87
nanus, Taoniscus 53
nanus, Vireo 586
napensis, Stigmatura 332
Napothera 420
narcissina, Ficedula 472
narcondami, Aceros 238
riarina, Apaloderma 224
Nasica 271
nasicus, Corvus 640
nasutus, Tockus 236
natalensis, Caprimulgus 197
natalensis, Chloropeta 443
natalensis, Cisticola 451
natalensis, Cossypha 396
natalensis, Francolinus 101
natalis, Zosterops 522
nationi, Atlapetes 553
nativitatis, Puffinus 58
nattereri, Anthus 358
nattereri, Phaethornis 206
nattereri, Pipra 312
nattereri, Selenidera 249
nattererii, Cotinga 309
naumanni, Falco 88
naumanni, Turdus 412
ndussumensis, Criniger 371
Neafrapus 201
nebouxii, Sula 60
nebularia, Tringa 126
nebulosa, Rhipidura 490
nebulosa, Strix 191
nebulosus, Picumnus 251
necopinus, Xiphorhynchus 273
Necrosyrtes 78
Nectarinia 512
nectarinioides, Nectarinia 517
neergaardi, Nectarinia 516
neglecta, Pterodroma 56
neglecta, Sturnella 592

neglectus, Anthrepes 511
neglectus, Phalacrocorax 61
neglectus, Phylloscopus 445
nehrkorni, Dicaeum 509
nehrkorni, Neolesbia 210
nelicourvi, Ploceus 616
nelsoni, Geothlypis 578
nelsoni, Vireo 586
nematura, Lochmias 284
nemoricola, Gallinago 127
nemoricola, Leucosticte 598
Nemosia 562
nenday, Nandayus 166
nengeta, Fluvicola 317
Neochelidon 350
Neochen 70
Neochmia 607
Neocichla 621
Neocossyphus 401
Neoctantes 292
Neodrepanis 341
Neolalage 484
Neolesbia 210
Neolestes 373
Neomixis 422
Neomorphus 178
Neopelma 311
Neophema 162
Neophron 78
Neopipo 311
Neopsittacus 156
Neositta 504
Neospiza 596
Neothraupis 559
Neotis 119
neoxenus, Euptilotis 222
Neoxolmis 314
Nephoecetes 199
nereis, Garrodia 58
nereis, Sterna 132
Nesasio 192
Nesillas 443
nesiotis, Gallinula 117
Nesocharis 603
Nesocichla 408
Nesoctites 252
Nesofregetta 58
Nesomimus 390
Nesopsar 590
Nesospingus 559
Nesospiza 545
Nesotriccus 322
Nestor 157
Netta 73
Nettapus 71
neumanni, Hemitesia 461
neumayer, Sitta 504
nevermanni, Lonchura 609
newtoni, Acrocephalus 442
newtoni, Coracina 360
newtoni, Falco 89
newtoni, Lanius 381
Newtonia 476
newtoniana, Prionodura 630
newtonii, Nectarinia 513

niansae, Apus 203
nicaraguensis, Quiscalus 593
Nicator 379
nicefori, Thryothorus 386
nicobarica, Caloenas 145
nicobariensis, Hypsipetes 373
nicolli, Ploceus 616
nidipendulum, Idioptilon 329
nieuwenhuisii, Pycnonotus 367
niger, Capito 241
niger, Certhionyx 528
niger, Copsychus 399
niger, Halietor 62
niger, Neoctantes 292
niger, Nephoecetes 199
niger, Pachyramphus 309
niger, Parus 500
niger, Phasidus 109
niger, Quiscalus 593
niger, Rynchops 133
niger, Threnetes 204
nigerrimus, Knipolegus 316
nigerrimus, Nesopsar 590
nigerrimus, Ploceus 615
nigra, Astrapia 632
nigra, Chlidonias 131
nigra, Ciconia 67
nigra, Coracopsis 162
nigra, Lalage 362
nigra, Melanitta 74
nigra, Melanocharis 506
nigra, Melanoperdix 103
nigra, Melopyrrha 549
nigra, Myrmecocichla 403
nigra, Penelopina 93
nigra, Phylidonyris 534
nigra, Pomarea 484
nigrescens, Caprimulgus 196
nigrescens, Cercomacra 296
nigrescens, Contopus 322
nigrescens, Dendroica 577
nigrescens, Pitohui 496
nigrescens, Rheinartia 109
nigrescens, Turdus 412
nigricans, Cercomacra 296
nigricans, Petrochelidon 353
nigricans, Pinarocorys 343
nigricans, Pycnonotus 366
nigricans, Rallus 113
nigricans, Sayornis 316
nigricans, Serpophaga 333
nigricapillus, Formicarius 301
nigricapillus, Lioptilus 433
nigricapillus, Thryothorus 386
nigriceps, Apalis 456
nigriceps, Choriotis 119
nigriceps, Eremopterix 344
nigriceps, Orthotomus 458
nigriceps, Ploceus 615
nigriceps, Polioptila 437
nigriceps, Serinus 594
nigriceps, Stachyris 423
nigriceps, Thamnophilus 290
nigriceps, Todirostrum 328
nigriceps, Turdus 412

nigriceps, Veniliornis 260
nigricincta, Aphelopcephala 467
nigricollis, Anthracothorax 207
nigricollis, Busarellus 84
nigricollis, Grus 111
nigricollis, Phoenicircus 306
nigricollis, Ploceus 614
nigricollis, Podiceps 55
nigricollis, Sporophila 547
nigricollis, Stachyris 423
nigricollis, Sturnus 622
nigricollis, Turnix 111
nigrifrons, Monasa 241
nigrifrons, Phylloscartes 331
nigrifrons, Telophorus 378
nigrigenis, Agapornis 163
nigrilore, Dicaeum 508
nigriloris, Estrilda 606
nigrimenta, Yuhina 435
nigrimentum, Ploceus 614
nigripectus, Machaerirhynchus 484
nigripennis, Gallinago 127
nigripennis, Oriolus 625
nigripennis, Pterodroma 56
nigripes,,Dacnis 572
nigripes, Diomeda 55
nigrirostris, Andigena 249
nigrirostris, Columba 138
nigrirostris, Cyclarhis 585
nigrirostris, Macropygia 140
nigrirostris, Phaethornis 205
Nigrita 602
nigrita, Hirundo 352
nigrita, Myzomela 527
nigriventris, Eupherusa 213
nigrivestris, Eriocnemis 217
nigrobrunnea, Tyto 181
nigrocapillus, Nothocercus 50
nigrocapillus, Tyranniscus 336
nigrocincta, Tangara 572
nigrocinereus, Thamnophilus 290
nigrocinnamomea, Rhipidura 488
nigrocristatus, Basileuterus 580
nigrocyanea, Halcyon 229
nigrofumosus, Cinclodes 277
nigrogularis, Clytorhynchus 485
nigrogularis, Colinus 97
nigrogularis, Cracticus 629
nigrogularis, Icterus 589
nigrogularis, Phalacrocorax 61
nigrogularis, Psophodes 414
nigrogularis, Ramphocelos 565
nigrolineata, Ciccaba 190
nigrolutea, Aegithina 374
nigromaculata, Phlegopsis 300
nigromitratus, Trochocercus 482
nigropectus, Biatas 290
nigropectus Eulacestoma 491
nigropunctatus, Picumnus 251
nigrorufa, Crateroscelis 470
nigrorufa, Ficedula 473
nigrorufa, Hirundo 352

nigrorufa, Poospiza 545
nigrorufa, Sporophila 548
nigrorufus, Centropus 179
nigrorum, Stachyris 423
nigrorum, Zosterops 520
nigroventris, Euplectes 618
nigroviridis, Sericornis 469
nigroviridis, Tangara 572
Nilaus 376
nilghiriensis, Anthus 357
nilotica, Gelochelidon 131
Niltava 473
Ninox 188
nipalensis, Aceros 237
nipalensis, Actinodura 431
nipalensis, Aethopyga 518
nipalensis, Alcippe 433
nipalensis, Bubo 185
nipalensis, Carpodacus 599
nipalensis, Certhia 505
nipalensis, Cutia 431
nipalensis, Delichon 354
nipalensis, Paradoxornis 436
nipalensis, Pitta 338
nipalensis, Pyrrhula 601
nipalensis, Spizaetus 86
nipalensis, Turdoides 425
nippon, Nipponia 68
Nipponia 68
nisoria, Sylvia 443
nisus, Accipiter 81
nitens, Lamprotornis 621
nitens, Malimbus 617
nitens, Phainopepla 382
nitens, Psalidoprocne 354
nitens, Trochocercus 482
nitida, Asturina 84
nitidissima, Chlorochrysa 570
nitidula, Lagonosticta 604
nitidula, Mandingoa 603
nitidum, Dicaeum 509
nitidus, Carpodectes 309
nitidus, Cyanerpes 573
nitidus, Phylloscopus 446
nivalis, Montifringilla 613
nivalis, Plectrophenax 538
nivea, Pagodroma 56
niveicapilla, Cossypha 397
niveigularis, Tyrannus 318
niveoguttatus, Hypargos 604
nivosa, Campethera 254
njombe, Cisticola 452
noanamae, Bucco 240
nobilis, Ara 165
nobilis, Chamaeza 301
nobilis, Francolinus 101
nobilis, Gallinago 128
nobilis, Oreonympha 219
nobilis, Otidiphaps 146
noctis, Loxigilla 549
noctivagus, Crypturellus 51
noctua, Athene 189
noguchii, Sapheopipo 267
Nonnula 241
nonnula, Estrilda 606

680

nordamanni, Glareola 123
notabilis, Anisognathus 567
notabilis, Lichmera 526
notabilis, Nestor 157
notabilis, Phylidonyris 534
notata, Campethera 254
notata, Carduelis 597
notata, Coturnicops 116
notata, Meliphaga 529
notata, Nectarinia 517
notatus, Chlorestes 208
notatus, Elanus 77
Notharchus 239
Nothocercus 50
Nothocrax 93
Nothoprocta 52
Nothura 52
Notiochelidon 350
Notiomystis 531
notosticta, Aimophila 543
nouhuysi, Melidectes 533
nouhuysi, Sericornis 468
novacapitalis, Scytalopus 306
novaeguineae, Dacelo 228
novaeguineae, Harpyopsis 85
novaeguineae, Mearnsia 201
novaeguineae, Philemon 532
novaeguineae, Toxorhamphus 525
novaeguineae, Zosterops 521
novaehollandiae, Accipiter 82
novaehollandiae, Anhinga 62
novaehollandiae, Ardea 66
novaehollandiae, Cereopsis 70
novaehollandiae, Coracina 358
novaehollandiae, Dromaius 49
novaehollandiae, Larus 130
novaehollandiae, Phylidonyris 534
novaehollandiae, Recurvirostra 122
novaehollandiae, Scythrops 175
novaehollandiae, Tachybaptus 54
novaehollandiae, Tyto 181
novaeseelandiae, Anthus 356
novaeseelandiae, Aythya 73
novaeseelandiae, Charadrius 125
novaeseelandiae, Finschia 470
novaeseelandiae, Hemiphaga 153
novaeseelandiae, Ninox 188
novaeseelandiae, Prosthemadera 535
novaeseelandiae, Falco 89
novaezelandiae, Cyanoramphus 161
novaezelandiae, Himantopus 121
noveboracensis, Coturnicops 116
noveboracensis, Seiurus 577
nuba, Neotis 119
nubica, Campethera 253

nubicus, Caprimulgus 197
nubicus, Lanius 381
nubicus, Merops 234
nuchalis, Campylorhynchus 383
nuchalis, Chlamydera 630
nuchalis, Garrulax 428
nuchalis, Glareola 123
nuchalis, Grallaria 302
nuchalis, Parus 501
nuchalis, Sphyrapicus 253
Nucifraga 639
nudiceps, Gymnocichla 298
nudicollis, Procnias 310
nudigenis, Turdus 413
nudigula, Pachycephala 494
nudipes, Otus 184
nuditarsus, Collocalia 200
nugator, Myiarchus 320
Numenius 126
Numida 109
nuttalli, Pica 638
nuttallii, Phalaenoptilus 195
nuttallii, Picoides 259
Nuttallornis 322
nuttingi, Myiarchus 320
Nyctea 186
nycthemera, Lophura 107
Nyctibius 193
Nycticorax 64
nycticorax, Nycticorax 64
Nycticryphes 121
Nyctidromus 195
Nyctiphrynus 195
Nyctiprogne 194
Nyctiornis 233
nympha, Tanysiptera 232
Nymphicus 157
nyroca, Aythya 73
Nystalus 240

oatesi, Pitta 339
obbiensis, Spizocorys 347
oberholseri, Empidonax 323
oberi, Icterus 590
oberi, Myiarchus 320
oberlaendari, Zoothera 406
obscura, Elaenia 334
obscura, Manorina 535
obscura, Meliphaga 530
obscura, Myrmotherula 293
obscura, Myzomela 526
obscura, Penelope 92
obscura, Pluvialis 124
obscura, Psalidoprocne 354
obscura, Sporophila 547
obscurus, Dendragapus 93
obscurus, Erithacus 395
obscurus, Hemignathus 584
obscurus, Myadestes 400
obscurus, Phaeornis 408
obscurus, Tetraophasis 99
obscurus, Turdus 412
obsoleta, Certhiaxis 281
obsoleta, Hirundo 351
obsoleta, Rhodopechys 599

obsoletum, Camptostoma 335
obsoletus, Crypturellus 51
obsoletus, Hemitriccus 331
obsoletus, Picoides 256
obsoletus, Salpinctes 383
obsoletus, Turdus 413
obsoletus, Xiphorhynchus 273
ocai, Pipilo 551
occidentalis, Aechmophorus 55
occidentalis, Catharus 408
occidentalis, Charadrius 125
occidentalis, Dendroica 577
occidentalis, Geopsittacus 162
occidentalis, Larus 130
occidentalis, Leucopternis 83
occidentalis, Pelecanus 60
occidentalis, Strix 191
occidentalis, Thamnomanes 293
occipitalis, Aegypius 78
occipitalis, Chlorophonia 569
occipitalis, Dendrocitta 638
occipitalis, Lophaetus 86
occipitalis, Phylloscopus 446
occipitalis, Podiceps 55
occipitalis, Ptilinopus 149
occipitalis, Yuhina 435
oceanica, Ducula 152
oceanica, Myiagra 487
oceanicus, Oceanites 58
Oceanites 58
Oceanodroma 59
ocellata, Agriocharis 93
ocellata, Leipoa 91
ocellata, Rheinartia 109
ocellata, Strix 190
ocellata, Turnix 111
ocellatum, Toxostoma 391
ocellatus, Cyrtonyx 98
ocellatus, Garrulax 429
ocellatus, Nyctiphrynus 195
ocellatus, Podargus 192
ocellatus, Xiphorhynchus 273
ochotensis, Locustella 440
ochracea, Sasia 252
ochraceiceps, Hylophilus 587
ochraceiceps, Pomatorhinus 419
ochraceiventris, Leptotila 144
ochraceiventris, Myiophobus 325
ochraceus, Contopus 323
ochraceus, Criniger 371
ochrocephala, Amazona 170
ochrocephala, Mohoua 470
ochrogaster, Penelope 92
ochrolaemus, Automolus 286
ochroleucus, Hylopezus 303
ochromalus, Eurylaimus 269
ochromelas, Melidectes 533
ochropectus, Francolinus 100
ochropus, Tringa 126
ochropyga, Drymophila 296
ochruros, Phoenicurus 399
Ochthoeca 315
Ochthornis 317

Ocista, Collocalia 200
ocreata, Fraseria 471
Ocreatus 218
octosetaceus, Mergus 74
ocularis, Glareola 123
ocularis, Ploceus 614
ocularis, Prunella 392
oculata, Emblema 607
oculea, Caloperdix 105
oculeus, Canirallus 112
Oculocincta 525
Ocyphaps 141
odiosa, Ninox 189
Odontophorus 97
Odontorchilus 383
oedicnemus, Burhinus 122
Oedistoma 525
oemodium, Conostoma 435
Oena 141
Oenanthe 403
oenanthe, Oenanthe 404
oenanthoides, Oethoeca 315
oenas, Columba 136
oenone, Chrysuronia 211
oenops, Columba 137
oglei, Stachyris 423
Ognorhynchus 166
olax, Treron 146
oleaginea, Pipromorpha 338
oleaginea, Psalidoprocne 354
oleaginea, Rukia 524
oleaginus, Mitrospingus 562
olivacea, Carduelis 597
olivacea, Certhidea 550
olivacea, Chlorothraupis 562
olivacea, Gerygone 465
olivacea, Lampribis 68
olivacea, Nectarinia 512
olivacea, Pachycephala 492
olivacea, Piranga 565
olivacea, Rhinomyias 471
olivacea, Stactolaema 244
olivacea, Tiaris 549
olivacea, Zosterops 524
olivaceiceps, Ploceus 516
olivaceofuscus, Turdus 409
olivaceum, Chalcostigma 219
olivaceum, Oncostoma 329
olivaceus, Amaurornis 117
olivaceus, Criniger 371
olivaceus, Geocolaptes 254
olivaceus, Linurgus 596
olivaceus, Mionectes 337
olivaceus, Phalacrocorax 61
olivaceus, Phylloscopus 447
olivaceus, Picumnus 250
olivaceus, Prionochilus 507
olivaceus, Psophodes 414
olivaceus, Rhynchocyclus 327
olivaceus, Telophorus 378
olivaceus, Turdus 409
olivaceus, Vireo 586
olivascens, Muscicapa 475
olivascens, Sicalis 546
olivater, Turdus 413

olivea, Tesia 438
olivetorum, Hippolais 443
oliviae, Columba 136
olivieri, Porzana 116
olivinus, Cercococcyx 173
olor, Cygnus 69
omeiensis, Liocichla 430
omissa, Foudia 617
Oncostoma 329
onocrotalus, Pelecanus 60
Onychognathus 620
Onychorhynchus 326
oorti, Megalaima 243
opaca, Aplonis 619
Ophrysia 106
ophthalmica, Cacatua 157
ophthalmicus, Chlorospingus
    559
ophthalmicus, Pogonotriccus
    331
opistherythra, Rhipidura 488
Opisthocomus 110
opisthomelas, Puffinus 58
Opisthoprora 219
Opopsitta 158
orbignyianus, Thinocorus 129
orbitalis, Pogonotriccus 331
orbitatum, Idioptilon 330
orbygnesius, Bolborhynchus
    167
Orchesticus 559
ordii, Notharchus 239
oreas, Picathartes 436
orenocensis, Knipolegus 316
orenocensis, Saltator 557
oreobates, Merops 233
Oreocharis 510
Oreoica 491
Oreomanes 573
Oreonympha 219
Oreophasis 93
oreophila, Catamenia 549
oreophilus, Buteo 85
Oreopsar 592
Oreopsittacus 156
Oreornis 530
Oreortyx 96
Oreoscoptes 391
Oreostruthus 607
Oreothraupis 555
Oreotriccus 337
Oreotrochilus 215
oreskios, Harpactes 224
orientalis, Acrocephalus 441
orientalis, Anthreptes 511
orientalis, Arborophila 105
orientalis, Batis 480
orientalis, Collocalia 200
orientalis, Eurystomus 235
orientalis, Meliphaga 528
orientalis, Merops 234
orientalis, Pterocles 135
orientalis, Streptopelia 138
orientalis, Vidua 610
Origma 470

orina, Coeligena 216
orinus, Acrocephalus 441
Oriolia 381
Oriolus 624
oriolus, Oriolus 624
oritis, Nectarinia 513
Oriturus 543
orix, Euplectes 618
ornata, Lophornis 208
ornata, Meliphaga 529
ornata, Myrmotherula 294
ornata, Nothoprocta 52
ornata, Poospiza 545
ornata, Thlypopsis 561
ornata, Thraupis 566
ornata, Urocissa 637
ornatus, Calcarius 538
ornatus, Cephalopterus 310
ornatus, Lamprotornis 621
ornatus, Merops 234
ornatus, Myioborus 580
ornatus, Myiotriccus 325
ornatus, Pardalotus 510
ornatus, Ptilinopus 149
ornatus, Spizaetus 87
ornatus, Trichoglossus 154
Ornithion 337
Oroaetus 87
orostruthus, Phyllastrephus 370
orpheus, Pachycephala 493
orrhophaeus, Harpactes 224
orru, Corvus 640
Ortalis 91
Orthogonys 562
Orthonyx 414
orthonyx, Acropternis 306
Orthorhyncus 208
Orthotomus 458
ortizi, Incaspiza 545
ortoni, Penelope 92
Ortygocichla 463
Ortygospiza 606
Ortyxelos 111
oryzivora, Padda 610
oryzivora, Scaphidura 594
oryzivorus, Dolichonyx 594
Oryzoborus 548
osburni, Vireo 586
oscillans, Rhinomyias 471
oscitans, Anastomus 67
osculans, Misocalius 174
osea, Nectarinia 516
oseryi, Psarocolius 588
osgoodi, Tinamus 50
ossifragus, Corvus 640
ostralegus, Haematopus 121
ostrinus, Pyrenestes 603
Otidiphaps 146
Otis 119
Otophanes 195
ottonis, Thripophaga 282
Otus 181
otus, Asio 191
oustaleti, Cinclodes 277
oustaleti, Nectarinia 515

682   *oustaleti, Phylloscartes* 331
ovampensis, Accipiter 80
owenii, Apteryx 50
owstoni, Rallus 114
oxycerca, Cercibis 68
Oxylabes 435
Oxypogon 219
Oxyruncus 338
Oxyura 74
oxyura, Treron 148

pabsti, Cinclodes 277
Pachycare 491
Pachycephala 492
pachycephaloides, Clytorhyn-
   chus 484
Pachycephalopsis 480
Pachycoccyx 172
Pachyptila 57
Pachyramphus 308
pachyrhyncha, Rhynchopsitta
   166
pachyrhynchus, Eudyptes 53
pacifica, Ardea 66
pacifica, Ducula 152
pacifica, Gallinula 117
pacifica, Gavia 54
pacificus, Apus 203
pacificus, Gabianus 129
pacificus, Puffinus 57
Padda 610
paena, Erythropygia 393
pagodarum, Sturnus 622
Pagodroma 56
Pagophila 129
palauensis, Rukia 524
palawanense, Malacopteron 418
palawanensis, Chloropsis 374
palawanensis, Hypsipetes 372
pallasi, Emberiza 537
pallasii, Cinclus 382
pallatangae, Elaenia 334
pallens, Vireo 585
pallescens, Neopelma 311
palliata, Falculea 381
palliatus, Cinclodes 277
palliatus, Garrulax 427
palliatus, Thamnophilus 290
pallida, Certhiaxis 281
pallida, Hippolais 443
pallida, Leptotila 144
pallida, Lonchura 609
pallida, Spizella 542
pallida, Zosterops 523
pallidiceps, Atlapetes 554
pallidiceps, Columbia 137
pallidigaster, Anthreptes 512
pallidinucha, Atlapetes 553
pallidipes, Cettia 438
pallidirostris, Tockus 236
pallidiventris, Anthus 357
pallidus, Apus 203
pallidus, Bradornis 470
pallidus, Camarhynchus 550
pallidus, Criniger 371

pallidus, Cuculus 173
pallidus, Turdus 412
pallipes, Niltava 474
palliseri, Bradypterus 440
palmeri, Phaeornis 408
palmeri, Tangara 570
Palmeria 584
palmarum, Charmosyna 155
palmarum, Corvus 640
palmarum, Dendroica 577
palmarum, Phoenicophilus 562
palmarum, Thraupis 566
palpebrata, Phoebetria 55
palpebrosa, Gerygone 465
palpebrosa, Zosterops 520
paludicola, Acrocephalus 441
paludicola, Estrilda 605
paludicola, Riparia 351
palumboides, Columba 136
palumbus, Columba 136
palustre, Pellorneum 416
palustris, Acrocephalus 441
palustris, Cistothorus 384
palustris, Megalurus 462
palustris, Microligea 579
palustris, Parus 498
palustris, Sporophila 548
pamela, Aglaeactis 216
pammelaina, Melaeornis 471
panamensis, Malacoptila 240
panamensis, Myiarchus 320
panamensis, Scytalopus 306
panayensis, Aplonis 619
panayensis, Coracina 361
panayensis, Eumyias 476
panderi, Podoces 638
Pandion 75
panini, Penelopides 237
Panterpe 210
Panurus 435
panychlora, Nannopsittaca 168
Panyptila 202
papa, Sarcoramphus 75
Paphosia 208
papillosa, Pseudibis 67
papou, Charmosyna 156
papua, Pygoscelis 53
papuana, Erythrura 608
papuana, Microeca 477
papuensis, Archboldia 630
papuensis, Chaetorhynchus 626
papuensis, Collocalia 200
papuensis, Coracina 360
papuensis, Eurostopodus 195
papuensis, Neositta 505
papuensis, Podargus 192
papuensis, Sericornis 469
Parabuteo 84
Paradigalla 632
Paradisaea 633
paradisaea, Sterna 131
paradisaea, Vidua 610
paradisea, Anthropoides 111
paradiseus, Dicrurus 628
paradiseus, Ptiloris 631

paradisi, Terpsiphone 482
paradoxa, Anthochaera 535
paradoxa, Eugralla 305
Paradoxornis 435
paradoxus, Paradoxornis 435
paradoxus, Syrrhaptes 134
paraguaiae, Gallinago 127
Paramythia 510
parasiticus, Stercorarius 129
Pardalotus 510
pardalotus, Xiphorhynchus 273
parellina, Cyanocompsa 558
parens, Vitia 463
pareola, Chiroxiphia 312
pariae, Myioborus 579
parina, Xenodacnis 573
Parisoma 461
parisorum, Icterus 590
parkinsoni, Procellaria 57
Parmoptila 602
parnaguae, Megaxenops 289
Paroaria 555
parodii, Hemispingus 560
Parophasma 434
Parotia 632
Parula 575
parulus, Anairetes 332
Parus 498
parva, Conopias 319
parva, Ficedula 472
parva, Loxops 584
parva, Microdynamis 174
parva, Porzana 117
parvirostris, Chlorospingus 560
parvirostris, Coloramphus 333
parvirostris, Crypturellus 52
parvirostris, Elaenia 334
parvirostris, Tetrao 95
parvula, Coracina 360
parvulus, Anthoscopus 498
parvulus, Camarhynchus 550
parvulus, Caprimulgus 196
parvus, Cypsiurus 203
parzudakii, Tangara 570
Passer 611
Passerculus 540
Passerella 538
Passerina 558
passerina, Columbina 142
passerina, Mirafa 341
passerina, Spizella 542
passerinii, Ramphocelus 565
passerinum, Glaucidium 186
passerinus, Forpus 168
passerinus, Veniliornis 260
pastazae, Galbula 239
patachonicus, Tachyeres 71
patagonica, Aptenodytes 53
patagonica, Thripophaga 282
Patagona 216
patagonicus, Cinclodes 277
patagonicus, Mimus 390
patagonicus, Phrygilus 544
patagonus, Cyanoliseus 166
paulistus, Phylloscartes 331

pauper, Camarhynchus 550
pauxi, Crax 93
Pavo 190
pavonina, Balearica 111
pavonina, Lophornis 208
pavoninus, Dromococcyx 177
pavoninus, Pharomachrus 222
paykullii, Rallina 115
pealii, Erythrura 608
pectardens, Erithacus 395
pectorale, Dicaeum 509
pectoralis, Aphelocephala 467
pectoralis, Caprimulgus 197
pectoralis, Cissomela 534
pectoralis, Coracina 360
pectoralis, Coturnix 103
pectoralis, Erithacus 395
pectoralis, Euphonia 569
pectoralis, Garrulax 427
pectoralis, Herpsilochmus 295
pectoralis, Hylophilus 587
pectoralis, Icterus 589
pectoralis, Lonchura 610
pectoralis, Notharchus 239
pectoralis, Pachycephala 493
pectoralis, Polystictus 332
pectoralis, Prinia 454
pectoralis, Rallus 114
pectoralis, Thlypopsis 561
pecuarius, Charadrius 125
Pedionomus 111
pekinensis, Rhopophilus 449
pelagica, Chaetura 202
pelagicus, Haliaeetus 78
pelagicus, Hydrobates 59
pelagicus, Phalacrocorax 61
Pelagodroma 58
Pelargopsis 227
Pelecanoides 59
Pelecanus 60
pelewensis, Ptilinopus 149
peli, Gymnobucco 244
peli, Scotopelia 186
pella, Topaza 215
Pellorneum 415
peltata, Platysteira 481
Peltohyas 126
Peltops 477
pelzelni, Aplonis 619
pelzelni, Elaenia 334
pelzelni, Granatellus 582
pelzelni, Myrmeciza 299
pelzelni, Ploceus 614
Pelzelni, Pseudotriccus 330
pelzelni, Tachybaptus 54
pembae, Nectarinia 516
pembaensis, Treron 148
penduliger, Cephalopterus 310
pendulinus, Remiz 498
Penelope 92
penelope, Anas 72
Penelopides 237
Penelopina 93
Peneoenanthe 479
Peneothello 479

penicillata, Eucometis 562
penicillata, Meliphaga 529
penicillatus, Phalacrocorax 61
penicillatus, Pycnonotus 367
pennata, Pterocnemia 49
pennatus, Hieraaetus 86
pensylvanica, Dendroica 576
Penthoceryx 173
pentlandii, Nothoprocta 52
pentlandii, Tinamotis 53
peposaca, Netta 73
peracensis, Alcippe 433
percnopterus, Neophron 78
Percnostola 298
percussus, Prionochilus 507
percussus, Xiphidiopicus 253
perdicaria, Nothoprocta 52
Perdicula 104
Perdix 103
perdix, Perdix 103
peregrina, Vermivora 575
peregrinus, Falco 90
Pericrocotus 363
Periporphyrus 557
Perisoreus 636
Perissocephalus 310
perkeo, Batis 480
perlata, Pyrrhura 166
perlata, Rhipidura 491
perlatum, Glaucidium 187
perlatus, Ptilinopus 149
Pernis 76
pernix, Myiotheretes 315
peronii, Charadrius 125
peronii, Zoothera 406
perousii, Ptilinopus 149
perreini, Estrilda 605
perrotti, Hylexetastes 271
personata, Agapornis 163
personata, Corythaixoides 171
personata, Heliopais 119
personata, Incaspiza 545
personata, Poephila 607
personata, Prosopeia 160
personata, Rhipidura 489
personata, Spizocorys 347
personatus, Artamus 628
personatus, Atlapetes 554
personatus, Coccothraustes 602
personatus, Pterocles 135
personatus, Trogon 223
personus, Turdus 413
perspicax, Penelope 92
perspicillata, Ducula 151
perspicillata, Hymenops 317
perspicillata, Melanitta 74
perspicillata, Pulsatrix 186
perspicillatum, Trichastoma 417
perspicillatus, Garrulax 427
perspicillatus, Hylopesuz 303
perspicillatus, Sericornis 469
perstriata, Ptiloprora 533
pertinax, Aratinga 166
pertinax, Contopus 322

peruana, Cinnycerthia 384
peruviana, Conopophaga 304
peruviana, Geositta 276
peruviana, Grallaricula 304
peruviana, Rupicola 310
peruviana, Sporophila 548
peruviana, Tangara 571
peruviana, Vini 155
perversa, Ninox 189
petechia, Dendroica 575
petiti, Campephaga 363
petiti, Psalidoprocne 354
Petrochelidon 353
Petroica 477
Petronia 613
petronia, Petronia 613
Petrophassa 141
petrophila, Neophema 162
petrosus, Ptilopachus 105
Peucedramus 582
Pezopetes 555
Pezoporus 162
Phacellodomus 283
Phaenicophaeus 177
Phaenicophilus 562
phaenicuroides, Hodgsonius 399
Phaenostictus 300
phaenocephalus, Criniger 371
phaenocephalus, Myiarchus 320
phaeocercus, Mitrephanes 324
Phaeochroa 206
phaeochromus, Oriolus 624
Phaeonotus, Junco 540
Phaeoprogne 350
phaeopus, Numenius 126
phaeopygia, Pterodroma 56
Phaeornis 408
phaeosoma, Melamprosops 584
Phaeotriccus 316
Phaethon 59
Phaethornis 205
phaeton, Neochmia 607
Phaetusa 131
Phainopepla 382
phainopeplus, Campylopterus 207
Phainoptila 382
Phaiomyias 335
phaionota, Pachycephala 492
Phalacrocorax 61
Phalaenoptilus 195
Phalaropus 127
Phalcoboenus 87
phalerata, Coeligena 216
Phapitreron 146
Phaps 141
pharetra, Dendroica 576
Pharomachrus 222
phasianela, Macropygia 140
phasianellus, Dromococcyx 177
phasianellus, Tympanuchus 95

684 phasianius, Centropus 179
Phasianus 108
Phasidus 109
phayrei, Pitta 338
Phedina 351
Phedinopsis 351
Phegornis 125
phelpsi, Cypseloides 199
Pheucticus 555
Phibalura 306
Phigys 155
philadelphia, Geothlypis 579
philadelphia, Larus 130
philadelphicus, Vireo 586
philbyi, Alectoris 99
Philemon 531
Philentoma 479
Philepitta 341
Philetairus 611
philippae, Sylvietta 461
philippensis, Loriculus 163
philippensis, Ninox 188
philippensis, Pelecanus 60
philippensis, Pseudoptynx 186
philippensis, Rallus 113
philippensis, Spizaetus 87
philippensis, Sturnus 622
philippii, Phaethornis 205
philippinensis, Pachycephala 492
philippinus, Hypsipetes 372
philippinus, Merops 234
philippinus, Ploceus 616
Philodice 220
Philomachus 129
philomelos, Turdus 412
Philortyx 96
Philydor 285
·Phimosus 68
Phlegopsis 300
Phleocryptes 283
Phlogophilus 215
Phodilus 181
phoebe, Metallura 218
phoebe, Sayornis 316
Phoebetria 55
phoenicea, Campephaga 363
phoenicea, Liocichla 430
phoenicea, Petroica 478
Phoenicercus 306
phoeniceus, Agelaius 591
phoeniceus, Pyrrhuloxia 556
phoenicius, Tachyphonus 564
phoenicobia, Tachornis 202
phoenicomitra, Myiophobus 325
Phoeniconaias 69
Phoenicoparrus 69
phoenicoptera, Pytilia 603
phoenicoptera, Treron 147
Phoenicopterus 68
phoenicotis, Chlorochrysa 569
Phoeniculus 235
phoenicura, Rhipidura 488
Phoenicurus 399

phoenicurus, Amaurornis 117
phoenicurus, Ammomanes 345
phoenicurus, Eremobius 283
phoenicurus, Phoenicurus 399
phoenicurus, Pseudattila 322
Pholidornis 610
Phonygammus 631
phryganophila, Schoeniophylax 278
phrygia, Xanthomyza 534
Phrygilus 544
Phylidonyris 534
Phyllanthus 434
Phyllastrephus 369
Phyllolais 457
Phyllomyias 336
Phylloscartes 331
Phylloscopus 444
Phytotoma 338
piaggiae, Zoothera 406
Piaya 175
Pica 638
pica, Fluvicola 317
pica, Pica 638
picaoides, Heterophasia 434
picata, Egretta 65
picata, Oenanthe 404
Picathartes 436
picatus, Hemipus 364
picazuro, Columba 137
picina, Mearnsia 201
pickeringii, Ducula 152
Picoides 255
picta, Chloephaga 70
picta, Conopophila 534
picta, Emblema 607
picta, Ispidina 226
picta, Oreortyx 96
picta, Psittacella 158
picta, Pyrrhura 167
picturata, Streptopelia 139
pictus, Calcarius 538
pictus, Chrysolophus 108
pictus, Francolinus 100
pictus, Myioborus 579
picui, Columbina 143
Piculus 261
Picumnus 250
picumnus, Climacteris 506
picumnus, Dendrocolaptes 272
Picus 265
picus, Xiphorhynchus 273
Piezorhina 545
pilaris, Atalotriccus 330
pilaris, Turdus 412
pileata, Halcyon 228
pileata, Leptasthenura 278
pileata, Nemosia 562
pileata, Notiochelidon 350
pileata, Oenanthe 404
pileata, Penelope 92
pileata, Pionopsitta 169
pileata, Timalia 425
pileatus, Atlapetes 553
pileatus, Chlorospingus 560

pileatus, Coryphospingus 555
pileatus, Dryocopus 264
pileatus, Herpsilochmus 295
pileatus, Lophotriccus 330
pileatus, Monarcha 485
pileatus, Pilherodius 64
pileatus, Piprites 311
Pilherodius 64
pinaiae, Lophozosterops 524
pinarocorys 343
Pinaroloxias 550
Pinarornis 394
Pinicola 600
pinicola, Zoothera 406
pinnatus, Botaurus 63
pinon, Ducula 152
pintadeanus, Francolinus 100
pinus, Carduelis 597
pinus, Dendroica 576
pinus, Vermivora 575
Pionites 169
Pionopsitta 169
Pionus 169
pipiens, Cisticola 453
pipile, Aburria 92
Pipilo 551
pipixcan, Larus 130
Pipra 312
pipra, Iodopleura 307
pipra, Pipra 313
Pipraeidea 568
Pipreola 307
Piprites 310
Pipromorpha 338
Piranga 564
pirit, Batis 480
piscator, Crinifer 171
pistrinaria, Ducula 152
pitangua, Megarhynchus 319
Pitangus 319
Pithecophaga 85
Pithys 299
pitiayumi, Parula 575
pitius, Colaptes 263
Pitohui 496
Pitta 338
Pittasoma 302
pittoides, Aterlornis 235
Pitylus 557
pityophila, Dendroica 577
Pityriasis 381
piurae, Ochthoeca 315
placens, Climacteris 506
placens, Poecilodryas 479
placentis, Charmosyna 1155
placidus, Charadrius 124
plancus, Polyborus 87
Platalea 68
platalea, Anas 73
platenae, Ficedula 473
platenae, Gallicolumba 145
plateni, Prionochilus 507
plateni, Rallus 113
plateni, Stachyris 422
platensis, Cistothorus 384

platensis, Embernagra 546
platensis, Leptasthenura 278
Platibis 68
platurus, Anthreptes 512
platurus, Prioniturus 159
Platycercus 161
platycercus, Selasphorus 221
Platycichla 409
Platylophus 633
platypterus, Buteo 84
platyrhynchos, Anas 72
platyrhynchos, Platyrinchus 326
platyrhynchum, Electron 232
Platyrinchus 326
platyrostris, Dendrocolaptes 273
Platysmurus 633
Platysteira 481
platyura, Schoenicola 462
plebejus, Phrygilus 544
plebejus, Turdoides 426
plebejus, Turdus 413
Plectorhyncha 534
Plectropterus 71
Plectrophenax 538
Plegadis 68
pleschanka, Oenanthe 404
pleskei, Locustella 440
pleskei, Podoces 638
pleurostictus, Thryothorus 386
plicatus, Aceros 237
Plocepasser 611
Ploceus 614
plumata, Prionops 375
plumbea, Columba 137
plumbea, Dendroica 576
plumbea, Euphonia 568
plumbea, Ictinia 77
plumbea, Leucopternis 83
plumbea, Polioptila 437
plumbea, Ptiloprora 532
plumbea, Sporophila 547
plumbeiceps, Leptotila 144
plumbeiceps, Oreotriccus 337
plumbeiceps, Todirostrum 328
plumbeiventris, Eulabeornis 112
plumbeus, Micrastur 87
plumbeus, Myioparus 476
plumbeus, Thamnomanes 293
plumbeus, Turdus 412
plumifera, Guttera 109
plumifera, Petrophassa 141
plumosus, Pinarornis 394
plumosus, Pycnonotus 367
plumula, Meliphaga 529
pluricinctus, Pteroglossus 249
pluto, Myiagra 487
Pluvialis 124
pluvialis, Piaya 175
Pluvianellus 126
Pluvianus 122
Pnoepyga 421
Podager 194
podargina, Pyrrhoglaux 184

Podargus 192
Podica 118
Podiceps 54
podiceps, Podilymbus 54
Podilymbus 54
podobe, Cercotrichas 394
Podoces 638
poecilocercus, Mecocerculus 333
poecilocercus, Phaeotriccus 316
poecilochrous, Buteo 85
Poecilodryas 479
poecilolaemus, Dendropicos 254
poecilonota, Hylophylax 300
poeciloptera, Geositta 276
poecilopterus, Rallus 113
poecilorhyncha, Anas 72
poecilorhynchus, Garrulax 429
poecilorrhoa, Cryptophaps, 153
poecilosterna, Mirafa 343
poecilotis, Moupinia 425
poecilotis, Pogonotriccus 331
Poecilotriccus 330
poecilurus, Knipolegus 316
poensis, Batis 481
poensis, Bubo 185
poensis, Neocossyphus 401
poensis, Phyllastrephus 370
Poeoptera 620
Poephila 607
Pogoniulus 244
Pogonocichla 394
Pogonotriccus 331
Poicephalus 162
poiciloptilus, Botaurus 63
poicilotis, Hylophilus 587
poioicephala, Alcippe 433
Polemaetus 87
Polihierax 88
poliocephala, Alethe 397
poliocephala, Chloephaga 70
poliocephala, Ducula 151
poliocephala, Geothlypis 578
poliocephala, Ortalis 91
poliocephala, Stachyris 423
poliocephalum, Todirostrum 328
poliocephalus, Accipiter 82
poliocephalus, Caprimulgus 197
poliocephalus, Cuculus 173
poliocephalus, Phaenicophilus 562
poliocephalus, Phyllastrephus 370
poliocephalus, Podiceps 54
poliocephalus, Tolmomyias 327
poliocephalus, Turdus 411
poliocerca, Eupherusa 213
poliogaster, Accipiter 83
poliogaster, Caryothraustes 556
poliogenys, Niltava 474
poliogenys, Seicercus 448

poliogenys, Spermophaga 603
Poliolais 458
poliolopha, Prionops 375
poliolophus, Batrachostomus 193
polionota, Leucopternis 83
poliopareia, Estrilda 605
poliophrys, Alethe 397
poliophrys, Synallaxis 278
poliopleura, Emberiza 537
polioptera, Coracina 362
polioptera, Dnyocichloides 397
poliopterus, Toxoramphus 525
Polioptila 437
poliosoma, Pachycephalopsis 480
poliothorax, Kakamega 418
polleni, Xenopirostris 381
pollenii, Columba 136
pollens, Campephilus 265
pollens, Coracina 359
Polyboroides 79
Polyborus 87
polychopterus, Pachyramphus 308
polychroa, Prinia 455
polyglotta, Hippolais 443
polyglottos, Mimus 390
polygramma, Meliphaga 530
Polyonymus 218
polyosoma, Buteo 85
Polyplancta 215
Polyplectron 108
Polysticta 74
Polystictus 332
Polytelis 160
Polytmus 211
polytmus, Trochilus 211
Pomarea 484
pomarina, Aquila 86
pomarinus, Stercorarius 129
Pomatorhinus 418
Pomatostomus 420
pompadora, Treron 147
pondicerianus, Francolinus 103
pondicerianus, Tephrodornis 365
Pooecetes 542
poortmani, Chlorostilbon 209
Poospiza 545
Popelairia 208
popelairii, Popelairia 208
porphyraceus, Ptilinopus 149
porphyrea, Ptilinopus 148
porphyreolophus, Tauraco 172
Porphyrio 118
porphyrio, Porphyrio 118
porphyrocephala, Glossopsitta 155
porphyrocephala, Iridosornis 567
Porphyrolaema 309
porphyrolaema, Apalis 456
porphyrolaema, Porphyrolaema 309

686 Porphyrospiza 558
portoricensis, Loxigilla 549
portoricensis, Melanerpes 252
Porzana 116
porzana, Porzana 117
praecox, Thamnophilus 290
prasina, Erythrura 607
prasina, Hylia 463
prasinus, Aulacorhynchus 248
pratensis, Anthus 357
pratincola, Glareola 123
preciosa, Tangara 571
presbytes, Phylloscopus 446
pretiosa, Claravis 143
pretrei, Amazona 170
pretrei, Phaethornis 206
preussi, Nectarinia 515
preussi, Petrochelidon 353
preussi, Ploceus 616
prevostii, Anthracothorax 207
prevostii, Euryceros 381
prigoginei, Chlorocichla 369
prigoginei, Phodilus 181
primigenius, Aethopyga 517
princei, Zoothera 407
princeps, Accipiter 82
princeps, Halcyon 231
princeps, Leucopternis 83
princeps, Melidectes 533
princeps, Ploceus 615
principalis, Campephilus 265
pringlii, Dryoscopus 376
Prinia 453
priocephalus, Pycnonotus 365
Prioniturus 159
Prionochilus 507
Prionodura 630
Prionops 375
Priotelus 222
pristoptera, Psalidoprocne 354
pritchardii, Megapodius 91
Probosciger 156
Procellaria 57
Procelsterna 133
procerus, Hemignathus 584
Procnias 310
procurvoides, Campylorhamphus
275
Prodotiscus 247
Progne 350
progne, Euplectes 618
promeropirhynchus, Xiphocolaptes 271
Promerops 535
propinqua, Synallaxis 279
propinquus, Hypsipetes 372
proprium, Dicaeum 508
proregulus, Phylloscopus 445
Prosobonia 127
Prosopeia 160
Prosthemadura 535
Protonotaria 578
provocator, Foulehaio 530
Prunella 392
prunellei, Coeligena 216

pryeri, Megalurus 462
przewalskii, Paradoxornis 436
Psalidoprocne 354
Psaltria 497
psaltria, Carduelis 597
Psaltriparus 497
Psamathia 438
Psarisomus 269
Psarocolius 588
Pselliophorus 555
Psephotus 161
Pseudalaemon 347
Pseudattila 322
Pseudeos 154
Pseudibis 67
Pseudobias 480
Pseudocalyptomena 269
Pseudochelidon 349
Pseudocolaptes 284
Pseudocolopteryx 332
Pseudocossyphus 405
Pseudoleistes 592
Pseudonestor 584
Pseudonigrita 611
Pseudopodoces 638
Pseudoptynx 186
Pseudoscops 192
Pseudoseisura 284
Pseudotriccus 330
pseudozosterops, Randia 462
psilolaemus, Francolinus 102
Psilopogon 242
Psilorhamphus 305
Psilorhinus 636
psittacea, Erythrura 608
psittacea, Psittirostra 584
psittacea, Treron 147
Psittacella 158
Psittacula 164
psittacula, Camarhynchus 550
psittacula, Cyclorrhynchus 134
Psittaculirostris 158
Psittacus 162
Psittinus 158
Psittrichas 160
Psittirostra 584
Psophia 112
Psophodes 414
ptaritepui, Crypturellus 51
pteneres, Tachyeres 71
Pteridophera 633
Pterocles 134
Pterocnemia 49
Pterodroma 56
Pteroglossus 248
Pteronetta 71
Pterophanes 216
Pteropodocys 358
Pteroptochos 305
Pteruthius 431
Ptilinopus 148
Ptilocichla 420
ptilocnemis, Calidris 128
ptilogenys, Gracula 623
Ptilogonys 381

Ptilolaemus 237
Ptilonorhynchus 630
Ptilopachus 105
Ptiloprora 532
Ptilorhynchus, Pernis 76
Ptiloris 631
Ptilorrhoa 415
Ptilostomus 639
ptilosus, Macronous 425
Ptychoramphus 134
Ptyrticus 418
pubescens, Picoides 259
pucherani, Guttera 109
pucherani, Melanerpes 252
pucheranii, Campylorhamphus
275
pucheranii, Neomorphus 178
Pucrasia 106
pudibunda, Thripophaga 282
puella, Hypothymis 483
puella, Irena 375
puellus, Hylophilus 588
Puffinus 57
puffinus, Puffinus 58
pugnax, Philomachus 129
pulchella, Charmosyna 156
pulchella, Heterophasia 434
pulchella, Lacedo 228
pulchella, Myzomela 527
pulchela, Nectarinia 517
pulchella, Neophema 162
pulchella, Ochthoeca 315
pulchella, Phyllolais 457
pulchellus, Caprimulgus 198
pulchellus, Mettapus 71
pulchellus, Ptilinopus 150
pulchellus, Vireolanius 585
pulcher, Calothorax 220
pulcher, Myiophobus 325
pulcher, Phylloscopus 445
pulcher, Spreo 622
pulcherrima Aethopyga 517
pulcherrima, Alectroenas 151
pulcherrima, Megalaima 243
pulcherrima, Tangara 572
pulcherrima, Carpodacus 599
pulcherrimus, Malurus 464
pulcherrimus, Psephotus 161
pulchra, Apalis 457
pulchra, Coturnicops 115
pulchra, Cyanolyca 635
pulchra, Incaspiza 545
pulchra, Macgregoria 631
pulchra, Pionopsitta 169
pulchricollis, Columba 136
pulitzeri, Macrosphenus 461
pullaria, Agapornis 163
pullicauda, Neopsittacus 156
pulpa, Mirafa 341
Pulsatrix 186
pulverulenta, Peneoenanthe 479
pulverulentus, Mulleripicus 268
pumilio, Indicator 248
pumilo, Cyanolyca 635
pumilus, Coccyzus 175

pumilus, Picumnus 251
punctata, Anas 73
punctata, Bowdleria 463
punctata, Tangara 571
punctatum, Cinclosoma 415
punctatus, Falco 89
punctatus, Pardalotus 510
punctatus, Phalacrocorax 62
punctatus, Thamnophilus 291
puncticeps, Dysithamnus 292
punctifrons, Anthoscopus 498
punctigula, Colaptes 262
punctulata, Hylophylax 300
punctulata, Lonchura 608
punctulata, Ninox 189
punctulatus, Chlorospingus 560
punctuligera, Campethera 254
punensis, Geositta 276
punensis, Grallaria 302
punensis, Thripophaga 282
punicea, Columba 136
punicea, Xipholena 309
puniceus, Carpodacus 600
puniceus, Picus 265
purnelli, Amytornis 465
purpurascens, Penelope 92
purpurascens, Vidua 610
purpurata, Querula 310
purpurata, Touit 168
purpuratus, Ptilinopus 150
purpuratus, Trachyphornus 246
purpurea, Ardea 66
purpurea, Cochoa 400
purpureicauda, Metallura 218
Purpureicephalus 160
purpureiceps, Lamprotornis 620
purpureiventris, Nectarinia 516
purpureus, Carpodacus 599
purpureus, Lamprotornis 621
purpureus, Phoeniculus 235
purpuropterus, Lamprotornis 621
purusianus, Galbalcyrhynchus 238
pusilla, Acanthiza 467
pusilla, Aethia 134
pusilla, Calidris 128
pusilla, Emberiza 537
pusilla, Eremomela 460
pusilla, Glossopsitta 155
pusilla, Pnoepyga 421
pusilla, Porzana 117
pusilla, Sitta 503
pusilla, Spizella 542
pusilla, Wilsonia 579
pusillus, Campylorhamphus 275
pusillus, Ceyx 227
pusillus, Chordeiles 194
pusillus, Lophospingus 544
pusillus, Loriculus 164
pusillus, Merops 233
pusillus, Pogoniulus 245
pusillus, Serinus 594
pusio, Micropsitta 157
pustulatus, Icterus 589

puveli, Trichastoma 418
Pycnonotus 365
Pycnoptilus 470
Pycnopygius 531
pycnopygius, Sphenoeacus 457
pycrofti, Pterodroma 57
pygargus, Circus 80
Pygarrhichas 289
Pygiptila 292
pygmaea, Aethia 134
pygmaea, Sitta 503
pygmaeum, Dicaeum 509
pygmaeum, Oedistoma 525
pygmaeus, Picumnus 251
pygmeus, Eurynorhynchus 128
pygmeus, Halietor 62
Pygoscelis 53
pylzowi, Urocynchramus 599
pyra, Topaza 215
Pyrenestes 603
Pyriglena 297
pyrilia, Pionopsitta 169
Pyrocephalus 317
pyrocephalus, Machaeropterus 311
Pyroderus 310
pyrohypogaster, Hypopyrrhus 592
pyrolophus, Psilopogon 242
Pyrope 314
pyrope, Pyrope 314
pyropygia, Hylocharis 211
pyrrhocephalus, Phaenicophaeus 177
Pyrrhocoma 561
Pyrrhocorax 639
pyrrhocorax, Pyrrhocorax 639
pyrrhodes, Philydor 286
pyrrhogaster, Dendropicos 255
Pyrrhoglaux 184
pyrrholeuca, Thripophaga 281
Pyrrhomyias 325
pyrrhonota, Petrochelidon 353
pyrrhonotus, Passer 612
pyrrhophanus, Cacomantis 173
pyrrhophia, Certhiaxis 281
pyrrhophrys, Chlorophonia 569
Pyrrhoplectes 602
pyrrhops, Stachyris 422
pyrrhoptera, Alcippe 433
pyrrhoptera, Philentoma 479
pyrrhoptera, Phylidonyris 534
pyrrhopterum, Trichastoma 417
pyrrhopterus, Brotogeris 168
pyrrhopterus, Lycocorax 631
pyrrhopygia, Halcyon 229
pyrrhopygia, Sericornis 469
pyrrhopygus, Copsychus 399
pyrrhothorax, Turnix 111
pyrrhotis, Blythipicus 268
pyrrhoura, Myzornis 435
Pyrrhula 601
pyrrhula, Pyrrhula 601
Pyrrhuloxia 556
Pyrrhura 166

pyrrogenys, Trichastoma 416
Pytilia 603
pytyopsittacus, Loxia 601

quadragintus, Pardalotus 510
quadribrachys, Alcedo 226
quadricinctus, Pterocles 135
quadricolor, Telophorus 378
quadrivirgata, Erythropygia 394
Quelea 617
quelea, Quelea 617
querquedula, Anas 73
Querula 310
querula, Zonotrichia 540
quinquestriata, Aimophila 543
quinticolor, Capito 241
quinticolor, Lonchura 609
quiscalina, Campephaga 363
Quiscalus 593
quiscula, Quiscalus 593
quitensis, Grallaria 303
quixensis, Microrhopias 295
quoyi, Cracticus 629

rabieri, Picus 266
rabori, Napothera 421
racheliae, Malimbus 617
radiata, Ducula 151
radiatum, Glaucidium 187
radiatus, Erythrotriorchis 80
radiatus, Nystalus 240
radiatus, Polyboroides 79
radiceus, Carpococcyx 178
radiolatus, Melanerpes 253
radiolosus, Neomorphus 178
radjah, Tadorna 71
rafflesii, Binopium 267
rafflesii, Megalaima 243
raggiana, Paradisaea 631
raimondii, Phytotoma 338
raimondii, Sicalis 546
Rallina 115
ralloides, Ardeola 64
ralloides, Myadestes 401
Rallus 113
ramphastinus, Semnornis 242
Ramphastos 249
Ramphocaenus 437
Ramphocelus 565
Ramphocinclus 391
Ramphocoris 345
Ramphodon 204
Ramphomicron 218
Ramphotrigon 328
ramsayi, Actinodura 431
Ramsayornis 534
Randia 462
ranivorus, Circus 79
rapax, Aquila 86
Raphidura 201
rara, Lagonosticta 604
rara, Lampribis 68
rara, Phytotoma 338
rarotongensis, Ptilinopus 149
raveni, Pachycephala 492

688   ravidus, Turdus 412
raytal, Calandrella 346
razae, Calandrella 346
rectirostris, Anthreptes 512
rectirostris, Automolus 287
rectirostris, Limnornis 283
rectunguis, Centopus 179
Recurvirostra 122
recurvirostris, Avocettula 207
recurvirostris, Esacus 122
recurvirostris, Halcyon 231
redivivum, Toxostoma 391
reevei, Turdus 413
reevesii, Syrmaticus 108
regalis, Buteo 85
regia, Nectarinia 516
regia, Platalea 68
regia, Vidua 610
regina, Ptilinopus 149
regius, Cicinnurus 633
regius, Cosmopsarus 622
reguloides, Acanthiza 468
reguloides, Anairetes 332
reguloides, Phylloscopus 446
regulorum, Balearica 111
Regulus 448
regulus, Machaeropterus 311
regulus, Prodotiscus 247
regulus, Regulus 448
rehsei, Acrocephalus 442
reichardi, Ploceus 615
reichenbachii, Nectarinia 512
reichenovii, Cryptospiza 603
reichenowi, Anthreptes 511
reichenowi, Nectarinia 517
reichenowi, Pitta 340
reichenowi, Streptopelia 138
reinhardti, Iridosornis 567
reinwardtii, Harpactes 224
reinwardtii, Selenidera 249
reinwardtii, Turdoides 426
Reinwardtipicus 268
Reinwardtoena 140
reinwardtsi, Reinwardtoena 140
reiseri, Xanthomyias 336
relictus, Larus 130
religiosa, Gracula 623
remifer, Dicrurus 627
Remiz 498
renauldi, Carpococcyx 178
rendovae, Zosterops 522
rennelliana, Rhipidura 489
rennelliana, Zosterops 522
repressa, Sterna 132
resplendens, Vanellus 124
respublica, Diphyllodes 633
restricta, Cisticola 451
reticulata, Eos 154
reticulata, Meliphaga 530
retrocinctum, Dicaeum 508
retzii, Prionops 375
revoilii, Merops 234
reyi, Hemispingus 560
reynaudii, Coua 178
rex, Balaeniceps 66

rex, Clytoceyx 228
Rhabdornis 506
Rhagologus 491
rhami, Lamprolaima 214
Rhamphocharis 507
Rhamphococcyx 177
Rhamphomantis 174
Rhea 49
Rhegmatorina 300
Rheinartia 109
rhinoceros, Buceros 238
Rhinocrypta 305
Rhinomyias 471
Rhinoplax 238
Rhinopomastus 236
Rhinoptilus 123
Rhinoptynx 191
Rhinortha 177
Rhipidura 488
rhipidurus, Corvus 641
Rhizothera 103
Rhodinocichla 562
rhodocephala, Pyrrhura 167
rhodochlamys, Carpodacus 560
rhodochrous, Carpodacus 560
rhodogaster, Accipiter 80
rhodogaster, Pyrrhura 166
rhodolaema, Anthreptes 511
Rhodonessa 73
rhodopareia, Lagonosticta 604
Rhodopechys 599
rhodopeplus, Carpodacus 560
Rhodopis 220
rhodopyga, Estrilda 605
Rhodospingus 555
Rhodostethia 131
Rhodothraupis 556
Rhopocichla 424
Rhopodytes 176
Rhopophilus 449
Rhopornis 297
Rhyacornis 399
Rhynchocyclus 327
Rhynchopsitta 166
Rhynchortyx 98
Rhynchospiza 543
Rhynchostruthus 596
rhynchotis, Anas 73
Rhynchotus 52
Rhynochetos 119
Rhytipterna 322
richardsii, Monarcha 486
richardsii, Ptilinopus 149
richardsoni, Eubucco 242
richardsoni, Melanospiza 550
ricketti, Paradoxornis 435
ricketti, Phylloscopus 446
ricordii, Chlorostilbon 209
ridgwayi, Aegolius 192
ridgwayi, Buteo 84
ridgwayi, Caprimulgus 196
ridgwayi, Cotinga 309
ridgwayi, Nesotriccus 322
ridgwayi, Plegadis 68
ridibundus, Larus 130

riedellii, Tanysiptera 232
riefferii, Chlorornis 559
riefferii, Pipreola 307
rikeri, Berlepschia 285
Rimator 420
riocourii, Chelictinia 77
Riparia 351
riparia, Riparia 351
risoria, Yetapa 316
Rissa 131
rivoli, Ptilinopus 150
rivolii, Piculus 262
rivularis, Basileuterus 582
rixosus, Machetornis 317
roberti, Conopophaga 304
roberti, Cossypha 396
robertsi, Prinia 454
robinsoni, Myiophoneus 405
roboratus, Otus 184
roborowskii, Carpodacus 600
robusta, Arachnothera 519
robusta, Cisticola 451
robusta, Coracina 360
robusta, Crateroscelis 470
robustirostris, Acanthiza 467
robustus, Campephilus 265
robustus, Eudyptes 53
robustus, Melichneutes 248
robustus, Poicephalus 162
rochussenii, Scolopax 127
rockefelleri, Nectarinia 516
rodericanus, Bebrornis 443
rodinogaster, Petroica 478
rodolphei, Stachyris 422
rogersi, Atlantisia 114
rolland, Rollandia 54
Rollandia 54
rolleti, Lybius 246
Rollulus 105
roquettei, Phylloscartes 331
roraimae, Herpsilochmus 295
roraimae, Myiophobus 326
roratus, Eclectus 160
rosacea, Ducula 152
rosea, Petroica 478
rosea, Rhodinocichla 562
rosea, Rhodostethia 131
roseata, Psittacula 164
roseatus, Anthus 357
roseicapilla, Ptilinopus 149
roseicapillus, Eolophus 156
roseicollis, Agapornis 163
roseigaster, Temnotrogon 222
rosenbergi, Amazilia 212
rosenbergi, Sipia 297
rosenbergii, Eulabeornis 112
rosenbergii, Myzomela 528
rosenbergii, Tyto 180
roseogrisea, Streptopelia 138
roseogularis, Piranga 565
roseus, Carpodacus 600
roseus, Pelecanus 60
roseus, Pericrocotus 363
roseus, Sturnus 622
rositae, Passerina 558

rossae, Musophaga 171
rossi, Anser 70
rostrata, Geothlypis 578
rostrata, Pterodroma 56
Rostratula 121
rostratum, Trichastoma 417
Rostrhamus 77
rothschildi, Astrapia 632
rothschildi, Buthraupis 566
rothschildi, Leucopsar 623
rougetii, Rougetius 115
Rougetius 115
roulroul, Rollulus 105
rourei, Nemosia 562
Rowettia 544
rowleyi, Eutrichomyias 483
rubecula, Erithacus 395
rubecula, Myiagra 487
rubecula, Nonnula 241
rubecula, Poospiza 545
rubecula, Scelorchilus 305
rubeculoides, Niltava 474
rubeculoides, Prunella 392
ruber, Ergaticus 579
ruber, Eudocimus 68
ruber, Laterallus 116
ruber, Phacellodomus 283
ruber, Phaethornis 206
ruber, Phoenicopterus 68
ruber, Sphyrapicus 253
rubescens, Carpodacus 599
rubescens, Gallicolumba 146
rubescens, Nectarinia 513
rubetra, Saxicola 402
rubetra, Xolmis 314
rubica, Habia 564
rubicilla, Carpodacus 560
rubicilloides, Carpodacus 560
rubicunda, Grus 111
rubida, Prunella 392
rubidiceps, Chloephaga 70
rubidiventris, Parus 499
rubiensis, Monarcha 485
rubifrons, Cardellina 579
rubigastra, Tachuris 332
rubiginosa, Ortygocicla 463
rubiginosus, Automolus 287
rubiginosus, Blythipicus 268
rubiginosus, Margarornis 284
rubiginosus, Piculus 261
rubiginosus, Ploceus 616
rubiginosus, Trichoglossus 154
rubiginosus, Turdoides 426
rubinoides, Heliodoxa 215
rubinus, Pyrocephalus 317
rubra, Crax 93
rubra, Eugerygone 477
rubra, Foudia 617
rubra, Paradisaea 633
rubra, Piranga 564
rubra, Rallina 115
rubricapilla, Megalaima 243
rubricapillus, Melanerpes 253
rubricata, Lagonosticta 604
rubricatus, Pardalotus 510

rubricauda, Clytolaema 215
rubricauda, Phaethon 59
rubriceps, Piranga 565
rubricera, Ducula 152
rubricollis, Campephilus 265
rubricollis, Charadrius 125
rubricollis, Malimbus 617
rubrifacies, Lybius 246
rubrigularis, Charmosyna 155
rubripes, Anas 72
rubrirostris, Arborophila 105
rubrirostris, Cnemoscopus 560
rubritorques, Anthreptes 512
rubrocanus, Turdus 412
rubrocapilla, Pipra 313
rubrocristata, Ampelion 306
rubrogenys, Ara 165
rubronotata, Charmosyna 155
ruckeri, Threnetes 205
ruddi, Apalis 455
ruddi, Heteromirafa 343
rudis, Ceryle 225
rudolphi, Paradisaea 633
ruecki, Niltava 474
rueppellii, Eupodotis 120
rüeppellii, Gyps 78
rüeppellii, Poicephalus 163
rufa, Alectoris 99
rufa, Anhinga 62
rufa, Casiornis 322
rufa, Cisticola 452
rufa, Climacteris 506
rufa, Coturnicops 115
rufa, Formicivora 296
rufa, Lessonia 314
rufa, Malacoptila 240
rufa, Mirafra 343
rufa, Ninox 188
rufa, Schetba 381
rufa, Tricocichla 463
rufalbus, Thryothorus 386
rufaxilla, Ampelion 307
rufaxilla, Leptotila 144
rufescens Acrocephalus 442
rufescens, Aimophila 543
rufescens, Atrichornis 341
rufescens, Calandrella 346
rufescens, Egretta 65
rufescens, Laniocera 322
rufescens, Otus 181
rufescens, Parus 499
rufescens, Pelecanus 60
rufescens, Rhynchotus 52
rufescens, Prinia 454
rufescens, Sericornis 469
rufescens, Sylvietta 461
rufescens, Trichastoma 417
rufescens, Turdoides 426
rufibarba, Estrilda 605
ruficapilla, Alcippe 432
ruficapilla, Grallaria 302
ruficapilla, Hemithraupis 561
ruficapilla, Nonnula 241
ruficapilla, Phylloscopus 447
ruficapilla, Spermophaga 603

ruficapilla, Sylvietta 460
ruficapilla, Synallaxis 278
ruficapilla, Vermivora 575
ruficapilla, Vitia 463
ruficapillus, Agelaius 591
ruficapillus, Baryphthengus 232
ruficapillus, Charadrius 125
ruficapillus, Enicurus 400
ruficapillus, Schistochlamys 559
ruficapillus, Thamnophilus 291
ruficauda, Aimophila 542
ruficauda, Chamaeza 301
ruficauda, Cichladusa 397
ruficauda, Cinclocerthia 391
ruficauda, Galbula 239
ruficauda, Histurgops 611
ruficauda, Muscicapa 475
ruficauda, Myrmeciza 299
ruficauda, Neochima 607
ruficauda, Ortalis 91
ruficauda, Ramphotrigon 328
ruficauda, Rhinomyias 471
ruficauda, Upucerthia 276
ruficaudatus, Philydor 285
ruficeps, Aimophila 543
ruficeps, Chalcostigma 219
ruficeps, Cisticola 452
ruficeps, Coua 178
ruficeps, Elaenia 334
ruficeps, Erithacus 395
ruficeps, Laniarius 377
ruficeps, Macropygia 1402
ruficeps, Orthotomus 458
ruficeps, Paradoxornis 436
ruficeps, Pellorneum 415
ruficeps, Poecilotriccus 330
ruficeps, Pomatostomus 420
ruficeps, Pseudotriccus 330
ruficeps, Pyrrhocoma 561
ruficeps, Stachyris 422
ruficeps, Stipiturus 465
ruficeps, Thlypopsis 561
ruficervix, Tangara 571
ruficollaris, Halcyon 231
ruficollis, Automolus 286
ruficollis, Branta 70
ruficollis, Calidris 128
ruficollis, Caprimulgus 196
ruficollis, Chalcites 174
ruficollis, Corvus 641
ruficollis, Eudromias 126
ruficollis, Garrulax 429
ruficollis, Gerygone 466
ruficollis, Hypnelus 240
ruficollis, Jynx 250
ruficollis, Madanga 524
ruficollis, Micrastur 87
ruficollis, Montifringilla 613
ruficollis, Myiagra 488
ruficollis, Pomatorhinus 419
ruficollis, Stelgidopteryx 350
ruficollis, Tachybaptus 54
ruficollis, Turdus 412
ruficrista, Lophotis 119
rufidorsa, Rhipidura 489

690   rufidorsum, Ceyx 227
rufifrons, Basileuterus 581
rufifrons, Formicarius 301
rufifrons, Fulica 118
rufifrons, Garrulax 427
rufifrons, Percnostola 298
rufifrons, Phacellodomus 283
rufifrons, Rhipidura 488
rufifrons, Spiloptila 457
rufifrons, Stachyris 422
rufigaster, Ducula 152
rufigastra, Niltava 474
rufigena, Caprimulgus 197
rufigenis, Atlapetes 554
rufigenis, Tangera 571
rufigula, Dendrexetastes 271
rufigula, Ficedula 472
rufigula, Gallicolumba 145
rufigula, Gymnopithys 299
rufigula, Petrochelidon 353
rufigula, Tangara 571
rufigulare, Idioptilon 329
rufigularis, Falco 89
rufigularis, Piaya 175
rufigularis, Sclerurus 288
rufilata, Cisticola 451
rufimarginatus, Herpsilochmus
   295
rufina, Netta 73
rufinucha, Atlapetes 553
rufinucha, Campylorhynchus
   383
rufinucha, Pachycephala 492
rufinus, Buteo 85
rufipectoralis, Ochthoeca 315
rufipectus, Arborophila 104
rufipectus, Formicarius 301
rufipectus, Leptopogon 337
rufipectus, Napothera 420
rufipectus, Spilornis 78
rufipenne, Trichastoma 417
rufipennis, Butastur 83
rufipennis, Geositta 276
rufipennis, Macropygia 140
rufipennis, Neomorphus 178
rufipennis, Petrophassa 142
rufipennis, Xolmis 314
rufipes, Strix 191
rufipileatus, Automolus 287
rufitorques, Accipiter 82
rufitorques, Turdus 414
rufiventer, Pteruthius 431
rufiventer, Tachyphonus 563
rufiventer, Terpsiphone 483
rufiventris, Accipiter 81
rufiventris, Ardeola 64
rufiventris, Euphonia 569
rufiventris, Monticola 405
rufiventris, Neoxolmis 314
rufiventris, Pachycephala 494
rufiventris, Parus 501
rufiventris, Piccumnus 250
rufiventris, Pipromorpha 338
rufiventris, Poicephalus 162
rufiventris, Rhipidura 490

rufiventris, Saltator 557
rufiventris, Turdus 413
rufivertex, Iridosornis 567
rufivertex, Muscisaxicola 314
rufivirgatus, Arremonops 552
rufoaxillaris, Molothrus 593
rufobrunneus, Serinus 596
rufobrunneus, Thripadectes 286
rufocinctus, Lioptilus 434
rufocinctus, Passer 612
rufocinerea, Grallaria 302
rufocinerea, Terpsiphone 482
rufocinereus, Monticola 405
rufocinnamomea, Mirafa 342
rufocrissalis, Melidectes 533
rufofuscus, Buteo 85
rufogularis, Alcippe 433
rufogularis, Anthochaera 535
rufogularis, Apalis 456
rufogularis, Arborophila 104
rufogularis, Conopophila 534
rufogularis, Garrulax 428
rufogularis, Pachycephala 492
rufolarvatus, Tachybaptus 54
rufolateralis, Smithornis 269
rufomarginatus, Euscarthmus
   332
rufonuchalis, Parus 499
rufopalliatus, Turdus 414
rufopectus, Podiceps 54
rufopicta, Lagonosticta 604
rufopictus, Francolinus 100
rufopileatum, Pittasoma 302
rufoscapulatus, Plocepasser 611
rufosuperciliaris, Hemispingus
   561
rufosuperciliatus, Philydor 285
rufula, Grallaria 303
rufulus, Gampsorhynchus 431
rufulus, Troglodytes 388
rufum, Conirostrum 582
rufum, Toxostoma 391
rufus, Attila 321
rufus, Bathmocercus 459
rufus, Campylopterus 206
rufus, Caprimulgus1 195
rufus, Furnarius 277
rufus, Neocossyphus 401
rufus, Pachyramphus 308
rufus, Philydor 286
rufus, Selasphorus 221
rufus, Tachyphonus 563
rufus, Trogon 223
rugiensis, Metabolus 485
ruki, Rukia 524
Rukia 524
rumicivorus, Thinocorus 129
rupestris, Chordeiles 194
rupestris, Columba 136
rupestris, Hirundo 351
rupestris, Monticola 405
Rupicola 310
rupicola, Colaptes 263
rupicola, Pyrrhura 167
rupicola, Rupicola 310

rupicoloides, Falco 88
rüppelli, Eurocephalus 375
ruppelli, Sylvia 444
rushiae, Pholidornis 610
ruspolii, Tauraco 172
russatum, Todirostrum 328
russatus, Chlorostilbon 209
rustica, Emberiza 537
rustica, Haplospiza 544
rustica, Hirundo 352
rusticola, Scolopax 127
rusticolus, Falco 90
ruticilla, Setophaga 577
rutila, Amazilia 213
rutila, Emberiza 537
rutila, Phytotoma 338
rutilans, Passer 612
rutilans, Synallaxis 280
rutilans, Xenops 288
rutilus, Cypseloides 199
rutilus, Otus 182
rutilus, Thryothorus 386
ruwenzori, Apalis 457
Rynchops 133

sabini, Dryoscopus 376
sabini, Raphidura 201
sabini, Xema 131
sabota, Mirafa 343
sacerdotum, Monarcha 486
sacra, Egretta 65
Sagittarius 87
sagittata, Sericornis 469
sagittatus, Oriolus 624
sagittatus, Otus 181
sagrae, Myiarchus 321
sakalava, Foudia 617
Sakesphorus 289
salamonis, Gallicolumba 146
salangana, Collocalia 200
sallaei, Granatellus 582
sallei, Cyrtonyx 98
salmoni, Brachygalba 239
salmoni, Chrysothylpis 562
Salpinctes 383
Salpornis 506
Saltator 557
Saltatricula 555
salvadorii, Cryptospiza 603
salvadorii, Eremomela 460
salvadorii, Onychognathus 620
salvadorii, Psittaculirostris 158
slavadorii, Zosterops 520
salvini, Caprimulgus 196
salvini, Crax 93
salvini, Gymnopithys 299
salvini, Pachyptila 57
salvini, Tumbezia 317
samarensis, Orthotomus 458
samoensis, Gymnomyza 533
samoensis, Zosterops 522
sanblasiana, Cissilopha 635
sancta, Halcyon 230
sanctaecrucis, Gallicolumba 146
sanctaecrucis, Zosterops 522

sanctaehelenae, Charadrius 125
sanctihieronymi, Panyptila 202
sanctithomae, Brotogeris 168
sanctithomae, Ploceus 616
sanctithomae, Treron 148
sandvicensis, Branta 70
sandvicensis, Thalasseus 133
sandwichensis, Chasiempis 484
sandwichensis, Passerculus 540
sanfordi, Haliaeetus 77
sanfordi, Niltava 474
sanguinea, Cacatua 157
sanguinea, Himatione 584
sanguinea, Rhodopechys 599
sanguineus, Pyrenestes 603
sanguineus, Veniliornis 260
sanguiniceps, Haematortyx 105
sanguinolenta, Myzomela 527
sanguinolentus, Rallus 113
sanguinolentus, Ramphocelus 565
sannio, Garrulax 429
santovestris, Aplonis 619
Sapayoa 310
Sapheopipo 267
saphirina, Geotrygon 144
sapphira, Ficedula 473
sapphirina, Hylocharis 210
Sappho 218
saracura, Eulabeornis 112
sarasinorum, Myza 533
Sarcogyps 78
Sarcops 623
Sarcoramphus 75
sarda, Sylvia 444
Sarkidiornis 71
Saroglossa 622
Sasia 251
sasin, Selasphorus 221
Satrapa 317
satrapa, Regulus 449
saturata, Aethopyga 518
saturata, Euphonia 568
saturata, Scolopax 127
saturatus, Caprimulgus 196
saturatus, Cuculus 172
saturatus, Platyrinchus 326
saturninus, Mimus 390
saturninus, Thamnomanes 292
satyra, Tragopan 106
saucerrottei, Amazilia 212
saularis, Copsychus 398
saundersi, Larus 131
saundersii, Sterna 132
saurophaga, Halcyon 231
Saurothera 176
savannarum, Ammodramus 541
savesi, Aegotheles 193
savilei, Lophotis 119
sawtelli, Collocalia 200
saxatilis, Aeronautes 202
saxatilis, Monticola 405
Saxicola 402
saxicolina, Geositta 276
Saxicoloides 404

saya, Sayornis 315
sayaca, Thraupis 566
Sayornis 316
scalaris, Picoides 259
scandens, Geospiza 550
scandens, Phyllastrephus 369
scandiaca, Nyctea 186
scansor, Sclerurus 288
Scaphidura 594
scapularis, Alisterus 160
Scardafella 143
Sceloglaux 189
Scelorchilus 305
Scenopoeetes 630
Scepomycter 459
schach, Lanius 379
scheepmakeri, Goura 146
Schetba 381
schifferni, Coracina 359
schistacea, Leucopternis 83
schistacea, Percnostola 298
schistacea, Sporophila 547
schistacea, Zoothera 406
schistaceigula, Polioptila 438
schistaceus, Atlapetes 553
schistaceus, Enicurus 400
schistaceus, Mayrornis 484
schistaceus, Thamnophilus 291
Schistes 219
schisticeps, Abroscopus 448
schisticeps, Coracina 361
schisticeps, Phoenicurus 399
schisticeps, pomatorhinus 419
schisticolor, Myrmotherula 294
schistisagus, Larus 130
Schistochlamys 559
schistogynus, Thamnomanes 293
Schizoeaca 278
schlegeli, Arremon 552
schlegeli, Eudyptes 53
schlegeli, Philepitta 341
schlegelii, Cercomela 401
schlegelii, Francolinus 103
schlegelii, Pachycephala 494
schneideri, Pitta 339
schoeniclus, Emberiza 537
Schoenicola 462
Schoeniophylax 278
schoenobaenus, Acrocephalus 441
schomburgkii, Coturnicops 115
Schoutedenapus 201
schoutedeni, Schoutedenapus 201
schrankii, Tangara 570
schreibersii, Heliodoxa 215
schulzi, Cinclus 382
schulzi, Dryocopus 264
schwartzi, Phylloscopus 445
scintilla, Selasphorus 221
scirpaceus, Acrocephalus 441
Scissirostrum 624
scita, Stenostira 463

sclateri, Ampelion 307
sclateri, Cacicus 589
sclateri, Eudyptes 53
sclateri, Forpus 168
sclateri, Hylophilus 587
sclateri, Lophophorus 106
sclateri, Meliarchus 533
sclateri, Myrmotherula 293
sclateri, Myzomela 527
sclateri, Nonnula 241
sclateri, Parus 499
sclateri, Picumnus 251
sclateri, Pseudocolopteryx 332
sclateri, Spizocorys 347
sclateri, Thripophaga 282
sclateri, Xanthomyias 336
Sclateria 298
sclateriana, Amalocichla 407
Sclerurus 287
scolopacea, Eudynamys 175
scolopaceus, Limnodromus 128
scolopaceus, Pogoniulus 244
Scolopax 127
scopifrons, Prionops 375
scops, Otus 181
Scopus 66
scoresbii, Gabianus 129
scotica, Loxia 601
Scotocerca 449
scotocerca, Cercomela 402
Scotopelia 186
scotops, Eremomela 460
scotops, Serinus 595
Scotornis 198
scouleri, Enicurus 400
scripta, Petrophassa 142
scriptus, Elanus 77
scrutator, Thripadectes 286
scutulata, Cairinia 71
scutulata, Ninox 188
scutatus, Augastes 219
scutatus, Malimbus 617
scutatus, Pyroderus 310
scutatus, Synallaxis 280
Scytalopus 305
Scythrops 175
sechellarum, Copsychus 398
sechellarum, Foudia 617
sechellensis, Bebrornis 443
seebohmi, Atlapetes 553
seebohmi, Bradypterus 440
seebohni, Dromaeocercus 457
sefilata, Parotia 632
segmentata, Uropsalis 198
segregata, Muscicapa 475
Seicercus 447
seimundi, Nectarinia 512
seimundi, Treron 148
Seisura 484
Seiurus 577
Selasphorus 221
seledon, Tangara 570
Selenidera 249
Seleucidis 632
seloputo, Strix 190

692   Semeiophorus 198
semibrunneus, Hylophilus 587
semicincta, Malacoptila 240
semicinerea, Certhiaxis 281
semicinereus, Hylophilus 587
semicollaris, Nycticryphes 121
semicollaris, Streptoprocne 199
semifasciata, Tityra 309
semiflava, Geothlypis 578
semiflavum, Ornithion 337
semifuscus, Chlorospingus 560
semilarvata, Eos 154
semilarvatus, Parus 502
Semioptera 632
semipalmata, Anseranas 69
semipalmatus, Catoptrophorus 126
semipalmatus, Charadrius 124
semipalmatus, Limnodromus 128
semipartitus, Empidornis 471
semiplumbea, Leucopternis 83
semiplumbeus, Rallus 114
semirufa, Cossypha 396
semirufa, Hirundo 353
semirufa, Thamnolaea 403
semirufus, Atlapetes 554
semirufus, Myiarchus 320
semitorquata, Alcedo 225
semitorquata, Streptopelia 138
semitorquatus, Lurocalis 194
semitorquatus, Micrastur 88
semitorquatus, Polihierax 88
semitorques, Spizixos 365
Semnornis 242
semperi, Leucopeza 579
senator, Lanius 381
senegala, Lagonosticta 604
senegala, Tchagra 376
senegalensis, Batis 480
senegalensis, Burhinus 122
senegalensis, Centropus 179
senegalensis, Dryoscopus 376
senegalensis, Ephippiorhynchus 67
senegalensis, Eupodotis 120
senegalensis, Halcyon 229
senegalensis, Hirundo 353
senegalensis, Nectarinia 513
senegalensis, Otus 182
senegalensis, Podica 118
senegalensis, Streptopelia 139
senegalensis, Zosterops 523
senegallus, Pterocles 135
senegallus, Vanellus 124
senegaloides, Halcyon 229
senegalus, Poicephalus 162
senex, Aerornis 199
senex, Sturnus 622
senex, Todirostrum 328
senilis, Myornis 305
senilis, Pionus 169
seniloides, Pionus 169
sephaena, Francolinus 102
sephanoides, Sephaniodes 217

Sephanoides 217
sepiarium, Trichastoma 417
septimus, Batrachostomus 193
serena, Pipra 312
sericea, Loboparadisea 631
sericea, Nectarinia 514
sericeus, Monarcha 485
sericeus, Orthotomus 458
sericeus, Sturnus 622
sericocaudatus, Caprimulgus 195
Sericornis 468
sericossypha 559
Sericotes 207
Sericulus 630
Serilophus 269
serina, Calyptocichla 369
Serinus 594
serinus, Serinus 594
serpentarius, Sagittarius 87
Serpophaga 333
serrana, Formicivora 295
serrana, Upucerthia 276
serranus, Larus 130
serranus, Turdus 412
serrator, Mergus 74
serrator, Morus 60
serriana, Coua 178
serrirostris, Colibri 207
serva, Cercomacra 296
setaris, Leptasthenura 278
sethsmithi, Muscicapa 476
setifrons, Xenornis 292
Setophaga 577
Setornis 372
severa, Ara 165
severa, Mackenziaena 289
severus, Falco 89
sewerzowi, Bonasa 95
sganzini, Alectroenas 151
sharpei, Erithacus 395
sharpei, Lalage 363
sharpei, Macronyx 355
sharpei, Smithornis 269
sharpei, Terenura 296
sharpii, Apalis 456
sharpei, Cinnyricinchus 621
shelleyi, Aethopyga 518
shelleyi, Bubo 185
shelleyi, Cryptospiza 603
shelleyi, Francolinus 102
shelleyi, Nectarinia 516
shelleyi, Nesocharis 603
shelleyi, Spreo 622
shorii, Dinopium 267
Sialia 399
sialis, Sialia 399
sibilans, Erithacus 395
sibilator, Sirystes 317
sibilator, Syrigma 64
sibilatrix, Anas 72
sibilatrix, Phacellodomus 283
sibilatrix Phylloscopus 445
sibirica, Muscicapa 475
sibirica, Zoothera 406

sibiricus, Uragus 599
Sicalis 545
sieboldii, Treron 148
siemiradzkii, Carduelis 597
siemssenii, Latoucheornis 535
sigillatus, Peneothello 479
signata, Eremopterix 344
signata, Erythropygia 394
signatus, Basileuterus 580
signatus, Myiotheretes 315
siju, Glaucidium 186
silens, Melaeornis 471
silvestris, Gallinula 117
silvicola, Otus 183
similis, Anthus 356
similis, Chloropeta 443
similis, Myiozetetes 319
similis, Saltator 557
simoni, Selasphorus 221
simplex, Anthreptes 511
simplex, Camaroptera 459
simplex, Chlorocichla 369
simplex, Geoffroyus 159
simplex, Myrmothera 304
simplex, Pachycephala 493
simplex, Passer 612
simplex, Phaetusa 131
simplex, Pogoniulus 244
simplex, Pseudotriccus 330
simplex, Pycnonotus 368
simplex, Rhytipterna 322
simplex, Sporophila 548
sinaloa, Thryothorus 386
sinaloae, Corvus 640
sinense, Chrysomma 425
sinensis, Centropus 179
sinensis, Ixobrychus 63
sinensis, Pycnonotus 366
sinensis, Sturnus 623
singalensis, Anthreptes 5112
sinica, Carduelis 596
sintillata, Chalcopsitta 154
sinuata, Cercomela 401
sinuatus, Pyrrhuloxia 556
sipahi, Haematospiza 601
siparaja, Aethopyga 518
Siphonorhis 195
Sipia 297
Siptornis 283
siquijorensis, Hypsipetes 372
sirintarae, Pseudochelidon 349
Sirystes 317
sissonii, Thryomanes 385
Sitta 503
Sittasomus 271
sitticolor, Conirostrum 582
sjostedti, Columba 136
sjostedti, Glaucidium 187
skua, Catharacta 129
Skutchia 300
sladeni, Gymnobucco 244
sloetii, Campochaera 362
Smicrornis 467
Smilorhis 244
smithi, Anas 73

smithii, Hirundo 352
smithii, Petrophassa 142
Smithornis 268
smyrnensis, Halcyon 228
Snethlagea 330
sociabilis, Rostrhamus 77
socialis, Pluvianellus 126
socialis, Prinia 454
socius, Philetairus 611
socotrana, Emberiza 536
socotranus, Rhynchostruthus 596
söderströmi, Eriocnemis 217
soemmerringi, Syrmaticus 107
sokokensis, Anthus 358
solandri, Pterodroma 56
solangiae, Sitta 504
solaris, Nectarinia 515
solaris, Pericrocotus 364
solitaria, Ficedula 472
solitaria, Gallinago 127
solitaria, Origma 470
solitaria, Tringa 126
solitarius, Buteo 85
solitarius, Cacicus 589
solitarius, Cuculus 172
solitarius, Harpyhaliaetus 84
solitarius, Monticola 405
solitarius, Phigys 155
solitarius, Tinamus 50
solitarius, Vireo 586
soloensis, Accipiter 82
solomonensis, Gymnophaps 153
solomonensis, Nesasio 192
solomonensis, Ptilinopus 150
solomonis, Ninox 189
solstitialis, Aratinga 165
solstitialis, Troglodytes 388
somalica, Mirafa 342
somalica, Prinia 454
somalicus, Lanius 380
Somateria 74
sonnerati, Chloropsis 374
sonneratii, Gallus 106
sonneratii, Penthoceryx 173
sophiae, Leptopoecile 449
sordida, Cercomela 402
sordida, Eumyias 476
sordida, Pitta 339
sordida, Thlypopsis 561
sordidulus, Contopus 322
sordidus, Cynanthus 209
sordidus, Pionus 169
Sorella 613
sorghophilus, Acrocephalus 441
soror, Batis 480
soror, Pachycephala 493
soror, Pitta 338
soui, Crypturellus 50
souimanga, Nectarinia 515
souleyetii, Lepidocolaptes 274
souliei, Actinodura 431
soumagnei, Tyto 180
souzae, Lanius 379

spadicea, Galloperdix 105
spadiceus, Attila 321
spaldingii, Orthonyx 414
sparganura, Sappho 218
sparsa, Anas 72
Spartonoica 283
sparverius, Falco 88
sparverioides, Cuculus 172
spatulata, Coracias 234
speciosa, Ardeola 64
speciosa, Columba 137
speciosa, Geothlypis 578
speciosa, Stachyris 423
speciosum, Conirostrum 582
speciosus, Odontophorus 98
spectabilis, Celeus 264
spectabilis, Dryotriorchis 79
spectabilis, Elaenia 334
spectabilis, Lonchura 609
spectabilis, Selenidera 249
spectabilis, Somateria 74
specularis, Anas 72
specularioides, Anas 72
speculifera, Diuca 545
speculiferus, Nesospingus 559
speculigera, Conothraupis 559
Speculipastor 621
Speirops 525
spekei, Ploceus 615
spekeoides, Ploceus 615
Spelaeornis 421
speluncae, Scytalopus 305
spencei, Heliangelus 217
Speotyto 189
sperata, Nectarinia 513
Spermophaga 603
Sphecotheres 626
Spheniscus 53
sphenocercus, Lanius 380
Sphenocichla 422
Sphenoeacus 457
Sphenostoma 414
sphenura, Treron 148
sphenurus, Haliastur 77
Sphyrapicus 253
spilocephala, Ninox 188
spilocephalus, Otus 181
spilodera, Petrochelidon 353
spilodera, Rhipidura 489
spilodera, Sericornis 468
spilogaster, Picumnus 250
spilogaster, Veniliornis 260
spilonota, Ninox 188
spilonotus, Laterallus 116
spilonotus, Parus 502
spilonotus, Salpornis 506
spiloptera, Porzana 116
spiloptera, Saroglossa 622
spiloptera, Zoothera 407
spilopterus, Centropus 179
Spiloptila 457
Spilornis 78
spilorrhoa, Ducula 153
Spindalis 565
spinescens Carduelis 597

spinicauda, Aphrastura 277
spinicauda, Chaetura 202
spinicollis, Carphibis 67
spinoides, Carduelis 597
spinoletta, Anthus 357
spinosa, Jacana 120
spinosus, Vanellus 123
spinus, Carduelis 597
spirurus, Glyphorhynchus 271
spixi, Synallaxis 279
spixii, Cyanopsitta 164
spixii, Xiphorhynchus 273
Spiza 555
spiza, Chlorophanes 573
Spizaetus 86
Spizastur 86
Spizella 541
Spiziapteryx 88
Spizixos 365
Spizocorys 347
splendens, Corvus 639
splendens, Malurus 464
splendida, Neophema 162
splendidissima, Astrapia 632
splendidus, Lamprotornis 621
spodiops, Idioptilon 329
spodioptila, Terenura 296
spodiopygia, Collocalia 199
spodiurus, Pachyramphus 308
spodocephala, Emberiza 537
sponsa, Aix 71
Sporophila 547
Sporopipes 613
spragueii, Anthus 358
Spreo 622
spurius, Icterus 590
spurius, Purpureicephalus 160
squalidus, Phaethornis 205
squamata, Callipepla 96
squamata, Drymophila 296
squamata, Eos 154
squamata, Lichmera 526
squamata, Tachornis 202
squamatus, Capito 241
squamatus, Francolinus 101
squamatus, Garrulax 429
squamatus, Lepidocolaptes 275
squamatus, Mergus 74
squamatus, Picus 266
squamatus, Pycnonotus 365
squameiceps, Cattia 438
squamiceps, Lophozosterops 524
squamiceps, Turdoides 425
squamifrons, Oculocincta 525
squamifrons, Sporopipes 613
squamiger, Margarornis 284
squamiger, Neomorphus 178
squamigera, Brachypteracias 235
squamigera, Grallaria 302
squamigularis, Heliangelus 217
squamipila, Ninox 189
squammata, Scardafella 143
squamosa, Columba 137

693

squamosa, Myrmeciza 299
squamosus, Heliomaster 220
squamulatus, Picumnus 250
squamulatus, Turdoides 426
squatarola, Pluvialis 124
Stachyris 422
Stactolaema 244
stagnatilis, Tringa 126
stairi, Gallicolumba 145
stalkeri, Tephrozosterops 524
stanleyi, Chalcostigma 219
starki, Spizocorys 347
Starnoenas 145
Steatornis 192
steerei, Pitta 340
steerii, Centropus 179
steerii, Eurylaimus 269
steerii, Liocichla 430
steinbachi, Thripophaga 282
steindachneri, Picumnus 251
Stelgidopteryx 350
stellaris, Botaurus 63
stellaris, Pygiptila 292
stellata, Brachypteryx 392
stellata, Gavia 54
stellata, Pogonocichla 394
stellatus, Batrachostomus 193
stellatus, Caprimulgus 198
stellatus, Margarornis 284
stellatus, Odontophorus 98
stelleri, Cyanocitta 634
stelleri, Polysticta 74
Stellula 221
Stenostira 463
stentoreus, Acrocephalus 441
stenura, Chlorostilbon 209
stenura, Gallinago 127
stephani, Chalcophaps 141
stephaniae, Astrapia 632
Stephanoaetus 87
Stephanophorus 567
Stephanoxis 208
stepheni, Vini 155
Stercorarius 129
Sterna 131
Sternoclyta 215
sterrhopteron, Wetmorethraupis
567
stewarti, Emberiza 536
stictigula, Modulatrix 397
stictocephalus, Herpsilochmus
295
stictocephalus, Pycnopygius
531
stictolaema, Deconychura 270
stictolopha, Lophornis 208
Stictonetta 70
stictoptera, Touit 169
stictopterus, Mecocerculus 333
stictothorax, Dysithamnus 292
stictothorax, Myrmeciza 299
stictothorax, Synallaxis 280
sticturus, Herpsilochmus 295
stierlingi, Camaroptera 459
stierlingi, Dendropicos 255

Stigmatura 332
stigmatus, Loriculus 163
Stiltia 123
Stipiturus 465
Stizorhina 401
stolidus, Anous 133
stolidus, Myiarchus 320
stolzmanni, Chlorothraupis 562
stolzmanni, Rhynchospiza 543
stolzmanni, Tyranneutes 311
stolzmanni, Urothraupis 555
strenua, Ninox 188
Strepera 629
strepera, Anas 72
strepera, Elaenia 334
strepitans, Garrulax 428
strepitans, Phyllastrephus 370
Streptocitta 623
Streptopelia 138
streptophorus, Francolinus 102
streptophorus, Lipaugus 307
Streptoprocne 199
stresemanni, Ampelion 307
stresemanni, Hylexetaste 271
stresemanni, Merulaxis 305
stresemanni, Zavattariornis 638
stresemanni, Zosterops 522
striata, Aplonis 619
striata, Coracina 359
striata, Dendroica 577
striata, Geopelia 142
striata, Kenopia 420
striata, Leptasthenura 278
striata, Lonchura 608
striata, Malacoptila 240
striata, Muscicapa 475
striata, Stachyris 423
striata, Sterna 132
striaticeps, Dysithamnus 292
striaticeps, Entotriccus 316
striaticeps, Macronous 424
striaticeps, Phacellodomus 283
striaticolle, Idioptilon 329
striaticollis, Alcippe 432
striaticollis, Mionectes 337
striaticollis, Myiotheretes 314
striaticollis, Phacellodomus 283
striaticollis, Philydor 285
striaticollis, Siptornis 283
striatigula, Neomixis 422
striatigularis, Xiphorhynchus
274
striativentris, Melanocharis 507
striatus, Accipiter 81
striatus, Amytornis 465
striatus, Butorides 465
striatus, Chaetornis 462
striatus, Colius 221
striatus, Garrulax 428
striatus, Melanerpes 252
striatus, Pardalotus 510
striatus, Pycnonotus 365
striatus, Rallus 113
striatus, Turdoides 426
stricklandi, Picoides 259

stricklandii, Copsychus 398
stricklandii, Gallinago 128
strigiceps, Aimophila 542
strigilatus, Myrmorchilus 295
strigilatus, Philydor 285
strigirostris, Didunculus 146
Strigops 171
strigoides, Podargus 192
strigula, Minla 432
strigulosus, Crypturellus 51
striolata, Emberiza 536
striolata, Hirundo 353
striolata, Leptasthenura 278
striolata, Stachyris 423
striolatus, Nystalus 240
striolatus, Serinus 596
Strix 190
strophianus, Heliangelus 217
strophiata, Ficedula 472
strophiata, Prunella 392
strophium, Odontophorus 98
struthersii, Ibidorhyncha 121
Struthidea 628
Struthio 49
stuarti, Phaethornis 206
stuhlmanni, Poeoptera 620
sturmii, Ixobrychus 63
Sturnella 591
sturninus, Sturnus 622
Sturnus 622
stygia, Lonchura 610
stygius, Asio 191
suahelicus, Passer 612
subaffinis, Phylloscopus 445
subalaris, Lipaugus 307
subalaris, Macroagelaius 592
subalaris, Philydor 285
subaureus, Ploceus 614
subbrunneus, Cnipodectes 326
subbuteo, Falco 89
subcaeruleum, Parisoma 461
subcinnamomea, Euryptila 459
subcorniculatus, Philemon 532
subcristata, Aviceda 75
subcristata, Certhiaxis 281
subcristata, Serpophaga 333
subcylindricus, Bycanistes 238
subflammulatus, Knippolegus
316
subflava, Amandava 606
subflava, Inexia 333
subflava, Prinia 453
subfrenata, Meliphaga 530
subgularis, Ptilinopus 149
subhimachalus, Pinicola 600
subis, Progne 350
Sublegatus 335
subminuta, Calidris 128
subniger, Falco 89
subochraceus, Phaethornis 206
subpersonatus, Ploceus 614
subplacens, Myiopagis 335
subpudica, Synallaxis 279
subruficapilla, Cisticola 451
subruficollis, Tryngites 129

subrufus, Turdoides 426
substriata, Prinia 454
substriatus, Pardalotus 510
subsulphureus, Pogoniulus 245
subtilis, Picumnus 251
subularis, Amblyornis 630
subulata, Cettia 438
subulatus, Philydor 285
subulatus, Todus 232
subunicolor, Garrulax 429
subvinacea, Columba 137
subviridis, Phylloscopus 445
sueruii, Lalage 362
Suiriri 335
suiriri, Suiriri 335
Sukatschewi, Garrulax 428
Sula 60
sula, Sula 60
sulaensis, Rhipidura 488
sulcatus, Aulacorhynchus 248
sulcirostris, Crotophaga 177
sulcirostris, Phalacrocorax 61
sulfuratus, Ramphastos 249
sulfureopectus, Telophorus 378
sulfuriventor, Pachycephala 492
sulphurata, Campephaga 363
sulphurata, Emberiza 537
sulphuratus, Pitangus 319
sulphuratus, Serinus 595
sulphurea, Cacatua 156
sulphurea, Gerygone 467
sulphurea, Tyrannopsis 318
sulphureipygius, Myiobius 325
sulphureiventer, Neopelma 311
sulphurescens, Tolmomyias 327
sulphurifera, Certhiaxis 281
sultanea, Melanochlora 502
sumatrana, Ardea 66
sumatrana, Bubo 185
sumatrana, Niltava 473
sumatrana, Sterna 132
sumatranus, Corydon 269
sumatranus, Rhopodytes 176
sumatranus, Tanygnathus 159
sumichrasti, Aimophila 542
sumichrasti, Hylorchilus 383
sundara, Niltava 473
sunensis, Myrmotherula 294
superba, Lophorina 632
superba, Menura 341
superba, Nectarinia 517
superba, Niltava 474
superba, Pitta 340
superbus, Ptilinopus 149
superbus, Spreo 622
superciliaris, Abroscopus 448
superciliaris, Burhinus 122
superciliaris, Camaroptera 459
superciliaris, Drymodes 394
superciliaris, Ficedula 473
superciliaris, Hemispingus 560
superciliaris, Leptopogon 337
superciliaris, Lophozosterops 524
superciliaris, Melanerpes 253

superciliaris, Ninox 188
superciliaris, Penelope 92
superciliaris, Petronia 613
superciliaris, Phylloscartes 331
superciliaris, Polystictus 332
superciliaris, Rhipidura 488
superciliaris, Scytalopus 306
superciliaris, Sterna 132
superciliaris, Sturnella 591
superciliaris, Tesia 438
superciliaris, Thryothorus 387
superciliaris, Xiphirhynchus 420
superciliosa, Eumomota 232
superciliosa, Ophrysia 106
superciliosa, Poecilodryas 479
superciliosa, Synallaxis 278
superciliosa, Vermivora 575
superciliosa, Woodfordia 524
superciliosus, Acanthorhynchus 535
superciliosus, Accipiter 83
superciliosus, Artamus 629
superciliosus, Centropus 180
superciliosus, Dasylophus 177
superciliosus, Merops 234
superciliosus, Orituris 543
superciliosus, Parus 499
superciliosus, Phaethornis 205
superciliosus, Plocepasser 611
superciliosus, Ploceus 616
superciliosus, Pomatostomus 420
superciliosus, Vanellus 124
superflua, Rhipidura 488
surda, Touit 169
surinamensis, Myrmotherula 293
surinamus, Pachyramphus 308
surinamus, Tachyphonus 563
Surnia 186
Surniculus 174
surracura, Trogon 223
suscitator, Turnix 110
sutorius, Orthotomus 458
svecicus, Erithacus 395
swainsoni, Myiarchus 321
swainsonii, Buteo 84
swainsonii, Chlorostilbon 209
swainsonii, Francolinus 100
swainsonii, Gampsonyx 76
swainsonii, Limnothlypis 578
swainsonii, Passer 612
swainsonii, Polytelis 160
swalesi, Turdus 4142
swierstrai, Francolinus 101
swinderniana, Agapornis 163
swinhoii, Lophura 107
swynnertoni, Pogonocichla 394
sylvanus, Anthus 357
sylvatica, Prinia 455
sylvatica, Turnix 110
sylvatica, Zoonavena 201
sylvaticus, Bradypterus 440
sylvestris, Rallus 113
Sylvia 443

sylvia, Tanysiptera 232
sylvia, Todirostrum 329
sylviella, Anthoscopus 498
Sylvietta 460
sylviolus, Leptotriccus 331
Sylviorthorhynchus 277
Sylviparus 503
Synallaxis 278
syndactyla, Bleda 371
Synoicus 103
synoicus, Carpodacus 600
Synthliboramphus 134
Sypheotides 120
syriacus, Picoides 258
syriacus, Serinus 594
Syrigma 64
Syrmaticus 107
syrmatophorus, Phaethornis 205
Syrrhaptes 134
szalayi, Oriolus 624
szechenyii, Tetraophasis 99

tabuensis, Aplonis 619
tabuensis, Porzana 117
tabuensis, Prosopeia 160
tacarcunae, Chlorospingus 560
tacazze, Nectarinia 516
Taccocua 176
tachiro, Accipiter 81
Tachornis 202
Tachuris 332
Tachybaptus 54
Tachycineta 349
Tachyeres 71
Tachyphonus 563
taciturnus, Arremon 552
tacsanowskius, Bradypterus 440
taczanowskii, Cinclodes 277
taczanowskii, Leptopogon 337
taczanowskii, Leucippus 211
taczanowskii, Montifringilla 613
taczanowskii, Nothoprocta 52
taczanowskii, Podiceps 55
taczanowskii, Sicalis 546
Tadorna 71
tadorna, Tadorna 71
tadornoides, Tadorna 71
taeniata, Dubusia 568
taeniatus, Peucedramus 582
taeniopterus, Ploceus 615
Taeniotriccus 330
tahapisi, Emberiza 536
tahitica, Hirundo 352
tahitiensis, Numenius 126
taitensis, Urodynamis 175
taivanus, Pycnonotus 366
takatsukasae, Monarcha 487
talaseae, Zoothera 407
talatala, Nectarinia 515
Talegalla 91
talpacoti, Columbina 143
tamarugensis, Conirostrum 582
tamatia, Bucco 240
tanagrinus, Lampropsar 592
tanganjicae, Zoothera 406

696   *Tangara* 570
tanki, Turnix 110
tannensis, Ptilinopus 149
Tanygnathus 159
Tanysiptera 231
tao, Tinamus 50
Taoniscus 53
Tapera 177
tapera, Phaeoprogne 350
Taphrolesbia 219
Taphrospilus 211
Taraba 289
taranta, Agapornis 163
tarda, Otis 119
tarnii, Pteroptochos 305
tasmanicus, Corvus 640
tataupa, Crypturellus 52
tatei, Margarornis 283
Tauraco 171
Tchagra 376
tchagra, Tchagra 377
tectus, Notharchus 239
tectus, Vanellus 123
teerinki, Longchura 610
teesa, Butastur 83
teijsmanni, Rhipidura 488
Telacanthura 201
telasco, Sporophila 548
Teledromas 305
telescophthalmus, Arses 487
Telophorus 378
temia, Crypsirina 638
temminckii, Calidris 128
temminckii, Coracias 234
temminckii 359
temminckii, Cursorius 123
temminckii, Eurostopodus 195
temminckii, Orthonyx 414
temminckii, Picoides 255
temminckii, Picumnus 251
temminckii, Tragopan 106
Temnotrogon 222
Temnurus 638
temnurus, Priotelus 222
temnurus, Temnurus 638
temporalis, Aegintha 606
temporalis, Ploceus 614
temporalis, Pomatostomus 420
tenebricosa, Tyto 181
tenebrosa, Chelidoptera 241
tenebrosa, Gallinula 117
tenebrosa, Gerygone 466
tenebrosa, Pachycephala 492
tenebrosa, Rhipidura 489
tenebrosus, Phyllastrephus 371
tenebrosus, Pitohui 497
tenebrosus, Turdoides 426
tenella, Neomixis 422
tenellipes, Phylloscopus 445
tenellus, Tmetothylacus 355
tenuirostris, Acanthorhynchus 534
tenuirostris, Anous 133
tenuirostris, Cacatua 157
tenuirostris, Calidris 128

tenuirostris, Coracina 360
tenuirostris, Geositta 276
tenuirostris, Inezia 333
tenuirostris, Numenius 126
tenuirostris, Onychognathus 620
tenuirostris, Puffinus 57
tenuirostris, Xenops 288
tenuirostris, Zosterops 523
Tephrodornis 364
tephrolaemus, Pycnonotus 369
tephronota, Sitta 504
tephronotum, Glaucidium 187
tephronotus, Turdus 410
Tephrozosterops 524
Terathopius 78
Terenotriccus 324
Terenura 296
Teretistris 579
Terpsiphone 482
terrestris, Phyllastrephus 370
terrestris, Trugon 146
Tersina 574
Tesia 438
tessmanni, Muscicapa 476
tethys, Oceanodroma 59
Tetrao 94
Tetraogallus 98
Tetraophasis 99
Tetrax 119
tetrax, Tetrax 119
tetrix, Tetrao 94
textilis, Amytornis 465
textrix, Cisticola 449
teydea, Fringilla 594
teysmanni, Treron 147
Thalasseus 132
thalassina, Cissa 637
thalassina, Eumyias 476
thalassina, Tachycineta 350
thalissinus, Colibri 207
Thalassoica 56
Thalassornis 75
Thalurania 209
Thamnistes 292
Thamnolaea 403
Thamnomanes 292
Thamnophilus 290
Thamnornis 443
Thaumastura 220
Thaumatibis 67
thayeri, Larus 130
theklae, Galerida 348
thenca, Minus 390
theomacha, Ninox 189
theresae, Montifringilla 613
theresiae, Metallura 218
theresiae, Polytmus 211
Theristicus 68
Thescelocichla 369
thibetanus, Serinus 594
thilius, Agelaius 590
Thinocorus 129
Thlypopsis 561
tholloni, Myrmecocichla 403

thomensis, Columba 136
thomensis, Estrilda 605
thomensis, Nectarinia 513
thomensis, Zoonavena 201
thompsoni, Hypsipetes 373
thoracica, Apalis 456
thoracica, Bambusicola 105
thoracica, Poospiza 545
thoracica, Stachyris 424
thoracicus, Bradypterus 440
thoracicus, Charadrius 125
thoracicus, Cyphorhinus 389
thoracicus, Dactylortyx 98
thoracicus, Hylophilus 587
thoracicus, Liosceles 305
thoracicus, Prionochilus 507
thoracicus, Thryothorus 386
Thraupis 566
Threnetes 204
threnothorax, Rhipidura 488
Threskiornis 67
Thripadectes 286
Thripophaga 281
Thryomanes 384
Thryothorus 385
thula, Egretta 65
thura, Carpodacus 600
thyroideus, Sphyrapicus 253
Tiaris 549
tibetanus, Syrrhaptes 134
tibetanus, Tetraogallus 98
tibialis, Lorius 155
tibialis, Neochelidon 350
tibialis, Pheucticus 556
tibialis, Pselliophorus 555
tibicen, Gymnorhina 629
Tichadroma 504
tickelli, Ptilolaemus 237
tickelli, Trichastoma 416
tickelliae, Niltava 474
tigrina, Dendroica 577
tigrinus, Lanius 379
Tigriornis 63
Tigrisoma 63
Tijuca 306
Tilmatura 220
Timalia 425
Timeliopsis 525
timorensis, Ficedula 473
timoriensis, Megalurus 462
Tinamotis 53
Tinamus 50
tinniens, Cisticola 453
tinnunculus, Falco 88
tiphia, Aegithina 374
tirica, Brotogeris 168
tithys, Synallaxis 279
Tityra 309
Tmetothylacus 355
tobaci, Amaziba 213
Tockus 236
toco, Ramphastos 250
tocuyensis, Arremonops 552
Todirostrum 328
Todopsis 464

Todus 232
todus, Todus 232
tolmei Geothlypis 579
Tolmomyias 327
tombacea, Galbula 239
tomentosa, Crax 93
tonsa, Platysteira 481
Topaza 215
torda, Alca 134
Torgos 78
tormenti, Microeca 477
torotoro, Halcyon 229
torquata, Ceryle 225
torquata, Chauna 69
torquata, Coeligena 216
torquata, Corythopis 338
torquata, Grafisia 620
torquata, Melanopareia 305
torquata, Myrmornis 302
torquata, Poospiza 545
torquata, Saxicola 402
torquatus, Atlapetes 554
torquatus, Celus 264
torquatus, Corvus 640
torquatus, Cracticus 629
torquatus, Lanioturdus1 376
torquatus, Lybius 246
torquatus, Melidectes 533
torquatus, Myioborus 580
torquatus, Neolestes 373
torquatus, Pedionomus 111
torquatus, Pteroglossus 249
torquatus, Rallus 114
torquatus, Thamnophilus 291
torquatus, Turdus 410
torqueola, Arborphila 104
torqueola, Sporophila 547
torquilla, Jynx 250
Torreornis 543
torridus, Attila 321
torridus, Selasphorus 221
torringtoni, Columba 136
totanus, Tringa 126
totta, Serinus 596
Touit 168
toulou, Centropus 179
townsendi, Dendroica 577
townsendi, Myadestes 400
toxopei, Charmosyna 155
Toxorhamphus 525
Toxostoma 391
tracheliotus, Torgos 78
Trachyphonus 246
tractrac, Cercomela 401
Tragopan 106
traillii, Empidonax 323
traillii, Oriolus 625
tranquebarica, Streptopelia 139
transfasciatus, Crypturellus 51
traversi, Petroica 478
Tregellasia 478
Treron 146
triangularis, Xiphorhynchus 274
tricarunculata, Procnias 310
trichas, Geothlypis 578

Trichastoma 416
Trichocichla 463
Trichoglossus 154
Tricholaema 245
trichopsis, Otus 183
Trichothraupis 564
trichroa, Erythrura 607
Triclaria 171
tricollaris, Charadrius 125
tricolor, Agelaius 590
tricolor, Alectrurus 316
tricolor, Atlapetes 553
tricolor, Ephthianura 470
tricolor, Erythrura 607
tricolor, Ficedula 473
tricolor, Furnarius 277
tricolor, Egretta 65
tricolor, Perissocephalus 310
tricolor, Phalaropus 127
tricolor, Ploceus 616
tricolor, Rallina 115
tricolor, Vanellus 124
tridactyla, Jacamaralcyon 239
tridactyla, Rissa 131
tridactylus, Picoides 260
trifasciatus, Basileuterus 581
trifasciatus, Carpodacus 600
trifasciatus, Hemispingus 561
trifasciatus, Nesomimus 390
trigonostigma, Dicaeum 508
Tringa 126
trinitatis, Euphonia 568
trinotatus, Accipiter 81
tristigma, Caprimulgus 198
tristigmata, Gallicolumba 145
tristis, Acridotheres 623
tristis, Carduelis 597
tristis, Corvus 640
tristis, Meiglyptes 268
tristis, Rhopodytes 176
tristissima, Lonchura 609
tristrami, Dicaeum 509
tristrami, Emberiza 537
tristrami, Myzomela 528
tristrami, Oceanodroma 59
tristramii, Onychognathus 620
tristriatus, Basileuterus 581
tristriatus, Serinus 596
triurus, Mimus 390
trivialis, Anthus 357
trivirgata, Conopias 318
trivirgatus, Accipiter 81
trivirgatus, Monarcha 486
trivirgatus, Phylloscopus 446
trocaz, Columba 136
trochileum, Dicaeum 510
trochilirostris, Campylorhamphus 275
trochiloides, Phylloscopus 446
Trochilus 211
trochilus, Phylloscopus 444
Trochocercus 482
Troglodytes 387
troglodytes, Cisticola 452
troglodytes, Collocalia 201

troglodytes, Estilda 605
troglodytes, Troglodytes 387
troglodytoides, Spelaeornis 421
Trogon 222
tropica, Fregetta 58
Tropicoperdix 105
tropicus, Corvus 641
trudeaui, Sterna 131
Trugon 146
Tryngites 129
tschudii, Ampelioides 307
tuberculifer, Myiarchus 321
tucanus, Ramphastos 250
tucinkae, Eubucco 242
tucumana, Amazona 170
tukki, Meiglyptes 268
tullbergi, Campethera 254
Tumbezia 317
tumultuosus, Pionus 169
Turacoena 140
turatii, Laniarius 377
turcosa, Cycanolyca 635
turcosa, Niltava 474
turdinus, Campylorhynchus 383
turdinus, Ptyrticus 418
turdinus, Schiffornis 310
Turdoides 425
turdoides, Cataponera 408
Turdus 409
Turnagra 497
turneri, Eremomela 460
Turnix 110
Turtur 141
turtur, Pachyptila 57
turtur, Streptopelia 138
tuta, Halcyon 231
Tylas 374
tympanistria, Turtur 141
tympanistrigus, Pycnonotus 365
Tympanuchus 95
typica, Coracina 360
typica, Nesillas 443
typicus, Corvus 639
typus, Polyboroides 79
Tyranneutes 311
tyrannina, Cercomacra 296
tyrannina, Dendrocincla 270
Tyranniscus 336
Tyrannopsis 318
Tyrannulus 337
tyrannulus, Myiarchus 320
Tyrannus 317
tyrannus, Muscivora 317
tyrannus, Spizaetus 87
tyrannus, Tyrannus 317
tyrianthina, Metallura 219
tyro, Dacelo 228
tytleri, Phylloscopus 445
Tyto 180
tzacatl, Amazilia 213

ucayalae, Philydor 286
ugiensis, Zosterops 522
ultima, Pterodroma 56
ultramarina, Aphelcoma 634

698   ultramarina, Vini 155
ulula, Surnia 186
umbellus, Bonasa 95
umbra, Otus 182
umbratilis, Rhinomyias 471
umbretta, Scopus 66
umbrovirens, Phylloscopus 447
unappendiculatus, Casuarius 49
unchall, Macropygia 139
uncinatus, Chondrohierax 76
undata, Sylvia 444
undatus, Celeus 263
undatus, Lybius 246
underwoodii, Ocreatus 218
undulata, Anas 72
undulata, Chlamydotis 119
undulata, Gallinago 128
undulata, Phylidonyris 534
undulatus, Aceros 237
undulatus, Crypturellus 51
undulatus, Melopsittacus 162
undulatus, Zebrilus 63
unduligera, Frederickena 289
unicincta, Columba 136
unicinctus, Parabuteo 84
unicolor, Aphelocoma 634
unicolor, Chamaepetes 93
unicolor, Chloropipo 311
unicolor, Collacalia 199
unicolor, Cosmopsarus 622
unicolor, Cyanoramphus 161
unicolor, Haematopus 121
unicolor, Haplospiza 544
unicolor, Meliphaga 530
unicolor, Mesitornis 110
unicolor, Myadestes 401
unicolor, Myrmotherula 294
unicolor, Niltava 474
unicolor, Paradoxornis 435
unicolor, Phrygilus 544
unicolor, Scytalopus 305
unicolor, Sturnus 622
unicolor, Thamnophilus 291
unicolor, Turdus 410
unicornis, Crax 93
uniformis, Chloropipo 311
unirufa, Cinnycerthia 384
unirufa, Synallaxis 280
unirufa, Terpsiphone 483
unirufus, Centropus 180
unirufus, Lipaugus 307
Upucerthia 276
Upupa 235
Uraeginthus 604
Uragus 599
uralensis, Strix 191
Uratelornis 235
urbica, Delichon 354
Uria 134
urile, Phalacrocorax 61
urinatrix, Pelecanoides 59
Urochroa 215
urochrysia, Chalybura 214
Urocissa 637
Urocynchramus 599

Urodynamis 175
urogallus, Tetrao 95
Uroglaux 188
Urolais 457
Uromyias 332
Uropelia 144
urophasianus, Centrocercus 95
Uropsalis 198
Uropsila 388
uropygialis, Acanthiza 468
uropygialus, Cacicus 578
uropygialus, Carduelis 597
uropygialis, Chirocylla 307
uropygialis, Melanerpes 253
uropygialis, Sicalis 546
uropygialis, Tyranniscus 336
uropygialis, Zosterops 521
urosticta, Myrmotherula 294
Urosticte 214
urostictus, Pycnonotus 367
Urothraupis 555
Urothriorchis 83
ursulae, Nectarinia 512
urubambensis, Thripophaga 282
urbitinga, Buteogallus 84
urumutum, Nothocrax 93
usambiro, Trachyphonus 247
ussheri, Muscicapa 476
ussheri, Scotopelia 186
ussheri, Telacanthura 201
usticollis, Eremomela 460
ustulatus, Catharus 409
ustulatus, Microcerculus 389

vaalensis, Anthus 357
vagabunda, Dendrocitta 638
vagans, Cuculus 172
vaillantii, Picus 267
viallantii, Trachyphonus 246
validirostris, Lanius 380
validirostris, Melithreptus 531
validirostris, Upucerthia 276
validus, Corvus 639
validus, Myiarchus 320
validus, Pachyramphus 309
validus, Reinwardtipicus 268
valisineria, Aythya 73
vana, Lonchura 609
vanderbilti, Trichastoma 417
Vanellus 123
vanellus, Vanellus 123
Vanga 381
vanikorensis, Collocalia 199
vanikorensis, Myiagra 487
varia, Grallaria 302
varia, Miniotilta 575
varia, Strix 191
varia, Tangara 571
varia, Turnix 111
variabilis, Emberiza 537
variegata, Mesitornis 110
variegata, Sula 60
variegata, Tadorna 71
variegaticeps, Alcippe 432
variegaticeps, Philydor 285

variegatus, Certhionyx 528
variegatus, Crypturellus 52
variegatus, Garrulax 428
variegatus, Indicator 247
variegatus, Merops 233
variolosus, Cacomantis 173
varius, Cuculus 172
varius, Empidonomus 318
varius, Gallus 106
varius, Parus 502
varius, Phalacrocorax 61
varius, Psephotus 161
varius, Sphyrapicus 253
varzeae, Picumnus 251
vasa, Coracopsis 162
vassali, Garrulax 428
vassorii, Tangara 572
vaughani, Zosterops 524
vaughanii, Acrocephalus 442
vauxi, Chaetura 202
velata, Philentoma 479
velata, Xolmis 314
velatus, Enicurus 400
velatus, Ploceus 615
Veles 195
velia, Tangara 572
velox, Geococcyx 177
velox, Turnix 111
venerata, Halcyon 231
venezuelanus, Pogonotriccus 331
venezuelensis, Diglossa 574
venezuelensis, Myiarchus 320
Veniliornis 260
ventralis, Amazona 170
ventralis, Buteo 85
ventralis, Gallinula 117
ventralis, Phylloscartes 331
venusta, Chloropsis 375
venusta, Dacnis 572
venusta, Nectarinia 515
venustulus, Parus 500
venustus, Charadrius 125
venustus, Granatellus 582
venustus, Platycercus 161
veraguensis, Anthacothorax 207
veraguensis, Geotrygon 145
veredus, Charadrius 125
vermiculatus, Burhinus 122
Vermivora 575
vermivorus, Helmithera 578
vernalis, Loriculus 163
vernans, Treron 146
veroxii, Nectarinia 512
verreauxi, Coua 178
verreauxi, Leptotila 144
verreauxii, Aquila 86
verrucosus, Phalacrocorax 61
versicolor, Amazilia 211
versicolor, Amazona 171
versicolor, Anas 73
versicolor, Ergaticus 579
versicolor, Eubucco 242
versicolor, Geotrygon 145
versicolor, Lanio 563

versicolor, Mayrornis 484
versicolor, Meliphaga 529
versicolor, Pachyramphus 308
versicolor, Passerina 558
versicolor, Phasianus 108
versicolor, Pitta 340
versicolor, Strepera 629
versicolor, Trichoglossus 154
versicolurus, Brotogeris 168
versteri, Melanocharis 507
verticalis, Creurgops 563
verticalis, Eremopterix 344
verticalis, Hemispingus 561
verticalis, Monarcha 486
verticalis, Nectarinia 513
verticalis, Tyrannus 318
vesper, Rhodopis 220
vespertinus, Coccothraustes 602
vespertinus, Falco 89
Vestiaria 584
vestitus, Eriocnemis 217
vetula, Muscipipra 317
vetula, Ortalis 91
Vetula, Saurothera 176
vexillarius, Semeiophorus 198
vicina, Meliphaga 528
vicinior, Scytalopus 306
vicinior, Vireo 585
victor, Philinopus 151
victoria, Goura 146
victoriae, Lamprolia 470
victoriae, Lesbia 218
victoriae, Ptiloris 631
victoriae, Sitta 503
victorini, Bradypterus 439
Vidua 610
viduata, Dendrocygna 69
viduus, Monarcha 486
vieilloti, Lybius 246
vieilloti, Sphecotheres 656
vigil, Rhinoplax 238
vigorsii, Eupodotis 120
viguieri, Dacnis 573
vilasboasi, Pipra 312
vilissimus, Tyranniscus 336
villanovae, Xiphocolaptes 272
villaviscensio, Campylopterus 207
villosa, Sitta 504
villosus, Myiobius 324
villosus, Picoides 259
vinacea, Amazona 171
vinacea, Streptopelia 139
vinaceigula, Egretta 65
vinaceus, Carpodacus 599
vincens, Dicaeum 508
Vini 155
vinipectus, Alcippe 432
viola, Heliangelus 217
violacea, Euphonia 568
violacea, Geotrygon 145
violacea, Hyliota 463
violacea, Loxigilla 549
violacea, Musophaga 171

violacea, Nectarinia 516
violaceus, Centropus 178
violaceus, Cyanocorax 635
violaceus, Nycticorax 64
violaceus, Ptilonorhycnchus 630
violaceus, Trogon 224
violiceps, Amazilia 213
violiceps, Goldmania 211
violifer, Coeligena 216
vipio, Grus 111
virens, Contopus 322
virens, Dendroica 577
virens, Icteria 582
virens, Loxops 583
virens, Megalaima 242
virens, Pycnonotus 368
virens, Sylvietta 461
virens, Zosterops 523
Vireo 505
vireo, Nicator 379
Vireolanius 585
virescens, Empidonax 323
virescens, Hypsipetes 373
virescens, Meliphaga 529
virescens, Phylloscartes 331
virescens, Pseudoleistes 591
virescens, Schiffornis 310
virescens, Tyranneutes 311
virescens, Xanthomyias 336
virgata, Aphriza 128
virgata, Ciccaba 190
virgata, Sterna 131
virgata, Thripophaga 282
virgaticeps, Thripadectes 286
virgatus, Accipiter 80
virgatus, Garrulax 429
virgatus, Sericornis 468
virginiae, Vermivora 575
virginianus, Bubo 184
virginianus, Colinus 96
virgo, Anthropoides 111
viridescens, Hypsipetes 372
viridicata, Myiopagis 335
viridicata, Pyrrhura 167
viridicauda, Amazilia 211
viridicollis, Tangara 572
viridicyana, Cyanolyca 634
viridifacies, Erythrura 607
viridiflavus, Tyranniscus 336
viridifrons, Amazilia 213
viridifuscus, Oriolus 624
viridigaster, Amazilia 213
viridigenalis, Amazona 170
viridigula, Anthracothorax 207
viridipallens, Lampornis 214
viridirostris, Rhopodytes 176
viridis, Androphobus 414
viridis, Anthracothorax 207
viridis, Artamella 381
viridis, Calyptomena 270
viridis, Centropus 179
viridis, Cochoa 400
viridis, Frederickena 289
viridis, Gecinulus 267
viridis, Gymnomyza 533

viridis, Laterallus 116
viridis, Megalaima 242
viridis, Merops 234
viridis, Neomixis 422
viridis, Pachyramphus 308
viridis, Picus 266
viridis, Psarocolius 588
viridis, Psophia 112
viridis, Pteroglossus 248
viridis, Ptilinopus 150
viridis, Sphecotheres 626
viridis, Telophorus 378
viridis, Terpsiphone 482
viridis, Tersina 574
viridis, Trogon 223
viridissima, Aegithina 374
viscivorus, Turdus 412
vitellina, Dendroica 577
vitellinus, Manacus 311
vitellinus, Ploceus 615
vitellinus, Ramphastos 249
Vitia 463
vitiensis, Clytorhycnchus 484
vitiensis, Columba 136
vitiosus, Lophotriccus 330
vitriolina, Tangara 571
vittata, Amazona 170
vittata, Graueria 461
vittata, Oxyura 75
vittata, Pachyptila 57
vittata, Petroica 478
vittata, Sterna 131
vittatus, Heterotrogon 224
vittatus, Lanius 379
vittatus, Picus 266
vitticeps, Chlorostilbon 209
vivida, Niltava 473
vocifer, Haliaeetus 77
vociferans, Lipaugus 307
vociferans, Tyrannus 318
vociferoides, Haliaeetus 77
vociferus, Caprimulgus 196
vociferus, Charadrius 125
Volatinia 546
vulvani, Junco 540
vulgaris, Sturnus 622
vulnerata, Myzomela 528
vulneratum, Dicaeum 509
vulpina, Certhiaxis 281
Vultur 75
vulturina, Gypopsitta 169
vulturinum, Acryllium 110

waalia, Treron 147
waddelli, Babax 427
wagleri, Aratinga 165
wagleri, Icterus 590
wagleri, Psarocolius 588
wahlbergi, Aquila 86
wahnesi, Parotia 633
waigeuensis, Anas 71
waldeni, Actinodura 431
walenii, Dicrurus 626
wallacei, Eulipoa 91
wallacei, Semioptera 632

700   wallacei, Todopsis 464
wallacei, Zosterops 521
wallacii, Ageotheles 194
wallacii, Ptilinopus 149
wallacii, Rallus 113
walleri, Onychognathus 620
wallichii, Catreus 107
wallicus, Pezoporus 162
wardi, Harpactes 224
wardi, Pseudobias 480
wardii, Zoothera 406
watersi, Coturnicops 115
watertonii, Thalurania 210
watkinsi, Grallaria 302
watkinsi, Incaspiza 545
watsonii, Otus 184
webbianus, Paradoxornis 435
websteri, Ceyx 227
weddellii, Aratinga 165
wellsi, Leptotila 144
westermanni, Ficedula 473
westlandica, Procellaria 57
wetmorei, Buthraupis 567
wetmorei, Rallus 114
Wetmorethraupis 567
weynsi, Ploceus 615
whartoni, Ducula 152
whiteheadi, Calyptomena 270
whiteheadi, Cettia 438
whiteheadi, Collocalia 200
whiteheadi, Harpactes 224
whiteheadi, Otus 183
whiteheadi, Sitta 503
whiteheadi, Stachyris 423
whiteheadi, Urocissa 637
whitei, Conopophila 534
whiteleyi, Caprimulgus 196
whiteleyi, Pipreola 307
whitemanensis, Melidectes 533
whitneyi, Cichlornis 463
whitneyi, Micrathens 188
whitneyi, Pomarea 484
whytii, Stactolaema 244
whytii, Sylvietta 461
wilhelminae, Charmosyna 155
wilkinsi, Nesospiza 545
willcocksi, Indicator 248
williami, Metallura 218
williamsi, Mirafa 341
williamsoni, Muscicapa 475
wilsoni, Coeligena 216
wilsoni, Hemignathus 584
wilsoni, Vidua 610
Wilsonia 579
wilsonia, Charadrius 124
winchelli, Halcyon 229
winifredae, Scepomycter 459
wolfi, Eulabeornis 112
wollweberi, Parus 499
woodfordi, Corvus 639
Woodfordia 524
woodfordii, Ciccaba 190
woodhousei, Parmoptila 602
woodi, Leonardina 418
woodwardi, Amtomis 465

woodwardi, Colluricincla 496
woosnami, Cisticola 425
worcesteri, Turnix 110
wrightii, Empidonax 323
wumizusume, Synthliboramphus 134
wyatti, Thripophaga 282

xanthocephala, Tangara 570
Xanthocephalus 590
xanthocephalus, Xanthocephalus 590
xanthochlorus, Pteruthius 431
xanthochroa, Zosterops 522
xanthogaster, Euphonia 569
xanthogastra, Carduelis 597
xanthogastra, Tangara 571
xanthogenys, Parus 501
xanthogonys, Heliodoxa 215
xanthogramma, Melanodera 544
xantholaemus, Icterus 589
xantholaemus, Pycnonotus 367
xantholophus, Dendropicos 255
xantholora, Amazona 170
xanthomus, Agelius 591
Xanthomyias 336
Xanthomyza 534
xanthonotus, Indicator 248
xanthonotus, Oriolus 624
xanthonura, Gallicolumba 145
xanthophrys, Oxylabes 435
xanthophrys, Phyllastrephus 371
xanthophrys, Pseudonestor 584
xanthophthalmus, Agelaius 591
xanthophthalmus, Hemispingus 561
xanthoprymna, Oenanthe 404
xanthops, Amazona 170
xanthops, Forpus 168
xanthops, Ploceus 614
Xanthopsar 590
xanthopterus, Dysithamnus 292
xanthopterus, Ploceus 615
xanthopterygius, Forpus 168
xanthopygaeus, Picus 266
xanthopygius, Heterospingus 563
xanthopygius, Prionochilus 507
xanthopygos, Pycnonotus 366
xanthopygus, Pardalotus 510
xanthorhychus, Chalcites 174
xanthornus, Oriolus 625
xanthorrhous, Pycnonotus 366
xanthoschista, Seicercus 448
xanthosterna, Petronia 613
xantusii, Hylocharis 210
xavieri, Phyllastrephus 370
Xema 131
Xenerpestes 284
Xenicus 340
Xenodacnis 573
Xenoglaux 188
Xenoligea 579
Xenopipo 311
Xenopirostris 381

xenopirostris, Xenopirostris 381
Xenops 288
Xenopsaris 308
xenopterus, Laterallus 116
Xenornis 292
Xenospingus 545
Xenospiza 541
Xenotriccus 324
Xenus 126
Xiphidiopicus 253
Xiphirhynchus 420
Xiphocolaptes 271
Xipholena 309
Xiphorhynchus 273
Xolmis 314

yanacensis, Leptasthenura 278
yarrelli, Carduelis 597
yarrellii, Eulidia 221
yaruqui, Phaethornis 205
yeltoniensis, Melanocorypha 346
yemenensis, Acanthis 598
yersini, Garrulax 430
yessoensis, Emberiza 537
Yetapa 316
yetapa, Gubernetes 316
yncas, Cyanocorax 635
ypecaha, Eulabeornis 112
ypsilophorus, Synoicus 103
ypirangus, Emberizoides 545
yucatanica, Cissilopha 635
yucatanicus, Campylorhynchus 382
yucatanicus, Otophanes 195
yucatanensis, Amazilia 213
yucatanensis, Myiarchus 320
Yuhina 434
yunnanensis, Sitta 503
yuracares, Psarocolius 588

Zanclostomus 177
zantholeuca, Yuhina 435
zanthopygia, Ficedula 472
zappeyi, Paradoxornis 436
Zavattariornis 638
Zebrilus 63
zelandica, Aplonis 618
zeledoni, Chlorospingus 560
Zeledonia 582
zena, Spindalis 565
Zenaida 142
zenkeri, Melignomon 247
zeylanica, Megalima 242
zeylanicus, Pycnonotus 365
zeylonensis, Ketupa 186
zeylonica, Nectarinia 513
zeylonus, Telophonus 378
zimmeri, Synallaxis 280
Zodalia 218
zoeae, Ducula 153
zonaris, Streptoprocne 199
zonarius, Barnardius 161
zonatus, Campylorhynchus 383
Zonerodias 63

zoniventris, Falco 89
Zonotrichia 539
zonurus, Crinifer 171
Zoonavena 201
Zoothera 406
Zosterops 519
zosterops, Idioptilon 329
zosterops, Phyllastrephus 370

Notes

Notes

Notes

Notes

Notes

Notes

Notes

Notes

Notes

Notes

Notes

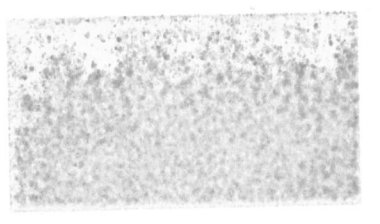